The PC-SIG
Encyclopedia
of Shareware

4th Edition

WINDCREST®

FOURTH EDITION
FIRST PRINTING

Library of Congress Cataloging-in-Publication Data

The PC-SIG encyclopedia of shareware / by PC-SIG, Inc. — 4th ed.
    p.   cm.
   Includes index.
   ISBN 0-8306-2669-7 (p)
   1. Shareware (Computer software)—Catalogs. I. PC Software
Interest Group (Sunnyvale. Calif.)
QA76.76.S46P33   1991
005.365—dc20   91-25481
                                    CIP

TAB Books offers software for sale. For information and a catalog, please contact TAB Software Department, Blue Ridge Summit, PA 17294-0850.

Acquisitions Editor: Ron Powers
Cover: Sandra Blair Design, Harrisburg, PA.   WP1

We dedicate The Encyclopedia of Shareware to the shareware authors whose considerable talents fill this book. Their extraordinary qualities of generosity and creativity have produced a unique asset for the personal computer community. As part of that community, we offer this expression of our gratitude and admiration.

We further wish to acknowledge the contribution of all the end-users of shareware software. Your interest in low-priced, quality software and your support of shareware authors with payment of registration fees make shareware work for everyone.

Acknowledgements

Richard Petersen *President*
Erv Slaski *General Manager*

Project Manager and Editor

Bruce R. Kent *Product Development Manager*

Special Contributors:

Steve Taylor *System Design*
Mike Coman *Art Director*
Debra Ashcraft *Contributing Editor*
Barbara Rittiman *Contributing Editor*
Joe Speaks *Contributing Editor*
George Pulido *Technical Editor*

Those responsible for getting this book to you:

Deborah R. Wheeler
Claudia Graziano
Steve Landau
Joe Nguyen
Jozelle Cox
Greg Harsh
Mike Coman
Ethan Thompson
Sandra Seymour
Kim Washington
Victoria Irwin
Ginger Otto
Sandy Whitaker
Carlos Talavera
Veronica Pulido
Anthony Castillo
Jonathan Robinson
Jesse Ugarte
Shiryl Taylor

ENCYCLOPEDIA OF SHAREWARE
TABLE OF CONTENTS

Program Categories (Alphabetically Listed)

Accounting, Billing
Accounting, Checkbook Management
Accounting, Educational
Accounting, G/L, A/P, A/R, Payroll
Accounting, Home Checkbook Management
Accounting, Home/Personal
Accounting, Inventory Control
Accounting, Job Costing and Bill of Materials
Accounting, Purchase Orders
Accounting, Time-Billing Management
Agriculture
Archive/Compression Utilities
Artificial Intelligence
Astrology and Fortune Telling
Astronomy and Space Exploration

Auto/Vehicle Management
Banner Makers
Barcodes
Bible Study
Bulletin Board Systems (BBS)
Business Specific Systems
CAD (Computer Aided Design) and Designing
Calculators
Chemistry and Physics
Children's Programs (ages 2-10)
Church Administration
Communication Programs
Conversion Programs
Copy Utilities
DOS Shells

DOS and PC Training and Education
Database, dBase Utilities
Databases
Desktop Organizers
Desktop Publishers and Desktop Publishing
 Utilities
Disk Catalogers and Disk Labelers
Engineering
Entertainment, General
File Management Utilities
Flying and Navigation
Food and Drink Preparation
Forms Packages
Fractals and Mathematic Based Graphics
Gambling
Games, Adventure and Text
Games, Arcade
Games, Arcade (Sports)
Games, Board and Dice
Games, Cards
Genealogy
Graphing Programs
Ham Radio
Hard Drive Utilities
Health Management
History, Educational
Home Management
Hypertext
Integrated (Wordprocessing, Database, and
 Spreadsheet)
Investment Management
Label Makers
Language Study, Foreign
Library, Dewey Decimal, etc.
Loan Calculators
Lottery
Mail Lists, Address Managers, and Telephone
 Organizers
Maps
Math and Geometry Programs
Menu Programs
Movie/VCR/Music Databases
Music
Network Software and Utilities
PCjr
Paint and Drawing Programs
Personnel Management

Photography
Practical Jokes
Presentation Graphics (Slides)
Printer Managers
Printer Utilities
Printer Utilities, Laser
Printing, Sideways
Programming Tools
Programming, (Specific Language)
Programming, Assembly
Programming, BASIC
Programming, C
Programming, Forth
Programming, Fortran
Programming, Modula-2
Programming, Pascal
Project Management
Quotes, Bids, and Estimating
Real Estate and Property Management
Reference Materials
 (Books/Articles/Information/Data)
Resumes and Job Search
Sales and Prospect Management
Schedulers, Calendars, To Do Listers and Ticklers
Security — File, Disk, or System
Spelling, Word, and Vocabulary Quizzes and
 Games
Sports Management
Spreadsheet Templates
Spreadsheet Utilities
Spreadsheets
Statistical Packages
Survey Tracking
Tax Preparation
Teaching, Grading Systems and Recordkeeping
Test and Quiz Preparation
Trivia
Typing, Educational
Utilities, Macro Programs
Utilities, System or Hardware
Visually Impaired, Programs
Word Processor and Text Utilities
Word Processors, Text Editors, and Outliners
Word Processors, Educational
Writing and Composition Aids

INTRODUCTION

Why an Encyclopedia of Shareware?

Have you ever spent your entire day running from one software store to another, talking to salesperson after salesperson, all in search of a good piece of software? Well, *The PC-SIG Encyclopedia of Shareware* takes the legwork out of finding the right software. As a guide to more than 2500 great shareware programs, this book introduces you to an entirely new way of buying software — a way that is both convenient and affordable.

Whether you need a program to help run your business, manage your home, keep your bowling league organized, trace your family tree, or even demonstrate molecular bonding, this encyclopedia has already found it for you. From powerful spreadsheets and databases to games and home accounting programs, it's all available for a fraction of what you might expect to pay.

This book chronicles the growing world of shareware, low-cost IBM PC software. With shareware, copying software and sharing it with friends is not only permitted, it's encouraged. Through free and open distribution, shareware finds its way into the hands of those who want it and are willing to pay for it. This revolutionary method of software distribution virtually eliminates costly marketing, promotion, and packaging associated with typical software retailing. You'll notice the savings in the low prices you pay for these outstanding programs.

PC-SIG has taken great pains to bring you this compendium of information in encyclopedia format. Only as an encyclopedia could this book deliver such comprehensive coverage of shareware. These pages provide you with a familiar system of organization so you can instantly find the information you need, no matter how specialized or obscure. In addition to program titles and general information, you'll find detailed program descriptions and product reviews to help you choose the right program for your needs. And since it's shareware, you can try these programs before you buy them.

The Third Edition of this Encyclopedia included two new ways to access this vast volume of information: an index by disk number and reprints of *Shareware Magazine* articles. For the Fourth Edition we have added a glossary of computer terms and symbols after the program title to indicate if a program has been updated ✍ or is a new entry ☆ since the Third Edition. We wish you a good voyage through the expanding world of our encyclopedia.

PC-SIG: A Tradition of Service

For over seven years, PC-SIG has bridged the gap between software authors and end-users by bringing fine shareware programs to the attention of software buyers. Books such as this, PC-SIG's SHAREWARE Magazine, and numerous other publications have helped users around the world discover a wealth of great shareware.

Yet PC-SIG is more than a respected publisher of shareware information. PC-SIG is also the world's largest distributor of shareware and public domain software. Virtually every shareware program ever released can be found in the PC-SIG Library of Shareware. Additionally, every program in the Library is available to the computing public through PC-SIG and its international network of authorized dealers. By acting as a source for both shareware information and shareware programs, PC-SIG has brought organization and convenience to the rapidly-expanding shareware industry.

PC-SIG prides itself on the completeness and intuitive organization of its library. Considerable time and effort goes into making the PC-SIG Library easy to manage and user friendly for all levels of computer users.

Beyond being an international source for quality shareware, PC-SIG provides a wide array of services. PC-SIG serves shareware users by providing technical support, customer service, and prompt order-processing for those taking advantage of the PC-SIG Library. Simultaneously, PC-SIG serves shareware authors with dynamic new avenues for promoting and distributing their software.

By working closely with each individual shareware author, PC-SIG is able to keep the PC-SIG Library accurate and current year after year. As authors release new programs or update existing ones, PC-SIG is among the first to receive a copy. And since all PC-SIG software comes directly from authors, you are insured that the most complete and up-to-date version of any program can be found in the PC-SIG Library.

What is the ASP?

The Association of Shareware Professionals (ASP) is an affiliation of shareware authors dedicated to the shareware concept. Since 1987 the ASP has played an important role in the shareware industry by creating standards and guidelines for shareware software and its distribution.

By defining good shareware and helping fellow authors create it, the ASP contributes to the overall quality of shareware programs. Through communication with shareware vendors, the ASP insures that shareware products are responsibly promoted to the software buying public. As an approved vendor and associate member of the Association of Shareware Professionals, PC-SIG is recognized for its adherence to all ASP distribution standards, and for its accurate representation of shareware programs.

You'll notice that many of the programs in this encyclopedia are marked ➤**ASP member** . This notation means the program meets strict ASP quality standards and the author is a member of the ASP. There are, however, many outstanding programs covered in this book that do not bear the ASP distinction. As the ASP continues to grow, more and more programs will likely be listed as ASP member programs.

ASP wants to make sure that the shareware principal works for you. If you are unable to resolve a shareware-related problem with an ASP member by contacting the member directly, ASP may be able to help. The ASP Ombudsman can help you resolve a dispute or problem with an ASP member, but does not provide technical support for members' products. Please write to the ASP Ombudsman at P.O. Box 5786, Bellevue, WA 98006 or send a Compuserve message via easyplex to ASP Ombudsman 70007,3536.

Call for Shareware Authors

Marketing your own software can be costly, competitive, and risky. It can also become a full-time job. Software publishers can help, but the battle for exposure is always intense. Thus PC-SIG invites you to take advantage of shareware distribution through PC-SIG. Become a shareware author and participate in the PC-SIG Library.

Regardless of whether a market is vertical, horizontal, or somewhere in between, more and more software authors are using shareware as their primary method of distribution. Through shareware distribution, software is made accessible to the entire computing community and at prices that reflect the quality of the program, not the package.

Programs in the PC-SIG Library enjoy many benefits and opportunities. Once your program is accepted into the Library it is listed in major PC-SIG publications such as this encyclopedia. Your program has the chance to be included in our national advertising campaigns. In-depth reviews of shareware programs appear in SHAREWARE Magazine. PC-SIG even pursues retail distribution and registered sales for some of the shareware products distributed through the PC-SIG Library. This is all part of the non-exclusive agreement that PC-SIG offers shareware authors.

As a contributing author you will join other shareware professionals who work closely with PC-SIG to bring great shareware and accurate product information to the public. You'll also be tapping into a source for a wide variety of shareware information: your free subscription to SHAREWARE Magazine provides industry information, the PC-SIG Author Newsletter keeps you in touch with other shareware authors, and PC-SIG itself provides feedback on your specific program and what users are saying about it.

PC-SIG is known for distributing the best that shareware has to offer. In keeping with that tradition, PC-SIG is seeking professional, fully functional software to complement its Library. Admission preference is given to full working versions and new or unique applications. No program that is crippled and could potentially frustrate a customer is allowed into the Library.

Regardless of how you are currently marketing your software, you should take a closer look at shareware marketing. Since shareware distribution is non-exclusive, it is compatible with just about any other marketing strategy you may be using. If you are just beginning to consider marketing alternatives, contact PC-SIG for an honest evaluation of your program and its potential as a shareware product.

Please see the Shareware Author Submission Form in the back of this book or contact the Library Submissions Department of PC-SIG.

How to Use This Book

Only an encyclopedia could give you instant access to every shareware program in the vast PC-SIG Library, so PC-SIG has created just that: The PC-SIG Encyclopedia of Shareware. This third edition of the Encyclopedia describes the contents of over 2,400 disks, considerable growth beyond the 1,484 disks of the premier edition.

The main body of the book consists of program descriptions which give in-depth information and highlight the usefulness and benefits of the programs. These descriptions are placed alphabetically within program categories, which are also arranged in alphabetical order. For example, all wordprocessors are grouped together, all spreadsheets are grouped together, and all databases are grouped together. For a listing of the program categories, see the Table of Contents.

Because there is no "one right way" to organize all the information in the book, we have tried to anticipate the different ways you might access this information by including keywords within the index. These keywords will refer you to the program categories in the Encyclopedia. For example, you may want to find information about "Adventure Games." Program descriptions are not listed under "Adventure Games," but a keyword in the index would refer you to the category "Games, Adventure." Also, if you looked under Text Adventure Games, you'll be directed to the category, "Games, Adventure."

Here is another example. If you are looking for a program to help you design and draw mechanical parts, you might start by looking under "Graphics Programs." Under graphics there are no specific programs listed, but you are advised to see either "CAD (Computer Aided Design) and Designing," or "Presentation Graphics," or "Paint and Drawing Programs." If CAD (Computer Aided Design) sounds more like what you want, you should look under CAD (Computer Aided Design) and Designing. We have tried to consider every possible way you might look for a program. No matter what word you dive in looking for, we think you'll be led to the information you need. If you do manage to approach a topic from an angle we didn't anticipate, please try another related word.

So whether you browse the book from front to back, or use it to find something specific, we think you'll find this book both informative and fun.

In addition, if you know the PC-SIG Library by disk number, there is an index in the back that will tell you the programs on each disk.

Sample Index Listings

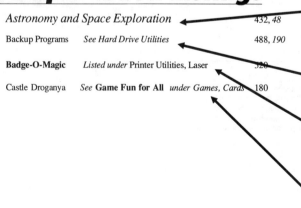

Astronomy and Space Exploration — 432, *48*

Backup Programs   *See Hard Drive Utilities* — 488, *190*

Badge-O-Magic   *Listed under* Printer Utilities, Laser — 320

Castle Droganya   *See* **Game Fun for All** *under Games, Cards* 180

This is a category reference. The number just after the category is the page in Volume II where this category begins. There you'll find detailed descriptions of all the new software in this category. The next number, in italics, is the page in the first volume, The Encyclopedia of Shareware, where this category begins.

This is a keyword reference. This word refers you to a category that is closely related to the word. You are instructed to "See" that category, then given the pages in each volume where that category begins.

This is a program title reference. The category under which this program is "listed" is included as a reference to similar programs. However, the number that follows is the exact page where you'll find a description of the program. If the page number only refers you to the first volume, look up the category instead. You'll be guided to similar programs in Volume II.

This is an associated program title reference. This program will be mentioned within the description of the main program (in bold type). Similar programs may be found in the category, listed next. The page number is where the main program description can be found.

ENCYCLOPEDIA LISTINGS

Copy Utilities

Dcopy

DCOPY is an enhancement of the MS-DOS COPY command. You can still copy files, but you control the copying process based on the file's creation/revision date. The program also pauses when the new disk becomes full, lets you put in another, and even formats it! If you want, you can ask DCOPY to prompt you before each file is copied. Wildcard copies are supported.
(PC-SIG Disk# 936)
Special Requirements: *None.*
Author Registration: *$35.00*

DiskDupe

DISKDUPE was made for folks who need to duplicate lots of programs or disks in various formats.
It's versatile! It copies 5.25" disks whether they are standard 360K, AT high-density 1.2M disks, or even CPM/86 with eight sectors. It also handles 720K and 1.4M 3.5" disks.
It's fast! It duplicates 360K disks in less than 58 seconds. Using pre-formatted disks, the time drops to less than 26 seconds. DISKDUPE uses your hard disk as a buffer so you can copy high-density disks exceeding your RAM memory without slowing down.
You can quickly format disks ahead of time, copy image files from a diskette onto your hard disk, and specify a list of hard disk image files to create or copy from. It runs manually, or along with special auto-loader hardware available from the author.
(PC-SIG Disk# 1279)
Special Requirements: *Hard drive.*
Author Registration: *$39.00*

▼ ▼ ▼

This program category heading introduces a grouping of programs with similar functions. These are also listed alphabetically throughout the Encyclopedia. For a complete listing of categories see the Table of Contents

This is the program name, complete description, and PC-SIG disk number. The PC-SIG disk number is our reference number and should be used whenever ordering or requesting information about a disk.

Here are any additional system requirements that exceed our assumed minimum requirements of 256K RAM, a single disk drive, and a monochrome (non-graphic) display. If the program requires a different computer configuration, only the differences from the standard configuration will be noted.

This is the author registration in US dollars. If you find the program useful, this fee is paid directly to the shareware author. The payment of the registration fee allows you to continue to use the program and in many cases you will receive added benefits such as printed manuals, additional support, and program updates.

This signifies the end of a program category.

Program Versions

Shareware authors continually improve their programs . Typically, authors associate a version number with each release or upgrade of their programs. In fact, authors so frequently update their programs that about one third of the programs in the PC-SIG Library change every six months. Because the programs are updated so frequently, we felt it was inappropriate to list program version numbers. PC-SIG always carries the latest version and if you need any information on program versions, please call.

BEGINNING WITH SHAREWARE

U sing shareware can be a great way for beginners to start computing. In addition to finding programs to help you learn computing, you'll be able to experiment with numerous shareware applications that cost nothing to try.

This beginners' section will get you started by introducing you to the different parts of your computer, showing you the most basic commands of DOS, and giving you special tips on how to use shareware.

Hardware: Parts is Parts

OK, so maybe you know the difference between your keyboard, your monitor and that big box known as the CPU or Central Processing Unit; but do you really know what they do and how they work together?

Let's look closely at the CPU. It is called the central processing unit because this is where all the real computing takes place. In most cases, this is the part people refer to as the "computer." The monitor merely lights up the screen based on what the CPU tells it. The keyboard can send only simple signals that the CPU is smart enough to understand. A computer can run perfectly without either of these devices—no computing takes place in the monitor or the keyboard. That is why these devices are called **peripherals**.

If you ever get the chance to get inside the case of the CPU, take a good look. You'll find the circuit boards that make up a computer are very intricate—you would need to know some electrical engineering to figure them out.

There are only about three or four of these circuit boards in a computer, and they fit together very easily. There are four or five other preassembled components that also go into every computer, including the case, but that's it. So next time someone tells you they built their own computer, don't be so impressed. Putting a computer together can be less difficult than assembling some children's toys.

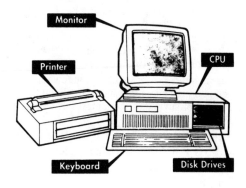

Above is a picture of a typical computer and its peripheral parts.

The Difference Between Hardware and Software

The physical parts of your computer are called hardware. Hardware is anything that you can touch, usually high-tech looking, and often expensive. Software, on the other hand, is information (usually stored on disks) that tells the hardware what to do, and if it's shareware it may not be expensive at all. Think of it like your favorite novel; the ink and paper are the hardware of a book, while the words and the story are the software that make it a best seller. But we'll worry about software later.

■ Memory Always Forgets

There are a couple of parts inside the CPU that are important to understand: memory and "secondary storage devices" (everybody else just calls them disk drives). The two are often confused by new users.

Memory is where the computer holds information that it is currently working on. Most computers today have 640K of Random Access Memory known as RAM. It is called RAM because the computer can instantaneously and randomly work with any one of the more than 640,000 pieces of information held in 640K of RAM. The computer works in RAM, and temporarily stores information in RAM, because RAM is the fastest place that a computer can store information.

But memory only works while the computer is turned on. Once the computer is shut off memory cannot hold any information. This is where disk drives come in handy.

■ Floppy Disks and Disk Drives

Floppy and hard disk drives are common types of "secondary storage devices," but they certainly aren't the only kind. The slot on the front of your computer where you slide in the floppy disk is the mouth of your floppy disk drive. Hard disk drives (called either hard disks, hard drives, fixed disks or sometimes Winchester drives) are usually mounted inside the CPU, out of sight.

Both floppy and hard disks work on the same principal. There are thin wheels of magnetic material that spin under a magnetizing head. The head writes information in its own strange language by magnetizing and demagnetizing designated spots on the wheel. Who cares? Well, you should, because information can be damaged by touching the magnetized portion, or exposing a disk to a magnet.

Above left is a 5 1/4" floppy disk. Above right is the newer 3 1/2" floppy disk. Even though the smaller 3 1/2" disks are made of a firm plastic they are still called floppy disks. Pictured are the disks. The disk drives which read the disks are mounted in the CPU.

Be aware that there are magnets in the few remaining phones that really ring instead of beep. There are magnets that drive your stereo speakers. Even the magnets on a purse button might be enough to ruin something important. Also, if a hard drive is dropped or shaken, the head can crash into the wheel and cause damage.

EXTREME TEMPERATURES WILL WARP THE DISK.

TOUCHING THE MAGNETIC PORTION OF THE DISK CAN LEAVE OIL AND SCRATCHES.

AVOID ALL MAGNETS.

No matter how careful you are, problems with hard disks and floppies can occur without warning. Remember: if something is worth saving once, it is worth saving a second time as a backup. This can be a painful lesson if learned the hard way.

Above are a few "no-no's" when it comes to caring for floppy disks.

Enough DOS to Get You Started

■ What is it?

Though you have heard of DOS you may not be aware that it stands for Disk Operating System. Its name is quite descriptive because DOS is a piece of software that tells the computer how to handle information on the disk drives. DOS also acts as an interpreter, allowing you to talk to the computer in relatively plain language.

Nonetheless, DOS is not smart enough to understand just anything you type. Like a dog, DOS only understands a few basic commands that it has seen before. You can tell your dog to "take a load off," but he won't do anything but tilt his head until you clearly say "Sit!". In the same way, DOS needs certain commands and even those must use the proper format (or syntax) if the computer is to understand your instructions. **DOS commands** are a collection of these specific instructions that you can use to tell the computer what you want it to do.

■ Speaking the Language of DOS

There are a couple terms and concepts that are so fundamental to working with DOS you should fully understand them before you try to learn commands.

Filename (and Extension)

This is simply the name of a file (obvious but important). Since it's just a name, let's apply some Shakespeare, "A rose by any other name would smell as sweet." Yes, it is relevant . . . a file by any other name would work the same. The name has no bearing on what *can* be in a file. The computer does not really care what you name a file—it's just a way for you and the computer to keep your files straight.

A filename can be from one to eight characters long and made up of letters, numbers, or even a few other characters like the dash and apostrophe. Most people use simple words as filenames; words that describe what is in the file.

Extensions are short little appendages that can usually be found on the end of filenames after a period. (MAC users would call them prehensal appendages . . . that's some techno-evolutionary humor that you beginners will understand in a year or so.) Extensions *can* be one to three characters long, but don't have to be there at all.

Though a filename has no real bearing on what can be in a file, computer people have grown fond of using certain extensions on certain types of files. It's a way of letting other computer users know what is probably in the file. Some common extensions are discussed on page 16, under **Using Shareware**.

LAURA.LET

Above is a typical filename. It could be any file, but by the way someone has named it, it is probably a letter to a friend named Laura.

A Capital Idea

You'll notice the above filename example is in all "CAPS" (upper case letters). You can type filenames in either upper or lower case, DOS only looks at what letters are typed, not whether they are upper or lower case. The point is, DOS sees **LAURA.LET** is identical to **laura.let**. In fact, everything done in DOS, even DOS commands, can be entered in upper or lower case without any difference in how DOS processes the command.

Prompt

You already know that prompt means to cue someone, or tell them they're on. In computing, it's the same. DOS will prompt you with the letter of a disk drive followed by the greater than (>) sign, as shown below. (The prompt that your computer cues you with may look slightly different from the one below.

That is because prompts can be customized using the DOS command **prompt**. Customizing your prompt is beyond the scope of these pages, though it is covered thoroughly in your DOS manual.)

A>

A prompt like the one above is your cue that DOS is ready for a command. The letter displayed at the prompt tells you which disk drive is currently your "default drive".

Default Drive

The default drive is the disk drive you are working on. If the prompt reads **A** then your default drive is **A,** your first floppy drive. The default drive is important because your computer, unless otherwise instructed, will look there every time it needs to get or give information.

You can **change your default drive** by entering a new drive letter at the prompt. For example, you are on drive A and you want to switch to drive B (a second floppy drive is most likely called B).

A>B: [ENTER]

To go from drive A to drive B you enter the new drive letter followed by a colon and press the ENTER key.

You should also know that even within the default drive, access to files is narrowed down to just the "root directory," or "subdirectory" you're in.

Root Directory and Subdirectory

DOS allows users to organize files into what can be thought of as individual departments, or directories. Like filenames, this is another tool that DOS gives us humans so we can keep track of our files. Directories can be likened to a tree. Think of the **root directory** as the trunk. The files can be thought of as the individual leaves. Now, imagine a tree with all its thousands of leaves growing directly out of its trunk—what a mess!

Holding the leaves and connected to the trunk are the branches, the subdirectories. By naming your branches or subdirectories, and placing certain files in certain subdirectories, you can keep all your files organized. For example, you might want to create a subdirectory called Letters and keep all your letters there. Like a real tree, subdirectories that branch off the main root directory can have their own smaller branches. Maybe they should be thought of as "sub-subdirectories," but they're simply called subdirectories, too.

Subdirectories are especially useful when working with hard drives. Hard drives have so much more storage space than a floppy disk; you literally could have thousands of files all in the same place. It would be impossible to keep all those files straight unless you use subdirectories. There are a few commands that give you the power to use subdirectories. (In these examples, the sample subdirectory "Letters" is used, though you could substitute anything in its place.)

A>MD LETTERS

A>RD LETTERS

A>CD LETTERS

Above are examples which use the three commands needed to work with subdirectories. The first **MD** *stands for Make Directory. With the command* **MD LETTERS** *given from the A prompt as above, you would create the subdirectory called "Letters" and it would be a branch off the root directory of A. The root directory generally doesn't have a name other than "the root."*

RD LETTERS *would Remove the Directory "Letters" when executed from the root drive. Directories can only be removed with this command when they are empty, when they contain no files. The root directory cannot be removed.*

CD LETTERS *will change your position from the root directory to the subdirectory named "Letters." Now this subdirectory is your "default directory." (Above we defined default drive as the drive you are currently on. Well, default directory is the subdirectory on the default drive that you are currently working in.)*

While subdirectories are a great way to keep files organized, they can also get confusing unless you have some shorthand way of telling DOS where to find your files. Well, there is a way—A:\LETTERS represents the "path" to the "Letters" subdirectory.

Path

A path is set of directions for how to get somewhere or how to find a certain file. Let's say that all your letters to friends are in another subdirectory stemming from the "Letters" subdirectory.

A:\LETTERS\FRIENDS

If you are asked what path to find your letters to friends, you could answer with the above path. No prompt is shown above, only the path itself. It states that your letters to friends are in a subdirectory called Friends, which is in a subdirectory called "Letters," which is off the root directory of A. A path can be linked to a filename to give the exact location of the file; think of the **path and filename** *as the complete, more precise, name for any file.*

A:\LETTERS\FRIENDS\LAURA.LET

Above is the **path and filename** *of the file LAURA.LET in the subdirectory called "Friends," which is in the subdirectory "Letters," which is off the root of A.*

As we move on to DOS commands, paths become important for specifying the right files. Whenever a path is not specified in conjunction with a filename, DOS assumes that the path of the file is the same as the path of the default directory. We'll be looking at examples of this with the DOS commands we are about to learn.

DOS Commands

■ Internal Commands

The only thing your computer hardware knows how to do without the help of software is look for a file called COMMAND.COM on either your hard drive or your A drive depending on your system. COMMAND.COM is an important part of your DOS software because it takes command of the computer upon startup (this process is called "Booting" your computer). As COMMAND.COM takes over the computer, it puts some of the most useful DOS commands into memory so they will always be available. DOS commands that are put into memory upon startup are called internal commands. Here are the most common internal commands.

Dir

Dir will list all the files in a specified directory or subdirectory. The normal directory listing provides you with five columns of information. The first column is the filename, the second column is the extension, the third column tells us the size of the file, the last two columns report the date and time that the file was created.

A>DIR\where

DIR *is the DOS command that can be entered from any prompt.* **Where** *is the path of the directory or subdirectory you want to list.*

A>DIR

When no path is specified, DOS will assume you want to list the default directory. The above command will list the contents of the root directory of A. The contents would be displayed as shown in Figure #1.

Figure #1

A>DIR /W

By adding the "switch" /W, we are requesting a **Wide** *display of the files. In other words, DOS will skip all other information and just list the filenames with extensions, five filenames across instead of stacked one on top of another as usual. You can see many more files in less space by using the /W switch. (Figure #2)*

The /W switch will help you look at more filenames on the screen at one time, but sometimes you need the rest of that file information. If your

Figure #2

directory is so long that it just scrolls off the screen before you have a chance to view it, there is another switch, **/P**, that tells DOS to list all the files one screen at a time. DOS will give you one screen, then wait until you strike a key before listing the rest of the directory.

Copy

This is perhaps the most common and most powerful command you will use in DOS. The copy command allows you to move files from one place to another. Below is the most basic way to understand the proper syntax of the copy command and what information is required when using it.

A>COPY *what where*

COPY *is the DOS command and can be entered from any DOS prompt regardless of where the files you are copying reside.*

What *is the file you wish to copy. This can include the filename and extension. Or it can also be the drive and path of the file. If no path is indicated, DOS will assume that the file is in the default directory. If no path is specified and the file is not in the default directory, DOS will let you know with an error message telling you the file was not found.*

Where *is the final destination for the information you are copying. The destination can be as simple as a different drive letter, or as complex as a new filename under a new path. (The* **where** *of the copy command can even send files to the printer by specifying the destination as* **PRN**.*)*

A>COPY LAURA.LET B:

This simple example of the copy command entered from the A prompt copies the file LAURA.LET, from the root of A to the root of B. Since there is no path with the filename LAURA.LET, DOS simply assumes that LAURA.LET is in the default directory. We know that the default directory is A, as indicated by the DOS prompt.

A>COPY C:\LETTERS\LAURA.LET B:\PERSONAL\DOUGLASS.TXT

Here is a more complex example of how to use the copy command. The file LAURA.LET from the "Letters" subdirectory on the C drive, is to be copied to a file called DOUGLASS.TXT in a subdirectory called "Personal" that is on the B drive. The file will be identical despite its new name. In this example, the subdirectory "Personal" must already exist before the file DOUGLASS.TXT can be copied to it.

B>COPY DOUGLASS.TXT PRN

This use of the copy command will send the file DOUGLASS.TXT to the printer (abbreviated PRN) where it will be printed. A printout of a file is referred to as "hardcopy."

Wildcards: * and ?

If you have ten different files in the root directory of A and you want to copy them all from one place to another, it would take a while to copy them one at a time. DOS allows you to copy many files at once using **wildcards**. Wildcard characters can stand for anything—like the blank tiles in the board game Scrabble.

A>COPY LAURA.?ET B:

The wildcard ? stands for any single character. In the above example, files named LAURA.LET, LAURA.BET, LAURA.GET, or LAURA.VET would all be copied to B.

A>COPY *.LET B:

*The wildcard * stands for any series of characters, not just one wild character but as many as eight. So here DOS would look in the root directory of A for all the files that have the extension .LET as part of their filename. All those files would be copied to the root of B. LAURA.LET would be copied from A, but DOUGLASS.TXT would not because it ends in .TXT and not .LET.*

A>COPY *.* B:

In this example every file in the root directory of A would be copied to the root of B. All files fit the description when wildcards are given for both the filename and extension.

Wildcards are just as useful with other DOS commands. If you plan wisely when naming your files and give similar types of files similar names, then you will be able to use wildcards efficiently with all types of

DOS commands. Here's how wildcards can help you get only the information needed from a directory.

A>DIR C:\LETTERS*.LET

This use of the DOS command Dir will list all the files that have the extension .LET which are in the "Letters" subdirectory, which is found on drive C. This example shows that filename specifications can also be given when using the Dir command.

Del (delete) or Erase

The delete command, abbreviated Del, is the same command as Erase. Either can be used in the same way to get rid of files. We will use Del. You can use the Del command to rid yourself of old files, or delete files after you have copied them to another location.

A>DEL *what*

DEL *is the command that instructs DOS to get rid of whatever follows.* **What** *is the path and filename of the file you wish to delete.*

A>DEL LAURA.LET

The above command would delete the file LAURA.LET from the A drive.

Wildcards can be used with the delete command to get rid of a number of files simultaneously. Del cannot be used to get rid of subdirectories; RD (Remove Directory) is needed for deleting subdirectories.

A>DEL B:LAURA.*

Everything in the root directory of the B drive that has the filename LAURA, regardless of the extension, will be deleted. For example, files LAURA.LET, LAURA.TXT, LAURA.WKS, and even LAURA would all be deleted from this directory if they were there.

A>DEL *.*

You should be careful when using wildcards. This command will permanently erase everything that is on drive A.

Ren (rename)

The rename command, abbreviated Ren, is used to change the name of a file from one name to another. The rename command leaves behind only one file with a new name. (If you wish to create a second file of a different name with the same contents, you should use the copy command.)

A>REN *what newname*

The rename command is first followed by **what** *you want to rename. A path and filename can be used to clearly indicate the exact file you wish to rename. If only a filename is given, DOS will assume that the file is in the default directory. You must also provide the* **newname** *you would like the file changed to.*

Wildcards don't really help at all when it comes to renaming files. Each file in a directory or subdirectory must have a unique name. It wouldn't make sense to be able to change multiple files to the same name using wildcards.

A>REN LAURA.LET DOUGLASS.TXT

This use of the command will give LAURA.LET a new name, DOUGLASS.TXT. Renamed files will continue to reside in the same subdirectory.

■ External Commands

The internal commands explained above are all placed in memory when the computer is turned on. They are placed in memory because they are so commonly used; it's convenient to have them available at all times. External commands, on the other hand, are less frequently used DOS commands that are not placed in memory. There are many external commands and to put them all in RAM would waste too much of your computer's limited memory.

External commands, like internal commands, do something when they are called from a DOS prompt. But with any DOS command, your computer must be able to find it. Internal commands are easy to find, they are in memory; external commands are either on your DOS disk if you are using a floppy-based system, or somewhere on your hard disk, if you have one. Whenever you attempt to execute an external DOS command (or any other program file for that matter) you must be certain that DOS can find the file by providing a path.

You can provide the path to the command file either by placing the proper path at the beginning of the command; by changing the default directory to the directory or subdirectory where the command file resides; or by including the subdirectory where the command file resides in your computer's "path."

A "Path" for Less Resistance

As described earlier, a path is the route to a file. It is perfectly adequate to provide paths for every file or command you work with, but DOS also allows you to program your system with one master path that can include several subdirectories. By **Setting a Path** you are giving your computer a list of different directories that are all to be treated as default directories.

If you don't understand the previous paragraph, don't worry. Setting a permanent path requires more information than we have presented. For our purposes we will assume that you are working with your DOS disk in drive A and that A is your default drive. DOS will always find the external command files it needs on that disk.

Format

All disks must be formatted before trying to write on them. A disk starts out as only a sheet of magnetic material with a hole in the middle. The disk drive can't find its way on all this open space. Formatting the disk is a way of putting up magnetic fences so the disk drive can tell one area from another. You are placing markers on the disk so the disk drive knows where one section of the disk ends and another begins.

Formatting a disk prepares the disk for information storage. That same process will also wipe out any information stored on a disk. Be careful not to format a disk that has valuable information on it.

A>FORMAT *drive*

Format is the DOS command, while **drive** *refers to a drive letter of the disk you want to format. This command does not have anything to do with files, so wildcards are irrelevant. Be aware that you can only format entire disks; individual subdirectories cannot be formatted.*

A>FORMAT B:

With this command you are asking to format the disk that is in drive B. DOS will then tell you to place the disk you want to format into drive B and press [ENTER]. Then DOS will proceed with formatting the disk.

There is one important "switch" you may want to use with the format command and that is the /S. This switch will place the DOS system files onto a disk as it formats it. The DOS system files include COMMAND.COM and other hidden files that are necessary to boot your computer. Once these files are on a disk, that disk can be used to start the computer, regardless of what else you put on that disk.

This is especially handy if you have a floppy-based system (no hard drive) and regularly work with one piece of software. Instead of fumbling with your DOS disk, then putting in your program disk, you could simply format a disk with all the system files on it using the /S switch and then copy all the program files to the same disk. You will have created one disk with both DOS and your favorite program on it. No more disk swapping.

A>FORMAT B:/S

This command will format the disk in drive B as in the earlier example, and it also will transfer all the system files to the newly formatted disk. That newly formatted disk then can be used as a boot disk.

Diskcopy

This external command does more than just copy files, it completely duplicates a disk. Not only file for file, but piece for piece. Everything about one disk is copied over to the other. The new disk doesn't even have to be reformatted when using the diskcopy command because diskcopy even clones the formatting of the original disk.

A>DISKCOPY *original newdisk*

The **Diskcopy** *command is followed by the drive letter of the original disk, then by the drive letter of the disk that is to become the clone. The two disks must be the same type of disk or DOS will give you an error message suggesting that the copy command is what you should be using.*

Diskcopy can accept the same drive letter for both the **original** and the **newdisk**. In such a case, DOS will prompt you to switch disks back and forth between the original and the newdisk as it replicates. If you only have one disk of a certain type, this command is a great way to make copies in one simple step.

A>DISKCOPY A: B:

This use of the command Diskcopy would duplicate the disk in A onto the disk in drive B. For this to work, the disk in A must be the same as the disk in B. Subdirectories cannot be Diskcopied to another subdirectory, only entire disks. Therefore, wildcards are irrelevant.

BASIC Basics

One of the special requirements for running some programs mentioned in this book is "a version of BASIC." Don't let this requirement scare you off—running BASIC programs can be simple. Besides, a version of BASIC is probably already loaded on your computer. The next few paragraphs will show you how to run a BASIC program without knowing a thing about programming.

■ What is a BASIC program?

When the filename of the program you want to run ends with a **.BAS** extension, you have a basic program on your hands (you can see the filenames on a disk by listing the directory with the DOS command DIR). The .BAS ending tells you this file was originally created using a programming language known as BASIC. More importantly, this file still needs the BASIC language to run.

■ Finding a Copy of BASIC

A copy of BASIC is usually included with your DOS files. Get out your DOS disks and place the one labeled *Supplement* in your disk drive. Use the command **DIR/P** to list the directory of that disk one page at a time. There will be many files on the disk, but you're looking for a particular file named either GWBASIC.EXE or BASICA.EXE. Both of these files are versions of the BASIC programming language, however BASICA.EXE only works with true blue IBM machines, while GWBASIC.EXE runs on other PC compatibles.

If you can't find your DOS disks but your computer has a hard drive, your DOS and BASIC files are probably on the hard drive in a subdirectory named **DOS** . Try to locate GWBASIC.EXE or BASICA.EXE there.

If you can't find your DOS disks, or your DOS disks don't include a version of BASIC, get in touch with your local computer dealer or users group. They may be able to help you get a copy. Unfortunately, GWBASIC.EXE and BASICA.EXE are not shareware or public domain so they can't be distributed by PC-SIG.

■ Getting it All Together

In order for your computer to run a BASIC program, it must be able to locate both the .BAS file you're trying to run, and your version of BASIC (GWBASIC.EXE or BASICA.EXE). The easiest way to make sure your computer finds both parts is to put them both on the same disk.

In most cases, you can simply copy your version of BASIC (GWBASIC.EXE or BASICA.EXE) onto the disk that the **.BAS** file is on. For example, PC-SIG Disk #105 PC-Professor (a BASIC tutorial that needs BASIC to run) has plenty of room on the disk to copy your version of BASIC right onto your working copy of the PC- Professor disk. Copy either GWBASIC.EXE or BASICA.EXE to the PC- Professor disk so your version of BASIC and the main .BAS file that runs PC-Professor (named INTRO.BAS) are both on the same disk and ready to be run.

Some PC-SIG disks are so full of programs there isn't enough room to copy GWBASIC.EXE or BASICA.EXE onto the disk itself as in the example above. As an alternative, you should figure out which .BAS file you want to run, copy it onto a blank disk, and then copy GWBASIC.EXE or BASICA.EXE onto that same blank disk. For example, suppose you have PC-SIG Disk #613 Managing Your Money and want to use the program DATEDIST.BAS (one of several programs on this disk) to figure out the distance between two dates in years, months, and days. Copy DATEDIST.BAS to a new blank disk. Then copy your version of BASIC (either GWBASIC.EXE or BASICA.EXE) to that same new disk. Now, both files needed to run the program are on that new disk.

Instead of using a new blank disk, hard drive users can create a new subdirectory on your hard drive, then copy all necessary .BAS files to that subdirectory along with your version of BASIC (GWBASIC.EXE or BASICA.EXE). As long as the .BAS files and your version of BASIC are in the same place, you will have no trouble running the BASIC program using the instructions that follow.

Read "Beginning With Shareware" earlier in this book if you're not sure how to copy a file or create a directory on your hard drive.

■ Starting a BASIC program

Once you've managed to put your .BAS file together with your version of BASIC (cither GWBASIC or BASICA.EXE) the hard part is done. Now all you have to do is go to the disk or directory where you put the two files, and issue a single command. This single command first tells your computer to start your version of BASIC, and then run the .BAS file you indicate.

For example, suppose you copied GWBASIC.EXE onto your PC-Professor disk which is in drive A. You would type the following command at the A prompt and press [Enter] to run the main PC-Professor file named INTRO.BAS:

A:\GWBASIC INTRO

Or if you copied BASICA.EXE onto your PC-Professor disk which is in drive A, you would type this command at the A prompt and press [Enter] to run the main PC-Professor file named INTRO.BAS:

A:\BASICA INTRO

In another example, suppose you copied all the files, including DATEDIST.BAS, from the Managing Your Money disk into a subdirectory named C:\MONEY on your hard drive. Then copied GWBASIC.EXE there too. You would start the program DATEDIST.BAS from the C:\MONEY prompt with this command:

C:\MONEYGWBASIC DATEDIST

It's really that easy! If you follow the examples above, your BASIC programs should start directly.

■ Hints and Tips

Though most BASIC programs will run according to the instruction above, there are a few common snags that might trip you up. Here are quick antidotes to typical problems.

If your BASIC program starts out fine but then bombs with an error message or a "line number" listing, it's possible that the program may need more than just the .BAS file to run properly. It may be looking for additional information in a data file that came with the original disk but you didn't copy to your working disk. If you can tell which data file is missing, add it to the disk or directory where you're running the program and try starting the program again.

If you want to exit a BASIC program while it's running you can either follow any exit instructions given by the program itself, reboot your computer by pressing the [Ctrl], [Alt], and [Delete] keys simultaneously (always a sure-fire method), or press the [Ctrl] and [Scroll Lock] keys simultaneously. This last method will take you out of the BASIC program, but it will return you to the BASIC programming screen instead of DOS.

If you exit the program by pressing [Ctrl]-[Scroll Lock], or if the program simply fails due to an incompatibility, you may find yourself at the BASIC programming screen (an unfamiliar sight with highlighted blocks along the bottom and "OK" above the flashing cursor). If you type the command **SYSTEM** at the cursor, you will return to the familiar DOS prompt where you can try starting the program again.

PC-SIG's technical support line is available to help you through any problems you might encounter while trying to run a BASIC program. Call them at (408)730-9291.

Using Shareware

Okay, you just received your first piece of PC-SIG shareware. You're very anxious to get it up and running, so let's get right to it. PC-SIG has spent considerable time and effort to make it easy for you to find instructions and start the program. Your time can be spent enjoying the program.

■ Making a Backup

Yes, you want to start the program right away, but there is one thing you should do first; make a backup copy. Some programs work by creating data files, or starting some sort of record keeping system linked to your clock, or any number of "self-altering" routines as soon as they are run. You may want to have an unaltered copy of the original program just in case you wish to start over. Besides, there is always the chance that you will accidentally delete or damage something on the disk while using it.

It's always safer to make a backup before you ever run the program. It's usually better to make a backup of a PC-SIG disk using the diskcopy command instead of the copy command. While PC-SIG disks don't contain any hidden files, sometimes they do contain subdirectories that wouldn't be copied with the simple **COPY *.*** command. Refer to the earlier section on DOS for how to use diskcopy.

Store the original in a safe place and only use the backup. This way, if your backup ever fails you can get the original and make a new copy.

■ What's on the Disk

You should start by listing all the files that are on the disk. Put the disk in drive A and list the directory.

A>DIR

Figure #3 is a directory from PC-SIG shareware disk #403, Computer Tutorial.

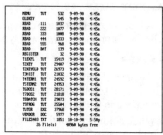

Figure #3

■ PC-SIG GO.BAT's

You'll notice in the above directory listing a file named GO.BAT. PC-SIG provides "GO.BAT's" as a quick and easy way to start nearly every disk in the PC-SIG Library. This file allows you to simply type GO at the DOS prompt and you'll instantly get instructions on printing the documentation and starting the program.

A>GO

A PC-SIG GO.BAT tells you how to start the program and how to print the documentation. (Figure #4) Then the GO.BAT returns you to the DOS prompt where you can do either.

GO.BAT's make PC-SIG Shareware simple to use right away, but a little closer look at what is on the disk may give you a better understanding of the program.

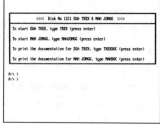

Figure #4

■ Extensions Tell All

When you are ready to dive into a PC-SIG Shareware disk, it is well worth the time to list the directory and look at the file extensions before starting the program. There are a few easily recognizable file extensions that software authors universally use to indicate certain types of files.

■ Text Files

Shareware programs are not distributed with printed documentation—it would be too expensive. But, shareware programs certainly do have documentation. Sometimes hundreds of pages worth. The documentation is in the form of text files.

Text files are simple files that can be sent to your printer so you can print your own documentation, or sent to your screen and read. They can also be called into most wordprocessors or text editors so you can browse through the text, even perform searches electronically.

Almost all text files will be listed in a directory in one of the following forms:

`*.TXT`

`*.DOC`

`README`

`READ.ME`

Files that match the formats above are meant to be read. The author has provided information and "documentation" (instruction manuals) in these types of files. This information will help you understand what the program is and how to use it.

In the directory listing of PC-SIG disk #403, you'll notice a file named FILES403.TXT. PC-SIG puts a file like this on every disk. Inside this file is a description of what programs are on the disk, as well as a listing of every file associated with thc program. With this information you can be sure you have the program you need, and that you have the entire program.

If you wanted to print this or any other text file to your printer, you could use the copy command and name the device PRN (printer) as your destination.

`A>COPY FILES403.TXT PRN`

You also have the option of sending text files to your screen so you can read them without printing them. The DOS command Type will type the text to your screen.

`A>TYPE FILES403.TXT`

If you try the above command on any text file you'll find that the text does go to the screen, but will continue to scroll up and off the screen before you have a chance to read it. There is a way to freeze the screen while you read and, then start it moving again.

While holding down the control key (labeled **Ctrl** on your keyboard), press the **S** key. Pressing the two simultaneously will freeze the screen. Pressing any key will start the screen again. It can be stopped as many times as necessary. There is no way to scroll backward within DOS. Using the **Ctrl-C** combination instead of the **Ctrl-S** combination will break you out (stop the file from being typed to the screen) and return you to the DOS prompt.

There are other ways to use text files. Most wordprocessors (probably including the one you now use) can import text files and work with them in the same way they work with any letter you write. Features such as searching and browsing can be used with the text files found on PC-SIG Shareware disks. (See your wordprocessor manual for exact instructions on importing a DOS text, or ASCII text file.)

■ Command and Executable Files

Now that you've read about a program, you are ready to start working with it. There are two types of files that can be used to start a program: Command and Executable files. These are files that actually do something when their filename (without the extension) is typed at a DOS promt. You can tell these files because they end in two common extensions.

`*.COM`

`*.EXE`

You can tell right away that these are command and executable files by their extensions.

If you look once again at our directory listing for PC-SIG disk #403, you'll see one program file (a file that ends in .EXE) in the directory. Some programs may have more than one command or executable file in the directory. You can usually tell by the filename (TUTOR.COM) which one is the main program file.

`A>TUTOR`

By typing this command, which was noticed in the directory listing of PC-SIG disk #403, the program will start working. If you happen to type in a command filename that isn't the main program, don't worry, you'll probably just get an error message.

■ Batch Files

Like command files, a batch file gets something going. Batch files can be recognized in a directory listing because they always carry the file extension .BAT. The PC-SIG GO.BAT's are common examples of batch files.

A batch file is actually no more than a series of commands that are executed one right after another. Someone else puts the commands into a batch file and names the batch file. Then, when you execute the batch file by typing the batch file's name (without the .BAT extension) at a DOS prompt, all of the commands that someone else programmed will be executed one after another. It is a way of saving you the trouble of typing the same series of intricate commands over and over again.

A>GO

This command would execute the batch file named GO.BAT. Some software authors use batch files to start their programs instead of .EXE or .COM files. When you are looking at a directory listing to find the right command to start a program, be on the lookout for .BAT files as well as .COM and .EXE files.

You may want to learn how to make your own batch files, especially if you find yourself typing the same series of commands over and over again. (See your DOS manual for additional information.)

■ Program Installation and Setup

Most PC-SIG Shareware programs are ready to be started as soon as you get them. However, there are a few programs that require some setup or installation before they will work the way you want them to. Generally the PC-SIG GO.BAT program will alert you to required installation.

If you are working with a hard drive, you may want to install the program to your hard drive for faster and easier operation. Read the documentation to find out if there are any special installation instructions for running from a hard drive. With most programs you simply make a subdirectory on your hard drive and copy all the files of the program into that subdirectory. Then you can go into that subdirectory and start the program just as you would from floppy. (See subdirectories in the earlier section on DOS.)

■ Troubleshooting

If you put in your PC-SIG disk, type the right command, and nothing happens, there are a few things you can do to try to determine what is wrong.

You should be aware of system requirements before you use a program. Many programs in The PC-SIG Library require color graphics, over 256K memory, or a hard drive. If the program calls for such extras and your system doesn't have them, then the program may not run on your system. Don't worry, no program will damage a system that does not meet the system requirements, it just won't work.

Your computer may answer your command with an error message instead of starting the program. If your computer responds with "Bad command or file name," it is telling you that it could not find the file you requested. First, check your spelling of the command—close doesn't count. Next, make sure that the command file is in your default directory, or that the proper path is provided.

If your computer gives you an "Error reading drive A" message, you may have a bad disk. First, be sure the disk is inserted properly and the door on your disk drive is closed. Quite a few calls to our technical support staff are resolved by having the user turn the disk over and reinsert it. Once in a while, a disk is defective. If everything else is working and your computer still can't read the disk, then send the disk back to PC-SIG with a letter and we'll send you a new copy.

If you have a problem that you can't solve, feel free to call our technical support line at (408)730-9291. PC-SIG technicians are especially helpful at getting you up and running with a new piece of software.

■ Programs for Beginners

The PC-SIG Library has many programs for beginners. Computer Tutorial, PC-SIG disk #403, is just one example of beginning tutorials. There are a number of different programs that will help you learn to use DOS commands.

If you want to learn BASIC, Pascal, C, or other programming languages, there are disk-based tutorials on all of these subjects. Interactive instruction is also available for popular software packages such as Lotus 1-2-3 and WordPerfect.

The PC-SIG Library also contains great applications such as spreadsheets, databases, wordprocessors, and utilities. Since they're shareware, you can try before you buy. If you are curious about a certain type of software, try it through PC-SIG.

Below is a list of programs recommended for beginners. Some are instructional, while others are recommended because they are easy for beginners to understand and use. Remember, the best way to learn about computers is to use them. Good Luck!

Galaxy Lite — A wordprocessor.

AsEasyAs — A spreadsheet.

File Express — A database.

PC-Deskteam — A desktop organizer.

Fastbucks — A home checkbook management program.

TUTOR.COM — A computer introduction.

PC-Learn — A computer introduction.

PC-Chess — Chess on your computer.

Nethack — An adventure game.

PC-Fastype — A typing tutor.

Pushbutton — A menu program.

Amy's First Primer — Children's games.

Crossword Creator — Create crosswords on your computer.

THE ENCYCLOPEDIA OF
SHAREWARE

Accounting, Billing

DAYO POS (Point of Sale) ✍   *by TJS Lab*

DAYO POS (Point of Sale) is a billing and invoicing application for any size business. It is the DAYO module that permits you to invoice out your products while keeping an accurate record of all your sales. Features include: multiuser (i.e., Novell), registers, quote interface (to DAYO Quotes), templates back orders, data entry validation, cash drawers (serial or parallel), databases are dBase™ compatible, HP laser special invoices, passwords (with DAYO Passwords), many reports, and much more!

DAYO is a collection of multiuser business applications that provide a means of managing inventory, purchasing, invoicing, customers, vendors, sales and more... All DAYO products are multiuser, designed to work on a Microcomputer (PC) Based Local Area Network (LAN), like Novell™. They can, however, work as a standalone running on a single PC. See the Network Software & Utilities section of the "Encyclopedia of Shareware" for a complete listing of all the Dayo modules.

(PC-SIG Disk#'s 2402, 2403)

Special Requirements: *640K RAM, a hard drive, and DOS 3.3.*
Author Registration: *$25.00*
➤*ASP Member.*

DAYO Price Book ✍   *by TJS Lab*

DAYO PRICE BOOK is a system of creating and maintaining specialized pricing for your customers/clients. Special printouts (price books/catalog) may be printed to a standard printer, or to a Hewlett Packard LaserJet or compatible. It requires DAYO INVENTORY and DAYO POS (Point of Sale) programs/databases. Customers are invoiced (with DAYO POS) using the price in the inventory database or with one of the special price book methods: fixed, margin, or list discount.

Customers are invoiced (with DAYO POS), using the price in the inventory database (INV.DBF), or with one of the special Price Book methods:

Fixed: Fixed Price for a Unique Item + Customer (1st Priority); Margin: "Cost Plus" (2nd Priority); List Discount: Discount off the List/Retail Price (3rd Priority)

(PC-SIG Disk# 2404)

Special Requirements: *640K RAM, a hard drive, and DOS 3.3.*
Author Registration: *$25.00*
➤*ASP Member.*

Fast Invoice Writer ✍   *by H&P Software*

FAST INVOICE WRITER is just what the small businessman ordered. A winner for everyone from landlords to health professionals!

This program provides invoices, purchase orders, requisitions, or any document similar in format to an invoice. Compute taxes or bill by the hour — the program does all the calculations.

Produce a numbered, professional-looking document in about 60 seconds and print as many copies as you want. Then print your mailing labels and inserts for 10-inch window envelopes. Your firm's name, address, and phone number are printed on the invoice in large letters. Taxes and shipping charges are handled. The program contains a customer database routine and cashbook file for printing periodic summaries.

(PC-SIG Disk# 1147)

Fast Invoice Writer (PC-SIG Disk#1147)

Special Requirements: *512K RAM, and DOS 2.11 or greater.*
Author Registration: *$39.95*
➤*ASP Member.*

Fast Statement Writer ✍   *by H&P Software*

FAST STATEMENT WRITER creates billing statements for your business in a quick and orderly fashion.

       ✍ = Updated Program
☆ = New Program

In about 60 seconds, FAST STATEMENT WRITER turns out a numbered, professional-looking statement and prints as many copies as you want. Then it prints mailing labels and payment return stubs. It also prints your firm's name, address and phone number on the statement in expanded or condensed characters.
(PC-SIG Disk# 1216)
Special Requirements: *384K RAM.*
Author Registration: *$29.95*
➤*ASP Member.*

GIST ✍ by *TypeRight Corporation*

If your small business invoices all your sales and uses an outside accounting firm, GIST may make your life easier and save you money. GIST's purpose is two-fold. First, it makes it easy to invoice sales and bill your customers. Second, it captures your sales information in a manner that your accountant will find easy to use. This makes you money through better control of your Accounts Receivables and minimizing your accounting fees. In addition to keeping Accounts Receivables and preparing your sales information for your accountant, GIST provides a great deal of very useful business information.

The following are just some of GIST's features:
❑ Shows customer's last sale date and total amount spent
❑ Prints a customer telephone directory
❑ Prints two customer address directories
❑ Prints customer mailing labels
❑ You can use handwritten or computer-generated invoices
❑ Prints Accounts Receivable statements with matching mailing labels
❑ Prints a list of invoices with totals for time period, salesperson, customer, or sales category
(PC-SIG Disk# 2466)
Special Requirements: *512K RAM. A hard drive is recommended.*
Author Registration: *$69.00*

Invoicer with Accounts Receivable by *Miccasoft, Inc.*

Designed for companies that sell products or services to a number of accounts, INVOICER quickly cranks out custom invoices, statements and overdue notices. Track billings and sales activities, maintain a journal of your customers and a list of your company's stock or service items, and produce a variety of reports, including aging. Invoices are automatically posted to Accounts Receivable (included with this program) using either the open-item or balance-forward system, and taxes and finance charges are calculated for you. An installation program makes it easy to put INVOICER on your hard drive.
(PC-SIG Disk# 1348)
Special Requirements: *None.*
Author Registration: *$59.50.*

Micro Register ✍ by *Micro Methods*

MICRO REGISTER is a point-of-sale and invoicing program designed to automate a retail or service-related business. MICRO REGISTER can be set up for many different types of business applications. Print invoices for customers, statements for charged sales or services, and even generate price quotations.

The program keeps track of inventory and customer account information and gives you the option of using a salesperson file that will automatically give you total commissions earned by each salesperson. Income is recorded on a daily, monthly, and year-to-date basis. These totals can be printed at any time and have password protection.

MICRO REGISTER produces many printed reports such as inventory item lists, item below reorder level, customer and sales personnel list, and will print price labels for your inventory. MICRO REGISTER can hold 65,000 inventory item numbers, 65,000 customer accounts, and 100 salespeople in its database.
(PC-SIG Disk# 1806)
Special Requirements: *A hard drive, 80-column dot-matrix printer.*
Author Registration: *$75.00*

PCBilling
by Bradley D. Strausbaugh

Free yourself from some of the necessary clerical tasks of running a small business with PCBILLING.

Using a simple data entry screen, PCBILLING prompts you to enter billing information — who your clients are and what they are being billed for, and then prints their invoices. Once an invoice is sent, PCBILLING remembers it. If payment is not received within 30 days, it automatically prints a past-due notice. If there is no payment after 60 days, a delinquent notice is printed.

Instruct PCBILLING to report on outstanding bills or summarize receipts, receivables, or bad debts.

PCBILLING is menu-driven for ease of use and comes with a set of demonstration files to assist you in getting started.

(PC-SIG Disk# 2255)

Special Requirements: *Standard continuous-feed paper printer.*
Author Registration: *$25.00*

▼ ▼ ▼

Accounting, Checkbook Management — Business

PC-Check
by Peninsula Software, Inc.

A menu-driven financial system for a small business or professional office, as well as for personal use. Why hire a bookkeeper when you can do it yourself?

PC-CHECK provides maintenance, with check-writing capabilities. It can handle multiple checkbooks and assign up to 78 payees and 100 ledger accounts. Sort data files, find payees, print checks, track income tax deductions, list data by month, quarter, payee or ledger account. Automatically assign the ledger account number when an assigned payee is selected.

Let PC-CHECK take the mystery and drudgery out of financial control and put you back in charge — where you belong!

(PC-SIG Disk# 275)

Special Requirements: *Two floppy drives.*
Author Registration: *$35.00*

PFAS (Personal Financial Accounting System) ✍
by PC Soft-E

PERSONAL FINANCIAL ACCOUNTING SYSTEM (PFAS) is a small business checkbook manager to make bank reconciliation much faster and easier. PFAS provides the necessary information to get through any bank reconciliation statement. It can handle 1000 transactions for each account for a full calendar year. An outstanding feature lets you configure a customized chart of accounts to properly track your expenditures. This is a strong plus at tax time.

PFAS has full edit, insert, and delete features. The current bank balance and true account balance are posted at the top of the screen. Issue date-specified reports to the screen and/or printer. Search and list transactions to screen only, or printer, by any whole or partial "issued to" name, by date, or by check number.

The screens look very similar to many dBASE programs in their style of screen prompting. As a result, PFAS offers good, clear-cut instructions to get any beginning user off the ground quickly.

(PC-SIG Disk#'s 2475, 2476)

Special Requirements: *Two drives.*
Author Registration: *$25.00*

▼ ▼ ▼

Accounting, Checkbook Management — Home

Bank Account Manager ✍
by SupremeSoft

BANK ACCOUNT MANAGER lets you keep track of all your bank accounts. It is intended for novice users who want to balance their checkbooks and/or keep track of up to ten active accounts. Use special codes to describe different types of accounts, such as checking, interest, savings, etc. BANK ACCOUNT MANAGER's interface is easy-to-use and menu-driven, with on-line Help. Extensive documentation is provided for reference. Get reports on account number, outstanding checks, reconciled checks, type of transaction, transaction amounts, and individual checks. A pop-up calculator is included to help with calculations.

(PC-SIG Disk# 1134)

Special Requirements: *None.*
Author Registration: *$55.00*

Bank Statement Tamer ✍   *by NursePerfect Software*

BANK STATEMENT TAMER provides a menu-driven, headache-free way to balance your checkbook against your bank statement. Step-by-step, you are led through the mechanics of how to arrive at the same ending balance as your bank. Avoid overdrawn accounts or happily discover that the bank actually goofed! It does happen!

Verify balances from the previous month, find checks still out, and mark off paid checks, deposits and other credits/debits. These values are entered into the program, a running balance is calculated and displayed, showing any difference between your register balance and the adjusted bank statement balance. Included is a feature that can help save you hours cleaning up your checkbook register. It searches through your checkbook entries and locates where you made any arithmetic error(s).

(PC-SIG Disk# 1435)

Special Requirements: *None.*
Author Registration: *$5.95*

BankBook   *by Atlanta Ideas, Inc.*

A truly easy-to-use checkbook manager — really intuitive. BANKBOOK was designed to make the management of your home finances easy and automated in a way that doesn't require an accountant to understand.

BANKBOOK makes the presentation of your home finances look just like your checkbook entries, and adds automated support for bill payment and budget analysis.

❑ Print checks on your PC printer
❑ Enter checks you have handwritten
❑ Enter ATM (automated teller) and EFT (electronic funds transfer) transactions
❑ Enter deposits from a variety of sources
❑ Go back in time to enter checks you wrote over the past several months to set up a history of spending trends
❑ Define a list of bills that you pay each month so they will be printed automatically on the proper date
❑ Associate each check with a spending category so you can divide your expenses into meaningful groups for later analysis
❑ Print reports and view displays of spending trends in various ways to see YTD spending patterns or patterns over other periods of time

(PC-SIG Disk# 1911)

Special Requirements: *512K RAM.*
Author Registration: *$15.00*

Cash Control   *by Adrian-Thomas Developments Inc.*

CASH CONTROL simplifies your home financial records by managing your accounts in the same manner as your standard checkbook register. Enter transactions from checking, savings or charge accounts, balance your account with your bank statement, remind yourself when payments are due, and prepare reports based on your recorded transactions. An easy to follow interface and good documentation make this program great for home use.

(PC-SIG Disk# 1966)

Special Requirements: *320 K RAM*
Author Registration: *$29.95 (US), $34.95 (Canadian)*
➤*ASP Member.*

CCI Home Budget   *by Joseph McMaster*

CCI HOME BUDGET is a menu-driven program to help you and your family monitor and control common everyday household income and expenditures. Make financial decisions without massive number-crunching.

Some of the helpful features included in CCI HOME BUDGET:

❑ 96 user-defined categories such as food, housing, utilities, etc.

❏ 16 transaction types such as credit, cash, check, refund, etc.
❏ 10 user-defined accounts in savings, checking, stocks, etc.
❏ 24 pre-defined common entries for faster posting
❏ Custom/automatic posting of paychecks to various categories
❏ Custom entry-sorting for bank reconciliation, trends, etc.
❏ Individual/automatic entry group editing
❏ Custom budget totals monthly, quarterly, annually, etc.
❏ Custom monthly totals in savings, utilities, automobile, etc.
❏ Prints entries, monthly totals and budget totals.

Track your expenditures and use the data you amass to analyze just where you and your family are financially.

(PC-SIG Disk# 1864)

Special Requirements: *None.*
Author Registration: *$25.00*

Charge Account Management
by M.P. Data

CHARGE ACCOUNT MANAGEMENT provides an easy and enjoyable way to manage all of your charge account records. This program determines your charged expenses by category and provides valuable accounting reports. Menus guide you through entering and maintaining charge account transactions. Each transaction can consist of charges, payments, or interest.

CHARGE ACCOUNT MANAGEMENT provides many valuable reports. Reports can be generated for one category, charges, payments, interest, or all categories for a particular date or a range of dates. Full editing functions are supported for all transaction fields. The program is menu-driven, fully documented, and provides an on-line Help facility. CHARGE ACCOUNT MANAGEMENT can support a maximum of 3000 transactions if the transaction data is kept on a separate disk, 2000 transactions if the program and the transaction data are on the same disk.

(PC-SIG Disk# 1167)

Special Requirements: *None.*
Author Registration: *$25.00*
➤*ASP Member.*

Check-King ☆
by Rickenbacker Software

Not just another pretty face, CHECK-KING combines power and simplicity in a practical, no-frills product. Convert your checkbook into a database, with minimal data entry. Keep track of all checking transactions, while easily balancing your checkbook against monthly bank statements.

Unlike a regular checkbook, CHECK-KING will automatically perform all calculations and produce a variety of reports for your review. Define up to 20 expense categories with up to 20 common payees for your checks. As each check is written, CHECK-KING automatically tracks the next check number. Simply enter the expense category (if any), the date, the payee, and the amount. There is no field to write comments about each check. Deposits and cash withdrawals can be entered. Reports of your checking transactions can be produced by a specifying a date range, checking amount, checking payee, expense category, or outstanding transactions. CHECK-KING always lets you know how much your balance is (or isn't).

CHECK-KING is for people who want to avoid the hassles of a regular checkbook, but still need an easy way to balance and reconcile all their checking transactions. If you don't need split checking, check printing and a tie-in to other accounts, this may be the perfect checkbook program for you.

(PC-SIG Disk# 2707)

Special Requirements: *No special registration.*
Author Registration: *$20.00*

The Checkbook
by Practical Solution

Tired of manually balancing your checkbook and trying to keep track of your charge accounts and budgets? Let THE CHECKBOOK free you from this drudgery. It's a menu-driven money management system designed for family or small business usage where the accounting system is based on checking accounts. The maximum amount of money that can be handled is $999,999.99.

✎ = Updated Program
☆ = New Program

Select checking accounts or budgets, load another account, reconcile statements, print checks, search a file, or use the on-screen financial calculator. The financial calculator provides four valuable financial tools. Calculate monthly loan payments, display/print amortization schedules, project future value of deposits, and calculate withdrawals from annuities.

All current transactions and budgets are maintained and manipulated in memory.

(PC-SIG Disk# 2238)

Special Requirements: *None.*
Author Registration: *$10.00*

Checkbook Management
by M.P. Data

CHECKBOOK MANAGEMENT is a complete checkbook management system which takes the check register one step further while helping you to maintain your budget. It's good for personal and small business checking accounts.

Record all forms of checking account transactions, including bank charges, ATM deposits and withdrawals, and interest. CHECKBOOK MANAGEMENT writes checks, but can also reconcile bank statements with a variety of reports on itemized transactions and periodic summaries. Keep up to 3000 transactions on floppies, or an unlimited number if you use a hard disk.

Establish budget categories and assign each transaction item to a budget classification. This flexible program lets you change these designations as needed. At last, you'll be able to find out just where it all goes!

(PC-SIG Disk#'s 393, 2049)

Special Requirements: *320K RAM, two floppy drives or a hard drive.*
Author Registration: *$35.00*
➤*ASP Member.*

CheckBooks & Budgets Plus
by Digital Processes

This disk has a full-featured checkbook database, check printing, and budgeting program to keep track of your personal checking and savings accounts with ease. CHECKBOOKS & BUDGETS PLUS helps you automatically set aside a portion of your income into each different category in your budget. The budgeting section of the program is completely flexible, letting you move budgeted funds from account to account at will.

Features include: an easy-to-use, windowed, menu-driven, checkbook and budgeting system; full multicolored displays with pop-up windows for easy readability; optional printing of industry-standard checks, built-in Help menu system; instant hot key listings at any time from anywhere in the program; data-input editing and error checking, up to 180 accounts (120 for expenses; 60 for income); and up to 192,000 check-register entries (limited by disk space available). It uses keyed index files for quick data storage and retrieval and provides multiple format listings to screen, printer, files or print spooler. It also makes financial reports, automatically balances your check register, quickly reconciles your check register with your monthly bank statement, and makes financial and loan calculations. The program can also exit to a DOS shell.

(PC-SIG Disk# 1126)

Special Requirements: *384K RAM.*
Author Registration: *$25.00*

Checkbooks and Budgets
by Digital Processes

CHECKBOOKS AND BUDGETS is the ideal household finance program for you, whether you live alone or with a family of 10 or more.

It is versatile, multi-featured, and is a universally useful program. It not only lets you keep close and careful track of your personal checking accounts, but also automatically sets aside portions of your income into different categories in your budget.

The budgeting portion of the program is completely flexible, and lets you move budgeted funds from account to account at will.

FEATURES:

❏ Easy to use, windowed, menu-driven checkbook and budgeting system
❏ Optional printing of industry-standard checks
❏ Built-in Help menu system
❏ Data input editing and error-checking

❑ Up to 180 accounts — 120 for expenses and 60 for income
❑ Up to 65,535 check register entries (limited by disk space)
❑ Keyed index files used for quick data storage and retrieval
❑ Multiple formatted listings to screen or printer
❑ Financial reports made, including bar graphs
❑ Automatic balancing
❑ Quick and easy bank statement reconciliation system
❑ Financial and loan calculations
(PC-SIG Disk# 735)

Special Requirements: *None.*
Author Registration: *$15.00*

Checkease
by Softwarr

CHECKEASE is an electronic checkbook that functions like a personal finance manager for the everyday tedious checkbook accounting details. CHECKEASE is fully menu-driven and intuitive to operate, with very little need to refer to printed documentation. First establish an account (maximum of 18), which consists of bank name, address, etc., and account balance. Then select one of several options to perform against that account. Write checks or make deposits and the account balance will be automatically adjusted. Mark checks as a tax item for use in calculating your yearly taxes. Search for past checks and even void invalid checks. Deposit slips listing all of your deposits can be printed.

CHECKEASE has a bill paying feature that will automatically print out the monthly bills that need to be paid. When you establish an account, enter your monthly bills, creditor name, payment amount, account balance, etc., and CHECKEASE will maintain these personal account balances as you write checks for payments on these accounts. Various reports can also be printed, such as a listing of bills due and bills paid, a listing of all checks and deposits, a listing of outstanding checks and deposits, and a listing of tax category items.
(PC-SIG Disk# 1677)

Special Requirements: *None.*
Author Registration: *$25.00*

CheckMate
by CTech

Keep an accurate account of your personal finances — without all the hassle. It records and maintains your checking and charge transactions while giving you full editing capabilities at your fingertips. It sorts and prints reports, searches for selected items, helps you reconcile your statements, and even prints your checks for you. CHECKMATE can also print checks and reports in any of three pitches, and reports can be printed in two different layouts.

CHECKMATE is very intuitive. It has a user's guide and built-in, context-sensitive Help menus.
(PC-SIG Disk# 784)

Special Requirements: *None.*
Author Registration: *$29.95*
➤*ASP Member.*

CHEKLIST SYSTEM
by Logic and Systems Design

A simple system for maintaining bank account records for the home that provides the functions you need to keep your bank-related information accurate and up-to-date.

Track up to ten bank accounts with 1000 entries, or transactions. Maintain ledger accounts, draw instant balances, bank statement reconciliations, and flexible search and sort options.

Convenient to use, this checkbook manager provides thorough recordkeeping for today's harried householder.
(PC-SIG Disk# 397)

Special Requirements: *None.*
Author Registration: *$35.00*

Cheque-It-Out

by Hooper International, Inc.

Quicker than QUICKEN, more intuitive than INTUIT, CHEQUE-IT-OUT is the choice for everyone who wants to do more than just balance their checkbooks. Here at last is a complete personal bookkeeping system that doesn't expect you to be an accountant to use it. Nor does it treat you like a child in its well thought-out explanations of how to keep track of your finances, balance the books and generate impressive statements of net worth, profit and loss, etc., — guaranteed to impress your banker or accountant.

The double-entry financial system creates financial reports, and tracks income and expenses, assets, liabilities and budgets. It prints checks, both standard pin-fed and individual personal checks. Easy-to-follow menus and context-sensitive pop-up Help screens guide you along. The optional sound effects actually make doing your books fun! More importantly, this is a program that puts you back in charge of your own finances — teaching you what you need to know to manage your money yourself!

(PC-SIG Disk#'s 1559, 1560)

Special Requirements: *448K RAM, one high-density floppy, or two 360K floppies.*

Author Registration: *$49.95; includes a manual and free unlimited technical support.*

➤*ASP Member.*

Cheque-It-Out (PC-SIG Disk#'s 1559, 1560)

CheX

by Rich Young

CHEX is a bookkeeping program for balancing checks, credit cards, and savings accounts. The program looks and feels just like the recording section in your own checkbook. For each item or check you write, you enter the date, check number, whether it is a debit or credit, who the item is written to, a short note, and a category code. As the amount for each check is entered, the program will keep a running total of your bank statement.

CHEX is easy to use because all information is entered and displayed in a list divided into columns on the screen. At any time, you may sort the checkbook by date, allowing you to enter checks in any order you please. Balance the checkbook at the press of a button. CHEX can print an individual check, the entire checkbook, or a financial graph and total for the last 60 months. CHEX will allow you to customize the standard print format for your own checks. Continuous forms are not required. Export the checkbook information into LOTUS 1-2-3. CHEX has on-line, context-sensitive Help, password and encryption protection, and an automatic Save feature which activates after a specified period of time with no input from the keyboard.

(PC-SIG Disk# 2015)

Special Requirements: *None.*

Author Registration: *$20.00*

CK System

by David M. Alexander

Use this personal and household financial management program to keep a close eye on income and expenses. You worked hard to get it — know what you're doing with it!

CK tracks your cashflow and financial obligations in checkbook form and prints checks and many types of reports. Repeating checks can be printed each month by changing the check number and date and re-printing the checks. Keep an orderly and accurate check register/deposit record. Prepare a month-by-month year-end summary of all your income and expenses for up to nine separate accounts. Draw up bar charts on income/expenses. Detailed documentation is provided for the new user.

(PC-SIG Disk# 462)

Special Requirements: *None.*

Author Registration: *$25.00.*

Exacct

by John P. Gangwisch

Monitor your finances and know where you are with EXACCT, a no-frills aid to financial control.

EXACCT records and keeps a running total of all your financial transactions and allows for flagging groups of transactions to perform various operations. EXACCT is functional, yet easy to use, and can be used for checking/savings/credit accounts, business income and expenses, and loan payments.

(PC-SIG Disk# 1306)

Special Requirements: *None.*
Author Registration: *$15.00*

Exchequer
by Left Coast Software

This checkbook program is designed primarily for home users and small businesses wishing to automate and simplify the process of paying their bills.

EXCHEQUER avoids the complexities of most small accounting programs, yet provides many features which support small business accounting. It also offers powerful and flexible reporting capabilities. Any part of the check register can be printed in chronological order, sorted by category, or sorted by payee. List all transactions in a single category or to/from a single party. EXCHEQUER even prints an income statement, and any report can be sent to a printer, the screen, or a file.

Features:

❑ Pay all of your regular monthly bills with one keystroke per check
❑ Looks and works just like a regular checkbook register
❑ Works with virtually all types of continuous-feed checks
❑ Supports an unlimited number of accounts
❑ Store up to 4000 transactions
❑ Assign each transaction to one of 255 user-defined categories.
❑ Reporting functions allow the user to sort the check register by category, making tax preparation a breeze!
❑ Offers ten different report types which facilitate record keeping and expense analysis
❑ Handle transaction amounts up to $99,999.99 and register balances up to $999,999.99 or down to -$99,999.99. The maximum expenditures or deposits to any single category can be as high as $999,999.99.

(PC-SIG Disk# 1786)

Special Requirements: *None.*
Author Registration: *$15.00*

ExpressCheck
by Expressware Corporation

EXPRESSCHECK has a simple goal — to help you manage your checking accounts. Without EXPRESSCHECK, you can either guess at where you spent all your money, or you can spend long hours with a calculator. With EXPRESSCHECK, find out in only a few seconds.

How much do you spend each month on food, car payments, electricity, gas, and entertainment? How much have you given in tax-deductible donations? Every check and deposit can be recorded with various user-defined budget codes. This makes it possible for you to see at any time during the year where you stand in regard to your spending.

Entering checks and deposits is fast and enjoyable. Enter recurring payments with two keystrokes. The screens look the same as real checks, deposit slips, and check registers, so you'll find the program extremely easy to learn and use. You can define budget codes on the fly, and windows show all currently-defined codes.

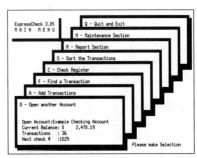

ExpressCheck (PC-SIG Disk#'s 1057, 2085)

EXPRESSCHECK even prints the checks for you on any kind of tractor-fed forms.

Print predefined reports that give you monthly or year-to-date totals for any or all budget codes, a check register with running balance, all transactions that have not yet cleared the bank, checks or deposits that included certain budget codes, or all checks made out to certain payees. Many of the figures that go on your tax return are at your fingertips.

(PC-SIG Disk#'s 1057, 2085)

Special Requirements: *320K RAM.*
Author Registration: *$34.95*
➤*ASP Member.*

✍ = Updated Program
☆ = New Program

FamTRACK
by Thomas W. Mcmaster

FAMTRACK is an effective management tool designed to make the unpleasant task of family budgeting — if not fun — survivable and profitable. It will accommodate every type of financial transaction common to modern families.

Produce screen or printed records of monthly and year-to-date performance in 40 different budget categories for both husband and wife. Handle as many as 20 separate financial accounts — checking, savings, bank cards or charge accounts — and reconcile each account at statement time. The payment activity for as many as 21 payees or income sources can also be tracked.

Menu-driven FAMTRACK can automatically reconcile your checkbook at any time during the month or whenever bank statements are issued. A database of all financial transactions is maintained and there is an automatic year-end closing procedure and data storage.

One of the most useful features of FAMTRACK is the loans calculator. You can easily calculate mortgage amortization, future values, present values, interest rates, payoff times, effective annual rates, and doubling times for any compounding period. These tools are extremely valuable in comparing different credit options when purchasing homes, automobiles, furniture, or other major items.

Take real financial control and plan your future.

(PC-SIG Disk# 889)

Special Requirements: *None.*
Author Registration: *$19.95*

FastBucks
by Software Expressions

FASTBUCKS is a menu-driven home-finance program that is easy to understand and operate.

FASTBUCKS supports up to 25 accounts each in checking, savings, charge accounts, and 25 cash sheets. With each account, you can update, list, reconcile, balance, or edit a record. List an account by month, year, or expense category. The program offers a graphic illustration of your expenses for a certain year, and shows your overall average expenditures.

Account listings can be displayed or printed. When listing a checking account and overall balance, the program will immediately show you if a check has bounced by displaying its line in inverse print. Each line gives the date, description, whether or not it is a credit or debit, and total balance to date.

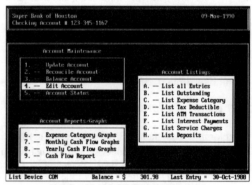

FastBucks (PC-SIG Disk#'s 855 et al.)

Use the recursive budget model to create a workable family budget. Calculate total income, for both the pay period and the year, and compute your "disposable" income. Allot transactions to your various expense categories or to your savings account.

There is a financial calculation section to calculate item depreciation, investments and loan information, plus a complete loan amortization generator.

Change initialization parameters for display type, printer, drive, data file path, and expense categories as desired. FASTBUCKS presently supports 141 printers and a user configuration, if your printer is not presently supported.

(PC-SIG Disk#'s 855, 1296, 7063)

Special Requirements: *Two floppy drives. Hard drive recommended.*
Author Registration: *$47.75*
➤*ASP Member.*

Finance + Plus
by Plano Computer Sales

Want to plan your financial future? FINANCE + PLUS can provide you with a complete financial planning system.

FINANCE + PLUS is everything you need to plan and track your personal finances, both present and future. An extensive budgeting system is available that can handle many types of income, earnings, IRA/Keogh, savings, etc. Track charge and savings accounts and plan savings goals.

FINANCE + PLUS lets you list registers for several checking accounts and print individual checks or batches of checks. Detailed transactions for taxes are maintained along with line entries for IRS schedules. Keep a detailed list of your assets, track capital gains and losses, record your investments, and evaluate investment performance.

With FINANCE + PLUS, you can keep your personal balance sheet, project cash flow, and build your own financial portfolio.

(PC-SIG Disk# 1873)

Special Requirements: *512K RAM, and two floppy drives or a hard drive.*
Author Registration: *$24.95*

Genesis: Series II
by Signature Software, Inc.

Turn your computer into a check-writing machine with GENESIS: SERIES II. It's an easy-to-use home check writing program. So simple, in fact, that anyone who now maintains a checkbook by hand already knows the basics. The display screens even look just like your checkbook — right down to the names on the checks.

GENESIS automatically does all the calculations that you now do by hand, but it won't make any mistakes. Balance your checkbook in a fraction of the usual time, and if you're out of balance, it will help you find and correct the error. Print your checks, configured to your specific printer. You don't even need special checks — the check on the screen will look similar to the one you are using.

Keep track of tax deductions or anything else that you want to categorize. Search for a check written months ago with only the barest of information, and then get a report on the findings. Checks that you write to the same companies over and over will be kept in memory, ready to be used at the push of a key. Tired of addressing envelopes? GENESIS does it for you. To keep prying eyes out, give GENESIS a password and your checkbook is locked. There is also multiple checkbook support.

(PC-SIG Disk#'s 2242, 2243)

Special Requirements: *CGA.*
Author Registration: *$10.00*

Home Budget Management System ✍
by Brentson L. Worrell

Financial record-keeping, a desirable and enlightening habit to get into, is usually a dreaded task and a prime target for procrastination. HBMS was created to make it as painless as possible.

HBMS is a double-entry ledger system that helps you set up a chart of accounts (such as rent, medical costs, clients, professional services, bank interest, office expenses, etc.) into which you post (record) all your expenses, income, assets and liabilities. At any time, particularly when figuring taxes, you can see your complete financial position, readily viewed on screen or printed in a variety of useful reports.

Daily financial transactions can be posted to as many as 254 accounts to generate monthly and yearly reports showing totals broken down by those categories. For instance, how much you spent on auto repair. You pick the codes (of one to four letters) for the various accounts, so it is relatively easy to remember them when posting entries without having to look up numbers, as is required by some ledger systems.

HBMS provides a budgeting function, easy editing for incorrect entries, checkbook balancing, and check printing. It can handle 12 separate checking accounts and up to 1140 transactions per month.

(PC-SIG Disk# 1302)

Special Requirements: *Printer.*
Author Registration: *$30.00*
➤**ASP Member.**

Home Management II
by MVP Software

HOME MANAGEMENT II (HMII) is five separate home/small business financial programs in one package:
❑ Budget — Checking account and finance manager
❑ Typewriter — Turns your computer printer into a no-frills typewriter
❑ Personal Budget Planning — Makes budget planning a breeze
❑ Quik Loan — Calculate monthly payments at various interest rates and repayment schedules
❑ Stock Broker — Track stock transactions and compare your portfolio action to the Dow Jones average

You don't need to be a CPA or a member of Mensa to control your household or small business finances. With five separate financial programs to choose from and 19 pages of well-written documentation, you simply take what you need and leave the rest.

Use HOME MANAGEMENT II and become a master of your finances!

(PC-SIG Disk# 1108)

Special Requirements: *384K RAM. Printer recommended.*
Author Registration: *$29.95*
➤*ASP Member.*

Home Money Manager IIa   *by MoneCraft Computer Products*

Enter transactions in up to 12 check registers, keep track of your balance and reconcile your bank statements. Void, search, edit, reconcile, mark as cleared, and consolidate your recorded transactions. HMM will support split transactions and keep running totals for each account.

You'll know the amount of money you are spending in any of 84 categories. This program also provides a variety of reports that can help you organize your records at tax time or just report on where and how much money was spent and on what. On-line Help screens are provided to guide you as you use the program.

(PC-SIG Disk# 837)

Special Requirements: *Two floppy drives, printer recommended.*
Author Registration: *$59.00*
➤*ASP Member.*

Mark's Checkbook Plus   *by Mark Alberts*

Designed for people who save a number of transactions before entering them into their checkbook, this complete checkbook manager will perform complex tasks that you thought you needed an accounting program to handle. It is well suited for those who use the automatic teller machines (ATMs) frequently and/or use the carbon copy type checkbooks. Also perfect for those with a number of credit cards or accounts that require a regular payment.

MARK'S CHECKBOOK PLUS handles two types of accounts: assets and liabilities. Track an unlimited number of accounts and transactions. The program allows the transfer of funds between accounts and keeps track of all outstanding credits and debits. It is very easy to reconcile, and print monthly reports or all transactions reports. You have control over all your accounts with browse and sort functions, which makes it easy to see where your money is going.

(PC-SIG Disk# 1793)

Special Requirements: *Hard drive recommended.*
Author Registration: *$25.00*

Multi Assistant   *by Jones Consulting*

MULTI ASSISTANT wants to be your personal executive assistant, and keep track of the myriad of necessary details in your hectic life! This PC whiz kid takes care of your finances, calculates lending figures, manages your telephone and mailing lists, inventories your investments, and keeps your calendar.

MULTI ASSISTANT prints checks for you, confirms checks/deposits (which it disburses into budget areas you select), finds and lists checks by category, and computes your account balance.

Track your personal investments, compute their investment value, and pull them up to view by name or number. Maintain multiple investment files with multiple categories per file. Track your debits, compute loan interest, and display and print payment schedules.

MULTI ASSISTANT acts as your personal secretary, maintaining telephone and mailing lists, and multiple directories. It can print addresses from your keyboard input or from list files, onto labels or directly onto envelopes — even inserting the return address. It ensures that you will never forget another appointment or important project deadline, by keeping your calendar for you. It displays daily and weekly events or the events between any two dates you choose.

(PC-SIG Disk# 1423)

Special Requirements: *384K RAM.*
Author Registration: *$29.00 or $39.00.*

PC Account
by Gulf Sierra

PC-ACCOUNT is a personal accounting system and checkbook ledger, preset for a total of 60 asset accounts and 15 checking, savings, or loan accounts. Search for all transactions against an account, a user-defined code, an amount, a text string, or a check number. A full year's transactions in specific categories can be retrieved at tax time.

Reconcile your bank statement swiftly and double-check entries and totals in your checkbook. A unique feature is the ability to print on any personal check. PC-ACCOUNT lets you create formats for 15 different checking accounts and specify the location of each data field on the check. Listings of accounts and transactions can be sent to the screen, printer, disk text file, or file that can be imported by LOTUS 1-2-3.

(PC-SIG Disk# 941)

Special Requirements: *None.*
Author Registration: *$45.00*
➤*ASP Member.*

PC MONEY2 ☆
by Conrad Button's Software

Each year it gets a little tougher to keep track of finances. One program figures out loans, the next is needed to plan retirement, and yet another is required to track mutual funds — until PC MONEY2!

PC MONEY2 will tell you anything about any loan you may be considering. Find the monthly payment, the largest loan you can afford, and the years required to pay off the loan — even if it has balloon payments. You can even print the loan payoff schedule.

For annuities, find out how much money you can put in or how much you can take out. If you have a fixed amount invested and you want to see how it will grow, PC MONEY2 will show you. Have a periodic investment plan? See the value of the plan at maturity, the number of years to reach a goal, and more. PC MONEY2 also keeps track of saving bonds or mutual funds and their performance.

Use the set of financial tools included in PC MONEY2 to plan your retirement. Calculate how much money you'll need to invest in order to receive a regular income after retirement. PC MONEY2 is one financial tool for all of your investment planning.

(PC-SIG Disk# 2717)

Special Requirements: *A graphics card.*
Author Registration: *$19.50*

PC-Billmaster
by John Davis

PC-BILL MASTER manages your checkbook for you. It was written because the author needed a system that was easy to use, had a regular checkbook register type display, and could handle recurring payments.

PC-BILL MASTER features:

❑ Familiar easy-to-use register type display
❑ Ability to enter items as posted (immediately balanced) or unposted (totaled into an unposted balance)
❑ Ability to merge multiple checkbooks
❑ Easy bank statement balancing
❑ Retrieval of items from all checkbooks on disk, with reports displayed, filed, or printed
❑ A search capability based on the contents of any field including a partial string search
❑ Up to 500 items per check register with an unlimited number of registers
❑ Up to 100 ledger account codes and titles

(PC-SIG Disk# 1021)

Special Requirements: *None.*
Author Registration: *$25.00*

PC-Flow
by Daniel Comeau

PC-FLOW, the personal cash-flow budgeting system, lets you forecast and evaluate your home or small-business budget, emphasizing daily cash-flow. Each transaction can be designated as once-only, daily, weekly, or monthly. The entries can be exact or estimated. Record incoming and outgoing activities and sort and categorize by group.

🖎 = Updated Program
☆ = New Program

Schedule future transactions within a user-defined time period. This approach to budgeting lets you observe the cash-flow situation as the transactions are scheduled to occur. Reports of starting resources, cash-flow, and transaction breakdown can be printed. Sort budget transactions by ID, frequency or ending date. There are three cash-flow reports: daily transaction detail; daily, weekly, monthly, or yearly cash-flow summaries; and breakdown by transaction classification.

(PC-SIG Disk# 957)

Special Requirements: *None.*
Author Registration: *$40.00*

PCMoney ✍   *by Keith Consulting*

PCMONEY is designed to maintain personal, family, and small business financial and tax records. It includes an accounting module that keeps records for a home (or small) business, a stock and bond portfolio management module, and a module that consolidates tax information from personal and home business tax records and then estimates federal income tax liabilities.

PCMONEY makes it possible to keep records for as many as nine bank accounts. Maintain an annual tax account which includes up to 44 categories for easy consolidation and compilation of like items for income tax estimating or preparation. Entries such as checks or deposits that affect both a bank account and your tax account are made in a single entry. Bank and tax records can be displayed (and printed) a number of different ways. All operations are selected by menus that are easy to use. All account data is entered via fill-in forms with editing capabilities.

(PC-SIG Disk# 532)

Special Requirements: *High-density drive.*
Author Registration: *$25.00*

Personal Ledger ✍   *by David M. Alexander*

PERSONAL LEDGER will help you keep track of all your financial activities.

Each transaction includes a check number or an entry number, a one-word description, payee/comment, amount, and date of the transaction. Entries can easily be sorted according to number or date. Automatic entry features are included to modify, delete, or search for previous entries. For personal sorting purposes, transactions may be grouped together in any of ten user-defined categories, with each category having up to 20 descriptions.

(PC-SIG Disk# 1482)

Special Requirements: *CGA.*
Author Registration: *$25.00*

QCHECK3 - Checking Account Management System ✍   *by Creative Resources*

QCHECK3 — Creative Resources's checking account management system is a menu-driven program set up to minimize errors and ease reporting of data on any checking account, either personal or small- to medium-sized businesses.

Menu selections include new check/charge entry, deposit entry, check cancellation, deposit cancellation, balance inquiry, screen listing of a portion or all of the check register file, listing of all uncanceled items, editing of any item, creation of a new register, a variety of reports on check and deposit activity, and a means of restarting the program for a different check register data file without the need to exit to the operating system. Also includes several DOS utilities for free disk space, free memory, etc.

QCHECK3 can export data to an electronic spreadsheet (PC-Calc, SuperCalc, Quattro, Lotus 1-2-3, etc.). It also provides for user-defined check memo code suggestions, user-defined function key macros for "pay to" entries, user-defined printer set-up strings, a handy calendar function for date look-up, and checks for adequate disk space prior to actions requiring more space.

(PC-SIG Disk# 968)

Special Requirements: *410K RAM and two floppy drives. Hard drive recommended.*
Author Registration: *$30.00*

QPacs ✍   *by Richard A. Williams*

QPACS is a personal accounting program that can handle up to nine different bank accounts, keep track of user-defined budgets, record investments, assets and liabilities, and estimate your Federal income taxes.

For each bank account, you may record check amounts, deposits, interest and service charges. QPACS can balance the bank statements, and print out a complete check register or a summary register by user-defined categories. The program can also print out a net worth calculation report, based upon the information from the checking accounts, the investments, and the assets and liabilities. QPACS also has a built-in address and phone number index card system which is very helpful for keeping track of the people and businesses that are important to your finances, as well as a household inventory file. The latest release also prints checks and includes a recurring check file.

(PC-SIG Disk# 1640)

Special Requirements: *None.*
Author Registration: *$22.00*
➤*ASP Member.*

Quick Check Book   by CanCom Computing Company

Balancing your checkbook and savings accounts can now be a breeze, with QUICK CHECK BOOK. QUICK CHECK BOOK is a menu-driven program that smooths the effort of maintaining a checkbook, paying bills, sticking to a budget, and writing checks.

The absence of accounting terminology, account numbers, and confusing methods make QUICK CHECK BOOK the perfect solution for those who like to keep things simple and smart. Each menu selection has a pop-up Help window.

QUICK CHECK BOOK has no limit to the number of checkbooks it can maintain, or the number of transactions in a checkbook. The amount of storage space available determines your limitations on the number of checkbooks and transactions.

QUICK CHECK BOOK is usable in various ways. If you want to write checks, it does so on your checks and your printer. If you only want to maintain a check database or budget, QUICK CHECK BOOK does that too. Balancing with the bank will no longer be the source of anguish. To balance with the bank, you simply confirm a transaction amount against your bank statement by pressing the return/enter key. QUICK CHECK BOOK does the rest.

A calculator, calendar, and other utilities are always a keystroke or two away. Mouse support is also available.

(PC-SIG Disk#'s 1721, 1731)

Special Requirements: *384K RAM.*
Author Registration: *$40.00*

Time and Money   by Daniel H. Marcellus

A simple financial record-keeping system for the home or small business. Finally, you can know just where all the money goes!

Design and keep a budget, create financial plans, track cash outlay, and analyze rent/buy options. Track bank accounts, manage your checkbook, and monitor your use of charge cards. Select menu options to project future plans and analyze specific financial alternatives. The system makes graphs of projected cash use for up to a year in the future. Use TIME AND MONEY to help take control of your financial life!

(PC-SIG Disk# 251)

Special Requirements: *320K RAM.*
Author Registration: *$25.00*

▼ ▼ ▼

Accounting, Education

DAC Easy Tutor   by Logical Business Systems

Learn to use the DAC EASY accounting system, plus gain knowledge of basic bookkeeping with lessons that lead you step-by-step through the program. The non-interactive tutorial can either be printed out, or read off the screen for quick reference by using the Read utility.

(PC-SIG Disk# 1294)

Special Requirements: *Printer.*
Author Registration: *$10.00*

▼ ▼ ▼

Accounting, G/L, A/P, A/R, Payroll

Account + Plus ✍
by Plano Computer Sales

Do you need an integrated accounting management system for your business? ACCOUNT + PLUS is the ideal choice, providing everything a small business needs in one package.

ACCOUNT + PLUS consists of individual modules: Payroll, Bookkeeping, Inventory, Checkbook, Receivables, Payables, and report generation.

The Payroll module handles all types of employee payroll. Deductions include Federal, state taxes, insurance, and pension. Earning may be by hour, week, month, or commission.

The Bookkeeping module operates as a General Ledger, keeping track of all of your income and expenses. It will also write the checks you need to issue to paying your bills.

The Inventory module lets you maintain an inventory database with add, delete, and change record functions. Many report generation options are available here.

The Checkbook module is a complete checkbook management system. It will keep track of your deposits, your withdrawals, your checks, balancing of your checkbook, and several report printing options.

ACCOUNT + PLUS is menu driven with an on-line Help facility that does away with the need to constantly refer to printed documentation. No small business should be without ACCOUNT + PLUS, the integrated accounting management system.

(PC-SIG Disk#'s 1871, 2662)

Special Requirements: *512K RAM, and two floppy drives or a hard drive.*
Author Registration: *$49.00*

Accounting 101 ✍
by Iddo L. Enochs

ACCOUNTING 101 is an easy-to-use, menu-driven accounting program designed for the average home user or small business owner. Do basic accounting operations such as recording deposits, making journal entries, recording accounts payable, and closing your accounts at the end of each month and year. ACCOUNTING 101 automatically lists your income and expense totals for the year-to-date and the current month. Change the accounting numbers and categories to suit your own financial situation.

ACCOUNTING 101 can print a variety of reports: a deposit journal, an accounting journal, a check journal, a trial balance, a balance sheet, your account numbers, an account activity report, and an income statement.

(PC-SIG Disk# 1193)

Special Requirements: *512K RAM and two floppy drives.*
Author Registration: *$25.00*

Accounts Payable Lite
by Hooper International, Inc.

The ACCOUNTS PAYABLE LITE module provides a simple way to keep track of all your payables. This module is essential to managing your cash flow as it allows you to pay invoices using seven payment selection methods. Checks are generated automatically by the computer or you may make payments by writing checks manually. Full integration into your General Ledger will save you hours of time and effort and avoids duplicate data entry. Proper use of this module requires the GENERAL LEDGER LITE PC-SIG Disk #151.

Features include: up to 2000 vendors, 32000 transactions; continuous form checks; enter miscellaneous debits or credits, pre- or post-dated transactions; easy to use or learn, easy to modify or delete transactions and vendors, prior period adjustments. Complete range of financial reports; select reports by month, quarter, year and year-to-date or trended. Pop-up windows, sound, mouse compatible; eight-digit invoice and reference number, departments; allows multiple distribution; post the G/L in summary or detail format; and much more.

(PC-SIG Disk#'s 1545, 1546)

Special Requirements: *512K RAM, two floppy drives, and PC-SIG disk #151.*
Author Registration: *$39.95 includes printed & bound manual, quarterly newsletter, and more.*
➤*ASP Member.*

C-A-S-E Accounting
by Custom Cycle Fitments

C-A-S-E ACCOUNTING offers a system of accounting functions that meet the needs of most small- to mid-sized businesses.

C-A-S-E maintains three journals: the General Journal and two subsidiary journals, Sales and Payroll. Sales are recorded in the Sales Journal because all sales transactions are basically similar. Payroll transactions are recorded in the Payroll journal because that provides confidentiality, if desired. Also, both kinds of transactions generate large numbers of detailed transactions with low dollar amounts, such as sales tax and deductions, that clutter up the General Journal when entered individually. Totals for these two subsidiary journals are entered into the General Journal whenever desired, usually at fixed accounting intervals.

C-A-S-E also maintains files detailing the transactions for cases or projects (using the name that you use in your business), for invoices and credit sales, for employee pay and deductions, for payables, and for capital equipment. Whenever a transaction is entered through any of these systems, the appropriate information is fed to the others that are affected and to the appropriate journal. This information is readily available, either on the screen or in printed reports.

C-A-S-E produces both the standard accounting reports and the management reports that are most useful to knowledge firms: Sales Journal, by profit line and tax class, between any two dates; Payroll Journal, by employee by month, with deductions, between any two dates; General Journal, between any two dates. Transactions in any General Journal account between any two dates, with totals and balance. C-A-S-E financial histories that detail every transaction for a case, line item by line item. These use an easy-to-remember coding system that enables you to match billings against expenses and partner's time. The total expenses, billings, partner's time, disbursements from retainers, unpaid invoices and balance are also shown. Accounts Receivable, by invoice. Accounts Payable, by commitment and by firm.

This is a straightforward and professional accounting program with every feature the small business will need.

(PC-SIG Disk# 1115)

Special Requirements: *640K RAM and two floppy drives.*
Author Registration: *$75.00*

CheckMate-GL   *by CTech*

Do you own a small business, or are you thinking of starting one — only to be frightened by the thought of all the financial homework you know it entails? If you want to keep track of your expenses and manage your finances wisely, you need an accountant — or CHECKMATE-GL.

CHECKMATE-GL is a powerful multiple-entry General Ledger package that operates on the principles of classic accounting. CHECKMATE-GL has turned the complicated world of accounting into a user-friendly task, and even has an introduction to the basic principles of accounting for anyone unfamiliar with them.

CHECKMATE-GL was designed to integrate with CHECKMATE, but does operate independently. The two programs have a unique interface, letting CHECKMATE become, in effect, a cash disbursements journal for CHECKMATE-GL. What is special about this

CheckMate-GL (PC-SIG Disk#785)

is you can operate your day-to-day finances with CHECKMATE, and not worry about accounting or expensing your checks except at specific times. In this way, you can separate your day-to-day finances from more critical accounting data. Home users will discover that you need only run CHECKMATE-GL once a week or so to quickly update your records. For businesses, personnel can work with CHECKMATE while you or your accounting professional can work exclusively with CHECKMATE-GL.

CHECKMATE-GL can support up to 256 accounts simultaneously and has powerful search-and-filter routines for all databases and reports. CHECKMATE-GL also has a user-friendly pull-down and pop-up menu system with on-line Help. Included in this menu system is a pop-up chart of accounts for quick reference, and a pop-up accountant's calculator with rolling tape. The system allows for 50 predefined journal transactions that can be called up at a keystroke. CHECKMATE-GL also has unique "quick-look" reports and flexible predefined reports with output control.

(PC-SIG Disk# 785)

Special Requirements: *Two floppy drives or a hard drive.*
Author Registration: *$39.95*
➤*ASP Member.*

       ✍ = Updated Program
                                                                    ☆ = New Program

CPA-Ledger
by Tronolone & Foster PC, CPA

A menu-driven general ledger and financial statement program designed for non-manufacturing businesses that offer products or services for sale.

Start your books and maintain them: post transactions; prepare unadjusted and post-closing trial balances, and income statements; print a list of all postings for any period; search for previously-entered transactions; and reconstruct specific GL accounts and add new ones.

CPA-LEDGER has plenty of muscle to record your daily transactions. Any single general ledger entry can have up to 30 debits and 30 credits, with total values of up to $999,999,999.99. A very powerful system. Some knowledge of double-entry bookkeeping is necessary to operate this package.

(PC-SIG Disk#'s 466, 468)

Special Requirements: *A version of BASIC.*
Author Registration: *$45.00.*

DAYO AP (Accounts Payable) ✍
by TJS Lab

DAYO is a collection of multiuser business applications that provide a means of managing inventory, purchasing, invoicing, customers, vendors, sales and more... All DAYO products are multiuser, designed to work on a Microcomputer (PC) Based Local Area Network (LAN), like Novell (tm). They can, however, work as a 'standalone', running on a single PC.

DAYO AP (ACCOUNTS PAYABLE) is the "final chapter" to the processing and maintenance of all your Payables. DAYO AP's key mission is to process/post your purchase orders. However, many other routines have been provided; i.e., Expense Maintenance, 1099 MISC Forms, Purchase Clearing, Vendor Maintenance, Hand/Manual Checks, Batch Checks, Recurring Checks, Unlimited Bank Accounts, Unlimited Check Printing Formats, and over 21 Reports. See the Network section of this encyclopedia for a complete listing of all the DAYO modules.

(PC-SIG Disk#'s 2411, 2412)

Special Requirements: *640K RAM, a hard drive, and DOS 3.3.*
Author Registration: *$25.00*
➤*ASP Member.*

DAYO AR (Accounts Receivable) ✍
by TJS Lab

DAYO AR (ACCOUNTS RECEIVABLE) is the "final chapter" to the processing and maintenance of all your Receivables. DAYO AR includes routines to handle cash receipts, customers, invoice types, terms, taxcodes, sales persons, and more. Many reports are included (i.e., Aging, Customer, Sales...). There is a routine to print Statements (i.e., SMART, 90, 60, 30 days), and another one to create and print 'non'standard invoices. HP Laser forms are provided as an option for Statements and Invoices.

(PC-SIG Disk#'s 2409, 2410)

Special Requirements: *640K RAM, a hard drive, and DOS 3.3.*
Author Registration: *$25.00*
➤*ASP Member.*

DAYO GL (General Ledger) ✍
by TJS Lab

DAYO GL (GENERAL LEDGER) provides a means to manage and report company finances. DAYO GL is totally integrated with the other DAYO packages. Features include computer generated posting, multiuser, double entry, export data, 20+ reports, budget management, and unlimited accounts.

(PC-SIG Disk#'s 2413, 2414)

Special Requirements: *640K RAM, a hard drive, and DOS 3.3.*
Author Registration: *$25.00*
➤*ASP Member.*

DAYO Payroll ✍
by TJS Lab

DAYO PAYROLL provides a system for the computation of payroll for businesses of any size and contains many features and functions not normally found in PC payroll applications.

Some of DAYO PAYROLL's features include: multiuser, unlimited employees, weekly, biweekly, and/or monthly payrolls, quarterly, year-to-date (YTD), and current summary databases, databases are dBASE-compatible, automatic payroll posting and computation, vacation maintenance, sickpay/days maintenance, check printing, SDI tax, overtime and premium hourly wages, up to eight deductions, exempt/non-exempt deductions, view reports on screen, printer setup and drivers, over 24 configurable options, and many reports.

(PC-SIG Disk# 2397)

Special Requirements: *640K RAM, hard drive, and DOS 3.3.*
Author Registration: *$25.00*
➤*ASP Member.*

Electric Ledger
by Try-Then-Buy Software

The ELECTRIC LEDGER is an extremely easy-to-use yet powerful double-entry bookkeeping system that will keep track of your assets, income, expenses, liabilities, and capital.

Basic functions include:

❏ ADD, DELETE, and REVISE accounts
❏ ADD, CHANGE, and DELETE transactions

Reports include Balance Individual Account, Trial Balance, Profit and Loss Statement (income statement), Balance Sheet, and List of Transactions.

Designed to be the easiest ledger program you will ever use. Excellent for personal use and for small and large businesses alike!

(PC-SIG Disk# 2219)

Special Requirements: *None.*
Author Registration: *$95.00*

FCP Accounting
by Flowsoft Custom Programming

FCP ACCOUNTING is an easy-to-use accounting program designed to work similarly to the double entry method of accounting. All you have to do is enter your journal entries (which entails debiting one or more accounts and crediting one or more accounts), and everything else is done automatically.

All journal entries are checked to make sure that they balance. After your journal entries are entered and posted, many reports are provided including: trial balance, income statement, balance sheet, capital statement, sales bar graphs, monthly balances line graphs with average line, Year-To-Date totals, Month-To-Date totals, and cash flow analysis.

(PC-SIG Disk# 1985)

Special Requirements: *None.*
Author Registration: *$10.00*

Finance Manager II General Ledger Lite
by Hooper International, Inc.

FINANCE MANAGER II is an extremely flexible and comprehensive accounting package for the non-professional accountant. It's easy to use and very cost-efficient for the small- to medium-sized business.

Outstanding features of FINANCE MANAGER II include:

❏ Maintaining up to 1999 accounts
❏ Recording up to 32,000 transactions per year (3,800 on floppies)
❏ Providing a listing of all transactions in a specified period of time
❏ Tracing account activity against Chart of Account numbers
❏ Displaying net income (or net loss) for specific period requested
❏ Showing balance sheet for assets, liabilities, and equity accounts
❏ Providing cumulative or trended source/use-of-funds statement
❏ Showing budget variance on expenditures
❏ Listing a current Chart of Accounts to be run after changes
❏ Listing of budgeted income or expense accounts

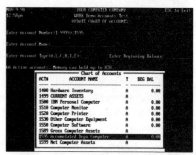

Finance Manager II General Ledger Lite
(PC-SIG Disk# 151)

✍ = Updated Program
☆ = New Program

(PC-SIG Disk# 151)
Special Requirements: *2 floppy drives.*
Author Registration: *$49.95; includes a manual, newsletters, unlimited technical help.*
➤*ASP Member.*

Finance Mgr II Accounts Receivables
by Hooper International, Inc.

If you don't get paid, you can't pay your bills. This critical module lets you remain in control easily and effortlessly. You can have up to 2,000 customers and send out invoices (using either pre-printed or blank sheets) and statements using balance-forward accounting. To allow correct interface with the income and other important accounts, the General Ledger module, FINANCE MANAGER II (PC-SIG disk #151) is required.

Important Features:
❑ Up to 2,000 customers
❑ Integrated with G/L
❑ Finance charges
❑ Miscellaneous debits/credits
❑ Custom message on statements
❑ Up to 32,000 transactions/year
❑ Post to G/L in detail or summary format
❑ Multiple G/L distribution
❑ Prior period adjustments allowed
❑ Post-dated transaction allowed
❑ Balance-forwarding accounting
❑ And much more

(PC-SIG Disk# 1107)
Special Requirements: *None.*
Author Registration: *$39.95, includes a manual, newsletters, unlimited technical help*
➤*ASP Member.*

Freeway
by Freeway Software LTD

This is a payroll management system built expressly for the European businessplace. FREEWAY PAYROLL programs can accommodate weekly, fortnightly, four weekly and monthly pay frequencies. The programs provide:
❑ Payslip stationery (obtainable from the author)
❑ Bank Giro's and payment lists
❑ Cheque printing
❑ Internal pension schemes with fixed sum or percentage contributions
❑ Additional voluntary contributions
❑ Up to 99 departments each with a coin analysis and cost of payroll total

Create your own headings for taxable and non-taxable additions to pay and post-tax deductions and produce lists of deductions under these headings. (Year-end documentation includes P35 and P60 forms, also obtainable from the author.) The system accommodates statutory sick pay, and password protection. The user may change tax rates and bandwidths, as well as earnings brackets.

Each employee may have attached to his record card, in addition to basic pay and hours, any regularly occurring payment or deduction. During entry of pay data, only these employees will have the variables entered. Calculation of pay and deductions is very flexible, permitting recalculation if necessary.

(PC-SIG Disk#'s 671, 672, 673)
Special Requirements: *Two floppy drives.*
Author Registration: *45 pounds.*

General Ledger II
by Peak InfoSystems, Inc.

In need of a basic, no-frills accounting system to handle your billable time? Then GENERAL LEDGER II is for you.

GENERAL LEDGER II can handle up to 300 accounts, grouped into 32 different categories. Define both the account names and category names. The number of vouchers (groups of account postings) that can be handled is determined by available disk storage. Transaction entry is simplified when you call for accounts by name (or partial name) as well as by account number.

Standard report formats eliminate the need to design reports. A check register automatically captures data on all checking account activity. A cash journal can create a double-posted petty cash journal with just a single entry for each transaction. Journaling has a pre-posting list feature that previews the posting results and makes corrections before final posting. The Reports menu includes an option that can print all of the mandatory end-of-month reports with a single keystroke.

(PC-SIG Disk# 2235)

Special Requirements: *Two floppy drives and a 132-column printer.*

Author Registration: *$50.00*

HDP Accounts Receivables   *by HDP (Holman Data Processing)*

HDP ACCOUNTS RECEIVABLES manages your customer accounts and transactions for your business. It not only stores, organizes, and retrieves customer information, but also lets you edit all data or transaction information kept on file for each customer. With HDP ACCOUNTS RECEIVABLES, you have full control over your transactions and invoices.

The Reports option lets you print and compute finance charges, print mailing labels, and process data at the end of the month. The system utilities of the program let you check data files and rebuild the various indexes, clear all transactions off accounts, selectively delete transactions on one account, and add new customer files.

This version of the program is limited to about 250 customers.

(PC-SIG Disk# 821)

Special Requirements: *None.*

Author Registration: *None. $25.00 for upgraded version.*

Medlin Accounting ✍   *by Medlin Accounting Shareware*

MEDLIN ACCOUNTING is a group of four companion accounting packages providing fast, easy-to-use accounting services for the small- to medium-sized business.

The main program, PC-GL, is a double-entry General Ledger module which allows up to 800 items in the chart of accounts and 6,000 transactions per period. It can be used by itself or with PC-AP. PC-AP is an Accounts Payable program which allows a maximum of 2,000 vendors and 2,000 invoices per month. PC-AR is a menu-driven Accounts Receivable module, supporting up to 2,000 customers and 4,000 invoices per month. PC-PR, the Payroll program, includes current Federal tax tables, support for most state taxes, and a W-2 program. All programs use similar commands and share the same operating features.

New features to this version includes:

❑ PC-GL — When scrolling through data, the active line is highlighted
❑ PC-AR — Faster save-to-disk, page numbering on most reports, customer codes on the AR ledger, select beginning and ending customer codes for reports, single key jump from enter invoices to enter customers
❑ PC-AP — Maintain and display current bank balance, automatic posting of offsetting entry in PC-GL, new accounts summary report totals unpaid bills by account number, select beginning and ending code for reports, single key jump from enter invoices to enter vendors
❑ PC-PR — 1991 Federal tax tables; supports tips, 401K plans, and cafeteria plans; skip prompts for unused deduction fields, export employee and payroll check data to ASCII files

In addition, all programs provide the following new features:

❑ A four-function pop-up calculator which can insert a result into a numerical field
❑ A new method of entering customer codes, vendor codes, and account numbers listing possible matches as codes are entered
❑ When customer codes, vendor codes, employee names, or account numbers are changed, all historical data is also changed
❑ PC-INV, an invoice writing program. PC-INV works directly with PC-AR data files to print customer invoices and post them on PC-AR
❑ The ability to calculate sales tax on taxable items
❑ Up to 50 lines for invoice detail
❑ Up to 42 characters per line for descriptions, with @ symbol to multiply item and automatically enter amount

❑ The ability to print invoices as you enter them

❑ The capability to print invoices on NEBBS form 9296, form 9292, or plain paper, 11" or 7" format

NOTE: All programs are run in RAM; the numbers of supported accounts quoted above are based on at least 512K RAM. Less RAM will allow the modules to run but will support a smaller number of accounts.

(PC-SIG Disk# 331)

Special Requirements: *Two floppy drives.*

Author Registration: *$35 for PC-GL; PC-AP; PC-AR; PC-PR. $25 for PCINV*

➤*ASP Member.*

Micro Accounting System
by SonShine Software, Inc.

Those looking for a single-entry General Ledger accounting program need look no further. Micro Accounting System (MAS) provides a service needed by many small businesses. In addition to the General Ledger functions, MAS has banking and budgeting functions. These additional sections are not included by many other programs.

Those who do not need invoicing, Accounts Receivable or Payable functions, and who need a simple-to-use General Ledger with ample report options, will like this program.

(PC-SIG Disk# 2030)

Special Requirements: *512K RAM. A hard drive is recommended.*

Author Registration: *$95.00*

➤*ASP Member.*

NonProfit General Ledger
by Reliance Software Service

If you are a service or nonprofit organization, the NONPROFIT GENERAL LEDGER (NGL) may serve your bookkeeping needs. It uses pre-defined account numbers to track service groups and their related fund accounts. NGL does not have online Help and does not use the function keys, but it does have a tutorial and start-up program which simplifies the installation process.

Installation is not difficult, although familiarity with accounting terms is a plus. NGL uses a six-digit account number system and you must use it. For those working in a nonprofit groups, NGL is especially useful since it is designed to work with multiple fund and service accounts. Various reports can be printed for these accounts which can help the group keep up with the various designated monies. However, there is only a consolidated report for these funds and service accounts. There are no fund or service tracking reports. On the up side, data is posted directly to the accounts for fast reporting of the status of the organization.

The NGL manual is thorough, and is especially useful to nonprofit groups. The manual alone may be worth the registration fee. The program can be used by anyone, regardless of the type of organization. This is a good package for anyone needing a General Ledger accounting program.

(PC-SIG Disk# 2055)

Special Requirements: *None.*

Author Registration: *$40.00*

Painless Accounting ✍
by Painless Accounting

If you are looking for a full-featured accounting program, then PAINLESS ACCOUNTING may be it. Similar to DAC EASY ACCOUNTING in the way the account numbers are used and in the way the menus are laid out. PAINLESS ACCOUNTING is business-oriented — good for those small businesses looking for an inexpensive accounting program.

PAINLESS ACCOUNTING is a fully integrated accounting package. The modules included consist of: General Ledger, Billing, Accounts Receivable, Accounts Payable, Purchasing, File maintenance, Reports, Closing, Utilities, and Beginning Balance setup.

Some of the major features include: user-definable invoice/statement/PO/received PO and check-printing formats; pull-down window interface, context-sensitive Help, network-compatible, job costing, build materials, departmentalization, password protection, check reconciliation, automatic beginning balance setup, multiple product price levels, salesman commissions, multiple companies, historical information maintained for all clients/vendors/products/services, and numerous reports including Balance Sheet and Income Statements, as well as budgeting capabilities.

This version of the program contains major modifications to the GST tax calculations for Canada, and now supports the Australian date format.

PAINLESS ACCOUNTING can be recommended to those looking for a good package to perform ledger, billing, Accounts Receivable, Payables and Purchase Order work, providing they have some knowledge of accounting. For those acquainted with DAC EASY, it will be a simple task to set up the chart of accounts. For all others, it is suggested that the sample accounts be used and printed out and then studied. The program will meet the business needs of the self-employed and small businesses everywhere.

(PC-SIG Disk#'s 2059, 2060, 2061)

Special Requirements: *640K RAM, and a hard drive.*
Author Registration: *$125.00*
➤*ASP Member.*

Painless Accounting/Payroll Companion Disk ☆   *by Painless Accounting*

PAINLESS ACCOUNTING/PAYROLL COMPANION is a custom graph/report/export-generating program designed to be used with PAINLESS ACCOUNTING (#2059 - #2061) and PAINLESS PAYROLL (#2607, #2608).

The modules include: graphs, reports, exports, and utilities. Create: Line, Bar, Point, Stacked-Bar, Pie, and High-Low Graphs. Display these graphs, print them, or save to .PCX files. Create custom line reports from any file in PAINLESS ACCOUNTING or PAINLESS PAYROLL. Export data to ASCII file formats.

Just like all the programs in this series, the PAINLESS ACCOUNTING/PAYROLL COMPANION DISK contains a pull-down windows interface along with context-sensitive Help throughout the program.

(PC-SIG Disk# 2609)

Special Requirements: *640K RAM and a hard drive.*
Author Registration: *$45.00*
➤*ASP Member.*

Painless Payroll ☆   *by Painless Accounting*

PAINLESS PAYROLL is a fully integrated payroll system. The modules include: payroll generation, reports, files, closing, and utilities.

Other major features: Federal and all 50 states withholding tax tables, automatic interface into PAINLESS ACCOUNTING (#2059 - #2061), multiple companies supported, context-sensitive Help, pull-down menu interface, user-definable check printing formats, password protection, as well as W2s and 1099s printed.

This version of PAINLESS PAYROLL contains the new Federal tax tables for 1991 including the changes to Medicare and FICA Taxes.

(PC-SIG Disk#'s 2607, 2608)

Special Requirements: *512K RAM and a hard drive.*
Author Registration: *$75.00*
➤*ASP Member.*

Payroll Lite   *by Hooper International, Inc.*

This easy-to-use module provides a very efficient way to record important information such as: hire date, earnings, deductions, vacation and sick time, overtime and holiday pay. It automatically calculates gross pay, net pay, deductions and liabilities, prints checks and W-2 forms, supports both hourly and salaried employees paid weekly, bi-weekly, semi-monthly or monthly, and fully integrates into the General Ledger Module. Allows manual override of deductions and includes user-modifiable tax tables you can keep current. Allows payroll after the fact. Proper use requires the FINANCE MANAGER II (PC-SIG Disk #151).

Up to 1000 employees, 32000 transactions, user-modifiable tax tables, user-modifiable tax calculations, three additional earnings categories and two additional deduction categories with separate tax options; can delete paid and posted payroll transactions; supports 80-column printers and HP LaserJet checks; generates a complete range of reports, such as: quarterly tax summary reports, quarterly tax payments, paid payroll recap for your 941 form, and SDI option for employee or employer.

(PC-SIG Disk#'s 1547, 1548)

Special Requirements: *512K RAM, two floppy drives, and PC-SIG disk #151.*
Author Registration: *$49.95 includes manual, quarterly newsletters, and technical support.*
➤*ASP Member.*

PC-Deal ✍ *by Kindred Spirits*

PC-DEAL is a double-entry ledger program, an application of cash accounting. The object is to keep track of cash or money. Where is it coming from? Where is it going? How much is available? How much is owed?

The basic mechanisms for doing this are the account and the transaction. PC-DEAL supports 300 accounts and up to 1,200 transactions per month. It maintains a journal of transactions entered and a separate ledger and transaction journal for each account.

PC-DEAL is designed for double-entry booking; that is, the specification of two account numbers (the To/Debit and From/Credit accounts), for each transaction. The transaction is recorded in two account ledgers and a balance is maintained between the cash coming in and the cash going out.

PC-DEAL maintains transaction journals and account ledgers for a period of 13 months — the 12 month accounting period and the first month of the next year.

Generate and print the following reports:
- Chart of accounts
- Cash flow
- Monthly transactions journal
- Trial balance
- Balance sheet
- Monthly income and expense
- Monthly activity in asset and liability accounts
- Change in net asset value
- Budget comparison
- Budget projection
- Annual income and expense
- Annual asset and liability account activity

PC-DEAL is fully menu-driven and intuitive to operate.

(PC-SIG Disk# 1870)

Special Requirements: *Two floppy drives.*
Author Registration: *$40.00*
➤*ASP Member.*

PC-General Ledger *by Charter Software*

PC-GENERAL LEDGER was written by a financial executive with over 25 years of experience in all areas of accounting, finance, and general management. The program makes it easy to add entries, maintain charts of accounts, print entries and general ledger updates, as well as print General Ledger and trial balances, financial statements, and month- and year-end closings. It handles up to five bank accounts and eight departments or cost centers, and also prints checks.

The program is easy to use and can be set up and running in less than 15 minutes.

(PC-SIG Disk# 237)

Special Requirements: *None.*
Author Registration: *$50.00.*

PC-Payroll ✍ *by Peninsula Software, Inc.*

PC-PAYROLL is a complete, menu-driven payroll system for moderate-sized companies.

It handles 80 employees on floppy-based systems and 200 employees on hard disk systems. PC-PAYROLL accepts hourly, salary, and tip wages, as well as bonuses and commissions. Federal, state and local taxes, FICA, pension and insurance withholding and user-defined deductions are automatically computed.

Paychecks and stubs can be printed according to several predefined formats. A full range of reports are included: monthly, quarterly and year-to-date summaries, federal tax reports (W-2, W-3, 941), and a complete pay period detail. PC-PAYROLL is well organized, and has as complete a list of facilities as commercial payroll systems.

(PC-SIG Disk# 565)

Special Requirements: *384K RAM and two floppy drives. A hard drive recommended.*
Author Registration: *$145.00*

PC-PAYROLL W-4 Module *by Peninsula Software, Inc.*

Compute the exact withholdings of Federal, FICA and state taxes for up to 30 different employees. The tax tables are valid for 1989 taxes in all 50 U.S. states.

PC-PAYROLL W-4 asks questions related to the IRS Form W-4 and automatically computes withholdings for each employee. It can also compute all taxes for the year 1989. It greatly reduces the amount of time normally spent on tax calculations, and prints individual W-4 worksheets.

Note that this program needs to be updated annually.

(PC-SIG Disk# 2124)

Special Requirements: *None.*
Author Registration: *$10.00*

PC-Payroll (PC-SIG Disk#'s 565, 1019)

Que Accounting General Ledger ✍ *by Que Accounting*

QUE ACCOUNTING GENERAL LEDGER (QUE G/L) is a full-featured General Ledger that supports multiple companies and multiple departments. While the QUE G/L is easy to use because of its menu-based design and context-sensitive Help screens, it is a serious accounting package. You must have accounting knowledge to use it.

QUE G/L includes the following features:

- ❏ Batch entry of transactions
- ❏ Automatic repeating entries
- ❏ Audit trails with batch dates
- ❏ Budget entries by company, department, and account
- ❏ Financial statements by corporation, company, and department
- ❏ Financial and budget comparisons between companies and periods
- ❏ Detailed listings with account and department totals
- ❏ Posting to closed periods
- ❏ 99 fiscal periods and transaction limit of $99,999,999
- ❏ dBASE file compatibility

QUE G/L comes with a functional practice set that quickly introduces you to its many features. The extensive report writer and query systems make it the type of system that's popular with CPA firms. QUE G/L integrates easily with the other QUE accounting modules and is a great way to get serious about your financial information.

(PC-SIG Disk# 2495)

Special Requirements: *512K RAM, two floppy drives or hard drive.*
Author Registration: *$45.00*

QUE Accounts Receivable ☆ *by Que Accounting*

QUE ACCOUNTING ACCOUNTS RECEIVABLE (QUE A/R) integrates with the QUE General Ledger or works alone. Like the QUE G/L, it is menu-driven and includes context-sensitive Help screens. It takes some accounting knowledge to operate. QUE A/R supports multiple companies and is a serious financial tool.

Some of its features include:

- ❏ Credit limits per customer and default credit terms
- ❏ Invoices with user defined formats (Bill To:, Ship To:, etc)
- ❏ Tracking of sales by salesperson and product with reports
- ❏ Aging (detail and summary) for any date
- ❏ Automated dunning messages
- ❏ Unlimited number of distributions per invoice
- ❏ Customer statements
- ❏ Uses dBASE-compatible files

The extensive report writer and query systems makes all information easily accessible. QUE A/R integrates with the other QUE accounting modules and is a great way to control your Receivables.

(PC-SIG Disk# 2496)

Special Requirements: *640K RAM, two floppy drives or a hard drive, and a printer.*
Author Registration: *$45*

RAMbase Accounting *by RAMbase Accounting*

Fast, faster, fastest are words that describe this program. RAMBASE ACCOUNTING is run completely within RAM and you can immediately see the difference in speed. Data is saved to disk, but only when you request it.

✍ = Updated Program
☆ = New Program

There are absolutely no delays to be found in the program. State-of-the-art technology is used to sort, index and merge all of the necessary data at keystroke speed. Switching is easy. Move between Payables, Receivables, Inventory, Checkbook, Point-of-sale and Reports simply by pressing a key. Each task is suspended until you return to it. In addition, invoices can be produced and printed quickly, which is something that many other accounting programs only dream about.

It is suggested that the user read the manual to understand the way the program has been organized.

(PC-SIG Disk# 2033)

Special Requirements: *None.*
Author Registration: *$35.00*

Rosewood Journal ✍   *by Rosewood Software*

ROSEWOOD JOURNAL is an invoice journal and Accounts Receivable "front-end" to be used in conjunction with any General Ledger program. It keeps track of cash and credit sales invoices, payments on account, sales tax (up to two levels), and complete Accounts Receivable. A General Ledger report tells the amounts to be entered, and the accounts in which to enter them. Accounts Receivable lists are aged (current, 30 days, 60 days and 90+ days). Customer statements are designed to be folded into a standard business window envelope. These statements are also aged. A label maker is built in. Screen colors and names of sales taxes are user-configurable. ROSEWOOD JOURNAL is simple to learn and easy to use. There is no need to understand accounting terminology. Entries are made quickly with the aid of softkey macros and intuitive data entry.

(PC-SIG Disk# 1309)

Special Requirements: *320K RAM and a printer.*
Author Registration: *$38.00 (U.S.); $45.00 (Canadian)*
➤*ASP Member.*

SBAS General Ledger ✍   *by Millrose Corporation*

Finally, an easy double-entry bookkeeping system designed around a General Ledger! SBAS (Small Business Accounting System) lets a small company track income and expenses and print reports on demand.

SBAS doesn't have modules for Receivables, Payables, and Payroll, but instead uses the General Ledger system to perform these tasks. Consequently you can't print invoices, but it does keep everything simpler.

Its on-line Help screen is very helpful. And it automatically checks for valid account numbers during entry and allows new accounts to be added during entry.

Installing the program isn't difficult. The manual and program provide the information to set up your books in a short period of time. Easy-to-read reports can be produced as needed. The system uses a five-digit account numbering system, and the manual suggests a certain way of setting up the accounts, but you can change it if you want. Overall, this is a good accounting package for businesses that don't need all the bells and whistles.

(PC-SIG Disk# 2178)

Special Requirements: *384K RAM.*
Author Registration: *$25.00*

SBW   *by Avi Rushinek*

SYSTEM FOR BUSINESS AND THE WORKPLACE (SBW) is a multifaceted integrated system that meets many common business needs. The system has five different functions and a separate module for each: Customer Information system, Human Resources (personnel) management, Accounting, Inventory, and Production system. It also has an extensive manual covering all five modules. The system is written in dBASE III+ and you will need dBASE III+ to run it. Also included is the dBASE source code.

The Customer file lets you maintain a complete customer database including purchase information and demographics about the customer. You can even print mailing labels or generate form letters. With the Human Resources management system, maintain detailed personnel records on your employees. Previous employment history, personnel reports, and payroll are all supported. The accounting system is also designed for the small business. It handles both Accounts Payable and Receivable. It maintains your chart of accounts and posts all expenses and income. Inventory management is for either manufactured goods or raw materials.

(PC-SIG Disk#'s 1094, 1095)

Special Requirements: *A printer, and dBASE III+.*
Author Registration: *$10.00*

Simple Bookkeeper ✍   *by A.P. Software*

The SIMPLE BOOKKEEPER is the easiest single-entry bookkeeping system available for home or small businesses. No accounting experience is required. Keep track of business expenses (40 categories) and income for the year. Three report formats include yearly profit/loss summary and YTD expenses. Information is entered on a monthly basis.

(PC-SIG Disk# 860)

Special Requirements: *None.*
Author Registration: *$15.00*

SOAR   *by SOAR Software*

SOAR (Service-Oriented Accounts Receivables) helps you simplify customer billing, generate meaningful management reports, and quickly get a snapshot of your business income and its sources. The program is menu-driven and easy to operate.

Some of SOAR's major features include:

❑ Simplified billing for businesses that provide services as well as products; three billing formats are supported — two industry-standard general-purpose forms, as well as a generic form
❑ Charges based on fixed-item (inventory item), services, hourly rates, fixed-cost, or variable-cost
❑ Customers assigned a late-charge rate so you can give special treatment to good customers; automatic billing of customers with fixed-rate service or support contracts; customer inquiries are rapid and provide an instant history of the customer's activities
❑ Mailing lists are generated from the customer database and labels can be prepared for customers billed, all customers, active customers, inactive customers or customers with past-due balances
❑ A tax-exempt status for dealing with government agencies or wholesale transactions; taxable and non-taxable sales are automatically stored and reported
❑ 22 categories to summarize your business activity
❑ Powerful reporting of specific areas of income; data files can be merged to have your business reported in quarters or other increments
❑ Easy identification of items or services that are profitable for your business
❑ Reports sorted by up to five keys to give you the specific information you need for your business and directing your areas of effort

SOAR does not teach accounting rules and assumes a certain level of expertise in accepted accounting procedures and protocols.

(PC-SIG Disk#'s 812, 813)

Special Requirements: *Two floppy drives.*
Author Registration: *$59.00*
➤*ASP Member.*

SPC-ACCOUNTS RECEIVABLE   *by I.J. Smith*

SPC-ACCOUNTS RECEIVABLE handles the Accounts Receivables for a small business. Separate account numbers for each payee track the person's address, phone number and tax code. Enter a short comment and six-line address labels will be printed for the records that you select.

Features:

❑ Virtually unlimited accounts and records
❑ Menu-driven and very easy to use
❑ Uses standard sized paper to print statements
❑ Generously-sized descriptions for statements

Make charge or payment entries, record the date, a reference (such as an invoice number), a description and the type of payment. Reports include charges, payments, detailed account and summary reports, period reports, general statements and a Past Due Accounts report listing all outstanding balances of 30, 60 or 90 days. Records may be selected for interest charges on overdue payments.

(PC-SIG Disk# 1715)

Special Requirements: *Unarchiving software.*
Author Registration: *$35.00*

    ✍ = Updated Program
☆ = New Program

SPC-Payroll
by I.J. Smith

SPC-PAYROLL is a payroll system designed for small companies which allow you to keep a payroll record and print out payroll forms for all your employees. For each employee, you may enter all the information for their wages, taxes and deductions from your checkbook stubs. SPC-PAYROLL can then print out transaction reports showing all the information entered. Various quarterly reports can be printed as needed. One report allows for maximum yearly earnings in which overages are listed separately. Allows for SDI deductions where needed. SPC-PAYROLL prints a Year-To-Date report and payroll W-2 forms for your employees.

(PC-SIG Disk# 1960)

Special Requirements: *None.*
Author Registration: *$25.00*

Takin' Care of Business ✍
by Hooper International, Inc.

A complete professional accounting system for non-accountants, TAKIN' CARE OF BUSINESS (TCB) improves on the top rated FINANCE MANAGER II by increasing speed, number of transactions and ease of use.

❑ User-definable data and time masks
❑ Ability to add/modify accounts while entering transactions
❑ Drop-to-DOS
❑ Context-sensitive Help
❑ Over 3,000 screen color selections
❑ Exploding windows
❑ EMS memory use for faster speed
❑ Full screen mouse support
❑ On-the-fly check writing
❑ Net subtotal type accounts for income statement
❑ User-definable check layout
❑ Automatic sales tax calculation
❑ Cash requirements report
❑ LaserJet compatible checks

❑ User-definable decimal and comma characters
❑ Unlimited number of transactions
❑ Seven-digit check numbers
❑ Greatly enhanced menuing system
❑ Pop-up, pull-down menus
❑ User-controllable sound effects
❑ Datafile backup utility
❑ Screen burn-in saver
❑ Check-like transaction input screen
❑ Alphanumeric account numbers
❑ Ten-character reference field
❑ Graphing capabilities (pie, bar, chart)
❑ Multiple state tax tables

(PC-SIG Disk#'s 2130, 2131)

Special Requirements: *640K RAM and a hard drive.*
Author Registration: *$39.95 to $49.95 per module, $149.00 for 6 modules, $299.00 for complete package including Payroll and Point of Sale/Invoicing.*
➤*ASP Member.*

TCB Accounts Payable Module ✍
by Hooper International, Inc.
(PC-SIG Disk# 2134)
Special Requirements: *640K RAM, a hard drive, and disks #2130 & 2131.*
Author Registration: *$39.95*

TCB Accounts Receivable Module ✍
by Hooper International, Inc.
(PC-SIG Disk# 2133)
Special Requirements: *640K RAM, a hard drive, and disks #2130 & #2131.*
Author Registration: *$39.95.*

TCB Accounts Reconciliation Module
by Hooper International, Inc.
Special Requirements: *640K RAM, a hard drive, and disks #2130 & #2131.*
Author Registration: *$14.95*

TCB General Ledger Module ✍
by Hooper International, Inc.
(PC-SIG Disk# 2132)
Special Requirements: *640K, a hard drive, and disks #2130 & #2131.*
Author Registration: *$49.95*

TCB Inventory Module ✍   *by Hooper International, Inc.*
(PC-SIG Disk# 2136)

Special Requirements: *640K RAM, a hard drive and disks #2130 & #2131.*
Author Registration: *$39.95*

TCB Payroll Module ✍   *by Hooper International, Inc.*
(PC-SIG Disk# 2135)

Special Requirements: *640K RAM, a hard drive, and disks #2130 & #2131.*
Author Registration: *$49.95*

TCB POS/Invoicing Module ✍   *by Hooper International, Inc.*
(PC-SIG Disk# 2137)

Special Requirements: *640K RAM, a hard drive, and disks #2136 & #2137.*
Author Registration: *$39.95*

W2/1099-Misc Generator   *by John Salmons*

Let W2/1099 print your W-2 and 1099 tax forms this year. The program is designed for the small business owner or tax preparer who needs to prepare these forms for their employees or clients.

W2/1099 accepts and stores employer, employee, and contractor information. When you need to print W-2 or 1099 forms, simply load your printer with preprinted continuous forms and away you go. Required subtotals are provided during the printing operation to aid in the preparation of other types of accounting forms.

(PC-SIG Disk# 1762)
Special Requirements: *None.*
Author Registration: *$49.00*

WYS-AR   *by I.J. Smith*

This Accounts Receivable program is based on a very simple concept, "What you see" in the data record windows "is what you get" in your statements and reports. Being able to see the account records in scrolling record windows makes the program very easy to use. The program also uses many lookup tables to further enhance its ease of use.

The concepts used eliminate many extra steps usually needed in programs of this type. No journals to post. No periods to close. No loss of your existing charges by month end closeouts. No 30-, 60-, or 90-day aged totals only. You decide the closing dates to print on your statements.

This program is designed to keep all outstanding charges in record tables for visibility and report purposes. The program offers virtually unlimited record capacities for maintaining large files if needed.

(PC-SIG Disk# 1856)
Special Requirements: *512K RAM.*
Author Registration: *None.*

ZPAY 3 ✍   *by Zpay Payroll Systems, Inc.*

Eliminate professional accountants while having complete control over your own payroll with ZPAY 3. Handle different pay periods; salaried, hourly, commissioned and salary with commission employees; tipped employees; non-employees; two overtime rates; bonuses; cost accounting; payroll computations; print your own checks and tax reports; automatic posting of pay periods! ZPAY 3 keeps track of multiple companies — as many as your disk will hold!

Eliminate costly programming updates with a built-in tax table editor for changing your own tax tables when necessary. A sample payroll allows you the opportunity to experiment without using your own payroll files!

ZPAY 3 is user-friendly, utilizing clear and simple menus with on-screen Help windows (at the touch of a key). The pull-down menus and pick lists are complete with mouse support!

(PC-SIG Disk#'s 2322, 2323)
Special Requirements: *375K RAM, a hard drive, and one floppy drive.*
Author Registration: *$69.95*
➤*ASP Member.*

▼ ▼ ▼

Accounting, Inventory Control

DAYO Inventory ✍   *by TJS Lab*

DAYO Inventory is a Multiuser inventory control, purchasing, and vendor maintenance application.

Since DAYO Inventory is multiuser, it is capable of operating on most of the PC based networks, ie Novell (tm). Other features include reports, labels, lists, and a graph. A simple database management module is also included to provide you with additional means to modify, view, and report your data. The ability to upgrade your system is available with the addition of supporting DAYO products (ie: DAYO POS, DAYO EOP, DAYO AP, and more...).

(PC-SIG Disk# 2401)

Special Requirements: *640K RAM, a hard drive, and DOS 3.3.*
Author Registration: *$25.00*
➤*ASP Member.*

DAYO Smart Reports ✍   *by TJS Lab*

DAYO SMART REPORTS contains many reports and routines that will help you to manage your purchasing, inventory, invoices, back orders, sales, and databases. There are 22 reports/lists/routines included in smart reports; i.e., Single warehouse, inventory zero price, valuation expanded, inventory zero retail, reorder (two weeks), reorder (four weeks), reorder (eight weeks), negative onhand, stock level shortage, vendor list, stock level over, customer list, inventory ASCII text, inventory item list, late P.O., checking account list, P.O - due in this week, check format list, inventory zero cost, and an expenses list.

(PC-SIG Disk#'s 2417, 2620)

Special Requirements: *640K RAM, hard drive, and DOS 3.3.*
Author Registration: *$25.00*
➤*ASP Member.*

Easy Inventory   *by I.J. Smith*

EASY INVENTORY brings small businessmen a near perfect stand-alone Inventory Control program. It can end the retailer's worst nightmare — too much of what is not selling stacked next to empty racks that ought to be holding the goods that sold like hotcakes. Instead, you can have the sweet dream of having on hand what the public wants, when it wants it, and for the best price volume purchasing can buy.

The basic Inventory Control chore of reporting what goods are on hand by numbers, locations and supplier is taken care of smoothly. With virtually unlimited capacity, it allows the businessman to quickly enter purchases and record sales. Then it reports what is on hand and where it is located. Lastly, you tell EASY INVENTORY what minimum quantity of each should be on hand and it will tell you what is needed, and how much you should buy from each supplier.

EASY INVENTORY offers nine reports. It tells you sales by time period or sales by both time period and location. It prints purchases and sales for the period, a useful tool for cash flow and usage monitoring. You can also print out total inventory. The Reorder report prints what you should order by item. Another report tracks backorders. You can print out a price list and an inventory by location and an inventory by supplier.

(PC-SIG Disk# 1996)

Special Requirements: *512K RAM and a hard drive is recommended.*
Author Registration: *$35.00*

Inventory Sort   *by Goose Lake Software*

Keep track of your inventory and other applicable information needed to analyze your inventory position.

INVENTORY SORT can handle multiple inventory lists which can have up to 1,000 part types in each. Maintain five fields of information per part type — including part number, part name, quantity, location, and cost. Sort records alphabetically, numerically, or by location. Update and delete part types, and get a formatted printout of the inventory list. Wholesale and retail cost values can be tracked as well.

(PC-SIG Disk# 961)

Special Requirements: *A version of Basic.*
Author Registration: *$25.00*

PC-Inventory+   *by TriSoft Enterprises*

An inventory program — not an accountant, not a computer cash register — just an inventory program. But if that's all you want, then this one is easy to use with lots of Help and good report features.

Pull-down menus make this program easy, especially if you are familiar with the inventory process. Configure the program at startup to handle your particular items, stock numbers, minimum inventory, prices, etc., and it will generate year-to-date sales reports, "low inventory reports" listing those items that fall below the minimum inventory level, and an "inventory price list" — a report of all items in the inventory showing your profit or loss margin on each item. If you have a mouse attached to your computer it will help you move around the Main Menu.

(PC-SIG Disk# 1910)

Special Requirements: *None.*
Author Registration: *$25.00*

Point-of-Sale/Inventory   *by Try-Then-Buy Software*

The POINT-OF-SALE/INVENTORY program is very easy to use. It functions as either a stand-alone inventory program or as a front-counter ticket system. Standard functions include enter, update and delete inventory, print tickets, edit the client list (updated automatically from POS), customize company information.

Reports include WTD/MTD/YTD sales, Catalog Printout, Full Inventory Listing, Client List, Company Information, Suggested Order. All reports are available in detailed and summary form.

An excellent program that is versatile enough to be used with your business.

(PC-SIG Disk# 2219)

Special Requirements: *2 floppy drives.*
Author Registration: *$95.00*

Pricebook, The   *by RJL System*

THE PRICEBOOK acts as a centralized item pricing log so you and your employees can instantly know what you are paying for any of the hundreds to thousands of items you carry. It also generates price quotes, acknowledgements, purchase orders and invoices. Each of these forms will have the prices automatically entered, extended and totaled, eliminating manual data entry and math errors.

(PC-SIG Disk#'s 1373, 1374)

Special Requirements: *None.*
Author Registration: *$99.95*

SPC-Inventory Plus   *by I.J. Smith*

SPC-INVENTORY is a business inventory program that will allow you to record an item's description, location, unit cost, last unit cost, unit price, quantity on hand, quantity on order, and up to three suppliers. For each item you may constantly update the sales and purchases to date. Update an item's price at any time. The program also allows for two other prices based on percentage factor of the standard price. This could be useful for fast sale lists. An inventory report can be generated using the last unit cost, thus representing the current value or replacement costs. Other reports include various sales and purchases reports, supplier listing, minimum order report, on-hand report, period usage report of quantities, and inventory report based on actual unit cost. The period reports generated could be especially useful to monitor profit from sales.

(PC-SIG Disk# 1961)

Special Requirements: *384K RAM and MS-DOS version 3.0 or higher.*
Author Registration: *$50.00*

Starbooks   *by Allsoft Computer Products*

STARBOOKS generates purchase orders, maintains stock levels based on sales rates, tracks and automatically updates your inventory, invoices and bills your customers and tracks their accounts, keeps tabs on backorders, and tracks sales trends and profits on an item-by-item basis.

It's a big, smart comprehensive program — and yet is surprisingly simple to run.

STARBOOKS does a lot more than similar programs costing over a thousand dollars. Set your proper inventory levels and STARBOOKS, through computer-generated SKU numbers, watches sales to make sure you order soon

      ✍ = Updated Program
      ☆ = New Program

enough, never forgetting to include backorders. It generates purchase orders by supplier and can automatically update stock levels. It prints out stock lists for inventories and lets you identify your shrinkage.

The Accounts Receivable menu lets you generate invoices and statements which list past due invoices. Posting payments takes seconds. While the program does not age accounts, it generates a customer list with account statuses. It watches backorders and lets you split payments among invoices. If a customer phones in a query, you can bring up the account in seconds. Almost unique to the program is its ability to generate long invoices with hundreds of items printed on it. Read the documentation carefully. This program has its own way of doing things and isn't very forgiving of experimental key pressing.

(PC-SIG Disk# 1250)

Special Requirements: *Hard drive strongly recommended.*
Author Registration: *$29.95*

Stock Inventory Control
by Declan Cowley

STOCK was created specifically for maintaining inventory control for businesses with a standard list of inventory items with specific order levels. (Businesses that stock one-of-a-kind items can use STOCK, but they must ignore references to order levels and year-to-date sales for each item.)

Items are listed as individual records in the database and each item has an order level. The program was written in dBASE III+, compiled and runs directly from DOS. For those who know dBASE and like to tinker, the source code is provided.

(PC-SIG Disk# 958)

Special Requirements: *None.*
Author Registration: *None.*

▼ ▼ ▼

Stock Inventory Control (PC-SIG Disk# 958)

Accounting, Job Costing and Bill of Materials

Cost Calculation
by MEABT Ltd.

Do you need to determine how much a product should cost your client? Do you need to know how much to charge customers for your new widget? If you do, then COST CALCULATION will help you. Tabulate activities, equipment, labor, indirect equipment, and materials used and arrive at a cost to be charged for your new widget or whatever you are manufacturing or making.

COST CALCULATION is a program for recording the costs involved in a small to large manufacturing and/or construction firm. Its objective is to provide itemized overhead costs and costs of each final product produced.

Installing the program is easy. Once done, read the manual carefully. This is necessary or the program cannot be used properly. For those in construction or manufacturing, COST CALCULATION is worth examining. The shareware version is limited to 20 pieces of equipment, 60 activities, 400 vouchers, and 10 consumers (not customers).

(PC-SIG Disk# 2035)

Special Requirements: *640K RAM. A hard drive is recommended.*
Author Registration: *$50.00*

Cost Effective II ✍
by Effective Software, Inc.

Are you having a hard time figuring the cost of that construction job? COST EFFECTIVE is here to help you out. COST EFFECTIVE keeps track of your raw materials and their prices. When you have a job to do, you tell the program what you will be needing and COST EFFECTIVE will tell you what the price will be.

Raw materials are never going to be the same price from day to day, this is why COST EFFECTIVE also allows you to enter new prices for your raw materials and get a new estimate. Reports like raw materials listings a prices can be printed from the program.

The program is fully menu-driven and there are Help screens available at any point in the program. You will find COST EFFECTIVE a great asset to your company if raw materials are a part of your productions.

(PC-SIG Disk# 845)

Special Requirements: *512K RAM. A hard drive is recommended.*
Author Registration: *$39.95*

COST-BIZ
by I.J. Smith

This job cost program is intended for those needing an easy-to-use, stand-alone job cost program. The program provides for four types of cost records: equipment, labor, materials and subcontractor costs. It also includes the option for percentages or quantities to be used in the cost items. Various reports are provided for either cost method used and both can be used if desired.

The program is very straightforward with four basic steps: add a job name record, add job cost records, enter and process transactions, and print reports as needed. The files used have virtually unlimited record capacities for large applications. It features automatic searching of tables and scrolling record windows for ease of use.

(PC-SIG Disk# 1984)

Special Requirements: *512K RAM. A hard drive is recommended.*
Author Registration: *$35.00*

DAYO MRP (Materials Requirement Planning)   ✍
by TJS Lab

This new version features increased memory management/availability and no more use of overlay files (.OVL). As a matter of fact, it is a totally rewritten program with many more features than 1.0. (Version 2.0 is not compatible with Version 1.0.) DAYO MRP (MATERIALS REQUIREMENT PLANNING) is a routine designed for manufacturers.

DAYO MRP builds items (end items) from items (components) in the inventory database. End items can later be placed into inventory for later sales. Supports a multilevel Bill of Materials. Features include automatic inventory posting and creation of inventory adjustment records. Databases are dBASE-compatible, multiuser, and many reports are available. See the Network Software & Utilities section of the "Encyclopedia of Shareware" for a complete listing of all the Dayo modules.

(PC-SIG Disk#'s 2398, 2619)

Special Requirements: *640K RAM, a hard drive, and DOS 3.3.*
Author Registration: *$50.00*
➤*ASP Member.*

Job Cost   ✍
by Micro Data Assist

JOB COST was made for the person who is responsible for monitoring and keeping costs under control on complex, expensive projects.

With this system you can:

❑ Set up multiple jobs each with its own unique set of cost centers
❑ Establish budget controls for each cost center for labor, material, and other expenses
❑ Edit and post transaction cost items to each cost center
❑ Post estimates of percent completions for each budget item
❑ Set up budgets for up to 99 unique change orders per job

JOB COST then provides you with cost variances, projected profit/loss at the detail budget level, cost center level, and total job. As expenses are posted, the overall job status is updated, keeping you

Job Cost (PC-SIG Disk# 1230)

informed of balance of funds available and projected profit/loss for the job's original estimate and change orders. You are provided concise reports for distribution to your client, foreman, and sub-contractors.

At the end of the job, after all reporting has been performed, you can back up the completed job to a floppy disk for storage, delete the job from your active job database, and if necessary, restore the job from backup for recording additional cost information after the job is completed. New jobs can be set up from existing job formats, requiring only the entering of the new job's unique budget information.

All functions are menu-driven with on-screen Help.

(PC-SIG Disk#'s 1230, 2674)
Special Requirements: *640K RAM, a hard disk, and a printer.*
Author Registration: *$45.00*

Takoff
by I.J. Smith

TAKOFF MINI ESTIMATOR was designed primarily for estimates and material take-offs for general contractors. A master file of the cost of up to 6000 items (materials and/or labor) is maintained and individual estimates can be printed out by combining these items. The menu system makes it easy to change stock prices and print new estimates. This program may be suitable for other professions which use items with established costs.

(PC-SIG Disk# 1715)
Special Requirements: *Unarchiving software.*
Author Registration: *$20.00*

▼ ▼ ▼

Accounting, Purchase Orders

Purchase Order System
by Ron Byxbe & Associates

PURCHASE ORDER SYSTEM is great for almost any kind of business. It makes it easy to enter and print purchase orders, and keep a record of all vendors. Enter a list of vendors with addresses and phone numbers, which you can later browse, edit, or delete. And you can print a vendor master list.

When entering a purchase order, the screen is divided into several columns for the account number, quantity, unit, item description, and price. Outstanding purchase transactions can be printed by account, vendor, or Purchase Order. Purchases received can be cleared immediately, and if a purchase transaction is accidentally cleared, it can be uncleared for recall.

(PC-SIG Disk# 741)
Special Requirements: *640K RAM, a hard drive.*
Author Registration: *$69.00*

▼ ▼ ▼

Accounting, Time-Billing Management

The Billing Statement
by A.P. Software

When you need a quick way to bill customers for time, services, or products, THE BILLING STATEMENT is an easy-to-use program for producing standard billing statements. The bills can be printed on plain or letterhead stationery. Track client accounts for one entire year. Individual charges and credits up to $100,000 and all balances and totals can be as much as $1,000,000.

(PC-SIG Disk# 2211)
Special Requirements: *None.*
Author Registration: *$35.00*

BillPower Plus ✍
by Integra Computing

BILLPOWER PLUS is an extremely powerful time-keeping, billing, and bookkeeping system designed specifically for small firms.

It's designed to help attorneys, accountants, and other professionals keep precise records and bill regularly. BILLPOWER PLUS tracks time worked on professional matters and calculates the amount owed by each client. It also keeps up with receipts and disbursements, and it maintains such accounts, allowing you to carry out simple bookkeeping functions. Most importantly, it automatically compiles service, disbursement, and receipt transactions for each client into monthly bills.

BILLPOWER PLUS offers a degree of integration not found in other time and billing programs. It can simultaneously update affected G/L accounts (as well as a client's balance and aged Receivables) at the time a disbursement or receipt is entered. This "real time" approach to bookkeeping saves you the time you would otherwise spend making duplicate G/L entries, posting transactions, and/or transferring files from one program to another.

BILLPOWER PLUS is designed as a unique "free entry" system. Open accounts at will, any time you want. Correct nearly any entry made at any time in the past. Also unique is BILLPOWER PLUS's ability to re-prepare bills. Transaction data is not destroyed when bills are prepared, therefore, it is easy to re-prepare bills that may be several months old. BILLPOWER PLUS can handle any combination of the following: 15 timekeepers/ employees (partners, secretaries, and others), 4000 cases, 4000 accounts, and 8000 transaction entries per month (services, disbursements, etc.).

(PC-SIG Disk# 1168)

Special Requirements: *512K RAM and a hard drive.*
Author Registration: *$150.00*

DAYO Time & Billing ✍ *by TJS Lab*

DAYO TIME & BILLING is a system of creating invoices for services and/or products. It has support for an Inventory, Receivables, projects/job/cases, and customers/clients. Other features include: multiuser, unlimited clients, unlimited projects/job/cases, project notes, customer notes, 30+ reports, onscreen reports, dBASE-compatible databases, laser formats for invoices and statements, two styles of statement/bills, printer setup and drivers, cash drawers, and over 46 configurable options.

(PC-SIG Disk#'s 2399, 2400)

Special Requirements: *640K RAM, hard drive, and DOS 3.3.*
Author Registration: *$50.00*
➤*ASP Member.*

Doing Time ☆ *by John Cope*

DOING TIME is a timekeeping and billing program that generates professional bills. Although it can be used by any company that is service-oriented, it is especially designed for companies whose employees bill by time worked (it was written for a law firm). DOING TIME maintains, among other things, the amounts billed, hours worked, and amounts due for each employee, each client, each case or project, and the company as a whole, for the current billing period and for the year. It also maintains up to 60 billing periods of history that are instantly available, from which bills can be reprinted.

Geared toward the more experienced computer user, documentation is limited, though not really needed to any extent as most options are fairly straightforward. DOING time could very well be the solution for service-oriented companies that have not had any luck yet with other software programs.

(PC-SIG Disk# 2783)

Special Requirements: *640K RAM, DOS 3.0+, and hard drive recommended.*
Author Registration: *$50.00+*

Mr. Bill *by David M. Alexander*

Money in the bank — a lovely phrase. Money owed to your company could be money in YOUR bank — if you collect it. MR. BILL does almost everything needed for your small- to medium-sized firm to birddog bills and increase collections with a minimum of labor and losses.

Highly flexible, MR. BILL handles taxes and charges of every sort. It automatically updates and sends client bills out monthly, prints your letterhead, and up to a 30-line message. You can charge different customers different rates for the same thing. Each file can have 16,000 entries. Get the client's name, address, phone number, and current balance from the operating system in less than four seconds.

Prepare itemized invoices/bills and generate a bevy of summary and in- depth reports including account aging and an excellent audit trail. The 28-page manual is adequate for experienced clerks.

(PC-SIG Disk#'s 469, 470)

Special Requirements: *Two floppy drives.*
Author Registration: *$40.00*

PC/BILL ✍ *by Radcliffe Shareware*

Here's a Time and Billing system for those who bill by hourly rates or dollar amounts for specific services.

✍ = Updated Program
☆ = New Program

With PC/BILL, all options are selected with a single key; it's completely menu-driven. Calculate fees based on either hours billed or a flat fee for services. Five different billing formats are available, allowing for varying amounts of detail in the bill for individual clients. Summary bills for clients with multiple accounts are generated automatically. Aging of Accounts Receivable and calculation of late-charge interest is optional for individual clients. Messages can be printed at the end of the bill with different messages available for accounts which are delinquent for 30, 60, 90, or over 90 days.

By using separate files, customized bills can be easily produced. Client information can be listed by account number or by client name. Each client's account can be checked for accuracy prior to generating any bills. If an error is found in a client's account, a bill cannot be produced until the error is corrected — an invaluable safeguard. Data security is assured by a file backup procedure carried out each month as part of the end-of-month procedures.

The package comes with a set of demonstration files that you can use to run the system and get acquainted with the billing operation.

(PC-SIG Disk# 2258)

Special Requirements: *Hard drive.*
Author Registration: *$100.00*

QUE Accounting Time & Attendance ☆   *by Que Accounting*

QUE ACCOUNTING TIME AND ATTENDANCE is a system for recording employee attendance.

Managers enter work schedules and work rules (rates, break times, overtime, late arrival grace period, etc.). The employees' In/Out times are entered from time cards or from an ASCII file created by a time clock system.

Three levels of reports are possible: corporate, company, and work rule. Reports include employee listing, time card validation, employees approaching overtime, employee schedules, period summaries, and more. The extensive report writer and query systems make information easily accessible.

Increase the accuracy of payroll calculations, reduce preparation time, improve labor allocation efficiency, get timely reports of errant behavior, and improve forecasting with the use of historical data.

QUE is completely menu-driven and includes context-sensitive Help, documentation, and a tutorial. QUE uses dBASE-compatible files and integrates with other QUE accounting modules. A great way to take control of payroll expenses.

(PC-SIG Disk# 2497)

Special Requirements: *640K RAM, two floppy drives and a hard drive.*
Author Registration: *$45.00*

Time Tracker   *by Superior Micro-Techniques*

Do you have to keep track of the amount of work you do for others? Are you a contractor, lawyer, consultant or other hourly professional? Here's an easy way for your to track your working hours and simplify the billing process.

TIME TRACKER keeps track of what you do for your clients and the time it takes to complete it. It keeps track of all of your accounts and bills them. It also records the receipt of money from your billings.

Since your Accounts Receivable is taken care of, the only thing you have to worry about is keeping track of your expenses. Moreover, it will let you know where you stand in terms of accounts receivable, income, and unbilled hours, at any time.

(PC-SIG Disk# 825)

Special Requirements: *512K RAM. A hard drive is recommended.*
Author Registration: *$69.00*

Time Tracker (PC-SIG Disk# 825)

TimeStax ✍   *by Johnson Technologies*

TIMESTAX is a personal time management tool like Timeslips-III, Time Card, and Timesheet. This low-cost time management program allows one or more users to systematically record and summarize time spent doing work.

Timecards are entered specifying user-defined clients, projects, and tasks along with the date, time, and an optional eight-line note describing the activity. Fully control the level of summary detail in a wide variety of management reports. Other features include an automatic timer to clock any given activity; flexible export, archive, and backup of timecards; on-line Help screens; full report selection and sorting criteria; sublists of projects and tasks specific to each client; up to 100 employees per database; and LAN compatibility.

By simplifying the important features and eliminating the less essential features, TIMESTAX offers full functionality at a lower price than the competition. Since most users will spend less than 20 minutes a week running the program, TIMESTAX relies on a simple intuitive interface that takes only ten minutes to learn.

(PC-SIG Disk# 2393)

Special Requirements: *None.*
Author Registration: *$49.95*
➤*ASP Member.*

▼ ▼ ▼

Agriculture

Agriculture Assortment   *by Dept of Agriculture & Appld Econ*

More tools for today's farmer!

The Department of Agriculture at the University of Minnesota has prepared this wide-ranging collection of BASICA decision aids for farm management.

Several conversion programs and calculators help the busy farmer with yield analysis, gestation dates, harvest and storage costs, probable feed requirements, maximum bid price for farmland, and more. Applicable information for small- to large-sized farms help you through the intricacies of farm management problems and opportunities.

(PC-SIG Disk# 459)

Special Requirements: *Two disk drives, CGA, and a version of BASIC.*
Author Registration: *None.*

File Descriptions:

AUTOEXEC	BAT	Automatic instructions to read this file
ACRSCALC	BAS	Analysis of federal depreciation computations
FARMBID	BAS	Determines the maximum bid price for land or a farm
DRYSTORE	BAS	Analysis of harvest and storage cost & alternatives
DATECALC	BAS	Computes future (gestation) dates & calendars
BESTCROP	BAS	Price & yield analysis of crop choices (equal-margin)
FEEDPIGS	BAS	Should I feed out a batch of feeder pigs
MENU	BAS	Menu program for BASIC pgms on this disk
FEEDVALU	BAS	Given corn & SBM values, what's a feed worth
FEEDSILO	BAS	Calculates likely dairy feed in a silo, given feed rate
STEERBID	BAS	Calculates equivalent FOB prices for fat steers at farm
SOWINDEX	BAS	Determines a sow index, relative to the group
SDIR	COM	Two-column directory
SCROLLCK	COM	Scroll lock - control with shift keys
RUN	BAT	Batch file requests date, loads BASICA & starts MINNAIDS
README	DOC	Documentation file
READ	BAT	Batch file to provide instructions for SCROLLCK.COM
PEARSON	BAS	Balances one ration nutrient from two feed sources
USERDOCS	BAS	Explains how to make hardcopy documentation of MINNAIDS
ULOGO	BAS	University of Minnesota logo — START HERE
TIMEC	COM	Help program

Agriculture Programs from Ridgetown College   *by Ridgetown College of Agricultural*

From Ridgetown College of Ontario comes this fine collection of farm management tools. Besides a handy metric conversion program, highlights include:

LUMBER — Welcome to the world of computer carpentry. Enter your basic design and constraints, if any. It produces reliable estimates of all the construction materials you will need for your project and keeps a running total of the costs.

USLE — Deal with the problem of soil loss evaluation on irregular slopes with this program. Get a fast, accurate estimate of such soil loss. As many, if not most, fields have irregular slopes, the farmer/conservation specialist can benefit from this aid.

WOODHEAT — Explore the economics of using wood as a primary source of heating.

The documentation also includes the code for Hewlett Packard (HP-41c) calculators.

(PC-SIG Disk# 461)

Special Requirements: *None.*
Author Registration: *None.*

▼ ▼ ▼

Archive/Compression Utilities

Arc
by Budget Software Company

A collection of file archiving utilities. Use the space on your disks more efficiently. Because file compatibility can change with different versions of ARC, four different versions are included.

(PC-SIG Disk# 609)

Special Requirements: *None.*
Author Registration: *$35.00*
➤ *ASP Member.*

ArcMaster ☆
by New-Ware

ARCMASTER is a slick program for users who need to manage, view, convert, or look into the contents of compressed files. Files that have been compressed by special computer programs such as PKZIP, ARCA, PAK, LHA, and ARJ, ARC, are all supported by ARCMASTER.

It is a complete and detailed archive program interface control system. ARCMASTER remembers all of the various command line switches and options that may be used with archiving programs. In addition, it is a powerful and flexible DOS shell to help you maintain and manipulate your DOS directory and file structures.

The ARCMASTER interface is about as intuitive as they come.

Features include:

❑ Full support for either keyboard or mouse
❑ File selection with scrolling cursor bars
❑ Launch other programs (such as your favorite word processor)
❑ Point-and-shoot or pull-down menus
❑ Directory tree structure for two drives or subdirectories
❑ File tagging

You must have one or more of the compression programs installed in your system in order to get the full benefits from ARCMASTER. Tag a group of files, use McAfee's SCAN to check them for viruses, keep a running total of their size, and create new or updated compressed files. ARCMASTER comes with a simple file browser that allows you to list the contents of archived files, and even print ASCII documents from inside the archive file. This is a great feature when you want to view the documentation of a program before you un-archive it.

In addition to the complete archiving systems cited above, ARCMASTER supports LZEXE, PKLITE, and DIET, all of which are designed for the specific purpose of compressing executable (.EXE) files.

(PC-SIG Disk# 2764)

Special Requirements: *PKZIP, ARCA, PAK, LHA, ARC, or ARJ.*
Author Registration: *$35.00*

ARJ ☆
by Robert K. Jung

ARJ is the newest file compression program with compression and speed as good or better than PKZIP. It has started to gain popularity on BBSs because it does a very good job of tightly archiving files. Watch out PKZIP, there's a new kid on the block!

Major features include;

❑ Ranks with the best in compression in terms of size reduction. Particularly effective with database files, graphics files, and large documents
❑ Archive and individual file comments with option of inputting comments from a file
❑ 32-bit CRC file integrity check

❏ DOS volume label support
❏ Empty directory support
❏ Option to test new archive before overwriting the original archive
❏ Archive multiple volumes with one ARJ command. Backup a full hard disk drive to multiple floppies
❏ File re-ordering facility. Sort by file size, file extension, CRC value, date-time modified, filename, pathname, compression ratio, file attribute and more
❏ String search with context display within archive files
❏ Recover files from broken archives
❏ Self-extraction feature internal to the ARJ runfile. The SFX module is full-featured with a built-in Help screen
❏ Internal string data integrity check in ARJ to resist hacking a la LHARC to ICE
❏ Archive security envelope feature to resist tampering with secured archives. This feature disallows ANY changes to a secured archive
❏ Password option to encrypt archived files
❏ File extraction to screen in a paged mode to permit browsing
❏ Specification of the files to be added to an archive via one or more list files
❏ Specify files to exclude from processing
❏ Sub-directory recursion during compression and extraction
(PC-SIG Disk# 2772)

Special Requirements: *None.*

Author Registration: *$30.00. Site licenses available.*

DStuff   *by TOADWare Software Systems*

It's a safe bet that one or more of these DSTUFF utilities will prove invaluable to programmers and other people who make their living with computers. Serious home computer users will also benefit from these speedy utilities.

D makes the DOS DIR command obsolete. Using color highlights, D displays directory information, sorted by file name in ascending or descending order. Switch from displaying the file size to displaying the DOS file date. Hidden files can no longer hide. If they're on your hard disk, D will find them for you.

DZIP displays the internal directory of members of PKWare ZIP files. Information is displayed in groups of 58 entries. DZIP will tell you what the individual file size will be after it is uncompressed. It can display the total compressed size and the total extracted size of all archived members of the file and the total disk space that will be used if all members are compressed or uncompressed.

DARC displays the internal structure of SEA ARC files and their compressed sizes or with a quickcommand line option see what the uncompressed sizes are! Also, you will be shown what compression method was used for each entry.

DDBASE will display all of the header information for any dBASE III, III+, or IV .DBF file. See all of the field names, their type and length in an easy to follow paged format. Also displayed is the total record size, number of records, and the date the file was created or last modified.

DICE shows what files are in an LH .ICE compressed file. You can see all of the files, or by using an optional command line mask, only the files you wish to see. Elect to see the compressed file sizes, or the uncompressed sizes. You will also be shown what compression method was used for each entry.

BIOSD is identical to D except the BIOS is used for screen writing to allow operation on DeskView and other multi-taskers.

SCRNPRT.COM allows you to redirect all LPT output to any other device or file. It is a Terminate and Stay Resident (TSR) program.

All of the programs in the DStuff Package can detect if they have been attacked by most viruses and will warn the user if this occurs. These programs also use fast direct screen writing and colors to display the needed information as quickly as possible in an easy to read format. All colors are user-configurable in a simple, easy to use, point-and-shoot manner that automatically detects the presence of a mouse and allows it to be used along with the cursor keys.

Users of any of these programs will find their lives made easier with these utilities.

(PC-SIG Disk# 1861)

Special Requirements: *CGA. A hard drive is recommended.*

Author Registration: *$25.00*

LHarc & Utilities
by Paul Anacker

This collection of archive utilities can make you the tightest, most effective archiver on the block.

LHARC compresses more tightly than other compression programs. It takes a little longer — but there are times when space is more important than speed.

2LZH converts ARC, PKARC, and ZIP files to LHARC format. LHDIR is a companion program to view and identify compressed LHARC files and self-extracting LHARC.

And if LHARC isn't all you need, the utility MAD (Mike's Archive Directory) can show you the contents of every popular archive-type available and their self-extracting executable (SFX) files. MAD currently supports ARC, PAK, ZIP, ZOO, LZS, DWC and LZH archives and all self-extracting .COM and .EXE files created by SEA ARC, PK-ARC, PAK, PK-ZIP, SEZ (zoo), LARC (lzs), DWC and LHARC (lzh).

ZIPNOTE rounds out the collection; it lets you attach comments to ZIP files. The utility is especially useful for BBS sysops who want to mark ZIP files for free advertising. ZIPNOTE's flexibility allows a comment to be typed from the keyboard, copied from an existing text file, or stored in a configuration file.

(PC-SIG Disk# 2018)

Special Requirements: *None.*

Author Registration: *Zipnote $10 , Mad $5 , other programs - no fee.*

LZE
by Fabrice Bellard

Can you imagine the space you could reclaim from your hard drive by compressing all the .EXE files? Well, LZE, a public domain program, compresses an .EXE file to almost half its size! This isn't compression that must be decompressed to use the file; this is compression of the code, so the program can be used as is.

LZE works with companion program COMTOEXE (which converts .COM files to .EXE files) to make a powerful compression package.

(PC-SIG Disk# 2316)

Special Requirements: *None.*

Author Registration: *None.*

LZESHELL
by Peter Petrakis

LZESHELL interacts with LZE and COMTOEXE (all public domain programs) to make those programs even better. LZESHELL changes .COM files to .EXE files with one command. LZE then compresses the code of .EXE files to regain space on your hard drive.

(PC-SIG Disk# 2316)

Special Requirements: *None*

Author Registration: *None*

PKLITE ☆
by PKWare Inc.

PKLITE is an easy-to-use file compression program. PKLITE increases your valuable disk space by compressing executable files so they will require much less disk space. PKLITE also has the ability to expand your files back to their original size.

PKLITE compresses your files much like PKZIP, but adds a small amount of extraction code at the beginning of the executable file. When you run an application that has been compressed with PKLITE, the program is automatically expanded into memory and run. The compressing process does not change the operation of the program; it merely reduces the disk space required to store it. No additional memory is needed to run most programs compressed with PKLITE. Running a PKLITE-compressed program requires a maximum of 4K of extra memory overhead to expand the application. Memory available to the application remains the same.

When you wish to use PKLITE to create compressed executables for commercial software, you can obtain the PKLITE Professional Package for $146. This version includes an extra compression option so that compressed executables cannot be uncompressed by PKLITE.

(PC-SIG Disk# 1364)

Special Requirements: *None.*

Author Registration: *$46 - $146 for Professional Package*

➤*ASP Member.*

PKPAK, PKUNPAK, and PKSFX   *by PKWare Inc.*

PKPAK, PKUNPAK and PKSFX are a set of archiving utilities that allow you to compress your files into an archive file which takes up less disk space for storage and helps reduce the transmission time when sending files over a modem. PKPAK compresses multiple files into an archive file, PKUNPAK extracts some or all these files from the archive for normal program usage, and PKSFX creates self-extracting archive files. Archive files may be updated, listed to the screen, annotated with comments, printed, and password-protected.

Other features include: extract only the most recent files when the same named file already exists on disk, extract files to the printer in both ASCII and binary mode, an easier to read listing of files, and updating archives which are larger than half your floppy disk storage area.

(PC-SIG Disk# 1330)

Special Requirements: *None.*
Author Registration: *$20.00*
➤*ASP Member.*

PKZFIND ☆   *by PKWare Inc.*

PKZFIND File Finder Plus works like other "where is" type programs, with an important plus. PKZFIND not only searches all directories on your floppy or hard disk, but searches through ZIP files too. Once the desired file is located, PKZFIND can automatically change to the subdirectory where the file was found! Find any file, zipped or not, simply and easily. PKZFIND requires only 32K of free memory to run and opens files in SHARE mode, which allows for compatibility with network software and LANs.

(PC-SIG Disk# 1364)

Special Requirements: *None.*
Author Registration: *$25*
➤*ASP Member.*

PKZIP, PKUNZIP, PKSFX   *by PKWare Inc.*

PKZIP is the new file compression system from PKWare which helps you cram more programs and data onto the precious, crowded real estate of your hard disk by shrinking that data into small archived ZIP files. When you take data on the road, zipping means fewer floppies to carry or lose. Downloads and backups of your system will be completed faster with the program. Zipped files take less time to transmit via modem — many BBSs use ZIP files as a standard.

PKZIP will handle all file maintenance needs, including the addition and deletion of files, and provides reports of technical information from within compressed files.

PKUNZIP is the complimentary program to reconstruct or extract compressed files. In addition to reconstructing a complete ZIP file, it can selectively release individual files, show files on the screen for fast viewing, or print them.

PKSFX creates self-extracting archive files. Archived files may be updated, listed, annotated with comments, printed, and password-protected.

Included on-disk is a 28-page manual telling you everything you ever wanted to know about how compression works.

(PC-SIG Disk# 1364)

Special Requirements: *None.*
Author Registration: *$25*
➤*ASP Member.*

PKZMENU ☆   *by PKWare Inc.*

PKZMENU is a menu-driven version of PKUNZIP. A quick and easy way to extract files from ZIPped files, the program provides a variety of additional functions. You can display zipped files of a given directory and view the contents; tag the specific files you want to work with.

Pull-down menus access a variety of features:

❏ View ZIP file contents   ❏ Use the easy but powerful tagging options
❏ Display technical information of zipped files   ❏ Extract, test, view, or print zipped files
❏ Use the built-in FAST! extraction code   ❏ Sort displayed files in a variety of ways
❏ Extract password-protected files   ❏ Create DOS directories from within the program
❏ Create PKZIP/PKUNZIP-compatible list files

PKZMENU also includes support for VGA 50 line-, EGA 43 line- and monochrome monitors, mice, networks and laptop computers. The program is DesqView-aware.

(PC-SIG Disk# 1364)

Special Requirements: *None. Hard drive recommended.*
Author Registration: *$39.50*
➤*ASP Member.*

TinyProg ✍ *by Tranzoa, Co.*

If you need more hard drive or floppy disk space (and who doesn't?), TINYPROG could be your disk space miser. TINYPROG compresses .EXE and .COM program files by as much as 30%. Compress the file once and forget about it. When you run the compressed file, it decompresses and starts right up. TINYPROG has command line option features for the programmer in all of us, like the /u option that allows you to put a personal message at the beginning of your favorite program. As a safety feature, TINYPROG makes a backup copy of your original .EXE or .COM file.

(PC-SIG Disk# 2018)

Special Requirements: *None.*
Author Registration: *$15.00*

▼ ▼ ▼

Artificial Intelligence

Decision Analysis System *by Armada Systems*

DECISION ANALYSIS SYSTEM, (DAS), is probably the best decision analysis package on the market. It utilizes a number of well established Multiple Criteria Decision Making algorithms in its analysis. This is not a "black box" program. Numerical results are provided for each stage in the analysis, so that the user can see what is happening and have confidence in the results.

DAS presents a scientific approach to decision making. It will replace intuition and speculation, while preserving such qualitative factors as experience and judgment. This innovative, yet remarkably easy-to-use package consists of two separate decision analysis programs: the Decision Matrix Method (DMM), and the Pairwise Comparison Method (PCM).

DMM is designed to be used primarily with tangible and easily quantifiable data. Employing a matrix of criteria and alternatives, DMM is extremely easy to use, providing you with an unbiased ranking of alternatives. The program begins its analysis by highlighting dominated or substandard alternatives. Remaining alternatives are then ranked in order of preference by using a number of popular and well respected decision analysis techniques. Some of these techniques include: LAM (Linear Assignment Method), NAW (Normalized Additive Weighting), ELECTRE (Elimination et Choice Translating Reality), and TOPSIS (Technique for Order Preference by Similarity to Ideal Solution). An aggregation and synthesis procedure follows which produces the final preference rankings of alternatives. The user's manual includes text book references where these techniques and algorithms are explained in full detail.

PCM is designed to deal specifically with subjective assessments and evaluations of alternatives and criteria. It is based on the well-known Analytic Hierarchy Process (AHP), developed by Thomas L. Saaty at the Wharton School, University of Pennsylvania. Here, problems are modeled using a hierarchical structure with elements in this hierarchy compared in pairs. The advantage of this is that it helps you to focus your attention on each part of the problem separately. Based on your inputs, PCM will calculate your judgment consistency, and it will quantify the impact of each element in the hierarchy on the overall goal. For example, it may quantify your preference of a set of alternatives based on some subjective criteria. PCM is not only useful in decision making problems, but also in any other area where you find it difficult to quantify subjective factors.

Applications include: location planning, cost/benefit analysis, strategic planning, employee selection, resource allocation, sales forecasting, taste testing, new product evaluations, and many more.

(PC-SIG Disk# 953)

Special Requirements: *None.*
Author Registration: *$100.00 per program, $150.00 for both.*

ESIE
by Lightwave

Put some smarts in your personal computer and turn it into your very own assistant. ESIE, the Expert System Inference Engine, is an artificial intelligence shell that lets you build a custom knowledge base, or expert system, to help you make decisions.

Simple but effective, ESIE operates by loading in a knowledge base and building inferences out of the rules contained therein. You define the rules that the system uses. This is especially good as an introduction to expert systems as well as having excellent on-disk documentation to get you started in AI. For the advanced student, ESIE can handle the normal gamut of expert systems building.

To see how ESIE works without building your own knowledge base, load ESIE and one of the three supplied knowledge bases (ANIMAL, DOCTOR, or GLASS) and try it!

(PC-SIG Disk# 398)

Special Requirements: *None.*
Author Registration: *$75.00. For $145.00, you get source code, telephone support and more.*

EyeSight
by Robots, ETC

Enter the world of artificial intelligence and learn about computer vision with EYESIGHT.

EYESIGHT is a vision processing program designed as an introduction to the field of computer vision. You do not need a camera or any prior knowledge of computer vision to use EYESIGHT. EYESIGHT provides an environment for reading and writing image files, performing various image processing functions, and displaying the results.

Computer vision is a branch of artificial intelligence attempting to give computers the gift of sight. Using EYESIGHT, you will learn how this is possible. EYESIGHT comes with sample image files that you can use to experiment and learn with. You will learn about region recognition and edge detection. EYESIGHT provides 17 different image processing functions with which you can experiment. Also included is a tutorial on computer vision. EYESIGHT is an exciting look into computer vision.

(PC-SIG Disk# 1678)

Special Requirements: *CGA or EGA.*
Author Registration: *$25.00*

Imp Shell, The
by Daniel H. Marcellus

IMP SHELL is a powerful expert system for the IBM-PC. It has all the utilities needed to develop, test, and run new expert systems.

An expert system is a program that has captured the expertise in some field and can deploy that expertise with seemingly intelligent behavior. This shell is useful for diagnostic problems — whether you're an auto mechanic with a client whose car keeps stalling, or a Test engineer with a batch of wafers that for some reason just won't pass QC. IMP SHELL can speed up your diagnosis process considerably. The IMP SHELL's functions are menu-driven and appear in windows. IMP expert systems are rule-based, backwards-chaining systems. They are very fast and not limited by an artificially small number of rules. It is especially good for classification tasks, troubleshooting, and alternative selection. It does not, however, have the proper architecture for applications that need a well-defined sequence of complex steps — applications such as cost estimation or equipment configuration. These should be done on a forward-chaining shell.

(PC-SIG Disk# 761)

Special Requirements: *512K RAM.*
Author Registration: *None.*

Management Action Expert
by Richard Eveille

MAE (Management Action Expert) is an expert system shell that can solve problems in a non-procedural manner from an application of rules and facts about a problem.

MAE reads a file known as a "knowledge base," and asks you a series of questions to determine the cause of the problem. Based on the answers and the information in the knowledge base, a recommended course of action is given.

Create your own knowledge base with a few simple commands and use the program for a variety of applications.

(PC-SIG Disk# 976)

Special Requirements: *None.*
Author Registration: *$25.00*

    ✍ = Updated Program
☆ = New Program

XLISP
by David Betz

XLISP is an experimental programming language combining some features of LISP with an object-oriented extension capability. It is written in C and is easily extended with user-written functions and classes. It assumes some knowledge of LISP and object-oriented programming. This version has both MS-DOS and PC-DOS specific code. This package represents an inexpensive opportunity to begin to tackle programming in the field of artificial intelligence.
(PC-SIG Disk# 148)

Special Requirements: *None.*
Author Registration: *None.*

XXXpert
by Performance Systems Group

XXXPERT lets you create question-and-answer diagnostic programs to help solve problems — an expert system.

An expert system can be used for just about any application that lends itself to a hierarchy of rules. Once a set of rules is created and entered into the expert system, it will let you make decisions more quickly and consistently than before. The same set of rules, used by another, should yield the same decisions.

XXXPERT lets you create a file of rules in an English language syntax. Then you enter questions into a file. Both rules and questions are compiled and then executed by the CONSULT program. This lets a person answer questions and make decisions.
(PC-SIG Disk# 883)

Special Requirements: *512K RAM.*
Author Registration: *$29.00*

▼ ▼ ▼

Astrology and Fortune Telling

Astrol96
by Halloran Software

Know what the stars have in store for you, your family and friends. ASTROL96 is a comprehensive astrology program that calculates the zodiacal positions of all of the planets and the sun, moon, and the 12 house cusps for any date, time, and place. Display the aspects and midpoints between the planets, ascendant, and midheaven and midpoint/planet conjunctions.

Calculate a person's transits for up to one year. Charts can be displayed in either graphic chartwheel format or in non-graphic format. The charts can be saved to disk, reviewed, deleted, sorted alphabetically, and compared with other charts.

Compare mutual aspects and indexes of communication for compatibility, as well as conduct rapid searches for compatible matches between charts.

So, what's your sign?
(PC-SIG Disk# 966)

COLORADO
MOUNTAIN ZONE 7 HRS
LONGITUDE = 104° 30'
LATITUDE = 40° 0'

Esc to Exit
Astrol96 (PC-SIG Disk# 966)

Special Requirements: *None.*
Author Registration: *$29.00*

The Astrologer
by Independent Computer Services

The ASTROLOGER provides a personal profile derived from a library of over 200 personality aspects. In exchange for your name, birthdate, time and place of birth, and latitude and longitude of birthplace, a report is generated that focuses on your individuality and your desire for self-improvement.

If you are curious about how the positioning of the planets at the time of your birth affected your personality, and how you can make a better you, you should try THE ASTROLOGER!
(PC-SIG Disk# 2453)

Special Requirements: *None.*
Author Registration: *$30.00*

Book of Changes ☆

by R.K. West Consulting

Do you have a question you just can't answer? Are you looking for advice? Consult the I Ching, the BOOK OF CHANGES, one of the classics of Chinese literature. Use its poetic messages for both fortune telling and insight into humanity's role in the natural world.

Toss computerized versions of coins or sticks. These coins or sticks create a pattern of six lines to form a hexagram. The hexagram is then interpreted by using the I Ching. The "yin and yang" philosophy of the I Ching is ideally suited to the "yes and no" or "0 and 1" organization of the computer.

Sit back and read its thought provoking messages. Edit the messages, add your own comments, and then print or save them.

(PC-SIG Disk# 2720)

Special Requirements: *420K RAM and two floppy drives.*
Author Registration: *$24.00*
➤*ASP Member.*

By the Numbers ☆

by R.K. West Consulting

BY THE NUMBERS is a complete personality report that uses the philosophy of Numerology to analyze your name and birthdate for their symbolic meaning and metaphysical vibrations. The Pythagorean system takes name changes into account, analyzes 10 separate personality elements, and provides your forecast for the coming year. Professional-quality reports can be saved and edited for a truly personalized reading. This program is used by many mail-order numerologists. This has been a most popular program for nearly three years!

(PC-SIG Disk# 2730)

Special Requirements: *420K RAM and hard disk or dual-floppy system.*
Author Registration: *$29.00*
➤*ASP Member.*

Chou I ✍

by Richard K. Thompson

If you're a Taoist, a student of the I Ching, or just curious about the I Ching and divination, you should have this program!

"Chou I: The Changes of Chou" is an original translation of the Book of Changes (often called "I Ching") of the Chou Dynasty (circa 1100 B.C.). This version provides an interpretation of the primordial symbolism of the archaic Chinese pictographs which reflect the Taoist and Shamanistic roots of the I Ching. The translation included is entirely new, made by an internationally recognized scholar.

The program allows one to study the text, perform divinations, and save the results (and your comments) to disk for later review. Windowing options allow one to view data about the relevant trigrams while viewing a hexagram. Also available (in a pop-up window) is a glossary of over 100 key terms, with descriptions and interpretations of the ancient Chinese characters. Complete instructions are provided in the on-screen manual.

(PC-SIG Disk# 2142)

Special Requirements: *None.*
Author Registration: *$10.00*

Crystal Ball ✍

by R.K. West Consulting

When and where will disaster strike? What will be a future scientific development and what good will it do? What will make international headlines? Who will win future elections?

Welcome to the first psychic computer program. Like human psychics, CRYSTAL BALL generates predictions about the future and answers any question you may wish to ask. Unlike human psychics, CRYSTAL BALL generates its predictions entirely at random. It makes no claim for accuracy. Nor does CRYSTAL BALL claim that what it says will make sense. But that's why it's fun. Just type in your question and sit back and watch for the answer on the screen. Great for New Year's Eve parties!

(PC-SIG Disk# 1492)

Special Requirements: *None.*
Author Registration: *$19.00*
➤*ASP Member.*

✍ = Updated Program
☆ = New Program

Fortune Teller ☆
by R.K. West Consulting

A potpourri of fortune-telling techniques. FORTUNE TELLER offers three divination methods: dice, short Numerology readings, and runes. Also included are explanations of each method and its history, as well as an ESP test.

(PC-SIG Disk# 2744)

Special Requirements: *400K RAM, hard drive or dual-floppy system.*
Author Registration: *$29.00*
➤*ASP Member.*

Geomancy
by R.K. West Consulting

Want to know what your future holds? Try this computerized version of GEOMANCY, an ancient system of divination.

Originating in Africa, GEOMANCY was officially outlawed by churchmen for its ties to the occult and witchcraft. For the daring computer buff, it offers a way to become a Querent and turn your questions over to four Mothers, four Daughters, four Nephews, and two Witnesses in a dozen Houses with a Reconciler to resolve conflicts.

You or your computer can create the needed 16 rows of dots found in a random field. Minutes later, you scroll through the dozen houses to see the truth revealed in ASCII interpretations. Save your answers to disk, chart them, or print them.

(PC-SIG Disk# 1275)

Special Requirements: *512K RAM.*
Author Registration: *$30.00*
➤*ASP Member.*

Mayan Calendar ✍
by R.K. West Consulting

Mesh the two ancient Mayan calendars with the Julian calendar and venture an understanding of your mystic horoscope on a level you have never suspected. Unto you may come the knowledge that on this date, warnings abound of the evils that lurk in the dark. Yet it may be a fine day for making war, love or money. Only the MAYAN calendar can bring you these arcane truths!

The ancient Mayans used a complicated system of two calendars running parallel with each other. One, like ours, was a solar calendar, based on the 365-day year. The other was a 260-day astrological calendar. Together, they formed a 52-year cycle of named and numbered days and months, and were the basis of festivals, predictions, and religious practices. (Imagine the two calendars as big gear wheels with intermeshing cogs, one with 365 cogs, the other with 260. It takes 52 years for a particular cog in one wheel to mesh again with a particular cog in the other, thus repeating the days in their original order.) Converting a modern calendar date to its Mayan equivalent requires complex calculations. This program performs the task quickly and even prints your Mayan horoscope! Not superstitious? Astronomers and anthropologists share great interest in the one solar calendar of 365 days and the second 260-day astrological calendar. Harmonic convergences lurk where they mesh!

(PC-SIG Disk# 1520)

Special Requirements: *None.*
Author Registration: *$29.00*
➤*ASP Member.*

Personal Tarot ☆
by R.K. West Consulting

Now you can enjoy professional-quality Tarot card readings on your computer!

Ask a question — PERSONAL TAROT deals and then describes the cards and their meanings. PERSONAL TAROT is customizable. Edit the card descriptions and add comments for truly personalized readings.

(PC-SIG Disk# 2521)

Special Requirements: *420K RAM, two floppy drives or a hard drive.*
Author Registration: *$24.00*
➤*ASP Member.*

Procon Fortune
by ProCon Software

An astrology program designed to provide a personality analysis according to both Western and Eastern astrology and numerology. Just enter birthdates and names, and you'll have complete personality descriptions and compatibilities with other signs. Results are displayed under both systems of astrology, and another report is provided based on numerology.

(PC-SIG Disk# 1054)

Special Requirements: *None.*
Author Registration: *$30.00 to $90.00.*

Richard Webster Programs ☆
by R.K. West Consulting

RICHARD WEBSTER'S AURA READING and RICHARD WEBSTER'S QUICK NUMEROLOGY: Based on the work and research of internationally-known psychic entertainer Richard Webster, WAURA helps you learn what to look for when attempting to see the human aura. WQUICK uses a special method of Numerology, popular in Australia and New Zealand, to give a quick but pointed personality profile. Great fun! Complete documentation included.

(PC-SIG Disk# 2716)

Special Requirements: *Hard disk or dual-floppy system.*
Author Registration: *$29.00*
➤*ASP Member.*

Rune-Caster
by Gesture Sotware

In RUNE-CASTER, the casting of runes, an ancient tool of divination, is used as a modern method to explore personal understanding and growth. Runes are ancient letterings, each of which stands for a concept or theme such as names, momentum, thorn, beach, path, torch, giving, joy, hail, need, ice, harvest, support, kind, star, sprouts, horse, people, water, awaken, and home. Following a quick display of all 24 runes with these one-word definitions at the onset, the RUNE-CASTER Menu appears. The first selection lets you randomly select a rune by pressing a key while you concentrate on the thought you want some insight on. You are then presented with an explanation of and thoughts about the rune on the left side of the screen, and its detailed graphic representation on the right. The second selection approaches problems from the present situation, the challenge to the situation, and the consideration of future potential. The third selection, the spiral five selection, uses five runes to explore a topic in terms of its initial seed or vision and processes its coming to fruition. This method delves into the perspective of each rune fully before proceeding to the next rune and so on through the five runes.

A brief history of rune usage is provided along with a bibliography covering the subject. The method of rune selection chosen is not a true random selection, but depends merely on the timing of pressing a key. Whether or not such timing yields divination is a matter for subjective speculation. However, the explanations and discussions of the runes are provocative and can lead to unique examinations of problems and decisions which could result in helpful insights.

This program is easy to use and an effective means for distracting one's attention away from the workaday world to more fundamental and spiritual areas.

(PC-SIG Disk# 1173)

Special Requirements: *Hercules graphics.*
Author Registration: *$10.00*

Sage-Past Life Tutor
by Wonderland Software

THE SAGE'S APPRENTICE - THE PAST LIFE TUTOR should liven up your next party or social gathering! First it was New Age music, then New Age videos, and now we have New Age software! Actually, this is a very intriguing program which focuses on the controversial subject of past lives or reincarnation.

Introductory screens take you through several guided visualization exercises and discuss the concept of past lives. If you wish to pursue a study of past lives, the program gives you four cultures to explore through visualization exercises: Ancient Egypt, Renaissance Europe, Ancient Greece, and Atlantis.

(PC-SIG Disk# 1486)

Special Requirements: *CGA and DOS 3.2 or higher.*
Author Registration: *$10.00*

▼ ▼ ▼

✍ = Updated Program
☆ = New Program

Astronomy and Space Exploration

Apollo Mission   *by Duckware*

The APOLLO MISSION SIMULATOR is an in-depth simulation of a manned lunar exploration in the year 2010. This is NOT a game, it is a simulation. There are no points to score; either you survive your mission or you and your crew are space dust!

In a typical mission, you begin in the Orbiting Laboratory, circling 150KM above the lunar equator. Enter the landing vehicle, undock and perform several orbital maneuvers, then land on the moon. Explore the surface using a long-range mobile base and a short-range roving vehicle. A permanent fixed base is also included. Names and locations of over 300 lunar features are listed in one of the documents, each of which is actually in the simulation, so you can become familiar with real lunar geography.

The APOLLO MISSION SIMULATOR is not "just another Lunar Lander." You participate in practically every aspect of a manned lunar exploration program. Set program goals, plan specific missions, and carry out those missions. Enough detail is provided so you can learn a great deal about lunar geography, orbital mechanics and physics in general.

(PC-SIG Disk# 987)

Special Requirements: *None.*
Author Registration: *$10.00*

Astronomy Programs   *by Larry Puhl*

Explore some of the mechanics of the solar system with these tutorials and calculators.

KEPLER solves Kepler's equation for elliptic, parabolic and hyperbolic orbits. SIDEREAL introduces you to the relationships between Julian calendar dates and solar and sidereal times.

J2000 converts stellar positions, proper motion, parallax and radial velocity from the standard epoch B1950 (FK4) to epoch J2000 (FK5). GALILEAN determines the position of the Galilean satellites relative to Jupiter.

(PC-SIG Disk# 921)

Special Requirements: *A version of BASIC.*
Author Registration: *$34.95*

Astronomy Star Catalogue   *by Michael G. Worst*

A valuable collection of useful programs for anyone with an interest in astronomy.

STAR CATALOGUE lists the named and designated stars of the 88 constellations — generally of the sixth magnitude or brighter. Others of interest are included along with dimmer stars within ten light years of Earth. About 1,700 stars are included in the data files. The statistics on each star include name, magnitude, spectrum type, distance, and other information. It also includes cross-referenced stars, whether the star is a binary, variable, or erratic variable, and the period of variation.

CONSTELLATION 88 presents a diagram of each of the 88 constellations, with their general coordinates, right ascension, and decline. SOLAR SYSTEM gives essential facts and figures on the planets, moons, asteroids, and satellites within our solar system. Information includes distance, diameter, rotation, revolution, orbit, eccentricity, and much more.

ASTRONOMY NOTES discusses general information concerning stellar astronomy such as spectral classes, Hubble's Constant, Kepler's Harmonic Law, and Hertsprung-Russell diagrams.

CONSTELLATION NAMES lists (surprise!) the names of the constellations, and ASTRONOMY CONVERSIONS contains information about different systems of distance, temperature, and time.

(PC-SIG Disk#'s 851, 852)

Special Requirements: *CGA.*
Author Registration: *$30.00*

Astrosoft Ephemeris (ACE)   *by Martin E. Morrison*

This program is a general-purpose astronomy software package with three separate parts — ACECALC, ACESOLAR and ACECAT.

ACECALC is a menu-driven astronomical ephemeris. Perform the most needed astronomical calculations involving the sun, moon and planets. The menu displays the local time, date and time zone name, universal time, local mean sidereal time, Julian day, and the name of the location designated in the installation. It also calculates astrophotography exposures, precession of coordinates, phases of the moon, equinoxes and solstices, and satellites of Jupiter.

ACESOLAR provides information on objects in the solar system such as numeric data on the sun, the planets and their satellites. Also available are narrative descriptions of the sun and planets and observational data.

ACECAT lets you search the sky catalog for objects by name, catalog number, and position — in terms of R.A./declination, object type, and constellation. This sky catalog provides data on over 2000 deep-sky objects, the entire Messier Catalog, 100 named objects, all bright stars to magnitude 2.0, and 100 prominent double stars, with detailed commentary on nearly 400 of these objects. Objects can be searched on the basis of one criterion or a combination.

(PC-SIG Disk#'s 692, 693)
Special Requirements: *None.*
Author Registration: *$25.00*

Deep Space 3-D   *by David Chandler*

DEEP SPACE 3-D is a powerful star mapping program that uses a database of over 19,000 stars (expandable to nearly 250,000 stars and 1100 comets), used by a number of serious astronomy publications to create their star charts.

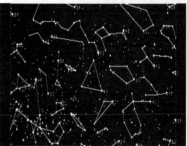

It can produce all-sky views or horizon views for any day and time anywhere on earth. Selected portions of the sky can be chosen by constellation or coordinates, then zoomed in for more detailed views. Comet paths can be computed and added to the star maps to create finder charts or to visualize the orbits of comets from any point in space. A new "What's Up" feature tells at a glance the times of sunrise, sunset, twilight, moon phases, and positions of the sun, moon, planets, and current comets for a given day and time. Once computed, the information is stored and may be added to the star maps.

Deep Space 3-D (PC-SIG Disk# 866)

The most unique feature of DEEP SPACE 3-D is depth. It can produce stereo 3-D printouts that show the stars or the orbits of comets in their true three-dimensional relationships when viewed with a stereo viewer. A 3-D viewer is included in the registration price.

Although DEEP SPACE 3-D has many features that will be attractive to experts, it is simple enough to be used easily by beginners. An extensive Help menu teaches the beginner as much about astronomy as it tells about the program. An improved user interface provides intelligent default values in case the feature is beyond the interest or knowledge of the user. It supports CGA, EGA, VGA and Hercules monitors.

This program is an ideal starting point for anyone who is looking for a reliable guide to observational astronomy. For centuries man has gazed at the night-time sky and wondered what was out there. DEEP SPACE will help answer some of those questions.

(PC-SIG Disk#'s 866, 867)
Special Requirements: *512K RAM, graphics card, two floppies, Epson-compatible printer*
Author Registration: *$59.00*

Earthwatch ✍   *by Larry Nagy*

EARTHWATCH is a graphic display program that displays a dynamic Mercator projection map of the world.

It includes almanac information such as:
❑ Graphical presentation of day and night areas of the earth
❑ Sunrise and sunset times for a specified location
❑ Comparison of sunrise/sunset time with those of previous day
❑ Days until the beginning of next season (solstices & equinoxes)
❑ Percentage of daylight for present date at specified location
❑ Time of day in each of the world's time zones
❑ Date on either side of the International Date Line
❑ Present sunrise and sunset zones throughout the world

❑ Position, age, and phase of the moon
❑ Position of the sun along the analemma path

Replace your ordinary calendar or screensaver program with EARTHWATCH. It's an informative and fascinating earth-monitoring clock.

(PC-SIG Disk# 2533)
Special Requirements: *CGA.*
Author Registration: *$25.00*

Launcher
by Robert Castle

LAUNCHER simulates a single stage-to-orbit launch vehicle. This is a very good quality simulation to learn the "feel" for orbital mechanics. Design your own vehicle, pilot it to orbit, and rendezvous with the space station. An interest in orbital mechanics is required (knowledge about it would be helpful, but is not mandatory). A documentation file is included.

(PC-SIG Disk# 945)
Special Requirements: *CGA.*
Author Registration: *$20.00*

Moonbeam
by Fred Mendenhall

MOONBEAM is a program that takes the date and time, as well as your time zone, and gives you general information regarding the position of the moon and its relationship to Earth. SUNSET accepts the date, time and location of position and displays general information about the sun in relation to Earth.

(PC-SIG Disk# 538)
Special Requirements: *None.*
Author Registration: *None.*

The Night Sky ✍
by A.C. Stevely

This computer planetarium is capable of plotting 24,000 stars to magnitude +7.49. THE NIGHT SKY is a very easy to use menu-driven program for the amateur astronomer. In fact, this program was written by an amateur astronomer who, when he is not looking at the stars, drives a London transport bus. He has spent many of his off hours working on this program, which originally started as an exercise in programming.

Use THE NIGHT SKY to draw a star map and move around the sky, show the night sky to a magnification and resolution of your choice, plot all the planets and the moon any time from January 1, 1600 to December 31, 3000; predict solar and lunar eclipses; and view your local sky. Also covered are comets, the minor planets, the sun, moon, and satellites of Jupiter. From the stars menu, you can choose the constellations, 21 brightest stars, bright star catalogue, map the night sky, star atlas, and deep sky.

(PC-SIG Disk#'s 1796, 1797, 2139, 2140)
Special Requirements: *Hercules graphics or CGA.*
Author Registration: *24.95 pounds.*

Particle Simulation
by Byoung J. Keum

Here are several programs that simulate the orbits of celestial bodies and small particles. Use them to simulate the orbit of a three-star system, the orbit of a comet approaching the Earth, and the orbits of the Earth, sun, and moon. PARTICLE SIMULATION also has programs that simulate the movement of a particle inside an ellipse or an ellipsoid. In addition, there's an explanation of the twin paradox of relativity — why people should cease to age as they approached the speed of light. Graphics are included in the explanation.

(PC-SIG Disk# 1070)
Special Requirements: *CGA or EGA.*
Author Registration: *None.*

Planets
by Larry Puhl

PLANETS computes the position, distance, magnitude, orbital view, and skyview for the planets, major asteroids, and Halley's Comet. The skyview and orbital view can describe forward or retrograde motion. The moons for each of the planets can be displayed.

(PC-SIG Disk# 298)

Special Requirements: *CGA.*
Author Registration: *$10.00*

Rocket Programs
by Larry Puhl

A trio of programs applicable to the performance of rockets and gliders, and the air in which they fly.

ATMOS determines properties of the standard atmosphere. ROCKET1 explores the flight performance of a single stage model rocket. GLIDER determines the maximum flight range and endurance conditions of boost and rocket gliders. This is also applicable to sailplanes, hang gliders, and radio-controlled gliders.

(PC-SIG Disk# 921)

Special Requirements: *A version of BASIC.*
Author Registration: *$19.95*

Satellite Programs
by Larry Puhl

SYNCSAT and TNODE help you determine the location of several Earth-orbiting satellites. You can use this information for radio tracking, communications and visual observations of Earth satellites.

(PC-SIG Disk# 921)

Special Requirements: *A version of BASIC.*
Author Registration: *$24.95*

Silicon Sky
by Larry Adkins

SILICON SKY is a planisphere that lets you study the night sky as it appears in any region of the world, looking in any direction, and as it appeared on any date you select. It offers two viewing options, Stars+Solar System Objects and Planetarium. There's even an optional cricket sounds accompaniment!

The program paints the stars on the screen for most horizons. Then two menus are available so you can request that solar system objects and constellations be highlighted. Specific planets and the moon are circled, and constellations are drawn in with dotted lines upon request.

(PC-SIG Disk# 1103)

Special Requirements: *CGA.*
Author Registration: *$10.00*

Silicon Sky (PC-SIG Disk# 1103)

Skyclock
by Ottawa University

A unique program, SKYCLOCK is an historical astronomical ephemeris and data conversion program. Unlike most other astronomical ephemeris programs, this program works with dates of both the Julian and Gregorian calendars and dates A.D. and B.C. Calculate the positions of the visible astrological houses for a specific date. With SKYCLOCK, you may also automatically convert dates between several calendars used at different times throughout history. On what day did Julius Caesar die according to the Roman calendar? With SKYCLOCK, you can find out.

As an astronomical ephemeris, SKYCLOCK allows you to calculate the positions of the sun, moon, planets, stars, comets, and astrological houses for any date back to several centuries B.C. Enter the date and time, and the latitude and longitude of your desired observation point. SKYCLOCK lists all the time variable elements entered, and the position of the celestial body. For the planets, SKYCLOCK lists the heliocentric and geocentric longitude and latitude, its perihelion, the right ascension, the declination, the azimuth, the altitude, the phase angle, elongation from the sun, the distance to the sun, and the distance to the earth. Other specific information is included for the sun, moon, comets and stars. SKYCLOCK can also list summary information of the positions for the sun, moon, and all the planets for a specific date all at once. For calculating the positions of the visible astrological houses, enter the longitude of mid-heaven, the geographical latitude, and the obliquity of the ecliptic.

SKYCLOCK will then list the positions of the visible astrological houses according to nine different systems used throughout history.

SKYCLOCK is not only an astronomical ephemeris, but also a calendar date conversion program. Easily convert dates between nine different calendars used throughout history. These include the Julian, Gregorian, Egyptian, Alexandrian, Roman, Nabonassar, Islamic, French, and Zodiacal calendars. Enter either the date or the Julian day number. SKYCLOCK will then list the Julian day number, the day of the week, the age of the moon, and the Roman indiction. You may also find the date of Easter Sunday and the date of lunar epact according to both Julian and Gregorian calendars.

(PC-SIG Disk# 1614)

Special Requirements: *None.*
Author Registration: *$25.00*

SkyGlobe ✍   *by Klassm Software*

SkyGlobe is fast, fun, and easy-to-use. The splendor of the heavens comes to life, especially on an EGA or VGA system.

The program also runs on CGA and Hercules systems, and creates printouts on Epson compatible printers. See up to 15,000 stars, over twice as many as are visible to the naked eye. Turn the constellation lines on or off with a single keystroke. Change viewing direction or location just as quickly. Use the Automatic Mode to watch the movement of the stars through the night. Since the planets, Sun, and Moon are also displayed, SKYGLOBE is the best way to learn about the wonderful show in our skies every night.

SkyGlobe (PC-SIG Disk #2604)

(PC-SIG Disk# 2604)

Special Requirements: *Graphics card.*
Author Registration: *$15.00*

Space Shuttle Tracking System   *by Robert L. LLoyd, Jr.*

Look to the heavens to find the space shuttle, but first consult your computer and the SPACE SHUTTLE TRACKING SYSTEM. You don't have to be an astronaut to successfully chart the course of the space shuttle and figure out what time of night it will be visible overhead. You'll be shown the flight pattern taken around the world on an impressive looking map of the globe. Plot the shuttle's location for any specified time into the flight, or watch the shuttle's progress during the real-time simulation of the flight. Speed up the flight to watch a simulation of several hours of flight time in just a few minutes.

This program is great for all ages. It doesn't require that you understand longitude and latitude lines, but merely asks for some basic flight information which varies with every flight: direction of the launch, orbit time or altitude, and inclination. This information is readily available through the media prior to the launch. By looking at the orbit charted on the map of the world, you can accurately predict when the shuttle will be overhead in your area. An excellent tool for science students or space enthusiasts.

(PC-SIG Disk# 1689)

Special Requirements: *CGA, EGA, or VGA.*
Author Registration: *$10.00*
➤*ASP Member.*

STARSIDE ✍   *by Virtual Srket Technology*

If you enjoy looking at the sky, use STARSIDE to view the stars in a new light. It's an educational astronomy program designed to generate star maps from any place and any time in the world. The positions of the sun, moon, and planets can be included in the maps you print from STARSIDE. It can also predict sun and moon eclipse dates.

Since STARSIDE has a large database of stars, it calculates the best times for viewing celestial objects. Merge, add, change, search, and create a customized database to fit your needs. This is a user-friendly tool for any person who wants to learn more about astronomy.

(PC-SIG Disk# 2180)

Special Requirements: *512K RAM, EGA, and DOS 3.0.*
Author Registration: *$20.00*

Auto/Vehicle Management

PC Mechanic ✍   *by Michael R. Busman*

Whether you run a hotel or heavy equipment yard, PC MECHANIC will insure that preventive maintenance for your company is properly handled. This integrated Preventive Maintenance system outperforms many programs costing several thousand dollars and will serve the needs of companies that process up to 200 work orders every day. It consists of five interactive modules: the Inventory system, Work Order system, Preventive Maintenance system, Equipment database, and Employee database systems.

The Inventory system tracks vendors, helps prevent parts shrinkage, cuts down on overstocking and helps make sure you have what you need when you need it. The system remembers what you paid for parts and adds that amount to the cost files on each job and piece of equipment.

The Preventive Maintenance system insures that vital maintenance is done in a timely manner and keeps track of who does the servicing. Work orders are printed along with schedules and work assignments. If someone abuses or neglects equipment, the program crunches the labor and parts numbers to generate costs for all to see.

PC MECHANIC lets you print daily or weekly reports showing what work was performed by who. List outstanding work orders and review them with respective trade supervisors and foremen. You get aging reports telling you where you stand on completing your work backlog.

The Employee database system stores basic information on employees and makes sure that performance reviews are done on time. It can print employee lists, alphabetically, including the ID numbers which are posted as part of preventive maintenance reports. It also lists workers by seniority.

The extensive use of lookup windows in the various database modules makes searching for specific data easy and greatly reduces keyboard.

(PC-SIG Disk# 1277)

Special Requirements: *640K RAM, CGA, hard drive, dot matrix printer.*
Author Registration: *$50.00*

Schedule Magic   *by Murray Spitzer Associates*

SCHEDULE MAGIC is designed to automatically calculate and optimize daily commercial vehicle schedules. The schedule optimizer finds vehicle routes that minimize the number of vehicles needed, thus reducing total fleet miles. Until now, the formidable mathematics of optimization needed mainframe computers for vehicle scheduling. This program uses a new method that allows the same calculations to be made on any IBM-PC or compatible.

Four sample scheduling applications are included as tutorial example problems:

❑ Service: plumbing, heating and air conditioning, appliance installation and repair, pest control, etc.
❑ Delivery: wholesale delivery of groceries, drugs, hardware, fuel oil, commodities, etc.
❑ Schools: bus routings
❑ Banks: courier vehicles for branch bank pick-up operations

SCHEDULE MAGIC offers a whole new approach and system design based on the concepts of grid coordinate locations of all points, automatically-calculated straight line distances and travel times, and getting started by use of a complete manually-calculated schedule.

(PC-SIG Disk# 1098)

Special Requirements: *A printer and LOTUS 1-2-3 or ASEASYAS.*
Author Registration: *$49.00*

TLC Truck Data System ✍   *by TLC Software*

Proper management of business vehicle fleets requires good record-keeping. This is an area where TLC FOR TRUCKS (TLC) really shines for small to medium-sized fleets (999 vehicles or less).

TLC makes a database that allows 19 different fields of data for each vehicle. A reporting function prints this data in various formats, making cost analysis easier.

TLC is very complete and easy to use. The documentation provided is both ample and understandable. Source code is available separately so you can customize the program to suit your needs.

(PC-SIG Disk# 1085)

Special Requirements: *512K RAM and a printer.*
Author Registration: *$25.00*

Vehicle Expenses/Maintenance

by Gary LaRonge

VEHICLE EXPENSES provides a means of writing, storing and maintaining files of four categories: fuel, scheduled, emergency, and other expenses related to the operation and maintenance of motor vehicles or other equipment.

Using VEHICLE EXPENSES is quite easy. The database is created by simply assigning a file name and adding the appropriate information. While the system is set to handle many different vehicles, it is best suited for the individual or small business with only a few cars.

VEHICLE MAINTENANCE provides a typewritten check-off sheet listing items to be serviced at pre-defined intervals. The check-off sheet may be used as a "memory jogger" to prevent overlooking items that should be maintained, or the sheet may be presented to a service agency in order to indicate the work you would like them to accomplish.

The database is created by inputting up to five maintenance intervals; i.e., 5000, 10000, 15000, 30000, and 60000 "miles" for vehicles, or you may use "hours" as the maintenance period criteria for items such as generators, snowmobiles, air compressors, etc. The maintenance period criteria is followed by a description of the maintenance items you would like serviced at each of the specified intervals; i.e., change oil, replace oil filter, replace air filter, check brake pads, etc. Any of the interval item descriptions may be added to, deleted from, or edited as required without leaving the program.

(PC-SIG Disk# 1748)

Special Requirements: *None.*

Author Registration: *$5.00 individual and for $20.00 commercial use.*

VRS PLUS (Vehicle Record System) ✍

by K-Jon Software

VEHICLE RECORD SYSTEM PLUS (VRS PLUS) by K-Jon Software is the comprehensive vehicle management system for homes and businesses. It tracks fuel, maintenance, insurance, registration, tires, loans, travel, cost per mile, and much more for any number of vehicles. Easily determine and analyze vehicle costs for any period of time, and VRS PLUS tells you when to service your vehicles. Customized maintenance schedules show you what maintenance operations need to be done, when they need to be done, and which ones are overdue.

The VRS PLUS can be customized for use in many countries and is currently being used in the United States, Canada, Australia, and England. Vehicles can be tracked by odometer or hours. The VEHICLE RECORD SYSTEM comes highly recommended by users and their comments are included. The step-by-step demo and tutorial will get you started quickly and make it easy to track the information you want and need to know.

(PC-SIG Disk# 733)

Special Requirements: *640K RAM and hard drive. A 286 system recommended.*

Author Registration: *$45.00*

▼ ▼ ▼

Banner Makers

Banner
by Glenn C. Everhart

Print long, large banners for birthdays, anniversaries, sales or announcements. Included is the MS-FORTRAN source code to customize the program to suit your needs. A straightforward program and a good addition to anyone's collection.

(PC-SIG Disk# 386)

Special Requirements: *Printer.*
Author Registration: *$5.00*

PC-Banner
by Sofstar

"Welcome Home" for the new baby, the traveller or the convalescent, "Sale Today" to boost your daily cash-flow, or "Hi Mom" from the football game. You can have them all and more with PC-BANNER.

Here is a simple, menu-driven banner program that lets you change the style of print from light to dark. And it uses the IBM graphics character sets for high-quality banners.

(PC-SIG Disk# 779)

Special Requirements: *Printer.*
Author Registration: *$2.00*

PrintPartner ☆
by Acropolis Software

Well it's finally been done. Acropolis Software has created an excellent clone of the popular graphics program, Print Shop. Create banners, posters, and calendars and print them with your dot-matrix or laser printer.

Create fun banners for birthdays, posters for lost dogs, or even monthly calendars for the office. Print the monthly calendar for any month in any year from 1980 to 2098.

The program supplies 11 fonts and 75 clip art pictures. Banners can have a graphic on either end and use any font you select. PRINTPARTNER will attempt to smooth the text and graphics to make them look better. Two graphics can be placed anywhere on the page. Options include multiple copies of each piece of clip art, in one of three different sizes. Each line of text can be a different font and may be sized to your specifications.

PRINTPARTNER comes with a picture editor to change the existing graphics or create your own masterpieces. Also included is a conversion program to take picture files from Print Shop and convert them to use in PRINTPARTNER.

Most major printer brands such as Epson, Panasonic, NEC, HP LaserJet and Citizen, as well as some generic 24-pin printers, are supported. Twenty printer drivers are included.

P.S. You can find more clip art pictures to use with PRINTPARTNER on the Cooper Graphics disks, PC-SIG #2100 to #2117. Each disk contains 100 individual clip art graphics.

(PC-SIG Disk# 2660)

Special Requirements: *A graphics card and printer.*
Author Registration: *$20.00*

▼ ▼ ▼

Barcodes

BarCode
by MicroGadgetry, Inc.

They're everywhere. On your soda can, at the grocery store, on the TV guide — those groups of lines with numbers under them. BARCODE allows you to print these bar code labels on your printer. It is designed to print code three of nine, a type of bar code which allows both alphabetic and numeric characters. Labels can be printed up to 15 characters in length.

Define the placement of the bar codes, place a description over each code, print single or multiple copies of one bar code, or print a run of sequentially-numbered bar codes. BARCODE can hold three different printer configurations, and can switch between these configurations with one key stroke. The three configurations can be modified to accommodate a multitude of printers and are pre-configured for IBM graphics, APA graphics, and Epson graphics printers.

(PC-SIG Disk# 877)

Special Requirements: *Printer.*
Author Registration: *$25.00*

DAYO Bar Code ☆

by TJS Lab

DAYO is a collection of multiuser business applications that provide a means of managing inventory, purchasing, invoicing, customers, vendors, sales and more. All DAYO products are designed to work on a LAN, like Novell. They can, however, work as a stand-alone, running on a single PC.

DAYO BAR CODE prints three of nine bar codes with an Epson or IBM compatible dot-matrix printer. It is integrated with the DAYO INVENTORY and the DAYO CUSTOMER databases.

DAYO Bar Code (PC-SIG Disk #2626)

Labels are printed onto standard labels (3.5 by $^{15}/_{16}$ inches at six lines per inch). The inventory bar code label consists of an item number and its bar code, with the option to print the vendor item number, description, unit of issue, weight, and bin/location. The customer barcode label supplies a customer number, its bar code, and has the option to print the customer's name and telephone number.

Inventory and customer bar codes can be printed by "browsing" through their respective databases using multiple indexes. When a desired item or customer is found, just print. Batch printing of item bar codes is possible based on the item type, class, location, receipts, and purchase orders.

(PC-SIG Disk# 2626)

Special Requirements: *640K RAM, a hard drive, and DOS 3.3.*
Author Registration: *$25.00*
➤*ASP Member.*

▼ ▼ ▼

Bible Study

A Bible Companion ☆

by Philip P. Kapusta

A BIBLE COMPANION is just that — a companion to assist you in your study of the Bible. An interesting variety of methods help you to relate to the setting and context of the passages.

When entering the program, you receive a suggested reading for the day. If you own a Bible on disk, read it using BIBLE COMPANION'S File View option while still being able to use the utilities of the program. Choices of visual aids include three different maps, chronology charts, the Jewish calendar, a summary of the Gospel, and a dictionary for the King James translation's many archaic and obscure words. Although the material is not exhaustive, A BIBLE COMPANION is a great way to understanding the Bible a little more.

(PC-SIG Disk# 2679)

Special Requirements: *Graphics card.*
Author Registration: *None.*

Bible Men

by SonShine Software, Inc.

BIBLE MEN is a wonderful little quiz program that tests your finer knowledge of the Word. Begin by telling BIBLE MEN whether you want it to focus on either the Old or New Testament. You'll be asked for each player's name (up to eight). The program will give you some significant passage, often written in the first person, and you'll be asked to identify the person.

For example:

"May the Lord show mercy to the household of Onesephorus, because he often refreshed me and was not ashamed of my chains."

Type the name of the person referred to. (In the above example, the reference is to Onesephorus, the scripture is II Timothy 1:16, and the author is the Apostle Paul.) When you don't know the answer, you can choose to see the verse, the answer, or move on to another question. Look at the answers to a question and move on without affecting your score. Scoring occurs only when you type an answer. BIBLE MEN displays your score as tries, wrong, right, and percent. Did you know the answer to the above example?

(PC-SIG Disk# 781)

Special Requirements: *None.*
Author Registration: *$15.00*
➤**ASP Member.**

Bible Men (PC-SIG Disk# 781)

BIBLE QUIZ PLUS ✍   *by C.A.B.T. Ministries*

BIBLE QUIZ PLUS is a religious trivia game with three different levels of play for one to six players. Questions are asked and answers can be in multiple choice, fill-in-the-blank, or answer-only format. These questions are from the Book of Psalms and the Book of Proverbs from the King James version of the Bible.

(PC-SIG Disk#'s 974, 2126)

Special Requirements: *None.*
Author Registration: *$10.00*

Bible-Q ✍   *by Robert S. Smith*

BIBLE-Q is a trivia-type game with 600 multiple-choice questions drawn from the Bible. Bible students and church school teachers will certainly want this in their collections.

Test yourself and others on a wide range of topics including geography of the Biblical lands, personalities, incidents, and teachings of the Gospels. Players can choose the category and difficulty level of the question. Combine with WORDWORKER (PC-SIG disk #'s 581, 582) and you have the foundation for an excellent on-line scripture study system.

(PC-SIG Disk# 628)

Special Requirements: *None.*
Author Registration: *$5.00*

Daily Bread   *by PTD Software Systems*

DAILY BREAD is a Bible program that will display a different verse or reading from the King James version for every day of the year. One can read the entire Bible by following DAILY BREAD's daily readings for a whole year.

(PC-SIG Disk# 1327)

Special Requirements: *None.*
Author Registration: *None.*

Destiny   *by PTD Software Systems*

DESTINY is a simple text-adventure game designed to teach Biblical truths. In each place encountered, you must make a decision in order to determine your destiny. The adventure has its own symbolism which must be interpreted to succeed in the game.

(PC-SIG Disk# 1327)

Special Requirements: *None.*
Author Registration: *None.*

Gospel Concordance   *by Biblesoft Co.*

GOSPEL CONCORDANCE lists every word of the four gospels of the Bible in alphabetical order and the passages where each is found. Of interest to Bible students and ministers, this research tool helps with word studies, finding a particular passage, and comparing the accounts of the four gospels. When unarchived, the GOSPEL CONCORDANCE occupies a total of three floppy disks.

✍ = Updated Program
☆ = New Program

LIST.COM, also included, allows you to directly view the concordance text files on your screen or you can use any standard word processor. All of the files pertaining to the GOSPEL CONCORDANCE are simply text files that you can view or print. Also on this disk is a catalog which lists other program study aids for the Bible.

(PC-SIG Disk# 1208)

Special Requirements: *None.*
Author Registration: *$9.00*

The Great Exchange ☆ *by Robert S. Smith*

This program presents, in a simple, straightforward manner, the basic message of the Bible. Using an interactive "slide show" with screens and text, THE GREAT EXCHANGE lends itself to both the person looking for the simple meaning of the Bible and to those who want to share it with others.

(PC-SIG Disk# 1327)

Special Requirements: *640K RAM and EGA.*
Author Registration: *None.*

King James Bible Search Program *by Raymond Ruppert*

If you're looking for a better way to find Bible references, this program can be your computer Bible concordance. It will search for a single word or a combination of words and then will display a list of verses that contain all of those words. Best of all, you don't need the entire Bible on-disk to do it. However, if you have a copy of the King James Bible on disk, then this search program will also display the actual verses and put them in a text file.

Do multiple word searches, search for specific verses, even copy the selected verses into your word processor for editing or inclusion into a document you're preparing. Utility programs are included to allow you to build your own concordance from any English version Bible you may have on disk. This program will prove invaluable for anyone who does Bible studies — preachers, teachers, Bible study leaders, and many people who study for their own enrichment. (Note: this product does not include the Bible, which is on PC-SIG disks #'s 766-772.)

(PC-SIG Disk#'s 1654, 1655, 1656, 1657)

Special Requirements: *Hard drive recommended.*
Author Registration: *None.*

Lexicon (Interfaces with Online Bible) ✍ *by Thomas S. Cox*

The world's first computer-based public domain Greek and Hebrew LEXICON is now available. This program is an add-on to the ONLINE BIBLE (PC-SIG disk #'s 2191-2197). The menu-driven program includes Strong's numbers and complete Greek and Hebrew Lexicons keyed to Strong's numbers. The LEXICON is based on Thayer's Greek Lexicon and the Brown et al Hebrew Aramaic English Lexicon. Search for any words, phrases, or Strong's numbers and access the definitions. Print a passage with all the numbers plus the definitions of words used in that passage. Saves hours of time during detailed Bible studies.

LEXICON is in text format and may be readily altered using facilities in the ONLINE BIBLE.

(PC-SIG Disk#'s 2204, 2205, 2206, 2485)

Special Requirements: *Hard drive, and PC-SIG disk #'s 2191-2197, 2482.*
Author Registration: *None.*

Online Bible ✍ *by Online Bible Ministries*

Did you ever wish that there was an easier and faster way to find words or phrases in the Bible? The ONLINE BIBLE is a full-function search and retrieval program for Bible students.

Search facilities include word, phrase, and multiple words. Add notes of any size to a verse using the supplied text processor. Cross-reference information may be stored in the notes for automatic recall. Verses may be printed or saved in ASCII format and from there, you can customize them with your favorite word processor.

Using the ONLINE BIBLE is a breeze with adjustable window size for viewing verses, drop-down menus, and context-sensitive Help screens.

Furthermore, visually challenged individuals can now use screen reader hardware to use the ONLINE BIBLE screens. These characteristics, plus the coupling of ONLINE BIBLE with the Greek and Hebrew LEXICON

(PC-SIG disk #'s 2204-2206, 2485) and ONLINE BIBLE CROSS REFERENCE (PC-SIG disk #'s 2483-2484), make ON-LINE BIBLE a powerful tool.

(PC-SIG Disk#'s 2191, 2192, 2193, 2194, 2195, 2196, 2197)

Special Requirements: *Hard drive and PC-SIG disk #2482.*
Author Registration: *None.*

Online Bible Cross References ☆　　　　　　　　*by Online Bible Ministries*

The authors of ONLINE BIBLE (PC-SIG disk #'s 2191-2197) now offer another add-on, ONLINE BIBLE CROSS REFERENCES, to make ONLINE BIBLE even more complete. Using over 550,000 cross-references from the Treasury of Scripture Knowledge and other sources, ONLINE BIBLE CROSS REFERENCES allows instant recall and display of cross-references. This makes for very rewarding Bible studies.

(PC-SIG Disk#'s 2483, 2484)

Special Requirements: *Hard drive & PC-SIG disk #'s 2482, 2196-2197.*
Author Registration: *None.*

Online Bible Installation Disk ✍　　　　　　*by Online Bible Ministries*

The ONLINE BIBLE INSTALLATION DISK is required to install ONLINE BIBLE (#2191-#2197), LEXICON (#2204-#2206, #2485), and ONLINE BIBLE CROSS REFERENCES (#2483-2484).

(PC-SIG Disk# 2482)

Special Requirements: *Hard drive.*
Author Registration: *None.*

Problems ✍　　　　　　　　　　　　　　*by Paul R. Godin*

What does the Bible have to say about abortion? Alcoholism? Humility? Vengeance? These, and 55 other topic areas, are instantly accessed through PROBLEMS. Pick your topic or problem of concern, such as "pride," and the relevant Bible verses pop up on your screen and/or printer. For example: PROVERBS 16:18 "Pride goeth before destruction, and an haughty spirit before a fall." Verses can be added or deleted, allowing you to customize this program according to your interests.

(PC-SIG Disk#'s 1526, 2661)

Special Requirements: *None.*
Author Registration: *$10.00*

Revelation Tutorial　　　　　　　　　　　*by Revelation Software*

This is a scriptural tutorial for anyone interested in exploring the Book of Revelations.

The author, a minister, offers a fresh perspective on this work for those who have studied the Bible and a measured overview for those with little or no background in Revelations.

Two methods of teaching are used. One type of question provides familiarity with, and tests for, details of the scriptural references covered in the eight lessons. Multiple-choice, fill-the-blanks, and yes/no quizzes test for knowledge of such items as: how many, who, or what? Details are referenced scripturally and, at several points in the program, the current material is summarized. At the end of the disk, a comprehensive self-test is provided.

The other type of question explores the meanings behind the details. Interpretive exercises are designed to aid insight into the references and symbols used throughout the book.

The author has used "The New International Version" of the Bible as the source document for the tutorial. Most of the lessons can be completed in an hour or less but some run longer. The user may leave the tutorial and reenter at the same point at a later time.

(PC-SIG Disk# 1554)

Special Requirements: *None.*
Author Registration: *$20.00*

Scripture　　　　　　　　　　　　　　　*by Gil Yoder*

A Bible Study program designed for easy use while providing some high-powered database functions for meaningful surveys and searches.

Advanced features include:

❑ Three windows display any portion of scripture desired
❑ A fourth window for simple text editing of files
❑ Move and resize these windows
❑ Verses/references automatically inserted into the editor window
❑ A quick search facility with three modes of search
❑ Mark books to include/exclude during a word search
❑ Compile lists of verses matching your search criteria
❑ All biblical words (over 12,000) displayed in alphabetical order
❑ Bookmarks to hold your place for another study period
❑ Context-sensitive Help system with more than 60 topics

EGA/VGA support for 43/50 line modes is supported. This version does not contain the entire set of scriptures.
(PC-SIG Disk#'s 1816, 1817)

Special Requirements: *Two MB of disk storage.*
Author Registration: *$50.00*
➤*ASP Member.*

Scripture Master ✐   *by PractiComp*

For anyone interested in Bible verses, the books of the Bible, the Disciples, or the Ten Commandments, here are 104 passages in each of the King James, New International, and New King James translations.

The program is menu-driven and easy to learn and use. It checks verses entered and displays errors, and can print on either index cards or 8.5" x 11" paper. Add verses to the translations or add new translations. There are activities to help memorize other biblical information — the books of the Bible, Ten Commandments and Disciples are also provided. Reports may be printed, or saved to disk and then viewed on-screen.

By utilizing two different study techniques, you can quote a verse given the reference or, given a verse, cite the reference. Study verses by topic, reference, or a combination of the two.
(PC-SIG Disk# 2268)

Special Requirements: *512K RAM. Printer recommended.*
Author Registration: *$25.00*

Scripture Memory   *by MVP Software*

Your computer can help with Bible memorization, taking you step-by-step through the processes of learning and review. Through an exclusive arrangement with NavPress, SCRIPTURE MEMORY comes with 66 verses on-disk, organized under the Navigators' Topical Memory System. Add as many verses as disk capacity allows.

SCRIPTURE MEMORY uses the technique of associating topic, reference, and verse to make it easy to memorize and retain what you have learned. The program uses two files to store both the verses you are currently memorizing and the ones you have already memorized. Each time you use the program, you will be working on the current review. In addition, SCRIPTURE MEMORY will choose from 5 to 40 back-review verses for you to go over. Once you have built up a sufficient number of verses in your review file, the program will randomly select different verses each time it is used.
(PC-SIG Disk# 1658)

Special Requirements: *None.*
Author Registration: *$15.00*
➤*ASP Member.*

Scripture Quest ☆   *by Philip P. Kapusta*

You won't be getting the same question very often with this Bible game. SCRIPTURE QUEST tests you with over 1600 questions from the Old Testament, the New Testament, or both.

Subjects include people, places, words, commandments, and doctrines of the Bible. Print-out quizzes, pop-up windows, referenced answers, and a "Top Ten" score chart are among its features. Play by yourself, or make it a group game for up to nine people! Play against the clock for better scores!
(PC-SIG Disk# 2680)

Special Requirements: *None.*
Author Registration: *None.*

SeedMaster ✍   *by White Harvest Software, Inc.*

SEEDMASTER allows you to find specific words and phrases in the King James Bible (included). Unlike traditional concordances (which provide verse references for a single word), SEEDMASTER can search for combinations of words with options to test for specific word order and case sensitivity. Logic searches (AND, OR, XOR, and NOT) are also available.

For Bible study, SEEDMASTER can display and scroll up to three Bible text windows side by side. The text can be scrolled one verse at a time, or the user can jump directly to specific verse locations. Selected Bible verses can be printed or saved to a disk file. All Bible books can be selected from a menu (you don't have to remember book abbreviations).

Additional features include:

❑ Commentary function to enter and recall your comments verse by verse
❑ Pop-up notepad to develop lessons within the program
❑ Copy and paste text
❑ Output can be viewed or sent to disk or printer

(PC-SIG Disk#'s 1591, 1592, 1593, 1594, 1595, 1596, 1597, 1598, 1599, 1600)
Special Requirements: *512K RAM and 4.5 MB of a hard drive.*
Author Registration: *$30.00 plus Bible version database price.*
➤*ASP Member.*

Verse   *by Frank Chin, M.D.*

Install VERSE on your computer and a different excerpt of the Bible will automatically be displayed every day when you start your PC. The program allows you to include your favorite verses. VERSE is a nice way to start your day right.

(PC-SIG Disk# 1511)
Special Requirements: *None.*
Author Registration: *None.*

WordWorker   *by The Way International*

This is an electronic New Testament Bible reference system ideal for writing sermons, doing research, and the serious Bible student.

Select any New Testament word or combination and then search and display the text of verses that meet your request. In memory-resident mode, verses can be copied into a word processor. Additional features include on-line Help, bookmarks, speed reading, word use and 14,800 references to research works. WORDWORKER also has a complete editor to create letters, sermons or other text with the information in the database.

(PC-SIG Disk#'s 581, 582)
Special Requirements: *Two floppy drives.*
Author Registration: *$45.00*

▼ ▼ ▼

Bulletin Board Systems (BBS)

CAPTAIN VIDEO   *by Cosmic Annex Software*

If you run a video store, or have a video collection the size of a store, CAPTAIN VIDEO will organize and keep track of every videocassette you own. For video sales and rental outlets, CAPTAIN VIDEO eases the burden of movie and game rental paperwork through the use of menus and forms for customers, rentals, inventory, maintenance, and employees.

Printed reports include forms (rental invoice, video in/out, games in/out, employee information, and service information), reports, labels, lists (customers, employees inventory) and letters.

If you're just starting a video rental business and you want to track your rentals and sales, check out CAPTAIN VIDEO.
(PC-SIG Disk# 2146)
Special Requirements: *512K RAM.*
Author Registration: *$50.00*

Electronic Information System
by American On-Line Systems

ELECTRONIC INFORMATION SYSTEM (EIS) is an electronic bulletin board plus. More than a way for people to post messages and read those posted by others, EIS is a complete information retrieval system. It is an invaluable electronic mail and communication tool for small businesses and BBS operators, with a complete security system to prevent intrusion.

EIS offers compatibility with many of the utilities and games written for a slew of other BBS systems. EIS offers support for the PCRelay BBS networking software, and offers support for a multi-node system. Supported file transfer protocols include Xmodem, Xmodem-CRC, Xmodem-1K, True Ymodem Batch, and Zmodem CRC-32 with MobyTurbo and Crash Recovery. EIS operates at baud rates from 300 to 38,400 bps on any com port that you have available. The ANSI Message Editor will allow your user to do full-screen message entry and editing. EIS can run up to 10,000 nodes on a local area network (LAN).

EIS will manage an unlimited number of message bases and file areas and can hold about two billion messages in each message base. EIS is 100% compatible with the MegaMail Off-line reader, and with the PCRelay BBS networking system. EIS will run doors designed to run with about 30 different BBS systems.

Installation is a breeze. There is no complicated copying or editing necessary to get a fully-functional system on-line. Before you know it, you will be logging into your own BBS.

EIS is perfect for your small business, too. There is a secure E-Mail system and support for general message bases. Display catalogs and take orders. You can keep secure and public file directories of files for your customers and staff to download. Your customers will love having BBS support, and your staff will love to be able to call in and grab that file they forgot at the office or send secure E-Mail.

If you want, you can emulate a traditional BBS. Or configure your system to be unique from every other information system on the market today and to match your own specific needs. If you are looking into BBS or information retrieval systems for any reason, EIS is exactly what you are looking for.

(PC-SIG Disk# 1627)

Special Requirements: *512K RAM, hard drive, and modem. Min. 8 Mhz computer recommended.*
Author Registration: *$119.00*

FindBBS
by George Campbell

FINDBBS provides you with quick access to hundreds of bulletin board systems' (BBS) phone numbers across the nation. Dial up and log-on. It also serves as the BBS search door for WILDCAT! BBS (PC-SIG disk #'s 745, 746).

(PC-SIG Disk# 1370)

Special Requirements: *Modem.*
Author Registration: *None.*

Free Speech BBS ✍
by Pinnacle Software

FREE SPEECH is a streamlined BBS designed for high message throughput. Installed in seconds, it supports up to three languages (English and French text provided), with full foreign-character translation. Can be run as a stand-alone BBS, a front-end, or as a door. Like all Pinnacle BBS products, FREE SPEECH is a zero maintenance system.

(PC-SIG Disk# 2382)

Special Requirements: *Modem. Familiarity with BBS terms.*
Author Registration: *$25.00*

Micro Serve
by Software Construction Co.

MICRO SERVE supports up to four users and a system administrator at a single time. Depending upon the host machine speed and number of ports used, 300 to 9600 baud can be maintained. With over 32,000 possible menus and nine options per menu, almost 300,000 different user options can be created. Such advanced functions as private mail, conference mode, questionnaires, and file transfer (ASCII and XMODEM and YMODEM protocols) are included.

This package is perfect for the small company or individual who wants to have a state-of-the-art BBS. Watch out, CompuServ!

(PC-SIG Disk# 1458)

Special Requirements: *One serial port per user, Hayes-compatible modem.*
Author Registration: *$39.00*

Personal Oracomm BBS ☆   *by Surf Computer Services, Inc.*

ORACOMM, the popular commercial multiuser bulletin board software, is now available in the shareware market. The shareware version of ORACOMM is a 1-line/1-user system. To get the 2-line/3-user (com1, com2, plus the console) you must register the program.

There is no limit to the number of user accounts or messages. PERSONAL ORACOMM BBS is easy to use. Commands such as R for "read", E to "enter a message", D to "download" make it easy and logical for new users. The space bar to control screen scrolling, ESC to return to the main menu from anywhere, and Immediate Commands can be entered while the menu is displayed.

ORACOMM provides networking between other Oracomms in the commercial version. The Personal and Basic Oracomm does not have the network feature. However, two utility programs that are available, TOFIDO and FROMFIDO, allow you to extract messages and create FIDO-style files which can be transmitted with other FIDO mailers.

Upload and download commands support xmodem protocol. Each sub-board has it's own upload/download directory to distribute files according to subject. Directories can be access level protected, and individual files can be access level, password, or account protected. A "download database" maintains up to 9000 byte description of each file, the date of last download, and number of times it was downloaded. The file management system makes it easy for the sysop to add, move, copy to/from floppy, or delete files on the system while other users are online.

All menus, help files, questionnaires, and prompts are changeable by the sysop. Menus have both an ASCII and an ANSI form. Users calling with color monitors can view Oracomm with color and graphics. All system management, customization, and installation commands can be done online with simple menus while Oracomm is running, so it can be operated remotely. The Personal Oracomm comes with an abbreviated sysop manual to allow it to fit on one disk. The registered Basic Oracomm comes with a comprehensive 120+ page system operator manual and 50+ page user manual on disk covering all aspects of operation, use, and management of Oracomm.

(PC-SIG Disk# 2651)

Special Requirements: *DOS 3.0+, 640K RAM, hard drive, and a hayes compatible modem.*
Author Registration: *$59.00*

RBBS-PC   *by RBBS-R*

The RBBS is the bulletin board system of choice for many IBM-PC BBSs. It's a large system on four disks and supports the PC-SIG LIBRARY ON CD ROM.

RBBS-PC's internal structure is modularized and structured. The program includes a File Management System for directories, additional file exchange protocols, support for managing subscriptions, configurable command letters, multiple uploads on a single command line, new A)nswer and V)erbose ARC list commands, and context-sensitive Help. It also can run as a local application on a network, use any field or define a new field to identify callers, and individualize callers having the same ID. The source code is included.

(PC-SIG Disk#'s 212, 334, 621, 622, 2092)

Special Requirements: *Hard drive and a modem.*
Author Registration: *$35.00*

Sapphire   *by Pinnacle Software*

Each brand of BBS suits a different kind of sysop. SAPPHIRE is specifically designed for stores, computer consultants, customer support lines, people who have never run a BBS before, and people who have run a BBS before and found it too much work.

SAPPHIRE is very easy to set up and maintain. A moderately experienced computer user can set it up in less than an hour and spend approximately one hour per week performing the various duties required of a sysop.

SAPPHIRE's design is quite flexible, so you can modify it to look the way you want. Multi-line systems are not supported by Sapphire. This is in keeping with the "install-and-forget" design of the system, but it does mean that Sapphire won't suit everyone.

(PC-SIG Disk# 1833)

Special Requirements: *512K RAM, two floppy drives or a hard drive, and a Smartmodem.*
Author Registration: *$45.00*

✍ = Updated Program
☆ = New Program

Searchlight BBS
by Searchlight Software

Looking for a bulletin board system that's both powerful and easy-to-use? Take a look at SEARCHLIGHT BBS.

Unlike other bulletin board systems, SEARCHLIGHT BBS is user-friendly for both you (the system operator) and those who call in to your system. It has an easy to understand menu command system, so users who call in to your system need no documentation or help from you to use the BBS. If any help is needed, the program has an on-line Help system. Moreover, it has some significant features, such as optional ANSI graphics and color selections for the screen, customized menus, public message boards, private mail, a full-screen text editor (compatible with WordStar commands), and a file transfer system with both Xmodem and Ymodem transfer protocols.

SEARCHLIGHT BBS has password protection and 255 levels of security, letting you control access to your system. Like other bulletin boards, this one can be left unattended while callers leave messages and transfer files to and from your board. Specify an upload/download ratio for all who use the file transfer system so there is a fair trade-off of programs.

There is a complete electronic mail system with up to 24 message subsections, each with up to 300 messages. SEARCHLIGHT BBS has enough system operator utilities so you can easily manage the system from a remote location and shell to DOS to run a program or DOS command.

(PC-SIG Disk# 1136)

Special Requirements: *Hard drive, a modem, DOS 3.1, and PKUNZIP.*

Author Registration: *$35.00 to $95.00.*

➤*ASP Member.*

Vari-Tale
by Pinnacle Software

VARI-TALE is a "branching authoring system" designed to run either locally on your computer screen, or as a "door" on BBS systems such as PCBoard, RBBS, NoChange, Fido, ROS, Sapphire, and so on.

You will be able to write stories (known in VARI-TALE as "books") that have alternate chapters. At any point, there is always an alternative. In VARI-TALE, each step (known in VARI-TALE as "chapters") can be up to 50 lines long. After each step, there can be up to five alternative chapters.

This allows you and other people to create "story-rounds," in which everybody contributes chapters to the tale. Story-rounds are quite popular on BBS systems, but there is a problem. Eventually somebody will take the story in the wrong direction and the other writers will get annoyed. And that is the end of that story.

With VARI-TALE, the writers can propose alternate chapters, either in response to an inappropriate effort by another writer or simply to explore a different facet of the story. This version is limited to three books.

(PC-SIG Disk# 1794)

Special Requirements: *BBS with "Door" capability.*

Author Registration: *$35.00*

Wildcat BBS ✍
by Mustang Software

A full-featured BBS with the easiest setup operation in the industry. In his review of the installation procedure John Dvorak says "...this is the way it's supposed to be done." A completely indexed documentation file is included which covers all program features. The message system includes private mail, forwarding, carbon copies, and return receipts. File transfers make use of Xmodem, Ymodem (batch), Zmodem (batch, Kermit, and any others as external protocols. A branching questionnaire allows formatted answers for order-taking or polling callers. WILDCAT! features specific internal support for multitasking operation. Baud rates up to 19,200 are supported. WILDCAT! lets you install an operational BBS and get a real feel for the power of the commercial multi-line/LAN release.

(PC-SIG Disk#'s 745, 746)

Special Requirements: *512K RAM and a hard drive.*

Author Registration: *$129.00*

▼ ▼ ▼

Business Specific Systems

Advertising Response Manager (ARM)   *by Argonaut Systems*

Advertisers, there is an easy way to see if your advertising dollars are paying off. ADVERTISING RESPONSE MANAGER (ARM) helps you keep track of the response to all types of advertising and promotional campaigns. ARM can handle advertisements, news releases, product surveys, technical articles, reply cards, or anything else you might use as promotional material. ARM gets you started with menus that prompt you for everything from product information to advertising costs. Once your advertising and promotional pieces are entered, another section of the program allows you, or your administrative support, to keep track of responses. You do not need to be a computer or advertising guru to effectively use ARM.

Look at how much you spent on advertising overall, or by publication, by product, by type of media, or by individual piece. You can look at responses based on the media name, issue, type, identification number, product advertised, last response date, or number of responses to date.

One of the best things about ARM is that it allows you to plug your data files into any other spreadsheet or database program that uses dBASE files. With ARM, you can finally see what you're getting for your advertising dollar.

(PC-SIG Disk# 1562)

Special Requirements: *512K RAM and a hard drive.*
Author Registration: *$25.00*

Call Master ✍   *by Micro Data Assist*

CALL MASTER is a simple-to-use service call management system with a full Accounts Receivable subsystem, specifically designed for pest control, lawn care, air conditioning, and other service businesses. CALL MASTER is completely menu-driven and extremely flexible. You define the service provided, the number of calls required by each service contract, and the frequency between each service call. Once defined, each service can be tracked in a wide variety of ways. Services are automatically rescheduled upon posting of invoices.

The capability of projecting current service contracts into the future will be an invaluable aid when planning vacations or projecting cash flow. Each client can be assigned to multiple service locations. Each location can have service contracts for every service you provide. Each provided service can have its own schedule and rate.

CALL MASTER also performs basic accounting functions. Reports are provided of all dollar activity in a format that allows you to prepare entries for any type of accounting system you are currently using. Standard reports of aged Accounts Receivable and monthly statements are only a few of the reports provided.

In addition to reports, CALL MASTER will print mailing labels, envelopes, Rolodex cards, service maintenance records, service call schedules, client telephone listings, and statements. CALL MASTER is everything you need to set up and run your own service business.

(PC-SIG Disk#'s 1622, 1623)

Special Requirements: *640K RAM, a hard drive, and a printer.*
Author Registration: *$175.00*

Chiro Patient Tracking System ✍   *by C&C Computer Support*

CHIRO was written in conjunction with several physicians to provide a specific service in a medical office. The system maintains a detailed patient database and eliminates the nuisance of typing claim forms. It uses friendly and colorful screens, is easily installed and no cumbersome manuals are required. It is completely menu-driven, with on-line Help always available. Backup, purge, and restore of patient data is provided.

Claim form data is printed directly on form HCFA-1500. Other printed output includes reports of outstanding claims and standard office statements. It provides automatic sort and merge of new patient records and can rapidly fetch any patient record for analysis or claim form processing. Similar medical products on the market retail for thousands of dollars.

New features include:
❑ Pop-up windows for procedures and diagnosis
❑ Aging report on payments
❑ New Patient Scheduler

(PC-SIG Disk# 1044)

Special Requirements: *384K RAM, DOS 3.0, hard drive, HCFA-1500 forms, and printer.*
Author Registration: *$295.00*

Club-Ez ✍ *by SoftSolutions*

CLUB-EZ is a simple-to-use program designed to handle any club or organization's recordkeeping, including membership, attendance, and financial information. The program is powerful enough for the experienced PC user and yet, because it is menu-driven, it allows the novice to be up and running in minutes.

CLUB-EZ is in full color, with no graphic cards or printer drivers needed, and is packed with features. It prints two kinds of club rosters, and will print dues statements on plain paper or letterhead for ANY billing cycle. It produces mailing labels for members, guests, and dues statements, tracks attendance, and easily handles meeting reservations. The financial module (sent free with your $45 registration) allows you to set up a budget and track income and expenses for any period. The module also allows you to set up your own income and expense categories.

CLUB-EZ is particularly advantageous in that years of club records can be saved for future reference and it eliminates compatibility problems when transferring records from one year (or person) to the next. CLUB-EZ is a good value and will be useful for years to come.

(PC-SIG Disk# 2477)

Special Requirements: *None.*
Author Registration: *$45.00*

Construction Estimator *by Michael O'Massey*

At last! An easy-to-use construction estimation program. This program is unlike all others because it actually calculates the cost and the quantities that are needed to order materials.

For the home handyman or amateur builder who likes to tackle major projects, CONSTRUCTION ESTIMATOR provides a menu-driven aid for estimating building project costs.

There are 12 common estimation calculations to choose from: concrete footings, stem walls, and floor slabs; block and wood walls; ceiling and floor joists; roof sheeting; rafters; sheetrock and wallsiding. Hardcopy of cost totals can be obtained by using the print command. Estimates can be converted to spreadsheet or ASCII files.

(PC-SIG Disk# 1159)

Special Requirements: *512K RAM and CGA.*
Author Registration: *$25.00 for ver 1.9, and $59.95 for ver 2.0*

Cut Optimizer 2 *by Donald P. Michelotti*

CUT OPTIMIZER 2 is a must for any manufacturer or hobbyist who needs materials cut from any bulk source. Whether you're a steel fabricator, machinist, carpenter, or work in storefront construction, you'll maximize your material by reducing waste. Easily generate piece layouts, manage inventory, and calculate the costs of materials. CUT OPTIMIZER 2 even has piece layout forms for frames with mitered or butt joints.

With the included database, you can print an inventory summary and a variety of nesting reports based on custom information. The pull-down menus, automatic inventory updating, and context-sensitive Help round out this system.

(PC-SIG Disk# 1062)

Special Requirements: *None.*
Author Registration: *$15.00 or $100.00 for business use.*

Dental P.M.S *by Suresoft*

DENTAL PATIENT MANAGEMENT SYSTEM (DPMS) tracks treatments and manages Accounts Receivable, insurance, patient billing, and follow-up information. Insurance company information, complete patient information, and procedure details are integrated. Information need be entered only once; data from insurance forms is automatically posted to a patient's Account Receivable records. DPMS uses common computer forms such as an Attending Dentist's Statement and the NEBS Patient Billing form. Entering a patient procedure automatically updates billing information including charges. Invoicing can be done in four keystrokes.

DPMS's biggest strengths are patient tracking and generating written and telephone follow-up reminders, as well as inactive patient lists. Patient files can be read by most word processors to generate labels and form letters. Most routine procedures are included, and more can be added.

(PC-SIG Disk#'s 1251, 1252, 1253, 1254, 1255)

Special Requirements: *512K RAM and a hard drive.*
Author Registration: *$125.00*

The Electronic Catalog Construction Kit ☆   *by Cerebral Software*

The Revolution is here! THE ELECTRONIC CATALOG replaces the traditional paper catalog. Create a personalized catalog of items for sale, including short descriptions and prices. Define such details as a company letterhead, state and Federal taxes (if applicable), methods of payment, and any shipping and handling charge to be added to orders.

This catalog is then "built" to a floppy disk. This built version contains the program to electronically display the catalog, the database of products offered, and a customizable README file with information about the program. All this is done without any user intervention.

The catalog can then be viewed from DOS. It allows the user (a buyer) to select the items s/he wants to purchase and enter quantities for each. The program keeps a running total of the price, taxes, and shipping/handling charges. It generates an invoice for the totals and provides space for entering the addresses for shipping and billing. The quantities for each of the items purchased and the shipping and billing information are the only things the user enters.

The Electronic catalog is written in PROLOG and takes advantage of the powerful features offered by the language. The inclusion of a Wordstar-like editor and the ability to import text files makes THE ELECTRONIC CATALOG a very efficient and powerful program.

(PC-SIG Disk# 2715)

Special Requirements: *Hard drive or high density floppy drive.*
Author Registration: *$45.00*

MIS Manager   *by The Micro Group*

This is an ex-commercial program that has now become available as shareware. The MIS MANAGER is a comprehensive package for tracking computer hardware, software, and applications. It is a powerful tool for the data processing department. It covers regular hardware maintenance, development requests, purchased or leased equipment, makes inventory labels, and it even has a database for software or hardware magazine reviews. It creates departmental bills for nearly every MIS application, and it tracks by department and budget codes. It can compute straight-line and ACRS depreciation. It also contains over 100 reports (including complete audit trails).

Special Requirements: *512K RAM, a hard drive, and a printer. 640K RAM recommended.*
Author Registration: *$99.00*

The Order Pro   *by Automated Systems*

If you run a mail order business, you know how important it is to track your daily operations. Here's a menu-driven program that's specifically designed to completely automate the mail order business. This program is the successor to the earlier OFFICE PRO. It offers a complete range of features including dBASE compatibility, order entry, inventory control, mailing labels, invoices, packing slips, Accounts Receivable, vendor tracking, financial reports, sales tracking reports, inventory reports, and back order reports.

THE ORDER PRO comes with a succinct five-page "getting started" manual. It clearly directs the startup and walks you through the beginning steps. Whether your business is established or just getting started, THE ORDER PRO can offer the kind of help that makes a computer pay for itself in time, money, and ease of use.

(PC-SIG Disk# 2263)

Special Requirements: *512K RAM, and a hard drive.*
Author Registration: *$99.95*

The Parcel Shipping Program   *by East Hampton Industries*

The PARCEL SHIPPING PROGRAM (PSP) is a menu-driven system that meets all UPS reporting requirements. It is designed to eliminate the tedious UPS paperwork needed to ship parcels.

All UPS shipping rates and tables are included. As you enter the shipping transaction, PSP calculates the UPS zone shipping charges. Produce shipping labels, COD tags, and UPS manifests. PSP maintains a shipping address file for frequently shipped-to customers, and a temporary file for one-time shipments that can be deleted at the end of the day. The format of the shipping data entry screen is similar to the UPS log book, making PSP very easy to use.

(PC-SIG Disk#'s 2262, 2319)

Special Requirements: *A hard drive, or high-density drives.*
Author Registration: *$125.00*

PC-Food ✍   *by Schreck Software*

PC-FOOD automatically calculates and maintains the food or beverage cost of each item on a restaurant's menu when any ingredient cost or portion cost changes. You can maintain a real profit when you know what it REALLY costs. PC-FOOD is used in small and large food service operations, including schools and hotels.

Of course, PC-FOOD not only deals with creating menus but guides the user through the program with its own easy-to-use computer menus. After describing the way inventory ingredients are purchased and used, the user "builds" each batch recipe simply and quickly by choosing from the defined ingredients and batch recipes. A batch recipe can contain up to 19 inventory ingredients in any quantity. Each menu item can contain up to 12 inventory ingredients or batch recipes in any quantity. One such menu item might be the "noon special" that includes a sandwich, soup and a cookie. How do you price it and make a fair profit?

PC-FOOD will maintain required selling prices for each menu item based on a desired gross profit percentage and/or dollar amount. Several reports can be printed, including required price changes. At the touch of a key, all uses of an ingredient or batch recipe can be displayed.

(PC-SIG Disk# 1809)

Special Requirements: *384K RAM and printer.*
Author Registration: *$49.00*
➤ *ASP Member.*

Pony Express ✍   *by Melisco Marketing, Inc.*

This program can help individuals or businesses to automate USPS (U.S. Post Office) and UPS (United Parcel Service) rate and fee calculations.

Enter the zip code of the destination, the value and weight of your package, and PONY EXPRESS will show you all the available rates and services. If you need to compare speed vs. cost, there's a function to display the ETA and the cost for each level of service.

Numerous USPS rate types and options are supported, such as First Class Express Mail, post office to addressee, Priority Mail, insurance, and COD fees. UPS options supported include Next-Day Air, Second Day Air, ground service insurance, and oversize package fees.

A nice feature is that it can be run as a stand-alone or a memory-resident program. If used in the memory-resident mode, it takes as little as 9K of RAM when used with expanded memory or disk swapping.

The next time you need to find out how much it costs to ship a 5 lb. parcel across the U.S., and how long it takes to get there, use the PONY EXPRESS.

(PC-SIG Disk# 2246)

Special Requirements: *None.*
Author Registration: *$80.00*

ReSearch ✍   *by Integra Computing*

Designed for attorneys, RESEARCH packs the power to document and sort through caseloads full of research material to find vital evidence.

A research, document, and evidence organizer, RESEARCH lets you enter notes on evidence or other research, and file up to an eleven-line summary according to source, page, line number and subject. Notes can be chained together if 11 lines are inadequate. Using up to 32,000 entries per hard disk, RESEARCH can file the data under 500 subjects or types. Keep tabs on documents or other evidence including who sent it, where it is located, and where and when it was found.

Scan-and-find tools are fast and accurate, and enable you to sort through massive files for obscure bits of incriminating data. The program uses ASCII, making it compatible with your word processor.

(PC-SIG Disk# 2271)

Special Requirements: *512K RAM and a hard drive.*
Author Registration: *$50.00*

Service Plus   *by ACS*

Maintenance and repair companies will find SERVICE PLUS a valuable system to organize, control and track service calls, and generate expense and billing reports. It converts easily-forgotten verbal commitments into focused, daily appointment and callback lists that result in extra business.

SERVICE PLUS generates appointment schedules with a tickler file, and billing and expense reports that can clock and cost each activity. Create an "industry-specific" Help screen with up to 15,000 characters of text about your industry, accessible anywhere in the program with a single keystroke. SERVICE PLUS standardizes your maintenance and service call information.

The following business types have found SERVICE PLUS to be a valuable system: heating/air conditioning repair, electrical maintenance, auto repair, computer/copier rental and repair, any equipment tracking or maintenance, plant preventive maintenance, plumbing, bus or taxi maintenance, any repair business with a service bay, plus any department that provides product service and support.

SERVICE PLUS comes with a tutorial and is extensively documented.

(PC-SIG Disk#'s 1270, 1271)

Special Requirements: *640K RAM and two floppy drives.*
Author Registration: *$99.00*

$hareware Marketing $ystem ✍   *by Seattle Scientific Photo*

The $HAREWARE MARKETING $YSTEM is a detailed two-part resource for shareware authors who need creative ideas and a RATED mailing list of over 800 major shareware distributors, large computer clubs and recommended BBS systems. The first part of the package, the shareware distributor's database, contains mailing addresses, phone numbers, a Shareware Distributor Rating and other detailed data which can be used to prepare envelope mailing labels or BBS calling uploads.

The database file is rated by shareware distributor so you can mail your shareware to vendors rated A, B or C. The database file is supplied in standard file formats such as dBASE and 1-2-3 which can be directly imported into your database! Sort lists of shareware distributors by zip, state or other criteria. Foreign and U.S. distributors and computer clubs are included.

The second part of the package is a detailed newsletter and marketing strategy guide, prepared by an established shareware author. It contains dozens of creative tips, tricks and traps which every shareware author should know. Written by the author of the PC-LEARN computer tutorial, the $HAREWARE MARKETING $YSTEM provides detailed and valuable information in a frank, candid and sensible style.

(PC-SIG Disk# 2315)

Special Requirements: *Database (.DBF files), or spreadsheet (.WKS files)*
Author Registration: *$25.00*

SheetCut ✍   *by Donald P. Michelotti*

If you have to cut it, you need SHEETCUT. SHEETCUT is a state of the art material optimization system which will save time and money by helping you get the most out of your raw materials.

Enter the raw material sheet size, list the size and number of pieces you need to cut, and SHEET CUT does the rest. The best way to cut the raw material can be graphically displayed on the screen or printed out as part of a "work order" which includes a diagram and a list of the cuts and their sizes.

By reducing your raw materials (plywood, glass, plastic, sheet metal, or any material that comes as a sheet) and labor costs, SHEETCUT reduces your product costs. Pull-down menus make this program a breeze to use.

You can easily recoup the registration fee of the program in the first week of use!

(PC-SIG Disk# 2509)

Special Requirements: *CGA.*
Author Registration: *$7.50 for individuals and $49.95 for companies.*

Software Sales Tracker ✍   *by TypeRight Corporation*

SOFTWARE SALES TRACKER is designed for software authors who sell and distribute their own products directly to the PC user. It assists by keeping track of the Who, What, Where, Why, and How Much involved in the sale of most products. Get the most mileage out of your program distribution dollar.

If used properly, SOFTWARE SALES TRACKER can save you a great deal of time, effort, and money. Organize your sales and program distribution into an intelligent and productive tracking system. As well as keeping track of registered users, you will come to know "Who is" producing sales for you and "Who is not."

SOFTWARE SALES TRACKER will organize your sales into a separate file for each different product. Switching files is fast and easy, through directory Pop-Up windows. As new entries are made, SOFTWARE SALES TRACKER will automatically issue a unique product serial number for each item sold. It will keep track of quantities sold, customer addresses, telephone numbers, product serial numbers, product versions or models, prices charged, shipping charges, sales tax, and the dates sold and paid (as well as Purchase Orders and check numbers).

Automatically patch any of your .EXE files with your customer name, date of sale, and registered serial number. Print options include customer statements, customer information, disk and mailing labels, and income statements. (PC-SIG Disk# 2376)

Special Requirements: *512K RAM, DOS 3.0, and a printer. A hard drive is recommended.*
Author Registration: *$39.00*

Winning Bid, The
by Precision Systems

I have a dollar, do I hear two dollars? Two dollars, two dollars... sold!

THE WINNING BID is a bonanza for both professionals and amateurs turning to auctions to raise big bucks. It lets you trace merchandise from donors or the house through to the purchaser, reporting who receives what, and how much the bid price was. The 70-page manual tutors hobbyists on how to set up and operate this profitable fundraiser.

THE WINNING BID records sellers or donors, and consigned merchandise, providing pre-sale receipts. Post-sale statements double as receipts for tax purposes and allow buyers to pick up merchandise. Merchandise lots are tagged with lot numbers, a description, and minimum bid if needed. Date, time and amount of sales are recorded along with the buyers' identities.

The program prints paddle numbers in advance, tracks buyers by paddle number and the merchandise they bought, and even adds sales tax where appropriate. It can combine lots, track bids made under the minimum, and record seller alterations to bid prices after the sale is complete. Buyers can close and pay for their purchases at any time during the auction or after its completion. Likewise, sellers can be paid at any time or limited to payment when the purchasers pay for of their merchandise. (PC-SIG Disk# 1388)

Special Requirements: *Printer.*
Author Registration: *$25.00*

▼ ▼ ▼

CAD (Computer Aided Design) and Designing

Curve Digitizer (Hercules)
by West Coast Consultants

CURVE DIGITIZER is a completely professional, two-dimensional CAD/CAM drawing tool for the personal computer. The interactive help screen, detailed documentation, and six menu screens make it easy to operate.

❑ Direct hi-resolution printer output with controllable width, length, resolution and an option for reverse field-printing.
❑ A wide-printer output option for printers with carriages up to 16" wide.
❑ A versatile line thickness controller has been added to the Select command. This allows for double lines, poly lines or filled lines with a selectable density.
❑ Distance and angle, or delta x & y readouts are available.
❑ Advanced features; e.g., scaling & rotation, hatching and area calculations of irregular polygons.
❑ A user-defined plotter driver routine is included.

(PC-SIG Disk#'s 2068, 2069)

Special Requirements: *Hercules graphics, two floppy drives, and a graphics printer.*
Author Registration: *$149.00*

Curve Digitizer EGA/CGA
by West Coast Consultants

CURVE DIGITIZER is a completely professional, two-dimensional CAD/CAM drawing tool for the personal computer. The interactive help screen, detailed documentation, and six menu screens make it easy to operate.

❑ Direct hi-resolution printer output with controllable width, length, resolution and an option for reverse field-printing.
❑ A wide-printer output option for printers with carriages up to 16" wide.
❑ A versatile line thickness controller has been added to the Select command. This allows for double lines, poly lines or filled lines with a selectable density.
❑ Distance and angle or delta x & y readouts are available.
❑ Advanced features; e.g., scaling & rotation, hatching and area calculations of irregular polygons.
❑ A user-defined plotter driver routine is included.

(PC-SIG Disk#'s 2066, 2067)

Special Requirements: *CGA or EGA, two floppy drives and a graphics printer.*
Author Registration: *$149.00*

DANCAD3D ✍
by Daniel H. Hudgins

DANCAD3D is a versatile drawing program for stereoscopic 3-D wire-frame drawing, 3-D vector graphic animation, and computer aided manufacturing as well as designing letterheads. Draw in two or three dimensions. Separate groups of lines into elements to be saved, loaded, magnified, rotated, flipped, offset (moved), and used over and over again.

DANCAD3D prints surprisingly sharp, crisp lines on Epson/IBM-compatible dot matrix printers. Use it for many different applications, including the following:

❑ Mechanical drawings and technical illustrations
❑ Business forms of many kinds
❑ Page layouts which combine text and drawings
❑ Automatic computer slide shows
❑ Engineering simulation to verify the fit of 3-D shapes

DANCAD3D also supports many plotters, PostScript, and LaserJet printers, as well as image setters such as the Linotronic 300. It works with a mouse, 3-D track ball, or cursor keys.

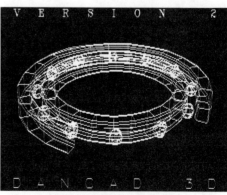

DANCAD3D (PC-SIG Disk# 701)

✍ = Updated Program
☆ = New Program

DANCAD3D includes the DANMOVIE program, a useful engineering tool. With it, you can program DANCAD3D to make an animated close-up of parts in a layout drawing. Use this close-up to confirm the fit of moving parts. Produce an animated perspective view of the entire assembly with all of the parts in motion. (PC-SIG Disk#'s 701, 702, 703, 704, 2498)

Special Requirements: *CGA, EGA, or Hercules, and a hard drive.*
Author Registration: *$45.00*

DANCAM/DANPLOT ☆   *by Daniel H. Hudgins*

DANCAM and DANPLOT are two programs that let you automate most types of machine tools. Make some connections between your computer's parallel port and motor driver modules, available from a variety of manufacturers, and Presto!, you can have your computer automatically make almost anything you like.

You will have to attach the stepper or servo motors to your machine if your machine is not already equipped with stepper or servo motors.

DANCAM and DANPLOT are simple to use once they have been configured to fit your machine tool, and can be operated from the DOS command line. DANCAD3D (Disks 701, 702, 703, 704, and 2498) can be used to produce the tool path file required by DANCAM and DANPLOT. Draw where you want the tool to go with DANCAD3D, save to tool path as an ASCII file, and run DANCAM or DANPLOT to make your part.

DANCAM is designed to do any kind of three-axis task such as vertical milling. DANPLOT is for 2-D work like drilling, or cutting out vinyl signs. DANPLOT can also be used to build a large plotter to make full size plans of ship or airplane parts.

DANCAM and DANPLOT is useful for many different applications:
❑ Full-size mechanical drawings and plans up to 100 yards long!
❑ Engraving signs and control panels
❑ Vertical milling and lathes
❑ Drilling printed circuit boards and pipe fittings
❑ Saber saw and knife cutting
❑ Cutting foam with hot wires
❑ Automated routing of wood or plastic
❑ Torch, laser, and plasma cutting of sheet material

DANCAM and DANPLOT have these features:
❑ Can be set up to work in any system of units, metric or inch
❑ Motor jog and position menu for manual positioning in X Y Z axis
❑ Motor testing utilities for reliable service
❑ Automatic feed rate changes and four control relays
❑ Automatic or manual pause for tool change
❑ Can be operated from DOS command line or DOS batch files
❑ Thirty pages on disk for complete hook up information
❑ Linear, circular, and curve interpolation when used with DANCAD3D
❑ Works on any PC or AT computer system with a parallel port
❑ Automatic backlash compensation for accurate parts

Connect several machines in parallel in order to make many parts at once with only one computer! DANCAM and DANPLOT use an easy-to-access ASCII data file format that you can read or write with DANCAD3D, a text editor, or a BASIC program.
(PC-SIG Disk# 2598)

Special Requirements: *Standard parallel printer port.*
Author Registration: *$1.00 for special mailings.*

Draft Choice ✍   *by Trius, Inc.*

DRAFT CHOICE is a powerful, fast, object-based, floating-point CAD program, for both novice and expert user.

The ease of pull-down menus is combined with the flexibility of vector-based elements to be scaled, modified, rotated, copied, or otherwise manipulated. There is a slide creation/replay option and, of course, printing to dot-matrix printers and plotting to HP-compatible pen plotters is supported.

Whatever the subject, whether it's your house plan, a drawing of an invention, or graphics for business presentations, you'll be glad to know that you can get the help you need from DRAFT CHOICE!

(PC-SIG Disk# 1760)

Special Requirements: *Hercules, CGA, EGA, or VGA.*
Author Registration: *$50.00*
➤*ASP Member.*

Droege
by Environmental Optics Corp.

DROEGE (Design Robot for Origination of Exacting Graphic Engineering) was created for designing printed circuit photomasters.

DROEGE is a manual CAD system, which means it has no automatic functions such as schematic capture, wire listing, routing, parts lists, etc. It does provide the computer-aided equivalent of a taped master or drawing board with the advantage of always having things in perfect registration and the ability to work on selected layers.

General features include a 65" x 65" working area, twelve layers deep, with a resolution of 0.001". The output can be scaled, however, so what is actually provided is a 65,000 X 65,000 point working space. Layers can be turned on and off and assigned any available color. Lines, pads, symbols, arcs and labels can be entered. The symbol feature is particularly powerful since symbols can be nested up to twenty levels deep, allowing the construction of very complex objects with a few keystrokes.

Note: This program has a limited documentation file, so it will be very helpful if you have prior experience with CAD systems and with designing printed circuit boards.

(PC-SIG Disk#'s 904, 905)

Special Requirements: *320K RAM, CGA, and Epson or compatible printer.*
Author Registration: *$25.00*

EDRAW
by Emark Systems

EDRAW is a sophisticated graphics program for drawing electronic schematics, block diagrams and flow charts. Originally designed for technical people such as engineers, teachers and students, it can even be used to lay out a printed circuit board!

EDRAW features several text fonts for incorporating into any drawing or diagram. Logic and electronic symbols have been included for drawing electronic circuits as well as lines, boxes, circles, and other icons. EDRAW is a must for anyone who has specific drawing or graphic needs.

(PC-SIG Disk# 828)

Special Requirements: *320K RAM and CGA.*
Author Registration: *$49.95*

MegaCad
by Megatech

This program, developed in Germany, has sold thousands of copies there and is twice as fast as AutoCad.

MEGACAD is a 2D CAD program for intermediate and professional use. It has all of the basic drawing elements such as points, lines, circles, arcs, text, grid, redraw, and zoom. MEGACAD also boasts more powerful drawing commands, such as dimensioning, hatching, macros, separate, layer, defaults, and group. This program offers the serious CAD programmer all of the options he or she will ever need.

Registered users receive plotter drivers, laser drivers, desktop publishing interface, additional fonts, and a program enabling the user to generate and edit original fonts.

MEGACAD — A software package for people who are serious about CAD.

(PC-SIG Disk#'s 2250, 2251, 2252)

Special Requirements: *512K RAM, graphics card, hard drive, and Microsoft-compatible mouse.*
Author Registration: *298 - 2280 DM*

NorthCad-3D ✍
by The Quest Company

NorthCAD-3D is a design and modeling program for creating, viewing, and editing three-dimensional objects and images in full color. Completely menu driven, the program can perform a variety of design and viewing tasks, and is easy to learn and use. Drawings may be created from any viewpoint, moved in any direction, and scaled along any axis.

Drawing units and rotation increments are user-selectable, and includes Absolute or Relative coordinate display functions. Pan and Zoom commands also enable specific sections of a drawing to be worked on in greater detail. On EGA and VGA systems, drawings may be created in 16 colors, an can be interactively selected from a 64 color palette. NorthCAD-3D comes along with a 170 page manual that contains a tutorial on the program.

A feature that would take this program from being merely good to excellent is the ability to print the created images. As it stands now, you need to do a print screen, or use a image capture program to print the designs. (PC-SIG Disk# 762)

Special Requirements: *512K RAM, DOS 3.0 or later and CGA, EGA, or VGA.*
Author Registration: *$79.95*

PC-Draft II   *by Natural Software*

A high-resolution, pixel-oriented utility for drawing and drafting. Built-in functions draw circles, lines and boxes; load and edit fonts; create bar, line and pie graphs; create patterns to fill areas; cut and paste objects; save objects to files for later use. Record graphic keyboard macros in files for playback and animation effects.

Maximum resolution is 1280 by 700 dots, which covers several screens and fills an 8.5" x 11" paper at 150 dots-per-inch resolution.

Capture screen images from other programs, save them in separate files and load them into PC-DRAFT II. Export portions of the screen, full screens, and/or full-sized drawings in GEM.IMG file format. Include graphics created with, or captured by, PC-DRAFT II directly into desktop publishing documents such as those created with Ventura Publisher. (PC-SIG Disk# 1060)

Special Requirements: *CGA.*
Author Registration: *$50.00.*
➤*ASP Member.*

PC-Draft-CAD   *by Natural Software*

PC-DRAFT-CAD is an object-oriented CAD program for drawing or drafting on a PC. PCD-CAD is different from most drawing packages because it can store drawings as basic elements (such as points and lines) in a database.

PCD-CAD has all of the standard functions for drawing circles, lines, curves, ellipses, boxes, etc., with or without a mouse. PCD-CAD goes further with the ability to change the scale of drawings (great for logos!) and create keyboard macros. Pull-down menus make it easy to use.

Drawings can be exported in .GEM or .WPG file format to be used in desktop publishing programs like Ventura Publisher and WordPerfect. Several text fonts are available, as well as a database of commonly used objects. (PC-SIG Disk# 1757)

Special Requirements: *CGA and an IBM, Epson, HP LaserJet, or HP DeskJet printer.*
Author Registration: *$65.00*
➤*ASP Member.*

Professional Cam Cad   *by James H. Graham*

PROFESSIONAL CAM CAD guides the novice or engineer through the complex calculations required to design cams. A cam is a rotating piece that imparts motion to a roller moving against its edge, transforming this rotary motion into a translating or oscillating motion. Requirements imposed on cams vary from machine to machine due to the speed changes and type of equipment they are to be used in. PROFESSIONAL CAM CAD helps you to select eight different motion contours from a table.

Various styles of cam contours are available in PROFESSIONAL CAM CAD. Harmonic, Cycloidal, 3-4-5, Polynomial, Constant Velocity, Matching Constant Velocity, and dwells are included. Input one motion contour for a sector and incorporate another motion for another sector in the same cam.

PROFESSIONAL CAM CAD will display the exact contour of the cam and allow you to view the cutter path. See the final shape using the cutter/cam follower of your choice. If necessary, re-plot the cam before actually manufacturing it, saving countless expensive hours of development time.

PROFESSIONAL CAM CAD does the hard work for you. It provides eight different displacement profiles for your selection, calculates the profiles, displays the contour of your cam and will even save the profiles to disk for future reference.

(PC-SIG Disk# 2372)

Special Requirements: *512K RAM, CGA, and a printer.*
Author Registration: *$35.00*

TURBODRAW
by Daytron Electronics Inc

An entry-level CAD program combining an easy point-and-click user interface with the ability to generate user symbol libraries. TURBODRAW produces professional-quality drawings for electrical, architectural, and mechanical engineers, as well as dataflow, program flow and structural charts for programmers, systems analysts, and database managers.

The menu access system and the spooling capability are handy features. Redirect output to a file instead of to a device. Print or plot output at a more convenient time or from a PC that is connected to the proper printer or plotter.

Unique features:
❏ Symbols can be generated and incorporated into symbol libraries   by the user
❏ Pop-up menus
❏ Automatic undo/delete, unlimited depth
❏ Pattern fill
❏ Supports all plotters, dot-matrix printers, LaserJet with 512K or 1.5MB
❏ Supports Hercules mono, CGA, EGA, VGA or MCGA
❏ Mouse driver included
❏ 300 dpi output, suitable for presentation artwork
❏ .TIF, .PCX, .PLT output for desktop publishing/wordprocessing.

TURBODRAW doesn't handle bit-mapped images like some painting/drawing programs and is best used to create technical drawings that consist primarily of lines and curves.

(PC-SIG Disk# 2151)

Special Requirements: *Hercules graphics, CGA, EGA, VGA, or MCGA.*
Author Registration: *$69.00*

VGACAD
by Marvin E. Gozum, M.D.

VGACAD is an all-purpose graphics editor, image processor and paint program to create, enhance, or colorize digitized images.

VGACAD provides 21 brush shapes with 5 different brush modes, normal, spray, air#1, air#2, and eraser. There are 256 color fills, border tracing, and pattern/gradient fills. Three modes of zoom editing are also available. Air#1 (airbrush) adds a color mixture as you paint over your picture, just like a real air brush. Air#2 mixes colors in more gradually. Spray, when used with the Mask feature, has the effect of placing a stencil over the painted area. Colorize grey images in the same way old movies are reborn in color. Cut and Paste functions are also fully supported.

VGACAD provides several ways of altering the size and orientation of an image. Rotate the entire screen 90 or continue to 180 to turn it upside-down. Create a mirror image, or an upside-down mirror image, of any defined area.

VGACAD supports .BLD, .PLT, .GIF and .CLP file formats. Utilities are provided to convert pictures to VGA from CGA and EGA, and from VGA to EGA. Also available is a VGA print utility that prints any viewable color picture in 7 user-selected grey shades. Shrink large-sized pictures. Edit large .GIF files (up tp 32K x 32K x 256).

VGACAD has been used by such institutions as Lawrence Livermore Labs, the University of Pittsburgh, Warner Brothers, and the New York Times.

(PC-SIG Disk#'s 1587, 1588)

Special Requirements: *VGA or EGA. A hard drive is recommended.*
Author Registration: *$27.95 or $42.95 outside USA.*

▼ ▼ ▼

✍ = Updated Program
☆ = New Program

Calculators

CMPCALC3
by UDH Enterprises Inc.

CMPCALC3 converts your PC into a programmable calculator for complex numbers. Using reverse Polish notation (RPN), like Hewlett-Packard calculators, complex numbers and functions become as easy to handle as real ones.

CMPCALC3 provides the arithmetical functions of addition, subtraction, multiplication and division, as well as the more complex exponential, logarithmic, trigonometric, hyperbolic, and square root functions. It has nine labeled storage areas, which are shown on the screen, and 41 numbered storage areas, which are not. CMPCALC3 can memorize programs

(PC-SIG Disk# 1951)

Special Requirements: *None.*
Author Registration: *$49.00*

HDBCalc
by Jim Lynch

HBDCALC is a 16-bit calculator made for programmers. Perform binary, decimal, or hexadecimal calculations or mix the three number bases and display the answer in all three. Convert a number from one base to another instantly. Handle both mathematical and logical operations including: ADD, SUB, SHR, SHL, AND, NOT, XOR and OR functions. The CPU's sign and carry flags are also displayed.

(PC-SIG Disk# 1385)

Special Requirements: *None.*
Author Registration: *$10.00.*

Morsoft Calculator
by Morsoft

If you own a computer but still find yourself looking for a pocket calculator, look no further. Here's a full-function calculator for you.

It may be used as an "adding machine" with the ability to sum up to 1,000 values. Each value is stored in the computer memory "tape" which may be scrolled forward or back, changed, and printed. Both sub- and overall totals are retained and displayed on the screen, and the "tape" may contain multiple totals.

Arithmetic and trigonometric functions are provided and calculation results may be added to, or subtracted from, the memory "tape." Values may be added, subtracted, multiplied, or divided to or from memory as they are entered. Enter and retain values in either decimal or hexadecimal number base. (All functions are available in either.) Try that on your pocket calculator!

(PC-SIG Disk# 1831)

Special Requirements: *None.*
Author Registration: *$14.95*
➤*ASP Member.*

PC/Calculator
by Micro Business Application

PC/CALCULATOR turns your PC into a programmable multi-function RPN (Reverse Polish Notation) calculator. It features 16 visible memories, seven function key modes, and 14 number display formats. Run it in stand-alone mode or keep it in RAM. Define a "pop-up" key and call your calculator from inside any of your other applications.

You'll always be able to add things up!

(PC-SIG Disk# 444)

Special Requirements: *None.*
Author Registration: *$10.00 - $25.00.*

Quick Calculators
by Phil Faircloth Software

Get four memory-resident calculators for the price of one with QUICK CALCULATORS: a powerful algebraic calculator, a programmer's calculator, a scientific calculator, and a financial calculator! Get them all in one program in as little as 10K of RAM with programmable hot keys.

The programmer's calculator allows you to enter values in either binary, octal, decimal, or hex formats and automatically convert these values to the other number systems.

The scientific calculator has access to 31 functions such as inverse tangent, hyperbolic cosine and sine of an angle.

All of the calculators have on-line help and a scrolling tape that can hold up to 500 entries, which can be saved when you exit the program.

(PC-SIG Disk# 2244)

Special Requirements: *Hard drive recommended.*
Author Registration: *$19.95*

QWIKMATH, The Complete Programming Calculator   by Advocate Enterprises, Ltd.

QWIKMATH is one of the most comprehensive programmer's calculator on the market today and provides a wide array of features.

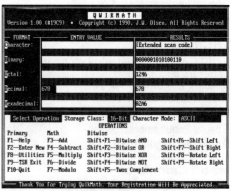

QUIKMATH (PC-SIG Disk# 2371)

Enter values in binary, octal, decimal, or hexadecimal. Results are displayed in all these bases, as well as the ASCII or extended scan code equivalents. A complete range of arithmetic and bitwise operators is supplied. Press any ASCII or extended scan code key and instantly see its value in all number bases. Perform calculations with 32-bit, 16-bit, and 8-bit values. A 16-level "undo" feature allows escape from most errors. Experiment freely in "what if" sessions without losing the results of prior operations. Need help? QUIKMATH has context-sensitive help screens.

QWIKMATH's Character Format is a feature not normally found in a programmer's calculator. Choose how you want the character output treated — in ASCII mode or extended scan code mode. See ALL the characters output to the screen.

QWIKMATH runs as a stand-alone or memory-resident program (instantly popped-up with a "hot key"). Now you can have all the functions you will ever need in a programmer's calculator, right on your screen.

(PC-SIG Disk# 2371)

Special Requirements: *None.*
Author Registration: *$24.95*

RPN   by Richard T. Behrens

RPN is a Reverse Polish Notation calculator based on a fully-visible stack, especially useful to busy programmers and computer specialists.

(PC-SIG Disk# 874)

Special Requirements: *360K RAM.*
Author Registration: *$10.00*

RPNCALC   by Richard T. Behrens

RPN allows your computer to function conveniently as a scientific calculator using Reverse Polish Notation, It can be used as an ordinary 'transient' program, invoked from the DOS prompt. It can also be installed as a Terminate and Stay Resident (TSR) program, and invoked from anywhere by pressing the Hot Key. As a TSR, it occupies about 40K of memory.

RPNCALC has the following features:
- Scientific notation or fixed decimal display
- Trigonometric functions and inverses (degrees or radians)
- Logarithmic functions and exponentials
- Additional mathematical and stack functions
- 6-byte floating point (about 11 digit internal accuracy)
- Pi key (3.14159 . . .)

🖫 = Updated Program
☆ = New Program

❏ TSR can be removed from memory without re-booting
(PC-SIG Disk# 2614)
Special Requirements: *None.*
Author Registration: *$10.00*

Smart Calculator
by Cobrasoft, Inc.

Ever use a calculator or an adding machine? You don't need ANOTHER machine. You don't even need a spreadsheet. What you do need is SMARTCALC, an intelligent four-function business calculator which can double as a state-of-the-art adding machine.

Display only and print display modes share billing with such advanced features as automatic repeat, store and recall, freeze display, on-line help, date/time stamped tapes, printed tape messages, tape entry count, double window, and stored memory display.

The program has a range of -99,999,999.99 to 99,999,999.99.

(PC-SIG Disk# 1784)
Special Requirements: *Printer recommended.*
Author Registration: *$20.00*

Xact Calculators ✍
by CalcTech Inc.

XACT brings you a trio of programs emulating three top Hewlett Packard hand held calculators — the HP-11C Scientific Calculator, the HP-12C Financial Calculator, and the HP-16C Programmer's Calculator.

All three programs have approximately 70 functions keys laid out in the standard HP format. The prefix key usage is the same on the computer and the calculator.

"When a program performs flawlessly, it makes writing a review hard. Such is the case with XACT-16C."— Jacques Benavente, PCM Magazine, August 1988.

"PC-12C's (an OEM version of XACT-12C) emulation of the HP-12C is exact.... Popular's PC-12C gets my vote." Jim Seymour, "The Best of the Best Utilities," PC Magazine, June 1987.

"XACT-16C... It has power to burn." Johnathan Matzkin, PC Magazine, May 29, 1988.

"It's (XACT-11C) just like my HP-11C. I use it all the time and keep it on my laptop computer when travelling." Bill Treneer, 1776 Corporation.

(PC-SIG Disk# 1502)
Special Requirements: *None.*
Author Registration: *$27.00*

ZYAC Calculator
by Gregory D. Elder

ZYAC will turn your IBM-PC or compatible into programmable scientific calculators.

ZYAC performs all common arithmetic functions from addition and subtraction to exponentials, square roots and logarithms. Other features range from trigonometric functions, including hyperbolics in radians or degrees, to statistical functions such as mean, standard deviation, population variance, etc., and metric-to-English conversions.

ZYAC uses the entire 80x25 computer screen, has online help and a menu. It's much easier to read and use than a normal hand-held calculator. Two memory registers and two programmable function keys, make it one of the most comprehensive calculator programs available.

(PC-SIG Disk# 1509)
Special Requirements: *CGA and a text editor.*
Author Registration: *$15.00*

▼ ▼ ▼

Chemistry, Biology, and Physics

BSIM
by Paul H. Deal

College and high school Biology instructors — You will find BSIM especially interesting. In classrooms equipped with PCs, BSIM can create simulated ecological systems to be used as models of actual biological systems. The program provides fun reinforcement of the basic subject matter covered in class and encourages the mental manipulation of conceptual elements well beyond standard calculation-phase gymnastics. The model for the program is an aquatic ecosystem, but the general features can be applied across a broad range of other ecosystems.

Sample stagnant and circulated flask environments, leave open or closed to oxygen and carbon-dioxide atmospheres, choose light or dark, depth, and choice of sample location according to a grid. Temperature and pH are assumed constant and optimum. Also available is a readout of solution elements for the sample taken.

"Pseudogenomes" are projections of real organisms, complete with physical structures and processes determined by 13 changeable elements set by the user. Organisms feed and grow, using a simplified carbon chemistry. They are capable of reproduction or reduction with sampling possible at each generation. BSIM allows for new organisms or the "reseeding" of old ones at first generation. BSIM has a simple printer facility and easy menus.

The registration fee provides the user with technical data and program utilities to assist program analysis, and an experimenter's manual for ten experiments. These experiments cover sampling techniques,

(PC-SIG Disk# 1725)

Special Requirements: *CGA, EGA, or Hercules graphics.*
Author Registration: *$29.95*

Chemical
by Larry Puhl

CHEMICAL — a molecular-modeling program for 3-D representations of chemical elements.

Select atoms from the Periodic Table and the program retrieves the electron orbital information. The atoms can be bonded into molecules, and the molecules bonded with other molecules to make large chemical structures. The chemical is displayed as it is constructed, and when formed, can be rotated and viewed. The Hybrid and Ionize commands can be used to alter the orbitals before bonding. Read, write and view a chemical data file from the disk. CHEMICAL also has a help function and a tutorial.

Included is CHEMVIEW (an EGA-only function), a companion program that shows three-dimensional animation of the models made with CHEMICAL.

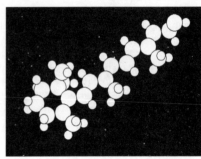

Chemical (PC-SIG Disk# 938)

(PC-SIG Disk# 938)

Special Requirements: *640K RAM, and CGA or EGA.*
Author Registration: *$20.00*

Crystal
by Larry Puhl

Generate and view 3-D models of crystals. The built-in editor allows you to modify crystal structures from the included library or construct entirely new ones.

Sample crystal files are included on this disk, and new crystal structures may be created by modifying these files or by creating a new file. CRYSTAL has a complete set of built-in editing capabilities. When viewing a crystal structure, use the cursor pads to rotate the model on the x, y and z axis. Also provided are data files of crystals for use by CHEMICAL and CHEMVIEW, two excellent companion programs to CRYSTAL. CRYSTAL operates independently or in conjuction with these programs.

(PC-SIG Disk# 1469)

Special Requirements: *None.*
Author Registration: *$20.00*

Electron ✍
by H&P Software

Great for electrical engineers, technicians and hobbyists. ELECTRON helps solve electrical equations, performs various electronic and electrical calculations, and displays many different diagrams of motors, transformers, etc., on a graphic monitor. Electronic calculations are available for the D.C. Ohm's law, parallel resister, resonant frequencies, decibels, and

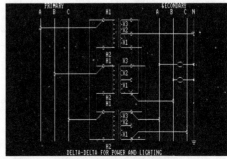

Electron (PC-SIG Disk# 1045)

✍ = Updated Program
☆ = New Program

resistance for ammeters. Electrical calculations are supplied for true power, watts, ohms, RPM, and frequency. Various tables, such as a standard wire size table, are also provided.

(PC-SIG Disk# 1045)

Special Requirements: *384K RAM.*
Author Registration: *$10.00*
➤*ASP Member.*

Element Study Aid ✍   *by Enchanted Tree Software*

Having recurring nightmares about flunking your chemistry class? Well, we've got good news for you! THE ELEMENT STUDY AID teaches you everything you need to know about all of the elements on the Periodic Table. Learn the element's name, atomic number and symbol, atomic weight, common valence, specific gravity, and the melting and boiling points of each. An option on the Periodic Table allows you to see where all of the elements fit into it. After you have studied the elements or the group of your choosing, run the test option to see how well you've learned them.

(PC-SIG Disk# 2184)

Special Requirements: *512K RAM*
Author Registration: *$34.95*

Labcoat (American version) ✍   *by Douglas Standing*

LABCOAT, a laboratory data and cost analysis program, can help you to manage a clinical lab. Calculate item depreciation and evaluate extensive-test cost data for your equipment. Routine lab statistics and Q.C. charting are included.

LABCOAT handles data entry and calculations for lipoprotein data. You can calculate numerical data, mean and standard deviation, and range. Also included is an evaluation program for prospective lab assistants, based on such criteria as job knowledge, judgment decisions, patient awareness, organizational skills, and more.

(PC-SIG Disk# 932)

Special Requirements: *CGA.*
Author Registration: *None.*

MSFORMS   *by Declan Cowley*

MSFORMS and its utility program, NAMES, read a QUAN report from a Finnigan(tm) mass spectrometer and produce a finished report for given classes of target compound analysis (TCA), suitable for presentation to a client.

Attach the RS232 communications cable that runs from the GC/MS NOVA computer to the Tektronix/Westward system terminal of the NOVA to the serial port of your PC. Load a suitable terminal emulator program in your PC and capture the Finnigan TCA QUAN reports as individual ASCII files.

MSFORMS is then loaded and the QUAN filenames are passed to the program, along with other information, including matrix type and dilution factors. MSFORMS processes it and prints an analysis form suitable for delivery to a client.

(PC-SIG Disk#'s 970, 1453)

Special Requirements: *512K RAM, two floppy drives, and a printer.*
Author Registration: *$50.00*

Nuclear Magnetic Resonance   *by Milton Johnson*

This highly-technical and useful nuclear magnetic resonance (NMR) analysis program is of interest to students of chemistry and physics. Written by a University of South Florida professor of chemistry, NMR allows the analysis of this technique, used in many advanced chemistry applications.

This unique program displays the calculated spectrum including adjustable peak broadening. Simulated plotting of very complex molecules, such as strong coupled proton spectra, is supported. Parameters for up to seven spins (nuclei) can be calculated.

(PC-SIG Disk# 590)

Special Requirements: *Printer.*
Author Registration: *$10.00*

PC-Calib
by Paull Associates, Inc.

Chemists, researchers, and other users of analytical instruments will find PC-CALIB a multifaceted aid to the sometimes tedious task of instrument calibration or verification.

PC-CALIB's curves can have up to eight points with three replicates each, and can be measured in any of 12 different standard units. They can be curve-fitted using linear, log-linear, linear-log, or log-log equations (log base 10) and either a first- or second-order polynomial least-squares fit. Experimental values or controls can be entered and checked against a generated curve.

View the results on screen, print them, or format them as ASCII files for import into other software. Documentation for this menu-driven program is 40-plus well-written pages, and telephone support is available.

(PC-SIG Disk# 1078)

Special Requirements: *512K RAM, CGA or EGA.*
Author Registration: *$55.00*

SCI-Calc
by Bill Joyner

SCI-CALC is a scientific calculator with a simple, direct approach. Various standard formulas are shown on the screen relating x and y. Enter the numbers you want and the program calculates the results.

(PC-SIG Disk# 1326)

Special Requirements: *None.*
Author Registration: *$4.00*

▼ ▼ ▼

Children's Programs (ages 2-10)

ABC Fun Keys
by Courtney E. Krehbiel

In our rapidly moving technological world, people are being introduced to the computer at younger and younger ages. ABC FUN KEYS teaches the alphabet, numbers, and keyboard skills to children, ages 2-6. Each letter is represented by colorful pictures and nursery rhyme melodies are played when the right key is chosen.

ABC FUN KEYS has four learning games designed around the alphabet. An adult control panel and menu allow you to select the letters to be presented, the order of presentation, and many other game options.

In the first game, a letter appears along with a picture of something that begins with that letter, and the child must find and press the key associated with the letter. Pressing the correct key causes the computer to play a song. Pressing the wrong key makes a buzzer sound.

Game Two is similar to the first game, except that the picture is gradually revealed, slowly at first and then at an increasing rate. If the correct key is not quickly pressed, the picture disintegrates and another begins to take its place.

Game Three, named Heaven and Mud, is a typing tutor for young children. Letters float in the "air" in the middle of the screen. When the correct key is pressed, the letter explodes into hearts that then float to heaven. "Unloved" letters fall and sink into the mud.

The fourth game is designed for very young children. It displays the letter of any key that is pressed and plays a randomly-selected song.

ABC FUN KEYS is educational and designed to make learning as fun and stimulating as possible.

(PC-SIG Disk# 844)

Special Requirements: *CGA, EGA, VGA, or Hercules graphics.*
Author Registration: *$15.00*

Amy's First Primer ✍
by Computing Specialties

Amy's First Primer is a collection of six fun games designed to teach basic skills to a pre-reading child, helping them with skills of countin letter recognition, simple problem solving, pattern recognition and keyboard use. The games stress positive reinforcement of these basic skills to promote a learning is fun attitude.

The documentation is well written and explains everything necessary. Repeated suggestions that the parent use the games with thier child adds a nice reinforcement toward family learning.

New features:

✍ = Updated Program
☆ = New Program

❑ Now Amy's First Primer can detect VGA, MCGA, and EGA graphics adapters and displays much more color if possible.

❑ The programs have been combined into one .EXE file which was compiled by Microsoft's Quick Basic 4.5.

❑ Smaller picture files with much more color are being used, but they've been compressed to take up only third of the disk space they used before.

❑ Also included, a full page of instructions for use with Hercules graphics (The shareware program HGCIBM by Athena Digital makes it poss- ible to run AMY and other CGA programs on a monochrome graphics).

(PC-SIG Disk# 646)

Special Requirements: *CGA, EGA, VGA or MCGA.*
Author Registration: *$15.00*

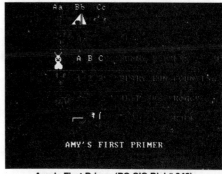

Amy's First Primer (PC-SIG Disk# 646)

Animated Math ☆
by Flix Productions

ANIMATED MATH teaches counting, addition and subtraction to children from pre-school through the first grade. Animated rewards are given every step of the way. Not just a drill, this fun tutorial gives graphic help to the children to provide a highly interactive and friendly environment to sharpen their math skills.

Several different types of games are provided as additional incentive. These include dinosaur connect-the-dot games, color games, a build your own rocket game, an animated piano and a mouse game. Animated Math uses over 100 animated sequences. Both keyboard and mouse support are provided.

This program is a joy to work with. Your child will like the animated scenes, and he/she will love the extra games provided when they complete a set of problems.

(PC-SIG Disk# 2644)

Special Requirements: *640K RAM, EGA or VGA, and a hard drive. A mouse is optional.*
Author Registration: *$10.00*

Animated Shapes ☆
by Flix Productions

ANIMATED SHAPES teaches shape and color identification using a colorful menu system designed for children pre-school through the first grade. Each shape correctly identified combines with other shapes to create a picture. Upon completion, the picture becomes an entertaining mini-movie.

When you register ANIMATED SHAPES, you're sent a version personalized with your child's name as well as fifteen new animations.

(PC-SIG Disk# 2640)

Special Requirements: *640K RAM, EGA or VGA, and a hard drive. A mouse is optional.*
Author Registration: *$7.95*

Balloon Speller
by KIDware

Your kindergarten or early elementary student will delight in these three happy games that teach spelling. Make 20-word lists of the words you want your child to learn and sit back while your PC turns into an infinitely patient tutor.

In one game, the word flashes for an instant on the screen. The child pilots a balloon around the screen, picking up the correct letters to rebuild the word. If the child forgets the word, you can flash it again by pressing the space bar. The second game is like the first, except that each flashing of the word costs a point. In the last game, the letters are scattered about the screen and the game resembles Hangman.

(PC-SIG Disk# 1333)

Special Requirements: *Hercules or color (CGA) graphics.*
Author Registration: *$11.95 or $12.95.*

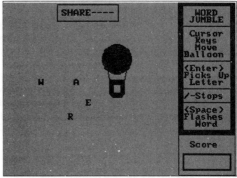

Balloon Speller (PC-SIG Disk# 1333)

Balloons ☆
by Assistware

BALLOONS displays balloons on the screen and creates notes of music as each key is pressed. Each balloon is randomly sized and differently colored. Pressing certain letter keys will cause a balloon of a specific color to appear. The Up arrow key enlarges a balloon while the Down arrow key shrinks a balloon. Enlarge or shrink a balloon until it pops or disappears, after which a star will be drawn and "Twinkle, Twinkle Little Star" will play. A colorful rainbow is then drawn across the screen. BALLOONS is a fun way for children 18 months or older to play on the computer.

(PC-SIG Disk# 2709)

Special Requirements: *CGA, VGA, or EGA.*
Author Registration: *$7.00*
➤*ASP Member.*

BRANDON'S BIG LUNCHBOX ☆
by JOEY ROBICHAUX

The entire Brandon's Lunchbox series on one diskette! 18 fun educational modules for children ages 3 to 7. Beginning and pre-readers learn keyboard skills, drill on upper/lower case alphabet, number sequences (greater than/less than), counting, problem solving, memory games, simple arithmetic, sight word drills with 184 different "sight" words — you can create your own custom word lists! Practice counting by two's or fives, learn US geography, watch your little ones discover deductive rea Plenty of flashy colors, wild sounds, and fun rewards like dancing bears Mardi Gras parades!

(PC-SIG Disk# 2669)

Special Requirements: *Hercules, CGA Graphics or Better.*
Author Registration: *$20.00*

DrawSome ☆
by Assistware

DRAWSOME allows children, 18 months or older, to draw simple designs and flowers using the keyboard and/or mouse. Move a hand around the screen to draw a line of various colors depending on what letter key was last pressed. The number keys will automatically draw a square, circle or triangle. Pressing a function key will draw a flower, creating a wonderful design on the screen for young children.

(PC-SIG Disk# 2709)

Special Requirements: *CGA, EGA, or VGA. A mouse is optional.*
Author Registration: *$8.00*
➤*ASP Member.*

EGA Coloring Book ✎
by David C. Swope

This is a computer coloring book with a selection of over 500 crayons (colors). There are five full-screen pictures that you can paint with the crayons. This program was originally made for children but anyone can enjoy it whether they're an adult or young at heart. It's just right for those times when your kids need something to do or when you need to color those blues away. Registered users get 10 more new pictures.

(PC-SIG Disk#'s 2233, 2676)

Special Requirements: *416K RAM, EGA or VGA. Optional hard drive; mouse recommended.*
Author Registration: *$20.00*

EGA Mouse Paint ✎
by Flying Mouse Software

If your children like to color pictures, EGA MOUSE PAINT will introduce them to using a mouse while coloring 17 pre-made pictures with 42 brilliant colors. A very nice feature is the ability to save a picture and restore it later. (This comes in handy when it's bedtime for the artist.) The program is very easy to use. Just point to the picture you want to color, choose a color, and have fun!

(PC-SIG Disk# 2366)

Special Requirements: *EGA, and a mouse.*
Author Registration: *$20.00*
➤*ASP Member.*

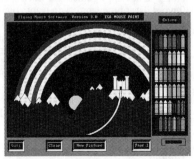
EGA Mouse Paint (PC-SIG Disk# 2366)

✎ = Updated Program
☆ = New Program

Fact Pack
by David G. Bodnar

FACT PACK is a pair of programs, TABLE and FACTRACE, designed to sharpen basic arithmetic skills (addition, subtraction, multiplication and division) for students in grades 1-8.

TABLE displays a multiplication or addition table minus the answers. The computer chooses problems at random which the student then calculates. The size of the table can be expanded to larger sums and products.

FACTRACE gives a timed quiz on a mix of addition, multiplication, subtraction and division problems. A report is generated of the problems answered correctly, the problems attempted, the percentage of correct answers and any errors made.

Both programs run in practice and test modes. In practice mode, the student can work on a problem at a leisurely pace. In test mode, both programs provide exciting challenges for the students as they race the computer in finding the answers.

FACT PACK supplies both fun and motivation for younger learners, and is an excellent tool for providing basic math skill drills.

(PC-SIG Disk# 1381)

Special Requirements: *CGA.*
Author Registration: *$10.00*

Fun With Letters and Words
by Wescott Software

For your youngster, aged 2-5. FUN WITH LETTERS AND WORDS provides a computerized First Reader with colorful graphics and personalized stories that can include your child's name and the names of friends, pets, and other family members. Varying reading levels are provided for, along with the option to add additional words for building vocabulary and spelling skills.

(PC-SIG Disk# 1278)

Special Requirements: *CGA.*
Author Registration: *20.00.*

Funnels and Buckets
by Data Sage

FUNNELS teaches math as a game, attracting young ones to the subject. A very effective tool since they'll be too busy having fun to notice they are learning!

Arithmetic problems fall from the sky and the idea is to solve them before they hit the bucket on the ground. A tap on the space bar while the problem is falling brings the solution. The "falling" speed can be adjusted for age. When the buckets are full, the game is over. Target ages: 5-11.

(PC-SIG Disk# 229)

Special Requirements: *None. (BASIC is required to run accompanying program.)*
Author Registration: *$10.00.*

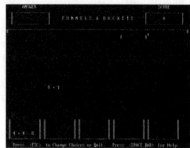
Funnels and Buckets (PC-SIG Disk# 229)

Googol Math Games ✍
by Paul T. Dawson

Here's a classic shareware program your kids will love. these three top-notch arcade-style math games are designed to make learning basic ma fun. Original twists on popular arcade themes allow these programs to do addition, subtraction, multiplication, and division. The games are so entertaining and colorful, the children won't realize they're learning. In fact, even parents enjoy them just for the games themselves.

At the lowest skill levels, the games are playable by very young children. If they are not yet able to read, parents can help them get started. Older children, 5-10, will usually be able to figure out all of the games by themselves. Finally, at the highest skill levels, the games are a challenge to everyone!

The graphics are better than many other math programs — complete color control, variable skill levels, and personalized congratulations for every correct answer are only a few of the features that make this a top-notch program.

New Features:

❑ New graphics.
❑ Higher scores for higher levels.
❑ Instant game switching.
❑ Level menu & lots more!
(PC-SIG Disk# 1768)
Special Requirements: *384K RAM, CGA or Hercules.*
Author Registration: *$10.00*

IQ Builder
by Public Brand Software

This set of educational programs is ideal for parents or teachers who want to work with youngsters to develop word and number skills. Each of these BASIC programs is separately loaded from a main program menu. The synonym and antonym programs are particularly challenging.

IQ BUILDER uses no graphics, but it does get the job done. The target group is children between the ages of 5-10.

(PC-SIG Disk# 18)
Special Requirements: *A version of BASIC.*
Author Registration: *None.*
➤*ASP Member.*

File Descriptions:

MENU	BAS	Menu to select programs for execution.
MASTER	BAS	MASTERMIND — guess the code.
READING	BAS	Improve your reading speed.
FRANK	BAS	HANGMAN by another name.
WORDS	BAS	Data for FRANK.
MATH	BAS	Drill of simple math problems.
NIM	BAS	Ancient game of skill and strategy.
BACKGAM	BAS	BACKGAMMON.
BLACK	BAS	BLACKJACK — 1 or 2 players.
TRUCKER	BAS	Make your fortune in the trucking business.
IQBUILD	BAS	Sub-menu to run the IQ-Builder Series.

Jem
by Chris Wiley

JEM LOGO was written to teach children the basics of computer programming. A very simple programming language, it teaches children the logic associated with a computer and how to combine commands to carry out complex tasks.

JEM has three basic modes: Help, Explain, and Run. The first mode you see is Run, when the logos are displayed. If you type Help, you get four pages of text, giving a brief description of the logo or word you indicated when you requested help.

(PC-SIG Disk# 922)
Special Requirements: *CGA.*
Author Registration: *$20.00*

Katie's Clock ✍
by TZK Publications

Teaching children to tell time from an analog (standard old time) clock can try the patience of most parents. That was before KATIE'S CLOCK was developed.

KATIE'S CLOCK displays a giant analog clock on your computer screen. As the dial changes position, you can quiz your child orally or have him/her enter the time digitally into the computer. During the testing, you can set the dials to move randomly or increment every five minutes. You can also test by inputting the time digitally and having the clock dials display the proper time. This program is a breeze to use and you'll be teaching time — in no time!

(PC-SIG Disk# 2463)
Special Requirements: *EGA.*
Author Registration: *$12.00*

Kid Paint
by Compass Systems

KID PAINT is an electronic coloring book, with a few added surprises, that is certain to keep any child entertained. Choose from a palette of colors and use a mouse, a joystick, or the keyboard arrow keys, instead of the more conventional crayons or fingerpaints. Throughout the coloring session, children will enjoy background music and at certain intervals, the pictures become animated. The simple concept is executed so beautifully that even a two-year-old can use it. All that's needed is a little eye/hand coordination and some imagination. A great way to introduce small children to the computer.

(PC-SIG Disk# 2065)

Special Requirements: *EGA or VGA.*
Author Registration: *$4.50*

Kid Paint(PC-SIG Disk# 2065)

KidGames
by Donald Pavia

KIDGAMES is a blast! This collection of games is specifically geared to KIDS, ages 2-10 years, and has a straight forward commitment to make learning fun. It also has excellent graphics and is a great program for introducing your kids to your home computer.

For education, HANGMAN in one of the best on this disk. It teaches basic spelling and allows you to expand the dictionary as the child's vocabulary increases. For pure fun, MOSAIC teaches pattern matching and encourages pattern building. Also on this disk are:

❑ ALPHABET, which teaches the alphabet and alphabetic sequence
❑ ANIMALS, which teaches simple preschool math
❑ CLOCKGAME, which teaches how to read an analog clock

(PC-SIG Disk# 705)

Special Requirements: *CGA.*
Author Registration: *$10.00*

KidGames (PC-SIG Disk# 705)

KinderMath
by Duong's Software

Up-and-coming computer hackers will love the sounds and colors of this educational math game. Basic enough for any age just starting to add, subtract, multipy, or divide. There are some quick instructions for Mom and Dad to get the child started, but once started, the child can easily run KINDERMATH.

The program will ask the child what he/she wishes to practice. KINDERMATH then runs a timed drill (time can also be specified by the user), keeping track of correct answers. Encouraging beeps move the child along. This is an excellent way to give a youngster a head start in today's technological age.

(PC-SIG Disk# 1629)

Special Requirements: *512K RAM.*
Author Registration: *User determined.*

Learn to Guess
by David G. Bodnar

LEARN TO GUESS is a set of four games that can help your child, grades 1-12, to learn basic arithmetic and develop problem-solving strategies. Each of the games is complete in itself. When used in sequence, skills already learned are honed and reinforced.

In GUESSME, for one to four players, students in grades 1-8 develop their problem-solving strategies by trying to guess the computer's secret number. There are eight levels of difficulty which sustain the challenge for most players. Other concepts used in the remaining programs are introduced here.

ROMAN GUESSME is identical to GUESSME, except the numbers used are displayed as, and must be entered as, Roman numerals. Grades 5-12.

At first glance, NEAREST (a game for two to four players) seems to be a simple number-guessing game, but it requires sharper thinking than is at first apparent. Appropriate for grades 2-8.

SUPERGUESS, for two to four players, challenges students in grades 3-12 to exercise their knowledge of prime numbers, composite numbers, factors, multiples, sums, differences, and products as they compete against one another in a race across the computer's screen.

(PC-SIG Disk# 1412)

Special Requirements: *CGA.*
Author Registration: *$15.00*

Math And Logic Games For Kids

by KIDware

MATH AND LOGIC GAMES FOR KIDS presents six programs that challenge a child's mathematics and thinking skills. The programs are aimed at grade levels K-6, but can be enjoyed by all.

TARGET MATH and JELLY BEANS are competitions between two players, or one player versus the computer. In TARGET MATH, take turns adding numbers trying to reach a target sum. In JELLY BEANS, take turns removing beans from a jar. (The one who takes the last bean loses!)

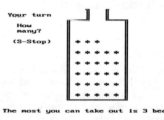

Math and Logic Games for Kids (PC-SIG Disk# 2344)

I SHOT AN ARROW is a simple simulation of an arrow flying through the air until the program introduces estimation and answer refinement skills. LEAKY TUB simulates filling a leaky bath tub with hot and cold water, and is just plain fun while teaching logical thinking. In MATH RACE, up to four players take turns answering arithmetic flash card problems. The faster you answer your problem, the further down the track your car travels. Each player can race at a skill level pretty pictures using the ideas of Fractal math.

(PC-SIG Disk# 2344)

Special Requirements: *CGA or Hercules graphics.*
Author Registration: *$11.95*

Math Tutor

by Tim Keller

This elementary grade level tutorial — targeted at grades 1-6 — supplies age-graded exercises and tests for a variable student body. MATH TUTOR also supplies the opportunity to redesign exercises for special problems.

If you're a parent, or are involved in a tutorial situation, these lessons and non-timed drills can be a lighthearted, challenging way to teach math principles. It seems more appropriate for home use. Tests are sent to the screen.

(PC-SIG Disk# 95)

Special Requirements: *A version of BASIC.*
Author Registration: *None.*

Number Magic

by Greenline Computing

NUMBER MAGIC teaches preschool children number recognition and counting skills. Favorite childhood songs reward success and the game encourages older siblings to share in the learning. After a parent gets things started, counting, matching, and maze games help your children learn, while making the learning a more rewarding experience for all.

(PC-SIG Disk# 1214)

Special Requirements: *CGA.*
Author Registration: *None.*

Play 'n' Learn

by MoneCraft Computer Products

PLAY 'N' LEARN is a delightful collection of six simple educational games for young children, ages 1-1/2 to 4. They help children acquire skills in letter recognition, simple counting, and computer usage.

AMANDA'S LETTER LOTTO teaches both upper- and lower-case alphabets; ZACK-A-DOODLE is a paint/draw game; COLOR SCREEN and COLOR MATCH help children to recognize colors; WORD WHIRL

🖎 = Updated Program
☆ = New Program

and NEXT NUMBER are perfect for learning words and simple counting from 1 to 9. PLAY 'N' LEARN also includes a game that helps a child learn shapes.

(PC-SIG Disk# 916)

Special Requirements: *None.*
Author Registration: *$10.00*
➤*ASP Member.*

Wizquiz
by Robert J. Farrell

WIZQUIZ is an educational program that offers randomly-generated problems across a wide area of the average elementary school mathematics curriculum including such disciplines as addition, subtraction, multiplication, division, lowest common denominator, greatest common factor, simple and advanced fractions, decimals and percentages, and reciprocals.

Each type of problem has 10 levels with a target score determined by the number of errors and the time it takes to solve all 10 problems of that level. Since WIZQUIZ asks for and remembers a player's age, it restricts access to easier problems by age.

After each set of 10 problems, the program calculates the new average, checks the score against the best ever and the player's own previous best performance, and announces the score. WIZQUIZ keeps a separate record for each player's best score and averages.

WIZQUIZ can be used both at home for personal studying and at school in the classroom.

(PC-SIG Disk# 922)

Special Requirements: *CGA.*
Author Registration: *$9.00*

Word Processing for Kids
by Sidney D. Nolte

WORD PROCESSING FOR KIDS (WPK) is a simple word processor especially designed for children, ages 5-10.

WPK was developed to help children build communication skills, develop computer expertise and make writing not only possible, but fun! In a distinctively bright and friendly environment, it features graphic menus, word wrap, and extra large characters — making it less intimidating and easier for the little ones to read. The on-line help function takes only a few moments to master. Well-written and thorough documentation completes the package for the budding author.

(PC-SIG Disk# 343)

Special Requirements: *CGA.*
Author Registration: *$10.00*

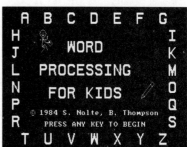
Word Processing for Kids (PC-SIG Disk# 343)

▼ ▼ ▼

Church Administration

Advanced Church Information System (ACIS) ✍
by John M. Phillips

ACIS (Advanced Church Information Systems) is a friendly system designed to increase church productivity by keeping relevant information about members, visitors, and organizations. This information can then be used to print mailing labels, Rolodex cards, and a variety of reports.

Menu-driven ACIS requires no prior experience with database programs in order to be productive right away.

ACIS was programmed by John M. Phillips for the First United Methodist Church of Allen, Texas, but has been adapted for use with most denominations. ACIS is divided into four distinct systems: the member information system, capable of storing 800 records; the visitor information system, also 800 records; the organization information system, 500 records; and the utility functions. The variety of reports the systems generate, together with an informative manual and easy program, fit in well with a church that wants to be the "home" church of its congregation.

(PC-SIG Disk# 2388)

Special Requirements: *384K RAM and a hard drive.*
Author Registration: *$49.00*

Church Accounting System   *by SonShine Software, Inc.*

Those looking for a single entry general ledger accounting program need look no further. CHURCH ACCOUNTING SYSTEM (CAS) provides a service needed by many churches or small businesses. In addition to the general ledger functions, CAS has banking and budgeting functions. These additional sections are not included in most other programs.

Those who do not need invoicing, accounts receivable or payable functions and who need a simple-to-use general ledger with ample report options will like this program.

Overall, CAS is a worthwhile program, and while churches will benefit from its approach, CAS is actually a "general" general ledger accounting program and can be used by any business looking for such a

(PC-SIG Disk# 1798)

Special Requirements: *640K RAM and a hard drive.*
Author Registration: *$95.00*
➤*ASP Member.*

Church Contribution System ✍   *by Vian Corporation*

This is an easy-to-use program that allows you to record pledged and unpledged contributions for each member of your church in 240 separate categories. Print out membership reports, mailing labels, pledges and contributions. Create data files of member time and talent resources, use these files in a word processor and print lists based on these talent categories. CHURCH CONTRIBUTION SYSTEM is currently in use by churches throughout the United States.

Features include:

❑ Easy entry of contributions
❑ Two formats for Member Summary
❑ Contribution List by date (Ledger Sheet)
❑ Contribution totals for period of time by category
❑ Mailing Labels
❑ Member Directories with any combination of the following: Name, Family Members, Address, Phone, Envelope Number, Pledge Amount, Contributions to Date.

(PC-SIG Disk# 659)

Special Requirements: *Two floppy drives or a hard drive, printer (optional).*
Author Registration: *$70.00*

Church Membership System   *by SonShine Software, Inc.*

The CHURCH MEMBERSHIP SYSTEM, designed as a database to keep track of members of your church, works equally well for your group, club, or business. Keep track of birthdays and anniversaries, or any other special or important dates. Some of the handy features include: modify/delete, browsing, and making multiple reports. Menu-driven and user-friendly.

(PC-SIG Disk# 742)

Special Requirements: *640K RAM and a hard drive.*
Author Registration: *$95.00*
➤*ASP Member.*

Church Shareware Software   *by Cedric Fairweather*

CHURCH SOFTWARE is an excellent database management program that organizes and maintains data about the church members.

Features:

❑ Maintain a database of current church members

      ✍ = Updated Program
                                                           ☆ = New Program

❏ Maintain a database of previous members and current prospects
❏ Easy system for tracking and maintaining prospect data
❏ Provides a fast and easy method of recording tithes
❏ Password protection for tithes data
❏ Maintain a complete log of video and audio tapes
❏ Print member lists, Deacon's list and mailing labels
❏ Print phone directory
❏ Select the mailing list for newsletters and notices
❏ Generates excellent screen or print reports
❏ Uses indexing techniques for quick data retrieval
❏ Customize the program to your church
❏ Thorough documentation.

Generate reports by categories. Specify a selected group (e.g., all members between the age of 25 and 32, or all active Sunday School members) and CHURCH SOFTWARE will produce the desired report.

(PC-SIG Disk# 1753)

Special Requirements: *640K RAM and a hard drive.*
Author Registration: *$1.00 donation per congregation member.*

Church Treasurer ✍ *by Vian Corporation*

CHURCH TREASURER automates most of the heavy responsibilities of properly overseeing and managing the finances of a large church. It helps track your budget, income, and expenses listed under 500 budget categories of your choosing. Up to fifteen separate bank accounts are supported, including: checking, savings, and CDs. Balance your bank statements. You can even post to previous dates with an audit trail.

Scores of standard and user-defined financial reports are provided to help you find exactly where funds are being expended. A handy utility allows you to translate budget item information into ASCII format for use with other programs such as your wordprocessor. This information can then be included in monthly church reports. A huge user manual is supplied on-disk along with an excellent tutorial.

(PC-SIG Disk# 1538)

Special Requirements: *384K RAM, two floppy drives or hard drive, and a printer (optional).*
Author Registration: *$85.00*

Church Visitation System *by SonShine Software, Inc.*

CHURCH VISITATION SYSTEM helps anyone active in their church keep track of their church contacts—visits, phone calls, or letters. Several information formats help you keep track of those who need you the most.

Printouts can be generated in the form of 3x5 or 4x6 cards, mailing labels, full contact lists or selected contact lists for organized follow-up and mailings. And anyone can learn this simple system.

(PC-SIG Disk# 2454)

Special Requirements: *640K RAM and hard drive.*
Author Registration: *$49.00*
➤*ASP Member.*

CMTS - Church Membership Tracking System ☆ *by Torbert Data Systems, Inc.*

Whether you're responsible for the entire administration of a large church or just need to keep track of members for a small one, the CHURCH MEMBERSHIP TRACKING SYSTEM (CMTS) will make your job easier.

Easy-to-use CMTS is completely menu-driven and lets you look up or enter data through friendly pop-up windows. Help screens are available everywhere in the system and extensive documentation is included.

Features of the CHURCH MEMBERSHIP TRACKING SYSTEM include:
❏ Print rosters and mailing labels for special church organizations like the choir
❏ Print mailing labels for all church members or individual families
❏ Maintain an inventory of church members' special skills (mechanic, carpenter, etc.)
❏ Record church members' special dates (birthdays, etc.)
❏ Record donations by member name or envelope number

❏ Includo an audit trail of all donations
❏ Print detailed donation reports
❏ Print quarterly members' donation statements
❏ Include password protection for all information
(PC-SIG Disk#'s 2541, 2542)
Special Requirements: *640K RAM, and a hard drive.*
Author Registration: *$129.00*
➤*ASP Member.*

Heritage Church System
by Heritage Micro Systems

HERITAGE CHURCH SYSTEM is designed to automate the most mundane clerical tasks of the local church. Record and access contributions and membership information in a quick and concise manner. Entries can be made for families in general and for each individual in a family.

Each entry includes the name, address, phone, and church status. An envelope number can be entered if pre-numbered envelopes are used for recording family giving. Contributions are entered separately and the program then processes the data in a weekly accounting system and prints contribution reports for each family.

Mail merge capabilities work with PC-WRITE and Microsoft WORD, allowing mass mailings to the congregations.
(PC-SIG Disk# 881)
Special Requirements: *Two floppy drives. Hard drive recommended.*
Author Registration: *$89.00*

Minister Assign Program
by Tom Hayes

MINISTER helps you schedule readers, altar boys, communion ministers, head ushers, and greeters for the Catholic Mass.

The scheduling process takes into account the preferences of the people scheduled, vacations, and assignments of other family members. The schedule is suitable for inclusion in the church bulletin. It can handle up to 600 people and any reasonable number of masses. Schedule Sunday masses, weekday masses, and special masses that appear on an irregular basis, such as Christmas and Easter.

Schedule an additional minister-type schedule of your own definition. Display and print labels, phone lists for substitutes, or the entire database.
(PC-SIG Disk# 954)
Special Requirements: *None.*
Author Registration: *$95.00*

Minister's Sermon Indexer
by SonShine Software, Inc.

MINISTER'S SERMON INDEXER is a simple database designed with the pastor in mind. Keep track of previous sermons as well as the date and location they were given. Store the title, subject, and scriptural references. A field is provided for a five-digit reference number, so you can refer to the text file where the actual sermon is stored.

The MINISTER'S SERMON INDEXER does not do anything that cannot be done with most available databases; however, it does have an excellent user interface. Also featured are pull-down menus accessed by your cursor control keys. The documentation is very good, although the program is so easy to use it is hardly needed.
(PC-SIG Disk# 790)
Special Requirements: *640K RAM and a hard drive or two floppy drives.*
Author Registration: *$49.00*
➤*ASP Member.*

ProDev*MEMBER ☆
by Pro Dev Software

PRODEV*MEMBER is an excellent Church Membership Giving, Attendance and Talent tracking system for any sized church. Pull-down menus and on-screen "what to do next" instructions with context-sensitive Help makes the system highly intuitive to learn and use. The system uses dBASE III+-compatible files and does not require the user to own the dBASE system.

Keep track of any number of members, non-members, former members, shut-ins, visitors, and affiliated missionaries. By using a relationally-linked child database, information can be kept on zero to any number of children per member. Givings or Offerings are easily posted and a complete range of Giving Statements can be printed. Enter the appropriate information on talents, duties, and teaching expertise.

(PC-SIG Disk# 2757)

Special Requirements: *Hard drive or high-density floppy drive.*
Author Registration: *$30.00*
➤*ASP Member.*

▼ ▼ ▼

Clip Art

ArtPak   *by Computer Completers*

If you use PageMaker, Xerox's Ventura, or similar desktop publishing software you know that being able to use electronic clip art can make it easier to generate professional looking bulletins, flyers, newsletters, etc.

This disk contains eight borders, ten headlines, ten pieces of electronic clip art, five accents, seven symbols, and eight bonus files with four major credit card symbols in .PCX and .TIF formats. The clip art can be used with Xerox's Ventura, PageMaker, CorelDRAW, WordPerfect 5.0+, Word For Windows, AMI, Arts & Letters, and many other programs that can import graphics. WordPerfect macros are included to aid beginning users in adding clip art to their documents.

The borders are in .WMF and .CGM formats. These files take up very little room and because they use vector graphics, they can be proportionally sized without losing resolution.

(PC-SIG Disk# 2280)

Special Requirements: *None.*
Author Registration: *$19.95*

COOPER GRAPHICS #01   *by Cooper Graphics*

Images representing each state (e.g., a desert cactus for Arizona) and various decorative borders to enhance publications comprise the first in this series of graphics disks.

The COOPER GRAPHICS series consists of 18 disks packed full of eye-catching images. Each image is stored in multiple file formats supporting all major paint programs including Print Shop, Printmaster, First Publisher, GEM, MacPaint, Microsoft Paint, and PC Paintbrush.

One or more of these formats mentioned will work with First Publisher, Express Publisher, Ami, Ami Professional, GEM Desktop Publisher, Page Perfect, Pagemaker, Print Magic, Publish-It, Finesse, Springboard Publisher, Microsoft Word 5+, WordPerfect 5+, and Ventura Publisher.

Each disk contains over 100 images. Get the whole set and you'll have your own graphics library.

(PC-SIG Disk# 2100)

Special Requirements: *A desktop publishing or graphics program.*
Author Registration: *$6.00*

COOPER GRAPHICS #02   *by Cooper Graphics*

Humorous and "scary" captioned images can compliment any report. This second disk in the COOPER GRAPHICS series makes it easy to integrate such graphics into your work.

The COOPER GRAPHICS series consists of 18 disks packed full of eye-catching images. Each image is stored in multiple file formats supporting all major paint programs including Print Shop, Printmaster, First Publisher, GEM, MacPaint, Microsoft Paint, and PC Paintbrush.

One or more of these formats mentioned will work with First Publisher, Express Publisher, Ami, Ami Professional, GEM Desktop Publisher, Page Perfect, Pagemaker, Print Magic, Publish-It, Finesse, Springboard Publisher, Microsoft Word 5+, WordPerfect 5+, and Ventura Publisher.

Each disk contains over 100 images. Get the whole set and you'll have your own graphics library.
(PC-SIG Disk# 2101)

Special Requirements: *A desktop publishing or graphics program.*
Author Registration: *$6.00*

COOPER GRAPHICS #03   *by Cooper Graphics*

From banner-type religious phrases, "FOR GOD SO LOVED..." to bumper sticker-style humor, "MAKE MY DAY" are available on this third disk in the COOPER GRAPHICS series.

Cooper Graphics #01 (PC-SIG Disk #2100)

The COOPER GRAPHICS series consists of 18 disks packed full of eye-catching images. Each image is stored in multiple file formats supporting all major paint programs including Print Shop, Printmaster, First Publisher, GEM, MacPaint, Microsoft Paint, and PC Paintbrush.

One or more of these formats mentioned will work with First Publisher, Express Publisher, Ami, Ami Professional, GEM Desktop Publisher, Page Perfect, Pagemaker, Print Magic, Publish-It, Finesse, Springboard Publisher, Microsoft Word 5+, WordPerfect 5+, and Ventura Publisher.

Each disk contains over 100 images. Get the whole set and you'll have your own graphics library.
(PC-SIG Disk# 2102)

Special Requirements: *A desktop publishing or graphics program.*
Author Registration: *$6.00*

COOPER GRAPHICS #04   *by Cooper Graphics*

These sign-style graphics get noticed in a powerful way. Warnings and messages include "U BREAK IT U BUY IT," "NO PARKING," and "DO NOT X-RAY."

The COOPER GRAPHICS series consists of 18 disks packed full of eye-catching images. Each image is stored in multiple file formats supporting all major paint programs including Print Shop, Printmaster, First Publisher, GEM, MacPaint, Microsoft Paint, and PC Paintbrush.

One or more of these formats mentioned will work with First Publisher, Express Publisher, Ami, Ami Professional, GEM Desktop Publisher, Page Perfect, Pagemaker, Print Magic, Publish-It, Finesse, Springboard Publisher, Microsoft Word 5+, WordPerfect 5+, and Ventura Publisher.

Each disk contains over 100 images. Get the whole set and you'll have your own graphics library.
(PC-SIG Disk# 2103)

Special Requirements: *A desktop publishing or graphics program.*
Author Registration: *$6.00*

COOPER GRAPHICS #05   *by Cooper Graphics*

COOPER GRAPHICS Disk #5 is full of funny faces for every occasion: the happy coffee drinker, upset boss, logical engineer, TGIF employee, and more. You need a face in your document? You've got it.

The COOPER GRAPHICS series consists of 18 disks packed full of eye-catching images. Each image is stored in multiple file formats supporting all major paint programs including Print Shop, Printmaster, First Publisher, GEM, MacPaint, Microsoft Paint, and PC Paintbrush.

One or more of these formats mentioned will work with First Publisher, Express Publisher, Ami, Ami Professional, GEM Desktop Publisher, Page Perfect, Pagemaker, Print Magic, Publish-It, Finesse, Springboard Publisher, Microsoft Word 5+, WordPerfect 5+, and Ventura Publisher.

Each disk contains over 100 images. Get the whole set and you'll have your own graphics library.

✍ = Updated Program
☆ = New Program

(PC-SIG Disk# 2104)
Special Requirements: *A desktop publishing or graphics program.*
Author Registration: *$6.00*

COOPER GRAPHICS #06   *by Cooper Graphics*

Roadside-type signs (white on black background) and astrological figures make up most of the images on this disk with a few other miscellaneous images thrown in for good measure.

The COOPER GRAPHICS series consists of 18 disks packed full of eye-catching images. Each image is stored in multiple file formats supporting all major paint programs including Print Shop, Printmaster, First Publisher, GEM, MacPaint, Microsoft Paint, and PC Paintbrush.

One or more of these formats mentioned will work with First Publisher, Express Publisher, Ami, Ami Professional, GEM Desktop Publisher, Page Perfect, Pagemaker, Print Magic, Publish-It, Finesse, Springboard Publisher, Microsoft Word 5+, WordPerfect 5+, and Ventura Publisher.

Each disk contains over 100 images. Get the whole set and you'll have your own graphics library.

(PC-SIG Disk# 2105)
Special Requirements: *A desktop publishing or graphics program.*
Author Registration: *$6.00*

COOPER GRAPHICS #07   *by Cooper Graphics*

COOPER GRAPHICS Disk #7 contains the flags of the 50 United States as well as the flags of Washington D.C., American Samoa, Puerto Rico, and the Virgin Islands. A few miscellaneous graphics round out this selection.

The COOPER GRAPHICS series consists of 18 disks packed full of eye-catching images. Each image is stored in multiple file formats supporting all major paint programs including Print Shop, Printmaster, First Publisher, GEM, MacPaint, Microsoft Paint, and PC Paintbrush.

One or more of these formats mentioned will work with First Publisher, Express Publisher, Ami, Ami Professional, GEM Desktop Publisher, Page Perfect, Pagemaker, Print Magic, Publish-It, Finesse, Springboard Publisher, Microsoft Word 5+, WordPerfect 5+, and Ventura Publisher.

Each disk contains over 100 images. Get the whole set and you'll have your own graphics library.

(PC-SIG Disk# 2106)
Special Requirements: *A desktop publishing or graphics program.*
Author Registration: *$6.00*

COOPER GRAPHICS #08   *by Cooper Graphics*

Sign language graphics, Indian-type symbols, Garfield faces, and a collection of funny faces for your desktop publisher fill the COOPER GRAPHICS Disk #8.

The COOPER GRAPHICS series consists of 18 disks packed full of eye-catching images. Each image is stored in multiple file formats supporting all major paint programs including Print Shop, Printmaster, First Publisher, GEM, MacPaint, Microsoft Paint, and PC Paintbrush.

One or more of these formats mentioned will work with First Publisher, Express Publisher, Ami, Ami Professional, GEM Desktop Publisher, Page Perfect, Pagemaker, Print Magic, Publish-It, Finesse, Springboard Publisher, Microsoft Word 5+, WordPerfect 5+, and Ventura Publisher.

COOPER GRAPHICS #09 (PC-SIG Disk #2108)

Each disk contains over 100 images. Get the whole set and you'll have your own graphics library.

(PC-SIG Disk# 2107)

Special Requirements: *A desktop publishing or graphics program.*
Author Registration: *$6.00*

COOPER GRAPHICS #09   *by Cooper Graphics*

This disk offers you a display of a various birds, Zodiac symbols (white on a black background within a circle), flowers, animals, and character figures.

The COOPER GRAPHICS series consists of 18 disks packed full of eye-catching images. Each image is stored in multiple file formats supporting all major paint programs including Print Shop, Printmaster, First Publisher, GEM, MacPaint, Microsoft Paint, and PC Paintbrush.

One or more of these formats mentioned will work with First Publisher, Express Publisher, Ami, Ami Professional, GEM Desktop Publisher, Page Perfect, Pagemaker, Print Magic, Publish-It, Finesse, Springboard Publisher, Microsoft Word 5+, WordPerfect 5+, and Ventura Publisher.

Each disk contains over 100 images. Get the whole set and you'll have your own graphics library.

(PC-SIG Disk# 2108)

Special Requirements: *A desktop publishing or graphics program.*
Author Registration: *$6.00*

COOPER GRAPHICS #10   *by Cooper Graphics*

With COOPER GRAPHICS Disk #10's ring insignia graphics, you can personalize your publishings just like royalty would! Also in this program are pictures of happy dogs, miscellaneous framed objects, and cute pictures.

The COOPER GRAPHICS series consists of 18 disks packed full of eye-catching images. Each image is stored in multiple file formats supporting all major paint programs including Print Shop, Printmaster, First Publisher, GEM, MacPaint, Microsoft Paint, and PC Paintbrush.

One or more of these formats mentioned will work with First Publisher, Express Publisher, Ami, Ami Professional, GEM Desktop Publisher, Page Perfect, Pagemaker, Print Magic, Publish-It, Finesse, Springboard Publisher, Microsoft Word 5+, WordPerfect 5+, and Ventura Publisher.

Each disk contains over 100 images. Get the whole set and you'll have your own graphics library.

(PC-SIG Disk# 2109)

Special Requirements: *A desktop publishing or graphics program.*
Author Registration: *$6.00*

COOPER GRAPHICS #11   *by Cooper Graphics*

Here's a great graphics program for the holidays! With COOPER GRAPHICS Disk #11, your publication is well-dressed for Halloween, Thanksgiving, Christmas, the New Year, and other holiday occasions.

The COOPER GRAPHICS series consists of 18 disks packed full of eye-catching images. Each image is stored in multiple file formats supporting all major paint programs including Print Shop, Printmaster, First Publisher, GEM, MacPaint, Microsoft Paint, and PC Paintbrush.

One or more of these formats mentioned will work with First Publisher, Express Publisher, Ami, Ami Professional, GEM Desktop Publisher, Page Perfect, Pagemaker, Print Magic, Publish-It, Finesse, Springboard Publisher, Microsoft Word 5+, WordPerfect 5+, and Ventura Publisher.

Each disk contains over 100 images. Get the whole set and you'll have your own graphics library.

(PC-SIG Disk# 2110)

Special Requirements: *A desktop publishing or graphics program.*
Author Registration: *$6.00*

COOPER GRAPHICS #12   *by Cooper Graphics*

This COOPER GRAPHICS disk includes a complete set of numbered and alphabetized "building blocks," an array of animal graphics, a baby carriage, and even a gazebo! A must if you publish for or about kids.

The COOPER GRAPHICS series consists of 18 disks packed full of eye-catching images. Each image is stored in multiple file formats supporting all major paint programs including Print Shop, Printmaster, First Publisher, GEM, MacPaint, Microsoft Paint, and PC Paintbrush.

One or more of these formats mentioned will work with First Publisher, Express Publisher, Ami, Ami Professional, GEM Desktop Publisher, Page Perfect, Pagemaker, Print Magic, Publish-It, Finesse, Springboard Publisher, Microsoft Word 5+, WordPerfect 5+, and Ventura Publisher.

Each disk contains over 100 images. Get the whole set and you'll have your own graphics library.

(PC-SIG Disk# 2111)

Special Requirements: *A desktop publishing or graphics program.*
Author Registration: *$6.00*

COOPER GRAPHICS #13   *by Cooper Graphics*

Do you need a wide assortment of Christmas graphics to choose from? COOPER GRAPHICS #13 has probably more than you can imagine to fit any creative Christmas occasion.

The COOPER GRAPHICS series consists of 18 disks packed full of eye-catching images. Each image is stored in multiple file formats supporting all major paint programs including Print Shop, Printmaster, First Publisher, GEM, MacPaint, Microsoft Paint, and PC Paintbrush.

One or more of these formats mentioned will work with First Publisher, Express Publisher, Ami, Ami

Cooper Graphics #13 (PC-SIG Disk #2113)

Professional, GEM Desktop Publisher, Page Perfect, Pagemaker, Print Magic, Publish-It, Finesse, Springboard Publisher, Microsoft Word 5+, WordPerfect 5+, and Ventura Publisher.

Each disk contains over 100 images. Get the whole set and you'll have your own graphics library.

(PC-SIG Disk# 2112)

Special Requirements: *A desktop publishing or graphics program.*
Author Registration: *$6.00*

COOPER GRAPHICS #14   *by Cooper Graphics*

Eye-catching numbered and lettered black and white cue balls are supplied on COOPER GRAPHICS Disk #14. Military stripes, old cars, cartoon characters, and other graphics populate this disk.

The COOPER GRAPHICS series consists of 18 disks packed full of eye-catching images. Each image is stored in multiple file formats supporting all major paint programs including Print Shop, Printmaster, First Publisher, GEM, MacPaint, Microsoft Paint, and PC Paintbrush.

One or more of these formats mentioned will work with First Publisher, Express Publisher, Ami, Ami Professional, GEM Desktop Publisher, Page Perfect, Pagemaker, Print Magic, Publish-It, Finesse, Springboard Publisher, Microsoft Word 5+, WordPerfect 5+, and Ventura Publisher.

Each disk contains over 100 images. Get the whole set and you'll have your own graphics library.

(PC-SIG Disk# 2113)

Special Requirements: *A desktop publishing or graphics program.*
Author Registration: *$6.00*

COOPER GRAPHICS #15   *by Cooper Graphics*

COOPER GRAPHICS Disk #15 displays a set of uppercase calligraphic letters, accompanied by a few kaleidoscope-style designs and some history and sports graphics.

Each disk contains over 100 images. Get the whole set and you'll have your own graphics library. (PC-SIG Disk# 2114)

Special Requirements: *A desktop publishing or graphics program.*
Author Registration: *$6.00*

COOPER GRAPHICS #16
by Cooper Graphics

CAOOPER GRAPHICS Disk #16 has a map of each of the 50 United States with the name and location of its capital city. Finishing this set are six "Freedom" graphics, dancing couples, along wih some other surprises. (PC-SIG Disk# 2115)

Special Requirements: *A desktop publishing or graphics program.*
Author Registration: *$6.00*

COOPER GRAPHICS #17   *by Cooper Graphics*

COOPER GRAPHICS Disk #17 is dedicated to the display of 100 national flags, beginning with the country of Afghanistan and alphabetically ending with the flag of Nepal. (The national flag set is continued on Disk #18.)

(PC-SIG Disk# 2116)

Special Requirements: *A desktop publishing or graphics program.*
Author Registration: *$6.00*

Cooper Graphics #17 (PC-SIG Disk# 2116)

COOPER GRAPHICS #18   *by Cooper Graphics*

COOPER GRAPHICS #18 completes Disk #17's display of national flags, beginning with the 13 States' Old Glory flag and ending with Zimbabwe's. Includes numbers and letters, each in their own sun dial. (PC-SIG Disk# 2117)

Special Requirements: *A desktop publishing or graphics program.*
Author Registration: *$6.00*

CROPGIF (GIF File Cropper)
by Alchemy Mindworks Inc.

Crop smaller fragments out of your .GIF files. Use the GRAPHIC WORKSHOP to convert other formats into .GIF files for cropping. CROPGIF uses a simple mouse interface to make cropping image fragments no more complicated than using a paint program. (PC-SIG Disk# 2277)

Special Requirements: *640K RAM, and a mouse.*
Author Registration: *$20.00*

GrafCat
by Alchemy Mindworks Inc.

Print a visual catalog of your image files, sixteen to a page. Drive all LaserJet and PostScript laser printers, and work with any mixture of .GIF, .MAC, and .IMG files. (PC-SIG Disk# 2277)

Special Requirements: *Laser printer.*
Author Registration: *$20.00*

Graphic Workshop
by Alchemy Mindworks Inc.

Need to convert .GIF or .PCX files for inclusion as halftoned art in desktop publishing, or use MACPAINT pictures for WORDPERFECT? Then try this program — the last word in image programs.

It converts, prints, views, dithers, transforms and halftones: MACPAINT, GEM/VENTURA, .IMG, .GIG, .TIFF, .WPG, .MSP, and .ESP files. Batch processing is featured if you need to convert many files. Extended and expanded memory are supported. It has an intuitive user interface and easy-to-follow menus. With GRAPHIC WORKSHOP, you can even convert color image files into superb black and white clip art for desktop publishing.

Other features:

❏ Rotate image files in 90 increments.

❑ Flip image files horizontally and vertically.

❑ Print to most laser and dot matrix printers.

❑ Support for .IFF/.LBM files allows pictures which originate in Amiga and Deluxe Paint files to be converted into more common PC formats.

(PC-SIG Disk#'s 2277, 2600)

Special Requirements: *None.*
Author Registration: *$35.00*

Grin Graphics (PCX) ☆ *by The Grin Graphics Company*

Over 150 humorous graphics drawn by a professional cartoonist in PCX format, compatible with desktop publishing programs such as Ventura Publisher, PageMaker, and First Publisher versions 2 and 3. Other formats available from the author include EPS (by special request), TIF, WPG, ART, IMG, LBM, GIF, and BMP. Customized work is also offered.

(PC-SIG Disk#'s 2803, 2804)

Special Requirements: *Desktop publisher and hard drive.*
Author Registration: *$15.00*

Kidpix ☆ *by R.K. West Consulting*

KIDPIX is a collection of children's drawings that have been adapted for displaying on your computer using Windows 3.0. The drawings are in 16 color bitmapped format and are suitable for use as "wallpaper" with Windows 3.0. The pictures come in both .BMP and .PCX format and can be displayed by any graphics program that can handle these formats. The drawings are similar, in style, to those found in children's books. A collection of twenty drawings is provided for your enjoyment: a flower, pig, pumpkin, fish, cat, rooster, puppy, snowman, farm house, a Christmas drawing, and several others.

The KIDPIX collection of drawings are easy to display. Simply open the file and select a drawing by either pressing the Enter key or clicking the mouse. The drawings can be edited, adding your own special touches, and saved away on the file for later viewing. Even though the drawings are in a child's format, eg. stick people, they can be enjoyed by any age level.

(PC-SIG Disk# 2793)

Special Requirements: *Windows 3.0*
Author Registration: *None.*
➤*ASP Member.*

New Print Shop Library ☆ *by Michael E. Callahan*

This disk contains a library of over 1000 pieces of clipart for the New Print Shop. It features people, places, and just about anything else you can think of.

(PC-SIG Disk# 2795)

Special Requirements: *New Print Shop.*
Author Registration: *None.*

SOFTSCENE PCX ☆ *by SoftScene*

Here are 29 PCX format pictures hand drawn by Stephen Hornback. The pictures can be used to enhance letters, newsletters, and other periodicals that are produced using desk top publishing programs or word processing programs that allow you to import PCX images.

(PC-SIG Disk# 2802)

Special Requirements: *Desktop publisher.*
Author Registration: *$10.00*

Wacky1 *by Cooper Graphics*

Just when you thought all the clip art you ever needed could be found in the 18-disk Cooper Graphics set, Cooper Graphics comes out with still another fun set of art, this time as WACKY1.

This graphics series introduces 2-inch tall by 7-inch wide graphic headers intended to top memos and notepads. All five pictures follow the theme of health and hair with pictures of men shaving, a man sneezing, the stork with a baby, a bedridden parrot, and a Bald is Beautiful Banner.

WACKY1's graphics can be printed on laserjets, deskjets, and other printers that suppport the .PCX and .MAC formats.

(PC-SIG Disk# 2443)

Special Requirements: *Printers that support .PCX and .MAC formats.*
Author Registration: *$6.00*

Wild Animals ☆

by Michael E. Callahan

Wild birds and animals make up this collection of 19 .PCX files

(PC-SIG Disk# 2791)

Special Requirements: *Desktop publishing program.*
Author Registration: *None.*

▼ ▼ ▼

Communication Programs

BACKMAIL

by Alethic Software

Turn your computer into the center of your own electronic mail network with BACKMAIL, a background communications program that will not interrupt your work or your incoming voice calls.

BACKMAIL can be used to compose and send messages, files and programs with other BACKMAIL users over regular phone lines using a standard modem while you are using your computer as you ordinarily would.

Operating in the background, BACKMAIL will call phone numbers to which you have addressed messages or files, deliver them at a preassigned time, collect any mail addressed to you from there, terminate the call and repeat this process for the next appropriate destination on your list. All of this without bothering you, and without interrupting the normal use of your machine.

BACKMAIL doesn't interfere with the normal use of your phone for voice messages. Turn down the bell on your phone and carry on with your work. BACKMAIL will use your modem to answer all calls. If it's a voice call, the program will ring the speaker on your computer and ask you to pick up the phone. If it's another BACKMAIL calling, the program will receive your mail, store it to disk, and send any pending mail that you have addressed to the person who called you.

(PC-SIG Disk# 1841)

Special Requirements: *Modem.*
Author Registration: *$30.00*

Boyan Communications ✍

by Boyan Communications

BOYAN is a top-rated communications package which provides all of the flexibility, speed, ease-of-use and features a person might desire while taking full advantage of the new world of electronic mail, computer bulletin boards, and telecommunications.

Features include:

❑ Works at 9600, 4800, 2400, 1200, and 300 baud
❑ Context-sensitive help screens available at any time
❑ "Back up" or cancel current actions any time with the Escape key
❑ Save time and money by uploading messages prepared off-line
❑ Supports terminal emulations including VT-1, VT-52, and ANSI-BBS.
❑ File transfers use a wide variety of error-checking protocols
❑ An extensive macro language with over 200 commands
❑ Every BOYAN keyboard command is user-definable
❑ Script files run communications sessions completely unattended.
❑ Use Host mode to dial into your computer from a remote system
❑ "Usage Log" to record the length of all modem connections
❑ Full file manager to scan directories, copy and view files
❑ Dialing directory and redialing queue
❑ Scroll-back buffer to scan through off-screen text

BOYAN is generally self-explanatory. Experienced users and new users alike find they can use the program without ever reading the on-disk manual. It's there, just in case!

(PC-SIG Disk#'s 1206, 1343)

Special Requirements: *A modem. A hard drive is recommended.*
Author Registration: *$40.00*

Brainstorm! *by Mustang Software*

BRAINSTORM is a new approach to group problem solving. It facilitates network group discussions by allowing users to respond to any number of organized "topics" instead of to individual people.

Most E-Mail packages allow user A to send a message to user B, and perhaps send a carbon copy to users C, D, and E. While this type of message management is ideal for individual communication, it falls short when the goal is to gather feedback from a group while keeping everyone abreast of the project status.

BRAINSTORM is "topic" structured, not "user" structured. Messages and replies don't even include a reference to the addressee. The focal point of a BRAINSTORM message is the "topic." Any user can go to any topic and read what others have written there. BRAINSTORM keeps track of what a user has already read and what's still unread.

BRAINSTORM is not a replacement to your existing E-Mail package. It is a supplemental program to structure communication between your network users. Network-compatible with Novell 2.0a and above, Banyan Vines 2.x or above, or any network which supports DOS 3.x file and record-locking, or the Share command.

(PC-SIG Disk#'s 1927, 2305)

Special Requirements: *448K RAM and netBIOS compatible LAN.*
Author Registration: *$349.00 for 25 user version.*

BSR *by Datamate Company*

Transfer files back and forth between computers using different sizes of disk drives; e.g., between laptop 3.5" disk drives and desktop 5.25" drives. BSR is particularly handy in situations where you don't have copies of the .EXE program on both 3.5" and 5.25" media. BASIC versions of the Send and Receive programs are included and can be typed into both computers relatively quickly. Then all that's needed is a version of BASIC to run the Send and Receive programs.

(PC-SIG Disk# 1987)

Special Requirements: *Serial ports, null modem cable, and a version of BASIC.*
Author Registration: *$20.00*

COMTOEXE *by Fabrice Bellard*

A companion program to LZE, COMTOEXE converts a .COM file into an .EXE file that can then be compressed by LZE (LZE compresses the code of .EXE files). With the combination of the two files, you now have the ability to reclaim a sizable amount of valuable disk space from both .COM and .EXE files.

(PC-SIG Disk# 2316)

Special Requirements: *None*
Author Registration: *None*

Dialer *by Lightwave*

An electronic phone dialer that maintains a list of names and phone numbers. Look through an unlimited number of names and instantly dial the correct phone number associated with the name you select. It's assumed that you're already using a modem and communications package. DIALER lets you interact and talk on a BBS, but does not support the uploading or downloading of files.

(PC-SIG Disk# 717)

Special Requirements: *Modem.*
Author Registration: *$49.95*

EZ-Reader ✍

by Thumper Technologies

EZ-READER reduces the time needed to read and create messages on BBS that use the Qmail, MarkMail, RoseMail, TomCat!, KMail, DJMail, RAMail, QWicKer, Jimmer, TriMail, MjrMail, and other QWK format compatible mail doors. PCBoard capture files and ProDoor ZIPM files are also supported.

Read and create messages off-line, saving you time and money on long-distance phone bills. EZ-READER is a total message management system allowing you to save messages for later retrieval. View the news, new files, and bulletins.

Features:

❏ The EZ-iest operation of any message reader available today
❏ Supports the Qmail message format
❏ One key operations
❏ Uses your favorite editor so you won't have to learn a new one. (If you don't have one, PC Magazine's TED editor is provided)
❏ Shell to DOS at anytime
❏ On-line Help screens
❏ Reconfigure EZ-READER at anytime
❏ Define and execute up to 66 DOS commands and programs from within EZ-READER
❏ Place replies in any conference
❏ Sort messages four different ways
❏ Access to 50 taglines at a time
❏ Address messages to 20 people. Unlimited number of addressees with mailing lists
❏ Edit and Delete replies
❏ Multiple mail packets
❏ Use your communications program's upload and download directories. No need to move any files
❏ Works with floppy disks

(PC-SIG Disk# 2721)

Special Requirements: *A modem. Hard drive recommended.*
Author Registration: *$25.00*
➤*ASP Member.*

FoneBook

by Wildcard Software

FONEBOOK lets you use your computer as your personal telephone directory and will even dial the numbers for you.

If you're like most people, you probably have names, addresses, and phone numbers scribbled on little bits and pieces of paper all over the place. FONEBOOK helps you organize all those bits and pieces into a single database of names, addresses, and phone numbers.

With FONEBOOK you can:

❏ Create and add names, addresses, and phone numbers
❏ Send your database to an ASCII file for easy editing
❏ Browse through the database
❏ Search on any field in the database
❏ Quickly find and dial (with modem) any phone number
❏ Print the entire database or only selected records or fields

(PC-SIG Disk# 1226)

Special Requirements: *Modem.*
Author Registration: *$10.00*

FoneBook (PC-SIG Disk# 1226)

GT Power

by P&M Software

GT POWER is an example of telecommunications at its finest. An easy set-up routine and quick simple-to-use commands make communicating with other computers and BBSs a snap. GT POWER is a set of programs and files that provide complete capabilities for your system. Designed for use on IBM/compatible micro-computers, it supports a wide variety of modems including all Hayes compatibles, USRobotics, and IBM.

Just a few of the features you will find on GT POWER are:

❑ ANSI standard terminal emulation
❑ ANSI.SYS style color graphics, without the need of ANSI.SYS!
❑ Multiple telephone directories with 999 entries each. Records the password for each BBS, as well as the date and time of last contact. The total number of calls, accumulated time, uploads and downloads are also recorded.
❑ Numerous protocols are supported, such as: SEAlink, Xmodem/CRC, WXmodem, Ymodem/CRC, Telink/CRC batch file, the CompuServe "B" protocol and more. Also, ten slots for external protocols to be added by the user. GT comes with several of these slots pre-setup for the most popular protocols; i.e., Zmodem, Ymodem-G, Kermit, Jmodem, Super8k, and BiMode. These can be changed easily or added to, by modifying the External Protocol Table in the GT configuration.
❑ ASCII file transmission, using XON/XOFF protocol and/or line-by-line pacing and/or inter-character delays.
❑ Full control of all communication parameters.
❑ 40 function keys, to store logon, passwords, etc.
❑ Full printer support, using XON/XOFF flow control with the host.
❑ DOS Shell. Exit to DOS and return, GT stays in the background.
❑ Interactive script language, to automate many repetitive tasks.
❑ Optional LOG file. Keeps a complete record of your calls.
❑ Detects BUSY, VOICE, NO DIAL TONE, and more, with modems that support extended result codes, such as the USRobotics Courier 2400 Modem.
❑ On-screen clock, so there is no need for a memory-resident clock program.
❑ Host mode. Allows user to set up a system to accept incoming calls.
❑ Support for the non-standard COM ports: 3 and 4.

A comprehensive Help menu is available at any time.

(PC-SIG Disk#'s 782, 783, 1549, 1550)

Special Requirements: *Two floppy drives or a hard drive.*
Author Registration: *$40.00*

Ideal Terminal (IT) ✍   *by Donald G. Harbaugh*

IDEAL TERMINAL (IT) is a VT-100 and VT-52 terminal emulator and a full-service communications program.

Features:

❑ Fast — suitable for screen editing at 9600 baud
❑ On-line help, including current macro definitions
❑ KERMIT, XMODEM, and ASCII file-transfer capabilities
❑ Wildcard file specs for KERMIT transfers
❑ Auto-dialing/auto-retry for Hayes-compatible modems
❑ Save and review screen images
❑ Log to printer or disk
❑ History of the most recent 16 screens of data
❑ Automatic screen blanking, after 30 minutes of inactivity
❑ Macro key definition and script files

(PC-SIG Disk# 679)

Special Requirements: *Modem.*
Author Registration: *$20.00*
➤*ASP Member.*

KERMIT   *by Kermit Distribution*

KERMIT implements a file transfer protocol for the MS/PC-DOS operating system family. The package has a complete program for IBM-specific machines, as well as generic MS-DOS selections. The Assembly language source code comes with the package.

KERMIT performs almost complete emulation of the DEC VT-102 terminal at speeds up to 19,200 baud. Full-speed 9600 baud operation is possible on 4.77Mhz systems. KERMIT is a popular file transfer protocol on many mini and mainframe computers, used daily in schools, colleges and many businesses.

Features:
- Local operation
- Remote operation
- Binary file transfer
- Filename collision avoidance
- Wildcard sending
- Eigth-bit and repeat-count prefixing
- Time out
- Alternate block checks
- Terminal emulation
- Session logging
- Local file management
- Advanced commands for servers
- Command macros

(PC-SIG Disk# 42)
Special Requirements: *Modem.*
Author Registration: *$29.95*

Message Master
by Brian Cieslak

Provide a message center in your computer. Several users of the same computer can leave messages and notes to each other.

Type, read, and delete messages of up to 1,000 characters using the Send and Read routines. MAIL lists the names of the people who have messages waiting for them and can be set up to be executed when the computer is first turned on. Although MESSAGE MASTER has limited text editing capabilities and no password protection, it is very easy to use and keeps a record of all messages sent until they are deleted.

(PC-SIG Disk# 988)
Special Requirements: *None.*
Author Registration: *None.*

Nouveau ✍
by Integra Computing

If you're searching for a simple, convenient E-mail system, look no further. This pop-up E-mail system is intended for small Local Area Networks (LANs). It only requires 7K RAM when operating in the background and is ideal for sending a quick memo to someone when he's out. When he returns, all he has to do is pop into NOUVEAU and press the PgDn key to view each of his new messages. If installed for use on a Novell network, NetWare's broadcast routines will be used to beep the destination's workstation whenever a message is sent to it.

(PC-SIG Disk# 2267)
Special Requirements: *Hard drive and a LAN.*
Author Registration: *$25.00 per workstation*

One-To-One
by Digital Transit

ONE-TO-ONE (121) is a unique, easy-to-use telecommunications program designed for interactive communications between two people (as opposed to calling a bulletin board service). Type messages back and forth by modem (chat) during file transfers. Separate windows of text are provided for both incoming and outgoing messages and each window can be scrolled by either user.

Other features include pull-down menus and a thorough series of easily accessible help screens.

(PC-SIG Disk# 1031)
Special Requirements: *A modem.*
Author Registration: *$20.00*

PILOT ☆
by Lead Technologies, Inc.

This is a good, fully funtional communcation program. With it you can call other PC's, BBSs, information services (CompuServe), or main frames to upload and download files. PILOT also allows you to have your PC receive calls.

This version of PILOT V1.1 contains the following features:
- On-screen help features. Function keys are defined on-screen.
- ANSI Terminal Emulation.
- Upload and Download file capabilities.
- Supports the major file transfer protocols including XModem, XModem 1K, YModem, YModem-g, YModem-g Batch, and Kermit.
- Dump any incoming data directly to the printer at the same time the data information is being displayed to the screen.
- Dump any incoming data directly to hard or floppy disks at the same time the information is being displayed to the screen. The program gives you the ability to create different file names for the information that you are saving.
- Supports the major extended modems such as Hayes, US Robotics HST, Telebit, MultiTech, GVC SM-96, Generic and others.
- Supports Baud Rates from 150 to 38.4k.
- The option to operate under a TSR (Terminate Stay Resident). The TSR capability allows PILOT to pop-up on top of most applications on the market. The software program you were running is frozen until you exit PILOT. Example: If you are working on a Lotus spreadsheet, you have the capability to load PILOT without leaving Lotus, transfer or receive files and then return to Lotus without actually exiting the Lotus program.
- Complete Host and Remote capabilities: 1. Answer calls. 2. Upload and download files. 3. Show files with wildcard capabilities in the current directory. 4. List sub-directories. 5. Change directories. 6. Make new directories. 7. Chat on-line with Host service.
- Ability to emulate a BBS and receive calls. Your PC can be left on to wait for a call from another PC, or a main frame.
- Supports up to 9 serial ports (1 at a time).

(PC-SIG Disk# 2664)
Special Requirements: *A modem.*
Author Registration: $25.00

Private Line, The  *by Everett Enterprize*

Information is the currency of today's world. Protect your data with THE PRIVATE LINE, an encryption/decryption program.

When encrypting or decrypting a file, THE PRIVATE LINE prompts you before overwriting an existing file. Single and double encryption is provided, the latter involving the encryption of an encrypted file, preferably with a different key.

An encrypted file usually contains binary data, but some bulletin boards, such as CompuServe and EasyLink, require ASCII text files. THE PRIVATE LINE can convert a file from binary format to printable ASCII and then print it. Included is an option which demonstrates compliance with the 171 tests required to meet the Data Encryption Standard of the NBS.

(PC-SIG Disk# 893)
Special Requirements: *None.*
Author Registration: $30.00

Procomm *by DataStorm Technologies, Inc.*

ProComm is a general-purpose program designed to provide easy and convenient access to a broad variety of telecommunications tasks. Included are features found in highly sophisticated telecommunications software:
- The ability to emulate these popular terminals: VT100, VT52, IBM3101, TV920, TV950, ADM5, HEATH19, ANSI, ADDSVP and WYSE100
- A dialing directory containing 100 entries
- Automatic redial facilities for connecting with hard-to-reach numbers
- A host mode that allows users to call your system for file transfer or conversation
- Several popular file transfer protocols including Xmodem, Kermit, Telink, Modem7, Ymodem, Ymodem Batch, ASCII, CompuServe B, and Wxmodem

Procomm (PC-SIG Disk# 499)

❑ Command files to control automatic logon and unattended operation

❑ A DOS gateway which allows you to execute DOS commands or other programs while you are still on line

There are a host of additional features in this top-rated program, including keyboard macros, disk and printer logging, and many others.

(PC-SIG Disk# 499)

Special Requirements: *A modem.*

Author Registration: *$75.00*

ProFonEdit Plus — Procomm Plus Directory Editor   by Sunflower Systems

PROCOMM PLUS is a good telecommunications program, but you can only edit single entries at a time. With PROFONEDIT PLUS, you can mark entire blocks of the directory for moving, deleting, inserting, exchanging, packing, and sorting telephone entries. Edit your PROCOMM PLUS dialing directory like a wordprocessor.

PROFONEDIT PLUS gives more editing capabilities on each line of the directory and can "undo" multiple-editing changes. A backup file can be created at any time and on-line help explains each command of the program menu. This program is a necessity for anyone using PROCOMM PLUS who wants to edit and reorganize their telephone directory.

(PC-SIG Disk# 956)

Special Requirements: *A version of Procomm.*

Author Registration: *$20.00*

QMODEM SST ✍   by The Forbin Project, Inc.

A fast and powerful telecommunications program for anyone using a modem. Expanded memory usage, windowing, Xmodem protocol and auto-redial are only some of the strengths of this package.

The "quick-learn" mode option is perfect for novices and further training is available with the context-sensitive Help function. Read and write ASCII files with the integrated text editor. X,Y and IMODEM protocols are fully supported as are multi-tasking environments such as Topview, Desqview, Taskview and Windows. The dialing directory can be sorted, printed, and searched. Terminal emulations for VT100, ANSI, TTY and Televideo 925 ensure further flexibility. LOG allows you to maintain usage records — who called, time called, time online and a Date/Time stamp for each log entry.

(PC-SIG Disk#'s 310, 1022, 1023, 1483)

Special Requirements: *Modem. A hard drive is recommended.*

Author Registration: *$30.00*

Qmodem SST (PC-SIG Disk #310)

Serial File Copy ✍   by MarshallSoft

SERIAL FILE COPY allows the transfer of files between any two IBM-PC compatible computers equipped with standard serial ports. SFC is particularly useful in copying files between PCs with 5.25" disks and those with 3.5" disks, such as the IBM PS/2 and the various IBM-PC compatible laptops.

Other features include:

❑ COM1 through COM4 ports are supported

❑ Baud rates of 1200, through 38400 may be selected

❑ Select groups of files with DOS wildcards

❑ Select entire directories

❑ Complete disk and transfer status on screen

❑ On-line help provided for all SFC commands

❑ Full 16-bit CRC checksum is used

❑ Bad file packets are automatically retransmitted

❑ Supports command line parameters

❑ Supports batch file lists

❑ Option to send or skip any file from selected group

❏ Print files on remote computer
(PC-SIG Disk# 2003)
Special Requirements: *Serial ports and a null modem cable.*
Author Registration: *$25.00*

SignOut ☆   *by Integra Computing*

SIGNOUT is a "pop-up" program designed to keep track of where the workers in an office have gone. It's the electronic equivalent of the centrally-located "SIGN-OUT" board that many offices have. The program will track up to 99 employees and display to anyone on the office's LAN a list of who's signed out, where he's gone, and when he'll be back. It will also allow the person departing the office to leave detailed instructions on how he can be reached, why he left, whom he's meeting, and so on.

SIGNOUT may be used on any IBM-compatible PC running DOS 2.1 or greater and any DOS-based Local Area Network. It requires about 180K when it's actually being used, but when it's just sitting in the background waiting for you to press its hotkey, it's memory requirements will be reduced to only 7K! Incidentally, there are some very good reasons that this simple little program requires 180K (call Integra Computing if you'd like an explanation), but since the background RAM requirement is a mere 7K, the larger figure is hardly important.

(PC-SIG Disk# 2267)
Special Requirements: *Hard drive and a LAN.*
Author Registration: *$60.00 - $800.00*

Supercom   *by Lightwave*

SUPERCOM is a standard asynchronous communications package, letting you communicate with other computers and transfer files over the phone lines. This is a simple, direct package for someone who doesn't need to bother with a lot of fancy features.

(PC-SIG Disk# 717)
Special Requirements: *Modem.*
Author Registration: *$49.95*

TapCis ✍   *by Howard Benner*

TAPCIS automates the use of CompuServe and, in the process, reduces connect time to a minimum. The time-consuming tasks of reading or replying are done using the facilities of your own computer where the computer time is "free."

This efficiency can save you a great deal of money. If it takes ten minutes to compose a message online, it could cost you two dollars or more. Prepared offline and sent with TAPCIS, the cost might be as low as 22 cents for the same message. TAPCIS makes it possible for you to actively participate in the forum without destroying your budget.

(PC-SIG Disk# 2051)
Special Requirements: *Access to CompuServe. Hard drive recommended.*
Author Registration: *$79.00*

TapCis (PC-SIG Disk# 2051)

Telemate   *by Tsung Hu*

TELEMATE is a full-featured and flexible communication program with an easy-to-learn and easy-to-use integrated environment. With TELEMATE, you don't need to use a separate editor, viewer and mouse driver for smooth communications. All these features are built-in and are accessible through the menus and windows.

TELEMATE has built-in multitasking features. While dialing or downloading, you can prepare messages, view files, scroll back to the last connection. Or you can have all of them at the same time, each running in its own window.

The editor allows you to prepare your messages, edit documents or type letters. And the viewer can display files as references without influencing the editor. The very large back scroll buffer works just like an editor, allowing you to save parts of the content to files, find text and even quote a message.

Through the clipboard, you can cut and paste text between windows. Prepare a message in the editor and then copy and paste it to the terminal.

TELEMATE has the most popular protocols built-in, including Zmodem, Ymodem-G, SEAlink and CompuServe QuickB. There are four slots for external protocols.

Easy-to-learn Script Language makes writing a TELEMATE script program as simple as writing a BASIC program. No programming experience? Don't worry. The Learn Script Mode can generate script files for you.

Telemate (PC-SIG Disk #2341)

Without any additional hardware, TELEMATE lets you select a screen height from 25 to 32 lines on your normal CGA adapter as well as 7 choices of screen height on an EGA or VGA adapter. TELEMATE accesses expanded memory, extended memory and EGA/VGA video RAM as virtual memory to store data.

(PC-SIG Disk#'s 2341, 2342, 2343)

Special Requirements: *480K RAM, and a modem.*
Author Registration: *$40.00*

Telix ✍   by Exis Inc.

This is a powerful communications program designed to meet the needs of almost any user. Features include a large range of built-in file transfer protocols, such as Zmodem, Compuserve Quick B, Xmodem, Xmodem-1k, Xmodem-1k-g, Ymodem (TRUE), Ymodem-g, Kermit, SEAlink, Telink, Modem7, and ASCII. Up to four "external" protocols can be defined and called from within TELIX, making almost any kind of file transfer possible.

Multiple dialing directories hold up to 1000 entries each. Also provided are: automatic queue redialing for hard-to-reach numbers, DEC VT100 and VT52 terminal emulation, full access to DOS including a DOS shell, a host mode, a chat mode, and even an extensive SALT script language to allow TELIX to perform automated logons. As an example of the power of script files, the TELIX Host Mode is written in the SALT script language.

Telix (PC-SIG Disk #2300)

(PC-SIG Disk# 2300)

Special Requirements: *Hard drive and a modem.*
Author Registration: *$39.00*

UNICOM ✍   by Data Graphics

A communications program for Windows. UNICOM performs data communication tasks in the background while other applications are running. UNICOM can even transfer Windows-unique data formats between computers, such as the contents of Window's Clipboard from one PC directly into the Clipboard of another.

UNICOM includes the following features:
❑ X/Y/ZMODEM, Kermit, CompuServe B, Quick B and ASCII file transfer protocols
❑ ANSI-BBS, VT52 and TTY terminal emulation
❑ Directory-assisted batch dialing for users with Hayes compatible modems
❑ An on-line help system
❑ Ability to record mouse and keyboard operations for later playback
❑ Script file processing for automatic logon to remote host systems
❑ Keyboard macros, file logging, file paste, and print screen.

UNICOM can transfer Windows-unique data formats between computers, such as the contents of Window's Clipboard from one PC directly into the Clipboard of another.

Operate your computer in a multi-user mode with UNICOM's Host mode. A built-in command processor lets a validated remote user examine or transfer files on a designated disk drive while remaining completely transparent to any user who may be at the keyboard operating other Window applications.

(PC-SIG Disk# 2127)

Special Requirements: *Modem, MS Windows*
Author Registration: *$45.00*

Weak Link
by Information Modes

Use WEAKLINK to transfer files between your PCs via RS232 serial ports.

Its primary use is to allow file transfers between two machines that have different or non-removable media. For example, file transfers can be made from the 3.5" floppy drive of one machine to the 5.25" drive of another. When installed and activated, the master unit can access and transfer files to or from any or all of the drives of the slave unit incuding RAM disks. Transfer speed of data is selectable from 1200 to 115K baud.

(PC-SIG Disk# 893)

Special Requirements: *RS232 serial port and cable.*
Author Registration: *$15.00*

Weak Link (PC-SIG Disk# 893)

XPort
by Digital Innovations

This utility uses the serial communication adapters (serial ports) in your PCs to transfer files from one machine to another. Serial transfer is much easier and faster than copying files from machine to disk to machine again. XPORT will allow you to transfer files between: a 5.25" disk drive on one machine and a 3.5" drive on another; or directly from one hard drive to another (regardless of file size); or between two drives that can't seem to read from each other's disks (common between 360K and 1.2MB drives).

Many full-blown communication packages will do this job. But if you just want a simple, inexpensive method of getting the files from one system into another with a minimum of fuss and as conveniently as possible, use XPORT.

Not sure about serial port parameters and how to set them? Forget it. The transporter sets them up the way it needs them. More than one port in your machine, but you're not sure which is COM1, COM2, COM3, and COM4? Don't worry. The transporter automatically detects which port you've got the cable plugged into.

XPORT also includes XCLONE. Because the XPORT program must be on both computers to operate, you may need a way to get the XPORT program file installed on another computer with incompatible disk drives. XCLONE is a nifty little utility that copies XPORT to the other computer without the use of the disk drives.

(PC-SIG Disk# 1775)

Special Requirements: *Serial ports on both machines and a null modem cable.*
Author Registration: *$24.95*

▼ ▼ ▼

Conversion Programs

CNVRT ☆
by Pat Anderson

CNVRT automates the process of converting archived files from one archiving method to another. CNVRT supports ARC, ZIP, LZH, and ZOO archiving methods.

CNVRT can operate in two different modes. In the Command Line mode, convert a single file or all files in a directory from one archiving method to another. In the Pick List mode, select files to be converted from a list by marking them.

CNVRT manages the conversion process, but does not actually perform unarchiving or rearchiving functions. CNVRT follows the same process you would be likely to use to accomplish the same task manually. For example, if you want to convert an ARC file to an LZH file, CNVRT creates a temporary directory, invokes

PKXARC.EXE to unarchive the file to the temporary directory, invokes LHARC.EXE to rearchive the file, copies the new LZH file back to the original directory, and finally erases the original ARC file and removes the temporary directory. CNVRT does not erase the original ARC file until it has confirmed that the new LZH file has been created and copied to the original directory.

You will need the following additional archiver/unarchiver programs; PKARC.EXE, PKZIP.EXE, PKXARC.EXE, PKUNZIP.EXE, PAK.EXE, LHARC.EXE, and ZOO.EXE.

(PC-SIG Disk# 2018)

Special Requirements: *None.*
Author Registration: *$10*
➤*ASP Member.*

CONVERT   *by Bryan Feldman*

CONVERT is a metric-English/English-metric conversion calculator.

Thirty-six conversions relating to length, weight, area, volume, and pressure are available. Select the type of conversion from the menu in the program or from the command-line.

(PC-SIG Disk# 960)

Special Requirements: *None.*
Author Registration: *$5.00*

Convert   *by Public Brand Software*

CONVERT is a conversion calculator that accepts arguments from the command line and shows a list of equivalent quantities of different units (English vs. Metric). This program is very useful because it converts a variety of units concerning distance, area, volume, time, rate, heat, energy, and force.

(PC-SIG Disk# 1183)

Special Requirements: *None.*
Author Registration: *$5.00*
➤*ASP Member.*

Units   *by Prowess INC.*

UNITS is a menu-driven, technical units conversion program that includes a review of six common systems of units and gives a number of physical constants and relationships. What this means, in English, is that the program converts units of measurement from one form to another. For example, do you need to know how many millimeters are in 14.0 inches? UNITS can answer that question (355.6mm) and more.

(PC-SIG Disk# 1014)

Special Requirements: *None.*
Author Registration: *$15.00*

▼ ▼ ▼

Copy Utilities

CopyMaster ✍   *by New-Ware*

COPYMASTER is a file copy utility that makes file and disk copying fast, easy, and effective through the use of the following features:

❑ Dual directory viewing of files
❑ Batch tagging of files for copying
❑ Move files across drives
❑ Selectable date criteria for copying
❑ Selectable file overwrite protection
❑ CRC file copy verification
❑ CRC disk copy verification
❑ File encryption/decryption

❏ Fast file search
❏ Two-drive cyclic disk copying
❏ File-by-file compare option
❏ Disk Compare on 360K/720K/1.2MB/1.4MB
❏ "Lotus"-style command menu
❏ Pop-up data-entry windows.

The program occupies approximately 150K RAM and will use expanded memory conforming to the LIM 3.2/4.0 Expanded Memory Specification (EMS), if available in the host machine. COPYMASTER supports the use of a two or three button mouse.

(PC-SIG Disk# 2176)

Special Requirements: *None.*
Author Registration: *$30.00*

Dcopy
by James Oh & James Oh Associates

DCOPY is an enhancement of the MS-DOS COPY command. You can still copy files, but you control the copying process based on the file's creation/revision date. The program also pauses when the new disk becomes full, lets you put in another, and even formats it! If you want, you can ask DCOPY to prompt you before each file is copied. Wildcard copies are supported.

(PC-SIG Disk# 936)

Special Requirements: *None.*
Author Registration: *$35.00*

Disk Duplicator ✍
by Jim Bilderback

DISKDUP makes it easy to make multiple floppy copies of all your favorite shareware programs for your friends. It is also handy for disk librarians, teachers, and others needing multiple copies of a disk. Written in Forth, the program is faster than the standard DOS DISKCOPY, with more user options. It allows the user to copy only allocated sectors as a time saving feature. It has options to format disks, verify copies and detect any write errors and will try three times to read a disk section before giving up in disgust.

Because DISKDUP loads the source disk to be duplicated into its virtual memory, it frees up both of your disk drives to crank out two copies at a time! The volume name of the source disk is always shown on the screen so you don't wind up duping a bunch of copies of the wrong program. An optional alert signal lets you do something else while DISKDUP takes care of the copying, calling you when it's time to pop in two more blank disks. A counter lets you know how many copies have already been made.

(PC-SIG Disk# 1451)

Special Requirements: *640K RAM.*
Author Registration: *$25.00*

DiskDupe
by Micro System Designs

DISKDUPE was made for folks who need to duplicate lots of programs or disks in various formats.

It's versatile! It copies 5.25" disks whether they are standard 360K, AT high-density 1.2MB disks, or even CPM/86 with eight sectors. It can also handle 720K and 1.4MB 3.5" disks.

It's fast! It duplicates 360K disks in less than 58 seconds. Using pre-formatted disks, the time drops to less than 26 seconds. DISKDUPE uses your hard disk as a buffer so you can copy high-density disks exceeding your RAM memory without slowing down.

You can quickly format disks ahead of time, copy image files from a diskette onto your hard disk, and specify a list of hard disk image files to create or copy from. It runs manually or with special auto-loader hardware available from the author.

(PC-SIG Disk# 1279)

Special Requirements: *Hard drive.*
Author Registration: *$39.00*

EZ-DISKCOPY ✍ *by EZX Publishing*

Once EZ-DISKCOPY reads the contents of a disk into memory, you can make as many copies as you want without your PC rereading the original disk. Make unlimited copies after a single master disk read. Just like a dedicated hardware duplicator (which can cost thousands), and just about as fast! The DOS DISKCOPY command spends about 27 seconds loading data on every copy. EZ-DISKCOPY does it only once, saving almost a minute every three disks. Even better, the program verifies the copy during each operation. Map disk usage and get sides and sectors information about a disk. If you choose, you do it all without typing in a single command. Just scroll across the pull-down menu and hit Enter. As an option, you can use single-character commands.

Other features include verify, format only, compare, directory information, extensive on-line help, and more. Extensive, easy-to-read documentation is included in the package. The only things to be wary of are memory-resident programs which chew into the memory needed for EZ-DISKCOPY.

(PC-SIG Disk# 1201)

Special Requirements: *PC/MS DOS 3.1+. A RAM disk or hard drive is recommended.*
Author Registration: *$139.00*

FormatMaster ✍ *by New-Ware*

FORMATMASTER exploits your 1.2MB high capacity 5.25" drive to get the most of your 360K low capacity floppies — it formats them to 800K. It forces the BIOS to treat the disk more like a 1.2MB than a 360K. This nifty formatting trick doesn't make the disk any less reliable and the disk can be read by most other 1.2MB floppies — even if they've never run FORMATMASTER.

Technically, when formatting a 1.2MB disk in a high-capacity 1.2MB drive, the BIOS sets the head stepping to the single-step mode, sets the data transfer rate to 500Kb/sec, and formats at 15 sectors per track. For a 360K floppy, the head stepping rate is normally double- step mode and the data transfer rate is usually 300Kb/sec.

To format a low capacity 360K disk to 800K, FORMATMASTER forces BIOS to set the stepping rate to the single-step mode, the data transfer rate to 300Kb/sec, and formats at 10 sectors per track. Most modern AT/PS2-compatible BIOS have no problem adjusting to the non-standard format of the 800K disk, but there are exceptions.

(PC-SIG Disk# 2176)

Special Requirements: *A 1.2M floppy disk.*
Author Registration: *$20.00*

FORMGEN'S DISK DUPLICATOR *by FormGen Corporation*

Need to make many copies of the same diskette and serialize them at the same time? DISK DUPLICATOR is the program that can do it.

With DISK DUPLICATOR, format, write, and verify can be done in one pass. Both format and verify can be turned off if needed, for preformatted disks and for maximum speed. An audible alarm even signals for disk change.

DISK DUPLICATOR is excellent for making distribution copies of diskettes. Serial numbers can be added to the disks for registration purposes. DISK DUPLICATOR supports both high and low density 5.25" and 3.5" diskettes.

(PC-SIG Disk# 1694)

Special Requirements: *HP LaserJet II.*
Author Registration: *None.*
➤*ASP Member.*

PCOPY *by Patri-Soft*

The DOS COPY command is one most used commands in DOS. Unfortunately, its abilities are very limited and are not sufficient to many disk maintenance chores. PCOPY is similar to the DOS COPY command in that it copies file data between disks and hard disk directories but PCOPY is greatly superior to DOS COPY in that it provides intelligent file selection and processing options. PCOPY options allow you to use a single PCOPY command to perform a function that would require many DOS COPY commands and much thought.

In addition to superior file copy functions, PCOPY provides a safer way to copy files than is provided by the DOS COPY command. Copy only newer files or update a directory with the contents of another. PCOPY will never overlay a file accidentally.

✍ = Updated Program
☆ = New Program

PMOVE is an option of the PCOPY command used to move files between disks and directories on disks. PMOVE combines the functions of DOS COPY and DELETE commands to make moving files easy. In addition to moving files, PMOVE also allows selection criteria to be specified to better qualify the files to be moved.

PMOVE automatically determines the environment the move is requested for and then determines if the data must be moved or if the file can be moved by renaming. Moving with rename is allowed if the move is to another directory on the same disk device. If a rename move can be done, it is much faster than moving the data, it helps to keep from fragmenting disk free space, and allows very large files to be moved between directories when they could not normally be moved with DOS COPY because of insufficient space.

Try PCOPY, the advanced replacement for DOS COPY.

(PC-SIG Disk# 2312)

Special Requirements: *None.*
Author Registration: *$20.00*
➤ *ASP Member.*

Playback ✍   *by RSE Inc.*

PLAYBACK is a task automator. It records keystrokes (including delays) and plays them back at a touch of a key, as a batch file, or by using the Menu program. PLAYBACK means you can run programs unattended at some later time.

(PC-SIG Disk# 2391)

Special Requirements: *None.*
Author Registration: *$25*

▼ ▼ ▼

Database, dBase Utilities

Colorset
by George Campbell

Select your screen color from a chart that lists all of the available colors for your CGA, EGA, or VGA system.
(PC-SIG Disk# 1370)
Special Requirements: *EGA.*
Author Registration: *None.*

Data Master ✍
by RKS Associates

DATA MASTER is not your run-of-the-mill dBase III and Lotus 1-2-3 file manipulator. Use functions like create, modify, browse, add, and copy to create dBase III databases from Lotus 1-2-3 worksheets, change the structure of the databases, and design your own custom reports.

The ability to build a powerful query (search filter) is a must for today's software needs. With DATA MASTER, you have the most sophisticated and easy-to-use query builder you will ever need for your data searches.

DATA MASTER can convert Lotus 1-2-3 worksheets into dBase III files and back again. With this program in your computer you can do everything you need to do, and more, with your dBase III, Lotus 1-2-3, and even Symphony worksheets. A full calculator, DOS commands and access to your text files anywhere on your hard drive is just a keystroke away.
(PC-SIG Disk# 2358)
Special Requirements: *512K RAM and a hard drive.*
Author Registration: *$35.00*

dbClean
by Practical Programs

DBCLEAN is designed to search for, and optionally delete, duplicate records in a dBase or compatible file. Finding and eliminating duplicate .DBF records can save disk space and program processing time.

DBCLEAN is completely menu-driven, using popular pull-down menus and on-line context-sensitive Help screens. A Help screen relating to the current operation is always available with a single keystroke, eliminating the need to refer to printed documentation.

DBCLEAN provides three modes of operation. In TURBO mode, the easiest to use, the selected file is searched based on every field in the database. Duplicate records are automatically deleted. In BATCH mode, select the fields you want to search on. If any duplicate records are found, a list is presented and you select the ones you want deleted. INTERACTIVE mode functions the same as BATCH mode except that duplicate records are presented to you as they are found and you must take action at that time.
(PC-SIG Disk# 2373)
Special Requirements: *None.*
Author Registration: *$20.00*

DBSCAN
by Maine Data & Financial Systems, Inc

DBSCAN is an easy-to-use browsing utility that lets you view the contents of dBase III files without having to enter the dBase program. If the information you need is simple, why are you waiting for dBase to load?

This is a stand-alone program accessed from DOS — you don't even need dBase, only dBase-type files. You can view the .DBF files but you can't change them. You do, however, have control of the fields displayed and their position on the screen.
(PC-SIG Disk# 2098)
Special Requirements: *None.*
Author Registration: *$40.00*

DBSCREEN ✍
by Tim Keller

DBSCREEN is a filter package that lets you create dBase II, III, and III+ screens. Instead of entering row and number designations into a format file, simply "paint" your fields on your display in a full-screen edit mode. See exactly what your screen is going to look like. DBSCREEN also lets you modify and print dBase II, III, and III+ s formats. Other programs let you modify character strings, change tabs into spaces, and encrypt/decrypt your files.

✍ = Updated Program
☆ = New Program

(PC-SIG Disk# 163)
Special Requirements: *None.*
Author Registration: *None.*

dBSearch
by Reliable Programming

DBSEARCH was written for people who inherit dBase III or compatible data files, but want an easier way to "get a handle" on their data. Edit dBase-type data files — without dBase.

Using dBSEARCH, do the following (and more) with dBase III data files:
❑ "Point and shoot" loading of any file, any path.
❑ Browse records in various view-styles.
❑ Search for records using a template which can include up to seven fields and their ranges or values.
❑ Sort files based on any three fields.
❑ Print current status (filename, number of records, finds, etc).
❑ Print records (some or all fields, indexed or not, finds-only or not).
❑ Construct and print address labels (indexed or not, etc.)
❑ Create a new database composed of fields from the original and containing records (indexed order or not, etc.).
❑ Save current (filename, path) settings to disk.

Load dBase III data files of any size. However, searching and indexing can only cover 32000 records at a time. Up to 128 fields can be displayed and selected. Memo fields (free-form dBase fields) are ignored by the program.

The search template is convenient and intuitive, as well as extremely flexible. Data files are not modified by the program, ensuring that data is not destroyed.

(PC-SIG Disk# 1995)
Special Requirements: *320K RAM.*
Author Registration: *$25.00*

dEdit
by The PC Solution

Need a faster, easier way to correct or update data in your database files? Then consider DEDIT. DEDIT allows direct editing of dBase III and the 100%-compatible data files produced by Clipper, Foxbase, and PC-File:dB without going into your database program.

Some database applications don't allow the user to quickly and easily correct mistakes made in data entry. DEDIT allows the user to access data files directly, find any errors, and correct them.

It's easier and faster to enter the database and edit information with DEDIT than to struggle with the maze of menus and editing screens that populate those applications.

Beginners will appreciate how simple it is to use the program. Experienced users will appreciate the access speed. No special knowledge of dBase, Clipper, Foxbase, or PC-File:dB is needed.

(PC-SIG Disk# 1569)
Special Requirements: *320K RAM and two floppy drives.*
Author Registration: *$20.00*

dLITE ✍
by Ward Mundy Software

DLITE brings powerful dBase III application tools to RAM memory, providing instant access to 10 powerful utilities. Applications "pop-up" at the press of a key while you are in another program.

DLITE has a natural home in the busy office where a majority of the computer time is spent running accounting or word-processing programs but instant access to database files is needed for telephone queries. It's like having a multiuser program without buying the expensive hardware and software necessary. An expensive and comprehensive mailing list manager comes with the package. Edit, add, select, delete/undelete records or paste the data from any dBase III file into spreadsheets or text files. Indexes can be altered at will.

DLITE includes three sample databases: the congressional directory, an index of PC Magazine articles for the last three years, and a mailing list manager.

(PC-SIG Disk# 1204)
Special Requirements: *None.*
Author Registration: *$25.00*
➤ *ASP Member.*

dProg
by University Research, Inc.

DPROG, a dBase III programming tool, creates programs and writes user manuals from your screen designs. A "must have" program for anyone who uses (or wants to use) dBase III or Clipper.

DPROG is a cluster of three programs controlled by a main menu. DPROG is a screen designer, the heart of the system. Simply draw the screen exactly as you want it, identify the fields (also very simple), and everything else is automatic. DPCOMP takes the screen layout you have created and produces all of the needed dBase III files. Then DPDOC prints out a 30-page step-by-step guide to your new database system.

DPROG is extremely easy to use and it produces impressive results while requiring very little knowledge of dBase.

(PC-SIG Disk# 2036)

Special Requirements: *Hard drive, and dBase III or Clipper.*
Author Registration: *$39.95*

EZWin
by Paul Jordan

EZWIN is a unique WYSIWYG dBase III window generator, allowing the user to create windows (with text) and move them anywhere on the screen. Change border designs and colors, and generate ready-to-run dBase code.

EZWIN was designed to be intuitive, easy, and fast. The edit feature is a simple line-editor for correcting mistakes and centering lines of text within your window. The ability to move windows without retyping all the SAY lines is one of the options that makes EZWIN a delight to use. Reload your window in any position on the screen. The windows generated can be called by, or merged into, any dBase III or dBase III clone program you create.

(PC-SIG Disk# 1947)

Special Requirements: *None.*
Author Registration: *$20.00*

Intelli-Trieve
by Richard Ray Viets

INTELLI-TRIEVE is a "weighted retrieval" utility for users of dBase III, dBase III+ and compatible database managers. Weighted retrieval is a way of sorting database records with greater flexibility than a simple sort. The weighted retrieval sorts on multiple fields, but it allows you to put numeric "importance" on different fields and then totals your database's "score" over several different fields.

INTELLI-TRIEVE performs weighted retrieval by comparing each record in a database to user-defined selection criteria and produces a copy of the database with the records arranged in descending order of acceptability. The result is an entirely new view of your data, one that cannot be attained through standard indexing, filtering or sorting operations.

A simple, menu-driven process helps you choose a database and the fields that are to be included in the weighted retrieval calculations. Decide how each field is to be judged and weighted, without reworking your database or program. The function is nondestructive and leaves the original files intact. New files are created with the data rearranged according to the sort criteria.

(PC-SIG Disk# 811)

Special Requirements: *None.*
Author Registration: *$19.00*

Recap ☆
by R.K. West Consulting

It can be very frustrating to find that some of your database records have been entered in caps when you didn't want them that way, or that some have not been entered in caps when you wanted caps. RECAP will go through any dBASE III-compatible file and make the desired adjustments. Save yourself hours of re-entering data.

(PC-SIG Disk# 2740)

Special Requirements: *dBASE III-compatible database file.*
Author Registration: *$15.00*
➤*ASP Member.*

SSQL
by SilvaWare

This program uses the Structured Query Language, fast becoming the standard among the top databases (ORACLE, dBase IV). It's a complete implementation of ANSI SQL with the exception of the security features.

Some examples of the program's features are:
❑ CREATE TABLE, CREATE VIEW.
❑ INSERT, UPDATE.
❑ DELETE, DROP, SELECT.
❑ Full support for nulls.
❑ Up to 14 tables in joints.
❑ Up to 14 levels of subqueries.
❑ Support for correlated subqueries.
❑ dBase compatible.

SSQL comes with sample databases to work with while you're going through the tutorial. You will need an understanding of databases in order to put SSQL to work for you.

(PC-SIG Disk# 2284)

Special Requirements: *None.*
Author Registration: *$35.00*

UltraSearch ✍   *by Index Applications Incorporated*

ULTRASEARCH is a search and editing tool that is easier to use than dBASE III, and gives you more capabilities than simple searches.

With ULTRASEARCH you can do a fast full text search of the data in any .DBF format file, construct a subfile of just the data you need, and tailor the screen displays to meet your needs.

Editing and adding records is simple. You don't even need to have dBASE loaded. The edit commands can be displayed on the screen for easy reference, and each user can adjust the editing commands with a couple of key strokes to fit their preferences. With full function editing, do any file maintenance necessary including flagging records for deletion.

ULTRASEARCH allows you to distribute your database throughout your organization without obtaining multiple copies of dBASE. Since it uses the same file format, you can use this program to add and maintain records in the database.

(PC-SIG Disk# 2324)

Special Requirements: *Hard drive.*
Author Registration: *$39.00*

The Volunteer Network ☆   *by The Micro Group*

THE VOLUNTEER NETWORK is an extensive dBASE III database, designed to organize volunteers to perform different tasks and assignments. It tracks special skills and the experience of each volunteer. Schedule assignments to match the time availability of each volunteer. Keep track of the hours that each volunteer has worked and what groups or committees they belong to.

THE VOLUNTEER NETWORK is most useful to any volunteer organization that has a large volunteer base or has many assignments that need to be met, subject to time availability or special skills that may be required. Sign-in sheets can be printed, as well as mailing labels for the volunteers.

Keep a record of specific information on each volunteer such as age, education, health condition, education, emergency phone number and contact, membership dues, tests taken, whether or not they can drive, if they have a car or truck, assignment interests, the times that they are available, and the total number hours that they have worked. The number of hours that each volunteer puts in is automatically updated as each work assignment is accomplished. Awards can be issued on the basis of the number of hours contributed, and you can keep track of the awards each volunteer has attained.

The skills and experience of each volunteer are entered in records separate from the personal information. Volunteer skills can be entered for each person, as well as all past experience and training courses completed. This will allow a volunteer organization to pool its resources more efficiently. Assignments can be scheduled and filled by individual volunteers or by a group of volunteers. Volunteers can be given regular daily assignments or special tasks that need to be performed. THE VOLUNTEER NETWORK will allow you to keep track of unfilled assignments and what hours are still open.

In addition to the search and review options, THE VOLUNTEER NETWORK can print out many reports.

Produce mailing labels for all volunteers, for specific groups or committees, for volunteers on a particular assignment, for members only, for board members only, or for inactive volunteers.

(PC-SIG Disk#'s 2587, 2588, 2589)
Special Requirements: *512K RAM, and a hard drive.*
Author Registration: *$99.00*

Workbase ☆   *by R.K. West Consulting*

Designed with the serious database developer in mind, WORKBASE provides an interactive environment for dBASE language commands, including some that may be new to you.

Features include:

❏ Create a DBF file; append a DBF file

❏ Edit and browse records

❏ Restore from and save to MEM files

❏ Display memory

❏ Display structure

❏ Modify structure

❏ and many other commands necessary for development, troubleshooting, and support

The current version includes a simple PRG interpreter. If your applications use dBASE-compatible DBF files, you'll love this handy utility. Unlike other "dot prompt" programs, this one works! Everything you need to create and manipulate dBASE III data, memo, and index files is here.

(PC-SIG Disk# 2740)
Special Requirements: *512K RAM. Knowledge of Clipper or dBASE recommended.*
Author Registration: *$49.00*
➤*ASP Member.*

XREF ☆   *by Jim Lynch*

XREF is a data dictionary documentation tool for dBASE-language databases. View and print database structures, index expressions, and cross-references between them. Add and edit descriptions for each database field to provide more extensive documentation.

Do a quick on-screen lookup, or print reports of all or selected databases and indexes. Reports may be directed to a file for off-line viewing or printing. With the cross-referencing function, it's easy to determine which indices belong with which database file, and to determine if there is an existing index on a particular field.

XREF is network-aware and can be used while your databases and indices are in use on other workstations. Multiple workstations may run XREF at the same time.

XREF is written almost entirely in Clipper. XREF also works with both NDX and NTX index formats.

(PC-SIG Disk# 2698)
Special Requirements: *360K RAM.*
Author Registration: *$15.00*

XTAB   *by Quality Data Systems, Inc.*

If you're using dBase and compatible database systems but require advanced analytical reports and graphs, XTAB can help. XTAB is a statistical package to directly access dBase III-compatible files.

XTAB features multiple regression and correlation, frequency analysis and crosstabulation, descriptive statistics, and graphics. XTAB also features on-line Help and pop-up menus as part of an interface designed for the dBase user. It is compatible with data files created by dBase III, dBase IV, Foxbase+, Clipper, dbXL, and other programs using .DBF files.

Since the interface is based on dBase, a dBase user can meet his/her statistical analysis needs without having to learn how to use a new program. Analytical variables can be fields, or they may be complex dBase expressions. Note that keyboard entry is not possible. .DBF data files are needed to operate the program.

(PC-SIG Disk# 1937)
Special Requirements: *512K RAM.*
Author Registration: *$25.00*

▼ ▼ ▼

✍ = Updated Program
☆ = New Program

Databases

A2Z ✍   *by TEXSYS SOFTWARE*

A2Z is a multi-link fixed-structure database. Dynamically link to any number of files under macro control. It is best suited to handle complex database operations where text-based or home data-filers dare not tread.

A2Z is an unusual database manager with simple relational capabilities linking files with a common record number. Its structure also enables very quick database operations. The power of this database can be used best by someone with a knowledge of Boolean logic or programming experience. Autocode, A2Z's macro compiler, uses editor-created external macro files to create very powerful and complex Boolean structures, including nested IFs, substring handling, and conditional access to link file data.

(PC-SIG Disk#'s 1740, 1741)

Special Requirements: *A graphics card and high density floppy drive.*
Author Registration: *$9.95*

ADDTEL   *by YHL Software*

If you need an easy-to-use name and address database, but don't want to spend any time learning a database program, ADDTEL is your answer.

Enter names, addresses, and phone numbers, specifying how you know each person with a "category" listing. If you like, insert foreign countries where necessary and record the date each record was updated; both features are extras not found in most address book packages. The main screen displays 14 records from a selected database. Page or scroll forward and backward through the database, selecting records to view or change.

ADDTEL has a fully-functioning, on-line Help facility that explains program operation, field definitions, etc., and is selectable from any place in the program, using a single keystroke. In addition, ADDTEL will print a four-line mailing label from any record in the database.

(PC-SIG Disk# 1674)

Special Requirements: *None.*
Author Registration: *$10.00*

The CardShop   *by Sofstar*

Keep all of your favorite baseball cards at your fingertips with THE CARDSHOP. THE CARDSHOP is an efficient and easy-to-learn baseball card collection database. Organize your baseball card collection by year, player name, condition (mint, fair, etc.), card count (four Mickey Mantles, three Ted Williams, etc.), type (Rookie, Hall of Fame, etc.) and manufacturer.

(PC-SIG Disk# 2161)

Special Requirements: *None.*
Author Registration: *$19.95*

Coin Collector's Database   *by Edward B. Toupin*

Coin collections can be fun. But if you need information on one of your coins, it's usually quite a chore. Not with the COIN COLLECTOR'S DATABASE.

COIN COLLECTOR'S DATABASE is capable of recording up to one million entries tracking the type of coin, year and place of mint, condition and quantity minted; face value; present value and country of mint — all with a couple of keystrokes. Once entered, you'll never have to thumb through a coin folder again. The system will report on the status of your collection just as easily.

COIN COLLECTOR'S DATABASE comes with a sample file of coins, context-sensitive help screens to assist you in finding your way around and, as a bonus, a text file viewer to ease documentation reading.

(PC-SIG Disk# 2166)

Special Requirements: *512k but 640k, hard drive, and EPSON compatible printer recommended.*
Author Registration: *$25.00*

Database Publisher   *by Neil Albala*

DATABASE PUBLISHER is a menu-driven program to record and track any kind of data you wish to store on the people in your life or the customers of your business.

DATABASE PUBLISHER handles data for up to 2,000 people, each with up to 100 categories. Records can be linked to multiple categories. Each record can contain information about a person, the status of an account, purchase history, demographic information or any other data you may need to manage. A telephone call timer even helps you charge customers for time spent on the phone.

Print out sorted mailing labels with any combination of selected categories. Format the database information into booklet form. The records can be printed either on a laser or dot-matrix printer.

(PC-SIG Disk# 854)

Special Requirements: *Hard drive recommended.*
Author Registration: *$59.00*

DREAM (Data Retrieval/Entry and Management) *by PC-Systems Inc.*

DREAM is a relational database program that comes in three diskettes, all three needed to complete the package. The archiving procedure was used to combine the contents of original five DREAM disks into three.

DREAM, produced by PC-Systems, is a relational database system with extreme power and flexiblity. Much like dBASE, it can custom design database applications, which include reports, sorting abilities, query abilities, and data entry and retrieval abilities without writing code. DREAM comes complete with over 200K worth of on-line and manual documentation which lead the user step by step through the program. DREAM can handle over 32,000 records per data file with over 1,500 characters per fixed record length.

Features:

- Two modes of operation: technical and end user.
- Multiple views of data.
- Edit, format, and range tests on input.
- Single data file reports - post or concurrent with data entry.
- Copying/moving data from one file to another.
- Windowing technique for multiple data files.
- Four character sizes for reports and labels.
- Multiple look-up and data transfer from outside files.
- Color selection.
- Five levels of user expertise.
- Computations on input/output, including computations with dates.
- Auto-generation and duplication of data fields and records.

- Three levels of data protection.
- Multiple record updates (batch processing).
- Data restructuring.
- Relational operations for multiple files.
- Screen painting for data entry and reports.
- Unique report layout features.
- On-line help and tutorial.
- Interrupt routines using function keys.
- ASCII file format and portability of data.
- Electronic note pad.

(PC-SIG Disk#'s 599, 600)

Special Requirements: *Hard drive.*
Author Registration: *$79.00*

DSKrak! ✍ *by SOFTreat*

Quickly organizes your software into a professional library with fast access to information about specific files or programs.

DSKrak manages your software by dividing your programs into "trays" of diskettes in the same way that you would use a tray to store disks. Each disk in a particular tray can be assigned a number from 0-999. Each record, which you can browse or print, contains a wide variety of important information that you can use to find your software. As well as tray and disk number, add title, comments, user-definable categories, and the total number of bytes available on a particular disk.

Create a comprehensive printed index listing for use outside the program. Sort by number, category, or file name. When you're looking for that specific program, or want to see exactly what game or utility programs you've got, you'll have complete information at your fingertips.

(PC-SIG Disk# 2209)

Special Requirements: *384K RAM. Hard drive recommended.*
Author Registration: *$24.95*

EZ-Forms DataBase ✍ *by EZX Publishing*

With EZ-INFORMA DB, you can turn forms created with EZ-FORMS (lite or executive) into a database.
Features include:

✍ = Updated Program
☆ = New Program

❑ Menu integration to EZ-FORMS EXECUTIVE or EZ-FORMS LITE.
❑ Handles information quickly and easily.
❑ Converts from several other popular data formats, like fixed-length, ASCII and "FileExpress."
❑ Reads/writes industry standard .DBF files.
❑ Will create an input screen from your .DBF file.
❑ Handles over 2.1 BILLION records, limited only by disk space.
❑ Full tutorial for the database novice. "DR" program is included to create a meaningful database of all the files on any hard or floppy drive.
❑ Quickly create from, or match to, a database from an existing form.
❑ On-line manual and extensive context-sensitive Help.
❑ Query, seek, find, and browse modes quickly scan your records.
❑ Print fancy labels using a form as a label.
❑ Modify database format to add/delete fields, change field sizes.
❑ Quick Report feature for on-the-fly counting, adding and averaging.
❑ Multiple indexes: Have your database sorted every way you can.
❑ Automatic indexing as new records are added.
❑ Duplicate search mode.
❑ Merge or append other database files.
❑ Keyboard macros for those repetitive tasks.
❑ Field validations: numeric, logical, date.
❑ Can be used as a fill-out only module for EZFX or EZFL.
❑ Forms printing with all the features supported in the source form.
❑ EZFX v2.4 or EZFL vE20 or higher is required to modify master forms. A number of pre-designed forms and applications are included, but they can only be modified with EZ-FORMS EXECUTIVE, or EZ-FORMS LITE.
(PC-SIG Disk# 2354)
Special Requirements: *Hard drive.*
Author Registration: *$239.00*

FastFile ✎   *by RD (Monte) Benham*

Here's a database that is small, simple, and just right for beginners and small businesses. Great for laptops or single floppy drive computer.

FASTFILE is a memory-resident database with "eyeblink" speed. It also works with a hard disk. Up to 2,000 records/file, 32 fields/file, and 32 files per directory without disk swapping.

It's easy to learn because the same screen is used to enter, edit, and search for data. Features such as record duplication, field blanking, and edit access to previous records are real time savers. Table and relative fields conserve memory and simplify data entry.

The 50-page manual uses "learn by doing" examples. Six files are provided: Checkbook with general ledger categories, a client list for mail merge and labels, two inventory examples — a consignment invoice and a teacher's gradebook. If a file suits your needs, erase the records, rename the file, and enter your own records. Want to create your own file? The manual gives a detailed example. Two reports that can be edited or created are included with each file and five sorting levels are available.
(PC-SIG Disk# 2548)
Special Requirements: *None.*
Author Registration: *$70.00*
➤*ASP Member.*

FFD ✎   *by Peter Campbell Software*

FFD is a free-form database which can store an unlimited amount of data and still access it almost instantly. FFD is different from most information retrieval programs because it does much more than that.

FFD is designed for inputting data — anything from client mailing lists and letters to full scale relational data. With some planning, FFD can be used to store client details, transactions and inventory with order details. Full relational capabilities are possible without actually defining any fixed structures.

FFD can also be used to store program source files. This is ideal for producing cross-reference lists and finding field names or procedures.

(PC-SIG Disk# 2058)

Special Requirements: *None.*
Author Registration: *$45.00*

File Express ✍   *by Expressware Corporation*

Expressware has dramatically enhanced its product flexibility by rewriting FILE EXPRESS in C and Assembler. Basic relational capability has been added to make it easier and more intuitive for the user to retrieve and place information in other databases.

Over 100 new features have been added to FILE EXPRESS. The functionality of nearly every aspect of data management — screen definition, import/export, database size, reports, form letters, sorts — has been expanded. Users can now edit records while in Browse mode.

Recognizing that one of the primary uses of a database is for mailing lists, FILE EXPRESS now has word processing capabilities. Users can write a letter from within the program and merge data from a database.

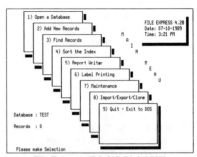

File Express (PC-SIG Disk# 287)

FILE EXPRESS features:

❏ Increased capacity, handling 2 billion records per database, 200 fields per record, 1000 characters per field, 4000 characters per record, and 100 databases per directory
❏ Context-sensitive Help screens to assist new users
❏ File locking for network use
❏ Mouse support
❏ Custom input screen design
❏ 36 definable macro keys
❏ Enhanced screen definition with features like color, automatic addition of field names, calculated fields, word wrap, and easy drawing of lines and boxes
❏ Search and replace or search and delete records; automatically search for duplicate records within a database file or between two databases
❏ Formats can be changed at any time; users can add new or remove existing fields, change field lengths or field organization
❏ Query and reporting facilities as well as a report writer that can generate reports in columnar or multi-line format
❏ Enhanced Import/Export features to transfer data from eight different formats, including dBASE, Lotus, and WordPerfect
❏ Mathematical calculation capability with 14 digit numerical accuracy; up to three levels of subtotals are available on any or all fields in the Report Generator
❏ Sorts up to 10 fields simultaneously
❏ Support for 280 printers
❏ All printing, including mailing labels, can be in regular or condensed mode

(PC-SIG Disk#'s 287, 288, 2555, 2672)

Special Requirements: *512K, 2 drives (1 high density). Hard drive recommended.*
Author Registration: *$99.00*
➤*ASP Member.*

FILEBASE ✍   *by EWDP Software, Inc.*

If your data needs constantly drag you between your database and mail list output, FILEBASE is the database for you. This powerful system keeps data in mail list format. You'll never have to generate mail list output again — it's already there!

For technicians, FILEBASE is a variable-length fields data manager, storing records in ASCII comma delimited format. This is the type of file created by many versions of the BASIC language, sometimes referred to as "MailMerge" format.

✍ = Updated Program
☆ = New Program

The files used by FILEBASE to maintain your database records can be used directly by the letter-merge functions of most word processors including: WordStar/Mailmerge, DisplayWrite, Multimate, Word, XyWrite, PC-Write, and others.

FILEBASE's strong database capabilities work with any MailMerge file. — even if it was created with some other program. Sort, merge, split, and modify. Apply functions like restructuring, indexing, appending new records, adding new fields, joining them, performing calculations, and generating reports and labels. Comma delimited format records can be converted to block format and vice versa.

Special sort features and full search capability is also supported. Look for a record by number or use logical tests to find numbers. Wild card searches are supported.

(PC-SIG Disk# 2152)

Special Requirements: *Two floppy drives.*
Author Registration: *$30.00*

Find-X ✍   *by Custom Cycle Fitments*

If you are looking for an easy way to catalog household goods, coins, photographs and slides, record albums and compact discs, computer programs, or some other collectible, FIND-X is the program for you.

Designed with the computer novice in mind, FIND-X is relatively easy to install and use. Once installed, FIND-X is totally menu-driven and very little computer knowledge is required to add or retrieve information. However, you probably will be able to use the program more effectively if you have some familiarity with how dBase programs create and handle files.

By taking advantage of the relational capabilities of the dBase language, FIND-X stores data in two small files rather than one large one, allowing it to find and retrieve information relatively quickly. The size of the catalogs is limited only by the available disk space.

Conduct exact or generic searches. Exact searches retrieve only those files containing identical text strings. (Entering "flower" will not yield entries for which the descriptor is "flowers.") Generic searches will yield all entries containing a descriptor beginning with the same text string as that specified by the use. (Entering "flow" will yield "flower," "flowers," "flowery," and "flowing.")

FIND-X is a friendly program that creates and searches catalogs with agility. For the home user in search of a bit more order in today's domestic life, it is worth a look.

(PC-SIG Disk# 1719)

Special Requirements: *384K RAM and two floppy drives.*
Author Registration: *$20.00*

Free File   *by Stilwell Software Products*

FREEFILE is a relational database system for anyone with little or no programming experience to determine how files are to be created, enter information, and print reports.

It is particularly useful for someone interested in maintaining a collection of information with the ability to set up "calculated fields" and import or export data to and from other packages. FREEFILE has on-line help and two tutorials. It allows 10 indexes per database, 2 billion records, 1000 characters per record, and 100 fields per record.

(PC-SIG Disk# 521)

Special Requirements: *None.*
Author Registration: *$45.00*

GIFTBASE ✍   *by NewLife Software*

How do you efficiently manage the records of an organization, group, or club in which members either pay dues or make occasional contributions? GIFTBASE, an integrated database program that manages a list of givers, tracks multiple gifts per giver, produces reports, statements, mailmerge files, and labels, and runs on a single user machine or a network.

GIFTBASE has two main parts, a master file for membership information and a gift file for contribution information which are linked through this relational database. All maintenance to the two files is done in the same program by zooming between master file and gift file with two keys. Membership information and donation/payment information is efficiently added to both files. For example, the addition of a donation in the gift file automatically updates the YTD total giving balance in the giver's Master File.

There are several reports and labels programs, such as a master file gift statement, a gift report, phone directories, or master file Labels, with "query-by-example" and user-defined titles for almost unlimited flexibility in reporting. Full sort capabilities by any field (such as gift date) or within a range of records (such as within two dollar amounts) is supported.

Other features include record capacities of 999,999 or more in nine different files, built-in security at the program level, storage of unlimited notes for each giver, online help screens, a "mini-editor" for field editing, batch programs for global updates of all or groups of records, importing and exporting capabilities, backup/restore from main menu, and network support — Novell or generic DOS 3.1 LAN.

(PC-SIG Disk#'s 1991, 1992)

Special Requirements: *None.*
Author Registration: *$20.00*

I Found It
by John Davis

I FOUND IT offers an absolutely simple database for people who keep lists of other people as well as things. For home or business, I FOUND IT sets up the database with 19 predefined fields that are perfect for things like Christmas mailing lists and Little League rosters.

All the user has to do is hit a couple of keys and begin entering names, addresses and phone numbers. I FOUND IT will print the data as mailing labels, records, or in tabular form. It will find individual records, print selected records, merge two files and user change the names of the fields. The menus and prompts are the nearest thing to total simplicity. Multiple files are allowed on each disk.

(PC-SIG Disk# 1607)

Special Requirements: *384K RAM.*
Author Registration: *$20.00*

IdeaList ☆
by Computer-ease

Are you the kind of person that writes notes and ideas on little pieces of paper which you can't find later?

Turn your computer into an amazing information manager. Instead of writing notes on paper, enter them into IDEALIST. Record, retrieve, and print ideas, notes, categories, or descriptions on virtually any topic you can identify.

Use it to catalog hobby information — stamps, coins, books, etc. Use it for recipes. Store all those great business ideas that will make you a fortune some day. The possibilities are endless.

IDEALIST is unique in the way it operates, using a colorful graphical interface to make information entry/retrieval easy and enjoyable. Using IDEALIST is as easy as selecting a picture of what you want to do.

IDEALIST is a great tool for exploring your creative ideas. Enter them when they first occur to you. Expand or extend them later after you've had a chance to think about them.

IdeaList (PC-SIG Disk# 2487)

(PC-SIG Disk# 2487)

Special Requirements: *EGA and a hard drive.*
Author Registration: *$20.00*
➤*ASP Member.*

ImageAccess
by Wierenga Software

IMAGEACCESS — a database program that associates a graphics image file with each text record. The result is a simple database of pictures that can be displayed on your monitor and printed on either a dot-matrix or laser printer.

IMAGEACCESS accepts image files in .MSP (Microsoft Paint), .PCX (PC Paintbrush), or .TIF (Tagged Image File) formats. The image files can be created by a hand scanner, a full page scanner, any of several paint programs, or a video digitizer.

Whatever the subject matter of the images or photographs, IMAGEACCESS will make their organization easier. Access to a specific image is only a few keystrokes away. Once entered, the database can be searched and images displayed or reports printed which include the data and images.

✍ = Updated Program
☆ = New Program

The potential uses of IMAGEACCESS are limitless. IMAGEACCESS can create an inventory of just about any collection or group of people, places, or things. Clip-art for desktop publishing can easily be organized by category, description, and size. Personnel files can contain photographs of employees for easy identification and security. Collectors, genealogists, historians, writers, archaeologists, photographs or images of interest.

(PC-SIG Disk# 2350)

Special Requirements: *512K RAM, and EGA. A hard drive is recommended.*
Author Registration: *$49.00*

ImageAccess (PC-SIG Disk# 2350)

Information Please! ✍ *by TexaSoft/Mission Technologies*

INFORMATION PLEASE! is a text storage and retrieval program that stores and retrieves full-text information, such as memos, catalogs, briefs, letters, invoices, product descriptions, articles, scientific papers, and so on. You can enter information from the keyboard or import it from an ASCII file. Search, display, and print entries using keyword or full-text searches that allow multiple AND and OR criteria. Relate text to a PCX graphic or another program. User interface is an easy-to-learn pull-down menu (Windows-like) interface. The program contains an example "textbase" with help for dealing with DOS disk problems.

(PC-SIG Disk# 2377)

Special Requirements: *364K RAM and CGA. Hard drive recommended.*
Author Registration: *$49.00*
➤*ASP Member.*

Itemized Calculator, The *by RJL System*

ITEMIZED CALCULATOR allows you to create an electronic list of item descriptions that automatically tracks quantities, prices, price extensions and totals. Whether you're making a shopping list, tracking inventory or updating stock portfolio transactions, the system does the job in a quick, straightforward manner.

Set up data files to define units to be tracked, the tracking category, and the unit costs. Call up the item and enter the number of units bought or sold and ITEMIZED CALCULATOR does the rest, calculating costs and totals. Sort and print item lists according to description, price, or price extension, in ascending or descending order. The 60-page on-disk manual is clear and comprehensive.

With the advent of low-cost laptop computers, ITEMIZED CALCULATOR has uses ranging from recording rack-jobbing inventory to listing sales, revenue and expenses for a flea market operation.

(PC-SIG Disk# 1375)

Special Requirements: *None.*
Author Registration: *$39.00*

Multifile-XL ✍ *by H&P Software*

MULTIFILE is a memory-resident database program designed specifically for mailing labels, membership files, or small inventories.

It is a small, versatile, menu-driven database that can arrange your data into from one to six equally-spaced columns. These can then be used for lists, mailing labels, envelopes, or printouts on paper for windowed envelopes. Columns can be sorted so data will appear in alphabetical or numerical order. The totals for each column can be calculated and printed. Other corresponding columns can be sorted by one particular column.

Delete, edit, or search for a particular entry. Each file can be saved or loaded from the disk. Two sample files are included to help you become familiar with the program.

MULTIFILE handles up to 500 records in memory and prints standard 3.5" one-across labels. You can also define the print format for odd sized

(PC-SIG Disk# 835)

Special Requirements: *384K RAM. Hard drive recommended.*
Author Registration: *$29.95*
➤*ASP Member.*

Muses
by Louie Crew

MUSE is a specialized database for authors and agents to organize the circulation of manuscripts to publishers, especially useful when sending multiple or simultaneous submissions. Keep track of queries, submissions, publishers' responses, acceptances and publications, as well as current mailings. Review the status of any manuscript at any publisher at any time. Mail merge the address in the files with appropriate form letters and print letters on one printer and envelopes on another.

(PC-SIG Disk#'s 635, 636)

Special Requirements: *Two floppy drives.*
Author Registration: *$15.00*

NewBase II
by Star Data Systems

NEWBASE is a menu-driven database manager for mailing lists, name and address lists, sales reports, expense account maintenance, and budget preparation and maintenance. The program is a data management system that makes it easy for you to organize and manage information. Thus, you can later order, change, or retrieve, and then print the data to suit a variety of circumstances. The database limits are: 36 fields per record; 32,000 records per data file, and a field size of 750 characters.

NEWBASE also interfaces with many of the most popular wordprocessing systems. NewBase is very easy to use.

Features:

❑ Multi-key sorting
❑ Global update/edit multiple records with a single entry
❑ B-tree indexing
❑ Single-keystroke entry of repetitive data
❑ Date fields
❑ Numeric accuracy to 16 digits
❑ Report and form library
❑ Searching for less than, greater than, equal to, included, not, etc.

❑ Lookup tables
❑ Statistical summaries.
❑ Macro keys
❑ Protected fields
❑ Invisible fields

(PC-SIG Disk# 233)

Special Requirements: *Two drives.*
Author Registration: *$39.00*

Newsbase
by Richard Ray Viets

NEWSBASE is a convenient and powerful database application to help you keep track of the contents of each issue of a periodical. It is great for publishers of journals, magazines, and newsletters, as well as radio and television broadcasters.

Articles, descriptions, synopses, or key words and phrases are entered along with the column number, page number, volume, and issue date. The search function can then find the article related to a particular subject by entering a key word or phrase, or it can list all the descriptions of articles entered within a certain time frame. Print the list or save it for later use to an ASCII file.

NEWSBASE is terrific for doing any kind of library research, such as for term papers (especially when used on a laptop). Reporters and editors will find it useful for keeping their "morgue" (files of old stories) organized and easily accessible. Whether you are an investigative reporter hot on a story, a bewildered publisher/editor needing to keep track of materials, or a student struggling on a term paper — NEWSBASE will help you stay on top of the information heap.

(PC-SIG Disk# 715)

Special Requirements: *None.*
Author Registration: *$19.00*

Papers ☆
by DBF Systems

PAPERS is a custom database for scientific literature intended for librarians, scientists, and graduate students. It has fields for author(s), title, journal (book), year, volume, pages, keywords (6), and notes (64K). The speedy text editor and search function work smoothly. Files can be sorted, merged, and are dBASE-compatible.

Other handy features include a DOS shell, storage in MedLine or ASCII formats, and a database size limited only by the available memory. PAPERS is intended for librarians, scientists, and graduate students.

(PC-SIG Disk# 2761)

Special Requirements: *380K RAM. A hard drive is recommended.*
Author Registration: *$60.00*

PC Data Controller
by Richware

If you are a moderately experienced user looking for a powerful and relatively easy-to-use flatfile database program, PCDC probably deserves your attention.

The program incorporates many advanced features, including limited relational capabilities which permit data from two files to be joined in a third. PCDC also permits the creation of "Action Files" which execute macros created by recording keystrokes, allowing you to perform repetitive tasks automatically.

PCDC is characterized by outstanding flexibility in the design of user's favorite word processor to generate elegant report forms.

(PC-SIG Disk# 1723)

Special Requirements: *None.*
Author Registration: *$29.95*

PC-File ✍
by Buttonware

PC-FILE is an all-purpose database that can organize, manipulate, update and retrieve information. It's ideal for customer and address fil invoicing and billing, customized form letters, sales tracking and analysis, itemized lists, inventory, and much more.

PC-FILE is an updated version of PC-FILE+ version 3.0 and PC-FILE:dB, and is packed with features, including:

❏ Versatile report writer for fast and easy custom reports.
❏ Graph line, pie, bar charts and more (Postscript output supported).
❏ Retrieve data from multiple databases.
❏ Mailing labels are a snap.
❏ dBase file compatibility. PC-FILE reads and writes dBase files.
❏ Customize up to five data entry screens, with up to 128 fields.
❏ Telephone dialing and phone log.
❏ Mouse support.

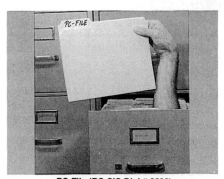

PC-File (PC-SIG Disk# 2082)

(PC-SIG Disk#'s 2082, 2083, 2084)

Special Requirements: *512K RAM, hard drive or two high density floppy drives, and DOS 3.0.*
Author Registration: *$149.95*
➤*ASP Member.*

Personal Secretary
by Superior Micro-Techniques

PERSONAL SECRETARY could become the best secretary you've ever had! You'll never lose a number again because you'll have a place to store your contacts. Keep track of all those customer and personal contacts with this easy-to-use database.

Log necessary information about a customer contact in a database that is foolproof and user-definable. Hold as many names and addresses as you want — PERSONAL SECRETARY has no size limitation. For each customer record there is room to enter a name, address, company name, telephone, and a note about the customer. And if that's not enough, add your own fields to the record.

Once the records are added, take advantage of the mini word processor to write letters and memos up to four pages long. The labeling and mail merge capability in PERSONAL SECRETARY can make mass mailings a snap. Don't waste any more time exiting your current database and entering your word processor because you need to write a letter — do it all from PERSONAL SECRETARY.

Personal Secretary (PC-SIG Disk #2198)

(PC-SIG Disk# 2198)
Special Requirements: *640K Ram.*
Author Registration: *$25.00*

Pirouette
by DeMars & Tilley

Take total control of your database entry screen and report formats without doing a lick of programming. This database lets you "paint" screens and reports, giving the user maximum control over the appearance of input screens and printed output.

Create databases of unlimited size. Data is loaded into memory one record at a time, so any file limitations are imposed by your disk size, not your system's memory. Files are in standard dBase format so they are compatible with other database software.

PIROUETTE even has "relational" power to help you work with multiple, interrelated databases simultaneously. In addition, all standard search and sort routines are fully implemented.

(PC-SIG Disk# 1746)
Special Requirements: *512K RAM and two floppy drives or a hard drive.*
Author Registration: *$59.00*

PopDBF ☆
by Bowen Software

POPDBF is a utility program which provides instant access to dBASE files at the press of a hotkey. A memory-resident program that takes a minimal amount of memory, it can also be run in non-resident "pass-thru" mode. Using PopDBF, you can browse, edit, append, delete and search records. You can also delete, pack, or zap database files.

Some of POPDBF's other features include: view index expressions (.IDX, .NDX, .NTX), copy structure, print file structures, print only selected fields, print only records which meet search, search entire record or selected field(s), and much more.

POPDBF is so intuitive even a novice user only needs to know the hotkey. Context-sensitive Help is available just by pressing F1.

If you need access to any dBASE.DBF file, you need POPDBF!

(PC-SIG Disk# 2504)
Special Requirements: *None.*
Author Registration: *$35.00*
➤*ASP Member.*

ProDev*BASE Data Base System
by Pro Dev Software

PRODEV*BASE DATA BASE SYSTEM is a multi-file data base system for those who want nothing hidden. The system allows you to define your single or multi-file random access data base and the system then generates BASIC language programs to operate your data base. The program definer/ generator has pull-down menus, pop-up F1 Help Screens, full on-screen editing and much more. The system will generate a variety of report programs that can automatically pull together data from one or many data base files as required. Since the system gives you customized BASIC language programs, you can modify those programs to add additional features as desired. The documentation disk includes a complete 144 page instruction manual and a 66 page on-disk "BASIC Primer" book for those who always wanted to learn BASIC, but couldn't find an easy-to-read manual.

Although designed with the BASIC programmer in mind, this system can also easily be used by non-programmers. The step-by-step examples show you how to create, run and report on your custom data base files without even looking at the BASIC language programs. Included is a flexible menu program for automatically running the BASIC programs.

(PC-SIG Disk#'s 396, 1025)
Special Requirements: *A version of BASIC and two floppy drives.*
Author Registration: *$40.00*
➤*ASP Member.*

ProFile Professional Filing System ✍
by National Software Design

PROFILE is a flexible, easy-to-use relational database manager. With PROFILE you may file and retrieve information, create comprehensive reports, print labels, and do much more. And, it can share information with other software programs, such as word processors and spreadsheets. It can also help you prepare bulk mailings with its 2nd and 3rd class bulk mail sort function, and mailmerge file creation.

PROFILE is designed so that the user can get started easily and quickly. It has over 150 online help screens and a large, indexed manual. No computer experience is needed to get started and help is always a keystroke away.

Profile supports many advanced features including calculated fields, relational lookups by linking multiple databases. data entry checking, unlimited database size, and up to ten index fields per database. A hot label and dialer function allows you to create a single label or dial a number while adding or editing records. For mailing list users, PROFILE supports 2nd and 3rd class sorts plus it has mailmerge file creation for many popular word processors (WordPerfect, PC-Write, etc...). The label function has been expanded to handle rotary cards, post cards, shipping labels and even special labels for laser printers.

(PC-SIG Disk#'s 1002, 1003)

Special Requirements: *320K RAM.*

Author Registration: *$39.95/ $49.95 including printed manual.*

➤*ASP Member.*

Questor   *by Random Tree Software, Inc.*

With QUESTOR, you can enter, edit, and catalog up to 2 billion videos — you're only limited by the space available on your hard or floppy disk. For each video entry, there is a field for title, actor(s), rating (G, PG, R), category, year, location, and five star rating. There's even a notepad field that gives you plenty of room to give a Siskel & Ebert type overview of the video.

Once you've entered the info for each video, you can use the Artificial Intelligence Language Interpreter to find a specific video! Talk to QUESTOR using ordinary English to tell it what videos to search for and display. QUESTOR is an easy-to-use, menu-driven program that has help screens at every turn. You'll never be at a loss as to what to do next.

(PC-SIG Disk#'s 2202, 2203)

Special Requirements: *Two floppy drives or a hard drive.*

Author Registration: *$29.95*

Quiksort   *by Omniware Corp.*

QUIKSORT is a high performance sort/merge utility for processing large data files.

Sort an unlimited number of files and merge up to 16 files. QUIKSORT supports file sizes of up to 32 megabytes. An unlimited number of key fields and many different key field types are allowed. Records can be fixed or variable-length, and record lengths can be up to 32 kilobytes. Extensive input record selection and output record formatting are supported.

QUIKSORT outputs records, key fields, pointers, or key fields and pointers. Even wild card characters are allowed in file names. It sorts Btrieve and dBase III files and also provides high-language interfaces for a called subroutine. An outstanding sort/merge utility, QUIKSORT comes with extensive documentation.

(PC-SIG Disk# 1152)

Special Requirements: *None.*

Author Registration: *$40.00*

Simplicity ✐   *by John M. Phillips*

SIMPLICITY is an easy-to-use record-keeping database system that also prints mailing labels and Rolodex cards. It is fully menu-driven, so there is no need to read lengthy documentation in order to begin and no prior experience with database programs is necessary. SIMPLICITY is perfect for organizations, small businesses, and home use.

SIMPLICITY supports a 500 record database, with each record having the following format: last name, first name, work phone, birthday, spouse name, work phone, up to six children's names and birthdays, street address, city, state, nine digit zip code, mailing zone, anniversary, personal note field, extended personal note card, and join date. All fields, except the first two, are optional. You can add, delete, or edit any record in the database using simple menu option selections. Search the database for matching records based on specific key fields.

SIMPLICITY provides nine reports, three Rolodex options, and eight mailing label options. Printing reports, cards and labels may be by date range, zip code, alphabetic by letter, mailing code, or by selected fields. A comprehensive record directory can be printed that is a complete list of the database content sorted alphabetically. A birthday report can be printed that will print a list of names who have a birthday on a given date or within a date range.

Mailing labels can be printed by first name, spouse name, or both names. Mailing labels can be sorted by zip code and up to six copies can be printed.

(PC-SIG Disk# 1581)

Special Requirements: *384K RAM and a hard drive.*
Author Registration: *$18.00*

Snap Filer
by Marty Franz

SNAP FILER is a compact, memory-resident database program with many of the features of a built-in spreadsheet for use with jobs too small or short-term to require a slower, more complicated database.

Organize data as a table or spreadsheet, with rows and columns displayed on-screen. Pull-down menus help make this program easy to operate. Keep track of names, addresses, sales, or anything else that can be kept in a list. Define and use dates, times, names, and dollar amounts for fields, with automatic proofing and formatting for each. Sort, search, and calculate the data in each file. SNAP FILER uses formula relationships in fields, with automatic recalculation after each entry. Print reports, either the current file or a certain block of data. Import and export files in .DIF format to other software packages such as Lotus 1-2-3.

(PC-SIG Disk# 1043)

Special Requirements: *None.*
Author Registration: *$25.00*

SR-Info ✍
by Sub Rosa Publishing Inc.

For anyone requiring a database, SR-INFO is capable of almost any database task from the most simple flat file application to complex relational database applications. SR-INFO is an upgrade of VP-Info, version 1.

A relational database working with up to six data files at one time, it also works with any DOS file in both sequential and random access modes.

A rich set of commands speeds the development of applications of any complexity. Programs compile to a special compact format and then run with blazing speed. Extensive on-line help and a comprehensive set of demonstration programs help new users get "up to speed" quickly.

Speed is a hallmark of SR-INFO. Programs are compiled before they are run. The compilation is to a special SR-INFO format that runs at the same speed as C code. Comments in program files have no effect on execution speed — a big plus when compared to database languages that interpret each line of code as it is read.

In addition to .DBF data files, SR-INFO can work with a variety of external formats including .SDF files. Any file can be processed one byte at a time, sequentially, or in random access mode. ASCII files can also be processed one line at a time. Data may be moved to and from serial ports.

(PC-SIG Disk#'s 2330, 2331)

Special Requirements: *400K RAM, high density floppy drives, and PC-SIG #1364.*
Author Registration: *$50.00*
➤*ASP Member.*

Unclaimed Funds Database
by IDP Systems Group

Did you know that there's millions of dollars out there that no one has claimed in years — money that could belong to you? Lost bank accounts, estates that have no heirs or heiresses, etc. Find out if you're one of the lucky ones by checking out the UNCLAIMED FUNDS DATABASE.

This is a menu-driven program that holds thousands of names and addresses of people that have left behind bank accounts for more than seven years. Not only are the names and addresses given, but also the amounts that were left behind in each of these accounts. You will also find a large list of people who have passed away and left a large estate to no one, no one who can be found anyway.

Enter a name, city, or street of a person that you think may have money coming to them and the UNCLAIMED FUNDS DATABASE will search through its list and give you all occurrences of your search criteria. Once a match has been made, just give the author a call and he'll be more than happy to tell you what is necessary to collect what is coming to you.

(PC-SIG Disk# 2294)

Special Requirements: *640K and a hard drive.*
Author Registration: *$35.00*

The PC-SIG Encyclopedia of Shareware ✍ = Updated Program
☆ = New Program

Videocat ☆

by William A. Jackson

Designed for serious collectors and large collections, VIDEOCAT is a feature filled program for cataloging videocassettes.

VIDEOCAT boasts both fixed information fields and free-form text comment areas in each record. Some categories can be configured by the user.

Available are: add, change, delete, search functions, screen or printer output options, label printing and statistical reports. Family API runs under either DOS or OS/2. Memory-intensive, this program may conflict with some TSRs.

(PC-SIG Disk# 2499)

Special Requirements: *None.*
Author Registration: *$20.00*
➤*ASP Member.*

VINO:FILE Cellar Master ✍

by Mark G. Christian

VINO:FILE CELLAR MASTER manages your wine cellar and tasting notes. Analyze your cellar — by variety, year, origin, peak drinking period and location. Identify future purchases, print reports, maintain an accurate inventory of your collection, locate wines and enter tasting notes using windows and pull-down menus. Includes a neat cross reference facility, help screens, an extensive on-disk manual and sample files.

(PC-SIG Disk# 2365)

Special Requirements: *640K RAM and a hard drive are recommended.*
Author Registration: *$25.00*
➤*ASP Member.*

Wampum

by Ward Mundy Software

One of the database granddaddys of the Shareware revolution, WAMPUM provides the richest assortment of database management functions for the lowest cost of any database product in the world!

WAMPUM can be loaded as a pop-up TSR, occupying less than 20K of RAM while your other favorite programs remain active in the foreground. It provides fully relational, menu-driven database management using dBase III-compatible databases. Virtually all features of the dBase language are supported, including dBase-compatible reports and labels. WAMPUM adds a host of features of its own, including PowerBrowse (a spreadsheet-like database manager), form letters, a phone dialer, and many other original touches. Now WAMPUM supports creation of graphics databases with picture fields using .PCX-compatible graphics files.

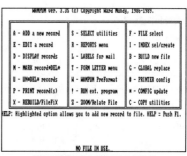

WAMPUM (PC-SIG Disk# 830)

COMPUTER SHOPPER hailed WAMPUM as, "a gift-horse you CAN afford to look in the mouth." Wampum's form letter generator was rated by DATA BASED ADVISOR as, "the only tool you'll ever need." And PC WORLD

(PC-SIG Disk# 830)

Special Requirements: *512K RAM and a hard drive. VGA, EGA, or Hercules recommended.*
Author Registration: *$50.00 per PC or $150.00 per network, User's Guide $20.00*
➤*ASP Member.*

Wyndfields ✍

by Wyndware

WYNDFIELDS is a good general-purpose database program for those of us who don't need all the fancy features. Yet it runs by pull-down menus making it even easier to use and understand.

Creating and printing mailing labels or detailed reports can be accomplished painlessly from within the program. Multiple indices are maintained automatically for you, and several methods are available for extracting the information you need. For more advanced users, WYNDFIELDS also offers extensive string and math functions for use in searches and calculated fields.

WYNDFIELDS has full mouse support; context-sensitive, cross-referenced help screens; import/export capabilities; and mail merge files compatible with most popular word processors — features you might not expect in such a basic database.

Databases created with WYNDFIELDS can have 70 different fields, 2 billion records, and 10 different indices, each with 10 key fields in either ascending or descending order.

(PC-SIG Disk# 2120)

Special Requirements: *512K RAM and Dos 3.0 or higher.*
Author Registration: *$70.00*

Wyndfields (PC-SIG Disk# 2120)

Zephyr ✍   *by Ward Mundy Software*

ZEPHYR is a fully relational, FoxPro-compatible database management system for non-programmers. It now can be loaded as a 20K TSR pop-up. Up to 25 databases can be manipulated simultaneously. Its performance is roughly 16 times that of dBase III and eight times that of dBase IV. Using a Mac-like interface, sophisticated database applications (including reports, labels, lists, and form letters) can be designed and generated in minutes, not months. ZEPHYR is the perfect database tool for both novice and experienced database users.

SPECIAL NOTE: The Shareware version of ZEPHYR is completely functional but the accompanying FoxPro run-time supports only 120 records. The author provides a $1 upgrade coupon with the Shareware version entitling the user to acquire an unlimited run-time for evaluation use. The unlimited run-time supports up to one billion records per database.

(PC-SIG Disk#'s 2215, 2216)

Special Requirements: *640K (470K free RAM), and a hard drive.*
Author Registration: *$50.00*
➤*ASP Member.*

ZoomRacks   *by Hyperracks Inc.*

Organize everything in your home or business with one of the premier information management systems in all the IBM PC world — ZOOMRACKS. More than just a great database, ZOOMRACKS uses its patented card and rack metaphor to allow you to organize everything from business letters to your finances. Whole businesses are running on ZOOMRACKS alone.

ZOOMRACKS is based on a simple, real world object: racks containing cards that have information on them. Imagine a rack hanging on the door of a doctor's examining room that holds cards containing the patients' medical records. The top of every card is visible when looking at the entire rack, so you look for the desired patient's record, then pull that card and view it. Essentially, this is how ZOOMRACKS operates on your computer.

This simple idea makes ZOOMRACKS one of the fastest and easiest databases to use, according to COMPUTE! MAGAZINE which bestowed its 1989 Choice award on ZOOMRACKS, as one of the 13 best products of the year, and the best database. With full text searching, a powerful macro language, online help and the multi-talents of database and word processor — as well as many of the functions of a spreadsheet — there should be little wonder why ZOOMRACKS is zooming into both homes and businesses as the "do all" program everyone wants.

Unlike a traditional database where you are limited by the specified fields, with ZOOMRACKS you have the option of putting anything you want on a card, including information into preset fields. If you want to write a letter, go to a card and start writing. Word processing is an integral part of ZOOMRACKS. If you want to organize class notes, maintain records of all business correspondence with your clients, or manage you home budget, ZOOMRACKS is a powerful solution.

Like a spreadsheet, ZOOMRACKS uses templates. You define what kind of information you will be storing in a rack by defining a rack template. Change the format of any rack at any time. Add fields, sort fields, rearrange and move fields, perform mathematical functions, change the names or the widths of fields, even change the name of the rack, if you like. You can easily build your own templates or use pre-designed templates (also available from PC-SIG) for home management, general business and accounting.

It does takes time to learn the initial commands, but the program is very convenient to use, once learned. Help screens and a tutorial are included. Works great with or without a mouse.

(PC-SIG Disk#'s 1287, 1288)

Special Requirements: *384K RAM.*
Author Registration: *$89.95*

✍ = Updated Program
☆ = New Program

ZoomRacks Business Kit   *by Hyperracks Inc.*

This Business Starter Kit for ZOOMRACKS, the database that uses the cards and racks approach, will allow you to computerize your company without changing the way you are used to doing business.

This collection of 37 templates, 47 output forms for printing, and 10 macros, works within ZOOMRACKS to help you do everything from inventory control to tracking corporate assets. Since this is a series of templates, you have the option of fine-tuning the package to meet your particular business needs.

(PC-SIG Disk# 1289)

Special Requirements: *Zoomracks, PC-SIG disk #1287 and #1288.*
Author Registration: *$49.95*

File Descriptions:

GENERAL	ZRX	General Information.
AGENDA	ZRX	Keep meeting agenda.
ARCHIVE	ZRX	Archive of old cards in MISCDOCS & TASK1.
AREACODE	ZRX	List area codes, states and cities.
ASSETS	ZRX	Keep track of business assets.
BCHECKS	ZRX	Keep track of checks and deposits.
BNAMES	ZRX	List of names and contacts.
BUSFORMS	ZRX	Output forms to use with the BUSINESS STARTER kit.
BUSKIT	ZRX	A list of all the racks in the BUSINESS STARTER kit.
CMPNYNOS	ZRX	Corporate ID numbers.
CORRESP	ZRX	Correspondence rack - same as MISCDOCS.
CUSTOMER	ZRX	Customers and prospects.
DAILY87	ZRX	Appointment calendar for 1987.
EMPLOYEE	ZRX	Employee records.
EXPENSES	ZRX	Keep track of daily expenses.
INVENTRY	ZRX	List of inventory items.
INVESTOR	ZRX	Keep list of corporate investors.
INVOICES	ZRX	List of invoices, sales orders, backorders.
MACBUS	ZRX	Macros used in BUSINESS STARTER kit.
MCHECKS	ZRX	List of regular monthly checks.
MEMOS	ZRX	Write brief memos and print them.
MISCDOCS	ZRX	Rack of miscellaneous documents.
OFFFORMS	ZRX	Catalog office forms.
OFFICEFL	ZRX	Record of office files.
OFFPROC	ZRX	Description of office procedures.
ORDERS	ZRX	Record list of sales orders received.
PAIDINV	ZRX	Your paid invoices/receivables.
PAYABLES	ZRX	List of payables, also purchase orders and paid bills.
PAYROLL	ZRX	Payroll records.
PHONELOG	ZRX	Log of incoming phone calls.
POLICIES	ZRX	Policies.
PRICEL	ZRX	Product price list.
PROSPECT	ZRX	Prospects. (Uses same template as customers.)
PURCHORD	ZRX	Outstanding purchase orders.
RACK27F	ZRX	General-purpose 27-field rack.
SHIPLOG	ZRX	Keep a log of things shipped.
TASK1	ZRX	Rack for a special task.
TICKLER	ZRX	Tickler items.
USINGZR	ZRX	Rack of hints and suggestions on using ZOOMRACKS.
VENDORQU	ZRX	Vendor quotations.
VENDORS	ZRX	Vendor records.

ZoomRacks Home Starter Kit   *by Hyperracks Inc.*

Get rid of those manila envelopes and those shoe boxes full of old records. ZOOMRACKS HOME STARTER KIT lets you painlessly put all your home management paperwork on a computer.

ZOOMRACKS, the program selected as The Best Database for 1989 by COMPUTE! MAGAZINE, uses a revolutionary but simple "cards and racks" approach to data management that will let you harness the power of computing without complicating your life.

This collection of 35 templates, 35 output forms for printing, and 2 macros, works within ZOOMRACKS to help you do everything from finding phone numbers to keeping track of the food in the freezer (and the decade it was out in there). All templates can be changed to best serve your particular needs. You will need ZOOMRACKS to run the HOME STARTER KIT.

File descriptions: APLIANCE ZRX Appliance records. BOOKS ZRX Library of books. CALENDAR ZRX Daily calendar of appointments, events, and things. CALLREC ZRX Record of phone calls and what was said. CAMPEQP ZRX Used to list camping equipment. CANNING ZRX List of home canned items, recipes, inventory. CKBKINDX ZRX Index to recipes in cookbooks. CLIPPING ZRX List of magazine and newspaper clippings, and location. CLOTHSIZ ZRX Keep track of people's clothing sizes and styles. CORRSPND ZRX Keep track of letters sent and received. COUPON ZRX List of grocery coupons. CRDTCRDS ZRX List of credit cards for limits and numbers. DISKINDX ZRX Index of Atari disks. EATERIES ZRX Where to go for dinner? Search and sort. Comments. FAMCNTRT ZRX Record family contracts and agreements. FAMHLTH ZRX Keep information on illnesses, vaccinations, sickness. FRZRINVT ZRX Keep freezer/ refrigerator inventory. GIFTS ZRX Record of gifts given and received. HCHECKS ZRX Used to balance checkbook and keep track of expenses. HFORMS ZRX Rack of output forms for use with HOME STARTER pack. HNAME ZRX Names, addresses, phone numbers, Christmas cards, etc. HOMEINV ZRX Home inventory records for insurance purposes. HOMKIT ZRX List of all of the racks on this disk. IMPDATES ZRX List important dates in date order. INVEST ZRX Keep track of stock investments. ITEMLOAN ZRX Record items loaned. LOCATOR ZRX List of locations of things (and who took them). PETS ZRX Keep updated on health information. PRESCRIP ZRX Keep list of prescriptions for family members. RECIPES ZRX Recipe card file. RECORDS ZRX Phonograph records catalog. SHOPPING ZRX Shopping List. SOURCES ZRX Keep track of information on subjects of interest. SUBSCRIP ZRX List of subscriptions and expiration dates. USINGZR ZRX Rack of hints and suggestions on using ZOOMRACKS. XSTITCH ZRX List of books with cross-stitch patterns.

(PC-SIG Disk# 1290)

Special Requirements: *Zoomracks, PC-SIG disk #1287 & #1288.*
Author Registration: *None.*

ZoomRacks Small Business Kit　　　　　　　　　　*by Hyperracks Inc.*

Whether you find accounting procedures confusing or, on the contrary, are an accounting professional but would like to save time and effort, the SMALL BUSINESS KIT, used as a template to ZOOMRACKS, may be the answer.

This is a strong general accounting package that has built itself around the advantages of ZOOMRACKS, the award winning "rack and card" database.

Templates are included for everything from accounts receivable to a cash journal and check register. Each template comes with field descriptions, usage notes, pre-designed report formats and more. All of these individual templates combine to form a complete accounting system.

(PC-SIG Disk# 1291)

Special Requirements: *Zoomracks, PC-SIG disk #1287 and #1288.*
Author Registration: *$49.95*

File Descriptions:

ACCKIT	ZRX	A list of all the racks in this kit.
ACHECKS	ZRX	Collection of checks to be printed.
ADJUSTS	ZRX	Rack of adjusting entry cards.
AFORMS	ZRX	Rack of output forms to use with this kit.
BALBLANK	ZRX	Company balance sheet—blank.
BALSHEET	ZRX	Company balance sheet—sample.
DIALY88	ZRX	Calendar for 1988.
LDGRACTS	ZRX	List of ledger accounts and account numbers.
MACACC	ZRX	Macros used in this kit.
NOTEPAY	ZRX	Notes payable register.
NOTERCV	ZRX	Notes receivable register.
PANDL	ZRX	Profit and loss (income) statement—sample.
PAYABLES	ZRX	List of payables (purchase orders and payments).
PAYROLL	ZRX	Payroll records.
PLBLNAK	ZRX	P and L (income) statement plus usage instructions. SALES
ZRX L	st	invoices, sales orders, and backorders.
TRIALBAL	ZRX	Trial balance.
USEAKIT	ZRX	Rack of notes on using this kit.
USINGSRX	ZRX	Rack of hints and suggestions on using ZOOMRACKS.

X8086	ZRX	Sample archived transactions for June, 1986.
XACTS	ZRX	Simplest form of recording business transactions.
ZACCTPAY	ZRX	Special-purpose accounting racks.
ZACCTRCV	ZRX	Special-purpose accounting racks.

▼ ▼ ▼

Desktop Organizers

Alt ✍   *by Instinct Software*

ALT combines the best features of several well-known utility programs to do just about everything.

Functions include a RAM-resident editor, a disk manager, calculator, address book, appointment book, calendar, a multitasking platform, and more.

Each of ALT's features is complete — from the disk manager, with disk information and file-tagging capability, to the calculator with more functions than most $35 hand-held units. ALT can record keyboard macros to save keystrokes. There is even a cut-and-paste feature to copy blocks of text from one program to another.

ALT's multitasking platform swaps programs in and out of memory. Work on a spreadsheet and write a business letter at the same time. A command menu for running frequently-used programs completes the package.

(PC-SIG Disk#'s 1189, 2551)

Special Requirements: *Hard drive.*

Author Registration: *$49.95*

Compass Desktop Manager   *by Jim Miille*

COMPASS is the first integrated program that combines six major programs and utilities into one program. It has the following modules:

❏ Database — A full-fledged database you can use to add, change and delete information.

❏ Word processing — A functional word processor with all the abilities you'd expect to find: automatic word-wrapping, text block editing, utilities, and more.

❏ Spreadsheet — A complete spreadsheet program, with 315 cells (A-G columns, 1-45 rows) that should meet any small to medium calculating needs you have.

❏ Accounting — A built-in, single-entry accounting package that can track up to 999 different income and expense sources, give you a month-to-date and year-to-date report, and show balances by account number. It has three report statements (an account number listing, a monthly transaction report, and an income statement), and an easy-to-use, end-of-period processing utility.

❏ Calendar — A module to keep track of all your appointments on your schedule, displaying them either by day or by month.

❏ Names — A built-in mailing list program

❏ Utilities — A set of five major built-in utilities: list empty disk space available, show a directory of the disk, copy files from one disk to another, run other programs without leaving COMPASS, and set up the parameters of COMPASS.

COMPASS is the perfect program for the lap-top computer user on the go. It is easy to use, runs from one floppy disk, and is completely self- contained. Great for beginners!

(PC-SIG Disk# 764)

Special Requirements: *320K RAM and CGA.*

Author Registration: *30.00*

Ez-Desk   *by Softlight Microsystems*

EZ-DESK transforms your computer into an integrated, on-line office.

This single program handles word processing, client lists, account tracking, scheduling, mailings, autodialing, telecommunications and filing.

EZ-DESK gives you an appointment calendar with notes. The word processor takes care of your letters and reports with the ability to run form letters with automatic mail merge. The mail-handling program generates mailing lists and labels, and works with your word processor. The mailing lists can be edited and merged. Build a client file, track your accounts, and get reports on their status. An agenda option lets you maintain personal agenda information as well as use an auto-dialer to call your office or home.

(PC-SIG Disk# 1256)

Special Requirements: *512K RAM and a hard drive.*
Author Registration: *$90.00*

Hal9000 *by UTopia Software*

Hal is back and he's in charge of your system! Hal, the mutinous, homicidal computer from the movie "2001, A Space Odyssey" will keep you organized and on schedule with unnerving prompts like, "I'm sorry, Dave, but ..." He'll not only tell your fortune, he'll fill you in as to what happened historically every day.

HAL9000 is an almanac, philosopher, clock/calendar, and a memo calendar all rolled into one. He comes complete with sound track music from the movie. When invoked, he displays time and date, what famous birthdays occur that date and a humorous, informative quotation. The opening screen can display a short memo the user designated for that date. HAL9000 has a separate pop-up screen to track appointments, and another screen displays a three month calendar.

To use the Almanac, enter any date and HAL will respond with what happened on that date in history. The Fortune Cookie generates an electronic fortune based on your sex and birth date.

(PC-SIG Disk# 1242)

Hal9000 (PC-SIG Disk# 1242)

Special Requirements: *None.*
Author Registration: *$20.00*

IMX Co-Pilot *by Micro Computer Technology Inc.*

IMX CO-PILOT is a desk organizer program that includes the following subsections:

❑ A calculator.
❑ Appointment calendars with alarms.
❑ Phone and address books with label-printing capability.
❑ A notepad for any type of messages.
❑ And several other features including disk management utilities.

IMX CO-PILOT is memory-resident and runs with most major software packages. It is invoked only when you call it up with a special user-defined keystroke. A must for the business person on the go. Keeps track of several different appointments and reminds you what time they are, freeing you to worry about other important tasks.

IMX Co-Pilot (PC-SIG Disk# 1020)

(PC-SIG Disk# 1020)

Special Requirements: *A hard drive is recommended.*
Author Registration: *$24.95*

Launch Pad by Brandyware ✍ *by Brandyware Software*

Forget DOS — now you can manage your computer and organize yourself with LAUNCH PAD. To manage your computer, LAUNCH PAD includes a DOS shell program to view, copy, delete, and move files, either in a group or individually. A complete menu system accesses word processors, databases, or any program, with one keystroke. Some clever extras include a program timer that executes a specified program at a preset time and a DOS spooler that executes a list of DOS commands.

But that's not all. To help organize your work, LAUNCH PAD includes a calendar and appointment book, name and address book (complete with labels), memo pad, and an alarm. Lots of documentation and on-screen Help makes LAUNCH PAD easy to start using.

(PC-SIG Disk#'s 2524, 2525)

Special Requirements: *CGA and a hard drive.*
Author Registration: *$29.95*

✍ = Updated Program
☆ = New Program

MemTool
by Holistic Health Group

If you're looking for a program to help you be more productive, MEMTOOL may be the answer. It's a memory resident program that only takes up 8K when properly installed. User-definable hot keys, LAN support, and optional diskswapping to save memory, are just a few of its functions. MEMTOOL will automatically use EMS memory if you have it.

MEMTOOL features include:

❑ Calculator.
❑ File editor.
❑ Diskview.
❑ Alarm clock.
❑ Screen ruler/grid.

❑ Calendar/Appointment pad.
❑ DOS quick guide.
❑ Phoneview.
❑ ASCII table.

The phoneview file can hold up to 500 entries. The file editor will handle a file up to 35K or 2500 lines, whichever comes first, and the calendar/appointment pad is limited only by disk space.

For those of you who aren't using a memory-resident program, MEMTOOL is an easy and useful set of utilities you can call on to help get your work done efficiently.

(PC-SIG Disk# 2175)

Special Requirements: *Hard drive recommended.*
Author Registration: *$30.00*

PC-DeskTeam
by Alternative Decision Software

Take control of your PC and manage your work more efficiently with this desktop manager. RAM-resident or stand-alone, PC-DESKTEAM maintains eight accessories — one keystroke away!

This menu-driven system keeps a calendar to remind you of appointments; an alarm clock to warn you of the time; a notepad for reminders and DOS access; a calculator whenever you need to run the numbers; an auto- dialer; and printer controls (all available from within your other applications). Use your printer as a typewriter. (Sometimes it's just faster.)

A super alternative to SIDEKICK, with full documentation and on-line help.

(PC-SIG Disk# 405)

Special Requirements: *None.*
Author Registration: *$29.95*

PC-DeskTeam (PC-SIG Disk# 405)

RAMdesk
by Integra Computing

RAMDESK is a memory-resident program for single PCs and networks. It maintains a programmable calculator; an address/phone directory; a mini-scheduler; a log for entry of income, expenses, and work done; and several mini-databases. If used on a Local Area Network, it can pass messages among workstations. All of these features are available on a pop-up basis.

If RAMDESK is installed without its RAM-resident alarm, it takes up only 7K RAM. With the pop-up alarm (which has a snooze feature and the ability to handle 20 alarms per day), it requires 45K. The scientific calculator alone is worth a look. It combines the most popular standard and scientific functions with 50-line "tape," on which you may back up to any entry to make a correction. The macro facility enables you to program a wide variety of formulas, such as interest, depreciation, amortization, etc.

Finally, RAMDESK can work hand-in-hand with TICKLEX and BILL-POWER, either in a network environment or on a single PC.

(PC-SIG Disk# 2271)

Special Requirements: *None.*
Author Registration: *$50.00*

▼ ▼ ▼

Desktop Publishers and Desktop Publishing Utilities

Code to Code ✍ *by AlphaBytes*

CODE-TO-CODE, the "Norton Utilities" of desktop publishing does two things to make desktop publishing (DTP) easier.

Edit your typesetting codes from .DTP programs like Ventura Publisher, XyWrite III, Magna, Penta, or any word processor that can produce an ASCII version of a file (most do).

To do this, it takes a .DTP file and separates it into two files — one with the typesetting codes and one with the written text. Edit the text file in your favorite word processor and use CODE-TO-CODE's Search and Replace features to make changes to the typesetting code file. When you're done making changes, CODE-TO-CODE will combine the two files the same way it split them.

CODE-TO-CODE also makes working with large files easier. It splits large files into smaller ones. Do this by either specifying a group of characters to split on, or the maximum size of the split files (64K maximum). Finish your editing and then CODE-TO-CODE easily recombines them.

(PC-SIG Disk# 2431)

Special Requirements: *None.*
Author Registration: *$29.00*
➤*ASP Member.*

Desktop Paint ✍ *by Alchemy Mindworks Inc.*

Integrating a picture into a document might be worth a thousand words — but only if it's the right picture. DESKTOP PAINT makes sure your images are perfect by giving you the power to edit and add text to any image you put on your page.

DESKTOP PAINT is a bit-mapped paint program designed especially for desktop publishing software like Ventura Publisher, PageMaker, Publish It, and other programs that integrate graphics such WordPerfect.

Quickly create and modify bit-mapped graphics, either for use as stand-alone pictures or for inclusion in other documents. DESKTOP PAINT features a wide variety of file formats, a powerful selection of drawing tools, an easy to operate windows-like interface and lots of room for customization.

DESKTOP PAINT supports the following image file formats:
❑ MacPaint .MAC (and PSF MAC files)
❑ Ventura .IMG
❑ PC Paintbrush .PCX
❑ .TIFF
❑ WordPerfect .WPG

Note: DESKTOP PAINT will only create and work with monochrome .WPG files which contain bit-mapped images.

DESKTOP PAINT is a paint program, rather than a drawing program. It does not support .GEM, Corel Draw, Designer, .DXF or .EPS files.

Complete EMS support, DESKTOP PAINT to handle enormous images, up to several megabytes if your system has enough expanded memory.

Among the advanced features DESKTOP PAINT are:
❑ Six picture "gallery" of image fragments
❑ Gradient and fill tools
❑ Rotation, scaling, and flip functions
❑ Full set of drawing tools
❑ Cut, copy, and paste
❑ Left, center, and right text justification

The basic DESKTOP PAINT package comes with a selection of three fonts in different point sizes, but more fonts can be added.

(PC-SIG Disk# 2546)

Special Requirements: *384K RAM. 640K RAM recommended.*
Author Registration: *$35.00*

DIEGO1
by Published Perfection!

DIEGO1 is a fully-functional PostScript font for Ventura Publisher users and Windows/PageMaker users with the .MGX PostScript driver. Complete character mapping is provided along with special symbols and foreign language characters. Example files and a mapping chart are provided for Windows/PageMaker users.
(PC-SIG Disk# 2282)

Special Requirements: *PKUNZIP. Window users must have .MGX PostSript drivers.*
Author Registration: *$10.00*

Dropcaps ☆
by The WRITE Desktop Publisher

A collection of ornate French capital letters, DROPCAPS is ideal for the raised first letters in book chapters and typesetting poetry. Since they are in .PCX format, DROPCAPS is compatible with many desktop publishing and graphics or paint programs.
(PC-SIG Disk# 2554)

Special Requirements: *Desktop publishing, graphics, or paint application.*
Author Registration: *$15.00*

Heidelbe
by Published Perfection!

HEIDELBE is the second fully-functional PostScript Font for Ventura Publisher users and Windows/PageMaker users with the .MGX PostScript driver. Complete character mapping is provided along with complete detailed documentation.
(PC-SIG Disk# 2282)

Special Requirements: *PKUNZIP. Window users must have the .MGX PostScript drivers.*
Author Registration: *$10.00*

Rubicon Publisher
by Rubicon Computer Labs

This comprehensive desktop publisher, modeled on traditional typesetting concepts, has over 120 features. This Postscript or LaserJet system has two LaserJet font families (Trajan and Renner) and supports many others. The batch processor is controlled by tags embedded in the input file. No mouse or graphics capability is required to run RUBICON PUBLISHER but an ASCII word processor is necessary. The LaserJet fonts require 1.4MB of disk space.
(PC-SIG Disk#'s 2334, 2335, 2336)

Special Requirements: *640K RAM, hard drive, and a Laserjet or Postscript printer.*
Author Registration: *$89.00*
➤*ASP Member.*

Typesetter PC
by XLENT Software

A single page desktop publishing program that lets you mix text and graphics anywhere on the page in a WYSIWYG environment. An unlimited number of fonts sizes and styles can be mixed on the page. TYPESETTER PC is also a full-featured drawing program, including functions such as pencil draw, line draw, k-line, circles, rectangles, rounded rectangles, polygons, fills, splines, fat bits, and more.

With TYPESETTER PC, you can import ASCII files to use in your newsletter or flyer. Graphics from other programs such as Dr. Halo and PC-Paintbrush can also be imported. A utility (CBEAM) allows screen capture from other programs on CGA systems.

The Near Laser Quality output to 9-pin dot matrix printers is a key feature. Because TYPESETTER PC literally draws all text and graphics to the design page, the user can control every pixel on the page with either a mouse or the keyboard.
(PC-SIG Disk#'s 2167, 2168)

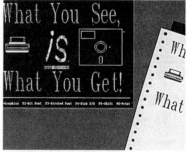

Typesetter PC (PC-SIG Disk# 2167)

Special Requirements: *640K RAM, Hercules graphics or CGA, and an Epson compatible printer.*
Author Registration: *$30.00*

▼ ▼ ▼

Disk Catalogers and Disk Labelers

BJ-FILES
by Robert G. Jensen Jr.

Easily create and maintain an inventory list of all those disks you have laying around. Now you can know exactly what's on them. BJ-FILES will record every file and what disk it's on. You can also use this program to provide a nice listing of the files on your hard disk, including a listing of duplicate files.

BJ-FILES automatically reads directory information from hard disks and floppy disks, and builds an inventory of your files. It updates the inventory by rereading the same disks. Several reporting options are available with your choice of output type (screen display, ASCII file, or printer).

Other features include optional changing of volume labels and an 30-character description for each disk. Reports can be generated with all files listed by disk and subdirectory, all files by file name, all files for one specified disk, or all disks and subdirectory locations for one specified file. Wild cards are optional for one file or one disk reports. User-selectable items from the inventory may be written to a delimited ASCII file for use in database software.

(PC-SIG Disk# 1804)

Special Requirements: *None.*
Author Registration: *$15.00*

Catalog
by Greenline Computing

Build your disk library catalog simply and easily.

CATALOG is a simple program that reads a disk volume label and directory and then formats the directory information into an ASCII file. This file can then be imported into your favorite database manager. It comes with sample file headers for use with PC-FILE+ to help you in designing your database.

(PC-SIG Disk# 1312)

Special Requirements: *None.*
Author Registration: *$20.00*

DBS-KAT File Librarian Package
by Applied Foresight, Inc.

DBS-KAT is a menu-driven file cataloger for hard drive users who want information about their diskettes in one compact database. It accommodates 9,999 floppies and/or up to 16 million filenames. No data entry is required!

Features include: inquiry by diskette ID, filename (or part of it), directory or comment (or part of it), location, or date range; backup and disk cleanup operations; file manager; programmer's print formatter (with special features for C programmers); menu-creator; on-line manual; file-viewing utility (supports mouse or keyboard); ASCII file-split utility (via the print utility); and batch file menu-maker program.

Source code is available. DBS-KAT is an internationally liked diskette cataloger for power users since 1986 and one of the "Best-Rated Shareware Programs, Honorably Mentioned Within the Computing Community Media" by DON'S DIRECTORY.

Now you can start using your disks to contain critically needed files and put off upgrading the hard drive capacity of your computer. You can start thinking of your disks as being as hard disk subdirectories, for you will be able to find out directory information about any file you have worked on.

(PC-SIG Disk# 537)

Special Requirements: *384K RAM and DOS 2.1 or greater.*
Author Registration: *$27.50*

Disk Cataloging Program
by Rosemarie Jabour

After collecting numerous programs on your hard disk or several floppies, finding a particular program can be a tremendous, dreaded problem. DISK CATALOGING PROGRAM is a simple utility designed to handle just that. It creates a catalog of all your files by reading the information from your disks as you insert them in your floppy drive. Add or change the disk label as each disk is read by the program and catalog over 500 disks in one catalog. View and modify a list of disks. Search for a filename and the program tells you all the locations for that file. Add individual file descriptions once the disk is cataloged.

(PC-SIG Disk# 1049)

Special Requirements: *None.*
Author Registration: *$19.00*

Disk File
by Alive Software

DISK FILE is a simple but complete database program for making your own disk labels. It supports IBM/Epson/compatible printers. Note: These are ONE-UP gummed labels.

(PC-SIG Disk# 1356)

Special Requirements: *None.*
Author Registration: *$5.00*

DiskCat
by Jeanne M. Nerwinski

DISKCAT is a floppy disk cataloging program for hard disk-based systems. Files from each disk are automatically read by the program and put into the catalog. The catalog records the file name, size, and extension. DISKCAT allows you to add your own description of the file and the file category. Afterwards, you may search for a file or print a report by disk, by file name, or by file category. DISKCAT will also print 1⁷/₁₆" x 5"-sized disk labels.

DISKCAT is not only a convenient way to keep track of what programs you have and where they are located, but it also allows you to describe each file so you can immediately recall the program's usage.

(PC-SIG Disk# 1320)

Special Requirements: *512K RAM, hard drive, and printer.*
Author Registration: *$30.00*

Diskette Manager
by Micro System Solutions

How would you like to catalog your hundreds of shareware disks by volume and program, and be able to locate any file or program in seconds? DISKETTE MANAGER can do the job. Simply slip your disks one-by-one into a drive, press a key and all the files on it are instantly listed in your catalog.

You can alter volume names, delete or add files, and search and find them instantly. Don't worry about archives. DISKETTE MANAGER reads archived files and records both the archive file name and its contents. You can even add a 40-character description to any record. File sizes are listed along with dates and attributes.

The program includes a 27-page user guide on-disk, and context- sensitive on-line help.

(PC-SIG Disk# 1393)

Special Requirements: *None.*
Author Registration: *$37.00*
➤*ASP Member.*

Diskmaster
by Robert W. Lennox

Tired of trying to read those scribbled labels on your disks? Print disk labels on 5" x 1⁷/₁₆" label stock. This is the ideal size for a floppy disk.

(PC-SIG Disk# 709)

Special Requirements: *None.*
Author Registration: *$10.00*

DiskScan
by Roy Mickelsen

DISKSCAN automatically builds a database of all your floppy disks!

Using DISKSCAN, a comprehensive list of all your files is compiled by a floppy number and a user-defined floppy name. The program does all the work as you feed your disks in one-by-one. When finished, you can browse through a sorted file list on screen, or search the database by disk name, file name, file extension, file size, date, or file attributes. You can also print a catalog of the entire database.

Updates and changes are quick and foolproof. Just insert the disks that have new or changed files into your PC, provide the disk number, and DISKSCAN does the rest.

(PC-SIG Disk# 1286)

Special Requirements: *MS-DOS 3.X, 640K RAM and a hard drive.*
Author Registration: *$15.00.*

Disk_Tag
by Wildcard Software

DISK_TAG allows you to print custom disk labels, directory listings, and even disk sleeves for your diskettes.

DISK_TAG is a disk label program with the added feature of being able to create sleeves for your disks. When you have those couple of disks that just don't seem to have any sleeves for them, it's nice to be able to make your own.

The program also makes sleeves for 3.5" disks. It's not necessary to have sleeves for the smaller disks but it also leaves you without a place for your directory listings. The sleeve the program prints for these disks has been tested in several disk holders and fits fine.

Sleeves or labels printed by DISK_TAG can include a complete listing of all the subdirectories on a disk, or only the root directory, in alphabetical or actual order, at your option. DISK_TAG will also print the contents of .ARC or .ZIP files, if necessary. A line for comments is provided as well, printed in condensed print to allow for longer comments.

(PC-SIG Disk# 1226)

Special Requirements: *Printer.*
Author Registration: *$10.00*

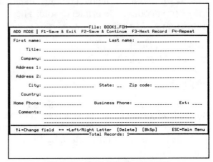

Disk_Tag (PC-SIG Disk# 1226)

FBNCAT ✍
by FBN Software

Here's a disk cataloger with pull-down menus, full search and sort capabilities by disk and file, and the power to print disk labels. Enter disk and file comments and save for later editing. Pull up reports on your own library, then edit the cataloger to keep it current.

FBNCAT was designed to be easy to use. The menus and dialogue boxes are self-explanatory and extensive context-sensitive help screens are included. At any point that help is required, simply press F1 and a

(PC-SIG Disk# 1934)

Special Requirements: *Two floppy drives or a hard drive.*
Author Registration: *$15.00*
➤*ASP Member.*

FlopCat
by W.R. Software

FLOPCAT is a menu-driven disk-cataloging system with 23 functions to organize and manage your ever-increasing inventory of floppy disks.

The disk labeling feature alone makes it well worth owning. Print labels with volume name, volume comment line, disk number, free bytes, file names and extensions. Build and update your catalog of disks. Look through the index or at the directory of a specific disk. Change the volume name, add a comment about the volume or make specific comments about individual files as you review the contents of each disk. Search through all floppy directories for volume names or wild card search strings. Volumes or files found are displayed on the screen or printer. A numerical or alphabetical listing of volumes is supported.

Print a disk label in 3.5" or 5.25" formats. This function takes the directory information and neatly prints it on self-adhesive labels. This makes your selection of disks uniformly labeled, numbered, named, and dated, with the free bytes listed as well.

FlopCat (PC-SIG Disk# 959)

New features include pop-up command windows, choice of file date record or comments, disk label path mask (allows labels to be printed only for selected drives), and expanded search functions.

(PC-SIG Disk# 959)

Special Requirements: *512K RAM and two floppy drives.*
Author Registration: *$15.00*

✍ = Updated Program
☆ = New Program

LaserLbl ✍ *by Williamsware*

LASER LABEL is a simple utility for printing diskette labels on an HP LASERJET II printer. The program reads the directory of files on a floppy disk and then sorts and prints them (along with a user-defined title and description) on AVERY #5161 laser printer diskette labels. LASERLBL allows the user to download different fonts for both the title and file name areas of the label. There are no documentation files on this disk. All of the information you need to use this program is included on the screen as you run it.

(PC-SIG Disk# 2028)

Special Requirements: *HP LaserJet II/IIP/III/compatible printer and ANSI.SYS.*
Author Registration: *$15.00*

Masterfile Disk Management System *by Masterware*

Stop searching through your floppies or hard disk trying to locate specific files.

MASTERFILE can describe the contents of a file without having to use the application that created the file, determine what each file is, and give a unique description of each file or group of files — up to 75 characters long.

Search for your files by name or description. Print a hard copy of your disk library with these descriptions.

(PC-SIG Disk# 981)

Special Requirements: *Two floppy drives.*
Author Registration: *$20.00*

MaxCat ☆ *by maxSoft*

MAXCAT is a menu-driven diskette cataloging program which creates an index of floppy disks. This catalog can reside on your hard disk or on another floppy disk. With one keystroke, diskettes are read and each file and subdirectory is automatically indexed. File names are also extracted from both .ARC and .ZIP files and added to the MAXCAT database. This index can be browsed on screen by diskette or by individual subdirectory. Searches by file name or extension are a snap to perform. Comments can be attached to both diskettes and subdirectories.

Printed reports include:

❏ a listing of all diskettes
❏ all files
❏ all files in a selected subdirectory
❏ all subdirectories
❏ all files on a selected diskette

Complete, helpful database statistics are always available, as well as context-sensitive Help.

MAXCAT indexes diskettes by volume label. Volume label is a logical label which is recognized by DOS (and MAXCAT) as the "name" of the diskette. MAXCAT (and DOS) provides the ability to add, change, or delete volume labels.

MAXCAT will provide you with an easy-to-use, highly effective means to catalog and track all of your floppy disks. The more floppies you have, the more valuable MAXCAT will be.

(PC-SIG Disk# 2579)

Special Requirements: *Two floppy drives. Hard drive recommended.*
Author Registration: *$20.00*

PC-Disk Label II *by Foto 64 Inc.*

PC-DISK LABEL prints out disk labels for 3.5" and 5.25" disks and saves them for later reference or reprinting.

PC-DISK LABEL (PCDL) is a simple program that can help organize a computer user's disk collection and, at the very least, make every disk label legible to the untrained eye. On each label, PCDL can print four lines of 22 characters and a fifth line of 74 characters in compressed mode. PCDL can even print multiple copies, invaluable for those who need to back up their hard disks often or the professional distributing software.

Labels can be produced in three sizes for 3.5" disks and three sizes for 5.25" disks. A routine is included which prints labels to match 25 stock label dimensions. PCDL is easy to use and works with IBM, Epson, Okidata, and Hewlett Packard printers.

(PC-SIG Disk# 1192)

Special Requirements: *Printer*
Author Registration: *$25.00*
➤*ASP Member.*

PmCat
by William Chris Scott

Finally, a nice looking disk cataloger. PMCAT+ is designed to allow you to arrange, track, and sort the file information DOS stores in the directories of any hard drive or multiple diskettes.

Detailed linking makes file searching and organization a snap. You can keep track of your disks, every file on those disks, or the layout of your hard drive. Categorize and organize your collection however you want, with as much detail as you need. Although PMCAT+ was originally intended to be used with small to moderate (50 - 200 diskettes) catalogs, it is quite capable of managing truly huge diskette collections.

PMCAT+ offers a DOS shell for command execution and has the ability to read, de-archive, and catalog files that have been archived in .ARC, .ZIP, .LZH, and .PAK formats.

(PC-SIG Disk# 1997)

Special Requirements: *None.*
Author Registration: *$25.00*

▼ ▼ ▼

DOS and PC Training and Education

DOS Practice ✍
by Skill Software

This program is a new approach to the development of proficiency and speed in the use of DOS. It is not a tutorial, and is not intended simply to teach the basic knowledge needed to use a personal computer. Its purpose is to increase practical knowledge, skill, and speed in the use of DOS by providing what people need most — practice.

Sessions of simulated interaction with DOS can be selected for whatever topic or level of expertise is desired, whether the student is a novice or has been using personal computers for years. DOS PRACTICE is also a very effective refresher in DOS usage, and complements computer tutorials, written courses, and classes taught by instructors. Interaction with the program is mostly self-explanatory, but context-sensitive help may be called at any time.

(PC-SIG Disk# 1950)

Special Requirements: *Hard drive.*
Author Registration: *$25.00*

DOS-Pro
by Prowess INC.

DOS-PRO is a menu-driven utility that lists the most commonly used DOS commands and is very helpful to novice users. Select the command you want to use with the cursor. If you are unfamiliar with the use of that specific DOS command, an on-line help function is ready to explain it to you. DOS-PRO's menu occupies only one screen, and is divided into directory commands, format commands, and other DOS commands.

(PC-SIG Disk# 889)

Special Requirements: *None.*
Author Registration: *$15.00*

DOSHelp
by JJL Enterprises

If you have ever become frustrated with any of the DOS commands or have had problems finding a command in the DOS manual, then DOSHELP is for you. DOSHELP is a menu from which you choose a DOS command. No more struggling with proper spelling or syntax. This program presents a quick summary of the command along with some examples of how the command is used. For even quicker help on a particular DOS command, type the command at the DOS prompt when executing the program.

DOSHELP has been updated to include all the commands through version 3.2 of both MS-DOS and PC-DOS.

Also provided with DOSHELP is a program that prints out a 17-page quick reference guide for all DOS 3.2 commands.

(PC-SIG Disk# 1067)

Special Requirements: *None.*
Author Registration: *$15.00*

✍ = Updated Program
☆ = New Program

Help/Pop-Help
by Help Software

Finally, the help that we've all been looking for! HELP!! And POP- HELP are a combined on-line reference manual to DOS that comes when it's called and is always there when you need it. Both HELP!! And POP- HELP are DOS utilities with a complete listing of DOS commands through DOS version 3.3. HELP!! Is available at the DOS command line. POP-HELP is memory-resident, so it is available anywhere you are. This is the program that every husband should give his wife (and vice versa) unless, of course, you wish to appear incredibly knowledgeable.

Both HELP!! And POP-HELP are easy to use. POP-HELP's command keys can be set so that they will not conflict with your program commands. There are very clear instructions to allow you to add extra information and your own commands.

(PC-SIG Disk# 1881)

Special Requirements: *None.*
Author Registration: *$15.00*

HelpDOS
by Help Technologies

A "help system" for learning and using the commands and functions of DOS version 2.0. HELPDOS has menus, reference information, a technical dictionary and a cross-reference feature which work together to show you what DOS can do and how to use it.

From the main menu, select brief or in-depth information on basic and advanced DOS commands, special keyboard keys, batch subcommands, and an overview of the DOS facilities.

The technical dictionary explains frequently-used terms with overviews of DOS facilities and personal computers. The dictionary also has additional reference information and usage notes.

When you select a category from the hint menu, HelpDOS will show you a menu of the DOS features relating to that category. The hints function is a unique and powerful aspect of HELPDOS.

(PC-SIG Disk# 686)

Special Requirements: *None.*
Author Registration: *$20.00*

PC-DOS HELP
by Chris Bailey

Lost in the wilds of DOS again? Here's real direction for you — an on-line help function for DOS commands in versions 2.0, 2.1 and PCjr. This is especially informative for the beginner.

How do you get there from here? Just type HELP, followed by the DOS command you are unsure of, and PC-DOS HELP shows you its proper usage and leads you back into the light.

(PC-SIG Disk# 254)

Special Requirements: *None.*
Author Registration: *$15.00*

PC-Glossary ✍
by Disston Ridge Software & Consulting

What is shadow RAM, an ALU, a Dvorak keyboard, and a bit-mapped graphic? Find these and the answers to many more questions about computer terms with PC-GLOSSARY.

This educational desktop reference program helps you keep abreast of the ever-changing terminology of microcomputers. Hundreds of terms, abbreviations, buzzwords, and acronyms are defined. Each entry is cross-referenced to other entries. PC-Glossary supports all monitors and graphics, including laptops with backlit screens.

(PC-SIG Disk# 2208)

Special Requirements: *DOS 2.1 or higher and a hard disk recommended.*
Author Registration: *$29.00*
➤*ASP Member.*

PC-Help! ☆
by DG Systems

Now you can quickly and easily create your own context sensitive help screens for programs, spreadsheets, — anything. It's easy with PC-HELP!, the memory resident program that lets you add help screens to any other application program!

How easy is it to make a complete help system? First type in the text you want to appear on your help screens. Then specify a key word or phrase that your application program (database, spreadsheet, etc.) is displaying when you want each help screen to appear. That's it — your done! Now start PC-HELP! and then your application program (PC-HELP! wi be memory resident). When the user presses the help key, PC-HELP will grab the proper help screen and display it. A complete help system without the time and trouble of programming it.

Special Requirements: *Two floppy drives.*
Author Registration: $25.00

PC-Learn ✍ *by Seattle Scientific Photo*

PC-LEARN opens the world of the personal computer to beginners. A collection of on-disk articles, it covers the essentials every new PC owner should know. Using PC-LEARN is simple. Select a subject from the menu and read it on the screen or print a copy and keep it near your computer for reference.

Subjects include: purchasing a new PC, DOS for beginners, advanced DOS, batch files, spreadsheets, hard disk drives, word processors, databases, computer history, display standards, upgrading a PC, software resources, glossary, modems, telecommunications, a detailed bibliography and suggested reading list.

Over 9,000 computer beginners have registered PC-LEARN. Users include many universities, government offices, and 350 computer clubs.

(PC-SIG Disk# 1399)

Special Requirements: *None.*
Author Registration: *$25.00.*

PC-Prompt *by Lake Medici Software*

PC-PROMPT is a unique, memory-resident DOS help program that automatically provides information for DOS commands as you type them. The F10 function key can display additional help whenever needed. Help screens can also be invoked for EDLIN, DEBUG, BASIC and Borland's Turbo Pascal editor.

Since PC-PROMPT is memory-resident, it stays loaded in memory until you reboot the PC. It automatically activates at the DOS prompt, and deactivates whenever you execute any DOS command, batch file, or program. Because of this, it is compatible with most software, even with programs which do direct screen memory operations without using DOS. It is even compatible with various other memory-resident programs such as RAM drive emulators, printer spoolers, and Borland's SideKick.

(PC-SIG Disk# 558)

PC-Prompt (PC-SIG Disk# 558)

Special Requirements: *None.*
Author Registration: *10.00*

PCHELP & Utilities ✍ *by COMPU.CON*

Imagine on-line help for DOS. This utility is a quick-and-easy reference guide to DOS commands, their uses and proper formats. When you need help, just type PCHELP plus the name of the command you are curious about. An explanation of the command and its proper usage come to the screen.

Also included on this disk are some of the most popular DOS-like utilities. These routines do things that DOS should: WHERE will find files on your hard drive, RENDIR will rename a directory, LOCATE will find text in a file, DIRCOMP will compare two directories, and more. You can find similar files elsewhere in The PC-SIG Library, but these versions are supported by PCHELP — you get an explanation and syntax help just like any other DOS command. You'll get helpful information without ever dragging out a DOS manual.

PCHELP uses no overhead memory and won't get in the way of normal DOS operations for those who don't need the help.

(PC-SIG Disk#'s 1774, 2026)

Special Requirements: *None.*
Author Registration: *$20.00*

✍ = Updated Program
☆ = New Program

QRef
by Associative Memory Systems LTD

A memory-resident utility that displays a list of all the DOS commands available and a detailed description of them.

Scroll through a display of all the MS/PC-DOS commands. The DOS prompt will always be displayed at the top. You can limit the list by typing in a letter — only the commands that begin with that letter will be displayed. Pressing another letter will limit the list to commands that begin with those two letters. Get a brief summary of the command or a detailed description.

(PC-SIG Disk# 875)

Special Requirements: *None.*
Author Registration: *$49.00*

TUTOR DOS ✍
by Kevin L. Cummings

TUTOR DOS was created by a professional computer instructor to assist beginners who are trying to learn DOS. It was written with the novice in mind, and starts with the basics of RAM and DOS before moving on to topics such as formatting disks, manipulating sub-directories, and creating batch files.

TUTOR DOS consists of 21 interactive lessons. Students are able to practice their newfound skills as they acquire them. TUTOR DOS will recognize a variety of answers to its questions and prompts users with hints. Each lesson ends with a short quiz to help students review what they have learned. At the end of the program, students take a multiple-choice test to evaluate their knowledge. Based on this test, TUTOR DOS either recommends lessons for review or rewards the student with a custom printed certificate.

(PC-SIG Disk#'s 2384, 2385, 2386, 2387)

Special Requirements: *None.*
Author Registration: *$10.00*

TUTOR.COM ✍
by Computer Knowledge

Did they laugh when you sat down at the keyboard? No more! TUTOR.COM is a collection of self-paced tutorials that cover the basics of a first course on computer usage and PC-DOS, the disk operating system.

Learn the basics of PC computing from the general information and historical aspect to the nuts and bolts, so to speak, of running and organizing a hard disk. Explore the twists and turns of DOS and learn how to write batch files. Do all of this at your own speed, in the privacy of your own computer, and without an instructor breathing down your neck.

(PC-SIG Disk# 403)

Special Requirements: *None.*
Author Registration: *$15.00*
➤**ASP Member.**

TUTOR.COM (PC-SIG Disk# 403)

Typing DOS Commands ☆
by Fred Howard

Typing in DOS commands — copy this, delete that. If you make a mistake and delete this and copy that — you got trouble! Let's face it; DOS is hard to use because the commands are hard to use. To get good at DOS commands, you have to practice. That's why TYPING DOS COMMANDS was developed; to give you practice.

It's easy to use. TYPING DOS COMMANDS describes the DOS activity and you type in the command that will accomplish it. For example, you may be asked to: "with C the current drive, copy all files that end with TXT from drive B to drive A." Now you type in the complete DOS command and the program will check it. If your answer is wrong, you will be shown the correct answer. After the test, all incorrect answers are printed out for your review.

While TYPING DOS COMMANDS is great for a beginner, even you DOS hotshots might learn something. Because not only are the answers correct, but they are also the shortest and most efficient version possible. Great for teaching yourself or others.

Special Requirements: *None.*
Author Registration: *$5.00*

▼ ▼ ▼

DOS Shells

DFM
by Don Retzlaff

Here's a DOS shell that gives you more than filenames and key commands. You can now include an English description with a file and DFM will keep track of it for you, even if you copy the file or change its name. The added description is very useful for remembering what is really in a file, yet does not get in the way of quick command operation from the DFM shell.

DFM provides easy-to-remember single keystroke activities for the most common file maintenance operations (editing, copying, renaming, printing, and deleting), as well as providing convenient features that cannot be found in many similar directory management tools. No longer will you fight through hard-to-understand DOS manuals trying to find the syntax of a command — just point to a file and your operation is only a single key away!

(PC-SIG Disk# 1899)

Special Requirements: *None.*
Author Registration: *$10.00*

DirectMaint
by Morsoft

A pox on DOS! If you believe that DOS file and directory commands were designed by demented hackers, you'll appreciate the simple, sane approach of DIRECT MAINT. Now you need not remember those obscure DOS commands. You can ignore paths and leave the DOS manual under one leg of your printer table. Instead, use a friendly highlighted bounce bar to decide what you want to do. If the program needs to know something, it will ask you. Works great on hard and floppy disks.

Load and run programs and batch files using the point-and-shoot menu. Easily find, copy, compare, erase, display, print, and change names, dates, times, and attributes of files. DIRECT MAINT copies all or selected files wherever you desire. You are prompted when target disks are full, so you'll never split files between disks. Physically move files wherever you want. Comparing old and new files is a snap. Erase multiple tagged files or whole directories, and print subdirectory names in a single directory or tree structure. View two disks or two directories on the same disk at the same time.

(PC-SIG Disk# 1497)

Special Requirements: *None.*
Author Registration: *$29.95*
➤*ASP Member.*

Directory eXtended
by Econo-Soft

Give yourself more power and freedom in managing your files operating totally from the DOS command line.

DIRECTORY EXTENDED (DX) allows you to easily select one file or multiple files, including hidden and system files if desired, which you may then copy, move, delete, rename, compare or append with another file. You can change a file's attribute or its date, and check if a group of files can fit on a disk.

Normal DOS files, as well as those within an archive (.ARC) file, can be directly sorted by name, extension, size, date, or file attributes. DX can perform a CRC or checksum test on your files to detect defects or alterations in files. DX commands can be incorporated into batch files.

(PC-SIG Disk# 1605)

Special Requirements: *None.*
Author Registration: *$25.00*
➤*ASP Member.*

Disk Navigator
by Stan C. Peters

DISK NAVIGATOR takes over for the ordinary DOS prompt on your computer and displays the files on your disk(s) in several display formats; copy, move and erase files on an individual or group basis.

Individual files can be browsed or renamed. There is a submit facility in which the commands and file names normally typed at the DOS prompt are now typed and automatically passed on to DOS. The benefit — no misspellings!

Context-sensitive help screens and pop-up windows make DISK NAVIGATOR easy to use. The program can show the files from a number of drives/ directories on the screen at the same time, giving your computer a "super" disk directory. Scan one disk directory or the entire disk directory structure.

✍ = Updated Program
☆ = New Program

(PC-SIG Disk# 810)
Special Requirements: *None.*
Author Registration: *$19.00*

Edicom-12   *by Edicom Systems*

No more memorizing of DOS commands, syntax or keyboard codes. EDICOM-12 converts DOS to a menu driven system that's easy to use and more productive. Typing commands are replaced by moving the cursor and pressing Enter.

(PC-SIG Disk# 1037)
Special Requirements: *360K RAM.*
Author Registration: *None.*

Disk Navigator (PC-SIG Disk# 810)

EzDoss   *by John Bean*

It's a DOS shell that the novice will love for its menus and verification prompts. The experienced user will appreciate it for "quick key" command execution, "expert mode" to let the more experienced user work faster, and a unique operational design that provides faster disk access.

One of the most annoying features of many DOS shells is each time a drive is selected, a time-consuming search for subdirectories takes place. With EZDOSS, this is greatly reduced by having the program create a disk file the first time it reads a hard disk. This disk file keeps track of where all the files are. When the drive is selected again, the disk file can be read faster without searching for subdirectories.

The power of a DOS shell is realized through features like multiple file manipulation, precise "tagging" control by pattern, masking, viewing text files, and locating files in any subdirectory by name.

(PC-SIG Disk# 1803)
Special Requirements: *None.*
Author Registration: *$10.00*

File Access   *by Peter Alachi*

FILE ACCESS is a powerful file and disk access utility that offers a wide variety of access options.

Major capabilities include:

❏ Menu-driven access to directories and files.
❏ Tag/untag a single file or group of files for copying, erasing, moving, renaming, or printing.
❏ Create, remove, and rename directories.
❏ Remove a specified file from all directories.
❏ Search for a misplaced file in all directories.
❏ Change or view current environment table settings.
❏ Sort the current directory.
❏ Access DOS command line.
❏ Count lines in text files.
❏ Test system configurations.
❏ Read or write to a specified disk sector.
❏ Execute or view files from within the environment.
❏ Extensive macro definition feature.
❏ Extensive help screens.

(PC-SIG Disk# 1860)
Special Requirements: *Hard drive.*
Author Registration: *$20.00*

File Friend
by ColePro Software

FILEFRIEND is a memory-resident file manager which can display files from up to 10 disks and subdirectories; add or remove files from the listed directory; sort by name, extension, date, time, size, or path; scroll through the directory or tag files to copy, rename, delete, type, dump, or change file attributes.

All commands are quickly executed by the ten function keys and the bottom line of the screen will display the options available to you. The top line of the screen shows the free disk space. View the date/time or change them.

Edit your DOS commands as you enter them, keeping your five previous commands in a buffer, allowing you to go back and execute a command without having to reenter it. A log of your 20 last commands are shown on the right side of the screen.

(PC-SIG Disk# 871)

Special Requirements: *None.*
Author Registration: *$34.95*

FileViewer
by George A. Yandl

FILEVIEWER — a alternative to the hassle of DOS. If you still can't find your magic DOS-decoder ring, try this file manager.

Every DOS command can be executed with a maximum of two keystrokes. Move smoothly from file to file, directory to directory. Sort entire directories for viewing on screen by name, extension, age, or size of files. Tag files for mass copying and deleting. A thoughtful touch is the confirmation prompt to protect against accidental deletion or copying over existing files.

FILEVIEWER provides an execution menu that calls application programs in two quick keystrokes. Flip between displaying 20 sorted files at a time with size and date information, or 80 files at a time with only the filenames.

(PC-SIG Disk# 1503)

Special Requirements: *None.*
Author Registration: *$25.00*

FLIST/PC
by Fire Crystal Communications

FLIST/PC is a selection menu for manipulating your files in a more efficient manner.

Copy, move, rename, delete, edit, and execute a file by simply indicating the desired action. Multiple actions can be executed with a function key. FLIST/PC can be used with your own word processor or text editor without exiting FLIST/PC. The disk file directory can be sorted by filename, extension, size, or date. You can easily scroll through a directory, display the tree structure of all subdirectories on the current disk drive, and select new paths and directories to be displayed.

(PC-SIG Disk# 933)

Special Requirements: *None.*
Author Registration: *$15.00*

Hard Disk Director
by Helpware

Highly recommended by Dr. Filefinder, this DOS shell and menu system will speed and ease all your program, file, and directory management tasks. The commands are logically presented on the menus and can also be accessed by the function and control keys. The mouse integration is so seamless that you can copy or move directories or files without a keystroke.

The four main modules are DL, DB, DA, and DM. DL gives you a pictorial view of a directory tree, highlighting the current directory. Want to move to a different directory? Cursor to it or simply type a few letters. DL will take you to the directory as you type. While in the directory view, mark selected directories for copying, moving, or removing. Make, hide and unhide, and rename directories as well as change drives, search for files and print a copy of the tree.

Hard Disk Director (PC-SIG Disk# 1219)

Highlighting any directory and pressing Enter will show you a sorted list of the files in that directory. From the file view, edit, view, copy, rename, change attributes, print, and resort any group of files. Run any program or batch file. DL can now handle drives with up to 500 directories and up to 1000 files per directory.

File viewers included with this version are:

❑ Wordperfect version 5 and greater files.
❑ Microsoft Word.
❑ Word for Windows.
❑ dBase, FoxBase, FoxPro, Clipper, Quicksilver and compatible DBF files
❑ Lotus 123, Quattro, Symphony and compatible spreadsheets.

❑ WordStar version 4 and greater files.
❑ Window Write.
❑ PCX pictures.

DB lets you sort and move your files with uncanny ease. Sort your files by filename, file size, modification date, and file extension. Move files from one directory to another with ease. The function keys are used to delete, rename and mark files. A special menu lets you print file lists or contents, change attributes, show disk usage, or get program information about DB.

DB is a stripped down version of DL — it gives you all the functions of DL, but only for a single directory. DB gives you a sorted file list for any directory. Pathnames, file specifications, and sort parameters can be added to the command line. Moving around a file list is a snap. Type the first letter of the file and the bar highlights it. Mark files for copying and when it's done, DB unmarks them to let you know they have been copied.

DA scans an entire drive and produces a listing of all the files on that drive. Add the files of additional drives to the view. In addition to the standard copy, etc., commands, DA will also show duplicate files, and write ASCII or .DBF files of the file list.

DM is a full-featured hard disk menu. Add up to 20 entries to the main menu with unlimited submenus of up to 19 entries each. DM can be run from the command line or also popped up in DL or DB. When running DM from DL, run programs and add the highlighted or marked files from DL and DB to the command line. In this manner you can also use DM to run archive programs and to act on the marked files in DL or DB.

(PC-SIG Disk# 1219)

Special Requirements: *None.*
Author Registration: *$35.00.*
➤*ASP Member.*

IDCshell/NARC
by Infinity Design Concepts

IDCSHELL and NARC takes you where no man has gone before — the nether world of archived files. First, you are provided with an understanding of the world of packing, squeezing, crunching, and squashing. Second, you are given the tools to view, edit, delete, move, print, and make changes without unarchiving.

The two programs operate in tandem — IDCSHELL provides the environment and NARC, the key to archived files. NARC is a menu-driven de-archive facility that allows you to move easily from file to file. Operated from a mouse or keyboard, NARC is called by IDCSHELL, a DOS-like operating shell. IDCSHELL can also call your editor to allow you to alter files at will.

The next time someone packs files to one-tenth of their original size, you can shrug your shoulders and treat the microfiles as if they were old-fashioned ASCII text. Documentation is extensive.

(PC-SIG Disk# 1205)

Special Requirements: *None.*
Author Registration: *$45.00*

MasterDOS ☆
by MasterSOFT Inc.

If you're tired of typing multiple keystrokes to execute common DOS commands, then MASTERDOS can relieve your keyboard-cramped fingers. DOS commands are reduced to single keystrokes making the overall operation of your DOS-based machine a breeze. Master configurations are stored as data files to eliminate re-entering of data. MASTERDOS has selectable terminal emulations and includes commands to copy files, change drives, erase files, locate files globally, reorder files on-screen, type files, and perform many other features.

Learning MASTERDOS requires minimal training time, and on-line help is only a function key away. Six pages of well-written documentation cover the basics of operation.

(PC-SIG Disk# 1101)

Special Requirements: *None.*
Author Registration: *$35.00.*

P-Cem
by Mohamad Suhor Ghafor

P-CEM is a program that displays the current directory and allows you to execute several DOS commands at the touch of a key. It simplifies complicated file and directory usage that would be more complicated using just the DOS command line.

With P-CEM you can use the cursor pad to select a file from the directory, and press a single key to copy, delete, rename, execute, view, print or wipe that file. Encrypt and decrypt files, and change file attributes. P-CEM can switch between directories and allows you to create and delete directories. For other operations, you may temporarily shell to DOS and immediately return to the program.

Additional utilities are included. COLOR is a program that allows you to change the border color on a CGA monitor, and CURSOR will allow you to change the size of the cursor so that it can be located on the screen more easily. DISKINFO will state what free space is available on a disk, and MEMORY will display your total computer memory and currently available memory. READSECT will allow you to view any disk sector. (This is useful for looking at the "raw" data of a program or finding a lost file.) SYSINFO will display general system information of your computer configuration, and REBOOT will reboot your computer (same as Ctrl-Alt-Del). REBOOT is a useful program if it becomes necessary to reboot the computer in a batch file.

(PC-SIG Disk# 1464)

Special Requirements: *None.*
Author Registration: *$9.95*

Point & Shoot Hard Disk Manager
by AMST

The POINT & SHOOT Hard Disk Manager addresses two of the most important needs of hard disk users — program execution and file/ directory management.

POINT & SHOOT includes all of the standard menu, file, and directory commands with a split-screen file list and directory tree. The program includes DOS access, floppy disk formatting, multiple hard drive support, mouse support, file and subdirectory undelete, passwords and time logging, text search, and much more.

(PC-SIG Disk# 930)

Special Requirements: *Hard drive.*
Author Registration: *$45.00*
➤*ASP Member.*

Power Shell
by Falconer Services Inc.

POWER SHELL brings you a way to manage hard disk files that can save you lots of time. A single screen displays an abundance of choices and information on your files. List your files by name, size, attributes, time and date. Quickly copy, delete, find, move, mark, and rename your files. POWER SHELL will climb the tallest directory tree on the plantation in seconds and tell you everything you need to know.

(PC-SIG Disk#'s 1878, 1879)

Special Requirements: *None.*
Author Registration: *$20.00*

Quick Directory
by Steven Roman

QUICK DIRECTORY makes the chore of cleaning up your disk storage space easy and fun. File commands such as copy, erase, make directory, locate, compare, rename and sort on date, size, name or extension are available at the touch of a key. Handle multiple files with one command. The commands are loaded with conformations and messages that makes them almost foolproof.

The copy command can accept two different targets or copy to the same target repeatedly. By using the mark and copy commands, selective backup is available. If you want to backup only changed files, you can do so with one copy command. Copy will even skip a file too big to fit on the disk and copy another, smaller file already marked for backup.

The QUICK DIRECTORY display can show time and date, summarize disk information, provide help for the function keys, and display different directories on the left and right sides of the screen. The typical directory entry is altered to indicate file attributes such as read-only, archive, system, or hidden files. Files that have been copied or erased are identified, allowing for easier tracking during the session.

The instruction manual is complete and includes examples for easier learning. QUICK DIRECTORY assumes the user possesses a familiarity with DOS file maintenance commands.

(PC-SIG Disk# 2081)

Special Requirements: *Hard drive.*
Author Registration: *$30.00*

Scout ✍ *by New-Ware*

SCOUT is a memory-resident disk file manager you can customize to your liking. Define paths and your favorite applications and change your options at any time.

Any program can be executed from SCOUT by scrolling through the directory and pressing the appropriate key. Tag files or scroll through the directory to copy, move, alter, delete, or rename the files. SCOUT can search for a particular file, and can change the file's date and time. Create a directory, create a volume label, format, or display disk memory information. Read text files and even display a directory listing of an .ARC file.

Special features include a displayable calendar and an ASCII character table. SCOUT also displays RAM memory usage, showing how much memory each memory-resident program is currently using. When exiting from SCOUT, you have the option of removing it from memory.

(PC-SIG Disk# 895)

Special Requirements: *None.*
Author Registration: *$30.00*

Scout-EM *by New-Ware*

Put your expanded/extended memory to good use with SCOUT-EM. This is the expanded memory version of SCOUT, the disk/directory/file manager and DOS shell. All of the functions of SCOUT are available and when loaded into EM, SCOUT-EM only uses 15.4K of normal memory.

Point-and-shoot menus, "hotkey" capability, user-designed menus and command files, assignable function keys, and immediate access to DOS are available from memory-resident SCOUT-EM. Format 5.25" or 3.5" disks from within your current spreadsheet or word processor, sort files five different ways, save screens to disk, and print CGA graphics screens. Perform DOS functions without leaving the comfort of your text editor.

SCOUT-EM is preconfigured to support 180 directories with 650 files each. More can be added as long as you have the memory to support

(PC-SIG Disk# 1706)

Special Requirements: *None.*
Author Registration: *$35.00*

Still River Shell *by Bill White*

The STILL RIVER SHELL provides an intuitive interface with your system that MS/PC-DOS has never provided the user.

Typical DOS functions of execute, find, copy, move, delete, or list are completed with significantly fewer keystrokes while still providing access to all DOS commands. It gives you a more comfortable and informative operating environment than DOS alone, and the friendly, visible nature of the display can actually help the new user to better understand the operating system.

Get things done with greater speed and precision. After all, isn't that the point of computing?

(PC-SIG Disk# 481)

Special Requirements: *None.*
Author Registration: *$25.00 to $59.00.*

StupenDOS *by PKWare Inc.*

STUPENDOS is a powerful disk management utility that goes beyond just displaying and manipulating files in a user friendly manner. In addition to sorted file lists, tree directory display, file tagging, disk and memory information, STUPENDOS has a mouse interface, a file-find function, a file-display filter, and a file-move utility to move files from one directory to another.

But the more subtle features are what sets STUPENDOS apart from other disk managers. When a batch copy of files stops because of lack of disk space, STUPENDOS can continue and copy smaller files in the batch list that might fit. STUPENDOS has a "view contents" function that can be customized to call any program (DISP, SHOW, a favorite editor, etc.) in place of the TYPE function to view the file.

(PC-SIG Disk# 1336)

Special Requirements: *None.*
Author Registration: *$35.00*
➤*ASP Member.*

Task Master ✍

by David Hoover

Looking for a slick alternative to XTree or your current DOS shell? TASK MASTER is an integrated set of utilities for disk, directory, and file management that gives you powers far beyond those of DOS alone.

More than a simple DOS shell, TASK MASTER allows you to log up to 26 disk drives, then graphically display your tree of subdirectories for any disk drive. It also provides for multiple file functions including attributes and date/time changes, file security, and backup onto multiple diskettes. You can recall 20 stored DOS or TASK MASTER commands. The fully indexed user's manual will guide you through the power of this program.

Perhaps the greatest strength of TASK MASTER is its ability to work with whole directories in ways DOS never dreamed of. Copy, move, or delete a directory or multiple directories with a single step — as easy as working with individual files.

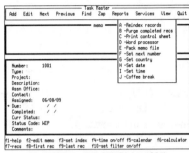

Task Master (PC-SIG Disk# 1635)

(PC-SIG Disk# 1635)

Special Requirements: *384K RAM.*
Author Registration: *$35.00*

TreeTop

by Kilgore Software

This is a multi-functional hard disk file and directory manager that provides an easy-to-use interface to DOS commands. A tree structured graphic image of the disk directory structure is first displayed when running TREETOP, then a point-and-shoot user interface is used to execute commands and navigate through the hard disk. It's fast and user-friendly, featuring pull-down menus, on-line context-sensitive help, a user-installable setup and full mouse support.

TREETOP helps you organize your files and directories so you can easily maintain your hard disk. You can rapidly search, sort, rename, add, delete or view files and directories with single key commands. The pull-down menus make changing the date/time stamp or file attributes easy. Files can be tagged by directory, filename, date/ time, file attributes, entire logical hard drive, or any combination of these items. Once selected as a group, you can mass copy, print, sort, delete, or move these files from directory to directory or disk to disk.

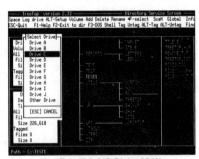

TreeTop (PC-SIG Disk# 2248)

Temporarily shell to DOS, or execute any .COM, .EXE, or .BAT file on your drive from within TREETOP. The user-installable setup provides a means for entering the name of your favorite text editor so TREETOP can automatically run your editor when you choose to edit a file.

(PC-SIG Disk# 2248)

Special Requirements: *Hard drive recommended.*
Author Registration: *$39.00*
➤*ASP Member.*

Treeview ✍

by Magee Enterprises, Inc.

Getting lost in your hard disk forest of files? Climb a tree, with TREEVIEW, to easily find your way about and make file operations a breeze.

Called up by a hot key, TREEVIEW displays disk and directory contents in up to six windows. Perform operations, such as deleting, on several files in several directories at once and select files by time, date, or

---

✍ = Updated Program
☆ = New Program

extension. A simple tree display graphically shows your directory structure, allowing you to zip about your files in ways you never thought possible. On-line help is available from anywhere in the program and an on-disk user guide provides in-depth instruction.

A "show-all" and "show-sub" display lets you access all files on the current disk as if they were in one directory. A file-viewing function displays files as ASCII text or hexadecimal format to permit use of listing and editing programs. Offering full mouse support, TREEVIEW exploits DOS command line macros to let users access complete file and directory pathnames using just one or two characters. Screen colors are user-selectable.
(PC-SIG Disk# 1243)
Special Requirements: *None.*
Author Registration: *$25.00*
➤*ASP Member.*

VDOS   *by Advantage Systems*

VDOS is a visual DOS interface (shell) for power-users that prefer to work from a command line, yet want a directory display, quick-key DOS commands, previous command recall, and other shell features. It provides direct access to all standard DOS features, plus features not available in standard DOS. These include a paging file directory display that lists all files in alphabetical order and shows their file attributes as well as a visual directory tree for hard drive users.

VDOS provides full command-line editing, and allows recall of the last 18 commands for entry or editing. On-line help is provided for common DOS operations and frequently used commands can be entered by pressing one of the function keys. The VDOS interface is user friendly and always displays the current disk drive, directory, and DOS version.
(PC-SIG Disk# 1914)
Special Requirements: *None.*
Author Registration: *$19.95*

Wyndshell ✍   *by Wyndware*

WYNDSHELL is a friendly, complete disk manager for users who fear the DOS prompt world. In addition to superior disk management, this menu-driven program can call programs or user-created macro commands (in lieu of batch files) with one keystroke, or mouse click. Never need to use the standard DOS prompt again.

The WYND-DOS section of the WYNDSHELL program graphically displays disk and directory information. Using pull-down menus you can execute all DOS file and directory commands. But WYND-DOS doesn't stop here. There are commands to move files, re-sort the directory listing, print disk info, and more. A superior feature is the ability to "tag" multiple files for a file operation such as copy or delete, saving many repeated steps. All of these features can be run with minimal keyboard strokes, or even more easily with a mouse.

The WYNDSHELL menu can be customized to directly call selected programs or execute a series of commands. A two-level menu is supported, letting you group programs by application. If you desire, WYNDSHELL pauses and prompts for parameters that the program may require. This is a feature many similar menu systems have left out.

All of WYNDSHELL's commands and prompts are straight forward and easy to use. There is on-line help available throughout the program. WYNDSHELL adds the ability to include passwords for any menu item, the ability to select screen colors, and includes a screen-blanking routine when at the main menu.
(PC-SIG Disk# 1190)
Special Requirements: *320K RAM and DOS 3.0 or higher.*
Author Registration: *$30.00.*

▼ ▼ ▼

Engineering

A-Filter
by Sitting Duck Software

This program calculates the resistor and capacitor values for various operational amplifier based active filter circuits. A-FILTER is menu-driven and covers high and low pass, equal value Sallen-Key filters to the 4th order.

Calculations will simultaneously include seven response curves for each filter (greater than 1st order); best delay, compromise, flattest, slight dips, 1db dips, 2db dips and 3db dips.

The screens are laid out in a format similar to the illustrations in "The Active Filter Cookbook" by Don Lancaster. The screens refer to pages in the book which show the shape of each curve. Although it is not necessary to have this book to run A-FILTER, the book provides valuable additional information.

(PC-SIG Disk# 1799)

Special Requirements: *None.*
Author Registration: *$35.00*

CC-Surveyor
by Civil Comp

CC-SURVEYOR is a geometric design program for civil engineers and land surveyors. It allows creation of point files with coordinates, elevations and descriptions, with import/export of points from/to most data collectors. It includes normal COGO routines plus radial stakeout, predetermined area, perpendicular and parallel offsets, topo reduction, vertical curves and grades, intersections, cul-de-sacs, and knuckles. Screen graphics include plotting of points, lines and curves, assigned to user-named layers with different linetypes and colors. Hard copy plotting may be done on Epson compatible dot matrix printers and on Hewlett-Packard or Houston Instrument pen plotters. Data may be transferred to CAD programs via DXF files.

(PC-SIG Disk#'s 926, 1029)

Special Requirements: *640K RAM, EGA or VGA, and a hard drive.*
Author Registration: *$300.00*

Chart
by Scott D. Nelson

If you are an electrical engineer who frequently has to use the Smith Chart for impedance and admittance calculations, for characterizing transistor parameters, or for creating high frequency matching networks, CHART is the one for you!

Forget the calculators and slide rules. Forget the rulers and triangles and manually drawing graphs. The chart is drawn for you on-screen, with the numeric results shown on the side.

Help is available throughout the program with examples built in. You can even use a mouse if you have one. If you are not using any similar program and still do calculations the old way, then CHART is a must-have.

(PC-SIG Disk# 1761)

Special Requirements: *256K RAM, and EGA or VGA.*
Author Registration: *$25.00*

CoGo
by Carl M. King

COGOWARE is a coordinate geometry surveying program for plat designers. Calculate coordinates of each point in the plane of the survey and of each point calculated by the plat designer. Each pair of coordinates is assigned a point number by the designer as the calculations progress. These designated coordinates are saved in batches of 100 points to a file. Any designated point can be recalled, and the survey extended as the design progresses. All calculations are carried out in double precision.

(PC-SIG Disk# 1013)

Special Requirements: *CGA.*
Author Registration: *$10.00*

The Electrical DBS disk ✍
by Future Systems

THE ELECTRICAL REFERENCE DATABASE gives electricians, engineers, designers, and panel shop operators one place on your computer where you can find those little notes that only experience produces. In this case a professional has given you his experience and created a forum for you to add your own.

Databases include:

✍ = Updated Program
☆ = New Program

❏ DC motors
❏ Three phase induction motors
❏ Three phase synchronous motors
❏ Motor frame sizes
❏ Single phase conductor ampacities
❏ Three phase transformers
❏ Recommended copper wire and transformer sizes.

❏ Single phase motors
❏ Three phase wound rotor motors
❏ NEMA data
❏ Three phase conductors ampacities
❏ Maximum conductors in conduit

Motor databases provide information as to full load currents, motor over current protection rating, the size or guage of the wire required to connect one motor of that particular horsepower in a general purpose application, the conduit trade size required to house the wire, the NEMA size starter recommended, the amperage and the recommended fusing.

The present data is referred to as "seed" data just to get you started. You may add and delete data as you like. Each data base can handle a maximum of 2.1 billion entries.

Each database is menu-driven and complete with its own help function and notes field. Use this data base as a tool — not as a replacement for the NATIONAL ELECTRICAL CODE manual. All information assumes a single motor installation. Consult your NEC manual for the details of your particular installation.

(PC-SIG Disk#'s 1977, 1978)

Special Requirements: *640K RAM and a hard drive.*
Author Registration: *$60.00*

PC-Ecap ✍ by Circuit Systems

An easy-to-use AC circuit analysis program which analyzes circuits consisting of resistors, capacitors, inductors, transformers, transistors (both bipolar and FETs), operational amplifiers and transconductance amplifiers. Anyone with an interest in electronics — hobbyists, students, HAM radio enthusiasts, teachers, electronics engineers or technicians will find this program useful.

Totally integrated in one package, PC-ECAP contains a full-screen text editor for preparing analysis input, an electronic circuit analyzer that calculates your circuit's frequency and phase response, a high resolution display plotter that supports all common graphics adapters and a high resolution plotter for IBM/Epson compatible printers.

Features:

❏ Completely menu-driven — very simple to use.
❏ Analyze circuits with up to 40 nodes — no limit on the number of components.
❏ On-line Help function.
❏ Free input format — common abbreviations such as P, U, N, M, K, MEG, G are recognized.
❏ Supports CGA, EGA, VGA, Hercules, and Monochrome Display Adapters. PC-ECAP will automatically configure itself for most adapters and displays.
❏ All calculations are done in double precision — 14 digits of BCD.
❏ Program may be configured to send its output to LPT1, LPT2 , LPT3 or a disk file.
❏ Bipolar transistor model-maker. Enter your transistor's operating parameters and PC-ECAP will create a Hybrid-Pi model.
❏ Does not need a numeric coprocessor.

(PC-SIG Disk# 2253)

Special Requirements: *None.*
Author Registration: *$79.00*
➤*ASP Member.*

PC-Schematics ✰ by John Mattern

PC-SCHEMATIC helps you to draw electrical schematics, create printed circuit artwork, draw electronic timing and clock diagrams, block diagrams, and more. To start drawing, simply use the cursor keys to draw lines on an empty drawing board. Select any of the standard characters or electrical components from the menus.

Use the standard components (336 are included) or create your own. Store up to 4096 components that can be used again and again. Copy, move, and automatically repeat components. Work on two drawings at one time.

When you're finished drawing, save to disk or print to a standard dot-matrix printer. Ample documentation and on-screen Help get you started— you decide where to stop.

(PC-SIG Disk# 2508)

Special Requirements: *512K RAM, CGA, and DOS 3.0+*
Author Registration: *$20.00*

PCBreeze II ☆   *by Kepic Pty Ltd.*

PCBREEZE II is a sophisticated yet easy-to-use tool for designing printed circuit boards (PCB). Create, view, modify, and output any one- or two layer PCB of up to 300 square inches (using a 50 mil grid system). It has two text layers for each PCB layer and a common silkscreen layer. Most operations can be performed directly through the keyboard or by pop-up menus. Microsoft compatible mice are also supported.

Simply specify the component pads and use the cursor keys to draw the traces. Pan and zoom to any part of the drawing. Move, copy, or delete any section of the artwork. Save sections to disk to create libraries and use repeatedly. Design is simple with the use of auto-routing facilities allowing an entire board to be routed by PCBREEZE alone, or interactively edited and autorouted to get precise control over the artwork generated.

The results can be output to a plotter or Postscript printer with the included plotting utility. PCBREEZE II can also produce prototype quality plots on a Epson FX/LQ or compatible printer.

(PC-SIG Disk# 2510)

Special Requirements: *384K RAM and CGA, EGA, VGA or Hercules graphics.*
Author Registration: *$95.00 Australian*

ResisPop   *by Notor Engineering Services*

RESISPOP is a simple resistor selection program that allows you to convert arbitrary resistance values between 1.0 ohm and 10 Mohm to standard values for 0.1, 0.2, 0.5, 1, 2, 5, and 10 percent tolerances. These standard values are the ones available from distributors. Both memory resident and non-memory resident versions are provided.

(PC-SIG Disk# 1884)

Special Requirements: *None.*
Author Registration: *None.*
➤*ASP Member.*

Survey Land Yourself ✍   *by CAVE, Inc.*

You can survey your land yourself — quickly, easily, and inexpensively. This is a simple compass and tape surveying system which can be used to plot deeds, find lost property corners and lines, calculate acreage and write land descriptions so that you can find your boundary again at a later time. You can also establish test plots, subdivide property, layout building foundations and gaming fields, hide and recover buried treasure, or even map a cave.

The surveying instructions (print them from disk files) are in plain English. They presume only a high school education. No magic. The catch is that the precision is only 98%, equal to the accuracy of drawing on graph paper with a protractor and ruler. BASIC is required for calculations, and with CGA or Hercules you can draw maps on the screen.

The intended audience is those people who need a good preliminary survey. Obvious users include buyers and sellers of land, and landowners who want to know their boundaries. Land use planners, developers, artists, landscapers, architects, foresters, geologists, prospectors, ecologists, hydrologists, pollution control engineers, and industrial espionage engineers estimate with this method.

Speleologists and other brands of -ologists use this method to measure points, lines, areas, and volumes on, above, and beneath the Earth. For 2% of the expense and trouble, they get 98% of the information.

(PC-SIG Disk# 1826)

Special Requirements: *A version of BASIC and a printer.*
Author Registration: *$5.00, or $75 with compass & tape.*

▼   ▼   ▼

Entertainment, General

The Animated Memory Game ☆
by Flix Productions

The ANIMATED MEMORY GAME uses animated pictures to test memory skills. By matching hidden pictures in pairs, you win the game and get animated rewards.

Many options are provided: select from 14 different tile patterns, change the background color, and even enjoy a mini-movie theater. Various difficulty levels provide a challenge for all ages. Adults can use it too! Both keyboard and mouse support are provided.

(PC-SIG Disk# 2645)

Special Requirements: *640K RAM, CGA or VGA, and hard drive. Mouse optional.*
Author Registration: *$6.00*

The Animated Memory Game (PC-SIG Disk #2645)

Cipher ✍
by Nels Anderson

If you are tired of word games which look dull and boring. Here's a colorful and challenging program that uses high-resolution graphics.

CIPHER is a "crypto-quotes" type of game. A quotation is enciphered and displayed on the screen in its scrambled form. Your challenge is to figure out the cipher by replacing the scrambled letters with the actual letters. As you go along, more and more of the puzzle will start to look like real words. Eventually, you should be able to solve the entire quotation.

CIPHER IS a word puzzle game, yet it uses hi-res VGA or EGA graphics for displays (mouse optional). It also will run in text mode. It includes over 30 puzzles to solve and the registered version comes with over 200 additional puzzles. You can also enter your own already encrypted puzzles.

(PC-SIG Disk# 2266)

Special Requirements: *None. Color monitor recommended.*
Author Registration: *$15.00*
➤*ASP Member.*

Compu-Nerd
by Try-Then-Buy Software

COMPU-NERD is a tongue-in-cheek diagnostic program used to determine whether or not the user has the dread malady COMPUTERUS-NERDITIS or BOZOITIS-JERKONUS. These terrible and sometimes lethal diseases creep up on one unexpectedly. By answering a few, simple questions the user can determine if he has either disease, its progress and the remedy for the current stage of development. This is a sure winner at computer club meetings and parties, or just to show off a bit of the absurd to your friends and prove that computers can be used for more than spreadsheets or Galaxy Noids.

(PC-SIG Disk# 2222)

Special Requirements: *None.*
Author Registration: *Contribution.*

Creative Chaos ✍
by R. Evan Lunde

CREATIVE CHAOS is made for those whose ideas are too predictable and whose minds are too logical. To enhance creativity, CREATIVE CHAOS uses random selection to help you create short stories, juggle menus, tell fortunes, generate silly phrases and funny nonsense sentences. But most of all, CREATIVE CHAOS can stimulate your imagination, help you create inventions, artwork, games, or engage in incredibly obtuse mental gymnastics.

Instead of deductive thinking, CREATIVE CHAOS stimulates intuitive thinking. The fundamental idea behind CREATIVE CHAOS is to use random selection in a very structured way to juggle lists of ideas, chores, and anything you can list. Sometimes the results are hilarious, other times they contain a real germ for change. And, sometimes they are plain old silly.

(PC-SIG Disk# 1691)

Special Requirements: *None.*
Author Registration: *$22.00*

Crossword Creator ✍ by PC Help-Line

CROSSWORD CREATOR can be used by anyone who enjoys designing or solving crossword puzzles. It provides the tools you need to lay out a puzzle on the computer's screen, define clues for each word, save your design on disk, and produce professional-looking printouts of your crosswords.

Enhancements include: 70 pages of context-sensitive available on-line, support for Wordfind (Castle Oaks Computing), desktop publishing conversion, support for all types of printers (including lasers), and an automatic word placement feature that will actually build a puzzle for you, using words you enter. Features include:

❏ Pull-down menus, dialog boxes, and mouse support
❏ Comprehensive, context-sensitive HELP
❏ National language support for French and Spanish
❏ Supports dot-matrix, and HP ink-jet and laser printers
❏ Type horizontally AND vertically
❏ 36 x 23 puzzle matrix; up to 4 lines of text per clue
(PC-SIG Disk# 819)

Crossword Creator (PC-SIG Disk# 819)

❏ Compatible with all popular networks.

Special Requirements: *320K RAM and printer. Mouse recommended.*
Author Registration: *$20.00, $35.00, $50.00.*
➤*ASP Member.*

CRYPTO! by Tom Gough

Are you a cryptogram junkie? CRYPTO! and CRYPTO MAKER give you the chance to solve and create challenging word puzzles. Test yourself and tease your friends with jumbled famous quotes.

Choose from a library containing 200 different puzzles. Ponder over the serious and funny quotations provided by the creator, Tom Gough, as you rack your brain trying to discover the next letter in the quote. Don't cheat! The program will give you hints, but try to unearth the answers for yourself. If you are stumped you can "cheat" by revealing a letter or use the hint key to tell you whether the letter is a vowel or consonant. The name of the speaker of the quotation appears when the puzzle is solved.

You can also create your own cryptograms to perplex your friends. Type in your favorite quote, change the letter sequence, and you're ready to play. Becoming familiar with playing CRYPTO! will help you in making your puzzles.

Function keys toggle colors and all puzzles can be printed. Easy-to-use instructions and menus give fast access to the game. A great game for all adults who enjoy word puzzles.

(PC-SIG Disk# 2141)
Special Requirements: *None.*
Author Registration: *$6.00*

Do-It-Yourself Promo Kit by Roxbury Research Inc.

Why send a piece of cardboard or paper to express your feelings, when you can send a disk that plays music? What a birthday surprise!

These programs are a perfect replacement for traditional birthday and Christmas cards — they play music and greet the recipient. With the included editor, you can write your own cards for any occasion. They run on either a monochrome or color system, without the need for a graphics card.

Add that personal touch that people never forget!

(PC-SIG Disk# 996)
Special Requirements: *Two floppy drives and a printer.*
Author Registration: *$24.95*

G.I.F.T.S. by Hulen & Associates

Having that same old trouble coming up with a gift for Aunt Gertrude year after year? How about Mom? Given her all the gifts you could think of already?

G.I.F.T.S. is a database designed to give you gift ideas for people. From a menu you select two key words for the price range of the present, the category of the item, and the type of person it's for. Gifts are then selected out of the database, which may be viewed on the screen or printed on the printer. Each listing will display the title of the gift, the approximate cost, the supplier, a description, and a comment.

Got that charge card ready?

(PC-SIG Disk# 876)

Special Requirements: *None.*
Author Registration: *$10.00*

Garden City Software Collection #1 *by Garden City Software*

Psychologists tell us that watching fish can reduce stress. They don't understand what a $150.00 fish, belly-up in the tank, can do to your blood pressure. Instead, try electronic fish. Not a game, FISHTANK is a soothing alternative to pet care and maintenance. With proper voltage, your fish will live forever. You get all the accessories complete with a snail and eel.

History buffs will love HIST-PAL, a simple timeline database that gives the years of birth and death, the occupations, and noted quotes ("Let them eat cake!") of over five hundred famous people. With a word processor you can add to the time line. Want to be among the "Rich and Famous"? Just drop yourself into this electronic "Who's Who" to impress your friends and enemies alike.

(PC-SIG Disk# 1421)

Special Requirements: *CGA.*
Author Registration: *$2.00 for each program.*

Garden City Software Collection #2 *by Garden City Software*

An even half-dozen programs that run the scale from mortgages to metronomes.

HYPNO brings onto screen colorful hypnotic images to induce relaxation or enhance meditation. Provides changing circles, spirals a swinging watch, etc. Of particular note is a visual that is combined with affirmations (positive statements) to help you change negative mental images or bad habits.

MORTGAGE is a neat package that will compute your proposed mortgage payments and homeowner's costs by considering things such as insurance, taxes and maintenance dues.

TIMEZONE tells you what time it is anywhere in the world, listing by country, area of country and cities. Useful when communicating with faraway places.

The next three are for musicians. PC-SOUND achieves the unbelievable: your computer can sound like a tuba, saxophone, fife or other instruments. Or, if you prefer, you get white or pink noise or the sound of a siren or ray gun or clock ticking or waves beating on the shore, and lots more. Depending on your PC's speaker, the effects range from entrancing to distracting.

How would you like to tune a guitar, violin, banjo, mandolin and other musical instruments with the help of your computer? Or, produce mathematically precise tones. Use TUNER.

METRON is an electronic metronome for musicians to set the beat.

(PC-SIG Disk# 1422)

Special Requirements: *None.*
Author Registration: *$2.00 for each program.*

Get Lucky! *by Glencoe Computing*

This disk has a multi-faceted adult-oriented game, featuring trivia (for one or two players), adult trivia, adult poker, and a poker machine like those in Las Vegas. The questions covered by the trivia section include entertainment, sports, general knowledge, science, and sex. Penalties for missing a question or losing a hand in either of the "adult" games include removing an article of clothing, taking a drink, performing a task, telling a joke, or trying to say a tongue twister — all of which can be considered optional... or mandatory, depending upon the players.

(PC-SIG Disk# 711)

Special Requirements: *CGA.*
Author Registration: *$24.99*
➤*ASP Member.*

Greetingware for Christmas and Birthdays
by Roxbury Research Inc.

This is one greeting card that won't get thrown in a shoebox after the occasion is over. Just think of the fun your friends and relatives will have when they receive a customized birthday or Christmas card-on-a-disk from you!

GREETINGWARE's CHRISTMAS MEDLEY and BIRTHDAY MEDLEY will let you send a musical and colorful electronic greeting card. The Christmas card entertains you with a Christmas tree with flashing lights, while the birthday card greets you with a cake and candles.

Each card plays six songs, which your family and friends can sing along with. The program will put the words on the screen and then... just follow the bouncing ball.

(PC-SIG Disk# 839)

Special Requirements: *None.*
Author Registration: *$14.95*

It's All In The Baby's Name
by Greenline Computing

Planning to have a baby? Then you will certainly want this program which helps you choose the right name to insure your offspring's future success! Great gift for your friends who are about to become parents!

Tell the computer the baby's last name and it will provide you with an almost endless list of combinations of first and middle names that you can view or print. Names are drawn from a large variety of ethnic backgrounds and sources and provide a great starting point for naming the next generation. Some combinations can be quite startling, some quite plain, and some will be recognized as relatives.

It's All In lhe Baby's Name (PC-SIG Disk# 1214)

Another option allows Mom and Dad to scan prospective first names and choose likely candidates. Your trusty computer then mixes and matches them and lists them out with your last name for comparison shopping. The result allows the proud parents-to-be to mull over the combinations which look and sound best and try to pick something even the child will like.

(PC-SIG Disk# 1214)

Special Requirements: *None.*
Author Registration: *$12.00*

Mastermind
by Dan Bartnik

How many guesses would it take you to figure out a secret six- or seven-digit number? How about if you got clues? Have fun and test your logical thought process with MASTERMIND. MASTERMIND determines the secret number and you have to guess it. Each time you guess, it tells you how many digits were correct, but not which ones! You take it from there and try to solve the secret in the fewest guesses.

Three different versions are included for all skill levels. MASTERMIND is easy to use, includes all the game instructions on help screens, and supports a mouse.

(PC-SIG Disk# 2468)

Special Requirements: *CGA.*
Author Registration: *$10.00*

Memor-E
by TO-Soft

A computer version of "Concentration." Match 18 pairs of pictures in a 36-square grid. Get on-line Help, hints, or even where all the pairs reside. The game can be played by one player against the clock, or by up to four players.

(PC-SIG Disk# 2276)

Special Requirements: *None*
Author Registration: *$10.00*

✍ = Updated Program
☆ = New Program

MOSAIX
by Data Assist

MOSAIX is a computerized jigsaw puzzle program that turns photographic quality color images into puzzles. The puzzles presented by MOSAIX may be created using a video image capture board, a black and white scanner, or a color scanner. Since MOSAIX can import standard PCX graphics files, puzzles may also be created using almost any PC paint program. Whether you scan your own PCX graphics files, create them in a paint program, have personal photo's scanned, or use included PCX files, you'll have high quality screen images in your jigsaw puzzles.

For those who do not have access to a color scanner or digitizing equipment, MOSAIX creators, Data Assist, provide a color image scanning service. Scan in your own photographs and custom create personal jigsaws. Since MOSAIX displays actual color pictures for its puzzles, a VGA, MCGA or EGA graphics system is highly recommended. The use of a mouse is optional.

(PC-SIG Disk#'s 1972, 1973)

Special Requirements: *384K RAM, CGA, EGA, or VGA, and two floppy drives or a hard drive.*
Author Registration: *$35.00*

OpenDoor
by Computer Resources

Finally, someone put the fun back into computing! OPENDOOR introduces a new category of software — the anti-program! It's for all those times when you need a break from the other "stuff" you do on your computer. The Seattle Times called this program "the Saturday Night Live" of DOS software.

OPENDOOR simulates the look of a real operating system, with single touch commands, using the Function Keys and other "live" keys. On screen help is provided at the touch of a key - any time. Wordprocessing, spreadsheet, graph, and multitask screens can be displayed when you don't feel much like working, but want it to look like your computer is.

The built-in programs of OPENDOOR are all geared toward the fun side of computing:

❑ Crystal Ball - a life reading index that can even be rigged.
❑ What To Eat Decision Maker - answers for "Where do YOU want to eat?"
❑ Jerk-O-Meter - rates a person's "irritation" factor.
❑ Lie Detector - provides ratings from "Outright Lie" to the "Truth".
❑ Ringing Phone - a perfect interruption to get rid of someone.
❑ Stars! - every imaginable character blasted all over your screen.
❑ Computer Lock - it even looks like it works.
❑ Death Simulator - a blank screen with an eternal message.

OPENDOOR is not for doing any serious work, because its main purpose is to provide plain and simple fun — all without doing harm to anyone's computer (or ego). You can use OPENDOOR to make it look like you are working very hard, for things like deciding where to eat, or even to play jokes on others.

(PC-SIG Disk# 2157)

Special Requirements: *None.*
Author Registration: *$49.95*

PARTYDOT ✍
by Rite Item

Generate colorful designs on your computer. Enjoy a kaleidoscope that you create, or let the computer originate one for you.

PARTYDOT allows you to use pre-defined geometric shapes, colors and graphic designs to create unique screen displays. Experiment with the various options and menu items and save the designs that you like for later viewing.

(PC-SIG Disk# 1553)

Special Requirements: *512K RAM and CGA, EGA, or VGA.*
Author Registration: *$10.00*

Tommy's Crosswords ✍
by Tommy's Toys

Does anyone know a four letter word for a Russian River? Hmmmm...once again you are racking your brain trying to figure out another clue to TOMMY'S CROSSWORDS, a sleek package which allows you to solve and/or create your own crossword puzzles. Either work on one of the 40 puzzles provided on the disk — choosing from an array of topics — or create your own puzzle, using your own imagination or typing in one from your favorite newspaper.

With the ease of the function keys, you are able to toggle sound, pop-up instructions, enter and exit puzzles, and much more. The program will track not only your score — but also will provide you with hints by filling in either single letters, or complete words within the crossword grid. If no hints are needed, a score of 10,000 points will be awarded for a solved puzzle, otherwise minus one point for each letter provided. A puzzle solving timer is also kept in the lower right hand corner of the screen.

Although not for younger children, TOMMY'S CROSSWORDS is an entertainment machine for all adults. A skillful challenge for the most avid crossword fan, you will be captured by the ease of play, the complexity of the puzzles provided, and use the program as a tool to build your own for years to come.

(PC-SIG Disk# 1711)

Special Requirements: *None.*
Author Registration: *$2.00*

Universe Analyzer
by Mark Mahin

What is the probability of an undesigned universe meeting all the requirements for a biologically favorable universe? UNIVERSE ANALYZER is designed to provide a limited answer to this important question. By "a biologically favorable universe," this program means a universe with plenty of heavy elements such as carbon, and a large number of bright long-lived stars like the sun.

After prompting the user for inputs, the program generates a list of seven requirements for a biologically favorable universe. Using a random number generator, the program then generates many "universe models" with various characteristics as a result of chance. The program does NOT involve any religious or philosophical presuppositions. However, the program does tend to reach the philosophically interesting conclusion that there is less than one chance in 1,000,000,000,000,000 that an undesigned universe would be biologically favorable.

(PC-SIG Disk# 1772)

Special Requirements: *None.*
Author Registration: *$15.00*

Word Play
by Charles A. Spence

This game is the third in a series of visual puzzles from the author of Maze Cube (PC-SIG disk# 1419) and Wreck Tangle (PC-SIG disk# 1836). If you enjoyed these programs, then WORD PLAY will give you an even greater challenge.

You're presented with shuffled letters that are required to create given words. Completion of each word displays a matching meaning. The game continues until exact placement of all letters is correct. Sound easy? You will be struggling to approach the top scores on any level without lots of practice. The exciting challenge is to achieve this in the least number of moves.

25 different puzzles of varying degrees of difficulty are included. The top ten scores for each puzzle are recorded and the Masters Scoreboard displays the scores of the world's best player for each level.

A nice feature is the Autoplay facility which replays your best game so you can see where improvements can be made. You can also easily design your own puzzles, up to a maximum of 99 different games. WORD PLAY is entirely menu-driven and provides thorough on-screen instructions.

(PC-SIG Disk# 2256)

Special Requirements: *None.*
Author Registration: *$15.00*

▼ ▼ ▼

✍ = Updated Program
☆ = New Program

File Management Utilities

4Edit
by XD Systems

4EDIT is a full-screen editor for 4DOS file descriptions. It is much more convenient than the 4DOS DESCRIBE command because you can see the descriptions for all selected files at one time. Create or edit descriptions for any grouping of files using multiple filenames and extended wildcards, like 4DOS. Works with all versions of 4DOS. Look for the companion utility, 4ZIP also.

(PC-SIG Disk# 2272)

Special Requirements: *4DOS*
Author Registration: *$15.00*
➤*ASP Member.*

ActaeOn ☆
by Jon Clempner

ACTAEON is a hard disk manager that replaces the DOS command line with a graphical, mouse-driven interface. ACTAEON includes a wide array of features such as context-sensitive Help and a text editor.

ACTAEON makes the chore of hard disk management easy with a mouse-driven point-and-shoot interface. With the standard views of the directory tree and the file directory, ACTAEON provides functions such as File Search and Text Search in a selected set of files.

Display the tree and file directories in scrollable windows and select files using the mouse or the keyboard. Also provided are context-sensitive Help for all commands and a Wordstar-like text editor.

ACTAEON supports all video modes and makes use of EGA/VGA if present. EGA/VGA users can also select the 43/50 line display modes. ACTAEON can also use Expanded Memory, if present.

ACTAEON is a newcomer in the world of hard disk managers that has created its own niche with a fresh interface and an accessible set of functions.

(PC-SIG Disk# 2667)

Special Requirements: *512K RAM, and a hard drive.*
Author Registration: *$39.95*
➤*ASP Member.*

Analyze
by Gary R. Pannone

ANALYZE verifies or determines the exact contents or format of files.

ANALYZE displays file character data and their ASCII values. It displays byte values of binary data (dump). It analyzes files to determine record length, type and internal (field) format. Fully configurable, ANALYZE lets you select the number base and numbering system. It supports several record types and scrolls up and down through data records and horizontally within records. It allows quick access to specific records by record number.

(PC-SIG Disk# 1619)

Special Requirements: *None.*
Author Registration: *$20.00*

ArgaUtilities: Argafind, ArgaMenu, Argacopy
by RGA Inc

Three related programs to simplify life on the hard drive!

ARGA-FIND is welcome relief for hard disk owners who forget in which directory, or sub-sub-subdirectory they left a needed file! A misplaced file lost somewhere on a 20 MB hard disk is the modern day "needle in a haystack"! Fortunately, this program does the searching for you and displays the located filename, length, date, time, and path to get to it. Since "wild-cards" are permitted, the full filename need not be known. This version can search a maximum of 512 directories, with 512 files per directory.

ARGA-MENU makes it easy for you to bring order to your countless files and programs on your hard disk by creating point-and-shoot menus. This means you can automatically call up a program on any drive or directory, without needing to know where it's located or defining its DOS path — all with one key-stroke. When you exit one of these files or programs, you are automatically returned to the menu. Menus are a great way of limiting other users to specific programs or files in your system where they can do no harm!

ARGA-MENU can hold up to 90 menu selections, organized as nine pages with 10 entries on each page. Menus in different directories can be "chained" to each other for greater flexibility. The program guides you through installation and updating, with all menu entries made from the menu, without using a text editor or wordprocessor.

ARGA-COPY is a DOS shell that lets you do the most common DOS operations (copy, delete, etc.) with the direction cursor keys or a mouse. When performing housekeeping chores on a hard disk, or even floppies — such as erasing no longer needed files, moving files from one directory to another, etc. — you will quickly appreciate not having to continuously type in DOS commands and path names! A click or keystroke selects any of eight of the most useful DOS commands, and three file sort functions.

(PC-SIG Disk# 1359)

Special Requirements: *Mouse optional.*
Author Registration: *$15.00 for each program.*

Baker's Dozen
by Buttonware

This disk of utility programs, from the author of PC-File+ and PC-Calc+, is a must for anyone who owns a PC. BAKER'S DOZEN is packed with more than 13 handy utility programs to run alone or from the menu.

Some of BAKER'S DOZEN utilities: a powerful disk program to recover deleted files, a calendar that can be memory-resident, a file finder that searches strings of text, a sideways printer, a mini-spreadsheet that supports formulas, trig, business functions and hexadecimal/decimal conversion, and much more.

(PC-SIG Disk# 800)

Special Requirements: *None.*
Author Registration: *$59.95*

➤*ASP Member.*

File Descriptions:

BTTNCALC	EXE	One-page spreadsheet.
DOZEN	BAT	Batch file to run BAKER'S DOZEN.
SWLPT12	COM	Switch printer ports for LPT1 and LPT2.
SWCOM12	COM	Switch RS-232 ports for COM1 and COM2.
SNAPSHOT	COM	Take pictures of any 80-column screen (not graphics).
SET-SCRN	EXE	Used to set screen border color and default screen colors.
CALENDAR	COM	Programmable date calendar.
RDIR	EXE	Remove subdirectory including all files and all children.
PRN-FILE	EXE	Redirects all information normally sent to your printer.
PC-SORT	EXE	Sort files with up to four fields.
P90	EXE	Print files at ninety degrees (also prints normally).
LOCATE	EXE	Find any file(s) on disk.
GKEY	EXE	Provides all keyboard information.
FILECOMP	EXE	Compare two ASCII text files.
DISKUTIL	EXE	Disk utility program.
BAKERS12	EXE	Menu program to run the dozen utilities on this disk.
CAL	DAT	Data for holidays in calendar.
DOZEN	TBL	Lookup table used by menu program.
SETSCRN	COM	Sets up screen.

Best Utilities
by Lewis Haupt

The programs here are a collection of some of our most popular utilities gathered from other disks in our library. Some of the high points include: a DOS command editor that remembers your last 15 DOS commands executed, a couple of selective copy-and-delete utilities to perform mass-file functions with ease and confidence, and utilities to let you BROWSE text files in a much easier manner than your DOS TYPE command.

(PC-SIG Disk# 273)

Special Requirements: *None.*
Author Registration: *BACKSCRL $20.00, and SP $15.00.*

File Descriptions:

BACKSCRL	COM	Retrieve what has scrolled off screen top — very useful.
BROWSE	COM	Browse through text files of any size.
BACKSCRL	DOC	Documentation for BACKSCRL.COM.
MEMBRAIN	EXE	Flexible RAMdisk.
MEMBRAIN	DOC	Documentation for MEMBRAIN.EXE.
GDEL	EXE	Selective delete utility.

✍ = Updated Program
☆ = New Program

GDEL	DOC	Documentation for GDEL.EXE.
GCOPY	EXE	Selective copy — changes date to current.
GCOPY	DOC	Documentation for GCOPY.EXE.
FILEDUMP	COM	Display disk sectors on screen.
BROWSE	DOC	Documentation for BROWSE.DOC.
MOVE	COM	Flexible copy, copy-and-erase utility with prompts.
NDOSEDIT	COM	DOS line editor, adapted from VMS.
MOVE	DOC	Documentation for MOVE.COM.
SP	DOC	Documentation for SP.EXE.
SDIR24C	DOC	Documentation for SDIR24C.COM.
SDIR24C	COM	Flexible screen directory display — many options.
NDOSEDIT	DOC	Documentation for NDOSEDIT.COM.
SP	EXE	Super spooler program — variable size.
ST	COM	Super type command — 2-way scrolling.
ST	DOC	Documentation for ST.COM.
VDEL	COM	Selective delete utility — prompts to delete each file.
WHEREIS	DOC	Documentation for WHEREIS.COM.
WHEREIS	COM	Find a file in any subdirectory.

Circle Software Utilities
by Circle Software

CIRCLE SOFTWARE is a DOS-level command shell with loads of utilities to help you get more from your PC.

Menus include:

❏ PMENU a comprehensive DOS level menu system

❏ ADVANCED BATCH MENU SYSTEM a point and shoot menu with help areas for each menu item

❏ ADVANCED MENU SYSTEM runs in BATCH or memory resident mode, help windows and multiple help pages

Utilities include:

❏ ATS change or read file attributes

❏ CDD change drive and directory with one command

❏ CHKFILE runs DOS CHKDSK to fix unlinked clusters, views and deletes or saves found files

❏ CLRCRT clears the crt, prevents burn in

❏ CLRPRT clears printer, advances paper

❏ COUNT counts words in ASCII files

❏ DELE deletes all files except the ones specified to be retained by date, filename, or file extension

❏ DSD delete subdirectory

❏ DSPTXT displays text in a file, can also show parts of a file

❏ DT set, reset a file's date and time

❏ EOF places DOS EOF character at the end of a file

❏ FE adds Circle Software searches to any other program

❏ FIND_ finds lines that have the searched for string and prints them

❏ FINDA (a combination of FINDF and PFIND) locates files by string within the name and then checks for string within the file

❏ FINDF finds character strings located anywhere in the file name

❏ FK changes keyboard delay and repetition rates

❏ LOG logs date and time, password protected

❏ MODE80 switches screen to 80-column color mode

❏ PCOMP compares files using partial file names, and/or dates

❏ PCOPY copies files using partial file names, and/or dates

❏ PFIND finds information between special markers

❏ PPRINT prints ASCII files with a header, addresses envelopes

❏ PRTCODE sends special user specified print codes to the printer

❏ PRTLBL prints address labels found using PFIND

❏ PSND sounds a speaker tone

❏ PSORT sorts blocks of data

❏ RUN_IT finds a program in any directory and runs it (path not needed).

Help files for each menu and command are presented on the screen in a window next to the command menu. The user can also create his/her own help files that show in the same way.

PURSUIT, a survey maker, is also included. The program allows the user to construct a set of questions and store the answers in a database for later analysis.

(PC-SIG Disk# 1331)

Special Requirements: *Hard drive and a printer.*
Author Registration: *$15.00 to $30.00.*

Dabutil ✐   *by Simian Id Software*

DABUTIL offers hard disk users a half-dozen valuable utilities to help them maintain their files and disks. A list directory command lists directories on any drive showing the number of files and the sum of their file sizes including hidden files. The find file utility lists all the occurrences of a file and the directories in which it is found. Disk information lists a variety of information about diskettes and fixed disks. It shows sector size, track size, cluster size, FAT, and root directory.

(PC-SIG Disk# 2625)

Special Requirements: *Hard drive.*
Author Registration: *$10.00*

Diredit ✐   *by Peter R. Fletcher*

Edit your DOS directories. DIREDIT helps you to sort your directories in various ways — by filename, extension, size, etc. Specify arbitrary order and move individual directory entries. Display each directory in a very compact manner with up to eighty filenames visible on the screen at once. Need more information? You can see the full file description for any entry simply by moving the cursor to the name.

Use DIREDIT to arrange your directories on disk for more efficient access. Resort them temporarily on the screen while searching for a file, all without disturbing the directory structures on disk.

(PC-SIG Disk# 908)

Special Requirements: *None.*
Author Registration: *$20.00*
➤*ASP Member.*

DIRUTILS   *by Advocate Enterprises, Ltd.*

Here is a collection of directory-related programs that will excite you. ADVOCATE SCOUT is a "file finder" with features such as simultaneous multiple searches and path-specific searching. Now you can find files if you know virtually anything about them — any part of the name, something like it, or just its approximate date. Comes complete with batch files to automate your most frequent searches. For example, simply type "TODAY" for all of today's files.

ADVOCATE DIR masquerades as a typical, modern DIR replacement, but when you want to compare several directories or sets of files, up to four can be displayed side by side as easily as one.

ADVOCATE TREE is the useful TREE replacement you've waited for. Far more informative than TREE, it includes size of directory and percentage of the drive it occupies, and operates at twice the speed.

CDX is a fast way to change directories with a single command. It also changes simultaneously drives and directories with one three-stroke command. All utilities work great within menus, but they're especially powerful for the command-line user.

(PC-SIG Disk# 1853)

Special Requirements: *None.*
Author Registration: *$30.00*

Disk Utilities ✐   *by Ulrich Feldmuller*

Disk utilites to easily copy and format disks.
❑ QFORMAT — Quickly format and verify disks in one or more drives. Supports 5 1/4 and 3 1/2, 180k, 360k, 720k, and 1.4meg drives.
❑ QCOPY — A very fast disk copy program which loads to disks in the sequence you specify, knows what formats to use and will do so from a command line or during the running of the program.

(PC-SIG Disk# 1914)

Special Requirements: *Hard drive or RAM disk.*
Author Registration: *$15.00*

☆ = New Program

Disk Wiz
by Computer Creations

DISK WIZ is a disk file manager, editor, and printer control center that pops up like magic at the DOS prompt or within running programs to provide an easy and convenient way to work with your computer. It is much easier and faster than DOS commands and provides many functions DOS doesn't, and is as simple to use as possible.

DISK WIZ displays up to 100 alphabetized file and subdirectory names at a time, including hidden ones, and basic disk information. Selecting files or switching directories is as easy as moving the highlight bar to the name and pressing "Enter" — no typing of names! Files may be selected in groups matching a pattern (i.e., ".BAK") or directories displayed with standard DOS wildcard matching. Files may be viewed "raw" or processed as text files, with word and line count and line numbering if wanted. ASCII files may be edited with the simple built in editor and text files can be printed out in several formats.

DISK WIZ's printer control features let you send special codes from a user customizable menu of 20 single keystrokes for commonly used commands, such as condensed print and formfeeds or strings of commands for those used less often. DISK WIZ can swap output between two printers, LPT1 and LPT2, change the cursor shape and display all the screen colors and characters available on your computer. There is also a screen blanking feature to extend monitor life.

A marvelous feature of the program is an interactive tutorial demonstration which leads you through the use of the program with lively sound effects and graphics.

(PC-SIG Disk# 1257)

Special Requirements: *None.*
Author Registration: *$25.00*

DiskSign ✍
by Dalicom Software

Are you looking for a nifty little gimmick to customize your own shareware release or perhaps the disks you share with friends or members of your local users group? If so, get DISKSIGN.

DISKSIGN is a simple, inexpensive package that lets you place a customized message of up to three lines in length into the DOS directory. The message is displayed each time someone uses the DIR command on the disk. The special title or business name is displayed in vertical columns and outlined in borders for emphasis. Operating this package is easy and uses very little memory. One of the more clever promotional or marketing ideas to come around in a while!

(PC-SIG Disk# 1101)

Special Requirements: *None.*
Author Registration: *$20.00*

DOS Extensions
by Daryll Shatz

An interesting series of extremely flexible and useful DOS enhancements. These are not meant to replace standard DOS commands, but to add versatility and utility as powerful supersets of these commands.

Features include: multiple file names on command lines; 16 new wild cards; visual file selection; more useful file/system information; retrieval of deleted files; measurement of elapsed time of programs or commands, and directory sorting. These extensions can also be combined to create new functions or process multiple files with one command.

(PC-SIG Disk#'s 585, 586)

Special Requirements: *None.*
Author Registration: *$55.00*

File Descriptions:
The First Disk Contains:

REF	DOC	Documentation — reference manual for DOS Extensions.
LS	EXE	DOS extension — directory lister.
USER	DOC	Documentation — installation and use of extensions.

The Second Disk Contains:

ATT	EXE	view or change file attributes.
WHEREIS	EXE	file locator.
VOLM	EXE	view or change volume name.
CAT	EXE	concatenate files.
ALARM	EXE	sound a controllable tone.
INP	EXE	input data to a DOS pipe.

INFO	EXE	display disk, or memory information.
GPM	EXE	find text patterns in files.
DIRSRT	EXE	directory sorter.
CP	EXE	copy files.
CMD	EXE	execute programs, commands, .bat files.
CLK	EXE	elapse time of programs or commands.
UNIQ	EXE	duplicate text line handler.
UNDEL	EXE	retreive a deleted file.
TXLAT	EXE	character translator.
TEE	EXE	DOS pipe output controller.
STAT	EXE	statistical text file information.
SLEEP	EXE	pause command.
SELECT	EXE	visual selector.
SED	EXE	file editor.
RM	EXE	delete files.
RENM	EXE	rename files.
RENDIR	EXE	rename a subdirectory.
PRNT	EXE	output selected text lines of files.
MV	EXE	move files.
MERGE	EXE	merge text lines from multiple files.

Dos-Ez
by Lansun Chang

DOS-EZ is a package of utilities to help make using a PC a little easier. Included are some extensions of existing functions, as well as some routines that DOS forgot.

❑ NOW — Displays both current date and time at once.

❑ SOUND — Makes the speaker in your PC sing or beep.

❑ VIEW — A full screen browsing program to view a specific file. Better than the TYPE command, contents won't scroll off the screen.

❑ XDIR — XDIR provides more functions than "DIR *.* | SORT". XDIR can search files before/after/within certain dates. XDIR also sorts the screen output.

❑ DTREE — Displays the tree structure of specific pathnames or disks.

❑ XDEL — Deletes all files and files in sub-directories. In addition, XDEL try to remove all sub-directories if it is possible.

❑ RNDIR — Renames a directory.

❑ MVFILES — Moves files from one directory to another directory. Wildcard and "?" can be used in files' name which MS-DOS lacks.

❑ FDATE — Change the date and time of specific files.

❑ SWAPF — Swap file or sub-directory without using "copy" and "delete."

❑ CRYPT — A DES algorithm to encrypt/decrypt your files.

❑ WIPEOUT — Writes zero to a file(s) and deletes it, completely erasing the contents of the file.

❑ XFIND — Search files for a keyword which may contain wildcard "*" and "?". Using Kunth-Morris-Pratt non-backtracking pattern searching algorithm.

❑ FGREP — Search files for multiple keywords. Using Aho-Corasick non-backtracking pattern searching algorithm.

❑ GREP — A superset of grep, fgrep, egrep. Support OR "|" operator and all regular expression operators.

❑ FINDF — Find one or more than one files in the specific disk.

(PC-SIG Disk# 1994)

Special Requirements: *None.*

Author Registration: *$25.00*

Eddy
by John Scofield

EDDY (EDit DirectorY) lets you edit the elements of a directory entry. These are filename, date, time, and file attributes.

The program has commands to copy and move a file, as well as delete and/or destroy a file (or files). Additional commands let you view the contents of a file, and patch the data. A provision is made for viewing the directory in hex or text, as well as a "bit-stripping" feature that translates WordStar into ASCII files.

A single keystroke inserts the current date and time into any directory entry. Changes made to directory entries are not written to disk until you choose to do so. Also provided is an undo function. EDDY has extensive help, available at any time.

✍ = Updated Program
☆ = New Program

(PC-SIG Disk# 1026)
Special Requirements: *Hard disk.*
Author Registration: *$15.00*

Elftree ✍   *by Elvish Consulting*

If you want to get the most out of your computer, here's an integrated file and directory manager to help you get the job done.

Copy, move, protect, edit, print, rename, locate and hide files quickly and easily. Rename, protect, hide, locate, copy, move, make and remove directories just as easily. Sort the file display 14 ways. You have eight ways of tagging a group of files for use. ELFTREE will remember your last 15 commands and give you a convenient way to retrieve them when desired. You may also attach short notes to files in any directory.

There's an editor that can handle as many files as will fit into RAM. It will let you edit multiple files by tagging them and selecting a menu option. It has 11 storable keyboard macros for complex editing, a speedy search-and-replace, many block commands (cut, paste, copy, save, print, convert to upper, lower, proper case), and it's small!

Elftree (PC-SIG Disk# 2286)

Instruct ELFTREE to run a program for you by simply pointing to it and pressing ENTER. ELFTREE can be programmed to recognize up to 40 extensions per directory, so your applications are automatically launched with the corresponding data file. When you use ELFTREE to run a program, it will reserve less than 3K for itself, leaving you with the room to run memory-hungry programs.

(PC-SIG Disk# 2286)
Special Requirements: *Hard drive.*
Author Registration: *$35 and $50.00*
➤ *ASP Member.*

Extend-A-Name ☆   *by World Software Corporation*

Whatever programs you use, DOS filenames are a common problem. There comes a time, sooner or later, when eight characters is just not enough to properly identify your files. Wouldn't it be nice to be able to describe a file with a longer word, maybe a phrase, or even a whole sentence? Now you can, if you use EXTEND-A-NAME, the 60-character filename utility.

EXTEND-A-NAME is a memory-resident utility giving you the freedom to describe, organize, find, manage, and retrieve files in ways you never thought possible. The DOS filenames don't get changed. The descriptive filenames are stored in a hidden file linked to the real DOS filenames. When your application requests a file, the EXTEND-A-NAME window pops-up. Choose an appropriate 60-character file with a scroll bar menu.

Select one of six configurations based on the number of files in your largest subdirectory. The five conventional memory configurations range in size from 40K to 65K. The sixth configuration uses Expanded Memory (LIM 4.0) and requires only 3K of lower memory.

The program has automatic installation for the following programs:

❏ Agenda	❏ AutoCAD	❏ DisplayWrite
❏ Enable	❏ Lotus 1-2-3	❏ Sprint
❏ WordPerfect	❏ Microsoft Word	❏ Microsoft Works
❏ Multimate Adv	❏ PC Write	❏ PeachText
❏ Symphony	❏ WordStar	❏ PFS Write
❏ Q & A	❏ Quattro	❏ Samma
❏ SmartWare	❏ Volkswriter	❏ XyWrite

(PC-SIG Disk#'s 2665, 2666)
Special Requirements: *Two drives.*
Author Registration: *$30.00*

EZDO   *by Sooner Software Inc.*

EZDO (Easy Disk Operations) is a file and directory utility that gives you additional capabilities to DOS.

With EZDO, you can sort the files within the present directory, find a file in the directory, change a file's attributes and mark a group of files to perform a certain operation. You can copy, delete, rename, change directories, and make directories. The screen display can be saved to a disk file. EZDO can invoke other programs to edit, view, and print a file. A general purpose user-definable program may also be invoked on any selected file.

(PC-SIG Disk# 1176)

Special Requirements: *None.*
Author Registration: *$12.95*

FC   *by Mike Albert*

FC compares ASCII text files and lists the differences between them line by line. FC provides the following benefits:

❑ shows word by word differences between lines that have changed.
❑ helps "C" programmers merge program changes. FC can compare two "C" programs containing separate sets of changes, and combine them automatically to make a single program.
❑ lets you do multiple comparisons in one run. Wildcards can be used to specify groups of files to compare.
❑ can ignore white space changes. This is useful when you want to ignore format changes in "C" programs or other text.
❑ never gets confused or "unsynchronized" (as some comparison programs can).
❑ always finds the smallest set of differences between files, and never misses matching lines.
❑ lets you list changes in ways that make sense to you by providing multiple display options. You can also customize FC to use your favorite options automatically.
❑ The difference listing can be put in a third output file, or displayed on the screen. Output to the screen can be controlled interactively; e.g.; show next screen, show next line, scroll continuously, etc.

FC works with any ASCII text file that contains up to 16,300 lines. Non-ASCII characters (e.g., line drawing characters) are handled correctly too.

(PC-SIG Disk# 1584)

Special Requirements: *None.*
Author Registration: *$25.00*

FCDOC   *by Mike Albert*

FCDOC is a file comparison utility that compares English documents and lists the differences between them, sentence by sentence. The program lists the changes applied to the first file to make the second file. The output listing can be put in a third output file, or displayed on the screen. Output to the screen can be controlled interactively; e.g., show next screen, show next line, scroll continuously, etc.

FCDOC works with any file that contains up to 16,300 sentences of ASCII English text. FCDOC ignores non-printable characters and white space when comparing sentences, so only differences in the content of the document are shown.

FCDOC always find a minimal list of differences (smallest number of lines or sentences deleted or added), and never misses matching sentences.

(PC-SIG Disk# 1584)

Special Requirements: *None.*
Author Registration: *$25.00*

File Patch   *by Morsoft*

FILE PATCH is a utility program designed for use by computer consultants, technicians, information centers, software developers and those individuals who "tinker" with files. It provides the ability, at the byte level, for on-screen viewing, dumping to the printer, modifying, extracting or creating any data or program file up to 10 megabytes in length.

When displayed on the screen each character within a file is shown along with its corresponding ASCII or Hex value. The screen may be scrolled one line at a time up or down, may be paged a screen at a time, or repositioning may be performed at any point within the file. Also, the file may be scanned for a specific occurrence of a string of values and the file will be automatically repositioned at the point where the values are found.

If a file is dumped to the printer all or only portions of the file contents may be printed and the values will be shown in either ASCII or HEX and optionally the corresponding characters may be displayed. The values in any file may be modified or new values appended to the end of the file in either character, ASCII or HEX. Any of the 256 ASCII or HEX values may be used. Values may not be inserted or deleted. All or portions of a file may be extracted to a new file or appended to the end of an existing file.

(PC-SIG Disk# 1945)
Special Requirements: *None.*
Author Registration: *$14.95*
➤*ASP Member.*

FILE/ARCHIVE ✍   *by Marcor Enterprises*

At last, a self-activating utility for analyzing and archiving files on a hard disk. Using criteria set by the user, the system looks for files which may no longer be active and offers the user the opportunity to either remove them completely or archive (move) them from their current location. Technically a hard disk is not required, but the system's value is in its ability to scan large amounts of data and automatically select data needing attention.

To use the system, pre-select directories to be periodically analyzed. A master configuration record tells FILE/ARCHIVE how often to look at directory entries to see whether they should be analyzed. By including the proper command in the AUTOEXEC.BAT file, the system can be made totally automatic. The only thing it will not do automatically is actually archive files — it merely presents the files that meet the selection criteria in a menu and asks if you would like to archive or delete any of them. Any files that are selected are then moved to a designated archive location, usually a floppy disk.

Customize several parameters such as a variety of default values, specify whether to include system or hidden files in the analysis (although it won't allow you to archive such files as long as they have those attributes), specify whether or not to use DOS' Write Verify feature, assign your own function keys, and more.

(PC-SIG Disk# 2287)
Special Requirements: *Hard drive recommended.*
Author Registration: *$50.00*

FileNotes ✍   *by RSE Inc.*

PC-DIRECTORY is PC-FileNote's big brother. A powerful file manager with advanced file management capabilities to help you remember what's in your files, PC-DIRECTORY lets you attach 160-character pop-up notes to file names. Disk management functions include one-touch menu commands to view files, rename, tag copy, tag delete, and tag move files. Other functions include search for file, search for text, search for FileNote, change file or directory attributes, tree listing of directories, change drives, print files, catalog floppies, and much more. PC-DIRECTORY is fast and includes both a TSR (33K) and non-TSR version.

(PC-SIG Disk# 2391)
Special Requirements: *None.*
Author Registration: *$25*

Find Duplicates   *by John Bean*

FIND DUPLICATES will search a specified hard drive and all subdirectories and locate all duplicate files. Once the duplicate files are located they are displayed on the screen. Files can be tagged for deletion, viewed, printed or deleted. This program is very easy to use and the documentation is excellent.

(PC-SIG Disk# 2029)
Special Requirements: *Hard drive.*
Author Registration: *$10.00*

FindFile   *by S.K. Data Inc.*

FINDFILE searches all your drives and subdirectories for a particular filename, then displays all its locations on-screen. You can interrupt the search at any time by pressing the ESC key. FINDFILE lets you use wild card characters when entering the filename.

(PC-SIG Disk# 1425)
Special Requirements: *None.*
Author Registration: *$15.00*

Findzz
by Aeius Corporation

FINDZZ locates misplaced files in the blink of an eye! Use wildcard characters to find files created at specified dates and times. FINDZZ is much faster than DOS because FINDZZ creates a disk index which allows for speedy access of up to 300 subdirectories.

FINDZZ consists of four easy to use screens: "find files;" "found files"; "selected file"; and "configuration file." Indicate search criteria in the "find files" screen, then see the list of files found in the "Files Found" screen. Highlight one of the found files, press return and the "selected file" screen allows you to edit this file using your text editor. Up to eight of your programs can be added to the "selected file" screen program menu. FINDZZ is convenient, and it's a great time saver for any hard disk owner!

(PC-SIG Disk# 2052)

Special Requirements: *None.*
Author Registration: *$19.00*

FreePack
by Stilwell Software Products

FREE PACK is a collection of six utilities which make any DOS user's life easier. Full screens, prompts and pop-up help screens make these utilities valuable additions to your utility library.

❏ COMPARE — Compares two files and shows exactly what the differences are.
❏ COPYF — Saves processing time by copying only files which have been changed or are not on the target disk. If files won't fit on disk, it prompts you for another disk.
❏ FP — Optional menu to run FREE PACK utilities. Displays descriptions of each utility. Great when using FREE PACK for the first time!
❏ MENU — Handy, easy-to-use hard disk menu program. Password protection.
❏ SHELL — Beats the DOS DIR command by a mile! Displays file listings. Options to tag files for delete, copy, move, print, rename, view or execution.
❏ VIEW — Displays ASCII text files to your screen. Options to scroll through text by line or by page.
❏ WHERE-IS — Searches all directories to find requested files. Can redirect to printer.

(PC-SIG Disk# 1727)

Special Requirements: *None.*
Author Registration: *$39.00*

Fugue Utilities
by Fugue Software

FUGUE UTILITIES is a package of useful file management utilities that are missing from MS-DOS: INFO, CAT, TELL, DIR, FI, CHD, EXCLUDE, ASK, YES, WHEREIS, FILTER, and XQT.

INFO lets you integrate descriptions of files (up to 66 chars) right into the directory listing. Descriptions you enter are stored in a file called INFO.DIR, in the directory where the files reside. When the program is run, the directory is displayed with each file's descriptive text. The list permits menu-like selection to run a file or edit its special narrative text. No more running or editing a file just to know what it's for.

CAT prints floppy diskette covers on EPSON compatible printers in compressed mode. A disk title is printed with available disk space, volume name, and all the filenames and sizes on the diskette. There are four columns of output and the files are grouped by directory. Note that these are diskette covers, not labels, so much more space is used.

TELL is a context sensitive help program for DOS. Put away your DOS manuals because DOS help is only a keystroke away. The help is invoked from the command line and gives a brief summary of DOS commands and utility programs (format, assign, etc). This is helpful if you have forgotten the order of the DOS chmod parameters and don't feel like digging through the reference manual.

DIR is half DOS shell and half menu system for running programs or batch files and changing directories. Activating DIR generates a menu of batch files, executable programs and directory names for the current directory. Depending on the item selected DIR will change the current directory or run a selected program, pausing to accept any command line parameters. All valid keystrokes are displayed at the bottom of the screen and there is online help. DIR is perfect for the novice user who just wants to run programs and is confused by the MS-DOS directory structure.

FI displays a browse list of files and allows the addition of descriptions to files in full screen mode. Press Return to edit the description of the highlighted file. The descriptions are stored in file FILEINFO.WF in the directory being browsed.

CHD changes to the directory starting with the letters typed for its first parameter, or goes to full screen mode and displays all directories for you to select. It saves the directory in a file CHD.DIR for quick start.

You can create new directories, delete them, or set them to be hidden from DOS commands, or Unhide them, or even rename them from the full screen mode.

EXCLUDE is used to exclude files from DOS commands.

ASK accepts a character from the keyboard and sets ERRORLEVEL accordingly.

YES accepts Y or N from the keyboard and sets the ERRORLEVEL accordingly.

WHEREIS searches your disk for a file matching the file specs.

FILTER filters an input file to produce an output file.

XQT calls batch files from within batch files.

(PC-SIG Disk# 1634)

Special Requirements: *Some utilities require Epson compatible printer.*
Author Registration: *$15.00*

Fugue Utilities #2 *by Fugue Software*

For those who program lots of batch commands, FUGUE UTILITIES #2 brings a disk full of helpful tools including a file editor and a memory resident DOS handler. This assemblage of eleven programs will make your programming day easier.

❑ ACCEPT takes a string as a parameter and appends the accepted information to the end of a string for display or redirection.

❑ ASK is similar to ACCEPT but is more suited to building a menu system from batching.

❑ YESNO is similar to ASK except it accepts only the letters Y, y, N, or n.

❑ BEEP emits a half second beep to alert you when a long job is finished.

❑ EDITENV helps set an environment variable from a batch file.

❑ XQT lets you run nests of batch files within other batch files.

❑ EXCLUDE will exclude a list of files from any command by setting hidden bits.

❑ RENAMED changes the name of a directory without the need to move files out of it, delete it and set it up again under a new name.

❑ SYSDATE remembers the last date you booted and is for those without battery-backed clocks.

❑ DOSH is a memory resident DOS handler that keeps a circular queue of commands and makes them available via arrow commands.

❑ ED is a simple editor with WordStar-like commands which handles ASCII files up to 64K with one window.

(PC-SIG Disk# 1755)

Special Requirements: *None.*
Author Registration: *$25.00*

FX - File eXaminer ✍ *by William Noble*

This program can be used by the novice to view any file, or by more experienced users to decipher, analyze, and understand file formats.

FX is a "byte-level" word processor. Scroll through any DOS file, (even damaged files). Request that the display be formatted in any of seven ways (any mix of ASCII, hexadecimal or decimal).

An important, and unique, feature is the "Numeric Display" that appears at the top center of the screen. Many database and word processing files contain integers and long integers in the file to indicate the number of records, offsets of certain information in the file, etc. FX continuously displays this information (the values of the byte, integer and long integer) in decimal, hexadecimal or binary, in both signed and unsigned forms. Without this feature, it can be tiresome to calculate this by hand, since the bytes are physically stored in reverse order.

Any possible series of file bytes can be located, counted or modified using FX, including ASCII 0.

FX has the built-in ability to automatically optimize its formatting parameters for dBASE database files, creating a binary "browse" for both the header AND data areas.

(PC-SIG Disk# 2249)

Special Requirements: *DOS 3.0 or above.*
Author Registration: *$30.00*

GetFile
by Tarbex Software

If you've ever experienced the frustration of looking for a rarely-used file on a crowded disk, you will appreciate this utility. GETFILE will immediately find a file on a disk drive, even if it is hidden!

Tell GETFILE the drive and filename and it will search all directories and subdirectories until it is found... and then switch you to that subdirectory! OK, so it's been a long time and you're not sure what the filename is. GETFILE can deal with wildcards. Get as close as you can to the vaguely remembered name and it will offer you a list of those files that match your request, and the subdirectory path to find them.

GETFILE is especially useful for finding files on a hard disk.

(PC-SIG Disk# 1503)

Special Requirements: *None.*
Author Registration: *$15.00*

Grep
by Bruce P. Douglass,PhD

GREP UTILITIES overcomes the limitations of the DOS wildcard expressions in matching files. They provide more power and flexibility with UNIX-like file searches, moves, and copies not possible with normal DOS. No longer are you limited to wildcards * and ?, now any number of letter and number combinations can be specified with ranges to search.

Here are examples of GREP wildcard expressions: "A[0-9]+Z" matches all files starting with an "A", followed by a string of one or more digits, and then a "Z", such as A0Z.PAS, or A99Z.MAP. You can also do "negative searches" such as finding all files that don't start with the letter "A."

Organizing files is made easier with GREP commands that search files using GREP wildcard expressions: "Grep Delete" uses a regular expression to select files for deletion. "Grep Grep" searches specified files for a text string. "Grep Move" is similar to Grep Copy, except that if the files are on the same drive, the file is not copied, but its directory entry is modified so that it is moved to the new subdirectory. "Grep Whereis" uses a regular expression to search for matching files in all subdirectories of the specified drive, or all drives. It includes an option to delete the files as they are matched. The GREP UTILITIES always prompt the user before overwriting or deleting an existing file, unless directed not to do so. Bundled with GREP UTILITIES are environment and path editors, and "Which.exe," a program that identifies executable files in the path.

(PC-SIG Disk# 1929)

Special Requirements: *None.*
Author Registration: *$25.00*

Handy Dandy Utilities
by Compu-teck

HANDY DANDY UTILITIES offers you a no-fuss alternative to learning complicated utility programs or frustrating DOS commands. This easy to learn set of file management utilities offers an uncomplicated approach to commonly used batch file and DOS commands.

❑ MOV — Moves files between subdirectories. A command DOS has long been lacking.
❑ CSR — Hides and unhides the cursor. Useful in batch file creation.
❑ SEEMORE — Displays text files to screen a page at a time.
❑ DIRTREE — Displays a diagram of your directory structure. Move cursor through diagram to select a directory to change to. Press return and you are automatically placed in that directory.
❑ FF — Causes printer to formfeed. Use in batch files or just to save trips to the printer.
❑ BOOT — Warm boots your computer. Convenient in batch file creation.
❑ CHOOSE — Allows multiple user choices in batch files.

(PC-SIG Disk# 1834)

Special Requirements: *None.*
Author Registration: *$25.00*

Hyde
by Dalicom Software

Protect your data — HYDE allows you to hide/unhide files. When you hide a file, it won't be accessible by DOS until you use the unhide program.

(PC-SIG Disk# 877)

Special Requirements: *None.*
Author Registration: *$15.00*

The HYPE Utilities ☆   *by Hyperkinetix*

Utility programs are a must for today's computer users.

Use THE HYPE UTILITIES to search entire disks for a particular file, display the free space on a disk, or even add a directory to your path. One very nice thing about these small utilities is that if you run the program with no parameters, a Help screen will appear explaining the format, what the program does, what it's intended for, and giving some examples.

THE HYPE UTILITIES are:

❏ ALL2DAY.EXE — Display all of the files created today
❏ APATH.COM — Add or remove a directory from your path. It will NOT change your AUTOEXEC.BAT
❏ BEEP.COM — Nothing fancy to this one, it just beeps
❏ DIRS.EXE — Display all of the subdirectories in current directory, (similar to DOS's DIR)
❏ FF.EXE — A handy file finder. Quickly search through a drive volume for that file you can't seem to find
❏ FREE.COM — Display available disk space, total disk space, and disk space in use on a specified drive
❏ MEM.COM — Display the amount of free DOS and EMS memory
❏ RESTPATH.COM — Change to a directory whose name was saved in a file with SAVEPATH.COM (Allows batch files to "remember" one or more directories)
❏ SAVEPATH.COM — Save the current directory for later use by RESTPATH.COM
❏ SHOWTIME.COM — Display the current time, day, month, date, and year.
❏ TIMER.EXE — Time program execution. For those who want to know how fast programs run
❏ TODAY.EXE — Display all files created today in a specified directory

The best thing about THE HYPE UTILITIES is that they are free.

(PC-SIG Disk# 2572)

Special Requirements: *None.*
Author Registration: *None.*

KYM-Disk Utility   *by Dirk Heydtmann*

KYM-DISK is a collection of utilities, including a copy program, a directory deleter, a file mover, a hard disk access time checker, and a program to display DOS's internal disk parameter table. Source files (Turbo 2.0) are included.

❏ MOVE enables you to move files and subdirectories from one directory to another. It does not copy physically, but rearranges the disk directory tree structure in a suitable manner.
❏ YCOPY, a DOS XCOPY-like copy utility, with which files and whole directory structures can be copied.
❏ KILLDIR erases a directory and its complete contents.
❏ HD-SPEED measures your hard disk's average cylinder access time.
❏ DISKPARA displays DOS' internal disk parameter table.

(PC-SIG Disk# 1904)

Special Requirements: *None.*
Author Registration: *None.*
➤*ASP Member.*

Leoce ToolKit ✍   *by Computer Sciences Corp*

Bring UNIX functionality to MS-DOS with the LEOCE TOOLKIT, a collection of utilities complete with textbook quality C source code that beginner programmers will find highly useful.

❏ DLT.COM — Routine to permit deleting of multiple files without wildcards (like UNIX RM command).
❏ ENTAB.COM — Converts spaces in files to tabs according to options specified or default processing using 8 spaces per tab.
❏ HEAD.COM — The UNIX HEAD command reads a number of lines (20 default) from the start of a file and writes them to the screen.
❏ MERGE.COM — Routine will read the .A output from the Turbo C compiler and read the .C source, and merge the two. This is useful to see how the compiler has translated individual code segments.
❏ PR.COM — The UNIX PR function generates formatted print files with carriage returns to a file or the printer.
❏ SIZEOF.COM — The UNIX SIZEOF routine counts the number of bytes in a file.

❏ STGMAP.COM — Traces through memory reporting the names and sizes of hooked vectors for all active load modules in memory. This is useful to determine if virus programs or renegade TSR programs are present.

❏ TAIL.COM — The UNIX TAIL function reads n (20 default) lines from the bottom of a file onto the screen.

❏ TEE.COM — The UNIX TEE function will copy a file both to the screen and to a designated file (with optional redirection for input an output). This is commonly called a FILTER function.

❏ TP.COM — Routine to replace the DOS TYPE command. This function will type a file onto the screen. There are a number of options supported to control output, such as tp/p file file file... files are output one group at a time followed by the " -More- " prompt.

❏ WILD.C = C Source for supporting file wildcard processing in a C program.

❏ CMDLINE.C — C source for supporting command line switch processing.

(PC-SIG Disk# 1533)

Special Requirements: *None.*
Author Registration: *None.*

LightWave Utility Disk *by Lightwave*

LIGHTWAVE UTILITIES is a large collection of useful programs; some are quite uncommon. WHERE looks in all the directories of a specified drive and reports where a filename occurs. LS and DR both give sorted directories listed in column form, but DR also includes file size information.

The other seven utilities are in BASIC, and they include the source code. They will:

❏ Show you all the screen attributes of your screen
❏ Show you all the screen characters
❏ Find all the active memory in your PC
❏ Tell you when your BIOS chip was designed
❏ Tell you when your BASIC chip was designed
❏ Show you the keyboard status bits
❏ Perform percent-change calculations from one month to the next.

(PC-SIG Disk# 736)

Special Requirements: *A version of BASIC.*
Author Registration: *$20.00*

ListBack and LstBack2 *by Gary R. Pannone*

LISTBACK is a hard disk utility that lists all the files and directories stored on a backup disk that was created using the DOS 3.3 BACKUP command. LSTBACK2 will do the same for backup disks created using DOS 2.0 to 3.2. If you do not know the backup disk number, LISTBACK displays it. If the backup disk is not the last one, LISTBACK will prompt you to insert the next disk. For each file listed you may optionally have the program display the full path specification the file was copied from.

(PC-SIG Disk# 1994)

Special Requirements: *None.*
Author Registration: *$10.00*

MASDIR ✍ *by Monterey Bay Disk Data Systems*

MASDIR takes the fumbling out of dealing with directories. You can display and sort your files alphabetically by name or by extension or size or date. You can display your files on two, four or six columns, allowing you to view up to 126 files on a single screen. Change the display with a single keystroke without returning to DOS. Page backward or forward through long listings. You can also print disk labels in small and tiny type faces and three lines of titles on disk sleeves. Create files of directory listings for cataloging. On-line help screens, a tutorial, demo, and the documentation make it easy to use. A setup program permits customizing all the features of this versatile program.

The disk also contains a public domain batch file enhancer and a utility to allow you to automatically use the pause command when browsing through ASCII files.

(PC-SIG Disk# 1876)

Special Requirements: *None.*
Author Registration: *$19.00*

✍ = Updated Program
☆ = New Program

Match-Maker
by Chris Williams

If you need to find duplicate files on you hard disk then MATCH-MAKER is for you. It locates duplicate files across as many drives as you specify and, if you wish, MATCH-MAKER will delete them for you. This may yield more space on your hard disk.

One unique feature of MATCH-MAKER is the use of match attributes. Files can be considered duplicates if they match on one or more of several attributes — file name, file size, file's time, and file's date. Select the match attributes before starting the search for duplicate files. Once you designate the drive or drives of your choice, MATCH-MAKER will perform an exhaustive search of all directories and produce a list of duplicate files.

MATCH-MAKER offers four distinct delete options. You can simply view (or print) the duplicate file list, selectively delete files from the list, delete one of the duplicate files or delete both of the duplicate files.

MATCH-MAKER provides a disk storage option to free up RAM in the event that the list of duplicate files is too large. It also has a file tolerance feature which lets you match two files that differ by a couple of bytes in size.

Let MATCH-MAKER do your hard disk housekeeping chores for you.

(PC-SIG Disk# 1791)

Special Requirements: *None.*
Author Registration: *Appropriate amount.*

Memos&More, The File Companion ☆
by JCK Enterprises

MEMOS&MORE, THE FILE COMPANION is a user productivity shell which provides file management, task documentation, file launching and file editing under one easy-to-use interface. It is designed to help get a handle on the ever-growing number of files generated by most computer users.

MEMOS&MORE provides such features as attaching up to 500 lines of user defined text for each directory entry, launch files into applications, QuickView into another drive/directory, store keystrokes to often-used applications in up to 26 hotkeys, edit files with your own editor, and find a file anywhere on a drive.

MEMOS&MORE can be used by both experienced and novice PC users. The experienced user will appreciate the memo feature to record notes on work-in-process and the hotkey to store tedious series' of keystrokes to run applications or perform other operations. The novice can use the memos as mini online manuals to become familiar with the available applications. (This can be a great time saver for PC Managers.) Everyone in between will find that having Help notes right with the files is a great memory jogger while the file launcher brings a file into an application in one keystroke.

MEMOS&MORE is not a DOS shell. It is a productivity shell to help you get your job done. It is designed to be the center of user interaction — a basic tool to make PC usage easier for all types of users.

(PC-SIG Disk# 2569)

Special Requirements: *370K RAM*
Author Registration: *$40.00*

MultiBak
by Gilbert Shapiro

MULTIBAK makes computer tasks requiring multiple file changes less frustrating and safer from disaster. Many programs, such as wordprocessors, database managers, and spreadsheets, provide for a single generation of backup, usually renaming the old version of "filename.ext" to "filename.bak" before writing a new "filename.ext" to disk. When a new revision is again saved, the old version again becomes "filename.bak," wiping out the backup file saved earlier.

But what if we change our minds about a major revision and need to return the document or spreadsheet to its state several generations earlier? Or if we later discover a major error and the loss of earlier versions could seriously set our work back? MULTIBAK allows for creation of backups whenever significant changes are made, accumulating them until a final version is completed and verified. MULTIBAK allows sequential creation of up to 99 backup versions of a file. These backup files can be conveniently erased later using the PURGE program.

(PC-SIG Disk# 2052)

Special Requirements: *None.*
Author Registration: *$20.00*

Nabbit ✍ *by RSE Inc.*

NABBIT lets you "nab" information from your screen and send it to your printer to print envelopes, labels, or do selective screen dumps. Store the information in a buffer and redirect it through the keyboard at a later time. Insert information into another application as though you typed it yourself. Transferring information between programs is a breeze.

The program is a very small TSR (2K) that's easy to learn and to use! The longer you use it, the more uses you'll discover and it won't be long before you'll wonder how you got by without it!

(PC-SIG Disk# 2391)

Special Requirements: *None.*
Author Registration: *$10*

PC-Directory ✍ *by RSE Inc.*

PC-DIRECTORY is PC-FileNote's big brother. A powerful file manager with advanced file management capabilities to help you remember what's in your files. PC-DIRECTORY lets you attach 160 character "pop-up" notes to your file names. Disk management functions include one-touch menu commands to view files, rename, tag copy, tag delete, and tag move files. Other functions include search for file, search for text, search for FileNote, change file or directory attributes, tree listing of directories, change drives, print files, catalog floppies, and much more.

PC-DIRECTORY is very fast and includes both a TSR (33K) and non-TSR version. Even if you have a file manager that you're comfortable with, you still owe it to yourself to check out PC-DIRECTORY.

(PC-SIG Disk# 2391)

Special Requirements: *None. Hard drive recommended.*
Author Registration: *$48.00*

PC-Util *by Abacus Computer Service*

PC-UTIL is an archived cornucopia of utility programs that can save programmers and serious computer users thousands of hours.

It includes:

❑ CAT — Concatenate files
❑ FILES — Extract a list of files from a disk
❑ PINDEX — Print a disk file index
❑ SEE — Display files containing nonprintable characters and make modifications to create a file usable by most text editors
❑ MLABEL — Print labels in five different character sizes and pitches. Automatically incremented serial numbers of up to 9 characters can be included on each label
❑ LPR — Print ASCII files with page headings, numbers, and more
❑ BSAVE — Save a byte image of the screen buffer
❑ BLOAD — Write a saved image back to the screen buffer
❑ CP — Copy, move, or delete files individually or in tagged groups for directory listings sorted by name, extension, size or date
❑ DR — Integrated file management facilities for sorting, renaming, deleting, and moving files to another directory
❑ KEYPRESS — Branch in a batch file to select and execute user options
❑ REPEATS - Search all drive subdirectories and list filename duplications with their directories
❑ RN — Create, remove, rename, hide and unhide files, and change directories. Set and reset read-only and archive bits in all files within a directory. Report file count and space allocated
❑ SWEEP — Cause a command to be successively executed in every subdirectory on a hard disk
❑ MENU — Modify batch files so each program will run without the user needing to remember where it and its related files are located
❑ M_MS-DOS — A mouse pop-up menu
❑ WHEREIS — Search for specified files through all directories and list matching files with their directories and subdirectories
❑ FINDEX — Generate an alphabetical list of hard and floppy disk files

✍ = Updated Program
☆ = New Program

❑ ECHO2 — Control screen display attributes such as bold, underline, blink, reverse video, color and cursor position by generating ANSI escape sequences

❑ BRACE — Display C source programs for error-checking

❑ HEX — Convert numeric value and ASCII characters to various equivalent decimal, octal, hex and ASCII values

❑ BEEP — Add sound to batch files so a variety of tunes can indicate the status of batch operations

❑ EDMCAMC - An editor of WordPerfect macro files.

(PC-SIG Disk# 1751)

Special Requirements: *None.*
Author Registration: *$40.00*

Peruse: An ASCII and Binary File Reader ✍   *by Falk Data Systems*

A file viewer that does it all! Now you can quickly and easily view any sized file, ASCII text or binary. In fact you can even look at groups of files and simply page through them. Looking for a particular word or phrase? Use PERUSE'S search functions. Print the entire file you are viewing or just a portion of it.

PERUSE can be customized to your computer. It supports the 43/50 line modes on EGA/VGA, extended and expanded memory, and will run almost every command with a mouse. It can even be loaded as a memory-resident program. The next time you need to look through a lot of files, just put your feet on your desk, and let PERUSE do the work.

(PC-SIG Disk# 2537)

Special Requirements: *None.*
Author Registration: *None.*
➤*ASP Member.*

PIK ☆   *by SPELLBOUND! Software*

PIK is a useful little 32K utility which allows you to pick files from the standard DOS "DIR" display to mark for Deleting, Copying, Moving or Zipping into a Zip format compressed file.

How many times have you typed "DIR" to examine the contents of a directory and seen several files which should be moved, deleted, or stored for later use in ZIP format. Typing the commands necessary to accomplish the task could take some time. By typing "PIK," you can select the files upon which to perform the necessary operation right from the display left behind by the "DIR" command. Once the files have been marked, you just press ENTER and you are on your way to keeping your files updated.

(PC-SIG Disk# 2650)

Special Requirements: *Hard drive.*
Author Registration: *$7.00/$15.00*

Process   *by Bill Newell*

PROCESS simplifies access to many small programs using a point-and-shoot technique. It can be started from either the DOS command line or a batch file.

(PC-SIG Disk# 1305)

Special Requirements: *None.*
Author Registration: *$20.00*

Professional Master Key ✍   *by Public Brand Software*

MASTER KEY is a powerful disk and file manipulation utility, comparable to programs like Norton Utilities.

Edit any part of any disk or file using a handy windowed hex and ASCII screen dump. Editing can be from the ASCII text or the hex dump. Menus and organization help you learn the package quickly. Many other utilities are included, such as duplicate file search, file renaming and erasing abilities, and unerasing of files mistakenly erased.

(PC-SIG Disk# 598)

Special Requirements: *None.*
Author Registration: *$35.00*
➤*ASP Member.*

Professional Master Key (PC-SIG Disk# 598)

Read My Disk! ✍

by DairySoft Custom Software

Anyone who works with ASCII-based databases, wordprocessors, or any program that stores its data in ASCII files will find this program useful. READ MY DISK! recovers ASCII data from a floppy or hard disk that has been severely damaged. This damage can be missing file allocation tables, missing directories, deleted files, magnetically-damaged disks and even disks with holes in them. In other words, if the disk will fit in your disk drive, then the damaged data can be recovered.

When READ MY DISK! recovers data, it writes the data to an undamaged formatted disk. If needed, you can specify the size of the file in case you have a wordprocessor with limits on the size of the files it can handle. You can also specify if you would like high-order bit characters saved. This helps if you have damaged a file that was saved in a format used by WordStar or any other program that uses its own characters.

READ MY DISK! works on all floppy and hard disks up to 32 megabytes in size.

(PC-SIG Disk# 1394)

Special Requirements: *Two floppy drives or one floppy drive and a hard drive.*
Author Registration: *$25.00*

Read My Disk! (PC-SIG Disk# 1394)

Read.Com ✍

by John Libertus

A fast text file reader, READ.COM pages, scrolls, and searches in ASCII files. The screen-switching option lets you prepare a table of contents for a file without direct switching to any screen. The program offers no written documentation and limited help on screen.

(PC-SIG Disk# 1687)

Special Requirements: *None.*
Author Registration: *$10.00*

SetAttr

by Tarbex Software

SETATTR makes it easy to set or change the attributes of your files.

With a single command, you can make a file normal, hidden, read only, or a system file. SETATTR saves time by supporting wild cards and directories. Change the attributes of entire blocks of files. It displays the names and new or old attributes of changed files. A help function is included. Networks are supported.

(PC-SIG Disk# 1503)

Special Requirements: *None.*
Author Registration: *$15.00*

Sorted Directory

by Fire Crystal Communications

SDR.COM provides more information than the resident DOS DIR command about the files on a disk, and lets you select, sort, format, and display the information in a variety of ways. You can specify a pattern name to select the desired files and by specifying any of a variety of command line switches. The default switch values have been carefully chosen to reflect their most common use, and for compatibility with the standard DIR command. Select files by attribute, age, or string match. Sort on any directory field. Global disk directories can be searched for files matching the specified criteria.

Use in stand-alone mode or as memory-resident. It is possible to use SD in an almost infinite variety of ways by using the switches in different combinations. Designed to be as transparent as possible in normal operation, it does not impose itself between the user and the operating system. Novices or experienced users both can profit from this utility.

(PC-SIG Disk# 933)

Special Requirements: *None.*
Author Registration: *$20.00*

✍ = Updated Program
☆ = New Program

SUP
by Anders Olsson

Another little victory in the battle against copy protection. SUP removes copy protection from most Sierra On-Line games, such as the popular KING'S QUEST and SPACE QUEST. Now, you can have a backup or install the program on your hard disk. It works only with games called up from DOS and does not handle self-booting disks.

(PC-SIG Disk# 1406)

Special Requirements: *None.*
Author Registration: *$10.00*

TechStaff Tools
by TechStaff Consultants, Inc.

This program is designed to be used in conjunction with the NORTON GUIDES, PC-BROWSE, and MicroSoft-compatible MAKE files that control the compilation of large projects. It reads the ASCII source code for any program and extract the comments which indicate the purpose, function, and expectations of the various building blocks of your program.

NG_MAKER will combine and assemble these comments in a database file compatible with the NORTON GUIDES or PC-BROWSE. Once completed, you can call up either program and review the various building blocks of the program you are working on.

(PC-SIG Disk#'s 2288, 2289)

Special Requirements: *640K RAM. Mouse and hard drive recommended for some utilities.*
Author Registration: *$29.95*

TwoDisks
by Barry L. Campbell

TWODISKS is a program for comparing and updating files on two separate disks or directories. Both directories can then be shown, and you may automatically copy or move files between the two directories. By selectively picking the individual files that are to be copied, moved or deleted, you may operate on whole groups of files at once.

When viewing the files that are on each directory, the files that are identical will be displayed on the same screen. If the files have the same name but different dates, the newer files will be displayed on the list for the directory where it is located. These files then may be copied easily or moved to the other directory being compared. Files that are not found on the other directory will be displayed on a separate list. Thus TWODISKS separates the files into three groups: those files that are identical, those files that have the same name but different dates, and those files that are completely different. TWODISKS will make it much easier to compare and update directories on both floppies and hard disks.

(PC-SIG Disk# 1636)

Special Requirements: *None.*
Author Registration: *$25.00*
➤*ASP Member.*

What
by Bill Newell

It's been three months since you used that file. You know it's in there somewhere, but where? And what the heck did you name it? If you had used WHAT, you'd be able to find it quickly.

If your filenames have lost their meaning, WHAT will make sense of them. This program maintains a listing of your files and directories and lets you attach descriptions of up to 61 characters for each. You then can use WHAT's search facility to locate that obscure file you know you have, somewhere....

(PC-SIG Disk# 1305)

Special Requirements: *None.*
Author Registration: *$15.00*

WiseDir
by Tarbex Software

WISEDIR streamlines and updates the old DOS DIR command. It shows ALL your files — including system, hidden, and read-only files — in ALL your subdirectories. Copy to the screen or print the file list of filenames with attributes, file size, and date and time of creation. WISEDIR also tells you the system date and time, and provides a summary of disk space available and used. WISEDIR can be used on networks.

(PC-SIG Disk# 1503)

Special Requirements: *None.*
Author Registration: *$15.00*

Xanadu Utilities
by Robert Woeger

XANADU UTILITIES has some very useful programs. HOTDIR, for example, is a colorful sorted directory program that displays different colors based on file extension. The directory listing can be sent to the screen, printer, or disk file. Files can be sorted by name, extension, date, size, or other criteria. It can automatically display all files: hidden, system, archive, directory, read-only, and normal.

PCSTAT3 displays disk/RAM statistics and is much more extensive and quicker than CHKDSK.

SFIND finds files quickly anywhere on the disk and then lists on the screen all the matching files. SFIND can list files found even in an archive file.

(PC-SIG Disk# 737)

Special Requirements: *None.*
Author Registration: *$25.00*

XCUTE
by Brainware Enterprises

Execute any program in any directory or subdirectory. Go immediately from application to application in different directories just by typing the name of the program — or even a partial name if you have forgotten the whole name. If there are several programs that match your partial entry, XCUTE will list each matching program individually and will ask you if that is the program you wish to execute. When using a hard disk and thousands of programs, XCUTE will do the work of finding your program and will even execute it for you.

(PC-SIG Disk# 818)

Special Requirements: *Hard disk or 1.2 meg drive, and DOS 3.10.*
Author Registration: *$20.00*

XDIR
by XD Systems

XDIR is a commented directory utility that replaces the DOS DIR command. With XDIR you can attach a descriptive comment of up to 65 characters to each file. The comment will appear in the directory display. Unlike other programs, XDIR makes sure that comments will stay with your files when you COPY, RENAME or MOVE them. Version 3.0 can RUN programs from the directory list and supports executable extensions. The run feature (e.g., XDIR /r *.exe) permits the user to select one or more entries from the directory list, and run them. The program prompts for program parameters. Also, XDIR will run other programs on files selected from the directory list. For example, XDIR /rlist *.doc would list all of the .doc files, allow the user to select from them, and then list each of the selected files. Finally, XDIR supports executable extensions. With proper setup, it will recognize the appropriate application to call for a given file extension.

A group of additional utilities is supplied to registered users. These include XDZIP and XDUNZIP, which automate inclusion of XDIR comments in PkWare ZIP files and restores them on unzipping. XDCount and XDUpdate keep track of the number of times your files have been accessed, as well as the date of last use.

(PC-SIG Disk# 2272)

Special Requirements: *None.*
Author Registration: *$25.00*
➤*ASP Member.*

XDOS
by Micro Business Application

A handy collection of DOS enhancements that will make your life a little easier.

ALARM is a RAM-resident alarm clock to remind you of those important appointments and commitments. Go ahead and work on your application. This clock will call you anyway.

CAT is similar to the DOS DIR command with some major exceptions:

❑ CAT pauses at the end of each screen of listings and waits for a prompt from you before proceeding
❑ Files in subdirectories are automatically listed — down to five levels of directories
❑ All files are displayed, including system and hidden files
❑ The display is more aesthetically pleasing than DOS

HELP is a text file that explains and expands on the use of DOS commands and syntax. Exit to DOS at any time.

LOCK lets you change two of a file's attributes — locked and hidden. Consider using this for sensitive or confidential information.

NOPRINT lets you divert data being sent to the printer and display it on your monitor. Helpful when developing and testing printed output without using a printer.

(PC-SIG Disk# 444)

Special Requirements: *None.*
Author Registration: *$10.00*

▼ ▼ ▼

Flying and Navigation

Cat System
by Building Bloc Systems

Tomorrow's airplane mechanics, CAT SYSTEM (Computer Aided Teaching System) is software to help you study for the FAA aviation mechanic written examinations which lead toward receiving the FAA Powerplant or Airframe Mechanic licenses. These tests can be tricky, so it is important to get the feel for how questions are asked on the exams. The more practice you get the better. With CAT SYSTEM, your computer administers and scores mock exams of the same questions that may appear on the actual test. Your computer gives the test, so you can concentrate on the questions. The software is easy to use, even for the computer novice.

The questions are drawn right from the the FAA "Aviation Mechanic Powerplant Question Book" FAA-T-8080-11B and the "Airframe & Powerplant Mechanics Powerplant Handbook" AC65-12A. Both are available from the FAA and other book resellers. Keep in mind that the FAA does not publish the correct answers, only the questions. CAT SYSTEM is your chance to get a working professional's insight into the best answers for these questions.

(PC-SIG Disk#'s 1681, 1680)

Special Requirements: *Hercules graphics or CGA.*
Author Registration: *$15.00*

Clearance Flight Planning System ☆
by Data-Plane Inc.

This program is all that a pilot could hope for in a pre-flight planner.

The CLEARANCE FLIGHT PLANNING SYSTEM allows a pilot to pick any starting point and destination within the U.S. and Canada and have a route displayed showing the MEA, MOA's, Victor airway, Jet airways, intersections, etc., along the route of flight.

It will:
❏ Generate a route from city to city using common names (e.g. Chicago to New York (not ORD to JFK)
❏ Once the flight plan is generated, the return flight is displayed with a single keystroke
❏ Generate a route from and including way points such as LAT-LONG co-ordinates, DME radial and distance, intersection names, and VOR-to-VOR
❏ The NavAid (navigational aid) frequencies and their LAT-LONG positions can be printed out and taken along the flight
❏ The distances between each point, its elevation, and MEA (or obstacle clearance) are also printed
❏ Up to 5000 flight plans can be stored for easy reference. Use as is or edit for any special circumstances that may arise.

CLEARANCE FLIGHT PLANNING SYSTEM, especially when linked with the WEATHER STATION (PC-SIG #2702) and WEIGHT AND BALANCE (available only through the author), will provide any pilot with the most thorough pre-flight planning imaginable.

This program is not for the novice pilot. Its best utility would be found in the higher performance, instrument-rated environment.

(PC-SIG Disk#'s 2699, 2700, 2701)

Special Requirements: *Hard drive.*
Author Registration: *$59.00*

Flight
by Patrick C. Roe

FLIGHT is a flight-planning program for private pilots.

Enter up to 20 waypoints by name and the estimated airspeed of the plane. The program matches the waypoints against data files, retrieves the latitude, longitude and magnetic variation for each point, and then calculates the magnetic course, the distance between the waypoints, and the estimated time between each set of waypoints.

The results are printed on the screen, together with the total distance and the total estimated flight time. You can then have a flight log printed. The files containing the waypoints for FLIGHT can be edited from within the program or with an ASCII wordprocessor.

(PC-SIG Disk#'s 939, 1476)

Special Requirements: *None.*
Author Registration: *None.*

Flight Plan System
by Charles L. Pack

Whether you fly a prop plane or a jet, FLIGHT PLAN SYSTEM lets you create a printed flight log with up to 1,023 route entries. Each entry includes a location identifier, name, latitude, longitude, magnetic variation, and site elevation. Information on locations can be added, but the program includes this information on most VORS and major airports in the 48 United States.

FLIGHT PLAN SYSTEM lets you save different routes for the same trip. Then the route can be used over and over with minimal changes.

By entering performance parameters for your aircraft, your flight plan can include minimum fuel burn, minimum flight time, and optimum flight altitude. An added feature lets you try "what-ifs" by experimenting with winds aloft, aircraft performance, and other factors. Complete documentation and lots of help screens make this program easy to use.

(PC-SIG Disk# 2474)

Special Requirements: *None.*
Author Registration: *$25.00*

The Loran Locator
by Fundamental Services

LORAN LOCATOR is an "electronic numbers book" for those mariners who accumulate LORAN numbers for their fishing and diving hot spots. Fifteen LORAN chains around the world are supported. Using the system requires prior knowledge of the Loran C navigational system, and the author suggests that a Loran manual be kept handy to enter GRI's. The package is configured to operate in any Loran chain in the United States and most chains worldwide, and is intended to be used ONLY as a guide.

LORAN LOCATOR calculates heading and distance between any waypoint entered. Multiple data files, scratch pad function, waypoint register, and float plans are all supported.

(PC-SIG Disk# 1542)

Special Requirements: *512K RAM.*
Author Registration: *$49.95*

MARNAV ☆
by C&E Associates

Are you a private plane or boat pilot? Do you need an easy way to add LORAN-C data to charts and maps? Well, here's the software solution!

MARNAV converts LORAN delays to latitude/longitude coordinates and vice versa. Other features include a heading and distance calculator from either LORAN delays or coordinates, a handy time/speed/distance calculator, and a LORAN Chains editor. The documentation is thorough and easy to follow. A sample chain file is included; the registered version has all chains worldwide.

(PC-SIG Disk# 2758)

Special Requirements: *None.*
Author Registration: *$35.00*

Passing Passages and GS-Testit
by Gordon Griffin

Trying for your wings? GS-TESTIT will give you practice to pass the Private Pilots' written examination administered by the FAA.

Using actual FAA questions, this quiz program lets you select from several subject categories, including: the physical aircraft, navigation, airports and air traffic control, FAA regulations, the weather, and the environmental effects of aircraft. GS-TESTIT then selects 40 multiple choice questions to quiz you on, tells you instantly which questions you may have answered incorrectly, lets you review the question and try again.

Included, also, is PASSING PASSAGES, an educational game where you are lost in a maze and confronted by FAA examiners who ask you test questions which you must answer correctly in order to move on! To survive, you must also find cash, food, and places to sleep. The right side of the screen shows a graphic representation of the hallways and doors, while the left side of the screen shows a map which is made as you explore the maze. May also be played without the questions.

(PC-SIG Disk# 1362)

Special Requirements: *CGA, hard drive recommended.*
Author Registration: *$30.00.*

Pilot Log Book ☆
by Data-Plane Inc.

The PILOT LOG BOOK eliminates the need for the traditional hard cover log book. The program tracks the pilot's flying experience and gives him or her quick and easy access to any currency requirement that might be desired. In addition to providing total flying time, THE PILOT LOG BOOK will also report any currency requirement by simply giving a start and end date. For those who fly infrequently, this is a valuable function in determining pilot legality. The program has printer support and even a set of columns to track expenses, whether rental or owner related. The program will track up to 300 entries per year, which should be more than adequate to satisfy the needs of any pilot.

(PC-SIG Disk# 2703)

Special Requirements: *No special requirements.*
Author Registration: *$59.95*

Weather Station ☆
by Data-Plane Inc.

This program can be an invaluable aid to those pilots who have problems understanding and deciphering the government's computer weather program (DUAT). The WEATHER STATION will collate and print, in plain English, any forecast a pilot could want for pre-flight planning.

The WEATHER STATION, when coupled with the CLEARANCE FLIGHT PLANNING SYSTEM (#2699-#2701), will retrieve the weather and forecasts, calculate and file a flight plan, and automatically provide the pilot with an accurate, weather-corrected flight plan.

As a stand-alone program, the WEATHER STATION is fully compatible with DUAT and can be customized for just about any weather vendor. All of the significant weather prognoses can be accessed by this program in an easily-understood format.

(PC-SIG Disk# 2702)

Special Requirements: *PC-SIG #2699-#2701, hard drive, modem, & DUAT member.*
Author Registration: *$49.95*

▼ ▼ ▼

Food and Drink Preparation

CALCOUNT/ ☆
by Kenneth R. Haeusler

Dieters rejoice! Track your daily calorie consumption, weight, and blood pressure. The extensive food and calorie lists make menu planning a breeze. CALCOUNT automatically calculates calories per serving and has an extensive editing capability. Graphs and printouts are also available.

(PC-SIG Disk# 2621)

Special Requirements: *Graphics capability and printer recommended.*
Author Registration: *$19.95*

Computer Baker
by B.M.W. Programs

THE COMPUTER BAKER is a computer recipe book containing 99 recipes for homemade — made from scratch — baked goods that are very quick and easy to prepare.

THE COMPUTER BAKER is completely menu-driven and you can select recipes from six categories: snacks (brownies and pastries), fudge and candy, muffins and biscuits, cookies, cakes and frostings, and pies.

(PC-SIG Disk# 1171)

Special Requirements: *None.*
Author Registration: *$5.00*

Edna's Cook Book   *by Specialty Microware*

EDNA'S COOKBOOK is a program that will store and organize all your recipes and even provides password protection to keep your guarded family recipes secret from prying eyes.

Now, you no longer have to deal with disorganized slips of paper and clippings thrown together in a drawer or box, only to be frustrated when you can't find that particular recipe. EDNA'S COOKBOOK is a program for collecting, filing, sorting, finding and printing recipes. Essentially, it is the equivalent of the cookbook in which you now keep all your recipes, except that it is electronic. The program may also be used in the preparation of cookbooks for publication.

The screen is divided into an ingredients section and a directions section, making it simple to enter your recipes along with a selected category (such as soups), a subcategory (lentil), a name (Mama's Hearty Soup), and a source where the recipe was obtained (my mom). Categories and subcategories can be changed to suit your own preferences. Once entered, recipes may be listed or printed individually, by category, subcategory, or all at once.

EDNA'S COOKBOOK automatically sorts and arranges your recipes for you alphabetically by category, then by subcategory, and then by recipe name — making it easy to find things. You can also encrypt any recipe you wish with a password, so that certain recipes may be kept private.

(PC-SIG Disk# 1229)

Special Requirements: *None.*
Author Registration: *$29.00*

Grocery   *by Synergy Software*

Save your budget and your diet. Never go into a grocery store without a grocery list and don't deviate from it once you're in the store. Know what you need, go get it, and get out while you're still in control. How? Use GROCERY!

The marketing specialists know that if we wander around without a specific idea of what to buy, we're more likely to "impulse buy." GROCERY keeps track of grocery items bought on a regular, or irregular, basis. Items are stored in aisles, and the program will handle up to 30 aisles with 36 items in each. Duplicate the floorplan and layout of your favorite store. Once all the data is entered, you can print out the entire list or only the items that you select. The printout is quick and organized according to aisle.

A few more words of advice — never shop hungry and don't look at the aisle end-caps!

(PC-SIG Disk# 856)

Special Requirements: *None.*
Author Registration: *$10.00*

Home-Bartenders Guide ✍   *by B.M.W. Programs*

You may not learn how to juggle bottles in the air like Tom Cruise did in the movie "Cocktail," but HOME BARTENDER will teach you the secrets to mixing all those hysterical drinks you saw being happily quaffed by his patrons!

Learn how to make drinks like a professional bartender, including the Alabama Slammer, Colorado Bulldog, Fuzzy Navel, Harvey Wallbanger, Orgasm, Rusty Nail, Singapore Sling, and 142 more libation favorites.

The drinks are divided into categories which include frozen drinks, Polynesian drinks, cream drinks, non-alcoholic drinks, martinis and Manhattans, champagne and wine drinks, and coffee drinks, etc. For each drink HOME BARTENDER provides the ingredients, the directions, and what type of glass should be used. All the drinks may be selected from a system of menus, or referenced from the index.

(PC-SIG Disk# 1516)

Special Requirements: *None.*
Author Registration: *$5.00*

Master Meal Manager ✍   *by Thomas C. Johnson*

One of the toughest parts of being in charge of family meals is deciding, week after week, what you're going to cook. Another tough part is trying to remember to put all the important ingredients down on one shopping list so you can actually cook the meals. If you're rich, you avoid the whole problem and get a housekeeper. If you're smart, you get MASTER MEAL MANAGER.

MASTER MEAL MANAGER is the program that home users dreamt about when the computer industry said, "... and you can keep recipes in it, too!" Now you really can. MASTER MEAL MANAGER stores up to 500 recipes, automatically schedules up to 14 days of meals, and creates and prints a shopping list of ingredients in all the meals on your schedule.

MASTER MEAL MANAGER is easy to get along with, too. You have total control over the recipes, schedules and lists. You can print any or all of your recipes and change the number of servings they're written for. You can easily edit your shopping list before you print it so it only shows the items you need to buy rather than everything you're going to cook.

Even if normal meal planning is a breeze for you, MASTER MEAL MANAGER can prove invaluable for those special occasions when you find yourself catering a family reunion or having to plan two weeks worth of meals for a nursery school program. Whatever size family you're feeding, MASTER MEAL MANAGER can make the process almost painless.

(PC-SIG Disk# 2128)

Special Requirements: *512K RAM.*
Author Registration: *$15.00 to $25.00.*

Recipe Index System
by Bill Kirby

The RECIPE INDEX SYSTEM lets you index your recipes and then search through that index to quickly locate the names of recipes containing specific ingredients or of a certain category. It does not store the actual recipes themselves. You enter the principal ingredients of each recipe, not the steps used to create the food. The reports created by the search function do not create shopping lists or give portion size.

The RECIPE INDEX SYSTEM is completely menu-driven and fully documented. The most common use of this software is by people who have many cookbooks and food journals. They enter the name of the recipes they like, the ingredients, a source (name of book or journal) for the recipe (including page number), and category and style fields. When they use the search function to look for recipes that meet certain criteria, the source and page number information are used to find complete details about the recipe. This saves having to enter into the computer endless details that are already in the books and journals.

```
┌─────────────────────────────┐
│  RECIPE MAINTENANCE - MODIFY │
└─────────────────────────────┘

Name: Garlic bread
Book: PC-COOK          Page:   10
Code:   164         Style:      Category:      Time: 1

Ingredients:
french bread, garlic, butter
```

Do you want to edit another record ? (Y/N)
Recipe Index System (PC-SIG Disk# 1317)

Although originally designed to work with food recipes, this system can also index other concerns — like contents of drawers and storage boxes, or books and the major topics they cover. Any endeavor that can be broken into entries and subparts (like ingredients) can be indexed. You could even use it to track the contents of video tapes.

(PC-SIG Disk# 1317)

Special Requirements: *320K RAM and two floppy drives.*
Author Registration: *$30.00*

Recipes
by East Hampton Industries

Use your PC to plan weekly meals, parties and special holiday dinners. RECIPES contains over 125 recipes for delicious appetizers, soups, salads, pastas, breads and desserts. RECIPES lets you find the recipes you want in seconds. However, you will not be able to add recipes of your own to the data file. Adjust serving sizes from one to 99, and print recipes to take to the kitchen. For a bonus, you can print a shopping list to take to the store.

(PC-SIG Disk# 1210)

Special Requirements: *None.*
Author Registration: *$15.00*

▼ ▼ ▼

Form Creation Programs

EZ-Forms Executive ✍   *by EZX Publishing*

Stop trying to satisfy your information needs by using someone else's idea of the "right" form. Make documents tailored to your specific requirements to answer your special questions.

You can print forms to fill out by hand, or to fill in before printing. Spreadsheet math functions automate numerical extensions such as multiple items/per item pricing and tax computation. Merge with information from a database and automatically insert dates and times as desired. Editing functions, such as word wrap, text centering and automatic justification, help you make professional-looking forms, quickly and easily.

Useful for small businesses or organizations that need few copies or store all data electronically. Especially valuable as a forms development tool for designing and streamlining before committing to a large print run.

Features include:
- ❏ Macros (keystroke record/playback makes form fill-out a breeze)
- ❏ ASCII data file merge
- ❏ Data Export in 8 different ASCII delimited formats
- ❏ Auto date, time, increment numbering
- ❏ Chain (multi-page forms) and multi-copy printing
- ❏ Handles forms up to 248 columns by 132 lines
- ❏ Enhanced printer support includes extensive user modifiable printer attributes and embedded characters, also double/single block/shade character line drawing and any character "drag" modes
- ❏ Italics, superscript, subscript, double wide, bold, underline, etc. are supported for properly equipped printers
- ❏ Laser Printer (HP and compatibles) support includes auto font downloading, graphics emulation and custom font support
- ❏ File encryption to protect sensitive files
- ❏ File compression to save valuable disk space
- ❏ Increment number counter (different number on each form) printing
- ❏ Auto-tab/fill-in and file (makes filling out pre-printed forms a snap)
- ❏ Field markers (lock out designated areas)
- ❏ Vertical typing
- ❏ Cut and paste
- ❏ Mouse support for Logitech and Microsoft mice.
- ❏ 101+ pre-designed and user modifiable forms (Basic Forms Pack) included.
- ❏ Search Mode: Like a mini free form database.
- ❏ Support for non-USA characters like etc.
- ❏ Basic Laser Fonts now included. 10 soft fonts (which include the line drawing characters not usually available in soft fonts) for the HP-LaserJet Plus.

(PC-SIG Disk# 404)

Special Requirements: *640K RAM and a hard drive.*
Author Registration: *$129.00*

EZ-Forms First ✍   *by EZX Publishing*

Take advantage of professional forms created with the popular EZ Forms form generator. Included in EZ FORMS FIRST are 13 standard business forms that you can customize with your own business data. These forms will help you track expenses, invoice labor, take a sales order, plan a meeting, bill a customer, keep track of appointments and more.

EZ FORMS FIRST is not a custom form generator such as EZ Forms or EZ Forms Lite. Instead, the job of creating the forms has been done for you. You can jump right into customizing these forms with your own data. Print these forms and use them as masters to be filled out in ink, or fill in the forms on your computer and keep each as a computer record. And if you find these forms useful, an additional registration fee buys 50+ more business forms.

(PC-SIG Disk# 1838)

Special Requirements: *Printer.*
Author Registration: *$39.00*

       ✍ = Updated Program
                                                    ☆ = New Program

EZ-FORMS Plus   *by EZX Publishing*

EZ-FORMS LITE solves the major problem for the business which needs a multitude of forms. EZ-FORMS LITE is a powerful forms generation and management system that helps you create forms on your screen, print and store them, edit them later, and, if you choose, use your PC to fill them out. The program allows you to use your PC to fill out other pre- printed forms and lets you preview the output on your screen to prevent errors. The person who currently spends too much to get a few thousand forms from a printer will find this program financially and aesthetically appealing.

With context-sensitive help screens, the program handles any IBM compatible printer, including the 24-pin and lasers. Extra fonts are available from the author (EZX) for lasers. Color controls are excellent and forms may be sized up to 88 lines by 132 columns. When this program is used, you can be prevented from typing in the wrong part of a form. Form numbering is available and time and date can be generated at time of execution, vital ways to prevent employee theft at the order desk. You can make up all your own forms — the time needed is brief — or order disks full of additional forms from EZX and alter them to fit your needs. The program allows you to print up to 255 forms at a time. The on-disk manual gives you extensive, well-presented documentation.

Features include:

❑ Solid borders, lines, shades, combs and numerous graphics with just a few key strokes
❑ Auto-time/date/sequence numbering
❑ Block cut/paste/copy, import/export
❑ Forms up to 130 columns by 86 lines
❑ Complete printer drivers included. Supports most printers including Epson(tm)/IBM and compatible printers; also the HP-LaserJet(tm) and compatibles ("Y" cartridge; other fonts may vary — see soft font pack below). Over 90 user modifiable forms also included
❑ Bolding and underlining
❑ 90+ basic forms template/style sheet pack included.

(PC-SIG Disk# 1202)

Special Requirements: *384K RAM and a printer.*
Author Registration: *$69.00*

EZ-Forms' Database   *by EZX Publishing*

EZ-FORMS' DATABASE adds a new dimension to data management and forms processing. It is the perfect marriage of the ever popular "EZ-Forms Executive" and "EZ-InFORMa dB"! (Both included.)

Imagine being able to enter information into a database as you fill out a form! Imagine searching for a particular form by typing keystrokes, instead of laboriously searching through endless file folders! Imagine being able to generate various printed reports from a single forms' data! Imagine being able to fill in forms by retrieving information that already exists in any database! Imagine no longer...EZ-FORMS' DATABASE is here!

Simply read in your form and create a database. The data you enter will automatically be stored into your own database! And guess what? EZ-FORMS' DATABASE reads/writes files in the industry standard ".DBF" file format. So, you can easily use data that has been created by other dBase compatible programs.

Whether or not you are currently using a forms processor or database, EZ-FORMS' DATABASE is the easiest inFORMation handler ever devised.

(PC-SIG Disk#'s 2439, 2440)

Special Requirements: *640K RAM and hard drive.*
Author Registration: *$239.00*

Form Master   *by CastleSoft*

FORM MASTER is a versatile, powerful, and easy-to-use tool for creating, modifying, completing, and printing specialized forms for a home or business. Once you create a form, you can fill it in on-screen and print it, or print it and fill it out manually. If you have pre-printed forms, they can be fed into the printer and the data fills the blanks. You can export FORM MASTER forms into other software. It includes capabilities for word wrap, field justify, look-up, math operations, plus automatic date, time and form sequence number insertion.

FORM MASTER is easily configured to support most printers with features including boldface, underlining, italics, super- and subscripts, expanded or compressed text, overstrike, and others. Should problems develop in printer configuration, registered users can get telephone assistance. Documentation is straightforward and clearly written, and learning FORM MASTER is easy, with examples and four on-disk tutorial lessons. You can even add customized help files for other people using your forms.

(PC-SIG Disk# 1099)
Special Requirements: *320K RAM.*
Author Registration: *$25.00*

Formgen ✍

by FormGen Corporation

FORMGEN works like a wordprocessor with graphics features for creating forms. The help screen makes it easy to begin producing your first form within minutes of sitting down. The program is easy to use and an effective tool for making forms which require only combinations of thin and thick lines and two type fonts and sizes.

You can easily mark and copy the contents of a part of your form, or move them to other areas in the document. You can print a form with options for pica (10 cpi) or elite (12 cpi). The wordprocessor has most standard functions plus easy access to reference help, and quick display of files. Call the operating system to load a secondary copy of DOS — this lets you copy files, format disks, and run other programs from within FORMGEN.

(PC-SIG Disk# 1561)
Special Requirements: *Printer.*
Author Registration: *$35.00*
➤*ASP Member.*

FormGen - Business Form Collection

by FormGen Corporation

A collection of business forms for use with FORMGEN. Standard invoices, purchase orders, credit applications, accounting forms, fax letters, etc., that you can use "as is," or modify to suit your needs. Over 70 commonly-used business forms.

(PC-SIG Disk# 2329)
Special Requirements: *Formgen #1695*
Author Registration: *$15.00*
➤*ASP Member.*

FormGen - Home Form Collection

by FormGen Corporation

A collection of 50 forms for use with FORMGEN. Includes many useful and innovative forms for groceries, hobbies, genealogy, and sports. Also included are forms for satellite dishes, VCR use, scanners, as well as golfing, ham radio, church and other activities. Quickly customize to your exact needs with FORMGEN.

(PC-SIG Disk# 2332)
Special Requirements: *FormGen #(1695)*
Author Registration: *$15.00*
➤*ASP Member.*

FormGen Fill (companion to FormGen) ✍

by FormGen Corporation

FORMGEN FILL is a powerful, yet easy-to-use package for filling forms. This companion system for FORMGEN lets you define data areas on a FORMGEN form. Once completed, the form can be filled and printed — perfectly every time. Handy features include: multi-line fields, system date and time support, calculated fields, and much more. The context-sensitive help function makes it easy to learn and use. Print forms on your Epson, IBM or HP-type printer. The results are amazing!

(PC-SIG Disk# 2328)
Special Requirements: *FormGen #1695.*
Author Registration: *$35.00*
➤*ASP Member.*

Home and Business Legal Guide ✍

by R Fringe Publishing

THE HOME AND BUSINESS LEGAL GUIDE AND FORMS GENERATOR is really three programs in one. It prepares custom legal documents from on-screen interviews, contains the full annotated text of important laws and regulations, and provides many nuts and bolts explanations of the law.

Users can prepare more than 150 different custom legal forms for personal, business, real estate, estate planning, and living trust use, all of which have been written by an attorney/consumer advocate. The program prepares legal forms specifically for your needs based on answers to on-screen questions.

Also featured are instructional tutorials that clearly explain various legal problems. In addition, the tutorials feature an on-line dictionary and the ability to examine both the full text of the laws and the explanation on screen.

(PC-SIG Disk#'s 2539, 2540, 2668)

Special Requirements: *448K RAM and a hard drive.*
Author Registration: *$39.00*
➤*ASP Member.*

PopForm ✍

by Integra Computing

Here's a RAM-resident program that can be called up from within nearly any application, grab information from the screen, and merge it into a form that you can send to a printer or a disk file.

Unlike the typical single-purpose label or envelope printer, POPFORM is actually programmable. Execute subroutines, perform comparisons and conditional procedures, and much, much more. It'll even do simple page formatting, including margins all around, word wrap, page numbers, and one-line headers and footers.

Prepare forms of nearly ANY complexity, as long as the information to be plugged into them can be found on your computer's screen.

If you have simple needs, you'll find POPFORM a dream come true. But it's nice to know that it also has the power to do heavy-duty chores.

(PC-SIG Disk# 2267)

Special Requirements: *None.*
Author Registration: *$50.00*

▼ ▼ ▼

Fractals and Mathematics Based Graphics

Cell Systems

by Charles Platt

CELL SYSTEMS creates linear cellular automata that are often beautiful and also have mathematical significance. The patterns simulate the growth processes of simple biological entities. The program has a library of patterns already installed, with room for many more. This program lets you create new growth patterns of your own, save them, re-run them, and edit them. Your new cell can die, flourish, create a mess, or make a beautiful pattern that can be stored on disk. View the parameters for the sample cells and edit them if you want a slightly different pattern. You can create the patterns on either a medium- or high-resolution monitor and can print them. An installation program configures the program to fit your printer needs.

(PC-SIG Disk# 1109)

Special Requirements: *CGA.*
Author Registration: *$18.50*

Chaos ☆

by Judson McCranie

CHAOS is a collection of five separate programs to generate different patterns. Vary the pattern parameters to investigate and explore the fascinating mathematical realm of Chaos Theory. Included are the Lorenz Butterfly, random triangles, the logistic equation, three-body orbits, and Henon diagrams.

Math buffs will appreciate the documentation which includes references for further study. The non-mathematically inclined will find CHAOS fun because of the tremendous variety of patterns which can be generated, even if they don't know why (or care)!

(PC-SIG Disk# 2704)

Special Requirements: *CGA, EGA, VGA or Hercules.*
Author Registration: *$10*

Demon ☆
by Judson McCranie

DEMON generates patterns of crystal-like growth. The inspiration comes from Scientific American's Computer Recreations, August 1989. The author thoughtfully provided many options so the patterns are very different, depending upon the values of the various parameters. Typical patterns are fully developed in a few minutes on AT-class machines while taking about an hour on a PC.

(PC-SIG Disk# 2704)

Special Requirements: *CGA, EGA, VGA or Hercules.*
Author Registration: *$5.00*

Fractal Grafics
by Cedar Software

FRACTAL GRAFICS is an easy, intuitive fractal drawing program that anybody can use. You don't need to know math or even be good at art, although both skills can be used to make state-of-the-art motion picture special effects. Create your own models of systems like rivers, trees, mountains, and natural disasters.

Use with the keyboard or a mouse. On-line Help and many examples will get you started quickly. Begin to explore the world of with a new and fascinating fractal-drawing program!

(PC-SIG Disk# 2217)

Special Requirements: *384K RAM and CGA.*
Author Registration: *$59.00*

Fractal Grafics (PC-SIG Disk# 2217)

Fractint ✍
by Tyler Software

FRACTINT plots and manipulates images of "objects" — actually sets of mathematical points — that have fractal dimension. Using integer math, these sets of points are generated by relatively simple calculations repeated over and over, feeding the results of each step back into the next, something computers can do very rapidly. FRACTINT lets you zoom into a small area created by the calculations to reveal intricate detail, from which you can assign colors to selected points and "animate" the images by quickly shifting those color assignments.

An advantage of FRACTINT over other fractal graphics programs is that, as formerly mentioned, it uses integer math, rather than the floating-point calculations. That means that you don't need a math coprocessor chip (aka floating-point unit or FPU), though it will recognize and automatically use an 80x87 chip if it's present.

FRACTINT works with many adapter and graphics modes from CGA to the 1024x768, 256-color 8514/A mode. Even "larger" images, up to 2048x2048x256, can be plotted to RAM, EMS, or disk: this bypasses the screen and allows you to create images with higher resolution than your current display can handle, and to run in "background" under multi-tasking control programs such as DESQview.

The program was born fast through an experiment in collaboration by Bert Tyler and many volunteers. The authors of this public domain program encourage further contribution of ideas to make FRACTINT even better than it already is: "speedy, versatile, and all-around wonderful."

(PC-SIG Disk# 2304)

Special Requirements: *CGA*
Author Registration: *Copyrighted freeware.*

Fractkal
by Quantrill Software

FRACTKAL combines the best of a fractal generator and a kaleidoscope. Similar to a kaleidoscope in that it can generate fractals at random, this menu-driven program is great for the novice.

Finished fractals, generated by you or by FRACTKAL, can be saved as PICT files and may brought up from disk at any time within the program. The documentation is excellent and a short step-by-step tutorial is offered.

While a higher-level user might find FRACTKAL's functions limiting, the beginner can spend hours experimenting with custom-designing fractals or seeing what the computer can come up with. All this, without having to deal with the mind-boggling bells and whistles of the more advanced fractal-generating programs.

(PC-SIG Disk# 2309)

Special Requirements: *EGA*
Author Registration: *$15.00*

Life Forms
by Charles Platt

LIFE FORMS is an enhanced version of the "Game of Life," developed by mathematician John Conway. The program creates a video pattern that evolves like biological cells, according to a certain growth rate. Many features have been added to Conway's simple game, including eight extra growth rules for producing whole new families of screen images.

LIFE FORMS is simple to use, with lots of on-screen help and self- explanatory menus. The "life forms" that you create can be stored, retrieved, edited, and deleted. More than 100 life patterns are supplied on the program disk, with room for 240 in all. You can "capture a specimen from the zoo," or design a life form according to your own specifications.

Control many factors that influence the growth cycle: complexity of development, species, pigmentation, habitat and original seed shape. There is a library of seed patterns which have been specifically chosen for the interesting results that they tend to produce. Choose one of these, edit it or devise your own seed form. As your life form starts to grow, control how fast each growth step is displayed on the screen and even pause your life form's development.

(PC-SIG Disk# 802)

Special Requirements: *CGA.*
Author Registration: *$15.00*

Mandelbrot & Julia Set Generator
by Wierenga Software

MANDEL generates and displays marvelously beautiful images based upon the recently developed area of mathematics called "fractal geometry." With this program, you can create an unlimited number of new images, change the colors of the images, and save the images to a disk file. Sample images are included, and on-line help suggests numerical values, making it easy to begin.

The program has two outstanding features: the assignment of color masks to create an unlimited range of color variations for each image, and the ability to zoom in and magnify selected portions of the screen.

MANDEL is a comprehensive program that takes some time to create a new image, but once saved to disk the image can be displayed on the screen more quickly. You can also generate Julia images, which are similar to the Mandelbrot images, but require different numerical values to create the image. The documentation has suggested readings for more information on Mandelbrot and Julia set images.

(PC-SIG Disk#'s 1076, 1241)

Special Requirements: *EGA or VGA.*
Author Registration: *$20.00*

Mandelbrot Magic
by Left Coast Software

Fractal geometry has been used in the past to create images of many different subjects. From three-dimensional pictures of landscapes to an accurate cross section of the heart, fractals are the wave of the future.

MANDELBROT MAGIC generates color displays of the Mandelbrot Set, a famous group of mathematical structures also known as fractals. Fractal geometry is a complicated field in mathematics, but this program is easy to use and will automatically create the fractal slides according to your specifications.

With this program you can create a new slide, or recreate a slide from an already existing one. A set of fractal slides will display a portion of the former slide in greater detail. Generating a slide is an intensive computational task and can easily take from three to 16 hours, but an 8087 math coprocessor will reduce the generation time by a factor of 10.

(PC-SIG Disk# 841)

Special Requirements: *CGA, EGA, or VGA.*
Author Registration: *$15.00*

Mandelbrot ZoomLens
by Peter Gwozdz

MANDELBROT ZOOM LENS lets you create, view, and magnify a Mandelbrot fractal and demonstrate the unique nature of these complex mathematical patterns which are found in nature. As a fractal image is magnified, the smaller details will still look like the same fractal. The more a fractal is magnified, the more hours it takes to fill in all the details on the screen.

(PC-SIG Disk# 1326)

Special Requirements: *CGA.*
Author Registration: *$20.00*

Recursive Realm    *by Austin Software Design*

Experience the fascinating beauty of fractals. Use RECURSIVE REALM to build and explore Mandelbrot sets, Julia sets (5 equations), Newton's method (13 equations), and models of magnetism from a detailed menu system.

RECURSIVE REALM uses expanded memory where available. Files are saved in .PCX format for use with many commercial and shareware packages. It features zooming, escape sequence tracking, easy coloring, slide show animation and more. Save designs at any stage of development and resume building at a later time. The program contains some sample pictures to get you started and help is available anytime.

(PC-SIG Disk# 2367)

Special Requirements: *EGA or VGA.*
Author Registration: *$20.00*
➤*ASP Member.*

Recursive Realm (PC-SIG Disk# 2367)

▼ ▼ ▼

       ✎ = Updated Program
☆ = New Program

Gambling

Cambridge Thoroughbred Handicapper ✐   *by Federal Hill Software*

CAMBRIDGE THOROUGHBRED HANDICAPPER attempts to predict a horse or dog's race performance by analyzing past performances in a consistent, scientific manner. It also gives you a strategy for betting on races based on your handicapping analysis.

The system blends sophistication and ease-of-use for the race fan who enjoys the sport but doesn't have hours to devote to handicapping. If you've never handicapped a race before, you'll find this informative. If you're an experienced handicapper, the data you collect is just as useful as the ratings themselves. Sharpen your own analytical thinking.

(PC-SIG Disk# 918)

Special Requirements: *None.*
Author Registration: *$20.00*
➤*ASP Member.*

College Football Pool   *by Critics Choice*

COLLEGE FOOTBALL POOL is designed to make football pool games easier to play/follow/bet each week.

A demonstration schedule is included. Pick the week you want, and all the games for that week will be displayed. Choose any fourteen games for the selection sheet. The object of the game is for each player to try to pick the most winners of the 14 weekly games. Selection sheets can then be printed showing all the players' choices.

After the games are completed, enter the winning teams and print a final report showing the number of games each player picked correctly. In the event of ties, the player who was the closest in guessing the total number of points scored in the last game on the selection sheet is declared the winner. Up to 300 players can be handled by this program.

(PC-SIG Disk# 892)

Special Requirements: *None.*
Author Registration: *$25.00*

Football Fun   *by Critics Choice*

FOOTBALL FUN (FFUN) is a complete office football pool management system — just what your office might need! It has the entire season schedule for professional teams, thus saving you the monotony of keying in all the team names every week when preparing weekly selection sheets. Just a few keystrokes are needed to make a weekly selection sheet.

Last year's schedule is on this disk for demonstration purposes, but you can order the current season from the author any time after June 1. The new season schedule also includes any new revisions to the program. The schedule costs $10 every year.

The program is easy to operate. A data-entry screen makes it simple to enter team selections of each participant. The participants' names do not have to be keyed in every week if they are stored in the seasonal database.

You win if you pick the most games right. If there is a tie, total points scored in Monday night's game is used for a tiebreaker. Player standing reports are printed after Sunday games and Monday games. Weekly results can be accumulated in a seasonal database which can be used to operate a separate pool for the whole season.

The program makes a playoff selection sheet that includes the four quarterfinal games, the two conference championships, and the Super Bowl.

(PC-SIG Disk# 747)

Special Requirements: *Two floppy drives and a printer.*
Author Registration: *$25*

Horses   *by Boots Software*

So simple to use that it makes reaching for a computer manual unthinkable, HORSES is a fast-out-of-the-gates, thoroughbred handicapping program. It was designed for the parimutuel player who loves both horses and betting at the track. Because it is objective and data oriented, HORSES offers you a leg up on touts and intuition. Taking up to eight entries per race on a dirt or turf track, HORSES lists projected race results numerically, according to odds and with a graphic bar chart.

Users should read the Daily Racing Form and know how to understand the past performance charts printed in it. The program asks for names of horses, type of race, distance, and whether the sexes or ages are mixed. Then it asks specific questions about the history of each horse. In a flick of a horse's tail, the screen is filled with hard data. The percentages are especially valuable: the greater the percentage difference between horses, the more certain the outcome.

(PC-SIG Disk# 1514)

Special Requirements: *None.*
Author Registration: *$17.50*

The Las Vegas EGA Casino ✍ *by Ted Gruber Software*

Take a trip to Vegas without spending a dime. THE LAS VEGAS EGA CASINO is a collection of three favorite Las Vegas casino games.

Las Vegas Casino Blackjack is a simulation of the table game, as played on the Las Vegas Strip. Las Vegas Video Poker is a re-creation of the popular video poker machines played in casinos, grocery stores, bowling alleys, airports, and other notorious Nevada hangouts. Las Vegas Dollar Slots (MicroBucks) is a colorful visual game of three-across slots.

(PC-SIG Disk# 2501)

Special Requirements: *EGA.*
Author Registration: *$15.00*

NCAAPool *by Tom Cunningham*

NCAAPOOL makes handling company pools for NCAA basketball a lot easier and less time consuming. Normally there are several people who would like to know their statistics after each round of games is played, and doing this may take hours of work. There is also the possibility of making a mistake in one of the records.

NCAAPOOL solves all that. All it needs are the first round team match-ups of the 64 basketball teams in the four divisions. You then enter the names of the pool players, and the choices of their teams they think will win in each of the rounds of games, until the final winner is reached. At any time afterwards you can enter the results of each round of the games, and immediately get a printout of the individual results for each pool player, showing which teams chosen won or lost. A summary report, showing the total winning teams each player guessed correctly, can then be sent to the screen, printer, or both.

(PC-SIG Disk# 1387)

Special Requirements: *None.*
Author Registration: *$20.00; joint registration with NFLPOOL $29.00*

NFLPool *by Tom Cunningham*

NFLPool does everything NCAAPool does and does it just as well for your local NFL football pool. It eliminates the long hours of handwork normally required to stay on top of the games.

(PC-SIG Disk# 1387)

Special Requirements: *None.*
Author Registration: *$20.00; joint registration with NCAAPOOL $29.00*

The Pool Manager *by American Systems*

It's a great day, sports fans! Here's something you've needed for years.

THE POOL MANAGER makes running a football pool a snap. Whether the featured event at a private party or the regular office pool, FPM does all the tedious work. Enter the basic information and it handles everything else, from generating a picksheet to printing the final standings.

It has complete flexibility to handle up to 18 games and 90 participants in a single pool. For NFL pools, the teams are already stored in the program, just indicate the opponents. You can maintain season-long standings, utilize a tiebreaker, and determine winning teams by applying the point spread. It can be used for pools in any sport.

So, who do you like for next week?

(PC-SIG Disk# 882)

Special Requirements: *Printer.*
Author Registration: *$25.00*
➤*ASP Member.*

SportsBook 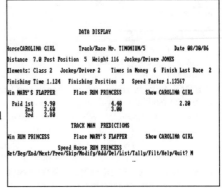   *by Robert Bentsen & Associates*

Want to be a bookie? Then fantasize with SPORTSBOOK. It's a bookie simulator that's entertaining and fun. If you want to make college and professional sports wagers and maintain records of those transactions, then SPORTSBOOK is for you.

The sports supported by SPORTSBOOK include NBA and NCAA basketball, hockey, and NFL, CFL, and NCAA football. SPORTSBOOK does all the necessary record keeping hardcopy generation, and calculations required for a bookmaking operation.

(PC-SIG Disk# 1132)

Special Requirements: *None.*
Author Registration: *$59.95*

Track Man Thoroughbred Challenge   *by B.L. Software, Inc.*

Here's one for the serious horse racing fan, a fully integrated and comprehensive thoroughbred handicapper and database manager. Handicap a race using actual racing data against TRACK MAN's favorite five. Learn how your personal computer can eliminate those tedious timne consuming manual calculations. This shareware version has all the features and functions of the commercial version except you handicap against TRACK MAN's favorite five horses. The commercial version allows you to handicap up to a ten horse field.

The program consists of two modules; a handicapper module and a database module. The handicapper module is designed to analyze certain elements and give predictions for win, place, show and speed. Data elements analyzed include winning time, post position, weight, distance, stretch run, track, class, jockey record, times in the money and last race finish position. These elements can be varied to fine tune predictions without reentry. Also included is a feature that displays and prints charts to compare data between all the horses in the race.

TrackMan Thoroughbred Challenge (PC-SIG Disk #1660)

The database module provides a variety of statistical data elements to be tracked including race date, track name/race number, post position, jockey or driver name, finishing time, distance, weight, last race finish position, if claiming race, jockey or driver rating, times in the money, speed factor, names of winning, place and show horse, prices paid, and finishing position. You can add, delete, modify, edit and search a record in the database and track your own predictions for win, place, show and speed. Once a horse is handicapped, only data for the horse's last race is required when handicapping a new race. Performance data for earlier races of the horse being handicapped is automatically added to the handicapper module from the database module for increased accuracy and decreased data entry time.

(PC-SIG Disk# 1660)

Special Requirements: *310K RAM and a hard drive.*
Author Registration: *$25.00*

▼ ▼ ▼

Games, Adventure and Text

Adventure Game Toolkit   *by Softworks*

Want to create your own text adventure games? Now, with the ADVENTURE GAME TOOLKIT (AGT) you can, and you don't need to know programming!

In text adventures, players assume the roles of characters in a story which they read. But unlike a book story, the reader is able to interact with the plot, go different directions, ask questions and do things which may lead them to treasure or doom.

Using AGT, game enthusiasts can now transform their wildest fantasies into high-quality adventure games — and teachers and parents, with a little imagination, now have a wonderful tool for making riveting games that can teach basic subjects, such as history, math, foreign langauges, vocabulary development, etc., in a fun and impactful way.

AGT can create complex worlds with up to 200 locations, 100 inanimate objects (swords, trees, cars, lasers, etc) and 100 animate objects (hobbits, orcs, famous persons, etc.). An AGT game can understand a 400-word vocabulary that can include complex (multiple actions) and function key macros for common commands for a polished result that conforms to the Infocom standard in adventure games so anyone can learn to play quickly.

AGT comes with complete instructions (100 page on-disk manual) and a sample mini-game that is walked through showing what can be created using AGT without requiring the game designer to have programming knowledge or experience. It also contains the source code files for the Colossal Cave adventure. This is an AGT version of the original game that was written by Crowther and Woods that was the first adventure game ever written. It is a classic! The AGT files for this game can be played and enjoyed simply as great entertainment or as a platform to build upon and/or learn from for the AGT game designer.

(PC-SIG Disk#'s 1231, 1232)

Special Requirements: *384K RAM and two floppy drives.*
Author Registration: *$20.00 to $50.00.*
➤*ASP Member.*

Adventureware
by Agency Automation

A fistful of text adventure games, ranging from a mystery adventure, to an episode of espionage, to a tale of horror. If you enjoy the challenge of puzzles and exploring the unknown, then you will be occupied for days with this quintet:

CRIME: Solve a crime and be a hero! You find yourself embattled in a world where the streets are not safe. Keep your back to the wall and look for allies!

HAUNTED MISSION: While on his way to a party, the world-famous Pumpkin Man was shanghaied by the evil Lady Winslow. Search the neighborhood, rescue him, and take him to the party.

ISLAND OF MYSTERY: Explore a tiny island in the middle of a vast ocean in search of 11 treasures. Locate each and then find the secret place where they must be stored.

THE NUCLEAR SUBMARINE ADVENTURE: To add to the growing threat of nuclear proliferation, the USS Nautilus has been reactivated and totally refitted with the most modern and lethal equipment. As a new crewman aboard the Nautilus, you have received extensive training but experience is still the best teacher, and you will learn much more during your stay onboard — if you survive!

TERROR IN THE ICE CAVERNS: The Soviets are developing a new death laser in the remote, frigid caves of Antarctica. Your mission (should you choose to accept it), is to enter the caves and the Soviet complex, locate the laser, steal the plans for it and then return to the surface to be picked up by a helicopter. Where are your mittens?

(PC-SIG Disk# 453)

Special Requirements: *None.*
Author Registration: *None.*

Alice In Wonderland
by Robin Johnson

ALICE IN WONDERLAND is an adventure game based on Lewis Carroll's novel, Alice's Adventures in Wonderland. Although you need not be familiar with the novel to play, there are occasionally places it would be helpful.

In this narrative adventure, you type in dialogue and directions as you wander through Wonderland as Alice, gathering special objects and talking with the odd creatures and other characters from the novel.

You will discover that your size can change in this game. You start out your normal size and then may grow or shrink, depending on your actions. At times, you will have to be very small to accomplish certain tasks. But be aware that the larger you are, the better your chances of evading death. Also, when you are very large, there is no weight restriction on what you can carry. When you are tiny and you encounter a danger, your chances of survival are pretty slim.

Winning consists of finding a particular valuable object and returning home with it. Along the way, there are many adventures to be had and many places to see. You will need to explore everything. Suitable for ages 9 through adult.

(PC-SIG Disk# 1495)

Special Requirements: *None.*
Author Registration: *$10.00*

✍ = Updated Program
☆ = New Program

Another Lifeless Planet and Me With No Beer   *by Try-Then-Buy Software*

NOBEER is a logical adventure game. It's a big one, too, created with the Gamescape adventure game generation system. The response has been incredible. If you like adventure gaming, this is a must have! In NOBEER, the player is an astronaut stranded on a hostile alien planet (sound familiar? Players of Marooned Again will recognize the character immediately). The goal: find a way to get to an alien space ship and rig it to blast off to safety. That's easier said than done; as the astronaut you will face perils such as deadly slurpers, air squids, bladderbeasts and the terrible pun palm tree!

Unlike many adventure games, ANOTHER LIFELESS PLANET AND ME WITH NO BEER is completely logical. Everything in the game has a reason (well, maybe) and everything you do has a purpose (most of the time) and above all, everything is logical (well, to an alien, anyway). This game is funny too. Do you know what happens when you eat a frog? Or the only way to get past an alien monster? Have you ever tried to munch a slimeball? Do you know what it feels like when you try to pick up slime? What does a dead astronaut's head look like? You'll find all this out in ANOTHER LIFELESS PLANET AND ME WITH NO BEER.

(PC-SIG Disk# 2138)

Special Requirements: *640K RAM.*

Author Registration: *Donation, or $59.00 if using for game creation.*

The Asian Challenge   *by Conrad Button's Software*

Attention geography teachers — teach your students about Asian geography in a text adventure setting. Make learning exciting.

The ASIAN CHALLENGE is an educational program, written for grades five through ten, which provides the student with information concerning the geography of the countries on the Asian continent. It is to be used as a supplement to text books and other instructional material. It uses the text adventure format to encourage the student to carefully read the information presented. The text adventure format is an effective means for holding the student's attention for prolonged periods. Learning becomes a fun experience and the student becomes much more interested in the study of geography. The use of this program also increases the student's reading and spelling capabilities.

This educational adventure is similar to a novel in which the student is the main character. The students will visit most of the countries in Asia. In each country they will be presented with important facts concerning the geographical features, early history, and animals native to the country.

(PC-SIG Disk# 1688)

Special Requirements: *None.*

Author Registration: *$15.00*

ATC - Air Traffic Controller   *by Cascoly Software*

AIR TRAFFIC CONTROLLER, simulating the duties of a sector air traffic controller, is a game that's perfect for a few minutes or hours of fun! Easy to learn, but difficult to master, this game tracks best scores at each of 20 levels of difficulty.

You must guide about 20 planes safely through your sector, symbolized as a 13 by 13 grid. Two airports are shown, as are six "fixes" which are the only safe exits and entries to adjacent sectors. Take off, change altitudes, land — each plane is shown as a letter with arrows that show current direction. Use the whole keyboard with this game (...if you're moonlighting as an atc, F10 allows quick escape when your real boss shows up!).

(PC-SIG Disk# 2087)

Special Requirements: *None.*

Author Registration: *$20.00*

➤*ASP Member.*

Basketball Simulation   *by Daniel Imamura*

BASKETBALL is a text-based simulation of basketball — not an interactive computer game. Once you have chosen the teams and players, the game begins and you are a spectator.

As play proceeds, the radio announcer's dialogue rolls across the screen. If you enjoy listening to games on the radio, you will enjoy this game! Rather than trying to capture the physical representation of basketball on the PC, this program effectively brings the thrill of the game to you the same way the radio sports announcer does.

The program comes with data for six teams: the Celtics, the Lakers, the Rockets, the '76ers, and the East and West All-Star teams. Play games with any combination of these teams or create teams of your own.

(PC-SIG Disk# 946)

Special Requirements: *None.*
Author Registration: *None.*

Battle Ground
by MVP Software

BATTLE GROUND is a World War II field-combat game/simulator for two players.

Each player is the general of either the U.S. or German army commanding 16 privates with various weapons, two medics, one sergeant, and a major. These men have varying abilities that often come in handy while engaging in hand-to-hand combat. Each soldier carries hand grenades, adding even greater realism to this war simulation.

At the beginning of the game, the players select the battlefield on which to compete. There are five different battlefields to choose from. As the battle begins, you start in separate corners and come out fighting. All troops are represented by small squares. Both players take turns moving, firing, and whatever other strategy they think of. A great feature is each player can do as much as he wants on any one turn, adding even more realism to the game of war.

(PC-SIG Disk# 1090)

Special Requirements: *CGA.*
Author Registration: *$15.00*
➤*ASP Member.*

Beyond the Titanic
by Apogee Software Productions

Lucky you! BEYOND THE TITANIC begins as you find yourself aboard the Titanic just seconds before she sinks!

Your goal is to survive and get back home. On the journey, you'll discover a long-forgotten secret under the sea, travel to the Earth's future, get chased by a three-armed monster and more!!

If you've played any of Infocom's games, you'll notice the similarity in style. To add to the realism, a 16-color display and sound effects are used throughout the game.

(PC-SIG Disk# 832)

Special Requirements: *None.*
Author Registration: *$5.00*

Big Three
by SDJ Enterprise, Inc.

In this WWII strategy game you control all the action from the desolate fjords of Norway to the scorching sands of Egypt, from the strategic Rock of Gibraltar to the frozen streets of Moscow. Recreate the epic and fiercely fought battles of Tobruk and Stalingrad. Decide to open your second front in Normandy or the "soft underbelly" of Europe (Italy). Build bombers to hit your opponent's cities or build tanks and fighters to encircle and destroy his armies at the front.

Detailed maps done in excellent graphics help you track your progress and plan strategy. Each player assumes supreme command of the Axis, Allied or Soviet forces in Europe during 1939-1945. Players who perform better than their historical counterparts will normally win, and those who under-perform will normally lose. Mouse and/or joystick(s) are recommended but not required.

(PC-SIG Disk#'s 1925, 1940)

Special Requirements: *512K RAM, and CGA, EGA, or VGA.*
Author Registration: *$17.00*

The Case of Crime to the Ninth Power ☆
by Patrick Farley

Presenting THE ADVENTURE TOOLKIT's (PC-SIG #1230 & #1231) 1990 text game contest winner. THE CASE OF CRIME TO THE NINTH POWER is the first in a planned series featuring Cliff Diver, a hard-boiled, ex-cop private eye who lives and works in San Francisco.

You must help Cliff escape from the Zamboni crime family's secret headquarters. Along the way, you and Cliff will face snarling Dobermans, two of Zamboni's goons (named Flash and Bonzo), and many other twists and turns. A captivating mystery to solve.

The game features a 400+-word vocabulary, a pop-up Help system, and a Save/Restore feature that should be used often.

(PC-SIG Disk# 2742)

Special Requirements: *None.*
Author Registration: *$10.00*

Cavequest
by Lightwave

A graphics adventure game, in the same vein as Epyx's Temple of Aphsai. You start as an immortal, choose your new mortal attributes, and travel to Earth to seek out fame, fortune, and excitement.

This is a rich and complex adventure with hundreds of hours of first-class entertainment in store for you. Onward!

(PC-SIG Disk# 451)

Special Requirements: *CGA.*
Author Registration: *$35.00.*

Dark Continent
by Conrad Button's Software

A text adventure game that takes you to the heart of Africa. In DARK CONTINENT, you are on a safari expedition in search of King Solomon's legendary diamond. Unfortunately, your native followers have mutinied and left you lost in the wilderness without a map. Not only must you find the diamond, but also, your way back to England. (And try not to get eaten by wildlife on the way!)

(PC-SIG Disk# 967)

Special Requirements: *None.*
Author Registration: *$20.00*

DRACULA In London
by SDJ Enterprise, Inc.

DRACULA IN LONDON is a spell-binding adventure game with outstanding graphics for one to six players.

The plot of DRACULA IN LONDON is to track down the blood-thirsty vampire and put an end to his evil menace. Each player assumes the role of one of six vampire hunters: Van Helsing — renowned metaphysician, Mina Harker — school mistress, Jonathan Harker — solicitor's clerk, Dr. Seward — head of a lunatic asylum, Arthur Holmwood — son of Lord Godalming, and Quincy Morris — wealthy young Texan. Provisions include sacred weapons, equipment, and animals.

Full of surprises and fast moving, DRACULA will provide you hours of excitement. Be sure to wear your garlic and bring your own stake.

Dracula in London (PC-SIG Disk# 1220)

(PC-SIG Disk# 1220)

Special Requirements: *CGA.*
Author Registration: *$9.00*

Dungeon
by Erik J. Oredson

Grab your torch and sword and step into the DUNGEON, a game in which you must explore a maze of pathways leading into the bowels of the earth, while fighting monsters, seeking treasure, and hoping to find your way back out alive!

Similar to HACK (PC SIG disk #1000), symbols and letters are used to represent you, the maze and its denizens, so you don't need a graphics card to play. But don't let it's simple graphics fool you. This is an incredibly complex and intriguing game that can trap you for long hours before you can battle free.

You use the curser keys to move and the function keys to cast 40 different spells, such as: cast fireballs at monsters, teleport, pass through walls, find traps, transmute the air into gold, summon a demon, and more — gadzooks! You start off with six character attributes, which determine your capabilities during the game. As you gain experience, you will be able to cast more spells, and live longer when fighting with monsters. As you

explore each dungeon level, a map is displayed on the screen, showing your position among the many hallways. At any time on-line help is available, giving a summary of all the keys and their functions. Age level: 10 to adult.
(PC-SIG Disk# 1437)

Special Requirements: *None.*
Author Registration: *$15.00*

Dungeons of the Necromancer's Domain   *by R.O. Software*

DND is a computer fantasy role-playing game inspired by Dungeons and Dragons — the "grandaddy" of all the computer games that was developed and played on mainframe computers back in the '60s.

Different than most games, it uses character graphics in the upper-right corner of the screen, instead of graphics. Become a wizard and fight evil monsters and ghosts with your growing power. Or become a fighter and go head-to-head with mighty dragons. Or a cleric and try to dispel the evil spirits of the dungeons. The object is to stay alive and venture deeper and deeper into the depths of the dungeons. You have five completed dungeons to choose from, with expanded screen displays, character spells, and room furnishings. No matter which character you choose to be, this is a game that will test all of your game playing skills. Registration of the program includes a copy of "The Domain Master" for creating and editing both characters and dungeons.
(PC-SIG Disk# 567)

Special Requirements: *None.*
Author Registration: *$25.00*

Eamon   *by Wisconsin Software Systems*

Become a character in a land of adventure and do great and marvelous deeds! In this fantasy role-playing game, your first goal is to stay alive while getting rich during your questing.

When you enter these different universes, you are no longer John (or Jane) Smith — a quiet, mild-mannered computer hobbyist. Instead, you are, ta-dah!, in the center of a tale of adventure — fighting orcs, trolls, dragons, knights, and mages with an arsenal of weapons and terrible magic.

An entire series of adventures await you, starting with The Main Hall and including Ice Cave — sagas with all the appropriate monsters and traps. The challenges are difficult, but not impossible to survive, and will keep you on the edge of your chair. The monsters are very mean and give up their lives to stop you from getting any further in your quest!
(PC-SIG Disk#'s 296, 297, 1038, 1039)

Special Requirements: *None.*
Author Registration: *$5.95.*

Ecomaster ✍   *by Cascoly Software*

Get in touch with nature and animals, through your computer! ECOMASTER's an ecology simulation in which you predict how animals will survive in a series of different environments. This is a game of skill and chance. Some of the areas where skill comes in include learning which animals perform best in various environments, or biomes, and guessing which biome will follow the current one.

This is a challenging game for everyone. Accompanied by a dictionary or encyclopedia, it can also be a great way to learn about different animals from around the world!
(PC-SIG Disk# 2147)

Special Requirements: *CGA or higher graphics board.*
Author Registration: *$20.00*
➤*ASP Member.*

Facing the Empire ✍   *by MVP Software*

If you like strategic war gaming, then FACING THE EMPIRE might be right up your intergalactic alley! Not an arcade game designed around speed, flashy graphics and high-speed joystick jockeying, FACING THE EMPIRE is more like a strategic board game — oriented toward reasoning, planning and logistics.

As a member of the Lyran Stellar Federation, you must prepare your fleets and probes for deployment and battle. Then you must seek out the seven randomly-placed Morte stars hidden in the sixty-four stars of the Lyran periphery. You can accumulate points through destruction of Morte ship groups, bases, and their invasion headquarters. All this must be accomplished while they're trying to get you first!
(PC-SIG Disk# 1075)

Special Requirements: *None.*
Author Registration: *$15.00*
➤*ASP Member.*

FallThru ✍ *by Paul H. Deal*

You and up to two other players stand only half a chance of making it home alive in this text adventure, called FALLTHRU!

You don't know how you got to this strange place, but you quickly discover that Faland is very large, comprising millions of square miles (all visitable) of farms, rangeland, forests, deserts, mountains, etc. Much of it is inhabited by dangerous wild animals, renegades, warriors, and demons.

You and your fellow players must find your way through the trackless wilderness, while quickly learning to recognize friend and foe, earning a living, and defending yourself by fist and weapon. And along the way you must gather information and solve various riddles and puzzles by talking to shop keepers, strangers, warriors, inn keepers, etc., and by exploring the many settlements, dark and treacherous caverns, catacombs, mines, castles and ruins scattered throughout this vast territory.

FALLTHRU recognizes several hundred words by which you can set your course, pick up objects, buy and sell things, fight, hunt, shoot, and speak to the odd characters you and your companions will meet as you try to go home! Age level: 12 to adult.

(PC-SIG Disk#'s 1389, 2611)

Special Requirements: *300K RAM and two floppy drives.*
Author Registration: *$10.00.*

Figment - The Imagination Processor ✍ *by Patch Panel*

FIGMENT is a full development environment for adventure games or other type of interactive fiction. Play roles in existing interactive fictions or write them yourself. FIGMENT does all the hard work of developing an interactive story so you can concentrate on the creative aspects.

You declare the objects, define the attributes, write the appropriate messages, and develop the game's logic. Programming is easy and quick with the full-screen editor and complete Help system.

One you've developed your games, you can use FIGMENT to play them and trade them with other FIGMENT users. Also included is a run-time version of the program so that you can distribute your games to anyone.

In addition to adventure games, FIGMENT can be used by writers to model plots, as a role-playing tool in business, and much more. FIGMENT takes the tedium out of fiction writing and lets you put the creativity in.

(PC-SIG Disk# 2581)

Special Requirements: *384K RAM and graphics card.*
Author Registration: *$35.00*

Finnish Games *by University of Vaasa*

A smorgasbord of programs from the University of Vaasa in Finland! Games, linear programming tools, lots of telephone modem help, and even a touch of Scandinavian PC key use make an interesting mix of utilities.

MANAGAME is a management simulation game from the Department of Business Studies. You are in charge of a small manufacturing company with a new widget to market. Fortune or bankruptcy await you!

HEXAGAME is the old number guessing game with a twist: you can try it in decimal, binary or hexadecimal! Each guess is also shown in its decimal equivalent. Great for computer students.

MLTIGAME provides timed competition for one or more students on multiplication tables. Winners' names go into the Hall of Fame. Suitable for ages 9 to 14.

LINSOLVE solves linear programming problems with up to 25 variables interactively. It also solves linear GOAL programming problems.

PCPFON tackles your special needs in using ProComm Plus, such as: 1) How to use Zmodem with ProComm Plus; 2) How to get the Scandinavian characters working; 3) How to transfer files between two PCs (when neither is a bulletin board) — both by modem and by direct cable connection. Other files explain how to ready ProComm Plus and the Worldport 2400 modem for the host mode; give routines for calling Finnish Opus Bulletin Boards, and more.

(PC-SIG Disk# 1536)

Special Requirements: *None.*
Author Registration: *See documentation.*

Frigate
by MK Systems

FRIGATE is a strategy game which pits you and your ship against a Soviet fleet of vessels. The object is to destroy as many of the opposing ships as possible while avoiding destruction of your own.

Points are awarded for destroying your enemy while avoiding their missiles. Your ship, a nuclear-powered guided missile frigate, has many advantages over its Soviet counterparts but you are outnumbered by a large margin. Operating in an area of 1,000,000 square miles, you have radar, sonar, jamming equipment, anti-missile capabilities and three types of ordnance at your disposal.

FRIGATE is played from three on-screen windows — a main window which gives you an overview of your ship's status, an options window which changes in accordance with the commands you select and a command window from which you issue those commands. Your ship's status and position, and the location of the enemy are updated frequently. FRIGATE is a challenging and stimulating game that will provide many, many hours of entertainment.

(PC-SIG Disk# 1467)
Special Requirements: *None.*
Author Registration: *None Specified.*

FRP Game Master Utility
by Software Mines

The FRP GAME MASTER UTILITY is set up to be generally compatible with Advanced Dungeons and Dragons and its many variants. FRP is very flexible in its structure, and sacrifices some compatibility to maintain flexibility.

FRP's utilities take the manual labor out of playing Dungeons and Dragons. Everything done with paper, pen, and dice can now be done with the keyboard. These utilities are compatible with Advanced Dungeons and Dragons.

DICE ROLLING UTILITY — critical hits, fumbles, double damage, D100, D20, D12, D10, D8, D6, D4, any number of dice with modifiers, display monster information, roll monster hit points, and edit hit points.

RANDOM ENCOUNTERS UTILITY — generates random encounters for 10 different areas, each with different probabilities.

RANDOM TREASURE UTILITY — treasure types A-Z, gem value, jewel value, edit, and view treasure data.

GAME PARAMETER UTILITY — lets you alter critical hit, fumble, double damage, and encounter probabilities. The timer can be set, and combat die is selectable for special damage tables (except fumble).

(PC-SIG Disk# 1063)
Special Requirements: *384K RAM*
Author Registration: *$20.00*

Gamescape ✍
by Try-Then-Buy Software

GAMESCAPE is the fantastic program that allows you to design and distribute your own adventure games! GAMESCAPE is a powerful "adventure engine" that allows you to describe locations and rooms, objects, recognizable words, messages, and occurrences that happen within the game. You can also include sound, music, and any of the standard IBM special graphics characters! GAMESCAPE encodes information so your game secrets cannot be deciphered by end users, and allows games to be "linked" so your adventures can be of any length.

Once the game is finished, registered users are allowed to distribute the games without worrying about any kind of distribution fee—the initial registration is all that's required!

(PC-SIG Disk# 1293)
Special Requirements: *None.*
Author Registration: *$69.00, $95.00*

Golden Wombat of Destiny
by Huw Collingbourne

Your quest is to discover the Forbidden City of the Great Lost Empire and unearth the mysteries it holds. Do you have a prayer of succeeding?

SCORE: Much as in life, there is no scoring in The Golden Wombat.

THE POINT: The point of THE GOLDEN WOMBAT OF DESTINY is destiny, itself. Obviously. You'll know when you've found it. Possibly.

✍ = Updated Program
☆ = New Program

What do you think?

This text adventure game can handle full-sentence commands and has a large vocabulary of verbs. Users with CGA are able to customize screen colors.

(PC-SIG Disk# 678)

Special Requirements: *CGA.*
Author Registration: *None.*

Grand Prix *by Wizard Games*

Manage your own racing team! During the race season you're in charge of finances, hiring and firing of drivers, design staff and mechanics. You must also purchase cars, engines, and other items necessary for a successful season. Since you start out as rookie team manager you have a limited amount of money with which to put together the best team possible.

Once you have a completed team it's time to start your engine. There are 16 races in the season and you must try to qualify for each. With a skillful driver you may win a race. With a good chief mechanic you could win more. If you have an experienced chief designer your car may last the whole season. And if you manage to put all the parts together, the championship awaits you.

If you have ever wanted to be like Roger Penzske and manage a racing team GRAND PRIX is made for you!

(PC-SIG Disk# 2172)

Special Requirements: *CGA.*
Author Registration: *$20.00*

Hack Keys *by Chris Shearer Cooper*

The keyboard mapper HACKKEYS and its accompanying database are helpful tools for the Hack (PC-SIG disk #452) game enthusiast.

Hack is a complicated Dungeons and Dragons game with many rules, weapons, and monsters to memorize. The Hack database is a Norton Guides on-line reference for all the complicated details of the game and even has some helpful hints. This saves endless paper shuffling when you encounter an obscure monster or potion. It should be noted that Norton Guides, a database that lets you create your own help files, is required for the database.

Hack requires keyboard input to move from dungeon to dungeon at the different levels. Unfortunately since HACK was developed on UNIX, obscure keys like h,j, or k are used to move around the screen. Most PC users find these keys awkward to use. HACKKEYS is a RAM-resident program that alleviates this problem and lets you use the arrow keys.

(PC-SIG Disk# 1417)

Special Requirements: *Norton Guides for Hack database.*
Author Registration: *None.*

Hogbear Adventure Game *by Hogbear Software, Inc.*

The next time you are walking, hear laughter, and notice a nearby mansion, run for your life. If the HOGBEAR lures you in, you have to face him, a vampire, blue devils, killer bees, an ogre, a bear, pecking falcons and other perils.

If you are swift, wiser than most, and persistent, you might even overcome the snake and spider as you roam about the huge mansion. As in life, some games are unwinnable. But there's hope. This text adventure/graphics game moves quickly when you learn the knack of searching and gathering the tools and weapons you need. Otherwise, you lurch about from room to darkened room, stumbling toward certain doom in an obscure mansion filled with deadly surprises.

An update of the classic game Castle, HOGBEAR is fun for all ages. It runs on both color and monochrome systems.

(PC-SIG Disk# 1269)

Special Requirements: *None.*
Author Registration: *$10.00*

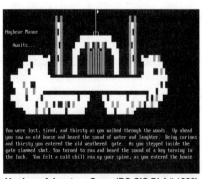

Hogbear Adventure Game (PC-SIG Disk# 1269)

The House At The Edge Of Time ☆   *by Pat Pflieger*

THE HOUSE AT THE EDGE OF TIME is a puzzle of time and space. Your eccentric uncle has died under mysterious circumstances and left you a fortune — IF you can survive a night in his enormous Pseudo-Tudor-Greco-Gothic-Byzantine mansion, where time and space are not exactly what they seem.

In this text adventure, typed commands allow you to move around the mansion, interact with those you meet, and find the key to...well, you'll find out. Play over and over again. This game is never the same game twice.

(PC-SIG Disk# 2769)

Special Requirements: *None.*
Author Registration: *$10.00*

Hugo's House of Horrors ✍   *by Gray Design Associates*

If you are looking for an exciting, fun filled game, HUGO's HOUSE OF HORRORS will fit the bill. Take your hero through an animated adventure, solving puzzles, finding hidden objects, and rescuing the sweet Penelope from the hosts of the demonic mansion. At the same time stay alive and don't let yourself be turned into dog food! The graphics are fantastic!

Programmmer David P. Gray creates a colorful and challenging world for the player. Full moving character pix, furnished rooms, hidden doors, a mad doctor, a vicious dog, and much more await any enthusiastic adventurer. Maneuver your character with the arrow keys while simple written commands let you take and use items, search and talk. As you solve the puzzles your score increases and is compared to the total score possible with the game. For registered users a free hintbook is available as well as the capability to play back previous games.

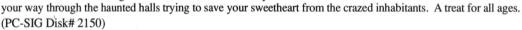

Hugo's House of Horrors (PC-SIG Disk# 2150)

Similar in concept to LucasFilm's Maniac Mansion, HUGO'S HOUSE OF HORRORS, though less complex, is as easy to use and as much fun. You will be glued to the screen for hours as you track your way through the haunted halls trying to save your sweetheart from the crazed inhabitants. A treat for all ages.

(PC-SIG Disk# 2150)

Special Requirements: *360K, EGA or VGA, and hard drive.*
Author Registration: *$24.00*
➤*ASP Member.*

Insanity   *by Wizard Games*

A huge maze based adventure game where INSANITY rules. Find clues, solve puzzles, and try to stay alive in a place where the unexpected is common, and pandemonium is found at every turn.

As you try to find the exit from INSANITY you'll encounter many strange things. You'll meet a wizard. Pass through the stars. Collect ammunition to defend yourself against little red men. Explore a castle and a church along the way. Play games like seven card challenge or a fast paced soccer match. Most things won't make sense, but if you can find a method to the madness, you could find the key to end your search for a way out of INSANITY.

(PC-SIG Disk# 2173)

Special Requirements: *512K RAM and CGA.*
Author Registration: *$20.00*

It's A Crime!   *by Adventures By Mail*

It's the late 1990's in New York City. You're a gang leader determined to build your gang into one of the richest, toughest and most notorious in the city on your way to becoming the Godfather. Compete with up to 500 other players, some of whom will be your enemies, while others will be your staunchest allies. Each turn, you will decide how to allocate your resources, what moves you should make. Mail your "turn card" with your moves. A computer will then process your information and send you a "results" sheet. It's your move!

(PC-SIG Disk# 1825)

Special Requirements: *None.*
Author Registration: *$12.00*

✍ = Updated Program
☆ = New Program

Kingdom of Kroz II ✍ *by Apogee Software Productions*

In KINGDOM OF KROZ, you are in search of a priceless amulet that lies somewhere within the mystical kingdom. Be careful, there are mysterious rooms and vicious monsters waiting for you. You are armed only with a whip and your wits.

As the intrepid explorer, you will venture through 25 unique levels of perils and treasures. In this combination game of arcade action, strategy and adventure, each level is patrolled by as many as 1000 monsters, all with a taste for your blood. 16-color graphics and sound effects add reality as you negotiate lava, rivers, earthquakes, pits, forbidden forests and more.

Three skill levels and a random playfield generator insure that no two games will be alike.

(PC-SIG Disk# 2001)

Special Requirements: *None.*
Author Registration: *$7.50*

The Land *by Riley Computer Services*

A fantasy role-playing game based on the book "The Chronicles of Thomas Covenant." Choose from six character classes, and explore towns, villages, and dungeons in search of treasure and magic.

Buy and trade armor, weapons, food, or magic items from the townspeople, who sometimes have helpful hints about the game. Mapping is simple in THE LAND since the program does it for you. As you search a town, a dungeon, or the outside world, an overhead view shows where you are, and how much is left to explore of that region.

You can save your game at any time — handy if you are about to do battle with a dragon, or Hydra. Like Ultima and Questron this game will take you many hours to complete as your character gains experience and knowledge in the place called THE LAND.

(PC-SIG Disk#'s 2158, 2159)

Special Requirements: *CGA or higher.*
Author Registration: *$25.00*

Landing Party ✍ *by Rick Pitel*

Captain!! The energy crystals that power our life-support systems are failing! We need to locate new ones before we all die! You'll have to count on your crew, now. Let's hope you chose them well.

Your favorite movie stars, historical figures, friends and relatives can become characters in this text adventure game if you choose them before you become captain. You must then deal with an assortment of monsters from the planet's surface before you can get those energy crystals you need so desperately. LANDING PARTY is menu-driven for ease of play. Individual games are short and different each time.

Hurry, Captain! The air... I... I can't breathe....

On the same disk is a two player trivia tic-tac-toe game. Each player must answer a trivia question to mark a square.

(PC-SIG Disk# 604)

Special Requirements: *None.*
Author Registration: *None.*

The Last Half of Darkness ✍ *by SoFTLAB*

Do you like graphic adventure games with sharp pictures, mouse support, save and restore game functions, and spine-shivering puzzles to solve? Then THE LAST HALF OF DARKNESS is for you!

When the game starts, you find yourself in front of your recently deceased aunt's mansion. In order to gain the title to her fortune and estate, you must find the ingredients to a potion she was working on before she was killed. It won't be easy as there are many strange denizens in the old mansion. Some will help you in your quest, while others would just as soon finish you off!

Choose one of the listed commands with either the keyboard or mouse. Use speaker sound or Covox's Speech Thing. Examine everything, take what you can, and don't forget to save your game

The Last Half of Darkness (PC-SIG Disk# 2438)

before you do anything dangerous which, in this game, can be a frequent thing.

What are you waiting for? Dust those cobwebs off your trusty old map notebook and take a journey to THE LAST HALF OF DARKNESS!

(PC-SIG Disk# 2438)

Special Requirements: *EGA, and A Hard Drive.*
Author Registration: *$20.00*

The Last Half of Darkness (CGA) ☆   *by SoFTLAB*

Do you like graphic adventure games with sharp pictures, mouse support, save and restore game functions, and spine-shivering puzzles to solve? Then THE LAST HALF OF DARKNESS is for you!

When the game starts, you find yourself in front of your recently deceased aunt's mansion. In order to gain the title to her fortune and estate, you must find the ingredients to a potion she was working on before she was killed. It won't be easy as there are many strange denizens in the old mansion. Some will help you in your quest, while others would just as soon finish you off!

Choose one of the listed commands with the keyboard or mouse. Use speaker sound or Covox's Speech Thing. Examine everything, take what you can, and don't forget to save your game before you do anything dangerous which, in this game, can be a frequent thing.

What are you waiting for? Dust those cobwebs off your trusty old map notebook and take a journey to THE LAST HALF OF DARKNESS!

(PC-SIG Disk# 2573)

Special Requirements: *CGA, and LHARC archiving utility (#2018)*
Author Registration: *$20.00*

Marooned Again ✍   *by Try-Then-Buy Software*

MAROONED AGAIN is not your standard text adventure. It's logical. It tells you this every time you try to do something illogical. The basic plot: You are marooned on an alien planet with a broken spaceship and a bunch of retarded clones who can only respond to two-word commands. There is hope however! Also on this planet is an alien spaceship that can be made to work with some minor repairs. All you have to do is use the clones to fix the alien ship, and take off.

MAROONED AGAIN is lots of fun, and does not bear the irritating "irrational" nature found in so many adventure games. This game has been highly acclaimed by our users, so much so that it even has a sequel!

(PC-SIG Disk# 1293)

Special Requirements: *None.*
Author Registration: *Contribution.*

McMurphy's Mansion   *by Don Higgins*

MCMURPHY'S MANSION is a text adventure game that begins when your Uncle McMurphy dies and leaves you his fortune. Unfortunately, the money is hidden somewhere on his estate. The object of the game is to find the money, using various clues and objects. Both a map and an inventory list are displayed on the screen, and you can save at any time.

(PC-SIG Disk# 1073)

Special Requirements: *None.*
Author Registration: *$16.00*

Megagopoly   *by Visual Data Communications Corp.*

MEGAGOPOLY is a game of high finance. The scenario: you have just inherited $100,000, now make millions more in the next 20 years. MEGAGOPOLY gives you the opportunity to create unlimited wealth by offering different investments. Depending upon how wisely or not you invest your money, you watch it grow or shrink. Types of investments include stocks, bonds, oil, real estate, and even betting. It also tracks your score so you can play against your friends.

But MEGAGOPOLY is more than that. Every five years of the simulation, you get a bar graph to show your progress down the

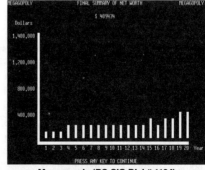

Megagopoly (PC-SIG Disk# 1194)

✍ = Updated Program
☆ = New Program

road to wealth. But don't get too complacent — you might find yourself in the middle of a recession, or trying to make out in the world of runaway inflation.

(PC-SIG Disk# 1194)
Special Requirements: *None.*
Author Registration: *$15.00*

Mix It Up   *by Mark Frank*

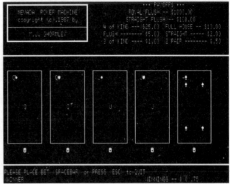

If you're in a gaming mood, here are four great entertainment programs in our library.

NEVADA POKER MACHINE is a simple-to-play, one-player poker game in which you may discard one to five unwanted cards of those dealt to you. The payoff odds are shown at the top right corner of the screen, and the winnings are shown at the bottom. If you've ever played a poker machine in Las Vegas or Atlantic City, NEVADA POKER MACHINE will be very familiar to you.

If poker is not your cup of tea, PRO LOTTO is designed to help you win lotteries ranging from a 6/15 through a 6/52 format. PRO LOTTO lets you store all the past numbers you have played and all past winning numbers. When choosing a

Mix It Up (PC-SIG Disk# 911)

lottery number you can put in your own number or a number produced by random generation. With PRO LOTTO your computer can also generate a number based upon the past record of winning lottery numbers.

PRO LOTTO can also produce a graphic screen showing what numbers are chosen most often, and can find the twelve most popular numbers for both you and your state's numbers. The program will print out the numbers you have chosen and the winning numbers from previous games. PRO LOTTO can show the money you have spent on the lottery and the odds of winning, and can look for all the matches you have made with the lottery for both matching and non-matching dates.

For those more analytical in their entertainment pleasures, and for those for whom a text-adventure is more to their liking, MUTANT INVASION is for you. This game puts you inside a science-fiction adventure in the year 2000. You're within a dome that covers the city to protect it from the firesky at nighttime. You can no longer hear the screams of the Outsiders, but you know they are very near. The atmospheric radiation storms are slowly quieting. Although most of the oceanic disturbances have run their course, tidal waves, typhoons and minor hurricanes occasionally come to claim a few more lives.

You are one of the survivors from the last war. But no one really knows what happened since all the radios, televisions and telephones went silent when the sky began to burn. The Outsiders, as you can guess, are not human. Most people call them mutants. They have more or less become used to living outside the city dome, out in the Burn. But there's no food or water fit for consumption, even for them. That's why they're coming again now. A few of the mutants have found a way into the dome. Do you feel ready to stop them? You must find their secret entrance and seal it off.

If you're more of a mystery fan than a sci-fi fan, the second adventure game is for you. INTERCEPT starts with you on the street in front of a car and a phone booth. If you look closely at your possessions, you see you have an ID card (not for buying alcohol) and a watch. Now, if you type in the correct command, you can get into the car. Once you're inside the car, what do you do? Get out, go into the phone booth, call your friend to find out how to start the car? You'll have to discover what to do on your own.

(PC-SIG Disk# 911)
Special Requirements: *None.*
Author Registration: *$2.00 for POKER, $10.00 for PRO LOTTO.*

Moraff's Revenge   *by MoraffWare*

Science fiction author Steve Moraff brings one of the most complex and beguiling dungeons and dragons games to shareware. Though called a beginners game, few will find it easy. With 70 levels, batallions of monsters and no clear cut rules, this adventure resembles life itself. This game has no single, simple object. Not even survival qualifies. Generally, the game involves equipping, fighting, exploring and healing.

New characters begin their odyssey with only a knife and no money. The characters must kill monsters, some of which are virtually indomitable, and find treasures to get money, weapons and cures. Even character improvement is a key to scoring in this game. The most exciting goal is to find the fountain of youth on the 70th level. A more typical expedition would call on a character to enter the dungeon and kill monsters and discover treasure. Then, the character returns and cashes in treasure at the bank, and sleeps at an inn to gain "spell points" and gain greater power. The character can then buy weapons with his extra money and reenter the dungeon to tackle even more powerful monsters.

Though this program uses simple ASCII graphics to represent the characters and rooms, the game's mapping system still adds to the excitement. The right side of the screen offers a three dimensional view of all four directions. Monsters become visible far down the corridor.

(PC-SIG Disk# 1641)
Special Requirements: *CGA.*
Author Registration: *$10.00*

Moraff's Stones ☆

by MoraffWare

What do they do in the taverns on Moraff's World? What a silly question! Play the strategy gambling/barter game called STONES, of course.

Here you are in a tavern on Moraff's World, the only human in the place. Don't worry, discrimination is against the law in this province. You're sure that the guys (guys? aliens, ETs, BEMs, whatever...) beckoning you to play STONES with them are nice enough creatures who just need a fourth player. You buy into the game and take a seat at the STONES table.

After a while, you aren't doing badly. In fact, you've just wiped out one opponent who leaves the game. Who's this taking her place? You gradually realize that each time one player gets wiped out, it gets replaced by somebody smarter and nastier.

This excellent game from Moraff supports all graphic cards from Hercules to 1024 X 768, 256-colors in super VGA resolution.

(PC-SIG Disk# 2767)
Special Requirements: *512K RAM, and a graphics card.*
Author Registration: *Varies*

Moraff's World ☆

by MoraffWare

MORAFF'S WORLD is an awesome fantasy role-playing game that may keep many players hacking and slashing monsters, night after night. It has 16-level dungeons with brick walls, wooden doors, ladders, and colorful monsters that you can see coming down the 3-D corridors.

Fight more than 20 classes of monsters, cast more than 100 spells, travel five continents, and explore many dungeons. Stores are located on the top levels of each dungeon where you can equip your character with weapons and armor. In the temples, you can buy spells to heal your wounds, and you can store your loot in the bank so its weight won't slow you down.

The main screen features a 3-D view for short distances, and a bird's-eye-view to show you where you are. MORAFF's WORLD has intelligent Help that realizes when you are confused, and makes appropriate suggestions. All commands are initiated with a single keystroke.

This game is part of the MoraffWare Elite Game Series. The games fully support Hercules (720 x 348), CGA (320 x 200), EGA (640 x 350), VGA (640 x 480, 16-colors), MCGA (320 x 200, 256-colors), VGA (360 x 480, 256-colors), 800 x 600, 16-colors, 1024 x 768, 16 and 256-colors!

(PC-SIG Disk# 2766)
Special Requirements: *640K RAM and a graphics card. Hard drive recommended.*
Author Registration: *Call 800-VGA-GAME for pricing.*

Nebula

by Conrad Button's Software

You are in a spaceship exploring the Orion Nebula for NASA. Your mission is to explore the three closest planets to your spaceship and collect one animal, one vegetable, and one mineral. How will you be able to tell? If you encounter an intelligent life form, how will you know? NASA has instructed you to capture it alive. Good luck!

(PC-SIG Disk# 967)
Special Requirements: *None.*
Author Registration: *$20.00*

Nirvana
by Wimsey Co.

When you enter this world of Wimsey, an incredible interactive fantasy awaits you. You will explore uncharted territory, solve ingenious puzzles, and talk to fascinating and sometimes deadly characters. Your quest: Destroy the Ice Maiden, Nirvana, and end the monthly disappearance of young men from the village.

Nirvana can only be destroyed by ringing a crystal bell. You must find the bell, enter her dark castle and destroy her. Otherwise, a fate worse than death awaits you. Here is a good thinking person's game with a vocabulary of more than 1,000 words you can use when speaking to the characters you meet.

This program can also be used as a door on some bulletin board services. Check your BBS software to see if it has this capability.

(PC-SIG Disk# 1281)

Special Requirements: *None.*
Author Registration: *$2.00*

Prince
by Media Methods

You have just inherited a small domain somewhere in the boundless tracks of central Asia. Each year you meet with your royal council and decide how many acres of land to cultivate, how much grain to reserve in the storehouses, and how much additional grain to buy or sell. Gold acquired from trade is needed to maintain your loyal troops, which can be used to defend your territory or to conquer new territory to accomodate an expanding populace. You can also send scouting parties to get information about the strength and potential threat of your surrounding neighbors. Above all, the main objective during your term is to build an irrigation system to guard against drought and make your crops more productive.

When making your decisions you must be careful not to tax your citizens too highly, since they might starve or grow rebellious. On the other hand, if you tax them too low, there may not be enough grain for planting crops next year. At the end of the year, your officers report to you a summary of the year's important events, such as harvest yields, balance in the treasury, population count, effects of drought or plague, territory captured, and information on the developments of any invasions from surrounding territories. The kingdom is in your hands. If you do well you will be honored, but if you do poorly you can always abdicate.

(PC-SIG Disk# 1140)

Special Requirements: *None.*
Author Registration: *$9.95*

Quantoids of Nebulous IV
by Kludgeware

To the Spaceport! If we don't hunt these madmen down, they'll destroy life as we know it today!

(C'mon, admit it. Would you want your daughter to marry an accountant or... Heaven forbid... an MBA?! Do you want your grandchildren calculating ROI?! Aha, I thought not!)

We must fight together and track down the QUANTOIDS OF NEBULOUS IV!!

You find yourself looking out the cockpit of your spacecraft while controlling ship maneuvers, varying your speed and firing at the enemy ships, filled with those nefarious bean-counters intent on enslaving us!

Look out! They have COMPUTERS!!

(PC-SIG Disk# 749)

Special Requirements: *CGA.*
Author Registration: *$25.00*

QuestMaker ☆
by Marietta Co-opware

If you have been dreaming of creating the next great animated adventure game, your dreams may come true with QUESTMAKER. More than two years in development, QUESTMAKER represents a giant step forward in animated game creation.

Even non-programmers will be able to create animated adventure games similar to popular games such as Kings Quest. This unique program allows the user to create fantasy, adventure, or even mystery games using .PCX images. QUESTMAKER is an excellent educational tool for creating subject-specific games. Make learning fun!

QUESTMAKER comes with a complete sample tutorial game called the "Adventures of Hero Harry." This game demonstrates most of the program functions. You won't need to worry about details such as Save and Restore operations, character movements, game Help, speed control, and inventory management since they are already built in. These automatic functions will reduce your game development time. Create a complete game in a couple of days instead of a couple of years.

Since many of the standard functions are already programmed, you can allow your imagination free rein to construct the ultimate animated game you've dreamed about.

All graphics used by the game are 640 x 200, 16-color .PCX images, which you can create using programs such as PC-Paintbrush or the QUESTMAKER II Toolkit, available after registration.

(PC-SIG Disk# 2746)

Special Requirements: *EGA, 286 or better, and a hard drive recommended.*
Author Registration: *$20.00*

Red Planet
by Don Higgins

The first manned expedition to Mars occurred in the year 2075. A lone astronaut, Captain Maltwee, successfully landed on the Red Planet and discovered that an advanced civilization had flourished there for thousands of years. Recent global wars had decimated the inhabitants, leaving but a few isolated bands of Martians intact. Through radio messages from Maltwee, the Earth Federation learned that he had gained the confidence of a religious order who inhabited the ancient city of Aukbaa. Maltwee soon learned that this order had collected the wealth of the old rulers and had hidden it in a secret underground vault. His last message to Earth indicated that he had discovered the secret vault and planned to steal the treasure.

It is now two years later. You have been selected by the Federation to travel to the Red Planet. Your mission is to find Captain Maltwee and return with the treasures of Aukbaa, to Earth.

(PC-SIG Disk# 1073)

Special Requirements: *None.*
Author Registration: *$12.00*

Return to Kroz
by Apogee Software Productions

RETURN TO KROZ is a fast-paced action/arcade style game which throws the player into a realm of dungeons and dangerous traps. Collect whips, gems, scrolls, keys, and other magical items as you make your way down further into the depths of Kroz, avoiding or killing the "text" icons that want to steal your gems and, finally, your very life.

RETURN TO KROZ is the first in a trilogy of games. Control your icon with the numerical key pad and press corresponding letters to use your whips and teleport scroll. Warning — this game is addictive fun — don't play if you have finals coming up or a business deal to close! Previous games by the author, Scott Miller, have won awards, and after trying your luck with RETURN TO KROZ, you'll understand why.

Special Requirements: *None.*
Author Registration: *$7.50*

Ringwielder ✍
by Try-Then-Buy Software

RINGWIELDER is an incredible non-computer role-playing game that features the worlds of both fantasy and science fiction! The full set of rules is included on this disk in text form.

In a "role-playing game," you take on the characteristics of someone (or something) from the realm of fantasy or science fiction and play the game as if you are that character. While RINGWIELDER uses both the worlds of fantasy and science, the occult and extreme violence so prevalent in other games are ommitted. This provides a viable alternative to those who are offended by such things.

RINGWIELDER is easy to play and fast-moving. The rules are easy to understand, but interesting enough to hold the interest of even the most advanced gamer. The entire rule section is contained within this disk, along with an offer to obtain the official, hard-bound collectors-item book and club membership!

(PC-SIG Disk# 1293)

Special Requirements: *None.*
Author Registration: *$10.00, $20.00, $30.00*

Robomaze II ☆   *by MVP Software*

ROBOMAZE II - THE LOBBY is the first in a series of three unique action arcade games, each one building on the other. You are a Freedom Fighter who must regain control of the Tower and the Dome to free your country from an oppressive dictator.

To accomplish this, you will be commanding the prototype Stalker robot. The Stalker is capable of moving left and right, as well as jumping. At the beginning of the game, you have only the limited firepower of a gun. As you acquire money and explore more levels, more powerful weapons become available.

ROBOMAZE II - THE LOBBY has 40 levels filled with 15 different types of robots whose job it is to protect the Tower. During your assault, you will encounter keys that open doors and chests, land mines and spikes that will hamper your progress, and moving platforms that can squash the stalker like an empty can. Along the way, you will find hearts that give you health, ammunition for your weapons, and even special attacks that do anything from making the enemy robots shoot each other to making you invisible for a short time.

Robomaze II (PC-SIG Disk# 2725)

ROBOMAZE II accepts keyboard and joystick input. However, some commands must be entered from the keyboard, while others can be executed using a joystick. The game can be played on a CGA system but the 640X200 16 color-resolution graphics really shine on EGA or VGA monitors.

(PC-SIG Disk# 2725)

Special Requirements: *Graphics card. Joystick compatible.*
Author Registration: *$15.00/$30.00*
➤*ASP Member.*

Secret Quest 2010   *by Eric Iwasaki*

SECRET QUEST 2010 is a graphic/text mystery that takes place aboard a starship in orbit around the Earth. You and a friend have been on a trip through space and are, just now, returning home. You wake up on the morning of your return and find that your friend is missing! You start searching the ship and begin to discover things in the process. Be careful! There are many traps for the unwary.

(PC-SIG Disk# 633)

Special Requirements: *CGA, two floppy drives, and a version of BASIC.*
Author Registration: *None.*

Skyland's Star ☆   *by Castle Software*

Skyland's Star is a science fictional text adventure game which draws its inspiration from classic prose adventures. The storyline is a follows: the Earth is in desperate peril. The rapid growth in population and need for energy has all but depleted the world's fossil fuels. Science has been unable to replace them with a safe and reliable alternative. The player, a member of a small group of scientists, is recruited to travel into the future to witness how the problem was solved - in the past. The bulk of the game takes place here, in a major metropolis of the future. The player must discover how the future solved the problem and retrieve the necessary information and items for the present to survive the crisis, so that the future he witnessed can exist.

The game is intended for anyone who wants a challenging, intelligent diversion from reality. The program would be particularly welcomed by people who long for classic text adventures in these days of graphic intensive programs.

There are several aspects of this game which make it superior to even some of the best known professional text adventures. First, Skyland's Star has an excellent vocabulary, recognizing nearly 1500 words, and a parser which can comprehend commands ranging from a single letter to complex English sentences. It contains a save and restore feature which can save up to 26 games to a single directory. Another feature of the game is its sheer size. There are nearly 150 separate locations for the player to explore, including the City of Skyland itself, the Moon, a lake, an underground sewer system, and the three story government complex. The game was the Grand Prize winner at the 1989 Rockwell International/LAUSD Computer Science Competition.

(PC-SIG Disk# 2796)

Special Requirements: *640K RAM. A hard drive recommended.*
Author Registration: *$25.00*

Sleuth   *by Norland Software*

This is an interactive text game you can populate with your friends, relatives and neighbors. As you begin a game of SLEUTH, a murder has just been committed!

You must explore the house, question the houseguests for alibis and locate both the weapon and the scene of the murder. The challenge is to solve the crime, gather all of the suspects together and accuse the guilty party — before the killer becomes suspicious and eliminates YOU!

This fascinating crime-solving game works on a monochrome monitor, and needs only the keyboard for input. And the killer is . . . .

(PC-SIG Disk# 694)

Special Requirements: *None.*
Author Registration: *$15.00*

The Soccer Game   *by Wizard Games*

Congratulations, you have just been hired as the new manager of a professional soccer team. Find out if you can handle this exciting job with THE SOCCER GAME, a sports managerial simulation game.

The object of this outstanding game is to become a successful manager of a soccer team. You start out managing a fourth division team and try to work your way up. You select the team players, team matches, and even the team scouts. You demonstrate your skills by trading and buying players, by selecting the best teams to play, by making the best team plays and the best deals.

THE SOCCER GAME uses a database of 1270 players, 100 teams, 100 scouts, 100 treasurers, 100 physiotherapists, 100 managers, and 100 assistant managers.

(PC-SIG Disk# 1695)

Special Requirements: *CGA.*
Author Registration: *$20.00*

Son of Stagefright   *by Softworks*

This is a text adventure game with a theatrical twist. Things just aren't going right for you. For starters, you're locked inside an old abandoned theater. The little voice inside you is screaming, "GET OUT OF HERE!" As you try to get out, you'll encounter creaky catwalks, raging rivers, mini-mazes, rogues, rats and a zookeeper. You'll also endure puns, perils, pratfalls, word play, bad jokes, and some mild innuendo.

This game was written using the Adventure Game Toolkit (PC-SIG Disk # 1231,1232) and was the winner of the text adventure contest sponsored by the authors of the Toolkit.

(PC-SIG Disk# 2299)

Special Requirements: *384K RAM.*
Author Registration: *$10.00*
➤*ASP Member.*

Super Game Pak   *by Apogee Software Productions*

SUPER GAME PACK contains six new games for you to explore and enjoy.

In the SHRINE OF KROZ, you are searching for the precious Crown within the mysterious kingdom of Kroz. Undoubtedly, the Crown must be guarded by unspeakable dangers. Armed with a whip and great courage, you decide to continue your journey.

WORD WHIZ is a word challenge game to measure your knowledge of the English language. For example, are you positive you know what the word "peruse" means? Most people believe it means "to skim" or "to glance over," but in fact it means "to read carefully." Most questions focus on a key word. There are four multiple choice answers to choose from.

Your quest in the ROGUE RUNNER is to recover the precious Heart of Courage, hidden deep inside the treacherous Ezam dungeons. The dungeons are populated by the lost souls of those who tried the journey before you. You may find maps and pick axes left behind by these adventurers. Keep an eye out for the scattered Teleport Scrolls. They will help you escape imminent death.

Test your knowledge in the world of Star Trek, one of the most popular TV series of all time, with TREK TRIVIA. There are 100 questions to pick your brain, each with four possible answers.

ASTEROID RESCUE has you put in command of the Space Eagle. Your mission is to rescue the crew members that have been blown from the USS Sagan during an uncharted asteroid storm. The crew members from the USS Sagan were able to get into their life suits, but their air supply will not last long. Help is needed immediately!

BLOCK FIVE is a simple game to learn, yet is quite difficult to master. The object is to place five of your Xs in a row while preventing the computer opponent from putting five Os in a row.

(PC-SIG Disk# 2296)

Special Requirements: *CGA.*
Author Registration: *$10.00*

Supernova   *by Apogee Software Productions*

SUPERNOVA is an interactive text adventure set in the future. As the dauntless adventurer, you will partake in an epic story that spans a galaxy and gives you the chance to save a civilization from an exploding star.

You begin the game on a remote mining planet with little to look forward to except another back-breaking day in the mines. From here on, you're on your own!

A 16-color display keeps you abreast of your injuries, hunger and thirst levels, sickness, and weariness, and displays necessary diagrams and signs. Sound effects are used throughout the game and over 1000 words are in the vocabulary. Included is a nice touch — a "clue" function when you are well and truly stuck.

Now, if you're going to save a civilization, you'd better get started!

(PC-SIG Disk# 952)

Special Requirements: *None.*
Author Registration: *$10.00*

T-Zero ☆   *by Dennis Cunningham*

Travel through time in T-ZERO, a text adventure in the grand style. Mix elements of fantasy and science fiction while exploring the nature of time. Explore a rustic but disturbing present, a bustling prehistoric era, and a damaged, bureaucratic future. Your task is to locate six round objects scattered across eras and landscapes, transport them to progressively future time-zones, and manipulate them in a fashion that will right the troubled times.

This game is dedicated to all gamers saddened by the premature death knell sounded for text adventures.

(PC-SIG Disk# 2691)

Special Requirements: *None.*
Author Registration: *$15.00*
➤*ASP Member.*

Tactical Combat Simulator   *by Michael J. Feldhake*

TCS (TACTICAL COMBAT SIMULATOR) is a wargame simulation.

This interactive utility program allows two players to control company-size combat units. Place mines, set spot zones, scout areas of a map, set obstructions (such as blown bridges), move units, call in artillery fire and direct ground support.

Design your own game or play a pre-made game like "Panzer Leader." The versatility of TCS is limited only by your imagination. Use different scenarios in different times of history. A nice touch is the dimension that most games forget — Hidden Moves. This program adds realism and versatility to wargaming. Each player has his own password and can only access his side of the game. You'll need to practice sound military tactics and intelligence to win. Use the Save feature and continue your game at a later time.

(PC-SIG Disk# 2378)

Special Requirements: *None.*
Author Registration: *$15.00*

Time Traveler   *by Conrad Button's Software*

You begin this text adventure in the Stanford University lecture hall in the year 2285. First, you must find the fabled Darnoc Time Machine. Then hurry back to the past to find the allaw allaw plant needed to save all civilization. Remember, you must be both smart and alert. Travel to the beaches of Normandy on D-Day. Visit revolutionary Philadelphia, the wild west, Sherwood Forest, the Egyptian pyramids, and an a prehistoric jungle. If you overcome the brontosaurus and other threats, you might save mankind. Remember that you alone have the burden of saving the world, one mistake and life on Earth as we know it will cease to exist.

(PC-SIG Disk# 1075)

Special Requirements: *None.*
Author Registration: *$12.00.*

Under the Gulf
by MK Systems

If you're a game player who's considered going pro, here's the test. UNDER THE GULF is a game which simulates the actions of a United States attack submarine. You are in control of the nuclear powered vessel while the computer controls an opposing fleet of ships and submarines. The game takes place in a 500nm x 500nm area of the Black Sea. In the south west corner, two land masses merge to form a natural canal into the Mediterranean Sea.

Your mission is to keep all of the opposing ships from reaching the open waters of the Mediterranean. UNDER THE GULF demands the highest level of concentration and forces you to stay on top of numerous variables — only the best of you will be able to hack this game, which relies heavily on your ability to keep track of your vessel's status.

Your submarine has complete radar and sonar systems, short and long range torpedoes, defensive systems, mining systems, and extensive navigational capabilities. Periodically, the weapons systems and the enemy ships will be updated. Unlike the enemy, however, your submarine is updated constantly and displayed with numeric status fields.

(PC-SIG Disk# 1852)

Special Requirements: *None.*
Author Registration: *$20.00*

World Generator
by Marcus L. Rowland

WORLD GENERATOR is a utility for referees of science fiction role- playing games such as Traveller(TM) and Space Opera(TM). It is not a game in itself.

It produces detailed descriptions and maps of solar systems and planets in three-dimensional space sectors, with data on lifeforms, atmosphere, geology, etc. You can quickly generate, store, and edit designs for individual planets and entire solar systems. Each sector of the universe can have up to 100 solar systems and each solar system is allocated a star and up to 17 planets, asteroid belts, dust clouds, or secondary stars.

WORLD GENERATOR is menu-driven and provides on-line help displays as well as a tutorial and a rolling demonstration to help you get started.

(PC-SIG Disk# 1133)

Special Requirements: *CGA.*
Author Registration: *$10.00*

▼ ▼ ▼

Games, Arcade

Adventures of Captain Comic
by Michael Denio

THE ADVENTURES OF CAPTAIN COMIC is a fast-moving arcade game with high- quality color graphics. The Captain's job, and you know he will accept it, is to recover three treasures of the planet Omsoc that were stolen and hidden on the remote world of Tambi.

Along the way he must face many dangers, including: dive-bombing birds, bugs, fireballs, beachballs, spinners, glow globes, blind toads, killer bees, sparks, atoms, saucers, and the dreaded space pollen.

But our hero is not one to go into battle unarmed. He carries a blaster to blow away any meanies that attack, a shield to protect him from their touch (temporarily), and the uncanny ability to jump amazing distances. He also finds many items that can help in his mission: keys, lanterns, corkscrews, boots, and cans of Blastola Cola.

If you decide to go adventuring with the Captain, all you need bring are quick reflexes, a good eye for detail and your ability to solve problems on the fly. Age level: 7-adult.

(PC-SIG Disk# 1450)

Special Requirements: *EGA with 256K of video RAM.*
Author Registration: *$10.00 to $20.00*

Alien Worlds
by Shannon Larratt

Here's an exciting game to show off your VGA screen. You're space walking in your space suit and you have to shoot aliens as they attack. The surreal view of outer space — its detail and color — make ALIEN WORLDS a unique action game. There are no documentation files with this program, but what you need to know is given within the program itself. The game is easy to grasp, but not as easy to master.

(PC-SIG Disk# 1939)

Special Requirements: *640K RAM, VGA, and a mouse.*
Author Registration: *$5.00*

Alive Sharks
by Alive Software

An underwater action arcade game that utilizes unique Artificial Intelligence, simulation and classic animation techniques to transform your computer screen into a realistic ocean floor.

You are the Frogman and your mission is to collect rare marine creatures and recover lost treasures from the bottom of the sea. Armed with your trusty stun-gun, you can retreat to your electromagnetic base that repels sharks and the rest of your dreadful enemies. Your diving uniform is state-of-the-art, but you can survive only a few shark bites and it is useless against the poison of the deadly jellyfish.

This is not your typical "shoot-em-up," "eat-the-dots" kind of game. Your enemies are crafty and independent and they surround you in clever formations. When you shoot at them from far away, they are smart enough to avoid your shot.

(PC-SIG Disk# 2231)

Special Requirements: *Optional mouse or joystick.*
Author Registration: *$20.00*

Arcade Series 3
by Tim Keller

A really fine collection of colorful arcade games. If you can't find a game to suit you here, perhaps you're just not a game player. This collection of games for the color tube will catch and hold your attention for hours. They work well on the PCjr also.

(PC-SIG Disk# 293)

Special Requirements: *CGA.*
Author Registration: *None.*

File Descriptions:

3-DEMON	EXE	A fascinating 3D Packman type game.
3-DEMON	HI1	Score keeper for 3-DEMON.
PC-GOLF	EXE	Plays golf on your color tube.
PANGO	EXE	Use blocks to squish the bees before they get YOU. PANGO
HGH Sc	re	eper for PANGO.
KONG	EXE	Jump the barrels and watch out for the gorilla.
FORTUNE	EXE	Word game like Wheel of Fortune (mono).
PYRAMID	EXE	Climb the pyramid and the blocks change color.
PITFALL	EXE	Diving down a long pit but don't touch the walls (mono).

Asteroid Field Battle
by Leithauser Research

ASTEROID FIELD BATTLE is a challenging battle against the dreaded Electronians within the confines of a computer screen.

Your ship is trapped inside an electro-barrier and the Electronians are hunting you down. Your sole defenses are a limited force field, a short range laser, and several asteroids also trapped in the barrier which can be used to pick off the enemy ships.

This game can be played with or without a joystick. There are five levels of play, but the speed is CPU clock dependent so faster hardware may need to be reset to play. Beware! As with any zap'em game, this one is highly addictive.

(PC-SIG Disk# 1523)

Special Requirements: *CGA.*
Author Registration: *None.*

Battle Fleet 🖉 *by Wade Corby*

A game similar to the Milton Bradley's Battleship. Deploy your BATTLE FLEET, and sink your opponent's ships before yours are destroyed. The program has nine levels of difficulty. Play against the computer, or another person via a modem.

(PC-SIG Disk# 2261)

Special Requirements: *EGA. Hayes compatible modem optional.*
Author Registration: *$15.00*

BEGIN: A Tactical Starship Simulation *by Clockwork Software*

This game is a battle simulation matching potential starship commanders against the computer. The candidate can represent any one of four possible nations: the Federation, Klingon, Romulan, or Orion. Several different ship classes with varying armament are available. The simulation is complete including damage, casualty reports (from Dr. McCoy), engine temperatures (from Scotty), phaser recharging times (Chekov), and even the variables involved in navigating large as opposed to small ships (Sulu). A player can command from one to a fleet of nine ships.

The degree of difficulty is controlled by the size of the opposing fleets; a player can configure the odds in his favor or to the computer's advantage. The computer strategy is quite effective; the novice captain probably will not win in a one-on-one confrontation. The starship captain has a great deal of responsibility in a battle situation, and this simulation will truly test a candidate's ability to command.

(PC-SIG Disk# 1692)

Special Requirements: *None.*
Author Registration: *$15.00*

Brian's Games *by Public Brand Software*

This disk has some of the better games in the PC-SIG library. Shoot the martians before they kill you in the arcade game, SPACEVAD. Hear Wocka, Wocka, Wocka as you play that old favorite, PACKMAN, and keep your eye on the ball when playing BREAKOUT. All these games run on the PCjr, so nobody is left out.

(PC-SIG Disk# 274)

Special Requirements: *Some programs require a version of BASIC and CGA.*
Author Registration: *None.*
➤*ASP Member.*

File Descriptions:

CASTLE	EXE	Find your way out of castle, get treasures, kill monsters.
CASTLE	RAN	Part of CASTLE game.
GAMES	TXT	Comments from the person who selected these programs.
XWING	BAS	Try to destroy the deathstar.
WIZARD	BAS	A role game to find the ORB of ZOT.
LIFE2	BAS	Source code for LIFE2.
LIFE2	EXE	Try to make your bacteria live.
BUGS!	SCR	Part of BUGS.
BUGS	EXE	Shoot crawling creatures before they get you.
LANDER	SCR	Part of LANDER.
LANDER	BIN	Part of LANDER.
LANDER	BAS	Land a space ship on a pad without crashing.
SPACEVAD	EXE	Shoot invaders before they invade earth.
BREAKOUT	BAS	Try to break out of a brick wall, like tennis.
PACKMAN	DOC	Documentation for PACKMAN.EXE.
PACKMAN	EXE	Gobble power pellets and eat monsters.

Casino Slot Machines *by Richard Metlen*

Here are three slot machine simulations for the casino lover. Besides a basic slot machine that matches dollar amounts three accross for your pay-off, there are also slot versions of keno and low-ball poker. These games would be ideal for someone planning their own casino night. While the ASCII graphics don't compare to the video slots you find in the casinos, the action is very much the same. And if you play long enough you might find these slots are a little loose... but we all like a loose slot, don't we?

(PC-SIG Disk# 1573)

Special Requirements: *None.*
Author Registration: *$10.00*

Caves of Thor
by Apogee Software Productions

On an expedition far within the icy mountains of Norway you discover a crevice leading deep into the jagged rock. You find yourself within a vast underground empire—an enormous network of caves, passages and chambers. Local legends reveal that a famous mythological deity once ruled these peaks, could you have stumbled across the mystical ruler's kingdom? You decide to find out....

CAVES OF THOR is a brilliant 16 color arcade/graphics game with a 4-way scrolling playfield. You'll need to explore seven huge levels for the three Symbols of Virtue. These three virtues are needed to finish CAVES OF THOR.

As you explore the empire you must overcome the many creatures that patrol it. Use your gun (unlimited bullets) to shoot creatures and creature generators. Other hazards include underground flowing streams (with currents that can drag you away!), bubbling lava pits and lakes, and the very dangerous Thor Beast, which creates creatures with devastating speed.

This program features some of the best music yet heard in a shareware game. Other notable features include a save/restore option, easy keyboard controls, a demonstration mode, permanent high score, and an easy playing cheat mode!

For those players looking for a game similar to the Kroz games... this is it.

(PC-SIG Disk# 2327)

Special Requirements: *CGA.*
Author Registration: *$10.00*

Commander Keen ✍
by Apogee Software Productions

Commander Keen pushes graphics to the limit. It's truly a "commercial quality" game that Nintendo and arcade fans will appreciate. It features ultra high-speed EGA graphics and superb sound effects. The animation and scrolling is updated at 60 frames per second (motion picture quality cartoons are filmed at only 24 frames per second).

The epic story of Commander Keen is in the style of the memorable matinee serials of Flash Gordon. You play the role of Billy Blaze, an eight year-old child genius who builds an interstellar ship when not working at home on his college fast-track degree. Among other household objects, Billy uses his Nintendo joystick for flight control and his mom's vacuum cleaner (heavily modified) for his ship's ion propulsion system (with pile height adjustment).

At the first hint of galactic trouble, Billy dons his brother's football helmet and becomes "Commander Keen" — defender of Earth! Ever on the side of justice, fairness, and high calorie junk food, Keen dispenses justice with an iron hand.

Commander Keen (PC-SIG Disk# 2505)

"Marooned on Mars" is Volume one of the Commander Keen trilogy. Each volume has its own unique appearance, with different goals, graphics, game characters, animation, and locations.

(PC-SIG Disk# 2505)

Special Requirements: *530K RAM, EGA/VGA, and high density drive.*
Author Registration: *$15.00 for each volume.*

Dark Ages ✍
by Apogee Software Productions

Once again the here is a superb game for all of you who like get away from it all and go adventuring to the DARK AGE.

Dark Ages is the first shareware game to support the Ad Lib and Sound Blaster music cards. It features a movie-style soundtrack of eight unique songs and themes. It also has sound effects that don't require an Ad Lib (or Sound Blaster) card to enjoy.

The EGA/VGA graphics are colorful and stunning, with fast scrolling screens and high-speed animation. Dark Ages has such demanding graphics and animation that it requires an 80286 (or 80386) machine to run at proper speed, otherwise it may run too slowly. Therefore, Dark Ages may only run on the newer, faster PCs and compatibles.

"Prince of Destiny" is volume one of the Dark Ages trilogy. Only part one is available via shareware distribution, the other two volumes ("The Undead Kingdom" and "Dungeons of Doom") may only be purchased directly from Apogee Software Productions (ASP). Each volume has its own unique appearance, with different goals, level designs and locations. Each volume has 10 huge scrolling levels packed with devious traps, creatures and treasures.

Other features include built in instructions, save and restore, permanent high scores, sound on/off, flexible keyboard configuration, and three skill levels. Registered players will also receive a secret password, which can be used to activate a "child level" mode, and also an auto-fire mode, so you can hold down the fire key for continuous shots!

(PC-SIG Disk# 2568)

Special Requirements: *286/386 PC, 400K RAM, EGA/VGA, and high density drive.*
Author Registration: *$15.00 per volume; $30.00 for set.*

Dino Picture Database   *by TO-Soft*

If you like dinosaurs, then you'll love the DINO DATABASE. DINO tells you the common and scientific names of a dinosaur and lists other dinosaurs in the same family. A world map graphically displays their habitats and the years they lived.

Kids will like the option to "paint" the dinosaurs and change the screen colors. A function to print the screen is also available. This program makes it fun and entertaining for kids or adults who want to learn about dinosaurs.

(PC-SIG Disk# 2276)

Special Requirements: *CGA.*
Author Registration: *14.95*

Duke Nukem ☆   *by Apogee Software Productions*

After the tremendous response to Commander Keen, Apogee's follow-up game had to be really spectacular. And Duke Nukem is just that—a superb showstopper with over one Meg of animation and graphics, four times more than Commander Keen had!

This is an arcade/adventure game that compares to the Sega Genesis home systems. (It's far superior to games typically seen on the Nintendo home system.)

Duke Nukem also has four-way, dual scrolling playfields, and does it better than any other IBM game. Features: Large animated characters, reflections, arcade sound effects, built-in hint mode, joystick support, cinematic sequences, self-running demo mode, save/restore, high scores, etc.

Rarely is a game released with such a well animated main character. Duke Nukem does realistic somersaults and uses his grappling hooks to hand-walk along ceilings. Duke is a hero everyone will like.

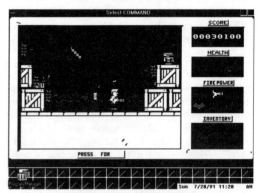
Duke Nukem (PC-SIG Disk# 2677)

Duke Nukem is rendered in vivid EGA graphics, with many special screen effects. As usual, Apogee offers two more episodes if players want to continue their adventures with Duke.

This is truly a game that will demonstrate the graphical abilities of your computer if you have EGA or VGA. Get ready for a fun time as you rescue the world from the latest madman, Dr. Proton.

(PC-SIG Disk# 2677)

Special Requirements: *640K RAM, EGA or VGA, and a hard drive.*
Author Registration: *$15.00 for each episode or $30.00 for all three.*

EGA Trek ✍ *by Nels Anderson*

You have been put in command of the Constitution Class Heavy Cruiser U.S.S. ENTERPRISE, naval construction contract number NCC-1701. Your mission as commander of the ENTERPRISE is to secure a 64 quadrant sector of the galaxy.

Since the collapse of the Organian Peace Treaty of 3199.5, a Klingon invasion fleet has been sighted in parts of the Federation territory. You have been instructed to eliminate any Klingon cruiser, command vessel, or Klingon starbase found in your area. Good luck, Captain!

This is an impressive EGA version of an old favorite.

(PC-SIG Disk# 1221)

Special Requirements: *EGA.*
Author Registration: *$15.00*
➤*ASP Member.*

EGL_RISE ✍ *by Esprit de E software design*

EGL_RISE comes is made up of two large games. Twenty game levels are similar to other arcade games such as Pac-Man, Donkey Kong, and Space Invaders. Each level is different enough to be a game in itself. The 25-level adventure series is called the "Rise & Fall of the Human Race". Both games offer excellent graphics

On each level you have a different objective to accomplish — collect all the treasures or objects, find your way to a certain destination, destroy all the monsters, defuse a bomb, etc. The level ends when you are hit by a monster or trapped so that you cannot escape. Some levels have a timer and you must complete the level before the time runs out. Some games are played like an arcade game, but in others you must take your time in order to plan your strategy.

EGL_RISE is compatible with all graphic cards, including CGA, EGA, VGA, Hercules and monochrome text adapters. Modify the graphics of the game characters with a draw function, creating your own style for each game. You can even create your own games when you register.

(PC-SIG Disk# 2673)

Special Requirements: *None.*
Author Registration: *$25.00 for game, and $39.00 for game creator.*

Frac ✍ *by Simsalabim Software*

If you think twisting, moving, and dropping different shaped blocks to form solid lines is fun, then FRAC, a new 3-D TETRIS-like program, will drive you completely over the edge.

The object of FRAC is deceptively simple. Pack falling blocks into solid layers as quickly and efficiently as possible. However, in FRAC you have to contend with not only moving and twisting the falling blocks, but also shifting them in space in order to place them in empty spaces on the 3-dimensional grid. If it sounds difficult, it is. The first couple of layers are relatively easy to complete, but with more than three layers, placing the many differently-shaped blocks can be a nerve-wracking fun experience.

If you've grown tired of 2-dimensional dropping-block games, enter the 3-D FRAC zone. Watch out for the huge 3x3x3 cube. It's the hardest shape to place.

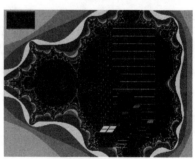
Frac (PC-SIG Disk# 2436)

(PC-SIG Disk# 2436)

Special Requirements: *EGA.*
Author Registration: *$10.00*

Games Galore *by Broad Street Photo*

Put your pedal to the metal! BIG-RIG is a text game which puts you behind the wheel of an 18 wheeler long-haul truck, where you must face various conditions pertaining to the road, your rig, and the weather. To make your deadline and make more money, you can skip sleep, drive faster, or increase your payload at the risk of getting into an accident or paying a fine. 10-4, good buddy!

GEMINI-2 is a tank war game which you may play against the computer's tank or that of another player remotely by modem. Colorful graphics put you inside your tank. The screen is divided into a radar map and a three-dimensional view showing the landscape and your opponent's tank.

NUKEWAR is a text game that lets you launch deadly nuclear weapons and wipe out whole cities. Choose sides. You can be the United States or the U.S.S.R. This is a game where no one wins.

In the colorful graphics game, SOPWITH, you pilot a World War I biplane. Your mission: bomb all the enemy outposts while using your machine guns against the computer's biplanes.

(PC-SIG Disk# 1328)

Special Requirements: *CGA and a modem for remote play.*
Author Registration: *$15.00.*

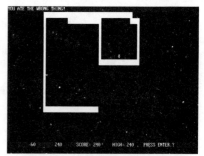
Games Galore (PC-SIG Disk# 1328)

Giant Space Slug ✍

by Try-Then-Buy Software

The classical game of WORMS with nothing special added—except blinding speed. The speed level is adjustable from very easy to absolutely impossible. This makes it more fun to play than previously existing games which typically offered only one speed level. This game uses joystick or keyboard input.

GIANT SPACE SLUG is excellent for building eye-hand coordination, especially among children. It utilizes all four directions of the screen, not just the typical back-and-forth motion of most arcade-type games. This game has been most popular among parents wanting good games for their children. It works on monochrome as well as color monitors.

(PC-SIG Disk# 1293)

Special Requirements: *None.*
Author Registration: *Contribution.*

Giant Space Slug (PC-SIG Disk# 1293)

Hugo II, Whodunit? ✍

by Gray Design Associates

It's adventure time again as HUGO and Penelope get swept up in another superbly animated 3-D EGA extravaganza! This time a murder mystery is afoot, with a couple of fiendish twists and a large helping of humor along the way.

Look what's in store — a revolving bookcase, a saucy French maid, and a murderer!! HUGO II, WHODUNIT? has the same look and feel of HUGO'S HOUSE OF HORRORS with more screens and characters.

If you enjoyed the original HUGO adventure, HUGO II has a real treat in store for you!

(PC-SIG Disk# 2571)

Special Requirements: *360K RAM, EGA, and a hard drive or high density floppy drive.*
Author Registration: *$20.00*
➤*ASP Member.*

International Game Collection

by PC Projects

PC PONTOON is a memory-resident blackjack type game with a few twists on the old classic.

The game is based on the original classic pontoon or blackjack, whichever you want to call it. From Ireland, it diverges from American casino blackjack in several significant ways. Like conventional casino blackjack, the object of the game is to get 21 or less, but PC PONTOON is for one player only. Some other rules of the game: if you and the computer get the same value, then the computer wins that game; Pontoon (blackjack, a natural) beats any other hands; a five-card trick beats all other hands except for Pontoon; and if both players go over 21 (bust) then both bets are returned.

PRINCE lets you rule your very own kingdom. Make decisions on how to rule it and face the consequences.

You have just inherited a small domain somewhere in the boundless tracks of central Asia. Each year you meet with your royal council and decide how many acres of land to cultivate, how much grain to reserve in the storehouses, and how much additional grain to buy or sell. Gold acquired from trade is needed to maintain your loyal troops, which can be used to defend your territory or to conquer new territory to accomodate an expanding populace. You can also send scouting parties to get information about the strength and potential threat of your surrounding neighbors. Above all, the main objective during your term is to build an irrigation system to guard against drought and make your crops more productive.

When making your decisions you must be careful not to tax your citizens too highly, since they might starve or grow rebellious. On the other hand, if you tax them too low, there may not be enough grain for planting crops next year. At the end of the year, your officers report to you a summary of the year's important events, such as harvest yields, balance in the treasury, population count, effects of drought or plague, territory captured, and information on the developments of any invasions from surrounding territories. The kingdom is in your hands. If you do well you will be honored, but if you do poorly you can always abdicate.

BALL CATCHER is a game where the object is to catch balls with a basket. A basket is moved below columns using the number keys one to eight. Balls move down columns called tubes slowly at first, but increasingly more rapidly. Every ball caught by the basket scores a point, and missing a ball registers a fault. A round ends when eight faults are accumulated, or the time allowed in seconds has elapsed. Points are determined by completed rounds versus the number of faults.

(PC-SIG Disk# 1140)

Special Requirements: *None.*
Author Registration: *$10.00 to $15.00.*

Islands of Danger! ☆ *by Richard Carr*

Your mission — Take your killer hovercraft, pass the Twenty Islands of Danger (and their missile launchers), and rescue Jean. Sound easy? Guess again, Rambo!

The author has used standard ASCII graphic characters and created an arcade-style game, complete with sound. Control your ship's path with one hand and shoot missiles with the other. Dodge enemy missiles and attack their launchers. The game can be played at different speeds for different abilities and also supports a joystick. Arcade fun at home!

(PC-SIG Disk# 2670)

Special Requirements: *Graphics card.*
Author Registration: *$13.00*

Jigsaw Mania *by United Innovations Plus*

Jigsaw puzzle fans rejoice! JIGSAW MANIA provides colorful fun for all who enjoy the challenge of a good jigsaw puzzle by scrambling an image on your screen and asking you to piece it back together.

You set the difficulty level by dividing the puzzle into a few big pieces or lots of little square pieces. The program mixes the pieces up and you put them back together. That may sound easy, but you know better.

JIGSAW MANIA counts the number of moves it takes to complete the puzzle. The shareware version contains two different puzzles, while athe registered version contains twelve. The puzzles are great for either childern or adults, simply just adjust the level of difficulty.

Don't worry about not having time to finish the puzzle. JIGSAW MANIA has a feature that lets you save the puzzle at any point and come back to it later. Not only is it fun, but it sure saves a lot of space on the dining room table.

(PC-SIG Disk# 2144)

Special Requirements: *384K RAM and VGA.*
Author Registration: *$18.00*

Jumpjet ☆ *by Montsoft*

Your mission: seek and destroy three enemy bombers. Sounds easy — but talk's cheap! This is one of many missions that will let you find out if you have what it takes to fly a JUMPJET.

Old fighter pilots will remember the "Defender" arcade series when they play this arcade-style fighter plane game. Use the cursor keys to fly over mountains, evade fighters, and attack tanks. Use the space bar to shoot your machine guns. Good arcade-style graphics make it easy to play — but challenging to win. JUMPJET also supports the Ad-Lib and compatible sound boards for realistic crashes, explosions, and the sweet sound of success.

(PC-SIG Disk# 2535)

Special Requirements: *CGA, EGA, or Hercules graphics.*
Author Registration: *$15.00*

Jumpjet (PC-SIG Disk# 2535)

Liberty Bell Slot ✍   *by TechStaff Consultants, Inc.*

LIBERTY BELL SLOT is very simple. You pull the handle and watch three barrels roll. Match numbers three across and score points. The sound and action is very much like an actual slot machine. The graphics are good considering it doesn't use anything other than ASCII characters.

(PC-SIG Disk# 2064)

Special Requirements: *448K RAM.*
Author Registration: *$7.95*

Linewars   *by Patrick Aalto*

LINEWARS is a two-user three dimensional space war game. It makes the most of your graphics display adapters with high definition graphics. You can play LINEWARS alone or against a friend using a modem or cable.

You are looking at your opponent from your Cobra Mark IV multi-purpose General Contact Vehicle. Your ship is equipped with an energy shield, up to six missiles and two beam lasers, front and rear.

The events of this game take place far away in intergalactic space, where stars are few and alien vessels common. Therefore, you should pay attention not only to your opponent but also to all other ships in your vicinity. And there is always the chance that your missile launching system may jam. If this happens, you cannot use missiles during the battle.

Supports a mouse and ports COM1 to COM4 and speeds of 300 to 19200 bps. It has an easy-to-use menu-driven interface for various game settings. Includes a terminal program with dialing and auto-answer features.

(PC-SIG Disk# 1764)

Special Requirements: *CGA, MCGA, EGA, or VGA.*
Author Registration: *$24.00*

Maze Cube   *by Charles A. Spence*

Remember magic squares — those little black and white plastic puzzles with the 24 numbered tiles and one empty space? You had to slide the tiles back and forth until you got all the numbers in the right order. This is the computer version and it's all grown up!

MAZE CUBE is an addictive puzzle strategy game for all ages. The object is to match a given pattern with the fewest number of moves. It is a great way to help younger players develop logical thinking and spacial relationship concepts. For the older player, it's just plum good fun! MAZE CUBE is entirely menu-driven and provides thorough on-screen instructions. Age level: 6-adult.

Also included are 25 different puzzles of varying degrees of difficulty. A nice feature is the autoplay facility that replays your best game so you can see where improvements are needed. The program also lets you design your own puzzle patterns, up to a maximum of 99 different games. This is the first game in the "Mind Maze" series, Wreck Tangle (Disk #1836) is the second.

(PC-SIG Disk# 1419)

Special Requirements: *None.*
Author Registration: *$15.00*

Minelayer ☆   *by Richard Carr*

A colorful fast-scrolling arcade game with on-line documentation. Your high speed minelayer can move in eight directions across a huge 24-screen ocean. Your mission: destroy (by ramming) all of the enemy bases. Your only defense against the enemy rammer ships are the mines you deploy. The advanced version has many variations that will keep you challenged, busy, and addicted for a long, long time.

(PC-SIG Disk# 2670)

Special Requirements: *Color adapter.*
Author Registration: *$10.00*

Miscellaneous Games
by Robert Castle

A collection of programs inspired by the Computer Recreations column in "Scientific American." Several data files are included.

❏ HYPER — a hyper cube (fourth-dimensional cube) drawing program.
❏ WALLPAP — an intricate patterns drawing program with a very simple numeric seed.
❏ WATOR — a biosphere simulation in which fish are eaten by sharks, which die and reproduce.
❏ CLUSTER — a simulation of the motion of star clusters of two or more stars.

(PC-SIG Disk# 945)

Special Requirements: *CGA.*
Author Registration: *$20.00*

Mix and Match ☆
by Richard Carr

If you liked Tetris, you'll love MIX AND MATCH. In Tetris, the goal is to arrange the blocks in the time allowed. In MIX AND MATCH, the goal is to match the random color in the fewest tries.

Match the color by choosing the correct intensity of the three primary colors of light (red, green, blue). A game the whole family will love! You'll also learn something useful — how the colors of light are made.

A great 640 by 480 high-res VGA game!

(PC-SIG Disk# 2670)

Special Requirements: *VGA.*
Author Registration: *$10.00*

Moraff's Blast I ✍
by MoraffWare

Remember the old Pong game? Use a paddle to hit a ball against a wall of bricks. MORAFF'S BLAST is the pong game of 90's. With 21 levels, you can have up to 14 balls in play at once! The game has many special effects such as changing the size of the paddle, splitting the ball into four, faster play, slower play, and advance to the next level when a special brick is hit.

MORAFF'S BLAST I is the first game ever to support SUPER-VGA 800x600 in 16 colors! Also supports HERCULES, CGA, EGA and VGA 640x480.

(PC-SIG Disk# 2227)

Special Requirements: *Graphics card.*
Author Registration: *$45.00*

Moraff's Entrap ☆
by MoraffWare

Moraffware brings yet another high resolution computer game to the shareware world, supporting everything from hercules monochrome to super VGA color monitors, including 1024x768 256 color graphics. Like Moraff's Pinball (the first high-res VGA game) and Morff's Blast (the first 800x600 16 color game), Moraff's ENTRAP reaches new video heights in both the shareware and retail market.

Moraff's ENTRAP is a three dimensional game with a spectacular view of a huge maze-like playing field littered with enemy robots programmed to capture you. Your objective is to reach the far end of the pathway. You'll have to use every ounce of your mental skill to entrap the enemy robots as you progress toward your objective.

(PC-SIG Disk# 2647)

Special Requirements: *Graphics card.*
Author Registration: *Varies.*

Moraff's Pinball
by MoraffWare

If arcade pinball is your game, then try MoraffWare's MORAFF'S PINBALL with all the elements of regular pinball including bumpers, side traps, double scores, flippers, and lots of lights and noise. Try to beat your best score and enter your name into MORRAF'S PINBALL Hall of Fame.

MORRAFF'S PINBALL loads easily onto any IBM or compatible. Use the up arrow key to play, putting the first of five balls into action. The TAB and Q keys control the left flippers, the SPACE BAR controls your bottom flippers, and the ENTER key controls the right flipper. Good eye and finger coordination will increase your score.

The shareware version only lets you play one ball each game.

(PC-SIG Disk# 2162)
Special Requirements: *EGA.*
Author Registration: *$10.00*

Moraff's Super Blast ☆
by MoraffWare

The sequel to the ultimate bricks and paddles is here. SUPER BLAST has 34 levels and up to 17 simultaneous balls. The game contains many special bricks that do things like move, multiply, eat balls, and explode into eight balls. Also included are one way bricks, tunnels to other levels, and paddle expansion and contraction bricks.

This game will work with any graphics card from Hercules to CGA, EGA, and even 800x600 VGA in 16 colors. The game only supports a joystick if you have an AT class computer.

(PC-SIG Disk# 2648)
Special Requirements: *Graphics card.*
Author Registration: *Varies.*

Nyet ☆
by None

If you haven't yet acquired Tetris, here's your chance to buy a "Tetris"-like program through shareware. The object of the game is to pack a 2-dimensional box with block-shaped figures as they come falling down from the computer sky. Try hard not to leave any spaces, but don't despair. You'll get it in time!

This game appeals to both computer game veteran and novice alike (it is quite addictive!). Once you think you're pretty hot stuff, NYET challenges you to make the game harder — drop those blocks faster! Now see what you can do!

(PC-SIG Disk# 2437)
Special Requirements: *None.*
Author Registration: *None.*

Paul's Games
by Paul Hilts

PAUL'S GAMES is a collection of three games: TANKS, BLASTER, and the card game MEMORY.

TANKS is a real-time, two-player game where you must manuever your tank through a maze to hit your opponent. The option to design your own maze adds unpredictability to the action. (The BASIC source code is included for your modification.) The secret to winning? Don't hit your own tank. Score is automatically kept by the computer.

BLASTER is a game that puts you in the cockpit of a spaceship. Your mission is to destroy as many enemy ships as possible within a certain time limit. With a front viewing screen and radar to track enemy spaceships and their missiles, you must defend your ship while attacking theirs. Look out behind you!

MEMORY is that childhood favorite, matching pairs of cards, brought up to date in this computer version. A multiple-player game with 32 pairs of cards, pick two cards that might match. If you're right, you score the points that are displayed on the card. Otherwise the cards are turned over for the next player's turn. At the end of the game the computer will anounce the winner. How's your short-term memory?

(PC-SIG Disk# 1814)
Special Requirements: *CGA.*
Author Registration: *None.*

Race!
by Carl Erikson

RACE! is a game of miniature car racing. The cars can accelerate, decelerate, or turn through the race courses while many obstacles block their progress, including walls, slopes, gates, tornadoes, and gas slicks. The more tracks a car successfully completes, the better the car becomes in areas such as acceleration, speed, traction, and helicopter speed. Also, RACE! lets the user design his own race tracks on which the cars compete.

This is a version of the old race program found in all the video arcades, and the quality is nearly as good. You get an overhead view, looking down on track where you are racing other cars. 20 different tracks are included. Great fun for kids, yet challenging for us older kids.

(PC-SIG Disk# 1892)

Special Requirements: *CGA or EGA.*
Author Registration: *$5.00*

Shooting Gallery *by Nels Anderson*

SHOOTING GALLERY is a colorful arcade game with several different levels to test your shooting skill.

Try your luck with traditional CARNIVAL SHOOTING. With 13 targets to test your aim. Shoot a whole row and get special points. Next is SKEET SHOOTING. Good aim is needed for this one. QUICK DRAW is the third round. Shoot when you get the green light. You'll need fast reflexes to get a good score here.

The program features practice for individual rounds, a hall of fame for high scores, and statistics for each round. A mouse is required to play this trigger-happy game.

(PC-SIG Disk# 2224)

Special Requirements: *450K RAM, VGA or MCGA, and mouse.*
Author Registration: *$15.00*
➤ *ASP Member.*

Slot *by Ted Gruber Software*

SLOT, by Ted Gruber Software, is a terrific slot machine simulation for your EGA systems. You bet from 1 to 5 coins and then give the one armed bandit a pull. If you're lucky enough you can make enough lucky bucks to pay for that new car you wanted. It's so much like the casino slot machines you'll forget you're playing at home. There are five ways to win, if you've got the guts to play 5 coins at a time that is, and the graphics alone make this program worth every quarter you put into it.

(PC-SIG Disk# 1544)

Special Requirements: *EGA.*
Author Registration: *$10.00*

Space Rescue *by Monte Giles*

A variation on the classic "Lunar Lander" theme.

Launch from Earth, maneuver your ship to dock with a space station, transfer the crew, return and land, preferably safely, on Earth again.

There are only a few commands to learn, which is good. You're not going to have a lot of time for practice. You'll be too busy trying to stay alive. Heads up!

(PC-SIG Disk# 749)

Special Requirements: *None.*
Author Registration: *$12.00*

Super Pinball *by Russ Fisher*

SUPER PINBALL is a collection of five great pinball games, each with a unique layout. You control the flippers with your left- and right-shift keys for realistic pinball action. The disk is menu-driven, letting you jump between games without exiting to DOS. No documentation is provided with this disk and none is needed — simply type GO and choose your game.

(PC-SIG Disk# 723)

Special Requirements: *CGA.*
Author Registration: *$10.00*

SuperFly ☆
by Nels Anderson

Who ever thought swatting flies could be so much fun? Chase flies and other crawling bugs through twenty different levels in this action game where strategy is almost as important as skill. On each level lurks different challenges.

This game has colorful high resolution graphics and fast action, even on slower machines. Three difficulty levels, sound effects, and a hall of fame compliment this fast paced game. Play SUPERFLY with the keyboard, a mouse, or a joystick.

(PC-SIG Disk# 2649)

Special Requirements: *EGA or VGA*
Author Registration: *$22.00*
➤*ASP Member.*

SuperFly (PC-SIG Disk #2649)

TechStaff Games Volume I ☆
by TechStaff Consultants, Inc.

TECHSTAFF GAMES VOLUME I is a collection of four games plus a small file viewer program.

Included are:

❏ SFV — A small file viewer program to display text files from any directory. SFV also allows the user to change the screen color.

❏ KENO — A game where the computer chooses twenty random numbers from a possible eighty. A player may choose from one to eleven numbers, and after each turn, the number of successful guesses is displayed.

❏ WILDCATTER — An oil drilling game. Guess where and how deep to drill, based on available geology reports. Site location is random, but the depth you drill to is determined by the reports. After each well is set up, you get an income statement. The game ends when you have no cash left OR you have a total of ten operating wells.

❏ SEA BATTLE — A battleship game where you must seek and destroy a submarine located in the depths below. Fire three depth charges for each torpedo fired on your ship. Specify the depth level and the location of the detonation for each depth charge. The game ends when the submarine is completely destroyed or your ship is hit by a torpedo.

(PC-SIG Disk# 2710)

Special Requirements: *Some games require graphics.*
Author Registration: *$5.00*

TechStaff Games Volume II ☆
by TechStaff Consultants, Inc.

TECHSTAFF GAMES VOLUME II is a collection of popular games for all ages.

Contained on this disk are the following games:

❏ HIQ1 — A puzzle with 32 pegs arranged in a cross with the center position empty. The object of the game is to remove all but one peg by jumping across pegs horizontally or vertically. The "perfect game" is when the last peg is located in the center of the cross.

❏ PCMAN1 — Another version of the popular game PacMan. Choose between one to four ghosts. The screen uses ASCII graphic characters while the program keeps track of the top ten scores.

❏ WHEEL3 — A version of the game Wheel of Fortune, for one to three players. A hidden phrase is given, and each player is given a turn to guess a consonant or buy a vowel. Spin a wheel to determine how much money each correct guess wins.

❏ STATES1 — A States and Capitals quiz game. Questions can be True - False, multiple-choice, or fill-in-the-blanks.

❏ ERULET1 — The game of European Roulette for one to four players. Thirty-six possible outcomes are on the wheel and each player makes bets on which number might come up next. Three separate bets are made on each turn — one on the specific number that will show up, another on whether the number is odd or even, and another on one of three blocks of twelve numbers. ERULET1 requires graphics.

(PC-SIG Disk# 2711)

Special Requirements: *Some games require graphics.*
Author Registration: *$5.00*

☆ = New Program

Tommy's Gorilla Balls ✍   *by Tommy's Toys*

TOMMY'S GORILLA BALLS is a quick game in which you must dodge "gorilla balls" that roll out onto the screen from the four corners of the game table. The game ends when you are rolled over by a gorilla ball, and you are given a score based upon the amount of time that you stayed alive. If you stay alive long enough, the game table will gradually begin to shrink and you will have less room to maneuver. The strategy of this game is to make two gorilla balls run into each other, causing both of them to disappear from the game board.

(PC-SIG Disk# 1604)

Special Requirements: *None.*
Author Registration: *$2.00*

Tommy's Meteors ☆   *by Tommy's Toys*

TOMMY'S METEORS has you avoiding falling meteors while your character gobbles up blocks of buildings for points. Periodically new buildings will appear on the screen to replace the previous ones. The game ends when you are hit by a meteor or when you are inadvertently caught underneath a new building that appears on the screen. Your score is based upon the amount of time that you are able to survive.

The game automatically keeps track of the top ten scores, has on-line instructions, and works with both color and monochrome monitors.

(PC-SIG Disk# 1604)

Special Requirements: *None.*
Author Registration: *$2.00*

Tommy's Saucer   *by Tommy's Toys*

Climb into a flying saucer cockpit to battle enemy saucers. Your mission is to destroy invading ships with the help of your ray beam. A point is scored every time you destroy an enemy saucer but the score reduces by one for every 30 clock ticks. The mission terminates when your shields are blasted and your ship is destroyed.

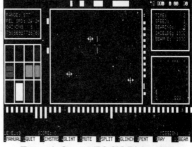

TOMMY'S SAUCER has various exotic alien display panels to show the energy and shield level, range, target crosshairs lock-in status, and aiming coordinates. You use a command panel at the bottom of the screen. The program has a sound effect toggle, a demo mode, function key control, an optional expanded view screen, and nine levels of difficulty. The sound and color show is nonstop and akin to a sci-fi movie. Runs on mono or color.

Tommy's Saucer (PC-SIG Disk# 1282)

(PC-SIG Disk# 1282)

Special Requirements: *None.*
Author Registration: *$2.00*

Tommy's Trek   *by Tommy's Toys*

Go to a galaxy far, far away and battle the Klingon forces as you captain the new improved Starship Enterprise. Use phasers and torpedoes, scan your enemies, lay space mines, put up your shields, navigate around your enemies and throw it into warp drive when the Klingon forces become too powerful.

This game is loaded, so read the manual carefully before starting — learn how to use all the function keys (for the various moves) and your key pad to move your ship through the 8x8 galaxy grid. Also important is the identification of the symbols — you don't want to attack the local Starbase! Travel through all 64 star systems as you rid the galaxy of the Klingons, and allow the Federation to bring peace throughout known space.

Remember, the game will start on autopilot, so be ready to control the real-time simulation of the Enterprise before you start seeing attackers and hearing the sound effects. Damage reports are flashed on the screens during attacks and an option menu is kept on the bottom of the screen to make your moves simpler. The graphics are easier to distinguish on a color screen, but monochrome also works well.

TOMMY'S TREK will bring hours of enjoyment to all who play. Ages 10 plus should take advantage of this smart package. Make the galaxies safe for ages to come, using all the skills the Federation has taught you as a captain of a star ship.

(PC-SIG Disk# 1718)

Special Requirements: *None.*
Author Registration: *$2.00*

TrainBall ☆
by David M. Alexander

TRAINBALL is a model train layout pinball game for all age groups. Create layouts with switches, tunnels, bumpers, and other features. Three trains can be designed with up to seven cars to a train. Objects on the user-designed screen affect the direction of the trains, which can fire missiles at other trains. Switching is randomly controlled by the computer but train speed is controlled by the user. If any of the trains collide, there is an explosion and the game ends.

TRAINBALL comes with two track layout files and three train files. Select from the existing files, edit them, or create your own. Creating screen layouts and trains can be difficult and confusing for those unfamiliar with ASCII characters. These files give inexperienced users an opportunity to practice and learn.

(PC-SIG Disk# 2712)

Special Requirements: *None.*
Author Registration: *$25.00*

VGA Concentration
by Alive Software

This is a fun and challenging picture matching game with novice and advanced levels. It tests the player's memory and concentration skills. This game has superb VGA graphics in 256 and 16 colors, derived from GIF files. There are four collections for a total of 52 great quality pictures.

The user interface is extremely simple. It's menu-driven and you can use it with the keyboard or a mouse. This is a special VGA version of CRAZY SHUFFLE. Register this program and get more pictures!

(PC-SIG Disk# 2232)

Special Requirements: *384K RAM and VGA.*
Author Registration: *$20.00*

VGA Jigsaw Puzzle
by Alive Software

VGA JIGSAW PUZZLE is game alive with color and brilliance in the 256 color mode that only VGA can produce. It loads a picture on the screen and then shuffles the pieces around. Your goal is to assemble the original picture!

The program includes three great quality jigsaw puzzles and features:

❏ Easy-to-use menu-driven operation.
❏ Keyboard or mouse option.
❏ Four levels of difficulty.
❏ Music.
❏ Scorekeeping.

Also provided is information on how to create your own VGA jigsaw puzzles using the popular .GIF and .PCX file formats in the 320 X 200 X 256 colors.

(PC-SIG Disk# 2229)

Special Requirements: *384K RAM and VGA.*
Author Registration: *$20.00*

VGA Sharks
by Alive Software

An underwater action arcade game that utilizes unique Artificial Intelligence, simulation and classic animation techniques to transform your computer screen into a realistic ocean floor. This the VGA version of ALIVE SHARKS.

You are the Frogman and your mission is to collect rare marine creatures and recover lost treasures from the bottom of the sea. Armed with your trusty stun-gun, you can retreat to your electromagnetic base that repels

✍ = Updated Program
☆ = New Program

sharks and the rest of your dreadful enemies. Your diving uniform is state-of-the-art, but you can survive only a few shark bites and it is useless against the poison of the deadly jellyfish.

This is not your typical "shoot-em-up," "eat-the-dots" kind of game. Your enemies are crafty and independent and they surround you in clever formations. When you shoot at them from far away, they are smart enough to avoid your shot.

(PC-SIG Disk# 2230)

Special Requirements: *384K RAM, VGA graphics display. Joystick or Mouse optional.*
Author Registration: *$20.00*

Willy the Worm
by Alan Farmer

Arcadiacs — Try WILLY THE WORM, a high-quality action game!

Like Donkey Kong or Lode Runner? Then you'll love WILLY. When you've exhausted the possibilities or grown weary of the screens as they are, use EDWILLY and create your own screens. Keep Willy moving and keep having fun!

(PC-SIG Disk# 445)

Special Requirements: *CGA.*
Author Registration: *$10.00*

Worthy Opponent
by FIT (Future Ideas Today)

WORTHY OPPONENT is a competitive, challenging, and entertaining game package that actually allows you to play games over your modem with other opponents.

What makes WORTHY OPPONENT unique are the sophisticated communications capabilities. Game competition occurs with an opponent miles away. You can still taunt and jeer at your opponent with every move. Discuss anything you like; strategy, good/bad moves, etc. with the specialized "talk" capabilities.

With excellent graphics, WORTHY OPPONENT is completely menu-driven and has on-line help screens to explain all functions. Four games are on the disk: Snake Pit, CornerStone, Checkers, and CannonBall.

Tournament play is also available where you can play against remote opponents using the on-screen clock.

(PC-SIG Disk# 1175)

Special Requirements: *Color monitor (CGA,EGA), modem recommended.*
Author Registration: *$15.00*

Wreck Tangle
by Charles A. Spence

WRECK TANGLE is a challenging strategy game for all ages. You have to match a given pattern by moving different shaped blocks in as few moves as possible. It will drive you crazy as you try to better the lowest scores and get your name on the master scoreboard. There are 25 different puzzles of varying degrees of difficulty. When you've mastered all 25, you can use the built-in puzzle generator to create your own WRECK TANGLE. Suitable for monochrome and color monitors. WRECK TANGLE is another game in the "Mind Maze" series (Maze Cube on disk #1419 is the first).

(PC-SIG Disk# 1836)

Special Requirements: *None.*
Author Registration: *$15.00*

▼ ▼ ▼

Games, Arcade (Sports)

Bass Class ✍
by Richard Olsen

Whether you are new to bass fishing or it's been your life, BASS CLASS will teach you the secrets of bass fishing. After you select your experience level and the location, you're out on a computerized lake, fishing for the biggest stringer in a six-hour fishing contest.

Sound tough? Don't worry, you're prepared! You have a modern, fully- rigged bass boat with six different fishing rods, 2300 different lure/color combinations, a nifty LCD depth finder, a trolling motor, and lots of accessories.

Select your rod and bait, navigate around the lake, and search for lunkers. Decide when to use the outboard motor and when to use the trolling motor, where to fish, which fishing poles and baits to use, and more.

BASS CLASS uses great graphics to show you the lake and even includes weeds and submerged stumps to trip you up. Remember, you are in a contest. If you don't make it to the weight-station before the end of contest, you lose.

BASS CLASS includes six different locations which are interchangeable with the locations in BASS TOUR, another program by the same author. Better bring your life jacket — some of the fish are incredibly big.

(PC-SIG Disk# 2500)

Special Requirements: *512K RAM, and EGA. A mouse is optional.*
Author Registration: *$15.00*
➤*ASP Member.*

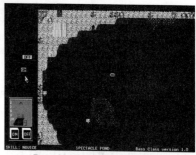

Bass Class (PC-SIG Disk# 2500)

Basstour ✍

by Richard Olsen

BASSTOUR is a fishing tournament game in which you captain a fully-rigged bass fishing boat. You control where the boat goes and how it gets there. Your bass boat has all the latest accessories, including a trolling motor, LCD chart recorder, a rod box containing six different fishing rods, and a fully-stocked tackle box. The object of the game is to catch the heaviest five fish limit on each of three days of the tournament. The fisherman with the highest total weight wins the tournament. As in real fishing, it's not always easy!

BASSTOUR has three levels of play: novice, intermediate and professional. In any of the skill levels, you are fishing against 30 of the top names in bass tournament fishing. You have six different bodies of water that you can fish. The fishing area is drawn on the screen, and the program randomly decides where fish should be placed. If you love to fish, you will love BASSTOUR.

(PC-SIG Disk# 1319)

Special Requirements: *512K RAM and graphics card. Mouse support provided.*
Author Registration: *$15.00*
➤*ASP Member.*

Budget Baseball

by Streetsong Software

Bring big league baseball to your den with BUDGET BASEBALL. Become one of baseball's great managers. You can replay a World Series game or pit a Series contender of one year against a team from another year.

Along the way, you can alter the course of the game by controlling batters, runners and pitchers. You can even alter infield placement, call for intentional walks and display the team rosters. You can tell the batter to bunt, take a pitch, try to fly out or go for a home run. On base, you can tell the runner to try and steal. A marvelous game for baseball fans.

(PC-SIG Disk# 1400)

Special Requirements: *CGA.*
Author Registration: *$19.95*

Cunning Football

by Cass Cunningham

You pick the plays, you run, you pass, you score! It's CUNNING FOOTBALL — a fast action game for mouse, keyboard, or joystick!

CUNNING FOOTBALL provides the "Saturday" quarterback a chance to try all of his winning strategies on a realistic playing field that includes interceptions, penalties, and an opposing team that wants to stomp you into the ground. On offense, you control the player with the ball. After the snap, you control the QB until you pass, lateral, or hand the ball off. On defense, you control the middle/inside linebacker. After selecting a play from the menu, you can display a diagram of the play to give you information about where you should move, who your available receivers are, and when you should pass. Go team!

(PC-SIG Disk# 1240)

Special Requirements: *320 K RAM and CGA, EGA, VGA, or Hercules.*
Author Registration: *$25.00*

✍ = Updated Program
☆ = New Program

Football Compu-Sched
by Cosoft Micro Systems

Keep track of your favorite NFL teams and their scoring records for the year with direct and simple menu structures. Add new scores as the games are played, week after week. Go back and look at history, running the program with only the function keys.

Last year's stats and standings are already included in the data files as well as the pertinent information from all 24 Superbowls. Compare seasons as well as teams. Print your results for convenient future reference.

(PC-SIG Disk# 2153)

Special Requirements: *Printer recommended.*
Author Registration: *$10.00*

Handicap Horse Racing ✍
by Data-Plane Inc.

Here's a horse racing simulation so real it practically leaves hoofprints. You control the horse registry, jockey, feed bills, stall rentals, liqudations, claiming races, auctions, and pari-mutuel betting. HANDICAP HORSE RACING has brought what used to be a simple game into the world of high stakes and heart-pounding finishes.

You're the marshal, or track commissioner, and you have a lot to do before, during and after the race. Before you even open the gates to the track, you must prepare the registry, see to your funds for race pay-offs, and rental and fees from your track stables. When your guests arrive, they'll be bringing their own money (play) for a day at the races. The system will make the race call and help you determine the payoff after a race.

With your registry changing as a result of each race, the excitment will grow every time you play. Your guests will look forward to playing their "Best of Breed" against the field. A limited number of horses running on an oval track with no betting action are supported. Registered users receive a track construction system, full betting action and a large stable of horses.

(PC-SIG Disk# 2145)

Special Requirements: *Hercules or better.*
Author Registration: *$74.95*

MONUMENTS of MARS! ✍
by Apogee Software Productions

Explore a secret underground city on Mars with THE MONUMENTS OF MARS, an arcade/adventure game set in the near future. In this first volume ("First Contact"), you will need to survive 20 unique and challenging levels filled with puzzles, traps, creatures, and useful artifacts.

Great graphics and sound effects make this a compelling and fascinating story. This is the first game to give you unlimited lives! You will never see a "Game Over" message in THE MONUMENTS OF MARS, since you simply restart the level whenever you die. Concentrate on solving each level without the hassle of cons tantly saving and restoring your game. Other features include save/restore, high score chart, sound on/off and keyboard configuration.

Because of the extensive animation, it cannot be played on 8088-based PCs.

This is the first of four volumes of THE MONUMENTS OF MARS, subtitled "First Contact." The other three volumes, available by registration only, are : "The Pyramid," "The Fortress," and "The Face." The volumes should be played in sequence, since they continue the story to a climactic and shocking ending.

(PC-SIG Disk# 2326)

Special Requirements: *8086 or better, 350K RAM, and CGA, EGA, or VGA.*
Author Registration: *$10 per volume; $25 for set.*

PC Pro-Golf
by CMA Software

PC PRO-GOLF is a game that graphically depicts in four colors an actual golf course with water-hazards, sand-bunkers, wooded areas, buildings, roads, etc. With each stroke the player may watch the course of the ball and see where it lands. When your ball comes within a certain distance from the hole, the program will display a close up view of the hole so that you may putt the ball in.

Penalty-strokes are added under the correct conditions and an updated score-card is available for review at any time, as are the help-screen and club-values list. An unfinished game may be saved for resumption at a later time.

Getting the program up and running is made easy by a very sophisticated installation program that was smart enough to know that we were testing this program on a Tandy SX1000! Also included is the printable 10-page manual, and AMHERST, another complete 18-hole course. Fore!

(PC-SIG Disk# 1344)

Special Requirements: *CGA.*
Author Registration: *$20.00.*

Pharaoh's Tomb ✍   *by Apogee Software Productions*

PHARAOH'S TOMB is an arcade/adventure game, set inside the heart of a huge Egyptian pyramid. Explore and (possibly) survive 20 uniquely dangerous levels, riddled with ingenious puzzles and traps. A special animation system called FAST (Fluid Animation Software Technology) provides flicker-free movement, even on older PCs.

You start with five lives and a few spears to overcome various dangerous denizens guarding the pyramid. Moving walls, bats, falling spikes, mummies, and magic winds are just some of the hazards to overcome. On each level, collect one or more keys to advance to the next level until, somewhere on the final level, you discover the prize of your journey.

No two levels have the same animated creature patrolling it, adding to the variety of the game. Sound effects are also used, but can be toggled off. The keyboard can be configured to use two alternate sets of keys. A five player permanent high score table keeps track of the all-time best explorers. Save the game on any level and restore at any time.

This is the first of four volumes of Pharaoh's Tomb, subtitled "Raiders of the Lost Tomb." The other three volumes, available only through registration, are: "Pharaoh's Curse," "Temple of Terror," and "Nevada's Revenge!" The volumes should be played in sequence, since they continue the story to the final encounter.

(PC-SIG Disk# 2326)

Special Requirements: *CGA.*
Author Registration: *$10.00 per volume; $25.00 per set.*

Pro Set Football ✍   *by Ed Hagen*

4th Quarter, two minutes left to play. Ball is on the 20 yard line, 4th down and 1 yard to go — as coach of your favorite football team it is up to you to decide the next strategy in Ed Hagen's PRO SET FOOTBALL. Choose from your favorite teams as you decide the offensive and defensive choices for your players. Pass, run, kick, score touchdowns and kick field goals. Get penalized for "off sides" or intercept a pass and run it back for 6 points!

Although PRO SET FOOTBALL is not a graphic game, its depth is made up in the format in which you play. First, either choose from pro or college teams. Second, play against the computer or a friend. Select from a menu of options for either the defensive or offensive plays — the computer then "plays" the results of your choices. Game time is held in 15 minute quarters and stats of all your players (real players from the 1987 pro teams and 1988 college teams) are displayed at half time and the end. Sound effects are minimal but do add a nice quality to the game.

Truly enjoyable, simple to use, PRO SET FOOTBALL will never be the same game twice. Enjoy playing the pros all year round — a nice addition to your computerized sports library.

(PC-SIG Disk# 1990)

Special Requirements: *None.*
Author Registration: *$15.00*

ProChallenge Baseball   *by JBE Ltd.*

PROCHALLENGE BASEBALL is a one- or two-player strategy game of computer baseball that has a variety of player options for every pitch of the game.

In this version the game simulates the 1987 World Series game between St. Louis and Minnesota, but in the registered version of the program you may choose between 26 Major League baseball teams. PROCHALLENGE BASEBALL is set up for you to be the manager giving signals to the players. The pitching team has the option to change its defensive formation, pick off a runner, and decide what pitches to throw. When a pitch is thrown, you can specify where the ball should be placed over the plate. The options for the team at bat include the choice to swing at the ball, bunt, steal a base, lead off a runner, hit and run, run and hit, and call the pitch.

PROCHALLENGE BASEBALL does everything to simulate the actual game, even to the point of using the statistics for each player of the team. Baseball fans will be pleased that the program allows them to play based upon the skill and strategy of the real game of baseball. PROCHALLENGE BASEBALL has graphic screens for the entire field with its players and the view from the pitcher's mound, not to mention the many colorful game menus to aid in game play. At any time you may let the computer make the signal, so that one player may play against the computer or even the computer against itself.

(PC-SIG Disk# 1207)

Special Requirements: *CGA.*
Author Registration: *$24.95*

Statistically Accurate Baseball

by Joe Damore

Being an armchair baseball manager is a tough job. For all the work you do during the season, the players on the screen never do what you tell them to do. You yell "run for third base" and they stay put at second, or you tell them to bunt and they strike out. Now there's hope.

STATISTICALLY ACCURATE BASEBALL lets you bring together two major league baseball teams, historical as well as current, and let them do battle on the diamond, with you as their manager. You can pit your managerial skills against the computer, a fellow armchair manager, or let two computerized managers go at it head to head.

STATISTICALLY ACCURATE BASEBALL provides you with players from The 1988 Cubs, A's, Bluejays and Giants, as well as The 1950 Red Sox and The 1936 Yankees (over 120 more teams are available from the author). It's the answer to the question of what to do after the World Series. Play ball!

(PC-SIG Disk# 2074)

Special Requirements: *A hard drive is recommended.*
Author Registration: *$14.00*

▼ ▼ ▼

Games, Board and Dice

Aggravation ✍

by Cutlass Software

At last, the PC has its own version of that old favorite board game, Aggravation. This is the same game that you played as a kid in summer camp or at the dining room table with the family. Play with up to three others or challenge the computer — you still get your markers sent back to the Start. Play is fast, the computer rolls the dice and you can always reach your men. The only thing missing is that little grin on your older sister's face as she sweetly inquires if you want to play again?

(PC-SIG Disk# 1590)

Special Requirements: *CGA.*
Author Registration: *$10.00*

Backgammon

by Software Creations

BACKGAMMON is finally here for your PC! Now you can play against a strong opponent on your own computer. If you've never played before, or you're the champion of your local club, BACKGAMMON will fill the role of instant opponent. For the true afficionado, the program keeps track of points, games, gammons, and backgammons.

(PC-SIG Disk# 708)

Special Requirements: *None.*
Author Registration: *$21.95*

Bingo

by Richard Metlen

Being the BINGO caller can be a thankless job, so let the computer do it! BINGO will print as many different bingo cards as are needed for your game, then pick and record the numbers for you.

The program picks numbers between 1 and 75, one number at a time, giving the number plus its line letter designation, as in a regular bingo game. The program keeps track of the called numbers on a "tote board," to be available for comparison with the numbers on the winning card.

(PC-SIG Disk# 1913)

Special Requirements: *None.*
Author Registration: *None.*

Board Games
by Helios Software

A trio of classic board games.

PC-PENTE is a game with its roots in the ancient game of Go. The playing field is a grid and the object is simple: either get five of your pieces in a row or capture 10 of your opponent's pieces by surrounding them with your pieces. It is assumed that you already know how to play the game, but in case you don't, Rules.com has a concise overview of the basic strategy of Pente.

PYRAMIDS is a strategy game based on an ancient Egyptian theme. You and the Pharaoh Cheops are vying to discover the other's pyramid before your own is found. The playing pieces include sphinxes, lions, bulls, rams, wolves, hawks, camels, cats, antelopes and a cobra — each with special powers. You can see your opponent's pieces and your opponent can see yours, but you do not know the rank and power of each until one of you attacks the other.

YAHTZEE is the classic dice game we've all played in which you try to collect pairs, three-of-a-kinds, full houses, and the like for points by rolling six dice. From each roll, you can pick up from one to six of the dice and re-roll them, to try to better the score you receive for the roll. Once a requirement has been filled, you cannot use that roll again. The winner completes his list with the highest total score.

(PC-SIG Disk# 993)
Special Requirements: *A version of BASIC.*
Author Registration: *$5.00 to $10.00*

Boggler ☆
by Solaris Systems

An addictive game that's great for get-togethers, BOGGLER is a word game for any number of players.

The game displays a 4x4 square of letters. All players try to build the longest and most unique words in three minutes' time. Connect any letter to any other adjoining letter to form large words. And the challenges lie in the restriction of being able to use each letter in the square only once each word. The only words that count as points are words with three or more letters that are unique to everyone else's!

(PC-SIG Disk# 2527)
Special Requirements: *Graphics card.*
Author Registration: *$10.00*

Border ✍
by Cascoly Software

BORDERS is a battle for turf — not in the city but on your computer screen. In this strategy game you try to claim more area than your opponent while blocking his attempts to do the same. Players take turns staking out their territory within a rectangular area. Claimed areas can only be in the form of triangles. Your aim is to make the largest triangles (thereby claiming the most area), while thwarting your opponent's attempts at making his triangles. The object is to outsmart your opponent by enclosing more than 40% of the available area to win.

You'll find this easy-to-learn game challenging and fun as you learn the various strategies that make or break your game.

(PC-SIG Disk# 2147)
Special Requirements: *CGA or higher graphics.*
Author Registration: *$20.00*
➤*ASP Member.*

CD Dot Challenge
by Cam-Don Group

CD DOT CHALLENGE is an easy-to-play game with over 75,000 different game variations. As easy as it is to play, it requires great strategy to win and is very addictive!

The game board consists of a grid of dots. The object of the game is simple... to draw a line between any two dots. Each time a player draws a line that "closes" a square, that player earns a point and another turn. As simple as this sounds, the strategy can be quite complex!

(PC-SIG Disk# 2421)
Special Requirements: *None.*
Author Registration: *$12.50*

✍ = Updated Program
☆ = New Program

Chess Tutor ✍

by Pep-Cal Software

Learn the subleties of famous chess games. Not a lot to read, but lots to learn as you play. CHESS TUTOR is an original and is meant to supplement PRAXIS I, although it is not necessary to run CHESS TUTOR. Improve your game painlessly.

(PC-SIG Disk# 2154)

Special Requirements: *None.*
Author Registration: *$14.95*

Civil War Battle Set

by W. R. Hutsell

Remember when you played "war" with your friends? CIVIL WAR BATTLE SET can help you relive those days, in the comfort of your home or office!

Chess Tutor (PC-SIG Disk# 2154)

CIVILWAR is a one-player re-creation of various battles from the American Civil War. Choose either side and command infantry, cavalry, artillery, and general units. Battles are affected by unit type, terrain, leadership, morale, attack type, and other factors. You may modify the game difficulty and the aggressiveness of the enemy, as well as visibility and artillery range. "Spy" on enemy troops, override orders of subordinate commanders, and control intensity of encounters. You can create or modify battle scenarios, including battle map, army type, strength, and other factors. Name units according to historical battles or choose your own names. And, if you get interrupted during an intense battle, save it and come back to it during your coffee break!

(PC-SIG Disk# 2430)

Special Requirements: *CGA*
Author Registration: *None.*

Conjecture ✍

by RSE Inc.

CONJECTURE is similar to a popular TV game show. Spin wheels, guess letters, and try to solve puzzles. The press called it "exceptional," and our customers rave over it.

The graphics are excellent and there is a mode for playing solo or with up to four others. It comes with plenty of puzzles and you can customize the game to suit yourself. CONJECTURE sold nationwide through major retail stores for $24.95 and is now being released as user- supported shareware. It's great fun.

(PC-SIG Disk# 2391)

Special Requirements: *Graphics Card.*
Author Registration: *$10*

Craps Complete

by United Innovations Plus

Craps is one of the most popular gambling games found in casinos throughout the world. Now craps can be played from your computer! CRAPS COMPLETE offers the player the same action as you would expect to find at the crap table. All the various wagers are explained in the documentation. These include: pass line, pass line odds, don't pass, don't pass odds, place bets, don't place bets, big 6 & big 8, field bets, come bets & come odds, don't come & don't come odds, proposition bets, hardway bets, craps/eleven, any craps, and the horn bet.

This is one way to become familiar with the game before going to the casinos and learning it the hard way. Enjoy it in your home with others or by yourself!

(PC-SIG Disk# 2418)

Special Requirements: *350K RAM, EGA, and MicroSoft compatible mouse. Hard drive recommended.*
Author Registration: *$15.00*

Crazy Shuffle

by Alive Software

Test your memory and concentration skills, no matter what your age. Match colorful cards with other cards or try to match a card with an associated word.

CRAZY SHUFFLE can be a joyful learning experience for young children, an educational program for teens and pre-teens and yet provide a formidable challenge to adults. Select three different games, with five levels of difficulty and three collections of pictures.

The game is menu-driven, provides score-keeping, has on-line help and optional mouse support. Variable speed control and great graphics add to the fun.

(PC-SIG Disk# 2014)

Special Requirements: *None.*
Author Registration: *$20.00*

Double TroubleTM ✍   *by Dickinson Software*

Anyone who loves puzzles will spend many hours trying to figure this one out!

DOUBLE TROUBLETM is a deceptively simple, yet challenging puzzle for young or old. Starting from a scrambled position, the user rotates two intersecting circles of colored balls, grouping them into four color groups. As the color groups are formed, the two intersecting circles promptly break up color groups already formed. Eventually, the balls will be grouped into their proper positions, completing the puzzle successfully. Try again, but for a lower score! The program counts each key press taken to move the balls into position. Help is available at a key stroke!

(PC-SIG Disk# 2437)

Special Requirements: *EGA*
Author Registration: *$15.00*

Crazy Shuffle (PC-SIG Disk# 2014)

DoubleCross ☆   *by Solaris Systems*

Here's a strategy game to keep two players busy for a while! Build a bridge that solidly connects both sides of the board...but you must do it while blocking your opponent's attempts to do the same!

(PC-SIG Disk# 2527)

Special Requirements: *Graphics card. Supports a mouse.*
Author Registration: *$10.00*

Five Dice Game   *by Fredric J. Smothers*

Get ready to roll! FIVE DICE GAME is a fun way to play dice. It is played by two or more players, with the object to attain a score of 5000 points or more. Each player rolls the dice, accumulating a score as long as he rolls scoring dice. If he fails to roll any score, he loses his turn and a "scratch" is posted against him. After any player has 5000 points, every other player gets one more chance to beat that score. The game can be played by up to 15 human or computer-controlled players (counting yourself). The computer can play any of three different strategies, from very conservative to fairly aggressive.

The program is very easy to run and instructions are included. This is an excellent program for any user — novice to expert. The Turbo Pascal source code is included in case you want to modify or write your own computer opponents.

(PC-SIG Disk# 743)

Special Requirements: *None.*
Author Registration: *$5.00*

Kaka! ✍   *by TelComm Associates*

Roll six die in competition to remain the highest scoring player in the game. Two to six players take turns to roll "scorable" combinations of numbers. Once a player's turn begins, play continues until the player chooses to quit and take the turn's score or until KAKA! is rolled — a non-scoring roll of the dice. Directions are provided online and context-sensitive help is a keystroke away. A new feature is saving your game where you left off.

(PC-SIG Disk# 2013)

Special Requirements: *Graphics card.*
Author Registration: *$15.00*

✍ = Updated Program
☆ = New Program

Mahjong

by ProCon Software

MAHJONG is a Chinese gambling game which arrived in the West in the early 1920's. The origin of the game is unclear but its development has touched on astrology, chess, gambling and, oddest of all, the Earth's magnetic field.

It is a fast moving, dynamic game that becomes addictive with its excitement and intrigue. The basic premise is a card game with 136 cards (or "tiles" as they are called in MAHJONG) requiring both skill and luck. Four players receive 13 tiles each and then pick up and discard tiles as they try to obtain four complete sets and a single pair of tiles.

The game is interesting because of the many combinations possible and the skill required to increase your score. To add further excitement, the fast pace provides little chance for contemplation — thus developing an "instinct" rarely seen in other games. Three levels of play are provided: beginner, advanced and professional. An entertaining game for the whole family.

(PC-SIG Disk# 641)

Special Requirements: *CGA, EGA, VGA, or Hercules graphics.*
Author Registration: *$30.00*

MahJongg

by Nels Anderson

MAH JONGG is based on an ancient Chinese game that has been around for centuries. The object of the game is to remove as many matching tiles from the playing board as possible. Sounds easy, huh?

Not quite. The board has five levels of tiles and the tile you may need might be at the bottom level, out of your reach. There are 65,535 different boards that can be played, which will keep you glued to your computer for many hours.

The game supports Hercules graphics as well as EGA. An UNDO facility, mouse support, and game statistics make it more interesting than ever.

(PC-SIG Disk# 1221)

Special Requirements: *Hercules graphics or EGA.*
Author Registration: *$15.00*
➤**ASP Member.**

MahJongg (PC-SIG Disk# 1221)

Micro Link Otra ☆

by Bob Lancaster

MICROLINK OTRA is a memory game, a cousin to "Simon," the electronic hit of the late 70's. Take turns replaying an ever-longer sequence of flashing squares generated by the computer. After four rounds, the player with the highest score wins.

Some features include:
❏ From one to seven players
❏ Accepts keyboard and mouse input and works on all monitors and display adaptors
❏ Top-ten scoreboard and statistics maintained on high/low/average scores in current session
❏ Sound on/off toggle
❏ "Fast" mode eliminates animation to speed up play

(PC-SIG Disk# 2493)

Special Requirements: *None.*
Author Registration: *Optional*

MicroLink Shut The Box ☆

by Bob Lancaster

MICROLINK SHUT THE BOX is an electronic version of the traditional boardgame of the same name.

A player rolls a pair of dice and then shuts numbered doors which add up to the total on the dice. If a roll cannot be used, the total of all shut doors is added to the player's score, and play passes to the next player. After five rounds, the player with the highest score wins.

Some features include:

❏ From one to seven human players or challenge a "PC Opponent"
❏ Keyboard and mouse input as well as MDA/Composite monitor support
❏ Top-ten scoreboard and statistics kept on high/low/average scores in current session
❏ Sound On/Off toggle and optional display of dice with dots or numerals
❏ "Fast" mode eliminates animation to speed up play

Enjoyed by adults, kids as young as five or six can play and benefit from the addition skills that the game exercises.
(PC-SIG Disk# 2493)

Special Requirements: *None.*
Author Registration: *$5.00 suggested*

MicroLink Yaht ☆   *by Bob Lancaster*

MICROLINK YAHT is an electronic version of the traditional dice game Yacht, now popularized as Yahtzee.

A player rolls five dice, attempting to score in a number of categories (full house, three of a kind, etc). The player may reroll any or all of the five dice for a total of three rolls per turn. After three rolls, the player enters the appropriate score into one of the categories on the scorecard, and play passes to the next player. When all categories are filled, the game is over. High score wins. Players of all ages will enjoy this game.

Some features include:
❏ From one to six human players or challenge a "PC Opponent"
❏ Keyboard, joystick, and mouse input plus color monitor support
❏ Top-10 scoreboard, statistics on high/low/average scores in current session and optional display of possible scores with each roll
❏ Sound On/Off toggle and optional display of dice with dots or numerals
❏ "Fast" mode eliminates animation to speed up play
(PC-SIG Disk# 2493)

Special Requirements: *None.*
Author Registration: *$5.00 suggested*

Mine Field ☆   *by Expert Systems Code Inc.*

MINE FIELD is a graphical game of logic, deduction and maybe a little luck. Mark all of the mines in a minefield so your troops can make it through safely. Mark all of the bombs or uncover all of the safe tiles and the game is over.

Some of the features of MINE FIELD include:
❏ Superb VGA graphics
❏ Mouse support
❏ 15 different boards to choose from
❏ User-selected number of mines
❏ On-line rules
❏ Sound toggle
❏ 640 x 480, 16-color VGA resolution
(PC-SIG Disk# 2765)

Special Requirements: *400K RAM, VGA, and a mouse.*
Author Registration: *$15.00*
➤*ASP Member.*

Miscellaneous Games and Lotto   *by Dedicated Software*

YES is the dice game Yahtzee for two players and has all the same rolls: full house, large straight, four of a kind, etc. The program randomly generates the dice rolls and automatically keeps score for each player.

RUN FOUR challenges two players to be the first to get four checkers in a row on a six-by-seven game board. Each checker must be placed at the bottom of the board or stacked on top of one another. A player wins by scoring four in a row either horizontally, vertically, or diagonally. RUN FOUR is supposed to have a different color for the checkers of each player, but on an EGA monitor both of the players' checkers are colored red.

ROBIN plays exactly like Bingo. Fun for parties, it prints up to 33 different cards for players and then randomly generates callouts. The player with the first winning card shouts, "ROBIN!"

LOTTO MAGIC WHEELER helps you select and wheel numbers to bet in a six- number lotto game. Wheeling is the technique of placing your numbers into combinations that guarantee a winning pick if any four of the six numbers are chosen. Options offered: computer random pick, and wheeling 7 to 12 numbers into as many as 42 different combinations.

(PC-SIG Disk# 1292)

Special Requirements: *Printer.*
Author Registration: *$10.00 to $19.50.*

NCRisk ✍   *by Neil Clasen*

This colorful strategy game, a clone of the Parker Brothers' game Risk, pits you and your army against the armies of up to five other players in a worldwide conflict.

Strategy involves trying to pick up extra armies by occupying whole continents. At the same time, you must protect yourself against unexpected moves by your opponents. Do not expect a short game if your foes are skilled. Conquering the world can be difficult!

(PC-SIG Disk# 1322)

Special Requirements: *Hercules graphics, CGA, EGA or VGA.*
Author Registration: *$10.00*

Nine Men's Morris   *by Travis Bailey*

Try a game that has its origins in ancient history! Layouts have been found in manuscripts and tombs, including one cut into roofing slabs in Germany (Muhle). Similar to the game Noughts and Crosses or Tic Tac Toe, it was most popular in the 14th Century, acquiring the name Morris in England. This was possibly due to the board resembling patterns made by Morris dancers.

Play takes place on the 24 intersecting points on the board. Each player attempts to arrange three of his pieces in a line on the board. Such a line is called a Mill. This entitles a player to remove any one of his opponent's pieces from the board, including any that are themselves forming a mill. A player who can reduce his opponent to two pieces or block him from making a legitimate move wins the game.

This strategic two-player game (the computer won't be an opponent) will make for a challenging and fun evening!

(PC-SIG Disk# 2185)

Special Requirements: *CGA.*
Author Registration: *$5.00*

OTH   *by Brett D. Bensley*

This delightful Othello-like game was created as a college class project. Well designed and speedy, it was written in Turbo Pascal. Fortunately, the students made the source code available as part of the package for those interested in programming. With four skill levels, the game permits up to four players. Othello devotees will find the computer is generally a mite smarter than expected when it comes to outflanking their squares. The game works well on both color and monochrome displays.

(PC-SIG Disk# 1523)

Special Requirements: *None.*
Author Registration: *None.*

PC Bingo   *by Bielkiewicz Computer Services*

Throw your next Bingo party at your home, church or school with Michael Bielkiewicz's PC BINGO. Easy to use, it plays like the real thing — no strings attached. Print out up to 8 Bingo cards per 8 1/2 X 11 inch paper, distribute among your players and let the computer choose the Bingo numbers.

A great party game, PC BINGO could actually be used to replace the old ping-pong ball method of the game — though that day is somewhat in the future. The ease of this package makes it accessible to all ages who share a love for the Bingo game.

(PC-SIG Disk# 1897)

Special Requirements: *Printer to generate bingo cards.*
Author Registration: *$10.00*

PC-Arena
by Mike & Jim Co.

Want to play chess against a Russian in the Soviet Union? Or how about a game of Othello against an Italian in Nice? Better yet, how would you like to do it without even leaving home?

PC-ARENA OTHELLO and PC-ARENA CHESS let you go up against fellow gamers with a PC and a modem anywhere in the world — limited only by your credit with the phone company!

PC-ARENA Chess play is governed by the International Chess Federation Laws of Chess. The gaming system validates all moves according to the rules of chess, supports castling, piece promotion, and en passant capture.

Othello, invented around 1888 and popularized in the local pubs, is played on a draughtsboard using sixty-four stone or wooden pieces. PC-ARENA Othello, developed in 1985 and popularized on electronic bulletin board systems and through user group libraries, is played on a PC equipped with a modem.

Let the games begin!

(PC-SIG Disk# 1518)

Special Requirements: *Modem.*
Author Registration: *$9.95*

PC-CHESS ✐
by Tim Keller

This program lets you play chess against the computer or a human opponent. The level of the computer's chess games are not particularly difficult, so it is not a challenge for experts. But when competing against human opponents, the program can store up to 26 games in-progress.

The graphics of the game only appear on systems using either EGA or CGA adapter cards. The program uses ASCII characters to depict the chess pieces on a monochrome or Hercules graphics systems.

(PC-SIG Disk# 120)

Special Requirements: *CGA, EGA, or Hercules graphics.*
Author Registration: *$15.00*

PC-Chess (PC-SIG Disk# 120)

PC-Jigsaw Puzzle
by Alive Software

PC-JIGSAW is an educational game of skill and intellect that starts out drawing an image on the screen and then it shuffles the pieces. The object of the game is to assemble the pieces to match the original image on the screen. You can use either the keyboard or a mouse to move the pieces.

PC-JIGSAW is completely menu driven and comes with an on-line help facility to quide you through the operation of the program. You select the image you want from the Images menu and then select Start from the main menu to begin playing. You can view the original image at any time to help you along. You can even change the level of complexity by making the PC-JIGSAW image pieces smaller or larger. The fewer pieces you swap, the better your score. Also, every time you view the image, points are subtracted from your score. PC-JIGSAW comes with four puzzles you can solve. If you like jigsaw puzzles, you will love PC-JIGSAW.

(PC-SIG Disk# 1558)

Special Requirements: *CGA, EGA, VGA, MCGA, or Hercules graphics.*
Author Registration: *$15.00*

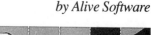

PC-Jigsaw Puzzle (PC-SIG Disk# 1558)

Peg Solitaire
by United Innovations Plus

PEG SOLITAIRE is played on a playing board shaped in the form of a plus sign. The board has 33 holes with 32 pegs. (The center hole of the board is left empty.) The object is to remove all but one of the pegs from the board jumping one peg at a time.

COLOR PEG is a second game. This board has 24 pegs divided into different colored groups of 6 pegs each. The object of this game is to jump pegs until all peg groups have exchanged positions. You win when the top and bottom peg groups have swapped places and the right and left peg groups have done the same.

Both of these games are simple to operate, but difficult to master. Use the keyboard or mouse to move around.

(PC-SIG Disk# 2223)

Special Requirements: *512K RAM and VGA.*
Author Registration: *$15.00*

Pentrix ✍
by Solaris Systems

It's Tic-Tac-Toe on steroids! Based on the board game GO-MAKU, PENTRIX will test your strategic thinking. You and an opponent take turns placing your game pieces on the board. Outflank your opponent by placing five of your pieces in a row and you've won. The Help screens explain the rules and make winning sound easy — but it's not.

PENTRIX works fine on any system, but has stunning graphics on EGA/VGA. Works great with or without a mouse.

(PC-SIG Disk# 2527)

Special Requirements: *None.*
Author Registration: *$10.00*

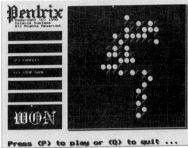
Pentrix (PC-SIG Disk# 2527)

Pig
by United Innovations Plus

All those who thought "Pig Out" only meant eating too much during the Holidays will be in for a surprise with Raymond Buti's simple, but delightful game called PIG. You take on the computer by rolling a single die, trying to reach the score of 100 or 200. You can accumulate a score as long as you don't roll a "1"—but if you do, you are awarded the title of PIG and loose all points scored up until that point! First to reach 100 or 200 is the winner and receives 10X the points ahead of the other player minus 5 points for each "Pig" received during play. Points accumulate after each round.

PIG is an exciting game for all ages. Anyone with an interest in dice games should enjoy it. Fun for the whole family, PIG will keep you occupied for hours as you try to match your wits with those of the computer.

(PC-SIG Disk# 1733)

Special Requirements: *None.*
Author Registration: *$15.00*

PowerChess ☆
by Werner Wild

POWERCHESS is one of the best chess playing games on the market today. POWERCHESS is a full screen, highly graphic chess game designed for both beginners and advanced players. Because of the clearly arranged screen and the complete implementation of international chess rules, POWER CHESS can also be highly recommended for chess classes.

POWERCHESS is filled with outstanding features. It obeys international chess rules, en'passant, 50-move drawing rule, three repetitions of a position recognizes stalemate, and technical draw. The screen displays the chessboard, as well as playing time for Black and White, an index of the last 21 moves, an index of all possible moves concerning the position on the board, announcement of a checkmate in N moves, with computer hints for the next move.

Using the computer hints, you can even have the computer play against itself. Chess moves can even be taken back, in case you

PowerChess (PC-SIG Disk# 2558)

change your mind. Different levels of play can be selected, for beginner to highly advanced. The chessboard can be set up in special positions so you can experiment with different types of play.

POWERCHESS provides a library of games and interesting positions which can be easily extended. POWERCHESS can be your own private chess tutor, providing you with hours of enjoyment and learning.

(PC-SIG Disk# 2558)

Special Requirements: *512K RAM and CGA, EGA, VGA or Hercules Graphics.*
Author Registration: *$42.00*

Puzzlers ☆

by Dennis J. Yelton

PUZZLERS is a puzzle game that has been described as a two-dimensional Rubik's Cube. PUZZLERS has a variety of numbered grids, each containing a colorful pattern, which the computer or another player can scramble by shifting individual rows and columns. Individual moves are shown on the screen as the pattern is scrambled. The object of the game is to unscramble the grid in the least number of moves.

PUZZLERS has two main patterns: checkered boards containing letters of the alphabet and quilt designs. The size of the grid square can range from 3 X 3 to 7 X 7.

(PC-SIG Disk# 2739)

Special Requirements: *512K RAM, EGA or VGA monitor.*
Author Registration: *$15.00*

Reversi ☆

by David W. Parsons

Someone once said of the board game Othello, "It takes minutes to learn, but a lifetime to master!" With REVERSI, a version of Othello developed by a nationally-ranked player, this is clearly true.

Othello, a game of great tradition, is a cross between checkers and backgammon. REVERSI, this computerized version, will instruct the beginner and challenge the master with hours of fun. Three playing levels and great graphics make it easy to learn, but difficult to master. What really sets REVERSI apart from other Othello games is its extensive instruction on strategy. Since the program was written by a top-ten U.S. Othello Association player, you learn the game from a master.

(PC-SIG Disk# 2520)

Special Requirements: *CGA, EGA, or VGA.*
Author Registration: *$15.00*

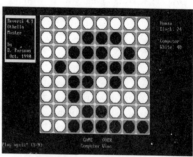

Reversi (PC-SIG Disk# 2520)

Roulette EGA

by United Innovations Plus

This game is for casino players, gamblers, and game players. The casino game of Roulette is played on a layout consisting of 38 spaces numbered 1 through 36, O and OO with 8 different types of wagers that can be made on the Roulette layout. They include a Straight Bet, Split Bet, Street Bet, Square Bet, Line Bet, Column Bet, Dozen Bet, and an Even Money Bet. There are 154 different betting locations on the Roulette layout which vary in payoff odds.

(PC-SIG Disk# 2381)

Special Requirements: *350K RAM, EGA, and a Microsoft compatible mouse.*
Author Registration: *$25.00*

Scramble

by Ted Gruber Software

Scramble plays like a familiar crossword board game of a similar name. It features stunning EGA graphics, optional mouse support, and a 33,000 word dictionary, along with utilities to modify the dictionary or use your own dictionary. Games can be played by one to four human or computer players. If all the players are computer players, Scramble will play against itself.

Roulette EGA (PC-SIG Disk# 2381)

An infinite undo feature is included to let you undo all the words back to the first word. A stats screen allows you to see what letters have been played, what words were made, and the point value for each word. Scramble can be played at two different skill levels. You've really got to see this one!

(PC-SIG Disk# 2448)

Special Requirements: *512K RAM, EGA, and true 100% compatibles.*
Author Registration: *$15.00*

Sherlock ☆   *by Gulf Sierra*

SHERLOCK is a game of deduction. Use the clues provided to logically determine the locations of 36 images.

SHERLOCK may be played by a single person, or organize a tournament with each person attempting to solve the same puzzle as quickly as possible.

Use the mouse to control this game. A time limit can add excitement and sharp graphics will help to keep you occupied for many sessions.

(PC-SIG Disk# 2684)

Special Requirements: *EGA or VGA, and a mouse.*
Author Registration: *$15.00*
➤*ASP Member.*

Sic Bo ☆   *by United Innovations Plus*

If you love to play dice and were in the Far East, you wouldn't be playing "craps," you would be playing SIC BO.

Now this fast-paced game (usually played with three dice) can be played anywhere you can put a computer! With SIC BO, the craps-type board is displayed on your computer in stunning graphics. Bet on dice combinations you think are winners — and roll 'em.

With 50 different winning combinations and payoffs up to 150 to 1, this is big time gambling fun.

(PC-SIG Disk# 2534)

Special Requirements: *EGA, and a mouse.*
Author Registration: *$15.00*

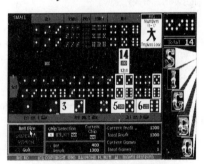
Sic Bo (PC-SIG Disk# 2534)

Solisquare ☆   *by Phil Paustian*

SOLISQUARE is a simple game of solitaire adapted from a certain card game. In SOLISQUARE, the screen is covered with squares of different colors. The object of the game is to remove all the squares by picking up pairs of squares that are next to each other horizontally, vertically, or diagonally.

Use the arrow keys (NumLock must be on) to move to any square that is next to another square of the same color. Then hit the "5" key to remove that pair of squares. When you do, all the remaining squares on the screen will slide left as far as they can, and then up as far as they can. Then the two spaces at the lower right corner will be filled in with two new colored squares as long as there are cards remaining in the "deck." If the square you choose is next to two or more squares of its own color, you will be asked to choose which one you want to remove. Just hit the number pad arrow key that points in the right direction.

In the standard game, the layout uses 15 colors laid out in 6 columns and 5 rows. The deck holds eight squares of each color, for a perfect score of 120 if you are able to remove all the squares. If you wish, you can choose different parameters. The program will ask you how many colors, columns, rows, and squares of each color you wish to use. (If you would like to play the game exactly like the original card game it was based on, choose 13 colors, 5 columns, 4 rows, and 4 of each color). The number of squares of each color must be an even number, obviously, or it will be impossible to win the game. Note that if you choose 0 of each color, the game will give an unlimited number of squares.

(PC-SIG Disk# 1524)

Special Requirements: *EGA.*
Author Registration: *$9.95*

Springer
by Ken Goodman

SPRINGER offers the beginning to intermediate chess player 10 levels of difficulty and plenty of options.

You can play against the computer, watch the computer play against itself, or play against another player while SPRINGER watches for illegal moves. You can take back a move you made, swap sides, and even interrupt the computer's thinking to force it to make a move. The maximum time SPRINGER takes to make a move varies from one second to a little over three minutes, depending on what level you are playing and your type of computer.

For games that are saved on-disk, SPRINGER can do an instant replay of the entire game or let you replay each individual move one at a time. It also prints a list of moves for each chess game, or prints a graphic display of the chess board at any time in the game. You select and move pieces with the cursor pad. On-line help is available for all options. You can play on either color or monochrome systems.

(PC-SIG Disk# 1434)

Special Requirements: *Epson or compatible printer.*
Author Registration: *$12.00*

Stained Glass
by Kent S. Brewster

Danger danger danger — imprudent use of STAINED GLASS may get you fired! Just ask the programmer's sister-in-law, who brought work to a standstill at a large New York investment banking firm after loading STAINED GLASS onto the company network server....

Simple to learn, yet devilishly difficult to master, STAINED GLASS is almost pathologically addictive. Remember the game you played with golf tees and a block of wood, jumping one tee over another into an empty hole and removing the tee you jumped, until there was only one tee left? STAINED GLASS takes that basic idea, substitutes colored panes of glass for golf tees, and adds primary and secondary colors and a very simple set of rules that you learned in kindergarten — blue plus yellow makes green, orange minus red leaves yellow, and so on.

Stained Glass (PC-SIG Disk# 2089)

STAINED GLASS has all of the bells and whistles you would expect with a top-of-the-line strategy game, including such options as load, save, undo, hint, restart, and a panic button, just in case the boss walks by!

Furthermore, the author is trying a very interesting experiment with the shareware registration system. He calls it "commissionware" — if you send him your $25 registration fee, he will send you your own serialized copy of STAINED GLASS. If you make copies and give them to your friends and one of them sends in his or her registration fee, you will receive a $5.00 commission.

(PC-SIG Disk# 2089)

Special Requirements: *CGA recommended.*
Author Registration: *$25.00*

Taipei
by Dave Norris

TAIPEI is an ancient oriental game of skill and chance. The game is played on a board and the object is to remove matching tiles. It is much harder than it sounds as the board can be up to five tiles deep, and you will not always have a matching tile easily available. The game has two modes, easy and expert. Beginners will appreciate the hint function to get them going, and experts can play the more than 60,000 different game boards for a real challenge. You can also save your game so you can play at a later time.

(PC-SIG Disk# 2455)

Special Requirements: *Windows 3.0*
Author Registration: *$10.00*

Triple Othello
by Reggie Howard

TRIPLE OTHELLO is an interesting variation on the classic strategy board game. Instead of playing one game against the computer, you play three games at once.

✍ = Updated Program
☆ = New Program

The object of TRIPLE OTHELLO is to win more pieces than the computer. Winning pieces is accomplished by "outflanking." "Outflanking" means you place your piece in such a way that you have your pieces on both sides (right and left, or above and below) of the computer's piece or pieces. Whatever piece(s) you "outflank" become yours.

(PC-SIG Disk# 1556)

Special Requirements: *None.*
Author Registration: *None.*

▼ ▼ ▼

Games, Cards

20TH CENTURY FARO
by Robert L. Nicolai

FARO is one of the oldest gambling card games ever to grace the casino. If you enjoy fast-moving casino games, you'll love this unique simulation called 20TH CENTURY FARO.

All bets which can be placed in the casino game are available in this program for one player. Even the casekeeper is displayed in the same way it would appear in a casino. A "Farobank" keeps track of all money lost by or paid to the player, letting you know how you're doing against the computer opponent. Like real Faro, it's the house that usually comes out ahead. But you never know — it could be your lucky day.

(PC-SIG Disk# 2088)

Special Requirements: *CGA.*
Author Registration: *$15.00*

Baccarat Professional ☆
by United Innovations Plus

Almost every self-respecting gambler knows how to play poker but how many know how to play Baccarat? Baccarat, while popular in European casinos, is unknown to many card players. Now BACCARAT PROFESSIONAL is available and anyone can learn it.

If you need to sharpen your skills, BACCARAT PROFESSIONAL will challenge you at a fast pace with clever graphics. If you need to learn how to play, you'll appreciate the detailed instructions, explaining all you need to know to become a "player." After just minutes, you'll be ready to take on your computer — for high stakes.

(PC-SIG Disk# 2722)

Special Requirements: *None.*
Author Registration: *$15.00*

BlackJack
by IBG Software

BLACKJACK provides hot action for one to six players with good quality card graphics. Options include insurance, splits, totes, opening player banks and game banks, and initial bet sizes. You can also set card-weight values and combine player names with levels of skill, as well as specify how the dealer and each player are to be treated during the game.

(PC-SIG Disk# 1329)

Special Requirements: *CGA.*
Author Registration: *$17.50*

BlackJack! ✍
by Glencoe Computing

BLACKJACK! is a tour de force in beating the casino dealer, and might help you line your pockets with green. Long overdue, it teaches you a basic blackjack strategy, adds an effective card counting system to it, and drills you on both the strategy and your counting ability. You play against world famous casinos or customize the rules the dealer follows. It's fun, quickly played, and could fatten your wallet on your next trip to Nevada, New Jersey, or Monte Carlo.

BLACKJACK! is a joy because you can alter the number of decks in the shoe and practice your count in the most difficult of circumstances. The rules on doubling down automatically change as you switch from single to multiple decks. You can play head on or add up to three players to your table. You watch your bank rise and sink with your luck and you can get instant advice on how to alter your betting strategy.

(PC-SIG Disk# 1283)

Special Requirements: *EGA, VGA, or Hercules graphics.*
Author Registration: *$29.99*
➤*ASP Member.*

BridgePal   *by WR Software*

Want a good game of bridge but lack the players? Want to improve your skill a bit before your next big game with your friends? This game's for you.

BRIDGEPAL is played just like a normal game of bridge, except the computer shuffles, deals, makes bids, plays the other three hands, and keeps score. You start bidding and playing from the south hand position. If your team wins the bidding, you get to play both the north and south hands; otherwise, you play defense with east or west as dummy. Optional besthand feature increases your chances for offensive play.

(PC-SIG Disk# 780)

Special Requirements: *None.*
Author Registration: *$9.95*
➤*ASP Member.*

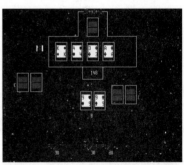

BridgePal (PC-SIG Disk# 780)

Card Game Collection   *by United Innovations Plus*

Bring your own deck and cut! Here's a lively collection of card games for your betting pleasure!

Going to Vegas or Atlantic City? Get in shape with Holdem Poker, the most popular card game in big casinos and card rooms across America. You play eight other players and start betting when you get two cards. The dealer displays three more cards which anyone can use. After betting, two more cards are displayed. This is a tough game and only the smart and the rugged survive.

Accordion Solitaire brings the battle-weary a game for rainy Sunday afternoons when time is as unimportant as winning. A gentle game with lots of instant gratification, it deals cards one by one. If cards next to each other are of identical rank or suit, pile one atop the other. Likewise for those spaced three cards apart. As the surf beats upon the shoals of Nirvana, you'll find your row of cards shrinking. Using serene strategies, you might in this, or some future lifetime, get down to a single stack and win.

Red Dog will delight any betting man or woman. A computerized version of the old Acey Duecy game, it pits you against the house. Professionally drawn and swiftly moving, it deals a spread of two cards. Your goal: draw a card numerically between the spread of the two dealt cards. You view a payoff table which tells you how much you will win if your draw is successful. You can raise your bet once.

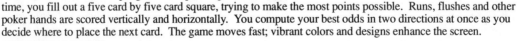

Card Game Collection (PC-SIG Disk# 1280)

Poker whizzes hone their betting skills on Poker Solitaire. On the surface, it looks like a simple game. Responding to cards dealt one at a time, you fill out a five card by five card square, trying to make the most points possible. Runs, flushes and other poker hands are scored vertically and horizontally. You compute your best odds in two directions at once as you decide where to place the next card. The game moves fast; vibrant colors and designs enhance the screen.

(PC-SIG Disk# 1280)

Special Requirements: *None.*
Author Registration: *$15.00 for each game.*

Computer Contract Bridge
by Small Business Software, INC.

COMPUTER CONTRACT BRIDGE is played by two teams, the we team and the they team. The we team consists of the North and the South. The computer is North and you're South. The they team consists of the East and the West, both played by the computer. All your interactions with your computer opponents are done through the keyboard, and you'll generally get a prompt on the screen to tell you what to do next. If you pay attention to the prompts and follow their lead, you will have no trouble playing. The computer plays a fairly good game, but in time you can learn how to win. This particular version of the program is meant for the novice bridge player. Though it is a game and not a tutorial, you will definitely learn a lot by playing it.

(PC-SIG Disk# 713)

Special Requirements: *None.*
Author Registration: *$4.95*

Computer Draw Poker
by Small Business Software, INC.

Walk away from your next game a winner! COMPUTER DRAW POKER is a fun and challenging program; an excellent way to increase your skill at poker. It is played as five card draw poker with no requirements for opening bet and no limit. Both the player and the computer start with 1000 chips. Each antes one chip before cards are dealt, and can raise the ante up to three chips per round.

This program is both a player and a tutor. It does not look at your hand to make its own playing descisions, and when it does check the cards you're holding, it doesn't remember them. It checks your hand only to see that you are playing by the rules — and tells you so when you're not. It also tells you when to bet, see, raise, call, fold, discard, and draw. The computer plays with a certain degree of sophistication and will bet high or low, as well as bluff, at random. When you can consistently beat the computer, you are playing with a good deal of skill.

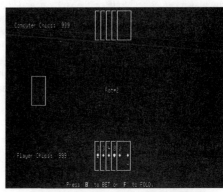
Computer Draw Poker (PC-SIG Disk# 714)

(PC-SIG Disk# 714)

Special Requirements: *None.*
Author Registration: *$4.95*

Computer Solitaire
by FreeBooter Software

The government should put COMPUTER SOLITAIRE on its list of addictive substances. The three games offer the compulsive obsessive card dealer all the variety and challenge you can handle. SPIDER is a tricky deal, the nearest thing to a solitaire strategy and skill game. Played with two decks, it's easy to learn but hard to master. You'll recognize KLONDIKE, today's most popular solitaire game. But you'll be taunted by three skill levels and a unique scoring system. CANFIELD, a voice from Saratoga's past, will haunt you. Originally, you bought a deck for $50 and got $5 for every card played in the field.

(PC-SIG Disk# 1177)

Special Requirements: *CGA.*
Author Registration: *$29.95.*

Cribbage by Crosby ✍
by Gary Crosby

If you've beaten everyone you know at cribbage or are looking for someone who doesn't make mistakes counting — CRIBBAGE BY CROSBY is here. Just start up the program and CRIBBAGE does the rest. With attractive color graphics, CRIBBAGE does the shuffling and deals the cards. Just cut for deal and your playing cribbage. Select cards for the "crib," play for points, and then the official will count'em up, keeping score on the on-screen cribbage board. Even though CRIBBAGE BY CROSBY doesn't teach you how to play, it can operate in either a fast or slow mode. Card fun has never been this easy.

(PC-SIG Disk# 2468)

Special Requirements: *CGA*
Author Registration: *$10.00*

Cribbage By T
by Ted H. Turner

A hand of Cribbage is fun, indeed, when played with the scoundrel (aka your computer). As you play, he comments on your play, the state of the game and the score needed to win.

Clear graphics add to the effect of natural play, while you concentrate on your strategy. The main menu will direct you to information about the rules, how to score and other material. If you get stuck or can't decide which play to make, use the hints function. Five hints per game can help if you need it.

(PC-SIG Disk# 1789)
Special Requirements: *CGA.*
Author Registration: *$20.00*

Cribbage Partner
by James I. Crowther, Jr.

Cribbage Partner is a complete and realistic simulation of the game of Cribbage. In all cases except the demonstration, the player opposes the computer. Shuffling, dealing and bookkeeping are done automatically so the player can concentrate on the strategy and scoring aspects of the game. A wide selection of options is provided so that players can gear the level and pace of play to their experience. Full documention and rules of cribbage are included.

Unique features of CRIBBAGE PARTNER:
- Cards, pegs, and Cribbage board are clearly represented
- Prompts and status messages explain the game situation and scoring
- Player can do scoring or have scoring done automatically
- Call for computer help on any play
- Any hand can be replayed
- "Muggins" option is available
- Full demonstration mode is included
- Function keys toggle among options during play
- Full color and monochrome options are included
- Will run on IBM PCjr.

(PC-SIG Disk# 1819)
Special Requirements: *None.*
Author Registration: *$10.00*

CROSSpro ✍
by JJO Software

LAS VEGAS EGA CASINO is a package of games that use the special features of your EGA monitor. Included are: Las Vegas Casino Black Jack, Las Vegas Video Poker, and Las Vegas Dollar Slots (MicroBucks). You can choose any of the three games to play from the program menu. It has great graphics and is so realistic you forget you're playing a computer.

XWORD lets you quickly create a crossword puzzle that can be saved to disk and printed. The crossword puzzle size can be from 15x15 to 23x23. You enter words with the cursor onto the puzzle grid. Afterward, the words can be "deleted," with the word placed on a "move" list where it can be recovered and placed in another location. This program maintains word lists for across and down, and clues which you can see at any time. XWORD lets you enter words on the puzzle grid even before the clue list is made. After you finish your puzzle, the program lets you print a blank crossword puzzle, a clue list, and the solution to the puzzle. Your crossword puzzle can be saved to disk. Thus, the amount of crossword puzzles you can create is limited only by disk space and your own imagination.

CASTLE DROGANYA is a reactive adventure game. The course of the game is dictated by your response to the situation. The goal is to free the souls of the townspeople who have been trapped by the evil Lord Droganya.

LIAR'S POKER is a game utility that simplifies playing Liar's Poker, a betting game in which each player's "hand" is a dollar bill serial number. The program generates random numbers that can be substituted to play the game. It keeps records on disk for up to 20 "liars" (players), each liar having up to 20 numbers which can be printed or displayed on the screen.

(PC-SIG Disk# 1074)
Special Requirements: *EGA and a version of BASIC.*
Author Registration: *$5.00 to $20.00.*

Draw Poker Professional
by United Innovations Plus

Keep your card skills polished and your poker face in training. Play DRAW POKER PROFESSIONAL in an eight-handed game of your favorite version of poker.

Whether you are a card game enthusiast, a neighborhood player or a professional, you can play poker just as it is played in a card club or casino. Seven of the eight hands are played by the computer. Play Straight Ante, Blind, Straddle, Anything Opens or a Jacks or Better game. Choose from the many configuration options to suit your playing preferences, mood or skill level.

(PC-SIG Disk# 1962)

Special Requirements: *None.*
Author Registration: *$15.00*

Games for EGA
by Spectrum Software

If you like computer games, you'll like EGA GAMES, with arcade quality graphics and playing style. EGA GAMES includes BlackJack, Poker, pac- man style Squasher, and a 3D version of TicTacToe.

Choose BlackJack and play with realistic looking cards. This version can improve your playing skills before your next trip to the casinos. Poker Square is a new variation of the traditional 5 card stud game. Each player has 5 hands and must place each card carefully in order to win this one. Squasher is a pac-man style game that combines action and strategy to retrieve the pots of gold before the monsters squash you. 3D TicTacToe is a variation of the original TicTacToe which opens up many more winning strategies.

(PC-SIG Disk# 1938)

Special Requirements: *880K bytes of free space, EGA, and a mouse.*
Author Registration: *$20.00*

Golf Solitaire
by United Innovations Plus

Here is yet another outstanding solitaire game from United Innovations Plus. GOLF SOLITAIRE is played with a standard deck of fifty-two cards. The layout is made by dealing out five rows of seven cards each, overlapping face up. A total of thirty-five cards form the layout. One more card is dealt below the layout, face up to form your base. The object is to clear away all the layout cards by building onto the base card. Building is done in sequence, in either direction, regardless of suit, and if you make a wrong move your computer will certainly keep you honest.

This top-notch software package comes with outstanding graphics plus all the features that make this a top-notch program. You can control the speed of dealing and elect to view the shuffling of the cards. You also choose the number of holes and which variation of the game you wish to play. The graphics are impressive, clear and easy to follow.

(PC-SIG Disk# 1700)

Special Requirements: *None.*
Author Registration: *$15.00*

Klondike
by Ted Gruber Software

KLONDIKE is a traditional gambling game similar to a card game most of us know as "Solitaire." KLONDIKE differs from Solitaire in that you can only go through the deck one time, cards are dealt from the deck one at a time instead of three at a time, and betting is an important part of the game.

The object of KLONDIKE is to put as many cards as possible on the "piles." This is accomplished by moving the cards around on the screen by using either the mouse or the keyboard. This game requires an EGA graphics adapter, which makes the graphics look so good it looks like you're playing with a real deck of cards.

(PC-SIG Disk# 1544)

Special Requirements: *EGA.*
Author Registration: *$10.00*

Lowball Poker Professional
by United Innovations Plus

The game of Lowball Poker is played with a fifty-three card deck, consisting of a standard deck of playing cards with one joker. This form of lowball is also known as California Lowball. The rank of cards are from the king (high) to an ace (low). The joker is wild and used as the lowest card in your hand so long as it doesn't make a pair.

In Lowball, your goal is to beat your opponents by trying to get the lowest hand. A complete reverse of what is normally played in high poker. The best hand is a 5-4-3-2-A known as a wheel or bicycle. Straights and flushes do not count. You watch your hand and the computer plays all the others. Good graphics and complete control over shuffling, dealing speed, and display of cards help make this program enjoyable.

(PC-SIG Disk# 1956)

Special Requirements: *None.*
Author Registration: *$15.00*

Memory ☆
by Steffen Mueller

MEMORY is the PC version of that challenging card game Concentration. Fifty cards are displayed face down. Players turn up two cards, one at a time, hoping to find a matching pair. If no match is found, the cards are turned face down again and the next player tries to find a match. Remember which cards are where in order to find the most matches. Play against a friend or five different levels of the computer.

MEMORY has excellent graphics, mouse support, optional sound, and a well-designed game board. This program is an excellent way to develop your visual memory. But beware — MEMORY is extremely addictive!

(PC-SIG Disk# 2705)

Special Requirements: *EGA or VGA.*
Author Registration: *$20.00*

Osmosis Solitaire
by United Innovations Plus

OSMOSIS SOLITAIRE takes the popular parlor game of solitaire and adds many new and interesting twists. Starting with a standard deck of 52 playing cards, the program creates 4 stock piles (3 cards down and 1 card up) and a base card which will be the key for starting the game. The rest of the cards are stored in the "waste pile." Each subsequent row can only be started by a matching base card of another suit. The object is to build upon each base card the other twelve cards of its own suit. Except for your starting stock row, you cannot play a card unless it can be found in the preceding row. To add to the fun, the 4 stock piles must also be used in play. The final outcome: hopefully, all cards will be played!

A great pastime for all who enjoy card games of any sort. Immediately accessible and easily understandable, OSMOSIS SOLITAIRE will soon be a popular game for your gaming library. Don't pass up this wonderful package created by Raymond M. Buti.

(PC-SIG Disk# 1913)

Special Requirements: *CGA.*
Author Registration: *$15.00*

Poker ✐
by Robert Gellman

Play draw poker head-to-head with the computer. POKER has a sophisticated style of playing and betting, and is intended to challenge the serious poker player.

It's honest. The computer does not know what is in your hand unless there is a showdown.

It's smart. The game has different patterns of betting and can observe your style of betting and modify its own behavior accordingly.

It's cagey. POKER can bluff in several ways and sometimes makes large bets with bad hands or no bets with good hands. Every action it takes has at least two possible interpretations. The randomness of the shuffling has been tested in simulations involving over half a million hands and the results mirror those expected in normal poker playing.

Ante up and deal 'em.

(PC-SIG Disk# 791)

Special Requirements: *None.*
Author Registration: *$20.00*

Poker Challenge
by WorkWare Company

Poker players, here are two games that will hone your skill while giving you lots of enjoyable practice. In Stud, you play against seven computer opponents — all smart and shrewd. In Texas Hold 'Em, you play against nine computer opponents who have lots of savvy. But Poker CHALLENGE does give you a break; poke a hot key and

　　　✐ = Updated Program
☆ = New Program

your odds of winning are instantly displayed on the screen, along with an abundance of information about the hand.

Not only are these games for the thoughtful, serious player, they also move fast enough to keep the beginner delighted. In fact, you can take advantage of the fast deal and then use the plus and minus keys to play the game so fast you can barely keep up with the moves. All face up cards are drawn on the screen, showing their ranks and suits. You control the ante and betting limits. For poker pros and amateurs, POKER CHALLENGE is a winner.

(PC-SIG Disk# 1642)

Special Requirements: *None.*
Author Registration: *$19.00*

Poker Slot ☆   *by United Innovations Plus*

POKER SLOT is a gambling game found in casinos in Nevada and New Jersey. Before playing POKER SLOT, choose one of four variations of the game — Second Chance Poker, Joker Wild, Deuces Wild, and Double Down.

The object of the game is to get a poker hand of Jacks or better. You will be paid off according to your poker hand. For each round, insert one to five coins worth $1.00 each. (POKER SLOT will keep track of the total coins bet.) You will be dealt five cards in each round and you may choose which ones to hold or discard.

POKER SLOT can be played with a mouse or keyboard, and has a detailed screen layout using EGA graphics.

(PC-SIG Disk#'s 2737, 2738)

Special Requirements: *360K RAM, EGA. Mouse optional.*
Author Registration: *$15.00*

Pro-Play Blackjack ☆   *by Bill Dobbing*

You have a King and a seven and the dealers has a nine showing. What do you do? I'll take another card! "Never hit hard 17 or more." That's something the advanced blackjack player knows and that something that PRO-PLAY BLACKJACK will remind you of. Have fun and learn the advanced concepts of blackjack with PRO-PLAY BLACKJACK; a blackjack simulation with great graphics.

If you have a basic understanding of blackjack, but want to take the next step and play like a "pro," here's your chance. PRO-PLAY includes all the help screens and the tables of strategies you'll need. PRO-PLAY uses the rules found in most casinos on the Las Vegas Strip to teach you concepts of hard/soft hands, splitting, double downing, and more. Once you have skills improved, invite six other friends to play and PRO-PLAY will keep the score.

Special Requirements: *512K RAM and CGA.*
Author Registration: *$12.00*

Pyramid Solitaire   *by United Innovations Plus*

The old game of pyramid solitaire is even better when your computer deals and keeps score — you just enjoy the game. Twenty-eight cards are dealt in the form of a pyramid. The pyramid has seven rows of cards. This is composed of successive rows of one to seven cards. Each card is overlapped by two cards of the row below. The last row, which contains seven cards, are turned face up. The object is to remove all cards from the pyramid and from the remainder of the deck by simple addition using any two cards available for play. The two cards must add up to 13 points.

This top-notch software package comes with all the extras. There is mouse support during the playing of the game. It allows dealing of the cards either face up or face down. There are two modes of play, multiple redeals or a single deal. It allows you to replay the previously dealt hand. You can even control the speed of dealing and elect to view the shuffling of the cards just to keep the computer honest. Graphics are impressive, clear, and easy to follow.

(PC-SIG Disk# 1701)

Special Requirements: *None.*
Author Registration: *$15.00*

SMSPOKER   *by Michael E. Lind*

SMSPOKER is similar to a Las Vegas poker machine. It's a solo game played against the deck/machine. You are dealt five cards in a horizontal row. The better the hands you get, the more $$$$ you can win. Between each poker hand, the game asks if you want to bet on whether a random card drawn from the deck is higher or lower than eight. Game features include adjustable playing speed, dealer/player interaction, and real awards to registered winners.

(PC-SIG Disk# 55)

Special Requirements: *CGA.*
Author Registration: *$10.00*

Solitaire
by IBG Software

SOLITAIRE is a computer version of the classic card game with additional features. Undo your last card played, select the number of cards to turn from the deck each time (usually three), and ask the computer whether or not there are any additional plays that can be made in a certain turn. There are several cheating options that you may or may not want to use, such as peeking at the first overturned card in each stack. On-line help is available to the player throughout the game.

(PC-SIG Disk# 891)

Special Requirements: *None.*
Author Registration: *$15.00*

Solitaire Card Games
by Richard Metlen

Attention escapist compulsive obsessives! Avoid this trio of solitaire games like the plague. Otherwise, you'll spend the rest of your life hunched over your PC enjoying these spiffy designer solitaire games. There's enough variety to keep you going for hours or eons. For those lonesome souls who need card games like Eleven, Even Out, and Block11 as a substitute for meditation or tranquilizers, this disk is worth its weight in gold.

(PC-SIG Disk# 1411)

Special Requirements: *None.*
Author Registration: *$5.00*

Thinking Man's Solitaire ☆
by United Innovations Plus

Are you familiar with the standard Solitaire game that builds a stack of cards from Ace to King? It's not so hard, especially if you don't have to stick to one suit. THINKING MAN'S SOLITAIRE presents a new twist: the order isn't as simple as Ace, 2, 3. In fact, you build four different stacks, each in a different order. Have trouble remembering what card comes next? Ask THINKING MAN'S SOLITAIRE to keep the order posted on your screen.

The documentation on the disk makes it easy to get started. Watch the colorful deck magically shuffle three times, cut, and stack. Deal the cards one by one, and see each one move to the stack you designate as your score mounts. If you have a mouse, you may use it. Otherwise, the keyboard does just fine. The hardest part of this entertaining game is stopping.

(PC-SIG Disk#'s 2759, 2760)

Special Requirements: *491K RAM and EGA.*
Author Registration: *$18.00*

Tommy's Gin Rummy
by Tommy's Toys

TOMMY'S GIN RUMMY implements the game allegedly invented in 1909 by E.T. Baker of the Knickerbocker Whist Club of New York, with optional automatic sorting of your hand to give the best score. You play against the computer, which plays a mean game. Your hand is displayed at the top of the screen, the computer's hand is displayed under yours. To learn the game, you can choose to play with open hands, meaning that you can see the computer's hand but it can't see yours. The computer shuffles, deals, and keeps all scores current.

You can choose from 3 different variations of GIN RUMMY; Standard, Oklahoma (Cedarhurst), and Tommy's Space Cowboy. A hot key demo mode is available, in which you can watch the computer play against itself, a great way to learn how to play this all-time favorite card game with plenty of music and color. It works both on mono and color screens.

(PC-SIG Disk# 1612)

Special Requirements: *None.*
Author Registration: *None.*

✍ = Updated Program
☆ = New Program

Ultima21 Deluxe
by Falconer Services Inc.

Play Blackjacks as it's played in the casinos with the computer as the dealer. ULTIMA21 keeps track of the hands played and who won each hand. It also shows your longest winning (and losing) streaks. In addition, you can set up your own options — resplit aces, double-down on any number of cards, make the dealer stand on 17, turn the sound on during play, and other things to keep it interesting.

Hit me!

(PC-SIG Disk# 791)

Special Requirements: *None.*
Author Registration: *$20.00*

UNO and Games ✍
by Garry Spencer

This games package mixes a new computerized version of a classic card game with a hard disk menu for your other computer games. This familiar card game — called UNO — centers on who can go out first by playing all cards dealt. You play against a relentless computer. Great for anyone who likes computer cards.

The GAME menu offers you a quick, easy way to reach your most popular games. You can edit the menu to allow access to any game on your hard disk. This is not as fancy as other menu systems in the library but it does the job.

(PC-SIG Disk# 1644)

Special Requirements: *None.*
Author Registration: *$5.00*

UNOSCORE ☆
by Suzanne Spencer Software

UNOSCORE is an eye-popping version of the card game UNO. In UNO there are four sets of numbered cards. Each set is a different color. You are dealt seven cards to start the game. Match the last card laid down, in color or number. If you don't have a match, draw a card. The winner is the first to play all of his cards.

Great graphics make UNOSCORE a joy to play. UNOSCORE is easy to learn, yet challenging for all ages. It's also a great way to teach young children pattern-matching skills while having fun!

(PC-SIG Disk# 2522)

Special Requirements: *CGA.*
Author Registration: *$5.00*

Vegas Johnny's Draw Poker
by Top Score Software

VEGAS JOHNNY'S DRAW POKER is a detailed simulation of a draw poker game. It plays all the other hands, gives you playing tips in plain English like "don't throw away good money — fold!" It will show you the odds of winning at any given time — makes play fun for the poker novice or pro. It works on all popular display adapters; a color monitor is optional, as is a mouse. Its features include:

❏ Bet limits, blind and ante amounts are user selectable
❏ Six levels of competition — user selectable
❏ Variable playing speed — user selectable
❏ On-line betting and drawing advice
❏ On-line odds and statistics
❏ On-line help with "what beats what"
❏ Scoreboard file to log big winners
❏ User interface allows fast and easy play.

(PC-SIG Disk# 1896)

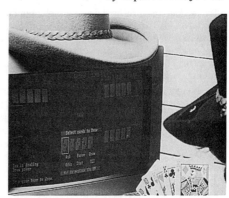

Vegas Johnny's Draw Poker (PC-SIG Disk# 1896)

Special Requirements: *None.*
Author Registration: *$7.00*

Vegas Pro Video Poker

by WorkWare Company

Video poker machines are the most popular "slot" machines in Las Vegas and account for almost forty percent of the billions of dollars that tourists spend in Nevada casinos.

VEGAS PRO takes you on a quick, happy trip to a casino to play the popular machine "five card draw poker." You bet and pull the handle and watch the cards line up. You can hold or draw each of the cards. Then you tell the machine to deal and get the good or bad news. Each game can be played in seconds.

Poker, to its afficionados, is not a card game, but a game of money management. VEGAS PRO lets you set the payoffs yourself to practice for different casinos. A draw tester allows you to try out different gambling strategies. The game will play on almost any monitor and provides superb graphics on EGA/VGA. The user can also control sound effects, speed of play, and other options.

(PC-SIG Disk# 1490)

Special Requirements: *None.*
Author Registration: *$19.00*

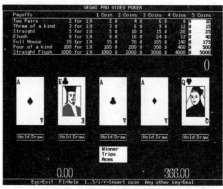

Vegas Pro Video Poker (PC-SIG Disk# 1490)

▼ ▼ ▼

Genealogy

Brother's Keeper Genealogy

by John Steed

BROTHER'S KEEPER helps you keep track of all your brothers, sisters, aunts, uncles, and other relatives going back generations!

In the hobby of genealogy, you never know just who or what you'll find once you start tracing your family tree! BROTHER'S KEEPER allows you to gather and organize the tidbits of ancestral history you uncover and will print the information in a variety of helpful ways. Included are: ancestor charts, family group sheets, alphabetical name lists, descendant trees, birthday lists, custom reports, and ahnentafel charts. (This is a chart which lists ancestors of a person, with standard code numbers that show relationships, such as parent, grandparent, etc., instead of using lines to graphically indicate the relationships.)

Two disk drives, or a hard drive, are recommended, but the program will work with one disk drive. You can record over 1000 names on a 360K disk, or 15,000 with a hard drive. For each person entered, you may include date of birth, date of death, and three other significant dates of your choosing. In addition, you may store place of birth, place of death, and three other places of important events. You also may enter two additional fields, which you define. Each person can have up to seven message lines of additional data, or a text file of unlimited size containing additional data that is linked to his record.

Up to eight marriages may be recorded for each of your more fickle forebears. Each record can hold a marriage date, a place of marriage, one additional date and place, and can store up to 24 children — very useful if you are related to the Waltons!

The GEDCOM file transfer standard is used so that data can be shared with other genealogists and amateur family tree-ers who use different programs. This is one of the most intriguing aspects of genealogy — the joining together of your research and family tree with others. You suddenly gain both entire blocks of ancestral data, as well as potential busloads of distant relatives you never knew you were related to coming to visit you!

A wide variety of printers are supported, including laser.

(PC-SIG Disk#'s 1504, 1505)

Special Requirements: *512K RAM and two floppy drives. A hard drive is recommended.*
Author Registration: *$40.00*
➤*ASP Member.*

🖎 = Updated Program
☆ = New Program

EZ-Tree
by MicroFox Company

EZ-TREE is a genealogy program to track and report on family trees. You can keep track of up to 16 marriages per person and up to 32 children per marriage. There is no logical limit to the number of generations you can have for each family tree. Each record contains first name, middle name, last name, maiden name, sex, birth date and information, death date and information, personal comments, marriage date and information, divorce date and information, and marriage and divorce notes.

From the main menu you can retrieve an existing family tree, create a new family tree, work on the current family tree, delete the current family tree, save the current family tree, or modify the program's configuration, such as colors, disk directory, and screen blanking timeout. You can easily add parents, spouse and children to the family tree. For convenience, function keys are used to select family tree options, such as: edit a record, find a specific record (person), zoom in on a particular person, etc.

EZ-TREE will produce three different reports, which can be directed to the screen or the printer. You can produce a report containing detailed information about a person, or a report on all people in a family tree, or a list of all descendants of a person.

(PC-SIG Disk# 1611)

Special Requirements: *None.*
Author Registration: *$10.00*
➤*ASP Member.*

Family History System   *by Phillip E. Brown*

Ever wonder who's lurking in the upper branches of your family tree? The FAMILY HISTORY system, a modular genealogy program, will help you organize and refine your search.

The system stores information about individuals, including all family relationships. You are not limited in the number of relationships that might exist for each individual, or the number of generations of ancestors or descendants. Information for up to 3200 individuals may be stored on a diskette and up to 9999 on a hard disk. You can produce ancestor, descendant, relative, and family group reports and ancestor (tree) charts. You may print out blank worksheets and charts to record information for entry into the system. Sample files are included for the descendants of Adam (as recorded in Genesis) and the family of Prince Charles. A GEDCOM export/import program permits sharing information with other genealogy software.

Research your roots and know where you came from. A great gift for the next generation.

Family History System (PC-SIG Disk# 361)

(PC-SIG Disk#'s 361, 632, 2291)

Special Requirements: *None.*
Author Registration: *$35.00*

Family Ties ✎
by Computer Service

FAMILY TIES is designed for the organized compilation of personal genealogical information.

All of the names entered in this program are automatically linked to each other, defining relationships. Starting with one individual (usually yourself) use the edit mode to enter your data. Then add a person linked to this first individual; for example, parents, spouse, other spouse or child, and enter their information. Start with any male person and then ancestors or decendants can be added in any order.

Please note: This program also has an optional mode which conforms to the preferences of The Church of Jesus Christ of Latter Day Saints (LDS) and maintains records according to sealings, baptisms, endowments, and temple dates.

(PC-SIG Disk# 465)

Special Requirements: *None.*
Author Registration: *$50.00*

Family Tree Genealogy
by Pine Cone Software

FAMILY TREE is a general purpose genealogy system designed for charting and maintaining family tree information and relationships between individuals. The system is menu-driven with single-keystroke commands, scrolling, mini-windows, and output to screen, printer, or disk file. You can change default options to select disk drive, screen colors, and printer control codes.

The maintenance function allows the entry of names, sex, dates/places of birth/death/marriage, and free-form text remarks. Spouse and parent/child relationships are established after data is entered.

The chart function uses the database to make reports by pedigree, ancestors, family groups, decendants, and relationships.

(PC-SIG Disk# 240)
Special Requirements: *Printer.*
Author Registration: *$35.00*

Family Tree Journal ✍
by Cherry Tree Software

Imagine having a book that chronicles the history of your family, going back generations! Here's your opportunity to create one for your great, great, great grandchildren!

FAMILY TREE JOURNAL provides a convenient way of collecting and compiling genealogical and biographical information. The output of this program is a formatted book with information about a virtually infinite family history. Just think, if you could locate the information about only your direct ancestors (not including any sisters, brothers, aunts, uncles, nieces, nephews, or cousins) for only 20 generations, you would find you're descended from over 1,000,000 people and over 500,000 of them would be your great, great, great grandparents!

FAMILY TREE JOURNAL takes information you uncover about your relatives and creates a document that lets others study the history without a computer. It has easy data entry and collates the information through various sort and merge routines into an informative family reference. Give copies as unique gifts to family members. An annual update of the book, based on new information accumulated throughout the year, could become a family tradition!

(PC-SIG Disk#'s 1535, 2094)
Special Requirements: *Printer.*
Author Registration: *$35.00*
➤*ASP Member.*

Genealogy on Display
by Melvin O. Duke

Genealogy On Display is an integrated, menu-driven group of 20 unprotected BASIC programs for IBM PCs (including the IBM-PCjr). The programs will help you organize, record, and report your own genealogical data.

As shipped, GENEALOGY ON DISPLAY provides for 500 persons and 200 marriages within its database, with no specific generation limit. These numbers can be increased to over 3000 persons and over 1000 marriages with sufficient storage space; i.e., a hard drive.

Output available for printing or displaying on the screen includes:
❑ Charts of ancestors (pedigree or family tree charts)
❑ Charts of families (family group charts)
❑ Charts of descendants (30 generations default)
❑ Detailed personal information
❑ Detailed marriage information
❑ Lists of persons (by number or alphabetized)
❑ Lists of marriages (by number or alphabetized)
❑ Lists of parent/child relationships

Note: A companion disk (PC-SIG disk number 594) is not necessary to run this disk, but it offers additional functions and smooths out the operation.

(PC-SIG Disk# 90)
Special Requirements: *A version of BASIC.*
Author Registration: *$49.00*

Micro-Gene
by Micro-Art

Want to find out who (or what) is swinging by one hairy arm from the branches of your family tree? MICRO-GENE is a thorough, comprehensive, well-documented software package to help you develop your family genealogical record. In addition to the data-recording capabilities, it has excellent printing capabilities so you can get hierarchical charts of your ancestors and other quality reports. Menu function selections simplify the use of the system and lets you concentrate on the family data rather than system functions.

Note that MICRO-GENE is a sophisticated, reasonably complex package and the quality of results you get are related to the level of energy expended in learning the program and acquiring data.

(PC-SIG Disk# 1068)

Special Requirements: *Printer.*
Author Registration: *$29.95*

MyFamily ✎
by PractiComp

Genealogical records and family histories can be easy to maintain. MYFAMILY puts an emphasis on flexibility and menu-driven ease of use. Records may be entered in any order. There are no limits placed on the number of children or previous marriages entered for each individual. The program accommodates children from previous marriages. When reports are produced children are automatically ordered by birthdate, and previous marriages by date of marriage. The programmable macro key feature allows the user to assign values to seven function keys to ease the data entry and editing processes.

MYFAMILY produces 14 different types of reports, including ancestor and descendant charts, individual and family sheets, various types of lists, and blank charts or sheets. Reports may be displayed on the screen, printed, or saved to a disk file. The file manager feature allows the user to copy files, erase files, and view a directory listing without leaving the program. Selected records may be copied from one genealogy file to another. The date calculator feature allows you to view a calendar for a selected date and perform arithmetic on dates. A sample genealogy file is included on the program diskette so that you may easily try out the program's various features.

(PC-SIG Disk# 1936)

Special Requirements: *384K RAM and a hard drive.*
Author Registration: *$25.00*

Notes and Sources on Display
by Melvin O. Duke

NOTES AND SOURCES ON DISPLAY is an extension of the GENEALOGY ON DISPLAY program (PC-SIG disk #90) and uses the "persons" file from that program. Enhance and organize the search for your ancestral past by saving notes on each new find. Keep track of your sources of information, the types of information you use, the event date, the research date and finally, the contents of the "note" itself.

(PC-SIG Disk# 594)

Special Requirements: *A version of BASIC and the PERSONS file from GENEALOGY ON DISPLAY.*
Author Registration: *$45.00 — $30.00 if a registered user of Genealogy ON DISPLAY.*

▼ ▼ ▼

Graphing Programs

CGA Screen Designer ☆
by Gene Coughlan

CGA SCREEN DESIGNER turns your keyboard or mouse into a drawing pen and your CGA monitor screen into an easel. With CGA SCREEN DESIGNER, you can draw your own pictures using graphics primitives such as lines, circles, and boxes. Use the numeric keypad or mouse to draw or move the cursor around the screen. Create eight different graph styles, save your pictures and graphs to disk for future editing, and print your pictures and graphs on any Epson-compatible dot-matrix printer.

Use the menu system or the Quick Command keys to operate CGA SCREEN DESIGNER. The Pen menu items include: Move, Draw, Erase, Pattern, or Pen Width (which can be 1, 3, or 5 pixels). Select the Shapes menu for options such as: Circle, Rectangle, Ellipse, Curve, or Line. Create eight different graphs. Choose from two types each of horizontal bar, vertical bar, and line graphs as well as three-dimensional bar graphs and pie charts.

CGA SCREEN DESIGNER supports all printers that emulate the FX/LX/MX/LQ series of Epson printers. This includes most of the dot-matrix printers on the market, and a few laser printers. Choose to print in Portrait, Landscape, or Oversize Portrait mode.

(PC-SIG Disk# 2696)

Special Requirements: *CGA.*
Author Registration: *$15.00*

EGA Screen Designer ☆

by Gene Coughlan

EGA SCREEN DESIGNER turns your keyboard or mouse into a drawing pen and your EGA monitor screen into an easel. With EGA SCREEN DESIGNER, you can draw your own pictures using graphics primitives such as lines, circles, and boxes. Use the numeric keypad or mouse to draw or move the cursor around the screen. Create eight different graph styles, save your pictures and graphs to disk for future editing, and print your pictures and graphs on any Epson-compatible dot-matrix printer.

Use the menu system or the Quick Command keys to operate EGA SCREEN DESIGNER. The Pen menu items include: Move, Draw, Erase, Pattern, or Pen Width (which can be 1, 3, or 5 pixels). Select the Shapes menu for options such as: Circle, Rectangle, Ellipse, Curve, or Line. Create eight different graphs. Choose from two types each of horizontal bar, vertical bar, and line graphs as well as three-dimensional bar graphs and pie charts.

EGA SCREEN DESIGNER supports all printers that emulate the FX/LX/MX/LQ series of Epson printers. This includes most of the dot-matrix printers on the market, and a few laser printers. Choose to print in Portrait, Landscape, or Oversize Portrait mode.

EGA SCREEN DESIGNER also includes a Pattern Editor Program, which can be used to change the patterns used by EGA SCREEN DESIGNER for filling in graphics images. The pattern is displayed in an eight-by-eight box, and you can change the color of each individual pixel by simply pressing the space bar.

(PC-SIG Disk# 2697)

Special Requirements: *EGA.*
Author Registration: *$15.00*

ExpressGraph

by Expressware Corporation

EXPRESSGRAPH is an easy-to-use business graphics program. Numbers can be analyzed much more easily and quickly when they are displayed in graphic form. It lets you display numbers in a variety of graphic formats. Then you can choose the display you like best, and print your graph.

Here are some examples of how people use EXPRESSGRAPH:

❏ Graphing sales dollars and gross profit on a weekly basis
❏ Displaying financial data graphically
❏ Analyzing budgets and expenses with a pie chart
❏ Spotting trends amid a "sea of numbers"
❏ Providing summarized data in graphic form to accompany financial statements, for quick analysis and trend spotting

The data for the graph can be imported from one of three formats, including DIF, or entered from within EXPRESSGRAPH. Save the data on disk and reload later for further changes or review. Graphs created with EXPRESSGRAPH can be displayed in one of 10 graphic formats (pie, line, bar, etc.), altered in various ways, and printed.

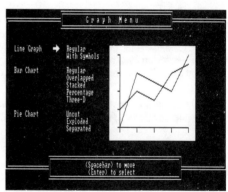

ExpressGraph (PC-SIG Disk# 1058)

(PC-SIG Disk# 1058)

Special Requirements: *None.*
Author Registration: *$29.95*
➤*ASP Member.*

✍ = Updated Program
☆ = New Program

Graphics Screen Designer ☆
by Gene Coughlan

Create pictures using lines, boxes, circles, and curves. Three line widths and many fill patterns are available. Create graphs (line, 2-D or 3-D bar, pie), and switch graph types to see which style best suits the data. Handy features are everywhere — scaling, reverse video, page switching, and a DOS shell. This smoothly-working program supports a mouse and Epson-compatible printers with such options as landscape or portrait. Sample files are provided, including data for graphs and a very nice map of the USA.

(PC-SIG Disk# 2777)

Special Requirements: *Hercules graphics.*
Author Registration: *$15.00*

Graphtime-II (CGA/EGA) ✍
by Computer Performance

GRAPHTIME-II is a business and technical graphics system with text and font editors. Designed for use with dBASE II/III, Multiplan, Lotus 1- 2-3 and ASCII files, it can also be used on its own with data entered from the keyboard into the built-in spreadsheet. Epson compatible, HP Deskjet and Laserjet printers are supported.

The package consists of six main modules:
❏ GRAPH — 19 types available with up to 10 graphs per screen
❏ DRAW — Full-screen color graphics editor
❏ FONT — Text generator and font editor
❏ FILE — External file input/output
❏ TEXTED — Text and macro editor
❏ PRINT — Printer driver

The graphics editor can create free-form diagrams or enhance a previously made graph. You can select arrow keys, joystick or mouse to control the graphics cursor.

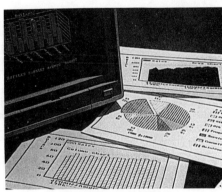
Graphtime-II (PC-SIG Disk# 669)

GRAPHTIME-II can be either menu or command-driven, with an emphasis on ease of use. All scales and labels are made automatically with manual override. A macro facility is included for commonly-used command sequences and to control slide shows. Macros can also be created by recording a sequence of commands as they are used.

(PC-SIG Disk#'s 669, 670, 7481, 7081)

Special Requirements: *640K RAM, CGA, and hard disk.*
Author Registration: *$49.95*

Graphtime-II (Hercules)
by Computer Performance

GRAPHTIME II is a business-presentation graphics program. GRAPHTIME II does various line, column and pie charts. The charts can be printed or plotted, viewed individually, or set up to run as an unattended "slide show" on the monitor. It accepts data from dBase II/III, Multiplan, and Lotus 1-2-3, or you can enter data directly. It has a font editor, macro editor and math functions including moving averages. There is even an "undo" function. A Microsoft mouse (or compatible) is recommended for the draw program.

This version will plot 24 data points and will print "paint" files or save them to disk.

(PC-SIG Disk#'s 833, 834)

Special Requirements: *Hercules graphics.*
Author Registration: *$20.00*

Picture Label ☆
by Terry D. Lustofin

PICTURE LABEL prints images from either PrintMaster, PrintShop, or The New PrintShop graphics libraries on address labels, and adds text — in one easy operation. Use any custom graphics created with these programs or other available clip-art (See COOPER GRAPHICS, PC-SIG Library).

NOTE: PICTURE LABEL is a stand-alone program and does not require either PrintMaster or PrintShop. Only the graphics libraries are required.

PICTURE LABEL is menu-driven with such features as:

❏ Four label heights — ¹⁵/₁₆", 1⁷/₁₆", 1¹⁵/₁₆", and 2¹⁵/₁₆"
❏ Standard six lines per Inch spacing provides up to five lines on a 1" label
❏ On-screen view of 12 graphic images at one time
❏ Selection of graphics libraries from a single screen display
❏ Special print features and font selection such as double wide, double high, italics, and enhanced
❏ Save label address data including fonts and printing enhancements for later use

Got a large mailing list? PICTURE LABEL can be used to "pre-print" just the graphics on your label stock. Use your database or mail label program to print the address lines later.

(PC-SIG Disk# 2550)

Special Requirements: *Graphics card and printer.*
Author Registration: *$10.00*

ZGraf ✎   *by John Jakob*

An easy color graphing tool for quickly creating informative presentations. Pull-down menus speed up the generation of several different kinds of graphs and charts.

The program implements a "quick-and-dirty" approach to graph construction. It is simple to use and supports the popular graphics display modes(Hercules, CGA, MCGA, EGA, VGA).

The program is designed to allow the user to create, display, and print X/Y Line, Log, Bar, Pie, and Area graphs, as well as graphs of functions of one and two variables [$Y = F(X)$ and $Z=G(X,Y)$]. It also provides some basic math/numerical analysis capabilities (integrals/derivatives/root-solving/linear regression/complex number calculations).

(PC-SIG Disk# 1967)

Special Requirements: *Graphics card. Hard drive recommended.*
Author Registration: *$10.00*

▼ ▼ ▼

Ham Radio

Ham Radio   *by Niel Wiegand*

Ham it up! Learn and practice your Morse with the variable speed sender and receiver programs. Other routines help the amateur radio operator compute various electronic formulas, design antennas, locate satellites and calculate orbits. RTTY and TTY are communication programs using Baudot, ASCII, or Morse code at varying speeds.

The USAT program provides real time tracking of the OSCAR 9, 10, and 11 and the RS 5, 7, and 8 satellites; the user specifies the date, time, length of time, and tracking interval. Several programs calculate coil inductance, coil properties, signals for varying frequencies, resistance and reactance. NETWORK provides analysis of user-specified circuits, to aid the amateur radio or electronic user. The great circle distance between any two points is computed by GRCIRDIS when the latitudes and longitudes are entered. An alphabetized list of all of the counties in each state can be found in the COUNTIES files.

(PC-SIG Disk#'s 436, 437)

Special Requirements: *A version of BASIC.*
Author Registration: *None.*

Ham Radio by Lynn Gerig   *by Lynn A. Gerig*

HAM RADIO offers three fairly technical programs to help the enthusiastic amateur radio hobbyist.

SCHART is a Smith Chart impedance matching program. Given a load impedance, the program calculates new input impedances for any combination of passive matching elements you choose. Outputs are listed in tabular form with resistive and reactive values given for each frequency of operation. If you want to analyze the impedances as a function of frequency, a graphics option is included which draws a Smith Chart and plots the impedances.

HFPROP calculates expected ground-wave communications ranges (in miles) from 3.5 to 50 MHz based on inputs of frequency, transmitter power, receiver sensitivity, antenna parameters, and type of terrain.

VHFPROP computes expected communications ranges (in nautical and statute miles) from 100 MHz to 3.5 GHz based on inputs of frequency, transmitter power, receiver sensitivity, and antenna parameters. Specs are included for ground-to-ground, ground-to-air, and air-to-air applications plus free-space line-of-sight information useful for satellite communications predictions.

(PC-SIG Disk# 1420)

Special Requirements: *CGA.*
Author Registration: *$15.00, $20.00 foreign.*

KB0ZP Message Handler   *by Larry Kebel*

The KB0ZP MESSAGE HANDLER aids the amateur radio operator, or Ham, with all the typing and organizational chores associated with recording radio traffic. Up to 10 "to and from" addresses can be saved in memory and recalled at any time. Time and date stamps are handled by the computer. Up to 225 individual messages may be saved on a single 5 1/4 inch floppy disk.

Help screens define HX codes, post office abbreviations, third party agreements and U.S. territories and possessions. Operators may send a single message to many addresses through a special booking option.

Finally, KB0ZP MESSAGE HANDLER can encode your messages for total privacy.

(PC-SIG Disk# 1887)

Special Requirements: *None.*
Author Registration: *$25.00*

KB0ZP Super Contest Log   *by Larry Kebel*

KB0ZP CONTEST LOG is an amateur radio contest logging program to help the radio operator log contest information in a suitable form for submission for awards. After entering the other station's call sign, you have the option of entering two more pieces of information (RST, Section, Grid Square, etc.). The CONTEST LOG takes over from there.

It dupes, calculates your score, and saves to disk or printer or both. The main screen shows date and time, name of contest, your station call sign, grand total number of contacts made by mode and band, elapsed time from last contact, total accumulated score, and the amount of free space available in RAM. Up to 4000 contacts can be made. Help screens show usable frequencies by band, class of license, and section abbreviations. All contacts can be listed on the screen during the contest for viewing and correcting. A "hurry up timer" can be set to time your contacts. The arithmetic for automatic scoring can be changed to suit the contest.

KB0ZP CONTEST LOG print program prints a list of the contacts made in almost any form you want, for submission for awards. It is to be used after the contest and at your leisure.

(PC-SIG Disk# 1096)

Special Requirements: *640K RAM, a hard drive, and a printer.*
Author Registration: *$25.00*

MiniMuf
by Carter Scholz

A MUF calculator for the amateur radio operator.

MINIMUF computes the Maximum Usable Frequency (MUF) for specified paths for a 24-hour period given in GMT (UTC). The program gives the MUF for one path and draws a graph. You can select from 15 pre-programmed paths or you can enter the latitude and longitude coordinates for any path in a setup data file. The graph is displayed in the text mode so it can be printed on all IBM compatible printers.

(PC-SIG Disk# 1315)

Special Requirements: *IBM printer or compatible.*
Author Registration: *$20.00*

Morse
by Patrick C. Roe

MORSE is a workable code-practice program for anyone who wants to learn Morse Code for their Amateur Radio Operator's license.

The program creates random-text groups of five characters each, then sends them in Morse code with the cursor underlining each word as it is sent. MORSE also sends individual random letters well spaced in time and reads text files prepared by your wordprocessor in capitals, then sends the text line-by-line.

(PC-SIG Disk# 939)

Special Requirements: *None.*
Author Registration: *None.*

Morseman
by Robin A. Gist

This is your chance to get private lessons in Morse Code. MORSEMAN is intended for amateurs, aspiring hams or anyone else who wishes to learn the International Morse Code or improve their performance and code speed. MORSEMAN will take you through the procedure of learning the Morse Code (or CW as called by hams) and help you to increase your speed.

You have the option of using MORSEMAN in teach or drill mode. You can start with the easiest characters and work your way up to small groups, later going back to the ones that gave you trouble. MORSEMAN is written with repetitiveness in mind, as the more often you hear the character and associate it with the sound, the easier it will be to recall it.

(PC-SIG Disk# 1759)

Special Requirements: *None.*
Author Registration: *$15.00*

PC-Ham
by Joe Kasser

PC-HAM is a set of amateur radio database programs. The program is based, in part, on programs described in, "Software for Amateur Radio," by Joe Kasser (G3ZCZ) and published by TAB Books.

PC-HAM has several features that are invaluable to any amateur radio operator with a computer. Some of the program's capabilities include:
❏ Display/print of your QSO's sorted by call-sign, alphanumerical order
❏ Search for and display of all QSO's with a specified prefix
❏ Automatic generation of your DXCC status
❏ Direct updating of award records from the log entries
❏ Analyze contest QSO's for duplicates and scoring contacts

❏ Automatic QSL 100% (after a contest or DX-Pedition) to all stations worked for one contact on each of five bands.
(PC-SIG Disk# 562)
Special Requirements: *A hard drive, a version of BASIC.*
Author Registration: *$36.50*
➤*ASP Member.*

PC-Track ✍

by Thomas C. Johnson

Here's a general-purpose satellite tracking package to take the complexity and confusion out of locating an earth orbiting satellite in space. It can also provide the antenna-pointing data necessary to transmit or receive signals.

PC-TRACK is intended for anyone who wants to monitor the positions of satellites — from amateur radio operators to professional weather satellite users. The program includes orbital data for a number of amateur radio and weather satellites, and position data for a number of observation points around the earth. Others can be added easily.

(PC-SIG Disk# 2241)
Special Requirements: *512K RAM, EGA, and two floppy drives. A hard drive is recommended.*
Author Registration: *$50.00*

SamfB - The Morse Code Program ✍

by Tranzoa, Co.

As you must learn hand signals before operating a vehicle, so must you learn Morse Code before firing up an amateur radio. You could begin with a healthy diet of how-to books, cassette tapes and LP records, followed by several weekends of personal instruction at a local Ham radio club. But that might get costly. What you need is a Morse Code instructor you can call on any time to teach you at your own pace.

SAMFB, The Morse Code Program, is such an instructor. SAMFB takes you through the basics of coding with hands-on keying right at your PC keyboard. SAMFB listens to your dits and dahs, types out what you keyed, and quizzes you with random words, all at a speed you set yourself.

If you get stuck, or bogged down, don't fret. SAMFB has an on-line, context sensitive help system. Several pull-down menus and configuration areas give further help.

(PC-SIG Disk# 1886)
Special Requirements: *None.*
Author Registration: *$20.00*

▼ ▼ ▼

Hard Drive Utilities

BackRem ✍

by Boreal Software

Do you back up your hard drive as often as you should? Like most computer users, you've probably been putting it off for months and would face heavy losses if your hard drive should crash tomorrow. You need a way to keep on your back-up schedule.

BACKREM reminds you when it's time to do a back-up, and then it runs the program. Just tell BACKREM how often you want the back-up to occur (e.g., every 5 days) and place it in your autoexec.bat file. On days you don't have to do a back-up, a message lets you know how many days have gone by since the last one. On the actual back-up day, BACKREM gives you the choice of doing the back-up or waiting until next time. If you need to do a back-up off schedule, you can make BACKREM run at any time. For those who need several copies to secure sensitive data, BACKREM allows up to five copies of the same back-up to be created at a time. BACKREM is a must for people who want to be sure to keep their data safe.

(PC-SIG Disk# 2445)
Special Requirements: *MS-DOS 3.0+, hard drive, and backup program.*
Author Registration: *$25.00*

BAKtrack
by Rockford Technologies Inc.

BAKTRACK provides an easy way to back up hard disk files to floppy diskettes. It is smart enough to make small daily backup chores fast and painless. BAKTRACK performs both full and partial backups, with directories and files easily excluded from the backup.

An index is maintained on your hard disk and on the backup diskettes. The index is a convenient navigation tool for locating files on the hard disk or the backup diskettes. The index allows fast recovery of one or more files. After making a full backup, daily partial backups are fast and easy since BAKTRACK keeps track of what files have changed or been added since the last backup and only backs up those files.

This program only works from the command line — there are no menus. BAKTRACK can be set to create a complete backup, prompted partial backup by looking for the DOS archive bit on a file, or a partial backup as specified by a control file named at startup.

(PC-SIG Disk# 1869)

Special Requirements: *Hard drive.*
Author Registration: *$15.00*

BatchMaker Plus ✐
by Northland Multisoft

BATCHMAKER PLUS has the convenience and versatility you've been looking for in a hard disk management system, and at the right price. This action-packed software includes a menu-driven full screen editor for building and changing batch files. Cut and paste (even to and from other files) and perform text searches. Making batch files is simpler than you may think and using just three DOS commands in your batch file will run most of your programs.

BATCHMAKER PLUS provides a complete DOS utility function with a double directory menu display, similar to Norton Commander. Manage your hard disk with the press of a button — Copy, Rename, Move, Erase, MkDir, and RmDir. Select and execute programs from the directory listing as well as change a file's attributes, view text and binary files, and display system information. Disk functions can be selected from the menu — Format, Chkdsk, Diskcopy, and Diskcomp. There's even a pop-up DOS Quick Reference so you never need to refer to the manuals.

BATCHMAKER PLUS includes a free program for figuring your savings and loan accounts. Figure a loan by payment or by loan amount. Calculate the amount needed to pay off a loan or plan for your future savings needs. A pop-up calculator is ready to help you with any calculations.

(PC-SIG Disk#'s 2692, 2693)

Special Requirements: *384K RAM, Dos 3.0+, hard disk drive, CGA or better.*
Author Registration: *$27.95*
➤*ASP Member.*

CopyAll
by Timothy O'Malley

Forget the DOS backup command. Now there's COPYALL which backs up hard disk files quicker and neater. COPYALL copies files in alphabetical order. That means folks with messy hard disks can use it to bring order to their files. Happily, it uses wild cards and shows the name of each file as it's copied. COPYALL works on any file as long as it is not larger than the diskette it is copied to.

(PC-SIG Disk# 1503)

Special Requirements: *None.*
Author Registration: *None.*

CUDUP
by Micro System Solutions

Do you have a zillion files on your hard drive? Are you getting close to your drive's capacity? Do you have archived documents that contain files that are probably also somewhere else on your hard drive? Take care of your problem with CUDUP, the duplicate file finder!

CUDUP is a menu-driven utility that reads up to 4000 files into memory and compares each file for any duplicates. The files can reside in any subdirectory, and can be normal or compressed format. Specify the filename or extension you're searching for, and CUDUP will locate them if they exist. If any duplicates are found, CUDUP will give you a list of those files and gives you the option of deleting them.

(PC-SIG Disk# 2199)

Special Requirements: *386K Ram.*
Author Registration: *$27.00*
➤*ASP Member.*

DOS Toolbox ☆

by Computer Tyme

DIRECTORY MASTER is a powerful hard disk managment utility. It brings up your hard disk files and allows you to mark selected files so you can copy, delete, or move them. It also allows you to rename files, change dates, and change attributes. You can run programs or set up your function keys to run programs on selected files.

DOLIST makes the DOS prompt an easier place to work. It gives you full line editing, like a word processor, for your commands. It also stores commands so that you can re-execute them. It remembers subdirectories and allows you to go back to them by pressing the TAB key. It offers programmable function keys, DOS extensions, multiple execution, and many more features DOS users need.

PICK DIRECTORY allows you to move through the directory system by displaying a graphic tree and letting you use your arrow keys to move around. It also lets you create, delete, rename, and hide directories.

TEDIT (a streamlined version of QEDIT from SemWare) is a powerful, easy-to-use full screen editor.

MARXTSR is a set of memory and TSR management utilities that lets you load and unload TSRs (terminate and stay resident programs) from memory. Utilities to list memory allocation are also included in this package.

Also included is D (a fancy directory listing program), WHEREIS (for finding stuff on your hard disk), SORT, MOVE, FIND, FREE, PIPEDIR, VERSION, and many more.

(PC-SIG Disk# 2639)

Special Requirements: *NONE.*
Author Registration: *$59.95*
➤*ASP Member.*

FLEXIBAK Plus ☆

by Shareable Software

FLEXIBAK PLUS, like its predecessor FLEXIBAK, is a flexible, easy-to-use hard disk backup system with a logical, simple and unique approach to the backup problem.

With the conventional backup system, you are required to complete a full backup approximately once a week with daily incremental backups, placed on separate disks. If you need to restore from the backup, you must first restore the full backup and then each of the incremental backups up to the last backup done. FLEXIBAK Plus, replaces the concept of full and incremental backups. Instead, you only need to do a full backup once with all subsequent backups placed on the same backup disks, providing some long-term speed increases, simpler file restoration, and an improved backup management capability.

Some outstanding features provided by FLEXIBAK PLUS:

❏ Selective backups allow you to specify, globally and by directory, which file groups should be included or excluded from the backup
❏ Incremental backups are placed on the same disks as the full backup
❏ The file management system keeps track of what has been backed up, and informs you if any files are missing from your hard disk since the last backup, allowing you to recover accidentally deleted files
❏ File compression is included as well as the ability to handle up to 20 hard disk drives
❏ The alarm system warns you that you have forgotten to do a backup for a specified number of days

(PC-SIG Disk# 2719)

Special Requirements: *None.*
Author Registration: *$39.95 + $4.00 S&H*
➤*ASP Member.*

Hard Disk Management

by TAB BOOKS Inc.

This disk is meant to be used with the book *Hard Disk Management with MS-DOS and PC-DOS* from TAB Books. The book gives you tips on how to run your hard drive at top efficiency. The following programs are included on this disk:

AUTOMENU — This is the solution to learning all the DOS commands to access different programs. No longer will you have to type in a list of commands to find the program you are looking for. With a single press of a key, almost any program can be made available. AUTOMENU gives you an easy-to-read and understandable menu of options to choose from. It automatically does the commands to run the program you have selected. AUTOMENU also lets you set up your own customized menu systems.

DISK TOOL — This program lets you look at and make changes to what is stored on your disks. You can work with individual files or the disk as a whole, and perform operations you normally couldn't do with DOS. In short, it lets you manipulate everything on your disks easily and with very few restrictions.

PACKDISK — You can keep your hard disk running at top performance by filling those empty sections on your hard drive with data from the outer edges of your hard disk. PACKDISK reintegrates lost clusters (file allocation units) into the available space on the disk and packs the root directory and subdirectories. It also has other features, such as an option to delete an entire subdirectory with one easy command, a HIDE/UNHIDE program, and a program to create a RAM disk in your computer's memory. And when you get to the point where you have too many subdirectories on your hard drive to keep track of, use the TREED program to map them all out on your screen.

And for that valuable information on your hard drive that you don't want anyone to touch, there is the LOCK program. This protects your data safely from accidental (or deliberate and unauthorized) viewing or editing.

(PC-SIG Disk# 786)

Special Requirements: *Hard drive.*
Author Registration: *$20.00 to $50.00.*

Hard Disk Utilities   *by GarMark Software*

This is a collection of utilities for the hard disk drive user, compiled from over 25 disks in our library. Some of the most famous: ALTER, used to change your file attributes; DISKPARK, for positioning your hard disk drive in the safety zone; and BACKSTAT to find out which files need to be backed up.

(PC-SIG Disk# 478)

Special Requirements: *None.*
Author Registration: *$5.00 to $50.00.*

File Descriptions:

ALTER	COM	Utility to change file attributes (Hidden/Readonly/etc).
ALTER	DOC	Documentation for ALTER.COM (4k).
BACKSTAT	EXE	Tells you which files need to be backed up.
CATALOG	COM	Make a sorted directory.
CDSECRET	COM	Go to a "secret" sub-directory.
DD	BAT	Sort directory by date (PART OF DNXSD.BAT).
DIR2	BAS	BASIC version of a directory sorter.
DISKPARK	DOC	Documentation for DISKPARK.EXE (1k).
DISKPARK	EXE	Position the hard disk drive head in a safety zone.
DISRTN	EXE	Undeletes and recovers lost first sectors.
DN	BAT	Sort directory by name (Part of DNXSD.BAT).
DNXSD	DOC	Documentation for sorting directory.
DS	BAT	Sort directory by size (Part of DNXSD.BAT).
DX	BAT	Sort directory by extension (Part of DNXSD.BAT).
DXSAVE	BAT	Sample change in .BAT to save sorted directory to disk.
FREE	COM	Displays amount of actual free space on hard disk.
GCOPY	DOC	Documentation for GCOPY.EXE (1k).
GCOPY	EXE	Menu type selective copy program.
GDEL	DOC	Documentation for GDEL.EXE (1k).
GDEL	EXE	Menu type selective delete program.
MDSECRET	COM	Make a "secret" sub-directory.
NDOSEDIT	COM	VM style editor for DOS commands.
NDOSEDIT	DOC	Documentation for NDOSEDIT.COM (5k).
POKING	TXT	Text file containing locations of information about disks.
RDSECRET	COM	Remove "secret" sub-directory.
READONLY	COM	Make a file read-only to make it un-erasable.
READONLY	DOC	Documentation for READONLY.COM.
READWRIT	COM	Return a read-only file back to normal read/write status.
READWRIT	DOC	Documentation for READWRIT.COM.
SDIR5	COM	Utility to list files by types and different formats.
SDIR5	DOC	Documentation for SDIR5.COM.
SEARCH	COM	Useful replacement for DOS path command.
SEARCH	DOC	Documentation for SEARCH.COM (2k).
SECRET	DOC	Documentation for RDSECRET, MDSECRET, and CDSECRET.
TREED	COM	Make a directory tree.
UNDEL	COM	Recovers erased files.
UNDO	BAS	Allows fixed disk users to read backup diskettes.
VDL	COM	File deletion utility.
VDL	DOC	Documentation for VDL.COM (2k).
VIEWDISK	DOC	Documentation for VIEWDISK.EXE.

✍ = Updated Program
☆ = New Program

VIEWDISK	EXE	Look at individual disk sectors.
WHEREIS	COM	Find a file on the hard disk regardless of location.
WHEREIS	DOC	Documentation for WHEREIS.COM (1k).
WRT	DOC	Documentation for WRTE.COM and WRTP.COM.
WRTE	COM	Make a read-only file copyable.
WRTP	COM	Make a read-only file.
DIARY	COM	System use logging program.
ADD	BAT	Batch file used by DIARY.COM.
LST	BAT	Batch file used by DIARY.COM.
OFF	BAT	Batch file used by DIARY.COM.
SEE	BAT	Batch file used by DIARY.COM.
READ_ME	1ST	Introductory text file for DIARY.COM.
PASSWORD	DOC	Documentation file for PASSWORD.EXE.
PASSWORD	EXE	Protect your system with a password.

Packdisk Utilities

by SoftPatch

PACKDISK utilities is a handy collection for file, floppy and hard disk management. Clean up your act!

❏ DELDIR — Deletes a subdirectory with its files and subdirectories.

❏ LISTFRAG — Lists all fragmented files in the drive.

❏ NAMEDIR — Renames a subdirectory.

❏ PACKDISK — Eliminates file fragmentation in the drive. Eliminates unallocated spaces between files. Reintegrates lost clusters (file allocation units) into available disk space. Packs the root directory and subdirectories. Frees trailing clusters.

❏ TRANSDIR — Transfers a subdirectory and its files and subdirectories into another directory in the same drive.

❏ PARK — Parks disk head before power off.

(PC-SIG Disk# 610)

Special Requirements: *None.*

Author Registration: *$30.00*

Point & Shoot Backup/Restore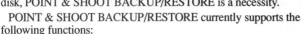

by AMST

Finally a program that makes backing up your hard disk so simple you'll wonder why you didn't buy POINT & SHOOT BACKUP/RESTORE sooner.

POINT & SHOOT BACKUP/RESTORE is a companion program for the POINT & SHOOT HARD DISK MANAGER (PC-SIG disk #930) but can also be used as a stand-alone product. It provides fast, easy backups of your hard disk data to floppy disks. Your involvement is minimized in the backup and/or restore process. If you own a hard disk, POINT & SHOOT BACKUP/RESTORE is a necessity.

Point & Shoot (PC-SIG Disk# 1188)

POINT & SHOOT BACKUP/RESTORE currently supports the following functions:

❏ Up to 10 user-defined backup configurations, each of which may contain a list of up to 10 subdirectory backup sources. Each backup source directory may include trailing directories for complete flexibility in backup definitions

❏ Each backup definition allows selection of matching file specs, modified files only, optional disk formatting and optional file compression during the backup process. A graphic directory tree display assists in the selection of backup source directories

❏ Files remain intact on backup disks (except when disk boundaries must be crossed, or compression is used)

❏ Required number of backup disks are automatically calculated

❏ Restoration options include source drive, restoration to other than the original path, prompts for duplicate or modified files, and selective file restoration. Again, a graphic directory tree assists in selection of restoration paths and files to restore

❏ Configuration options include colors, an hourly chime, and drive designations

❏ Backup speeds approach 1 Megabyte per minute with 1.2 MB or 1.44 MB disks, 0.5 Megabyte per minute with 360K or 720K disks.

(PC-SIG Disk# 1188)

Special Requirements: *320K RAM and hard drive.*

Author Registration: *$35.00*

➤*ASP Member.*

System Master ☆   *by Medley Data Services*

SYSTEM MASTER is an excellent application launcher with multiple menu levels, password protection, and excellent DOS support. With over 300 pre-defined menu items covering all DOS commands and extensive documentation, this disk makes it one of the best in this category.

SYSTEM MASTER'S multiple menu pages in a four-dimensional setup give it a unique look among DOS shells. With 16 menu pages and menu items, this hard disk organizer is a must for PCs with multiple users and security levels.

SYSTEM MASTER provides not only the standard shell options such as mouse control, custom color setup, and screen blanking, but also timed execution of programs, parameter passing to menu options, and a great context-sensitive Help system. Users can define over 85,000 menu items within the menu pages.

SYSTEM MASTER matches most commercial disk management packages in its documentation. More than 100 pages of documentation provide operating instructions as well as a brief description of how DOS commands have been implemented in SYSTEM MASTER.

Although SYSTEM MASTER doesn't have an automatic Search and Install option, the addition of new menu items isn't difficult. (The program does not currently support networks.)

(PC-SIG Disk# 2623)

Special Requirements: *384K RAM.*
Author Registration: *$42.00*

▼ ▼ ▼

Health Management

The Better Diet Analyzer ✍   *by John H. Byrd*

Have you been advised to keep an eye on your calorie, fat, cholesterol, and/or sodium consumption? Or, are you the lucky one who monitors someone else's diet?

THE BETTER DIET ANALYZER is an interactive nutritional database with records on more than 1,000 foods, including packaged brands and fast food restaurant menu items. All data gathered is from U.S. government sources and food manufacturers/vendors. Users can track calories, fat, percentage of calories from fat, cholesterol, and sodium, as well as their weight. Personal logs, with daily lists, daily summary, and a weekly summary can be kept indefinitely.

THE BETTER DIET ANALYZER can handle up to approximately 9,000 days worth of dietary summaries of the day's calories, fat, cholesterol, and sodium consumption, plus your weight, if entered.

THE BETTER DIET ANALYZER is extremely fast, flexible, and easy to use. There is no need to remember or enter food categories. For instance, if the user enters "cheese," THE BETTER DIET ANALYZER instantly displays a list of data records containing the word "cheese." The database is user-expandable. Add your favorite foods...if you dare!

(PC-SIG Disk# 2586)

Special Requirements: *384K RAM and hard drive recommended.*
Author Registration: *$24.95*

Biorhythm Monthly Schedule Program   *by Bill McGinnis Publications\Software*

Many people believe that the human body experiences a number of cycles every month or so. Three major cycles run simultaneously but have differing periods so that one cycle may be expressing the beginning of a curve while another will be at the peak of its own curve at the same time. It is believed that the overlapping and timing of these cycles or curves can be used to predict how you will perform in the future.

BIO can calculate these biorhythm cycles for any person born after the year 1753. The physical, emotional and intellectual cycles are marked by letters in columns for each day of the month, each letter showing how high or low that particular cycle is. An asterisk indicates a critical day for that cycle.

BIOCOMP.EXE compares the biorhythms of two persons, and will display the percentage of compatibility for each cycle.

(PC-SIG Disk# 879)

Special Requirements: *None.*
Author Registration: *$25.00*

Diet Balancer
by Nutridata Software Corporation

Need to lose weight, or reduce your sodium and cholesterol intake? With this program you may be able to determine your appropriate diet based on weight loss goals, sex, age, and exercise levels.

THE DIET BALANCER can:

❑ Chart your dietary performance over a 60-day period.

❑ Analyze your diet for 26 different nutrients, including calories, fat, sodium, and cholesterol.

❑ Save meal plans, and have instant access to previous day's diets and meal plans.

❑ Look at the nutritional contents of any foods in the database, including brand names, and fast foods.

❑ Add any new food to the database.

❑ Analyze your personal recipes for nutritional contents and save in the database for use in future diets.

Whether you are looking to lose a few pounds, watch your nutrient intake, or monitor your food intake, THE DIET BALANCER can help you get on the road to a more healthy body.

(PC-SIG Disk# 2283)

Special Requirements: *512K RAM.*
Author Registration: *$59.95*

Diet Disk and Weight Control 🖨
by Micro Development Software

WEIGHT CONTROL has several utilities to help you lose weight. The programs can test your dieting skills through a questionnaire; calculate your average weight loss over a period of dieting; calculate how long it will take to lose a certain amount of weight depending on how much weight you believe you will lose each week; and calculate how many calories of food to take daily to maintain or lose your weight. Also included is a diet shopping list with a list of foods and their calorie amounts. Choose items on the list to make a shopping list you can print. Three short essays on the principles of dieting, reasons to diet, and dieting at home alone are also included.

Diet Disk and Weight Control (PC-SIG Disk# 1077)

(PC-SIG Disk# 1077)

Special Requirements: *None.*
Author Registration: *$20.00*

DietAid 🖨
by Shannon Software Ltd.

DIETAID is a diet and menu planner in which the user consults tables of calorie, fat, protein and dietary exchange equivalents for each of the items in his diet/menu/recipe. The system can provide a daily allowance based on height, weight, age and activity level and compare them to actual meal plans or meals consumed. Personal recipes can be entered in the database for future use in menu planning. The table of foods can be amended and will support up to 3000 items.

DIETAID is valuable to anyone who is interested in diet, meal planning and good nutrition. Doctors, nutritionists and dietary specialists would be interested not only in using this program, but could also encourage their clients to utilize it in food and menu planning.

(PC-SIG Disk# 1578)

Special Requirements: *512K and a hard drive.*
Author Registration: *$15.00*

EKG/Tracings/Pump
by Anna Sall

EKG FOR NURSES provides review and practice tests for studying the electrical system of the heart and interpreting tracings made by an electrocardiograph. This program also correlates EKG waves with the anatomy of the heart and shows the proper placement of EKG electrodes on the body.

TRACING tests medical students on their knowledge of heart functions by displaying an EKG tracing and asking for the cardiac rhythm to be identified. Each answer then shows the correct cardiac rhythm with a short description.

PUMP tests nurses on the math of administering proper dosages of medications in I.V. fluids.

(PC-SIG Disk# 1513)

Special Requirements: *CGA.*
Author Registration: *$5.00*

Headache Free
by Groff Software

HEADACHE-FREE presents information about the different types of headaches and offers a comparison between migraine and cluster headaches. This tutorial is divided into five chapters and each chapter has a quiz at the end so you can check your knowledge absorption. Seven different types of headaches and related illnesses are presented along with 14 possible cures.

HEADACHE-FREE gives you detailed information on the following types of headaches; migraine, cluster, tension, pre-menstrual, hangover, low blood sugar, and pseudo-migraine. After reading about the selected headaches, take a quiz to verify what you have learned.

HEADACHE-FREE offers you the following 14 possible cures for your headaches; Acupuncture, Alexander technique, Astrology, Homeopathy, Chiropractic, electro-convulsive therapy, faith healing, health tonics, herbal medicines, hypnosis, indirect hypnotic, K'ai Men, standard medical, and vitamin therapy. The section on standard medical cures is much more comprehensive than the other possible cures. It includes foods to watch out for, relaxation techniques, and appropriate drugs.

HEADACHE-FREE also provides a Headache Diary to keep a 60-day record of your moods and activities because everything you do affects the way you feel. Along with the Headache Diary is a Diet Diary to keep track of your meals and note any foods that may trigger headaches.

(PC-SIG Disk#'s 2374, 2375)

Special Requirements: *512K RAM, and a printer. A hard drive is recommended.*
Author Registration: *$39.95*

Health Risk ✍
by Tim Keller

A PC conversion of the CDC Health Risk appraisal program that helps medical and health-care professionals — doctors, nurses, public health administrators, etc. — continue to deliver quality care.

A questionnaire helps you assess and evaluate risks to the patient's health. This program should only be used by qualified health professionals who have the experience and training to adequately interpret individual results.

For further information on HEALTH RISK, contact the Center for Disease Control directly in Atlanta, Georgia.

(PC-SIG Disk# 192)

Special Requirements: *None.*
Author Registration: *None.*

Insulin
by Anna Sall

INSULIN, BOTTLE, and NO6 are computer tutors that can teach student nurses to determine IV rates and measure insulin dosage correctly. Repetition of the task with simple on-screen instructions, explanations and user-response feedback makes it easy to learn with these programs.

MAKEFILE is a complimentary program to INSULIN that allows for entry of new insulin dose values or viewing of students names and scores. Determining IV rates for both plain solutions and medication additive solutions are covered.

(PC-SIG Disk# 1311)

Special Requirements: *None.*
Author Registration: *$5.00*

Kinetics
by Rick Tharp, RPH

KINETICS calculates dosages of several commonly-used drugs such as Aminoglycosides, Theophylline, Heparin and Vancomycin. Estimate initial doses based on calculated lean body weight, body surface area, and/or creatinine clearance. Calculate individualized maintenance dosage based on serum-level data.

Included are general drug-dosing recommendations for 82 drugs which require dosage reduction in patients with diminished renal function. Print a chart-ready dosing consultation form. KINETICS also features a comprehensive patient database management.

These programs should be used by a clinical pharmacist or a physician with training in pharmacokinetic dosing of drugs.

(PC-SIG Disk# 947)

Special Requirements: *None.*
Author Registration: *$100.00*

Managing Your Food ✍   *by Greg Aakhus*

MANAGING YOUR FOOD (MYF) gives you complete control over your diet. Plan your shopping list according to cost and nutritional value. MANAGING YOUR FOOD is designed for use by food manufacturers, restaurant managers, dietitians and the home user. It is friendly enough for novice and comprehensive enough for the professional dietitian.

The program will track cost, protein, carbohydrates, fat, calories, cholesterol, fatty acids, fiber, vitamins, minerals, exchanges, percent RDA, and two user-defined fields. An ingredient database of USDA Handbook 8 (4500 ingredients) is available to registered users.

There are over 100 ways to display the information in the files, including a shopping list arranged by store and aisle.

Managing Your Food (PC-SIG Disk# 1056)

Using your own recipes, you can find the nutritional information and cost for all ingredients in a meal. The information can be totaled and reported in appropriate percentages. Since you enter the information about your eating habits, MANAGING YOUR FOOD is customized to you. It's not just another diet, but a way to plan your own intake.

(PC-SIG Disk# 1056)

Special Requirements: *384K Ram. A hard drive is recommended.*
Author Registration: *$35.00*
➤ *ASP Member.*

Mealmate   *by DO-Dat Industries*

On a diet? Need some help?

MEALMATE is a planning aid for preparing meals for people on a carefully controlled diet. Although primarily designed for those 10% of us who are diabetic, it can be a big help to anyone preparing meals that have to meet strict requirements for calories, proteins, carbohydrates and fats. In today's health and nutrition-conscious society, that means everyone including you and your family.

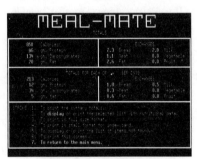

Combine information from meal plans or menus to verify the total nutritional content of a meal. Can't look another head of lettuce in the eye? Help is provided to plan more varied meals and to choose substitutes for disliked or hard to find items.

Mealmate (PC-SIG Disk# 700)

Let's face it. Nothing's going to make a diet fun but at least you can get help with some of the more dreadful aspects. MEALMATE is easily operated and presents nutritional information on many common foods.

Pass the salad, please.

(PC-SIG Disk# 700)

Special Requirements: *None.*
Author Registration: *$30.00*

Med#1 ✍   *by MEDshare*

MED#1 is a new medical office management system that will increase efficiency in the daily administration of the business side of your medical practice. It is designed with special features unavailable in other medical systems and is very 'user friendly'. MED#1 is one of the easiest systems to use, especially if you are already acquainted with computer operations. But even if you aren't, MED#1 will take you through operations with simple one-key functions that follow the logical progression of your normal routine.

No special forms are required for printing. All reports will be printed on 8 1/2" by 11" standard stock paper. Custom statement forms, and the standard insurance HCFA-1500, are available through MEDshare, but the system will print without them.

Features:

❑ Statements can be printed for all accounts with a balance due on your schedule.
❑ Patient ledgers are automatically updated at time of transaction posting - no need to maintain manual ledgers.

❑ Superbill and/or Insurance claim form can be printed as patient checks out or any time needed.

❑ Standard Insurance form HCFA-1500 can be printed automatically for insurance assignment with less mistakes, less manual re-input, saving time.

❑ Instant access to account/patient ledger information to help collect at the time of the office visit.

❑ Reporting to help you run your practice:

A) Daily charges and receipts recap. B) Month-to-date summary recap. C) Aged accounts receivables. D) Statements. E) Recall letters. F) Special Recall selection that will help you keep in touch with your patients. G) Insurance claim forms.

Now, more than ever, computerization is a part of every medical practice. It's faster, more accurate and opens you up to the opportunities of future technical advances. So what are you waiting for, try MED#1, and launch your small medical practice into the next century.

(PC-SIG Disk#'s 2478, 2479, 2480)

Special Requirements: *640K, hard drive, and a dot matrix printer.*
Author Registration: *$395.00*

The Nutritionist
by Sitting Duck Software

Put down that Twinkie and pick up THE NUTRITIONIST: a high-powered package for health-conscious hackers! THE NUTRITIONIST has just about everything you could possibly want to know about bringing health and nutritional balance into your daily diet.

Massive amounts of useful data are provided. Some topics covered are: food items, caloric content, ideal body weight, minimum daily requirements (MDR's), meal planning, calorie consumption calculations for various types of physical activity, portion planning, and recipe creation. A handy printer routine uses condensed type to print on tractor-feed 4x6-inch file cards for easy kitchen counter reference. Give THE NUTRITIONIST a look if you want a full-featured package for improving dietary habits.

If you're not going to eat that Twinkie...

(PC-SIG Disk#'s 1148, 1675)

Special Requirements: *None.*
Author Registration: *$36.00*

Parents Home Companion: Managing Colic
by Patrick Dance

This installment from the multi-part PARENTS HOME COMPANION (PHC) series is based on managing colic problems in infants. The PHC series provides parents and those responsible for childcare with expert assistance in a range of commonly-encountered problems.

The need for documentation has been eliminated in the PHC series through the program's structure. This is similar to the "expert systems" seen in artificial intelligence applications, in which you are guided from screen to screen by your answers to questions.

(PC-SIG Disk# 1100)

Special Requirements: *None.*
Author Registration: *$25.00*

PC-NurseWorks ✍
by NursePerfect Software

Nurses, make your job easier! Automate some of the routine tasks that take up much of your time. NURSEWORKS consists of seven modules that nurses in clinical practice and nursing students will find helpful.

Module 1 facilitates speedy and accurate tallying of intake-and-output (I & O) sheets. Module 2 makes short work of all sorts of drug dosage calculations: solid and liquid forms, children's dosages using the body surface area method, and individual doses of drugs that are administered in mg/kg/day. Module 3 computes I.V. flow rates using standard solutions and administration sets. Module 4 calculates I.V. flow rates for solutions of drugs that are ordered in mcg/kg/min such as are frequently given in critical care units. Module 5 instantly displays all of the conversions for temperature, weight, and volume that nurses use every day. Module 6 determines desirable body weight for a person's sex and height.

Get the most out of those computers at work. Suggest that NURSEWORKS be installed!

(PC-SIG Disk# 1776)

Special Requirements: *None.*
Author Registration: *$9.95*

Pregnant
by Kowa Engineering

PREGNANT can help a woman with unstable menstrual cycles track the times when she is most likely, and least likely, to become pregnant.

PREGNANT takes into account age, height, weight, the dates of each menstrual cycle and body temperature for each day of the past two months. It then displays on the screen the average length and stability of the menstrual cycle and the period of ovulation. Using this data, the program can predict with a high degree of accuracy when the next menstrual and ovulation periods will begin. Data for up to two people can be stored and analyzed.

(PC-SIG Disk# 1325)

Special Requirements: *CGA.*
Author Registration: *$25.00*

Psychotropic Drugs and The Nursing Process ☆
by Nursing Software Systems

Student nurses and registered nurses can learn or review the basics of psychotropic drugs. Easy to use tutorials and quizzes cover antipsychotic agents, sedative-hypnotic agents, antidepressants, mood stabilizers, and anti-parkinsonian agents. For each of these drug groups the study aids include the history, chemical type, effects, benefits and limitations, reactions, and much more. Site licenses are available for nursing schools.

(PC-SIG Disk# 2790)

Special Requirements: *None.*
Author Registration: *$30.00*

Remedies (Feeling Good with Herbs)
by B.M.W. Programs

Whether you have a sore throat, colic, cramps, gas, a headache, or a hangover, REMEDIES has some down-home ways to make you feel better. REMEDIES is not meant to replace a doctor, but it does offer some healthy natural advice for many common ailments. Select a listed ailment and REMEDIES recommends herbal cures. Select a listed herb and REMEDIES will tell you what it cures. Over 60 herbs and 60 ailments listed. By the way, what are licorice and ginseng good for?

(PC-SIG Disk# 2463)

Special Requirements: *None.*
Author Registration: *None.*

Slimmer ✍
by George D. Summers

SLIMMER is a computerized diet program that makes calorie-counting easier than ever before.

SLIMMER will calculate your ideal weight and proper caloric intake and provide you with an extensive menu of recommended foods and their calorie values. Food lists can be created for each day of the week and printed for reference. SLIMMER also provides information on the calories consumed by various forms of exercise. The SLIMMER program is menu driven so it's easy to use, and the food database can be expanded for those with exotic tastes.

(PC-SIG Disk#'s 1489, 2637)

Special Requirements: *425K RAM, DOS 3.0 or higher, and a hard drive with 1.5 meg. available.*
Author Registration: *$35.00*

Weight Control
by Micro Development Software

WEIGHT CONTROL is a collection of dieting utilities to help you in your weight-loss program.

Assess your dieting habits through a questionnaire. Calculate your average weight loss over a period of time; how long it will take to reach a certain weight based upon the amount lost each week; daily caloric intake to maintain or lose weight; and how many calories you have been consuming each meal of the day. A printout may be obtained for the calculations concerning your average weight loss and your calorie consumption.

(PC-SIG Disk# 1325)

Special Requirements: *CGA.*
Author Registration: *$20.00*

▼ ▼ ▼

History, Education

Classroom Jeopardy
by DEC Software

Answer: An excellent new teaching aid for your classroom.
Question: What is CLASSROOM JEOPARDY?

If you feel your students are getting bored with the same old routine, try this new program from DEC Software. Important subjects such as history, math, and science become classroom fun instead of classroom headaches. Teachers may design their own questions (or rather, answers) with the registered version, or use answers provided by the program.

Answers will be presented in gigantic letters on the screen and can be seen by students up to sixty feet away. Select your teams (two or three are suggested by the programmer) and divide your classroom into corresponding groups. CLASSROOM JEOPARDY will prompt you for a team name and then ask you to assign them any key on the keyboard to ring in for their responses. Repeat this process for each team.

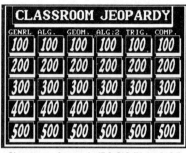

Classroom Jeopardy (PC-SIG Disk# 2164)

Two rounds of CLASSROOM JEOPARDY are played along with a final CLASSROOM JEOPARDY answer. Correct responses can be printed through the DOS print command. Point values range from 100 to 500 for the first round, 200 to 1,000 for the second round. Final CLASSROOM JEOPARDY wagers are based upon points available and daily doubles are found in each round. You need to keep score manually for each team. The team with the most points is the winner.

Registered users receive the current version of CLASSROOM JEOPARDY, a module that allows customizing answers to fit course content and a complete user's manual. An entertaining yet challenging game.

(PC-SIG Disk# 2164)

Special Requirements: *Hercules graphics or any color graphics card.*
Author Registration: *$20.00*

The Presidents
by Hubbard C. Goodrich

Test your knowledge of each U.S. president. In the first part, view the biographies of each president on the screen. You can page through the text, search for a particular word or phrase, and write parts of the bibliography to other disk files.

The second part quizzes and tests on the biographies of the presidents using 20 randomized multiple-choice questions. Typical questions include: the president's name, sequence, inaugural year, birthdate, party affiliation, political party, state affiliation, and eventful associations. Several versions can be produced on the screen or sent to the printer, each with its own answer key.

(PC-SIG Disk#'s 1065, 1066)

Special Requirements: *Two floppy drives.*
Author Registration: *$10.00*

▼ ▼ ▼

Home Management

Assets Inventory System
by Rokmar Computer Systems

The ASSETS INVENTORY SYSTEM is an inventory log program from Rokmar that enables you to keep track of your home or office assets.

In case of fire, theft, etc., your insurance company will want an itemized list of each piece of merchandise, the model numbers, the serial numbers, the location where the article was kept, the purchase/ replacement cost, etc. This information can be difficult to piece together with any amount of accuracy after the disaster strikes.

The ASSETS INVENTORY SYSTEM keeps track of all you own, allows for easy updating on a regular basis, and provides a detailed inventory report of assets sorted by type, location or user defined index. It is also able to generate customized files for importing to spreadsheets or financial analysis programs.

✍ = Updated Program
☆ = New Program

You may be amazed to find out how much money you have tied up in household/office assets, in what areas this money is concentrated, and in what type of merchandise! This information is useful for capital budgeting, tax planning, developing reasonable precautions against losses due to theft and fire, and, of course, documentation for insurance claims.

The INVENTORY SYSTEM also provides helpful guidance on how to take inventory, such as hints concerning often overlooked items: expensive clothing articles, landscaping purchases, books, telephones, computer software, lighting fixtures, custom curtains, hot water heater, kitchen appliances and utensils, tap water filters, children's articles, outside articles, items loaned to someone else, important papers, etc.

(PC-SIG Disk# 1227)

Author Registration: *$15.00 (includes updates).*

BTU Analysis ✍
by Enchanted Tree Software

Now you do-it-yourself handypersons can figure out which heating or cooling system is best for your home. A properly sized furnace or air conditioner is essential for efficient temperature control. BTU ANALYSIS puts the brain power of heating and cooling professionals to work for you.

This program, while useful for professionals, is especially helpful to those who know very little about BTU analysis. Self prompting pop-up help screens, on-line instructions, and complete explanations help you build an accurate picture of your home. "Worst case" methodology is used in analyzing your heating and cooling needs.

(PC-SIG Disk# 1832)

Special Requirements: *512K RAM.*
Author Registration: *$99.95*

The Christmas Helper
by Mark Harvey

Santa has helpers, so should you. Turn your computer into a little elf with CHRISTMAS HELPER, a Christmas-specific database that helps you organize the holidays. CHRISTMAS HELPER keeps your Christmas card list organized and alphabetized — there is even a special category to help you remember children's names while you write greetings. Of course it also provides for printing addresses on card envelopes or mailing labels.

CHRISTMAS HELPER also organizes and edits your christmas gift list with gift ideas for your friends and family. There is a place for last year's gift and ideas for the present year. A similar list of your Christmas supplies, candles, stamps, wrapping paper, etc., is also maintained for your shopping convenience.

(PC-SIG Disk# 1840)

Special Requirements: *None.*
Author Registration: *$20.00*

Computer Gardening Data Disk ☆
by Keith Owens

Throw those gardening books away! Now you can add information on over 400 flowers to your favorite database. The information included covers: botanical name, best use, light needs, height and colors, soil, season, cultural information, and more. The COMPUTER GARDENING DATA DISK isn't a database — it is data on flowering bulbs in standard comma delimited format. This format, also called Data Interchange Format (DIF), can be imported to almost all popular databases.

(PC-SIG Disk# 2724)

Special Requirements: *A database with DIF import capabilities.*
Author Registration: *$4.00/$10.00*

Coupon
by Fred Mendenhall

The GROCERY STORE COUPON ORGANIZER SYSTEM keeps track of grocery store discount coupons. Coupons can be added, modified, deleted or just browsed through. There is also a feature to delete all the coupons that expire before a user-defined date.

(PC-SIG Disk# 724)

Special Requirements: *None.*
Author Registration: *$15.00*

Crafty Li'l Helper
by Herbert I. Fuller

Here's a home business system that lets you concentrate on your craft, not your paperwork. Its menu system guides you painlessly through tracking costs, supplies, customers, and products counted.

The lure of running a business, making some extra money, or helping with a charity, has overcome all of us at one time or another. So what went wrong? We didn't have CRAFTY LI'L HELPER doing all the hard work! This is a very crafty helper, and the only thing that's "little" about it is its registration fee. Among its features is an easy-to-use menu system that guides you painlessly through inventory and invoicing, sales tax, and UPS shipping rates.

CRAFTY LI'L HELPER keeps track of your inventory size and cost; tracks your retail, wholesale and consignment customers; and follows all outstanding orders and billing. Although it can run on just one floppy drive, its record number is limited only by your disk storage size. With CRAFTY LI'L HELPER, all of the really difficult parts of running your own small business have been taken care of, and you're left with all the fun!

CRAFTY LI'L HELPER is a big help for small businesses with items to sell. It carefully shows where money is spent and how much has been made. Plus, it is very easy to use, with clear instructions on moving around in the program and encouraging words when you make a sale! Especially if you are going into a craft business, take along CRAFTY LI'L HELPER.

(PC-SIG Disk# 2149)

Special Requirements: *384K RAM*
Author Registration: *$30.00*

Garden Productivity Calculator
by Taxonomic Computer Research

Grow-your-own, and be profitable. GARDEN PRODUCTIVITY CALCULATOR helps you track the expenses and productivity of your home or small commercial garden, and analyzes its financial profitability.

This program works on the assumption that the cash value of the crop you produce should equal the total expenses of your garden to break even. Expenses are labor, seed, water, mulching materials, etc. GARDEN PRODUCTIVITY CALCULATOR calculates relative to the break even point, where your expenses match the value of your crops at the market. The statistics provided about your garden and needs for production are very thorough and informative.

Even if profit isn't the reason for your garden, you should still know which crops save you money and which ones cost you. Computing this information will help you choose the best crops for next year.

(PC-SIG Disk# 1894)

Special Requirements: *None.*
Author Registration: *$19.00*

The Gardener's Assistant
by Shannon Software Ltd.

This is a system for planning a garden. Describe where you live, the size of your garden and choose what vegetables and fruits you want to grow. THE GARDENER'S ASSISTANT helps you to:

❏ Calculate how many of each type of plant you need to grow in order to yield a certain sized crop
❏ Design your garden layout while considering space availability, planting density and expected yield
❏ Calculate planting dates and expected harvest times
❏ Add to/modify planting information and vegetable chart

THE GARDENER'S ASSISTANT is easy to use and can be a valuable tool for designing and managing your garden.

(PC-SIG Disk# 1125)

Special Requirements: *None.*
Author Registration: *$25.00*

The Gardener's Assistant (PC-SIG Disk# 1125)

Home Applications
by None

HOME APPLICATIONS has such a wide range of programs that almost everyone will find something of interest. You can track everything from your biorhythm to hurricanes. For gambling fans, there is a lottery number-generating program as well as an NFL point spread calculator. Of special interest is the HOME

✍ = Updated Program
☆ = New Program

APPLICATIONS program which lets you keep a record of all your possessions. This can be very useful for insurance purposes.

(PC-SIG Disk# 321)

Special Requirements: *A version of BASIC.*
Author Registration: *None.*

Home Control Primer
by Taegan D. Goddard

Have your computer turn your lights and appliances on and off! Build yourself a computerized home.

Someday all homes will be intelligent. You can get on-board now with the HOME CONTROL PRIMER, an excellent introduction to home automation. Light and appliance control is accomplished by using the X-10 Powerhouse Computer Interface. The HOME CONTROL PRIMER consists of three independent programs:

❑ SENDX10 turns lights and appliances on/off from the DOS command line or from batch files.
❑ SYNCHX10 synchronizes the clock inside the X-10 Powerhouse Computer Interface with that of your PC.
❑ GAMEPORT explores the analog and digital input capabilities of the PC gameport. The Game Port Monitor lets you hook up sensors to your PC's game port so you can begin to experiment with environment monitoring. You can measure light intensity in a room, monitor windows and doors, measure temperature, and observe human movement through open spaces.

Taken together, these programs will teach you the fundamentals of computerized home control. Move your home into the 21st Century today!

(PC-SIG Disk# 2169)

Special Requirements: *X-10 Powerhouse Computer Interface*
Author Registration: *$25.00*

Home Helper ☆
by Torbert Data Systems, Inc.

HOME HELPER computerizes routine household tasks. It includes an electronic phone book (with labels), a recipe filer, audio and video tape library database, and a record system for the valuable appliances in your home and more.

Your commitments and personal appointments can be recorded with the Personal Scheduler. HOME HELPER stores invaluable credit card information if your cards are ever lost or stolen. Emergency telephone numbers are a keystroke away.

The program is completely menu-driven with context-sensitive pop-up Help screens.

(PC-SIG Disk# 2544)

Special Requirements: *512K RAM. 640K RAM, and a hard drive recommended.*
Author Registration: *$15.00*
➤*ASP Member.*

Home Insurance
by MoneCraft Computer Products

HOME INSURANCE lets you keep track of what you own, where items are located, and how much it would cost to replace any items if lost or stolen. Unfortunately, most of us do not find out how much property insurance we need until after we suffer a major loss. All too often it isn't until such a loss that we discover that our insurance coverage, although based on replacement value, was not sufficient to cover the complete loss. Or, worse yet, we discover we are unable to document the true value of our possessions, resulting in a reduced and sometimes insufficient claim return.

HOME INSURANCE gives protection against these tragedies in several ways. First, it helps you determine whether or not you have adequate property insurance by comparing the actual replacement values for your possessions against the given limits in your policy. For example, many policies limit the coverage for special items such as jewelry, collectibles (coins, stamps, plates, dolls, etc.), guns and furs. You categorize items by type, including the total replacement value of each, and HOME INSURANCE lets you easily compare these amounts with the limits specified in your policy.

HOME INSURANCE holds 10,000,000 entries, provides over 250 possible cross references, and is completely menu-operational. It is easy to learn and simple to use. Three user-selectable levels of operation and user-customized field names let you modify HOME INSURANCE to meet individual requirements.

(PC-SIG Disk# 796)

Special Requirements: *None.*
Author Registration: *$59.95*
➤*ASP Member.*

Home Inventory Program

by Itasca Softworks

The HOME INVENTORY program lets you keep a database of your important possessions. The number of entries is limited only by disk space. HOME INVENTORY is completely menu-driven and very easy to operate. You begin by creating a new inventory file or loading an existing one. Then choose "add a record" to add records to the database. It's just that simple to build your own home inventory database. You can change or delete a record in the database with the "find a specific record" option. There are also three search options: search on the item description field, a specific field, or all fields. Print options are also provided for a listing of your entire database, or just a single record in the database.

The HOME INVENTORY program has on-line help to assist you in using the various options. This program provides an excellent way to gather and maintain an inventory of your valuable possessions.

(PC-SIG Disk# 1349)

Special Requirements: *None.*
Author Registration: *None.*

Home Inventory Program (PC-SIG Disk# 1349)

Home Inventory Record Keeper

by Professional Automated Systems

You may never figure out where all that stuff in your house came from, but as long as you have it, you might as well keep track of it. The HOME INVENTORY RECORD KEEPER lets you do just that, room by room.

It's not dramatic, but it is a handy way of keeping track of everything you have in your house. You can, of course, give a location for everything, and indicate the actual or estimated value of each item. This will be essential should you ever suffer a loss by theft or fire. You can also print a list of your possessions and tuck it away for safekeeping.

There is no manual on the disk, because you won't need one — that's how easy this program is to use. If you need help at any time, just press the F1 key and you'll see a context-sensitive help screen.

(PC-SIG Disk# 1811)

Special Requirements: *None.*
Author Registration: *$25.00*

Home Maintenance and Repair

by Home Maintenance Software

Don't you just hate it when you have to call a repairman but you think he may take advantage of you? Wouldn't it be nice to have some basic knowledge of your home and auto systems just so that you could ask the right questions and at least sound like you know what you're talking about? If you don't happen to have a brother-in-law to double-check with, you can learn basic home and automotive maintenance and trouble shooting techniques from HOME MAINTENANCE AND REPAIR.

HOME MAINTENANCE AND REPAIR has maintenance tutorials and trouble shooting charts for air conditioning, home electrical systems, heating, plumbing, appliances and automobiles. HOME MAINTENANCE AND REPAIR gives you tool lists, illustrations, and schematics of the systems. It allows you to print maintenance forms. It offers step-by-step support for doing regular maintenance on your home and car — the simple kinds of tasks that help to keep those expensive repairmen away from your door. And when something does go wrong, look to HOME MAINTENANCE AND REPAIR's trouble shooting charts for a suggestion of what the problem is and what you should do about it. In both the trouble shooting guides and the general maintenance tutorials, HOME MAINTENANCE AND REPAIR takes special care to alert you to all dangers, gives cautions and advice on working safely, and lets you know when it's time to call in a professional.

Depending upon your interest and skill level, HOME MAINTENANCE AND REPAIR can be a beginner's tutorial and guide book for dealing with mechanics and repairmen, or a ready guide for hands-on maintenance and repair. If you are among the thousands of people who don't really understand much about plumbing, wiring, how your furnace works, or just what you're supposed to do to keep your car in good condition, HOME MAINTENANCE AND REPAIR does.

(PC-SIG Disk#'s 2072, 2073)

Special Requirements: *None.*
Author Registration: *$15.00*

✍ = Updated Program
☆ = New Program

Household Register ✍   *by TurboSystemsCo.*

HOUSEHOLD REGISTER maintains a detailed list of everything you own. Each item is automatically categorized by location, category, owner and item. The user can easily customize the pop-up menus for the Location (24 selections), Category (24 selections) and Owner (8 selections) fields. The pop-up menus can be turned off if desired and data can be typed directly into the three fields rather than using menu selections. Each database can hold 99,999 items and there can be an unlimited number of databases. On screen help is provided for each screen and help lines are automatically displayed for each data entry field.

The comprehensive reports section of the program lets the user examine every aspect of his/her possessions. The total value report lists the inventory items and computes the total value of the inventory using purchase price or replacement price. A five page summary report computes the total value by category, location or owner and provides many valuable statistics about the inventory, such as the percentage change between the purchase price and replacement price. A warranty report is also provided that will prove invaluable in tracking warranty information. A total of seven reports are available which can be listed to the screen, printer or a disk text file. Also reports can be printed on continous form index or Rolodex cards

The full featured and comprehensive search/selection module lets the user list only those items that meet the specified criteria.

A sample database is included to allow quick examination of the program.

(PC-SIG Disk# 2187)

Special Requirements: *384K RAM and a printer.*
Author Registration: *$34.95*
➤ *ASP Member.*

Learn IBR Heatloss   *by Harold Kestenholz*

Now there's a way to figure out where all your heat is seeping on those cold winter nights. Or if you're about to build — this program may help keep your future home toasty warm. For the homeowner or heating professional who understands a little about heating, this program can be used to calculate heat loss.

The IBR HEAT LOSS program asks a series of questions. The first questions pertain to conditions the house will be exposed to at the coldest time of year. Then questions are asked which will determine the dimensions of a specific room. Further questions are asked in order to determine the size of openings in walls exposed to the outdoors. Answers to the final questions are used to derive the actual amount of heat that will flow through the room.

If help is required, pressing Alt and Period together will pop up an in- memory screen to provide more information. As the operator answers heat flow questions, the heat losses through the walls, ceiling, floor, or openings appear. The room's total loss appears below the answers. A copy of the room's loss may be kept using the DOS printscreen keys.

(PC-SIG Disk# 1647)

Special Requirements: *None.*
Author Registration: *$20.00*

Letter of Instruction Writer ✍   *by Lingua Systems, Inc.*

LETTER OF INSTRUCTION organizes information about your finances, property, and personal affairs. It provides this information to whoever you designate to handle or manage your affairs in the event of your death, or if you are unable to manage your affairs yourself.

This can include physical or emotional disability, travelling away from home, or other similar circumstances. It also provides you with a recordkeeping tool for financial and estate planning.

NOTE: LETTER OF INSTRUCTION is not a Will, nor does it give advice on how to manage your affairs. However, it can provide you with essential information at your fingertips when seeking advice from a qualified professional.

(PC-SIG Disk# 2538)

Special Requirements: *None.*
Author Registration: *$25.00*
➤ *ASP Member.*

PAR
by Micro System Solutions

If your home were to burn down tomorrow, would you have enough information documented and available on your belongings to prove their worth and to satisfy your insurance company? Is your estate documentation in good shape? If you were to die unexpectedly, would your family or your lawyer know what your assets and liabilities were? If you answered "no" to any of these questions, you need the PERSONAL ASSET MANAGER (PAR).

PAR provides a record of your personal or business assets. The program can track the following areas:

- ❏ Insurance policies
- ❏ Household inventory
- ❏ Safe deposit boxes
- ❏ Book inventory
- ❏ Software inventory
- ❏ Video cassette recordings
- ❏ Art, jewelry, and collectibles
- ❏ Credit card inventory
- ❏ Safe deposit box inventory
- ❏ Computer inventory
- ❏ Investment portfolio

Each area has a set of applicable characteristics you can use to document your belongings. You may add, delete, or modify subjects or characteristics to meet your unique needs. PAR allows up to 18 areas with an unlimited number of records (up to memory capacity).

(PC-SIG Disk# 2199)

Special Requirements: *386K RAM.*
Author Registration: *$37.00*
➤*ASP Member.*

Point & Shoot Home Manager
by AMST

HOME MANAGER helps you manage the details of operating a home and its (sometimes complicated) day-to-day finances.

Create a database of your assets and liabilities, budget and track your home finances, print addresses on envelopes (laser printers only) or labels, calculate various payments and interest earnings, schedule and track maintenance on your home, create a list of things to do, track your vehicle maintenance and make lists of general items, names, addresses and phone numbers, and your important data. Print any or all of these records. There is also a built-in calculator and calendar to view each month of any year. Also includes a complete double-entry accounting system that is easy enough for beginners yet sophisticated enough for small businesses.

(PC-SIG Disk# 940)

Special Requirements: *320K RAM and two floppy drives.*
Author Registration: *$35.00*
➤*ASP Member.*

QuickList
by KSSD

A great program for any homeowner or renter who wants accurate records of possessions for insurance reasons. Keep track of each piece of your furniture, its current replacement price, who uses it, and where it is located in your home. The list is categorized by room and can either be printed by room or in its entirety.

(PC-SIG Disk# 1033)

Special Requirements: *None.*
Author Registration: *$35.00*

Refund
by David M. Alexander

REFUND is a database which keeps two types of information — refunds that have been sent out and refunds that have been collected. Each of these data categories will hold up to 998 refund records. All records can easily be coded per type of merchandise, and after being coded, the records may be sorted according to date or code.

(PC-SIG Disk# 1323)

Special Requirements: *CGA.*
Author Registration: *$12.00*

✍ = Updated Program
☆ = New Program

Room
by Sitting Duck Software

This program helps you find the best location in your stereo room for the loudspeakers and the "sweet spot" listening position.

Properly locating the speakers and listening positions avoids the low frequency intensity variations caused by room generated standing wave patterns. Hand calculating the best positions is tedious. This program will allow you to find several acceptable set-ups which can avoid the overbearing bass and poor transient response due to improperly situated speakers. Not for use with dipole radiators.

(PC-SIG Disk# 1898)

Special Requirements: *CGA or Hercules graphics.*
Author Registration: *$30.00*

RootDirectory - FLOWERS Knowledge Base
by GardenTech

Successful gardening is no longer dependent on the use of a green thumb. With ROOTDIRECTORY-FLOWERS, even novice gardeners can produce beautiful flowers and shrubs, ideally suited to the environment.

ROOTDIRECTORY-FLOWERS is a new kind of communications tool. Using Hypertext (hot buttons) and expert knowledge, it lets the personal computer become a medium to communicate ideas and information to others.

The uses for ROOTDIRECTORY-FLOWERS are many. For example, in a nursery, complex gardening information can be effectively communicated to customers and new employees. Plant material, pest control, sales aids, and staff training are a few of the areas that can benefit from this system.

RootDirectory - Flowers (PC-SIG Disk #'s 2362-4)

For individuals, ROOTDIRECTORY-FLOWERS offers an exciting new possibility. You don't have to decipher complex information from a wide variety of gardening books any more. Select the growing zone, blooming season, plant form and color, growing situation, plant type, and height. It searches its knowledge base of more than 400 flower species and varieties to find the flowers that best meet your needs. The information, while accessible to beginners, can get very technical and advanced.

(PC-SIG Disk#'s 2362, 2363, 2364)

Special Requirements: *None.*
Author Registration: *$39.95*

RootDirectory - TREES Knowledge Base
by GardenTech

Successful gardening is no longer dependent on the luck of a green thumb. With ROOTDIRECTORY, even inexperienced gardeners can produce beautiful, lush trees, flowers and shrubs, ideally suited to the environment.

ROOTDIRECTORY is a new kind of communications tool. Using hypertext (hot buttons) and expert knowledge, it lets the personal computer speedily communicate the ideas and information the user choosers.

The uses for ROOTDIRECTORY are many. For example, in a nursery, complex gardening information can be effectively communicated to customers and new employees: plant material, pest control, sales aid and staff training are a few of the areas that can benefit from ROOTDIRECTORY.

RootDirectory -Trees (PC-SIG Disk#'s 1941-3)

For individuals, ROOTDIRECTORY offers an exciting new possibility. Now a person doesn't have to decipher complex information in gardening books. With ROOTDIRECTORY you can landscape your own yard or create picture perfect gardens without professional help or months of research. The information, while accessible to beginners, is thorough and can get very technical and advanced.

(PC-SIG Disk#'s 1941, 1942, 1943)

Special Requirements: *640K RAM, EGA, and a hard drive.*
Author Registration: *$39.95*

Shop
by Robert Bullen

Whether it's groceries, clothes, or supplies, SHOP can help make your shopping a little easier by keeping track of the money you spend.

SHOP will store lists of items, their prices, and the date last purchased. It is organized by store and by item category. After a few diligent months using SHOP, you will have an accurate database of everything you regularly purchase. Using the selection feature, items can be selected and then printed to produce an ordered shopping list with an estimated total cost.

SHOP tracks household spending and cost inflation while making sure you always have the right amount of cash on hand, thereby saving you from those potentially embarrassing times at the checkout counter. SHOP is quick and painless to use. A hard drive is suggested for the serious shopper.

(PC-SIG Disk# 1648)

Special Requirements: *None.*
Author Registration: *$15.00*

Smart Home Shopper ✍
by Torbert Data Systems, Inc.

Get organized for grocery shopping expeditions before you set foot in the store! SMART HOME SHOPPER allows you to prepare a grocery store shopping list, quickly and conveniently.

Add items to the list as needed and print a handy shopping list by category before store visits. The program maintains prices for up to five stores and automatically "comparison shops." Pop-up context- sensitive Help screens and complete documentation are included.

SMART HOME SHOPPER will help you make the most of your shopping dollar. Ideal for large groups.

(PC-SIG Disk# 2543)

Special Requirements: *640K RAM, and a hard drive recommended.*
Author Registration: *$20.00*
➤*ASP Member.*

The Weather Channel
by Martin E. Morrison

Everybody complains about the weather, but nobody does anything about it. Well, now you can complain with authority! THE WEATHER CHANNEL provides detailed information about temperature, rainfall, and atmospheric pressure, giving you a day-by-day listing of high, low and average statistics for date ranges you specify. All you have to do is compile the data and enter it in an ASCII file according to THE WEATHER CHANNEL's specifications. This simple program will do the rest, offering output to screen or printer.

The program provides high, low, and average temperatures, atmospheric pressures, and rainfall for any year and city entered in the database. Sample databases and template provided.

(PC-SIG Disk# 1903)

Special Requirements: *None.*
Author Registration: *None.*

Wine Cellar
by KCS Software

WINE CELLAR is a simple database designed to keep track of all the wines you have encountered, good and bad, and your evaluation of each one. This database allows you to store practically every bit of information about the wine: each record contains fields for the name of the winery, the variety of wine, the color of the wine, the vintage year, the place the wine was grown and where it was bottled, the date the wine was bought, the cost of the wine, the percentage of alcohol, and a one line comment concerning how the wine tasted.

WINE CELLAR allows you to edit, search, and print the records. The wine records may be selectively searched by any field of the records, and the results may be sent to the screen or the printer. A floppy disk will contain all the working files and about 1300 wine records, but the number of wine records that WINE CELLAR may store on a hard disk is practically unlimited.

(PC-SIG Disk# 2080)

Special Requirements: *None.*
Author Registration: *$25.00*

Your Very Own Home Inventory

by Melvin O. Duke

Keep track of everything you own; furniture, heirlooms, paintings, silver, collections, etc. Know where everything is, where it came from and what it is worth. Perfect for insurance coverage and claims.

Use your own words or specialized expressions to describe all the data you record. You can store and retrieve by various categories such as room or chairs or "Mother's." Record serial numbers or other identification.

The documentation for this menu-driven program is extensive and very thorough. Routines are included to print complete inventories or reports on specific categories. A must for every homeowner!

(PC-SIG Disk# 395)

Special Requirements: *A version of BASIC and printer.*
Author Registration: *$35.00*

Your Very Own Home Inventory (PC-SIG Disk #395)

▼ ▼ ▼

Hypertext

Black Magic

by Ntergrid

Wordprocessors, databases and spreadsheets all manipulate and structure information in specific, but different ways. Hypertext systems, such as BLACK MAGIC, enable you to expand information in another way — by dynamically linking keywords, graphics and blocks of information to one another.

For example, you are creating a document and need to define a concept or word but the detail of the definition would distract the reader from the main text. You can tag a keyword that will indicate that the definition is available. An area of the screen opens and you type the definition or explanation. To explore the definition, the user triggers the tag and the reference is displayed. This is a simple illustration of hypertext.

BLACK MAGIC can shell to DOS, and link and transfer information between hypertext and other applications. Build context-sensitive help systems, link specific items in text documents to technical drawings or illustrations and expand obscure references with detailed explanations. A screen grabber has been added to integrate graphics into BLACK MAGIC. The extended ASCII character set is supported for the use of international characters.

If you are currently using a document generator for live electronic documents such as: computer-based training guides, foreign language tutorials, interactive catalogs, or educational courseware, then you should be moving over to BLACK MAGIC hypertext writing. You will find BLACK MAGIC to be more than you ever imagined.

(PC-SIG Disk#'s 1120, 1121, 1122)

Special Requirements: *384K RAM and CGA, HGA, EGA or VGA.*
Author Registration: *$89.95.*

Desert Storm - Farewell to Babylon ✍

by OEDWARE

DESERT STORM - FAREWELL TO BABYLON is a hypertext information system from OEDWARE, makers of PC-KEY DRAW. This program includes maps of the mideast countries involved, weapons specifications, background information and much more. $5.00 of the $15.00 registration fee will be donated to the American Red Cross.

(PC-SIG Disk# 2549)

Special Requirements: *CGA, EGA, or better and a hard drive.*
Author Registration: *$15.00*

Desert Storm (PC-SIG Disk #2549)

Hyper Helper
by Bryan Flamig

HYPERHELPER lets you make special "hypertext" pop-up windows or help screens from an ordinary ASCII file created by your wordprocessor. Each window is linked together by highlighted words in the text with other windows, which users can pop up for even more detailed information. Windows may be positioned to any part of the screen.

(PC-SIG Disk# 1332)
Special Requirements: *None.*
Author Registration: *$20.00*

HyperPAD ☆
by Brightbill-Roberts

HYPERPAD is an object-oriented application development tool to make you more productive with your PC. More than two dozen personal applications are offered, each designed to help you manage information and data easily.

You can easily personalize these applications, even if you are not a programmer. If you're a non-programmer, HYPERPAD's powerful tools give you the ability to do things with the PC that you never thought you could do. If you're a programmer, HYPERPAD is a rich environment that gives you a huge head start towards your finished product.

When you set up HYPERPAD, you create buttons on your "home" pad that link you to your MS-DOS software. After setting up your home pad to launch applications, you'll never have to look at the DOS prompt again. Push a button and HYPERPAD shrinks to 4K and launches DOS programs such as Lotus 1-2-3 and WordPerfect or Windows software such as Microsoft Excel, PageMaker or Corel Draw.

Launch applications, manage information, and plan work in an intuitive, easily personalized desktop environment without the expensive upgrades required to migrate to Microsoft Windows, OS/2 PM or other graphical environments. HYPERPAD protects your investment in DOS software by modernizing your DOS environment. Get all of the benefits of graphical systems without the headaches and costs.

HYPERPAD features information-filled fields and buttons that can be used again and again. Create a button that launches your word processor, and then copy/paste it to any HYPERPAD application you build. There are many different flavors of buttons and fields from which to choose, plus pop-up menus, dialog boxes, modifiable system menus, and more...

Powerful and easy-to-use character-based painting and drawing tools are built-in to create colorful pads that will keep the interest and win the respect of your audience.

Link information by association to create powerful "hypertext" systems. Create interactive tutorials and computer-based training (CBT) systems. Build flat file databases or front ends to corporate database systems. The more you use HYPERPAD, the more new applications you'll discover.

(PC-SIG Disk#'s 2731, 2732, 2733, 2734, 2735)
Special Requirements: *390K RAM, and a hard drive.*
Author Registration: *$99.00*
➤*ASP Member.*

HyperShell ✍
by Text Technology

HYPERSHELL offers a powerful yet straightforward method of linking different text files and graphics (.PCX files) by key words. By placing codes within your text you can allow others to follow their interest from one file to another. Maneuvering of key words creates a type of on-screen menu which allows users to quickly move through documents directly related to their interests or needs.

For example, you are reading a text file called "Personnel" searching for information regarding severance policies. The document doesn't tell you enough about severance policies so you access other documents on your system regarding this subject until you find the right one. Once you designate reference words which link related files together, these links can be bridged easily by anyone. In the example above, "severance" would be the reference word and would appear as a highlighted word in the file "Personnel." Using cursor keys or a mouse, move to "severance" and press return. All text files you have tagged as related to the topic are now at your fingertips without leaving your original document.

HYPERSHELL assists you in the initial set-up of a hypertext system by providing a hypertext editor, syntax checker, and formatted printer program, as well as several helpful utilities.

(PC-SIG Disk#'s 1720, 2597, 2685)
Special Requirements: *Two floppy drives (hard drive recommended).*
Author Registration: *20 to 100 Pounds.*

The PC-SIG Encyclopedia of Shareware ✍ = Updated Program
☆ = New Program

Hypersketch

by Eastham Software

HYPERSKETCH is a program that helps you to create "layered" diagrams which can include boxes, lines and/or text. Create colorful diagrams with text for explaining a concept, giving instructions or documenting a program. The layered diagrams can be used as a menu system to execute your programs or perform DOS functions. HYPERSKETCH can be used for educational purposes, dataflow diagrams, and screen prototyping.

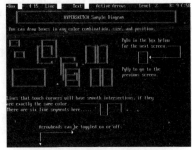

Hypersketch (PC-SIG Disk #1473)

Each diagram occupies a full screen. Boxes can be drawn in any combination of color, size and position. Text can be displayed in different colors and the lines can turn corners and have arrow heads. Any object of the diagram can contain a layered diagram beneath it on a totally separate screen. Layered diagrams can be accessed by pressing a key while the cursor is on the object which has the diagram beneath it. A maximum of 99 levels of diagrams may be created per file, depending upon available computer memory.

Any diagram on the screen can be printed, or written to an ASCII file for later use with a wordprocessor. The program has extensive editing features: objects can be moved, cut and pasted, edited, saved and read from a disk file into memory. You have two independent working areas allowing you to work with two diagrams at the same time.

(PC-SIG Disk# 1473)

Special Requirements: *384K memory. Printer with IBM line drawing character set.*
Author Registration: *$19.95*

Hytext ✍

by Medical Decisions Software

HYTEXT brings hypertext — the latest development in computer learning and information retrieval — within the means of every interested author, teacher or electronic publisher.

HYTEXT, using the new hypertext technique and electronic texts, may be the solution to the age old problem of forcing a reader to wade through an article or book sequentially, line-by-line, page-by-page. HYTEXT allows for skipping, dodging and darting along a reader's interest or learning curve.

Hypertext enables an author of computerized texts to designate specific words as hot words, highlight them in the text, and link them to related topics, footnotes, explanations or other programs. Readers can then instantly jump off from the main article or chapter at any of the hot words to delve deeper into subjects they need refresher information on or want to study further, and then jump back to where they were reading.

For example, the sentence, "Amphibians of the Amazon rain forest have survived relatively unchanged for centuries," might generate several hypertext jumping off points for the reader interested in knowing more about amphibians, the Amazon or rain forests. Authors need no longer worry about being too technical and losing the beginner, or too simple and boring for the more advanced. Readers are able to obtain just the right level of information they need, when they need it.

Hot words are displayed as highlighted text which may be selected using the cursor control keys. Readers simply point-and-shoot to go off on new tangents of learning. The Enter key is used to jump to the next topic. The End key is used to return to a previous topic.

HYTEXT uses simple control codes imbedded in any document to create hypertext links or scripts. These scripts are maintained using a text editor or word processor. Authoring tools such as file/path info, trace mode and hot word search are provided. An individual hypertext may span multiple files.

Several hypertext levels are supported:

❏ Topics containing hot words
❏ Cards for notes, definitions, etc.
❏ External text to link to other documents
❏ External programs to link to other programs

(PC-SIG Disk# 1234)

Special Requirements: *Text editor (plain ASCII text mode).*
Author Registration: *$50.00*

inView

by Integrasoft Corporation

The key to INVIEW is its simple notepad metaphor; you can jot down notes as you would on a real notepad, in whatever format you like. Using hypertext technology, any entry on an INVIEW page can be linked to another INVIEW page, any DOS application and associated file such as word processors, spreadsheets, DOS commands, or even browsers that allow you to examine the contents of a word processing document or spreadsheet without loading the actual application.

With INVIEW, you can access and organize your PC in a way consistent and in tune with the way you work. Launch applications or quickly locate any file with INVIEW's high speed text search-and-retrieval. The built-in time manager traces your appointments and reminds you of upcoming events two minutes or two years from now.

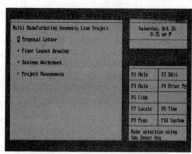

inView (PC-SIG Disk #2226)

You'll never be at a loss for what to do next; INVIEW constantly indicates what state it is in and shows you the currently available functions. A context-sensitive Help system explains the system as well as providing menu assistance.

(PC-SIG Disk# 2226)

Special Requirements: *512K RAM. Hard drive recommended, or high density floppy.*

Author Registration: *$45.00*

▼ ▼ ▼

✍ = Updated Program
☆ = New Program

Integrated (Wordprocessing, Database, and Spreadsheet)

SS1
by Gary Reysa

This combo of programs solves 70% of your computing needs! This integrated program combines a wordprocessor, a list/data manager, communications, a mid-size spreadsheet (64 columns by 255 rows), and a file and directory browser. To make the program even more comprehensive, pop-up aids are a keystroke away anywhere in the system. These include a calculator, an aid for graphing data, file/directory viewing, DOS shell interface, and a utility to make macros or smart keys.

Packed with features, the wordprocessor offers functions normally found only in the top of-the-line packages. The commands are unique to this program, but are easy to learn and fast. The mailing list manager uses standard text files, can edit columns, and sort, select and print records as reports or mailing labels. The spreadsheet has all the standard functions, plus handling multiple pages.

The communications program is one of the broadest on the market. It can communicate through almost every modem. However, this tremendous flexibility requires you to configure it for your particular system the first time you use it. The file and directory browser/manager, on the other hand, is fairly easy to use and a great help in dealing with hard disk housekeeping. All the commands found in many separate programs are at your fingertips: backups, deletions, printing, viewing and directory alterations.

The pop-ups include a calculator, file and directory checker, a print screen utility, a graph maker, and programmable "hot" or "smart" keys (macros). The calculator supports decimal, hex, and binary for basic arithmetic functions. The help system provides instant access to more than 100 screens of context-sensitive help.

(PC-SIG Disk#'s 1414, 1415)

Special Requirements: *360K RAM.*
Author Registration: *$50.00*

▼ ▼ ▼

Investment Management

APEX Financial Markets
by N-Squared Computing

APEX FINANCIAL MARKETS allows you to analyze market indexes/averages, foreign exchange rates, interest rates, industry groups, and market breadth data.

APEX FINANCIAL MARKETS is easy to set up, easy to use, and effective for the individual with some prior experience in the market. The manual explains how to use the program but does not train the novice in learning the "markets game." APEX lets you create strategies using single or double moving averages, based on buying long, selling short, or both. A valuable feature is the charting of optimization trials, allowing you to see the most effective choices for short and long term moving averages.

There is no registration fee, no start-up fee, but there is a per quote fee. You can enter your own data or download it by modem from Warner Computer Systems, Inc. Apex users can waive Warner's standard $48 sign-up fee. Warner currently has over 330 items that can be downloaded. Most of the data goes back at least 10 years. There is a sample database on disk two of this program, allowing some initial experimentation.

For those active in the market, the program provides a quick means to gain access to current rates and to plot them on the screen for review. For such investors, APEX FINANCIAL MARKETS is a valuable program. All the programs in the Apex series are easy to use, easy to set up, and useful. The manuals explain how to use the programs but do not train the novice in learning the "markets game."

(PC-SIG Disk#'s 2038, 2039)

Special Requirements: *512K RAM, DOS 3.0 or higher, and a modem.*
Author Registration: *None.*

APEX Futures & Commodities
by N-Squared Computing

APEX F/C will let you analyze futures/commodities with open- high-low-close bar charts and volume and open interest. Futures files will keep the open, high, low, close, volume, and open interest values for each day in the data. APEX lets you create strategies using single or double moving averages, based on buying long, selling short, or both. A valuable feature is the charting of optimization trials, allowing you to see the most effective choices for short and long term moving averages. For those active in the market, APEX FUTURES & COMMODITIES provides a means of data access with the added feature of plotting out the information easily.

There is no registration fee, no start-up fee, but there is a per quote fee. You can enter your own data or download it by modem from Warner Computer Systems, Inc. There is a sample database on disk two of this program, allowing some initial experimentation.

(PC-SIG Disk#'s 2040, 2041)

Special Requirements: *512K RAM, DOS 3.0 or higher, and a modem.*
Author Registration: *None.*

APEX Mutual Funds   *by N-Squared Computing*

APEX MUTUAL FUNDS allows you to plot and compare any of over 1600 mutual funds. For those active in the market, APEX MUTUAL FUNDS provides a means of data access with the added feature of plotting out the information easily.

There is no registration fee, no start-up fee, but there is a per quote fee. You can enter your own data or download it by modem from Warner Computer Systems, Inc. There is a sample database on disk two of this program, allowing some initial experimentation.

(PC-SIG Disk#'s 2042, 2043)

Special Requirements: *512K RAM, DOS 3.0 or higher, and a modem.*
Author Registration: *None.*

APEX Point & Figure   *by N-Squared Computing*

APEX POINT & FIGURE enables you to do complete point and figure analysis for any stock. Stock files will contain the high, low, close, and volume for each day.

There is no registration fee, no start-up fee, but there is a per quote fee. You can enter your own data or download it by modem from Warner Computer Systems, Inc. There is a sample database on disk two of this program, allowing some initial experimentation.

(PC-SIG Disk#'s 2046, 2047)

Special Requirements: *512K RAM, DOS 3.0 or higher, and a modem.*
Author Registration: *None.*

APEX Stocks/Options   *by N-Squared Computing*

If you own any stocks and want to stay up with the daily or weekly information, then APEX may be what you are looking for. This program will assist any investor in examining, analyzing, comparing, plotting or charting their stocks, bonds, funds, and more. APEX S/O will let you analyze any stocks or options using the popular high-low-close bar format with volume displayed below the price. If you have stock files, the data will be kept in individual files with high, low, close, and volume value for each day.

APEX lets you create strategies using single or double moving averages, based on buying long, selling short, or both. A valuable feature is the charting of optimization trials, allowing you to see the most effective choices for short and long term moving averages. If you have option files, open interest will also be stored in the file.

There is no registration fee, no start-up fee, but there is a per quote fee. You can enter your own data or download it by modem from Warner Computer Systems, Inc. There is a sample database on disk two of this program, allowing some initial experimentation.

(PC-SIG Disk#'s 2045, 2044)

Special Requirements: *512K RAM, DOS 3.0 or higher, and a modem.*
Author Registration: *None.*

Finance Analyzer ✍   *by Constantine Roussos*

This menu-driven program does loan analysis, time deposit analysis, annuity analysis, and interest rate conversion (APR, yield, add-on). If you are comparing different options, and want to get the best return on your money, FINANCE ANALYZER will do the number crunching for you. Get all the information you need to make a sound decision.

FINANCE ANALYZER features on-line context-sensitive help that can be customized by the user. Great if you want to offer special help files unique to your business.

(PC-SIG Disk# 2016)
Special Requirements: *None.*
Author Registration: *$25.00*

Finance Plus   *by RAMbase Accounting*

Finance Plus provides the user with a means to calculate sophisticated financial problems for return on investments, periodic deposits, periodic withdrawals, financial planning, loan evaluation, and bond analysis.

Easy to follow screen design and clear information make this multi-function investment/loan calculator a quick and easy way to weigh your financial options. Changing variables for "what if" comparisons is a snap.

Within each module you can calculate a number of unknowns. For example, in the loan analysis module you may calculate loan payments, loan amount interest rate or payoff time. If you choose the loan payment option, a data input window is displayed prompting you for the term, number of payments per year, loan interest rate, and loan principal. Upon entering the prompted value, the loan payment is computed.

(PC-SIG Disk# 1919)
Special Requirements: *384K RAM.*
Author Registration: *$25.00*

Financial Wizard ☆   *by Silva Corp.*

FINANCIAL WIZARD is a slick financial calculator for investment and loan analysis. Twenty-two options cover not only standard financial calculations such as future and present value, interest rate, and amortization schedule, but also depreciation (straight-line, double-declining balance, and accelerated), discount rate, Treasury Bills, and tax-free investments.

A trio of calendar options makes short work of yield analysis. Results from one calculation can be copied to a notepad for use in another calculation. Short-cut keys and a pop-up calculator further enhance this well-designed program. FINANCIAL WIZARD handles any amount less than $10 million. And, as you might suspect, the documentation is terrific!

(PC-SIG Disk# 2606)
Special Requirements: *None.*
Author Registration: *$25.00*

FPlan - Retirement Planner ✐   *by First Financial Software*

Not sure about how much money you'll have when retirement comes? Don't depend on someone to tell you — find out yourself with FPLAN. First, enter your the amount of money you would like to receive monthly when you retire. Then enter when you would like to retire and then the savings, pensions, IRA's, social security, and other retirement information. FPLAN will display or print an analysis of how your existing plans compare to your goals.

Developed by a Certified Financial Planner, FPLAN gives you the power to control your retirement planning.

(PC-SIG Disk# 2471)
Special Requirements: *None.*
Author Registration: *$30.00*
➤*ASP Member.*

The Manager's Toolbox ✐   *by Management Solutions*

If you know your business, you know you need these strong business management tools for financial statistical analysis. Included are menu-driven applications for breakeven analysis, predicting bankruptcy, inventory analysis, make or buy decision, queuing theory, financial analysis, forecasting, and sampling for defects.

Most of the methods are very versatile in that they will offer you several ways of working the same problem. This allows you to solve for the exact information you need. If you wish to obtain a printout of any screen, press the shift key and the print screen key at the same time. This program does not store any data; when you move to the next screen all data is lost.

On-line instructions provide basic information on how to use the tools. A documentation file that explains the application of tools is included. A prior understanding of finance and statistics is helpful, but not necessary.

(PC-SIG Disk# 1928)
Special Requirements: *None.*
Author Registration: *$25.00*

MarketPLUS ✍   *by F2S Enterprises*

    MARKETPLUS is a full-featured stock/mutual fund tracking package with strong graphics capabilities. It is written especially for the individual investor to display the price action of individual stocks or mutual funds of a portfolio with ease. With MARKETPLUS you can easily create a database for up to 50 individual stocks or funds, and up to 130 trading days (26 weeks) of data can be readily displayed. You can develop several different database files, and each file can be used to store, print, and plot an additional 50 stocks or funds. In addition, historic information for your assets can be saved covering 26 weeks at a time.

    MARKETPLUS is completely menu-driven and fully documented. A powerful zoom feature allows you to concentrate on the critical days for detailed analysis. Easy-to-use indicators help you separate real trends from the zig-zags. Multiple moving averages, overbought/oversold, universal indexes, convergence/divergence, relative strength Williams Oscillator, trend lines, and trading bands are all supported. It is an outstanding program that performs sophisticated technical analysis on stocks, mutual funds, and commodities.

(PC-SIG Disk# 1153)

Special Requirements: *640K RAM, and CGA or EGA.*
Author Registration: *$45.00*

Owl Personal Portfolio Manager   *by Otto-Williams Ltd.*

    OWL PERSONAL PORTFOLIO MANAGER is a program that can manage and analyze investments and finances for individual investors. With this program you may keep a record of your security investment transactions and other assets and liabilities, and produce charts and reports to assist you with investment decisions, tax reporting, and loan applications.

    From the data entered, the program can produce on-screen or printed reports on security transactions, dividend income, security performance rankings, portfolio status summaries, and net worth. You can even select which portfolios to include in a given report.

    This program can display several charts and graphs on-screen for analysis. These include price/volume graphs with multiple moving averages, relative performance charts which show the price strength of a security relative to the overall market or other securities, and stock and index correlates. The correlation charts allow the user to see how much the price of a security is influenced by the larger market index and helps pinpoint abnormal price changes known as breakout points.

    OWL PERSONAL PORTFOLIO MANAGER has documentation which either can be printed or read screen-by-screen on the monitor. Also included on this disk is sample data to allow you to become familiar with the program without having to enter your own information.

(PC-SIG Disk# 1639)

Special Requirements: *CGA, EGA, or Hercules graphics.*
Author Registration: *$25.00*

PC-Chart   *by Guru Systems Limited*

    Bullish on the market? Or bearish? This program will help you decide!

    PC-CHART brings you a comprehensive set of technical analysis tools to help you decide when to buy and sell stocks and commodities. Mathematical algorithms help you determine what action to take. The spreadsheet-like interface permits easy editing and manual updating of up to 400 price files. For anyone who prefers automatic updating, PC-CHART lets you use HAV-INFO, a low-cost data vendor to get price updates via modem.

    The analysis section permits use of price/volume, relative strength, moving averages, parabolic system, logarithmic plot, point and figure, stochastics, weekly charts, monthly charts, on-balance volume, money flow and other parameters. Menus and a 52-page user guide on disk help you get started.

(PC-SIG Disk# 1436)

Special Requirements: *512K RAM, Hercules graphics or CGA, and a modem.*
Author Registration: *$99.00*

PC-Chart (EGA Version)   *by Guru Systems Limited*

    See description above.

(PC-SIG Disk# 1704)

Special Requirements: *512K RAM, EGA, and a modem.*
Author Registration: *$99.00*

        ✍ = Updated Program
                                                                ☆ = New Program

PC-Portfolio
by Glenn C. Everhart

PC-PORTFOLIO is a database designed specifically for the collection and analysis of financial data for blocks of stocks, bonds, notes, mutual funds, and other securities.

While it does not make buy-or-sell recommendations, it does allow the investor to collect and view financial data from three aspects: the data can be inspected through a history editor; the last 53 records in a portfolio can be graphically viewed on screen; or closing prices and hi-low prices are graphed while volume of sales are shown. In addition, summary reports are compiled.

(PC-SIG Disk# 1310)

Special Requirements: *CGA.*
Author Registration: *$25.00*

PC-Stock
by Charles Overton

PC-STOCK finance program is a stock evaluation and tracking system. It will help you analyze stock trends with an easy to use, menu-driven system and informative graphics. Support is also included for graphics printers, enabling you to save your analysis to hard copy. Produce line graphs for: high, volume, composite, on-balance volume and average high/low analysis.

(PC-SIG Disk# 575)

Special Requirements: *CGA.*
Author Registration: *None.*

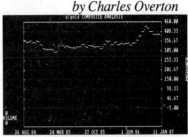
PC-Stock (PC-SIG Disk# 575)

Personal Portfolio Analyzer
by Charles L. Pack

THE PERSONAL PORTFOLIO ANALYZER performs record-keeping, analysis and reporting on any number of portfolios containing mutual funds, stocks, bonds, time deposits and other securities.

This program calculates market values, realized and unrealized gains and losses, holding periods, annual percentage returns, expected annual income and yield before and after taxes. Reports, which can be displayed on screen or printer, include income and taxability analysis, realized (tax) gains and losses, and current market value analysis. In addition, a list of expected income payments can be printed for the next 12 months. Expected income can be broken down monthly for budgeting purposes, and by security type and taxability (non-taxable, taxable Federal and taxable State) for tax planning. Total market value can be broken down by security type, portfolio name or industry category. Up to four portfolios may be combined in all reports.

THE PERSONAL PORTFOLIO ANALYZER is designed to be easy to use for individuals and small fund managers. Entry of the market price for one security, or application of a stock split or other distribution for one security, in any portfolio, automatically applies to that security in all portfolios. Security sales may be applied on a first-in first-out or last-in first-out basis, or applied to a particular purchase lot. When necessary, a purchase lot is automatically split into two parts.

(PC-SIG Disk#'s 2006, 2007)

Special Requirements: *None.*
Author Registration: *$25.00*

PFROI ✍
by Techserve, Inc.

Now you can track your investments daily. How often have you analyzed just how much of an increase, (or, sadly, a decrease), from the original cost, that daily value represents? PFROI helps you to maintain and manage a securities (stocks, bonds, mutual funds, CDs, etc.) portfolio and periodically measure the return on investment.

Several reports and analyses are available: gains, dividends, interest, miscellaneous income, open lots, transactions, account position, relative strength, valuation plot, portfolio ROI, security ROI and client statement. Focus on those marginal investments in order to make well-informed GO/NO GO decisions. PFROI does not download electronic stock data. A demonstration data file is included. All the tools are provided to manage an extensive portfolio and plan and prepare your taxes.

(PC-SIG Disk# 360)

Special Requirements: *None.*
Author Registration: *$29.00 - $49.00*

PORTRAC

by EDCO Software Concepts

PORTRAC is perfect for any investor who needs a versatile and flexible investments tracking program. PORTRAC keeps track of investments and evaluates their true return on a time-related basis. It can handle 999 individual investor accounts with up to 396 investments for each account.

PORTRAC tracks all transactions of any investment, whether a stock, a bond, fixed dollar-denominated investment, or an appreciable dollar-denominated investment such as real estate. It reads an individual investment report and quickly computes the internal rate of return. It produces a portfolio showing the investment name, file name, cost, present value, and gain or loss of the portfolio. It graphically and numerically presents the risk balance of the portfolio. You can get the total portfolio or selected portfolios by investment type. PORTRAC also produces net worth statements, amortized loan tables and provides six additional interest rate programs.

A major feature of the program is it can read an investment file and quickly compute the internal rate of return of the investment. With complete and accurate records of investments, along with a measure of the true time-related return of an investment, you can determine your future investment policy. The multiple account capability lets you set up an account for investment studies. With hypothetical investments, you can measure the internal rate of return on the forecasted investment. It is very difficult to manually evaluate the true return of an investment that had investments at different times, cash flow at variable intervals and in varying amounts, and sale of the investment at various time intervals and prices. PORTRAC will do this for you.

PORTRAC is menu-driven and easy to use. It has a demonstration account with files for quick familiarization. You can view reports and print them. These features and others make PORTRAC the perfect investment tracker and counselor.

(PC-SIG Disk# 754)

Special Requirements: *None.*
Author Registration: *$30.00*

Portworth Package

by George Wall

The PORTWORTH PACKAGE is an interesting set of programs that you can use to monitor and evaluate your stock portfolios. All of the programs are written in BASIC and so, are not overly fast, but they do the job. Portfolios of up to 25 stocks can be processed. It has graphing capabilities, and includes documentation and sample files to illustrate its usage. Source code is included.

(PC-SIG Disk# 101)

Special Requirements: *A version of BASIC.*
Author Registration: *$15.00*

Retire ✍

by George A. Bunson

A versatile, easy-to-use retirement planning tool that offers a simple way to take a hard look at personalized retirement prospects. Project retirement income based on company savings plans, IRAs, personal savings and social security.

RETIRE prompts you to enter details of projected retirement living expenses. Find out how long your savings will last. Income, taxes, and expenses are broken down and a year-by-year status of savings is shown. Major planned expenditures, cash collections, and special adjustments such as the sale of your house are provided for. "What if" analysis can be made for items like age at death for you or your spouse, rate of inflation, etc.

This version deals with a normal single life annuity pension option as offered by most companies.

(PC-SIG Disk# 2240)

Special Requirements: *None.*
Author Registration: *$29.95*

Retirement Annuity Calculator ☆

by Income Tax Aid

Will you be able to retire on the retirement funds that you have set aside or will inflation eat away at them leaving you in a disastrous position? Alternatively, how much can you withdraw each month from your retirement accounts without over-depleting them during your projected retirement period?

The RETIREMENT ANNUITY CALCULATOR calculates the amount you may withdraw each month, with subsequent annual increases to adjust for your assumed inflation rate. All you need to enter is the amount of your retirement funds, the interest or growth rate you expect to obtain on these funds after your retirement, and your anticipated inflation rate, retirement age, and life expectancy age.

(PC-SIG Disk# 2174)

Special Requirements: *None.*
Author Registration: *$25.00*

✍ = Updated Program
☆ = New Program

Social Security Calculator ✍ *by Income Tax Aid*

Will you receive the maximum Social Security retirement benefits? If you're uncertain, SOCIAL SECURITY CALCULATOR will tell you. It will estimate what your monthly retirement payment check will be for you and your dependent(s) for both retirement at age 65 and for optional retirement at earlier or later ages of your choice. It will also show the reduction in your monthly payment if you have continued earned income and/or if you have a pension based upon wages which were not subject to Social Security deductions.

Although there is no manual, the program is easy to follow. Data is included for those born between 1917 and 1949.

(PC-SIG Disk# 2174)

Special Requirements: *None.*
Author Registration: *$10.00*

Stock *by Thomas Charles Dawson*

STOCK tracks an unlimited number of stock portfolio files with up to 200 entries each. You fill out basic information, and the program generates loss or gain figures and annual and total percent value changes. Record keeping and evaluation meets most personal information needs, including tracking data required for income tax filing.

(PC-SIG Disk# 1159)

Special Requirements: *None.*
Author Registration: *$10.00*

Stock Charting System *by Charles L. Pack*

The STOCK CHARTING SYSTEM draws or prints "volume/high/low/close" charts for any stock, bond, commodity, or security that has a high/low/close price. Short- and long-term moving averages can be included on the chart and temporarily changed for "what-if" calculations. The STOCK CHARTING SYSTEM is menu-driven and comes with a complete set of context-sensitive help screens.

(PC-SIG Disk#'s 246, 1354)

Special Requirements: *CGA or equivalent, works with EGA and most VGA, two floppy drives*
Author Registration: *$25.00.*

Stock Charts *by David Lee Todd*

STOCK CHARTS is for the investor with an eye towards technical analysis of stocks or mutual funds. STOCK CHARTS graphically displays the price and volume action of stocks or mutual funds by producing charts similar to those found in books on technical analysis of the stock market. The program charts high, low, close, volume, and moving averages of stocks, mutual funds, or stock averages such as the Dow Jones Industrial Average. STOCK CHARTS is designed for the small investor who keeps track of day-to-day stock prices and volume movements through sources such as the Wall Street Journal or some other financial publication.

STOCK CHARTS is fully menu-driven and intuitive to operate. From the main menu you can choose to draw charts, list stocks, add/delete/insert data, or view data. Each option presents you with a sub-menu for ease of operation. Three charting options are available: chart high, low, close, volume; chart close only; and chart moving average. The list stocks option will show you all stock symbols that are currently in the database. STOCK CHARTS produces high resolution black and white CGA graphics and full color EGA graphics. Charts can also be printed.

(PC-SIG Disk# 1528)

Special Requirements: *CGA or EGA.*
Author Registration: *$20.00*

Stock Market Timer *by Ron West*

When should you buy and when should you sell your stocks? What numbers should you watch? The STOCK MARKET TIMER uses figures from your daily newspaper to time your actions to ongoing trends, not whims. This market analyzer is based upon M. G. Zahorchak's book entitled "The Art of Low Risk Investing." Mr. Zahorchak's main idea was to help the individual investor to protect himself from himself. That is, to give the investor a method of investing other than investing on hot tips or a stock some "guru" is touting that week.

To that end, he presented guidelines to investing based on several moving averages. If followed, the investor could expect to at least approach future investments with some discipline in his trading activities.

The data STOCK MARKET TIMER uses is quite simple and readily available. Market direction is determined from three sources: the weekly closing DJIA; the weekly number of Advancing and Declining stocks on the NY Stock Exchange; and the S&P500 weekly closing figures. Individual stocks are selected by the system user and are thus unique to the individual.

(PC-SIG Disk# 1800)

Special Requirements: *Hard drive recommended.*
Author Registration: *$29.00*

The Stock Trader ✍   by FreeBooter Software

STOCK TRADER tracks selected stock performances and generates buy and sell signals according to trends over user-selected periods of time. There are 8 stocks at the start for demo purposes. Stocks may be added and deleted, and the DOW performance, or an other accepted market average is also displayed. Stock performance is graphed in x-y mode, and graphs may be printed. The program is menu-driven requires color graphics.

System Requirements: 128K memory, two disk drives and color graphics.

How to Start: Load DOS and type STOCK to enter the main program. Consult READ.ME for program information.

Suggested Registration: $35.00.

(PC-SIG Disk# 644)

Special Requirements: *448K RAM, CGA/EGA/VGA, and two disk drives.*
Author Registration: *$35.00*

Wall Street - The Bottom Line ☆   by STANCOatlanta

WALL STREET - THE BOTTOM LINE is a custom database manager for stocks and bonds. It can store the details of each transaction, track your portfolio's performance, and graph the results. The program includes an impressive array of analysis tools and even accommodates short sells. The pop-up windows make the edit and search options a snap. A sample data file is included to help the user quickly learn the many features. The program can handle MCGA, CGA, EGA, and VGA graphics and a wide choice of printers. This is a great tool for investors, stockbrokers, and accountants.

(PC-SIG Disk# 2792)

Special Requirements: *320K RAM. Hard drive, graphics card, and printer recommended.*
Author Registration: *$49.95*

Your Networth   by Richard C. Rychtarik

Turn your PC into a personal financial planning assistant with YOUR NETWORTH, a 1-2-3 template that lets you take snapshots of your investment portfolio and forecast your financial future. It's your personal financial planning and analysis tool.

YOUR NETWORTH provides the means to track, manage, and assess your overall net worth. It provides fixed income management, financial forecasting, tax estimation, and has record keeping capability for all forms of assets and liabilities. YOUR NETWORTH is not a stock port- folio manager, a check writer, or a bill payer. This system provides the means by which you can track and manage your accumulation of all assets in order to achieve your total financial goals.

Although YOUR NETWORTH is a spreadsheet template for Lotus 1-2-3, very little 1-2-3 knowledge or experience is required. Use it to record and manage your financial assets and liabilities such as bank accounts, retirement plans, stocks, bonds, mortgages, and other personal assets. You can inventory and analyze anything of value.

You can also use the program to forecast "what if?" financial situations. Its goal seeking capability predicts your future financial condition. You can project how changing monetary conditions, inflation rate, investment yields, and personal tax liabilities impact your current and future net worth.

YOUR NETWORTH automatically provides help and/or hints if you incorrectly enter critical information.

(PC-SIG Disk# 2186)

Special Requirements: *Lotus 1-2-3*
Author Registration: *$15.00*

▼ ▼ ▼

✍ = Updated Program
☆ = New Program

Label Makers

Easy Labels
by Foto 64 Inc.

There has never been a simpler, quicker label program. Whether it's one or 99 labels you need, EASY LABEL is up to the job. It pops onto the screen in seconds, so straightforward help is not needed.

A screen asks you to type in the contents of the label, line by line. It asks you the size and if you need a label printed for alignment purposes. Flick a key and the label is on the way. What you see is exactly what you get an instant later.

The price for the simplicity is that nothing is saved to disk and you don't get sorting or all the other things complicated label programs offer. But if your job requires a few labels now and then and you hate reading user manuals, this is the program for you.

(PC-SIG Disk# 1683)

Special Requirements: *None.*
Author Registration: *$10.00*
➤*ASP Member.*

Fancy Label Maker
by David Simpson

Most computer users have a need for a simple utility which can print their labels for them. And whether those labels are going to be used on disks, letters, or something else, FANCY LABEL is the program for you.

Save and retrieve a specific label and print as many copies as you want. All the labels are saved into a data file on the drive of your choice. For each line you may choose either normal, double width, condensed, normal compressed, or double compressed. Each print style can be either in italics or regular print mode.

FANCY LABEL is designed to work with single-feed fanfold labels. You can use either $3\frac{1}{2}$" x $\frac{15}{16}$" labels, on which you can print up to five lines, or 4" x $\frac{7}{16}$" labels, on which you can print up to eight lines per label.

(PC-SIG Disk# 871)

Special Requirements: *Printer and labels.*
Author Registration: *$10.00*

Label CMT
by Consolidated Micro Technology

This simple program prints labels in any size up to 5.2 x 2.3 inches including regular address labels (3.5" x 0.7"), or file folder work labels (3.2" x 2.3").

Labels are shown on the screen letting you see what you are going to get. Size of type is standard with no options. You can save labels to a library, print one or more copies of the same label, and optionally pause the printer after each label is printed. LABEL CMT is most useful for creating labels that do not need to be part of a database, such as return address, file folder, or inventory/bin type labels. The program is menu-driven with on-screen help.

(PC-SIG Disk# 1297)

Special Requirements: *None.*
Author Registration: *$20.00*

Label Maker ✍
by Fort's Faceting

A simple menu-driven labelmaker, perfect for novices. Print labels for your library of floppies on the labels that come with your blank diskettes.

The program automatically reads and prints all file names, subdirectories, a large title, up to eight lines of comments, the date, number of files, disk format, and bytes used/free on three different 5.25 inchdiskette label sizes ($3\frac{1}{2}$ x $\frac{15}{16}$, 4 x $1\frac{7}{16}$, and 5 x $1\frac{7}{16}$) and on two 3.5 inch diskette label sizes ($2\frac{3}{4}$ x $2\frac{3}{4}$ and $2\frac{3}{4}$ x $1\frac{15}{16}$).

Options include printing multiple labels, and printing without listing file names. Supports LQ printers as well as Epson dot matrix printers, the IBM Proprinter or Graphics printer, and compatibles. Will also work on any printer capable of enlarged and compressed print modes. Printer, screen colors, label size, size of title, and other options can be configured to your specifications.

(PC-SIG Disk# 284)

Special Requirements: *None.*
Author Registration: *$25.00*

Label Master ✍ *by RKS Associates*

LABEL MASTER is a program for maintaining, sorting, and printing lists of names and addresses (mailing lists), with a couple of added twists. You will find all the regular capabilities of a labeling program such as full search and replace on all fields, full screen records browsing, accommodation for international addresses, and a larger phone field to accommodate any size phone number. The extra added twists you will find is a pop-up help system, pop-up calendar, pop-up digital clock, and pop-up calculator. There's even a coffee break game built into the program for times of over-stress and under pay.

LABEL MASTER will automatically date-stamp each new record in a "notes" field for future reference. Label Master will print multiple labels across te page, and will pause after each page, if requested (great for single sheet labels). The documentation consists of a brief description of each of the menu selections and a couple of paragraphs on installing the program on your system.

You will find LABEL MASTER to be one of the easiest-to-use mailing list management programs around.

(PC-SIG Disk# 750)

Special Requirements: *512K RAM, and a hard drive.*
Author Registration: *$35.00*

Label Utilities *by George Campbell*

A pair of programs that will take some of the headaches out of label- making.

LABELIT is for printing duplicate labels on any kind of printer that accepts label forms. This program is direct and simple. It can print any number of labels with the same information such as company names, return addresses, diskette labels, etc. These labels can be up to 12 lines of text and LABELIT will center or left-justify each label if desired. Print one-up or two-up and LABELIT accepts printer control codes for custom effects. The labels can always be re-used since LABELIT will save these custom formats to disk.

BAKLABEL does one thing — it prints sequentially numbered and dated labels for the diskettes used in backing up hard disks. The user selects the number of labels, a title line, and the name of the drive being backed up.

(PC-SIG Disk# 1866)

Special Requirements: *None.*
Author Registration: *$15.00*

Labels Plus! ☆ *by Westcoast Software*

Hate writing mailing addresses by hand? LABELS PLUS! will do so much for you that you'll wonder how you ever lived without it. Print and address envelopes, shipping labels, address labels and postcards. Design, save, and print your own labels and postcards. There is a names and addresses database with 1000 records. LABELS PLUS! is a very easy-to-use program.

(PC-SIG Disk# 2768)

Special Requirements: *Printer.*
Author Registration: *$15.00*

Mr. Label *by DataWave Software*

A labeling program that offers some very useful features. Create everything from simple reports to custom labels and print on any type of single-sheet or continuous form.

Use your printer like a typewriter to create one-time labels, or retrieve and print information from lists.

MR. LABEL offers professional features especially useful to secretaries, sales people, and businesses:

❑ Address envelopes — individual or continuous feed
❑ Print the return and destination addresses in one operation
❑ Design labels any size and position text anywhere on the label
❑ Vary type fonts between lines
❑ Print letterheads, price tags, ID badges, file folder labels, name tags, inventory slips, and disk labels
❑ Create mass-mailing applications
❑ Design print formats for database records
❑ Print promotional messages on mailers as they're addressed
❑ Plan formats to print checks and complete forms

✍ = Updated Program
☆ = New Program

❑ Print in any font supported by your equipment
❑ Avoid typing repetitive lines with fixed text
❑ Increase a printed number with the auto-increment feature
❑ Adjust screen colors, automatically center, and make multiple copies
❑ Design printing formats and save them to disk
❑ Includes a powerful text editor.
(PC-SIG Disk# 1673)
Special Requirements: *Printer.*
Author Registration: *$29.00*

PostNet   *by NE Inc.*

Save money at the post office by taking advantage of "bar code bulk rates." POSTNET will allow you to add bar codes to labels or envelopes so you can qualify for lower postage rates. Any database or other label program you might currently be using can feed addresses to POSTNET in an ASCII file. As long as your addresses are three lines long and all have the zip code on the third line POSTNET can automatically print your labels on one-up label stock.

POSTNET is your first step to getting the most out of your postage dollar. Your Postal Office bulk mailing representative can show you how to do the presort, and how to convert your old five digit zip codes to the +4 format. This program supports most dot matrix printers including 24-pin printers and the Okidata 192.
(PC-SIG Disk# 1758)
Special Requirements: *Graphics dot matrix printer.*
Author Registration: *$25.00*

Power Label   *by Starvector Software*

Print custom-designed labels, envelopes, and index cards.

For printing jobs where the size of the item is unusual, there is an "All-purpose" mode, with no restrictions on dimensions or spacing, allowing customization. Some features include:
❑ Custom print styles for each line by using any combination of the 12 print modes available: draft, elite, compressed, horizontally expanded, vertically expanded, subscript, italics, underlined, emphasized, doublestrike, letter quality, and proportional printing.
❑ The ability to change print styles on any line at any time.
❑ Editing of line text.
❑ File-saving option for storing label/envelope/card data on disk for later use.
❑ DOS shell.

Designed for use with Epson FX-compatible printers, but most near-compatible printers will work with all of POWER LABEL's features.
(PC-SIG Disk# 2293)
Special Requirements: *None.*
Author Registration: *$20.00*

PRTLabel   *by Mustang Software*

PRTLABEL prints multiple copies of a single label or single labels with a new address each time. It prints as many labels as you like in a given run, up to six labels across, 10 lines per label.
(PC-SIG Disk# 744)
Special Requirements: *None.*
Author Registration: *$25.00*

Simply Labels III   *by Simpleware*

SIMPLY LABELS is a unique free form label program that lets you design your own label formats and maintain files containing your labels.

Each label format you create can have its own standard background text, which can include graphics characters. In this way you can create labels with blank lines or boxes for data entry. You can also specify the length of the label and the number of lines each label has. Each line of the label you create can have a different kind of typeface, such as normal print, condensed, elite, etc. You can create mailing labels, tape labels, VCR labels, filing labels, or any kind of label for whatever you need.

Designated keys can be used to enter commonly used text with a single keystroke. Labels can be imported into SIMPLY LABELS from a text file or dBase III or PC-File database files. Labels are defined by selecting database fields from a menu and placing them directly into a label format.

Several predefined label formats are included in the program, and you can design up to 25 different label formats. SIMPLY LABELS sends the labels to the printer, a disk file, or the screen. You can print single or multiple copies of labels, and print multiple labels across the printer. Powerful searching and sorting routines allow you to select and organize your labels any way you like.

(PC-SIG Disk#'s 1150, 1679)

Special Requirements: *Printer.*
Author Registration: *$25.00*
➤*ASP Member.*

▼ ▼ ▼

Language Study, Foreign

Cantonese Tutor
by Louie Crew

Cantonese is an extremely hard-to-learn language spoken by more people than any other language in the world. This program can help you learn it. It is menu-driven, with menus for both the student and teacher. Lessons can be tailored by the teacher for drilling in certain areas.

CANTONESE is designed for use with other forms of Chinese language study, since it does not provide actual spoken Cantonese as an example. The documentation can be somewhat difficult to follow at times, but has all the needed information to run the program.

(PC-SIG Disk# 755)

Special Requirements: *None.*
Author Registration: *$10.00*

Hebrew Quiz and Tutorial
by David Rapier

HEBREW QUIZ is a Biblical Hebrew language tutor that teaches the Hebrew alphabet, vocabulary, verbs, and grammar. It is designed for use with Thomas O. Lambdin's "Introduction to Biblical Hebrew" from MacMillan & Co.

Learn the vocabulary by a certain word type, frequency of occurrence in the Hebrew Bible, and cognate groups. You can learn verbs by verb type, conjugation, tense, person, gender, number, or suffix. You can also choose the part of grammar to review.

In addition to the quiz program, HEBREW QUIZ comes with a tutor for each section that tracks your scores. Hebrew words are shown one at a time with an English translation. A menu on the screen displays all the options available.

(PC-SIG Disk# 902)

Special Requirements: *None.*
Author Registration: *$20.00*

Learning Japanese 1. The Hiragana
Symbols(PC-SIG Disk #2545)

Learning Japanese 1. The Hiragana Symbols ☆
by Australian Systems Co.

Have you ever wanted to learn Japanese? LEARNING JAPANESE 1 will teach you the Hiragana symbols. Hiragana is like a code, with symbols representing syllables. Learn to recognize the 75 Japanese Hiragana symbols using flash cards, literal conversion of English sounds, and a tutorial with recognition practice. Control the program with mouse or keyboard.

(PC-SIG Disk# 2545)

Special Requirements: *EGA.*
Author Registration: *$25.00*

✍ = Updated Program
☆ = New Program

OLE! 2000 SET 1 ✍   *by Robert H. Walker*

OLE! 2000 SET 1 is a novel way of learning a language — in short bursts and with a lot of variety. Various complete phrases are presented as expressions, with alternative verb usage, and even in short stories. By selecting one unit of 20 translations at a time, the user has unique control over the material covered, and his/her learning progress.

The program's unique integration of rewarding statements and musical tunes makes for an enjoyable learning experience. It's for the serious student or teacher who wants a challenging but rewarding tool for learning written Spanish. When you've learned the material presented in the 40 units of this introduction, a nominal registration fee will get you 60 additional units of advanced material (all of which span the first college semester). Besides this material and also receiving additional program tools for constructing and editing your own additional units, a special tourist disk and audio cassettes are also available.

(PC-SIG Disk# 2129)

Special Requirements: *None.*
Author Registration: *$15.00*

▼ ▼ ▼

Library Record Keeping (Including Dewey Decimal)

Book Minder   *by MoneCraft Computer Products*

BOOK MINDER is a book-cataloging system designed for both personal and business use. It can be used with books, magazines, newspapers, or almost any other published material. BOOK MINDER allows you to catalog a library and then locate a book or article in a magazine, by any one of up to 21 characteristics. Entries can be made for individual articles. This allows you to list the individually unique information contained in each article.

BOOK MINDER is completely menu-driven, easy to operate, and allows three levels of information cataloging. The three levels are: standard, research, and librarian. Each level provides a progressively greater detail of information that can be stored for each entry.

BOOK MINDER can be used to run a database search business, providing different levels of information to customers.

(PC-SIG Disk# 1178)

Special Requirements: *Hard drive recommended.*
Author Registration: *$59.95*
➤*ASP Member.*

Cassy   *by Diakon Systems*

CASSY is a versatile, inexpensive Dewey Decimal System-based program that helps keep books and audiovisual materials in order. Operation is menu-driven, simple, and intuitive. Printer support lets you print sets of catalog cards, accession lists, and shelf lists.

About 1,400 items can be stored on a single 360K disk and up to five subject headings are maintained per item. All catalog card data is printed in proper upper- and lower-case combinations. Also, catalog cards are printed in library order sets (AACR2) for easy filing.

(PC-SIG Disk# 1091)

Special Requirements: *Two floppy drives.*
Author Registration: *$20.00*

Pro Librarian   *by Soft-Slick*

PROFESSIONAL LIBRARIAN is an information-retrieval system for storing citations of articles and books in your own library.

Add, delete, edit, sort, and search citations in your database. Each record includes the author, date, title, citation, number, four subject categories, and a short description. A listing of the database can be output to the screen, a file, or the printer.

(PC-SIG Disk# 1313)

Special Requirements: *None.*
Author Registration: *$25.00*

Textbook Inventory
by Barry Alpern

TEXTBOOK INVENTORY CONTROL SYSTEM is designed to keep track of books issued to students, but it can be easily adapted for use by businesses that check out reference materials to employees, or in your own library to help you recall who borrowed that favorite book of yours! Completely menu-driven and extremely easy to use, the program allows you to update existing book records, record books returned, print all book inventory records, or print the records for books not yet returned.

The database record format for each textbook consists of: file name, book title, author's name, book cost-new, book code, book condition, student name, student identification number, date book issued, and date book returned. A sample of a book checkout form is included for hardcopy input. In all, an excellent method for handling small library inventory tracking!

(PC-SIG Disk# 1532)

Special Requirements: *None.*
Author Registration: *$50.00*

▼ ▼ ▼

Loan Calculators

AMORT ✍
by Micro Data Assist

AMORT generates loan amortization schedules for those of us without our Ph.D. in mathematics. A major purchase such as a home or a car can be confusing enough, let alone trying to figure in your loan payments. With AMORT, you provide either the loan principal (in dollars), annual interest rate, loan period (in months), or monthly payment (in dollars). As long as you provide three of the four, AMORT can calculate the missing element. In this way AMORT can help you answer questions about how much you can spend assuming a fixed monthly payment, or how much it will cost you each month assuming a certain overall price.

AMORT assumes the annual interest rate is compounded monthly (ordinary or exact interest). Loan amortization schedules can be sent to the printer, to the display screen, or both. Printed output also can be customized with titles, additional fields indicating who the schedule is prepared for, and a description of the schedule. These features make this an ideal tool for accountants, real estate agents, and anyone planning on buying or selling property.

AMORT is menu driven, easy to use, and fully documented.

(PC-SIG Disk# 1646)

Special Requirements: *512K RAM.*
Author Registration: *$15.00*

Amort70
by Burgess Enterprises Ltd.

This loan amortization program also specializes notes. You can calculate monthly or weekly home or personal loan amortization, and daily, weekly, or monthly interest on notes with a set repayment amount.

Both the loan and note menus will walk you through the numbers by prompting you for information. Who is the report prepared for? What is the amount? The interest rate? The period? The calculations are fast and easy to understand. Great for the professional who does a lot of calculating.

(PC-SIG Disk# 1805)

Special Requirements: *None.*
Author Registration: *$20.00*

Amortization Calculator
by Edward B. Toupin

Thinking of taking out a loan on your house, or buying a new house? Let the AMORTIZATION CALCULATOR calculate and print the payment amount and schedule for you.

Calculate loans of up to $500,000 for a term of up to 480 months (40 years). Taxes and insurance costs can also be entered as needed to calculate the total monthly payment, giving you a true monthly payment amount. Since all loan information is on the main screen and is updated as you enter amounts and rates, you automatically see the results of your loan. This is great if you are interested in doing "what-ifs" to find the right loan.

(PC-SIG Disk# 1693)

Special Requirements: *640K RAM.*
Author Registration: *$20.00*

Amortization Table 🖎
by H&P Software

AMORTIZATION TABLE calculates the monthly or periodical payment for a loan of between one to forty years and then prints a schedule showing the interest and principle for each period. Regular, discounted, and interest-only schedules are available, and optional APR calculations may be done for schedules that are not ballooned. Schedules may be ballooned at any payment period.

AMORTIZATION TABLE will amortize principals up to $999,999,999.00 and bases its schedule on the 360-day year.

(PC-SIG Disk# 1027)

Special Requirements: *384K RAM.*
Author Registration: *$29.95*
➤*ASP Member.*

Amortize
by J. Gordon Rowe

Would you like to know what a loan costs before talking to your banker? Would you like to know how much profit you could make before loaning your money to someone? Would you like to compare the cost of a loan using different interest rates? If these or other questions are important to you, then AMORTIZE can help. It helps solve such matters before you make a loan.

For example, if you know the principal (amount to be borrowed), the interest rate, the payment amount, and certain other data, then AMORTIZE will compute the number of payments to be made. AMORTIZE will compute for principal, interest, number of periods, payments, fixed principal amount, and for the balloon payment.

Amortize (PC-SIG Disk #2177)

AMORTIZE will save your worksheet for future reference, and also print to your printer or to a disk file (ASCII format for transfer purposes).

It doesn't handle simple interest formulas, bond value and yield information, and advance payment adjustments. But what it does do, it does easily and quickly.

(PC-SIG Disk# 2177)

Special Requirements: *None.*
Author Registration: *$20.00*

AZ Real Estate Finance
by Curtis E. Falany

Are you a real estate professional, broker, attorney, or investor who would like to do his or her own closings more quickly? This program will allow you to generate most of the financial information needed for a standard real estate or loan closing as well as allow you to check the work of others.

If you are a consumer who would like to better understand and check the work on those "TRUTH IN LENDING" documents you sign when you borrow money, this program will allow you to check your lender's work to the penny.

It calculates annuity payments or periodic amortization of loans, interest rates on a given monthly amortization for a flat payout, or for a balloon payment. It also displays and prints amortization schedules for payments to be made.

This program has been "ported" from commercial software written by the author for attorneys, real estate brokers, title insurance companies, and other professionals dealing in real estate and real estate finance. This experience in the "real world" means that special attention is always given to accuracy and presentation. The results are generally acceptable to law, real estate, and finance professionals.

(PC-SIG Disk# 1882)

Special Requirements: *None.*
Author Registration: *$15.00*

Banker
by Basic Soft

BANKER is a financial program that computes just about anything involving loans, savings, bonds, securities, and credit. Surpassing the needs of most laymen, BANKER meets the majority of computational needs of the finance professional. It computes commercial and installment loans, savings, etc., and provides information and definitions of various financial instruments.

Under commercial and installment loans, you find the payment per period, compute the principal, annual percentage rate, and find early payoff amounts (rule of 78's). Savings information includes the time required to save a given amount, nominal-to-effective rates, and interest on savings. General applications are present value (simple interest), present value (compound interest), and the present value of an annuity in advance.

Bonds and securities calculations offered are: the yield of discounted securities, yield-periodic interest payments, yield-interest at maturity, future value (compound interest), future value of an annuity, and a comparison of interest to discount rate.

(PC-SIG Disk# 1159)

Special Requirements: *None.*
Author Registration: *$35.00*

BuyAHome ☆
by Shareable Software

Fixed rate, adjustable rate, points, closing costs — these days you have to be a banker to figure out if you can afford a home. That was true until BUYAHOME was developed.

Enter loan information such as: loan amount, down payment, type of loan (fixed rate, adjustable rate, price level adjusted, and two step loans are supported), closing costs, and points. Then, enter expenses like insurance and property taxes. Finally, enter your income and tax information. BUYAHOME calculates the costs of owning the home, projected payments, and your potential loan approval rating. You can change any of the numbers and recalculate the loan information to do "what-if" analyses. When you're finished, get a detailed printout of your information.

BUYAHOME takes all the mystery out of buying a home and applying for a loan. These are the same calculations loan officers do. Now you can do them at home.

(PC-SIG Disk# 2506)

Special Requirements: *None.*
Author Registration: *$29.95*
➤*ASP Member.*

Drew's Amortization System
by Try-Then-Buy Software

AMORT is an excellent, easy-to-use amortization program. Figure the total cost and status of mortgages and loans. This program figures by either TIME OF PAYMENTS or PAYMENTS PER MONTH basis and keeps both current and total track of payments, interest, and principal. Unique in its simplicity, AMORT will help you understand what your loans really cost!

(PC-SIG Disk# 2219)

Author Registration: *Contribution.*

Financial Calculator
by Southern Electronics

FINANCIAL CALCULATOR is a simple, menu-driven program that calculates interest on loans, savings, or payments.

Calculate your monthly payments, total interest, and the total amount you will pay to the bank at the end of the loan. Get a month-by-month breakdown of your monthly payments, interest for that month, payment on the principal and the ending balance for that month. You can also figure the approximate annual interest rate for a loan. A metric conversion utility is included.

Financial Calculator (PC-SIG Disk #994)

(PC-SIG Disk# 994)

Special Requirements: *None.*
Author Registration: *$6.00*

✍ = Updated Program
☆ = New Program

Financier ✍

by Virtual Srket Technology

Use FINANCIER to calculate amortization schedules when considering that big purchase.

Schedules can be scrolled, printed, and stored in a file. Load a previously stored schedule and include balloon payments, if necessary. Perform interest iteration, term determination, and present value determination. Accrued and compound interest can be calculated along with bond present value, annuities, and sinking fund.

Directory listings are available if you forget a file name. Trend analysis and days between dates are also available. The output window keeps track of your calculations. A calendar and calculator are handy for quick date and calculation checks.

FINANCIER uses text-based windowing featuring pull-down menus and online Help. It has an easy-to-use interface with a short learning curve.

(PC-SIG Disk# 2492)

Special Requirements: *512K RAM and CGA or EGA.*
Author Registration: *$15.00*

Genamort

by KMA Systems Corp.

Thinking of taking out a loan for a house, new car, etc? Let GENAMORT calculate and print the payment amount and schedule for you. Find out how much that loan is really going to cost you.

Calculate loans of up to $10,000,000 for a term of up to 999 months, which is over 83 years. A balloon payment can even be added to the calculation. Payments can be calculated on a monthly, quarterly, semi-yearly, and yearly basis. All input fields are contained on one input menu, using single keystroke entries. Subtotals of interest, payments, and principal are calculated to aid in preparing your taxes.

The loan amortization schedule can be viewed on the screen or sent to the printer. The program can also calculate a periodic payment without printing a schedule.

(PC-SIG Disk# 1874)

Special Requirements: *None.*
Author Registration: *$15.00*

INTCAL

by Glenn C. Everhart

INTCAL (INTEREST CALCULATOR) can determine the present and future values of a series of equal payments for capital recovery or for a specific future amount.

The program explains compound-interest transactions, what things will cost and earn, and can help make difficult financial decisions easier. Asking only two or three questions, INTCAL accurately calculates the answer.

(PC-SIG Disk# 1310)

Special Requirements: *CGA.*
Author Registration: *$10.00*

Loan Warrior

by Brian & Colleen Lawson

LOAN WARRIOR is a full-featured loan amortization program that not only calculates monthly payments but also helps you make decisions about a loan by letting you compare different terms or early payoff. It works with both fixed and variable interest rates. Given the principal, the interest rate, and the term of the loan, LOAN WARRIOR gives a complete monthly amortization schedule, yearly interest payments, yearly principal payments, and both a detailed and summary report. An accelerated payoff option is included, analyzing money that can be saved by making larger payments.

(PC-SIG Disk# 1055)

Special Requirements: *CGA, EGA, or VGA.*
Author Registration: *$6.00.*

LoanCalc

by James A. Ray

A user-oriented loan and mortgage calculator with a variety of options. Compute interest paid for any given year and output a complete or partial amortization table on a screen or printer. Calculate the balance payment at any given date.

(PC-SIG Disk# 960)

Special Requirements: *None.*
Author Registration: *$10.00*

LoanPMT ✍

by Data Language Systems

LOANPMT is a multi-functional loan calculation program. Payments, principal, APR, and term of loan can all be calculated when given the other three. Additional loan costs and loan points can optionally be added to the principal. It is a good program for comparing different loans.

Amortization tables can be printed, displayed, or saved to disk for all loans computed. Early loan payoffs can be computed for existing loans. Loan information can be saved to or loaded from disk.

(PC-SIG Disk# 1854)

Special Requirements: *None.*
Author Registration: *$15.00*

LoanStar

by Michael R. Kenley

LOANSTAR is an easy to use loan calculator and amortization program for fixed and variable rate loans. LOANSTAR allows for advance payments to be paid at any month and shows any savings incurred as a result of making advance payments. Annual interest paid is also displayed to aid in tax calculations.

LOANSTAR is an excellent menu driven program for calculating and tracking any loan. The program solves for payment, interest rate, length of loan, or amount of loan. The amortization schedule displays on the screen or printer the monthly balance, equity, principle, and interest. Also shown on a monthly basis are advance payments, rate changes, and payment changes, if any. LOANSTAR displays on an annual basis total interest paid for income tax purposes. The amount of time and money saved as a result of making advance payments is shown on the last year of the schedule. All of this can be saved to disk for later recall and update. LOANSTAR is great for keeping track of a long mortgage.

(PC-SIG Disk# 1580)

Special Requirements: *None.*
Author Registration: *Any amount.*

Monamort

by Entrepreneurs Software

MONTHLY LOAN AMORTIZATION calculates and prints a monthly loan schedule.

It prompts you for essential information such as loan amount, percentage rate and length of loan. Then the program prints a report of the monthly loan payments showing the amount of the payment, the amount left due on the loan, and how much is going toward the principle of the loan.

(PC-SIG Disk# 960)

Special Requirements: *None.*
Author Registration: *$3.50*

MortPlan

by Mustang Software

MORTPLAN provides menu-driven ease for calculating home loans. It calculates a standard mortgage for principle amounts up to $99,999,999.99 and interest rates up to 35.000%, and saves the results to disk. Random additional payments can be used and the results analyzed. It has a section for comparing a range of interest rates and a range of loan amounts at the same time. There is also provision for variable rate loans. All output can be directed to either the screen or the printer.

(PC-SIG Disk# 1342)

Special Requirements: *None.*
Author Registration: *$30.00*

```
JUN  8, 1989            MORTPLAN 3.01              10:41 am

                      MORTGAGE PART ANALYSIS
                     ==> UNREGISTERED COPY <==
              Original loan amount .......... [$   5,555.49]

              Interest rate ...................... [54.000%]

              Length of loan ........ Years [23] Months [ 0]

              Principal & Interest payment .. [$   1,000.00]

              Number of payments per year .............. [ 3]

              Total Interest ............. [$   63,444.51]

              Number of payments ..................... [   69]

              Press ANY key to start over ... Esc to exit.
```

MortPlan (PC-SIG Disk# 1342)

PCLOAN 5

by Bottom Line Software

PCLOAN 5 was designed by a retired bank president who negotiated, originated and collected over 30,000 commercial loans.

PCLOAN 5 provides analysis data for amortizing loans with output to the screen, disk or printed reports. Perform almost any calculation needed for a business or personal loan which is amortized in multiple payments. It is menu-driven and includes quite a bit of on-line help.

✍ = Updated Program
☆ = New Program

Use PCLOAN 5 functions to project just what a loan is going to cost and when. Know what you're getting into, financially, before you take that final plunge.

(PC-SIG Disk# 399)
Special Requirements: *512K RAM.*
Author Registration: *$79.95*

Pelton Computer Consultants
by Pelton Cumputer Consultants

Here are five utility programs with five different purposes, but all helpful, easy to use, and well-documented.

Given a starting balance, interest rate, term, and an ending balance (lower than the starting balance), DISTRIB will immediately calculate the amount of money that you may take out of your interest-bearing account (withdrawal amount) so that your money decreases to the ending balance over the term.

FUTURE does the same problem but calculates the deposit amount when the ending balance you desire is higher than the starting balance. Both of these equations can be tricky with interest bearing accounts.

PAYMENTS is used to print range-and-spreads to the screen or to your printer. You are asked for a starting interest rate which forms a spread in increments of 0.5 across the top, and you are asked for a starting value of another quantity which is spread in appropriate increments down the left column. In between is a checkerboard of values around which your eye may peruse so that you may hone in on an interest rate that's best for you.

The SED utility program is a "stream editor." You run the program with three qualifiers: the name of the file to be worked on, the old string, and the new string. The stream editor then transforms the old string into the new string without having to enter a wordprocessing program. The SED program works only with ASCII files.

THINGS-TO-DO is a program to help you organize your lists of things to do, for example, lists of prospects, appointments, repairmen, phone numbers, action items for work projects, events leading up to a closing, lists of parts to buy for repairing your house or remodeling, grocery lists, lists of friends and their telephone numbers, party supplies, or any list limited only by your imagination.

(PC-SIG Disk# 1944)
Special Requirements: *None.*
Author Registration: *$10.00*
➤*ASP Member.*

Varamort
by David M. Alexander

VARAMORT is an amortization program that calculates the monthly payments for variable or fixed loans.

You specify the amount of the mortgage, the length in years, and the interest rate. For variable loans, you can specify the interest rate for each year or specify a certain range within which the interest rate may fluctuate. In all cases, VARAMORT will calculate the monthly payment, principal, interest amount, balance, cumulative principal and the cumulative interest amount. Each year may be separately displayed on the screen, or the entire loan information may be printed to the printer.

(PC-SIG Disk# 1323)
Special Requirements: *CGA.*
Author Registration: *$25.00*

Your Financial Advisor ✍
by MoneCraft Computer Products

YOUR FINANCIAL ADVISOR is a versatile financial management package with major financial modules — loan calculator, equity calculator, amortization table generator, and financial planner.

The loan calculator allows you to calculate monthly loan payments based on interest, loan amount, and the loan term. (You can enter any three of the values and the module will calculate the fourth value.) A payment table is displayed to reflect the interest or term change on your loan payment.

The equity calculator keeps track of the equity in your home and calculates the amount you can borrow against your home and keep the interest tax deduction.

The amortization module generates an amortization table of loan payments for each payment, a table displays the amount of the payment that goes towards the interest and the amount that covers the principle. Prepayments and balloon payments can be included.

The financial planner performs annuity, present value and future value calculations for your investments. This module provides specific tables for retirement planning, college cost planning, and IRA planning.

YOUR FINANCIAL ADVISOR has an additional feature for professional users which allows you to print your name, address, and phone number on all hardcopy reports. The program is completely menu-driven and has pop-up help screens for all modules.

(PC-SIG Disk# 1613)

Special Requirements: *None.*
Author Registration: *$35.00*
➤**ASP Member.**

▼ ▼ ▼

Lottery

Lottery Analyzer and Picker
by Jim Mooney

LOTTERY ANALYZER AND PICKER is a program that analyzes statistics on previous winning lottery numbers and randomly chooses lottery numbers for you. The winning lottery numbers can be updated and changed at any time.

Display a listing of the last 48 winning numbers, showing the number of repeats from the previous drawing, the total odd and even numbers, the sum of all six numbers, and the difference and average between the numbers drawn. Find out how many times each number was picked in previous drawings. Display a graph of the previous winning numbers and a graph of the frequency of each winning number.

Besides giving statistics on previous winning lottery numbers, LOTTERY ANALYZER AND PICKER can randomly select lottery numbers for you. Set limitations on the random selection to include or exclude certain numbers, set the average frequency, set the total sum of all six numbers, have consecutive or double numbers, include previous winning numbers and more. After you pick numbers from the random selection, LOTTERY ANALYZER can display a graph of all the numbers that were chosen.

(PC-SIG Disk# 1750)

Special Requirements: *None.*
Author Registration: *None.*

Lottery Player III 🖎
by Suzanne Spencer Software

LOTTERY PLAYER III offers a variety of systems you can use to try to win the lottery! A database for each of the 27 different lotteries is included.

LOTTERY PLAYER III is completely menu-driven and provides the following options by lottery:

❑ Trends/patterns — displays recurring numbers and probabilities
❑ U-pick your numbers — you select your own "lucky" numbers and the program analyzes your chance of winning
❑ The hot numbers — which numbers appear the most often as winners
❑ Most frequent digits — which numbers are most often selected
❑ Quick pick numbers — let the program pick your numbers for you
❑ Performance analysis — an extensive analysis is performed on the entire database
❑ Hot and cold numbers — which numbers occur the most often/least often

Lottery Player III (PC-SIG Disk# 1485)

LOTTERY PLAYER III includes databases for the following lotteries; Arizona, California, Colorado, Connecticut, Delaware, Florida, Iowa, Illinois, Kentucky, Kansas, Lotto America, Maryland, Massachusetts, Michigan, Missouri, Ohio, New Jersey, New York, Oregon, Pennsylvania, Tri-State, Virginia, Washington, Washington DC, and West Virginia.

(PC-SIG Disk# 1485)

Special Requirements: *None.*
Author Registration: *$15.00*

Lotto Buster ✍   *by FreeBooter Software*

If your dream has always been to strike it rich in the Lottery, maybe FreeBooter's LOTTO BUSTER can help you reach that goal. Lotto Buster now has the 12 most popular U.S. Lotteries along with an easy-to-use database program that will allows you to store your local Lotto drawings so you can track which numbers are hot and which numbers are not! With a little bit of research — the program works best when you can investigate at least the last 100 Lotto drawings — you may be able to turn the odds into your favor by examining the patterns in your Lotto series.

An easy-to-follow setup menu configures the program to your particular system before you can begin — after that it's up to you to enter the correct Lotto information. Color screens (if available on your system) and pull down menus also add to the usability of this program. Different "types" of information can be viewed — frequently picked numbers, less frequent numbers, and the "hot" sheet which selects the hottest numbers based upon the last twenty weeks of history. You can also pick your own numbers to wheel. Remember, without history, this program is valueless!

(PC-SIG Disk# 1735)

Special Requirements: *312K Ram.*
Author Registration: *$29.95*

Lotto Challenger ✍   *by Data Solutions*

LOTTO CHALLENGER is a commercial quality lottery number selection program designed for use with all Pick-5, Pick-6 and Pick-7 lottery games. Some of its functions can also be used with Daily 3 or 4 digit number games.

Using statistical analysis, LOTTO CHALLENGER analyzes the numbers drawn in previous drawings. Numbers are broken down into several categories: hot, cold, overdue, last drawing, 1 to 12, 13 to 31, and 32 and up. Averages and percentages are calculated from all the previous drawings for the above categories. A quick picks menu option generates numbers to play based on previous drawing statistics. A "winner's circle" menu option compares the numbers on your tickets to the numbers drawn.

All program functions are menu driven and easy to use with the keyboard or a mouse. Data entry screens prompt the user and will not allow invalid entry, and a pop-up help window is always available. All this, combined with colorful sliding screens, make LOTTO CHALLENGER an enjoyable program to use.

LOTTO CHALLENGER can be easily configured for any state lottery. It is distributed with two current Florida state lottery data files which can be used to explore and learn how to use LOTTO CHALLENGER. A state data file of your choice will be mailed to you at no charge when you register.

(PC-SIG Disk# 1906)

Special Requirements: *None.*
Author Registration: *$29.50*
➤ *ASP Member.*

Lotto Fever   *by L and H Enterprises*

LOTTO FEVER is a synthesis of astrology and lottery simulation with a sprinkling of numerology. Told the date and year of your birth, it gives your astrological forecast and a description of your personality. Next, it asks for the range of numbers for the lottery you are playing. LOTTO FEVER chooses numbers and shows your lucky lotto numbers, based on the data you have given it.

NOTE: The program will not display your lotto numbers on a monochrome monitor. If your system has a monochrome monitor, you must have a printer in order to see your numbers.

(PC-SIG Disk# 929)

Special Requirements: *CGA.*
Author Registration: *$9.00*

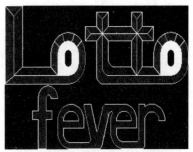

Lotto Fever (PC-SIG Disk# 929)

Lotto Magic Wheel ✍   *by Herb Rose*

One of the most effective ways to play the lottery is to "wheel" a set of numbers. Wheeling numbers involves playing a large selection of numbers and combining them into bets to cover all or most of the possible combinations of numbers. This produces the widest possibility of having some kind of a winning ticket. Serious lotto players have known about this for years. Unfortunately, setting up your own wheeling system can be very tedious work, especially if you play several lotteries.

That's where LOTTO MAGIC WHEEL and your computer come to the rescue. They will take the drudgery and guesswork out of wheeling numbers and provide sophisticated selection techniques such as balanced sets, odd/even distribution, number range selection and Key number usage. These selections are appropriate for any PICK-5, -6 or -7 lottery.

Now you can concentrate on the important things — such as how to spend your winnings.

(PC-SIG Disk# 1552)

Special Requirements: *Hard drive recommended.*
Author Registration: *$15.00*

Lotto Master Professional
by JPM Computer Products

LOTTO MASTER PROFESSIONAL is a multifeatured menu-driven program that assists you in making decisions about placing Lotto bets. The program is primarily designed for use with California Lotto 6/49, but can be used with other five or six-number lotteries, as long as the number field does not exceed 54.

The extensive program is designed to maintain and track LOTTO bets, check bets against the LOTTO drawings, maintain a history of winning numbers, analyze historical numbers for significant information, generate bets based on statistical history, support bets based on user- selected numbers with statistical backup, and perform "wheeling" based on nine built-in systems.

LOTTO MASTER PROFESSIONAL has a utility option that allows you to customize your game set up. This program is accompanied by an on disk user's guide.

(PC-SIG Disk# 1318)

Special Requirements: *None.*
Author Registration: *$25.00.*

Lotto Prophecy
by Charles P. Staats

LOTTO PROPHECY is a new and interesting lottery prediction program. It contains two prediction systems which allow you to use the program with any lottery that has a "pick 6" format. LOTTO PROPHECY also contains a wheeling system, which lets you choose a large group of numbers in any lottery game, play a special set of combinations of those numbers, and get a minimum win guarantee.

(PC-SIG Disk# 1616)

Special Requirements: *512K RAM.*
Author Registration: *$15.00*

Lotto Prophet by DataMicro ✍
by DataMicro, Inc.

LOTTO PROPHET has been completely redesigned, rewritten and expanded to become a very complete lottery software package. Point-and-shoot screens and well-documented programs make it nice to look at and easy to use. The best just got better. PROPHET is a lottery statistical compiler and forecaster.

The program has four main parts:

❏ Allows for file control, update, editing, and it sorts and prints the files showing repeat numbers
❏ Produces statistical reports based on the most frequent numbers, current HOT numbers, numbers that have appeared the most with other numbers, and numbers that have appeared the most in a specific month. Prints prophet cards, graphs, trend charts, and more.
❏ Stores numbers and checks for winners for up to three different lotteries at a time. Each lottery can have eight players, with up to six scores each. Prints a report on the players and their scores plus the results of the drawing—four out of six, etc. Great for groups of players.
❏ Selects numbers for you with the Prophet's Prognosticator, if you prefer, and expresses an opinion of them. Works on all the state LOTTOS, Australian Gold and Canadian 6/49.

LOTTO PROPHET can help you predict, store and check your numbers using the latest scientific methods or you can let the opinionated randomizer pick them for you. Good fun!

(PC-SIG Disk# 1006)

Special Requirements: *Two drives and a printer recommended.*
Author Registration: *$39.50*
➤*ASP Member.*

Lotto-Magic
by Gary J. Vigue

Track your state lottery and watch your computer calculate the next most likely winning numbers, generate random numbers or compute your lucky numbers based on astrological information.

The astrological option uses today's date and your birthdate to compute your lucky numbers, according to the stars. This is not a random number generator and your numbers will change from day to day.

Random picks are just that. Numbers generated at random. Many subroutines have been included to ensure a well-randomized output.

The scientific calculations are compiled by analyzing existing data of past winners. As each lottery occurs, enter that information into your lottery database. LOTTO-MAGIC will work with any lottery using from two to six numbers and will track up to five different games simultaneously.

(PC-SIG Disk# 1815)
Special Requirements: *None.*
Author Registration: *$10.00*

Lotto-Trax
by Paul Plosila

LOTTO-TRAX is a menu-driven system which helps you analyze, compare, forecast, display, store and maintain all your lottery numbers and those numbers selected by up to three different games. This package fits virtually every variation of lottery. No matter how your state changes the rules, you can quickly adjust LOTTO-TRAX to match. The system provides clear, on-disk documentation. If you're serious about the lottery, LOTTO-TRAX will give you lots of insights about what is happening.

(PC-SIG Disk# 1391)
Special Requirements: *CGA.*
Author Registration: *$15.00*

Lottopiks
by CrystaLines Ltd

LOTTOPIKS is a random number generator for playing six-number format state lottos. It sorts the numbers into ascending order and displays a screen of games. The Illinois and Missouri lottos are menued for the basic games, but other states' games can be easily configured with the program by setting that game's maximum high number (6 to 255).

(PC-SIG Disk# 789)
Special Requirements: *None.*
Author Registration: *$10.00*

Smart Money
by M.E. McCan

SMART-MONEY promises to pick lucky numbers for you for any state lottery, horse race, Keno, etc. This random number generator comes with a sense of humor and an odds calculator to show the probability of winning.

For team play, it offers a formatted agreement covering trustee, names of players, amount paid, number of weeks and how the money ought to be split. It can generate up to 100 sets of numbers and the largest number of each set can be up to 10 million.

(PC-SIG Disk# 1329)
Special Requirements: *CGA.*
Author Registration: *$15.00*

Super Lotto-Master
by Morris L. Bower

Anyone who believes no lottery system is truly random will find a friend in SUPER LOTTO-MASTER.

Not a random-number generator, but rather a historically weighted system, this program lets you enter past winning numbers for whatever lottery you are tracking. It then computes the odds of the numbers being picked again. SUPER LOTTO handles three, four, five, six and seven-number games and prints its choices in a list that ranks best to worst. You can also add in your own lucky number with the computer's — to hedge your bet. The program is menu-driven and requires no mathematical or computer skills to operate. As soon as you've entered at least 10 numbers, the program is ready to make predictions for you.

(PC-SIG Disk# 1407)
Special Requirements: *None.*
Author Registration: *$15.00*

Winning Edge-Lotto
by Fusion Software

THE WINNING EDGE-LOTTO is a complete system of lottery game management, providing the eight most popular methods of lottery number selection and explaining the theory for each. The program is extremely easy to learn and use and could improve your chances to become a better lotto player.

Choose from a selection of lottery numbers using the eight most popular methods: non-random analysis, hot numbers, cold numbers, hot & cold numbers, random numbers, defensive random theory, trend analysis and numerology.

Record lottery tickets purchased and lottery numbers drawn in the past 52 drawings. The tickets bought will be checked for winning numbers after each drawing. Statistical tools are provided to analyze past data. An automatic or manual wheeling system is also available.

THE WINNING EDGE-LOTTO can be used for all lotteries ranging from Pick Four of 40 to Pick Eight of 80. The program is completely menu driven and extensively documented.

(PC-SIG Disk# 1865)

Special Requirements: *None.*
Author Registration: *$35.00*

▼ ▼ ▼

Mail Lists, Address Managers, and Telephone Organizers

Address Book
by Aubrey L. Paverd

ADDRESS BOOK is an efficient way to keep the names, addresses, and phone numbers of your customers and vendors in good order and up-to-date. It is designed for a small to mid-sized company. Included is a way to add, edit and delete your addresses, and a printer menu to print any or all of your addresses. Keep track of your personal and business address and telephone lists with ease.

(PC-SIG Disk# 988)

Special Requirements: *None.*
Author Registration: *$25.00*

Address Manager
by CastleSoft

ADDRESS MANAGER helps you keep multiple databases of names, addresses, phone numbers, and useful comments. You can add new entries and delete or update current ones easily.

The program is especially designed to address envelopes — always a problem area, as well as print labels and even entire mailing lists. Labels can be printed on sheets from one to four across, and all entries can be sorted by zip code before printing.

ADDRESS MANAGER menus are function-key driven. On-line help is available from each menu. This provides a quick and user-friendly interface, one that is easy to learn and use.

(PC-SIG Disk# 218)

Special Requirements: *None.*
Author Registration: *$20.00.*

Bulkmail
by Peak InfoSystmes, Inc.

Made for businesses and nonprofit organizations, BULKMAIL is a heavyweight mailing list manager designed to make the job of preparing U.S. domestic bulk mail as fast and easy as possible.

Written in C language for maximum speed, BULKMAIL is a work horse able to handle the management, sorting, and printing of up to 32,767 address and name records. And it has well thought out features to help you churn through the tiresome process of getting 3rd class mail out the door.

Filters allow you to select records by a starting name or an ending name, a starting zip code or an ending zip code, a starting date or an ending date, two flags, and an alphanumeric category field. Add to this sixteen switches in each record that can be used in any combination to select or reject records. All records are maintained in both name and zip code sequence. You can re-sequence at any time to refilter records to include those only of interest. You can sort by telephone number.

Well crafted templates speed record updating. Template changes can be made on the fly. When you print using zip code order, BULKMAIL marks labels so you'll know when to tie off bundles without counting. BULKMAIL lets you protect your data disks with passwords.

If you use form letters, BULKMAIL data files can be created to be compatible with Micropro International's MailMerge form letter feature along with a number of other word processors.

The program allows you to configure your printer output to a specific label output. It will also transfer a subset of one mailing list to another. It imports ASCII files and allows you to purge subsets of records from a mailing list.

(PC-SIG Disk# 1527)

Special Requirements: *None.*
Author Registration: *$50.00*

CataList ✍
by Automation Consultants, Intl.

CATALIST is a comprehensive list manager to produce labels, envelopes, Rolodex cards, and bulk-mail flyers. It formats data from each entry that is easily merged into more than 15 of the most popular wordprocessing packages, including PC-Write. The program can also format for foreign addresses, including postal codes for 106 countries.

At least one help screen is given for each main screen in the system, giving beginner and intermediate users plenty of needed help. For data entry and modification, a legend is shown at the bottom of each screen defining the function keys and their specific functions.

ASCII file format is used thorughout the entire database system, which helps in compatability with most other software in the computer world.

(PC-SIG Disk#'s 864, 865)

Special Requirements: *Two floppy drives or a hard drive.*
Author Registration: *$69.00*

Catalist (PC-SIG Disk# 864)

Contact Plus ✍   *by E Trujillo Software*

If you are looking for a client tracking system for your business, your dream has come true. Introducing CONTACT PLUS, an electronic rolodex which will do everything at a push of a button.

CONTACT PLUS features:
- ❑ full-featured Word Processor
- ❑ mail/merge for mass mailings
- ❑ multiple databases
- ❑ rolodex cards
- ❑ user-defined date fields
- ❑ mailing labels
- ❑ user-defined index fields
- ❑ autodialer
- ❑ elapsed phone call timer
- ❑ phone call history
- ❑ colorful calendars and screens
- ❑ phone call graph
- ❑ automated follow-up schedules
- ❑ correspondence history
- ❑ ticklers/reminders
- ❑ unlimited date-stamped notes
- ❑ call analysis reports (who didn't you call?)
- ❑ extensive online help (over 2000 lines of help)
- ❑ 24 categories to classify your contacts
- ❑ Boolean search compatibility on categories
- ❑ interface to word processor with form files
- ❑ interleaved letter/envelope printing
- ❑ local and long distance dialing prefixes
- ❑ popup lookup and data entry windows
- ❑ keeps track of holidays/vacations
- ❑ reschedules your outstanding ticklers.

(PC-SIG Disk# 2190)

Special Requirements: *Hayes compatible modem. CGA and hard drive recommended.*
Author Registration: *$79.00*

Dmail   *by Telemedica*

DMAIL makes advanced mailing list functions a snap because of its new pull-down menus. DMAIL makes mailing list management a breeze. Create any number of master and subsidiary lists, tag addresses with key words, sort on any of nine fields and target mailings down to the city block. Print addresses directly on envelopes if you prefer not using computer labels. It also prints Rolodex cards as well as two different kinds of quick-reference lists. If you are sending personalized letters DMAIL will also create name and address files for Word Perfect, Microsoft Word and Wordstar.

✍ = Updated Program
☆ = New Program

DMAIL makes it a snap to identify and locate those individuals in a master list who have something (anything) in common. Through the key word tagging feature you can automatically create a sub-list of people who satisfy any condition you choose. Lists can be joined, split, and sorted according to your particular needs.

DMAIL is being used by institutions and businesses that need to organize mailings to as many as 15,000 people. It eliminates repetitive typing, and has added reporting features, and a streamlined envelope printing function. It is completely menu-driven. The number of addresses stored is limited only by disk space.

Features include:
❏ Copy selected addresses from one list to another.
❏ Target your mail by City, State, Zip Code, Area Code, key word etc.
❏ Classify addresses with key words or your own coding system.
❏ Perform key word searches and duplicate checking.
❏ Print with any dot matrix or daisywheel printer.
❏ Print addresses on one-up or two-up labels.
❏ Print from 1 to 99 copies of each label.
❏ Automatically record mailing date when addresses are printed.
❏ Redirect printer output to a disk file.
❏ Uses dBase/FoxBase compatible address files.
❏ Uses pull-down menus — the choices available are always on the screen.
❏ Provides automated file backup and restore.
❏ Displays in monochrome or color.
(PC-SIG Disk# 1172)
Special Requirements: *640K RAM and a printer.*
Author Registration: *$35.00*

Doctor Data Label ✍ *by Doctor Data Software*

DOCTOR DATA LABEL is a professional mailing list manager designed for adding, editing, organizing and printing mailing lists, including international mailings. Print on any size label (up to nine labels across), rolodex cards, postcards, and envelopes. Print multiple copies of a single label.

DOCTOR DATA LABEL has an optional carrier route presort number for all its data entries for bulk mailings. You can index, filter, or sort using all fields, as well as rename, copy, delete, join, divide and backup the data files. Also included is a 47,000+ city, state and zipcode database. It automatically inserts cities, states and area codes upon the zip code you enter. If there is more than one city for the zip code, selection is allowed.

Other features include:
❏ Files created with DOCTOR DATA LABEL are compatible with dBASE III.
❏ Allows up to one billion records per database file with unlimited files.
❏ Up to five automatically updated indexes per database.
❏ A notes field to store up to 64K of miscellaneous information.
❏ Allows international addresses.
(PC-SIG Disk# 943)
Special Requirements: *512K RAM and two floppy drives.*
Author Registration: *$59.00*

Easy-Plan *by AAA Data Systems*

EASY-PLAN stores names, addresses, telephone numbers, and comments. This program can be used to create mailing lists of customers and suppliers for your business or for personal mailing labels.

In addition to mailing labels, you can print a variety of reports from the data entries. Each record contains the company name, personal name, address, home and work phone, and an additional note or memo. Records can be added, edited, deleted, viewed, and searched. Sort according to one of the selections provided or according to your own customized index.
(PC-SIG Disk# 1541)
Special Requirements: *300K RAM, and a printer and labels.*
Author Registration: *$99.95*

EasyDial ☆
by Patri-Soft

Use your computer modem to dial your telephone for normal voice communication. Too many numbers to remember? EASYDIAL is for you.

Use EASYDIAL to call your bank — EASYDIAL remembers both the bank phone number and your account number. A few keystrokes will do it. Run from either the command line or in full menu mode. Track the total time of a call and enter a comment for each one.

(PC-SIG Disk# 2778)

Special Requirements: *None.*
Author Registration: *$20.00*
➤*ASP Member.*

Fone: Business
by Eugene L. Woods, PE/EE

If you are a small business or home computer user looking for a way to bring long distance telephone bills under control, FONE™ BUSINESS can help you reduce and track telecommunications costs. FONE™ is a mature telephone call pricing database program for point-to-point, voice, FAX, E-mail, and BBS calls.

FONE™ will display the approximate prices for national interstate long distance calls. Several major business telecommunication vendors are represented (AT&T, ITT, MCI, US SPRINT, etc.), including many services for each vendor. For each query, FONE™ will display the point of origination, time, point of destination (over 1200 cities are in the national database), approximate call BEFORE IT IS PLACED, the vendor ID, effective date of the rates, call billing periods, and applicable times for the lowest rates. At the press of a button, FONE™ will track the price of an ongoing call in real time.

Several user options, using F-keys, are available, including adjustment of sample call times, volume discount calculation, the ability to temporarily exit to DOS while the timer is running, plus many other features. A personal directory with notepad, for tracking contacts, is provided, and the user can get a printed report for each call displayed on the rate screen.

FONE™ is very easy to use, features hot menus, and an extensive help facility.

(PC-SIG Disk# 1729)

Special Requirements: *None.*
Author Registration: *$6.95 per disk, or $14.95 for the set of three disks.*

Fone: International
by Eugene L. Woods, PE/EE

If you are a home or small business computer user looking for a way to bring international telephone bills under control, you might be interested in FONE: INTERNATIONAL. FONE™ comes in three versions, each on its own disk; one for business users, one for residential users, and a third for international callers.

FONE will display the approximate prices for international calls to over 130 countries. Several major telecommunication vendors are represented (AT&T, ITT, MCI, US SPRINT, etc.), including many services for each vendor. For each query, FONE™ will display the point of origination, time, point of destination (several major cities in each country are in the international database), approximate call cost BEFORE IT IS PLACED, the vendor ID, effective date of the rates, call billing periods, and applicable times for the lowest rates.

At the press of a button, FONE™ will track the price of an ongoing call in real time. Several user options, using F-keys, are available, including adjustment of sample call times, volume discount calculation, the ability to temporarily exit to DOS while the timer is running, plus many other features. A personal directory with notepad, for tracking contacts, is provided, and the user can get a printed report for each call displayed on the rate screen.

The menu prompts can easily be used by someone with little computer experience, so the lack of a manual is not a problem.

(PC-SIG Disk# 1728)

Special Requirements: *None.*
Author Registration: *$6.95 per disk, or $14.95 for the set of three disks.*

Fone: Residential
by Eugene L. Woods, PE/EE

If you are a home computer user looking for a way to bring long distance telephone bills under control, FONE™ RESIDENTIAL can help you reduce and track telecommunications costs. FONE™ is a mature telephone call pricing database program for point-to-point, voice, FAX, E-mail, and BBS calls.

✍ = Updated Program
☆ = New Program

FONE™ will display the approximate prices for national interstate long distance calls. Several major telecommunication vendors are represented (AT&T, ITT, MCI, US SPRINT, etc.), including many services for each vendor. For each query, FONE™ will display the point of origination, time, point of destination (over 1200 cities are in the national database), approximate call BEFORE IT IS PLACED, the vendor ID, effective date of the rates, call billing periods, and applicable times for the lowest rates.

At the press of a button, FONE™ will track the price of an ongoing call in real time. Several user options, using F-keys, are available, including adjustment of sample call times, volume discount calculation, the ability to temporarily exit to DOS while the timer is running, plus many other features. A personal directory with notepad, for tracking contacts, is provided, and the user can get a printed report for each call displayed on the rate screen.

FONE™ is very easy to use, features hot menus, and an extensive help facility.

(PC-SIG Disk# 1730)

Special Requirements: *None.*
Author Registration: *$6.95 per disk, or $14.95 for the set of three disks.*

Lst-Mgr   *by Donald G. Harbaugh*

LIST-MGR searches for a text string or set of strings and selects records from a text file such as a list of addresses, clients, customers, members, etc.

Each retrieved record can have up to five labeled fields (e.g., name, street, city-state-zip, expiration date, notes). The number, length, or sequence of fields need not be the same for different records.

You can send selected records to screen, printer, a new disk file, or any combination of these. You can change the within-record field sequence in the output records, omitting some fields altogether if you want.

(PC-SIG Disk# 935)

Special Requirements: *None.*
Author Registration: *$15.00*
➤*ASP Member.*

M-Label ☆   *by R.K. West Consulting*

M-LABEL customizes labels, index cards, continuous-feed envelopes, etc., when working with mailing lists created by MAILLIST (PC-SIG #1506).

Choose from 1 to 4 labels across, 1 to 100 lines long, widths up to 250 characters, top and left margin padding, and distance between labels. Pick exactly which fields go on which line. User-defined fields allow you to insert any text into the printed output.

(PC-SIG Disk# 2745)

Special Requirements: *PC-SIG #1506 and 360K RAM. Hard drive recommended.*
Author Registration: *$39.00 (includes MAILLIST)*
➤*ASP Member.*

Mail It!   *by Itasca Softworks*

Print mailing labels without investing in an expensive or hard-to-learn database program. With point-and-click menus, it's perfect for small businesses, churches, interest groups, etc.

MAIL IT is flexible enough for most mailing needs. It lets you enter up to 1,000 individual records and search most fields for information to be printed. Several label-printing options are offered, but label printing is limited to single-column labels. And, there's even a help file of state abbreviations.

(PC-SIG Disk# 1064)

Special Requirements: *None.*
Author Registration: *$15.00*

Mail Monster ✍   *by PTD Software Systems*

MAIL MONSTER is an extremely flexible mailing label manager for any sized application. You can define the categories to fit your lists of people and/or organizations.

You can organize your mailing lists and print highly specialized selections. You can add, edit, sort, and print mailing labels in many different configurations. For example, print only those labels that need to reach a specific group — by targeted organization, zip code area, etc. Also included is a mailmerge feature to merge-print letters, as well as a personal telephone directory.

(PC-SIG Disk# 483)

Special Requirements: *384K RAM and hard drive.*
Author Registration: *$15.00.*

Mailing List Management DataBase   *by Edward B. Toupin*

Does your business need to track customer contacts and print mailing labels for customer information? The MAILING LIST MANAGEMENT DATABASE can do both jobs for you.

The MAILING LIST MANAGEMENT DATABASE uses a single entry screen and a series of pop-up windows, selected by function keys. These pop-up windows allow you to see the main entry screen as you select a particular function. You'll never lose sight of your data.

The database can maintain an unlimited number of files with up to 1,000 records per datafile. A fast search function will search through the selected data file for a particular record number, name, company, state, category, and/or ID number. A file backup feature is included to safeguard against data corruption. A file export function will allow the data to be sent to a file that can be imported to dBASE III+, LOTUS 1-2-3, or any word processing system with an ASCII import feature.

(PC-SIG Disk#'s 1702, 1703)

Special Requirements: *640K RAM and a hard drive.*
Author Registration: *$25.00*

Mailing-Made-Ez   *by Computeledge*

This address manager/mailing label system is so easy to use that you won't even need to read the instructions. Intuitive design and pop-up menus will guide you through the entire program.

The pop-up menu command consists of self explanatory choices like add, browse, delete, edit, find, print, and a few more. These are all you need to work with most mailing lists. If you should ever need more power, your data files can be crunched by any database software that uses standard dBASE file format.

(PC-SIG Disk# 1795)

Special Requirements: *512K RAM, and two floppy drives or a hard drive.*
Author Registration: *$25.00*

Mass Appeal   *by Mass Appeal Software*

MASS APPEAL doesn't just address envelopes and print mailing labels, it creates mail merge files for all the major word processors, dials the phone, allows you to disable fields you don't need, and utilizes macros to speed data entry, and reduce errors. Many powerful features found only in high-end multiuse databases have been fully integrated into MASS APPEAL such as field default values, copy fields from the previous entry, and advanced sort capabilities.

MASS APPEAL is a fully menu-driven program, requiring little or no knowledge of database management programs. All the "grunt" work has been done for you, allowing you to concentrate on maintaining your mailing list. Don't worry about how to generate a report — reports are plentiful.

A companion program Zipp Appeal, PC-SIG disk #1921, allows you to enter the name of the city and state by simply typing the zip code. Or you type the city and the zip code is found.

(PC-SIG Disk# 1920)

Special Requirements: *512K RAM, and two floppy drives or a hard drive.*
Author Registration: *$49.95*

MAST Mail   *by Micro Automation Software Tech.*

MAST MAIL's focus is on making the interaction between user and computer smooth and simple, yet it is an advanced and versatile mailing list manager. The commands for elementary tasks essential to a mailing list, such as adding, editing, finding, and deleting data, are direct and straightforward. More powerful features include an unlimited comment area for each record, user-definable group and company number fields, as well as prefix, suffix, and salutation fields. There is even an undelete function.

Clear menus list and describe the command options on the screen and point to the on-line manual, which is just one keystroke away. MAST MAIL also provides command level functionality for other essential tasks such as reports, labels, envelopes, Rolodex cards, merging, exporting, and importing.

MAST MAIL works well as a contact, lead, or direct mail program for salespersons. With MAST MAIL's comment field you can store and track pertinent information on each of your clients. A complex record selection feature makes MAST MAIL a productive tool for anyone who needs to phone, write letters, or send memorandums to selected people in the database. You can also create multiple lists that are separate from one another.

MAST MAIL is also an automated on-line Rolodex card system. Names, addresses and phone numbers can be accessed in a fraction of the time of conventional Rolodex cards. MAST MAIL can even speed dial your phone with only the touch of two keys.

Data files are fully compatible with dBase III/III+ data files, making it possible to use your MAST MAIL data with any other database program that makes use of this file structure. For mail merge, the secondary merge format of WordPerfect is supported, as well as two merge formats for PC-Write.

(PC-SIG Disk# 1564)

Special Requirements: *512K RAM, and a hard drive or two floppy drives.*
Author Registration: *$35.00*

MEMBERSHIP LIST
by Lloyd C. Bowen Jr.

MEMBERSHIP LIST AND MAIL LABEL PROGRAM will keep track of the members of any club and will print out address labels. Each member record includes name, address, home and work phone number, whether or not dues are paid, the date when the dues are up, and the committee the member belongs to. Each record may be edited, viewed, searched for, or deleted. The program can print the addresses on mail labels (single and multiple), mail envelopes or folders, cards or large labels, or customized labels. MEMBERSHIP LIST AND MAIL LABEL PROGRAM allows you to print the address records by any field of information, including by a particular date fees are due. You may also print the addresses by selected members or by members sorted according to those who have paid their fees and those who have not paid their fees.

(PC-SIG Disk# 1696)

Special Requirements: *None.*
Author Registration: *$20.00*

NamePal
by WR Software

NAMEPAL is the complete automatic address book. It keeps lists of names, addresses, phone numbers, and related comments, and prints them in a pocket-size "book" you can use anywhere. NAMEPAL works on plain paper with any printer — even lasers. You can optionally print on both sides of each page, and you can code your data to keep track of club members, birthdays, babysitters, or any other grouping. It also performs other handy tasks, like printing mailing labels, Rolodex card files, and full-page rosters. NAMEPAL is also completely menu-driven, and has on-line help screens.

(PC-SIG Disk# 706)

Special Requirements: *None.*
Author Registration: *$19.95*
➤**ASP Member.**

NamePal (PC-SIG Disk# 706)

PC-Mail
by Foto 64 Inc.

PC-MAIL is a menu-driven mailing list and address management program which will print mailing labels, keep track of addresses and allow you to delete the older ones.

PC-MAIL's sort function alone makes it worth the money. With this, you can sort on any field in a matter of seconds. All menu routines provide a listing of the options available to the user, making the program easy to use. Each program function opens with an introductory screen, explaining the functions provided. Just follow the instructions on the screen and it will explain what to do next.

The type and size of labels are user-specified. Widths can run from 2½" to 5" and height ranges from 1" to 2½."

PC-MAIL is not just another mailing list program, but a fully-functional package which will greatly assist you in your home or business.

(PC-SIG Disk#'s 868, 869, 1475, 7072, 7404, 7447)

Special Requirements: *Two floppy drives and a printer.*
Author Registration: *$30.00*
➤*ASP Member.*

PC-Mail (PC-SIG Disk# 868, et al.)

PC-Names   by WR Software

Tired of looking through your little black book only to find the numbers have faded or are so messy you have no idea what they are? Well, you're in luck! PC-NAMES, a combination mail list manager and address book program, stores an unlimited number of names and prints many mailing label and report formats. In addition, it prints pocket-sized address books in several sizes and styles. And it even prints address books on both sides of the page.

PC-NAMES features a phone dialer, mailing labels, Rolodex cards, automatic sequence by name or zip code, five report formats, envelopes, automatic vertical address centering and blank line suppression, large five-line address formats, personal and business name formats, hot key for individual label or envelope printing, two phone numbers per name, portable pocket-size address book, mail merge with five levels of salutation defaults, export, import, categories for grouping names, duplicate search, documentation on disk, user-defined custom label sizes, and support for dot matrix, laser, and impact printers.

(PC-SIG Disk# 2181)

Special Requirements: *512K RAM.*
Author Registration: *$18.00*
➤*ASP Member.*

PC-Names (PC-SIG Disk #2181)

PC-Postcard Plus 🖎   by Foto 64 Inc.

PC-POSTCARD PLUS uses standard dot-matrix printers to produce and address postcards with your custom business announcements, reminders and social invitations. The program even handles double postcards!

With first-class mail costs rising skyward, postcard mailings have suddenly become the darling of thrifty businesses and organizations. Get first-class delivery and immediate attention for postcard prices. Here's a program that lets you produce customized postcards — both singles and doubles, with or without a mailing permit — and even individually addresses them.

Using standard-sized (4x6) pin-fed postcards, PC-POSTCARD PLUS prints a message 22 lines by 55 characters, an address, and an optional header for the return address, postal mailing permit stamp, etc. It has formats for messages on both sides of a single or double postcard. (Double postcards are great because they allow for a tear-off response card for orders, RSVPs, etc.)

PC-Postcard Plus (PC-SIG Disk# 1361)

Addresses are automatically inserted as each card prints. Mailing lists can be built, added to, and sorted by up to 10 different fields.

Since PC-POSTCARD PLUS was written by Carl Mieske, author of PC-MAIL (See PC-SIG disks #868, #869), PC-MAIL mailing lists are compatible for use with this program, but are not required.

(PC-SIG Disk#'s 1361, 2561)

Special Requirements: *Pin-feed index card stock, a dot-matrix printer with tractor feed.*
Author Registration: *$25.00*
➤*ASP Member.*

🖎 = Updated Program
☆ = New Program

PC-Speedy Mailer
by Foto 64 Inc.

Have you ever wondered how those credit agencies, schools, and other businesses get the carbon envelope message mailers produced? Well wonder no more because it's easier than you might think.

PC-SPEEDY MAILER is a self-prompting menu-driven program which supports the development, printing, and addressing of continuous feed message mailers measuring $5^1/2$" x $8^1/2$". With PC-SPEEDY MAILER you may create a mailer message consisting of up to thirteen lines consisting of 60 characters. This message may be edited, saved to a disk file, and be recalled at a later time for editing or printing.

With PC-SPEEDY MAILER, businesses can recognize a significant saving in mail costs when communicating with clients. In a matter of minutes a message can be typed and printed for mailing. There is no need for art work production, printing, and envelope stuffing. The cost of labor and materials savings can be significant.

PC-SPEEDY MAILER was designed as a companion program to PC-POSTCARD. During printing, the user may merge address files developed with this program.

PC-MAILER was designed for use by the inexperienced because little is required of the new user. It makes liberal use of information and help screens, is menu-based, and is interactive with the user.

With PC-MAILER, your computer will become a powerful tool for maintaining contacts with friends, clients, and business associates.

(PC-SIG Disk# 1557)

Special Requirements: *IBM or compatible printer.*
Author Registration: *$30.00*
➤*ASP Member.*

PCFDial ☆
by Barn Owl Software

PCFDIAL, a 7K swapping TSR, dials phone numbers displayed by other programs (such as your favorite database software). It can dial "vanity" numbers like 800-IBM-DISK, keep a log of calls, and display the local time for any area code. Additionally, PCFDIAL pops up at regular intervals to let you know how long you've been on the phone (especially useful to salesmen who must "close the deal" in a certain length of time). Context-sensitive Help is available.

(PC-SIG Disk# 2689)

Special Requirements: *Hayes compatible modem.*
Author Registration: *$19.00*
➤*ASP Member.*

Phone
by Jose R. Pico

PHONE is a simple, easy-to-use telephone dialing program that delivers as much, or more than, it promises. The author says he tried to make his program fast, simple, versatile, easy-to-use, fun, useful, and colorful. And he did! PHONE makes phone calling fun. The program is easy and straightforward to use, and the screen is well organized and attractive.

PHONE will hold 19 separate databases with 21 phone numbers per database. It is usable from a floppy or hard disk. It was intended to avoid "ram wars" by being non-resident, but you can use the PHONE from DOS without actually entering the program.

(PC-SIG Disk# 1726)

Special Requirements: *Modem.*
Author Registration: *$10.00*

Phone by Vision Computing ☆
by Vision Computer

PHONE is a custom database manager with a little extra pizzazz. Besides tracking names, addresses, and phone numbers, PHONE can print labels, tell you the postal abbreviation for any state, and run on a network. PHONE has the usual database features for editing and searching, plus handy extras such as record backup and automatic directory creation.

(PC-SIG Disk# 2763)

Special Requirements: *None. A hard drive and printer are recommended.*
Author Registration: *$20.00*

Phone Caddy ✍ *by Micro Data Assist*

PHONE CADDY is a complete mailing list manager. It lets you update and maintain your mailing list and prints addresses on labels, rolodex cards (two sizes), and standard office envelopes. You can even specify the size of the labels.

Each PHONE CADDY address record includes fields for an ID number, group code, whether it is for an individual or business, first and last name, spouse name, address, and home and work phone number. For businesses, an extra address line is included along with a contact name. You select the order of printing according to any field in the record and also select the group of addresses to print according to the group codes.

(PC-SIG Disk# 1154)

Special Requirements: *512K RAM and two floppy drives.*
Author Registration: *$15.00*

PHONEMAN Personal Phone Book Manager ☆ *by TASCS Company*

Throw away those note pads and paper scraps with scribbled addresses. PHONEMAN helps you to computerize your phone number list.

Type in names, addresses, and phone numbers — PHONEMAN does the rest. Each phone book holds up to 1,000 entries, and you can have multiple phone books. Once the names and numbers are in PHONEMAN, it's easy to make changes with this completely menu-driven system. Create mail lists or phone lists with any printer, including HP-laser printers. If you have a modem, PHONEMAN will dial numbers for you. Includes a screen saver and mouse support.

(PC-SIG Disk# 2514)

Special Requirements: *None.*
Author Registration: *$22.00*

Pocket Filer & Pocket Notes *by CBT Horizons*

POCKET FILER and POCKET NOTES are two programs that make double-sided pocket address or note booklets from the entries in the program.

Entries can be edited, deleted, sorted, searched, and saved. Print a hard copy in a pocketbook format that will fit into a checkbook cover. Each program also allows you to page through and browse the records.

(PC-SIG Disk# 896)

Special Requirements: *Printer.*
Author Registration: *$25.00*

PRO-DEX Database Management System *by ISS Technologies*

PRO-DEX is a Rolodex tracking system that stores and maintains an index of names, addresses, telephone numbers, and other vital data.

Add, edit, delete, search, view, or print information. Search by name, address, city, state, firm/company, or title/position. Each entry includes a standard industrial code, a business/home phone, date of contact, a staff initial of connected person, and a comments section.

Flag each entry for mailing and labels, or to call again on a future date. The entry will appear on the appointments screen when the date is within two weeks of the current date. Print single mailing labels, all names flagged for mailing, or all names flagged with a particular status. The utilities menu lets you backup files, update the index, specify the drive/path setting, and enter your company name to be displayed on the logo of the program.

(PC-SIG Disk# 927)

Special Requirements: *512K RAM and two floppy disk drive.*
Author Registration: *$50.00*

Reliance Mailing List *by Reliance Software Service*

RELIANCE MAILING LIST is a fast and sophisticated mailing list program that should be useful to many groups, including political parties, charitable organizations and small businesses.

Print mailing labels four-across, select groups of people from the database by specifying up to eight criteria and create a mailmerge file. Handle as many records as you have disk space for.

(PC-SIG Disk# 503)
Special Requirements: *Two floppy drives and a printer with 132 column mode.*
Author Registration: *$25.00*

Zipkey ✍ *by Eric Isaacson*

With ZIPKEY no one with a PC will ever again have to manually type in the name of a United States city or town (at least not one big enough to have its own zipcode).

When run as an ordinary program, ZIPKEY allows you to instantly access any of the 43000+ zipcodes in the directory by searching by zipcode, by state-and-city, or by city-only. But ZIPKEY is at its best when installed permanently in memory. In this "memory-resident" mode, you can invoke ZIPKEY from within any other program (a wordprocessor, a database manager, etc.). You can type just a 5-digit zipcode, and ZIPKEY will fool the program you're running into thinking that you have typed any or all of the following: the city name, the state name and/or abbreviation, the zipcode, and any other combination of fixed keystrokes. This "keystroke output" can be in any format you wish.

ZIPKEY is completely configurable. You can specify any combination of keystrokes (the "hotkey") that will invoke ZIPKEY. You can also specify alternate hotkeys to allow differing configurations of ZIPKEY to be available at the same time.

(PC-SIG Disk# 1767)
Special Requirements: *Hard drive recommended.*
Author Registration: *$30.00*
➤*ASP Member.*

Zipp Appeal *by Mass Appeal Software*

ZIPP APPEAL is a companion product to Mass Appeal mailing manager, PC-SIG disk #1920. Essentially, ZIPP APPEAL is a large data file that links cities to zip codes and zip codes to cities. While working in Mass Appeal, if you enter the zip code ZIPP APPEAL will find the city and state and automatically insert them into the data entry screen.

With ZIPP APPEAL installed, you can also enter the name, or partial name of a city, and browse through a list of possible zip codes and states for the entry. You are allowed to page forwards, backwards, and even find another city if you like.

When ZIPP APPEAL is on your hard disk, Mass Appeal automatically senses the presence of the zip code data file, and inserts the city and state for over 95,000 U.S. zip codes (Also available in a smaller, 40,000 version)!

(PC-SIG Disk#'s 1921, 1922, 1923)
Special Requirements: *Hard Drive and the Mass Appeal Mailing Manager, PC-SIG disk #1920.*
Author Registration: *$39.95*

▼ ▼ ▼

Maintenance, Record Keeping

EIMS *by I.J. Smith*

This program maintains an equipment inventory, user-defined maintenance costs, and scheduled maintenance for each equipment item. Maintenance can be scheduled for almost anything. Although based on time schedules, this can still be used for periodic checks of other maintenance-based systems.

With EIMS, a quick check can be made periodically to see what maintenance is due, or you can print scheduled maintenance reports on a timely basis to stay on top of things. A date prompt is provided to enter a future date to plan a schedule for perhaps a week or month ahead of time.

The program offers virtually unlimited record capacities. It also uses auto lookup tables and scrolling record windows for ease of use. It will even blank your monitor screen after 10 minutes of inactivity.

(PC-SIG Disk# 1843)
Special Requirements: *512K RAM. A hard or high density drives are recommended.*
Author Registration: *$35.00*

Maintenance DBS
by H&P Software

MAINTENANCE DBS is ideal for the person in charge of maintenance for a large corporation or building. It records what maintenance was done, who did it, and where it was done. Then it keeps a running record of maintenance due: where, when, and what is needed. It tracks purchase orders by date, number, and the department to which the work is charged. Basically, MAINTENANCE DBS covers most of the important paperwork a maintenance director faces.

Simple to run, MAINTENANCE DBS allows you to set up your own fields and records if the suggested ones do not match your operation. It tracks up to 120 records per file. Each file tracks records for a month-long period and contains up to 414 characters, or six lines of data, at 69 characters per line.

(PC-SIG Disk# 1625)

Special Requirements: *None.*
Author Registration: *$10.00*
➤*ASP Member.*

▼ ▼ ▼

Maps

Vacation Planner ✍
by Ron Volkmar

The nicest thing to happen to car trips since highways, VACATION PLANNER gives you personalized trip information on the shortest route, cities en route, mileage, and travel time. It takes your starting city, all the interesting intermediate spots where you want to sightsee, and your destination city, and calculates the shortest route. It also tells you the distance between each town along the way, and the time and distance it takes.

VACATION PLANNER manages to give you all this information quite painlessly. There is step-by-step documentation if you feel you need it, and a special two page "Easy-Doc" instruction set for all of us impatient people. VACATION PLANNER offers clear menu choices and an option that keeps the instructions on screen while you follow them. VACATION PLANNER comes with a general USA map and detailed California state map.

VACATION PLANNER doesn't ask much of you and gives back a lot. If you're planning any trips out of town this year, plan to consult VACATION PLANNER first. Don't leave home without it!

(PC-SIG Disk# 2148)

Special Requirements: *None.*
Author Registration: *$20.00*

World City Distance Computer
by GeoGraphics Software

The WORLD CITY DISTANCE COMPUTER is designed to provide distance and travel time information between more than 400 different world cities, including most major US cities. The program is windowed, menu-driven and self-explanatory.

(PC-SIG Disk# 1127)

Special Requirements: *None.*
Author Registration: *20.00*

The World Digitized
by Allison Software

The WORLD DIGITIZED is a compilation of more than 100,000 points of latitude and longitude that form the outlines of the entire world's coastlands, islands, lakes, and national boundaries in great detail.

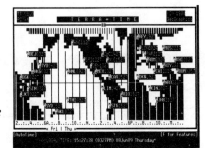

World City Distance (PC-SIG Disk# 1127)

The data is organized by continent. Disk 494 is required to expand the data to ASCII and also contains Africa, Antarctica, Australia, and South America. Disk 495 contains Asia and Europe. 496 contains North America and Greenland.

As distributed it is a pure database and has no programs to display the data. The basic display disk is made available to those who register. It contains two display programs: a user-modifiable BASIC version and a more advanced windowing version written in C and requiring a mouse. It also contains programs to reduce the number of data points and to transform the data for Mercator projection.

It really is a small world and now you can have it all.

(PC-SIG Disk#'s 494, 495, 496)
Special Requirements: *Hard drive recommended.*
Author Registration: *$12.00*

World29 by Robert L. LLoyd, Jr.

The world at your fingertips! Just like having a globe and atlas in your computer. View any place in the world in various scales. Learn national capitals. Track hurricanes or anything that has location. Single track mapping. Find distance between locations. Point to a location and get an expanded view. Play "Name the City, over 200 cities pinpointed. You can even add your own cities to the maps or your own maps.

World29 (PC-SIG Disk# 1392)

(PC-SIG Disk# 1392)
Special Requirements: *CGA, EGA, or VGA.*
Author Registration: *$10.00*
➤*ASP Member.*

▼ ▼ ▼

Math and Geometry Programs

Algebrax by Professor Weissman's Software

Cringe no more when menaced by that ominous-looking algebra problem! You now have ALGEBRAX to help you overcome your fear of mathematics. Some of the enhanced features in this package which are hard to find in other tutorials are:

❑ Random generation of all problems — you will never have the same problem twice
❑ There are five levels of difficulty for each lesson plan with five questions at each level
❑ After each correct answer, you will be branched to a more difficult problem
❑ There are no multiple choice problems (sorry, no guessing)
❑ Alternate answers are accepted. Most programs will allow one correct answer only, but ALGEBRAX knows there are different ways to write mathematical solutions
❑ When a wrong answer is given, ALGEBRAX will take you through the problem step-by-step
❑ All lesson results are saved by the program and can be reviewed on screen or printer

Most important of all, ALGEBRAX was written by a math professor with over 25 years of experience.

(PC-SIG Disk# 1456)
Special Requirements: *CGA card.*
Author Registration: *$30.00*

AnyAngle ✍ by Rite Item

Pythagoras would be proud! But if you don't know who Pythagoras is, you probably don't need this program. Ancient Greeks notwithstanding, most people do not appreciate the mathematical beauty underlying the simple triangle. If you yearn to become enlightened, though, this is the place to start!

ANYANGLE takes the drudgery out of capitalizing on the mathematical elegance of the triangle. If you provide a minimum amount of data about a triangle, this program computes the rest, solving for unknown angles or side lengths given what you have available.

Even if you're not a surveyor or trigonometry buff, you could use this program to calculate the height of the trees in your yard, plan your next woodworking project more rationally, or even landscape in the Greek tradition (Thomas Jefferson did, the hard way!).

Triangle aficionados will appreciate the analysis section of the program which provides such esoterica as area, perimeter, altitude, coordinates of vertices, and data about the inscribed circle and circumcircle.

(PC-SIG Disk# 1756)
Special Requirements: *384K RAM and CGA or Hercules graphics.*
Author Registration: *$19.95*

Are You Ready For Calculus?
by David Lovelock

A well-written pre-calculus tutor program designed to help students review the basics of algebra and trigonometry.

These programs give quizzes on those sections of algebra and trigonometry essential to calculus. There are two programs, one to prepare you for Calculus I, and another for Business Calculus. The differences are that the quizzes are easier in the Business Calculus section and there are fewer topics to review.

You'll have several choices to choose from. The instructions are written so you can start using the program right away. The quizzes are multiple-choice and the different answers are well chosen. The program is conveniently presented to the user with different window layouts.

If you don't know how to answer a particular question, ask for help. You'll get a help screen which covers the topic of your quiz.

Are You Ready For Calculus? (PC-SIG Disk# 858)

If you want to take calculus next quarter or semester, this program is for you.

(PC-SIG Disk# 858)

Special Requirements: *None.*
Author Registration: *None.*

Curvefit
by Thomas S. Cox

Burnt out on Euclid? Got the Newton blues? If you're a weary mathematician or a bogged-down high-level math student, CURVEFIT is an excellent program for you. CURVEFIT performs a least-squares curve fit on X, Y data. Curves for 25 equations are fitted. Equation coefficients, correlation coefficient, and best fit are computed with your data. CURVEFIT can make predictions for Y in any of the 25 equations. Residuals are calculated. The program does not include any graphics.

(PC-SIG Disk# 707)

Special Requirements: *None.*
Author Registration: *$10.00*

DAN (Data Analysis) ☆
by Jeffrey Kochy

DAN allows entire data files to be used as variables in formulas! What an idea! List, print, or plot the "manipulated" data in a fraction of the usual time.

DAN comes with 21 sample algorithms ranging from the mundane (gas and electric bill data) to the sophisticated (biorythms, 3-D equations, and electrical filters). This is a top-flight, well documented package for math students and teachers, engineers, and scientists. Combine math operators, including log and trig functions, with constants and data file names in algebraic expressions. Graphs can be plotted in linear, log, or polar coordinates. A wide range of printers is supported.

(PC-SIG Disk#'s 2602, 2603)

Special Requirements: *384K RAM and graphics card. A hard drive is recommended.*
Author Registration: *$40.00*

DataPlot
by Peter Ho

Here's a useful two-dimensional plotting system for scientific and engineering data which is powerful enough to produce publication quality graphs.

Capabilities include:
- Polar and linear plots
- Menu-driven operation
- Full-function graph setup editor
- Support for a variety of graph types, axis and plot styles
- Spline curve smoothing

✍ = Updated Program
☆ = New Program

❑ Linear and single-cycle/multiple-cycle log plots
❑ User definable graph types, axes styles, grid scales, data legends
❑ Plot up to 25 curves with unlimited data points
❑ Plot graphs can be saved to disk or sent to dot matrix or laser printer or HPGL compatible plotters
❑ Supports CGA, EGA, VGA and Hercules displays
❑ Supports optional mouse and math coprocessor.

(PC-SIG Disk# 1059)

Special Requirements: *HPGL compatible plotter and CGA, EGA, or Hercules Graphics.*
Author Registration: *$68.00.*

Differential Equations and Calculus   *by Byoung J. Keum*

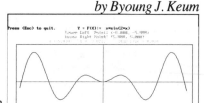

These programs visualize and solve high-level mathematical equations, conveniently graphing them for you on an EGA monitor. Great for students, scientists, or anyone who just enjoys math.

The DIFFERENTIAL EQUATION program can solve a variety of both ordinary and partial differential equations. You can also integrate factors of an equation, and create a graph of power series solutions.

Use the CALCULUS program to find the derivatives of an expression in x and/or y. Other features include graphing functions of y=f(x), graphing first and second derivatives, solving and graphing parametric equations, finding the integral of simple functions, and finding the surface contour of a function z=f(x,y). An MS-Windows version is available for registered users.

Differential Equations and Calculus (PC-SIG Disk #1072)

(PC-SIG Disk# 1072)

Special Requirements: *EGA.*
Author Registration: *$30.00*

EPISTAT   *by Epistat Services*

EPISTAT has a set of routines for analyzing small data sets, and is for users well-versed in math and computer operations. The entire package is fairly complicated and definitely not recommended for the casual user. However, for anyone with a special interest — chemistry, biology, or psychology students who need a number-crunching routine in their workflow — it can be a boon.

All of the programs are written in BASIC and the source code is included.

(PC-SIG Disk# 88)

Special Requirements: *A version of BASIC.*
Author Registration: *$25.00*

File Descriptions:

AUTOEXEC	BAT	Batch file to auto boot program.
ANOVA	BAS	One and two way analysis of variance.
CORRELAT	BAS	Calculates Pearson's correlation coefficient.
CHISQR	BAS	Chi-square test.
BINOMIAL	BAS	Binomial distribution.
BAYES	BAS	Bayes theorem to calc rates of false + and - tests. DATA-
ONE BAS	Mai	data entry program.
EPIMRG	BAS	Used by every EPISTAT program.
EPISETUP	BAK	Backup for EPISETUP.DAT.
EPISETUP	DAT	Used by every EPISTAT program.
FILETRAN	BAS	Transfers data from one data file to another.
EPISTAT	BAS	Guides user to proper program to use.
FORTRANS	BAS	Transfers FORTRAN to EPISTAT files.
FISHERS	BAS	Fisher's test to evaluate 2X2 tables of discrete values.
LNREGRES	BAS	Two variable linear regression.
HISTOGRM	BAS	Graphs data sample on CGA screen. NORMAL BAS
Calculat	s	
normal d	str	ution.
MHCHISQR	BAS	Mantel-Haenszel Chi-square test.
MHCHIMLT	BAS	Mantel-Haenszel Chi-square test for multiple controls.
MCNEMAR	BAS	McNemar's test or paired Chi-square test.

SELECT	BAS	Select subset of a data set.
SCATRGRM	BAS	Graph scattergrams.
SAMPLSIZ	BAS	Calculates sample sizes for statistical significance.
RATEADJ	BAS	Rate adjustment program.
RANKTEST	BAS	Three tests - signed rank, rank correlation and rank sum.
RANDOMIZ	BAS	Random sample generator.
PRINTDOC		Documentation file (25K).
POISSON	BAS	Calculates Poisson distribution.
T-TEST	BAS	T-test compares mean of 2 samples (paired and unpaired).
XTAB	BAS	Print crosstab reports.
EXAMPLE		Sample data set.

Equator
by Fernandez Enterprises

EQUATOR's purpose is to help you learn the function, use, and application of various general purpose formulas used in the fields of finance, math and science. It consists of 63 equations divided equally among the three subjects. Each equation appears on its own menu-driven screen or worksheet. EQUATOR is designed to let you experiment with each equation as much as you like. The more you work with an equation, the easier it is for you to understand it, remember it, and use it at home or at school.

The following are some of the equations in the math menu of EQUATOR:

❏ Area of a square, rectangle, circle, and triangle
❏ Circumference of a circle
❏ Volume and surface area of a cone
❏ Distance between two points

❏ Hypotenuse of a right triangle
❏ Volume and surface area of a cylinder
❏ Volume and surface area of a sphere

The following are some of the equations in the finance menu of EQUATOR:

❏ Simple and compound interest
❏ Payoff balance on a loan
❏ Earnings per share
❏ Years to 2X investment and return needed to keep up with inflation
❏ Monthly mortgage payments and annual simple interest rate on loans

❏ Equivalent taxable return of a non-taxed investment
❏ Gross and net profit margins
❏ Price/earnings ratio

The following are some of the equations in the science menu of EQUATOR:

❏ Celsius to Fahrenheit; Fahrenheit to Celsius
❏ Average velocity
❏ Acceleration
❏ Work
❏ Pressure

❏ Density ratio
❏ Metric to English; English to metric
❏ Force
❏ Power

(PC-SIG Disk# 249)

Special Requirements: *None.*
Author Registration: *$35.00.*

Equator by Pulse Research ☆
by Pulse Research

EQUATOR facilitates quick and easy entry, storage, and evaluation of equations. The program automatically decodes the equation on the screen, recognizing functions and standard constants. Greek and special characters are available. Once entered, the equation is stored in a categorized file for easy future access. Graphs of the results or other text data files may be plotted with linear or logarithmic axes on the screen, graphics printer, or on an HPGL plotter. EQUATOR helps by calculating optimum ranges for the axes which the user may accept or redefine before plotting the graph.

Features:

❏ Symbolic equations
❏ Inspection of each graph data point with cursor
❏ Complex numbers
❏ Variables and constants stored for reference
❏ Automatic graph scaling
❏ Graphs on HP LaserJet, IBM, and Epson printers.

❏ Report-quality linear or logarithmic graphs
❏ Trigonometric and hyperbolic functions
❏ Greek and special characters
❏ Context-sensitive Help system
❏ Menu-driven

(PC-SIG Disk# 2770)

Special Requirements: *CGA, EGA, or VGA, and a hard disk or high density drive.*
Author Registration: *$29.00*

Evaluate ✍ *by Dirk Heydtmann*

EVALUATE fills a niche in the computer mathematical analysis market. Although there are many calculator emulators, there are not many programs that allow you to enter complex equations as they are written and then, by hitting the return key, get them solved. In fact, EVALUATE solves as you write, providing intermediate results whenever there are enough logical operators entered.

EVALUATE will solve problems such as pi^2*sin(log(tan(x1))) if you enter them as written. This can be accomplished via a dialogue box or simply by entering the formulae at the command line. A very wide variety of operations are supported, including sophisticated date and statistical functions. It can operate in terminate and stay resident (TSR) pop-up mode, and can print its results.

(PC-SIG Disk# 1904)

Special Requirements: *None.*
Author Registration: *$15.00*
➤*ASP Member.*

Formula I ☆ *by Intelligent Educational Software*

FORMULA I is the first part of a two-part program which teaches a complete Algebra course — from basic addition to imaginary numbers. Written for high school and college students, its design makes it available to anyone who wants to acquire Algebra skills.

FORMULA 1 is the joint effort of a physicist with many years of experience in teaching and tutoring math, and a psychologist who specializes in the use of the computer as a teaching tool. State of the art Artificial Intelligence techniques imitate the actions and recommendations of a human tutor. The tutor checks your progress and guides you through the course, the same way a human tutor would.

You may choose not to use the electronic tutor. Decide which topics you want to study and in what order. The tutor will not prevent you from doing this, but it will make a comment if it "thinks" there is a better choice you could make!

The shareware version contains three of the nine tutorials which make up the entire course. The "Introduction to Numbers," the "Introduction to Fractions" and the "Quadratic Equations" tutorials have been included in full. The Pre and Post Tests for the other six tutorials are included to allow you to assess what the tutorials on these topics will cover.

(PC-SIG Disk# 2787)

Special Requirements: *None.*
Author Registration: *$49.50*

Graph *by Pacific Software Design*

GRAPH allows you to generate a myriad of strange two-dimensional shapes by plotting two individual waveforms on a cartesian (or two dimensional) plane, even if you don't understand the math behind how it works!

Most of the shapes this program produces are by nature abstract. However, with some practice it is possible to gain a talent for creating shapes that are easily recognizable to us as familiar objects.

From the main screen you will fill four boxes with basic trigonometric waveforms, their durations and amplitudes. Each one of these boxes makes up one user controlled "oscillator." Despite the technical terms, GRAPH looks (and acts) a lot like a video game, because the "controls" are easy to operate and the program in itself is extremely interactive.

The program is then ready to plot. Relax and enjoy the show, you'll be entertained and may even learn something.

(PC-SIG Disk# 1909)

Special Requirements: *512K RAM, EGA, VGA, or Hercules graphics (math coprocessor recommended).*
Author Registration: *$25.00*

Interactive Matrix Calculator *by Mountain Home Software*

Data collection for statistical analysis is made easier with MATRIX CALCULATOR. Twenty matrix areas, numbered from 1 to 20, can store 150 elements each. Since the matrices are in contiguous blocks, the capacities may be enlarged by, for instance, using every other matrix. This strategy results in 10 matrices with a capacity of 300 each. One operation at a time is performed; i.e., only one multiplication, one addition, etc. Results may be displayed at any time using the Print command.

The idea of the INTERACTIVE REGRESSION program is that the researcher knows his data best. Rather than provide canned variable selection routines, the researcher is prompted for the next step each time the model changes due to the addition or deletion of a variable. At any particular step, variables that are in the equation may be deleted, or variables which are not in the equation may be added. No provision is made for residual analysis since no data is stored. This is a serious limitation of the program in terms of modern regression analysis procedures.

(PC-SIG Disk# 823)

Special Requirements: *None.*
Author Registration: *$25.00*

Laser Graph   *by J.M. Baden*

LASER GRAPH is a group of programs, useful to engineers, for producing high resolution data plots using an HP LaserJet II printer. The types of plots LASER GRAPH is capable of producing are: single line, multiple line, three dimensional surface plots, X-Y plots, and scatter diagrams. The plots may be saved to a disk file; a program is included to review previously generated plots. It can print with a resolution of up to 2500 X 3000 dots (pixels), depending upon your printer. LaserJet soft fonts are supported, providing a high level of flexibility in font choice.

All of the elements of a really good data plotting system are here. It requires patience and diligence to become familiar with how it works but LASER GRAPH does produce stunning results on your laser printer. All plot commands may be entered on the DOS command line. This allows a string of plot commands to be put in a batch file for execution without requiring constant user intervention.

(PC-SIG Disk#'s 2027, 2308)

Special Requirements: *512K RAM, CGA, EGA, or VGA, hard drive, and DOS 3.0 or higher.*
Author Registration: *$49.00*

LSTSQR   *by George Wall*

LSTSQR carries out a least-squares fit of data to a variety of functional forms including linear, logarithmic, polynomial and exponential. It allows multiple fits of the same data using the same or different functions without exiting the program. LSTSQR87 supports the 8087 math co-processor.

The program has many measures of quality-of-fit, including standard deviation and the 95% confidence interval. The program also graphs and prints the fit if desired. You can input data by keyboard or from data files.

(PC-SIG Disk# 925)

Special Requirements: *CGA.*
Author Registration: *None.*

Math Pak III ✍   *by Dalal Publishing Co.*

MATH PAK III is a set of tutorials to help improve your problem-solving skills plus mathematical conversion routines to speed up some math operations.

It contains a range of tutorials — from the very basic arithmetic functions of addition, subtraction, multiplication and division to solving quadratic equations, computing geometries and understanding trig functions. MATH PAK III will also read your own data files to solve quadratic equations, derivatives, linear equations, DEC-BIN-HEX-OCT conversions, trig functions, determinants and more.

MATH PAK III (PC-SIG Disk# 394)

It offers 80x87 math coprocessor support, context-sensitive help screens, fast execution and printing of trig tables and sample problems to solve. Registration includes a 50 page manual with examples and solved problems.

This set of programs can be used as an educational program to help expand your knowledge and appreciation of mathematics.

(PC-SIG Disk# 394)

Special Requirements: *None.*
Author Registration: *$9.95*

✍ = Updated Program
☆ = New Program

Math Tool ✍

by MJM Engineering

MTOOL is an easy-to-use mathematical tool used to define and analyze functions of a single variable. The speed, power, and ease of use make it ideal for science, engineering, and math students.

This program can evaluate a function for a range of points or for a single point of the independent variable. It can numerically evaluate derivatives and integrals. It can find solutions for the function, and it can plot the function using CGA, EGA, VGA, or Hercules Graphics.

(PC-SIG Disk# 1183)

Special Requirements: *CGA, EGA, VGA, or Hercules graphics.*
Author Registration: *$10.00*

Mathplot

by J.H. McCrary

MATHPLOT is a set of graphics-aided programs designed to help scientists and engineers analyze data. Routines are included for least-squares fitting polynomials to sets of data points, solving simultaneous linear equations, numerically integrating a curve defined by a set of data points, calculating simple statistical parameters for data sets, and for calculating the coefficients of a Fourier series for a periodic function described by a set of data points.

Programs are also included for calculating and plotting Fourier spectra and Bessel functions, for plotting data sets and for plotting and comparing user-specified functions with data sets.

(PC-SIG Disk# 1863)

Special Requirements: *CGA, EGA, VGA, or Hercules graphics and a graphics printer.*
Author Registration: *$25.00*

Mercury ☆

by Real Software

MERCURY is a program for solving equations similar to Borland's Eureka. Easy-to-use, interactive, and powerful, MERCURY evaluates mathematical expressions, solves for the roots of an equation, solves a system of equations, and maximizes or minimizes a function, with or without constraints. In addition, you can evaluate derivatives and definite integrals, plot one or more functions, and print a report or a graph.

MERCURY has a built-in editor, pull-down menus, online Help, and all the conveniences necessary to make it accessible to computer novices.

Find out why this program made the Top 10 Shareware list two months in a row!

(PC-SIG Disk# 2646)

Special Requirements: *640K RAM, hard drive, and graphics monitor.*
Author Registration: *$49.00*
➤*ASP Member.*

Plot

by Prowess INC.

PLOT is a set of quick, easy-to-use tools for technical plotting. It can handle rectilinear, polar and vector plotting. After plotting, you can review a tabulation of all plotted points (except for the vector program).

(PC-SIG Disk# 1013)

Special Requirements: *CGA and a version of BASIC.*
Author Registration: *$25.00*

Polymath

by Lobster Software

POLYMATH is a programming language much like Forth in structure, and developed to bridge the gap between programmable calculators and personal computer languages. Anyone in the scientific or technical fields will find this program extremely useful for its number-handling abilities and ease of use.

This language works much like the Hewlett Packard programmable calculator and can be used as a calculator. Those familiar with the HP Reverse Polish Notation (RPN) know how simply complex formulas can be entered into the calculator. POLYMATH uses this same scheme, but with defined words or functions. Most words are defined with very simple tasks and then used and integrated with other words to build more powerful functions. An entire programming dictionary of function words can then be developed.

POLYMATH has a wide variety of applications and special uses. It has strong on-line documentation which takes the first-time user through a menu-driven tutorial. It also has files that explain the syntax and use of any word currently in its main dictionary.

Included are a few dictionaries and application programs. A review of these programs will be very helpful when learning the language. It also features full graphics to round out the package.

(PC-SIG Disk# 606)

Special Requirements: *CGA, EGA, VGA, or Hercules.*
Author Registration: *$40.00*

SPlot ✍   by William Hood

SPLOT plots two and three dimensional data to the screen of a PC with CGA, EGA, VGA or Hercules graphics. The plot can be sent to an IBM/Epson compatible printer or a DHPGL compatible plotter.

It can produce these types of plots: line, smooth curve, scatter, step or histogram of up to 16,000 data points. Up to 200 sets of data can be plotted on the same 2-dimensional plot; multiple data sets can also be plotted as a 3-dimensional plot. Axes can be linear, log or normal probability with auto or manual scaling. Data can be fit by a spline or a least squares polynomial or exponential.

The program creates the plot by executing a set of plot commands which can be typed at the keyboard, selected from a menu or read from a command file. On most PCs, the program detects the type of graphics card and uses the highest resolution available.

(PC-SIG Disk# 2024)

Special Requirements: *CGA, EGA, VGA, or Hercules and Epson or compatible printer.*
Author Registration: *$20.00*

Symbol-Quest ☆   by Steffen Mueller

Test your logic (and luck) with SYMBOL-QUEST, a delightful combination of mathematics and mystery. Numerals encoded as symbols in simple arithmetic problems make very challenging puzzles. Ample on-line Help is available, so you can enjoy this game without being a math whiz.

(PC-SIG Disk# 2705)

Special Requirements: *EGA or VGA and a mouse.*
Author Registration: *$20.00*

Vibrating, Rotating, and Cooling   by Byoung J. Keum

VIBRATING, ROTATING, and COOLING is a program that allows you to view and manipulate surfaces that are created according to a mathematical function. This should be of interest to the math and engineering student and teacher.

The main program, SURFACE.EXE, has six predefined functions plus an option to create a mathematical function of your own. Once a function is chosen, the program graphically demonstrates the results of the function on a plane surface. During the graphic mode you can change the speed, the axis of rotation, and the magnification of the image. The program also has the option to include a trace of the image on the screen and a help window.

VIBRATING, ROTATING, and COOLING is a versatile program that is compatible with CGA, EGA, CGA with a monochrome monitor, and VGA. In addition to the main program, this disk has two demonstration programs for computers that have smaller memory. An MS-Windows version is available to registered users.

(PC-SIG Disk# 1182)

Special Requirements: *CGA, EGA, or VGA.*
Author Registration: *$30.00*

Vision Free Software   by Vision Information Services

VISION is a collection of six mathematical programs which will help ease the pain of certain sequential computations:

❑ DTF converts a real number into a series of fractions, each more accurate than the preceding one until the error is less than one part per ten million.

❑ FACT calculates the factorial for any input number and FFFF defines all prime factors and powers of a given factorial.

❑ GCD computes the greatest common divisor for any two integers.

❑ REDUCE defines a fraction as a product of prime factors and its real number equivalent.

❑ FACTOR determines the prime factors of a given number or declares that number to be prime.

❑ TEMPCONV converts temperatures between units Kelvin, centigrade, Fahrenheit, and Rankine.

All of these programs can be installed and used with or without a math coprocessor. Documentation is included on disk.

(PC-SIG Disk# 1378)

Special Requirements: *DOS 3.0 or later. Math coprocessor recommended.*
Author Registration: *None.*

XYPlot   *by Argonaut Systems*

XYPLOT provides you with a precise graph of your data for better visualizing mathematical, scientific, engineering, or business information.

This versatile program displays and prints fully calibrated XY graphs of up to 1500 plotted points drawn from equations, individually inputted data, or imported "fixed length record" data files common to most spreadsheets and databases. X versus Y plots can be produced in a variety of line textures. X and Y axes may be linear or logarithmic. The aspect ratio of the graphs may be selected as 1.5 or 1. This permits complex data such as a sine versus a cosine to be displayed as a circle rather than an ellipse. Display resolution can be 640 x 350 pixels (EGA) or 640 x 200 pixels (CGA). Mouse compatible, but not required.

Program Limitations: HP Laser printing, curve approximations, and bar graphs only available in registered version.

(PC-SIG Disk# 1515)

Special Requirements: *CGA and an Epson compatible printer.*
Author Registration: *$25.00*

XYSee   *by Insight Advantage*

Teachers will welcome this computer-aided instructional system when designing interactive tutorials and tests for high school and college level algebra, geometry and trigonometry. At last, here's a method for time-crunched teachers and concerned parents to provide special, individualized help for the struggling student and enrichment for the advanced student!

XYSEE enhances students' understanding by incorporating high resolution graphics to help them visualize the curve represented by a given equation, and the effect upon the form of the curve when parameters within the equation change. Tackles such subjects as points and lines, intermediate quadratics and trigonometrics, and advanced parametrics and composites. In addition, interactive coverage is extended to forms such as triangles, user defined polygons (structured spline and free-form), and designs utilizing artistic mathematics.

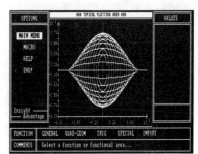

XYSee (PC-SIG Disk# 1507, 1508)

XYSEE's game module challenges the student to solve puzzles consisting of graphic representations of standard formulae. Imagine the excitement of a "Math Bee" or "College Bowl" pitting opposing teams in solving puzzle sets exhibiting complexities from ho-hum to horrific. The student's progress in solving each piece of the puzzle is displayed and special help is available for identifying boundaries and zeroing in on solutions. Teachers will appreciate the performance reporting module which tracks solution attempts by the student as well as difficulty levels attained.

The secret of this menu-driven instructional system lies in its use of macros which allow the instructor to formulate problems which demonstrate mathematical principles. All of XYSEE's macros, data-sets, and puzzles may be prepared with the "smart" capabilities of its fully integrated application sensitive editor. The intuitive structure and automatic validation abilities of the editor endow even casual users with the ability to quickly create scripts of any level of complexity.

System features include moving window displays, function-specific statistics, auto-scaling, and context-sensitive help screens. With progressive overlays and multiple import facility, the package offers plot enhancement techniques, and sound and color control. Both graphic and non-graphic printers are supported. A demonstration tutorial highlights program features and an extensive and well-written instruction manual is included.

(PC-SIG Disk#'s 1507, 1508)
Special Requirements: *CGA.*
Author Registration: *$30.00*

XYSolve
by Insight Advantage

Teachers will welcome this computer-aided instructional system for the design of tests and exercises for high school and college level Algebra, Geometry and Trigonometry.

XY-Solve challenges the student to solve a puzzle consisting of mathematical functions. Each piece of the puzzle represents a graphic solution to a standard formula. Puzzle complexity may be varied from simple displays of individual points or lines to extremely complex combinations of quadratics, trigonometrics, parametrics, and composite functions.

The student's progress in solving each piece of the formula is displayed and special help is available for identifying boundaries and zeroing in on solutions. A function teachers will appreciate is the performance reporting module which tracks the number of solution attempts by the student, and difficulty levels reached.

XY-SOLVE has seventeen "puzzle files" and the instructor can formulate additional problems by using the macro facility. Other system features include moving window displays, function-sensitive statistics, and context-sensitive help screens. Data can be imported in a variety of formats. Selectable sound and color options add impact to the lessons. An extensive on-disk instruction manual is provided.

See also XYSEE (PC-SIG disk number 1507 and 1508), a companion program.

(PC-SIG Disk# 1493)
Special Requirements: *CGA and a text editor.*
Author Registration: *$20.00*

▼ ▼ ▼

Menu Programs

Advanced Menu
by CMB Systems

Do you have problems in properly executing a DOS command, or getting immediate access to various programs and utilities on your computer? Are you tired of staring at a screen with no instructions to guide you? If this is so, you should take a look at ADVANCED MENU.

Most menu control programs use regular batch files to execute programs and DOS commands, but ADVANCED MENU also uses special command files that have more options.

Among these options are:

❑ Password protection for any menu selection, including DOS access
❑ Complete DOS commands entered
❑ Uncompleted commands finished
❑ Conditional command execution

A command file is created with the menu selections for the program. Each command file can have up to 32 menu selections with custom titles, and a menu command can load another command file. Command files can execute most DOS commands and work faster than regular batch files. ADVANCED MENU can handle an unlimited number of command files.

(PC-SIG Disk# 1050)
Special Requirements: *Hard drive recommended.*
Author Registration: *$39.95*

Automenu ✍
by Magee Enterprises, Inc.

AUTOMENU helps you control your computer in ways you only dreamed of before. Use the Menu Definition Language to create menus for accessing frequently-used programs. Forget obscure parameters while you perform DOS commands — execute application programs, batch files, and DOS commands with single keystrokes. Personalize your own menus.

AUTOMENU can prompt you for needed input for application programs. Chain from menu to menu with no limits on the number of menus. Demand different and unique passwords for different menu selections and use optional encryption of menu files. Take a nap while your computer executes menu selections according to the time of day. Short of memory? You can remove AUTOMENU from memory prior to starting an application program. Confused? Press "H" anywhere in the program for on-line help.

CGA, MDA, EGA, VGA, Hercules graphics displays and their compatibles are all supported. Try real-time switching between color and monochrome monitors. Use your mouse's sensitivity to navigate among menus. Prevent image-burning of your screen with automatic screen blanking and a periodically-displayed user message.

Highlight and select menu options: function keys, number and arrow keys, numeric keypad, spacebar, mouse or voice controller, date and time display. AUTOMENU features redirection capability and support for the ANSI.SYS driver. Five sections of the 114-page user guide are tutorials for inexperienced computer users. The option to network is available to advanced users.

Automenu (PC-SIG Disk# 608)

(PC-SIG Disk# 608)

Special Requirements: *Hard drive recommended.*
Author Registration: *$69.95*
➤*ASP Member.*

Awesome Menus (EGA)   *by Brian & Colleen Lawson*

AWESOME MENUS lets to start 20 of your favorite programs from a set of "Windows-like" set of pull-down menus. To add your favorite program to the menus, simply enter the title of the program, the exact name of the program file, and the path to the file. It's just that easy.

Another unique feature of this program is that it was made specifically for computer with EGA displays. This allows AWESOME MENUS to display a high quality digitized picture in the background of the pull-down menus. Choose your programs as you look at an astronaut on the moon, an elephant, a warrior, or a number of other pictures.

(PC-SIG Disk# 2469)

Special Requirements: *EGA or MCGA.*
Author Registration: *$6.00*

DAYO Brain ☆   *by TJS Lab*

DAYO BRAIN is a Job Scheduler and/or Menu system. Use the BRAIN to run any program or batch file during the day or night, manually or according to a schedule. Keep your computer(s) busy, even when you are not around!

The BRAIN can be scheduled to run jobs daily at a specific time, or every so many minutes, or run the jobs once, at a specific date and time. The BRAIN can also act as a Menuing system, allowing you to select and then run the job/program.

Features include: Multiuser, schedule report to printer or file, dBASE-compatible schedule database, PC Paintbrush or Micro Paintbrush (.PCX) screens and windows, passwords (4-digit code), keyboard locking, usage graph, disk status, variable speeds for the schedule, and more.

DAYO Brain (PC-SIG Disk# 2627)

(PC-SIG Disk# 2627)

Special Requirements: *512K RAM, EGA or VGA, a hard drive, a mouse, and DOS 3.3.*
Author Registration: *$50.00*
➤*ASP Member.*

DAYO Menu (Clock & Setup) ✍   *by TJS Lab*

DAYO MENU is a menu system for use with the DAYO line of business applications, as well as any other program on your computer. While it is multiuser when used on a PC-based LAN/Network, it can be run (like all DAYO products) as a 'standalone' application. The program is a QBASIC menu program and a DOS batch file that you can modify/edit. DAYO CLOCK is a simple clock display and optional alarm that can act as a job scheduler.

SETUP of the DAYO MENU (CLOCK & SETUP) disk is the setup system for the DAYO modules and is recommended, especially when the entire DAYO system is being installed.

DAYO is a collection of multiuser business applications that provide a means of managing inventory, purchasing, invoicing, customers, vendors, sales and more... All DAYO products are multiuser, designed to work on a Microcomputer (PC) Based Local Area Network (LAN), like Novell™. They can, however, work as a "standalone," running on a single PC.

To date, large and complex mulituser business applications required Mini and Mainframe computers, but because of products like the PC based LAN/ Network, they can now be run on microcomputers. DAYO is one of the first microcomputer based business applications designed to handle such a system.

DAYO Business Applications grow with your company. The ability to upgrade your system is available with the addition of other DAYO products. Source to DAYO is also available, allowing you to make further modifications and enhancements. DAYO Clock was written with Qbasic™; all others were written with Clipper™.

Current Modules:

❑ Inventory
❑ Smart Reports Point of Sale
❑ Materials Requirement Planning Price Book
❑ Menu Quotes
❑ Clock Index
❑ Payroll Passwords
❑ Update & Conversion Time & Billing

❑ Back Orders
❑ Accounts Receivable
❑ Accounts Payable
❑ General Ledger
❑ Look Up Databases
❑ End of Period/Purge

DAYO databases are all dBASE™ compatible, thus providing an additional or alternative source of support and reporting.

(PC-SIG Disk# 2395)

Special Requirements: *640K RAM, hard drive, and DOS 3.3.*
Author Registration: *$25.00*
➤*ASP Member.*

Directory Freedom ✍ *by Bit Masons*

DIRECTORY FREEDOM is intended for the person with a basic working knowledge of subdirectories, etc., by remembering filenames when, for example, they wish to selectively copy some files from a hard disk subdirectory.

It's a fast, compact (12K) alternative to a DOS shell and provides for selective file and directory operations (e.g., copying files), a scrollable environment for examining the contents of directories, and user-defined keys to operate on selected files. For example, define the CONTROL-F1 key to be an editor (e.g., QEDIT). Highlight a file in the directory, press CONTROL-F1 to move immediately into the editor and operate on the file. Colors, directory sort order, and the setting of the DOS Verify flag can all be customized.

(PC-SIG Disk# 2228)

Special Requirements: *DOS 3.3 recommended.*
Author Registration: *$20.00, $25.00, or $40.00*
➤*ASP Member.*

Easy Access ✍ *by Tengware Enterprises*

EASY ACCESS is an easy-to-use hard disk menu system that gives you usage logging, a screen saver, a calendar, and reminder functions. It lets you build your own custom menus and then select options, rather than having to remember specific program names, in order to run that program. You can control your system with just a few keystrokes.

EASY ACCESS gives you 16 options per menu, with unlimited submenus. You can set up user log-on ID's which restrict usage to users you've chosen. You can also track the use of particular options such as how many times an option is used, by whom, date and time, etc. A screen-saver option blanks the screen after a predetermined length of inactive time to prevent damage to the monitor.

You never have to miss another important date or appointment with the calendar and reminder option. The reminders can be set for: one time only, annually, monthly, quarterly, weekly, semi-annually, or every day.

(PC-SIG Disk# 1409)

    ✍ = Updated Program
☆ = New Program

Special Requirements: *None.*
Author Registration: *$25.00*
➤*ASP Member.*

EasyDOS
by Theodore D. Means

EASYDOS provides an easy-to-use menu for performing simple DOS operations. You do not have to know the complicated DOS syntax or command line parameters.

Select the letter of your choice on the menu to copy, erase, and rename files. Get a directory of a disk to view the files it contains. Change your CONFIG.SYS and AUTOEXEC.BAT files on your boot-up disk. View each file and either change it or leave it as it is. An on-line help function explains in detail each menu option in the program, and is very useful for DOS novices.

(PC-SIG Disk# 1176)
Special Requirements: *None.*
Author Registration: *$25.00*

EZ-Menu
by Micro Business Application

Show your PC who's in charge here anyway! EZ-MENU gives you a quick and easy way to run your programs while ending the clutter and confusion of scanning through directory and file listings. Handle 200 .EXE, .COM, .BAT and .BAS programs without breaking a sweat.

(PC-SIG Disk# 444)
Special Requirements: *A version of BASIC.*
Author Registration: *None.*

Front End
by Innovative Software Design

FRONT END is a fairly technical menu-development system of primary interest to programmers. Menus can be created for hard disks, or crowded floppies, allowing easy access to each program from the menu. The system lets you use nested menus (menu within a menu) for many more choices than would fit on the screen at once. You can also change the display colors and the size of the menu window.

FRONT END uses a unique programming language, similar in style to dBase III, and if you want to use this system's full potential, you should have at least brief exposure to some sort of programming; e.g., BASIC, dBase, or Pascal. The documentation concerns itself mostly with command syntax reference rather than programming techniques. There is a way provided to create menus without learning the language, but the full flexibility of the system is not truly available. The documentation provided (23 pages) is technically-oriented.

(PC-SIG Disk# 1301)
Special Requirements: *384K RAM.*
Author Registration: *None.*

HDM IV: Hard Disk Menu System 🖾
by MicroFox Company

HARD DISK MENU IV or HDM is a hard disk menuing utility of the finest commercial quality in a shareware package. Access and execute up to 100,000 different programs with this utility. HDM IV offers a multitude of features including multiple and independent menu modules with each having its own color and other set up characteristics, multiple levels of security, color and border control, mouse sensitivity, macros, command line arguments and the most striking ability to accomplish timed execution of programs; this latter feature being enough of a reason to purchase this utility! HDM IV can be operated within about 90% of it's abilities without ever consulting the documentation and the only confusion the user may encounter is centered around the use of macros and switching from one menu module to another. You will especially like the ability of HDM IV to execute programs at any time of day or week with it's "timed" program execution option. This feature alone is reason enough to purchase this splendid shareware utility. Jim Hass, the program author, offers various levels of licensing for HDM IV, beginning with a single user package rate of thirty-five dollars; the printed manual is an additional fifteen dollars. HDM IV offers all of the features of DIRECT ACCESS, a commercial hard disk menuing program, and a good deal more; a substantial value for your dollar!

(PC-SIG Disk# 631)
Special Requirements: *Hard drive.*
Author Registration: *$50.00*
➤*ASP Member.*

Icon Menu Selection Program ✍

by Vic Falgiano

Most menu programs are just a list of program names — BORING! That was until the ICON MENU SELECTION PROGRAM. Now your menus can include pictures (icons) to represent program selections, instead of just lines of text. It's also fun. Use the cursor keys or the mouse to select the icon/program you want to run, and off you go!

Icons are included for generic applications (word processing, kids games, etc.) and many specific applications (Lotus 1-2-3, Harvard Graphics, etc). In addition, you can create icons if you're using a paint or graphics editor that supports PC-Paintbrush files. While it takes a little more time to set up than other menu programs, the ICON MENU SELECTION PROGRAM is a great way to jazz up a computer or make it accessible to a child or anyone else who has trouble reading text-based menus.

Icon Menu Selection Program (PC-SIG Disk# 2516)

As an added extra, a disk catalog and label program for both 5.25 and 3.5 in. disks accompanies the package (currently supporting Epson or compatible printers only). The unique features of this program are the intuitive user interface ("pop-up" style windows), the ability to enter a bin number (for people with more than one disk box), and the ability to use more than one database file. Also, the program allows you to print a custom footer on the label such as "Property of: ..." as well as disk name, catalog number, and bin number.

(PC-SIG Disk#'s 2516, 2517)

Special Requirements: *512K RAM (EGA - 256K RAM). Hard drive & mouse recommended.*
Author Registration: *$24.95*

Instant Access Menu System

by Prodigy Technologies

INSTANT ACCESS MENU SYSTEM allows you to organize your software from one central program. Menu-driven and colorful, it can help you get the most out of your computer with the least amount of hassle.

Access any program you have on your disk from a menu. A one-letter selection will move you through the wilds of DOS paths, find your selection and start it. When you are done, it returns you to the control menu. A certain degree of experience with DOS will help you to configure the menus when you first set up the system, and provide you with the incentive to set up the system.

Included on the main menu with the system is a notepad, a text editor, a DOS shell, a time log and a screen dimmer. INSTANT ACCESS can be included in your AUTOEXEC file, and provision has been made to assign passwords to each program if you need to control access to specific software.

(PC-SIG Disk# 1577)

Special Requirements: *Epson compatible printer.*
Author Registration: *$10.00*
➤*ASP Member.*

LOGIMENU ☆

by Logivision Inc.

This is the new generation of DOS menu systems. Whether you want to access a few programs quickly and easily or need to turn on all the bells and whistles, LOGIMENU should satisfy you.

Extensive on-line Help, EGA/VGA 43/50 line mode, mouse, passwords, screen saver, hidden hot keys, and customizable Help. All this, plus an attractive presentation.

LOGIMENU can remind you of important dates with the Event Tracking feature. Furthermore, LOGIMENU does not use a single byte of memory while your own programs run. The automatic installation process scans your hard drive for popular programs. One of its three levels of installation will suit your needs perfectly.

With up to 50 items per menu, 50 sub-menus (multiple levels), 80 commands per item, and 30 general hidden hot keys. LOGIMENU has enough room to satisfy the most demanding user.

(PC-SIG Disk# 2622)

Special Requirements: *384K RAM and DOS 3.0+.*
Author Registration: *$50.00 + $5.00 S&H*
➤*ASP Member.*

    The PC-SIG Encyclopedia of Shareware   ✍ = Updated Program
☆ = New Program

Magic Menus
by CTech

MAGIC MENUS is a program that allows you to operate DOS and all your programs from simple pop-up menus. Specific DOS commands are also included for changing and listing directories, copying files, deleting files, renaming files, and setting the time and date. You can also run any other DOS command that you wish from MAGIC MENUS, or optionally return to DOS temporarily. MAGIC MENUS also has a DOS window in which you can execute DOS commands. It even remembers the last 10 DOS commands entered so that you do not need to retype them.

With this program you may also create up to 10 menus that can automatically execute up to 100 programs. These menus may include a short menu description, prompts to switch disks, prompts for additional command line information, and a password level to restrict usage.

Additional functions in MAGIC MENUS include menu options for sending printer control codes to the printer and a pop-up financial calculator. MAGIC MENUS can also define up to 10 options for your AUTOEXEC.BAT and CONFIG.SYS files.

A setup menu is included for screen blanking, screen colors, the video mode, a password system for the program, and general file paths. MAGIC MENUS also has context-sensitive help to further simplify the operation of DOS and other program applications.

(PC-SIG Disk# 1196)

Special Requirements: *Two floppy drives.*
Author Registration: *$29.95*
➤*ASP Member.*

Menu Construction Set
by Optimal Solutions of New Hampshire

This isn't merely another menu program, rather it is software that lets you construct customized and detailed menus. With MCS, you can create extremely clean menus, with no unnecessary distractions on the screen. The menus are not memory resident, and therefore use no additional memory.

Create attractive colorful menus with shadowing effects. Your menu choice can run a batch file, display an informational screen you create, or display another menu. MCS allows up to 100 items per menu and there's no limit on the number of menus in a given menu set.

The edit/construct mode uses "1-2-3 like" commands to walk you through the process of creating your own menu design. There are no documentation manuals with this program — that's how easy it is to use! Ideal for the system consultant or computer pro who needs to create a user friendly environment for computer neophytes. Full mouse and LAN support is provided.

(PC-SIG Disk#'s 1924, 2119)

Special Requirements: *384K RAM and a hard drive.*
Author Registration: *$47.50*

Menu Master
by No Sweat Software

Create customized menus to be "control centers" for running application programs and frequently-used DOS routines. For the novice, it saves a lot of frustration. For the more experienced user, it saves a lot of time.

You can run applications at the touch of a single key instead of typing in commands. No more forgetting commands or DOS directory names — all these are entered one time only and MENU MASTER remembers the commands for you. It frees you from having to remember and type those complicated commands — letting you concentrate on getting your work done.

Major features include:
- ❑ Menu settings entered directly from program — no text editor needed
- ❑ Ability to "chain" multiple menus together
- ❑ 24 menu items with user-defined prompts, passwords and paths
- ❑ Up to seven command lines per menu item
- ❑ Custom screen colors and individual menu prompt colors
- ❑ Personalized menu title with your own or company name
- ❑ Custom on-screen user notes
- ❑ Optional date and time display and clock chimes every hour
- ❑ Menu screen blanks after three minutes to prevent screen burn-in

❑ System password with extensive protection flexibility
(PC-SIG Disk# 1043)
Special Requirements: *None.*
Author Registration: *$30.00*
➤*ASP Member.*

Menu Master By Morgensen
by Phil Morgensen

MENU MASTER was designed specifically with ease of use and simplicity in mind. It can be set up or revised in just minutes, even if you have never used a hard drive before.

MENU MASTER has a total of sixty entries available to you. Thirty on the first menu and thirty on the second. You may not need all of these, but it's nice to know you have the capacity. MENU MASTER allows you to select either monochrome or color.

MENU MASTER lets you view any entry that has already been set up. In viewing you see the name that appears on the menu, the path to the subdirectory and the start-up command you entered at setup. If you desire to move the positioning of the entry to another entry location, you can.

(PC-SIG Disk# 1946)
Special Requirements: *Hard drive.*
Author Registration: *$10.00*

Menu, The
by Bill Joyner

THE MENU is a memory-resident program organizer that lets you access your programs with a single keystroke from a system of menus.

You can easily update and revise the menus with the editor provided. You can tailer the main menu, submenus, and keystrokes can be tailored to fit your needs. The editor can also edit batch files used for calling software programs while viewing the menu that uses them.

Included is an audible and visual appointment reminder which can be set for daily, weekly, monthly, and yearly intervals.

(PC-SIG Disk# 960)
Special Requirements: *None.*
Author Registration: *$9.95*

Menu-Matic
by BC Enterprises

MENU-MATIC is a hard disk menuing program that lets you access various programs on a hard disk by selecting a menu choice. The program allows you to have 80 options per menu file, with an unlimited number of menu files.

Some menus require a computer expert to set them up. Then, the user is stuck if he or she wants to add another menu option, or change the menu in any way. MENU-MATIC is written with the computer novice in mind; with its "Auto Generate" feature, you don't need to know complicated DOS commands to add another menu option. You type in the name of the program you want to add, and the rest is done for you.

Other features include screen-blackout, system statistics, time and date display, optional password protection, run-time parameters, usage tracking, timed execution of menu options, and keyboard macros.

(PC-SIG Disk# 1141)
Special Requirements: *Hard drive.*
Author Registration: *$35.00*

MenuEase ✍
by Creative Computer

MENUEASE is a program designed to help the user easily access application programs present on your hard disk. You can also create menu items which move an application program through up to 16 steps whenever you start it. Great for plowing through intro screens, or instantly getting to the portion of an application you usually use.

Features:

❑ Ability to save up to 16 command sequences per menu
❑ A menu can call any other menu

❏ Custom title setting for every menu choice
❏ Instant DOS access from within MENUEASE
❏ Colors customization for the menu display
❏ Passwords can determine access to menu items, menu maintenance, DOS access, and configuration
❏ Automatic screen blank after six minutes
❏ Context-sensitive help
❏ Logging of user, project, menu selection, date, time spent.
(PC-SIG Disk# 1835)
Special Requirements: *Hard drive.*
Author Registration: *$45.00*
➤*ASP Member.*

Menueze
by James Oh & James Oh Associates

Make menus to automatically load programs on your various disk drives. Put an automatic menu on each of the disks you use regularly.

You are prompted for the names of the programs you want included in a particular menu, then asked for the commands needed to run them. MENU-EZE lets you choose the colors for your menu screen and you can make a different menu for each of the disks in your library (including your hard disk).

(PC-SIG Disk# 936)
Special Requirements: *A version of BASIC.*
Author Registration: *$10.00*

MenuShow
by Superior Software Inc.

The PC programmer who needs a way to create professional menus will enjoy the colorful presentation of MENUSHOW. A viewer-paced demo shows how ASCII files are created and converted into a menu with the nice finishing touches you admire. MENUMAKE shows you how to create your own ASCII files. MENUSHOW then converts those files into a very attractive menu. While not recommended for the novice, it is well within the capability of programmers with mid-range skills. For anyone who wants quality output, it's worth the effort.

(PC-SIG Disk# 1410)
Special Requirements: *None.*
Author Registration: *$35.00*

MenuX
by Phil Faircloth Software

MENUX is a menu system that allows up to 4 menus on the screen at one time, and up to 10 options in each menu.

Features:
❏ 10,000 different options allowed
❏ Edit system colors
❏ Edit each menu's colors
❏ Save screen feature
❏ Password protection for each menu option
❏ Edit and change menu titles, prompts, and batch files
❏ Changing the date
❏ Changing the time
❏ Shell to DOS.
(PC-SIG Disk# 1788)
Special Requirements: *Hard drive recommended.*
Author Registration: *$19.95*

Mr. Menu
by Michael Dunne

MR. MENU can help you easily create simple menus for quick access to programs, files, and DOS functions.

You run programs by selecting a number from a menu or by highlighting a selection. You can also execute batch files. MR. MENU has multiple menus that let you easily move from menu to menu or return to the main menu. A maintenance program constructs new menus or modifies existing ones. You can either issue commands that are immediately executed or enter commands that require more input or parameters.

MR. MENU is memory-resident and is automatically returned to after the program or command is done. A configuration function lets you change the colors, default drive and directory, and opening screen titles.

(PC-SIG Disk# 944)

Special Requirements: *Hard drive.*
Author Registration: *$20.00*

Mymenu
by James Oh & James Oh Associates

MYMENU creates a start-up menu for your hard disk. A BASIC program is created by the program, and you provide a directory and the program name for each option in the menu. The menu can have up to 18 options, each having a short description of the program.

After the BASIC program is created, a few lines are entered into your AUTOEXEC.BAT file, and your menu is ready to go!

(PC-SIG Disk# 936)

Special Requirements: *A version of BASIC.*
Author Registration: *$10.00*

Navigator, The
by Edward Garrett

Steer your way around your hard disk with a sailor's ease. No need to keep your sextant at hand — NAVIGATOR knows how to direct you there. With this hard disk menu program, you'll get around without having to remember DOS commands.

You can access programs and directories with point-and-shoot menus. The program lists up to 200 directories, programs, and files when you boot up. Twenty-three files are displayed at a time. To access a directory, or run a program, point an arrow at it and press Enter. A handy command lets you instantly move to the root directory. You can quickly display or erase files and empty directories.

Ahoy, matey! Is that a .BAT file just above the horizon?

(PC-SIG Disk# 1279)

Special Requirements: *Hard drive.*
Author Registration: *$10.00*

Nifty
by Integra Computing

NIFTY helps new and casual PC users to create personalized menus to run programs, copy, or read files, and do other computer tasks at the touch of a key. It even offers password protection to submenus.

Memory-resident, NIFTY can be called up from DOS or popped-up by pressing a hotkey. When called, a help life jacket splashes onto the screen ready to save the new PC user faced with a formidable array of programs and a flat learning curve.

You can make easy-to-use menus that allow novices to quickly perform complicated computing tasks with little or no training. On-screen help files can be inserted to guide even the "first day" user through any computerized office operation. Passwords and security levels are available to control access to submenus.

Automatic program scheduling is another useful feature; you can set timers to cue and begin processing long or slow sorting and processing programs for the dead of night or other slow times.

(PC-SIG Disk# 1709)

Special Requirements: *None.*
Author Registration: *$50.00*

One View ☆
by COMEDIA

ONE VIEW is a complete DOS and hard disk management utility for MIS Managers and System Administrators. Monitor and control the activity of a computer station for up to nine different users.

Each user can quickly define their own menu to run specific application programs or issue DOS commands. Specify additional arguments on the command line for each application. Define whether or not ONE VIEW should automatically transfer to the directory of the program in order to access all subsidiary program files. As a DOS utility, ONE VIEW has easy-to-use pull-down menus and a directory tree display. Make, remove, rename and even hide directories. Tag specific files to copy, move, delete, rename, or change the attribute. Files can be encoded so that they can not be read or executed by other users. ONE VIEW has file-searching capabilities that work across all directories. Select a file and automatically execute the application program.

ONE VIEW is more than a typical DOS shell or file management utility — it is the type of complete management tool for a PC computer station that has previously only been available on mini- and mainframe computers. With ONE VIEW, an administrator can control and monitor all computer activities. The system administrator and each user must use a password to access their own menu, but the system administrator has complete access to the menu of each user. The administrator may set up all application menus for users who are not familiar with the system.

Reports and statistics can be generated recording the user name, the application, the date and time of execution, the amount of time the program was executed, and the amount of time there was activity with the application. The report or screen display of user activity can be sorted by user, by application, by amount of time in use, by amount of time working, or by date and is available in ASCII or LOTUS 1-2-3 format. ONE VIEW is the perfect program for all managers who need to monitor all computer activity, and while allowing each user to work independently.

ONE VIEW has an excellent file security system. For each application program or file, the administrator can restrict access to certain users. Even if a user exits to DOS, uses another bootable disk, or copies the program elsewhere, access to that program will be restricted. All invalid access attempts are recorded in the computer usage statistics.

ONE VIEW is a perfect way to let users have access to their own system and yet prevent unauthorized copies of software from spreading within the company.

(PC-SIG Disk# 2708)

Special Requirements: *Hard drive.*
Author Registration: *None.*

PC System Manager ☆   *by Morsoft*

PC SYSTEM MANAGER is a hard drive menu system to make life easier for any hard drive user. No more typing long DOS and program commands. Enter the command just once in PC SYSTEM MANAGER and have access to that command with just the touch of a key!

PC SYSTEM MANAGER remembers when it's time to run routine applications. Start up to 30 programs automatically based on time, date, day of week and day of month. Use password protection at the menu and/or program level to keep confidential files in the right hands. The user ID feature keeps track of who, when, and what was done on your PC.

The program produces four tracking reports. Other features include: window screens, pop-up messages, and a screen blanking option to prevent screen burn-in. PC SYSTEM MANAGER allows "reminder" notes regarding printer setup, disk insertion, etc., to be displayed before a program starts.

Customized prompts for command line replaceable parameters may be created. To get you started, a DOS menu is included with 16 useful commands. PC SYSTEM MANAGER is loaded with options but is surprisingly easy to learn. There's no need to learn a sophisticated menu language. The PC System Maintenance Manager walks you through adding, editing or deleting menu entries.

(PC-SIG Disk#'s 2502, 2503)

Special Requirements: *Hard drive.*
Author Registration: *$19.95*
➤*ASP Member.*

PC-Dashboard   *by No Sweat Software*

PC-DASHBOARD is a program menu system to make the operation of programs on a hard disk much easier and quicker. The program consists of a main menu and a virtually unlimited number of submenus, and each menu can have up to 24 choices. From the menus you can perform DOS commands, execute your favorite programs, go to other submenus, or shell to a specific directory.

PC-DASHBOARD allows you to customize your own menu choices and easily design a system of submenus to suit your own needs. You can type in your own personalized menu prompt for each entry used to execute a program. Once you have also included a directory path, a command, and an optional password, your menu choice is created, and all you have to do is type in the letter of the entry to execute the program.

You can design your menu entry to include up to 10 separate commands, giving you the capability to execute multiple programs or commands in succession from a single menu entry if you so desire. You can also design a command so that it prompts the user for more information to complete the command. Besides all this, PC-DASHBOARD lets you change the screen colors, turn the automatic screen blank (four min.), on or off, edit the menu titles and the on-screen notes, and choose the number of columns (1-4) for each menu.

PC-DASHBOARD's effective password protection system extends to the option to change the settings of the menus, exit from the program to DOS, specific menu entries, or access to entire submenus. In this way, several people can use the same computer yet have only restricted access to the system.

PC-DASHBOARD simplifies the operation of programs on your hard disk and controls the access to them. (PC-SIG Disk# 1165)

Special Requirements: *Hard drive.*
Author Registration: *$39.95*
➤*ASP Member.*

PC-MasterControl

by JTL Associates

PC-MASTERCONTROL (PCMC) is an in-depth custom menu and file management system for hard drives.

PCMC runs programs or DOS commands from menus, which you create, to help you stop fighting with your computer and become its friend. The menu section lets you access your programs with a single key. You no longer have to remember complex commands to run the many programs on your hard drive. You create and name your own custom menus. Then simply point to the menu you want and you're there — without a tremendous headache! The hard disk manager section lets you do all the complex DOS commands, and more, in a simple and easy-to-use format. Set up this powerful package once and let it run your PC forever.

PC-MasterControl (PC-SIG Disk# 1351)

Here are some of PCMC's features:

❑ Exits memory when running a menu and returns when finished — freeing up memory for your programs
❑ Extensive help keyed to each screen guides you through the program, as well as AutoHelp, a tutorial
❑ Hundreds of command menus (macros) for the demanding user
❑ Built-in editor to make menus (no fancy macro commands needed)
❑ Built-in screen saver to avoid screen burn-in
❑ Insert, delete or swap menus and macros with the press of a key
❑ Set the colors of any screen
❑ Check the total space and free space on any drive
❑ Copy, erase or move one file, or hundreds of files at a time
❑ Find any file on any drive with the global file finder
❑ And much, much more!
(PC-SIG Disk# 1351)

Special Requirements: *Hard drive.*
Author Registration: *$30.00 or $45.00.*

PC-Menu

by David Bird Computing

This menu system is for those who want the convenience of a menu, yet need to keep an eye on their computer's vital signs. When you run PC-MENU the date and the time will appear at the top. The bottom left of the screen will show the name of the current drive, the number of free bytes on the disk and the percentage of total free space.

The lower right corner will show the current status of the Caps Lock, Num Lock, Scroll Lock and INS keys. Below this is the size of the computer's memory, including any AT extended memory. There are four function keys and several other keys active when executing a menu. These keys offer you on-line help, the ability to edit menus, and the capability of changing colors. This is a menu that's easy if you're a novice, and still functional if you're not.

(PC-SIG Disk# 1810)

Special Requirements: *None.*
Author Registration: *$50.00 Australian.*

PC-SuperMenu Plus
by Foto 64 Inc.

SUPERMENU PLUS allows users to group programs by program functions rather than by the drive directories. Special libraries may be created for word processing, database, finance, DOS functions, CADD, graphics, etc. Up to 25 program libraries consisting of 9 programs each may be created and read by the SUPERMENU system.

The system is designed for the inexperienced user. It is 100% menu-driven and requires little instruction to set up. SUPERMENU may be operated from any floppy or hard drive and can access up to 225 programs or functions.

(PC-SIG Disk#'s 1975, 1976)

Special Requirements: *None.*
Author Registration: *$30.00*
➤*ASP Member.*

PC-Wizard PowerMaster II ✍
by Systematic Concepts

PC-WIZARD POWERMASTER II is a menu program to run all of your application programs and automatically perform backups on your hard disk.

Application programs and hard disk backups are executed by using the function keys in a series of custom menus. Up to ten different menus may contain up to 90 different programs. For application programs that may require additional input from the user, PC-WIZARD lets you specify whether or not each command allows user entry on the command line. After completing all activities, PC-WIZARD automatically takes you to the appropriate menu to backup each hard disk drive and information is given about the last backup.

PC-WIZARD will educate the user on how to use DOS commands. A menu of 20 common DOS commands is provided, and PC-WIZARD provides a Help menu and examples of each command. The user can become proficient in basic DOS commands and manage the computer system without becoming dependent on a specific menu program.

PC-WIZARD also has an activity log to record all programs and DOS commands that are executed. The activity log shows the date and time of execution, the amount of time the program was in execution, and the name of the command that was executed.

A complete network version is available from the author, plus a multi-user version that allows a standalone computer to handle up to 45 separate users.

(PC-SIG Disk# 2706)

Special Requirements: *Hard drive.*
Author Registration: *$34.95*

Pushbutton
by Acme Data

Access programs quickly and easily with PUSHBUTTON, a menuing system that runs programs at the press of a key. The main menu has 26 submenus, and each submenu has 26 choices for your programs and path information. This gives you the capability for 676 programs. PUSHBUTTON also provides password protection for your programs.

(PC-SIG Disk# 1041)

Special Requirements: *Hard drive and DOS 3.0 or higher.*
Author Registration: *$10.00*

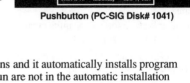

Pushbutton (PC-SIG Disk# 1041)

QuikMenu ✍
by On-Site Computer Services

QUIKMENU is a great menuing system with beautiful graphics and color. It works with a keyboard or mouse, has 3D command buttons, uses up to 10 menu pages, has password protection, text viewer, date and time display, and is network-compatible.

QUIKMENU uses only 4k of memory while running other applications and it automatically installs program main menu buttons for most major applications. If the programs you run are not in the automatic installation program, QUIKMENU will guide you through adding them. This menuing program rates a 10 for ease of set up and use without sacrificing power.

(PC-SIG Disk# 2361)

Special Requirements: *None. Mouse optional.*
Author Registration: *$35.00 (upgrades from 1.05 are free).*

Rokmar Floppy Disk Menu System
by Rokmar Computer Systems

Attention floppy disk users! Have you ever been frustrated by cumbersome DOS syntax? Have you ever accessed a floppy only to discover you didn't remember the commands to start your program? ROKMAR FLOPPY DISK MENU SYSTEM is a program designed especially for you!

With ROKMAR FLOPPY MENU DISK SYSTEM you enter DOS commands, program names, or batch files on a menu only once. Now, they are always available at the touch of a key! Easy to use and to set up. No need to spend hours learning a complicated menu language. Only DOS and batch file commands are used.

Not a lot of room to spare on those floppies? ROKMAR FLOPPY DISK MENU SYSTEM comes in two compact sizes, 14K or 25K and allows you to save different menus on each floppy. In addition, eight convenient utilities are included to help you manage your files.

(PC-SIG Disk# 1739)

Special Requirements: *None.*
Author Registration: *$6.95*

QuikMenu (PC-SIG Disk# 2361)

Sam's Menu
by Wilfred H. Moshier

SAM'S MENU is designed with large hard drives in mind, although it will run just as well on a 10MB hard disk as it will on a 360MB hard disk. Run applications can be at the touch of a single key. All commands or subdirectory names are entered once and SAM's MENU remembers them for you. Don't worry about remembering and typing those complicated commands; concentrate on getting your work done.

If several people use the same PC, each one can have their own menu screen with password protection. Want all your utility programs on one screen by themselves? Would you like to let your children use your computer but you don't want them in your files? Put all their games on one of the menu screens, and restrict their access to the rest of the menuing system. This and more is possible with SAM's MENU.

(PC-SIG Disk# 2212)

Special Requirements: *A hard drive.*
Author Registration: *$25.00*

SIMS
by Synergy Development

SELECT I MENU SYSTEM (SIMS) is a memory-resident program to design, edit, and maintain menus for your computer system providing user-friendly access to programs.

Menus are created from an ASCII text source file converted into menu format. These menus greatly simplify computer operation and program access for new and unfamiliar users of your system. Not only does this program help you save time in training other users, but it also eases personal use.

A security feature can be selected that requires a password for certain options on the menu. Total freedom is given to the menu creator regarding screen layout and options specified. The number of menus that can be incorporated into the system is only limited by available disk space. The screen design controls the colors, windows, menu options, placement of options, procedure for execution, user-defined fields, and security for the menus.

In other words, you can be quite creative with this program and use it for any application you wish.

(PC-SIG Disk# 895)

Special Requirements: *Two floppy drives and an ASCII wordprocessor.*
Author Registration: *$15.00*

✍ = Updated Program
☆ = New Program

Software Manager
by Richard Eveille

Here is a menu program that gives you real freedom over what your menu can look like. Its unique "paint" feature lets you determine how large different menu choices will be, which choices will blink, and what color each part of your menu will be. Besides a flexible appearance, you'll find the features you would want in any good menu program including password protection, multiple menu access, and an easy menu building facility.

Another advantage to SOFTWARE MANAGER is that it doesn't require you to create elaborate batch files to get your programs to run. It simply asks you where your program files are and what command needs to be issued to start the program. It does the rest automatically. Take the first step to making your PC easier to use.

(PC-SIG Disk# 1828)

Special Requirements: *None.*
Author Registration: *$20.00*

SuprMenu
by COMRES

Tired of wasting time searching through subdirectories on your hard drive to find the name of the program you wanted to run? Don't want to spend hours and hours trying to outwit a complicated menu system? SUPRMENU offers a comprehensive hard drive menu system basic enough for those interested in using minimal DOS commands to organize their files, yet with capabilities advanced DOS users will appreciate.

SUPRMENU offers an on-line pop-up help menu, file name search, subdirectory name search, a batch editor, runtime parameter ability, and a subdirectory menu structure. Menu choices can be nested as deep as 50 sub-menus down, and full support is provided for the Microsoft mouse. Both beginners and experienced hard drive owners will find SUPRMENU an efficient hard drive management tool.

(PC-SIG Disk# 2053)

Special Requirements: *None.*
Author Registration: *$25.00*

Systems Manager ✍
by MiCord

Easily manage both DOS and a hard disk system while using the computer for home and business. SYSTEMS MANAGER is a fast point-and-shoot one-screen menu system of up to 60 entries for application programs and DOS commands.

The menu has an easy loading feature as well as advanced loading for DOS batch files. It is not memory-resident so the maximum computer memory is available for big application programs.

SYSTEMS MANAGER will automatically generate time records and reports with business productivity value. Display date and time, use password protection, and customize the display and choice of records.

(PC-SIG Disk# 2239)

Special Requirements: *Hard drive.*
Author Registration: *$10.00*
➤*ASP Member.*

Tag_Along
by Triple-T Software

Are you finding it difficult to control and manage the files on your hard drive? TAG_ALONG can free you from this frustrating task. TAG_ALONG is a DOS enhancement tool and Menuing system, similar to Xtree, that is used to control and manage your hard drive. As a Disk Operating System DOS is fine but does have some shortcomings. With TAG_ALONG you have all of DOS's commands and some DOS forgot to give you. TAG_ALONG is a Two Level program. Level One is a Hard Disk Management/DOS enhancement program and Level Two is your Menuing system.

The DOS enhancement portion of TAG_ALONG displays a directory listing of your hard drive, in a tree format, showing all subdirectories. Along with this display is a list of the DOS commands that operate on files and directories, such as Mkdir, Rmdir, Copyfile, Delfile, View, Search, etc. You no longer have to remember the DOS command you need or have to type it in. Simply select the command you need from the menu. Special commands are available such as Shoot, which allows you to shoot to any of your last ten accessed subdirectories instantly. TAG_ALONG makes it easy to traverse the directories and subdirectories and maintain the files on your hard drive. Keyboard locking with password is also provided so that you can prevent someone from accessing your system when you have to leave it unattended.

The Menuing system portion of TAG_ALONG is designed to isolate you and others from complicated DOS commands. With TAG_ALONG you can operate your system completely from menus. The number of menus you can have is limited only by the amount of disk space available. Each menu can have up to 12 entries and can be password protected. Using TAG_ALONG is an excellent way to set up a computer system for use by novices.

(PC-SIG Disk# 2351)

Special Requirements: *Hard drive recommended.*
Author Registration: *$20.00*

Window Menu
by Texas Computer Cattle Company

WINDOW MENU is an advanced menu program with state-of-the-art screen windowing. This sophisticated program will organize your computer system. For the user with networking or a high performance PC, plus a color monitor and a mouse, WINDOW MENU delivers its fullest control over files and programs. It even includes features DOS lacks, such as automated backup and restore.

With WINDOW MENU, you see menus as you build them, including titles, options, selections and colors. In fact, you create the full program without ever leaving WINDOW MENU. Complete mouse support is built in with an actual mouse cursor and point and click capability, not just emulated keystrokes. You can have up to 105 menu selections categorized under as many as seven window titles across the menu bar. You can chain to other menus, allowing an unlimited number of menu options.

Menu selections can be assigned their own immediate execution keys for one-key access from any point in your personalized menu. Any character from the menu selections can act as a hot key, not just the first character of the selection name.

Each menu option can prompt for up to four parameters to be passed on to applications. You get password protection for every menu option, including exiting to DOS, menu modifying and displaying new menus. WINDOW MENU provides a help text window for each menu selection so you can enter your own descriptions. And, because it supports networks, multiple systems can share the same WINDOW MENU files.

WINDOW MENU contains context sensitive on-screen help at the touch of a single key.

(PC-SIG Disk# 1637)

Special Requirements: *Hard drive.*
Author Registration: *$40.00*

YourMenu
by MoneCraft Computer Products

YOURMENU is a menu-driven menu maker — a quick and easy way to use your computer. Once the menuing system is set up, you no longer need to hassle with typing out lengthy subdirectories or worrying about finding the correct command to start a program.

With some menuing systems you almost need to learn a programming language before you can set up the menu. Not here. When you want to add a selection to the menu, you are asked for the program title, the path to your program, and a one line description of the program selection. That's it. YOURMENU will hold up to ten pages of menu selections with twenty selections available on each page — a total of 200 selections allowed. This is certainly an easy menuing system to set up and use.

(PC-SIG Disk# 1638)

Special Requirements: *None.*
Author Registration: *$25.00*
➤*ASP Member.*

▼ ▼ ▼

Movie/VCR/Music Databases

Abstract
by RL & Associates

ABSTRACT is designed for cataloging and labeling photographs and other similar items such as sound recordings, video tapes, motion pictures, computer disks, paintings, etc. It can also be used for other database applications such as addresses, suppliers, lists, etc.

Each photo/tape/disk is described in a record that has four sorting fields and fits on a single line for easy printing and reviewing. The four fields represent categories of your choice, such as roll number, item number, frame number, name, description, date, subject matter, etc. Records can be sorted, edited, searched, viewed, and printed as reports, as well as labels to fit both slides and prints.

Each database holds 950 entries, but multiple databases can be joined for searching. Pull-down menus and help screens lead you through every option. Mouse compatible.

(PC-SIG Disk# 1300)

Special Requirements: *Dot matrix printer.*
Author Registration: *$15.00 to $50.00*

AlbumMaster ☆   *by Unicorn Software Ltd.*

Organize your record album library with ALBUMMASTER, a custom database manager. Data entry is a breeze. Edit, sort, and search. Print catalogs, listings, labels, 3 X 5 index cards, even cards for your Rolodex! ALBUMMASTER is well thought out and can make an album collector's chores almost fun.

(PC-SIG Disk# 2773)

Special Requirements: *None. A printer is recommended.*
Author Registration: *$25.00*
➤*ASP Member.*

Audio II   *by Rod Whisnant*

AUDIO II prints nice-looking and easy-to-read label inserts to identify your personal recordings on audio cassettes. The program is designed to help you organize your music collection, but can also be used to neatly label recordings of lectures, notes, sound clips, etc.

Eliminated, from this point forward, is the tedious process of writing on the cassette inserts supplied with the blank audio cassettes. All your recordings can now have custom printed inserts that make finding particular selections less of an eye strain, while bringing a professional look of quality to your entire collection.

Each cassette insert has: two title lines (for names of artists or groups), head A/B (for the headings on the two sides of the insert), date A/B (the current date is used or you can change it), and songs (a list for each side of the cassette).

AUDIO II is menu-driven with on-line help to answer your questions.

(PC-SIG Disk# 1438)

Special Requirements: *Printer.*
Author Registration: *$10.00*

Becknervision Video Database Manager   *by ATS Business Computers Inc.*

Get your video library in shape with BVIDEO, the database for cataloging and organizing records for your video tapes. Each entry includes a tape number, title, start and end memory number, machine number, category, rating, date entered, tape type, and search parameters. For each entry you can write short comments or notes in the memo section. Records can be added, deleted, edited, or searched. The reports option can print a list of tapes by catalog, rating, tape number, or alphabetical order. You can also print a list of categories and machine types.

(PC-SIG Disk# 1030)

Special Requirements: *None.*
Author Registration: *$20.00*

Cassette!   *by Logika*

CASSETTE! is a full screen editor that is specifically configured to create the paper inserts one puts in audio cassette boxes. Four different label formats are included in the program, as well as a printing program for high quality output.

This program generates enthusiasm and interest; if your interest is in creating high quality cassette labels, diligence will pay off in having a customized labeling system, capable of creating exactly the label you want.

(PC-SIG Disk# 1734)

Special Requirements: *None.*
Author Registration: *$20.00*

CDMaster    *by Unicorn Software Ltd.*

CDMASTER catalogs all your compact discs, letting you quickly search for and find a specific title, tune, or artist. Each entry in the catalog has compact disc number, title, artist, and up to 15 tunes per CD. This same information can be printed as labels, disc case inserts, 3x5 index cards, and Rolodex-style cards.

(PC-SIG Disk# 1439)

Special Requirements: *A printer, pin-fed labels (3 x 15/16").*
Author Registration: *$20.00*
➤*ASP Member.*

db-VCR   *by Michael R. Guffey*

Have you ever found yourself searching through a zillion video tapes to figure out which tape has, let's say, "Top Gun" on it? And when you find it, you have to fast forward for about 10 or so minutes to find out where it starts on the tape? Well, here is the answer you've been waiting for.

db-VCR helps you keep track of all your videos, whether they are movies, instructional videos or music. The program maintains a database of all your VCR tapes with titles, comments, where each entry on each tape starts, and so forth. db-VCR is completely menu-driven, letting you easily add entries, search for and view specific titles and print sorted lists of your collection. Mouse support is also provided. db-VCR looks great on color systems and the menus are wonderful. It is so easy to use that it actually makes using the program fun.

db-VCR (PC-SIG Disk# 1347)

(PC-SIG Disk# 1347)

Special Requirements: *320K RAM.*
Author Registration: *$17.95*

Disk Drive-In Theater   *by Drive Industries, Inc*

Here's the answer for anyone who needs a simple, structured way to keep track of all the movies and tapes they own.

DISK DRIVE-IN THEATER has an ergonomic and efficient data-input screen (one of the easiest anywhere), and a wealth of reports and searches, all of which are accessible within three keystrokes. Search by title, star, movie type, tape number, and retrieve data such as remaining room on tape. Print two differently configured labels for your tape library. With all these features and a database controller faster than most, it is a clearly superior video library manager.

(PC-SIG Disk# 493)

Special Requirements: *Printer recommended.*
Author Registration: *$15.00.*

For Record Collectors    *by MoneCraft Computer Products*

If you're a private collector, professional disc jockey, or radio station owner with a large record, CD, or audio tape collection, FOR RECORD COLLECTORS (FRC) gives a comprehensive searchable, sortable database for your collection. In fact, FRC gives you three programs: The Collector, The Advanced Collector, and The Professional Librarian.

Data fields include: song title, artist, label, producer, and up to 19 other characteristics, such as run length and year produced. FRC can handle up to 32,000 song titles per data file and an unlimited number of data files. An additional security feature prevents unauthorized file access.

(PC-SIG Disk# 1104)

Special Requirements: *None.*
Author Registration: *$59.95*
➤*ASP Member.*

Home Movie Librarian
by Jeff Thorness

HOME MOVIE LIBRARIAN provides you with a database and catalog of your home movies which can include movie titles, movie starting and ending positions, and quality of the recording. Another valuable feature is the ability to list movies that have a certain cast character. For example, you could list all the movies that Eddie Murphy is in. It will print several types of reports sorted by title or tape number.

The program includes a partial listing of home video movies from A-AN which can be browsed through, added to or printed out by type, such as drama, comedy, etc.

(PC-SIG Disk# 1266)

Special Requirements: *Hard drive.*
Author Registration: *$20.00*

Movie Database, The
by Packet Press

Old movie buffs and videotape collectors — here's a database of nearly 2,000 older movie titles now available on videotape. You can search each entry by title, MPPA rating, major cast members, writer, director, and other information. As you add to your collection, you can add new movies to the list with a wordprocessor or text editor.

(PC-SIG Disk#'s 311, 774)

Special Requirements: *A word processor to add data.*
Author Registration: *$15.00*

Movie Guide
by Sandd Software Systems

MOVIE GUIDE is a relational database for almost 200 movies featuring .PCX picture supports. It provides a unique actor/director lookup and displays the film history of the stars. Mouse-supported pull-down menus make accessing your data a snap. Many fields with user-defined series make the database flexible. Written in Pascal and Assembly.

(PC-SIG Disk# 2379)

Special Requirements: *384K RAM, graphics card. AT, 640K RAM, EGA, and hard drive recommended.*
Author Registration: *$29.95*
➤*ASP Member.*

Record Finder, The
by Brent Hanson

Can't remember if you already have that album or cut of music? Maybe you have too large a music collection — or maybe you just need the help of THE RECORD FINDER!

THE RECORD FINDER helps you organize your record or compact disk collection by building a database. Record information is cataloged by record accession number, record title, performer, composer, composition title, subject heading, and record label number. Menu-driven, THE RECORD FINDER supports basic edit and search functions. Index lists of recordings and compositions can be printed when you go out shopping for more music!

(PC-SIG Disk# 1276)

Special Requirements: *Two floppy drives.*
Author Registration: *$15.00*

Records & Tapes Database
by Christopher J. Noyes

RECORDS & TAPES organizes and catalogs all your records and tapes.

Ideal for anyone with large collections, this database can store up to 400 albums on a single disk and up to 32,000 on a hard disk. It lets you search for a particular album or cut by title, artist, music style, or other categories of your choice, and print lists of your entire collection sorted alphabetically or by category. It can even print individual "library cards" for each album, designed to fit in a rolodex file.

You can display the database in several modes, two of which are hide and dim. In the hide mode, only those records meeting the search criteria are displayed. In the dim mode, the selected records are shown on the screen in bright characters, while all others appear in dim characters.

(PC-SIG Disk# 1413)

Special Requirements: *Printer.*
Author Registration: *$25.00*

ShowLog ✍   *by Roy Mickelsen*

SHOWLOG is for all of us who record movies and soaps off the air, but then go crazy trying to keep track of them all!

Here is a complete system that not only prints out labels for your collection of nameless black boxes but also helps you catalog them in a database for easy retrieval.

Reports can be printed in a number of different sort orders containing information such as title, speed, show time, tape address, star of show, rating, category, producer, and more. All information is maintained in database format with an index for each sort order, thus providing quick and easy retrieval.

(PC-SIG Disk# 1274)

Special Requirements: *640K RAM and CGA. Hard drive recommended.*
Author Registration: *$22.00*

Video Librarian   *by TurboSystemsCo.*

VIDEO LIBRARIAN is a menu-driven database for VCR (VHS/BETA) users who want to catalog their video cassette libraries. VLB records 18 fields of information about each movie selection, performs powerful cross-referenced searches, and prints reports to the screen, printer or disk.

You can find any title, star, co-star, director or tape number in the datafile which can hold up to 64,000 selections — about 1000 on a 360K floppy. The program also lets you create and print professional-looking cassette labels to identify your nameless black boxes and keep your collection neatly organized. A tutorial helps you get started.

(PC-SIG Disk# 1424)

Special Requirements: *Dot matrix printer.*
Author Registration: *$25.00*
➤*ASP Member.*

Video Tape Control   *by Micro Methods*

Automate the rental and membership operations of your retail video store! VIDEO TAPE CONTROL's many unique features, such as a tape library, pop-up windows and the ability to take advantage of your computer's maximum processing speed, let you handle movie rentals and returns quickly and easily. Keep track of membership, rental revenue, film inventory and reservation information vital to your store's operation.

Reservations can be made on tapes and items for more than a week in advance and you're reminded of the reservations when the tape is rented or returned. Late fees are automatically calculated and you're alerted when fees are due. Customer receipts are generated with each transaction. Included is the opportunity to simplify your operations even further by connecting VIDEO TAPE CONTROL to your cash register drawer. Accounting data is collected regarding daily, monthly and annual rental revenues.

Print reports on member rental activity, revenue by member, film reservations, late returns, and tape inventory. Mailing labels for all members or specific categories of members may be generated. VIDEO TAPE CONTROL's timesaving and efficient transaction processing assists you in increasing your store's profitability.

(PC-SIG Disk# 2189)

Special Requirements: *512K, hard drive, and 80 column printer.*
Author Registration: *$95.00*

VideoMaster ☆   *by Unicorn Software Ltd.*

Organize your videotape library with VIDEOMASTER, a custom database manager. Data entry is a breeze. Edit, sort, and search. Print catalogs, listings, and even labels for both the videotape front and spine. VIDEOMASTER is well thought out and can make a videophile's chores almost fun.

(PC-SIG Disk# 2774)

Special Requirements: *None. A printer is recommended.*
Author Registration: *$25.00*
➤*ASP Member.*

▼ ▼ ▼

✍ = Updated Program
☆ = New Program

Music

Christmas Concert Volume 1
by Nancy Moran

Using shareware's PIANOMAN (PC-SIG Disk #279), Nancy Moran produced two self-running, outstanding 20-minute Christmas concerts. In Volume One, Ms. Moran took the basic bread-and-butter Christmas carols and brought a multiphonic majesty to them not often heard in computer-generated music. The carols can be played one at a time or as a concert.

Christmas favorites included are:
- ❏ "O Come All Ye Faithful"
- ❏ "Angels We Have Heard On High"
- ❏ "Away In A Manger"
- ❏ "The First Noel"
- ❏ "God Rest Ye, Merry Gentlemen"
- ❏ "Hark the Herald Angels Sing"
- ❏ "Joy to the World"
- ❏ "Deck the Halls"
- ❏ "O Holy Night"
- ❏ "Jingle Bells"

(PC-SIG Disk# 1211)

Special Requirements: *None.*
Author Registration: *None.*

Christmas Concert Volume 2
by Nancy Moran

This is the second of Nancy Moran's outstanding 20-minute, self-running Christmas concerts. In Volume Two, Ms. Moran explores Handel's Hallelujah Chorus and shares little-known carols such as Buxtehude's "A Christmas Canon" and the French "Pat-A-Pan." The carols can be played one at a time or as a concert.

Other selections are:
- ❏ "We Wish You A Merry Christmas"
- ❏ "It Came Upon a Midnight Clear"
- ❏ "We Three Kings of Orient Are"
- ❏ "Here We Come A-Caroling"
- ❏ "Bring A Torch, Jeanette Isabella"
- ❏ "Rudolph the Red-Nosed Reindeer"
- ❏ "I Saw Three Ships"
- ❏ "La March des Rois"
- ❏ "What Child Is This?"

(PC-SIG Disk# 1212)

Special Requirements: *None.*
Author Registration: *None.*

Composer
by Bob Aman

OK, Schroeder — I mean Beethoven — here's a program for you. COMPOSER is a simple music editor that lets you create music and then integrate your creation into a batch file or a program written in Turbo Pascal. A visual display of a piano keyboard lets you play and "record" your music from the computer keys. COMPOSER is a great way to bring musical life to programs you have written. It has a three-octave range and requires some knowledge of music terminology to create original music. Eleven prewritten songs come with the program.

Though it lets Turbo Pascal access the songs, it does not put the files into source code. By calling the file TRBOTUNE.SYS in your Pascal program, you can access your songs.

(PC-SIG Disk# 722)

Special Requirements: *CGA.*
Author Registration: *None.*

Composer by Oak Tree Software

by Oak Tree Software

If you're like most people, you've always had the urge to create music. But for some reason you never picked up that first instrument and really learned how to play it. COMPOSER makes your computer that first instrument.

COMPOSER is a graphics-based music editor that lets you compose, edit, play, save, and print single-voice music on your PC. Since COMPOSER is a graphics-based editor, you can actually see the notes that make up your music. You do not have to work with a confusing mixture of letters and numbers. Once your music looks correct on the screen and sounds correct, you can print your music with any dot matrix printer.

COMPOSER is easy to use and very flexible. If you have a PCjr, or compatible three-voice machine, COMPOSER can also create music files that later can be combined to make three-part sound. This lets you create harmony and chords.

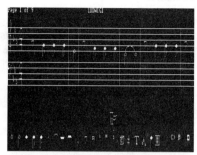

Composer by Oak Tree Software (PC-SIG Disk# 794)

COMPOSER's editing features make music entry easy. By using COMPOSER's block insert and delete mode, you can manipulate large sections of music quickly. Includes Beethoven's Symphony Number 5 and Minuet in G, John Phillip Sousa's Stars and Stripes Forever, and Scott Joplin's Maple Leaf Rag.

(PC-SIG Disk# 794)

Special Requirements: *CGA.*
Author Registration: *$20.00*

Lap Dulcimer Tuner and Sheet Music Sampler

by Marji Hazen

LAP DULCIMER TUNER AND SHEET MUSIC SAMPLER has five traditional songs arranged for lap dulcimer in DAA tuning and an electronic tuner with instructions for beginners on how to tune the dulcimer. The five songs are "Amazing Grace," "Boil Them Cabbage Down," "I'll Fly Away," "The Frozen Logger," and "Happy Endings on the Banks of Ohio."

The music screens can be printed with the Shift and PrtScr keys. The dulcimer tuning program helps beginners learn to tune their instruments with an electronic tuner. Instructions are included in the program, and tones can be repeated if desired.

(PC-SIG Disk# 967)

Special Requirements: *None.*
Author Registration: *$5.00*

Music Minder, The

by PC Works

THE MUSIC MINDER is a comprehensive music library management system. Schools, churches, civic organizations and individuals use it to keep track of music orders, music library inventory and performances.

Compositions in your music library are posted through the library system with all data concerning the composition available for editing. The library is displayed and various reports can be run against the database. Performance data can be posted and maintained, allowing the music director to view the performance history (three previous performances) for any composition. THE MUSIC MINDER also supports multiple music libraries.

Some of the features provided are: a music library filing system, complete ordering information system, individual 3x5 library card printing, performance tracking, establishment of multiple libraries, performance history reports, and other reports based on composer, keywords and title. Browse the library by keyword, composer or title. This program is fully menu-driven and easy to operate.

(PC-SIG Disk# 1472)

Special Requirements: *512K memory, 2 disk drives or hard drive, and CGA.*
Author Registration: *$20.00*

✍ = Updated Program
☆ = New Program

Musical Blocks
by Alan L. Moyer

MUSICAL BLOCKS is a fun paint program that also plays music. Each color of the pallet is a musical note of your design. Paint on a screen with two dimensional patterns which are played like sheet music. MUSICAL BLOCKS allows you to:

❏ Input existing music into the computer, save it and play it
❏ Break an existing composition into pieces and build new music from it
❏ Play either melodies or two part harmonies
❏ Create random music
❏ Experiment with two dimensional music
❏ Experiment with non western scales
❏ Create musical games and puzzles.

You can also type text onto the pallet. This can be used to add a title to a tune you compose. Need a little starter? Examples of musical blocks are included on the disk!

(PC-SIG Disk# 2451)
Special Requirements: *None.*
Author Registration: *$15.00*

NOTEable
by Try-Then-Buy Software

NOTEABLE is an easy to use program which teaches music students the notes of both the treble and bass music scales. It does so in a "competitive game" format, giving scores for quick and accurate recognition of notes. One can even compete with oneself, trying to improve previous scores. The top ten high scores are kept for each separate scale. NOTEABLE may be used in both personal and professional environments.

(PC-SIG Disk# 2222)
Special Requirements: *None.*
Author Registration: *$25.00*

PC-Musician
by Chris Wiley

PC-MUSICIAN is a tool for the beginning composer. It lets you enter musical notation and then plays it back. It needs no extra keyboards or instruments attached, as it uses only the keypad.

Playback is on the one voice of the computer. This program is more for the aspiring musician than for the technically-proficient musician/computer operator.

(PC-SIG Disk# 127)
Special Requirements: *None.*
Author Registration: *$20.00*

Pianoman
by Support Group, Inc.

Play your computer keyboard as if it were an electronic piano! More than just a simple note-playing routine, PIANOMAN can help you shape a true musical composition.

Playing music is simple. You'll see a picture of the keyboard on your monitor, with the notes written on the keytops. When you press a key, it lights up on the screen and sounds a tone for as long as the key is held down. You can record and edit music, insert and delete notes, adjust pitch and length, make global changes, and save/retrieve files. The maximum number of notes PIANOMAN can keep in memory is 63,488 if you have over 450K of RAM. Three octaves are available at a time and you can shift those octaves up or down.

Create lovely music with this versatile composition tool. Record your songs on disk and send music to your friends. They'll smile when you sit down at the computer!

(PC-SIG Disk# 279)
Special Requirements: *PC-DOS.*
Author Registration: *$25.00*
➤ *ASP Member.*

Pianoman Does Beethoven
by Nancy Moran

PIANOMAN DOES BEETHOVEN is an exquisite translation of Ludwig van Beethoven's artistry for the IBM-PC and compatibles. Five compositions, approximately 23 minutes of music, have been adapted by Nancy

Moran with finesse and accuracy. The music files were created using PIANOMAN and the author has included a detailed description of the advanced techniques she used in their transcription.

Selections include: Moonlight Sonata, Minuet in G-Major, Six Variations on a Duet from the Opera La Molinara, Seven Variations on the National Song, and the Sonata Pathetique.

(PC-SIG Disk# 1396)

Special Requirements: *None.*

Author Registration: *$7.50 brings a disk of additional music*

Pianoman Goes Bach
by Nancy Moran

PIANOMAN GOES BACH contains 12 musical selections by Johann Sebastian Bach: the first three two- and three-part inventions, Well Tempered Clavier (both preludes and fugues), and three suite movements. All were transcribed and adapted for IBM-compatible PC using PIANOMAN (PC-SIG Disk #279). The main menu offers the user many options in playing the 12 works and is easy to use, even for beginners.

The files are run from a menu as singles or in various sequences and provide approximately 30 minutes of Bach's work. Each selection is a rich piece of music, even through a PC speaker.

(PC-SIG Disk# 1395)

Special Requirements: *None.*

Author Registration: *$7.50*

Pianoman Goes Baroque
by Nancy Moran

Baroque music lovers will treasure this latest PIANOMAN artistry by Nancy Moran. Ten 18th Century compositions by Scarlatti, Telemann, Wagenseil and Karl Philipp Emanuel Bach are transcribed and adapted for the PC. Under Ms. Moran's hand, these 32 minutes of delight prove the ordinary PC to be a musical instrument of great range and diversity.

Ms. Moran, who also authored PIANOMAN DOES BEETHOVEN, PIANOMAN GOES BACH, and CHRISTMAS CONCERTS, takes PIANOMAN to soaringly complex heights while seeming to give the PC a new voice.

(PC-SIG Disk# 1397)

Special Requirements: *None.*

Author Registration: *$7.50*

Speaker
by Steve Platt

This program performs Thiele-Small alignments for any given speaker in a vented enclosure. This means it will determine the optimum cabinet and vent size for the driver entered. It requires the Thiele-Small parameters for the driver (available on most data sheets) to perform the analysis.

It will graph the speaker's response on screen along with all the calculated results. It can also graph the speaker's thermal and displacement limit curves and a simulated square wave response. The user can request the screen to be printed. The program includes a data file that contains almost every driver made by JBL. New drivers can be added to this file from within the program.

(PC-SIG Disk# 2019)

Special Requirements: *CGA or Hercules graphics and a graphics printer.*

Author Registration: *$10.00*

✍ = Updated Program
☆ = New Program

Network Software & Utilities

DAYO AP (Accounts Payable) ✍   *by TJS Lab*

DAYO is a collection of multiuser business applications that provide a means of managing inventory, purchasing, invoicing, customers, vendors, sales and more... All DAYO products are multiuser, designed to work on a Microcomputer (PC) Based Local Area Network (LAN), like Novell™. They can, however, work as a "standalone," running on a single PC.

To date, large and complex mulituser business applications required Mini and Mainframe computers, but because of products like the PC based LAN/ Network, they can now be run on microcomputers. DAYO is one of the first microcomputer based business applications designed to handle such a system.

DAYO Business Applications grow with your company. The ability to upgrade your system is available with the addition of other DAYO products. Source to DAYO is also available, allowing you to make further modifications and enhancements. DAYO Clock was written with Qbasic™; all others were written with Clipper™.

Current Modules:

❑ Inventory	❑ Back Orders
❑ Smart Reports	❑ Point of Sale
❑ Accounts Receivable	❑ Materials Requirement Planning
❑ Price Book	❑ Accounts Payable
❑ Menu	❑ Quotes
❑ General Ledger	❑ Clock
❑ Index	❑ Look Up Databases
❑ Payroll	❑ Passwords
❑ End of Period/Purge	❑ Update & Conversion
❑ Time & Billing	

DAYO databases are all dBASE™ compatible, thus providing an additional or alternative source of support and reporting.

(PC-SIG Disk#'s 2411, 2412)

Special Requirements: *640K RAM, a hard drive, and DOS 3.3.*
Author Registration: *$25.00*
➤ *ASP Member.*

DAYO AR (Accounts Receivable) ✍   *by TJS Lab*

DAYO AR (ACCOUNTS RECEIVABLE) is the "final chapter" to the processing and maintenance of all your Receivables. DAYO AR includes routines to handle cash receipts, customers, invoice types, terms, taxcodes, sales persons, and more. Many reports are included (i.e., Aging, Customer, Sales...). There is a routine to print Statements (i.e., SMART, 90, 60, 30 days), and another one to create and print 'non'standard invoices. HP Laser forms are provided as an option for Statements and Invoices.

(PC-SIG Disk#'s 2409, 2410)

DAYO Bar Code ☆   *by TJS Lab*

DAYO BAR CODE prints three of nine bar codes with an Epson or IBM compatible dot-matrix printer. It is integrated with the DAYO INVENTORY and the DAYO CUSTOMER databases.

Labels are printed onto standard labels (3.5 by ¹⁵/₁₆ inches at six lines per inch). The inventory bar code label consists of an item number and its bar code, with the option to print the vendor item number, description, unit of issue, weight, and bin/location. The customer barcode label supplies a customer number, its bar code, and has the option to print the customer's name and telephone number.

Inventory and customer bar codes can be printed by 'browsing' through their respective databases using multiple indexes. When a desired item or customer is found, just print. Batch printing of item bar codes is possible based on the item type, class, location, receipts, and purchase orders.

(PC-SIG Disk# 2626)

DAYO BO (Back Orders) ✍   *by TJS Lab*

DAYO BO (BACK ORDERS) is the maintenance module for the processing of all your customers sales back orders. DAYO BO (working with DAYO POS) determines and manages the filling (allocation) of your customers' back orders. It does this through an allocation process that determines what back ordered items are "fillable" because of receipts into the inventory. Creates the same type invoices as DAYO POS.

(PC-SIG Disk# 2408)

DAYO Brain ☆ *by TJS Lab*

DAYO BRAIN is a Job Scheduler and/or Menu system. Use the BRAIN to run any program or batch file during the day or night, manually or according to a schedule. Keep your computer(s) busy, even when you are not around!

The BRAIN can be scheduled to run jobs daily at a specific time, or every so many minutes, or run the jobs once, at a specific date and time. The BRAIN can also act as a Menuing system, allowing you to select and then run the job/program.

Features include: Multiuser, schedule report to printer or file, dBASE-compatible schedule database, PC Paintbrush or Micro Paintbrush (.PCX) screens and windows, passwords (4-digit code), keyboard locking, usage graph, disk status, variable speeds for the schedule, and more.

(PC-SIG Disk# 2627)

DAYO EOP (End of Period) ✍ *by TJS Lab*

DAYO EOP (END OF PERIOD PACK & INVENTORY) contains routines that are normally run at the end of a reporting period. DAYO EOP permits you to permanently remove deleted records from the Accounts Receivable (AR) and Accounts Payable (AP) databases, and to erase old report text files. There is also a routine for performing a physical inventory. Many reports are included (i.e., AR ageing, AP summary, inventory movement).

(PC-SIG Disk# 2416)

DAYO GL (General Ledger) ✍ *by TJS Lab*

DAYO GL (GENERAL LEDGER) provides a means to manage and report company finances. DAYO GL is totally integrated with the other DAYO packages. Features include computer generated posting, multiuser, double entry, export data, 20+ reports, budget management, and unlimited accounts.

(PC-SIG Disk#'s 2413, 2414)

DAYO Index ✍ *by TJS Lab*

DAYO INDEX is a program designed to manage the indexing of the DAYO databases. DAYO applications all have multiple indexes, and because it is recommended that they be reindexed at least once daily, DAYO INDEX was created to simplify this process.

(PC-SIG Disk# 2406)

DAYO Installation ☆ *by TJS Lab*

DAYO INSTALLATION was created to ease the process of installing the many DAYO programs. DAYO INSTALLATION 'drives' the process of copying all of the files onto the hard disk and then checks the configuration of each DAYO module to insure integration. Put your company name and address into each module and create all required databases and indexes.

Note: DAYO INSTALLATION is useful only for first-time installation.

(PC-SIG Disk# 2751)

Special Requirements: *DAYO modules, 530K RAM, hard drive, and DOS 3.3.*
Author Registration: *None.*

DAYO Inventory ✍ *by TJS Lab*

DAYO Inventory is a Multiuser inventory control, purchasing, and vendor maintenance application.

(PC-SIG Disk# 2401)

DAYO Look Up (Database Look Up) ✍ *by TJS Lab*

DAYO LOOK UP is a routine for DAYO users to view data from any DAYO database or dBase™ compatible database (.DBF). No editing is allowed. This provides a "safe" tool for users that do not have the need to make changes to the databases. Has multi-level passwords.

(PC-SIG Disk# 2415)

✍ = Updated Program
☆ = New Program

DAYO Menu (Clock & Setup) ✍ *by TJS Lab*

DAYO MENU is a menu system for use with the DAYO line of business applications, as well as any other program on your computer. While it is multiuser when used on a PC-based LAN/Network, it can be run (like all DAYO products) as a 'standalone' application. The program is a QBASIC menu program and a DOS batch file that you can modify/edit. DAYO CLOCK is a simple clock display and optional alarm that can act as a job scheduler.

SETUP of the DAYO MENU (CLOCK & SETUP) disk is the setup system for the DAYO modules and is recommended, especially when the entire DAYO system is being installed.

(PC-SIG Disk# 2395)

DAYO MRP (Materials Requirement Planning) ✍ *by TJS Lab*

This new version features increased memory management/availability and no more use of overlay files (.OVL). As a matter of fact, it is a totally rewritten program with many more features than 1.0. (Version 2.0 is not compatible with Version 1.0.)

DAYO MRP (MATERIALS REQUIREMENT PLANNING) is a routine designed for manufacturers.

DAYO MRP builds items (end items) from items (components) in the inventory database. End items can later be placed into inventory for later sales. Supports a multilevel Bill of Materials. Features include automatic inventory posting and creation of inventory adjustment records. Databases are dBASE-compatible, multiuser, and many reports are available.

(PC-SIG Disk#'s 2398, 2619)
Special Requirements: *640K RAM, a hard drive, and DOS 3.3.*
Author Registration: *$50.00*

DAYO Passwords ✍ *by TJS Lab*

DAYO PASSWORDS provide DAYO Business Application users with a system of database security through the use of passwords. Its use is optional, but recommended in areas where more than one person has access to the data.

(PC-SIG Disk# 2407)

DAYO Payroll ✍ *by TJS Lab*

DAYO PAYROLL provides a system for the computation of payroll for businesses of any size and contains many features and functions not normally found in PC payroll applications.

Some of DAYO PAYROLL's features include: multiuser, unlimited employees, weekly, biweekly, and/or monthly payrolls, quarterly, year-to-date (YTD), and current summary databases, databases are dBASE-compatible, automatic payroll posting and computation, vacation maintenance, sickpay/days maintenance, check printing, SDI tax, overtime and premium hourly wages, up to eight deductions, exempt/non-exempt deductions, view reports on screen, printer setup and drivers, over 24 configurable options, and many reports.

(PC-SIG Disk# 2397)

DAYO POS (Point of Sale) ✍ *by TJS Lab*

DAYO POS (Point of Sale) is a billing and invoicing application for any size business. It is the DAYO module that permits you to invoice out your products while keeping an accurate record of all your sales. Features include: multiuser (i.e., Novell), registers, quote interface (to DAYO Quotes), templates back orders, data entry validation, cash drawers (serial or parallel), databases are dBase™ compatible, HP laser special invoices, passwords (with DAYO Passwords), many reports, and much more!

(PC-SIG Disk#'s 2402, 2403)

DAYO Price Book ✍ *by TJS Lab*

DAYO PRICE BOOK is a system of creating and maintaining specialized pricing for your customers/clients. Special printouts (price books/catalog) may be printed to a standard printer, or to a Hewlett Packard LaserJet or compatible. It requires DAYO INVENTORY and DAYO POS (Point of Sale) programs/databases. Customers are invoiced (with DAYO POS) using the price in the inventory database or with one of the special price book methods: fixed, margin, or list discount.

Customers are invoiced (with DAYO POS), using the price in the inventory database (INV.DBF), or with one of the special Price Book methods:

Fixed — Fixed Price for a Unique Item + Customer (1st Priority)

Margin — "Cost Plus" (2nd Priority)

List Discount — Discount off the List/Retail Price (3rd Priority)

(PC-SIG Disk# 2404)

DAYO Quotes ✍ *by TJS Lab*

DAYO Quotes creates sales order quotes based on the DAYO Inventory, Customer, and other DAYO databases. Quotes can be printed on a standard printer or a Hewlett Packard™ Laserjet compatible printer. The quote can be printed on a pre-printed form, on the Laser printer in a special laser format, or as a standard/default form. DAYO Quotes closely models itself after the DAYO POS (Point of Sale) application and is totally integrated with that application. Templates (kits or bundles), are supported.

(PC-SIG Disk# 2405)

DAYO Smart Reports ✍ *by TJS Lab*

DAYO SMART REPORTS contains many reports and routines that will help you to manage your purchasing, inventory, invoices, back orders, sales, and databases. There are 22 reports/lists/routines included in smart reports; i.e., Single warehouse, inventory zero price, valuation expanded, inventory zero retail, reorder (two weeks), reorder (four weeks), reorder (eight weeks), negative onhand, stock level shortage, vendor list, stock level over, customer list, inventory ASCII text, inventory item list, late P.O., checking account list, P.O - due in this week, check format list, inventory zero cost, and an expenses list.

(PC-SIG Disk#'s 2417, 2620)

DAYO Time & Billing ✍ *by TJS Lab*

DAYO TIME & BILLING is a system of creating invoices for services and/or products. DAYO TIME & BILLING contains many features and functions found in many of the other DAYO modules.

It has support for an Inventory, Receivables, projects/job/cases, and customers/clients. Other features include: multiuser, unlimited clients, unlimited projects/job/cases, project notes, customer notes, 30+ reports, onscreen reports, dBASE-compatible databases, laser formats for invoices and statements, two styles of statement/bills, printer setup and drivers, cash drawers, and over 46 configurable options.

(PC-SIG Disk#'s 2399, 2400)

Special Requirements: *640K RAM, hard disk, and DOS 3.3.*
Author Registration: *$50.00*

DAYO Update & Conversion *by TJS Lab*

DAYO UPDATE & CONVERSION is a program that was created to update and convert earlier versions of DAYO databases and memory files. It is required when attempting to upgrade any existing DAYO module.

(PC-SIG Disk# 2396)

Special Requirements: *640K RAM, hard disk, and DOS 3.3.*
Author Registration: *$5.00/Free with upgrade (or included in $399.00 Basic DAYO Package)*

EasyMail - Network Email *by Superior Micro-Techniques*

Here's a very easy-to-use electronic mail program for networks which offers most of the features that commercial programs provide.

The interface consists of pull-down menus and single keystroke access to all functions with extensive on-line Help. EASYMAIL provides each authorized user with a complete environment for creating documents, selecting addressees, reading mail, and tailoring the program to their specific needs. Other features include text importing, document printing, and mail archiving. It works on all NetBIOS compatible networks (all popular networks). This version allows up to five users.

(PC-SIG Disk# 2279)

Special Requirements: *384K RAM, and Netbios network.*
Author Registration: *$65.00*

✍ = Updated Program
☆ = New Program

MarxMenu ☆ *by Computer Tyme*

MARXMENU is a very powerful menu/job control language with nearly 500 commands. MARXMENU gives you complete screen control, supports conditional menu options, supports math and string functions, lets you design professional looking exploding and shadowed windows, and uses no RAM! MARXMENU is especially good on networks.

This menu is intended for users with enough knowledge to write batch files. While it certainly isn't the easiest menu program around, MARXMENU might be one of the most powerful.

(PC-SIG Disk# 2638)

Special Requirements: *Hard drive.*

Author Registration: *$59.95*

➤*ASP Member.*

Topware Lan O.S. ☆ *by Micro-Mart*

TOPWARE NETWORKING OPERATING SYSTEM is the software needed to create a local area network (LAN) between two computers. Imagine accessing programs on one computer from the other. TOPWARE will run programs that are designed to run on the IBM PC Network, like dBASE III+, WordPerfect, and many others.

To run TOPWARE you have to install an ARCNET card (available from TOPWARE) in each computer. String some cable between them, install the TOPWARE NETWORKING OPERATING SYSTEM and you have a two-computer LAN.

Please note this is an involved process and the documentation is limited. It's definitely not for the computer novice!

(PC-SIG Disk# 2507)

Special Requirements: *DOS 3.0+, and ARCNET cards. 640K & HD in one PC.*

Author Registration: *$19.95 for two users, $295.00 for four users.*

▼ ▼ ▼

Paint and Drawing Programs

Charts Unlimited
by Graphware Incorporated

CHARTS UNLIMITED integrates graphics and text processing into a single system to allow creation, editing, and printing of flow charts, organization charts, floor plans, electrical diagrams, Gantt charts, business forms, and many other documents. Highly versatile, CHARTS UNLIMITED is valuable to engineers, architects, programmers, system analysts, teachers, and anyone with a need to draw charts.

Charts are drawn on a worksheet 256 columns wide up to 1,000 rows long, a graphics area of four million pixels or dots. A few keystrokes will bring up various geometric shapes, bar graph designs, flowchart arrows, math symbols, and more. They can be displayed, moved, stretched, shrunk, saved, and replicated.

Text can be entered anywhere as lowercase, uppercase, or boldface with most text editing features. You can load text files from spreadsheets and wordprocessors into your chart.

Most dot matrix and laser printers are supported. You can print your chart horizontally or vertically. A magnification feature allows you to expand your chart or a portion of it up to 100 times. A printer buffer lets you go on creating or editing a chart while you print another one.

(PC-SIG Disk#'s 1496, 7085)

Special Requirements: *512K RAM and CGA.*
Author Registration: *$35.00*

Cycloid ✍
by Phil Paustian

If you enjoyed spiralling away hours with Spirograph(tm) as a kid, you won't be able to resist this computerized version of the famous drawing game! And with CYCLOID, you won't have to worry about your pen slipping at the last minute and ruining your artistic efforts!

At first CYCLOID is a little more difficult to use than the actual game since the effect of the "disks" and "rings" can be tough to visualize. But after some experimentation anyone can become a pro at creating the telltale spirograph spirals. CYCLOID is very versatile; it permits adjustment of image size and shape, and has the ability to rotate an existing drawing or even create nested spirographs.

Images can be saved and reloaded for later display and there is a more limited version of the program for those of us more artistically inept. Great fun for the young, or bored, computer user.

(PC-SIG Disk# 1524)

Special Requirements: *Hercules graphics, CGA, or EGA.*
Author Registration: *$9.95*

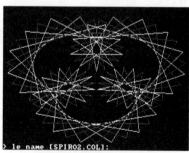
Cycloid (PC-SIG Disk# 1524)

Drawplus
by Eric Iwasaki

A Graphics/Drawing program written especially for the PC and PCjr.

Pull-down menus and a joystick control the various functions which include: Line, Circle, Paint, View, Cut-and-Paste/Delete, Fatbrush and Airbrush with varying color-width-density. Source code is included.

(PC-SIG Disk# 633)

Special Requirements: *CGA, two floppy drives, and a version of BASIC.*
Author Registration: *None.*

Fantasy
by Bill Newell

Create your own animated art and interesting designs with FANTASY.

Paint flowing, colorful pictures or designs as you move the mouse or press the cursor keys. As the images are created, the art is saved to a disk file so to replay on the screen whenever you want.

(PC-SIG Disk# 1305)

Special Requirements: *CGA. Mouse optional.*
Author Registration: *$20.00*

Finger Maps
by Poisson Technology

FINGER MAPS is an object-oriented drawing package supplemented with a comprehensive database of world geographical coordinates. It can serve as a standalone object drawing program, a world map maker, or simply a .PCX paint image file editor.

The finished drawing or map can be saved and converted into a. PCX bitmap or a proprietary object format. FINGER MAPS can read other .PCX files as a background image and draw objects on top of it. The screen image can be printed to an HP-compatible LaserJet in 300 dpi.

The map database contains geographical coordinates of all country borders, U.S. state borders, major rivers and lakes, U.S. state capitals and other major U.S. cities, and foreign capitals.

(PC-SIG Disk# 2420)

Special Requirements: *384K RAM and EGA.*
Author Registration: *$15.00*

Finger Painting Program
by Poisson Technology

FINGER PAINT, reminiscent of some programs for the Macintosh, is an easy-to-use, straightforward paint program for either home or office use.

FINGER PAINT has most of the bells and whistles you would find in a print program, such as variable drawing functions (dots, lines, rectangles, circle, arcs, etc.). But it also has a few that are rare in a program of this price — animation, variable text fonts, 3-D drawing, and more. The Movie command can serve as a slide show or animation program. 19 demo pictures are included to demonstrate this feature. One of its major advantages is its Hercules graphics compatibility. This means it can run on many computers. The picture file format is PCX which can be used by almost all paint programs. The non-registered copy of FINGER PAINT works only with the HP LaserJet printer and produces a 150 dot-per-inch output.

Finger Painting Program (PC-SIG Disk #763)

(PC-SIG Disk# 763)

Special Requirements: *256K RAM and CGA, EGA, or Hercules graphics.*
Author Registration: *$29.00*

Finger VGA ☆
by Poisson Technology

Let your creativity run free with FINGER VGA and create and animate your next masterpiece. FINGER VGA is a color image processing, painting and animation program that works in VGA graphics mode (320 X 200, 256 colors). (A Microsoft or Logitech compatible mouse is required.) Files are loaded and saved in .PCX format and can be printed to a LaserJet in 300 DPI (dots per inch) density.

Image editing features include: cut, copy, paste, inverse, rotate, flip horizontally/vertically and scaling to enlarge or reduce the selected image.

The drawing toolbox includes: freehand drawing, line, rectangle, triangle, brush, spray, eraser, flush, dupArea, dupPoint, fill an enclosed region, and draw a 3-D pyramid.

The curve drawing tools include: bezier curves, circle, ellipse, arc, arrow, thick line and text with four different scalable fonts. Text entry can be written either horizontally or vertically.

There are nine fill patterns which can be used to fill rectangle, circle, ellipse, pie and polygon with up to 200 vertices. The screen zoom-in feature (fat bit) is also proved to work on individual pixels at 16X or 64X level. Flip the whole screen either horizontally or vertically, clear, or inverse the screen image. Color image to grayscale conversion is also supported. There are 256 colors available for drawing and for background use.

(PC-SIG Disk# 2653)

Special Requirements: *384K RAM, VGA, and mouse (Microsoft or Logitech compatible).*
Author Registration: *$32.00*

FloDraw ✍
by George Freund

FLODRAW is a graphics editor that produces black and white full-page diagrams. It is designed to handle symbols quickly and easily and is ideal for documentation such as flowcharts, organization charts, system diagrams and other symbol-oriented materials. It combines text and graphics and is equipped with a basic graphics editor for lines and circles, plus pixel editing.

FLODRAW has symbol libraries for flowcharts, HIPO charts, and electric diagrams. Design your own symbols, save them, and combine them into new libraries, or add them to an existing library.

(PC-SIG Disk#'s 912, 913)

Special Requirements: *512K RAM, graphics card, DOS 2.0-3.3, and a Printer.*
Author Registration: *$37.50*
➤*ASP Member.*

MacPaste
by Brad Taliaferro

Read, edit, save and print pictures orignally drawn with MacPaint on the Apple Macintosh. MACPASTE lets you do this on your IBM-PC.

It has many features such as: cut-and-truncate, line-drawing, paint, scroll, magnify and much more. Printer parameters can be set from MACPASTE for printing ReadMac pictures. MACSHOW shows sequential ReadMac pictures on the same drive and MANYMAC combines four ReadMac pictures into one. MACBLANK creates a blank ReadMac picture which can then be edited with MACPASTE. When printed, a ReadMac picture is surprisingly realistic and detailed in nature.

(PC-SIG Disk# 1001)

Special Requirements: *CGA.*
Author Registration: *Any amount.*

Megadraw
by Logika

MEGADRAW is designed to create 12-frame animation sequences which can be incorporated into any program. MEGADRAW can write self-standing QuickBasic code (for CGA and EGA) which you can then insert into your own program, modify and use as you wish. These animation sequences can be used by any language.

In addition to animation, this program can be used to create typefaces/fonts. Having your own typeface adds a level of professionalism not found in many programs. Create fonts in multiple colors and, if you like, animate them. Stunning business or game graphics can be created by having full color text move around the screen.

(PC-SIG Disk# 2360)

Special Requirements: *EGA.*
Author Registration: *$40.00*

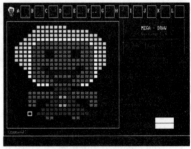

Megadraw (PC-SIG Disk# 2360)

MonoDraw
by Frank G. Pagan

MONODRAW provides full-screen 740x348 pixel monochrome graphics uncluttered by on-screen menus. All the features commonly available in "paint" programs are included. Full-screen resolution is maintained by keeping the intuitive menus in a separate window that is readily and instantly accessible. Full documentation is provided.

(PC-SIG Disk# 1092)

Special Requirements: *Hercules graphics and an Epson-compatible printer.*
Author Registration: *None.*

Painter's Apprentice
by R. Nelson

PAINTERS APPRENTICE is a bitmap editor like PC Paintbrush or Dr Halo. MacPaint users will find its black and white screen and pull down menus familar. For those who want to create detailed images that take advantage of high resolution printers, this program is faster and intuitively easier to use than its commercial counterparts.

PAINTERS APPRENTICE has all the functionality one would expect from the newest generation of quality paint programs. Mouse control and full use of drawing icons make for easy image manipulation. Cut and paste, zoom and expand, multiple paint texture and painting tools (brushes and spray cans) are all at your fingertips. Special drawing tools for circles, rectangles and other geometric shapes are also available. There is even the ability to rotate and flip selected images.

(PC-SIG Disk# 1645)

Special Requirements: *EGA, a mouse, and an Epson, IBM, Okidata, or HP printer.*
Author Registration: *$35.00*

PC-Art
by Mike Stone

PC-ART is a graphic-drawing program that lets you create color pictures and designs using the standard color graphics adapter on the IBM-PC.

This is a solid graphics package that does not depend upon the use of a mouse, light pen, koala pad or joystick. You can do everything from the keyboard. The following features are available to you:

❑ Crayon function for free-hand drawing in any color
❑ Paint brush function in any color using any one of 15 patterns
❑ Line and box functions with four different line patterns
❑ Circle function with a concentric repeat feature
❑ Text function in two fonts in any color and in 10 character sizes
❑ Retrieve or save an entire picture for later processing
❑ Snapshot function to take a picture of the screen and store it
❑ Image library to store and later retrieve drawn figures
❑ Easy-to-use window panels to select functions, colors, etc
(PC-SIG Disk# 629)

PC-Art (PC-SIG Disk# 629)

Special Requirements: *CGA.*
Author Registration: *$25.00*

PC-Key-Draw
by OEDWARE

PC-KEY DRAW combines the features of CAD, paint, slide show, and desktop publishing programs into one powerful and flexible drawing package. Fast and easy to use, with or without a mouse.

Create a wide variety of graphics such as:

❑ Mechanical design   ❑ Country quilt design
❑ Landscape architecture ❑ Graphics game development
❑ Business presentations   ❑ Graphic art

Drawing features include:

❑ Lines — parallel, spoke
❑ Circles — arcs, pie slices, ellipse
❑ Curves — sine, rose, spiral
❑ Others — dots, vectors, polygon, fillets and arrows

Paint features include:

❑ Spray paint   ❑ Shading
❑ 29 colors   ❑ Modify color
❑ 64 fill patterns   ❑ Fade/shift/strip colors
❑ Reverse video

PC-Key-Draw (PC-SIG Disk#'s 344, et al.)

Maximum drawing size is 55120 x 1600 with 64 layers.
Thirty-six text fonts are included in the registered version, four fonts in the shareware version, with the ability to create your own. It can read and write HP soft fonts. Text can be placed at the cursor location, justified, moved, rotated, and imported a an ASCII file. Screen modification includes all standard options and a few unusual ones.

Additional features include object area calculation, animation, templates, banner/poster printing, macro language, and powerful slide-show system.

The newest version of PC-KEY-DRAW also includes HYPERDRAW. HYPERDRAW provides a means to link related screens of information together in a database structure that is ideal for a variety of tasks such as teaching aids, interactive slide shows, image organization, drawing detailing, project scheduling, cataloging, process diagraming, and much more. There is also a full interactive tutorial that uses the linked screens of HYPERDRAW to teach the basic drawing commands of PC-KEY DRAW.

(PC-SIG Disk#'s 344, 345, 1032, 1124)
Special Requirements: *swo floppy drives and CGA.*
Author Registration: *$100.00*

PictureThis
by HortIdeas Publishing

Quickly and easily prepare professional-looking drawings for printing on PostScript-compatible laser printers and imagesetters with PICTURETHIS. Do them either freehand or by tracing "template" screens captured with a companion program, CAPTURETHIS.

Use PICTURETHIS even if you don't know how to program in the PostScript page description language. View a screen representation of your drawing as you prepare it, easily making additions and alterations. Print PICTURETHIS drawings at lower resolution on some dot-matrix printers, using the graphics screen dump program supplied with DOS.

PICTURETHIS doesn't need a lot of fancy hardware — just an IBM PC, XT, AT, or compatible. It doesn't even require direct access to a laser printer. Drawing files can be sent by mail or modem to a laser typesetting service bureau for overnight return of low-cost prints with 300, 1270, or even 2540 dots-per-inch resolution.

(PC-SIG Disk#'s 1130, 1474, 2301, 2302)

Special Requirements: *320K RAM, CGA, and PostScript or compatible printer.*
Author Registration: *$65.00*

Printer Art
by Galaxy Systems Corp

This PRINTER ART package is a collection of ASCII text files, that when sent to your printer, create many wondrous sights such as a clown, Schroeder of Charlie Brown fame, the Enterprise, and more. Some of these sights may not be suitable for young eyes to view, so please use your own discretion.

(PC-SIG Disk# 154)

Special Requirements: *A version of BASIC, a printer, CGA, and 384K RAM.*
Author Registration: *None.*

Ready Set Draw
by Jesse Rosenzweig

Looking for a small paint program that does the basics without all the frills of a full-blown computer studio? READY SET DRAW has the simple functions you want, and it works with or without a mouse. READY SET DRAW is a fun, easy drawing program with features like copy, paint, color, loading and saving pictures, and other basic operations.

Once loaded you will find a small X in the middle of the screen — that's your drawing pen. In the top left hand corner of the screen it has the pen status (up, down, erasing). When the pen is down it will draw, when the pen is up it won't draw, and when the pen is erasing it will erase each dot in the middle of the X. Eight direction keys, up, left, down, right, and diagonals, move the X the corresponding direction.

From there, you can fill in enclosed areas, cut and paste portions of your drawing, automatically draw various sized circles and rectangles, even change the color of your pen — all with simple key strokes.

(PC-SIG Disk# 1851)

Special Requirements: *CGA. A mouse is optional.*
Author Registration: *$5.00*

Spiro
by Stephen Sander

In the early 60's kids spent hours spinning out complex colorful spirals with the "Spirograph," a set of colored pens and plastic rings. Now you can put the designs on your EGA screen and not have to scrub your hands afterwards. Extremely simple to use, just choose three numbers and which color you would like to use.

The registration fee is reasonable and makes this a pretty safe bet for anyone wishing to find some entertainment for their restless "artists" at home.

(PC-SIG Disk# 1986)

Special Requirements: *EGA.*
Author Registration: *$3.00*

TurboFlow
by Daytron Electronics Inc

TURBOFLOW is a flowchart drawing program that generates ANSI X3.5-1970 and ISO 1028 flowchart symbols. It is a member of the EZCAD family of CAD packages. Similar in user interface and sharing basic device and graphics drivers, it produces professional quality drawings for electrical, architectural, and mechanical engineers, as well as dataflow, program flow, and structural charts for programmers, systems analysts, and database managers.

✍ = Updated Program
☆ = New Program

TURBOFLOW is menu-driven. The spooling capability redirects output to a file enabling you to print or plot output at a more convenient time, or from a PC that is connected to the proper printer or plotter.

(PC-SIG Disk# 1824)

Special Requirements: *Printer or plotter, and a mouse is recommended.*
Author Registration: *$69.00*

VGA Paint ☆   by David Evans

Produce screen images with up to 248 colors at once on a VGA system with VGA PAINT. Fourteen brush shapes and four automatic shapes such as boxes and circles are provided. Image handling capabilities include: sizing, flipping, moving, copying, and saving images to disk.

Although the resolution of the screen is only moderate (320 x 200), the careful use of color mixing can produce images with near-photographic realism.

VGA PAINT was written for a three-button mouse, but will work with just the keyboard or the keys plus a two-button mouse. Like VGACAD, this program is designed for working on screen images and no provision is made for printing.

(PC-SIG Disk# 2553)

Special Requirements: *450K RAM, VGA, and MSDOS 3.2+. 3-button mouse recommended.*
Author Registration: *None.*

▼ ▼ ▼

Amy's First Primer jr   by Computing Specialties

This is a collection of a half-dozen games designed to teach basic skills to children, ages 3-8. They stress positive reinforcement and promote a "learning is fun" attitude.

The collection includes a sing-along alphabet, a letter-matching game, an alphabet tutorial, a numbers-counting game, a maze game, and a pattern-matching game.

Repeated suggestions that the parents use the games with their child add a nice reinforcement toward family-based learning. This version is especially designed for the PCjr.

bSPECIAL REQUIREMENTS: PCjr with BASICA Cartridge.

(PC-SIG Disk# 647)

Special Requirements: *PCjr with BASICA Cartridge.*
Author Registration: *$15.00*

PC-Calc jr   by Victoria Irwin

This is Jim Button's famous spreadsheet program PC-CALC, specifically recommended for the PCjr. Perfect for small to mid-size applications such as financial analysis and simple accounting.

(PC-SIG Disk# 625)

Special Requirements: *None.*
Author Registration: *$48.00*

PCjr Educational Games   by Allendale County Schools

This is an excellent collection of games for kids aged 6 through 60 and beyond. There are games to tease and tantalize the intellect, and some that are just plain fun. For anyone with a PCjr, this package of fun really works overtime to exploit the strengths of this computer, its sound, and graphics.

(PC-SIG Disk# 241)

Special Requirements: *None.*
Author Registration: *None.*

File Descriptions:
2   BAS   Alphabetize a word list.

1	BAS	Spelling Bee.
3	BAS	Fun arcade-type bowling game.
4	BAS	A graphics display program.
5	BAS	Maxit, a strategy/numbers game.
6	BAS	Othello, an old standby.
8	BAS	Find-a-Word puzzle (requires printer).
7	BAS	Word Problems game.
10	BAS	Finds your age in days.
9	BAS	Creates a unique maze each time (requires printer).
12	BAS	Black and white version of word matching game.
11	BAS	Word matching game, similar to Concentration.
15	BAS	Word Scramble (1).
14	BAS	Word Scramble Number 1.
13	BAS	Hangman, an old favorite.
MENU	BAS	Menu that allows selection and calls up the games.
GRADE-*	LST	Wordlist for grade 1 through 5 (5 files).
BRIEFLY	BAS	Part of titles used by TITLE.BAS.
AUTOEXEC	BAT	A batch file that helps create a working disk.
ACS	PIC	Picture file — used by *.
20	BAS	Program descriptions — called from menu.
17	BAS	Mazes number 2.
16	BAS	Screen machine, a draw program (requires color graphics).
README	DOC	Documentation by authors.
TITLE	BAS	Title page and pointer to other documentation.

▼ ▼ ▼

Personnel Management

The Complete Office ✍   *by The Write Stuff*

Until now, you could either keep your office organized by using hundreds of forms printed on tons of paper, or select numerous different software applications for the various tasks related to office management. THE COMPLETE OFFICE is designed to be a better solution. This is a fully menu-driven program which integrates the important functions necessary to any office operation into one application.

You can record and track personal records, such as client files, or employee files. You can organize such files using several different field types — name, code, etc. A complete letter writing and mail merging function is included, you don't even have to go to your wordprocessor to handle those one-page letters. An envelope and label printing function is provided that accesses the data from your personal records and prints those envelopes for you automatically. To help you manage your time, important business and personal dates can be kept in the calendar. You can also record birthdays, anniversaries, and holidays. You can keep track of petty cash, inventory, office supplies or other resources, and even make inventory orders. A function for backing up your files to another disk for safe keeping is also provided. This will protect your important business information. For most offices, this program covers all the bases.

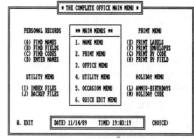

The Complete Office (PC-SIG Disk#'s 1585, 1586)

The main menu presents all the primary functions to choose from such as personal records, printing, calendar, editing, various office functions, and utility operations, but it also lists key commands to directly execute specific functions. This allows you to move through the program directly from the main menu, thereby bypassing several submenus.

(PC-SIG Disk#'s 1585, 1586)

Special Requirements: *512K RAM and a hard drive.*

Author Registration: *$35.00*

Employee Management System   *by Try-Then-Buy Software*

The EMPLOYEE MANAGEMENT SYSTEM 4.3 is a highly-accurate personality analysis system that is designed to reduce employee turnover and improve management/ employee communications. It is also excellent for use in personal relationships.

✍ = Updated Program
☆ = New Program

Reducing employee turnover is a very important consideration to the business owner/ manager; employee turnover is extremely expensive. EMS works in 5 ways: 1. It helps you to know the work personalities of your job applicants. 2. It presents to you the preferred work characteristics of your employees. 3. It presents motivational and demotivational factors. 4. It shows job personality characteristics, those traits that can be used to strengthen the work environment. 5. The history function helps you refer back to previous applicants and employees when additional information is required. EMS is intended to improve communications between people and enhance the ability of the personnel manager to interview potential employees, as well as improve current employee relations. EMS is also valuable as a personal communications tool between friends, marriage mates and any other relationship where personality is a strong component.

(PC-SIG Disk# 660)

Special Requirements: *None.*
Author Registration: *$95.00*

Hire   *by Louie Crew*

HIRE is a must for any manager or personnel officer who has a need to keep track of applications and resumes. HIRE lets you monitor all the people who apply for specific jobs, grants, or any other positions.

HIRE uses merge files to help you respond professionally in writing to everyone. It writes letters to send to applicants, acknowledging their applications, alerting those who have not sent all support documents, and rejecting those who don't qualify. You can personalize the merge files, by including the applicant's personal data, such as title, name, address, etc. HIRE can handle from 300-500 applicants, and can help you screen them according to your criteria.

(PC-SIG Disk# 1004)

Special Requirements: *A printer and FIND.EXE and SORT.EXE from your DOS disk.*
Author Registration: *$10.00*

Management Mentor   *by Gerald DeJaager*

MANAGEMENT MENTOR helps you evaluate management skills and fine tune them. A comprehensive self-assessment inventory, MANAGEMENT MENTOR uses questionnaires to evaluate your strengths and weaknesses in 12 management categories. A separate emphasis-selection process helps decide which questionnaires are most relevant to you. Results can be read on screen and printed.

For an additional fee, registered users get expert consultation in any of 244 management skill areas.

(PC-SIG Disk# 1156)

Special Requirements: *None.*
Author Registration: *$35.00*

Managing People ✍   *by Micro Development Software*

MANAGING PEOPLE is a set of questionnaires designed to help you assess and improve your management skills. The program is designed as a management course which should be used periodically, not just once. Areas covered are decision making, employee evaluation, communication skills, planning improvement, motivating employees, time management, getting projects done, and other areas. Additional documentation is provided for each area of management. A sample job interview file is included, as well.

(PC-SIG Disk# 1316)

Special Requirements: *None.*
Author Registration: *$25.00*

PC Shift   *by Bottom Line Software*

PC-SHIFT helps organize your employee shift schedule. PC-SHIFT allows you to divide the jobs by location or category and then lets you describe each job required for each area. The job descriptions consist of the beginning date, the location or department, the job title or description, the minimum and maximum qualification level, and the minimum and maximum security level.

PC-SHIFT then lets you enter a schedule for each job, showing a chart of each hour of the day divided into 15-minute intervals. Once all the data is entered, you may display or print a report on a 12-hour schedule, a 24-hour schedule, a 24-hour chart, or a report on all the job descriptions.

(PC-SIG Disk# 1195)

Special Requirements: *Printer.*
Author Registration: *$39.95*

PC-Punch 🖉   *by Genesoft*

Don't spend another dime on the most hated business machine in the
office — the time clock. PC-PUNCH does a better job of keeping
track of your employees, yet it doesn't break down, run out of ink, or
offend those employees who don't like the idea of punching a clock.

Your employees will spend no time learning the new system because
it uses the same punch-in and punch-out concepts. They may even
find it easier since they won't have to locate their card on the crowded
wall; PC-PUNCH keeps all information internally. Imagine, there will
be room for a nice picture where the time cards used to hang.

PC-Punch (PC-SIG Disk# 1589)

Best of all, payroll becomes easier. PC-PUNCH eliminates errors
caused punching the wrong card or the wrong space. It also calculates
the time an employee works between the time they punch in and the
time they punch out. All that's left for you to do is add. You set up the
employees' records and, with password protection, only you have
access to the records. Never again will a time card turn up missing or
mysteriously altered.

If your employees work on computers, install PC-PUNCH at their desks and let them "punch in" when they sit
down. PC-PUNCH and your computer will do a better job than your time clock ever did.

(PC-SIG Disk# 1589)

Special Requirements: *512K RAM. A hard drive and clock card are recommended.*
Author Registration: *$49.95 plus $5.00 for shipping.*

QuickTrax Employee Rollcall! 🖉   *by Discovery Graphics*

Automate your employee data, save time and improve your personnel management with QUICKTRAX
EMPLOYEE ROLLCALL! QRC! takes the pain out of employee data management by organizing your
information in an easy access format. Eliminate manual tracking and reporting with QRC!

With pull-down menus, pop-up screens and over 40 Help screens, learning to use QRC! is a breeze. The
program lets you track 9,999 employee files with EEOC and key events reporting, hourly scheduling and
attendance reporting. With two-level password protection, your employee data will be secure. Other convenient
features include a calendar, notepad, file backup, and report setup utilities.

Five Lookup code tables allow you to customize employee information to fit your company needs and ensure
accurate data entry.

Any one of 17 standard reports can be viewed on the screen, printed, or saved as a file. The disk user guide can
be viewed or printed from within the program. Customize your report with titles, shaded frames, italics, bolding
and size. Print continuous or sheet-fed return address labels.

The installation program loads and configures QRC! Setup is as simple as choosing a printer, customizing your
code tables and entering employee information. Produce quality company reports in less than one hour.

(PC-SIG Disk#'s 2591, 2592)

Special Requirements: *CGA, EGA or VGA. 640K and a hard drive recommended.*
Author Registration: *$39.00*

SuperTraq ☆   *by Hilary Neal Hooks*

SUPERTRAQ utilizes pull-down menus and pop-up windows to provide an easy-to-operate user interface with
no cryptic commands to remember.

SUPERTRAQ implements expense management much differently from other expense tracking products.
SUPERTRAQ recognizes that each individual's daily routine, activities and habits are different and supports the
Franklin International Institute Day Planner system. The Day Planner system easily and quickly records expenses
and files your receipts. At your leisure, enter the recorded expense information into your SUPERTRAQ software.

Many features help manage expenses simply and quickly. Track expenses by project, employee, client, or any
number of defined expense files. One of the more powerful features is its ability to track and manage separate
expense files. Expenses are categorized by Credit Cards, Checks, Cash and Mileage. Each expense category
includes the expense date, description, type code, tax status, daily entry number, amount and daily total for each
entry.

Various reports can be generated for tax preparation, accounting, project planning and tracking purposes, company and individual expense management, etc. Print to the screen, to a file name, or to the printer. Generate reports daily, weekly, monthly, and annually.

Reports can be generated individually for each expense category. Also available is a Batch Printing mode to automate the printing of each report file if and when it is necessary to print.

The SUPERTRAQ works with virtually any day organizer or daily/monthly calendar system.

FEATURES:

❑ Easy-to-use pull-down menus and pop-up windows
❑ Manage separate expense files
❑ Set up permanent credit and checking accounts
❑ Allow for user-defined expense types
❑ Output reports to ASCII file, display screen or printer
❑ Designed to work with day organizers such as the Franklin Day Planner System
❑ Generate reports daily, weekly, monthly and annual expenses reporting.
❑ Generate reports for each expense category (i.e., CREDIT, CHECKING, CASH and MILEAGE)
❑ Virtually no limit on the number of transactions and entries

(PC-SIG Disk#'s 2755, 2756)

Special Requirements: *Hard disk drive, 512K RAM, and DOS 3.0 or higher.*
Author Registration: *$39.95*

▼ ▼ ▼

Photography

Computer Darkroom
by Benjamin M. Kacenas

For those who develop their own pictures, calculating exposure times that are dependent on many factors can involve tedious (and expensive) guesswork. COMPUTER DARKROOM calculates new settings for you quickly and accurately.

Once you have one acceptable exposure with test prints, this program gives you the proper exposure times for any changes you decide to make in paper speed, contrast, magnification, or filter factors for all black and white prints, color prints, or color slides for f/stop values from f/2 to f/32.

(PC-SIG Disk# 1313)

Special Requirements: *None.*
Author Registration: *$25.00*

For Photographers
by MoneCraft Computer Products

FOR PHOTOGRAPHERS is a three-level menu-driven program for the amateur or professional photographer to aid in cataloging photographs. Since the entire program is menu-driven, little experience or training is required to be proficient in its use. Consequently the manual is rather brief.

The first level, Basic, is recommended for minimal record-keeping. You can store the most basic information about a photo, slide, or negative. But record-keeping is not restricted to these data. For instance, you could (if you painted) store valuable data about your paintings or drawings. The second level, Photographer, extends the information storage capability to include data such as processing and printing and any other data you might want to save. The third level, Professional, adds on client information in addition to the above information.

FOR PHOTOGRAPHERS allows you to create, edit, save, search, delete, and update any data files in the system.

(PC-SIG Disk# 1164)

Special Requirements: *Two floppy drives.*
Author Registration: *$59.95*
➤*ASP Member.*
➤

PC-Foto
by Foto 64 Inc.

Use PC-FOTO to create labels for your libraries of slides, prints, or any other objects that are classified and described like pictures. Both professional and amateur photographers will appreciate the extensive information that can be included on labels. All labels can have at least an account number, photographer's name, description of content, and location. Up to nine sets of labels can be printed with four labels per set. Also, a variety of label sizes are possible, so you can use it with a variety of photo products. It works with IBM, Epson, Okidata, and Hewlett Packard printers.

(PC-SIG Disk# 1040)

Special Requirements: *None.*
Author Registration: *$30.00*
➤*ASP Member.*

PC-Foto (PC-SIG Disk# 1040)

Photo Pack
by Wash and Ware Software Products

PHOTO PACK is a collection of programs for amateur and professional photographers guaranteed to improve your picture taking skills.

With PHOTO PACK, your PC helps you pick the right filters (called diopter lenses) for closeup photography, calculates your camera's settings for shooting moving objects, determine film image size for printing pictures, figures enlarger head to paper distance for blowing up an image, and calculates proper flash settings and depth-of-field information.

Impressed? Well, zoom in on this: PHOTO PACK also turns your PC into a darkroom processing timer, a label maker, and a negative/slide database. It also prints model releases!

The TIMER can be programmed to handle up to 16 separate processing steps. These steps may run in a darkroom or in a "lights-on" mode. The darkroom mode uses a black screen background with red digits. You can set tones or "beeps" to help you with developing and printing.

The LABEL MAKER prints return address labels, equipment identification labels, slide labels, or whatever other labels you can think of.

The DATABASE helps you keep track of all those shoeboxes full of slides and negatives. Describe your transparencies with multiple keywords in different categories. Later, retrieve photos by category and keyword. Each database can hold 65,000 records. If you use floppy disks for your database, you can use multiple disks for an unlimited number of records. (NOTE: You can average from around 1400 to 1800 records per floppy disk.)

(PC-SIG Disk# 1249)

Special Requirements: *None.*
Author Registration: *$10.00*
➤*ASP Member.*

Slide Manager ✍
by Robert W. Eppstein

SLIDE MANAGER organizes and catalogs your photographic slides or prints to make retrieval easy — with special features for artists who photograph their paintings for submissions to competitions.

For each slide or work of art, this specialized database stores the title, subject matter (12 categories), the medium (20 categories), dimensions of photo print or object, date created, ID number and special keywords. An additional history of where and when the slide has been shown, sent, sold or given an award can also be recorded.

The database allows you to search for a particular slide or group of slides by name, ID, or any of the other categories you've chosen. It can also produce a printed catalog of your collection sorted in a variety of ways, such as by subject, alphabetically by title, etc.

(PC-SIG Disk# 1390)

Special Requirements: *None.*
Author Registration: *$54.95*

✍ = Updated Program
☆ = New Program

SLIDE.PC
by Lynn A. Gerig

SLIDE.PC gives shutterbugs an efficient way to print caption information on labels to identify slides and photos, and at the same time store the information to disk for exporting to a database or spreadsheet.

Besides the printed label information, the program lets you include tech notes and comments in the data file. The data file format is compatible with Quattro, Lotus 1-2-3, dBase III, PC-File, and several other popular databases. The data file can also be converted to ASCII text format to export into any wordprocessor. You can then print a complete catalog of your photo collection. Because each slide entry takes up one long line, you need to use a wide carriage printer in condensed font, or a standard dot matrix printer using a sideways-printing utility.

The menu-driven program prints 7/16" by 1 7/8" pin-feed labels. A thoughtful routine helps you line up the labels before you execute the print function.

(PC-SIG Disk# 1418)

Special Requirements: *7/16" x 1-7/8" pin-fed labels and a dot matrix printer.*
Author Registration: *$25.00*

▼ ▼ ▼

Practical Jokes

A_Curse
by Conrad Button's Software

Cursed PC! More than an epithet, A_CURSE is a practical joke program that causes the victim's computer to start spouting macabre curses, such as, "May a one-eyed pigeon nest in your hard drive!" "May raunchy pitbulls kidnap your spreadsheet!"

A_CURSE displays up to ten random curses on your chosen one's screen. Each one is different (with millions of possible combinations) and they vary from the absurd to the disgusting. What a way to start the day!

(PC-SIG Disk# 1523)

Special Requirements: *None.*
Author Registration: *$10.00*

CrazyDos
by Compu-teck

A wisecrack response for every DOS command, for your own entertainment or a practical joke. CRAZYDOS is a temporary "replacement" for DOS with some interesting responses to commands. There are some alarming looking "error messages," but don't worry, there are no aliens, molasses, or problems reading drive Q:. All "system crashes," "Chinese keyboards," etc., are imaginary and temporary, and can be ended by a keypress in some cases, or ENTER in others. To exit CRAZYDOS you must tell your computer "I love you."

(PC-SIG Disk# 1912)

Special Requirements: *None.*
Author Registration: *$10.00*

Curses! ☆
by R.K. West Consulting

A humorous and creative "insult generator" with a twist. A single keystroke switches from insults to compliments! You control the contents so the program can be used to generate descriptive phrases on any subject. Phrases are randomly generated, based on your vivid vocabulary!

(PC-SIG Disk# 2741)

Special Requirements: *360K RAM.*
Author Registration: *$10.00*
➤*ASP Member.*

Hard at Work ☆
by R.K. West Consulting

HARD AT WORK (HAW) has eight different screens to make your computer appear busy while you are away. These dynamically changing screens produce a busy effect for the casual eavesdropper.

The screens supplied are those of a system test, a database re-index, a spreadsheet FILL option, disk optimization using Speedy Disk, a virus scan, and a speaker integrity test. All of the screens are amusing and provide laughs when the truth is discovered.

Definitely for the office computer. Use as a joke on a co-worker who may be fooled into believing that the computer is at work while you take a break!

(PC-SIG Disk# 2728)

Special Requirements: *No special requirements.*
Author Registration: *None.*
➤*ASP Member.*

Hotboot and Insults
by Vertical Software

A couple of practical jokes that are fun for the PC user and, possibly, the PC victim.

HOTBOOT is a public domain version of a classic. If you like this one, get the original from Left-Handed Software. Load HOTBOOT into the system of your victim. From here on out, it's a flirtation of sorts between the PC and the user. As the user attempts to work with the computer, the computer issues increasingly more personal remarks. How real is this to the victim? You'll have to watch and see if you can figure it out.

INSULTS can randomly generate 22 million insults on the unsuspecting PC user — some of them even make sense. Not for the weak-stomached.

(PC-SIG Disk# 619)

Special Requirements: *None.*
Author Registration: *$14.00*

LoveDOS ✍
by R.K. West Consulting

This program gives a whole new meaning to "personal" in personal computer. Pre-install LOVEDOS on a friend's machine and sit back and watch 'em blush! With each keystroke, a provocative remark flashes to the screen, line after line, putting the moves on the operator. A sexy rework of the old INSULTS program. Nothing too suggestive, but choose your victim carefully anyway. At last, a truly user friendly computer!

(PC-SIG Disk# 1403)

Special Requirements: *None.*
Author Registration: *None.*
➤*ASP Member.*

Program Grab Bag
by James Hill

For the PC practical joker, here are several safe (but insane) scams to play on some unsuspecting user's computer. Place them in a batch file or on his hard disk. When he comes back and touches a key or boots up his computer, look out! One trick makes his machine sound like it's filling with water and then it goes into a spin drive cycle! Fun galore. Don't blame us, though, if your victim gets even!

Other programs included here are a bit tamer: Convert almost any U.S measurement to the metric equivalent and vice versa; covers temperature, liquid, weight, linear distance, speed, and square and cubic volumes. CHK4BOMB checks a program to see if it does any disk writing or formatting and also displays any text it finds in the program code. SCRAMBLE and UNSCRAM can be used to encrypt and decrypt sensitive and private files. OBLITER8 totally deletes a file so it will be unrecoverable. SHOW provides a graphics demonstration of the PC-SIG logo. Lastly, read a very uplifting text by Pythagoras, a famous early Greek philosopher and mathematician.

(PC-SIG Disk# 1314)

Special Requirements: *CGA and a version of BASIC.*
Author Registration: *$15.00.*

Tommy's Insults
by Tommy's Toys

"You Hare-Brained Import of Slimy Maggot Fodder!" "You Premature Hamper of Gummy Toe Jam!" These are just a taste of the callous offenses you can view in TOMMY'S INSULTS. Aliens from another world have a favorite pastime of trading insults to gain friendship, and they want to teach you their customs. A rather odd premise, but also a rather odd program. Although not a "player's" game (it is more like a nickelodeon), it does offer the user uncounted thousands of insults ranging from the gross to the absurd.

While viewing, enjoy the many TV show tunes being played, as well as other jingles. Function keys allow you to change screen and border colors, while the space bar allows you to freeze the current insults on the screen, so you can print them for future use on your friends. Also supported is the Covox Speech Thing, an external speaker unit, to bombard your ears with insults.

TOMMY'S INSULTS is not recommended for the very young — some language is rated PG-13 and you have to read well to keep up with it all. Do not expect any interaction with this program. You can add adverbs and adjectives to the dictionary bank, but this is the only input you can have with the toy. If you enjoy viewing obscure and ridiculous phrases, you will enjoy the program; if not, as a gift it would convey the same message as a can of deodorant.

(PC-SIG Disk# 1736)

Special Requirements: *None.*
Author Registration: *$2.00*

TV/Volapuk
by Gustafsson Data

VOLAPUK is a combination practical joke and look-busy program. Start the mock debugger and your memory is seemingly reconfigured, your hard disk is diagnosed, and all errors are cleared from existence — in reality the screen messages are the only things that are changing.

TV simulates the late-night movie "War of the Ants" (that's where the screen "fuzzes out" after the national anthem). Then, when you press a key, the loudspeaker is silenced and the random pattern turns into a beautiful person with the message "Dear User, I Love You." In a few seconds the dreamgirl/dreamboy vanishes, the "War of the Ants" continues. Another keystroke takes you back to DOS. The programs are self-testing against viruses for security.

(PC-SIG Disk# 1912)

Special Requirements: *TV requires CGA.*
Author Registration: *None.*

▼ ▼ ▼

Presentation Graphics (Slides)

Collage
by Chip Consultancy House for Info.Pr.

A computerized show and tell software package to create colorful graphic pictures on your computer. Create and save slides, combine created slides, and present the created and combined slides as a show on your computer screen. COLLAGE also lets you create and maintain text files (upper ASCII included) with several good editing and block features.

(PC-SIG Disk# 975)

Special Requirements: *None.*
Author Registration: *$10.00*

CompuShow ✍ *by Canyon State Systems and Software*

Compushow (PC-SIG Disk #1461)

Display any of the popular graphic image formats by scrolling through your directory. COMPUSHOW is a graphics display program for CompuServe GIF and RLE, MacPaint, PC Paint, PC Paintbrush, Dr. Halo, Ega Paint, and ColoRix graphics images. It supports Hercules, CGA, PCjr/Tandy-1000, EGA, "Super-EGA", MCGA, VGA, "Super-VGA", the IBM Professional Graphics Controller and 8514/A adapters. Super-VGA support includes Ahead Systems, ATI, Chips & Technologies, Everex, Paradise, AST, Compaq, Dell, Genoa, Orchid, STB, Trident, Logix, ZyMOS, and Video7 adapters (and compatibles). CompuShow also provides 16 color graphics displays on a CGA, and Tandy 1000SL/TL 640x200x16 color mode.

Files are selected for display from an on-screen file directory, which may be sorted by name, extension, size or date, in ascending or descending sequence. You may log to a different disk drive, change sub-directories, copy, rename, and delete files. The program will automatically select the best display mode for any graphic, or you may display it in any mode available on your graphics adapter. Images larger than the screen may be panned vertically and horizontally. Colors may be adjusted on EGA, MCGA, and VGA systems, and the adjusted palette saved to disk.

The registered version of the program provides printing on monochrome and color dot matrix and laser printers and includes an automatic slide show, and a system configuration program.

(PC-SIG Disk# 1461)

Special Requirements: *Hercules, CGA, EGA, EGA-480, MCGA or VGA.*
Author Registration: *$25.00*

Gemcap
by Bill Newell

GEMCAP is a memory-resident utility that helps you capture screen images from programs, save them in separate disk files and load them into other programs. The disk files are compatible with any program that reads GEM.IMG files, regardless of whether the original screen was in text or graphics mode. These include WordPerfect, Ventura Publisher, and many other popular programs.

(PC-SIG Disk# 1305)

Special Requirements: *CGA or EGA.*
Author Registration: *$20.00*

Grabber ☆
by Gerald A. Monroe

GRABBER is a program that saves screen images to a disk file. GRABBER makes it very easy for you to summon the images to your screen at a later time, exactly as they were originally displayed.

GRABBER is memory-resident. After you start it, it's always waiting in the background while you run other programs. Tell GRABBER to capture the image currently being displayed by pressing a combination of keys.

GRABBER "captures" the screen to an .EXE file on your disk. When you want to view the screen, run this .EXE file like an ordinary program. GRABBER can also convert the captured screen file to .GIF, .PCX, and .PIC formats.

(PC-SIG Disk# 2775)

Special Requirements: *None.*
Author Registration: *$59.00, $29.00*

The Magic Font Machine
by REXXcom Systems

Want to make some eye catching electronic bulletin board advertisements, notes, or screens? If so, THE MAGIC FONT MACHINE will help you create and display brilliantly colored screens with 20 combinations of foreground/background colors. You can have the whole screen in poster mode (non flashing) or electric mode (flashing). The screens you make are saved in files and can be used one at a time or all together to make a slide show. You can even upload screens to computer bulletin boards for advertisements or messages.

We listed the directions below so you could see how easy THE MAGIC FONT MACHINE is to use!

❏ Type first line of text.
❏ Text appears instantly in mammoth superfonts.
❏ Select mode and background/foreground colors from the menu.
❏ Position text with Right and Left keys.
❏ Try different color combinations before saving the line.
❏ Select Edit to retype the line if necessary.
❏ Save the line when satisfied, and go on to the next line or screen. Thaaaaats all folks! Be creative and have fun with THE MAGIC FONT MACHINE!

(PC-SIG Disk# 2452)

Special Requirements: *Color monitor recommended.*
Author Registration: *$14.95*

PC-Demo Graphics Presentation Package
by Helios Software

PC-DEMO is a graphics package that lets you create demonstrations featuring graphics animation, program interface capabilities, and slide shows.

Use the full range of characters and colors on your computer. Choose between big or small characters. Fill in a box, move it, copy it, and even rotate it. Use the cursor keys to draw your picture without the need for a mouse or pad. Slides can be organized into an interactive demo which accepts input from users.

(PC-SIG Disk# 914)

Special Requirements: *Two floppy drives.*
Author Registration: *$35.00*

PC-FOIL
by Wally Anderson

PC-FOIL consists of two routines - FOIL-EDIT and PC-FOIL. These programs combine to provide a multi-purpose tool for the creation of overhead transparencies and attractive documents.

When the large print, bold print, and boxes are combined with your own creativity and agenda, the effect can be dramatic. You develop the presentation or document using FOIL-EDIT, a general purpose full-screen editor, and then print it. Use it as a word processor, creating programs or modifying standard DOS files. Fast and easy to use, it offers both menus and commands appropriate to your skill level. Complete with on-line Help.

You have the information you want to present. Now, here's the program that can do it!

(PC-SIG Disk# 347)

Special Requirements: *Two floppy drives and graphics printer.*
Author Registration: *$25.00*

PC-Images ✍
by RSE Inc.

Capture images from your computer screen and group these "pictures" into carousels that can run as a TSR. Pop them up at will, even during other programs. Would you like a picture of your kids, or the company logo, to be automatically displayed instead of the blank DOS screen? No problem with PC-IMAGES.

Registered users can also create stand-alone carousels that will run without using PC-IMAGES. This is excellent for creating user-paced business presentations or "slide shows." Use a carousel as a "screen-saver", automatically popping up after a period of keyboard and screen inactivity. Business users will appreciate PC-IMAGES' practical side, but it's a great way to personalize your computer and have a little fun too.

(PC-SIG Disk# 2391)

Special Requirements: *None.*
Author Registration: *$35.00*

Slide Generation
by John R. Lehmann

This program produces medium-quality slides and overhead transparencies. Images can be created, edited, saved, displayed, and printed using this program. Overhead transparencies are produced by photocopying the printed output onto transparent material. Photographic slides are produced by photographing the display or printed output.

(PC-SIG Disk# 244)

Special Requirements: *None.*
Author Registration: *$25.00.*

Vuimage ☆
by Offe Enterprises

If you work with .GIF/.TIFF/.PCX graphic files, you need VUIMAGE! VUIMAGE lets you display or print .GIF files and bilevel/grayscale .TIFF files. It's fast and uses only 150K of free memory.

VUIMAGE automatically configures for your monitor with excellent color rendition on CGA, EGA, VGA, MCGA, and Super VGA (Hercules monochrome is also supported).

Automatically scale a graphic to the size of your screen or manually scale from 1% to 999%. Zoom in and out, pan to different parts of a large graphic, and easily adjust brightness while the picture is on screen.

Print out any graphic (with six dithering options) and VUIMAGE will automatically size it for your printer. (Some .GIF images are provided.)

In addition, you can specify a list of files to be automatically viewed to eating great slide shows and demos.

Vuimage (PC-SIG Disk #2585)

(PC-SIG Disk# 2585)

Special Requirements: *Graphics card.*
Author Registration: *$30.00*

▼ ▼ ▼

Printer Managers

Bradford
by Contorer Computing

You don't need an expensive laser printer to output pages in beautiful fonts. With BRADFORD, you can print any ASCII or WordStar file in different types of fonts (typestyles) on your dot-matrix printer. The fonts include Greek text, double-height fonts, typewriter quality print, a variety of italics, and much more. There are over 40 fonts included and you can create additional fonts.

BRADFORD is excellent for printing other languages, such as Russian or Hebrew. Print reports and memos. The font commands can either be issued when BRADFORD is executed, or can be inserted into text files.

BRADFORD also has commands for page formatting. These include adjustable margins, center text, adjustable page length, underline, double underline, boldface, superscript, subscript, and proportional spacing.

(PC-SIG Disk# 1053)

Special Requirements: *IBM or Epson compatible or Gemini-10X printer.*
Author Registration: *$25.00 or $39.95.*

Exciting New fonts and
a new level of format control.

Choose from 42 different fonts
including greek αβξδε and hebrew אבדד,
or create your own.

Enhance a document with
Underline, Double Underline,

Bradford will even help you
center, justify, and set your margins.

Bradford (PC-SIG Disk# 1053)

Disk Spool II
by Budget Software Company

Don't waste valuable computer time waiting for a report, a memo, a spreadsheet or any other printing job to finish printing. Send your print files to a spooler. The spooler will hold your file until the printer is available while you go on with your work. DISK SPOOL II has two main parts: a spooler and a writer. The spooler intercepts data going to the printer, and redirects it to disk. The writer takes data from the disk and sends it to the printer.

The pop-up menu lets you control whether or not the spooler and/or the writer are active. You can, for example, start the spooler and not the writer, sending the printed output to disk and nothing will be printed. This mode is particularly useful if you don't have a printer attached to your computer. You can still do your work and transport the spool file to a machine that has a printer attached.

Change spool and writer ports as needed, drive more than one printing device at a time, and fine-tune your system for optimal printing speed.

(PC-SIG Disk# 609)

Special Requirements: *None.*
Author Registration: *$44.00*
➤*ASP Member.*

Epset
by George Campbell

EPSET offers you a nifty collection of batch commands to set the print parameters on the Epson MX, LX and FX series. One command, TINY.BAT, produces the smallest print you've ever seen from your dot matrix!. It works with most Epson compatibles, (but experiment first).

(PC-SIG Disk# 1370)

Special Requirements: *None.*
Author Registration: *$5.00*

FXmaster
by Brian Raub

FXMASTER uses one menu to let you select all 160+ Epson FX-series fonts from your keyboard or batch files. WSASCII converts WordStar files to ASCII and vice versa. MMSTAT computes statistics for field lengths in a mail merge file.

FXMASTER uses one menu, or command line parameters, to let you select all Epson FX-series fonts from your keyboard or batch files. It can issue a reset, line feed, or form feed, and can variably set margins, line spacing and form length, international character sets, and skip over perforation. It also allows you to toggle on/off your printer's sheet-feeder, paper-out sensor, typewriter and quiet (half-speed) modes.

🖎 = Updated Program
☆ = New Program

WSACII converts WordStar files to ASCII and vice versa. Several special options allow you to customize the conversion: strip dot commands, expand taps, strip leading spaces, and compress spaces.

MMSTAT computes summary statistics, average/maximum/minimum lengths, and number of empty or zero-length fields, for each field in a mail merge file.

(PC-SIG Disk# 1369)

Special Requirements: *Epson printer.*
Author Registration: *$10.00 to $15.00.*

Garc's Utilities
by George Campbell

Need to find a name or other text in a long file? Set up print parameters for your Epson compatible printer? Choose screen colors on CGA, EGA and VGA systems? Or find a BBS phone number quickly and easily? If so, GARC'S for you!

Give TEXTSRCH a filename and the text, name or data you are trying to locate. Go warm your coffee and by the time you get back, this program will have numbered the lines in your file and listed those which contain the text you are searching for.

EPSET offers you a nifty collection of batch commands to set the print parameters on the Epson MX, LX and FX series. One command, TINY.BAT, produces the smallest print you've ever seen from your dot matrix! EPSET works with most Epson compatibles, but experiment first.

COLORSET displays a chart of available colors from which you can choose your screen settings on CGA, EGA and VGA systems.

FINDBBS provides you quick access to hundreds of bulletin board systems' (BBS) phone numbers across the nation. Dial up and log-on. It also serves as the BBS search door for WILDCAT! BBS (PC-SIG disks # 745, 746).

(PC-SIG Disk# 1370)

Special Requirements: *None.*
Author Registration: *$5.00 each.*

LQ Printer Utility ✍
by Granny's Old Fashioned Software

So you want letter quality, but you're stuck with that old nine-pin dot matrix printer? Don't just resign, join the club; discover LQ PRINTER UTILITY! It is an impressive printer utility program that lets you use your inexpensive dot matrix printer to print a variety of fonts in near-letter quality. It can be loaded as a memory-resident program to filter the data from your wordprocessor or other programs, or it can be used alone to process individual files. But if you have the 80K or so of RAM, the memory-resident mode is the most convenient way to use this program.

LQ PRINTER UTILITY includes pre-defined fonts of Courier, Greek, Helvetica, Roman, and many others (italics for each font are included). A character editor is also provided to let you modify or create your own font sets. Each font character is 10 by 24 dots so there is enough resolution to make some fairly decent fonts.

Like all programs of this sort, LQ PRINTER UTILITY uses a graphics mode for your beautiful new fonts and printing takes longer — but it's worth the wait. It also provides a print spooler, and this optimizes graphics printing.

Included is the program BIGPRINT, which lets you print large-letter banners (using any of the same fonts that LQ uses). If your printer is an Epson (or compatible), the banner letters are made using the block graphics characters; otherwise, they are created with asterisks. (Just make sure you don't have LQ loaded when you run BIGPRINT, or your printer will be running forever.)

A new feature of LQ is a program that lets you create and edit your own letterheads. LETHEAD is a graphics editor that works with LQ to produce high-resolution letterheads consisting of 1" x 1" pictures and up to four lines of accompanying text.

(PC-SIG Disk# 718)

Special Requirements: *Epson or compatible printer.*
Author Registration: *$35.00*
➤*ASP Member.*

Print Control Program
by Blanchard Software

PRINT CONTROL PROGRAM (PCP) is a time saver for busy computer users. Memory resident, it gives your PrtScr command all the power of your printer with a few keystrokes.

Pop it up while running any other program. PCP menus let you send control codes to the printer to select print modes. Print any rectangular area of the screen. Set margins on the printed page. The printed image shows underlining, high intensity, reverse video and high order ASCII characters - whatever your printer can support.

PCP lets you type anywhere on the screen. You can use this to edit or annotate displays before printing. The original screen is restored when you leave PCP.

PCP is a handy way to enhance reports, make documentation more readable, or just to get access to the full capability of your printer.

(PC-SIG Disk# 1522)

Special Requirements: *Printer.*
Author Registration: *$10.00*

Prn Set
by c/o Hire Education

PRNSET is a universal nonresident printer-setting program that takes its configuration information from a file, which you can make with any text editor. This feature makes it possible to set the print control symbols for any printer and select and organize the instructions you want to have in PRNSET's repertoire. It can operate interactively through a menu, from a batch file, or directly from the DOS command line.

(PC-SIG Disk# 1303)

Special Requirements: *Printer.*
Author Registration: *$15.00*

ProMenu32
by NewLife Software

A memory-resident printer-control menu for Epson and compatible printers.

PMENU3 gives you control codes, such as condensed, double strike, or underline, on command. Once loaded, you can access PMENU3 while running your program and enter codes one at a time, or combinations of codes such as "bold and italics".

Smarter than your average printing program, PMENU3 does not display or send conflicting codes to the printer, and can also be removed from memory.

(PC-SIG Disk# 779)

Special Requirements: *Printer.*
Author Registration: *$15.00*

SetPrint
by Ponderosa Software

SETPRINT is a menu-driven printer-setting utility. Used before printing a file, you can set pitch and weight, set a special printer mode such as underlining, or just reset the printer. Commands can be embedded within the file to be printed to further change modes. In addition, you may pause the printing for manual feeding.

(PC-SIG Disk# 1312)

Special Requirements: *Two floppy drives and Epson-FX compatible printer.*
Author Registration: *$10.00*

TPOP
by Big John Software

TPOP is a memory-resident printer utility to use with any application. TPOP lets you use your printer directly as a typewriter or you can edit a full screen of text. While editing, you can mark blocks of text to send to the printer.

The left margin of the text is located wherever the print head is positioned before printing and lets you line up the printer for envelopes and labels. Control codes can be sent to the printer. You can direct the output from TPOP to any port (parallel or serial — LPT1, LPT2, COM1, or COM2), and you can permanently swap the addresses of printer ports.

(PC-SIG Disk# 1026)

Special Requirements: *A hard drive and a printer.*
Author Registration: *$10.00*

🖙 = Updated Program
☆ = New Program

Typerite
by Chris Wiley

Turn your PC and its printer into an electric typewriter. TYPERITE is simple, straight-forward and faster than using a wordprocessor for some day-to-day jobs.

(PC-SIG Disk# 860)

Special Requirements: *Printer.*
Author Registration: *None.*

Versa-Spool
by Jeff Newbro

VERSA-SPOOL brings a memory resident multi-printer spooler with big buffers and a bunch of options to the PC. You get multiple buffers with adjustable output speeds. If you're in a jam, you can redirect a printer output stream from one printer to another. That lets you use two printers at once to print the same file, a bonus for people dealing with big database files. It can also be a lifesaver for users who have a word processor whose output goes to a device other than the location of a letter quality printer.

While useful to beginners, VERSA-SPOOL permits sophisticated adjustments and monitoring of its performance through command line arguments computer veterans are comfortable with. It even allows the computer- wise to exploit memory locations beyond the 640k barrier that DOS was written to accommodate by specifying the location of RAM memory which VERSA-SPOOL will use for its buffers. People with light programming experience can usually find between 64k and 192k of unused RAM lurking in a PC equipped with 640K RAM.

(PC-SIG Disk# 1606)

Special Requirements: *None.*
Author Registration: *$20.00*

▼ ▼ ▼

Printer Utilities

BothSides ☆
by SPELLBOUND! Software

As its name indicates, BOTHSIDES formats text files of any pagination method so they can be printed to both sides of your printer paper. The program can send your file directly to the printer. First it prints the odd numbered pages, then stops to let you turn the paper over and prints the even numbered pages.

It can also format your text files by paginating them and printing a footer containing title line and page number at the bottom of every page. In addition, you can specify an inside margin to leave more room for binder holes!

Imagine how much paper you could save and how much thinner your documentation will be from all the shareware packages you print out!

(PC-SIG Disk# 2650)

Special Requirements: *Hard drive.*
Author Registration: *$10.00/$15.00*

Citizen Printer Utilities ✍
by R.K. West Consulting

CITIZEN allows you to change the pitch (characters per inch) at which you want to print your document on your Citizen printer. It handles 10 (pica), 12 (elite), 17, 20, 8.5, 6 and 5 pitch and lets you quickly type one or more addresses from the keyboard without having to enter a wordprocessor.

(PC-SIG Disk# 1543)

Special Requirements: *Citizen MSP-10, MSP-15, MSP-40, or MSP-45 printer.*
Author Registration: *None.*
➤*ASP Member.*

FXMatrix
by Jimmy Paris Software

Are you sick and tired of printing the same old characters over and over again on your Epson FX or JX printer? Or maybe you've decided to come up with your own alphabet. Well, FXMATRIX can add some spice to your printouts.

FXMATRIX is a matrix program that permits you to design user-created characters, store them in a file, and download them to the Epson FX and JX dot matrix printers. These created characters can then be used from any word processor, even if your word processor resets the printer upon execution.

(PC-SIG Disk# 485)

Special Requirements: *Epson FX or JX printer.*
Author Registration: *$18.00*
➤*ASP Member.*

Letrhead   *by Technical Service Associates*

You have a small startup business with more time and ambition than bucks — but you need classy-looking letterhead stationery and impressive envelopes and can't afford a graphics designer or expensive printing. LETRHEAD gives you a way to look real good, real cheap!

Create your own custom letterhead stationery and envelopes using a standard dot matrix printer. Design your own distinctive company logo using the built-in font editor.

A mail merge feature makes it easy to print custom envelopes complete with mailing addresses drawn from your ASCII files. Or crank out fancy labels to dress up your shipments.

(PC-SIG Disk# 1519)

Special Requirements: *Graphics printer.*
Author Registration: *$10.00*

LQMatrix ☆   *by Jimmy Paris Software*

LQMATRIX is an editor for user-made characters (soft fonts) for Epson LQ 24-pin dot-matrix printers and compatibles. It comes with the editor, a downloader, LQ.EXE, and over 40 complete fonts including a wide variety of common fonts, serif, script, etc. as well as old English, Gothic, two Cyrillic fonts, and classical Greek.

LQMATRIX and fonts are designed to use the text mode for printing user-made fonts. This mode is as fast as using the default letters and is useful for printing long texts. In the text mode, the printer accepts a soft font into memory and uses it rather than the built-in font. In fact, when instructed, it can switch back and forth between the two. If you have written a paper in English but wish to cite examples in the Greek alphabet, you can 'download' the Greek font and use it only when necessary.

Two types of users need these programs. First are those who wish to use a variety of ready-made fonts for different purposes or just for variety's sake. These users may not be interested in creating their own fonts. For them, all that is needed is the LQ.EXE program. With it, any of the premade fonts included here can be downloaded to the printer.

Others may wish to create their own fonts, modify others, or create a small number of special characters for a specific task. LQMATRIX.EXE provides just the environment these users need.

It is an easy-to-use program with many features that permit the user to create characters, store them in a file, and download them to the Epson LQ family of 24-pin dot-matrix printers. Design Draft, NLQ (10 CPI), and proportional characters.

(PC-SIG Disk# 2654)

Special Requirements: *Epson LQ 24-pin dot-matrix printer or compatible.*
Author Registration: *$19.50 ($24.00 overseas)*
➤*ASP Member.*

Multi-Print   *by Gerald P. Doyon*

Looking for a better alternative to the DOS PRINT program? Something that will give you more control over your printing? MULTI-PRINT accepts several different parameters for such added features as printing multiple copies of a document, left margin adjustment, page length, page width, and the ability to add page numbers and time stamps to the printout. Like PRINT.COM which comes on your DOS disk, this program has a print queue for multiple files, but MULTI-PRINT can also work in batch mode accepting a list of documents (with command options) from a file. MULTI-PRINT prints a file in interactive mode constantly displaying what is being printed, the files in the print queue, and a helpful estimation of print time.

The added control and flexibilty that come with MULTI-PRINT make it a necessary part of any user's utility library.

(PC-SIG Disk# 1661)

Special Requirements: *None.*
Author Registration: *$15.00*

PPRINT
by Patri-Soft

An extensive file printing system with many configurable options. PPRINT has an external definition file which can be tailored to support any printer. Many options are available to the user: Headers, footers, line/page numbering, lines per inch, maximum amount to print, start page xx, end with page xx, and many more. Great support for HP LaserJet II and other similar printers with a special option for printing C source code.

PPRINT is special and unique because it is customizable to any printer type. It also allows you to access printer features not normally available for printing normal text files.

(PC-SIG Disk# 2275)

Special Requirements: *A hard drive, and a printer.*
Author Registration: *$20.00*
➤ *ASP Member.*

Print-matic
by Software Brewing Company

PRINT-MATIC alleviates the hassle of sending setup control codes to your printer. It consists of two separate utilities: PMATIC and PMACRO. With PMATIC, you can press a pre-defined hot key inside any application, and a window pops onto the screen from which one of the 16 user-defined control codes may be sent to the printer. PMATIC will work inside most application programs.

With PMACRO, printer features that you couldn't use before become accessible, allowing you to embed printer control codes in a document to control the print output. You can define up to 100 macros as control codes, each up to 25 characters long.

(PC-SIG Disk# 2048)

Special Requirements: *None.*
Author Registration: *$20.00*

Printer
by Alan Jones

The printer utilities in this package are for Epson and compatible printers. Control your printer from the keyboard. Specify a variety of print modes and fonts such as compressed, italics, emphasized, underline, and more — from within other applications.

SP is a print spooler used to hold data intended for the printer. It works like the buffers that can be installed in the printer but the data is stored in RAM storage instead of in the printer. The buffer is unloaded to the printer at the printer's speed while DOS proceeds at its speed. You can specify the the size of the buffer from 1k to 62K, the number of copies desired, and also which printer port you want to use.

(PC-SIG Disk# 186)

Special Requirements: *Epson MX80 or compatible printer.*
Author Registration: *None.*

Printer Art 2 & YAMP, TMAC
by Galaxy Systems Corp

Here's another collection of art from the author of PRINTER ART (disk #154). This disk has a wide variety of art that can you can print without any type of graphics needed on your system. You'll find everything from a dragon or Snoopy to the Statue of Liberty. There are also some pictures that are not suitable for children, so parental discretion is advised.

Another program that has been included on this disk is TMAC100. With this program, you can convert a drawing that's been made with ASCII characters and convert it to a ReadMAC format. After your drawing has been converted, you can then display it on any system that has graphics capabilities. Any utility that can read ReadMAC format drawings will be able to read the drawings made with TMAC100.

(PC-SIG Disk# 2295)

Special Requirements: *384K RAM, and CGA.*
Author Registration: *None.*

Printer Utilities 7
by Dalicom Software

X-PRINT is a memory-resident printer utility for Epson and compatible printers. It lets you change the printing style to pica, elite, compressed, or near letter quality. You can also change the lines per page to 66, 51, or 33. Once loaded, X-PRINT stays in memory and can be activated at any time, even if you are in the middle of executing a program.

LINES takes any ASCII text file, and converts certain selected characters into line drawing characters. These line-drawing characters are part of the IBM extended character set that can be used to make professional-looking forms and charts on the screen or the printer.

DISK LABELER makes disk labels using one of three different sizes of labels: 1" x 3", 1" x 3.5", and 2.75" x 2.75". It's menu-driven and easy to learn (requires CGA).

SETIT is a menu-driven BASIC program that sets up an Epson FX series or compatible printer. Don't change the printer's dip switches or use BASIC to set up your printer. SETIT can set the printing style to near letter quality (NLQ), draft, proportional, condensed, double-wide, double-high, emphasized, double strike, superscript, subscript, and underline. You can also select the character set to be used from Epson character graphics, italics, or one of the international character sets.

GIFTWRAP lets you make custom wrapping paper. Just enter a short and personal message and the program prints it in slanted stripes or a zig- zag pattern.

(PC-SIG Disk# 1069)

Special Requirements: *IBM or Epson compatible printer and CGA.*
Author Registration: *$15.00.*

Printer Utilities 8 *by Small & Associates*

ATTENTION Star, Gemini, Epson and Panasonic printer owners — Here's a set of utility programs to exercise some of the more popular printers and really take advantage of their special capabilities. Jazz up your printing!

(PC-SIG Disk# 438)

Special Requirements: *Star, Gemini, Epson, or Panasonic printer.*
Author Registration: *$13.00*

PrintGL ✍ *by Cary Ravitz*

PRINTGL prints an HP-GL (Hewlett-Packard Graphics Language - HP 7475 subset) plotfile on a matrix printer. HP-GL is widely supported by graphics programs including AutoCAD, Generic CADD, MathCAD, SAS, MICROCADAM, Schema, and many more. PRINTGL has native mode drivers for Epson and NEC compatible 9 and 24 pin dot matrix printers, HP Laserjet, Deskjet, and PaintJet, and IBM 9 and 24 pin Proprinters, Quietwriter 2 and 3, and LaserPrinter. It will also display plots with a CGA, EGA, VGA, enhanced VGA, or HGC and output a bit map or GEM .IMG file.

Even if your graphics program supports your printer, you may find that PRINTGL gives better print quality. PRINTGL uses the best graphics modes available for each printer that it supports. If you need printed graphics output from personal software, you can output HP-GL and use PRINTGL to do the printing. This gives immediate support to a wide range of printers.

PRINTGL Menu Interface (PMI), included with PRINTGL, gives you easy access to PRINTGL's many options, and lets you select a list of plotfiles to print.

(PC-SIG Disk# 2481)

Special Requirements: *A printer.*
Author Registration: *$40.00*
➤*ASP Member.*

PrintPlus ☆ *by Lambert Klein*

PRINTPLUS gives you a powerful and easy way to view and print all of your ASCII text files. List all your files and simply select any text file to view or print. View files, tag and copy, move, delete or redirect output to an ASCII file. PRINTPLUS features pull-down menus and optional mouse support. Print files from specified page numbers, print line numbers, preview number of pages to print, and replace IBM box characters with user-defined characters. Configurations are possible for printer setup, screen colors, mouse functions, text output, etc. Print filename, current date/time and file date/time at the top of the first page.

(PC-SIG Disk# 2718)

Special Requirements: *No special requirements.*
Author Registration: *$19.00*
➤*ASP Member.*

✍ = Updated Program
☆ = New Program

Prntest
by Harry P. Calevas

PRN-TEST provides for testing the complete instruction sets of Centronics 102A printers, standard Okidata printers, or any printer compatible with the IBM graphics printer. Also, makes your printer show you ALL the possible characters it can print!

(PC-SIG Disk# 1522)

Special Requirements: *Printer.*
Author Registration: *$15.00*

Rstprint
by Harry P. Calevas

The on/off switch is often the first thing to fail with computer products; so quit shortening the life of your printer when RSTPRINT will reset your printer without ever reaching for the switch. This easy to use program quickly resets any printer on a parallel port on your system. It does not check for any other operation, just issues a reset.

RSTPRINT is unique in that it does not require the printer to be ready, or on-line. If the printer is powered on and not ready, off-line, it will be set to a ready condition, on-line, after RSTPRINT is run. RSTPRINT causes the printer to do a power-on reset, which is the same as turning the printer power off and back on. RSTPRINT is an excellent program to use after you have done some fancy printing because it sets the printer back to its default settings.

(PC-SIG Disk# 1842)

Special Requirements: *CGA.*
Author Registration: *$15.00*

Utilities Galore
by JJO Software

Make your printer serve you better with this collection of utilities. There's even a game thrown in for fun!

DIRPRN prints a disk directory sorted in various ways to make it easy to find a file. ENVPRN turns your computer into an electric typewriter for quickly dashing off addresses on an envelope in a variety of fonts. LABPRN works similarly but is specifically formatted to handle labels, such as for binders/drawers. MERPRN merges several separate text files into one formatted printed text. SETPRN sets the printer parameters prior to using a print spooler. XTRPRN extracts and prints call declarations and comments from Turbo Pascal source files.

All the programs let you select the print quality, text style, margin width, page numbering, printer port, and line spacing. They can be added as batch files to run whenever needed.

COLORE lets you choose the colors your monitor will display when your system first boots-up. You can select from 16 different colors for the foreground, background, and border of your monitor.

SURVIVAL is a game that requires quick reflexes. With a boxing glove you must punch monsters before they descend to the bottom of the screen, sending them back to the top.

LABEL computerizes your personal address/telephone directory for easy reference and printing of reports and labels. Menu options let you print: address labels (using standard $15/16$" x $31/2$" wide labels), list of all records (done with two entries side-by-side on $81/2$" x 11" paper), telephone list (only those records with a telephone number are printed), and individual records you select. Handles both three and four line addresses, automatically suppressing blank lines.

DOCFORM lets you add printing instructions to any text file to specify boldface print, underlined print, margins, double or triple spacing, headers, and footers — which then print correctly on almost every printer.

(PC-SIG Disk# 1299)

Special Requirements: *DataProducts DP8070, Epson MX/FX, IBM Proprinter, or compatible.*
Author Registration: *$20.00 for LABEL*

VPrint - Virtual Printer Utility for the IBM PC ✍
by Whitman Software

This disk has a set of utility programs useful in many printer applications. There are programs to print banners, print data sideways for wide documents, use print spoolers, do graphic screen dumps to a wide variety of printers, permit output that would normally go to the printer to be redirected to a disk file, and change printer settings. The ever-popular SIDEWAYS program rounds out the disk.

(PC-SIG Disk# 411)

Special Requirements: *None.*
Author Registration: *Various Amounts.*

Zapcode
by Morton Utilities, International

This is the ultimate printer control utility to burn them all away. Use ZAPCODE to select fonts, reset the printer, change margins, advance the page, and anything else your printer is capable of doing. It runs as memory-resident or standalone. ZAPCODE supports all types of printers: laser, dot-matrix, ink-jet, and even plotters! Drivers are included for all the popular printers. The printer driver editor allows you to easily customize or create your own, or the author will create yours for free.

There is no longer a need to hunt for your printer manual for control strings. Simply pop up ZAPCODE, select the desired printer option(s), and let the program enter the control strings for you — just as if you had typed them at the keyboard. It works with all programs.

(PC-SIG Disk# 2236)

Special Requirements: *None.*
Author Registration: *Single-user license = $19.95*
➤*ASP Member.*

▼ ▼ ▼

Printer Utilities, Laser

2Faced ✍
by Petersen Programming & Consulting

Who wants a two-faced software program? You do, if you want to save money or precious elbow room when printing files you plan to keep.

2FACED allows the HP LaserJet II+ and compatibles to scrunch two pages of text on each side of a single 8-1/2x11 sheet of paper — making it ideal for saving paper, storage space, and toner when printing hard copies of documentation or source code.

Options let you print the filename of the text file as a header, along with the file's creation time and date and the time and date of the printing. It also can draw a box around each page or add grey halftone bars which resemble the bars on fanfold computer paper. You also get a count of pages reported as they print.

(PC-SIG Disk# 1487)

Special Requirements: *HP LaserJet II+ or compatible printer.*
Author Registration: *$35.00*

4Print
by Korenthal Associates, Inc.

If you're a professional programmer or a home hacker who's "gone laser", 4PRINT is a simple-to-use, paper-conserving, laser printer utility that can ease program code documentation. 4PRINT lets the HP LaserJet, LaserJet+, Laser Jet II, and compatibles print title lines plus four 66-line, 80-column pages of ASCII text on 8-1/2" X 11" sheet of paper.

4PRINT helps you maintain source code by automatically recording a program listing's file name, date, time, and page count. It allows 264 lines of contiguous code to be visible at once in an opened three-ring binder, and can print multiple source files with a single invocation. 4PRINT handles tabs, form feeds, and end-of-file characters like a pro!

(PC-SIG Disk# 1079)

Special Requirements: *HP LaserJet, LaserJet+, LaserJet II, or compatibles.*
Author Registration: *$25.00 or $35.00.*
➤*ASP Member.*

Badge-O-Magic
by Ward Mundy Software

BADGE-O-MAGIC is a dBASE-compatible badge and nametag generator designed for use with an HP LaserJet II or 100% compatible laser. Using any dBASE III or IV data base (one is included with the software), BADGE-O-MAGIC generates one to four line badges with an optional header and footer line. The badges can be printed using type styles of 20 to 40 points. Five fonts are included with the program. Each badge is 3" x 4" with six badges being printed on each 8-1/2 x 11 inch page. BADGE-O-MAGIC also includes the necessary software to download the soft fonts to your laser printer and to print a perforation template suitable for ordering perforated name tag stock from your local printer. The perforated paper and badge holders also are available from the author when you register. .

BADGE-O-MAGIC also includes powerful file management utilities which permit you to edit and add data to any dBASE file without leaving the program.

Typical uses for this software would be to prepare name badges for participants at a conference, convention, family meeting, social event, etc.

The 18 page on-disk manual which comes with BADGE-O-MAGIC is organized very well with simple instructions to install and use the program quickly. Running the program is very simple, with all functions available from a main menu.

(PC-SIG Disk# 2034)

Special Requirements: *384K RAM, and HP LaserJet II or compatible laser printer.*
Author Registration: *$45.00*
➤*ASP Member.*

Dear Teacher HP Laser Font   *by Daniel Ross*

DEAR TEACHER is a sloppy handwriting soft font for the HP LaserJet II. LISTING LEVEL: Unsupported programs and disks

PROGRAM ID: 12242 Disks: 4502 PROGRAM NAME: Dr. File Finders Guide to Shareware #2 LONG DESCRIPTION:

(PC-SIG Disk# 1228)

Special Requirements: *HP LaserJet II.*
Author Registration: *None.*

DeskJet Softfonts & Utilities ✍   *by Elfring Soft Fonts*

HP Deskjet owners rejoice! Now a complete soft font package is available for the DeskJet. ELFRING DESKJET SOFTFONT PACKAGE (EDSP) has 25 different fonts and a lightning fast download program written especially for the DeskJet or DeskJet Plus with a 128K or 256K RAM cartridge.

EDSP offers more fonts for the deskjet in more sizes than any other package (including HP's own). The download program is fully-functional, loading fonts at nearly three times the speed of the HP package. EDSP fonts are available in 6 to 30 point size ranges while HP fonts stop at 12 points. Included in this package is an unusual symbol font that permits the inclusion of character sized airplanes, umbrellas, trade marks, and more in documents.

Soft fonts for the DeskJet are not compatible with LaserJet fonts, so many applications, such as MS-WINDOWS, do not support soft fonts for the DeskJet. With some adjustments this package enables DeskJets to fully emulate LaserJets, making the DeskJet RAM cartridge worth the price. Printer drivers for WordPerfect 5.0 and 5.1, Word 5.0, and PC-Write are included.

(PC-SIG Disk# 1462)

Special Requirements: *HP DeskJet with 128K RAM cartridge.*
Author Registration: *$25.00*
➤*ASP Member.*

Download   *by Elfring Soft Fonts*

DOWNLOAD is an utility program that manages the process of downloading soft fonts to a Hewlett Packard LaserJet, DeskJet, or compatible printers. DOWNLOAD can also select fonts as they are being sent. DOWNLOAD can send a font, or group of fonts, through the standard parallel printer port to your LaserJet or DeskJet printer. You have optional control over the soft font ID number, whether the font is permanent or temporary, and whether it is a primary or secondary font. A list of fonts may be sent to the printer by specifying the individual fonts names in an ASCII text file. All fonts resident in your laser may be optionally deleted before new fonts are downloaded, or you can reset the printer first.

(PC-SIG Disk# 1769)

Special Requirements: *HP LaserJet, HP DeskJet, or compatible printer.*
Author Registration: *$15.00*
➤*ASP Member.*

EFS's European LaserJet Soft Fonts ✍   *by Elfring Soft Fonts*

This is a collection of 12 soft fonts that will print almost any European language.

The fonts are for any HP LaserJet II or compatible printer and include Garamond, Helv, & Roman 12-point medium/bold/italic, plus 18-point bold versions. The package also supplies utility programs for downloading and printing sample sheets of fonts. Printer drivers are included for WordPerfect 5.0 & 5.1, Ventura, and PageMaker.

The fonts come with the PC-850 symbol set and directly support German, Spanish, French and many other languages.

(PC-SIG Disk# 2575)

Special Requirements: *HP LaserJet II printer*
Author Registration: *$25.00*
➤*ASP Member.*

Font "Tiles"   *by Daniel Ross*

TILES is a soft font for the HP LaserJet II printer. It is not an "Alpha-Numeric" font, instead it replaces the normal character set with a series of random graphic symbols. The font is used in the "Portrait" orientation. Installing the font is very simple; just copy the file TILES.LOD to your laser printer and you are ready to go. Also on the disk are all of the programs used to create the font or modify it. Using these programs to modify the font or to create your own requires some 'C' programming knowledge.

(PC-SIG Disk# 2028)

Special Requirements: *HP LaserJet II or compatible laser printer.*
Author Registration: *None.*

Laser Letterhead plus ✍   *by Consultant Pharmacist Services, Inc*

This program is an easy-to-use laser printing program that will let you create letterhead stationery and matching envelopes on your HP LaserJet printer. This includes all Hewlett Packard printers except the original LaserJet Model. Supported models are the LaserJet Plus, LaserJet 500 Plus, LaserJet 200, Series II, Series IID, Series IIP, and the new Series III. A closely compatible laser printer may also be used.

All font handling is automatically done for you. Copy your fonts into the directory with the program files, place the font names in the Setup program, and you are ready to go. With a few menu choices you can create stationery that looks as though it came from a typesetter's workbench.

Any laser printer using Level IV (page formatting feature) HP Printer Command Language (PCL) can use LASER LETTERHEAD. Using proportional fonts of your choice you may select centered or left justified groupings with ten variations of borders and shadings precisely formatted and calculated. You do not need bold type: the program will make bold type from your light or regular fonts.

Create not only a business letterhead, but a personal version also. You do not have to calculate each line of print, nor worry about the difficult task of centering proportional fonts. The program does it all for you. Boxing in lines is a snap, and shading the letterhead is a matter of choice. Everything is menu-driven to make it easy.

Addresses placed on envelopes can be saved to the address database and used again. This dBASE-type file can be exported to a wordprocessor and used to write form letters.

(PC-SIG Disk#'s 2037, 2616)

Special Requirements: *640K RAM, DOS 3.0+, hard drive, laser printer, soft fonts/cartridge.*
Author Registration: *$25.00*

LaserEnvelope ✍   *by Williamsware*

LASERENVELOPE is a very simple utility to print address information on envelopes using an HP LaserJet II printer. This program is extremely easy to use; the user is allowed 3 lines of text for the return address and 5 lines for the destination. The program will save your return address on disk, and will import an ASCII mailing list file when named on the command line. There is no documentation with this program and none is needed; simply run the program and follow the instructions on the screen. LASERENVELOPE uses whatever font you have selected from your printer keypad - internal, soft, or cartridge.

(PC-SIG Disk# 2028)

Special Requirements: *HP LaserJet II/IIP/III/compatible printer and ANSI.*
Author Registration: *$15.00*

LaserJet Soft Fonts and Utilities ✍   *by Elfring Soft Fonts*

SOFT FONTS AND UTILITIES is a boon to laser printer owners. Imagine a great font downloader, handy utilities, and a wealth of incredibly useful soft fonts — all in one package!

For headlines, you get 21 point Broadway font with a Ventura width table and matching EGA screen font. To complicate things, try a set of 24 point symbols such as copyrights, bullets and circled numbers.

Next, drop down to 10 or 12 point typefaces. You get proportionally spaced Roman Times in bold, italic and medium. Likewise, you get proportionally spaced Helvetica fonts in bold, italic and medium. If that's not enough, try Garamond in medium, bold and italic. For headlines try the 18 point Helvetica and Roman fonts.

An elegant Century Legal is buttressed by an extended character set with a number of useful symbols. It includes printer drivers for MS Word and WordPerfect. The proportionally spaced Script soft font and the Greek font will give your documents variety. Programmers can document routines with the font filled with keyboard characters.

The download program is as elegant as the typefaces. You can use it to download any HP compatible font. If you prefer, it will assign an ID number of your choice and designate primary or secondary and permanent or temporary status for a font. The utility can download directly from archived files.

Print a sample sheet of any particular font — a handy utility if you've come across a disk full of fonts. Another utility will print out the sort of technical information on typefaces graphic artists delight in. A final program gives you information on LaserJet and DeskJet font formats.

(PC-SIG Disk# 1463)

Special Requirements: *HP LaserJet or compatible.*
Author Registration: *$25.00*
➤*ASP Member.*

P4UP   *by Hexagon Products*

P4UP compresses 4 normal page images onto one page (four quadrants) of output, using its own fonts, with an HP LaserJet II printer. P4UP is very easy to use in command line form (just like DOS print) and has several options to change the order of the quadrants. No soft font expertise is required. It is ideal for printing large documents or program source files. Since four pages are shrunk to one piece of paper a lot of desk space (and paper) can be saved.

(PC-SIG Disk# 1460)

Special Requirements: *LaserJet printer.*
Author Registration: *$29.95*

Pamphlet   *by Martin C. Beattie*

PAMPHLET is a printing utility for HP LaserJets that creates 5-1/2" x 8-1/2" mini-booklets or pamphlets.

PAMPHLET divides any ASCII file into mini-pages, and then prints them in landscape (sideways) mode, two-up on a single sheet. A second pass through the printer to print the opposite side and — VOILA! You have a mini book. Page arrangement is automatically determined by the program so the resultant sheets are in correct order. Just fold down the middle and staple to form useful little pamphlets, booklets, or documentation manuals. PAMPHLET is also great for parents wanting to create personalized story books for their children.

Users can select from any of 25 resident fonts, upload additional soft fonts, place page breaks, automatically number pages, underline, and more. There is even a built-in editor, and a configuration for using the program with European metric A4 paper size.

(PC-SIG Disk# 1222)

Special Requirements: *HP LaserJet II.*
Author Registration: *$25.00*

Qfont ☆   *by Jamestown Software*

LaserJet users, prepare to be amazed. QFONT is a mouse-driven font editor to enlarge, shrink, or slant any HP-compatible soft font. Turn bit-mapped fonts into outlines or shadows. Make fonts bolder or lighter, or fill a character with a pattern. Using the built-in paint program, create an entirely new font or design a logo (a set of master fonts helps get you started).

QFONT offers pull-down menus, mouse support, "fatbit" editing, and even a "smooth" feature to remove "jaggies" from enlarged characters. Modify the font header, download a font, and much more.

If you have a LaserJet printer, use QFONT to edit current fonts, or create entirely new characters to suit your taste and creativity.

(PC-SIG Disk# 2529)

Special Requirements: *512K RAM, and a LaserJet printer. A mouse is recommended.*
Author Registration: *$80.00*
➤*ASP Member.*

SEND2LJ
by Daniel Ross

SEND2LJ is a printer utility program used to send commands, fonts, and text files to your HP LaserJet II printer. The operation of the program is simple, just enter your commands into a text file (using your favorite text editor) following the documented format, and the program will add the needed escape character wherever you have indicated when sending the command file to the printer. The documentation is fairly simple, and the disk contains a sample command file for you to try (provided you have the softfont specified in the command file handy). The program, as designed, is set up to work on printers hooked up to the LPT1 port; to change this requires some programming knowledge.

(PC-SIG Disk# 2028)

Special Requirements: *HP LaserJet II or compatible laser printer.*
Author Registration: *None.*

Tiny Fonts for HP Laser Jet
by Daniel Ross

As its name suggests TINY FONTS is a set of programs that generate very small character fonts for the HP LaserJet series II printers — so small in fact, that you might need a magnifying glass to read them.

There are two aptly named fonts, MYOPIA and FLYSPECK. MYOPIA crams 128 lines, with up to 200 characters each, on to one sheet of paper. It saves you reams and reams of paper, excellent for those long text files that you have to print on a daily basis. FLYSPECK outputs even smaller, 188 lines with up to 260 characters each per page.

In addition to dense printing of text files, these tiny fonts are suitable for labeling schematics and other technical diagrams. C source code as well as tips on how to generate custom fonts are also included for those who want to experiment on the micro-small level.

(PC-SIG Disk# 1224)

Special Requirements: *HP LaserJet II.*
Author Registration: *None.*

TSR Download ✐
by Elfring Soft Fonts

TSR DOWNLOAD is a memory resident soft font manager. (The program also works from the command line.) Once installed TSR DOWNLOAD will:

❑ Pop up in any non-graphics mode application
❑ Locate your soft fonts automatically
❑ Translate the fonts into an easy to read English language format
❑ Download individual or lists of fonts fast (100K in 16 seconds!)
❑ Select any soft font
❑ Create a soft font list for you
❑ Remember what fonts have been sent to your printer and how much memory they require
❑ Warn you when you are about to exceed your printer's memory limits
❑ Control basic printer operations like form feeds, resetting the printer, deleting soft fonts in the printer, returns back to the default font of your printer, changes between 10 & 16.6 cpi or between portrait and landscape modes, force true 66 lines per page, set line spacing, and switch between manual and tray feed
❑ Download DeskJet soft fonts by order of size
❑ Occupy 34K of RAM and supports 100 soft fonts.

(PC-SIG Disk# 2031)

Special Requirements: *HP LaserJet+, Series II, DeskJet, or compatible laser printer.*
Author Registration: *$35.00*
➤*ASP Member.*

▼   ▼   ▼

Printing, Sideways

ON-Side   *by Expressware Corporation*

ON-SIDE prints reports down the page (on their side), instead of across, in a variety of character font styles. It is useful for a presentation which looks perfect on the screen, but when you attempt to print it, it's too wide to fit on the paper. If a report overlaps onto two or three pages, the perforations can be left connected so a really wide report folds up nicely for filing. ON-SIDE is perfect for use with a spreadsheet, wordprocessor or any other program that can write its printed output to a disk.

(PC-SIG Disk# 1184)

Special Requirements: *Dot matrix printer.*
Author Registration: *$19.95*
➤*ASP Member.*

ON-Side (PC-SIG Disk# 1184)

Pivot!   *by Trius, Inc.*

AS-EASY-AS users take note! If you've experienced the frustration of trying to print a worksheet that has become too wide — even with your printer set to compressed mode — you need PIVOT!

This unique printing program from the people who brought you AS-EASY-AS allows you great flexibility in printing your finished worksheet. Choose the font of your choice, portrait or landscape orientation, characters per inch, lines per page, and many other options from the simple menu system and then relax as PIVOT! takes charge of putting your work on paper.

PIVOT! also comes with a graphics character editor which allows you to customize/create a character, or a whole character set, to be used with PIVOT!

Ease of use is just the first benefit of using this program — the real payoff comes when you see the finished product. PIVOT! produces high-quality printing on the lowliest of dot-matrix printers and gives you a document worthy of the time you spent creating it.

This is a MUST HAVE for all AS-EASY-AS users.

(PC-SIG Disk# 1763)

Special Requirements: *EPSON compatible dot matrix printer.*
Author Registration: *$15.00*
➤*ASP Member.*

Side Writer   *by Dea Software*

Are your spreadsheets too wide to print in one piece? Have you had to resort to cut-and-paste methods to tie your outline together? Try SIDEWRITER.

SIDEWRITER lets printers output sideways on paper. This lets you print reports and other materials that do not fit across a page, because it prints down the length of the sheet instead of across the width. It works much like SIDEWAYS.

SIDEWRITER prints existing text sideways, allowing unlimited print width. Spreadsheet columns can be printed on one continuous page. The function keys and menus make it easy to learn and use.

(PC-SIG Disk# 523)

Special Requirements: *IBM/Epson or ThinkJet printer*
Author Registration: *$15.00*

▼ ▼ ▼

Programming, (Specific Language)

C++ Tutor
by Coronado Enterprises

C++ TUTOR is a comprehensive tutorial for the C++ programming language which assumes the user has a moderate amount of programming experience.

The C++ source code is included to illustrate how to use C++ in a practical sense. This example is meant to be studied, compiled, and run by the student.

All of the points of C++ language, including properly-structured programming techniques, are covered at the elementary level. The description and instruction are applicable to Borland's implementation of C++.

(PC-SIG Disk#'s 2368, 2369)

Special Requirements: *C++ compiler.*
Author Registration: *$39.95*

Fastgraph/Light ☆
by Ted Gruber Software

Fastgraph/Light 1.04 is a powerful programmer's graphics library. The zipped format is appropriate for BBS distribution. Please note that your customers only need a set of disks in one specific format, that is, it is not necessary to send somebody both the zipped and unzipped formats. For the unzipped formats, the Fastgraph/Light installation program asks for the disks by the names printed on the labels. For this reason, please include the exact disk names on any labels you affix to the disks yo distribute.

(PC-SIG Disk#'s 2797, 2798)

Special Requirements: *640K RAM, and a Compiler.*
Author Registration: *$49.00*

The JORF Interpreter & Tutorial ☆
by The JORF Company

If you've been wondering about the world of object-oriented programming (OOPs), JORF is an OOPs language to get you started. It includes one data type, three key words, and 80 standard library functions. Although it uses a simple syntax and very few key words, JORF supports arrays, pointers, database storage, expert system rule chaining, bit and substring manipulation, recursion, and much more. JORF uses all of the conventions of OOPs languages: classes, encapsulation, inheritance, and polymorphism.

The JORF programming environment includes an interpreter, editor, debugger, tutorial, hypertext Help, and a class browser. The Help screens include a fine explanation of OOPs principles. This is high- level programming and a great way to learn OOPs.

(PC-SIG Disk# 2523)

Special Requirements: *Tutorial requires 512K RAM, and a hard drive.*
Author Registration: *$45.00*

▼ ▼ ▼

Programming, Assembly

A86/D86 Assembler/Debugger ✍
by Eric Isaacson

A86 is an excellent assembler that actually performs better and is easier to use than Microsoft's MASM 4.00. It also assembles your programs a lot faster than MASM. It lets you leave out all segmentation directives, if you want. The segmentation default model is compatible with most high-level languages. You can also access subroutines from your own libraries and, if you register, you receive the A86LIB tool for creating your own libraries more easily than with MASM. You can use floating point operands in assembly-time expression arithmetic. This is an A86 exclusive.

The manual (included on the disk) is excellent. You can learn 8086 or 80286 Assembly language programming with it. The debugger is great. It has a floating point display window for use with the 8087 or 80287 that will knock your socks off.

(PC-SIG Disk# 1111)

Special Requirements: *Hard drive recommended.*
Author Registration: *$40.00 each.*
➤*ASP Member.*

The PC-SIG Encyclopedia of Shareware ✍ = Updated Program
☆ = New Program

Assembly Utilities
by Tim Keller

A variety of Assembly language programs gathered for the convenience of the programmer. Source code is in Assembly language. Many routines improve handling of screens, disks and printers. See file descriptions for a real appreciation of the breadth of this collection.

(PC-SIG Disk# 309)

Special Requirements: *An Assembler.*

Author Registration: *None.*

File Descriptions:

ASM	TXT	2 tips from Boca Raton.
BEEP	ASM	Sound effect generator.
CLEAR	ASM	Sample clear screen routine from CHASM.
CLOCK	ASM	Print date and time on screen.
CLOCK	DOC	Documentation for CLOCK.
CO	DOC	Documentation for COENDP and COPRNT.
COENDP	ASM	Part of program to list disk contents.
DISASM	BAS	A BASIC program that disassembles assembly programs.
DISKDIRL	ASM	Part of program to list disk contents.
DISPTEXT	ASM	Displays a line on screen without BIOS.
DOS-EDIT	ASM	Assembly language text editor.
DOSERROR	DOC	Lists error return codes.
DSK	ASM	Returns the number of free sectors on a disk.
FREE	ASM	Shows available free space on a disk.
FREE	DOC	Documentation for FREE.
GETSP	ASM	Lists free space on disk.
INIT	ASM	Assembly Source Code..
INITMEM	ASM	Initializes memory between 544k and 576k.
LIST80	ASM	Lists the first 80 characters in a line of ASCII text.
MEMDRV	ASM	Faster bootup and use ALL of your available memory.
MEMDRV	DOC	Documents MEMDRV.
MORERAM	ASM	Use all of available RAM.
NOLF	ASM	Deletes extra linefeeds from some printer files.
OBJSNOOP	COM	Displays label references in object files.
PAGE	ASM	Demonstrates multiple screen pages.
PARTBIOS	LIS	Partial listing of BIOS low memory.
PASSWORD	ASM	Password protection of system.
PRTPATH	ASM	Prints current directory path.
PUT_DEC	ASM	Puts decimal point in ASCII string.
PUT_DEC	OBJ	Object code for PUT_DEC.
ROMBIOS	ASM	ROM BIOS information.
SCRN	ASM	A variable time screen saver.
SCRN	DOC	Documentation for SCRN.ASM.
SCROLL10	ASM	Tests DISPTEXT.
SKELETON	ASM	Skeleton of a minimal Assembly language program.
SL	ASM	Tests program that scrolls screen.
SPEDUPDK	ASM	Changes some disk drive parameters.
TABS	ASM	Replaces blanks with tabs in ASCII text files.
TALK1	ASM	Dumb terminal for IBM PC.
TEXT	DOC	Documentation for TEXT.EXE.
TEXT	EXE	Several text conversion options.
UPDIR	ASM	Moves the user up one directory level.
UPPATCH	ASM	Patch of another program.

CHASM
by Whitman Software

CHASM (Cheap Assembler) is a prime weapon for programmers who want to learn to program in Assembly language. The program comes with clearly- written documentation and has a tutorial built in for users lacking detailed experience with Assembly language.

CHASM is a compiler only and there is no editor included. You use an ASCII word processor to create your source code file, then use CHASM to compile it.

(PC-SIG Disk# 10)

Special Requirements: *Two floppy drives.*

Author Registration: *$40.00*

Doug's Programming Language (DPL)   *by Doug Cody*

DPL, or DOUG'S PROGRAMMING LANGUAGE, is a macro language which uses high level language syntax for its instructions.

DPL's language does not limit the programmer from using native 8088 code, but makes programming easier by automatically declaring segments and the program entrypoint. All return codes except end-of-file are standard DOS return codes. The program handles 64K of code and data and stack segments. Variables are automatically declared.

DPL supports simple data types and still permits the programmer to build other types. Basic data types supported are 16 bit integers and ASCIIZ strings. The 16 bit integers are considered to be signed integers and therefore will be manipulated appropriately. Files are supported which allow the program to address any disk file or logical device, such as the keyboard and screen.

Extensive documentation is available on disk in both standard ASCII and WordStar format. Also available is the DPL source program written in TURBO C. Many application routines and application routine construction files are provided, along with a demonstration of the use of shade and how to manipulate it.

(PC-SIG Disk# 1262)

Special Requirements: *Microsoft MASM, MAKE, LINK, and LIB, v3.0 through 5.0.*
Author Registration: *$25.00*

Hextodec & Dectohex   *by M.O. Embry*

HEXTODEC & DECTOHEX are two programs for assembly language computer programmers interested in converting decimal numbers to hexadecimal numbers and vice versa. Entries are displayed on-screen for user approval, then the entry reappears with its corresponding conversion number.

(PC-SIG Disk# 1650)

Special Requirements: *None.*
Author Registration: *None.*

The PC Assembler Help & Tutor   *by Nelsoft*

The PC ASSEMBLER TUTOR is an assembler tutorial that covers all 8086 instructions. Starting with the simplest instructions, it works its way through the whole instruction set. TUTOR also covers details of the hardware involved with the 8086.

The PC ASSEMBLER HELPER (ASMHELP.OBJ) is an object file which does I/O for assembler-level routines. It also displays the 8086 registers and flags, if desired, and allows each arithmetic register to be independently formatted.

The intended users are people who are already competent programmers in a high-level language and either are just starting to learn assembler, or know fewer than 60% of the assembler mnemonics and want to learn more. TUTOR assumes that the user has a general knowledge of the DOS commands, subdirectory structure, and pathnames. It is also helpful if the user has already linked object modules to form an executable file.

This is the only manual on the market that systematically covers the assembler mnemonics system, allows easy input and output of data at the assembler level, and allows you to see the arithmetic registers in the way they are being used.

(PC-SIG Disk#'s 2337, 2338)

Special Requirements: *None.*
Author Registration: *None*

PC/370 Cross Assembler   *by Don Higgins*

PC/370 is a cross assembler that lets you compile and run IBM 370 Assembly language programs on a PC, XT or AT.

These programs are well-documented with a good demonstration program. This is one of the most complete emulations of the VM370 assembler around. A generous debugging and erase facility is also included to help you complete development cycles without the big blue box.

Features included:

❑ PC/370 assembler subroutines can be called from Micro Focus COBAL/2 programs running either in extended memory-protected mode or normal MS-DOS real mode. Standard linkage conventions are supported.

❑ PC/370 run-time emulator can be made resident to eliminate loading it for each program or subroutine execution. As part of making the emulator reusable, debug supports restoring traces

---

❏ Hardware assist is available for the CVB and CVD 370 instructions using the math co-processor to speed up the instructions by a factor of four

❏ Two new supervisor calls are included: SVC 36 will load into a predefined area of memory (useful for overlays); SVC 37 defines user SVC exits for modifying native SVC support without requiring an emulated interrupt driven shell

❏ The cross assembler supports the copy statement to include source code files

❏ The linkage editor supports option U to allow external unresolved references.

(PC-SIG Disk#'s 402, 859, 1352)

Special Requirements: *None.*
Author Registration: *$45.00*

PseudoSam 18 and 65 *by Pseudo Corp*

PSEUDOSAM 18 and 65 are machine language cross-assembler programs for the RCA 1802, 4, 5, 6, and 6502 microprocessors. These programs let you construct 1802 and 6502 code on your IBM PC, to be transferred to an 1802 or 6502-based system for use.

The PSEUDOSAM (Pseudo brand Symbolic AsseMbler) assemblers conform to common syntax based on the UNIX system V assembler syntax. The opcode and addressing syntax is compatible with the manufacturer's, but label, directive, and expression operator syntax will differ.

The author of PSEUDOSAM chose this syntax because of UNIX's popularity, and to avoid the problem of maintaining compatibility with the many OEM assemblers. The documentation is well organized and easy to understand, although no attempt is made to teach 1802 or 6502 programming. You should have a good understanding of machine language programming and also be familiar with basic DOS functions.

(PC-SIG Disk# 776)

Special Requirements: *None.*
Author Registration: *None.*

PseudoSam 48 and 51 *by Pseudo Corp*

PSEUDOSAM 48 and 51 are machine language cross-assembler programs forthe INTEL 8748 and INTEL 8751 microprocessors. These programs let you construct 8748 and 8751 code on your IBM PC, to be transferred to an 8748- or 8751-based system for use.

The PSEUDOSAM (Pseudo brand Symbolic AsseMbler) assemblers conform to common syntax, based on the UNIX System V assembler syntax. The opcode and addressing syntax is compatible with the manufacturer's, but label, directive, and expression operator syntax will differ.

The author of PSEUDOSAM chose this syntax because of UNIX's popularity, and to avoid the problem of maintaining compatibility with the many OEM assemblers. The documentation is well organized and easy to understand, although no attempt is made to teach 8748 or 8751 programming. You should have a good understanding of machine language programming and also be familiar with basic DOS functions.

(PC-SIG Disk# 777)

Special Requirements: *None.*
Author Registration: *None.*

PseudoSam 68 and 685 *by Pseudo Corp*

PSEUDOSAM 68 and 685 are machine language cross-assembler programs for the Motorola 6800, 01, 02, 03, 08, and 6805 microprocessors. These programs let you construct 6800 and 6805 code on your IBM-PC so it can be transferred to a 6800 or 6805-based system for later use.

The PSEUDOSAM (Pseudo-brand Symbolic AsseMbler) assemblers conform to common syntax, based on the UNIX System V assembler syntax. The opcode and addressing syntax is compatible with the manufacturer's, but label, directive, and expression operator syntax will differ.

The author of PSEUDOSAM chose this syntax because of UNIX's popularity, and to avoid the problem of maintaining compatibility with the many of OEM assemblers. The documentation is well organized and easy to understand, although no attempt is made to teach 6800 or 6805 programming. The user should have a good understanding of machine language programming and also be familiar with basic DOS functions.

(PC-SIG Disk# 775)

Special Requirements: *None.*
Author Registration: *None.*

PseudoSam 80z and 85 🖉   *by Pseudo Corp*

PSEUDOSAM 80z and 85 are machine language cross-assembler programs for the ZILOG z80, NATIONAL SEMICONDUCTOR NSC800, and the INTEL 8085 microprocessors. These programs let you construct 80z and 8085 code on your IBM PC, to be transferred to an 80z or 8085-based system for use.

The PSEUDOSAM (Pseudo-brand Symbolic AsseMbler) assemblers conform to common syntax, based on the UNIX System V assembler syntax. The opcode and addressing syntax is compatible with the manufacturer's, but label, directive, and expression operator syntax will differ.

The author of PSEUDOSAM chose this syntax because of UNIX's popularity, and to avoid the problem of maintaining compatibility with the many OEM assemblers. The documentation is well organized and easy to understand, although no attempt is made to teach 80z or 8085 programming. You should have a good understanding of machine language programming and also be familiar with basic DOS functions.

(PC-SIG Disk# 778)

Special Requirements: *None.*
Author Registration: *None.*

Sofa 🖉   *by Peter Campbell Software*

SOFA is a CHASM-compatible 8088 assembler that assembles about 350 lines per second on a 4.77Mhz PC. SOFA, like CHASM, builds .COM files, which accounts for its speed. Modular programming is possible with SOFA because it can include any number of source files, a valuable feature. However, the size of a .COM is still limited to 64KB. SOFA also supports conditional assembly.

(PC-SIG Disk# 2058)

Special Requirements: *None.*
Author Registration: *$20.00*

TASM 🖉   *by Speech Technology Inc.*

TASM is an assembler that runs on an IBM-PC/XT/AT or compatible and creates codes for any of the following processors: 8048, 8051, 8085, Z80, 6805, 6502, TMS7000, TMS32010, or 6801/6803.

Features of TASM include: 17 operators for expression parsing, support of a subset of C preprocessor commands, macros, multiple statements per line, support of three object file formats, only absolute code generation, uniform syntax across versions, and support for PROM programming. The source code is available. Customize TASM to produce codes for other processors by creating a proper instruction definition table for the target chip.

(PC-SIG Disk# 643)

Special Requirements: *None.*
Author Registration: *$40.00*

▼ ▼ ▼

Programming, BASIC

ACSORT   *by T.N.T Software, Inc.*

This program will sort data files with fixed-length records and fields. The output file will be a list of record numbers (an index to the data file in sorted order). The index itself can be read as either a sequential file or a random file with a record length of 12. The data file being sorted may be of any reasonable size.

You may sort data of any type commonly used in any Microsoft language. Other sort programs may have difficulties with Microsoft random files. ACSORT will not, because it will not sort sequential data files; it is only intended for use with true random files. Because of this, it will not sort dBase data files.

(PC-SIG Disk# 1959)

Special Requirements: *None.*
Author Registration: *$25.00*

     🖉 = Updated Program
☆ = New Program

BASIC Development System by Betatool
by BetaTool Systems

A completely functional version of BetaTool's BASIC Development System for programs of less than 6500 bytes. BetaTool's system works with the BASIC interpreter to add easy file editing, instant cross-reference lists, selective line renumbering, variable dump and program expand/compress. If you program in BASIC you should try this package.

(PC-SIG Disk# 269)

Special Requirements: *BASICA or GW-BASIC.*
Author Registration: *$99.00*

BASIC Games
by Kevin Carr

Most of the games presented here are written in BASIC and represent an excellent example of game functions for the student programmer in BASIC to study. Most use ASCII graphics, so you can use any monitor.

(PC-SIG Disk# 174)

Special Requirements: *A version of BASIC. Some programs require CGA.*
Author Registration: *None.*

BASIC Games & Programming Intro
by DataCARE

This is a handy and interesting tool for getting acquainted with the world of microcomputers and programming.

It has an easily-understood tutorial on computers and does a good job on BASIC — introducing the beginner to the elemental concepts of the language. A big plus is a series of practice sessions so you can actually see the programs operate!

A set of simple games are included that will engage you in a lot of keyboard practice. They include a simple word processor and several number games as well as varying levels of anagrams.

(PC-SIG Disk# 595)

Special Requirements: *A version of BASIC.*
Author Registration: *None.*

BASIC Language Games
by Tim Keller

A wide ranging example of "games that were." If you're interested in BASIC programming, this could be an interesting set of programs to analyze. You might want to find out how to do a certain procedure, or adapt a given procedure to your own BASIC project. You'll find ample and diverse examples of game procedures in this package.

There are several educational games on this disk, plus a couple that will still keep you guessing. However, the games on this list are essentially out of date now, and, given the advances in programming over the years, there are many more up-to-date variations on the themes available in the PC-SIG library.

(PC-SIG Disk# 45)

Special Requirements: *Some programs may require CGA and a version of BASIC.*
Author Registration: *None.*

File Descriptions:

MINIMATH	BAS	BASIC math program.
BACCRRT	BAS	BASIC card program.
ANTONYMS	BAS	Learn your antonyms.
AWARI	BAS	Classic African sticks and stones.
BACCRRT	BAS	Card game.
SYNONYMS	BAS	Learn your synonyms.
TAXMAN	BAS	Beat the taxman.
WEATHER	BAS	Predict the weather.
TRADE	BAS	Intergalactic trading game.
GALAXY	BAS	Behold the stars.
FOOTBALL	BAS	Football simulation.
BASEBALL	BAS	Baseball game.
IQUEEN	BAS	Problem solving with chess pieces.
HIDESEEK	BAS	Search for hidden objects.
GREEKRTS	BAS	Match Greek words with their meaning.
GALAXY2	BAS	Behold the stars and be inspired.

DRAGRACE	BAS	Race the circuit.
DOTS	BAS	Connect the dots and make a picture.
CLOUD-9	BAS	Educational game.
BIO	BAS	Biorythms for printer.
CLIMATES	BAS	Educational game.
CIVILWAR	BAS	The blue against grey.
BOMB	BAS	Find the bomb.
BIRTHDAY	BAS	Find the day of the week you were born.
MEMBRAIN	BAS	Keep cells alive.
SHOP	BAS	Go shopping.
REVERSE	BAS	Arrange the numbers correctly.
SNOOPY	BAS	Print Snoopy on printer.
SQUARE	BAS	Competitive square building.
SWARMS	BAS	You are attacked by bees.

BASIC Programs in Finance and Inventory
by David R. Moffatt

The financial portion of this disk has 20 useful, easy-to-use progams, including such handy routines as loan amortization, asset depreciation, and bond yield. The inventory portion of this disk is well documented and includes routines to take cash register input data, generate pick lists, and report inventory.

The package also represents a wide range of excellent adoptable or adaptable applications of BASIC source code for financial functions for anyone studying the BASIC programming language.

(PC-SIG Disk# 171)

Special Requirements: *A version of BASIC.*
Author Registration: *None.*

BASIC Programs in Math and Statistics ✍
by Tim Keller

This collection of math and financial analytical tools, intended for the professional or student, or anyone interested in math or statistics, represents an outstanding "living laboratory" for studying applied BASIC source code in those areas of endeavor. A great opportunity to take it apart and see what makes it tick.

(PC-SIG Disk# 180)

Special Requirements: *A version of BASIC.*
Author Registration: *None.*

File Descriptions:

TRADENET		TRADENET network sampler.
M1	BAS	Greatest common denominator.
DATANET		DATANET network sampler.
M2	BAS	Prime factors of integers.
M4	BAS	Analysis of two vectors.
M3	BAS	Area of polygon.
M5	BAS	Parts of a triangle.
M6	BAS	Operations on two vectors.
M7	BAS	Coordinate conversion.
M8	BAS	Coordinate plot.
M10	BAS	Plot of polar equation.
M9	BAS	Angle conversion.
M12	BAS	Linear interpolation.
M11	BAS	Plot of function.
M14	BAS	Integration: Simpson's rule.
M13	BAS	Curvilinear interpolation.
M18	BAS	Roots of quadratic equation.
M16	BAS	Integration: Trapezoidal rule.
M17	BAS	Derivative.
M15	BAS	Integration: Gaussian quadrature.
M26	BAS	Matrix inversion.
M25	BAS	Matrix multiplication.
M24	BAS	Matrix add, subtract and scalar multiplication.
M23	BAS	Linear programming.
M22	BAS	Simultaneous equations.
M21	BAS	Trig polynomial.
M20	BAS	Roots of polynomials: half interval sear.
M19	BAS	Real roots of polynomials: Newton.

✍ = Updated Program
☆ = New Program

MATH	BAS	Menu for above math programs.
NCCLSPRE	BAS	Calculates a sample's precision.
MATRIX	BAS	Solves simultaneous equations.
S2	BAS	Mann-Whitney U test.
S1	BAS	Permutations and combinations.
REGRESS	BAS	Regression analysis.
NORMAL-Z	BAS	Normal distribution routines.
S6	BAS	Normal distribution.
S5	BAS	Poisson distribution.
S4	BAS	Binomial distribution.
S3	BAS	Geometric mean and deviation.
S8	BAS	Chi-square test.
S7	BAS	Chi-square distribution.
S10	BAS	Student's T test.
S9	BAS	Student's T distribution.
S12	BAS	Linear correlation coefficient.
S11	BAS	F-distribution.
S16	BAS	Geometric regression.
S15	BAS	Nth order regression.
S14	BAS	Linear regression.
S13	BAS	Multiple linear regression.
S17	BAS	Exponential regression.
S18	BAS	Mean, variance, standard deviation.
STAT	BAS	Menu for above S**.BAS statistics programs.

Basic Windowing Toolbox For BASIC Programers — *by Image Computer Systems*

BASIC WINDOWING TOOLBOX (B-WINDOW) is a collection of functions that give windowing capability to a BASIC programmer. Windows can be opened over sections of the screen and, when closed, the overwritten section of the screen is restored. With B-WINDOW, BASIC programs look more visually exciting and professional. B-WINDOW works with both QuickBASIC and interpreted BASIC. Special windowing cursor control and string character display, and border drawing are included. Everything happens at top speed because B-WINDOW was written in C, converted to assembler, and hand-optimized.

(PC-SIG Disk# 527)

Special Requirements: *None.*
Author Registration: *$20.00*

BASICXREF — *by Excelsior Software, Inc.*

The BASIC CROSS REFERENCE UTILITY is for the serious BASIC programmer. It helps in the programming and debugging of BASIC source language programs by building a complete cross-reference of all variables.

The utility provides list of the the following: all line numbers, showing all references by other statements; an alphabetic listing of all reserved words and line numbers where they appear; an alphabetic listing of all variables that are not reserved; and a listing of the BASIC source which might include both numbered and un-numbered statements. You can remove unreferenced statement numbers from compiled programs, remove REM statements from the source code, and unprotect source programs saved as protected programs.

(PC-SIG Disk# 358)

Special Requirements: *None.*
Author Registration: *$25.00*

Baslin — *by Amaryllis Software*

BASIC LINE NUMBERING removes unreferenced line numbers from — or adds line numbers to — BASIC programs saved in an ASCII format.

You can delete line numbers, use an ASCII editor to move sections of a code, and then add line numbers to produce a usable interpreted BASIC code. Add line numbers to a BASIC file while leaving any existing line numbers unchanged and add new numbers to unnumbered lines in the same way as existing line numbers. Line numbers can be added to a file written in compiler BASIC for debugging purposes. Switch easily between interpreters that require line numbers and compilers that do not require line numbers.

(PC-SIG Disk# 989)

Special Requirements: *A version of BASIC*
Author Registration: *$9.99*

CrossRef
by Harry P. Calevas

CROSSREF is a variable listing program for Turbobasic files (only). If you try to list a standard BASIC program you will get a very long list of line numbers (all of them). This program is for Turbobasic programs that use line numbers only as labels. And the program only takes up 8K.

(PC-SIG Disk# 1968)

Special Requirements: *CGA.*
Author Registration: *$15.00*

The Designer
by Tim Keller

THE DESIGNER is a programming tool for IBM BASIC users working with animated graphics. The source code in BASICA for each of the example programs is included, for study or modification by anyone who wants to write graphics games or experiment with animation. At least a beginning knowledge of programming and the BASIC language are recommended for using this package. It cannot use a mouse or joystick.

Features:

❏ Full PC function key use to control programming functions
❏ On-line help
❏ Printable reference card

(PC-SIG Disk# 69)

Special Requirements: *A version of BASIC and CGA.*
Author Registration: *$20.00*

DISAM
by Robert Pearce

DISAN is a GW-BASIC programmer's answer to random access. No block numbers to translate. No hashing formulas. Just pass the character key of the record and let DISAM do the work. A resident file handler, DISAM handles variable length records up to 255 bytes. Easy as: Open,filename; Get,Jim Jones; Close;.

You can open up to five DISAM files at one time. Assembler programs with record lengths in excess of 8K can also use DISAM. With loads of documentation, DISAM includes test files and a test program with structured BASIC source code. DISAM accesses records by assigned character key and will read records sequentially in ascending key order.

(PC-SIG Disk# 1617)

Special Requirements: *None.*
Author Registration: *$10.00*

EDFIX2
by T.N.T Software, Inc.

This program will read, edit, write and transfer random-access files up to two billion bytes, with individual records up to 2048 bytes. It will work on any file, even if the file is not truly a random-access file. With EDFIX2, you can manipulate dBase data files—except that EDFIX2 records will probably not match up with dBase records. You may also use EDFIX2 on spreadsheet files and files created by various other software packages.

(PC-SIG Disk# 1959)

Special Requirements: *None.*
Author Registration: *$25.00*

EZ-Windows Pull-Down Menu Library ✍
by John C. Strong

EZ-WINDOWS is a complete menu system for the QuickBASIC 4.x compiler that saves you from having to write your own pull-down menus. Modeled after the pull-down menu used in the QuickBASIC 4.x environment, EZ-WINDOW is very easy to integrate into your QuickBASIC programs.

All that is required to use EZ-WINDOWS are a few arrays containing formatting information for the pull-down menu and an array containing the actual text used. A simple CALL statement will take care of the rest. Loading the arrays is uncomplicated and worth the effort. Use EZ-WINDOWS for the ease and appearance of a professional program.

There is one disadvantage — the code size is rather large. However, programs that need such a pull-down menu system are the ones that present a multitude of options to the user and will be naturally large anyway, so the relative code size of the pull-down menu system shouldn't make a big difference.

     ✍ = Updated Program
☆ = New Program

StrongSoft Engineering's EZ-WINDOWS has demo programs to demonstrate the power and flexibility of the pull-down menu system.

❏ All routines use a mouse
❏ Works with Professional Development System 7.x
❏ Source code is available
❏ E-mail customer support available

(PC-SIG Disk# 2559)

Special Requirements: *QuickBASIC 4.0+ Compiler.*
Author Registration: *$5.00 and $30.00*

Funky ToolBox
                                                              by PeopleSystems

FUNKY TOOLBOX (function key toolbox) contains a large number of utilities for the programmer in you. Along with the utilities are a lot of miscellaneous BASIC programs and text files, to be used as examples for doing a specific programming procedure, or even used as subroutines within a program you are creating. See file descriptions for explanations of individual programs.

(PC-SIG Disk# 907)

Special Requirements: *A version of BASIC.*
Author Registration: *None.*

File Descriptions:

AINK$	TBX	Controls KYBD for opening files correctly.
ANYKEY	TBX	Advanced routine for any key to continue.
ARAYCOMP	TBX	Compute ARRAY size overhead in DEFSNG-DEFDBL-DEFSTR.
ALLCHARS	TBX	Displays a hexadecimal table of all screen characters.
ASCKEY$	TBX	ASCII Numbers for all keys.
AUREVOIR	TBX	Flashing panels say a big good-bye.
BLACKOUT	TBX	Example of a screen black-out.
SOUNDZ	TBX	Unusual sounds and musical effects.
SONGRITR	TBX	Easy music from score to CPU.
NICELEGS	TBX	How to make legs for your printer.
BANANA2	TBX	Error-trapping alternative.
BANANA1	TBX	Error-trapping ON-OFF routine.
ERROR2	TBX	Tough tests CPU for accuracy.
ERROR1	TBX	Fun tests the IBM-PC CPU for accuracy.
TESTEROR	TBX	Error-trapping demo.
COLRTOGL	TBX	Switches between mono and color.
LOKATE	TBX	Flashes screen address and points location.
SCRNMAP	TBX	Creates a map of the computer screen.
MARKSCRN	TBX	Roadmap your display for convenience.
FLIPPIES	TBX	How to use both sides of your disks.
INDEX1	BAS	Index on the files on this disk.
ABSECTOR	TBX	Converts track-sector to absolute sector for DEBUG use.
DEBUG	DOC	How to use DEBUG and error trapping.
GSBMUSIC	TBX	Background music for your programs.
GOBANANA	DOC	How to error-trap your programs.
PEEKFILE	DOC	How to peek into files and ROM with DEBUG.
HORNBOOK	DOC	Information on DOS for programmers.
ERORNUM	DAT	Data file for ERRMESAG.TBX.
ERRMESAG	TBX	Shows ERROR messages.
CURSER	TBX	Demo of CRSLIN and POS(0) for bookmarking.
INDEX2	BAS	Index of the files on this disk.
LETTER	BAS	A letter from PeopleSystems.
TALKPAGE	BAS	Why talking pages make reading easier.
BROWSE	COM	Utility for viewing text files.
STUFCHIP	DOC	How to protect your chips.
DOLABEL	TBX	Self-producing label program. Uses printer, but no labels.
DISKLABL	TBX	Label your disks with wide Directory. No labels needed.
PEOPLSYS	TBX	Big screen opening and closing. Chains to AUREVOIR.TBX.
INPUTEST	TBX	Trap KYBD entry with easy INSTR routine.
NOTENUMB	TBX	Makes octave shifts easy.
F5ERRMSG	TBX	Print out error messages by pressing F5.
README		How to get started.

WHATISPS	DOC	Information on PeopleSystems.
SOFTKEYS	TBX	Loads new F keys for color/mono then erases program.
WPROT	TBX	How to unprotect a file to list and save it.
MACHLANG	TBX	Using poke and machine language complete easy computation.
HEXSCALE	TBX	Graphics for addressing-nibbles-bytes-segment: offset.
FUNCTKEY	TBX	How to use your function keys.
MEMTEST1	TBX	Tests your computer memory.
COLORBOX	TBX	Displays various colored boxes.
MONO	BAS	Separate subroutine to run mono.
COLOR	BAS	Separate subroutine to run color.
COMO	TBX	Merge this color/mono subroutine into your program.
IBMKEYS	TBX	Reloads the F1 to F10 keys the way they were.
README2	DOC	Information on PeopleSystems.
HEX2DEC	TBX	Automatically convert any HEX address to decimal numbers.
SCRNCHRS	TBX	Now see all screen chars, some unmentionables.
BASUNPRO	TBX	Create machine language to unprotect files.
SAVEDLIN	TBX	Recovers lost EDLIN file when disk is full.
PROTECTD	TBX	A protected file for you to practice on.
PEPLSYST	BAS	The system of people and computers.
DAMNTRIV	DOC	Information on PeopleSystems.
FRIENDLY	TBX	How to be friendly.
CLUSECTR	TBX	DOS 2.0 conversion of start cluster to absolute sector.
SENSITIV	DOC	How to work with people.
DISKMOD	DOC	How to modify a disk with DEBUG.
BOOBOO	DOC	Improvement for the IBM-PC.
XMASTREE	TBX	Mono graphics and music for the season.

Managing Your Money   *by Amihai Glazer*

All the BASIC programs in the book "Managing Money With Your IBM PC," by A. Glazer, an economics professor at the University of California. (Prentice-Hall, 1985).

Among other things, you can determine the after-tax cost of a loan, demonstrate the advantages of an Individual Retirement Account, compare loans which have different interest rates and different origination fees, and calculate the amount of monthly savings necessary to finance a college education. Many different types of loans are also well demonstrated and made easier to understand.

Includes BASIC source code. Anyone interested in short, useful investment calculation programs, with the source code, will find this package very valuable.

(PC-SIG Disk# 613)

Special Requirements: *CGA and a version of BASIC.*
Author Registration: *$10.00*

File Descriptions:

AMORTIZE	BAS	Amortization schedule for a mortgage loan payment.
———	—	MANAGING YOUR MONEY (v1.0).
TERMDEPO	BAS	Balance in a savings plan any number of years.
SIMPINV	BAS	Analysis of an investment that produces no annual income.
SAVHISTO	BAS	Annual balance in a savings program with deposits.
RULEOF78	BAS	Amortization schedule for consumer and automobile loans.
README		General information and file information.
POINTS	BAS	Effective interest rate on a loan that charges points.
BALREM	BAS	Balance remaining on a mortgage.
CREDITCA	BAS	Gains from using a credit card instead of paying cash.
CHARGEHI	BAS	Monthly status of a revolving charge account.
PERTERM	BAS	How many deposits to make to reach a goal.
PERRATE	BAS	Interest rate to earn on your savings to reach goal.
PERDEPOS	BAS	How much to deposit each month or year to reach goal.
PERBALAN	BAS	Balance in savings account after any number of deposits.
PAYBACK	BAS	How long it takes to recover an investment.
CREDITPU	BAS	Minimum payment schedule for a credit purchase.
NUMDAYS	BAS	Number of days between two dates.
DAILYODO	BAS	Date that is a specified number of days away.
MONTHLYO	BAS	Date that is a specified number of months away.
MNTHINCM	BAS	Monthly income obtained from a specified amount of money.
LOANTERM	BAS	How many payments you must make on a loan.

✎ = Updated Program
☆ = New Program

LOANQUAL	BAS	Size of loan at interest rate and monthly payment.
LOANCOST	BAS	After tax cost of a loan.
IRA	BAS	The benefits of saving in an IRA.
INVYIELD	BAS	Annual rate of return on an investment.
INVVALUE	BAS	Present value of an investment.
INVPRICE	BAS	Sales price of an asset that yields a specified ROR.
INVINCOM	BAS	Annual or monthly income that yields a specified ROR.
INVHISTO	BAS	Annual description of an investment; value, ROR.
INTRATE	BAS	Interest rate on a loan.
DEPGROWS	BAS	Balance in a savings program with deposits.
DAYOFWEE	BAS	Day of week on which a specified date falls.
DATESINM	BAS	Dates in a month which a specified day of the week falls.
DATEDIST	BAS	Number of years, months, and days between two dates.

PBWindows 🖉 *by Barry Erick*

PBWINDOWS is a wonderful windowing utility for users of Spectra Publishing's PowerBASIC. Just include PBWINDOW.INC in your program and start creating all types of windows and menus.

With PBWINDOWS, you can create any size window with a variety of colors. Add titles and shadows to your window and you have an enviable display screen. Make menus with a variety of selection options: scrolling, non-scrolling, arrowed, single-key selection. And when you're finished, pop the windows off the screen with RemoveBox and you're back where you began.

PBWINDOWS comes with easy-to-read documentation. Programming with PBWINDOWS is simple and gives your display screen that professional look. Registered users receive additional source code to add personal touches to PBWINDOWS.

(PC-SIG Disk# 2182)

Special Requirements: *Power Basic program, V2.10.*
Author Registration: *$25.00*
➤ *ASP Member.*

PC-Professor *by Eagle Software, Inc.*

PC-PROFESSOR is a popular tutorial for teaching the BASIC programming language. It has an easy-to-understand, well-organized presentation and a comprehensive keyboard tutorial, although it is not overly interactive. The program also offers four chapters of indexed documentation for quick-referencing capability. It might be helpful to have at least a fundamental knowledge of BASIC before using this tutorial, but it is primarily for beginning programmers.

(PC-SIG Disk# 105)

Special Requirements: *A version of BASIC.*
Author Registration: *$30-$50.00.*

PC-Talk III *by Headlands Press*

This early-days telecommunications program (the first shareware program ever) is as straightforward and unfancy (by today's standards) as they come. Nevertheless, it can keep phone number records, dial them for you, and generally perform the connection functions you need to tie your computer to another through a modem over phone lines. If your interests lean toward programming, all of the programs on this disk provide great examples of BASIC applications. Something for beginning programmers to dig into!

(PC-SIG Disk# 16)

Special Requirements: *A version of BASIC and modem.*
Author Registration: *No longer supported as shareware.*

PowerBASIC BBS Library ☆ *by Lloyd Smith*

If you are a PowerBASIC user, check out this set of programs and routines. They will most likely save you programming time, giving you examples of code that can be incorporated into your application.

(PC-SIG Disk#'s 2631, 2632, 2633, 2634, 2635, 2636)

Special Requirements: *PowerBASIC compiler.*
Author Registration: *None.*

File Descriptions for Disk #2631, PowerBASIC BBS Library #1:

LIBRARY	DOC	Detailed descriptions of the ZIP files
BTRIEV	ZIP	BTRIEV.ZIP: An interface to Novell's BTRIEVE
CCTRAN	ZIP	COCOTRAN — BASIC token to ASCII converter
EMSFRM	ZIP	EMS Analysis Program for PowerBASIC
EQUIP	ZIP	EQUIPment shows how to use OBJ files with PB
ERROR	ZIP	v1.00 - Describes PB run-time error codes
EXAMP1	ZIP	PowerBASIC Book Examples
EXAMP2	ZIP	PowerBASIC Book Examples
EXISTS	ZIP	Exists, Findfile and how to access strings
FNDFIL	ZIP	Find First, Find All of the files to a filespec or filemask
GRAPH1	ZIP	Graphic applications, display system clock in large numbers, scrolling sign, capture and display Deluxe Paint images
EMSINF	ZIP	Enhanced version of EMS.ZIP

Disk #2632, PowerBASIC BBS Library # 2

Among some of the programs included are graphics programs, TB/PB files, a Windows application, upgrade information from PB 2.00a to PB 2.00b, fix and enhancement installation and adding 96K more memory for compilation.

GRAPH2	ZIP	Graphics animation using PowerBASIC.
GRAPH3	ZIP	More interesting graphics applications, pcopy replacement 8-day Industrial recording chart, how to load flash code screens
LIST	ZIP	Utility that will list ASCII or binary files in ASCII or hex
LISVAR	ZIP	When your PowerBASIC units contain external variables, you have to declare them all public in the main file. This utility does it for you.
LJL.BAR	ZIP	CODE39 barcode LaserJet font print subroutines
MAKE2	ZIP	Make utility - Upgrade
PATCH1	ZIP	To install fixes and enhancements
PATCH2	ZIP	To install fixes and enhancements
PBPLUS	ZIP	96K more memory for compilation
PTOUCH	ZIP	"Touches" a file's date and time
PW200	ZIP	Windows program
PWRBAS	ZIP	PowerBASIC 2.0: Its history, features, advantages
SPOOL	ZIP	Use DOS's PRINT spooler from within PowerBASIC
TB2PB	INF	Converting from TB to PB
TODAY	ZIP	Retrieve today's date, weekday, month, year
TOOLFX	ZIP	FIX file to allow TB toolboxes to run under PB.PROGRAM

Disk #2633, PowerBASIC BBS Library #3

ViewPrint for PB, how to do barcode printing from PB, serial port programs, a demo program of screen trends, a simple masking entry routine, and a complete explanation of all errors documented in PowerBASIC.

VPRNT	ZIP	ViewPrint for PowerBASIC
WHACPU	ZIP	Determines what CPU is in your machine
APLIB	ZIP	All-purpose PB programmer's library 11-90 version
BARCODE	BAS	How to do barcode printing from PB
COMSET	ZIP	Comset set COM3 & COM4 in memory for XTs and ATs. Used with PB 2.1, allows access to ports 3 & 4
CRSBAS	ZIP	Reads a PB source file and creates an alphabetized cross-referenced listing of non-reserved words and the physical line numbers where they appear
DIABLO	ZIP	TSR driver that will provide X-On & X-Off support with your serial port
ERASCN	BAS	Erase from cursor location to end of line, erase in the middle of line and erase a vertical column
FACTORY	BAS	Demo program of screen trends. Source included
MASKIN	ZIP	Simple masking entry routine
NATINST	BAS	Demo program screen, constructs Nat Inst look-alike screen. Source included
OPSYS1	ZIP	DOS multi-config menu utility
PASSWORD	ZIP	Changes password in your own .EXE files. No recompiling for new password
PATCH4	ZIP	Fixes serial port timeouts and problems with Chdriv$ command
PBERR	ZIP	Complete explanation of all errors documented in PowerBASIC

✍ = Updated Program
☆ = New Program

Disk #2634, PowerBASIC BBS Library # 4

Windows for PB, information on setting up addresses for COM1 - COM4, code to assist in reading Lotus files, translating tool for PB 2.10, printing and graphics applications, print spooling toolbox, an addition of DIR$ function, and an all-purpose PB programmer's library.

PBWND2	EXE	Windows for PowerBASIC 2.10
PORT4	BAS	Info on setting up addresses for COM1 - COM4; w/ source
READ123	BAS	Code to assist in reading Lotus files
RESWOR	ZIP	Translating tool for PowerBASIC 2.10 w/P
SCANP2	ZIP	Print EGA 640x350 graphics on Citizen compatible printer
SPECTERN	BAS	Demo graphics process control screen, includes source
SPOOLK	ZIP	Print spooling toolbox for PowerBASIC
TTDIR1	ZIP	Addition to DIR$ function of PowerBASIC
APLIB	ZIP	All-purpose PB programmer's library 11-90 version

Disk #2635, PowerBASIC BBS Library #5

Disk #2635, PowerBASIC BBS Library #5 — Routines for mouse usage in PB programs, an Epson-type printer barcode utility, disk routines for PB, Windows applications, and the PowerBASIC Newsletter, Issue #3.

BAR39	ZIP	Print three of nine barcodes on an Epson-type printer
DEFSEG	ZIP	Get current DEF SEG
DISK	ZIP	Disk routines for PowerBASIC
GETCWD	ZIP	Displays the current drive and directory using PB
HUFFMA	ZIP	Huffman encoding file compression
INDENT	ZIP	Indents PB source code
LBOX	ZIP	A vertical selection listbox
LRWIND	ZIP	Window PBU for PowerBASIC
LSTRAN	ZIP	Reads Lotus 1-2-3 named ranges
MAKE	ZIP	Make utility (Upgrade)
MICE	ZIP	Routines to enable mouse usage in PowerBASIC programs
PATCH3	ZIP	To install fixes and enhancements
PBNEWS	ZIP	The PowerBASIC Newsletter - Issue #3
PBWNDO	EXE	Windows for PowerBASIC

Disk #2636, PowerBASIC BBS Library #6

Disk #2636, PowerBASIC BBS Library #6 — Programs included on this disk are a file compressor/uncompressor, Parse command line, the source code for a screen builder program with mouse support, and the routine to reboot your computer from a PB program.

PKZ102	EXE	File compressor/uncompressor
PRSCMD	ZIP	Parse command line: Get parameters and the number
RATS	ZIP	Source code for a screen builder program w/ mouse support Make calls to the mouse driver. Has a screen saver and & scroll routine/exit.
REBOOT	ZIP	Routine to reboot your computer from a PB program

QB4CREF   *by T.N.T Software, Inc.*

This is a cross-reference program for Quickbasic programs. It's very easy to run. If you don't remember how to use it, just type in QB4CREF at the DOS command line and the program itself will tell you what to do. The program can handle up to 1,000 variables, 1,000 labels, 1,000 subprograms, and 1,000 functions (up to 4,000 items total).

(PC-SIG Disk# 1959)

Special Requirements: *None.*
Author Registration: *$25.00*

QBSCR Screen Routines   *by BAD Software*

Want to make your screen displays look like the professional programs, fast and dazzling? You can, with very little effort, using QBSCR SCREEN ROUTINES.

QBSCR SCREEN ROUTINES is a collection of utilities for the discriminating QuickBASIC programmer. With these routines, and very little effort, your own programs can be extremely professional in appearance. The screen routines are especially useful if you are in a hurry. The QBSCR package can cut development time of any project in half, since all the display routines are already written for you. Incorporate the QBSCR routines into your program with a single line of code, and all of the QBSCR resources are at your disposal.

Screen routines are available for building menus, windows, banners, color control, pop-down windows, exploding/imploding displays, text input and control, etc. You also get a complete ASCII color screen editor program to help you design complex screens for fast loading. A demo program is included to demonstrate all the features available to your programs.

The screen routines are more than just a toolbox, they can also fill the role of tutor. By reading through the source code of these routines, you will quickly find yourself learning how to do new things with QuickBASIC.

(PC-SIG Disk#'s 1714, 1713, 1712)

Special Requirements: *None.*
Author Registration: *$15.00*

Reformat
by Harry P. Calevas

REFORMAT will reformat a TurboBASIC source file by removing extra line feeds so that there is only one blank line between statements. Blanks in sets of 8 will be replaced with tabs to save space, and some other spaces will be removed. Also, all characters not in quotes will be changed to upper case. Try this program on a few work files first to be sure you like the way it formats a program's source code.

(PC-SIG Disk# 1842)

Special Requirements: *CGA.*
Author Registration: *$15.00*

Sounds in BASIC
by Tim Keller

SOUNDS is BASICally just good fun. It is a collection of routines written in BASIC that produce sounds ranging from TA-DAH to exploding bombs. Actually, since the routines produce no graphics — nothing on the screen at all — they work best with another, probably fun, project. A little something to add that "extra" touch.

On the other hand, SOUNDS represents an excellent study tool for the BASIC programmer looking to determine the details of a given sound routine.

(PC-SIG Disk# 53)

Special Requirements: *A version of BASIC.*
Author Registration: *None.*

Super Basic Programming Language
by Dennis Baer

The SUPER BASIC PROGRAMMING LANGUAGE a.k.a. Structured Programming Language (SPL) is a hybrid of structured BASIC, with its easy-to-use commands, and a Pascal-styled architecture.

This compiler takes an input source code and produces an ASCII file that can be executed in BASIC or compiled using the BASIC compiler. SPL has powerful commands that let you build of procedures, functions and structured programming blocks which are enclosed by BEGIN and END statements. SPL has graphics ability, mathematical operators, strong string-manipulation commands, and the ability to handle arrays and disk input and output routines.

It offers a way to create structured programs with a fair amount of ease although it is not intended for the novice computer user. SPL comes with a user's manual which has an error code list as well as a feature index.

(PC-SIG Disk# 666)

Special Requirements: *A hard drive and a version of BASIC.*
Author Registration: *$42.00*

TsrBasic Interpreter ✍
by Anthony F. Stuart

TSRBASIC lets you write Terminate and Stay Resident (TSR) programs in BASIC. It supports both pop-up applications that are recalled with a user-defined hotkey sequence and background tasks that are recalled after a specified period of time has elapsed. The entire interpreter can be recalled as well, giving you a powerful programmable calculator at your fingertips.

TSRBASIC simplifies BASIC programming by relaxing data type checking restrictions. This means you do not have to use special suffixes like $ and # to specify the type of data a variable will hold. Any variable can hold any type of data, either text or numeric. Conversions are performed when necessary.

Structured programming is a snap with TSRBASIC's IF...THEN...ELSE...END IF statement, which supports multiline THEN and ELSE clauses and nested IFs. The conventional form of the IF...THEN...ELSE statement is supported.

TSRBASIC's powerful screen handling functions let you select video attributes, define text windows for input and output, and save and restore portions of the screen. TSRBASIC supports direct video access for speed or ROM-BIOS/DOS mode for compatibility with nonstandard video adapters. You can execute the contents of a character string so that you can evaluate arithmetic expressions on the fly. You can also use this feature to construct powerful user-defined functions.

TSRBASIC compiles your program into intermediate code and interprets the intermediate code. This results in fast and efficient program execution. Display the intermediate code if you wish. TSRBASIC also lets you convert your BASIC program into an executable (.EXE) file that can be invoked from DOS.

(PC-SIG Disk# 2570)

Special Requirements: *None.*
Author Registration: *$15.00*

VRef
by W. Kremer

BASIC programmers — VREF (Variables Cross-Reference) is a programming utility which will show all lines where a specific variable is located in a BASIC program.

VXREF works with all BASIC programs written in GW/PC BASIC or BASICA and saved in an ASCII format. It can distinguish between variables and arrays of the same name and will ignore type declarations and system variables. Each occurrence of a variable in a line is mentioned once. The list may be printed on a printer or saved to a disk file.

(PC-SIG Disk# 875)

Special Requirements: *None.*
Author Registration: *$5.00*

▼ ▼ ▼

Programming, C

"c_wndw" and "c-ndx" Libraries
by Marietta Systems, Inc.

The "c_wndw" and "c_ndx" libraries are designed for both novice and intermediate C programmers who want full screen, color, cursor control, windowing abilities and relational database facilities without programming complex escape sequences or DOS-level interrupts. They are designed for experienced programmers who need a set of fast I/O windowing and disk access functions. A full set of file access functions are given that trap and handle all usual errors.

The "c_wndw" library provides input and output windowing abilities that operate at professional speeds. The output windowing facilities use memory mapping for instant screen display. Full advantage is taken of color monitors, and automatic editing of entry and output fields id provided. Pull-down and pop-up menu functions, help screens, and multi-layered windows provide a sophisticated user interface.

The "c_ndx" library provides multiple B-tree access to data files and supports intelligent relational access to multiple data files via hashed random file access. The database file is the familiar dBase standard, and the indexes are fully compatible with the dBase NDX format.

With these libraries you can develop superior programs in C in less time than in the dBase language.

(PC-SIG Disk#'s 1007, 1705)

Special Requirements: *A version of Turbo C or Microsoft C.*
Author Registration: *$79.00*
►*ASP Member.*

C Adventure
by Tim Keller

Welcome to C ADVENTURE, a classic text adventure game. You are standing at the end of a road before a small brick building. Go into the cave and gather as much treasure as possible without getting dismembered, eaten or otherwise maimed. And, of course, escape with your loot!

Since the C source code is included, the game players can explore and the hackers can change things to suit themselves. Features a good English language parser. Games can be saved in progress and restored for later playing.

(PC-SIG Disk# 259)

Special Requirements: *None.*
Author Registration: *None.*

C Communications Library ☆ *by MarshallSoft*

The C COMMUNICATIONS LIBRARY is an asynchronous communications library designed for experienced software developers programming in Microsoft C or Turbo C.

Sixteen communications functions as well as six support functions are provided.

Included are:

❏ Set Baud Rate for a selected port
❏ Monitor CTRL-BREAK key
❏ Write Char to screen,
❏ Set/Clear/Read the data terminal ready bit
❏ Delay
❏ Terminate selected port
❏ ...and many more

Communications rates from 300 to 115,200 baud are supported. The Receive queues are adjustable from 8 bytes to 16KB. All four ports, COM1 through COM4, are supported. (Most libraries only provide support for COM1 and COM2.) Additionally, two ports can be run concurrently.

The C COMMUNICATIONS LIBRARY provides complete modem control and status.

Eleven different communications errors can be trapped and reported. There is even support for the CTRL-BREAK error exit. The library supports all memory models and was written in optimized assembly language for small size and fast speed.

The source code for a simple terminal emulator program is provided as an example of the use of the library functions. This sample program can be used to call up bulletin board services and mainframe computers, or even to build a specialized communications interface for your application.

The C COMMUNICATIONS LIBRARY can be called from any language that supports the C-language calling convention and FAR arrays and functions.

(PC-SIG Disk# 2695)
Special Requirements: *C compiler and modem.*
Author Registration: *$35.00*

C Tutor *by Coronado Enterprises*

C TUTOR is a comprehensive instructional course for the C programming language which assumes the user has a moderate amount of programming experience.

The C source code is included for each of several examples discussed throughout the tutorial. These examples are meant to be studied and then compiled and run by the student. The examples are short and focus on specific topics.

All of the points of C language, including properly-structured programming techniques, are covered at the elementary level. The description and instruction are applicable to most compilers with some slight differences.

(PC-SIG Disk#'s 577, 578)
Special Requirements: *None.*
Author Registration: *$15.00 to $39.95.*

C Utilities 2 *by Leigh Cuthbertson*

This hard working, time-saving set of utilities and functions for the C programmer includes many screen-handling routines to draw boxes, clear lines, move the cursor, etc. Some DOS interfaces let you access DOS time (to hundredths), convert date formats, interface with BIOS, and more. If you'd like some help with your own programming projects, or only want to investigate how others have done the job, be sure to check out this one!

(PC-SIG Disk# 216)
Special Requirements: *None.*
Author Registration: *None.*

File Descriptions:

README	DOC	Notes about programs on this disk.
READS	C	Reads string from stdin.
WEEKDAY	C	Gives the day of week a given Gregorian date.

SCRATT	C	Toggles screen attributes (ie BOLD, blink, reverse video).
SCRINIT	C	Initializes screen and keyboard arrays.
JTOJ	C	Returns Julian day from date in form (yddd).
DOSDATE	ASM	Returns DOS month, day, year as integers.
JTOG	C	Function to convert Julian date to Gregorian date.
ELINE	C	Function to erase line of screen.
CHOSIT	C	Displays menu, prompt for a response and validate.
SCONTROL	H	Header file used by screen and keyboard control library.
FRAME	C	Function to draw box given two corners.
CURSOR	C	Function to move cursor to a specific r,c position.
GTOJ	C	Converts Gregorian date to Julian date.
CVTDATE	C	Unpacks Gregorian date (1/1/84) to (01/01/84).
GETLINE	C	Read record from file to string.
CURDOWN	C	Function to move curser down y relative lines.
GETDATE	C	Gets date in string form MM/DD/YY.
GETTIME	C	Gets time in form HH:MM:SS (24 hour clock).
DOSTIME	ASM	Gives DOS time in hours, minutes, seconds, 1/100 seconds.
ESCREEN	C	Function to erase line from screen.
CURUP	C	Mover cursor up y lines.
PAUSE	C	Pauses a program for period of time.
CURBACK	C	Move cursor back x columns.
CURFOR	C	Move cursor forward x columns.
BIOSIO	ASM	Assembly routines which interface directly with BIOS.
READC	C	Function to read string from stdin.
WRITES	C	Function to write string to stdout.
WRITEC	C	Function to write character to screen using DOS function.
COMM	MNU	Menu for communications program.
MENCON	C	Function to open menu file and display it on screen.
???	BAT	Batch files to emulate UNIX commands (9 files).
IBMTTY	C	Terminal emulation program with file upload & download.

CBase: The C Database Library ✍ *by Citadel*

This is a C database file management library. Records may be accessed both randomly and sequentially through indexes stored in B+-trees. Records may also be accessed sequentially in the order in which they are stored. Multiuser access is supported under any operating system with file locking capabilities.

Designed to be extremely portable, it's written in strict adherence to the ANSI C standard and can still be used with the K&R C compilers. All system dependent code is isolated to make it easy to port to new operating systems.

CBASE is actually made up of four individual libraries, each complete and independently accessible. At its foundation is the block buffered I/O library which models a file as a collection of blocks made up of fields. The linked sequential file library provides all the facilities necessary for the creation and manipulation of doubly-linked sequential files. The btree library provides the same for B+- tree files. The program's library uses the linked sequential file and btree libraries to perform all structured file management operations. The linked sequential library is used for record storage and the btree library is used for inverted file key storage. Database size is limited only by available disk storage.

CBASE comes complete with all source code, and a demo database is included to demonstrate its capabilities.
(PC-SIG Disk# 2247)

Special Requirements: *None.*
Author Registration: *$77.00*

CHTREE C Program Flow Analyzer ☆ *by Fowler Software Engineering, Co.*

CHTREE is a unique C program flow analyzer. It can be used to interpret C source code that someone else wrote, find in what file a function is defined and/or called, and to search for function names, strings and labels.

The program has its own way of doing things, like only accepting input in lower case. But if you need to maximize the speed of your program, CHTREE will find the functions that are called most often so you can optimize your program code.
(PC-SIG Disk# 2599)

Special Requirements: *640K RAM, CGA, Microsoft C. Hard drive recommended.*
Author Registration: *$25.00*

CTRLCLIB - The CTRL + C Library ☆   *by Trendtech Corporation*

CTRLCLIB - The Ctrl+C Library, contains C-language functions that programmers can use to manage user-initiated interrupts.

Using functions from CTRLCLIB, programmers can have full control over the following kinds of user-initiated program interrupts:

All types of program # "breaks" — CTRL-c, CTRL-break, CTRL-2, and ALT-3.

The "pause" keys — CTRL-s, and 'pause' (or CTRL-NUMLOCK).

The print screen keys — print-screen, CTRL-p, CTRL-printscreen, and others.

Trap the system reset keys, and/or force either warm or cold reboot. Capture and control the setting of all '-lock' keys such as Caps-lock and Num-lock. Facilities exist for capturing keyboard make/break codes, if needed, and popular C-compilers are supported. Registration includes full source code and additional memory-model libraries.
(PC-SIG Disk# 2574)

Special Requirements: *Microsoft or Borland C & C++ compilers and #1364 PKUNZIP.*
Author Registration: *$30.00*
➤*ASP Member.*

Extended Library   *by Maine Data & Financial Systems, Inc*

EXTLIB is a library of over 50 C run-time video routines for the advanced MS-DOS C programmer.

It features windows, pop-up and pull-down menus, menu bars, scroll bars, direct video memory I/O, and cursor control routines to be used with Microsoft C or QuickC. In addition to these video routines, there are formatted display input routines (dollars, for instance) and advanced error handling functions. The small, medium, compact, and large memory models are all supported. EXTLIB also comes with the floating point emulator or 80x87 packages.
(PC-SIG Disk# 1324)

Special Requirements: *Microsoft C or Quick C.*
Author Registration: *$20.00*

FlashPac C Library ✍   *by SimpleSoft Inc.*

Add blinding speed and style to your C programs with the FLASHPAC C LIBRARY. Your programs will run faster and look better than anything you can buy.

The FLASHPAC C LIBRARY provides C programmers with low level routines that access the video display, keyboard, printer, disk, and mouse devices. These routines are not intended to replace the standard features of C. They were created to add to and extend the C programming environment for MS-DOS and PC-DOS operating systems. In keeping with good programming practice, global variables within the Library have been kept to a minimum. All the functions in the Library are written in assembly language, for speed, using the Pascal parameter passing conventions.

The FLASHPAC C LIBRARY contains routines for DISK — many DOS functions that use byte STRAMS when accessing the disk files; VIDEO — direct access for saving and restoring the screen, framing windows, cursor control, etc.; MOUSE — basic support plus an event handler; BIOS print functions; and both DOS and BIOS keyboard functions.
(PC-SIG Disk#'s 1872, 2306)

Special Requirements: *None.*
Author Registration: *$50.00*

Indent   *by PTD Software Systems*

INDENT is a C program formatter that reformats any C program in the input file according to the switches or command options. Make your source code more readable and appear in an acceptable format. The C source code for the main program is included so you can modify it to fit your exact needs.
(PC-SIG Disk# 962)

Special Requirements: *320K RAM.*
Author Registration: *None.*

     ✍ = Updated Program
☆ = New Program

LE_C - C Library Functions ✍   *by ProBATE Software*

The LE_C LIBRARY is a set of C run-time functions that allow you to easily create programs that implement many of today's standard user interfaces such as menus, box menus, data entry, help facility, line drawing, border drawing (including exploding boxes), and more.

What makes the LE_C LIBRARY unique is its integrated help facility. All of the menu and input functions support help screens. Specify help screens unique to each menu selection and even move the help window within the screen. Help screens are an important part of any program, especially those using data-entry. The LE_C LIBRARY provides you with the help functions you need to build professional-looking programs.

Specify up to 40 special function keys (Ctrl-F1, Ctrl-End, etc.) for use with the menu and input functions. These 40 keys are in addition to the pre-defined commonly-used function keys. The screen functions write directly to video memory resulting in exceptional display speed.

You can increase the functional and aesthetic value of your programs with the LE_C C LIBRARY functions. A demonstration program is included to illustrate the value of this library.

(PC-SIG Disk# 2314)

Special Requirements: *QuickC or Microsoft C Compilers.*
Author Registration: *$30.00*

MPLUS Graphic Interface Library   *by Michael Yam*

MPLUS is a graphic interface library for Microsoft C version 5.0 and up. If your application generates business or scientific plots, or if you need to wrap an interface around an art program or your favorite fractal generator, MPLUS will simplify your task.

It provides four basic tools. The first is a graphic window which can display both text and graphics. The second tool provides three dialogue boxes to display a general message, a warning message, and an error message. The third tool is a bar menu with pull down windows. Functions and menu titles are easily plugged in. The bar menu also recognizes input from either the mouse or the keyboard. Finally, there is mouse support. These mouse routines are not purely a rehash of the mouse interrupt, 33H. You'll also find an event handler and a function which retrieves input from the keyboard and mouse. The documentation is 80 pages long and provides a complete reference to all of the functions provided.

MPLUS is a user-supported program. The shareware version contains only the small model library, but registration provides the medium, compact, and large models, a laser printed manual (double sided and in a Times Roman font), two free upgrades, and support via U.S. mail, Compuserve and voice mail.

(PC-SIG Disk# 2032)

Special Requirements: *CGA, VGA, or EGA, Microsoft C version 5.0, and mouse is optional.*
Author Registration: *$50.00*

Panels For C   *by Jay Brown*

Perform screen oriented input and output easily and quickly with PANELS FOR C. PANELS FOR C is a set of routines which can be called by your C programs to do screen oriented input and output. Screen layouts, or panels, are simple text files that you can create with any ordinary word processor.

PANELS FOR C demonstrates the ease with which panels can be created and linked into your programs. Included programs are sound generation, time display, screen attributes, personal telephone directory and auto dialer, a panel tutorial, and a panel display routine.

The PANEL.OBJ set of routines have been compiled using the Microsoft C 5.1 Optimizing Compiler under a small memory model.

(PC-SIG Disk# 1717)

Special Requirements: *None.*
Author Registration: *$29.95*

PC-GRAPHICS C   *by Robert Becker*

PC GRAPHICS is not just for HP BASIC types who need to port code to the IBM-PC. These software tools provide an intuitive and powerful method for graphics programming that makes up for shortcomings in the standard Microsoft C library.

PC GRAPHICS is a subset of the library primitives available in Hewlett-Packard workstation BASIC. Here are procedures for soft-clipping, scaling, line patterns, pen colors, and text rotation that let you write two-dimensional graph plotting programs in Microsoft C. The scaling feature is especially useful as it lets you create your own scale, removing the need to think in pixels. The package can also be used for simple animation.

(PC-SIG Disk# 1433)

Special Requirements: *CGA and Microsoft C, version 5.0.*
Author Registration: *None.*

PCC Personal C Compiler   *by C Ware Corporation*

The PERSONAL C COMPILER (PCC) is a fast and compact C compiler package with a lot of power.

PCC builds "small model" only: 64K of code, 64K data (which can be bypassed), and 64K stack executables from Kernigan and Ritchie standard C language source. It comes with compiler, Assembler, linker, library utility, standard library, debugger, editor, and includes sample files. PCC is not a bare bones system; it supports overlays, has an 8087 library, a library of supplemental screen I/O routines, and a special data type to break the 64K limit. The documentation is indexed, very complete and is a good learning tool for the beginning C programmer.

Most importantly, PCC produces small and efficient code very quickly, and even though it is not a fancy "optimizing" compiler with lots of bells and whistles, it's all a true programmer really needs.

NOTE: The librarian and the Xarray memory capability are not included with shareware version.

(PC-SIG Disk# 1337)

Special Requirements: *None.*
Author Registration: *$30.00*

QC_BAT (QC_TOOLS) ☆   *by Luis Larzabal*

Accompanying QC_UTIL in QC_TOOLS is QC_BAT, a collection of files that shows you how to exercise total control over your Microsoft QuickC compiler. Command-line compilation enhances the overall performance of your programs. It allows you to specify exactly what you want the compiler to do.

The proficient C programmer should be able to command-line-compile his programs. Understanding it, however, can be a tedious task. The many options available are confusing.

The purpose of QC_BAT is to introduce you to it. The documented batch files include page numbers that reference the QuickC manuals. The files cover the majority needs:

❑ Tiny memory model (64K of data and code) [.com @ QC 2.5 up]
❑ Small memory model (64K of data and 64K of code)
❑ Compilation extent (compilation, assembly, and linking)
❑ Software floating point (few can afford a math co-processor)
❑ Choice of 8088/8086 or 80286 native processors (PC/XTs and ATs)
❑ Optimization of the compilation process
❑ Display of most warnings
❑ Compilation to ANSI C standard extensions

(PC-SIG Disk# 2171)

Special Requirements: *Microsoft Quick-C compiler.*
Author Registration: *$10.00*

QC_UTIL (QC_TOOLS) ✍   *by Luis Larzabal*

A collection of C utilities that allow implementation of interrupt calls to DOS or to the BIOS of a PC, XT or AT. QC-UTIL of QC_TOOLS gives you the ability to control cursor movement, paint the screen, draw boxes and windows, control the keyboard buffer, and much more. The documentation correlates with, and references by page number, Peter Norton's "The New Peter Norton Programmer's Guide to the IBM PC and PS/2".

Source and object files are supplied for several C compilers, for example QuickC, MicroSoft C and Let's C. Programmers will find QC_UTIL routines to be a convenient addition to their programming tool libraries.

(PC-SIG Disk# 2171)

Special Requirements: *Microsoft Quick-C Compiler.*
Author Registration: *$10.00*

SDB ✍

by Tim Keller

SDB is a relational database system written in the C programming language. SDB is a simple database manager developed to provide a relatively low overhead system for storing data on machines with limited disk and memory resources.

While it performs very well as a somewhat limited database, the program has the source code in the C language included. This represents opportunities for programmers to get a look at how the functions have been constructed.

(PC-SIG Disk# 147)

Special Requirements: *None.*
Author Registration: *None.*

Steve's Library for Turbo-C ✍

by SEM Software

Do you want to speed up your C programs and reduce their size at the same time? STEVE'S TURBO C LIBRARY is a set of direct video functions that can do the job.

STEVE'S TURBO C LIBRARY provides a complete facility for direct writes and reads in video memory. This allows you to produce extremely fast screen displays, with full control over colors and attributes. With direct video access you can create the rapid, sparkling displays that attract users.

A special feature of STEVE'S TURBO C LIBRARY is the "ticker" interrupt handler function. With this function, you have the ability to install a special routine of your own to intercept DOS interrupt 1CH. This allows you to perform operations relative to the system's clock.

Several utility functions are also included in the library; search the current path for an excutable program, compare two ASCII files, count words, lines, characters, etc in a file, time and date formats, and a file dump to aid in debugging.

(PC-SIG Disk# 1737)

Special Requirements: *Hard Drive.*
Author Registration: *$25.00*

TesSeract CXL User Interface Development System ☆ *by Innovative Data Concepts*

The TCXL library is a supplement to your C compiler's standard run-time library. It contains over 375 multipurpose functions which provide a variety of capabilities. It is available for several popular C compilers including Microsoft C, QuickC, Turbo C/C++, and Zortech C/C++

These routines were written in highly-optimized C and assembler code, ensuring maximum program speed, minimum program size, easy modification and increased portability.

Use customized bar menus to create pop-up, pull-down, and Lotus-style menus, as well as any other custom menu that you can define. Features full mouse support, non-selectable items, global hotkeys, and more.

Multi-field formatted data entry creates data entry forms with one or more input fields. You have full control over user input and can tie validation functions into each input field.

Context-sensitive Help can index Help files for speed, category, and cross-referencing. Help can be applied at the global, window, menu item, and input field levels.

TCXL has scrollable pick menus to select from a list of items. Full mouse support and scroll bars are used in a dedicated file picker.

Full-featured window control allows as many open windows as memory permits. Windows can be stacked, tiled, shadowed, moved, resized, and changed in many ways. There are more than 75 functions designed to handle windowed output.

User-defined input system provides a consistent interface between the hardware-dependent input devices and TCXL's output systems. Features both formatted and unformatted user input, with varying levels of output control.

Nonstandard video sizes EGA 43 and VGA 50-line modes are supported.

TCXL has a full set of routines for access to Expanded Memory through the EMS specification, and for access to Extended Memory through the XMS specification. TCXL also recognizes the presence of advanced memory management schemes such as VCPI and DPMI.

(PC-SIG Disk#'s 2583, 2584)

Special Requirements: *A hard disk and C compiler.*
Author Registration: *$50.00*
➤*ASP Member.*

Utilities for Programmers

by Hal-PC

A collection of handy utilities for programmers and computer users in general. Check out the list — there's something here for almost everyone.

ENVED2 — Configure the DOS environment. Make changes more conveniently than using the manual SET command.

PASTILS — There are 52 various utility routines for the Pascal language in this source code written in Pascal. Some of these routines: return the various coordinates of an active window; turn on/off reverse video; produce a single click from the PC speaker; calculate a loan payment amount; get time/date from system; get password; convert strings to lower/upper case; has an auxiliary device driver and serial port input/output; save/restore a current/previous screen; and more.

87DTEC — This utility comes with two versions of source codes to be compiled. One is coded in the C language and the other in Assembler. Once compiled and linked, 87DTEC gives you the features, video features, and CPU type of your machine. It can also determine your machine's compatability, illustrate timing delays, test for the presence of the ANSI.SYS file and the presence of a math co-processor (8087 or 80287).

TC-HELP — This program is a reference guide to the library function of Turbo C version 1.0. TCHELP searches the reference guide (a file named TC.DAT) for the specified function, and displays the information about it to the console.

TC10PAT — This program reads a text from a .DIF file and applies the patch to the program file. The .DIF file is relatively free-format.

TPC — TPC reads a Turbo Pascal source file and converts it into the corresponding C source code. It does about 90% of the work required to do the translation (a macro header is included).

UCTURBO2 — This is a library that contains over 200 functions written in C and Assembler. There is a wide selection of graphics functions, general purpose functions and functions to control the graphics dot matrix and a daisy wheel printer.

C-WINDOW — A special windowing-cursor control-string, character display and border drawing included. Everything happens at top speed because C-WINDOW was written in C, converted to Assembler, and hand-optimized. The C-WINDOWING TOOLBOX (C-WINDOW) programs on this disk perform the same function for the programming language C (Lattice C or Microsoft C version 3 or 4).

(PC-SIG Disk# 885)

Special Requirements: *Two floppy drives.*
Author Registration: *Various.*

Window Boss ✍

by Star Guidance Consulting

WINDOW BOSS enhances and accelerates the development of systems and applications programs in the C language.

Create programs that have the same look and feel as the top-selling spreadsheet, database, and desktop accessory packages. Pop-up windows, pull-down menus, status lines, and in-context on-line Help functions can be implemented easily. Your applications can drag windows around the screen and automatically sense the video card installed. All of this without snow, flicker, or delay!

Includes support for Microsoft 6.0, Microsoft QuickC 2.5, shadowed windows, super titles, and graphics character text input. The WINDOW BOSS now supports Microsoft, Borland, Lattice, Watcom, Mix Power C, Computer Innovations, Datalight, Zortech, and Aztec C!

(PC-SIG Disk#'s 873, 1113, 2556)

Special Requirements: *C compiler.*
Author Registration: *$55.00*
➤**ASP Member.**

▼ ▼ ▼

Programming, Forth

Laxon & Perry Forth

by Tim Keller

A Forth Language system from Henry Laxon and Mike Perry. A compiler, L&P FORTH is portable and convenient, and especially good for novice programmers. This is a well-structured introduction to the Forth

---

✍ = Updated Program
☆ = New Program

language and includes an introductory text file for beginners. Documentation is brief and recommended reading is "Starting FORTH", by Leo Brodie.

(PC-SIG Disk#'s 263, 264)

Special Requirements: *None.*
Author Registration: *None.*

MVP-FORTH   *by Tim Keller*

MVP-FORTH (Mountain View Press Public Domain FORTH) is the programming language FORTH intended primarily for advanced FORTH programmers on the college or graduate level. This program was developed to accompany the book "Starting Forth," by Leo Brodie. This program is an interpreter, not a compiler and, as such, will not create stand alone EXE files.

(PC-SIG Disk# 31)

Special Requirements: *None.*
Author Registration: *None.*

▼ ▼ ▼

Programming, Fortran

ACM Volumes 1-5   *by Cullinet Software Inc.*

Here is a collection of Fortran routines/procedures for solving various problems in the areas of science, engineering, and numerical analysis.

Some of the many routines covered:
❏ Solution of zeros of polynomials
❏ Various partial differential equation solvers
❏ Linear equation solvers for over/under-determined problems (L1, L2 and Chebyshev norms)
❏ Eigenvalue solvers
❏ Function integration
❏ Minimization of unconstrained multivariate functions
❏ Curve-fitting in Chebyshev norm
❏ Dependence of solution of nonlinear systems on its parameters
❏ Sorting
❏ Global error estimation for ordinary differential equations
❏ Matrix bandwidth and profile reduction
❏ Spline interpolation
❏ Solution of linear systems for special matrices
❏ Cubic curve-fitting using local data
❏ Computation of condition numbers of a matrix without computing eigenvectors
❏ Bessel functions
❏ Statistical functions
❏ Revised simplex method for constrained resource network scheduling
❏ Exact solution of integer systems of linear equations
❏ Convex hull algorithm for planar sets
❏ A multiple-precision arithmetic package
❏ Adaptive smooth curve-fitting
❏ Basic linear algebra subprograms (BLAS)
❏ Optimized mass-storage fit
❏ Efficient one-way enciphering algorithm
❏ And more

(PC-SIG Disk#'s 1008, 1009, 1010, 1011)

Special Requirements: *A version of the Fortran programming language.*
Author Registration: *Any amount is appreciated.*

Automatic Fortran Format Statements
by Gerard E. Dallal

FMT takes the drudgery out of writing FORTRAN FORMAT statements by automatically generating FORMAT statements for you. Simply use a wordprocessor or text editor to create an ASCII file that looks just like the output you would like your program to produce. FMT turns your data into a set of FORMAT statements that can be pasted into your FORTRAN program. This is a great tool for any FORTRAN programmer.

The input to FMT is an ASCII file containing the output that is to be transformed into FORTRAN FORMAT statements. The file should look just the way it is to appear on screen. FMT automatically adds the leading blank character required by FORTRAN. FMT can be instructed to treat each line in the input file as a separate FORMAT statement.

(PC-SIG Disk# 1685)

Special Requirements: *None.*
Author Registration: *$7.00*

D-Access
by Olympic Software

D-ACCESS provides access to all the functions available in the IBM DOS and BIOS, access to the I/O ports including the mouse and direct memory operations, all from FORTRAN. No longer are you restricted to the functions provided by the FORTRAN compiler. Use as high level or as low level a function as you need.

D-ACCESS is a set of interface modules which you can call from within FORTRAN with the appropriate parameters. In most cases these parameters are 8086/80286 register values. The modules in turn call DOS, BIOS or the mouse driver, or perform direct I/O or memory operations. Applications where D-ACCESS will be extremely valuable include graphics programs, database programs, sound programs, mouse based user interface programs, communication programs, and printer oriented utilities.

Since effective use of DOS, BIOS, I/O, mouse or direct memory requires some knowledge of the 8086 family of CPUs, the IBM PC microcomputer family architectures, PC-DOS (or MS-DOS), BIOS and the mouse driver MOUSE.SYS, this program includes a recommended reading list for the serious programmer.

(PC-SIG Disk# 1930)

Special Requirements: *FORTRAN compiler.*
Author Registration: *$25.00*

GRAFX - Graphic Extension Library for FORTRAN 77
by Ridge Technology

The GRAFX library consists of over 50 FORTRAN 77 callable routines, which allow FORTRAN programs access to the PC's graphic and other capabilities. The graphic routines find application where emphasis is on ease of implementation and rapid presentation of numerical data. Three levels of capability are included. The top level requires no knowledge of the PC or computer graphics, and is suitable for pedagogical applications such as numerical methods instruction, quick-look analysis of computational progress, and for the professional who is not primarily a programmer. The middle level operates in problem space and suports display of points, lines, circles, ellipses, boxes, etc. to allow creation of custom displays such as map projections, multiple graphic windows, and 3D displays. The lowest level consists of primitives implemented in assembly language which operate in display space to directly access display memory and access to selected DOS and BIOS functions.

Many miscellaneous routines are included in the library. These provide bit level access, shift, and logical (AND, OR, NOT, EOR) operations required by some applications. A standard pseudo-random number generator, routines to get time-of-day, time in seconds, and date are included. A vector clipping routine is included which can be used to clip a problem space vector before drawing lines. If you really want to get down to the bits and bytes, PEEK & POKE routines are included to access any location in the 8086 address space.

In addition several illustrative example FORTRAN 77 programs are included to demonstrate usage.

(PC-SIG Disk# 1699)

Special Requirements: *CGA and a Fortran 77 compiler.*
Author Registration: *None.*

Graph For Fortran
by David I. Hoyer

This collection of FORTRAN subroutines will make it simple for you to plot high quality scientific and engineering graphs on dot matrix printers which have the ability to print graphics. These subroutines can be incorporated easily into any FORTRAN program, so that your own programs can automatically print high resolution graphs as part of the program output.

✍ = Updated Program
☆ = New Program

Also included is a sample program to illustrate the use of the subroutines. This sample program works as a stand-alone graph plotter for plotting graphs from a data file. As an alternative to incorporating the graph plotting subroutines into your own programs, you could instead get your program to write a data file to disk for later plotting using the sample program supplied.

Features include resolution options, vertical or horizontal plotting, linear or logarithmic axes, labelling of axes, overlaying grid lines on the graph, joining points with straight lines or a cubic spline, plotting user-defined functions, passing a list of parameters to the user-defined functions, and placing text on the graph.

(PC-SIG Disk# 1926)

Special Requirements: *FORTRAN 77 compiler, and a dot matrix printer w/ 8 pin graphics.*
Author Registration: *$30.00*

▼ ▼ ▼

Programming, Modula-2

Calutil
by Custom Cycle Fitments

Enhance the standard Modula-2 library with this useful toolkit. Though heralded academically, Modula-2 has some noticeable short-comings, especially in the I/O functions arena. CALUTIL will alleviate some of these difficulties.

CALUTIL provides modules for improved I/O, date and calendar functionality, string handling, screen display, and math routines (trig. and log. functions). For improved file I/O, CALUTIL comes with a model program to handle a sequential record datafile. CALUTIL also provides an alternate programming environment that enables the user to edit, print, compile, link, and run a program without explicitly typing each command.

CALUTIL comes ready for use with the Logitech Compiler, but all source is included so the modules can be adapted for other Modula-2 environments.

(PC-SIG Disk# 1649)

Special Requirements: *Hard drive and Logitech Modula-2 recommended.*
Author Registration: *$30.00*

M2JFTOOLS
by Custom Cycle Fitments

This collection contains library modules that provide new, useful procedures to be incorporated into Modula-2 programs, to either produce new effects or make it easier to achieve older effects. Also included are programs to make the programming process easier. This system offers control over:

❑ Date and time information with user-selectable formats
❑ File reading and writing of strings, numbers and Booleans
❑ Printing of strings, numbers and Booleans
❑ Printer control codes
❑ Additional string procedures.

Other features include comprehensive screen control: cursor control, partial or total clearing, Boolean prompts, inverse video boxes for data input, including decimal point, data entry, editing and display of reals, screen editing of strings, and integers.

The data functions provide keyboard entry, FileInOut, printing of all types of data items, and entry of logical variables. The Math1 library module provides the trigonometric functions. Those modules that employ real arithmetic are presented in two versions, one for those with a math coprocessor and the other for those without. There is even an improved programming environment that liberates you from constant mouse use, and gives you greater editing control. All the tasks that are necessary when developing a Modula-2 program can be executed from one menu.

(PC-SIG Disk# 1895)

Special Requirements: *Modula-2 compiler.*
Author Registration: *$30.00*

Modula-2 Compiler
by Fitted Software Tools

The MODULA-2 COMPILER (M2C) proves you don't have to buy a commercial package to get a full-featured compiler! M2C features the compiler combined with an integrated editor and "make" facility, a program linker, an execution profiler, and a makefile generator.

Code generated by the M2C suits either the Intel 8086 "huge" or "large" memory models. More restrictive memory models are not supported. For the "huge" model, each module has its own data and code segment. Each of the segments can be up to 64K in size. For the "large" memory model, static data from all the modules is combined into a single data segment. For either model, pointers are four bytes long and all remaining memory is available for the "heap".

The package includes 37 pages of well-written and indexed documentation.

(PC-SIG Disk#'s 1080, 1081)

Special Requirements: *512K RAM, and two floppy drives.*
Author Registration: *$25.00*

Modula-2 Tutorial
by Coronado Enterprises

MODULA-2 TUTORIAL teaches you the fundamentals of this complex language and will have you up and programming by the end of it.

The first part of this tutorial is composed of those features that are common to PASCAL and MODULA-2 and are also of a fundamental nature. You will need to study all of Part I in order to write meaningful MODULA-2 programs. If you are already a fairly experienced Pascal programmer, you should absorb this material very quickly.

Parts II and III teach those features that are new in MODULA-2 — advanced topics and features that allow the programmer to use the full power of the language and write larger and more complex programs. File

(PC-SIG Disk#'s 814, 815)

Special Requirements: *Printer.*
Author Registration: *$15.00 to $39.95.*

▼ ▼ ▼

Programming, Pascal

DML & XREF
by DML Software, Inc.

Turbo Pascal programmers, take note! Here are 87 Turbo Pascal routines not found in the standard version 4.0 or 5.0 library. Full source code and documentation is included for each routine.

The library is divided into four functional modules containing:

❑ 42 general purpose procedures for such things as system programming extensions, file I/O and protection, text encryption, general purpose video and video messages, disk and memory sizes, instruction timing, general purpose file, math, DOS and version control

❑ 18 numeric procedures for handling general numeric formatting and conversion, and date and time formatting and conversion

❑ 14 string procedures to handle general purpose string functions and conversion

❑ 13 keyboard procedures for controlling and accessing the keyboard and keyboard buffer.

The entire library can be accessed by a single statement or the four unit modules can be accessed individually. A demonstration is included that shows the action of each routine.

An additional utility included is XREF, a Pascal source code cross-reference and formatting program.

(PC-SIG Disk# 1697)

Special Requirements: *Turbo Pascal version 4.0 or 5.0, and a hard drive or high density drive.*
Author Registration: *$10.00*

Eissinger Programmer's Utilities
by Microcomputer Consultant

A passel of useful tools for Turbo Pascal programmers, as well as some batch utilities that do not require any programming language to use. Batch File Utilities:

❑ PASTE — Concatenates two files together line-by-line, butted together end-to-end. A line from the second file is appended to the first file to make a longer line for the new file.

❑ BLDBAT — Creates a text file containing directory's filenames specified by a file masking parameter. Similar to Unix's LS command to file.

❑ MELD — Merges two text files by interleaving lines of each file. The new file receives a line from the first file, then a line from the second, then one from the first, etc..

❑ PUTCURS — Moves the cursor to a designated line on the screen. Extremely useful for batch file I/O.

Pascal Utilities:

❑ INDENT — Reformats and standardizes PASCAL source files for indents and case. Useful when two or more programmers with different writing styles work on code for a program.

❑ EXTRACT — Pulls out and prints the names of all procedures and functions along with all in-line comments from source files. This is invaluable for documentation and cross-referencing.

❑ SGCVERT — For Screen Genie users, reveals how to take advantage of an undocumented feature in this popular window generator that permits the use of the Screen Genie work file as a screen in an object file or in a Turbo Pascal TPU unit.

(PC-SIG Disk# 1539)

Special Requirements: *Turbo Pascal 4.0 and higher.*
Author Registration: *$25.00*

FlashPac Pascal Library ✍   *by SimpleSoft Inc.*

These low level Turbo Pascal routines access the video display, keyboard, printer, disk, mouse devices, and a couple of DOS functions. These routines are not intended to replace the standard features of Turbo Pascal, but add to and extend the Turbo Pascal programming environment for the MS-DOS operating system.

To simplify the use of these routines, the number of global variables needed for this library has been kept to a minimum. All functions in the library were written in Assembly language using the Pascal parameter passing conventions.

FPDISK supports several DOS function calls that use byte streams when accessing disk files. FPKBD supports BIOS and DOS keyboard function calls. FPMOUSE supports basic mouse functions, including a mouse event handler. FPPRT supports BIOS printer functions. FPVIDEO consists of several video routines that provide direct access to the video display. Routines include saving and restoring the screen, framing windows, setting the absolute position of the cursor, and more.

(PC-SIG Disk#'s 1982, 2093)

Special Requirements: *A version of Turbo Pascal.*
Author Registration: *$50.00*

The Helper   *by David I. Hoyer*

Create hypertext-like programs and Help files to be used as information documents for interrelated topics, or as controller programs in their own right. Nice features include: many Help screens; easy movement between categories; backtracking; animated screens using time-delay overlays; text search, print screens; window size control; position and colors for each page; program cursor to execute specific DOS commands or shell (for menu programs, auto- installation routines, etc); use files independently or interface to Turbo Pascal for context-sensitive help and user-specified functions.

Note that you do NOT require Turbo Pascal to use The Helper, although sample TP programs are supplied to demonstrate how you can add the Help files to your own programs.

(PC-SIG Disk# 2383)

Special Requirements: *None.*
Author Registration: *$38.00*

Minigen   *by MiniGen Products*

MINIGEN is a screen generator that creates Turbo Pascal code for either color or monochrome displays. You can paint data-entry screens (constants areas and data fields), open and close windows with borders and cursor memory, perform controlled data entry, and create pull-down menus.

MINIGEN produces Turbo Pascal code which you can later add to your programs. It is entirely written in Turbo Pascal using the same source code routines provided on the disk. Also included is a TPU for accessing Microsoft-compatible mouse drivers.

Since this is a programming aid, the documentation assumes you already know how to program in Turbo Pascal. It also assumes knowledge of DOS and jumps right in describing the various functions and how to use them.

This program is primarily for intermediate to experienced users, and not the novice.

(PC-SIG Disk# 760)

Special Requirements: *None.*
Author Registration: *$10.00*

Mouse Tools   *by Nels Anderson*

If you are a Turbo Pascal programmer, this set of utilities provides most of the necessary procedures to use a mouse in your own programs, including:
❑ Display of the mouse cursor.
❑ Reading of mouse and button positions.
❑ Display of various prompts with "push buttons."
❑ Selection of filenames.

To use the tools, you will need Turbo Pascal 5.5 and the TP5.5 units Crt, DOS, drivers, fonts, and GRAPH available. Two example programs are provided along with the .TPU files for all the mouse tools. This should be enough to get you started writing mouse programs. The source code for the units is not included in this version.

(PC-SIG Disk# 2278)

Special Requirements: *Turbo Pascal 5.5*
Author Registration: *$10.00*
➤*ASP Member.*

Mystic Pascal   *by Mystic Canyon Software*

MYSTIC PASCAL is an integrated programming environment that rigidly follows the ISO Pascal Standard.

MYSTIC PASCAL combines editing, compiling, program testing, and debugging in to one unit. The traditional pattern of program development — the edit/compile/test cycle — is greatly speeded up with an integrated programming environment. You do not need to return to the operating system and reload each program at each phase of the cycle.

MYSTIC PASCAL is an "interactive compiler" and can compile entire Pascal source files. It also lets you key in Pascal statements, as well as instantly compile and execute then at the global level. This is similar to the Direct Mode of BASIC interpreters, with a critical difference: MYSTIC PASCAL is a true object-code compiler. It is not an interpreter or a pseudo-code compiler.

(PC-SIG Disk# 965)

Special Requirements: *None.*
Author Registration: *$10.00*

Numerical Recipes in Pascal ☆   *by Numerical Recipes Software*

A collection of Pascal procedures originally published as the Pascal Appendix to the FORTRAN book "Numerical Recipes: The Art Of Scientific Computing" (Cambridge University Press, 1986). Also included are test driver programs originally published as the "Numerical Recipes Example Book (Pascal)" (Cambridge University Press, 1986).

These procedures form a complete Pascal library for scientific computation. More than 200 procedures perform integration, linear algebra, differential equations, Fourier methods, data analysis, statistics, lots of special functions, random numbers, sorting, root finding, optimization, and much more.

(PC-SIG Disk# 2491)

Special Requirements: *A Pascal compiler.*
Author Registration: *None.*

P-Robots
by Softworks

P-ROBOTS is a game that helps teach programming in Pascal. The objective is to design and program a "robot" that can triumph over similar robots designed and programmed by others in a real-time battle of wits and flying missiles.

You control your robot by writing a procedure in Pascal to specify your robot's behavior and strategy in its efforts to vanquish up to three other robots in a battle to the death. A variety of pre-defined P-ROBOTS Pascal functions allow your robot to track its position on the battlefield, monitor its health or damage condition, and calculate the distance and angle to opponents from its current battlefield position. Each robot is equipped with a cannon to fire missiles, and a motorized drive mechanism to either close in to kill a hapless opponent or flee from a fierce foe.

P-ROBOTS is an excellent way for the novice programmer to sharpen his/her Pascal skills and have fun at the same time. However, P-ROBOTS does assume that the robot designer/programmer already knows the fundamentals of programming in Pascal.

For the experienced programmer, P-ROBOTS offers a chance to see just how well you program in a programming environment where "bad" code can lead to graphic and ignoble defeat and "brilliant" code can bring triumph and glory.

(PC-SIG Disk# 1386)

Special Requirements: *NONE.*
Author Registration: *$20.00*
➤ *ASP Member.*

P-Robots (PC-SIG Disk# 1386)

Pascal Translator/Interpreter ✐
by Victor Schneider PHD

The package consists of a Pascal to p-code translator and a p-code interpreter. The translator accepts standard Pascal programs with C masking and shifting extensions and produces text assembly language files that the interpreter program executes directly.

Programs can be compiled from a user's text file or directly one line at a time from the keyboard (keyboard input allows only the current line to be edited). This introductory version allows seven files to be open at a time, limits sets to 64 members, and allows string constants of up to 80 characters.

(PC-SIG Disk# 1321)

Special Requirements: *None.*
Author Registration: *$65.00*

Pascal Tutor ✐
by Coronado Enterprises

PASCAL TUTOR is a text-based tutorial on programming with the Pascal language. The assumption is that you know nothing about Pascal in particular and programming in general.

It begins with the most elementary aspects of programming and takes you through each step from dynamic allocation to the use of linked lists. The program was specifically written for use with Turbo Pascal versions 3.0, 4.0, and 5.0. Version 5.5 is also supported through two additional chapters covering object oriented programming. The Pascal source code used for examples throughout the tutorial is included.

(PC-SIG Disk#'s 579, 580)

Special Requirements: *Printer.*
Author Registration: *$15.00 to $39.95.*

PopText
by Tone Zone Computing

This help-screen generation utility for Turbo Pascal and Assembly language programmers allows programmers to easily integrate pop-up style help windows into their own programs.

POPTEXT features an easy to use editor, a unit to include in Turbo programs, and three bonus units, including some fast writing routines, routines to enhance CRT, and a unit with all of the key definitions.

Each help window is a record consisting of 15 lines and 15 links. The lines are displayed on the screen, and the links are hidden in the background. In addition to being linked by line, windows are linked by the page up and page down keys. Using the editor, you can create new files, and append the files up to 256 records each.

(PC-SIG Disk# 1935)

Special Requirements: *Hard drive recommended.*
Author Registration: *$25.00*

ScnDsign
by Iddo L. Enochs

In Turbo Pascal, designing screens for inputting data is often a very tedious task. However, with SCNDSIGN you can design with very little effort, creating screens on the monitor exactly as they'll appear in your program. Then, SCNDSIGN handles the complicated part of creating the source code in Turbo Pascal. The screens can also be saved for later use.

(PC-SIG Disk# 1092)

Special Requirements: *None.*
Author Registration: *$25.00*

T-Ref
by Synergy Software

If your programming language of choice is Turbo Pascal, you'll find that you won't be able to resist this one.

T-REF is a lister/cross-referencing program that makes your programming easier and quicker. Features include a full-screen driver with switch- selectable options; context-sensitive help windows to speed the learning process; and output directable to file or printer. You can also reform words in the lister along with line numbers, lexical and block-level numbering; cross-reference selection by object type and usage; error analysis; procedural table of contents; and much, much more.

(PC-SIG Disk# 827)

Special Requirements: *None.*
Author Registration: *$20.00 - $45.00*

TechnoJock's Turbo Toolkit
by TechnoJock Software Inc.

TechnoJock's Turbo Toolkit (TTT) is a comprehensive set of procedures and functions for Turbo Pascal and Quick Pascal programmers. The Toolkit is designed for professional programmers, as well as newcomers to the Pascal programming environment.

The main focus of the Toolkit is to give programs a polished and professional appearance. There are routines providing: formatted screen output, windows, many menu routines including pop-up and pull- down, form input procedures, string formatting, a Sidekick Plus style directory lister, and much more. These units are compact and very easy to manipulate and implement. The manual is clear and instructive. All source is included.

The abbreviated manual is included on disk (over 100 pages).

(PC-SIG Disk#'s 1651, 1652)

Special Requirements: *Turbo Pascal 4.0 (or greater), or Quick Pascal, and unarchiving program.*
Author Registration: *$49.95*
➤*ASP Member.*

Turbo Designer
by MMI Computers

TURBO DESIGNER is a programmer's toolbox for the Turbo Pascal compiler. TURBO DESIGNER helps you create pull-down menus, pop-up menus, and sophisticated hypertext help screens in your applications. It is very easy to use. The program asks you to input your data (what you want to appear when the program runs), on a series of "what you see is what you get" full-screen editors. Once you have set up your menu work environment, which includes windows, icons, and even a trash can, TURBO DESIGNER creates a Pascal source file according to your data. This new file can be compiled using Turbo Pascal. The result is a program with a complete environment, and a sophisticated user interface.

Using a price/performance ratio, TURBO DESIGNER is one of the best code generators of its type in the market today. Its screen routines are as fast as they possibly can be, and the algorithms used cannot be surpassed on the IBM-PC. TURBO DESIGNER is better than "just a library," since it creates actual code, and has routines for a pop-up directory listing, trash can, sophisticated help screens, and much more. It maintains an easy-to-use environment, including icons, pop-up windows, and pull-down menus. TURBO DESIGNER detects a monochrome monitor and corrects the display. A new palette of black and white colors are used, so all data is displayed correctly. This is a great utility for shareware developers, since it creates an easy-to-use environment, perfect for the first-time user.

(PC-SIG Disk# 1353)

Special Requirements: *512K RAM, hard drive, and TURBO Pascal v4.0 or higher.*
Author Registration: *$25.00.*

Turbo Pascal Modulating Printing Filter ✍   *by Dennis DiBartolomeo*

TPMPF prints Turbo Pascal source code files in an easy to read formatted outline. TPMPF first prints the filename and the file's creation date at the top of the page and then proceeds to print the formatted source code.

Procedure and function names are emphasized and underlined, index numbers are printed on the right side of the page, global variables are double-striked, and local variables are italicized. After printing the source code, TPMPF will print a listing of procedures and functions with their index numbers. You can elect to create source code files stripped of one or both comment types allowed in Turbo Pascal.

(PC-SIG Disk# 1531)

Special Requirements: *Printer.*
Author Registration: *$15.00*

Turbo-Lessons   *by Lyle M. Faurot*

Here are 16 different lessons in Turbo Pascal that teach you more than the elements of the language — you'll also learn programming technique and gain experience through practice. Each TURBO-LESSON is a bite-size tutorial which introduces one or more new concepts. Each of the lessons is presented in the same format, clear objectives followed by an organized tutorial. Most lessons direct you to work with a sample program which is provided with these lessons.

Programmers who had difficulty learning Pascal from reference books will find they are able to make better progress. The programming techniques you learn will save you time and frustration in your future programming. The lessons are designed to encourage you to try things on your own.

Lesson titles include:

❏ Essential editing skills
❏ Declarations, input
❏ Conditional processing
❏ CASE statement
❏ WHILE statement
❏ A function to detect errors
❏ Introduction to procedures
❏ Real numbers.

❏ Program structure
❏ Integer expressions
❏ REPEAT statement
❏ FOR statement
❏ Introduction to functions
❏ Strings
❏ Interactive screen handling

(PC-SIG Disk# 1932)

Special Requirements: *Pascal compiler.*
Author Registration: *$10.00*

Turbo-Screen System   *by The Connelly Brothers*

A tool for Turbo Pascal programmers who wish to develop screen I/O procedures quickly, TURBO SCREEN SYSTEM generates source code directly from "screen panel" files which you can design. The generated code will handle field editing, cursor movement, placement of messages and prompts, and passing field values to appropriate variables within the program. In addition to the application code, sample code for calling the generated procedures is also created. This makes integration into your main program easier.

Screen panels conform to the Common User Access terminology (IBM SAA) that some programmers may already be familiar with, but is intuitively logical if they are not. Using this program will virtually eliminate common development bugs and help a programmer maintain consistent standards throughout all applications.

(PC-SIG Disk# 2257)

Special Requirements: *Turbo Pascal 4.0 (or greater).*
Author Registration: *$33.00*

TurboMenu System
by Maxx Data Systems, Inc.

The TURBOMENU SYSTEM toolbox is a set of routines designed for use in the Turbo Pascal language to define and manipulate pull-down menus. The menus can be defined in a text or graphics mode in one or two dimensions.

This system supports an auto-tracking feature that helps the programmer by keeping menu-tracking to a minimum. It also comes with support for mouse-tracking. The data structure used by the system uses stack and heap memory very efficiently.

A sample program is included on the disk to demonstrate the type of menus that may be defined. The toolbox supports versions 4.0, 5.0, and 5.5 although this version is not object-oriented. The program is written in Pascal and is available to registered users.

(PC-SIG Disk# 1983)

Special Requirements: *A version Turbo Pascal.*
Author Registration: *$25.00*

▼ ▼ ▼

Programming, Tools

ADA-TUTR
by Software Innovations Technology

ADA-TUTR, the interactive ADA tutor, will teach you to be an excellent ADA programmer in minimum time.

ADA is an ideal programming language because Ada programs tend to have fewer errors, to be easier to read, and to be much easier to modify later. The U.S. Department of Defense mandated the use of ADA in mission-critical systems (DoD Directive 3405.2, 1987).

Not just a "quiz," ADA-TUTR is a thorough course of interactive instruction that even checks "homework" assignments. ADA-TUTR concentrates on teaching good program design, not just syntax, so that programs will take advantage of the features of ADA that make them more reliable and easier to maintain. ADA-TUTR was written by John J. Herro, Ph.D., who taught a graduate course in Ada at the State University of New York at Binghamton, and taught ADA to employees of General Electric Co., Grumman Aerospace Corporation, and Harris Corporation.

When ADA-TUTR is run on a PC, an ADA compiler is helpful, but not required. A list of ADA compilers available for the PC is included. Since ADA-TUTR comes with ADA source code, it will run on other computers with ADA compilers — even on mainframes.

(PC-SIG Disk# 1529)

Special Requirements: *A hard disk.*
Author Registration: *$25.00*

BOX
by Nescatunga Software

BOX is a screen-designing tool that lets you quickly create entry screens, help screens and menus.

You start with a blank screen, and using simple commands, you can draw lines, boxes, enter text, and change foreground and background colors. You can repeat an entry, paint an area, copy or move portions of the screen and select special characters from an ASCII table. Boxes are incredibly easy to design, and several different border lines are provided to create them.

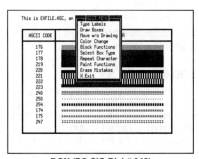

BOX (PC-SIG Disk# 842)

Any screen can be saved in any of three formats, (ASCII, memory, or packed), depending on the use of the screen. ASCII format lets you save your screen so it can be edited by a word processor.

Memory or packed format screens can be loaded directly and popped instantly on the monitor from a Pascal or C program. This disk also contains all the source code routines that you need to incorporate BOX in your Turbo Pascal programs.

(PC-SIG Disk# 842)

Special Requirements: *None.*
Author Registration: *$20.00*

   🔎 = Updated Program
   ☆ = New Program

CAPP
by Sooner Software Inc.

CAPP (C and Pascal Print and Check) helps you find errors in your C or Pascal program by printing a formatted output of the source code. This output contains visual aids that include source lines, blocks, comments, and possible errors. Nine simple semantic error checks are made, some intended to bring to your attention programming situations that may give you unintended results. The error file contains the line number of source lines which have an error or a probable error.

(PC-SIG Disk# 1176)

Special Requirements: *None.*
Author Registration: *$7.95*

ColorSet
by Nipper MicroServices

This program makes it easy for programmers to experiment with various background/foreground color combinations on-screen during the development of programs. This terminate-and-stay-resident (TSR) program is set up for programmers who work in Clipper or dBase.

(PC-SIG Disk# 1808)

Special Requirements: *None.*
Author Registration: *$20.00*

Creating User-Friendly Software
by Bill Kuhl

This utility set should be in the haversack of everyone trying to write attractive, user friendly BASIC or Turbo Pascal programs.

Some utilities will make your programs more attractive, most will make them quicker and more friendly. Source code is available for most. Users should understand ASCII.

Included are a batch of ways to help you write easy-to-use programs to get input from users, especially multiple data input. One utility helps set up one-sentence prompts for each input. Another enhances the use of default values. A third makes BASIC and Pascal understand upper and lowercase inputs identically. Other utilities help you deal with arrow key inputs, setting up data input screens, using lines and boxes, and displaying a message to buzz off when the computer is busy.

(PC-SIG Disk# 1609)

Special Requirements: *None.*
Author Registration: *$5.00*

EDITRAND
by CMD Data Services

Browse and edit random files produced by any program, regardless of record structure. EDITRAND can be used to analyze random data in ways not possible using the program that created the data. Data can be viewed exactly as it exists on disk, allowing speedy verification of program output and intelligent troubleshooting of problem situations. EDITRAND is intended for programmers or other persons with intimate knowledge of DOS files and random files in particular.

Avoid long hours of testing; use EDITRAND to peek at those random files and find the exact fields and records that are suspected of being corrupt or invalid. Have you found that an application will not allow a change that is desired? Load the data file into EDITRAND, swiftly make the desired changes, and put the data back into operation without a lengthy waiting period.

EDITRAND offers many features including full text, hexidecimal, and ASCII data editing; cursor key navigation just like ordinary text editors; standard editing functions such as search, replace, word count, cut and paste; full featured binary number operations, based on IEEE (the default) and Microsoft binary formats (for BASIC programers); undo/undelete changes to records; works on files of unlimited size; works on random files created by any language.

(PC-SIG Disk# 1918)

Special Requirements: *None.*
Author Registration: *$20.00*

Extended Batch Language - Plus
by Seaware Corp

Extended Batch Language adds additional features to the batch processing capabilities already supported by DOS. The program will guide you in the creation of batch files that prompt for responses and keep track of variables. Use it to set up printers, keep configuration parameters up-to-date, initialize programs or create other batch files. Optional floating point, enhanced string and arithmetic operations and file I/O support is provided. It is well documented and includes example batch programs.

(PC-SIG Disk# 124)

Special Requirements: *None.*
Author Registration: *$79.00*
➤*ASP Member.*

Fast ✍
by Peter Campbell Software

FAST is a completely new language for PC compatibles. FAST provides many new commands and options supported by your computer, but not supported by other languages. The main feature is speed. FAST produces code which runs faster than any other high-level language including C, Pascal, and compiled BASIC.

FAST supports multiple files, conditional assembly, word aligned variable and compiler directives. FAST has built in commands, fully optimized, that support windows, sprites, very fast screen printing, integer arithmetic, and file handling. FAST even comes with a source code debugger.

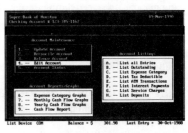

Fast (PC-SIG Disk 2058)

(PC-SIG Disk# 2058)

Special Requirements: *None.*
Author Registration: *$30.00*

Fixer
by Don Rooney

Edit your WordStar, WordPerfect, or ASCII files so they can contain the 255 character ASCII set. Press your ALT key along with the decimal code that denotes the character you desire and it will be put into your file. The program has a full screen editor and on-line help is available to you from a pop-up window.

(PC-SIG Disk# 978)

Special Requirements: *None.*
Author Registration: *$20.00*

Font Editor
by Synergy Software

Design and display your own special font characters. Two font editors have been provided: one for medium-resolution modes and the other for high-resolution mode.

After a font file is loaded or created, the entire font set is displayed at the bottom of the screen (all 128 characters) and the upper-right corner displays the bit mapping of a single font set. You can edit each bit or pixel of a certain character. The character can be rotated, moved, inverted, copied, and saved for future use.

The upper-left corner contains a menu of function-key commands for easy reference. Once you have created a font set to your satisfaction, you can access and use the file with Assembler, Pascal, C, BASIC or any other language that allows you to load the font file into a specific location in memory and then program DOS to acknowledge that location.

FONT EDITOR will not only help you to create your own fonts, but it can also help you design game graphics characters that make moving screen objects easier and neater to code.

(PC-SIG Disk# 856)

Special Requirements: *CGA or EGA.*
Author Registration: *$10.00*

FONTED
by MJM Software Design

Want to change the fonts that are normally displayed on your EGA or VGA screen? FONTED lets you change the size and shape of characters to suit your taste; create foreign language fonts like Russian, Hebrew or Arabic; or make custom fonts to suit other special uses.

✍ = Updated Program
☆ = New Program

You can reduce the size of a screen font to increase the number of text lines displayed on the screen. You can also save custom screen fonts in an executable COM file and recall them later. And custom fonts can be made "sticky" with an installation procedure so you can use the fonts with your favorite application such as a wordprocessor. Works great with or without a mouse.

(PC-SIG Disk#'s 2096, 2097)

Special Requirements: *EGA or VGA.*
Author Registration: *$15.00*

Hacker *by Ted Wray*

Want to write truly interactive and intelligent batch files? HACKER can add a whole new dimension to batch file programming.

HACKER is a multi-function utility for programmers. It communicates with both the user and the system, and performs many useful tasks. Most HACKER functions are for use within batch files, but command line processing is also supported. HACKER returns information to a batch file through DOS's errorlevel.

HACKER functions include:

❑ ASK a question from the user,
❑ BOOT causes a warm or cold re-boot,
❑ CLEAR clears selected portions of the screen,
❑ FIX changes the shape of the cursor,
❑ IS gives drive/directory control.
❑ NOTE sends notes to the screen,
❑ SHOW lists hidden files and directories,
❑ SOUND gives ability to produce tones or music,
❑ WAIT adds time delays,
❑ WHAT provides information about date/time/drive/mode.

HACKER also provides an extensive on-line help command that explains the use of each function.

(PC-SIG Disk# 1902)

Special Requirements: *None.*
Author Registration: *$20.00*

Hexcalibur *by Gregory Publishing Company*

This powerful hex editor provides a full set of editing commands for use with any file, text or code, in either hex mode or in ASCII mode. Character insertion and deletion — as well as overtyping — are all supported. In addition, both find and replace operations are supported in either ASCII or hex. Block mode operations like move, copy, and delete are also supported.

This hex editor stands out because it supports character insertion and deletion, as well as finding, replacing, and block mode operations, at the Hex level. It is a RAM editor, so the file you wish to edit must fit into main memory.

With HEXCALIBUR, you can: examine and change the contents of WordStar or other specially encoded files; filter incompatible codes out of files; convert Unix or BTOS text files (line terminator = 0a) to MS-DOS format (line terminator = 0d0a) or to MacIntosh format (line terminator = 0d), or vice versa; and much more. HEXCALIBUR provides a convenient tool for making the kind of changes that, until now, were extremely difficult to do!

(PC-SIG Disk# 1782)

Special Requirements: *None.*
Author Registration: *$30.00*

HexEdit *by Steve Platt*

This program allows the user to view, modify, and write any file. It edits the file in hex so it can edit .EXE, .COM, or data files. It provides basic editing functions such as insert, delete, search, insert/overstrike mode, load new file, save, and a 100-level undo. Help is available with the F1 key. It can edit any size file up to the limit of available memory.

(PC-SIG Disk# 2019)

Special Requirements: *None.*
Author Registration: *$10.00*

HXED ☆
by Anthony F. Stuart

HXED is a fast and easy-to-use editor for binary files that can be customized for your video and processing preferences. By using disk and memory very efficiently, HXED consumes less than 30K of memory and it can edit files of up to two megabytes in less than 100K of memory. HXED supports Insert and Overwrite modes and character delete, as well as Search and Replace functions. File data is displayed in a hexadecimal format: addresses on the left, hexadecimal representation in the middle, and character representation (ASCII) on the right. The current location in the file is marked by a pair of cursors, one for the hexadecimal data and one for the character data.

HXED provides on-screen Help, always available with a single keystroke.

A DOS shell is also available, returning to HXED using the standard EXIT command. Customize the way HXED operates by specifying command line options. Set cursor and text colors, specify fill characters and display characters for unprintable character values, set the number of memory buffers to use, and specify video BIOS instead of direct video access for speed improvement.

HXED is unique because it comes with the complete source code. See how file editors are constructed and perhaps even create one of your own.

(PC-SIG Disk# 2683)

Special Requirements: *None.*
Author Registration: *$15.00*

Icon Maker
by Jimmy Paris Software

ICON MAKER is a menu-driven program that allows you to create graphical icons and cross-stitch graphics interactively in any of three graphical modes supported by the IBM PC family. These three modes include the high resolution 640 X 200 two color, the 320 X 200 four color, and the 160 X 100 sixteen color. The icons you create can then be used directly in your program data area instead of having to be accessed as an outside file by your program.

All icons created can be saved in an ASCII file which will than be used in a form that is acceptable by the macro assembler (in the form of dw and db statements) and can be used in the data segment of your program to define your shape.

(PC-SIG Disk# 485)

Special Requirements: *CGA and an Epson-FX printer or compatible.*
Author Registration: *$10.00.*
➤*ASP Member.*

Loadkey
by Dick Wingerson

LOADKEY is a utility for batch files that allows you to customize and accelerate the execution of an application program by preloading a string of key strokes to the BIOS keyboard buffer.

LOADKEY operates in two modes — direct entry and hot key. In direct entry, you can invoke LOADKEY in a batch file by supplying a string of key strokes as a parameter to the call. When the batch file is run, LOADKEY executes and preloads the keyboard buffer. LOADKEY then terminates and the batch file now loads the application program. When input is requested by the program, it is immediately obtained from the keyboard buffer. In the hot key mode, LOADKEY allows you to assign an ASCII code to the entire string. This code can be used later to replace the batch parameter(%n) in the batch file.

LOADKEY limits the strings to 15 key strokes and only accommodates 80 individual strings.

(PC-SIG Disk# 1834)

Special Requirements: *None.*
Author Registration: *$15.00*

MMake
by Micro Systems

Programmers — automate the process of compiling and linking a program that is contained in several (or numerous) source files. MMAKE can be used with any programming language and with any compiler that can be run from the MS-DOS command line. It can speed-up program development enormously, both by making recompilation of a program go much faster, and by preventing errors when a changed file is not recompiled. Based on the UNIX "make" utility.

(PC-SIG Disk# 978)

Special Requirements: *None.*
Author Registration: *$20.00*

Model-S
by PC-Systems Inc.

MODEL-S is a CASE tool for developing database applications. This is a quality product that can rival any commercial package in its class. In fact, our research indicates that MODEL-S is unique in its design and functionality.

MODEL-S is a powerful piece of software that automates the development process yet does not require data processing expertise. It utilizes the rapid prototyping approach to application development, integrated with automatic generation of the dBASE III Plus programs and data files (.PRG and .DBF).

MODEL-S was designed to enable end users and data processing professionals to engage in a true joint application development, which promotes active participation of both in most aspects of the development process. It helps producing systems on time, within budget, and with complete user satisfaction — all that at a fraction of the traditional development cost.

Special Requirements: *No special requirements.*
Author Registration: *None.*

NG_Maker Programmer's Tool
by Steven W. Kurtz

This program is designed to be used in conjunction with the Norton Guides, by Peter Norton Computing, and PC-Browse, by QuickSoft. It reads the ASCII source code for any program and extracts the comments which indicate the purpose, function, and expectations of the various building blocks of your program.

NG_MAKER will combine and assemble these comments into a database file compatible with the Norton Guides or PC-Browse. Once completed, you can call up either program and review at a glance the various building blocks that make up the program you are working on.

The program is designed to work in cooperation with MicroSoft- compatible MAKE files that control the compilation of large projects. Using NG_MAKER will require that you make small changes in your MAKE file and to the source code for your project. In each case, the changes are all "hidden" behind remark symbols, so they are completely invisible to your compiler/assembler.

(PC-SIG Disk# 2290)

Special Requirements: *PC-Browse or Norton Guides.*
Author Registration: *$25.00*

OVL
by Devore Software & Consulting

OVL is a powerful overlay manager system for use with Microsoft LINK. Overlays are portions of program code which are loaded from disk into memory on an "as-needed" basis. Overlays allow a very large program to use a relatively small amount of memory.

LINK.EXE, Microsoft's Overlay Linker, included with MS-DOS and Microsoft languages, versions 3.x, 5.x, and some 2.x versions, allow creation of overlaid programs. However, LINK only inserts software interrupts and some overlay information in the program for an overlay manager to use. LINK doesn't provide the actual code that loads the proper overlay from disk and passes control to it. That's a job for an overlay manager, and that's where the OVL overlay managers come in.

OVL "manages" overlays. OVL loads overlays from disk at the appropriate time and jumps program execution to the overlay code. OVL managers have been tested with MASM 4.0 and 5.0; Turbo C 1.0, 1.5 and 2.0; QuickBASIC 4.0 and 4.5; Microsoft's BASCOM 6.0; and Clipper (PRONK.EXE, an included support utility, must be used with Clipper programs). Other languages that compile to standard Microsoft Overlay LINKable object modules may also work with OVL.

(PC-SIG Disk# 1933)

Special Requirements: *A compiler and Microsoft Link.*
Author Registration: *$80.00*
➤*ASP Member.*

PC-Tags
by Moderne Software

PC-TAGS is a DOS and OS/2 source-code retrieval system and source browser that will locate and retrieve a function or procedure definition from a text file written in C, Pascal, BASIC, dBASE, Assembly, Modula-2 or any other language (including English). After locating the correct source file, PC-TAGS will load the file into your editor and place the cursor at the retrieved function or procedure's beginning.

PC-TAGS can be used in conjunction with any text editor or programming environment. There is no need to change your current method of working. Further, if you use a MAKE facility or version-control system, PC-TAGS can be integrated easily into your current system.

(PC-SIG Disk# 2011)

Special Requirements: *None.*
Author Registration: *$34.95*

Personal Apt   *by Digital Manufacturing Systems*

Want to learn Numerical Control programming? This exciting and expanding field can be opened to you with PERSONAL APT. Need programming help? With its totally integrated working environment, including screen editor and graphic tool path display, PERSONAL APT is very helpful in teaching and learning this exciting and expanding field and yet powerful enough for significant industrial productivity improvement.

APT (Automatically Programmed Tools) is the oldest and most widely used Numerical Control programming language in use today. APT development was initially sponsored by the US Air Force, and later the AIA (Aerospace Industries Association), and has evolved into a universal programming language. PERSONAL APT is a subset of this powerful programming language, but is powerful enough to handle most requirements.

The minimum hardware requirements and features of PERSONAL APT make it an ideal program for schools and individuals to use in teaching and learning the APT language.

PERSONAL APT can be a very productive tool for engineers, draftsmen and others who spend time on complex mathematical and geometric computations. PERSONAL APT provides preprogrammed functions for the solution of intersection and tangency problems, transformation of dimensional data between coordinate systems and vector functions to aid computations.

(PC-SIG Disk# 1722)

Special Requirements: *512K RAM, CGA, EGA, VGA, or Hercules. Two drives recommended.*
Author Registration: *$49.00*

PowerBatch ✍   *by CSD, Inc.*

POWERBATCH creates standalone (.EXE) compiled batch files. POWERBATCH has all of the functionality of standard DOS batch files plus 40 additional commands to perform functions not available in a standard batch file. Executes any .COM, .EXE (including other POWERBATCH programs), or DOS intrinsic commands entered as a POWERBATCH source statement. Control screen colors, draw boxes, get input from the keyboard, access system information, string manipulation and comparison, and much more.

(PC-SIG Disk# 2425)

Special Requirements: *None.*
Author Registration: *$30.00*
➤*ASP Member.*

Pro-Inst   *by Input Software Development Co.*

Programmers, here is a program that allows you to automate even the most complex application installations. One command starts this program which walks users through the entire installation — complete with prompt screens and help text that you create.

Make it easier for your customers to install your software on their fixed disk without having to run a Batch file or follow intricate instructions buried in a read.me file.

Your end users have the option to accept/or change the following: which drive to install from; which drive to install to; which directory and/or sub-directory to install in; whether to add path statement; whether to change buffer statement; whether to change file statement.

This program does take up 200K of disk space itself. Therefore, it is most appropriate for applications with lots of disks.

(PC-SIG Disk# 1765)

Special Requirements: *High density floppy drive or a hard drive.*
Author Registration: *$20.00*

Probat I ✍ *by Mark Tigges*

Do you spend hours making batch files and wish there were a more comprehensive way to construct your own user friendly batch interface. Well, PROBAT has revolutionized the way complex batch files are built. This sophisticated program gives you the power to create batch files with chaining screens, graphic screen layout, keyboard input acceptance, and informational prompting. It is great for the programmer or system designer who currently uses a mixed bag of tricks to get batch files looking even halfway decent. With PROBAT you will work in one comprehensive batch file creator complete with pull-down menus and extensive editing options. Though PROBAT takes some time to learn, the results are the most professional batch files possible.

You can use PROBAT to save batch file formats or screen designs to be recalled and edited later. Create your own library of batch formats to be recalled and modified for different purposes. PROBAT lets you draw boxes, set screen colors, and create menus. There is even a handsome graphics menu screen that can be integrated into the batch files you create. If you are serious about batch files, PROBAT is an involved and indepth program that will allow you to create the best in batch files.

(PC-SIG Disk# 1565)

Special Requirements: *Hard drive recommended.*
Author Registration: *$35.00 ($45.00 Canadian)*
➤ *ASP Member.*

Programmer's Super-Maint ☆ *by EmmaSoft*

Programmer's SUPER-MAINT is the Make utility to simplify your program-building chores when using Microsoft, Borland, Aztec, Clipper, and Mix compilers. SUPER-MAINT builds your Make and Response files for you. It remembers all of your command flags and even the name of the Make file, so all you need to remember is "sm." Automatic installation, user-configurable context-sensitive Help, mouse support, online manual, and more! Builds Make, Response, PC-lint "indirect" and Clear + "list" files.

(PC-SIG Disk#'s 2726, 2727)

Special Requirements: *Dos 3.1, hard drive, and 640K RAM recommended.*
Author Registration: *$55.00*
➤ *ASP Member.*

Q4Tool - Programming Tools for QuickBASIC 4.x ☆ *by CareWare*

Q4TOOL LIBRARY is a collection of innovative and direct programming tools for Microsoft, QuickBASIC 4.xx. These library routines are intended for use by individuals with some QB programming experience. All of the routines are easily incorporated into almost any QuickBASIC 4.xx source without greatly increasing the size of the stand-alone program.

A summary of key services:

❏ Mouse support includes most of the routines needed to add mouse services into any application
❏ Window support uses screen routines developed with machine code for fast, clean appearance
❏ Screen save/restore routines save and restore the contents of any screen
❏ Other services include screen display, screen string centering, program delay, and other routines for access to system interrupts

While Q4TOOL doesn't contain routines for data input or manipulation, it does provide a solid foundation from which to build your own personal libraries.

(PC-SIG Disk# 2560)

Special Requirements: *QuickBasic 4.x.*
Author Registration: *$25.00*
➤ *ASP Member.*

Qparser Plus *by QCAD Systems, Inc.*

Here is the public domain version of QPARSER, a tool for writing translators, compilers, assemblers, and other language parsing programs. This disk has the full QPARSER software but it is limited with a top limit of 25 production/parsing rules. QPARSER is an excellent way to experiment with language design and compiler development. Very useful for computer science students.

(PC-SIG Disk# 419)

Special Requirements: *Hard drive recommended.*
Author Registration: *$10.00*

SCRDES
by c/o Hire Education

SCRDES is a full-screen text/graphics editor designed to ease the coding of custom screens — such as menu screens, data-entry forms and help screens — into programs. The editor was created for use with CGA and EGA, but will also function with a monochrome card, although with less distinctive effects.

The program was designed primarily to produce binary files of the type "character, attribute, character, attribute" for inclusion in Assembly language programs, or to be read directly from a file to the screen buffer in a high-level language. It will also produce ASCII text files of the form character, character, CR/LF, character, character, CR/LF (25 lines) suitable for use in interpreted languages such as BASIC or dBase III.

(PC-SIG Disk# 1303)

Special Requirements: *CGA, EGA, and DOS 3.x.*
Author Registration: *$15.00*

Screen Debut
by Willie Robinson

SCREEN DEBUT is a program used to build and develop text screens in any of four languages. Ansi code for use with dos, Basic code with and without line numbers, C code for Turbo Pascal, and compressed binary format for use with Fast Screen.

Fast Screen is included with SCREEN DEBUT and is used to view your screen. If you build screens in any of the formats mentioned, SCREEN DEBUT will make your task much easier. It is so fast to learn and use that you'll be producing screens instead of mulling over a thick manual. This manual is just an F1 key away. The program uses few commands, but the ones used are all you need; commands like cursor border, select color, box junctions, load screen, save screen, cut and paste, copy and paste, and recolor.

(PC-SIG Disk# 2359)

Special Requirements: *CGA recommended.*
Author Registration: *$10.00*

Screen Machine 🖫
by ASMicro Co.

Would you like to save time generating screens for your programs? SCREEN MACHINE is an excellent tool to free you from the dull and boring work of designing screens.

This screen editor can generate actual source code for BASIC, C, assembler, Turbo Pascal and dBASE. Editing screens is a snap with support for macros, box and line drawing, color, text centering, extended character set, and even an "undo" function for line and block operations.

SCREEN MACHINE has a memory resident utility to capture screens from other programs. The captured screens then can be changed into binary code to be edited with this program or into a text file that can be altered with a text editor or word processor. Creating interactive demonstration programs can be done very easily with SCREEN MACHINE. Different screen images can be linked to create a "slide show", a prototype, or demonstration program. SCREEN MACHINE manages to offer a complete solution to reduce your program development time, create screen prototypes, and generate source code for your programs — all for a very low registration fee.

(PC-SIG Disk# 2303)

Special Requirements: *None.*
Author Registration: *$9.95*

Screen-Do
by Port-of-Call Software Inc.

SCREEN-DO lets you design and create screens for use in BASIC programs. Each screen that is saved to the disk can be accessed through the BLOAD command in BASIC.

SCREEN-DO simplifies the process of editing screens through commands that let you easily delete, insert, move, and copy certain sections of the screen. Another function displays the ASCII characters numbered 126 to 254 and let you display them on the screen. One option lets you move the cursor across the screen to trace a certain character you selected. SCREEN-DO has on-line help that makes it easy to learn, in addition to simplifying the designing of screens for use with BASIC programs.

(PC-SIG Disk# 1118)

Special Requirements: *None.*
Author Registration: *$50.00*

Screen-Do (PC-SIG Disk# 1118)

🖫 = Updated Program
☆ = New Program

ScreenPaint
by Kai Laurinolli

SCREENPAINT lets you design lightning-fast batch file based hard-disk menus, help facilities, pop-up windows, and prototype screens for applications programs. Screens can be quickly "painted" in a full- screen editing environment, complete with pulldown menus, help screens, automatically connecting lines, and a wide variety of drawing and editing tools.

Completed screens can then be called from a DOS batch file and displayed quickly rather than scrolled using the extremely slow DOS ECHO command. Another feature allows screens to be displayed and key codes to be returned to the calling batch file where they may be used to control the operation of the batch file. Unlike other menu creation systems, SCREENPAINT gives you complete control over the style of menu displays.

(PC-SIG Disk# 1510)
Special Requirements: *None.*
Author Registration: *$25.00*

SEBFU ✍
by Scanlon Enterprise

Create professional, powerful batch files with SEBFU. SEBFU permits you to improve your batch file menus by giving you the option to control the position of text and colors (or monochrome intensity), create windows and boxes and to scroll text across the screen. SEBFU increases the potential of your batch files by allowing you to make decisions based upon your system configuration. Error levels are returned which indicate configurations such as presence of ANSI.SYS, disk drives, memory usage, mouse driver, printer status, cursor location, keyboard type and much more! SEBFU is a must for software developers or those who want to greatly improve the efficiency and power of their batch files.

SEBFU also includes the Business Control System (BCS), a simple telephone log database/telecommunications program. BCS dials your number, records who you called, the time and date, as well as any messages. BCS is easy to learn and is a handy organizational tool.

SEBFU includes 51 batch utilities, plus BCS. You can receive an additional 49 batch utilities with registration.

(PC-SIG Disk# 2081)
Special Requirements: *None.*
Author Registration: *$19.95*

Snobolyt Utilities
by Noah Systems

Programmers — Here's a diskful of handy utilities to take over some of the drudgery of programming for you.

Assembler source utilities include ASMGEN2 and MAKASEQ, two disassembly aids for the program ASMGEN (not included on this disk). ASMRECOV recovers assembler source from listing files, and PUBLBL is a debugger for assembly language.

ASMSTAT generates assembler program statistics, GENTBLS generates program source code tables, and SAPREF appends the assembler cross-reference to the listing file. CASE is a text file utility that converts files containing upper and lower case characters into all upper or lower case characters. DIFFER finds differences in two text files, and LIST displays any text file.

MSCRIBE produces a handy formatted version of a text file for easy reading. OVER shifts a print file to the right, and REPAGING repaginates a text file. PLAYCVMS, PLAYCUT, and PMUSCVT are utilities for the program DRVSPKR.SYS (not on this disk). DELALL deletes all matching files, DIRCMP2 compares files in different subdirectories, and DIRTREE makes a file of subdirectories present.

Among the other utilities on this disk are MELIZA, a psychoanalysis program, and SPACE, a disk-space management and recover utility.

(PC-SIG Disk#'s 928, 1128)
Special Requirements: *Hard drive.*
Author Registration: *Varies.*

SPA:WN
by University Computing Activities

Learn the concepts of nodal or structured programming with SPA:WN, Structured Programming Automated: Warnier Notation.

Tutorials are provided on the concepts of structured programming, and a program for use during design, documentation, and long-term maintenance of structured programs in any high-level language.

Warnier notation provides a graphic description of relationships between various components. SPA:WN provides the framework that lets you track these relationships. It then produces target language source code, again in any high-level language, as well as automatic layout and pagination of a Warnier diagram. The SPA:WN system provides the technical support which enables life cycle program/system management to be done entirely from Warnier diagrams.

The concepts of structured programming are also applicable to computer or other complex system design.

(PC-SIG Disk# 442)

Special Requirements: *None.*
Author Registration: *$50.00*

Temescal   by Kowa Engineering

Bring that next software development project in on time, and under cost. TEMESCAL is the tool that can do it for you. With TEMESCAL your project can be on time and on budget!

TEMESCAL is a tool for planning and managing software development projects. Software development projects are notorious for getting bogged down in unforeseen delays and costs. The reason, all to often, is that they are planned by guesswork. TEMESCAL brings you the experience of thousands of development projects. There is a more orderly approach to planning a software project and it is based on the "software equation." The "software equation" was developed after studying over 800 large development projects performed by many different companies and government agencies. The "software equation" has been improved and refined to include data on today's popular languages, such as ADA, C, Pascal, etc., and 8, 16, and 32 bit computers.

With TEMESCAL you can: compare a change in development time for a corresponding change in the number of man-months needed for a development project, evaluate the development time required in a software project when different languages are used, Calculate the efficiency of each and every programmer and monitor their productivity as the project progresses, and if you have a deadline to meet, you can calculate the number and efficiency level of the programmers required to meet it.

The languages supported by TEMESCAL are ADA, Assembly, BASIC, C, COBOL, Forth, FORTRAN, Modula-2, and PL1. If you plan or manage any software project, you need this program.

(PC-SIG Disk# 1952)

Special Requirements: *None.*
Author Registration: *$35.00*

TesSeRact   by Innovative Data Concepts

TESSERACT provides both the tools and the instructions for the programmer who desires to try his hand at TSR (terminate and stay resident) programming.

TESSERACT comes with extensive and in-depth documentation that is insightful and gives the first-time TSR programmer a good knowledge base. Included in this excellent package is a library of routines and data structures that will aid in developing RAM-resident programs and a set of routines that attempt to standardize TSR-to-TSR communication. The library is compatible with Microsoft C, Turbo C, Turbo Pascal, and assembler languages.

Interrupts and BIOS bugs have made TSR programming an extremely difficult and dark area of programming — TESSERACT makes the task far more manageable, both for the expert as well as the brave novice. The manual alone is worth the price!

(PC-SIG Disk# 1491)

Special Requirements: *Hard drive.*
Author Registration: *$25.00 for source code and $10.00 for newsletter.*
➤*ASP Member.*

Turbo ScrEdit ✍   by iHn Systems

As a Turbo Pascal programmer you may enjoy screen design, but dread the hours of coding required to get the screen to look the way you want. Many screen library packages help, but still require that you write a considerable amount of code. With TURBO SCREDIT, you create screens with the built-in screen editor; create menus, help, and data entry screens by using cut, paste, paint, lines, and boxes. TURBO SCREDIT automatically generates the code - no syntax errors and repetitive debugging.

The package mainstay is a special editor for designing screens. Tedious tasks such as programming in screen color, data field location, data field length, data entry order, and line and box drawing are easily manipulated in the screen editor. Data input, conversion, and error checking are all controlled with a simple macro sub language. No photographic memory or scratch work is necessary since the screen design is done as it would appear in the application. The generated code is even commented to make customization easier.

TURBO SCREDIT can be used by programmers at any skill level. It comes with extensive on-line help, a tutorial, a programmer's reference manual, and example programs ready to compile and run.

(PC-SIG Disk#'s 1653, 2220)

Special Requirements: *640K RAM, graphics card, two drives, Turbo Pascal 5.0+, Turbo C2.0, C++.*
Author Registration: *$39.95*

Ultimate Screen Manager
by MDFlynn Associates

The ULTIMATE SCREEN MANAGER makes it easy for you to design colorful screens that can be displayed from both batch and executable programs. Windows, menus, and data entry screens with different data entry types are supported. Full mouse support can be included in any screen you create. Screens can be designed to support both monochrome and color attributes. The attribute mask is automatically adjusted to the type of display monitor currently active. The ULTIMATE SCREEN MANAGER provides the ability to display screens from a batch file using environment variables to communicate data. Information entered or changed on the screen will be present in the corresponding environment variables when control is returned to the batch file. The screen editor lets you design screens to look exactly like you want them to look.

The ULTIMATE SCREEN MANAGER comes with a demo program and screens to demonstrate the value and ease of its use.

(PC-SIG Disk# 2345)

Special Requirements: *A hard drive is recommended.*
Author Registration: *$39.00*

UniScreen ✍
by Ebnet Software

Programmers, would you like to build your input format screens interact- ively? UNISCREEN is a true universal screen format generator, usable in any language.

The key to professional looking programs is the screen formats. However, producing such screens is often a tedious and time consuming task. UNISCREEN is a complete screen management system that offers: interactive format generation, windows, menus, popups, pulldowns, variable field and text attributes, alphanumeric and numeric selectable fields, mouse and printer support, and monochrome and color display support. Most importantly, UNISCREEN supports all the major languages and compilers, such as, C, Pascal, BASIC, Cobol, Fortran, Assembler, Prolog, Clipper, and dBASE III Plus.

UNISCREEN is invaluable to anyone wanting to improve the appearance of their programs. It even comes with a DEMO program to illustrate its ease of use.

(PC-SIG Disk#'s 2056, 2057, 2624)

Special Requirements: *None.*
Author Registration: *$49.00*

Vanilla SNOBOL4
by Catspaw, Inc

VANILLA SNOBOL4 is an easy-to-learn, flexible language used for non-numeric applications, such as artificial intelligence, database analysis, text formatting, data conversion, identifying data patterns, searching text files, and more.

This version of SNOBOL4 does not have real numbers, and the object program and data cannot exceed 30K in size. Otherwise, VANILLA SNOBOL4 provides the entire SNOBOL4 programming language as described in textbooks. Source programs for SNOBOL4 are typically 5 to 10 times smaller than equivalent C or Pascal programs. A 150-page language tutorial and reference manual are included.

(PC-SIG Disk# 980)

Special Requirements: *None.*
Author Registration: *None.*

VBug
by Advantage Systems

VBUG is a visual debug program interface for all users of the debug program, providing an improved "screen oriented" interface using standard debug commands. VBUG provides full command line editing features, including recall of the last 10 commands for entry or editing. On-line help is provided for all commands, and frequently used commands (such as trace and proceed) can be entered by pressing a function key. VBUG provides

"paging" dump and unassemble commands and always shows the file currently being debugged. VBUG also allows saving the file size via function key and later resetting the file size, also by a function key.
(PC-SIG Disk# 2012)
Special Requirements: *None.*
Author Registration: *$19.95*

X-Batch
by Gary R. Pannone

X-BATCH is a bunch of utilities that can serve as commands in batch files for the busy, no frills programmer.

While some of the X-BATCH commands can be started at the DOS prompt, they are most useful as part of batch commands. BOX displays boxes with optional borders. CHECKENVIR tests environmental variables. CHKSCREN searches for text, while CLRSCRN clears screens with selected colors.

COMPFILE compares data, time and file size. CREATE creates files and CURSOR positions the cursor. DISPFILE displays file text in a box, while DISPLAY shows it on the screen. GETCHAR awaits specific keys and report. SHOW displays date, time or day of week. SOUND beeps a tone for N seconds, while WAIT waits for time of day, key or N seconds.
(PC-SIG Disk# 1619)
Special Requirements: *None.*
Author Registration: *$20.00*

▼ ▼ ▼

Project Management

9 O'Clock Personal Time-Tracking System
by Advocate Enterprises, Ltd.

Now you can manage your time far better than ever before! 9 O'CLOCK PERSONAL:

❑ Tracks up to nine simultaneous activities, each with its own attached-note capabilities. You can even do so with 9 O'CLOCK entirely removed from your computer's memory—even with your computer turned off! And, of course, you may pause, restart, save, and reset clocks at any time.

❑ 9 O'CLOCK may be run like any other ordinary program or as a "stay-resident" program instantly available with a "hotkey" of your choice.

❑ An alarm clock "beeps" and "pops up" your own message at the chosen time.

❑ The accompanying 9OLOGP Data Base Manager provides total control of clock data you file in 9 O'CLOCK's data base. Edit, print, and otherwise manipulate all clock data—even create data for an activity which catches you unexpectedly without 9 O'CLOCK handy. Records may be grouped for printing, editing, etc., quickly and easily by date range and more—or individually selected at any time. Sophisticated report format options are provided.

❑ The data base for filed clock information may be of virtually unlimited size.

❑ Want to use 9 O'CLOCK's data with another program? No problem. 9 O'CLOCK provides automated export to formats usable by virtually any external data base, spreadsheet, or word processing program.
(PC-SIG Disk# 2449)
Special Requirements: *Hard disk recommended.*
Author Registration: *$29.95*

Automated Planning Form (APF)
by Prowess INC.

AUTOMATED PLANNING FORM (APF) is a menu-driven set of planning tools. You can quickly make, store, retrieve, and update project schedules.

APF uses CGA graphics, and via DOS GRAPHICS.COM, can quickly produce presentation-quality printouts on most dot matrix printers. Plan projects, and communicate plans and progress to management, clients and those working on the project.

APF features:

❑ Up to 17 action items with subschedules for more detail
❑ Works in weeks, months, quarters, or years
❑ Automatically translate from weeks to months to quarters to years

---

　　　　✍ = Updated Program
☆ = New Program

❑ Shows percent completion of each task (action item)
❑ Shows dependencies in critical path
❑ Full edit ability
❑ Automatic origination and revision dating
(PC-SIG Disk# 955)
Special Requirements: *CGA.*
Author Registration: *$39.00*

BestGuess
by Notor Engineering Services

BESTGUES is a task planning tool intended to complement the increasingly popular scheduling programs which have proliferated in recent years. BESTGUES is based on the PERT time estimating technique (as opposed to the PERT task charting technique found in many planning packages), helping you to conveniently estimate how much time to assign to each scheduled event.

PERT time estimating using BESTGUES is a statistically based approach. You break each major schedule item into subtasks (up to 15) and assign a minimum, typical and maximum time estimate for each. On your command, BESTGUES then calculates probability data for your entries. This data helps you to estimate the task duration with a statistically determined confidence of success.

BESTGUES has been designed specifically to make the PERT estimating process easy to use. The menu prompts virtually eliminate the need for a manual or chart of commands. BESTGUES uses a simple function key based menu system and provides several data samples to show just how simple the program is to use. Whether you are estimating labor costs, lead times or have to estimate the duration of an event, with BESTGUES you can make an intelligent, prudent guess.

(PC-SIG Disk# 1889)
Special Requirements: *CGA or Hercules graphics.*
Author Registration: *$29.95*
➤*ASP Member.*

Easy Project ✍
by Parcell Software

For the office manager on the go, EASY PROJECT is a comprehensive project management, tracking, and controlling system. Context-sensitive help screens are a standard feature of this menu-driven package, and the files it creates are compatible with dBase III.

EASY PROJECT supports up to 20 user-defined project phases and an unlimited number of resources. It uses variable-scale Gantt charts to show planned-versus-actual dates of completion, and has extensive reporting abilities. It has two automatic installation programs, which simplify the setup process for either hard disk or dual floppy disk installations, and 11 pages of understandable documentation.

(PC-SIG Disk# 1082)
Special Requirements: *512K RAM, DOS 3.3+, and a hard drive.*
Author Registration: *$59.00*
➤*ASP Member.*

Gantt Charting
by Glenn C. Everhart

Keep track of that project, know where your resources are and how they've been committed. Analyze your progress with a Gantt chart.

Produce Gantt charts lengthwise on paper. Plot up to 20 tasks with timespan ranges from 24 to 36 months. If space allows, timespan increments can be in weeks. The program is self-explanatory and checks extensively for invalid input.

(PC-SIG Disk# 1306)
Special Requirements: *CGA, SIDEWAYS, and dot-matrix printer.*
Author Registration: *None.*

Gantt Pac
by HITT Personal Software Co.

This is a group of project management aids that produce presentation- quality Gantt charts — graphic displays of schedules — from a list of projects, dates and times.

Four primary applications are provided: Gantt chart transparencies for meeting displays, the ability to directly drive a video projector from a PC for meeting displays, Gantt charts for insertion into the text files of word processors, and direct use to view project status. These types of displays are commonly used throughout industry for management presentations of project status and resource use.

(PC-SIG Disk#'s 593, 1198)

Special Requirements: *Printer recommended.*
Author Registration: *$295.00*

GANTT2   *by HITT Personal Software Co.*

Are you an executive who needs real time schedule status displayed graphically? Though you may be at some distance from the activities, computer networks can show you the project's status at electronic speeds. While it does not create or modify the information, GANTT2 allows you to examine that status.

GANTT2 is a fully functional program designed to make Gantt charts from lists of dates and times. It can also be used with a project management program such as SCHEDULE for planning and tracking. Accompanying the GANTT2 package is an educational version of SCHEDULE and a starter set of batch and command files.

GANTT2 (#2472) was designed for the hard disk personal computer. Personal computer users working with floppy drives can achieve the same results with GANTT CHARTING (#1306).

(PC-SIG Disk# 2472)

Special Requirements: *CGA, SIDEWAYS, and dot-matrix printer. Mouse is optional.*
Author Registration: *$10.00*

MT-Tracker   *by Integra Computing*

MT-TRACKER is an integrated productivity system for tracking clients, projects or jobs, planning projects, scheduling appointments of all kinds, keeping a complete log of expenses, receipts and accomplishments, and producing a variety of schedules and reports. MT-TRACKER will handle up to 8000 clients or projects, 8000 appointments and 8000 receipts or expenses, which means that MT-TRACKER can keep track of an office full of people, projects, schedules and expenses.

Several copies of MT-TRACKER can run on a LAN system. Best of all, MT-TRACKER manages to accomplish all this without destroying anyone's sanity. Simple, clear menus and a very supportive help system escort you through the entire program. Prepare to become efficient, prepare to know what's happening — here comes MT-TRACKER!

(PC-SIG Disk#'s 1744, 1745)

Special Requirements: *512K RAM and a hard drive.*
Author Registration: *$75.00*

PC-Project   *by Big Picture*

PC-PROJECT lets you organize and control complex projects. It uses the critical path method to produce a project schedule displayed in the form of a Gantt chart. It is designed to help you manage complex jobs so you can finish them on time and under budget.

PC-PROJECT views a project as a group of tasks or activities. When you supply the estimated duration of each task and the relationships between the tasks (the predecessor tasks and successor tasks), it automatically calculates a schedule for you and displays it as a Gantt chart. With the chart, you can see when each task should begin and end, the current status of each task and whether or not the task is on the critical path. Like a spreadsheet, PC-Project can immediately show you how any change alters the project's finish date and cost. This allows you to try repeated what-if scenarios until you have reached the optimal project schedule.

PC-Project also has a resource worksheet to track payroll,supplies, and equipment costs. The worksheet allows you to list your employees and equipment and assign them to tasks, so you can coordinate your resources efficiently. The resource worksheet tracks costs to date, anticipated costs, final cost, and cashflow.

The program is completely menu-driven and contains excellent on-line help, plus a detailed 75+ page on-disk manual. If you are moderately familiar with project management and critical path method, you will be able to use this program with relative ease. It is written in C for increased speed.

(PC-SIG Disk#'s 1340, 1341)

Special Requirements: *None.*
Author Registration: *$25.00.*

Production Control Schedule
by Robert L. Flowers

Captain Bly should've had this program for a first mate. It keeps track of who is to do what and when, and prints out a daily work log for such activities as swabbing the decks and polishing the brass.

SCHEDULER helps you supervise the daily activities of numerous individuals and departments working on a variety of projects. The program remembers activities that recur daily, weekly, monthly, and quarterly. It takes into account up to 36 holidays and generates to-do lists to start the day of each person and department.

Your calendar is never carved in stone. Change work days, alter holiday schedules or revise anything, and the global or specific changes are made automatically.

You can adjust work weeks from one to seven days and tell it to skip days like the first of each month. One activity can be set to trigger other activities. Just tell SCHEDULER to set activities a variable number of days prior to or following some scheduled activity and watch it take care of the details.

Its project planning ability helps prevent goofs. If the stockholder meeting is set for the third of next month, tell SCHEDULER who has to do what and when. First, it prints out a chronological checklist of all the activities that need to be done. Then, day-by-day, it coughs up to-do lists insuring that everything that needs to be done, gets done!

The fat on-disk user guide is crammed with useful information, but you may never need to consult it due to the simple-to-understand menus used to guide you along.

SCHEDULER will help keep your organization shipshape and that may just lower the odds of employee mutiny!

(PC-SIG Disk# 1244)

Special Requirements: *None.*
Author Registration: *$55.00*

Project Management
by Potato League Sports

A complete interactive project management system using the critical path method of project control. Know where your project stands at all times. Identify those bottlenecks and deal with them before your planning is affected.

Handle 500 inter-related and dependent tasks, subcontractors, variable start dates, and holidays. Calculate the critical path, cash-flow, cost reports, Gantt charts, and precedence networks.

The system is designed to handle all necessary functions internally or to let experienced users build and modify files using system-editing software.

A sophisticated tool for anyone who needs a good planning utility.

(PC-SIG Disk# 423)

Special Requirements: *132 column printer or printer with compressed print mode.*
Author Registration: *$50.00*

RKS Task Master
by RKS Associates

TASK MASTER helps you stay on top of all types of projects, assignments, tasks, schedules, correspondence, etc. It allows you to set up a database with customized forms/records that represent your activities, such as individual tasks and schedules for a particular project. Custom reports can be printed, including a list of all past-due assignments, all assignments for a particular project, which assignments are due for completion on a specific date, etc.

TASK MASTER is completely menu-driven, using pull-down menus for selected options. A pop-up calendar and calculator are also provided to help you build and edit your records/forms. The program is compatible with standard dBase III+ database files and supports an unlimited number of records.

(PC-SIG Disk# 1380)

Special Requirements: *384K RAM and a hard drive.*
Author Registration: *$35.00*

Simple Project
by William H. Roetzheim & Associates

Here's a project management program that features Gantt charts, outline mode, risk analysis, pro-forma financial statements, ROI/ATO analysis and cash flow analysis.

This is not a fancy-looking program — there are no flashy screens or displays — but it's a very workable one. The program is run by command lines throughout its various different screens, each with a prompt line that explains the purpose of the highlighted item.

SIMPLE PROJECT could prove to be an invaluable tool for a project manager or a student of the field.

(PC-SIG Disk# 2265)

Special Requirements: *384K RAM.*
Author Registration: *$25.00*

Udecide ✍ by Cascoly Software

We all know the best way to make tough decisions is to make a list of options, assign relative values to them, and choose the option with the highest score. But how many of us really do that? That was before UDECIDE!

UDECIDE helps you make tough decisions - for example, which database program to purchase. The options could be PC-File, File Express, and Wampum. When looking at the different programs (purchase options), you would develop categories of comparison like: power, flexibility, ease of use, and dBase compatibility. You would then assign number values to their relative importance of each category. Now evaluate each program and determine how they score in each category. Some would be easier to use and others more powerful, etc.

By entering the importance you associate with each rating category and how each program is rated in that category, UDECIDE determines a weighted average score for each program. The program with the highest score is the best one for your needs. You can then either print out the complete analysis or change the ratings and perform a "what-if" analysis. Use UDECIDE to decide which project to pursue, which college to select, which stocks to buy, or just about anything. It can't make the actual decision, but it can help you think it through more clearly!

(PC-SIG Disk# 2473)

Special Requirements: *None.*
Author Registration: *$35.00*
➤*ASP Member.*

▼ ▼ ▼

Quotes, Bids, and Estimating

BID-BIZ   *by I.J. Smith*

If you're a contractor looking for an inexpensive but powerful estimating program, try BID BIZ. This program is for those who bid jobs or estimate costs based on a number of different components, phase costs, or various items. The program uses windows for viewing multiple records, editing, and various searches. All files have virtually unlimited record capacities.

The program allows for two types of burden factors, direct and indirect. The direct burdens are applied directly to the unit amounts used in the estimate listings. This can be useful for such purposes as sales taxes or storage costs on materials, or other increased costs as needed. Indirect burdens are used as overhead factors and added at the end of the direct cost extensions. They are used for the normal taxes and insurance, bond premiums, general overhead, etc.

The program allows you to enter notes and comments with various factors used in estimating. It also makes it easy to compare between the different alternatives you have to do a job.

(PC-SIG Disk# 1855)
Special Requirements: *512K RAM and a hard drive.*
Author Registration: *None.*

DAYO Quotes ✍   *by TJS Lab*

DAYO Quotes creates sales order quotes based on the DAYO Inventory, Customer, and other DAYO databases. Quotes can be printed on a standard printer or a Hewlett Packard™ Laserjet compatible printer. The quote can be printed on a pre-printed form, on the Laser printer in a special laser format, or as a standard/default form. DAYO Quotes closely models itself after the DAYO POS (Point of Sale) application and is totally integrated with that application. Templates (kits or bundles), are supported.

DAYO is a collection of multiuser business applications that provide a means of managing inventory, purchasing, invoicing, customers, vendors, sales and more... All DAYO products are multiuser, designed to work on a Microcomputer (PC) Based Local Area Network (LAN), like Novell™. They can, however, work as a "standalone," running on a single PC.

To date, large and complex mulituser business applications required Mini and Mainframe computers, but because of products like the PC based LAN/ Network, they can now be run on microcomputers. DAYO is one of the first microcomputer based business applications designed to handle such a system.

DAYO Business Applications grow with your company. The ability to upgrade your system is available with the addition of other DAYO products. Source to DAYO is also available, allowing you to make further modifications and enhancements. DAYO Clock was written with Qbasic™; all others were written with Clipper™.

❏ Current Modules: ❏ Inventory
❏ Back Orders   ❏ Smart Reports Point of Sale
❏ Accounts Receivable   ❏ Materials
❏ Requirement Planning Price Book   ❏ Accounts Payable
❏ Menu Quotes   ❏ General Ledger
❏ Clock Index   ❏ Look Up Databases
❏ Payroll Passwords   ❏ End of Period/Purge
❏ Update & Conversion Time & Billing

DAYO databases are all dBASE™ compatible, thus providing an additional or alternative source of support and reporting.

(PC-SIG Disk# 2405)
Special Requirements: *640K RAM, a hard drive, and DOS 3.3.*
Author Registration: *$25.00*
➤*ASP Member.*

Easy Quote   *by I.J. Smith*

Do you need an easy-to-use price quoting program and only need to keep track of products with a single unit cost and price? EASY QUOTE will make your price quoting easier and faster. The program is designed to allow the printed quote to be used as a billing invoice. Automatic search tables and scrolling windows give you instant access to your products and prices.

The program provides a customer name and address file, product file, multiple company file and quote files. These files are maintained by the system, giving you a built-in record keeping system. You won't have to fumble through documents trying to find a quote you prepared last week, you can simply go into the system and retrieve the quote. EASY QUOTE offers virtually unlimited record capacities. It will even blank your monitor screen after 10 minutes of inactivity to protect it from burn in.

Well maintained costs and prices will make it easy for you to provide accurate quotes.

(PC-SIG Disk# 1812)
Special Requirements: *512K RAM. A hard drive is recommended.*
Author Registration: *$35.00*

PC-Bid+ *by I.J. Smith*

PC-BID, developed for contractors, is a database program for bid items, but it can also be useful to others for obtaining cost estimates. For each bid-item, you may record the costs for labor, equipment, materials and sub-contractors, along with the prices. PC-BID also provides for various percentage overhead factors such as insurance, taxes and other costs based on the various bid cost items. You may edit or delete bid records individually. The program also allows you to change all bid unit costs by a percentage factor. A standard labor rate for each bid can also be used for those using time based labor records. After the data is entered you may print out reports for bid estimates, bid analyses, bid proposals, and master listings of each bid category.

(PC-SIG Disk# 1955)
Special Requirements: *384K RAM.*
Author Registration: *$35.00*

PC-Estimator ✍ *by CPR International, Inc.*

PC-ESTIMATOR helps you estimate building costs for projects of all sizes and kinds, from skyscrapers to kitchen remodeling. Developed by construction professionals, the program can be changed to be as large or small, as complex or simple as you want. The bottom line is custom cost estimates with your markup and choice of detail included.

You begin with pull-down menus, lots of help, documentation and sample files. You will build material price lists and cost data that keeps accumulating. The databases are unlimited, growing as your application grows. They include markups, labor and equipment rates, standard cost codes and vendor tracking. You can have different markups for individual estimates or multiple estimates carried out simultaneously.

The program produces reports for several levels of detail in estimates including itemized and built-in markup applications, and allows for "what if" type analyses. An on-screen takeoff calculator with memory is available at the touch of a function key. The data files are 100% compatible with dBase III+ application programs and are translatable by Lotus and Symphony. Lookup windows allow you to view any file at any time.

Wage rates for a number of construction trades are included with the program. They are tied to four-digit codes commonly used by the construction industry. Based on union rates, they are the average of several major U.S. cities and can easily be customized to fit your area.

(PC-SIG Disk#'s 1383, 1384)
Special Requirements: *448K RAM, two floppy drives, and a printer.*
Author Registration: *$99.00.*

Power Quote ✍ *by Power User Software*

Give your business a professional look and save yourself hours of paperwork with this quotation/invoice system. PC-QUOTE is a customizable quote/invoice generator for any business with a customer list and a product line of goods and/or services. You enter customers and items into a database using online screens. The system automatically creates an index for the customers and items entered. The system produces quotations and invoices using the customer and items that you select.

A text editor is supplied with the system to allow customization of the document templates to your unique format. On-line help is available from any screen and a manual is provided on-disk. PC QUOTE supports the use of a mouse.

(PC-SIG Disk# 1575)
Special Requirements: *512K RAM and a hard drive. DOS 3.0 or greater for mouse.*
Author Registration: *$50.00*

ProDev*EPRICE ☆   *by Pro Dev Software*

An electrical, plumbing, heating and air conditioning contractor's price maintenance system designed as companion software to the PRODEV*QUOTE (PC-SIG #533) system. This allows contractors to take advantage of weekly/monthly price updates from either the National Price Service (USA), Trade Service Corporation (USA), Trade Service Of Australia, Trade Service Information (UK), or Plumlee Custom Publishing (USA).

(PC-SIG Disk# 2754)

Special Requirements: *PC-SIG #533 and a hard drive.*
Author Registration: *$35.00*
➤*ASP Member.*

ProDev*QUOTE   *by Pro Dev Software*

PRODEV*QUOTE is an excellent full-featured Quotation or Bid Estimating system for any type or size business. Consulting services can even use the Auto Labor feature to create labor only quotes without material, or any combination in between. An unlimited number of Labor Groups can be associated with any quotation. Using dBASE compatible files for the Supplier, Labor and Material costs, you can browse the material data base 4 different ways with a Point & Shoot browse method to rapidly build a customized quote. The latest in pull-down menus and constant on-screen and F1 Help "what to do next" instructions make the system highly intuitive to learn and use. You can use the system's natural defaults to build simple quotes or use all of the many bells and whistles to build complex quotes. The stand-alone program does not require the user to own Ashton-Tate's dBASE III Plus or dBASE IV systems.

To support your sales efforts, you can print complete catalogs of your products and services with either your prices, List prices or both. You can even include unlimited sized Specifications for the material items in your data base and optionally print them on the quote. Material items can also carry automatic multi-rate labor units so that labor can optionally be pulled in with the selected material items. You can place notes anywhere in the quote as desired. Sub-assemblies can be rapidly merged to a quote to save time and increase accuracy. When modifying a large quote, you can instantly jump to any item. At the low registration price, PRODEV*QUOTE is a best buy.

This group of programs helps you quickly and accurately prepare quotations for projects based on your databases with the elements required for the project; i.e., materials, processes, parts, labor rates, markups, etc. If you need quick analysis and production of financial data, this could be a great help. A very professional package for small to medium-sized businesses needing analysis and projection tools.

(PC-SIG Disk# 533)

Special Requirements: *512K RAM, hard drive recommended.*
Author Registration: *$45.00*
➤*ASP Member.*

ProDev*QUOTE Utility Programs ☆   *by Pro Dev Software*

PRODEV*QUOTE UTILITY PROGRAMS — The TRACKING program is used to track actual costs for a quotation, and print exception reports that allow you to see all variances between the quote estimate and the actual costs. The BROWSE program allows you to rapidly browse/edit the PRODEV*QUOTE (PC-SIG #533) material, labor, supplier and quotation data files via overlaid pop-up windows.

(PC-SIG Disk# 2752)

Special Requirements: *PC-SIG #533 and hard drive or two floppy drives.*
Author Registration: *$15.00/$10.00*
➤*ASP Member.*

SC-Estimate   *by I.J. Smith*

SC-ESTIMATE is a billing program for general contractors. Separate entries are made for different types of work completed and the information is used to update an estimate. The program allows you to enter costs and payments to date as jobs progress, and progress estimates can be printed as necessary.

(PC-SIG Disk# 1715)

Special Requirements: *Unarchiving software.*
Author Registration: *$25.00*

▼ ▼ ▼

Real Estate and Property Management

Crisp ✐
by James W. Funsten

CRISP is a bookkeeping system that can support 250 individual databases, making it perfect for property management of multiple commercial or investment properties, or for individual accounting for several separate projects or companies.

CRISP is completely menu-driven. You select the property, or account, you want to operate with from a menu and then select the operation you want from another menu. Each database has its own journal of receipts and disbursements of up to 9,999 entries, chart of accounts of up to 250 accounts, and payor/payee list of up to 250 names (plus unlimited special payor/payees).

For each database, you can display up to three bank account balances, create income and expense reports, print checks (with or without payee's address for window envelope), reconcile bank statements for each property or project, and display delinquency reports. You can also backup all account data to another file for safe keeping. In addition, CRISP can export files of up to a year of monthly account totals to Lotus 1-2-3. CRISP makes written reports including all transactions, selected transactions, and annual and monthly totals of accounts.

(PC-SIG Disk# 1346)

Special Requirements: *312K RAM.*
Author Registration: *$55.00*

Easy-Manage
by Bradley T. Shovers

EASY-MANAGE is a property management program to monitor your real estate investments. EASY-MANAGE keeps track of all expenses by property and category, automatically posts rent and late charges, calculates rent balances due, and maintains tenant information in a separate file.

The ledger system lets you add and delete rental units and properties, with rent and tenant records. The tenant information file contains rent history records for each tenant, past and present. Keep track of when a tenant moved in and out, each one's rent payment history, and more. The size of the ledger is limited only by the available disk space.

EASY-MANAGE provides the type of reports you need to fully manage rental properties; monthly profit/loss, annual profit/loss, rent records for individual properties, late rent listings, tenant status reports, and even a rent past due form letter.

A unique feature of EASY-MANAGE is the ability to manage the smoke detectors installed in your properties. You can keep track of which units have smoke detectors and when their batteries need to be changed. In some locations this is a mandatory responsibility of the property manager.

(PC-SIG Disk#'s 2348, 2349)

Special Requirements: *512K RAM. A hard drive recommended.*
Author Registration: *$99.00*

Home Finder
by Martin C. Dore

A sophisticated database program specifically for Real Estate Agents and property consultants, HOME FINDER puts your listings at your fingertips.

It sets up three databases: properties for sale, properties for rent, and properties currently rented. Each database can have up to 250 records (the registered version holds 20,000 records). Search quickly for properties that match a customers requirements in size, number of bedrooms, location, type of dwelling, swimming pool, parking, and many other criteria. Add and change criteria to meet your needs.

Home Finder (PC-SIG Disk #2163)

The program is sophisticated enough to also search for properties that almost match a customer's requirements as well. Searches can also be done by address or any keyed word or phrase. Results are displayed on the screen or you can print them . Impress your clients with personal reports of the properties they are interested in. HOME FINDER's client report format never prints vital property information that would let a customer simply go to the property owner.

✐ = Updated Program
☆ = New Program

HOME FINDER is an easy-to-use program that lets you move easily through its series of menus using your cursor keys. Help screens either automatically appear as you move through the operations or can be called up whenever you need them. You can print reports in five different formats.

(PC-SIG Disk# 2163)

Special Requirements: *A hard drive.*
Author Registration: *$65.00*

Mini-Minder   *by Jess Hillman*

MINI MINDER is an easy-to-use rental property management system written specifically for managers of mini-warehouses or locker rental areas. (With a little imagination, the program could be adapted to fit almost any rental property situation.)

Track information such as size (or other description), rental rate, various tenant data, payment records, and expense of operation on a property. Perform other tasks, such as producing mailing labels in record sequence and billing tenants. Run daily reports, list all outstanding units (those who have not paid yet), view the status on a single unit, or list the status of all units.

(PC-SIG Disk# 961)

Special Requirements: *None.*
Author Registration: *$50.00*

OverLord   *by GUIA International Corporation*

OVERLORD can help you manage your apartment building, condominium, club, parking garage, church, homeowners association, or any other type of organizations that tracks members by a "unit" such as a lot or apartment number, license number or serial number. OVERLORD is a multifunction program designed to help you organize and control your member records and accounts.

OVERLORD prepares and prints bills with an optional late charge feature, percentage or dollars. You can specify the current balance above which late charges should be billed. You can specify different late charges for billing and for delinquencies. You can do the billing all at once for all clients or you can use cycle billing and specify the billing interval period by month, quarter, half year and year, you can do mixed interval billing for each account.

You can send customized letters to clients; spelled contract start and expiration dates, current balance, and lien or deposit amount are imbedded within the text. Choices for salutation can be selected. You can choose to print on your own preprinted stationery or have the program generate the letterhead for you. You can do selective mailing to clients, based on contract dates, current balance, deposits or liens, etc. Generate mailing labels or print addresses on envelopes. All mailings are prepared to fit window envelopes. If the user has a hard drive, an audit trail is automatically activated showing current user, transaction amount, old balance, new balance, and transaction type.

Other Features:

❑ Handles up to nine different organizations on a hard drive
❑ Unit (apartment) availability is checked; also the availability by date
❑ Produces delinquency and YTD credited reports
❑ A financial summary is offered showing the overall income and source by category
❑ Maintains a year-to-date credit history, even after an account is closed
❑ Measures outgoing expenses to budget items every day
❑ Description of the "unit" detail, seven fields, with the option to customize the field names and print a report
❑ Has a flexible fiscal/budget year, the default is from January 1 to December 31.

(PC-SIG Disk#'s 2008, 2009, 2010)

Special Requirements: *Two floppy drives. A hard drive is recommended.*
Author Registration: *$29.00*

PC-Agent   *by RDP Services*

PC AGENT is one of those rare, focused programs that performs with speed and elegance. This no-nonsense program helps sell real estate by serving as a prospect card filing system for realtors.

Everything important about the prospects and their desires is in the file. Single family residence, townhouse or condo? What price range? Location? Do they want a garage? When a home pops up on the market, it quickly calls up everyone on the list who wants a property like that and has the money, or credit line, to afford it.

Sixteen fields for data cover: name, address, phone numbers, price range, income, cash down, number of bedrooms, style, garage, land, area desired, and comments. A user guide is available, but the screen prompts are so self-explanatory you'll be in business in minutes.

(PC-SIG Disk# 1405)

Special Requirements: *None.*
Author Registration: *$45.00*

Professional Real Estate Analyst   *by The Forbin Project, Inc.*

PROFESSIONAL REAL ESTATE ANALYST is designed for multi-family and commercial real estate analysis. All files in the ANALYST are interrelated, operate via Lotus-like menus, and have help screens.

The main program, Cash Flow Analysis, has LOTUS worksheets that perform 13 measures of investment, including Cap Rate, IRR, FMRR, Cash on Cash, NPV, and Debt Coverage Ratio. Determine purchase price with IRR, CR, GRM and more. It has been updated to comply with current tax laws.

The 130-page manual includes menu maps. You don't need to know Lotus to use this program.

(PC-SIG Disk# 923)

Special Requirements: *Lotus 1-2-3 v1A.*
Author Registration: *$55.00*

PropMan   *by PropMan*

PROPMAN will do property management accounting and record keeping for individual owners with up to 50 rental units. These may be 50 individual houses or one 50-unit building or any combination in between. Financial records are kept individually for each building. PROPMAN is an on-line accounting system. All data is updated throughout the system each time new information is entered. Displays and reports are always current. There are no transactions to post or trial balances to run. PROPMAN maintains monthly and year-to-date data about properties. Historical data is also kept about past tenants.

PROPMAN does move-in and move-out prorates, calculates mortgage payments, schedules rent changes and can also print three-day notices and rent change notices.

PROPMAN is completely menu-driven and has on-line help to guide you through its operation.

(PC-SIG Disk#'s 1179, 1180, 1452)

Special Requirements: *512K RAM and a hard drive.*
Author Registration: *$135.00*

Real Estate Systems ✍   *by MicroServices*

RES is an asset for any professional real estate office. It helps you maintain and organize information on properties for sale, as well as information on the agents in the company.

Keep detailed records of sales and search for pending/closed sales at any time. Keep agents's records of current/previous year commissions, add an agent, or search records of an agent. Generate valuable reports on office/agent commissions, projected income, pending/closed sales, and unsold property listings. An added feature is year-end processing which purges all closed sales from the system.

Spend your time and energy on selling real estate and leave the tiresome bookkeeping to RES.

(PC-SIG Disk# 656)

Special Requirements: *None.*
Author Registration: *$25.00*

RealQuik ✍   *by Princeton Economics, Inc.*

REALQUIK is a "property management" program that will allow you to form a real estate database for all of your listings. Entries in the database may be recalled rapidly based on the format of the Multiple Listing Service books. For example, if you want to recall all houses in the 80 to 100,000 dollar range, or all houses with pools, only a few keystrokes and a couple of seconds later and you will have your data. REALQUIK allows for complete market analysis of properties and allows you to make your own listing screen to suit your needs.

REALQUIK performs numerous functions: listing management, recall homes/ properties based on price/area/street or any number of search parameters, market analysis, agent sales analysis, buyer qualification, produce amortization schedules, produce mortgage comparison tables, calculate balloon payments, calculate commissions/fees/company dollars, and many more.

(PC-SIG Disk# 1620)

Special Requirements: *356K RAM, MS-DOS 3.0+, and two floppy drives.*
Author Registration: *$54.00*

REIPS ✍ *by Thomas R. Brent*

Real estate professionals — evaluate prospective real estate investments and keep track of them for your clients.

Evaluations are based on measurements produced by REIPS, such as the financial management rate of return, internal rate of return, net present-value profitability index, debt coverage ratio, and gross income multiplier. Compare these measurements with competing investments to help in making investment decisions personally or for clients. NOTE: The comparison between competing potential investments is the important concept, not an exact prediction of future results for an individual investment.

REIPS is designed around current Federal income tax law, although certain simplifying assumptions, such as those regarding the alternative minimum tax and passive losses, are made. The manual provides information in terms that are easy to understand.

(PC-SIG Disk# 860)

Special Requirements: *None.*
Author Registration: *$35.00*

Your Real Estate Partner ✍ *by Niche Software Inc.*

Whether you're a homeowner financing your first home or an investor making informed decisions about multi-unit properties, YOUR REAL ESTATE PARTNER can save you money.

Quickly determine your best total investment from purchase to resale. Evaluate five types of mortgages. Cash flows are adjusted for taxes and inflation so you can compare properties and financing options.

YOUR REAL ESTATE PARTNER was designed with the novice in mind. It's user-friendly and comes with an easy-to-read manual complete with real estate definitions.

(PC-SIG Disk#'s 2617, 2618)

Special Requirements: *512K RAM. 550K of hard disk space.*
Author Registration: *$35.00*

▼ ▼ ▼

Reference Materials (books/articles/information/data)

AC - Area Code Hunter ✍ *by Pinnacle Software*

Finding the area code for a city or finding the city for an area code can be frustrating. Find the phone book, look for the page with area codes, look for the city — someone tore out the area code page — arrghhhh!

This will never happen to you again when you use AC HUNTER. Just type in either the city, or state (full name or postal abbreviation), and AC HUNTER returns the following: city, state, postal abbreviation, time zone, and area code. Type in the area code and AC HUNTER displays all the main cities in the area code.

AC HUNTER even includes the access codes for all countries and routing codes for all their major cities. With AC HUNTER, matching telephone area codes with cities and states will never be easier.

(PC-SIG Disk# 2564)

Special Requirements: *None.*
Author Registration: *$15.00*

Animal Farm ✍   *by Steve Herbert*

Once again, the author of the shareware programs MACBETH and LORD OF THE FLIES demonstrates his expertise in English Literature, this time with the book, ANIMAL FARM. Giving full credit to the good teacher, the author's purpose with this and other programs like it is to facilitate learning, to make it as fun and as painless as possible.

Geared to the high school level, the student is given background material on George Orwell. The style of the book, the characters and themes of the story are discussed. The student is given various exam tips, study questions are suggested and a section is included on how to take an essay test.

A teacher himself, the author of ANIMAL FARM is out to help you win!

(PC-SIG Disk#'s 2428, 2429)

Special Requirements: *512K RAM and CGA.*
Author Registration: *$15.00; Site license $60.00*

Atlas of the World ☆   *by Ken Calman*

What are the 565 tallest mountains in the world? How about the deepest ocean? There was a time when questions like these would have sent you scurrying off to the library to find an atlas. That was before ATLAS OF THE WORLD came to your computer.

ATLAS OF THE WORLD does not have maps of the world but it does have the size and location of cities, countries, lakes, rivers, seas, oceans, mountains, and even meteor craters. Print lists and rankings of continents, cities, oceans, and more.

Atlas of the World (PC-SIG Disk #2536)

The ATLAS OF THE WORLD is not just a reference book. It's also a study aid. With the included trivia game, quiz yourself on atlas trivia and current events. Although ATLAS OF THE WORLD doesn't come with instructions, it's easy-to-use.

(PC-SIG Disk# 2536)

Special Requirements: *A hard drive.*
Author Registration: *None.*

Ballistic   *by William R. Frenchu*

BALLISTIC is a program used to calculate bullet trajectories, remaining energy, velocities, etc., for small arms. It will generate ballistic tables, calculate point blank range, and many other useful functions. Several may be plotted vs. range on systems with VGA, EGA, CGA, MCGA or Hercules graphics adapters. A built-in database makes storage of personal data easy.

The purpose of this program is NOT to teach the fundamentals of reloading small arms ammunition, but rather to aid the hobbyist in assessing the performance of the ammunition he has produced. It is assumed from the outset that the user of this program is acquainted with basic reloading techniques. For review, a list of references is supplied.

This program is very thorough and complete. The documentation is over 35 pages long and extremely informative. It discusses the variables considered in calculations, how they are to be derived, and why they are so important. The appendix even has definitions on key words, making BALLISTIC a fine learning tool.

(PC-SIG Disk# 1802)

Special Requirements: *None.*
Author Registration: *$15.00 basic or $30.00 deluxe.*

The Bates Directory of U.S. Public Libraries ☆   *by International Features*

If you need to contact libraries around the United States, you'll find the BATES DIRECTORY OF U.S. LIBRARIES a real time-saver. This database contains the names, addresses, phone numbers, and number of people served for the nearly 9,000 main public libraries in the U.S.

The BATES DIRECTORY couldn't be easier to use. Select the view function to page through the entire list of libraries or see information on individual libraries. While you can't add new libraries, you can update existing information. Print a list of the libraries either as a group or by state. Print labels (one or two across) for either the entire list or by state.

✍ = Updated Program
☆ = New Program

(PC-SIG Disk#'s 2512, 2513)
Special Requirements: *Hard drive.*
Author Registration: *$25.00*

BLCC - Building Life-Cycle Cost Program ✍ *by United States Dept. of Commerce*

BLCC is a comprehensive program for conducting life-cycle cost analyses of buildings and building systems. Designed to provide the LCC analysis required for energy conservation projects in federal buildings, it can be used for private sector LCC analyses as well. It calculates tax and mortgage information and complies with ASTM standards for building economics.

Using the program, you can evaluate alternative building and subsystem designs which might lower operating and maintenance costs.

U.S. Department of Energy projections of energy price increases are included to facilitate the economic analysis of energy-related projects. BLCC allows up to nine simultaneous alternative designs to be evaluated and generates year-by-year cash flow analyses as well as present-value analyses. (Each building design can be divided into as many as six subsystems, and up to four types of energy can be evaluated in each alternative design.)

DISCOUNT, included with BLCC, is a stand-alone program which provides individual calculations of present values, future values, and annual values for use in life-cycle cost analysis when the extensive analysis and reporting capabilities of BLCC are not needed.

(PC-SIG Disk#'s 572, 983)
Special Requirements: *None.*
Author Registration: *None.*

Business and Moral Values, 4th Edition *by Bus. Admin. Department*

BIBLIOGRAPHY OF BUSINESS ETHICS AND MORAL VALUES has a list of periodical references, texts, books, syllabi collections, and audiovisual materials compiled by Dr. Kenneth Bond of Humboldt State University. This is the fourth edition and it is updated about every year and a half.

Some subjects included are: energy, environmental issues (strip mining, toxic chemicals and water pollution), worker issues (discrimination, sexual harassment, whistle blowing, etc.), privacy, distribution of wealth, third world issues and more. An incredible resource!

(PC-SIG Disk#'s 506, 1018)
Special Requirements: *None.*
Author Registration: *None.*

Chronos ✍ *by Cascoly Software*

How old was Paul Revere when he rode into history? How many years separated Michelangelo and Cortez? With CHRONOS, you can sort and select by individual people and events, or groups and factions; develop new insights and trace patterns across different eras and cultures. CHRONOS will be useful to history and art students, teachers, genealogists, writers or anyone interested in exploring historical relations or cultural events.

Display time lines of history's important people and events. Sort by people, event, group or faction. Trace patterns across different eras an cultures. CHRONOS comes with two sample files to demo this program's many features. Details on any person or event can be displayed via hot keys; reports can be printed on all or selected portions of the database. CHRONOS is very easy to learn and use, works with any graphics card, including color and Hercules, and supports a mouse.

(PC-SIG Disk# 2528)
Special Requirements: *None.*
Author Registration: *$30.00*
➤*ASP Member.*

Code-Blue *by Sofstar*

If you tend to make long distance telephone calls during periods of computer use, CODE-BLUE (CB) might be able to save you some of those annoying telephone company directory assistance fees!

CODE-BLUE is an on-line telephone area code reference system. No documentation is provided, or needed, with this system. It lets you cursor-select a state and get its telephone area code. For larger states, CB breaks down the area code listings to the city level. These city listings tend to include all the major population centers, but for area codes of smaller cities you will still have to call long distance information.

(PC-SIG Disk# 1083)

Special Requirements: *None.*
Author Registration: *$14.95*

Computer Buyer's Best Price Database ☆   *by Business Computer Systems*

COMPUTER BUYER'S BEST PRICE DATABASE has already done the research for you for the best prices on computers, drives, printers, modems, fax boards, video boards, monitors, mice, scanners, and tape backups.

The database also includes names and phone numbers of vendors. Search by name or specification. Comprehensive, easily-used, and current, the information on this database is selected from the many PC magazines and computer vending sources available. Computer groups, businesses, and individuals can save a bundle — of both time and money — with this package!

(PC-SIG Disk# 2630)

Special Requirements: *None.*
Author Registration: *$150.00 annually (12 issues)*

Credit Fix   *by E.A.P. Co.*

Having problems with the credit bureaus? CREDIT FIX has all the information you will need to know in order to change your credit rating. Use the laws and the flaws in the system. Reverse the trend for derogatory information to accumulate in your credit report. Apply the techniques in this informative file to improve your credit rating and keep it that way. Clean up those "little problems" the mortgage company wants explained. You'll find these valuable tips are a real a time saver for major purchases!

(PC-SIG Disk# 2433)

Special Requirements: *None.*
Author Registration: *$29.95*

Damn the Trivia - Our Priorities are Drowning," Edition II   *by PeopleSystems*

More than just programs and data come on disks nowadays. The controversial new book "Damn the Trivia" fills two disks about Peoplesystems (PS) — the methods for tomorrow, that control our lives today.

Systems sort into two categories — systems for people — Peoplesystems (PS) and systems for things — technology. There are also hybrid or mixed systems, but it's easier to first understand the pure, simple forms before looking at the more complex.

Peoplesystems (PS) are simple patterns of people events that guide, control or affect our daily lives. This book shows how to create better Peoplesystems that will free us from old fashioned ideas.

(PC-SIG Disk#'s 972, 973)

Special Requirements: *Printer.*
Author Registration: *$10.00*

DIVORCE - Animated Strategy for Men   *by Self Help Law*

CALIFORNIA DIVORCE is designed to educate men on their rights and the procedures they should know about and follow — in California — in case of a divorce.

This program presents a series of graphic screens along with text concerning the legal matters of divorce, and is written in a humorous manner, entertaining and educational. Since it was written by a man for other men, it does have a slight bias against women and marriage in general. Once viewed, the educated user can then choose a course of action on a self-help basis or with the assistance of legal counsel.

(PC-SIG Disk# 886)

Special Requirements: *360K RAM and CGA.*
Author Registration: *None.*

Divorce (PC-SIG Disk# 886)

🖎 = Updated Program
☆ = New Program

Education of Handicapped Act

by ARC of Tennessee

This disk contains the Education for all Handicapped Children Act Regulations, which can be used to help ensure that handicapped children receive free appropriate public education. There is accompanying documentation that explains how to use the Code of Federal Regulations, and how to find later revisions and updates. Official indexes are included with the regulations. Knowledge of these regulations will help states and localities provide proper education for handicapped children, and a special education administration guide is included on this disk.

(PC-SIG Disk# 1690)

Special Requirements: *A wordprocessor or other program to view the ASCII files on this disk.*
Author Registration: *$12.00*

The Electric Almanac ✍

by Matrix Software

THE ELECTRIC ALMANAC is an elegant computerized book that offers in- formation and advice on the best dates and times for accomplishing many different tasks. Like the traditional almanac, it looks to the moon and stars for the proper times for planting, asking for a raise, starting a new relationship, or any of the other really important questions of life — including when to go to the dentist. Like the traditional almanac, but with far more depth, it offers information on astrological charts, tables of planetary hours and astronomy tables. You can not only insert your choice of time and date, but also your longitude, latitude and the meteorological zone so that the ELECTRIC ALMANAC can give readings specific for your area.

And like a traditional almanac, THE ELECTRIC ALMANAC offers tidbits of important information such as metric conversion tables and a variety of oracles from I-Ching and Tarot to the not-so-traditional "Almanac Oracle." Best of all, THE ELECTRIC ALMANAC accomplishes this in a clear, self explanatory format — all entries are available by high- lighting and entering. You may miss the 19th century illustrations and the bad riddles and puns, but THE ELECTRIC ALMANAC makes up for the loss with a friendly interactive approach that makes opening up this book similar to a chat with a very knowledgeable old friend.

(PC-SIG Disk# 1724)

Special Requirements: *None.*
Author Registration: *None.*

ERB

by Carter Scholz

EXTERIOR RIFLE BALLISTICS (ERB) is an aid for those sportsmen who reload their own ammunition.

Determine expected bullet rise if the target is before the adjusted ZERO point, and bullet drop downrange beyond the adjusted ZERO point. It saves deciphering of ballistic tables to estimate the correct combination of powder and primer for a bullet.

(PC-SIG Disk# 1315)

Special Requirements: *None.*
Author Registration: *$5.00*

EthInves

by Jerry Whiting

ETHINVES is a biannual, published database and almanac filled with articles concerning ethical investing. This edition of ETHINVES includes lists of top defense and nuclear contractors, all the SDI contractors, companies still in South Africa, companies that own nuclear power plants, and financial profiles of several types of investment opportunities. Also included in this edition of ETHINVES are useful lists of bulletin boards, government phone numbers, readings for ethical investing, and the 100 best companies to work for in America. Other information includes how your tax money was spent by the government in 1987, and the full statement by Rev. Sulliman concerning American divestment in South Africa.

(PC-SIG Disk# 1307)

Special Requirements: *Nor*
Author Registration: *$20.00*

EVERGLADE

by Hyperion SoftWord

Programming as a performance art? Experimental computer composition? EVERGLADE is the first work of hypertext poetry ever written, the creation of an internationally recognized poet — author of five books of poetry and a forthcoming novel — who designed and coded his own display program in order to achieve the optimal combination of speed, beauty, and friendliness.

Unlike help systems and knowledge bases (what hypertext is usually used for) in this work, the hypertext links are full of magic and humor, enticing the reader to explore for the sheer enjoyment of it. Reading EVERGLADE is like opening door after door in an endlessly intriguing mansion. The poetry was written over a period of four months in the spring and summer of 1989, using a technique that gave the poet the same freedom to explore that hypertext gives the reader.

Starting from the idea of hypertext — the world of choices before us and what happens when we choose — the poem moves first into the past, memories of childhood, adolescence and hippiedom, marriage, children, discoveries of oneself and of community. Here and there we meet other people, explorers like ourselves, and the stories they tell draw us onto the paths of their lives into the present and the future.

The author, Rod Willmot, is one of the first innovators to recognize the creative potential of hypertext and the art of hypermedia.

(PC-SIG Disk# 1901)

Special Requirements: *None.*
Author Registration: *$10.00*

EZhelp Reference ✍   *by Brain Child Systems*

Build your own Help system (complete with overlapping pop-up windows) to use as a stand-alone, link with software, or use as an on-line reference. Why dig for a manual when you can pop-up a menu to investigate different topics? Select a menu item and an overlapping menu appears with more subtopics. Text on the subtopics can run to several informative pages.

EZHELP REFERENCE is your tool for linking your own Help facility with existing software or for building on-line reference manuals into your programs. A companion program helps you choose colors for borders, backgrounds, text and highlights. Eight different border styles are available. No programming is necessary—just occasional one-line commands to tell EZHELP REFERENCE how to list menu items.

(PC-SIG Disk# 2531)

Special Requirements: *None.*
Author Registration: *$25.00*

Findata Corporate Profile ✍   *by Comp U Print Co.*

FINDATA CORPORATE PROFILE is a well-documented, two-disk set of data on over 4,000 publicly-traded corporations. It operates as a database within any system that reads dBase III files or can use its own built-in database system. Corporate data supplied includes: ticker symbol, name, address, city, state, zip code, telephone, president's name, type of industry, industry code, stock exchange code, year of latest data, company's fiscal year, annual sales, after-tax profits, earnings per share, average number of shares outstanding, sales margin, the high and low stock market price, and the high and low price-to-earnings ratio.

(PC-SIG Disk#'s 1051, 1052, 2612, 2613)

Special Requirements: *System that reads dBASE III, a hard drive with 3.0 MB available space.*
Author Registration: *$75.00*

FLAGS ✍   *by Wyndware*

Now you can have a display of colorful flags of every independent nation in the world (as of 1989), and information about each nation. The flags of cities, states, and dependencies are also included.

Enjoy full-color representations of over 250 different flags. And take a "Flag Quiz" to test your knowledge of national flags. The program can also run on its own, displaying each flag briefly. There are special sections which graphically illustrate the history of the British and U.S. flags. And, just for fun, you can change the colors of any of the flags.

(PC-SIG Disk# 2125)

Special Requirements: *DOS 3.00 or higher and CGA.*
Author Registration: *$25.00*

Gleaners Index ☆   *by Gleaners Printing*

GLEANERS INDEX is an index of National Geographic articles, January 1957 through October 1990, to be searched, edited, and printed. Search for any keyword in the People, Place, Event, Animal, Vegetable, or Object categories. List the titles of all articles using the keyword as well as the volume, number, month and year of publication. GLEANERS INDEX works easily and permits new databases to be written.

(PC-SIG Disk# 2762)

Special Requirements: *None.*
Author Registration: *$15.00*

The Legal Pad   *by Arthur J. Eierman*

THE LEGAL PAD is an informational resource for lawyers or law firms who use computers in their individual practice or business. THE LEGAL PAD provides a comprehensive catalog of software designed for lawyers or law offices. For each program, THE LEGAL PAD will give you a description, system requirements, an author or company address, phone number, and the price. The program categories in this catalog include information management and retrieval systems, simulated lessons of legal courses, programs for creating everyday legal documents, time and billing systems, law firm accounting, electronic communication services for lawyers, legal wordprocessing and utilities, programs for lawyers who have a specialized practice, client information systems, and more. Each software category has a separate menu from which you may choose the program that suits your personal or business needs most accurately.

(PC-SIG Disk# 1624)

Special Requirements: *None.*
Author Registration: *$25.00*

Lord of the Flies   *by Steve Herbert*

You're studying *Lord of the Flies* by William Golding. They say it's a classic, that it's a statement about society. You find it to be an interesting, sometimes boring, sometimes fascinating, sometimes you-can-see-yourself-in-the-character sort of book. What is Golding really saying?

The author of the shareware programs MACBETH and ROMEO AND JULIET sheds some more light for the high school English literature student. In a captivating way and from many angles, he draws the student into the story, familiarizes the reader with the characters, plot, and themes, and leaves the student with a new comprehension of *The Lord of the Flies*.

(PC-SIG Disk#'s 2426, 2427)

Special Requirements: *512K RAM, CGA, and GWBASIC or BASICA.*
Author Registration: *$15.00; Site licence $60.00*

MacBeth ✍   *by Steve Herbert*

Studying Shakespeare can be tedious. Do you really understand the language? The plot? The characters? This program can help you get through the play *MacBeth*, and have fun too.

MACBETH is an easy-to-use program designed as an aid for high school literature students. Using a simple menu system, students are taught about the play via quizzes, games, graphics, riddles, and notes on a wide variety of topics.

The games are designed to be fun and at the same time provide a painless way to memorize quotations, learn important speeches, and, in general, to become familiar with the plot, characters, and themes of the play. Definitely a worthwhile investment for those seeking to get the most from the play *MacBeth*.

(PC-SIG Disk#'s 2200, 2201)

Special Requirements: *512K Ram and CGA recommended.*
Author Registration: *$20.00*

Maptab World Culture Database ✍   *by World Cultures*

MAPTAB is a menu-driven data-management program that lets you search for data on different cultures — their beliefs, practices, and religions across the world.

This version of MAPTAB has a partial but useful sample of the ethnographic data on 186 societies worldwide. 177 variables pertaining to these cultures are provided, including kinship, social structure, incidence of aggression, climatic information, and types of marriage customs. In addition to these items, the documented societies range in time from 1750 B.C. to the present.

(PC-SIG Disk# 920)

Special Requirements: *None.*
Author Registration: *$30.00*

MoneyMaker ☆   *by Thinking Software*

How can you make money with your PC? We would all like the answer to that question. MONEYMAKER has some of the answers. Choose those that suit you best.

Easy-to-use and menu-driven, MONEYMAKER tells you what kind of PC to buy, some computer do's and don'ts, and discusses the peripherals available for your system.

MONEYMAKER presents ideas for making money in desktop publishing, accounting and tax return preparation, writing, the shareware business, consulting, custom programming, bulletin board systems, an ad agency, a research service, and others. MONEYMAKER suggests more than ten realistic ways to make extra money with your PC while keeping your present job.

(PC-SIG Disk# 2784)

Special Requirements: *None.*
Author Registration: *$10.00*

Operation Desert Storm ☆   *by The Unlearning Foundation*

OPERATION DESERT STORM is an electronic book about the recent war in the Persian Gulf as told by American soldiers who were there.

This book is published in a form that is new, easy and fun to read on a computer system of any kind. Also included is a catalog of more electronic books by this new non-profit corporation dedicated to promoting the use of computers for information.

(PC-SIG Disk# 2594)

Special Requirements: *None.*
Author Registration: *$10.00*

PC Reviews ✍   *by David Batterson*

PC REVIEWS is a collection of original "hands-on" reviews that can save you lots of money! How? By telling you what PC software and hardware to buy and what to avoid!

PC REVIEWS features professional evaluations by a computer journalist and consultant. The reviews are concise, to-the-point, and tell you exactly what you need to know about the products. This is a menu- driven program, and easy to use. The author uses a handy five-star rating system, too. All reviews are pure ASCII files and can be printed easily.

PC REVIEWS can help the MIS professional, office PC guru, or home user make the right PC purchasing decisions.

(PC-SIG Disk# 2392)

Special Requirements: *None.*
Author Registration: *$10.00*

PC-Card Catalog ✍   *by Diakon Systems*

Look up your books and magazines with the simplicity of the traditional card catalog, but with the efficiency of a computer! PC-CARD CATALOG (PCCC) is a cataloging program designed to provide your personal, church, school, or corporate library with a powerful on-line catalog that is easy to use, yet sophisticated enough for academic research.

Search by title, author, and subject. Items may be scrolled through, using the Arrow and age keys. Search for specific strings by simply typing them on-screen. Searches are not case-sensitive and misspellings are usually "close enough." The user may jump between catalogs (AUTHOR, TITLE, SUBJECT) with a single keystroke.

Librarians will appreciate the fast, efficient entry and edit of cataloging information plus the intuitive menu access to all activities. PCCC automatically files items in AACR2 (that is, "library," not strict "ASCII-") order.

(PC-SIG Disk# 2590)

Special Requirements: *None.*
Author Registration: *$39.00*

Personality Analysis System
by Try-Then-Buy Software

A highly-accurate personality analysis program designed to help the individual better understand his own personality and those of friends, acquaintances and loved ones.

PAS is based on the same principles and report system as the EMPLOYEE MANAGEMENT SYSTEM but has been modified to work more on the personal and business rather than strictly business level. PAS can help in several ways:

❏ 1. ACCURATE. The program is extremely accurate. Trained and licensed psychologists and psychiatrists have marveled at the sophistication and accuracy of such a low-cost program.

❏ 2. IMPROVE YOURSELF. PAS helps you know yourself by describing your strenghts, motivational factors and demotivational factors. Knowing thes things can help you improve yourself as a person. You can also work with your strengths and build them to your advantage.

❏ 3. OPEN SYSTEM. PAS is a POSITIVE ANALYSIS system (it doesn't pull skeletons out of the closet). The 5-page report is so amazing that people literally request a report to be run on their own personality as soon as they see it run on someone else. The PAS report is intended to be shared and thus opens communications and strengthens good will among people.

❏ 4. JOB MATCH helps you to determine whether or not a job fits in with your basic personality. Is the environment one that will encourage you to work and motivate you to produce your best? Will it allow you to use your personal skills to the utmost? PAS can help you determine this.

❏ 5. IMPROVE COMMUNICATIONS. PAS encourages open communication between adults and teens, helping to bridge the "generation gap."

PAS reports on the two greatest influencing factors of your personality. It also describes management style, decision making style, stamina, and personality characteristics. The final page deals in motivational and demotivational factors that would cause you to like or dislike the environment in which you work and live.

PAS is intended to improve communications between people and enhance your ability to improve your lifestyle. PAS is valuable as a personal communications tool between friends, marriage mates, business acquaintances and any other relationship where personality is a strong influencing factor.

PAS is a very accurate program and is a valuable personal tool.

(PC-SIG Disk# 2221)

Special Requirements: *None.*
Author Registration: *95.00*

Radiation
by Larry Lovell

RADIATION EXPOSURE CALCULATOR calculates your approximate yearly radiation exposure from a variety of sources, including your computer monitor! The radiation data used by this program was compiled from a recent study by the Department of Commerce.

(PC-SIG Disk# 1432)

Special Requirements: *None.*
Author Registration: *$6.00*

Radio Repair
by Larry Lovell

"Who knows what evil lurks in the hearts of all men? The Shadow knows!" Old radio shows are again playing on the air, capturing the ears and imaginations of a generation that has never heard of a cat's whisker tuner or a carbon arc transmitter! Now, what could be better than listening to these great moments from the Golden Age of radio on an antique radio you've restored yourself?

RADIO is a preliminary course on "How to service and restore antique radios." Fixing up old radios can be a rewarding hobby, particularly as antique radios have become collectors items! The quintessence of nostalgia, many of these old radios are lying around in attics and at junk shops—waiting for someone to see past the dust and bring them back to life!

This how-to booklet on disk reveals the simple test equipment you will need and guides you, step-by-step, through the process of checking and repairing each component of an antique radio to restore it to top-notch condition. A vacuum tube guide is provided, as well as the RMA color code for power transformers, audio-frequency transformers, intermediate-frequency transformers, and speaker field coils.

(PC-SIG Disk# 1432)

Special Requirements: *Wordprocessor or text editor needed to read the file.*
Author Registration: *$5.00*

ReadFast! *by Larry O'Rear*

Don't believe in "speed reading?" READFAST! is here to prove you wrong.

READFAST! first explains some of the causes of slow reading and then shows you how reading and comprehension can be improved. In addition to theory, READFAST! will measure a user's reading speed and then introduce exercises that will help improve upon that benchmark.

READFAST! can be used with any book; for some of the exercises, you will need to mark up the book. Anyone who reads should investigate this educational bonanza.

(PC-SIG Disk# 1630)

Special Requirements: *None.*
Author Registration: *$12.00 for individual version and $25.00 for the professional version.*

Reference Management System - RSX ✍ *by P. Douglas Goodell*

Reference Management System is a self-explanatory, menu-driven system for handling bibliographic references: data entry, viewing, searching, tabulation, and reporting. It provides data and index file compatibility with dBase III and III+, and it is compiled to provide operational speed. It is organized in five basic menus covering related operations. Searches include scanning, single and multi-item, and output can be sent to printer or disk in linear or card formats, with user control of included fields.

(PC-SIG Disk#'s 2213, 2214)

Special Requirements: *512K and two floppy drives. A hard drive is recommended.*
Author Registration: *$45.00*

Romeo and Juliet ✍ *by Steve Herbert*

Romeo and Juliet is a true classic. But was it meant for only the elite few who can figure out what all those words and flowery phrases really mean?

This program, from the author of the shareware program MACBETH, proves that Shakespeare can actually be understood and enjoyed by the non-Shakespearean fan! Geared to aid students of English literature at the high school level, ROMEO AND JULIET accomplishes this seemingly impossible trick through the use of menu-driven quizzes and games, notes, and a 'tour' through the Globe Theatre where the plays were first seen by audiences.

As with his other programs, the author also offers his students The Competition! — a chance to win prizes of cash and computer products, achievable only through a close knowledge of the play. Definitely a win-win program!

(PC-SIG Disk#'s 2422, 2423)

Special Requirements: *512K RAM and CGA.*
Author Registration: *$12.00*

Save the Planet ✍ *by Save the Planet Software*

SAVE THE PLANET is for anyone concerned about the future of our global environment — An environmental database on global warming and ozone depletion. SAVE THE PLANET can educate you about the real dangers to our world and show you how you can take positive action to curb its effects.

SAVE THE PLANET presents beautifully illustrated tutorials on global warming and ozone depletion, along with a bibliography and list of recommended reading for further study. Play a "Global Roulette" simulation which projects global temperatures for the next 60 years, based on various greenhouse warming sensitivities and energy policy choices.

Save the Planet (PC-SIG Disk #2370)

Also provided are the environmental voting records of all members of congress along with information on new environmental legislation, recycling, and energy saving tips. A built in "Write to Washington" word processor is ready to write quick letters to Washington. Select the politician's name from menus of the entire congressional delegation for each state. What better way to let your congressional representative know of your concern about our planet?

✍ = Updated Program
☆ = New Program

SAVE THE PLANET can explain and demonstrate the real danger our planet is facing AND it gives you a way to easily and effectively inform the government of your concern.

(PC-SIG Disk# 2370)

Special Requirements: *512K RAM and a graphics card.*
Author Registration: *$16.00/$30.00*

Select-A-College ✍ *by Decision Systems*

SELECT-A-COLLEGE sorts through over 1000 accredited two-year and four-year colleges and universities based on criteria you select, and tells you the 25 schools that come closest to meeting your requirements. Factors you can select include: major field of study or degree, specific courses, maximum tuition, maximum room and board costs, desired geography, Masters or undergrad programs, and more.

Processing takes around six minutes, and can save you hours of research. Includes an automatic letter-writing feature for contacting the schools to request further information and application materials. Surprisingly, some of the best rated schools in the nation have some of the lowest tuitions. Good news for parents!

(PC-SIG Disk# 1345)

Special Requirements: *None.*
Author Registration: *None.*

ShareDebate International #1 *by Applied Foresight, Inc.*

This shareware disk magazine has caught the world by storm! After just one issue, it is being distributed by 425 shareware dealers in 25 countries!

The magazine is a quarterly debate forum for PC users concerned about the present and future. Ben Bova, author and former editor of *OMNI* and *ANALOG*, wrote: "Electronic publishing is here! ShareDebate International is a bold, exciting venture that deserves the attention and support of everyone who seeks to create a better tomorrow." The debate forums established in this first issue deal with a National Interest Project-Level Stock Market; Occupational Representation vs. Geographical Representation for Voter Districting; Computer Modeling Future Cities to Fight the Greenhouse Effect and Strengthen the Economy; Japanese vs. U.S. Patent Law; Economic Impact of Corporate Income Tax; and the Existing Cost of Government Intervention in Health Areas.

A unique commission/subscription feature is built into ShareDebate International to encourage people to distribute, participate, and profit from the disk-based magazine.

(PC-SIG Disk# 2121)

Special Requirements: *384K RAM.*
Author Registration: *$25.00 for four future issues.*

ShareDebate International #2 *by Applied Foresight, Inc.*

This shareware disk magazine has taken the world by storm — after one issue, it is being distributed by 425 shareware dealers in 25 countries. The magazine is a quarterly debate forum for PC users concerned about the present and future.

Ben Bova, author and former editor of *OMNI* and *ANALOG*, wrote: "Electronic publishing is here! SHAREDEBATE INTERNATIONAL is a bold, exciting venture that deserves the attention and support of everyone who seeks to create a better tomorrow."

Issue two introduces four new debate topics and Ben Bova contributes! New topics: Supreme Court's 3/27/90 ruling that the majority of voluntary assemblies do not have free speech rights; Entrepreneurial Democracy; Futuristic currency systems to fight drug abuse; A private insurance plan for S&L depositors. Includes a built-in note- processor.

A unique commission/subscription feature is built into SHAREDEBATE INTERNATIONAL to encourage people to distribute, participate, and profit from it.

(PC-SIG Disk# 2260)

Special Requirements: *384K RAM.*
Author Registration: *$25.00*

ShareDebate International #3   *by Applied Foresight, Inc.*

Issue 3's Headlines:

NOBEL PRIZE WINNER IN ECONOMICS PARTICIPATES IN A DEBATE!

❑ Milton Friedman debates a National-Interest Project-level Stock Market (NIPS) NIPS privatized — Now called FIPS (Future-Interest Project-level Stock market)

❑ Science Fiction author, Ben Bova, leads Electronic Media Debate with fiction

ShareDebate International, a ShareWare diskette magazine distributed in over 430 shareware channels in 25 countries, is a quarterly debate forum for PC users concerned about the present and future. About it, Ben Bova, author and former editor of *OMNI* and *ANALOG*, wrote: "Electronic publishing is here! ShareDebate International is a bold, exciting venture that deserves the attention and support of everyone who seeks to create a better tomorrow."

Issue 3 introduces two new debate topics, and Ben Bova and Nobel Prize winner, Milton Friedman, contribute. New topics: Electronic Digital Media Publishing, with an excerpt from Bova's novel, Cyberbooks; and, Against Value-less Education. Friedman analyzes the National Interest Project-level Stock Market proposal.

A unique commission/subscription feature is built into ShareDebate International to encourage people to distribute, participate, and profit from the disk-based magazine.

(PC-SIG Disk# 2390)

Special Requirements: *384 K RAM.*

Author Registration: *Multiple registration plans from $5 through $25.*

ShareDebate International #4 ☆   *by Applied Foresight, Inc.*

Issue #4 Headlines — 6 GUEST AUTHORS & 7 NEW DEBATES!

Jerry Pournelle, Milton Friedman, Ben Bova, George Gilder, J. Neil Schulman, Murray Rothbard

Writing about...

NASA, Laws That Do Harm, Future of Science, Freedom and High Technology, Natural Law & Copyrights, Economic Spin Doctors, and Future Voting Methods.

SHAREDEBATE INTERNATIONAL, a disk magazine, is a quarterly debate forum for computer users concerned about the present and future. Issue #4 includes material by InfoWorld's and Byte's Jerry Pournelle, Ben Bova (President, Science Fiction Writers of America), Nobel Laureate Milton Friedman, Prometheus-winner J. Neil Schulman, economists George Gilder and Murray Rothbard, and futurist R.H. Martin. Seven more debate topics have been added to the 12 previous topics. The full text of a recent law authorizing government involvement with Shareware and public domain software is also included.

A unique commission/subscription feature is built into SHAREDEBATE INTERNATIONAL to encourage people to distribute, participate, and profit from this disk-based magazine.

(PC-SIG Disk# 2753)

Special Requirements: *384K RAM.*

Author Registration: *Multiple registration plans from $5 through $25.*

ShareDebate International #5 & #6 ☆   *by Applied Foresight, Inc.*

This is ShareDebate International's first double-disk issue, Spring/Summer 1991 (Issue #5 & #6). It features 11 popular authors including Jerry Pournelle & the League for Programming Freedom. SHAREDEBATE INTERNATIONAL is a debate forum for computer users concerned about the present and future and is carried by up to 1,444 BBSs or Shareware Dealers.

This shareware disk magazine was formerly published quarterly. Starting with this issue, it is now semi-annual. Of course, this also halves the subscription costs!

Prior to this edition, there were 19 debate topics (listed in issue #4). Five new debate topics have now been added. Three are related to the Gulf War and the Palestinian problem. One is a catch-all topic, used by Sysop-Attorney Paula Goldman in her coverage of recent FCC actions impacting the computer industry. The other topic covers intellectual property law and programming freedom. Four position papers of the League for Programming Freedom, including one written for ShareDebate International, kick off this debate.

Benston and Kaufman review the history of S&Ls. Bova writes about freedom of information over the satellite waves. General Graham writes on the political limitations imposed on the Patriot. The 28 Americans killed by the Scud missile didn't need to die. Pournelle discusses how government hurts progress. Smith assesses the National Interest Project level stock market proposal. Schulman's Prometheus-winning novel, Alongside Night, is excerpted (7 chapters). Martin writes on the Gulf War and viruses. McAfee Associates' latest version of its virus detector SCAN76-C is also included.

(PC-SIG Disk#'s 2749, 2750)

Special Requirements: *384K RAM.*

Author Registration: *Several registration plans from $5.00 and up.*

Storm ✍ *by UTopia Software*

Meteorology buffs and people living in hurricane country will find this program of great interest. Input storm statistics and see the historic path of a hurricane or the likely path of an on-going weather situation.

Specific storm statistics cause STORM to plot the path and movements of a hurricane on a map of the Caribbean and southeast North America. Warnings are issued if it comes close to a major city.

(PC-SIG Disk# 1372)

Special Requirements: *Graphics adapter. Hard disk recommended.*

Author Registration: *$25.00*

Storm (PC-SIG Disk #1372)

TEMPLEXX: The Template Multiplexer ☆ *by Henson Scientific, Inc.*

Keyboard templates are those little plastic instruction lists that lay on your keyboard or around your function keys. They can be a lot of help — if you can find one.

TEMPLEXX is a program that ends searching and fumbling for templates or other program helpers. TEMPLEXX is a memory resident (TSR) program that lets you "pop-up" a helpful template while you're using your favorite word processor, database, or any other application program.

TEMPLEXX is smart! Press the hotkey for a Help template and TEMPLEXX automatically senses the program and grabs the correct template to display. It finds the help you need to quickly return to your application program.

Create a template for any application if it is not already included in the completed templates. Templates for the following programs are supplied:

❏ dBASE IV
❏ Lotus 1-2-3
❏ Multimate
❏ QuickBasic and QuickC
❏ SuperCalc
❏ WordStar and others.

❏ DisplayWrite
❏ Microsoft WORD
❏ PFS Professional Write
❏ R:BASE
❏ WordPerfect

(PC-SIG Disk# 2580)

Special Requirements: *A hard drive and an application program*

Author Registration: *$15.00*

Terra*Time *by GeoGraphics Software*

TERRA*TIME tracks and displays the local time in hundreds of cities around the globe.

It considers not only time zone effects, but also daylight savings time at each city. Information comes up on a full-screen color non-graphics display. Windows and menu-driven commands are used for program modifications and program options let you tailor the display for their specific needs. As many or as few cities as you want can be displayed. The military or 12-hour clock can be selected and the layout of the world map can be varied to suit you.

Additional program features include time zone differences, great circle distances between cities, and a special alarm feature that can be set for any world city time.

(PC-SIG Disk# 1127)

Special Requirements: *None.*

Author Registration: *$20.00*

Twenty Greatest Ideas in Human Relations

☆   *by Bill McGinnis Publications\Software*

Terra*Time (PC-SIG Disk# 1127)

THE TWENTY GREATEST IDEAS IN HUMAN RELATIONS is a computer-assisted instruction course to give the user a working knowledge of the 20 greatest ideas ever developed for getting along with people.

As each idea is presented, the user provides feedback to demonstrate his/her understanding of each idea. The program will not allow the user to continue until all answers are correct. Once the proper feedback has been given, the user is allowed to continue until all of the material has been covered. To complete the course, a perfect score must be made on a 20-question test. Less than a perfect score implies that the user has not mastered the course, and the test must be taken again.

The course is easy to understand and takes about an hour to complete.

(PC-SIG Disk# 2713)

Special Requirements: *No special requirements.*
Author Registration: *$15.00*

Virtual Library, The
by Harvey Wheeler

This is THE VIRTUAL LIBRARY, a book about the electronic society of the future, based on an archival interpretation of human cognitive development.

The book discusses how the electronic society will trigger new developments in knowledge and education, and explores other changes which might develop from an easily-accessed databank: how research is done, how academic and scientific findings are published and read, how knowledge is transmitted, and how people relate to each other.

(PC-SIG Disk# 979)

Special Requirements: *None.*
Author Registration: *$5.95*

Wisdom of the Ages
by Micro Computer Resources

Find out how to attract success, wealth, power, happiness, friendship, and fame; how to avoid danger, fear, failure, ruin, pain, and sorrow; see what's been said about non-being, the eternal, creation, thought, soul and time and other important issues perplexing or ruling your life!

WISDOM OF THE AGES brings you the insightful thoughts and advice of the most significant philosophers, artists, scientists, writers, and leaders in history. In this four disk set, you are provided a capsulized collection of mankind's wisdom spanning over 2,000 years, covering subjects of endless fascination and importance.

If you are a writer or public speaker, you'll glory in a fountainhead of adages, aphorisms, and unforgettable sayings of 1,000 of the world's greatest minds. Perk up your writing and speaking and get your creative juices flowing with powerful ideas, quips, and insights from ancient civilizations to modern writers. Tap into the priceless treasures of the greatest thinkers of all time.

Organized in 81 subject areas, each subject is further divided into seven sections including: positive, negative, and advice. Easy-to-use menus let you dive into any subject area. You can also filter your selections to be limited to sayings from ancient times, short selections, Americans only, and other parameters.

(PC-SIG Disk#'s 1498, 1499, 1500, 1501)

Special Requirements: *None.*
Author Registration: *$54.00*

World Time
by Alan Hobesh

Need to know the time in London, Beijing or Bangkok? WORLD TIME can tell the time in 100 cities across the 24 world time zones.

✍ = Updated Program
☆ = New Program

WORLD TIME is fun for the curious and a must for international businessmen who want to avoid miscalculations that might result in embarassing overseas phone calls or faxes. WORLD TIME is simple to use: just type "WT" and the city name at the DOS prompt, and the local and international time appear on screen. (PC-SIG Disk# 1669)

Special Requirements: *None.*
Author Registration: *$10.00*

Writer's Namebase ✍   *by Robin Johnson*

Looking for a first name that suggests wealth and beauty for that great novel you're writing? How about a name that suggests intelligence and honesty for that newborn. WRITER'S NAMEBASE has hundreds of great suggestions.

Either specify a first name or select the qualities that you want in a first name and NAMEBASE will make suggestions. It will also list out nicknames and related names — some in other languages. If you are a writer, NAMEBASE allows you to change the existing database of names and add names of your own. The registered version includes names for different nationalities and science fiction characters.

Also included is a companion program called HEROINE. This program takes a male name and creates a tongue-in-cheek female name for use in romance novels. For the name "George" it returns: Georgette, Georgetta, Georgeen, Georgeanne, Georgina, and Georgia. (PC-SIG Disk# 2467)

Special Requirements: *CGA.*
Author Registration: *$20.00*

Zip Insulation ✍   *by United States Dept. of Commerce*

Save money on your home's heating and cooling bills! The National Institute of Standards and Technology wrote this program to help you determine how much insulation your home really needs to be both comfortable to live in and provide you energy savings of at least a seven per cent return over inflation on your cost of insulating.

To have the program calculate your insulation needs for having a warmer/cooler, more energy efficient home, you simply answer a few basic questions: whether your home is new or used, what components can be insulated (such as attic, walls, floor), costs of insulation, how your home is heated and air-conditioned, and the efficiency of your furnace. (PC-SIG Disk# 1468)

Special Requirements: *None.*
Author Registration: *None.*

▼ ▼ ▼

Resumes and Job Search

Apply   *by Louie Crew*

Keep track of the applications (for jobs, grants, contests, etc.) you have sent out. APPLY stores the relevant data and merges it with text files you create. It orders dossiers and prints your letters, resumes, and envelopes. APPLY also maintains a record of any past experiences you might have had with the person/institution. (PC-SIG Disk# 1005)

Special Requirements: *A printer and SORT.EXE and FIND.EXE from your DOS diskette.*
Author Registration: *$10.00*

Resume Shop   *by gSoft*

Take advantage of menu-driven help in doing that pesky but absolutely vital job of getting together a credible, attractive, and persuasive resume. RESUME SHOP prompts you to enter every item you need to construct your resume, including your name, address, job objective, education, work experience and references. The result is a concise, one page presentation of your background and credentials. The bottom line is that an adequate resume can be put together quickly and customized versions easily created to send to each prospective employer. A fourteen-page user guide offers advice on improving your resume writing skills. The program even includes a sample cover letter to be mailed with the resume.

(PC-SIG Disk# 1667)

Special Requirements: *None.*

Author Registration: *$10.00*

```
██████ Resume Shop Main Menu ██████          19:24

A▶ Personal Data          P▶ Display Resume
B▶ Education               G▶ Print Resume
C▶ Work Experience         H▶ Create ASCII File
D▶ References              P▶ Cut and Paste Menu
D▶ Job Objective           S▶ DOS Shell
              Q▶▶  Exit Program

gSOFT v Summer 88      F10-Registration      F1-Help
```

Resume Shop (PC-SIG Disk #1667)

Resumebest   *by Richard N. Wisan*

For most of us, the first contact a prospective employer has is not with us but with our resume. This is truly a first impression and we should take care that it is the best we can present. RESUMEBEST can help you create a good-looking, properly-prepared resume.

RESUMEBEST presents several different formats. You choose the one that best fits your past experience and the particular job you are seeking. Not only does it show what you should do for each resume section, but it also gives information concerning the proper order of presentation, the correct wording, the amount of copy you should write, the type of paper to use, how to make a cover letter, and more.

(PC-SIG Disk# 1097)

Special Requirements: *A version of BASIC and a printer.*

Author Registration: *$29.95*

▼ ▼ ▼

✍ = Updated Program
☆ = New Program

Sales and Prospect Management

The Complete Sales Automation System ✍ *by Software Innovations*

THE COMPLETE SALES AUTOMATION SYSTEM, an inclusive program for salesmen and business owners, offers sales-oriented databases in an easy-to-use menu-driven interface to track clients, product inventory, vendors and orders. Generate invoices, quotes, and order-detail tickets from information obtained and merged from each database.

Nice touches include the ability to work with profit margins, and discreetly view comments about clients. The report function prints summaries of sales and orders, as well as lists of clients, vendors, and products. Print out unsold quotations to follow up potential leads. THE COMPLETE SALES AUTOMATION SYSTEM is also compatible on many network systems: Novell, 3COM, IBM Token Ring, Banyan, LANtastic (read only), and PC/MOS.

(PC-SIG Disk# 2511)

Special Requirements: *640K RAM and a hard drive.*
Author Registration: *$69.00*
➤*ASP Member.*

Contact Tracker ✍ *by Wedge Marketing Communications*

CONTACT TRACKER packs just about every function a small businessman or crack salesman needs to record every prospect or key person he meets. It stores those contacts in a crisp database and converts your computer to a neat phone dialer. An arranger and organizer, CONTACT can maintain your calendar and schedule while prioritizing your chores. It lets you sort those contacts in a variety of ways, write a letter, and then its mail merge function makes sure the letter gets out to the right people.

You can set up CONTACT TRACKER to track important appointments, calls, meetings, dates, people and projects. You can send out price updates to selected customers or memos to selected employes. The program boasts it can churn out up to 60 letters in an hour and then print mailing labels. When needed, it will dial your telephone and let you make notes of your calls and store them with each contact file.

(PC-SIG Disk# 1880)

Special Requirements: *Two floppy drives. Hard drive recommended.*
Author Registration: *$50.00*

The Front Office ✍ *by Inter Active Micro*

Open the door to more opportunity with THE FRONT OFFICE (TFO). TFO is a marketing and sales productivity system for prospecting and lead tracking, telemarketing and call reporting, follow-up and sales performance.

TFO is menu-driven and uses a single data-entry system for all data. Data entered in one area is automatically copied to all other applicable areas — cutting down on data-entry costs, time, and errors. It comes with its own word processor and works with others, as well.

Letters, envelopes, labels, and reports are selectively produced by prospect code, salesperson code, zip code, follow-up date, customer code, product code, or your own user-defined fields for efficient and flexible prospect tracking and follow-up. Call reports include telephone time, sales forecasts, and potential sales volume for management analysis and sales support.

(PC-SIG Disk#'s 697, 698)

Special Requirements: *640K RAM and a hard drive.*
Author Registration: *$129.00*

IN-CONTROL ✍ *by ACS*

IN-CONTROL is a well-rounded business prospect/contacts and activity-tracking system. It provides a Rolodex, activities list, management reports, expense reports and an appointments tickler.

Everything is on-line with fast search capabilities. You get 60 on-line help screens, and has a unique built in zip code/area cross referen feature. The Rolodex features names, addresses and notations retrieval and a graphic "layer-in" ability which lets you temporarily merge mail lists. In addition, it is network-ready. The system also includes: appointments tracking, expenses, graphics, free-form data search, labels management and reports. A built-in telephone dialing system uses your modem and frees your phone for incoming calls. A built-in proposal and invoice generator is provided. The program standardizes your prospecting and follow-up information and converts forgotten verbal commitments into a focused daily list of appointments and callbacks that nets you extra business.

```
┌──────── Prospect and Activity Tracking System ────────┐
│                          ACS                          │
│  ┌──────────┐   ┌────────────────┐   ┌─────────────┐  │
│  │07/28/1989│   │ Please Choose one│   │ 09:51:00 AM │  │
│  └──────────┘   └────────────────┘   └─────────────┘  │
│ ┌ Records: ─       Main Program Menu for Friday, July 28, 1989  │
│ │ [ 10 ]      1)  Prospect File and Mailing Labels     │
│ │ [ 17 ]      2)  Activities File and Proposals/Invoices│
│              3)  Reports for Prospects and Activities  │
│              4)  Revenue/Expense Report and Statements │
│              5)  Other Options                         │
│              6)  Search Through Data, Memos, and Memo Status│
│              7)  Appointments and List of Priorities   │
│              8)  Select, Move, Delete, and Undelete Category│
│              9)  Base Station/Remote Site Consolidation│
│              A)  Create an on-line Help/Data screen [ now Off]│
│              B)  Output to external word processor/merge/data file│
│              C)  Economic Value of the Portfolio of Prospects│
│              D)  Automatically Create Future Activities │
│                                                        │
│              X)  Exit System                           │
│         Category Selected [defaults to ALL]: ALL       │
└────────────────────────────────────────────────────────┘
```
In-Control (PC-SIG Disk# 687)

IN-CONTROL requires registration after you have placed 50 records in the Prospect file. If not registered, this program will lock you out from access to the program, though the data files are always intact.

(PC-SIG Disk#'s 687, 688, 2686, 2687)

Special Requirements: *512K free RAM. Hard drive recommended.*
Author Registration: *$99.00*

Phoebe
by Crest Systems, Inc.

PHOEBE is designed to help you manage contacts effectively. In making a sale, you need to match the strategy to the prospect and supply the goods the moment the opportunity arises.

Prospecting is important to bring in new business, but without a system to manage these and prior contacts, prospects are useless. PHOEBE is an extremely powerful system designed to help you as a client management tool. Because of the amount of flexibility built into this system, it can help anyone with several contacts to manage.

Track clients by company name, date of last appointment, date of next appointment, year-to-date sales, salesperson, geographic area, and by eight user-definable fields called "relationship fields." Use these relationship fields to custom tailor PHOEBE to your own needs.

There is a comments section which you can use for important information about the last conversation, the next meeting, or anything else that will help you in dealing with that particular client.

The real power of any database is the information provided from it in the form of reports, and PHOEBE provides you with many options. PHOEBE can furnish reports with over 1,000 select and sort pattern combinations. Report capability includes tracking of calls, printing prospect lists, advertising sources where leads are generated, and more.

(PC-SIG Disk# 1790)

Special Requirements: *384K RAM and two floppy drives.*
Author Registration: *$69.00*

Sales Call Reports
by Argonaut Systems

SALES CALL REPORTS (SCR) enables a sales representative to easily and effectively use a computer to automate the reporting and customer list functions that are usually performed manually or not at all. SCR will help sales reps organize and document their relationships with a customer, while helping a company keep records of what their sales reps are doing. And all without ever actually filing reports.

SCR becomes an effective central data source for customer status, contacts, specific sales notes, address information, and other pertinent data for every sale call. Mailing labels, Rolodex cards, and sales reports are instantly available. Paperwork is saved, and important customer contacts and personal notes won't be lost if a salesperson leaves the staff. Best of all, the program is menu driven and so simple, even computerphobes will find it easy to use.

SCR will increase the efficiency of your organization and provide better documentation on which to base business decisions.

(PC-SIG Disk# 1610)

Special Requirements: *512K RAM.*
Author Registration: *$35.00*

Sales Tools
by DDK Software

If you are looking for a dBase program that keeps track of your sales calls, appointments and expenses, try SALES TOOLS. This program is a detailed sales management application that can be used as is with your copy of dBase II, dBase III, or dBXL, or (if you know how to program in dBase) the template can be customized to fit the unique needs of your particular business. Good screen layouts and logical program design make this program useful.

🖚 = Updated Program
☆ = New Program

SALES TOOLS provides menu items that, when selected, perform the desired function.

All creation, deletion, and editing functions, as well as reports, address labels, and appointment functions can be retrieved from within the database manager.

(PC-SIG Disk# 1582)

Special Requirements: *dBase III or compatible, two floppy drives or a hard drive.*
Author Registration: *$20.00*

SALES-BIZ
by I.J. Smith

This program is for those who need a sales tracking program to maintain customer and product sales information. It also maintains a directory of sales contacts and sales logs. Various daily, period, and to date sales reports are provided.

The program uses table searches and scrolling windows to make it easy for you to access your sales information. Sales can be entered by dates, customers or products. The program even has a screen saving feature that will blank the monitor after 10 minutes of inactivity.

(PC-SIG Disk# 1839)

Special Requirements: *512K RAM, and two floppy drives or a hard drive.*
Author Registration: *$35.00*

Sell More Software ✍
by Droege Computing Services, Inc.

The SELL MORE SOFTWARE program is designed to facilitate the marketing, sales, and administrative activities involved in selling computer software. Created specifically for software developers and value-added re-sellers, the program helps to plan projects, track contact with prospects and clients, track support, and print custom letters and forms.

The program saves you time by simplifying many routine tasks. For example, when you enter a client's order, the program makes it easy to create a product label, mailing label, and invoice. The revenue information is then passed to the General Ledger module.

The program's extensive set of reports help you to review trends in sales and support, plan future projects, control expenses, and manage your time more effectively.

The SELL MORE SOFTWARE program is part of the Droege Software Series, a complete line of information management programs.

Important features are:

❑ Complete contact histories   ❑ Next contact date
❑ Software support tracking   ❑ Project planning
❑ Mail merge   ❑ Reports
❑ Flexibility

(PC-SIG Disk#'s 2595, 2601)

Special Requirements: *640K RAM, and a hard drive. 80286 or better recommended.*
Author Registration: *$100.00*

▼ ▼ ▼

Schedulers, Calendars, To Do Lists, and Ticklers

Active Life for MS-DOS ✍
by 1Soft

Think a computer is too much hassle to replace your DayTimer? Or maybe your current appointment calendar doesn't have the strength you need? ACTIVE LIFE is an extremely powerful system for planning, managing, and tracking one's active business and personal life that takes advantage of your mouse (though a mouse is not required).

The flexible schedules manage workflow effectively and all types of recurring activities need be entered just once. Plus, the ACTIVE LIFE Notebook provides an indexed text/graphics database manager featuring telephone auto-dial. ACTIVE LIFE also includes pop-up calendars, alarms, and week-at-a-glance. Printed schedules provide reference and notation.

This DOS version uses a look-alike windows format. While you can use ACTIVE LIFE with only a keyboard, a mouse is highly recommended.

(PC-SIG Disk#'s 2022, 2021)

Special Requirements: *Hard drive and a mouse is recommended.*
Author Registration: *$149.00*

Active Life for MS-Windows ✍   *by 1Soft*

ACTIVE LIFE is an ambitious daily scheduling program which makes the desk calendar obsolete.

Keep track of all of your daily time commitments. Entering individual items is as simple as noting on a desk calendar. There is a great deal of flexibilty in that an event can occur at a specific or "floating" time frame.

Active Life for MS-DOS (PC-SIG Disk #2021)

Rescheduling events is a matter of one or two keystrokes. Daily, weekly, monthly, or even annually recurring events can be automatically added to the system saving repetitive entries. Comments can also be associated with events using ACTIVE LIFE's helpful notepad editor.

ACTIVE LIFE will generate printed reports of up to three months of activity and automatically saves past events for easy retrieval. Since ACTIVE LIFE is a MS Windows application, it can be run quickly from any other Windows application, is easy to use and is mouse-compatible. This program is the cure for the congenitally disorganized.

(PC-SIG Disk# 1481)

Special Requirements: *Microsoft Windows. 512K RAM. Hard drive and mouse recommended.*
Author Registration: *$149.00*

Active Life for OS/2 PM ✍   *by 1Soft*

Think a computer is too much hassle to replace your DayTimer? Or maybe your current appointment calendar doesn't have the strength you need? ACTIVE LIFE is an extremely powerful system for planning, managing, and tracking one's active business and personal life that takes advantage of your mouse (though a mouse is not required). Also, if you have MS-Windows, there is a version especially for you (disk #1481).

The flexible schedules manage workflow effectively and all types of recurring activities need be entered just once. ACTIVE LIFE also includes pop-up calendars, alarms, and week-at-a-glance. Printed schedules provide reference and notation.

While you can use ACTIVE LIFE with only a keyboard, a mouse is highly recommended.

(PC-SIG Disk# 2023)

Special Requirements: *512K RAM, a hard drive, Windows/286,/386, or OS/2 1.1+.*
Author Registration: *$149.00*

Ample Notice ✍   *by Granny's Old Fashioned Software*

AMPLE NOTICE is a calendar and alarm clock program that helps organize your schedule of appointments. Appointments and notes are entered into a standard text file in any of a variety of simple formats. Each day, you view a calendar of commitments taken from this file. This text file can be edited from within the program or from an ASCII wordprocessor.

You can specify that a birthday occurs each July 17, or that you have a meeting every other Tuesday at 4:00 for five meetings, or that Father's Day is the third Sunday in June.

Ample Notice (PC-SIG Disk #872)

Appointments that include a time can automatically set a pop-up alarm clock to notify you at a given advance interval. Print a specified range of dates to keep track of your appointments while away from your computer. These can be in a variety of print styles including a "tiny" option of very compressed listings for your wallet or purse. You can also print a calendar for any range of months for a particular year. The sorting and archiving options let you keep track of past activities for business purposes. Searching for a given appointment (future or past) is fast and easy. Also included is a program for addressing envelopes sideways from data on the screen or from a file.

(PC-SIG Disk# 872)

✍ = Updated Program
☆ = New Program

Special Requirements: *None.*
Author Registration: *$30.00*
➤*ASP Member.*

APPTracker   *by Software Innovations*

Keep track of all of your appointments whether they're this afternoon, next month or next year. Clean, crisp screens and a direct, effective approach make this datebook a pleasure to use.

All of your commitments are available from one screen, with on-line help a key-stroke away. Save all of your datebooks for record-keeping and instant retrieval. Never miss another appointment because you "forgot."
(PC-SIG Disk# 1792)
Special Requirements: *None.*
Author Registration: *$20.00*
➤*ASP Member.*

Big Event   *by Friendsware of Friendswood*

BIGEVENT warns you 10 days in advance of special events on your social calendar such as birthdays, anniversaries and special days of the year such as Mother's Day. After all, it's your memory — not your heart — that needs a hand. You enter all your special events in a text file according to a special program format. Once the data is entered, every time you turn on your computer it will tell you which events are coming up soon.
(PC-SIG Disk# 1900)
Special Requirements: *None.*
Author Registration: *$10.00*

Calendar Keeper ☆   *by Dataphile Software*

Looking for an easy yet elegant way to maintain, print, and distribute your household, business, or association's appointments or schedule of events? CALENDAR KEEPER is your answer.

Draw wall calendars, week-at-a-glance calendars, and year-at-a-glance calendars to include the events you need to remember. Keep up to 10 different calendar databases so you don't get things mixed up. Easy data entry of five different event types including: permanent events; one-time events; events which span consecutive days; events which occur every "n" days: and events which occur monthly on a day-of-week (as in second Tuesday).

There is a utility included to create printer driver for any printer (seven common drivers are included). Context sensitive Help and pop-up calendar is always available.
(PC-SIG Disk# 2655)
Special Requirements: *512K RAM, DOS 3.0+, and high density floppy drive.*
Author Registration: *$33.00*
➤*ASP Member.*

Calendar Mate   *by Hawk Software*

CALENDAR MATE can print a monthly calendar with your scheduled events. The strength of this program is its ability to interpret repeating events. Repeating cycles such as yearly, weekly, fortnightly are easily handled. More complicated cycles such as "3rd Sunday of the month," "2nd workday in September" can also be scheduled.

Flexible date formats allow users to enter dates in a variety of comfortable formats. There is context-sensitive help available from anywhere in the program and a help panel will be displayed.

The program can be customized by the user. All the window colors can be changed and saved. There are a number of system parameters that can be changed by the user. Things like whether or not to include the Julian date on a printed calendar, whether or not to automatically delete expired events, how often to save the data file, and many others are available to be tailored by the user.
(PC-SIG Disk# 1907)
Special Requirements: *384K RAM, printer for printing calendars, and DOS 3.0+.*
Author Registration: *$22.00*
➤*ASP Member.*

Calendar Program   *by A Little Software Company, Inc.*

Do you find yourself constantly flipping through a calendar to answer questions like, "How many days until . . . ?" or "What was the number of days between this date and that?" or "How many days ago was this?" Or maybe you just want to have a yearly calendar, for any requested year, pop up on your screen. CALENDAR PROGRAM is a quick, no nonsense way to help people whose lives are tied to dates.

If you need to see a full year of monthly calendars, tell the computer which year and touch the return key. If you have 90 days in which you must do something, tell CALENDAR PROGRAM the starting date. After a few seconds, it will tell you the date the 90 days are up. You can determine the number of days after a date, or before just as easily. Want to know how many days are between two dates? Type in the two dates and presto. CALENDAR PROGRAM works with dates for any year between 1901 and 1999.

Note that this program is not a scheduler, and is NOT intended to keep track of your appointments.

(PC-SIG Disk# 1571)
Special Requirements: *None.*
Author Registration: *None.*

Calendar Program by Small   *by Small & Associates*

Print a year's worth of calendar, four months per 8½ x 11 sheet of paper, for any year from 1990 through 1999. The program was designed to print the output using the Epson or Epson-type printer codes. The operating instructions are quite simple and prompts are available where needed.

(PC-SIG Disk# 1963)
Special Requirements: *Epson or compatible printer.*
Author Registration: *$5.00*

Comtrac   *by E Trujillo Software*

COMTRAC keeps track of your appointments, commitments, phone calls, and letters to other companies. It is the perfect support program for sales prospecting, or coordinating other business-to-business activities. The program can work with your modem to perform autodialing and log the time spent on each phone call.

COMTRAC maintains records on each company you deal with and organizes such information as the company name, the address, two phone numbers, the SIC number, the product, and whom to contact. Within a split second you can search for and find a company's record which includes logs of your last 15 phone calls, letters, and appointments with the contact. Each record also has a six-month, three-month, and one-month calendar showing your commitments, scheduled meetings, etc., with the company.

You can export any of this information to your wordprocessor to create form letters, Rolodex cards, envelopes and mailing labels. COMTRAC can also print reports such as the day's and week's appointments, a list of client companies, a telephone list, a phone log, and a letter log.

(PC-SIG Disk# 1530)
Special Requirements: *None.*
Author Registration: *$30.00*

DARN! Don't Forget! ☆   *by EmmaSoft*

A simple program with a simple task — to remind you of events that occur only once a year. We all know the trouble we can get into when we miss a tax deposit, a birthday, or even worse — an anniversary! Never let that happen to you again. Add important dates into DARN! once, and the rest is easy. Run DARN! once a day (or put it in your AUTOEXEC.BAT file to do this automatically) and it will remind you a week in advance of any important dates. See dates as far as 300 days in advance.

DARN! makes it easy to add, change, or delete dates. Keep multiple lists, print out your database of events, or export it to other databases. DARN! is so easy to use, you'll never again have a excuse for missing that special date.

(PC-SIG Disk# 2723)
Special Requirements: *None.*
Author Registration: *$10.00*
➤*ASP Member.*

DayMaster ☆   *by Unicorn Software Ltd.*

Never forget a date or appointment again. And have fun doing it! With DAYMASTER it's easy to enter up to five special events, three birthdays or anniversaries, and five appointments for any day. Run DAYMASTER at the beginning of the day or anytime. It will immediately display your schedule and list any birthdays or events. For fun it includes a number of historic events, famous birthdays, and some "quotes of the day." DAYMASTER is so easy to use you'll make all your appointments and have fun doing it.

(PC-SIG Disk# 2736)

Special Requirements: *None.*
Author Registration: *$20.00*
➤*ASP Member.*

DFStickl ✍   *by Dan Fisher Software*

A menu-driven calendar/tickler program designed to display certain previously-entered memos on certain dates.

Once the program is called, the screen immediately shows you any memos for that particular day. DFSTICKL can also be executed by putting this file in an AUTOEXEC.BAT file so the memos for that day will be displayed upon start-up. After you've read them, exit to DOS and get on with your business.

DFSTICKL is designed to remind you of personal priorities, important dates, and things that need to be done for the day. There is a "nag" option that will haunt you about a certain memo five days prior to the date or deadline.

You can add, edit, delete, and display any memos in the system. This program is very useful not only for personal use, but also for leaving notes, memos, and reminders to the other people who use the same computer.

(PC-SIG Disk# 818)

Special Requirements: *Hard drive.*
Author Registration: *$5.00*

EVENTMAN Personal Event Manager ☆   *by TASCS Company*

EVENTMAN makes it easy to remember the important dates in your life.

Whether it's birthdays, anniversaries, holidays, deadlines, business meetings or anything else, EVENTMAN will search for upcoming events whenever you type "whatsup" and will tell you what events are coming in 30, 60, or 90 days.

Record your important dates in an easy-to-use "windows-like" event database. Print lists of your events, and run the program from your AUTOEXEC.BAT file to automatically see what important events are coming up. EVENTMAN's on-line Help makes it easy for anyone to use. Includes screen saver and supports a mouse.

(PC-SIG Disk# 2519)

Special Requirements: *A hard drive or high density floppy drive.*
Author Registration: *$17.00*

Flexical ✍   *by Custom Cycle Fitments*

FLEXICAL tracks your business or social engagements and events, with up-to-date efficient and flexible calendars — complete with explanations of where to go, what to do, and when to do it. You will always have a calendar on your desk or wall, available to go with you when you travel. The calendars expand to hold as many events as you choose, for any time period, with as many details as you want. Print on standard 8-1/2" x 11" paper.

Flexical (PC-SIG Disk #1106)

The FLEXICAL system has two different types of calendars, the engagement calendar and the annual calendar. Both are used to plan a new engagement. The annual calendar gives you an overall view of the year, the engagement calendar shows you which time is free. When making engagements while away from your computer, make notes on your paper copy for later data entry. You can mark the annual calendar as you please, knowing that you can always print a new one whenever you like.

Calendars can be kept for as many people or purposes as necessary. Events are presented on-screen and printed in date order, with up to 20 lines of description per event. Reschedule any event, change its description, or delete it. Repetitive events can be entered once and are repeated each time period.

FLEXICAL also keeps track of your runs or hikes and gives both summaries and detailed reports for up to 20 runners for any time period. Details include route descriptions, elevations and average speeds.

The calendars and the runner's diary are independent of each other and can be used individually or together.

(PC-SIG Disk# 1106)

Special Requirements: *384K RAM, hard drive, and a printer.*
Author Registration: *$20.00*

The Gregorian Calendar
by Mektek Software

Enter any date between 1583 and 2100 and THE GREGORIAN CALENDAR will tell you what day of the week it was or will be. It also displays calendars six months at a time.

(PC-SIG Disk# 2155)

Special Requirements: *None.*
Author Registration: *$15.00*

H&P Calendar
by Patomac Pacific Engineering, Inc.

H&P CALENDAR creates a monthly calendar on screen with graphic designs or a yearly wall calendar without graphics.

Edit the monthly calendar by using the arrow keys to move the cursor anywhere on the screen to enter holidays, special dates, anniversaries, etc. When the calendar is completed, it is dumped to the printer using DOS "GRAPHICS.COM." A database is included to save the data to disk. The data for a particular month may be printed before filling in the boxes.

(PC-SIG Disk# 995)

Special Requirements: *CGA.*
Author Registration: *$5.00*

H&P Calendar (PC-SIG Disk# 995)

Instacalendar
by James M. Shellem

INSTACAL can produce a full-page calendar for any month, or entire year, from 1600 to 2050 A.D. You can print the calendar or show it on the screen. The documentation is brief but gives all the help needed to use the program.

(PC-SIG Disk# 709)

Special Requirements: *Printer.*
Author Registration: *$1.00*

Judy, the Memory Resident Calendar
by InterFact Software

We've all wanted a personal secretary to keep track of our appointment schedule for us. Let PC-SIG introduce you to the answer to your wish: JUDY CLONE, a memory-resident desktop organizer that keeps your schedules and appointments for years to come.

JUDY maintains the full-screen interactive calendar. She takes appointments, has editing functions, makes hard-copy, and goes through your notes and records, doing the daily filing tasks. She fills your computer's memory, does her job, leaves and then returns her space to the memory pool. She even wishes you "Happy Birthday" when that day rolls around.

(PC-SIG Disk# 848)

Special Requirements: *None.*
Author Registration: *$29.95*

LCG/Remind
by Levin Consulting Group

LCG/REMIND is a tickler program that can display a message or execute a program at a specified time interval, certain day of the week or on a day of the month.

This program can determine the date of the last backup of your hard disk from the backup log and will display a reminder to backup at predetermined intervals.

Clear the screen before displaying a message, choose your favorite colors for the display and specify how long the message will be on screen. When executing LCG/REMIND all of the program options are specified from the DOS command line.

(PC-SIG Disk# 1867)

Special Requirements: *None.*
Author Registration: *$12.95*

MakeMyDay
by Universal Business Concepts

A quartet of time-management systems for today's super-busy people. Beat Father Time at his own game.

APPOINTMENT CALENDAR lets you keep track of all of your appointments. Never forget another meeting or dinner engagement.

JOB SCHEDULER maintains your "to-do" list, in categories you define. Print a work-in-progress report the next time the boss asks, "Where are we on the Wombat project?"

EXPENSE ACCOUNT MANAGER monitors your expenses and provides the detailed account information necessary in the categories you specify.

TIME LOG tracks the billable time you spend on each client or project and provides the necessary documentation when you need it. Attorneys, accountants, consultants and other service professionals will appreciate it.

(PC-SIG Disk# 618)

Special Requirements: *None.*
Author Registration: *$50.00*
➤ASP Member.

Moe
by Integra Computing

A memory-resident datebook/desktop manager, MOE schedules events, reminds you of appointments, logs expenses and time, acts as a calculator, maintains and dials phone numbers, lets you establish lots of pop-up databases and lists, and offers an easy way to send printers new codes.

MOE schedules upcoming events, allowing up to 20 daily memory prompts, with alarms. It maintains up to 1,000 expense and time entries by project. The pop-up calculator offers a 20-line tape and the ability to transfer results to your wordprocessor or text editor. It does basic calculations, plus exponentials and inverse, and offers two memory keys.

You get a pop-up phone directory that dials for you, helps you with communications, and even prints mailing labels. You can establish numerous mini-databases, such as to-do lists and general ledger account numbers, and search them if needed. Sending codes to change printers, fonts, or format is made easier.

(PC-SIG Disk# 1225)

Special Requirements: *None.*
Author Registration: *$20.00*

MOMSYS
by Greg Gillock

Do you need to keep track of birthdays, anniversaries, events, and other re-occuring activities? MOMSYS is the ideal program for the individual, small business, or organization that needs to plan and track activities that occur on a regular basis.

Activities can be tracked on a date of the month, such as birthdays or anniversaries, or on a day of the week for meetings, or on a weeks of the year frequency for activities that occur during specific weeks.

MOMSYS is menu driven and consists of three components, a detail screen for entering/changing/deleting an activity, an inquiry system for locating activities quickly, and a reports function for daily or calendar reports.

(PC-SIG Disk# 1716)

Special Requirements: *None.*
Author Registration: *$20.00*

Names & Dates ✍
by WR Software

Do you ever find yourself switching back and forth between your address manager and your calendar program? Why not integrate both programs into one tidy application. NAMES & DATES keeps track of addresses and dates, and allows you to print mailing labels, envelopes, address books, and rolodex cards as well as wall calendars, and full page reports — all from the same print menu. With this one program you can set up a meeting, then generate a mailing label for a confirmation letter.

The address records have extra large entry fields for a person's title, first name, last name or business name, address, two phone numbers, category, salutation, and eight lines of notes. Data may be imported or exported from the program, and mail merge files can be created for letters.

NAMES & DATES also has a date reminder system, where you may enter the month, day and year of important events or appointments. A monthly calendar will flash the important days that you have entered, or you can print these dates on a wall type calendar. Printing can be done on either conventional or laser printers. Complete documentation is included on the disk, as well as context sensitive help screens.

NAMES & DATES can handle an unlimited number of records.

(PC-SIG Disk#'s 1566, 1568)

Special Requirements: *512K RAM.*
Author Registration: *$25.00*
➤*ASP Member.*

PAL
by PAL Software NY, Inc.

PAL is a handy scheduling tool, as well as a to-do list generator. PAL shows you sorted lists of upcoming appointments to help you use your time more efficiently and remember vital appointments.

PAL maintains a to-do list which prods you if you fail to do something after a specified date. You can set a virtually infinite number of alarms. PAL automatically repeats appointments and deletes old appointments. Secular and religious holidays are automatically displayed. You can also display calendars for any month in the 20th or 21st century.

Help is on-line from any place in the program. PAL can also interface with SIDEKICK appointment files.

(PC-SIG Disk# 1259)

Special Requirements: *Hard drive.*
Author Registration: *$49.95*

Personal Calendar ☆
by FunStuff

PERSONAL CALENDAR graphically displays a running clock, the current three months of calendars, and your appointments on the screen. The calendar's months can be scrolled back or forward a month at a time or moved to any date in a 10,000 year range, instantly, with the touch of a key. The calendar's digital and analog clock updates every second, and displays the date and time in 12- and 24-hour formats as well as Julian date.

Many options for events are available: one-time, daily, weekly, bi- or multi-weekly, monthly, specific week day of the month, quarterly, and yearly. Events may be scheduled to repeat indefinitely, or to repeat a specific number of times. Once an event or a note "becomes history," it is stored in a history file for your later reference (and modification if you choose).

The print capability will print a list of events separated by weeks, notes (optionally turn it off), and history (optionally turned on), along with the three current calendars, just perfect for folding up into your pocket or purse! Print options work well with single sheet or fanfold paper. Special support for the newest HP and IBM laser printers is also included.

Monochrome and color monitors are supported. The program can work by itself, or will run in the background as a TSR.

(PC-SIG Disk# 2593)

Special Requirements: *None.*
Author Registration: *$35.00 + $4 S&H USPS Ground in US*
➤*ASP Member.*

Phone Message
by E Trujillo Software

PHONE MESSAGE is a memory-resident utility that allows you to quickly record phone messages. Once the program is installed in memory, press the "hot-key" to activate this handy phone jotter. A small screen will appear allowing you to record who the phone call is for, who sent the phone call, the phone number of the caller, and a short message. All the information is then automatically transferred to an ASCII text file for later viewing or editing.

(PC-SIG Disk# 1530)

🖅 = Updated Program
☆ = New Program

Special Requirements: *None.*
Author Registration: *$10.00*

ProDex Plus   *by Prodex Development Company*

If your telephone is your livelihood, PRODEX-PLUS may ring your bell by combining a telephone directory, report log, and things-to-do scheduler to make you more productive.

Names and phone numbers of your personal and business contacts become a snap to keep track of and change as needed using the automatic telephone directory function. Auto dial is also included.

The report log allows you to record the date and time of calls, and make "folders" which act as electronic notepads and mini data files for keeping track of important information and follow-up on your phone conversations.

The things-to-do scheduler lets you set appointments, planned activities and ticklers to remind you of dangling commitments.

With PRODEX-PLUS, you can selectively sort and print mailing labels, address lists, phone directory lists, to-do lists, and folders. The program is memory-resident and so stays out of your way until needed, and is menu-driven for ease of use.

(PC-SIG Disk# 1248)

Special Requirements: *None.*
Author Registration: *$50.00.*

Remember-It ✍   *by W.R. Software*

REMEMBER-IT is a multi-featured date/memory manager program for PC/MS DOS computers that is designed to ensure that important events, payments due, billings, birthdays, or (heaven forbid) anniversaries, etc. are not forgotten. Business associates, relatives, friends, and others will be impressed at how thoughtful and organized you are by remembering those important dates year after year; you need not give the credit to your computer.

More than a calendar, REMEMBER-IT searches your list of events and when the date is within your predetermined warning window alerts you that the event is coming up. Only events that are pertinent to a particular day's warning window are displayed. You do not have to scan your calendar ahead for upcoming events. Determine the appropriate lead time for action when entering the event and your computer will remind you as the event approaches. This program is not memory resident but is designed to run every time your computer is powered up. Events within the warning window will be displayed and you may continue on to other applications with one keypress or utilize several other program functions before exiting REMEMBER-IT.

Program functions allow reminders to be entered based on annual, one-time, or monthly frequency. The menu based program allows reminders to be added, deleted with a single key press, displayed, or sorted by date. Additional features include a calendar capable of displaying any month in a 200 year period, a date computer that will determine a date future or past from your given number of days, and a Julian day calculator. Documentation is included on the program disk.

(PC-SIG Disk# 1217)

Special Requirements: *None.*
Author Registration: *$15.00*

Remind   *by Robert M. W. Tsou*

A lean and mean date reminder. Just put REMIND into your AUTOEXEC.BAT and always know when a holiday will occur and never forget another birthday or anniversary.

Enter "reminder" dates, such as your anniversary, your mother's birthday, and doctor's appointment into the program along with the number of days that you would like REMIND to start flagging you ahead of the event. Run the program from AUTOEXEC.BAT and each time you turn on your computer, the current date will be compared to the entries in the data file. If a date matches, a window will pop out, with the important reminder. If no date matches, the program will simply end inconspicuously, letting you proceed with your daily work. You may have multiple entries for each date and enter the dates to be reminded up to one year in advance of the current date.

(PC-SIG Disk# 2160)

Special Requirements: *None.*
Author Registration: *$10.00*

Remind Me! ✍ *by RSE Inc.*

REMIND ME! reminds you of the important events life before they occur. Also included is a calendar that displays any date in any year. It's unbeatable for keeping track of birthdays, holidays, paydays, bill due dates, business meetings — anything you need to be reminded of in advance. Enter the event, its date, and how far in advance you want to be reminded of it. REMIND ME! does the rest. Easy to learn and use, REMIND ME will never let you forget an important event again.

(PC-SIG Disk# 2391)

Special Requirements: *None.*
Author Registration: *$10*

Reminders *by Micro Data Assist*

Completely menu-driven, REMINDERS is a perpetual calendar, coupled with a tickler file for reminding you of important activities and dates. All date reminders are organized on a month and day of date basis: enter a date for a birthday, anniversary, or accounting deadline once, and that date reminder is shown on the correct day of the month, year after year.

Ten codes are used to group reminders under specific headings such as holiday, birthday, meeting, deadline, etc. REMINDERS can be displayed or listed to the printer by date, code, date range, code and date range, or in summary form, and calendar format, for any one month. REMINDERS is ideal for newsletters, clubs, groups, organizations, or use as a personal appointment/activity calendar.

(PC-SIG Disk# 1162)

Special Requirements: *512K RAM and a dot matrix printer.*
Author Registration: *$20.00*

Supercal and EGAcal *by Dan L. Davis*

SUPERCAL and EGACAL are calendar programs that let you keep track of dates and print out monthly and yearly calendars. Both programs are the same, but EGACAL takes advantage of EGA monitors and displays 43 lines on the screen. When first started, the program reads the date from DOS and immediately shows the month and puts the cursor in the box for that day. Holiday and history information for every day of the year can be displayed, and the programs can also print out a yearly calendar on one sheet of paper for any year after 1903.

(PC-SIG Disk# 1308)

Special Requirements: *An EGA card for EGACAL and a printer for both calendar programs.*
Author Registration: *None.*

TickleX ✍ *by Integra Computing*

TICKLEX is the ultimate scheduler/calendar. There is no more powerful or feature-laden program available. Equally at home on single PC's or LAN's, TICKLEX may be invoked as either a stand-alone program or as a pop-up. The program sports a multitude of screen displays, reports, and features, and it's capable of handling the scheduling needs of one person or a whole office.

TICKLEX handles appointments, deadlines, expectations, reminders and timetables, with each item having up to four reminders linked to it. Linking reminders to appointment deadlines or expectations is helpful when you need to change the original date. When a change is made, all the linked reminders are automatically changed. Among the handy features — find the day of the week for any date in the next half century, set up to 20 alarms for any day, and drag unmet deadlines (to-do's) forward from one day to the next. Keep this program in pop-up mode and it will service all your planning needs by reminding you on the fly.

(PC-SIG Disk# 934)

Special Requirements: *A hard drive and printer.*
Author Registration: *$50.00*

Tikler ✍ *by Richard Olsen*

If you are faced with the problem of organizing and remembering many appointments and dates, TIKLER will be of great assistance. This menu-driven scheduler generates full or partial print lists and also lets you view events, past, present, or future, on the screen. Four distinct delete options are provided. You can delete all events prior to a certain date, selectively delete one event at a time, delete a single event, or delete all the events.

(PC-SIG Disk# 1571)

✍ = Updated Program
☆ = New Program

Special Requirements: *None.*
Author Registration: *$15.00*
➤ *ASP Member.*

ToDo
by Northern Spy Computing

Keep a "things to do" list in your computer and in your pocket where you need it.

Each item or activity is a maximum of 38 characters to insure that the printout will fit into a daily diary or "day-timer"-type format. TODO automatically loads your list of up to 100 items when you run the program and stores any changes you make on the list. When you finish, TODO sorts your items by due date first, then by priority, then by key. If this sort pattern does not fit your needs, you can customize it.

(PC-SIG Disk# 917)

Special Requirements: *Printer.*
Author Registration: *$25.00*

TrackStar I
by 786 Systems, Inc.

If you have regular appointments and your current calendar is making you enter each one separately, TRACKSTAR specializes in repetitive scheduling. The repetition cycles can be defined by the number of days, the number of months, twice a month (15 days apart), or three special monthly cycles. Great for reminding yourself of when your bills are to be paid each month. You can even set an early reminder prompt for any number of days in advance. Of course the calendar is just as effective with one-time appointments.

(PC-SIG Disk# 1963)

Special Requirements: *None.*
Author Registration: *$15.00*

YCAL/DCAL
by Garry Spencer

Calendars are like police, there's never one around when you need one. Until now! YCAL lets you print out a yearly calendar, for any year, from 1582 to 9999. Just type in the year and YCAL creates a file with a bold heading for that year. You only have to copy that file to your printer with a DOS command and you have a smart looking calendar that fits on standard letter-sized paper.

Just want to check a date? DCAL displays the any-three-month calendar on your screen. If you don't specify a date, DCAL uses your DOS system date. Use YCAL/DCAL and never waste any more time looking for a calendar!

(PC-SIG Disk# 1644)

Special Requirements: *None.*
Author Registration: *None.*

Year Planner
by Flowsoft Custom Programming

YEAR PLANNER will help you and your staff organize your personal and business time month to month, or throughout the year. It lets you create your own wall planners which are laid out like the familiar "write-on, wipe-off" wall planner calender system. The system allows you to write deadlines and appointments and other important information in the "day blocks" of monthly calendars of your choice.

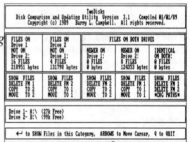

Year Planner (PC-SIG Disk# 1626)

The large standard calendar format lets you quickly update and erase appointments. Moving from date to date takes only seconds. You can list your appointments by the hour, or use a special wrap-around feature to put major task descriptions and deadlines within each day block.

An overlay template lets you enter similar messages in multiple day blocks. You can even get an on-screen year summary to see the whole year at a glance. The large calendar printouts already have major holidays built into each month. Your own important dates may be stored in a file for automatic insertion into next year's file.

(PC-SIG Disk# 1626)

Special Requirements: *520K RAM.*
Author Registration: *$10.00*

▼ ▼ ▼

Security — File, Disk, or System

b-Crypt
by b_Ware Software Series

A peace of mind program, B_CRYPT is a file encryption/decryption utility to protect your data files from unauthorized access. Whether sensitive personnel files, confidential financial data, or super secret research information, this program prevents prying eyes from gaining access. It will put the lock on any MS-DOS file structures including hidden files, no matter what the extension reads.

You supply a password and it converts your data into an incomprehensible binary form based on a pseudorandom algorithm. With a password from five to 32 characters in length, the chances of someone breaking the code file is greater than one to the 256^32. And that assumes the hacker has a copy of B_CRYPT. To complicate matters, you can encrypt a file more than once.

With lots of documentation and screen help, the program is painless to use, and fast: a 17K hard disk file is processed in from 10 to 40 seconds, depending on your PC's speed. A RAMdisk further speeds up encryption and decryption.

The author includes a challenge: break his encrypted message and win a cash prize!

(PC-SIG Disk# 1382)

Special Requirements: *None.*
Author Registration: *$25.00*

Cipher by Albert ☆
by Mike Albert

Keep sensitive data protected with CIPHER — a powerful encryption package that can turn any file into an unintelligible jumble of random characters. Only you have the key to unscramble it back into a readable form. Each encoding can have up to 50 printable characters. And, unlike most other file encryption schemes, CIPHER is very difficult to uncode because it's based on sophisticated techniques similar to those used by U.S. Government agencies.

(PC-SIG Disk# 1101)

Special Requirements: *None*
Author Registration: *$40.00*

Clean-Up ✍
by McAfee Associates/Interpath

The last in VIRUSCAN's trilogy of defense, CLEAN-UP kills and removes computer viruses, and in most instances, repairs infected files, reconstructs damaged programs and returns the system to normal operation. It works for all viruses identified by the current version of VIRUSCAN.

CLEAN-UP searches the entire system looking for the virus that you wish to remove. When found, the infected file is identified, the virus is isolated and removed, and for the more common viruses, the infected file is repaired. If the file is infected with a less common virus that can't be separated from the file, the infected file is wiped from the disk and deleted from the system.

(PC-SIG Disk# 2095)

Special Requirements: *None.*
Author Registration: *$35.00*

DosLock
by Haxton PTY Ltd.

File security is a difficult problem when more than one person has access to a PC. DOSLOCK provides complete file security for up to 26 users, as well as some very useful accounting tools.

With the DOSLOCK the system administrator can create file access, application access, and access to DOS. After installation the machine can only be used by those with a valid password. After logging on, a main menu appears showing the user all his valid options; there is no control key sequence to break out of DOSLOCK. On-line help is available which can be customized by the system administrator.

As most system administrators know, verbal reminders to back up data are often ignored by users. DOSLOCK's automatic backup feature solves that problem: before logging out users will be prompted to place a disk in the floppy drive and DOSLOCK does the rest. DOSLOCK also provides an audit report listing the users' activities with time stamps. This will help the administrators monitor application use and any improper system use (i.e. not logging out).

It should be noted that DOSLOCK has an impressive customer list, including Westinghouse and Readers Digest. Security like this has been available at the mainframe level for quite some time. MIS professionals will find DOSLOCK a welcome, and long overdue, relief.

(PC-SIG Disk# 1698)

Special Requirements: *Hard drive.*
Author Registration: *$90.00 for single user.*

EZ-Crypt-Lite   *by EZX Publishing*

If file privacy and security is a priority, EZ-CRYPT-LITE is a powerful encryption/decryption package that anyone can use. EZ-CRYPT-LITE will encrypt a source file using any one of several methods, and only decrypt the file using a confidential key. And do it all without cryptic commands!

Ideal for use with electronic information services and almost any type of file transfer (both electronic and mail service). Extensive menus, on-line manual, and context-sensitive help make it easy to use. And if you want file statistics to determine how well your file is encrypted (frequency/distribution, mode, mean, median, and more) they are available from within EZ-CRYPT-LITE. There is even a "file wipe" option to completely erase all traces of your file after deletion.

(PC-SIG Disk# 1771)

Special Requirements: *384K RAM and DOS 3.0+.*
Author Registration: *$39.00*

File-Safe ✍   *by Marcor Enterprises*

You know you should back up your files regularly, but you never seem to get around to it. FILE-SAFE will help you remember. Loaded in your autoexec.bat, it will tell you what files need backing up according to how often you told it to remind you.

You pre-select directories/files to be backed up and frequencies for each. When this backup program is included in the autoexec.bat file, the system automatically scans a master file of backup schedules and presents only those items needing backup. If no backups are needed, the program returns directly to DOS.

Entries needing backup are presented in menu form with single key selection of backup parameters along with information about previous backups. Parameters are saved with each backup and offered as the default selection on successive backup runs until changed. At any time, the program can be forced to display, for backup action, all directories/files in its master configuration file.

Results of every backup attempt are saved in a history file containing date and time of activity, results (successful, or if not, why not), and, for successful backups, the label of the backup disk. You also have full control over maintaining your backups and restoration.

(PC-SIG Disk# 1993)

Special Requirements: *Hard drive is recommended.*
Author Registration: *$50.00*

The Guardian ✍   *by Marcor Enterprises*

THE GUARDIAN is a security system designed to protect an entire disk (either a hard disk or a floppy disk) against unauthorized use. THE GUARDIAN uses an algorithm that logically "locks" a disk so that NO files, programs, or directories on the disk may be accessed. This can be an added security to files that may already be encrypted or password protected.

Many security programs load themselves from the AUTOEXEC.BAT file. Such programs are easily skirted with a floppy boot. THE GUARDIAN keeps disks locked tight until the "unlock" program is run.

When a disk is locked by THE GUARDIAN, the files on that disk are not physically altered. Rather, what is altered is the information that tells DOS where those files are. An anti-virus file check is also built into the system. Under no circumstances should this program be used before reading the instruction manual!

(PC-SIG Disk# 1787)

Special Requirements: *None.*
Author Registration: *$50.00*

Locktite Plus
by Ansoft

LOCKTITE is a file and program protector that's easy to use and requires no special hardware. Although your files or programs are locked, you can still copy them, transport them to home or office, where you can unlock the files and continue your work.

Best of all, LOCKTITE works with any DOS file, whether it's an executable file, a document file or even a compacted file. The program can read in your file or program, encrypt it using your password and then write it out to disk, along with a small header. Your information is locked tight!

Also offered is disaster insurance. Should the awful happen and you forget your password, follow the instructions included and the author will unlock your program.

(PC-SIG Disk# 1682)

Special Requirements: *None.*
Author Registration: *$39.95*

Login
by Arts & Sciences Company

LOGIN restricts access to the computer by requiring each user to enter an authorized user name and password.

A menu with up to 45 choices is then displayed from which each person can execute programs and DOS commands. Users can temporarily exit the program to DOS, to do other functions. If nothing is done by the user after a certain amount of time, LOGIN automatically logs off the user and blanks the computer screen. Each time a user makes a selection, LOGIN asks whether it is for business or personal use and the user is allowed to make a short comment. After the user is done and logs off, LOGIN records everything that was done into a special text file. This text file lists the user's name, date and time of each action, menu choice that was selected, whether or not it was for business or personal use, and a short comment by the user. LOGIN automatically creates separate monthly log files, according to the date entered when the computer boots up.

(PC-SIG Disk# 1146)

Special Requirements: *Hard drive.*
Author Registration: *$25.00*

Memoirs
by Bright Ideas Consulting

We all need a private place to keep our thoughts and notes, a place safe from prying eyes. At one time, it was a small book with a lock on it. But with the advent of the computer era, a better way has been made.

MEMOIRS is a private diary program that lets you encrypt your personal diary and store each encrypted line on disk as fast as it's typed. MEMOIRS also lets you view the encryption taking place as you go. The encryption method is quite fast and effective, with no redundant patterns — thus making it virtually impossible to crack the code.

MEMOIRS also encrypts and decrypts ASCII text files or documents. As with the personal diary, you can watch the encryption taking place.

(PC-SIG Disk# 756)

Special Requirements: *None.*
Author Registration: *$29.00*

MI-Log
by MiCord

MI-LOG adds two valuable features to your computer: multiple password control of computer access and automatic recording of PC usage by user, time, and purpose. The bottom line is access security, the information needed to document business use of your PC for tax deductions, and a powerful tool to measure worker productivity.

Each user may be assigned his or her own password. You can then display or print a report that tells you who used the PC according to date, time, hours, reason for use (business or non-business), and specific purposes of each use. MI-LOG also gives you cumulative totals of hours for each use. The program is not memory resident and will not affect any resident programs.

(PC-SIG Disk# 1494)

Special Requirements: *None.*
Author Registration: *$5.00*
➤*ASP Member.*

✍ = Updated Program
☆ = New Program

PC-Cryp2
by James Demberger

Is computer security important to you? Look into PC-CRYP2. First, it explains and demonstrates the Vernam encryption and decryption process of using a password as a numeric seed for encoding computer information. Second, it performs the encryption and decryption of your files.

No one will be able to access your data except you!

(PC-SIG Disk# 709)

Special Requirements: *None.*
Author Registration: *$15.00*

PC-Encrypt
by David Lincoln

PC-ENCRYPT keeps unauthorized users from peeking at your files!

Whether you work in a profession where you are required to keep information about clients or projects confidential, or you just want a little more privacy for that computerized diary of yours, PC-ENCRYPT puts a zipper on your files that only you can open.

The program accepts a password key of up to 255 characters, including spaces, and then makes an encrypted copy of a designated file. The copy cannot be decoded, without a supercomputer, unless it is decrypted by PC-ENCRYPT with the appropriate password.

Also includes HEXDUMP that translates a file into hexadecimal numbers and displays them page-by-page.

(PC-SIG Disk# 1533)

Special Requirements: *None.*
Author Registration: *$27.50 (Australian).*

PC-Iris ✍
by Digital Crypto

A file containing sensitive information may be encrypted by IRIS, effectively precluding unauthorized disclosure. The (encrypted) file may be copied to floppy disk and sent via public mail (an insecure channel) to another party, who, having access to IRIS and the "KEY" used to encrypt the document, will be able to decrypt the file, producing the original spreadsheet.

IRIS implements these commercial cryptographic techniques:

❏ ADFGVX
❏ DES
❏ VERNAM (XOR)
❏ BAZERIES
❏ CRC (checksum) generation

❏ RSA public key cryptography
❏ LITTLEWOOD
❏ PLAYFAIR
❏ VIGENERE
❏ Secure file erasure.

(PC-SIG Disk# 2004)

Special Requirements: *None.*
Author Registration: *$39.00 for PC-IRIS, PC-MERLIN, and PC-LOCK.*

PC-Lock ✍
by Digital Crypto

PC-LOCK allows the user of a PC to "lock" a DOS session, thereby inhibiting unauthorized usage of the machine during short absences such as lunchbreak. The PC-LOCK program prompts the user for a password (and re-prompts for verification), and then prevents any further use of the machine until the correct password is re-entered.

(PC-SIG Disk# 2004)

Special Requirements: *None.*
Author Registration: *$39.00 for PC-IRIS, PC-MERLIN, and PC-LOCK.*

PC-Merlin ✍
by Digital Crypto

PC-MERLIN integrates the DOS "copy" program with data encryption. This allows the user to copy multiple files to a target disk or directory, encrypting the data as the copy proceeds. Such a function is particularly useful to users who only need to encrypt data that goes offsite to remote users, or backups.

(PC-SIG Disk# 2004)

Special Requirements: *None.*
Author Registration: *$39.00 for PC-IRIS, PC-MERLIN, and PC-LOCK.*

PC-Scrambler ☆
by Shamus Software Ltd.

PC SCRAMBLER permits secure communications between two computer users. Using a modified version of the "Exponential Key Exchange" method, PC-SCRAMBLER sets up a secure communications link using a pseudo one-time pad based on an unpredictable random number generator.

This method uses calculations based on a 200-digit number in the negotiation of the encryption key in a way that will frustrate any intruder, active or passive (e.g. phone tapper). The encryption key used exists only in the computer, and only for the duration of the link. The user does not need to remember it or even be aware of it. Unauthorized Read access to the program source code does not compromise the security of the method. Nothing needs to be kept secret. There are no passwords to remember.

A 25-digit random number is used to initialize the system. The security of the method depends entirely on the inability of any intruder to guess this number. Both ends of the communication use different numbers and a new key will be generated for each new communication.

PC-SCRAMBLER works in conjunction with a Hayes-compatible modem. Once communications is established and the key has been negotiated, the system enters "chat mode," so the users can type messages to each another. Fresh keystrokes appear in normal video, successfully transmitted keystrokes appear in reverse video. Enter Voice Communications mode at any time with a single keystroke. Return to Transmit mode when ready.

PC-SCRAMBLER comes with full source code for inspection.

(PC-SIG Disk# 2694)

Special Requirements: *Modem.*
Author Registration: *None.*

Security
by Robert Wallingford P.E

Now you can protect your computer from unauthorized use. With SECURITY, only you know the password and only you can change it.

SECURITY lets you add password security to your computer through your CONFIG.SYS file. While this is safer than programs that use your AUTOEXEC.BAT to add password protection, it will not keep the sophisticated hacker out. However, it is a quick and easy way to keep most people off your computer. Assembly language source code is included.

(PC-SIG Disk# 2465)

Special Requirements: *None.*
Author Registration: *$7.00*

System Guardian Package
by EJC & Associates

SYSTEM GUARDIAN PACKAGE consists of SYSGUARD, ATTRIB, and EXECHECK, three programs which help keep your files safe from disaster.

Activate SYSGUARD and these potentially destructive commands cannot be performed: 1) disk format (including diskcopy); 2) disk write which bypasses DOS; 3) removal of a files read-only attribute; and 4) write to a read-only file. If any of these actions are attempted, a message is displayed and the operation is prevented from taking place. A simple command deactivates SYSGUARD and you again have access to any of the above actions. SYSGUARD is an efficient terminate-stay-resident program using only 1K of RAM and can be used alongside other TSR programs.

ATTRIB allows you to change the attribute of your files to read only, hidden, system, or archive. ATTRIB is similar to the DOS ATTRIB command but includes the capability to change attributes to hidden or system. Use ATTRIB to make your program files read only, so SYSGUARD can keep them safe from sabotage.

EXECHECK, available only to registered users, searches for .EXE programs that may have been patched or contaminated with a virus. If discovered, EXECHECK can attempt removal of the virus.

(PC-SIG Disk# 2444)

Special Requirements: *None.*
Author Registration: *$40.00*

Time Master ✍
by Geoffrey Broadhurst

Have you ever wondered how much your computer is used? Or what it is used for? TIME MASTER answers those questions.

✍ = Updated Program
☆ = New Program

Simply start TIME MASTER each time you start using your computer and "log-in." Then exit TIME MASTER and start using your other application programs. Do your word processing, accounting, etc. Each time you exit an application, enter TIME MASTER and "log-off." Tell TIME MASTER your name, what program you used, and how much time was used for business and personal reasons.

At the end of any period (day, week, year, etc.); TIME MASTER will display or print out reports that tell you who used what program, how long they used it, and how much time was used for business and personal reasons.

This program is perfect for any individual who needs to track, for taxation puposes, the time their computer is used for business and personal tasks. Also for the company or government department seeking management information on the use of their computers.

(PC-SIG Disk# 2465)

Special Requirements: *None.*
Author Registration: *$30.00*

VCOPY ✍   *by McAfee Associates/Interpath*

VCOPY is a replacement for the DOS Copy command that adds virus checking to the copying process. VCOPY checks the source and destination diskettes for boot sector and partition table viruses, as well as the files being copied for file-infecting viruses. VCOPY prevents infected viruses from entering your system and, if it finds one, identifies which virus it has detected and its location. Furthermore, VCOPY will check for viruses inside LZEXED files and will tell you if the infection is internal or external to the file.

(PC-SIG Disk# 2095)

Special Requirements: *None.*
Author Registration: *$15.00*

Virus Checker   *by Douglas K. Bell*

VIRUS CHECKER is designed to alert you to viruses that add themselves to command files. You create and maintain a list of the .BAT, .COM, and .EXE files that are on your disk drive. CHECKER takes notice of the size of those files and each time it is run, it lets you know if anything has been added to them, the first sign of a virus.

(PC-SIG Disk# 1785)

Special Requirements: *None.*
Author Registration: *$25.00*

Viruscan ✍   *by McAfee Associates/Interpath*

Stop viruses in their tracks! VIRUSCAN scans diskettes or entire systems for known viruses, identifies the intruder, removes the virus, and often repairs any damage to the system.

VIRUSCAN looks for any preexisting PC virus infection. Over 95 different virus strains and numerous sub-varieties for each strain can be identified by this program. These viruses include the ten most common viruses that account for over 95% of all reported PC infections. The documentation lists all the viruses by name (and what a list), for example: "The Do-Nothing Virus, Lisbon Virus, Ghost Virus-Ghostball, New Jerusalem, Disk Killer-Ogre, Dark Avenger, 1514- Datacrime II, Icelandic-II, and the Pakistani Brain, to name a few.

Viruscan (PC-SIG Disk# 2095)

It indicates the specific files or system areas infected and identifies the virus strain that's caused the infection. Removal can then be done automatically, or as a separate step.

(PC-SIG Disk# 2095)

Special Requirements: *Two floppy drives.*
Author Registration: *$25.00*

Viruschk   *by Carl Deneke*

VIRUSCHK, a computer virus alarm, helps protect your system from viruses that can lay dormant and suddenly destroy all your files. Days, weeks, or months of effort can be lost. It detects any change to your files and reports this to you before the virus can do its damage.

VIRUSCHK reads each file and performs a summing and encryption algorithm on each byte in the file. A special data file is created containing this information and is used to recheck all files upon command for any changes.

(PC-SIG Disk# 1279)

Special Requirements: *Hard drive.*
Author Registration: *$39.00*

VSHIELD (formerly Scanres) ✍   *by McAfee Associates/Interpath*

The memory resident version of VIRUSCAN, VSHIELD prevents viruses from getting into your system in the first place. It monitors and scans programs as they're loaded and prevents infected programs from executing. It also scans specific areas of the system — the boot sector, partition table, hidden files, command interpreter and itself, when it is first executed. It's your first line of defense against virus attacks.

(PC-SIG Disk# 2095)

Special Requirements: *None.*
Author Registration: *$25.00*

▼ ▼ ▼

Spelling, Word, and Vocabulary Quizzes and Games

ARIONX: Seeker of Gans   *by Dalal Publishing Co.*

Light on graphics but heavy on challenge, ARIONX: SEEKER OF GANS is the third in a six-part game series for math wizards.

If you love cryptographics, logic, math puzzles, and code-cracking, then you'll probably enjoy all six games in this series. Each game should be tackled and solved in consecutive order, as the preceding games' correct answers are required somewhere in the current game to arrive at the correct answer. However, it is possible to play each separately.

(PC-SIG Disk# 1090)

Special Requirements: *CGA.*
Author Registration: *None.*

ARIONX: Seeker of Gans (PC-SIG Disk# 1090)

Fictionary ✍   *by Cascoly Software*

What is the definition of bebung? Could be "an Indian dessert made with custard and honey." Then again it might be "an alchemist's distillation apparatus." Wrong again, it's "a sustained musical note having a pulsating effect. " Sounds like fiction, but it's actually FICTIONARY, a game of strange and unusual words designed by Steve Estvanik.

FICTIONARY can be played in two ways - either in a group where you try to fool each other into choosing the incorrect definition, or individually, where the game becomes a vocabulary guessing game. Playing with a group brings out the best playability in this program. You receive points for either selecting the correct definition or by having someone select your definition. You decide the final number of points needed to finish a game.

Easy-to-use menus make playing FICTIONARY a breeze. Load FICTIONARY on any IBM or compatible and the fun begins. Having a pencil and a piece of paper around may also come in handy. During each round of play, the word-giver sees the actual definition, then enters a paraphrase. The others see only the word and make up their own definitions. All players then vote for the definition they think is correct. If this appears similar to the board game Haberdash, it is, plus you now have the assistance of the computer.

A great party game, FICTIONARY will test both your intelligence and creativity. Adults will appreciate the difficulty, though children may find the words too difficult to enjoy. Nonetheless, hours of fun await those who dare to take the challenge.

(PC-SIG Disk# 2087)

Special Requirements: *None.*
Author Registration: *$20.00*
➤*ASP Member.*

Flash Cards: Vocabulary & Spelling
by Patomac Pacific Engineering, Inc.

A menu-driven 7,500-Word Vocabulary Builder and Spelling Teacher for the high school and college-level student. The flash card format has proved to be an effective teaching mechanism for improving spelling and vocabulary skills.

The dictionary does not include the 4,000 most basic words but, rather, the 7,500 next most commonly-used words. BASIC source code is included. While you're polishing your spelling, learn the parts of speech and the definition of each word.

(PC-SIG Disk#'s 367, 368, 369, 370)

Special Requirements: *None.*
Author Registration: *None.*

Foreign Language Hangman (Spanish)
by Norland Software

Norsoft FOREIGN LANGUAGE HANGMAN is an excellent educational program for learning Spanish, or for learning English for people who speak Spanish. While being educational, this program is very entertaining. It includes three variations on the basic Hangman game. The first is guessing what the secret word is, while in the second version you must guess an entire phrase. The last is Personalized Hangman, which can be played by two to nine players who enter a word or phrase to try to stump the others. This program is quite useful for building up your vocabulary or for learning basic grammar.

(PC-SIG Disk# 708)

Special Requirements: *None.*
Author Registration: *$15.00*

Gramarcy
by Robert L. Nicolai

GRAMARCY is a find-the-word-within-a-word game for children or adults. It has several thousand words, ranging in length from four to 11 letters.

You've seen this kind of game in the newspapers: locate all the words hidden in a given word. Each word given is randomly extracted from one of seven files in a word database. You compete against the clock to find all the words you can. Then you are scored for the number of correct words found versus the actual number of words hidden in the key word.

GRAMARCY is an excellent tool for anyone who wants to hone his or her skills at finding patterns in letters.

(PC-SIG Disk# 1158)

Special Requirements: *None.*
Author Registration: *$25.00*

Guess IT II
by Stat Software

Game players beware, it's addictive. If you like word or spelling games GUESS-IT may get you hooked. Like hangman, you get several guesses to figure out all the letters in the mystery word. In itself that might not sound too rough, but the 30,000 word list that comes with GUESS-IT will challenge even the most developed vocabularies.

As you make your guesses, the Guess-IT display keeps track of your progress. The scoreboard displays how many guesses you are allowed and how many you have used. The scoreboard also displays how many words or phrases you have tried and how many you have solved. There's a "peanut gallery" that makes comments, and also asks you if you want to try another word. You'll be kept abreast of the letters you have used and your progress with the current problem. If you run out of guesses, the secret word will be displayed for you.

GUESS-IT can be customized to use your own word or phrase lists. By making your own lists, GUESS-IT becomes a great tutorial for any topic. Build a list of your favorite spelling words, great historical figures, important geographical points, or famous quotes.

(PC-SIG Disk# 1563)

Special Requirements: *None.*
Author Registration: *$10.00*

Hangman by Norsoft
by Norland Software

HANGMAN is a game that enhances spelling and vocabulary. The program picks problems for you to solve from a diversified collection of data files. The vocabulary of words and phrases is extensive, keeping things from getting boring through repetition. You play against yourself, so at least you know the quality of the competition, although some players have been known to be surprised even then.

(PC-SIG Disk# 153)

Special Requirements: *None.*
Author Registration: *$10.00*

Hangman by Victor
by Victor Mux

Remember all the fun times you had trying to stump your friends playing hangman? Now, with Victor Mux's new computerized version of HANGMAN, you can test your own knowledge of music, science, computers and much more as you try to escape the fate of the gallows.

You can either use the keyboard or a mouse to play the game. HANGMAN can be played by 1 to 4 players, and follows the standard rules which we all have come to know over the years. Pick your letters one at a time, trying to keep body parts from appearing under the noose. Once the word is either discovered or missed, a small definition/description appears, providing the user with some background for the solution. Easy to play and simple to use, HANGMAN can provide hours of enjoyment for "children" of all ages.

In addition, you can create your own libraries. The program is able to contain 500 libraries and each library can contain 500 words. If a child is having difficulty in a particular area in school, you could use this program to help him with spelling and guessing words within a specific subject.

HANGMAN is a wonderfully easy and fun program which can be used by the whole family!

(PC-SIG Disk# 1965)

Special Requirements: *None.*
Author Registration: *$15.00*

Letter Shift
by Konstantin Articus

Puzzle people will be very happy with this one. Imagine, if you will, a square made of 16 smaller squares, four to a side. In each of these is placed one of the first fifteen letters of the alphabet, leaving one square empty. You define how many times the computer will shuffle these letters. Now, arrange them alphabetically while the computer counts your moves. Sounds simple, doesn't it?

(PC-SIG Disk# 1556)

Special Requirements: *None.*
Author Registration: *None.*

NameGram
by Support Group, Inc.

What do Lewis Carroll, Vladimir Nabokov, Jim Morrison, and Roman Polanski have in common? They all played with anagrams. Lewis Carroll rearranged politician William Ewart Gladstone's name to spell "wild agitator! means well." Nabokov named a character in Lolita "Vivian Drakbloom," an anagram of his own name. Jim Morrison of "The Doors" was "Mr. Mojo Risen." And in the movie Rosemary's Baby, an anagram is an important clue. Picture these creative artists hunched over a desk with a big dictionary arranging Scrabble titles to form words. If only they had NAMEGRAM! With NAMEGRAM, creating anagrams is a breeze.

NAMEGRAM takes a name or phrase, of up to 40 characters, and, using each letter only once, creates anagrams. The output, 1 to 16 letters each, are real English words. A curious, but fascinating exercise.

(PC-SIG Disk# 477)

Special Requirements: *None.*
Author Registration: *$25.00.*
➤*ASP Member.*

PC Cryptograms ✍
by Blanchard Software

NB BYDNSKMYFX AE E BIFTTLJMAJM NZPPTL MFXL! Oh, excuse me — you caught me talking cryptalk. Baffling riddles of letters await the most ardent of cryptogram fans. Cryptograms are the aristocrats of word puzzles. PC CRYPTOGRAMS gives you 50 of them in a program that takes all the disagreeable labor out of

✍ = Updated Program
☆ = New Program

solving. Type a guess anywhere the letter appears in the puzzle, and PC CRYPTOGRAMS makes the substitution throughout. Change a letter anywhere, and the program makes the corrections throughout.

PC CRYPTOGRAMS shows encrypted text and substitutions in the style of newspaper puzzles. It shows letter frequencies at the top of the puzzle. Function keys let you "SOLVE, "CLEAR," and "SAVE PARTIAL SOLUTIONS." The puzzle texts are well chosen quotes from famous authors.

PC CRYPTOGRAM will provide hours of challenging puzzle fun for young adults and older. Improve word association and other skills. A must for cryptogram lovers and a painless introduction for those who would like to try cryptograms.

(PC-SIG Disk# 1964)
Special Requirements: *None.*
Author Registration: *$15.00*

Phrase Craze   *by Excelsior Software, Inc.*

A word game that's great fun for the whole family. If you've ever seen "Wheel of Fortune" on TV, then you already know how to play PHRASE CRAZE. (Sorry, Vanna is NOT included.)

This is a phrase-guessing game where you fill in letters as outlined on the screen in a series of words that make up a well-known phrase. Can I have an "R," please?

(PC-SIG Disk# 385)
Special Requirements: *None.*
Author Registration: *$35.00*

ShareSpell ☆   *by ACROPOLIS SOFTWARE*

SHARESPELL is an excellent, easy-to-use Spell-Check system. Among the best anywhere, it is a stand-alone system that works with ASCII files. It shows the word in context with a list of possible replacements. Highlight the best choice for direct overlay into the document. Choose to ignore a word once or throughout the document, or add the word to the dictionary.

SHARESPELL has a 112,000+ word dictionary that is quite good. The system is very fast and the dictionary is compressed to take less space.

Included is a word-adding utility for merging your own word lists or for deleting words after they have been added to the dictionary.

(PC-SIG Disk# 2682)
Special Requirements: *None. Hard drive or 2 floppy drives recommended.*
Author Registration: *$20.00*

Spell Games   *by TexaSoft/Mission Technologies*

SPELL GAMES is a spelling game set in the scenario of the World Olympics.

The program temporarily flashes a word in the corner of the screen, and you must type it correctly in order to win the round. If a mistake is made in typing, you immediately lose the round. SPELL GAMES has four levels of difficulty in its selection of words to spell and you can select the amount of time the word flashes on the screen each time.

You have eight countries to choose from to represent your team and your opponent. SPELL GAMES has interesting color graphics and even plays different types of music depending on the country you choose to represent your team.

(PC-SIG Disk# 1144)
Special Requirements: *CGA.*
Author Registration: *$19.00*
➤ *ASP Member.*

The SPELLBOUND! Spelling Tutor ☆   *by SPELLBOUND! Software*

THE SPELLBOUND! SPELLING TUTOR provides a complete environment for improving your spelling skills. This thorough program meets virtually all the criteria to which educational software is held by the educational community.

Besides providing a full battery of teacher's tools, it prints individual and class reports, providing many types of useful information. As it teaches spelling, a personal difficult word list is created for each student. SPELLBOUND also allows you to create and format your own word lists. Use any text file as a source for words!

SPELLBOUND! features word list creation, editing, viewing, and maintenance functions as well as a full battery of teacher tools, grading, and reports. This, combined with an impressively simple user interface, makes SPELLBOUND! the wisest choice among even the most popular commercial programs.

The SPELLBOUND! Spelling Tutor (PC-SIG Disk #2656)

Adding to its appeal, SPELLBOUND! is for everyone. If you need to learn the spelling of esoteric words, such as for the medical and legal professions, this is the ideal system for you. For children, there are graphics in the form of animated Smileys who cheer the child on and shed tears when a word is misspelled. (Most adults run the program with the Smileys on!)

(PC-SIG Disk# 2656)

Special Requirements: *384K RAM, CGA/VGA/EGA, DOS 3.0, and two floppy drives.*
Author Registration: *$15.00*

Tommy's Wheel of Misfortune ✍ *by Tommy's Toys*

We've all said "I can do that" when it comes to guessing the letters on that game show. Here's your chance to prove it, but there are a couple of twists added to the situation.

TOMMY'S WHEEL OF MISFORTUNE is a one- to six player game in which players compete to guess a puzzle consisting of a word or phrase. The wheel has 24 slots, each with a money value or a special slot. Landing on a special slot can cause bankruptcy, give you a free spin, or make you lose a turn. Landing on the other slots earns you money if you guess a consonant of the puzzle correctly; if you guess a wrong letter that amount is subtracted from your winnings, thus giving you an incentive to be correct every time! The standard rules are available as an option.

The player who wins the first three rounds of the game goes on to the bonus round with a chance for the BIG money. There are more than 1,200 phrases packed into this fast paced and addictive program which features pop-up instructions, mute switch, and a moving Vanna.

(PC-SIG Disk# 891)

Special Requirements: *None.*
Author Registration: *$2.00 ($24.95 for expanded version with more game phrases)*

VMS Vocabulary Management System *by David G. Bodnar*

Create customized learning games for your children or students to help them improve their vocabularies, sharpen their spelling and learn new subjects. A variety of educational games can be created suitable to any age level from six year olds to adult and covering almost any topic.

The EDITOR allows you to compile facts and word lists you want used in the five different games.

WORD SEARCH makes printed word search puzzles and anagram puzzles. TEST PRINTER makes printed match-the-word-to-its-definition puzzles. A sample included is STATES which challenges students to match the states of the United States with their associated capitals, mottos, state flowers and state birds. Similarly the program could be used to learn other subjects, such as: presidents/important acts; foreign vocabulary words/English words; metric units of measure/English units; dates in history/important events; famous writings/their authors, etc.

The other three customizable games are played on the computer. QUIZZER tests players on words and their definitions. FORTUNE provides a "Wheel of Fortune" game format where players compete to identify a word by guessing the letters of its definition. SPELLER quizzes students on the spelling of words and includes the games FLASH and ANAGRAMS.

(PC-SIG Disk# 1379)

Special Requirements: *None.*
Author Registration: *$20.00*

✍ = Updated Program
☆ = New Program

Word Gallery ✍

by David C. Swope

This educational program helps children to associate the printed word with the object it describes. Word Gallery is a set of colorful word-object flashcards. Children 4-7, will enjoy watching the screen fill with color as they match the words with their pictures. The program has four separate "games" or "levels."

When a child first gets started, he selects a picture, the computer colors it, and its word will be displayed.

After becoming familiar with the word that describes the picture, the child can advance to the next game. Here, the computer displays a word at the top of the screen. When the child selects the picture described by the word, the picture is colored.

The third game reinforces what has been learned in the first two levels. A picture is displayed and when the child selects the word which describes the picture, the picture is colored.

The last level is the real test. One of the pictures is highlighted and puts the word which describes the picture at the top of the screen. The word, however, is missing one of the letters. When the child types the missing letter on the keyboard, the picture is colored and the complete word displayed.

In all levels, when correct answers are given and the screen has been colored, a song will play. This is a fun program for kids with lots of rewards and lots of learning!

(PC-SIG Disk# 2225)

Special Requirements: *350K RAM, MCGA or CGA. VGA or EGA recommended.*
Author Registration: *$17.50*

Word-Part Dictionary

by Edicom Systems

Get ready for your placement tests while you enhance your word power with WORD-PART Dictionary. The database of this system boasts 500 word parts and 2,000 related words with concise definitions.

The program enables you to learn new words with ease and speed since it allows you to study a group of related words at a time, each stemming from a common root word part. For example, a search of the root "retro" brings up on the screen: retroactive, retrocede, retroflex, and retrograde — along with their definitions. You get a highly selected list of word parts related to about 70 percent of the tough words in a typical SAT, ACT, CBAT, or GRE verbal test. The system is menu-driven and has on-line instructions.

(PC-SIG Disk# 1534)

Special Requirements: *None.*
Author Registration: *$24.00*

Word-Part Dictionary (PC-SIG Disk# 1534)

Wordfind

by Castle Oaks Computer Services

What's an eight letter word that starts with a "W" and means "a terrific puzzle-aid"? If you haven't guessed, the answer is WORDFIND, a sensational program for anyone who loves puzzles but doesn't always have all the answers.

WORDFIND assists in finding words for crossword puzzles and other types of word puzzles such as acrostics. Type in the word with a wild card symbol for the letters you don't know. WORDFIND searches its files and tells you every word that meets the letter requirements. You decide which word meets the crossword's definition.

WORDFIND contains a dictionary full of words, from two letters to 20 letters long. This program is perfect for frustrated crossword players and budding cryptogram pundits.

(PC-SIG Disk#'s 2434, 2435)

Special Requirements: *None.*
Author Registration: *$15.00*

Words
by BAD Software

Get the edge in school or business with this precisely done vocabulary enhancement tool! You know that people judge you by the clothes you wear, but did you realize that they also judge you by your vocabulary? Well, now's the time to use this smartly designed software to increase your working vocabulary to further your career in the business world or in school!

This well designed package allows you to test yourself by seeing either the word itself or the word definition in the quiz format. You can use the author's initial 100 word starter vocabulary set to familiarize yourself with the software. With registration, you'll receive the 500 word vocabulary file. You can create your own specialized vocabulary files for specific learning tasks, whether it be a foreign language or a specialized interest area, such as computers! With a separate utility you can also define the screen colors most appealing to you. The program is fast, and elegant in its simplicity; a must for students!

(PC-SIG Disk#'s 1998, 1999)

Special Requirements: *A hard drive is recommended.*
Author Registration: *$15.00*

Words*Words ✍
by Blanchard Software

A sophisticated word game, WORDS*WORDS is a logical deduction puzzle in which puzzle words are linked to quotations and proverbs. You have to deduce five-letter puzzle words by guessing no more than 18 words. For each guess WORDS*WORDS tells you how many letters are common to the puzzle word. For example, if the puzzle word was "drums" and you guessed "stump" the program would tell you that "3" letters match. The program uses a 6000 word dictionary to check your guess words.

The instructions are simple to follow. Function keys let you save letters that are part of the word or discard letters that are not part of the word, which helps you organize your thoughts.

There are no flashy colors or graphics, but if you love intellectual exercise, the 50 carefully chosen puzzle words and quotations will amuse you and challenge you for many hours.

This program could be used for helping children with spelling and word associations. An amusing yet challenging game for ages 12 and up, WORD*WORD breaks through its simple format with its tough puzzle solving.

(PC-SIG Disk# 1897)

Special Requirements: *None.*
Author Registration: *$15.00*

▼ ▼ ▼

Sports Management

BikeInfo ✍
by Constantine Roussos

If you're into cycling and want accurate performance statistics about your bike and your ride, BIKEINFO is a program which generates speed and gear ratio characteristics of a multi-speed bicycle (such as a 10, 12 or 18 speed bicycle).

The user is required to input the size of the tires in inches and the number of gear teeth in the front and rear gears (i.e. the chain rings and the sprockets). The program will then generate information like the gear ratios for the different speeds, and the miles per hour for different cadences such as 60 and 90 pedals per minute.

(PC-SIG Disk# 2017)

Special Requirements: *None.*
Author Registration: *None.*

Bowl - 101 ✍
by Randy Stowe

At long last, some help for all of you overworked bowling league secretaries. Let BOWL-101 handle the drudgery of maintaining the records.

Completely menu-driven, this was written with the novice PC user in mind. BOWL-101 pairs teams for you. Enter the three or four games for each bowler in the order they bowled, and it does the rest.

✍ = Updated Program
☆ = New Program

BOWL-101 handles high team and individual games and series. Scratch and handicapped, mixed or not, are done automatically. Keeping individual averages for several weeks is no problem. Errors are easy to correct: any team, bowler, sub, high game, name, or score may be changed with just a few keystrokes. It can handle 36 teams, 100 substitutes, 10 bowlers/subs per team. Auto lane assignments are totally configurable for match points, scratch, handicap, or mixed league in any combination. There are over 70 pop-up help screens, and easy edit features. Data can be sent to screen, printer or disk.

(PC-SIG Disk# 1246)

Special Requirements: *384K RAM*
Author Registration: *$49.95*

Bowling League Secretary
by William W. Klaproth

So you've been fingered to run the company bowling league, eh? No problem. This software, aptly called BOWLING LEAGUE SECRETARY, will make your job a snap. The package includes 12 programs that cover everything needed to run a league.

This highly generalized system handles league name, team, configuration, handicap basis, and schedule. As distributed, the system can handle 24 teams, up to nine bowlers per team, and up to a 50-week season.

Programs are provided to start all master files, enter scores and print standings (weekly), as well as prepare book average listings, final team/bowler standings, and display or print individual team/bowler record sheets.

(PC-SIG Disk# 23)

Special Requirements: *none.*
Author Registration: *$25.00*

Bowling League Secretary's System
by Lloyd C. Bowen Jr.

Take the tedium out of a time-consuming task.

BOWLING LEAGUE SECRETARY'S SYSTEM takes information like league name, bowling place, league type, team configuration, handicap basis, and schedule, compiles the data and starts all master files, prepares weekly standings, book average listings, final team/bowler standings and individual team/bowler record sheets.

The system can handle 40 teams, up to ten bowlers per team (400 total), and up to a 50-week season. BOWLING LEAGUE SECRETARY is menu-driven and has on-line help.

(PC-SIG Disk# 884)

Special Requirements: *None.*
Author Registration: *$25.00*

BowlSTAT ✍
by Kevin J. Stone

Bowling statisticians relax, BOWLSTAT keeps track of up to 300 bowlers on as many as 99 teams. Supports Tenpin, Candlepin, and Fivepin bowling games. Generates bowling schedules, nightly captain sheets, weekly, monthly, and yearly statistics for each bowler, and printouts as needed.

Most "standard" league individual awards have been included along with an option for saving of average sheets to the disk drive for wordprocessor integration. The program is completely "SMART MENU" driven so there is no need to learn a bunch of commands.

Keeps track of the individual statistics — name, pinfall, number of strings bowled, average, high single, high triple, high no mark, 69's, and team statistics — name, points won, points lost, total pinfall, team high pinfall, and percent of wins vs losses.

(PC-SIG Disk#'s 1953, 1954)

Special Requirements: *512K RAM.*
Author Registration: *$35.00*

Diver's Logbook
by RTD Software Systems

DIVER'S LOG is for the active scuba diver or scuba club to record information about each dive for future retrieval and analysis. Keep track of dive number, location, date, weather, and surface conditions.

Now you can back up your paper log in case of loss, theft or damage. It's an insurance policy for your dive log. Or, simply use it to review locations for the name of that great dive spot you want to dive again. The program is completely menu driven. You can store up to 1,024 dives in a single directory.

(PC-SIG Disk# 2050)

Special Requirements: *None.*
Author Registration: *$15.00*

Double Bogie Killer   *by Midwest Software Systems*

DOUBLE BOGIE KILLER is a golf stats/database used to track on-course performance.

For each hole played, three data items are recorded: gross, putts and fairways. Course data such as yardages, hole pars and course ratings are taken from the scorecard and recorded into the course database. Your stats for each round are entered into your player file.

The following reports can be run at any time after the first hole has been entered: overall summary, course by course review, USGA handicap and nine-hole handicap report, scoring percentages and efficiency Analysis. Send reports to a disk or printer.

(PC-SIG Disk# 984)

Special Requirements: *Two floppy drives.*
Author Registration: *$25.00*

Fantasy Sports Drafter ✍   *by Potato League Sports*

What is more fun than collecting and trading baseball cards; permits you to rub elbows with owners, starters and free agents; provides you the opportunity to compete against other players; and, doesn't stick to most dental work? It's Fantasy Leagues!

FANTASY LEAGUES are springing up across the country, covering baseball, football, basketball — all major league sports. Developing your fantasy team from the real players in the major leagues, you earn points depending on how a real player performs during a season. But how do you put your team together?

FANTASY SPORT DRAFTER provides you with a computerized opponent in the team draft arena. You can go up against it as many times as you wish, learning the ins and outs of actual fantasy drafting. When you're finished, you'll have assembled your own team from the best of the major leagues in that sport. You'll hardly be able to wait for the start of the season.

After you have developed your team, FANTASY SPORT DRAFTER allows you to submit your picks to a fantasy sports center to compete in an actual drafting contest. Your team may win the title of Fantasy Team Champion.

(PC-SIG Disk# 2078)

Special Requirements: *Hard drive is recommended.*
Author Registration: *$19.95*

Fish-N-Log Plus ✍   *by Taysys*

Want to catch a lot more fish? Want your fishing excursions to be more productive today and far more productive tomorrow? The serious angler will find this computerized fisherman's logbook the answer to an empty creel.

FISH-N-LOG lets you log important facts about your fishing trip by answering questions asked by the program. You are queried in detail about each fishing trip as to weather conditions, water levels and conditions, moon phase, feeding times, "hot spots", methods used, lures or bait used, depth, and much more. Angling sophisticates who use solunar time as a means of predicting when fish bite will find FISH-N-LOG very helpful. With this information you'll be able to duplicate successful fishing trips in the future.

You can enter an "endless narrative" regarding situations you want to detail. Reports to refresh your memory of previous trips are recalled by location, month, or location and month with the results listed on screen. The registered version offers a print option.

(PC-SIG Disk# 1659)

Special Requirements: *None.*
Author Registration: *$9.95*

✍ = Updated Program
☆ = New Program

FishBase II

by Richard Olsen

FISHBASE lets devoted fishermen, amateur and professional, keep track of their favorite fishing holes — to catch more, bigger fish in the future. It's a database diary in which you record all the important facts about the fish you catch, so you can return to the scene of your success. It holds up to 1000 fishing trips. In addition to location, you can record weather conditions, water temperature, size of fish caught, and which lures you used to catch them. You can even note items such as the phase of the moon, in order to find out when the bass are likely to spawn. You can also print many reports from your data.

Currently in use by several "pros," this program will also be of interest to fishing clubs for competitions. The many help windows move the program along swimmingly, and they are backed up by a hefty user guide guaranteed to hook you.

FishBase II (PC-SIG Disk# 1358)

(PC-SIG Disk# 1358)

Special Requirements: *Graphics card.*
Author Registration: *$15.00*
➤*ASP Member.*

Foursome Generator

by Software Assistance Co.

FOURSOME GENERATOR automatically calculates foursomes (teams of four) for golf tournaments based upon their handicaps. The program allows you to keep a running roster of members eligible to play, including address, phone number, and handicap. Information can be updated at any time. From the roster you mark those who are going to play in a tournament. FOURSOME GENERATOR generates foursomes so all teams will have an equal or almost equal handicap total. Other options include:

❑ Link players who want to play together while maintaining equal foursomes
❑ Produce mixed foursomes (male and female pairing)
❑ Up to 24 trial calculations (no repeats if same players participate week after week)
❑ Generate low/high foursomes
❑ Generate random foursomes
❑ Players can be ranked in four different groupings
❑ Tee times generated automatically
❑ Sort roster on any field
❑ Print address labels and print reports to printer, disk, or screen.

(PC-SIG Disk# 1174)

Special Requirements: *None.*
Author Registration: *$69.95*

Golf Handicapper

by Leithauser Research

GOLF HANDICAPPER is a combination golf score database and handicap calculator. It can hold the most recent 20 scores of up to 1000 players. When a player enters a new score, the program automatically calculates his or her current handicap, their net score for this game, and their handicap for the next game. The program can be used by an individual player, a team of players, or an entire golf club.

The program is easy to figure out, even if you haven't used any type of database before. The program is also complete, even taking into account the rating of your home course.

(PC-SIG Disk# 1827)

Special Requirements: *None.*
Author Registration: *$25.00*

Golf Scorekeeper

by Brian Squires

If it were just you and three close friends going out to the links once a week for a game of golf, keeping track of everyone's score would be easy. But if the rest of the men and women in your department, or the members of your club, found out about your weekends on the local courses, scorekeeping could get to be a burden. If this nightmare has come true, there's no need to sell your clubs for a skiing outfit. Now there's GOLF SCOREKEEPER.

Some of the features of GOLF SCOREKEEPER are: The ability to record an unlimited number of players and courses in its definition area; Player history reports, either full history or by course; team definition and scorekeeping; player and course ranking reports and a foursome or fivesome report generator. All players and golf courses defined are maintained in RAM for fast access and are shadowed on disk in case of any unexpected power loss.

In addition to all this, GOLF SCOREKEEPER provides pull-down menus, special hot-keys, context-sensitive help screens and full mouse support.

Probably the only thing GOLF SCOREKEEPER won't do is remind you to keep your head down.

(PC-SIG Disk# 2086)
Special Requirements: *None.*
Author Registration: *$25.00*

Graphic Coach
by Dunnigan Designs

GRAPHICS COACH gives serious runners of all levels an easy way to monitor their training, progress, and plans for improving fitness and race performance. Personal advice is given that establishes a training schedule based upon the runner's time for a 5K or a 10K run.

Monthly and yearly graphs and tables display the runner's pace, average speed, and total distance run. A practical, useful program for any runner who wants to improve and pace his/her running ability.

(PC-SIG Disk# 849)
Special Requirements: *CGA.*
Author Registration: *$24.95*

High Points
by Carter Scholz

HIGH POINTS belongs at your next meet or sporting event. Designed to assist in judging competitive events, it calculates and provides judges (and journalists) with tallies and standings, instantly.

The program handles events of one to 10 rounds with up to 400 participants grouped by one to 10 classes. The data entry screen is self explanatory and the documentation contains many useful hints and precautions for the actual events.

Save data to a file or print results of a round or current standings at any time. There is even a supplementary program to help resolve ties when the judges are required to include secondary criteria.

(PC-SIG Disk# 1315)
Special Requirements: *None.*
Author Registration: *$20.00*

PC-Golf
by E. H. Chandler

PC-GOLF is a score analysis program for all levels of golfers and golf instructors. Don't throw your clubs in the water hazard! Analyze your failings and fix your game.

Enter your game scores and course ratings for the courses you play to find the problem areas in your game. Keep track of how you do by course and by hole. Record practice games and handicaps. Compute gross and adjusted scores and average strokes for each player for each hole. Nine tables and graphs illustrate areas needing improvement.

Improved player performance is the focus so let your PC do the analysis while you concentrate on your game. And keep your head down!

(PC-SIG Disk# 262)
Special Requirements: *A version of BASIC.*
Author Registration: *$20.00*

PC-Sport
by Geoffrey Celic Monkley

You have just been awarded the position of sports director at your local club and your first responsibility is the club's annual all-county table tennis tournament. Twenty members from seven clubs will be arriving and it's your job to figure who plays who and when. The local sport store has never heard of table tennis statistic books and no one in your club knows anything about producing player charts. What do you do?

🖉 = Updated Program
☆ = New Program

You call on PC-SPORT. In one easy-to-use program, PC-SPORT takes information on your club or organization, the type of sport activity you will be dealing with, the number of players involved, their names and their organizations, etc., and prepares a database entry screen for statistic recording. PC-SPORT will also help you prepare those round robin, or ladder-style play charts. PC-SPORT is the sports directors' assistant.

(PC-SIG Disk# 2079)

Special Requirements: *None.*
Author Registration: *$40.00*

Pro Football Linemaker ✍ *by American Precision Instruments*

The PRO FOOTBALL LINEMAKER program uses the results of past football games to project the results of future games. You update the database with stats from this week's games (available in most national and local newspapers), then scores and expected statistical results for next week's games can be projected. The program will project the expected results of a game between any two teams selected.

In addition to providing you with the expected point spread between the two teams, you are provided with valuable information such as: projected passing, rushing, and total play yardages, projected first downs, projected lost fumbles, projected time of possession, projected times sacked, and much more.

You can generate a printout showing a detailed analysis of how the projections were calculated, select a less detailed printout of the projections, or have the projections displayed only to your monitor. The program also allows you to get involved in the development of the spreads, projections, and statistical categories used.

(PC-SIG Disk# 1905)

Special Requirements: *384K RAM.*
Author Registration: *$17.00*

Pro Football Picks ☆ *by ALC Software*

Attention football fanatics! PRO FOOTBALL PICKS (PFP) is a football handicapping program that takes into account the 'Betting Spread' (Points) to predict winning teams. Data required to use PFP is readily obtained from the daily newspapers.

According to the author, it has been used for five years with an accuracy of up to 73%! For those preferring under/over betting, the probable points scored is also provided. PFP is compatible with all 1991 season changes. All relevant statistics from the 1990 season are included to improve accuracy. Additional information, such as 1991 team schedules and a database of how each team performed vs. the spread over the past three years, are just a few keystrokes away.

(PC-SIG Disk# 2675)

Special Requirements: *None. Mouse supported.*
Author Registration: *$28.00*

SailScor *by Softab*

SAILSCOR is a very powerful and comprehensive sailboat race scoring program. It's a quick and easy way to score sailboat races, print results and maintain seasonal standings. It features automatic prompting of race results on a boat-by-boat basis, thereby eliminating the need to enter a boat's description more than once. Ties are automatically broken using the standard tie breaking rules. Multiple copies of the results are generated without a copier or running the program multiple times.

Easy-to-use menus simplify each step, from the creation of a fleet, to the printing of individual race results, regatta results and seasonal standings. This program also contains an extensive set of editing capabilities so that fleet information easily can be updated and corrected. It uses the three standard methods of scoring races: the high point method, the low point method, and the olympic method.

(PC-SIG Disk# 1801)

Special Requirements: *None.*
Author Registration: *$19.95*

SimBase *by Philip M. Smith*

SIMBASE is a baseball simulation program. It contains data for two teams. This program gives you a tool to analyze the value of a particular player or a group of players to the team over the course of one or more full seasons. It lets you review the pluses and minuses of different player lineups. And it provides a framework where you can forecast the likely outcome for a full baseball season. To really use SIMBASE productively, you must run a large number of games and look at the averages. Once you are familiar with the program, you will want to amend the LINEUPS.DAT file by shuffling or adding and subtracting players. This is easily done with any wordprocessor that reads and writes ASCII files.

(PC-SIG Disk#'s 1186, 1187)

Special Requirements: *None.*
Author Registration: *$50.00*

Soff Balls ✍   *by Jeffrey Gene Elwood*

SOFF BALLS was designed to make life easier for you. Keep records for a softball team, baseball team, or a whole league. Enter game results and SOFF BALLS keeps all the statistics.

SOFF BALLS is also easy to use. At the beginning of the season, enter team names and rosters. As each game is played, enter the game score and statistics for each player. Display or print the team's or player's current hitting statistics.

Though SOFF BALLS does not produce standings for leagues, it tracks the following statistics for 20 teams and up to 9,999 players: TAB, OAB, H, R, D, T, HR, SAC, B, SO, SA, BA.

(PC-SIG Disk# 2486)

Special Requirements: *270K RAM and video board*
Author Registration: *$25.00*
➤*ASP Member.*

Sports League Management   *by Sports League Mgmt Assoc*

Go ahead and volunteer to be your kid's team manager or coach. The work will be easy with this software package. SPORTS MANAGER helps you manage any sports team — Little League, Pop Warner, American Legion, etc.

It consists of three modules. The main module, TeamMgrM, contains information on players that is considered necessary for proper administration. Module TeamMgrC is to be used by the manager or coach for maintaining running comments on the performance of the various players on his team. Module TeamMgrD maintains information on the league and team required for day to day administration. Three packages designed for maintaining statistical information on baseball/softball, football, or basketball teams and players are immediately available from the author.

(PC-SIG Disk#'s 1844, 1845)

Special Requirements: *PKUNZIP unarchiving program (PC-SIG disk #1364).*
Author Registration: *$20.00*

Sports Statbook, The   *by RJL System*

If you're in charge of tracking stats for hockey, soccer, volleyball or other team sports, STATBOOK will significantly reduce the time and effort you spend. Appropriate for pro, semipro, high school, college and company-sponsored teams, it automatically tracks and provides year- to-date and/or historical player statistics. This software is currently used by such teams as Hockey Central of Philadelphia and the LA Kings. The documentation is extensive and helpful.

(PC-SIG Disk#'s 1426, 1427)

Special Requirements: *None.*
Author Registration: *$40.00*

▼ ▼ ▼

Spreadsheet Templates

Lotus Financial Worksheets   *by Tim Keller*

Lotus 1-2-3 financial worksheets for a small business — powerful enough for the veteran 1-2-3 user, yet friendly to beginners. Accounting templates include a check book controller, cash flow managers, an EOQ inventory mananger, depreciation and loan calculators. The macro library is sophisticated and requires reading of the included documentation.

(PC-SIG Disk# 304)
Special Requirements: *Lotus 1-2-3.*
Author Registration: *None.*

File Descriptions:

ADC	WKS	ACRS Depreciation Calc.
ARC	WKS	Accounts receivable collections tracker.
CBB	WKS	Check book balancer.
CFM	WKS	Cash flow manager.
CDB	WKS	Cash disbursements.
EIO	WKS	EOQ inventory ordering.
CFP	WKS	Cash flow projection.
FFS	WKS	5-in-1 financial statement.
GCC	WKS	Growth capacity calculator.
IIB	WKS	Interactive income statement.
IRR	WKS	Internal rate-of-return.
LCT	WKS	Line-of-Credit tracker.
LNP	WKS	Loan payoff calculator.
LNA	WKS	Loan amortization.
MACRO_1	DOC	Documentation for MACLIB.WKS (5K).
MACLIB	WKS	Lotus 1-2-3 Macros Library-combined into most worksheets.
OLDBULL	DOC	Doc file of all bulletins from the Capitol PC BBS.
NVB	WKS	New venture budget.
QA1	WKS	Queue analysis (single-station service facility).
PVA	WKS	Price volume analysis.
STC	WKS	Statistics calculator.
RAR	WKS	Ratio analyzer.
QGN	WKS	Quote generator - form and tracker.
QAM	WKS	Queue analysis (multi-station service facility).

Lotus Worksheets and Macros   *by F. CHARLES LOPPINCOTT*

A broad-ranging collection of Lotus 1-2-3 technical notes, utility programs, operation hints and templates for both the power user and the novice.

Features:

- Create address labels
- Make menu macros
- Import files
- Learn about /Xl macros
- Construct a macro library
- A for-next loop
- Learn to document formulas
- Build a table for range names
- Understand the /datafill Function
- Tech notes on many Lotus capabilities

(PC-SIG Disk# 301)
Special Requirements: *Lotus 1-2-3.*
Author Registration: *$15.00*

The Retirement Financial Projector   *by George R. Anderson*

Retiring soon? You need to plan your retirement finances if you want to enjoy the good life. THE RETIREMENT FINANCIAL PROJECTOR is just the program that can do it for you.

The RETIREMENT FINANCIAL PROJECTOR is designed primarily for the person who is contemplating retirement in a few years. However, if your retirement is far in the future, or if you have already retired, you will also find it useful. If you plan to retire soon, the projector provides a guide that leads you through the process of analyzing your retirement assests and needs, so that you can determine what you must accomplish in order to achieve the retirement lifestyle you desire. The RETIREMENT FINANCIAL PROJECTOR consists of two unique Lotus 1-2-3 templates, an expenses template and a projection template.

The projection template allows a parametric evaluation of investment growth through your retirement years. Investment returns, inflation, and retirement income are built-in parameters. Investment options, such as annuities, life insurance, and tax deferred investments also may be studied parametrically. The capability of incorporating other parameters is limited only by your imagination and spreadsheet skill.

The expenses template tracks and projects the expenses you have today and what they will be during your retirement years.

The RETIREMENT FINANCIAL PROJECTOR can provide you with the opportunity to plan and project your retirement finances so that you can really live the good life.

(PC-SIG Disk# 1875)
Special Requirements: *Lotus 1-2-3.*
Author Registration: *$25.00*

Scientific & Engineering Tools for Lotus
by K.I.T.A.L. Software

This is a template for people who are already well-versed in Lotus 1-2-3 and are interested in applying it to solving more advanced statistical problems. Among other things it simplifies the use of simple arithmetic, facilitates statistical macro programming, calculates frequency distribution and normal distribution of data, and does four types of curve-fitting. The template taps Lotus' mathematical abilities to solve complicated problems and to permit the user to customize it to his or her particular needs.

It is similar in concept to other spreadsheet templates in that it makes the macro language and advanced formula functions more accessible to the user. However, it is specialized in the area of engineering-type statistics.

(PC-SIG Disk# 1988)
Special Requirements: *Lotus 1-2-3 version 2.01, and a hard drive is recommended.*
Author Registration: *$20.00*

Whiterock Alternative
by New York Lotus Disks

The WHITEROCK ALTERNATIVE is a macro-driven worksheet shell (AUTO123.WKS) for Lotus 1-2-3 worksheets with four very useful applications: a checkbook manager, mailing list, loan amortizer and a jobcosting/time management worksheet.

AUTO123.WKS is a worksheet manager that allows access to other 1-2-3 worksheets. Supported by clever screen graphics, the WHITEROCK ALTERNATIVE applications are a pleasure to use. A library of 1-2-3 macros is also included.

(PC-SIG Disk# 583)
Special Requirements: *Two floppy drives and Lotus 1-2-3 v2.0.*
Author Registration: *$15.00*

▼ ▼ ▼

Spreadsheet Utilities and Education

Lotus Learning System
by ECC Learning Systems

THE LOTUS LEARNING SYSTEM is designed to teach the novice computer user how to use LOTUS 1-2-3. The program starts by how to use the tutorial and its menu structure.

Choose the option you would like to start with. From this menu you may choose spreadsheet background, applications for LOTUS 1-2-3, keyboard features, menu structure, commands, access system, control panel features, and more. Practice copying, moving, formatting, inserting, retrieving, saving, columns, and more in a look and feel simulation of Lotus 1-2-3. A 130-page workbook comes with registration. A must for anyone about to buy, or who already has, LOTUS 1-2-3.

Lotus Learning System (PC-SIG Disk# 846)

(PC-SIG Disk#'s 846, 847)
Special Requirements: *512K RAM and two floppy drives.*
Author Registration: *$79.95*

Menu-Range for Lotus 1-2-3
by K.I.T.A.L. Software

MENU-RANGE is a spreadsheet template which works with Lotus 1-2-3 and Quattro and allows the user to designate any range in the spreadsheet as an active menu. This allows the construction of custom applications in which the user selects from menu options, without the usual limitations in the number of options available at one time. Thus, it is possible to avoid complex nested menus which increase the possibilities for error. A helpful feature is the inclusion of different versions of the template for users of Lotus 1-2-3, and Quattro. In fact there are three different versions; one for 1-2-3 users, one for Quattro users, and one for users who run Quattro in 1-2-3 menu emulation mode.

This powerful program is best suited to those already well versed in Lotus 1-2-3 or Quattro. MENU-RANGE will appeal particularly to sophisticated users of Lotus 1-2-3 and Quattro who must build spreadsheets containing a large number of complex calculations that are repeated frequently. They will find MENU-RANGE a very useful tool. Normally these people rely heavily on the programs' macro abilities. MENU-RANGE will allow those macros to be listed on a menu and selected by moving the cursor/light bar to the appropriate entry and pressing ENTER.

MENU-RANGE can also be helpful to users responsible for building spreadsheets to be updated or analyzed by people who are not expert in the spreadsheet program itself. The process of updating may be automated through the creation of macros that may then be selected from the menu. Less experienced users can then take advantage of the powerful features of 1-2-3 and Quattro which would normally be beyond their reach.

Like any template, MENU-RANGE will add to the memory overhead of a spreadsheet, so users with scarce memory may find that they cannot

(PC-SIG Disk# 1989)

Special Requirements: *Lotus 1-2-3 or Quattro.*
Author Registration: *$20.00*

Templates of Doom
by Solar Systems Software

Learn how to use Lotus 1-2-3 with an adventure game! TEMPLATES OF DOOM makes learning spreadsheets fun and entertaining. DOOM makes learning spreadsheets fun and entertaining. It's a self-paced guide that helps teach the beginning user how to select and use spreadsheet commands such as: erase cells, change column widths, create graphs and even more.

Whether your're an experienced computer spreadsheet user or an eager beginner, TEMPLATES OF DOOM is a whole new learning adventure. A clever alternative to a stuffy spreadsheet manual, this easy-to-use program presents you with 25 related but increasingly complex and challenging puzzles.

You solve the puzzle against a ticking clock and piece together a story full of colorful characters, wild events and exotic places, using a variety of spreadsheet commands and formulas. If you get stuck, there are four levels of programmed help to rescue you.

(PC-SIG Disk# 2156)

Special Requirements: *LOTUS 1-2-3, QUATTRO, or VP-PLANNER*
Author Registration: *69.95*

▼ ▼ ▼

Spreadsheets

ALITE ☆
by Trius, Inc.

The folks that brought you AS-EASY-AS have a new "lite"version of their popular program. ALITE is a powerful spreadsheet program with graphics and minimum hardware requirements. The program should run on any IBM or compatible computer with 256K or more (that's right, only 256k), equipped with a Mono, CGA or EGA monitor. It's ideal for laptops where memory space is at a premium.

Graphics may be printed on any 9-pin Epson or graphics compatible printer, or .PIC files may be created for inclusion in other programs.

Features:
- 2048 rows by 128 columns
- Mathematical, logical, statistical, financial, string, user-defined, and date functions
- Macro Command Language
- Five types of graphs with Merge and Split Screen features
- File Merge, File Extract and File Linking

ALITE (PC-SIG Disk #2557)

❑ .WKS and .WK1 file compatibility
❑ Data Sort
❑ Data Regression and much more...
(PC-SIG Disk# 2557)
Special Requirements: *256K RAM.*
Author Registration: *$20.00 + $5.00 S&H*
➤*ASP Member.*

AsEasyAs ✍

by Trius, Inc.

ASEASYAS is an enhanced and refined spreadsheet program that
supports 256 columns and 8,192 rows. It has a high degree of command
compatibility with Lotus 1-2-3, lets you use Lotus files and includes a
broad range of formulas and functions.

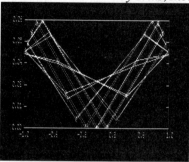

Unlike many other spreadsheet programs, however, ASEASYAS can
plot 11 different types of graphs from within the program. ASEASYAS
is very easy to use because you enter commands through on-screen
menus, unlike Lotus. Other unique features include direct dBase III
import/export, spreadsheet auditing, search and replace, macro record
and playback, goalseeking, spreadsheet linking, and a full complement
of macro commands. There is also a linked calculation sequence that
saves considerable time when recalculating.

(PC-SIG Disk# 751)

AsEasyAs (PC-SIG Disk# 751)

Special Requirements: *384K RAM.*
Author Registration: *$50.00*
➤*ASP Member.*

ExpressCalc

by Expressware Corporation

EXPRESSCALC is a spreadsheet with a wide variety of applications ranging from business forecasts to
mortgage calculations.

It does not require programming background to be able to use it, and will interface with other files and databases
— allowing an exchange of information. Included is a tutorial, good documentation and the option to configure
the package to specific systems. EXPRESSCALC supports spreadsheets up to 64 columns by 256 lines. Each
column can be up to 75 characters long.

(PC-SIG Disk#'s 524, 525)

Special Requirements: *512K RAM.*
Author Registration: *$59.95*
➤*ASP Member.*

EZ-Spreadsheet ✍

by EZX Publishing

You too can become a spreadsheet pro in 20 minutes or less! EZ-SPREADSHEET won't confuse you, try your
patience, or force you to learn 457 commands to get started. What you get is a spreadsheet that will produce 64
columns by 512 rows; more than enough for 99% of users' needs. For Epson type printers, a sideways printing
program is supplied. Includes printed manual/tutorial plus 5 sample spreadsheets.

Construct your own spreadsheet or use one of the templates included. The applications provided range from
budget worksheets and loan calculators to savings plans and financial statements. A good tool for home and
business.

(PC-SIG Disk# 695)

Special Requirements: *None.*
Author Registration: *$49.00*

Freecalc

by Stilwell Software Products

FREECALC is a mature spreadsheet program with numerous features. While it lacks some of the features and
power of a product like LOTUS 1-2-3, it also lacks LOTUS's high price. As a better than average spreadsheet, it
is quite adequate for most applications. Like LOTUS, FREECALC uses all available memory (up to 640k) and is

command bar driven. FREECALC also allows for a color monitor. The disk manual is very complete and is 106 pages long.

Features:

- ❏ 250 rows by 25 columns
- ❏ Text can be entered
- ❏ Display 0 to 6 decimal places
- ❏ Print spreadsheet by disk
- ❏ Load ASCII text files
- ❏ Up to 15 significant digits
- ❏ Move, copy, delete and insert columns/rows

- ❏ Column width of 0 to 70 characters
- ❏ Left or right justified
- ❏ Macros
- ❏ Export spreadsheet to other programs
- ❏ Support for 8087 and 80287 coprocessors
- ❏ Wordprocessing mode

(PC-SIG Disk# 574)

Special Requirements: *Two floppy drives.*
Author Registration: *$47.50*

Instacalc ✍ ︎ *by FormalSoft*

INSTACALC, a recipient of *PC Magazine* Editor's Choice award, is a high-power standalone spreadsheet, yet it can be run as a TSR (pop up) spreadsheet in less than 15K of RAM. INSTACALC can then be popped up inside your word processor to cut and paste data.

INSTACALC 3 introduces standard and new features:

- ❏ Standalone or TSR operation
- ❏ Cut and paste data
- ❏ Direct 1-2-3 import/export
- ❏ Worksheet database querying
- ❏ Business graphics
- ❏ 100 @functions
- ❏ Macro recorder
- ❏ Point & shoot file manager
- ❏ Sort on 9 fields at once
- ❏ Database entry forms
- ❏ Cell protection
- ❏ EGA 43 line support
- ❏ Auditing
- ❏ EMS support
- ❏ Context sensitive help

- ❏ Pop up through other programs
- ❏ TSR uses K RAM
- ❏ Querying of dBase files
- ❏ Goal seeking
- ❏ Larger sheet (256 by 4096)
- ❏ Powerful macro language
- ❏ Macro editor/debugger
- ❏ File linking
- ❏ Password file encryption
- ❏ Search & replace
- ❏ Matrix math
- ❏ Frequency distributions
- ❏ Options setting sheets
- ❏ Mouse support
- ❏ Much, much more

(PC-SIG Disk# 710)

Special Requirements: *Two drives.*
Author Registration: *$49.00*
➤*ASP Member.*

PC-Calc+ *by Buttonware*

If value means good product for the "right" price, then PC-CALC+ is outstanding value raised to the nth power. You will find a multitude of capabilities in this power package that makes for an unbeatable spreadsheet combination.

Math functions like absolute value, integer, modulo, natural log, round, sine, square root, true integer, 14 different trigonometric functions, and more are included. 8087/80287/80387 math coprocessors are automatically utilized if detected. You will find all the basic and not-so-basic statistical functions included, such as average, weighted average, count, maximum, minimum, standard deviation, sum, linear regression, binomial distribution, normal distribution, and Poisson distribution.

Data can be imported and exported from files from PC-File:dB, PC-File+, PC-Type/ASCII files, DIF, Lotus 1-2-3, and comma-delimited files. You can also import blocks from other PC-Calc+ spreadsheets. Printing options include printing entire spreadsheet or selected range, print to disk or printer, print sideways, use escape codes, pause between pages, and using single-, double- or triple-spacing. You can save 25 macros per file to eliminate repetitive keystrokes. PC-CALC+ spreadsheets can handle 256 columns and 8000 rows with 255 characters per cell. After you're done with your number crunching, create bar and pie charts, or line and scatter diagrams. Also, multiple variables can be graphed and accumulated.

PC-CALC+ combines number-crunching power, graphing and flexible report options for an ideal spreadsheet. PC-CALC+'s pop-up menus and context- sensitive help screens make it a pleasure to use

(PC-SIG Disk#'s 199, 1016, 1017)

Special Requirements: *280K RAM and a hard drive.*
Author Registration: *$69.95*
➤*ASP Member.*

Power Sheets
by Al Baker

PC Magazine calls POWER SHEETS "the most powerful, pure spreadsheet on the market" and labels it "easy to use." Corporations such as Ford, AMOCO and First Chicago are using it to develop sophisticated turnkey applications beyond the capabilities of other spreadsheets.

POWER SHEETS offers three-dimensional data presentations with the ability to rotate the data cube to view slices in other orientations. A special language gives POWER SHEETS programmability. Pop-up menus guide users through all functions.

Other spreadsheets operate on ranges; POWER SHEETS goes further, using lists involving a combination of ranges, cell references, or formulae. Another feature allows it to base the bounds of a range on the values of other cells, and provides for true date and time math. All functions are fully recursive and can be nested to any depth. The upshot is the availability of 16 million cells.

POWER SHEETS reads and writes .DIF files either row-wise or column-wise. It reads and writes ASCII files either non-delimited or delimited with any choice of delimiters. Its rich function library includes trig and log functions, statistical and Boolean functions, yes-no-maybe logic, and sophisticated case function.

(PC-SIG Disk#'s 1284, 1285)

Special Requirements: *None.*
Author Registration: *$19.95.*

▼ ▼ ▼

Statistical Programs

Easy Stats by Langley ☆
by Russell Langley, Dr.

EASY-STATS provides a menu of 21 programs which compute over 100 statistics, including most major research tools up to two-way ANOVA, regression with two predictors, and one-way ANCOVA. It also provides a number of unique features that make it extremely valuable even for devotees of mainframe or larger commercial packages. Unique features include a dandy matrix operations program that provides 18 routine matrix manipulations familiar to statisticians (e.g., eigenvalues and eigenvectors). If you have ever been caught without your statistical tables handy, you'll also appreciate the program that computes critical values of z, t, F, r, and Chi-squared for specified p-values. The program also makes it easy to obtain higher-order partial correlations simply by entering the known zero-order correlations.

Permutations, combinations, factorials, and a great number of other useful procedures make this program a fine addition to the armamentarium of anyone who uses statistics. And the intuitive, interactive, menu-driven interface will encourage you to turn to it regularly — even if you are typically committed to a different program.

Limitations to 400 cases and 20 variables, as well as some procedural omissions (no MANOVA, Factor Analysis, etc.) may make EASY-STATS inappropriate for some research users. As a teaching/learning tool, though, this program has a great deal to offer. For instance, each program allows you to test the assumptions underlying the analysis, encouraging this often- neglected step. In addition, the author's sophistication about the drawbacks of null-hypothesis significance testing is revealed by his routine presentation of confidence intervals and the provision for experiment-wise error rate protection (Bonferroni procedure). And if that's not enough incentive, the programs are written in a standard BASIC that can be customized or studied easily, and both a 120-page explanatory book and program notes on diskette are available to registered users.

(PC-SIG Disk# 2671)

Special Requirements: *A high density or hard disk drive.*
Author Registration: *$60.00*

Football Scoreboard NFL 1970-1989 ☆
by Cosoft Micro Systems

You probably thought the only thing that could make Sunday football better was a large pepperoni pizza, extra cheese. That was before FOOTBALL SCOREBOARD. FOOTBALL SCOREBOARD gives you access to the results of more than 4,200 games since the NFL was merged in 1970.

Every NFL game has been included with such information as: the teams that played (and their conferences), the week and year the game was played, the home/visiting team, and the final score. Specify any combination of the data and display it on your computer or send it to your printer.

FOOTBALL SCOREBOARD provides:

❑ Conference records and standings of the teams for a week, range of weeks, a year, a group of years, or all the years since 1970

(What's the 49'ers record since 1970? How about from 1980 through 1989? How do they compare to other teams? What was the conference standing in week seven in 1977?)

❑ Results of games, selected by favorite team, opponent, year, or location

(What are the results of the Browns' games against the Bengals since 1985? How about when the Browns were the home team? What were the results of the Browns' conference games in 1983?)

❑ Games won and lost, the win/lose percentage, and total points statistics of any team based on when they played, who they played, and where they played

(What is the Packers' record at home since 1985? Just in conference games? What about just against the Bears? Against the Bears when they were the home team?)

FOOTBALL SCOREBOARD lets you slice and dice the football stats any way you want it. It's a great way to make your own trivia questions!

(PC-SIG Disk# 2488)
Special Requirements: *None.*
Author Registration: *$20.00*

KS Probability and Statistics
by Joseph C. Hudson

The following programs are included:

KSPROB computes probabilities, percentage points, reliability and hazard functions for 23 probability distributions. It is menu-driven, can output to the screen, printer or disk. An 80x87 is used if present, but is not required.

KSSTAT has modules for exploratory regression (CFIT), testing for normality (LILFOR) and crosstabulations (XTAB), as well as for summary statistics and histograms with breakdown variables and test mode scatter plots. Missing values can be handled; column names can be specified and are used in output.

KSPDAT produces date files that can be used for producing probability tables and graphs. Output formats can be specified by the user. Output can be either multicolumn files or multiple two column files.

KSPRBAS is a BASIC program with accurate approximations for probability distributions commonly used in introductory courses. Intended for use in hand held computers, it is very compact.

SIMCORR produces pseudo-random samples from a bivariate normal population. It illustrates the meaning of the correlation coefficient.

An extensive chart showing interrelationships between distributions is included. There are examples of graphs produced with KSPDAT output. All programs are documented.

(PC-SIG Disk#'s 985, 2123)
Special Requirements: *512K RAM, CGA, two floppy drives, DOS 3.2, and Epson compatible printer.*
Author Registration: *None.*

KwikStat ✍
by TexaSoft/Mission Technologies

KWIKSTAT is a menu-driven, Statistical Data Analysis package written by a professional statistical consultant. Used by thousands of people in over 30 countries. It contains the most commonly used data analysis procedures such as descriptive statistics, t-tests (independent group and paired), ANOVA (independent group and repeated measures), simple and multiple linear regression, crosstabulations, Chi-Square, non-parametric statistics, and survival analysis. Pixel graphics include histogram, box-plots, scattergrams, 3-D bar charts, pictograms, time series plot, pie chart, and more. KWIKSTAT contains a database system to allow you to enter and manipulate your data, including subsetting datasets and transforming data. Supports missing values. Reads and writes dBase

and ASCII files, allowing you to import data from virtually any other program. PC WEEK calls KWIKSTAT the "Number's Game Winner." John Sweeney (Tech. Analysis of Stocks and Commodities) says, "KWIKSTAT is God's answer to SPSS. It's simple to use, fast, cheap, and powerful."
(PC-SIG Disk#'s 654, 655)

Special Requirements: *384K RAM and CGA. Hard drive recommended.*
Author Registration: *$49.00*
➤*ASP Member.*

KwikStat Simulation & Concepts ☆   *by TexaSoft/Mission Technologies*

The KWIKSTAT SIMULATIONS AND CONCEPTS module can be run independently or be merged into the KwikStat menu (PC-SIG #654, #655) and be used as a regular KwikStat module.

SIMULATIONS AND CONCEPTS allows you to:

❑ Create data sets for use in KwikStat (a scientific statistical analysis system complete with graphics. You can import ASCII files, dBase III files, or build your own databases.)
❑ See simulation of Confidence Interval Estimation
❑ See simulation of the Central Limit Theorem
❑ See simulation of a Coin Flip (Probability)
(PC-SIG Disk# 2615)

Special Requirements: *CGA. PC-SIG #654 & #655 optional.*
Author Registration: *$5.00*
➤*ASP Member.*

Micro Statistics Package   *by Elmo Keller*

Here is a powerful statistical package — lots of muscle, but an unintimidating look and feel. THE MICRO STATISTICAL PACKAGE (MSP) is an integrated system consisting of a command line interpreter and a set of statistical procedures with many utility routines. Together they are used to perform analyses and mathematical operations on data stored in the program's worksheet.

This package is intended to be used by students and researchers dealing with small or medium size data analysis problems. It allows the user to perform a wide variety of statistical analyses on columns of data contained in a worksheet. The user manipulates data in a typical statistical worksheet by typing in English commands indicating actions to be taken on the column or columns of data. Commands are also provided to edit data contained in the worksheet.

There are over 100 commands, including procedures for regression, analysis of variance, correlation, Chisquare analysis of count data, plotting, sorting, transforming data, stem and leaf displays, boxplots, nonparametric statistics, cross tabulation, save and retrieval of files, letter value displays, condensed plots, pop-up reverse Polish calculator with combinations and permutations and over 25 functions, pop-up distribution calculator to compute Normal, T, F and Chisquare distribution P values and help commands.
(PC-SIG Disk# 1931)

Special Requirements: *None.*
Author Registration: *$39.95*

Stat   *by Ohio State University*

STAT is a set of data-manipulation and analysis programs developed at the University of California, San Diego, and at the Wang Institute of Graduate Studies. They were designed under the UNIX philosophy that says individual programs should be designed as tools to do one task well and produce output suitable for input to other programs.

There are two sets of STAT programs: data manipulation and data analysis. The data manipulation programs are general utilities that cooperate with other programs. The data analysis programs compute the most widely-used descriptive and inferential statistics. Although these are independent programs, the output from one program can be used as input to another. A solid knowledge of statistics and computers is assumed.
(PC-SIG Disk#'s 990, 991, 992, 2292)

Special Requirements: *None.*
Author Registration: *$15.00*

STAT
by Gerald Mele

STAT is a program that analyzes, plots and displays statistical data from internal data files or imported DBASE III and LOTUS 1-2-3 files.

The data files created may have up to 800 records, 10 fields (variables) per record, and 10 characters for the name of each variable. They can be viewed, edited, sorted, manipulated, and printed. The program can analyze the data and produce a number of graphs, including histograms, scatter plots, line plots, multi-line plots, X-Bar and R Charts, pareto charts and bar charts. STAT can also calculate the mean, median, mode, range, standard deviation, standard error of the mean, and more.

(PC-SIG Disk# 1618)

Special Requirements: *None.*
Author Registration: *None.*

The STATHELP Package ☆
by Hawkeye Softworks

STATHELP is really three independent programs: WATSTAT, a clever guide to statistical procedures that are appropriate for your data; LOOKUP, a probability calculator for z, t, F, chi-square, and binomial tests; and RANDO, a pseudo-random number generator for uniform and normal distributions plus exotica like lottery numbers, random binary, and random integers.

All three programs are menu-driven with context-sensitive Help. WATSTAT also has extensive documentation and a terrific tutorial to lead you through the steps to choosing an appropriate statistic. A great package for statistics students and teachers!

(PC-SIG Disk# 2614)

Special Requirements: *A printer for RANDO.*
Author Registration: *$20.00*

Statistical Consultant
by Dept. of Geography

The STATISTICAL CONSULTANT is an expert system to help you select the right statistical test for your problem.

The system asks you a series of questions about the variables and goals of the measurement. Based on your responses, the system chooses a statistical test or measure. Should your problem require a deeper analysis than can be addressed within CONSULTANT, the system indicates references for further study.

The program assumes a level of technical knowledge greater than that offered in a first course in statistics.

(PC-SIG Disk# 949)

Special Requirements: *None.*
Author Registration: *$8.00*

Statmate/Plus
by The Software Hill

A statistical analysis package for handling numerical data, operated by entering one-line commands and subcommands. Command "batch" files can be created for automatic execution, along with explanatory screen remarks.

STATMATE operates on information contained in a database, generated by the program. A user ID is required before entering a database, and for every new user ID, an empty database is created. This feature permits multiple users to work with STATMATE while keeping the data files separated.

Extract data from an ASCII text file and load it into the database for operation. Data is stored in columns and rows, and you can extract portions of the data according to your specifications. As you manipulate the data, the results can be displayed on the screen, printed, or saved on a disk file.

The main analytic features are elementary statistics, scatter plots, cross tabulations, histograms, data comparison using the T-Test, correlation, arithmetic operations, distribution functions, curvilinear regression, multiple regression, nonlinear regression, data recoding, and data transformation and manipulation. An on-line help facility is included to give you a detailed description of all the STATMATE commands.

(PC-SIG Disk#'s 861, 862, 863)

Special Requirements: *Two floppy drives.*
Author Registration: *$35.00*

▼ ▼ ▼

Survey Tracking

Opinion Master ✍ *by Superior Micro-Techniques*

SURVEY SYSTEM is a useful program for creating attitude or climate surveys. Anyone with minimal skills on the IBM-PC or compatible can create their own survey. You can create the kind of survey that makes a general statement and the reader then chooses one of five levels of agreement about that statement. You first create a pool of general survey statements/questions in a master file. The statements are then incorporated into your specific survey. They can be modified, deleted or moved around once on the specific survey. A neat feature of the program is it can place the survey output into text files. Once in these files, you can exit the program and use any wordprocessor with them. They print in a usable format, but if you want to get fancy or use Ventura Desktop Publishing on them, this could be useful.

(PC-SIG Disk# 1035)

Special Requirements: *320K RAM and a hard drive.*
Author Registration: *$35.00.*

▼ ▼ ▼

Tax Preparation

AM-Tax ✍   *by AM Software*

AM-TAX helps you prepare your federal tax return. It does most calculations for you and, where possible, checks if the information you entered is consistent and valid.

Because it's powerful, you can try "what if" situations. Change an income or deduction and instantly see the result on your tax balance or refund. Many commonly-used forms and schedules are supported, as well as worksheets for specific situations such as capital gains, partnership and corporate income, and estate or trust income. Information entered or calculated for a supporting form is automatically transferred to the appropriate line it supports. All the forms can be printed and filed directly with the IRS.

(PC-SIG Disk# 479)

Special Requirements: *None. Printer recommended.*
Author Registration: *$20.00/$40.00/$65.00/$125.00*

Home Office Tax 1990 ✍   *by ParyTech Associates*

LONG DESCRIPTION If you have a home office, you'll find HOME OFFICE TAX 1989 especially useful. Using simple data entry sheets, you can determine amount of your Home Office tax deduction. Once computed, it can be attached to your SCHEDULE 2106 [EMPLOYEE EXPENSE SHEET], or the amount can be entered on your SCHEDULE C [SELF-EMPLOYED PERSON] tax form.

The data forms ask for such information as: Do you own your home or rent? If owned, you'll enter mortgage information, interest, property taxes paid, and other information. If rented, you'll enter the monthly payments. In addition, you'll enter the utilities and other maintenance costs. You'll also enter the total square footage of the home and the amount of office square footage being used.

The beauty of the program is it will generate reports in far less time than it takes you to gather the data for it.

HOME OFFICE TAX 1989 is simple, functional, and beneficial to those looking for a program that determines the tax benefit of having and maintaining an office in the home.

This is not a tax preparation program. It produces only this one set of reports.

(PC-SIG Disk# 2183)

Special Requirements: *384K RAM, graphics card, DOS 2.11, and two floppy drives.*
Author Registration: *$18.00*
➤*ASP Member.*

Tax-Planner   *by William Mirabello*

TAX-PLANNER is a question-and-answer program to help you estimate the income tax you'll owe Uncle Sam. Then, you can fine-tune your paycheck deductions so you'll have enough withheld when you file your returns the next year.

You can easily modify the withholding options, such as marital status, number of exemptions and additional taxes for withholdings. You can also estimate deductions from various employers and print reports each time an estimate is completed.

(PC-SIG Disk# 982)

Special Requirements: *None.*
Author Registration: *$20.00*

▼ ▼ ▼

Teaching, Grading Systems and Record Keeping

Aeius Gradebook   *by Aeius Corporation*

AEIUS offers teachers and administrators with multiple classes a versatile way to keep grade records of every sort. A fast, comprehensive program, AEIUS GRADEBOOK handles up to 20 classes of 48 students each, with 64 assignments per term.

Teachers can grade by letters, numbers, or virtually any known grading system. Student names can be encoded for privacy and security. Individual and class grades can be averaged, and adjusted to curves with different weights given different assignments and tests. It keeps tabs on missed assignments. Makeup grades are found at the touch of a key. Missing grades can be optionally excused or counted into grade averages. Weekly, monthly, and semester averages are generated, displayed, and printed for individuals or classes, if desired. Grade distributions can be calculated and graphed, and the teacher's comments printed.

Using a window system to display every facet of the program, AEIUS GRADEBOOK guides the user every step of the way. Help screens are always at hand. Finding and correcting errors is easy. The ability to print out individual and class report cards gives AEIUS an A+. The small amount of RAM memory used permits AEIUS GRADEBOOK to be used on nearly any PC. The 20-page on-disk manual assumes virtually no computer knowledge on the part of users, teaches basics, and works its way into the program.

(PC-SIG Disk# 1239)

Special Requirements: *None.*
Author Registration: *$35.00*

Class Record ✍   *by Software Assistance Co.*

CLASS RECORD is a spreadsheet-style program for maintaining grades and averages over the course of the school year.

A record of each student's name and grades is recorded. Give grades different weights, omit grades for absent students, and drop or change grades at any time. Calculate the total averages for each student and the total class average. You can also calculate a subset average for each student, such as the student's average for quizzes, tests, labs, etc. Printouts are available for many record combinations.

(PC-SIG Disk# 1071)

Special Requirements: *384K RAM.*
Author Registration: *$39.95*

Classbook Deluxe   *by J&K Programming*

CLASSBOOK DELUXE is a multi-function, menu-driven package that helps teachers keep track of attendance, homework, and test scores just as in a regular classbook. It accepts raw scores, percentages, or letter grades.

You can calculate grades, as well as create and print progress reports, class lists, and seating charts. Get the complete status on any student at the touch of a few keys!

(PC-SIG Disk# 951)

Special Requirements: *Two floppy drives.*
Author Registration: *$25.00*

Gradease   *by Softwarr*

Let GRADEASE do a teacher's dirty work. This software will calculate grades, print out class lists, print seating charts and gradebook pages, and print a summary of grades and progress reports for each student. The program can handle as many separate classes as your disk can hold.

For each class, you may have up to seven separate grading categories. These categories can be divided between quizzes, tests, homework, etc., and you may define categories that will not count in the final grade.

GRADEASE has several grading options. The program can calculate the overall grade for each grading category, with the final grade based either on the averages of these grades or on the weights of those averages. Each category of grades can be weighted by percentage or multiples. Missing grades may or may not be included in the final grade. You may drop the lowest grade or change all grades below a certain score.

GRADEASE can print out an immediate seating chart with the students arranged alphabetically or randomly. The student list may be updated and can be sorted alphabetically or by an assigned group number.

Spend your time teaching and let GRADEASE do the bookkeeping for you.

(PC-SIG Disk# 1862)

Special Requirements: *None.*
Author Registration: *$39.95*

Grader   *by NursePerfect Software*

Teachers — GRADER makes statistics that let you evaluate test quality and helps you establish grade breakdowns.

Just enter the number of problems in an exam and GRADER displays a table of possible scores based on the number of either right or wrong answers. GRADER can give standard statistics including range, midrange, median, mean, standard deviation, mode, skewness index, and a distribution of scores according to letter grade. The grade ranges are set by the program, but can be changed at any time. GRADER also displays listings of standard (Z) scores and all raw scores ranked in descending order.

Other features include: Rapid computation of the score a student needs on a final exam in order to pass the course; random number selectors to determine the correct answers on multiple-choice questions and to draw items from a test item bank; and difficulty and discriminability indices.

(PC-SIG Disk# 1071)

Special Requirements: *None.*
Author Registration: *$9.95*

Grades
by SupremeSoft

GRADES is a very simple database designed to track school grades. It is primarily for students who want to keep track of all the courses they have taken and pertinent data for each class. This information includes the class name, section name, course number, teacher name, amount of credits, test scores, and grade. Using the test score information you can predict the grade, and even see how a grade curve would effect your grade. This makes it very easy to determine one's current standing in a class. Allowing the program to decide the most likely grade, you can then see how this grade affects the overall GPA.

(PC-SIG Disk# 2025)

Special Requirements: *None.*
Author Registration: *$20.00*

Gradescan
by Crofton Binary Concepts

GRADESCAN is a menu-driven grade-keeping system designed with the busy teacher in mind. Its operation is so simple that it can be used with full confidence the very first time. Menu selectable options include: create/select class, enter assignments, enter grades, add new students, examine class data, and print reports.

GRADESCAN allows up to 17 classes to be created. Each class can contain 50 students and 41 assignments. The assignments can be weighted and student names can be copied into more than one class.

GRADESCAN was developed for teachers by a teacher. The program includes complete instructions on disk, self-explaining menus, and provides several sample class exercises for the new or timid user to experiment on without hurting anything.

(PC-SIG Disk# 1233)

Special Requirements: *None.*
Author Registration: *$20.00*
➤*ASP Member.*

Grading Assistant ✍
by Jim Reid

Here's some quality help for harried teachers. GRADING ASSISTANT churns out student grades throughout the grading period with a minimum of effort and study. The well crafted menus let computer-wise teachers skip most of the manual and plunge into program installation. To aid in tracking, GRADING ASSISTANT produces a bonanza of student and class average reports.

Teachers can use up to 12 grade categories such as work, homework, projects, tests and quizzes for each class. Different weights can be assigned to each category, but categories and weights can be changed at any time.

Grading Assistant (PC-SIG Disk# 1632)

Compute both numeric and letter grade averages. You define your own match of numeric grades to letter grades with pluses and minuses. You can automatically drop the lowest score for each student in a class for a particular grade category.

A thunderstorm of reports awaits the number conscious teacher. You get current grade average reports for each student in each class. You can get student averages for up to 12 different categories of grades per class. You also get the class grade distribution counts by letter grade.

An interim grade report lets you produce a listing for each student whose average is below a cut-off numeric grade. This helps the teacher notify both parent and child that things need changing. The class roster is handy for taking attendance or manually recording select grades. You get year-to-date grade average reports by student and by class and the overall average for each of the past grading periods of the school year. Then you get an overall school year average for each student in each class. You can compute a yearly class grade average at the end of the school year.

A special subprogram lets a teacher display current grade averages or grade averages from previous grading periods as a simple bar graph. And, another included program file lets teachers maintain a file of each student's address and telephone number.

(PC-SIG Disk#'s 1632, 2678)

Special Requirements: *640K RAM and 2 floppies or a hard drive.*
Author Registration: *$20.00*

Mark Record Plus
by W. A. Phillips

MARK RECORD PLUS allows teachers to harness the power of their PCs to avoid much of the drudgery involved in calculating and recording their students' marks.

MARK RECORD PLUS can handle up to 50 students per course and up to 50 grades per student. Reports can be generated using either the students' real names or their aliases (for privacy). Any combination of reports such as student ranking, weighted marks, and distribution curves can be printed or saved to disk. The teacher can easily generate bar graphs for visual representations. Includes 17 page on- disk guide.

(PC-SIG Disk#'s 1512, 2310)

Special Requirements: *Printer.*
Author Registration: *$20.00*

The Noble Gradebook ☆
by Noble Software Co.

THE NOBLE GRADEBOOK is a teacher's gradebook that can handle the most complex grading tasks. Based on a familiar spreadsheet format, THE NOBLE GRADEBOOK lets you quickly enter up to 150 scores for as many as 150 students.

Set up NOBLE to handle 18 different categories of tests, quizzes, or homework. NOBLE lets you enter the percent of final grade for each category, the maximum grade, the number of low scores to throw out, and any extra credit/no credit available for each category.

Once grades are entered, THE NOBLE GRADEBOOK does the rest. It sorts by any item (name, ID#, final grade, etc.); creates a bar graph on any item; and calculates statistics such as average, median, and standard deviation. Print the entire gradebook or a grade summary for all students or selected students.

THE NOBLE GRADEBOOK isn't the simplest gradebook program around, but it's not intended to be. This is serious power for the teacher who demands total control over even the most complex grading systems.

(PC-SIG Disk# 2515)

Special Requirements: *None.*
Author Registration: *$49.95*

The ProGrade System
by William E. Peace

THE PROGRADE SYSTEM is a full-featured grading program for educators. It was designed by an educator and has been rigorously tested by "non-computer expert" educators to meet their specific needs. The documentation manuals are complete. Once you've read the documentation and figured out how the system works, you will find that the system's power and flexibility is worth the time it takes to learn.

THE PROGRADE SYSTEM will accept letter or numerical grades and lets YOU decide the letter grade numerical equivalents. THE PROGRADE SYSTEM lets you enter grades in ANY order — any assignment for any student at any time. THE PROGRADE SYSTEM calculates weighted grades or unweighted grades, points, percents, or letter grades. And every floppy disk can store dozens of class files, each with up to 35 students, 45 assignments per student.

PROGRADE computes class averages, comparisons of grades, ranked or alphabetical class lists, averages of all tests, homeworks, etc. It will provide individual progress reports with averages for all assignment categories. Your students and their parents can know where they stand at all times, and you can, too.

(PC-SIG Disk#'s 1778, 1779)

Special Requirements: *348K RAM, and two floppy drives or a hard drive.*
Author Registration: *$45.00*

🖾 = Updated Program
☆ = New Program

The Progress Report

by A.P. Software

Teachers, now the task of writing classroom progress reports is academic. THE PROGRESS REPORT computerizes the process so that progress reports for five different classes, each with up to 50 students (250 student total), can be generated and printed along with a summary list. THE PROGRESS REPORT is completely menu driven and intuitive to operate. You can enter up to 28 progress report comments, which are saved to a file, and can then be individually selected for inclusion in a student progress report. This greatly simplifies the job of writing progress reports.

Each progress report consists of student name, comment number selections 1 - 28 (you may select up to 24 of the 28 comments for any one progress report), test grade option, and an additional teacher comment. The test grade option allows you to enter up to 8 test grades, which will appear in the report along with the average grade. The last item in the progress report is an additional teacher comment for each individual student. The progress reports are automatically printed along with a summary list of names for all students processed and their class or subject area.

(PC-SIG Disk# 1633)

Special Requirements: *None.*

Author Registration: *$10.00*

School-Mom

by Motes Educational Software

SCHOOL-MOM is one of the most comprehensive children's educational programs available. SCHOOL-MOM is a complete educational tool for children, ages 4 to 14.

Multilevel modules are provided for Math, Music, English, Spelling, Art, and Time.

The Math module contains four levels of addition and subtraction, multiplication and division, and four levels of pre-algebra math. It also contains two arcade math games. The first, Laser Blast, is a counting game that teaches quantity. The second, Applespider, is an exciting game that drills the student in basic addition, subtraction, multiplication, and division.

Three music modules let you use the keyboard to write tunes as you watch the notes appear on the screen. The first level allows eight notes to be played in seven octaves. The second level allows the note duration to be changed. The third level allows sharp and flat notes. Tunes can be edited, played back and stored.

School-Mom (PC-SIG Disk# 2530)

The English module contains three learning levels. The first level teaches children how parts of speech such as nouns, verbs, adjectives, and adverbs are used in sentences. The second level teaches sentence structure. The third level teaches subject-verb agreement.

The Spelling module contains three sub-options — Alphabet, Random Word and Homework Exercises. The Alphabet option is used to teach upper and lower case alphabet letters. The Random Words option flashes words on the screen and gives you three seconds to spell them. It has four levels. The Homework Exercises option can be used to enter the daily spelling homework so the computer can drill the student on the words.

The Art module gives students the chance to be creative. Draw, Spider Webs, Space Tunnels, Space Worms, and Space Ribbons are the five options available in the art module. The Draw option allows the student to draw freehand with either the joystick or the mouse. The Spider Webs option allows the child to control the actions of a spider who leaves a web behind him. The last three sub-options allow the student to create beautiful screen art with three-dimensional qualities using either a joystick or the keyboard.

The Time module has four learning levels that teach children to tell time. A ticking clock is shown on the screen and the student must choose the correct time from a list of three answers.

The Exam module allows the teacher or parent to create and score multiple choice examinations. Two exams on US Capitals and US Presidents are already provided.

(PC-SIG Disk# 2530)

Special Requirements: *CGA or better.*

Author Registration: *$25.00*

➤*ASP Member.*

Teacher Works ✍   *by R&G Software*

TEACHER WORKS is for teachers and school administrators who want to do it their way. TEACHER WORKS lets people use their favorite type of grading system, not conform to a grading method understood by a programmer. Requiring a minimum of keystrokes, the program tackles classes of up to sixty students.

TEACHER WORKS lets teachers grade by points or grade averages, using either letter or numeric grades. With a maximum of 240 grades per semester per student, teachers can weight grades within six categories and give extra credit. Calculated grades can be adjusted for the student who really worked but barely missed achieving a certain grade.

The teacher can edit one grade or the whole class on a single screen, adding grades in any order. Complete student records can be displayed and edited. Student records can be formatted and printed to meet the requirements of most districts. Students, and their records, can be transferred between classes.

You can use quarterly, trimester, or year round grading. Grades can be calculated by what the student has been assigned, so new check-ins are not penalized for grades they missed — unless you choose to do so. Class, student, and individual grades can be searched. Class grade averages are generated. Students are automatically assigned ID numbers which can be changed later. Grade printouts can be done by ID numbers to protect student anonymity. Data files are dBase III compatible so that they can be used by other commercial programs such as dBXL, FoxBase, PCTools, FormWorx, Quattro, or PC-File.

(PC-SIG Disk# 1521)

Special Requirements: *515K RAM, two floppy drives or a hard drive.*

Author Registration: *$25.00*

Teacher's Database   *by David G. Bodnar*

TEACHER'S DATABASE is designed particularly for teachers to organize information on their students. The database can track up to 500 students, each student having as many as 80 individual items of data in his record.

Store names and addresses, alphabetize or reorder records based on their contents, sort by homerooms or subjects, and print individual student progress reports, class gradebook sheets, and student seating charts.

Student test scores may be weighted, averaged, statistically analyzed, changed to a percentage or a letter grade. Graphs of student test results may be created using the computer's high-resolution graphic screen. Grade distribution can be displayed numerically or as a histogram. A spreadsheet-style editor makes data entry and editing a snap.

Let the computer do the paperwork while you focus on teaching. After all, that's why you became a teacher.

(PC-SIG Disk# 878)

Special Requirements: *None.*

Author Registration: *$35.00*

TutorialWriter ☆   *by Intelligent Educational Software*

Teachers, Parents, Trainers — TUTORIALWRITER is an educator's toolkit for computer-based training.

The computer is the ideal tool for the classroom, but in order to use it to the fullest, you have to learn how to program. Many people have knowledge to share but do not want to learn computer programming in order to do so. TUTORIALWRITER has closed this gap. Anyone who can use a word processor can create full color computer tutorials with Hypertext, pop-up windows, menus, online Help, tests, quizzes, branching on answers, graphics, mouse support, and more.

Harness the computer's power. Decide what you want to present, type it into a standard (ASCII) file with a word processor and then enter TUTORIALWRITER's codes where you want them. Put a title in a fancy box at the top of the screen. Put CONTINUE and QUIT boxes at the bottom of the screen. It is that simple. There are more than forty codes that give the author tremendous control of the computer. Give the ready-to-run tutorial disk to the people it was written for.

(PC-SIG Disk# 2788)
Special Requirements: *None.*
Author Registration: *$49.50*

VAR GRADE ✐   *by Dennis Revie*

VARGRADE is designed for teachers sho want to keep a computerized record of their students' grades. It tracks an unlimited number of students and up to 99 sections of students per class for up to 240 days of attendance. There is no limit to the number of classes.

VAR GRADE supports several grading methods, including weighted exams, use of letter or number grades, and the ability to throw out the lowest exam score(s). Several statistical features are also available through the program: calculation of mean, median, and mode for exams; correlation of two exams; and the ability to sum, average, or take the percentage of any combination of exams. Plot the exam results on your printer.

(PC-SIG Disk#'s 903, 1357)
Special Requirements: *384K RAM, a graphics card, two floppy drives, and a printer.*
Author Registration: *$30.00*
➤*ASP Member.*

▼ ▼ ▼

Test and Quiz Preparation

Besttest ✐   *by Wiseware*

BESTTEST takes the drudgery out of preparing tests so teachers can have more time to teach. Excellent documentation and a complete tutorial make this powerful program easy to use. Features are accessed through function keys or menus.

Questions are easily created with templates and can have various formats, including multiple choice, true/false, fill-in, matching, or essay. By assigning reference fields to each question, the questions can be sorted or filtered to create tests with a set number of questions, one format only, difficulty level, etc. The order of question and answer choices can be automatically shuffled at each printing.

Questions are stored in files on disk for future editing and printing. Other features include user-defined screen colors and macros. Daisy wheel, dot-matrix and laser printers are supported, with a user-defined printer option.

BESTTEST is the upgrade to both TESTMAKR and EXAMBANK. Import files from those programs into BESTTEST. BESTTEST even includes hints for writing good questions.

If you teach the same material over and over and hate making up tests, this program is a lifesaver!

(PC-SIG Disk# 2532)
Special Requirements: *384K RAM.*
Author Registration: *$50.00*
➤*ASP Member.*

Exam Bank ✐   *by Education Software*

Teachers give EXAM BANK an A+ because it takes the hassle out of testing. Its ability to quickly change test questions means that teachers will never again need to give the same examination twice. With one extra keystroke, teachers can scramble the sequence of questions, thus preparing two tests for the same class. The program even generates printed answer sheets.

Crossmatch questions are produced without hassle. Matches are entered side by side. Each time the question is printed the program scrambles both columns into a different order and then prints a correct answer sheet.

EXAM BANK stores examination questions of the type most commonly used by teachers and professors: multiple choice, true/false, short answer, essay and cross match. It allows for complete editing or deletion and replacement of previously written questions. Best of all, EXAM BANK's question entry screens have wordprocessing features and full cursor control key usage.

(PC-SIG Disk# 1631)

Special Requirements: *300K RAM.*
Author Registration: *$30.00*

NewQuiz/QuizWhiz
by Paul R. Godin

NEWQUIZ lets you make tests, quizzes, and trivia games as fast as you can type. Just type in a question, add the multiple choice answers (only one correct answer of course), note the correct answer, and you have a quiz. Make up one question; make up as many as your disk will hold — it's that easy.

Then, using QUIZWIZ, take the quizzes you made and test yourself or friends. QUIZWIZ lets up to four people take the same quiz at the same time. It keeps track of right and wrong answers, and the percentage of correct answers.

To get you started, QUIZWIZ comes with an example quiz with 900 questions about the Bible. Use it to make your own quizzes or just to brush up on your Bible trivia. Either way NEWQUIZ/QUIZWIZ is a winner.

(PC-SIG Disk# 2464)

Special Requirements: *None.*
Author Registration: *$10.00*

PC-CAI ✍
by TexaSoft/Mission Technologies

PC-CAI is a computer language for the easy creation of computer-driven tutorials, tests or demo programs.

Using the PC-CAI language, professional-looking graphics can be mixed with questions and text to produce a polished interactive program in minutes. The PC-CAI language has commands for interpretation of answers, responses to anticipated wrong answers, limiting the number of answer attempts and more. The graphics tools provided permit color selection and suitable screen manipulation, as well as the ability to create and animate images.

PC-CAI provides a simple environment that even the computer neophyte can use to design helpful educational programs or games. The system comes with on-line help and a built-in word processor to create programs — although any ASCII processor can be used. There is even a PC-CAI generated tutorial on how to program with PC-CAI.

(PC-SIG Disk# 1470)

Special Requirements: *360 K RAM. Color monitor and hard disk recommended.*
Author Registration: *$49.00*
➤*ASP Member.*

PC-Quizzer
by Data Assist

PC-QUIZZER is an educational program for instruction in almost any subject including foreign languages, history, science, math, vocabulary, trivia, and word definitions. PC-QUIZZER is an excellent educational tool and a must for anyone involved with learning or teaching, as it lets you create your own computer lesson. You can create quiz files using any standard ASCII text editor or wordprocessor.

You can create graphic images to use in the program with any graphics or painting package or a BASIC program. PC-QUIZZER lets you use color text, color graphics, and music. An ECHO speech synthesizer can also be used to produce speech. The questions used in a lesson can be true/false, fill-in-the-blank, or multiple choice. Various levels of help and other information can be included and are displayed when the student needs help or has entered a right or wrong answer.

(PC-SIG Disk# 1143)

Special Requirements: *384K RAM.*
Author Registration: *$29.00, $59.00, $129.00*

Pop Train
by Computer AXL

POP TRAIN is a trainable ram-resident help system able to display help screens depending on the page and field location of the cursor. Screen capturing enables later display for further help system development, briefings, etc. POP TRAIN is useful in employee training, telephone sales, general computer education, or other situations where a personalized help screen is needed.

POP TRAIN is especially useful when screens from mainframe programs can be downloaded to PC's. The problem screens that baffle many newcomers can be captured to disk. POP TRAIN will let you place hidden explanatory help messages in each area of difficulty. The bewildered beginner touches a hot key and the explanation appears at the cursor. Touch any other key and the message disappears.

The system is also invaluable when an older application is updated or expanded. Update the help system at the same time and many puzzled phone calls will never be made.

A PC-based, customizable, pop-up help and training system. Perfect for new and updated applications for PCs and mainframes. Training for novices.

(PC-SIG Disk# 1471)
Special Requirements: *None.*
Author Registration: *$49.00*

Quiz-Maker ☆   *by Intelligent Educational Software*

QUIZ-MAKER is an educational tool and a Trivia game. Take quizzes in three formats — match the question with the answer, type in an answer to the question or choose the correct answer from the four or five answers listed.

QUIZ-MAKER has two modules. QUIZPLAY lets you play the quizzes. QUIZMAKE is the Development module used to create quizzes. Of course, there's no challenge to solving quizzes you've created yourself, so create them for others — your spouse, children, friends, colleagues or the world at large. Give them a copy of QUIZPLAY and the quizzes you've created, and let them have fun meeting your challenge.

Upload quizzes to your favorite Bulletin Boards or Compuserve (the IBM NEW WordGames Forum or the Education Forum). Become known for your ability to create Trivia quizzes. (Your name will be displayed on the files you create!)

The user-friendly nature of the menus and the online hints make this an easy program to use.

(PC-SIG Disk# 2786)
Special Requirements: *None.*
Author Registration: *$24.50*

rse Explorers   *by Hubbard C. Goodrich*

Here's a great tool for anyone at high school or college level with an interest in early American history. This program has two parts: the EXPLORER HISTORIES and the EXPLORER QUIZ.

EXPLORER HISTORIES contains information about 45 explorers who touched American shores and are considered to have made important historical contributions to America's growth. Page through the explorers one by one until you have found the one you are interested in. Once the explorer has been chosen, you will be shown his/her full biography, including birth/death date, accomplishment, and other interesting tidbits.

It is best if the user has a good map of the U.S. for tracking the various expeditions.

The EXPLORER QUIZ asks a series of questions on the 45 explorers. The main menu provides a choice of subjects such as names of explorers, explorer dates, accomplishments and a fourth named POT LUCK.

(PC-SIG Disk# 2298)
Special Requirements: *None.*
Author Registration: *$10.00*

Test and Train ✍   *by Frank Lendaro*

Whether you're a teacher wanting to give tests on the computer, or a student who needs to drill for tests or courses, or a manager who needs to administer training drills to your employees, TEST and TRAIN can help you do the job.

You enter the questions and TEST AND TRAIN displays them on the screen. The program offers slightly different scoring options for testing and training. In both cases, the program accepts valid answers and rejects inappropriate ones, showing the correct answer with an optional comment when the answer is incorrect. You can put incorrectly answered questions on hold, and view them again until the correct answer is given. TEST keeps score of points associated with correct answers, and counts the number of incorrect answers entered. At the end of the test the program displays an optional evaluation, and stores the results in a permanent file on your disk.

(PC-SIG Disk# 797)
Special Requirements: *A word processor.*
Author Registration: *$11.88*

Test Maker ✍ by R. Allen Hackworth

Teachers, teacher's aides, and parents — TMAKER is here to help you at test time. Tell TMAKER the subject and how many questions should be in the test and stand back! Produce a quiz for the fourth period civics class and a quiz for the sixth period class, cover the same material and yet, have two different tests. Someone miss a test? Generate one for him to take as make-up. No need to worry if people have been comparing notes.

Create a database of up to 200 questions and answers in each file with as many files as you have the memory to support. You don't have to enter them all at once. As you create test questions and answers, put them in the database. The next time you create a test in that subject, enter any new questions and answers into the same database.

Tests can be printed and taken in a group or the computer can run a single test for a student. This one-on-one version is also good for tutorials and can be used by the students to create personalized study guides. (Optional password protection keeps private information private.) Exact answers are required for the computer-driven option so it's ideal for questions with exact answers such as names, dates, numbers, yes or no, multiple choice and fill-the-blanks.

The software is menu-driven, has a full help function and requires no special computer expertise to operate.

(PC-SIG Disk#'s 1551, 2596)

Special Requirements: *Hard drive. A printer is recommended.*
Author Registration: *Single $29.95; Network $49.95; School License $75.00*

Test Management System by Marshall Woolner R.N,

TMS stands for TEST MANAGEMENT SYSTEM, and the name is descriptive. TMS is a software system, or system of programs, which automates many of the routine and tedious chores of administering multiple-choice and true/false tests.

❑ Maintain a test bank of up to 999,999 questions.
❑ Browse through the test bank and mark questions at will for inclusion in a test; you can let the program search for the questions by author, by the class or course from which it is derived, or by the topic or area of the questions.
❑ Print the test directly on a printer, with a face sheet, a coded student answer sheet, and an overlay key template for correcting the student answer sheets.
❑ Save a test in ASCII text form, to load into your favorite word processor for additional editing or special effects such as boldface or italics.
❑ Print a reference key version of the test, which contains all the questions of the regular test, plus a graphic indication of the correct answer, the level of difficulty, area of the question, class, author and bibliographic citations.
❑ Administer the test by computer, by placing the test on a single diskette; the test will be scored automatically, and if you choose, the program will show the student his/her score and even review the test, with the correct answers and the student answers shown.
❑ For each test you administer by computer, print a report which contains the name and score of each person who took the test, and a tally of the distribution of answers for the test.

(PC-SIG Disk#'s 1890, 1891)

Special Requirements: *512K RAM and a hard drive.*
Author Registration: *$75.00*

TestWriter by Fred Glahe

Here's a riddle. What do teachers love that's easy to crunch and "red" all over? Give up? It's TESTWRITER! TESTWRITER takes the hassle out of making up tests. Well, not all the hassle, you still have to write the original questions or copy them out of the teacher's manual. But once that is done, you'll never have to type them again.

TESTWRITER is a full fledged word processor which can be used for preparing a file containing examination questions and for almost any other task that word processors can handle. Its fast, easy-to-use, and may just take the sting out of test writing. TESTWRITER offers a command structure very similar to WordStar as well as pull-down menus, function key commands and an "undo" key.

TESTWRITER prints the examination and also prints the corresponding answer sheets. Nobody loves tests, but TESTWRITER makes test writing easier to take.

(PC-SIG Disk# 2264)

Special Requirements: *None.*
Author Registration: *$25.00*

Total Recall ✍   *by Zoft Systems*

If you've ever had to study a foreign language or memorize a lot of words, terms, phrases, facts, acronyms, formulas, or dates, you've probably had to do it the hard way. You've enlisted unwilling friends to flash index cards at you, or test you until you became friendless. Wouldn't it be nice if there were a better way to memorize? Now there is with TOTAL RECALL.

TOTAL RECALL is a complete, computerized learning environment designed to help adults learn and memorize almost any subject. TOTAL RECALL is not a game or a children's educational program, but a powerful learning tool.

You enter everything you need to learn or memorize into TOTAL RECALL. It then helps you drill, review, and test on the material quickly and effortlessly. TOTAL RECALL automatically keeps track of where your weaknesses are and gives you the most practice in those areas, thus saving you hours of time and work. It helps you organize and manage your learning, too: you can print, edit, add, copy, merge, etc. Multiple users can study multiple subjects. In this shareware version, files are limited to 50 entries but you may keep as many files as disk space will allow.

Use TOTAL RECALL to study any subject where you have to learn or memorize terms, words, ideas, concepts, names, places, or dates. It may even help you raise your scores on the GRE, LSAT, GMAT, SAT, or ACT. Information and quizzes included are: states and capitals, English vocabulary, computer terms, and U.S. presidents.

(PC-SIG Disk# 1917)

Special Requirements: *512RAM, and two floppy drives or a hard drive is recommended.*
Author Registration: *$29.95*

Verbal Vanquish ☆   *by James Bair*

VERBAL VANQUISH is a program designed to help prepare for the verbal portions of exams such as the SAT, ACT and the GRE. The program walks the student/user through sample questions, strategies and hints to solve them and ends with sample exercises from previous years' examinations.

The program has a lot to offer to anyone from high school to college age preparing for the entrance examinations. Verbal sections of these exams can determine admission and scholarships and are therefore very importan VANQUISH acknowledges this need and provides a unique and inexpensive method preparation - Computer Aided Instruction.

VERBAL VANQUISH provides results to each exercise completed by the student provides guidence for similar questions through generic examples and questions. This is definitely a program for those preparing for the entrance examinations and does a wonderful job of helping remove a part of the anxiety.

(PC-SIG Disk# 2729)

Special Requirements: *512K RAM.*
Author Registration: *$25.00*

▼ ▼ ▼

Trivia

Astrosoft Trivia Game — Science and Entertainment Edition   *by Martin E. Morrison*

Astrosoft's Trivia is truly a trivia game to tempt the science (and science fiction) genius. In addition to astronomy, science, words, and grab bag questions, they added Star Trek and Star Wars questions. If you think "pon farr" is a vegetable dish, you had better check out the Star Trek trivia on this disk.

(PC-SIG Disk# 329)

Special Requirements: *None.*
Author Registration: *$10.00*

EZK-Quizzer   *by EZK Data Systems*

Since 1800, who are the only two brothers who have served in the Senate at the same time? What is a hematophagouse? What was the first X-rated film to win the Best Picture Oscar award? What building is on the back of the five dollar bill? Who cares? EZK-QUIZZER does!

EZK-QUIZZER is a computer trivia game that uses various subjects to get its questions. Before answering a question, you are asked what category tickles your fancy and then you must answer the question before time runs out. The categories range from television to mathematics, sports to history, and a potluck category where you never know what type of question will pop up. There are three rounds of questions and each round gets harder, so the points given when you answer a question correctly get higher also. After the first round, you can start to wage your points against the computer so hopefully by the end of the third round you have enough points to be in the Hall of Fame.

By the way, this program is so good I hear Alex Trebek has it on his computer at home.

(PC-SIG Disk# 1449)

Special Requirements: *None.*
Author Registration: *$15.00*

Have You Read That Movie? ☆ *by George Tylutki*

Have You Read That Movie? is a game of trivia on movies and related literature. The questions are multiple choice, and there are three levels of difficulty. The game has 91 easy questions, 141 medium questions, and 136 hard questions. The game can be played by one or two players. In two player games you can alternate turns or compete on each question simultaneously. The game can be set up so that you may have up to three tries before guessing the right answer. After the correct answer is given interesting facts are displayed about the movie or literature that should enhance the knowledge of all trivia buffs and movie fans. The game has pull down menus and online help.

Special Requirements: *None.*
Author Registration: *$10.00*

Know-It-All *by David Morlitz*

Everybody loves trivia, but nobody loves a know-it-all. That is, until they've experienced KNOW-IT-ALL, the trivia question game that goes beyond most traditional trivia games.

Star Trek, TV Shows, Science, and Slogans are just a few of the categories of questions that you'll find. Start out with the questions that KNOW-IT-ALL has to offer and after you've mastered these, use the editor in KNOW-IT-ALL to add questions to your own customized data file. The questions can be multiple choice or fill-in-the-blank.

KNOW-IT-ALL keeps a running tally of how many questions you've answered and returns your score. Since you can add your own questions to KNOW-IT-ALL, you could also use the program as an educational computerized tester.

(PC-SIG Disk# 2297)

Special Requirements: *CGA.*
Author Registration: *$10.00*

The Last Word *by Bit Masons*

Who said "I disapprove of what you say, but I will defend to the death your right to say it."? This, and hundreds of other famous quotations, are the basis of the trivia game, THE LAST WORD.

Answer questions about quotations by selecting either who said it, why it was said, where it was said, or what it was said about. Your answers are matched against a set of acceptable responses with a sophisticated pattern-recognition algorithm. You don't even have to spell every name perfectly to receive credit, and bonus points are given for quick responses.

While this is not a game for children, it can be used as an educational tool for young adults. Quotations are taken from old movies (Garbo, Bogart, etc.), humorists like Robert Orben, songs from Gilbert and Sullivan, and writers like Kipling, Nietzsche, Frost, Shakespeare, and Hemingway. (Ans: Voltaire.)

(PC-SIG Disk# 2432)

Special Requirements: *None.*
Author Registration: *$15.00*
➤*ASP Member.*

✍ = Updated Program
☆ = New Program

Opus 1 Brain Teasers Trivia Game
by Roxbury Research Inc.

Have you worn out your edition of Trivial Pursuit? Wish you could have more than six categories to test your brain cells? OPUS 1 BRAIN TEASERS fill this need.

OPUS 1 is a trivia-oriented game for up to four people. There are 25 different categories to choose from. A few of the diverse categories are: body talk, tv & film, 1-2-3, two-way words, books, and plays.

The game is played much like you would play Charades, with the clues brought up as a graphic clue. For example, The Graduate has the clue "GRADUUUUUUUU" (Grad + eight U's = Grad-u-eight). Have fun!
(PC-SIG Disk# 997)

Special Requirements: *None.*
Author Registration: *$19.95*

Trek Trivia
by Apogee Software Productions

TREK-1 is the first of ten volumes that measures your knowledge of the world of Star Trek, one of the most popular television series of all time.

You may need to be part Vulcan to win this game! The 100 True/False and multiple choice questions are provocative. The game moves swiftly, the challenge is great and the random questions beguile and sometimes frustrate even the most devout Trekkie.
(PC-SIG Disk# 1278)

Special Requirements: *None.*
Author Registration: *$4.00 per volume, or $30 for all 10 volumes.*

Tune Trivia
by Lanke Software

Remember "Name That Tune"? Here's a new version.

TUNE TRIVIA plays songs on your PC so you can try to guess the songs' titles. Once you've answered correctly, you are then challenged with trivia questions about musical history.
(PC-SIG Disk# 475)

Special Requirements: *None.*
Author Registration: *$30.00.*

▼ ▼ ▼

Typing, Education

PC-FASTYPE/CGA
by Trendtech Corporation

Don't let your lack of speed at the keyboard make computing a drag for you. Try this graphics-oriented, menu-driven touch-typing instructor for typists of all skill levels. Improve your keyboard typing speed and accuracy.

Keyboard displays of both the AT-Style keyboard and the 101-key Enhanced Keyboard are provided. Also available are keyboard images for the Old- Style IBM PC the Tandy-1000 and the BTC-5339. Use the self-paced drills and exercises to refresh old skills and learn new ones. Customize your drills by selecting the keys YOU want to learn. Import your own text files for additional typing exercises. After each test, check out your score on words per minute, number of errors made and other data concerning your typing performance.
(PC-SIG Disk# 320)

Special Requirements: *CGA.*
Author Registration: *$25.00*
➤*ASP Member.*

PC-Fastype/Mono
by Trendtech Corporation

A menu-driven interactive typing tutorial designed for use by computer enthusiasts who want to improve their typing skills. The program displays a character graphics image of the keyboard and prompts you to use the correct keys. You can have any kind of monitor (color or mono) to run this program. It's ideal for laptops and portables.
(PC-SIG Disk# 2254)

Special Requirements: *None.*
Author Registration: *$28.00*
➤*ASP Member.*

PC-Touch   *by Fernandez Enterprises*

PC-TOUCH is a typing tutor with varying levels of difficulty ranging from the very easy, for the beginner, to the difficult, for the expert who wants to brush up his or her typing skills. The program gives you the line to type into the system, and all your statistics — typing speed, errors, and test-adjusted scores — are maintained along the bottom of the screen.

(PC-SIG Disk# 249)

Special Requirements: *None.*
Author Registration: *None.*

Touch Type Tutor ✍   *by Gray Design Associates*

TOUCH TYPE TUTOR is going to make you the fastest typist in town. Or if you don't know how to type, this program will teach you.

The program has three teaching modes. The first is for the person who knows how to type, but wants to be faster. It provides four different letters on which you are tested. After you have become proficient on these, you can add your own letters for variety. The second mode is a graduated series of lessons that allow you to move along at your own pace. The third mode is a game for the beginning typist that teaches the keyboard layout.

Touch Type Tutor (PC-SIG Disk# 1334)

(PC-SIG Disk# 1334)

Special Requirements: *None.*
Author Registration: *$10.00*
➤*ASP Member.*

TP-ET ✍   *by Thumb Print Software*

Looking for a program to fill the void between the electric typewriter and a full-blown word processor? Then TP-ET is the program for you.

TP-ET turns your computer and printer into an electric typewriter. All margins (top, bottom, left, and right) are programmable.

Set tab stops. Decide if you want an End Of Line bell. If your printer is IBM/EPSON-compatible, pick from six printer font/quality settings, or enter your own printer codes. Save a configuration file to disk to be read every time you start TP-ET. Edit an entire line of text before sending it to the printer.

Adjust any parameters such as tabs, margins, etc. from the 1-2-3 style Main Menu. Thirteen Help screens explain all setting options.

(PC-SIG Disk# 2748)

Special Requirements: *A printer.*
Author Registration: *$19.50*

Typing   *by Larry Ryder*

Get those fingers of yours warmed up! Here is a new test for them. TYPING is an easy-to-use program that gives feedback on your typing performance. It displays the text on the screen, and you start typing — quickly, now! — and no mistakes! The timer starts as soon as you hit the first key.

TYPING does not display any statistics while you are typing. When the timer runs out, the screen clears and your typing performance is displayed in words per minute, total errors, and adjusted words per minute. The nice thing about TYPING is you can either type from the screen or print the test file and type from that. You can also supply your own file to type if you want.

(PC-SIG Disk# 793)

Special Requirements: *None.*
Author Registration: *$20.00*

▼ ▼ ▼

✍ = Updated Program
☆ = New Program

Utilities, Macro Programs

4ZIP *by XD Systems*

4ZIP is a utility for 4DOS. Used with the PKWare file-compression program PKZIP, it save 4DOS file descriptions along with the files as they are compressed. The included program 4UNZIP, calls PKUnzip, and restores the descriptions to 4DOS as each file is uncompressed. Select files to Zip or Unzip from a full-screen list with extended wildcards, like 4DOS. Works with all versions of 4DOS. Also look at companion utility, 4EDIT.

(PC-SIG Disk# 2272)

Special Requirements: *4DOS and PKZIP.*
Author Registration: *$15.00*
➤*ASP Member.*

Function Key Helper *by Sunshine Peripherals Inc.*

Make lists of the uses of function keys for various programs and add or edit a function-key template. Many are already included on this disk — Lotus 1-2-3, WordStar, WordPerfect, Multimate, PROCOMM, SuperCalc, RBBS, Turbo Lightning, and more.

Once a template is created, you may print the function-key assignments for quick and easy reference. Up to eight templates may be printed on a page and they include the Shift, Ctrl, and Alt-function key sequences in addition to the normal uses.

(PC-SIG Disk# 856)

Special Requirements: *None.*
Author Registration: *$20.00*

Hotkey *by Micro Business Application*

Have your keyboard do more of the work for you. Program specific keys to perform specialized functions, enter text strings or series of lengthy repetitive keystrokes. Do more computing and less typing! The program is both command line and menu-driven. You can create your own files which instantly reset the function keys to your own definitions.

(PC-SIG Disk# 444)

Special Requirements: *None.*
Author Registration: *$15.00*

NEWKEY ✍ *by FAB Software*

simplifies the entry of common keystroke sequences by letting you assign these sequences to any key desired. Once assigned to a particular key, whenever that key is struck the predefined sequence of keystrokes are returned. For example, the Alt-C key combination might be defined as "copy" and whenever you strike Alt-C, the string "copy" is displayed.

NEWKEY lets you customize software packages, readily create boiler plate passages, redefine your keyboard, and perform other useful tasks. You can even redefine your keyboard to the DVORAK keyboard if you wish. Several sample key definition files are included.

NEWKEY provides many features, including:
❏ Ability to define almost any key
❏ Menu macros
❏ Display macros
❏ Fixed-length pauses during key translation
❏ Nested key translation
❏ Translation bypass for native entry of defined key
❏ Dynamic display of the macro directory
❏ Dynamic display of macros
❏ Full-featured macro editor
❏ Easy change of any macro
❏ Ability to copy/move one macro to another
❏ Ability to move keyboard buffer into macro

❑ Ability to load, merge, and save macro files from within other applications
❑ Screen blanker
❑ Dynamic modification of the control keys
❑ Dynamic clear macros from memory
❑ User-defined dynamic define area length
❑ Time delay pauses during key translation
❑ Ability to toggle NEWKEY on/off
❑ Slow typing mode
❑ 128 keystroke type-ahead buffer
❑ Ability to speed up keyboard repetition rate
❑ Improved macro definition facilities
❑ And much more.

(PC-SIG Disk# 181)

Special Requirements: *None.*
Author Registration: *$43.00*

Painless Event Processor ☆

by Painless Accounting

The PAINLESS EVENT PROCESSOR allows your PC to work 24 hours a day!

Simply tell the event processor when to execute programs, batch files, tasks, utilities, etc. and at the specified time, the keystrokes will be entered into your computer as if you were sitting at the keyboard yourself.

The PAINLESS EVENT PROCESSOR sits in memory (using only 10K) waiting for the real-time clock to trigger an event or task. An event is a series of keystrokes that can be entered to run a program or a series of programs. When an event occurs, the PAINLESS EVENT PROCESSOR recalls what you keyed and enters the data directly into your PC, just as if you were there. Be productive even while you're away!

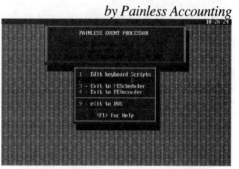

Painless Event Processor (PC-SIG Disk #2652)

If your task is a one-time, daily, weekly, monthly, annual, or even an erratic event, it will be done like clockwork.

If you ever have projects that keep you busy with various tasks like communications with remote sites, printing, backing up, or waiting for spreadsheets to finish calculating, then you have just been saved!

If you think remembering all the keystrokes you need to perform a task might be tedious, you're right. Included is a feature called the Key Stroke Memory. It allows you to go into an application and activate the PAINLESS EVENT PROCESSOR to start remembering your keystrokes. Execute your normal routine for later replay. When you've finished the task, the keystrokes are saved.

(PC-SIG Disk# 2652)

Special Requirements: *None.*
Author Registration: *$45.00*
➤*ASP Member.*

▼ ▼ ▼

Utilities, System or Hardware

400

by Matt Visser

Attention, programmers — 400 inspects the BIOS communications area and the DOS communications area and displays them in human-readable form. It also displays some brief comments describing each byte of the communications areas.

(PC-SIG Disk# 874)

Special Requirements: *360K RAM.*
Author Registration: *$5.00*

4DOS 🖊 *by JP Software*

4DOS is designed to make DOS more powerful and easier to use by replacing your COMMAND.COM file with a new command interpreter. You'll find 4DOS provides a wide variety of capabilities that regular COMMAND.COM can't — like an enhanced DIR command, point-and-shoot file selection for any command, or the ability to completely redefine your system's commands. It provides enhancements to most of the DOS commands and introduces more than 40 new commands. Yet 4DOS is fully compatible with COMMAND.COM. You'll wonder how you ever got along with DOS alone.

It is compatible with virtually all pc hardware and software, including most networks and most TSR (memory resident) programs. It requires less than 3K of RAM while applications are running (less than COMMAND.COM).

4DOS is a "DOS shell" but is unlike most DOS shells on the market. It doesn't isolate you from the DOS command line; it makes you more productive while working at the command line. If you're tired of the limitations of DOS, you'll love 4DOS.

(PC-SIG Disk# 1773)

Special Requirements: *None.*
Author Registration: *$50.00*
➤*ASP Member.*

An Ounce of Prevention ☆ *by Pete Maclean*

OZ protects your data by preserving deleted and overwritten files so that you can recover them. Provided that you have some unused disk space, this function is far more powerful than that provided by "unerase" programs such as those found in Norton Utilities or PC Tools.

OZ also performs other valuable tasks related to disk and file safety, including:

❑ Protection against attempts to format your hard disk(s).
❑ Optional protection against all attempts to write to a hard disk.
❑ Trapping critical DOS errors, providing additional information about them, and more power to recover from them.
    OZ offers several levels of data protection:
❑ File Security - OZ automatically preserves deleted files so that they may be instantly restored if needed. Up to eight generations of each deleted file can be preserved, all under the same name.
❑ Reformat Trapping - Oz prevents accidental or malicious attempts to reformat a hard disk.
❑ Write Protection - Oz allows you to write-protect a disk if you suspect the presence of a virus, or other rogue program, that might try to damage your system.
❑ Full-Disk Protection - Oz traps "full disk" conditions and offers you a helpful set of options to free some space for your work.
❑ Critical Error Handling - Oz recognizes a number of critical disk errors, tells you what is wrong, and offers a range of options for dealing with them.

(PC-SIG Disk# 2771)

Special Requirements: *A hard disk drive.*
Author Registration: *$35.00*
➤*ASP Member.*

ANARKEY *by Moderne Software*

Tired of having to retype the DOS command when you make a spelling error? Reduce the number of keystrokes you make when entering DOS commands by using ANARKEY.

ANARKEY is a commmand-line editor that will significantly reduce the keystrokes you make when entering DOS commands. ANARKEY provides one of the most powerful, compact, and flexible command-line environments available on a DOS machine.

ANARKEY is a memory resident program that intercepts your DOS commands. When you make a typing error, you can move the cursor backwards, without erasing characters, and make the correction. You can't do this with DOS. The shape of the cursor also changes to indicate overwrite or insert mode. ANARKEY will save all the commands you enter so that you can recall them for later use. This saves you from having to reenter commands that are used repeatedly. Simply press the F4 key until the command you want appears and then press enter.

ANARKEY also provides improved program and directory search functions, and the ability to control environment variables. It will also run in expanded memory so that it requires less than 1K of DOS memory space.

(PC-SIG Disk# 1877)

Special Requirements: *None.*
Author Registration: *$30.00*

AT-Slow   *by Better Software Co.*

Sometimes your speedy AT has a little too much speed for a game or older application you may want to run. AT-SLOW is your solution. This easy- to-use program will pull back the reins on your AT or 386 without any hardware modification — even if the original manufacturer only intended the machine to run at top speeds.

AT-SLOW uses the high resolution timer found in a PC-AT or close clone to slow down games and other programs which run too fast on PC-ATs. Your machine can run at almost any slower speed thanks to a variable startup command. Play around with different speeds until you find a speed that keeps both you and your computer happy. AT-SLOW can also be turned off or set to a different speed without rebooting your machine.

(PC-SIG Disk# 1834)

Special Requirements: *80286 or 80386 processor based PC.*
Author Registration: *$10.00*

Back & Forth ✍   *by Progressive Solutions, Inc.*

BACK & FORTH is a versatile program management tool that allows you to load up to 20 programs at once and instantly switch between them. Move between your word processor, spreadsheets, databases, and utilities at will without having to exit, reload, or wait.

BACK & FORTH delivers a flexible task management environment for up to 50 programs. Each program provides as much memory as needed but occupies only 17-23K of memory in your computer. If the high memory loader is used, less than 1K of memory is used. Accepting the definition of 50 programs for selection and use, BACK & FORTH uses Expanded Memory (EMS), cleaning up what's left by opening, executing, and closing programs within BACK & FORTH. RAM disks, hard disks, and conventional memory can be used to store swapping programs.

The color environment is easy to use, supporting CGA, Hercules, EGA, VGA and all video modes by UltraVision. Customize it, choosing colors that suit your own needs. Supports graphics well and uses a Microsoft-compatible mouse.

Run a selected list of programs automatically when BACK & FORTH is first loaded. Word processing capabilities are included. Select hot keys used to pop up BACK & FORTH, the Cut & Paste commands, and all defined programs. Text can be cut from a running program and placed in a clipboard for later pasting, can be printed, or written to a separate file.

BACK & FORTH sets up DOS environments for use in executing programs, utilities, and/or DOS commands. Use your modem to dial a number from the screen, and get global support for the following programs: 4DOS, PCED/VSTACK, QEMM, 386-to-the Max, etc.

(PC-SIG Disk#'s 2641, 2642)

Special Requirements: *100% IBM-compatible PC and DOS 3.0+.*
Author Registration: *$69.95*

Batutil   *by CtrlAlt Associates*

BATUTIL is a program with two purposes: to give you power inside your batch files and to give you more control over the DOS environment. It is non-resident and has almost 100 commands.

(PC-SIG Disk# 2207)

Special Requirements: *None.*
Author Registration: *$30.00*
➤*ASP Member.*

Blank-It ☆   *by Rhode Island Soft Systems, Inc.*

BLANK-IT is a program that will black out the computer display after a certain "timeout" period to prevent screen burning. "Burn-in," not an uncommon problem, results from allowing a computer screen to display the same image for long periods of time, and can ruin a monitor.

As long as the computer keyboard is in use, there's no evidence that BLANK-IT is even running. However, if the keyboard is left untouched for several minutes (customizeable from 1 to 59 minutes), then the screen will automatically blank. When the space bar is pressed, the screen will reappear and the user will be right where he or she left off.

BLANK-IT contains several advanced features, such as a quick-blank "hot key" (sometimes referred to as a "Boss Key"), and the ability to enable/disable BLANK-IT while it's loaded. It uses only 528 bytes of memory, works during high speed communication, and has added support for graphics mode.

(PC-SIG Disk# 2650)

Special Requirements: *Hard drive.*
Author Registration: *$10.00/$15.00*
➤*ASP Member.*

BOOT.SYS ☆   *by Hans Salvisberg*

If you currently edit your CONFIG.SYS and AUTOEXEC.BAT files and then reboot to change your system configuration, you're doing the work that BOOT.SYS should be doing for you.

BOOT.SYS makes it possible to display one or more menus at boot-up time. Execute different parts of your CONFIG.SYS and/or AUTOEXEC.BAT files, depending on which options are chosen from a configuration menu.

Need different drivers or memory configurations in your CONFIG.SYS file for different applications? In the past, you either had to rename or edit your start-up files and then reboot to get a different setup. This process is now much easier and safer, using BOOT.SYS.

The following features make BOOT.SYS a must-have for every sophisticated PC installation:

❑ Easy installation with detailed examples at every level of complexity
❑ Up to nine options per menu (one line per option) with a definable prompt area at the top of the screen
❑ Up to 25 consecutive menus, each defining a different aspect of system configuration
❑ Up to 25 levels of nested menus (submenus), simplifying the approach to systems configuration
❑ Only one version of CONFIG.SYS and AUTOEXEC.BAT. Rename files; no rebooting
❑ User-definable timeout and default option for each menu
❑ Edit individual CONFIG.SYS lines on the fly while booting up
❑ Insert comments into CONFIG.SYS without generating error messages
❑ Uses less than 200 bytes of resident DOS memory
❑ Warm or cold boot features from the DOS command line or from a batch file
❑ Includes PAUSE.SYS for debugging complex CONFIG.SYS set-ups.

(PC-SIG Disk# 2547)

Special Requirements: *None.*
Author Registration: *$39.00*
➤*ASP Member.*

BriteLine ✐   *by RSE Inc.*

Have trouble locating the cursor on your laptop? BRITELINE is the answer. It highlights the entire line the cursor is on, making it a breeze to find the cursor and read the data on the cursor line.

BRITELINE is a tiny TSR (less than 1K) that you can turn on or off. Registered users can make the cursor line any of 127 different color combinations and even change the size of the cursor. Quit squinting — give BRITELINE a try today.

(PC-SIG Disk# 2391)

Special Requirements: *None.*
Author Registration: *$10*

Burn-In
by George Campbell

BURN-IN tests your new PC to the limit to make certain that if there is a problem, it shows up before your warranty runs out.

BURN-IN makes your computer and drives do electronic pushups and deep knee bends for 24 to 72 hours. By then, the PC will either conk out and you can use your warranty or it will last until it's obsolete. The basic rule is that electronic devices usually break during their first couple of dozen hours of heavy use or else they will last a long, long time.

This program first runs a routine displaying ASCII characters. Then it runs graphics to exercise your CGA, EGA or VGA card. As soon as it's finished, it generates random numbers and stores them on your disks and displays them. Then it erases the numbers and repeats the whole exercise over and over and over again.

(PC-SIG Disk# 1335)

Special Requirements: *None.*
Author Registration: *$10.00*

Capacity
by Trevor Michie

Upon execution CAPACITY displays free disk space in bytes and kilobytes, disk capacity, cluster size, and a horizontal bar graph display of the free space as percentage of the whole disk. Helpful hardware information like the CPU speed, type of display adapter, I/O port detection including a mouse or joystick, installed memory, and DOS version is also displayed.

(PC-SIG Disk# 1682)

Special Requirements: *None.*
Author Registration: *$10.00*

Clock
by Ray Mathes

CLOCK displays a full analog clock face on the screen of your computer, including second hand, in real time taken from DOS. A menu-based help function is available to allow sizing and positioning of the clock on the screen, but the default is full screen size. The C source code for the program is included.

(PC-SIG Disk# 875)

Special Requirements: *CGA.*
Author Registration: *None.*

Clock (PC-SIG Disk# 875)

CloneRom
by PC Technotes

Watch out, Big Blue! CLONEROM helps the dedicated hobbyist make his PC/XT/AT absolutely, totally IBM compatible, right down to the programming of the chips in the motherboard. To obtain system-level compatibililty, you must install a true blue ROM-BIOS. The full text from the IBM-PC Read-Only-Memory Backup Manual is ready to print to tell you how. Two utility programs are available to help you finish the job.

If you already own an IBM or clone, how would you like to have backup ROM and EPROM chips that cost less than IBM-programmed ICs? You can do it with CLONEROM. Save your entire ROM on disks as insurance against disaster.

(PC-SIG Disk# 1408)

Special Requirements: *None.*
Author Registration: *$9.95*

CMOS-RAM/CHEKCMOS
by Thomas Mosteller

Eventually the batteries in your AT will run out! What happens then, you ask? Well, your computer just won't boot up. CMOS_RAM is the closest thing to having AT insurance. It stores all battery maintained information on a disk file then allows you to easily restore it once you've replaced your battery.

Not only the date and time depend on charged batteries, vital system configuration information is also held in CMOS RAM by battery power. Your computer is lost without it. This program keeps a record of all that information. It should be run, then stored away on floppy disk until the inevitable day comes when you need it.

✍ = Updated Program
☆ = New Program

On that day you won't have to panic or hire a technician. You'll just slip this diskette in your A drive, boot your computer from floppy, type CMOS_RAM, press return, and after a short but delightful introductory screen the program will let you restore your CMOS RAM information from a disk file.

This program also comes with a lookout utility that keeps an eye on your configuration file. If you ever change your configuration, it will prompt you to update your CMOS RAM backup. This lookout utility, called CHEKMOS, is also smart enough to watch your battery voltage and alert you if it starts to fade.

(PC-SIG Disk# 1781)

Special Requirements: *AT-compatible or any computer that stores setup infomation in CMOS RAM.*
Author Registration: *$5.00*

Date and Time
by Brown Enterprises

For those of you who do not have a clock card in your computer, here's a utility that quickly lets you enter the date and time during a computing session. The BASIC source code is provided.

(PC-SIG Disk# 908)

Special Requirements: *None.*
Author Registration: *$3.50*

DiskTest
by Steve Platt

This program performs read and write tests on any floppy or standard hard disk. If it detects any errors, it shows the exact error that occurred and the sector in which it occurred. When finished it shows how many errors were corrected by retries or recalibration. It allows the user to specify the starting and ending sectors to test and the number of test loops. It allows the user to choose read-only, write- only, or write and read testing. The user provides the data pattern to be written.

(PC-SIG Disk# 2019)

Special Requirements: *None.*
Author Registration: *$10.00*

Drivechk & Align
by John L Dickinson

This package should occupy a prominent place on the reference shelves of any computer repairman! Just about everything you'd ever want or need to know about disk drive diagnosis and adjustment is included in DRIVECHK & ALIGN. The diagnostics provided are quite easy to learn and operate. However, be warned that both special tools and some level of hands-on technical experience in the repair field are necessary to use all the power built into this package!

The two separate documentation packages included are very thorough and obviously written by an expert in the field of drive repair and adjustment. Subjects are approached in an understandable step-by-step manner. You can't go wrong at the price, even if you're a rookie who only uses the program for periodic tests of proper drive function.

(PC-SIG Disk# 1087)

Special Requirements: *Xidex/Dysan diagnostic diskettes.*
Author Registration: *None.*

Easy Format ✍
by Falk Data Systems

The fun floppy disk formatter. Powerful, flexible, fully customizable, and easy to use. Gives you complete control over every formatting detail. Supports all common diskette sizes.

EASY FORMAT is designed to meet all your diskette formatting needs, providing four different methods of disk testing and six different options for marking bad spots to make floppy disks more reliable. Or you can turn all disk testing off for very fast formatting.

EASY FORMAT makes it possible to format two disks simultaneously in two different drives, even if they're different capacities. You can place a volume label on each disk formatted and still make the disk bootable with the DOS "SYS" command. You can even put your own custom "boot message" onto the disk.

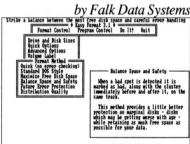

Easy Format (PC-SIG Disk# 2143)

EASY FORMAT makes it easy to format a 360K disk in a 1.2M for use in other 360K drives. It can produce diskettes with either one or two copies of the File Allocation Table (FAT). It won't format hard disks, so there is no danger in accidentally choosing the wrong drive for formatting.

Everything from drives and disk sizes, format options, screen colors, sound effects, and more can be customized. Set up EASY FORMAT once and it will remember your preferences the next time it is used. Or just flip a switch and EASY FORMAT changes languages. English, German, and Spanish are supported. These are all the extras you only get from the best.

(PC-SIG Disk# 2143)

Special Requirements: *None.*
Author Registration: *$40.00*
➤ *ASP Member.*

EGA Screen Save
by Max D. Teuton

A screen-blanking routine that shuts your EGA screen off after three minutes of keyboard inactivity. This helps prolong the life of your screen by preventing "image burn-in." Striking any key restores your video display.

(PC-SIG Disk# 789)

Special Requirements: *EGA.*
Author Registration: *None.*

Fansi-Console
by Hersey Micro Consulting, Inc.

A sophisticated memory-resident program which replaces the standard IBM PC console drivers.

Full support is provided for: IBM PS/2 product line for both video and keyboard; VGA and Super-EGA, including 132 column and 60 row display drivers; enhanced 101/102 key keyboards, including foreign and "Brand X" keyboards.

FANSI-CONSOLE extends and speeds up the ROM BIOS and processes ANSI X3.64 control sequences. Keyboard macros are supported — program specific keys to perform complex series of keystokes. Reconfigure your keyboard however you wish — even a Dvorak layout. Experiment with different drivers.

(PC-SIG Disk#'s 356, 650)

Special Requirements: *Two floppy drives.*
Author Registration: *$49.95 — use license; $75.00 — user manual and updated version.*

From CP/M to and Almost-DOS to DOS ✍
by Sydex

22DISK — Converts, formats, and manipulates diskettes in over 150 CP/M 2.2 formats (300 in registered version) to/from DOS files. ASCII diskette description file allows "roll your own" specifications for really hard-to-find systems. May require a 1.2M diskette drive.

22NICE — A companion product to 22DISK. 22NICE emulates the CP/M 2.2 operating system and permits most CP/M programs to run under DOS. Once installed, the DOS-CP/M integration is seamless. It will make use of NEC V20 or V30 CPU chip if one is present. 22NICE emulates most terminals and provides a keyboard-remapping function to obtain the best operation using the PC keyboard. (Includes 22DISK)

RAINDOS — The flagship of the DOS compatibility series, just made for those DEC Rainbow MS-DOS diskettes. Use this driver to read your diskettes, transfer files, even format new diskettes for your Rainbow.

EAGLE16 — Another driver in the DOS compatibility series, this product provides a solution to diskettes from this extinct-owner species. This driver lets you read and format Eagle 16 diskettes, and transfer files t your PC-compatible.

HP150 — Need to have HP 150 files on a PC-compatible? The third produc in the DOS compatibility series offers an alternative to the null modem method.

COTDOS — The fourth driver in this DOS compatibility series handles diskettes from the Sears/British Apricot, easier than special cabling an communications for file transfer to your PC-compatible.

(PC-SIG Disk# 2355)

Special Requirements: *High density drive recommended.*
Author Registration: *$15.00 to $40.00 per program.*

✍ = Updated Program
☆ = New Program

Garths Shareware Utilities
by Garth Braithwaite

GARTH'S SHAREWARE UTILITIES is a collection of utilities for copying disks, printing, and listing directories.

COPYDISK is a multiple 360K disk copying program that makes several disk copies after reading the source disk only once. If there are two floppy drives, you have the option to alternate between the two for writing onto the copy disks.

D is a utility that allows you to change directories without having to look for the "\" key.

DDIR is a date directory utility that lists files of a particular date, before a date, after a date, or in a particular date range. Change the dates and times of specified files. DDIR automatically searches every directory and can also be used as an ordinary file finder without the date options.

PRINTER sends printer codes to the printer for changing the line spacing and the printing style. The codes can be written to a file, which may be later used to set up the printer without the use of the program.

DIRLABEL prints out a disk's entire directory in a small compact form. The program allows you to specify the drive, the printer port, the size of paper or label to be used, and the top and ending spaces for each label.

(PC-SIG Disk# 1859)

Special Requirements: *None.*
Author Registration: *$20.00*

gBlink
by Glen Osborne

gBLINK is a simple utility to blank your pc's screen after a specified period of inactivity on the keyboard. The program also includes an onscreen clock which can be turned on and off from the keyboard (the clock is positioned in the upper right corner of the screen). The program is extremely simple to install and uninstall, and comes complete with documentation to help you get started.

(PC-SIG Disk# 2029)

Special Requirements: *None.*
Author Registration: *None.*

GEM Utilities ☆
by George McLam

A collection of many utilities, GEM UTILITIES was written with the technical person in mind, but has a little something for everyone. Included is a program to show your computer's equipment, disk's parameters, generate TV test patterns, control your printer, display a running clock, capture screens, display disk and (all) memory capacity/usage, encode/decode files, display today's saying, test your keyboard, split a file, display an ASCII table, CGA & VGA border color control programs, remove tabs or control Zs from a file, etc....

(PC-SIG Disk# 2419)

Special Requirements: *None.*
Author Registration: *$15.00; $50.00 site license.*

File Descriptions:

ADD	Append two or three files into one file.
ADDPATH	Modify PATH without retyping it or rebooting computer.
ASCIIHEX	Display ASCII character, hex value, decimal value & more.
BLANK	TSR to blank screen, show running clock, capture screens.
COLORS40	Display color palette in 40 column text mode.
COLORS80	Display color palette in 80 column text mode.
COMSWAP	Swap COM1: and COM2:.
DIRECT	Display only subdirectories of the current directory.
DIS	Like DIR, but only displays the files you want.
DSKCHK	Display technical data about a disk.
FORTUNES	Display a fortune, saying, or quote.
FREE	Display capacity and free space of memory and disks.
GETNUM	Use with batch files to create simple yet powerful menus.
HELP!	HELP! for DOS, utilities, and general info.
KEYTEST	Check out your keyboard.
LISTEQ	List equipment installed on your computer.
MENU	User configurable menu program, uses keyboard or mouse.
MOVE	Move files from one directory to another, allows wildcards
NODIR	Display files *. (optionally include subdirectories).
NODIS	Display files or directories except ???.

NOTABS	Expand tab characters into spaces and/or remove Cntrl-Zs.
PRINTERS	Use your printer's special features, user configurable.
PCONFIG	Use to create or edit overlay files for printers.
PORTSTAT	Show status or LPT1:-LPT4: & COM1:-COM4:.
PROCOLOR	Create special color (or B&W) prompt (requires ANSI.SYS).
SAYINGS	Displays multiple fortune files optionally in color.
SECRET	Encode/decode files (DOS & XENIX).
SPLIT	Split one file into two files.
ZDEL	Remove control Z characters from the end of a file.
NTSC	A collection of NTSC TV test patterns (requires color).
BORDER	CGA & VGA border color control programs.

Hdtest ✍   *by Peter R. Fletcher*

HDTEST performs a read/write test on your hard disk without disturbing the data currently on it!

HDTEST writes 20 different test patterns to every cluster on the disk, checks that they can be read back correctly, and then carefully restores your original data! Extremely sensitive, it can even detect errors which are minor enough to be corrected by the disk controller's own error-correcting code (ECC). These errors are normally invisible to the user but may be the first signs of future disk problems.

The program is also useful for automatic disk repair when you get intermittent or persistent read errors. Because HDTEST tries harder than DOS alone, it can often recover almost unreadable data from both hard and floppy disks and rewrite it — a real life saver when your backup fails you.

Simple to use, the program was written to minimize the likelihood of user error causing data loss on a good disk. HDCHEK, a companion program, gives you a quick compatibility report to tell you if HDTEST will run on your system.

(PC-SIG Disk# 1209)

Special Requirements: *None.*
Author Registration: *$35.00*
➤*ASP Member.*

Hercules   *by ProCon Software*

Run programs requiring a CGA card on a Hercules Graphics adapter. This emulator allows such programs as PC-Paint, Printmaster, Flight Simulator and many others to run with no visible difference.

(PC-SIG Disk# 641)

Special Requirements: *Hercules graphics.*
Author Registration: *$30.00*

HGCIBM   *by Athena Digital*

If you're the owner of a computer with a Hercules monochrome graphics adapter card, and have been lusting after a nice piece of color graphic (CGA) software, but can't run it because of your current computer set- up, this software will solve your problems.

HGCIBM provides owners of Hercules graphics cards with a means to run software written for the IBM Color Graphics Adapter. You need no additional hardware to run this emulator — HGCIBM works by "tricking" programs into thinking you have a color card when you don't.

With HGCIBM, a color program won't shut itself down but instead, will continue to send video output to your monochrome screen. This program is one of the few "must-own" programs for all Hercules users.

(PC-SIG Disk# 870)

Special Requirements: *Hercules graphics.*
Author Registration: *$10.00*

Hide-it ✍   *by RSE Inc.*

HIDE-IT is a great way to keep private data private. It's the most secure way I know of, short of encrypting your files. But what makes HIDE-IT so nice is it's virtually transparent to the user. When you firs boot up your computer you enter a password. If you don't, or the password is incorrect, then you won't find, or be able to work on the hidden files. It's as if they didn't exist. However if you enter the correct password then you'll have access to all the hidden files and you can go about your business as if they were normal old files. You do nothing except enter the password when the computer fist boots. From there HIDE-IT takes care of everything. Couldn't be easier, could it?

(PC-SIG Disk# 2391)

Special Requirements: *None.*
Author Registration: *$20.00*

InteMenu
by JC Systems

INTEMENU is an interactive, intelligent and integrated menuing system. Not just another pretty menuing program, INTEMENU is a command, control, and communications center for up to four LAN users. A Graphical User Interface (GUI) takes up 12K of memory, and is compatible with EGA, VGA, and monochrome monitors.

Three of the key features are:

❑ An Application Launch Pad — A traditional menuing feature which lets you organize your applications into manageable groups. Selection of any desired application is just one keystroke away.
❑ A Message Center — A revolutionary feature for a menuing system. Send and automatically receive simple messages interactively with other INTEMENU users without the trouble of invoking an E-Mail package.
❑ A Group of 26 Broadcast Stations — Tune in to the latest information, whether departmental news, sports and entertainment, gossip, etc. This feature provides a means to broadcast "important" news and creates a sense of community among Local Area Network users.

(PC-SIG Disk# 2353)

Special Requirements: *Any Local Area Network (Novell, etc.)*
Author Registration: *$100.00*

MakeSYS
by Denver MicroData

Still not sure why your CONFIG.SYS file is so vital, or not sure exactly how to make or change the one that's on your system? MAKESYS finally explains what your CONFIG.SYS file does and helps you build one. This program gives the non-technical user the power of the professionals. It may also be a time saver for those who often find themselves editing a CONFIG.SYS file with a cumbersome editor.

(PC-SIG Disk# 1994)

Special Requirements: *None.*
Author Registration: *$5.00*

MAXI Form
by Herne Data System, Ltd.

Like to increase the amount of storage available on your floppy disks? Format your disks with MAXI FORM and you can expand storage on your 360K disks by one-sixth: you get 420K bytes free. On 1.2 Meg drives, you get 1.4 meg; on 720K 3.5 inch drives you get 800K; and on 1.44 Meg 3.5 inch drives you get an incredible 1.6 Meg per disk! You also get 800K on a normal 360K 5.25 inch disk in a 1.2 Meg drive.

It's as simple as putting a disk in a slot and typing MAXI A: (with a few command line options, if you wish). The default "fast format" method can create a 420K disk in under 40 seconds, while an optional verify switch lets you check each track as it is formatted. MAXI created disks are not bootable.

(PC-SIG Disk# 1503)

Special Requirements: *DOS 3.2 or later.*
Author Registration: *$10.00 individuals; $100.00 corporate site license.*
➤*ASP Member.*

MicroMacroBat
by Sitting Duck Software

MICROMACROBAT lets your batch files perform tricks for which DOS makes no provision. Simple batch file commands allow for box drawing, scrolling, printing, fadeout, printing of big text and a plethora of other functions; all in color. Mix MICROMACROBAT commands freely with the batch file commands to which you are accustomed. For example, putting the command MB BOX/1/1/25/80/1/31/C in your batch file draws a white on blue box around the entire screen and clears the inside to blue. There are no complicated commands to learn and there no compiling steps. MICROMACROBAT is useful for installation programs, back-up batch files, tutorials, demos, slide shows and any occasion for which you need snappy batch files. MICROMACROBAT is a worthwhile utility for batch file creators and programmers.

(PC-SIG Disk# 2165)

Special Requirements: *None.*
Author Registration: *$35.00*

Montage2
by CrystaLines Ltd

MONTAGE2 is in this library for one reason: it's fun. It presents a colorful line display rivaled only by '60s music videos — a good way to show off your EGA system. You configure parameters that determine the color and pattern of the lines. It's self-documented with a help display during execution.

(PC-SIG Disk# 789)

Special Requirements: *EGA.*
Author Registration: *None.*

Patch
by Imaginative Software Concepts

PATCH lets you view and modify disk files in memory or peruse and change the computer's memory as if it were a disk file.

Display the contents of a file in memory, 256 bytes at a time. Move around in the file, modify its contents, cancel modifications and search for specified strings. Move immediately to the beginning or end of a file or jump to a portion of the file that is a certain offset, in bytes, from the beginning of the file.

The file contents are displayed in both ASCII and hexadecimal. You can do searches and modifications in either format. Both formats of the file are viewed at the same time, with the hexadecimal on the left and the ASCII on the right.

(PC-SIG Disk# 779)

Special Requirements: *None.*
Author Registration: *$20.00*

PC General Use Utilities ✍
by Sydex

CONFORMAT — A "pop-up" diskette formatter that allows you to format diskettes while doing more productive things. Has received rave reviews from its users and some very nice words in the press (see June, 1989 PC Magazine, pg. 48). An all-time "most popular" program.

COPYQM — A diskette duplicating machine. Formats, copies, and verifies all in one pass. Up to four drives supported at once; features color icon-type interface, drive-status sensing (no keyboard entries). Record/playback image files from hard disk, serialize copies, even copy non-DOS formats in "Blind Copy" mode. All standard DOS formats supported.

FORMATQM — Mass diskette formatter in the same "no hands" tradition of COPYQM. Formats and verifies faster than anything else around. Supports all standard DOS formats, up to four drives at a time.

TELEDISK — A diskette "fax" machine. Turn any diskette into a compressed data file and vice-versa. Allows you to send and receive entire diskettes via modem. Great for those bootable game diskettes and for diskettes with subdirectories. Even works with some "copy-protected" diskettes. This one is licensed by IBM!

(PC-SIG Disk# 2356)

Special Requirements: *None.*
Author Registration: *$15.00 for ConFormat & CopyQM. $10 for FormatQM. $20.00 for TeleDisk.*

PC Hunter ☆
by Thinking Software

PC HUNTER is a lean and mean file finder. Specify a file name (partial name with DOS wildcards) or text from a file, and PC-Hunter will search all the directories on any drive for the file. Then it lists the files and their locations or displays the text. And does it all FAST!

Special Requirements: *None.*
Author Registration: *$10.00*

✍ = Updated Program
☆ = New Program

PC-Kwick
by Multisoft Corporation

Speed up disk-intensive programs with memory cache. Great for programs like WordStar that use overlay files. Redundant disk accesses are eliminated by storing frequently-read data in RAM memory. This RAM can be accessed instantaneously, unlike mechanical drives. The concept is similar to a RAM disk; however, you can gain more performance with less RAM requirements because PC-KWICK is smart enough to store only repeatedly-accessed code in memory.

PC-KWICK automatically allocates memory above 360K that is not used by DOS or other memory-resident programs. The program is designed for DOS 2.0 through 3.3.

(PC-SIG Disk# 1037)

Special Requirements: *384K RAM*.
Author Registration: *$5.00 to $26.00*.

PC-Zipper
by Lawrence Software

Why not speed up your computer? PC-ZIPPER is software that will do exactly that without sacrificing performance. The speed of a PC, XT, AT or even a 386 (and their clones) is rather arbitrarily determined by the manufacturer. In actuality, if all the memory in your computer is sound there is no reason why you can't be running a little faster. And who doesn't want to run a little faster?

Ziptest is the first of two programs that come with PC-ZIPPER. This utility calls procedures, executes a routine, times it, and then records the results. Upon completion, Ziptest checks to find which procedure resulted in an increase in processor speed. The results create a curve, where the optimum system performance is at the "crest" of the curve. Zip, the main program, then can be set to maximize the speed of your computer.

If you didn't understand all that, then just believe it works. PC-ZIPPER increased the speed of this reviewer's AT by nearly one full MHz according to Landmarks Speed test (note that no speed testing software is included with PC-ZIPPER). You don't have to understand it to use it — it's easy to install and control even for the beginner. PC-ZIPPER will check for weak or faulty memory, it can be turned off without rebooting, and it can be used to slow your computer slightly. And, best of all, it uses NO memory.

(PC-SIG Disk# 1572)

Special Requirements: *None*.
Author Registration: *$9.95*

PDELETE
by Patri-Soft

PDELETE is an advanced DELETE command to be used in DOS systems. It may be used in place of the DOS Erase and Delete command or instead of it. Like other Patriquin utilities, PDELETE gives you more control of command processing and provides a much safer way to process files. PDELETE also provides several features not found with the standard DOS command.

Unlike other delete utilities, PDELETE supports DOS paths and wildcards. It keeps you aware of what files are being processed and provides an emergency stop feature just in case you have started something you feel is wrong.

PDELETE's file selection parameters provide you with numerous options for specifying the files to be deleted. You may select by directory, file, date, attribute, size, and even starting and ending filename.

Features:
❑ Advanced file selection.
❑ Emergency STOP by pressing any key.
❑ Delete entire directories and remove them from disk.
❑ Optionally wipe file data from disk during delete to prevent it from being recovered by unauthorized person.
❑ Optional verify feature lets you approve each file before it is deleted.
❑ Optionally deletes HIDDEN / SYSTEM / READONLY files.
❑ Delete files until specified freespace is available.
❑ Advanced DOS Pattern capability.
❑ Test feature allows you to try a command before actually deleting any files.
❑ Deletes from multiple disk drives with a single command.
❑ Accepts a list of files to be deleted.

❏ Exclusion capability allows files to be protected from deletion.
(PC-SIG Disk# 2312)
Special Requirements: *Hard drive.*
Author Registration: *$20.00*
➤*ASP Member.*

PDVIM
by PTD Software Systems

PDVIM, is the shareware version of VIM (VIrtual Machine), an interpreter/debugger that can simulate and/or allow access to the hardware of an XT or AT in an addressing space independent of the normal hardware.

This debugger can stop execution at any point, examine or alter memory or registers, examine the program, determine where the program has been, and much more. Unlike DOS DEBUG and other debuggers, these functions are accomplished by a program outside the addressing space of the program or system under test, so VIM can never be altered or destroyed by the errant program.

VIM also can trace DOS itself, or the ROMs, and set breakpoints within ROM or on data. When a faulty interrupt code is reached, the breakpoint stops VIM, so the code can be traced and variables examined. VIM's virtual approach allows it to debug programs that others can't, including terminate-and-stay-resident programs and device drivers.

(PC-SIG Disk# 962)
Special Requirements: *320K RAM.*
Author Registration: *$49.00*

Personal C - Screen
by Ebnet Software

The key to professional-looking programs is the screen design. However, producing such screens is often a tedious and time-consuming task. With PERSONAL C-SCREEN the implementation of a professional screen layout into your C program becomes a simple task. It has the following functions; interactive format generation, windows, menus, pop ups, pull downs, variable field and text attributes, alphanumeric and numeric selectable fields, mouse and printer support, and monochrome and color display support.

PERSONAL C-SCREEN includes a set of screen management modules to generate the screen formats. These interface modules let you use PERSONAL C-SCREEN with major C compilers such as Microsoft C, Microsoft Quick C, Turbo C, and Lattice C.

PERSONAL C-SCREEN is invaluable to anyone wanting to improve the appearance of their C programs, and even comes with a demo program to illustrate its ease of use.

(PC-SIG Disk# 2188)
Special Requirements: *C Compiler.*
Author Registration: *$17.00*

pKDisk
by Nun-Hong Lin

pKDisk is a compact terminate-stay-resident compression program which reduces the size of your .EXE or .COM files by 10 to 30 percent. Includes five utilities to aid in compressing your programs.

(PC-SIG Disk# 2446)
Special Requirements: *None.*
Author Registration: *$25.00 or $45.00*

Prism ☆
by The Brass Cannon Corporation

PRISM is a utility that will reset the color attributes on your VGA screen. Instead of using DOS's 16 garish colors, create more pleasing palettes of colors to use with ANY non-graphics program.

PRISM contains nearly 60K of Help screens. These Help screens will teach you everything you need to know in order to use the program effectively. Create bright new colors for your VGA system within minutes.

PRISM is written in Turbo Pascal 6.0, from Borland International, and makes use of the Object Professional library from TurboPower.

(PC-SIG Disk# 2747)
Special Requirements: *VGA, and a hard drive or high-density disk drive.*
Author Registration: *$25.00*

Procon Utilities
by ProCon Software

PROCON UTILITIES is a handy collection of memory resident utilities from Down Under — Australia that is!

❏ BLANKS — Automatically blanks the screen after 1 to 9 minutes of no keyboard or screen activity to preserve your monitor. Works with Mono/Hercules and CGA.

❏ HERCULES — Permits CGA graphics on a PC with a Hercules card. Works with many programs, including PC-PAINT, PRINTMASTER, and FLIGHT SIMULATOR (minus the Esc screen)!

❏ CLOCKON — A memory resident on-screen clock that works in all CGA modes and can be turned on and off from the key board.

❏ CLOCKSET, CLOCKGET, SETCLOCK — Quick fixes for the Real Time Clock bugs of the MM58167 RTC (leap year and year counter) chip and its interface with the system clock in your PC! Use to replace Timer.Com.

❏ SWAP, SCREEN, DUALS — Programs for PCs with two display cards and monitors. SWAP will toggle the active display and SCREENS will ensure both displays are initialized at boot-up. DUALS permits dual screen functioning from GWBASIC and is very useful for graphics demonstrations and debugging.

(PC-SIG Disk# 1537)

Special Requirements: *None.*
Author Registration: *$20.00*

Programmer's Productivity Pack
by Falk Data Systems

PROGRAMMER'S PRODUCTIVITY PACK provides the utilities and reference most frequently needed by programmers.

PROPAK provides you with:

❏ A programmer's calculator that works in decimal, hexadecimal, binary, and octal, simultaneously.
❏ Addition, subtraction, multiplication, integer division, and modulus mathematical functions.
❏ SHL, SHR, ROL, ROR, SAL, SAR, RCL, RCR bit manipulation functions.
❏ An ASCII color attribute chart.
❏ A keystroke reference utility that returns both the BIOS scan codes, and the dBASE INKEY() values.
❏ Keystroke recording and playback allowing up to 100 keystroke recordings of 1000 keystrokes each.
❏ A screen grabber utility that grabs text from the screen and plays it back like a keystroke recording.
❏ A screen capture facility allowing filtering for screen or printer.
❏ Access to the DOS background PRINT facility.
❏ A screen-blanking facility that will park your hard drive(s) while the screen is blanked.
❏ A pop-up DOS shell capable of shelling to DOS from any program, with up to 600K bytes of memory available.
❏ Complete control of all the hot keys, colors, sound effects, file extensions, memory usage, and more through PCUSTOM, the customizing program.

All this in one smoothly integrated package. PROPAK has tools which can run stand-alone, memory-resident (even with Sidekick), memory- resident with swapping, or as a background task in a multitasking environment. Since PROPAK provides you with the ability to customize every detail, it not only helps you to be more productive, it gives you the freedom to adapt it your particular needs and preferences.

(PC-SIG Disk#'s 2339, 2340)

Special Requirements: *None.*
Author Registration: *$79.00*
➤*ASP Member.*

PSEARCH
by Patri-Soft

PSEARCH will quickly locate any file by a name or text the file contains! You can have many search criteria, patterns like *TOM*.* to find files with TOM in the name, or ^REVIEW to find filenames sounding like REVIEW. Search for files containing 1-5 strings or words. Look for filenames in .ARC, .ZIP, .LZH. Search algorithm is fast! Search a directory, path, or all disks on your system automatically. Menu or command line driven.

Some of the many possible uses for PSEARCH:

❏ Wildcard searches.
❏ List files and text lines containing specified text strings.

❑ Compile all C programs referring to a specific include file.
❑ Locate document containing specific text strings.
❑ Delete any files containing specific text strings.
❑ Locate all Readonly files on a disk.
❑ List all files by date criteria.
❑ Search multiple drives for text or a file name
❑ Search for a file name archived into .ZIP, .ARC or .LZH formats.
❑ The ability to exclude files from the search process greatly improves search performance. Limit text search to words, prefixes, or suffixes. This greatly enhances the search by returning only the data you want.

(PC-SIG Disk# 2313)

Special Requirements: *None.*
Author Registration: *$20.00*
➤*ASP Member.*

Read
by clySmic

If you are a batch file writer who needs interaction and the use of DOS' environment variables, here are utilities to make your life easier.

Most batch file utilities return results in the ERRORLEVEL. These utilities set an environment variable, which means direct character results can be communicated between programs. If you ask for a Y or N you can test for a Y or N.

READLN and READKEY are programs that get input from the keyboard and place it in environment variables. They're perfect for making interactive batch files and much easier to use than utilities that use ERRORLEVEL to communicate the results.

READLN displays the prompt and waits for input. All input up to an ENTER is placed in a specified environment variable. If the first letter of var is capitalized, the input will be also.

READKEY displays the prompt and waits for input. ONE character is read (no ENTER is needed) and it is placed in the environment variable var. If the first letter of var is capitalized, the input character will be also. If an extended key (function key, arrow keys, &c.) is pressed, the ASCII representation of the hexadecimal scan code for the key is placed in the variable. If a Carriage Return, Escape, BEL, or TAB is pressed, the ASCII representation of the character's ASCII code is placed in the variable.

(PC-SIG Disk# 2234)

Special Requirements: *DOS 3.3 or 4.0*
Author Registration: *None.*

Reconfig
by Karl Freburger

RECONFIG is a handy utility for quickly reconfiguring your AUTOEXEC.BAT and CONFIG.SYS files. Multiple AUTOEXEC.BAT and CONFIG.SYS files can be stored by RECONFIG and accessed by a batch file that automatically switches files for alternative computer set-ups. The utility can also reboot your computer.

(PC-SIG Disk# 1037)

Special Requirements: *None.*
Author Registration: *None.*

Reconfig by Optimal
by Optimal Solutions of New Hampshire

For the beginner, RECONFIG demystifies the combination of AUTOEXEC.BAT and CONFIG.SYS — two files which tell your computer what to do when you first turn it on (anything from setting your path to loading memory resident programs).

A great tool for the hard disk user, RECONFIG lets you create and quickly change to a different DOS configuration. Instead of grabbing your DOS manual when you need to swap printers or drop your programs from memory, you'll make the needed change in minutes. You can maintain multiple sets of your AUTOEXEC.BAT and CONFIG.SYS files, quickly transforming your DOS machine to a whole new environment.

✍ = Updated Program
☆ = New Program

The program can maintain a database of up to 100 different configurations with its built-in editor and easy-to-use drop down menus.

(PC-SIG Disk# 1218)

Special Requirements: *Hard drive.*
Author Registration: *$39.50.*

ScreenSaver
by Signature Software

This memory resident screen blanking utility requires less than 2K of memory. It works with MDA, HGC, CGA, EGA, and VGA type displays. Unlike other screen blanking utilities that will only blank your screen at a DOS prompt or after a certain period of inactivity, SCREENSAVER will blank your monitor either instantly or automatically while you are in almost any application program.

(PC-SIG Disk# 1777)

Special Requirements: *Works with all display adapters.*
Author Registration: *$14.95*

SCRNOFF3 & KYLOCK
by Ocean

Here are a pair of protective utilities.

SCRNOFF3 blanks your screen after three minutes of keyboard inactivity. This avoids etching your monitor. Pressing any key brings the screen back into view.

KYLOCK blanks your screen and locks the keyboard from others. When the keyboard is locked, not even a Ctrl-Alt-Del routine reboots the computer.

(PC-SIG Disk# 779)

Special Requirements: *None.*
Author Registration: *$1.50*

SEL
by clySmic

SEL is an ANSI color selector for DOS or OS/2 for those who use any ANSI screen driver (ANSI.SYS, NANSI.SYS, &c. under DOS; ANSI ON for OS/2).

The program has easy color selection using mnemonics instead of numbers, a random color selection mode, and sets the prompt to a contrasting color.

(PC-SIG Disk# 2234)

Special Requirements: *CGA, and ANSI driver.*
Author Registration: *None.*

Snoop
by clySmic

This utility is not for beginners; it's for programmers and advanced users who wish to snoop around the VGA BIOS.

SNOOP shows various EGA and VGA pointers maintained by BIOS, and displays the contents of the tables these pointers point to. These tables include the user palette override table, the alpha character override table, and the SAVE_PTR table. The program also displays the current contents of the VGA color registers.

(PC-SIG Disk# 2234)

Special Requirements: *EGA, or VGA.*
Author Registration: *None.*

Soft87 ☆
by Multiix Inc.

SOFT87 is a memory resident math coprocessor emulator that emulates floating point calculations(80287, 802387) on your 286, or 386 computers. It is one of the cheapest ways to acquire math coprocessing capabilities.

SOFT87 is designed for those who do not have an 80x87 (8087, 80287,80387) installed on their computers, but want to use programs that require an 80x87, or write programs with 80x87 instructions.

This program will work with MS-DOS, PC-DOS, MS Windows or DESQview SOFT87 is a Once loaded into memory, SOFT87 stays there until you turn off the computer. After loading SOFT87, the 80x87 instructions can be executed directly even without an 80287 or 80387 installed in the computer. Then you can run programs that require an 80287 or 80387, such as AutoCAD R9, AutoCAD R10, PSpice, PC-MATLAB, ASYST, Auto sketch and PC-SIMNON.

The registered version of SOFT87 provides 57 extended instructions that cannot be found in other coprocessors. These extended instructions will simplify program design and shorten programming time.

With typical co-processors costing between $200(80287-10) to $500(80387-33), you can't afford not to try SOFT87, since it will save you money even after you register it.

(PC-SIG Disk# 2481)

Special Requirements: *286, 386, or 386SX.*
Author Registration: *$59.00 for 287 - $79 for 287/387 - $49 for developer kit*

Speech
by Timothy McIlwee

SPEECH can make your computer talk — in a robotic tone of voice, of course, and you can have it say anything you want!

The memory-resident program can be added via a batch file to any of your programs so they will give a talking introduction. It reads from any standard text file but the words need to be written phonetically. Several phonetic texts are included to give you an idea of how to write your own, and to get your computer talking right off.

Sixteen speeds are provided so you can use it on nearly any computer no matter what its processor speed, such as 8, 10 or even 33 megahertz. To start you just pick one of the versions of SPEECH#.COM you think is close to your machine's speed, load it and type READ (demo file of your choice). Unfortunately, you do have to reboot each time to try a different speed.

Depending on your computer's speaker, the results can be amazing or really bad. Getting your IBM-PC to talk, without adding additional hardware is kind of like dancing dogs. It's not that they do it very well that amazes us...it's that they can do it at all!

(PC-SIG Disk# 1377)

Special Requirements: *None.*
Author Registration: *None.*

Speech (by Vincent Poy)
by Vincent Poy

SPEECH is a program which generates speech and makes it possible for your computer to actually speak to you through its internal speaker. SPEECH is a "terminate and stay resident" program which becomes available as a background function, usable by other programs. An additional program is included, SAY, which passes its command line arguments to the SPEECH function, thus allowing batch files to generate speech.

SPEECH supports thirty-six phonemes, which are specified as one of two character codes, such as, a, ae, ah, b, ch, etc. Phonemes may be given either upper or lower case. Phonemes are separated with a dash and words are separated with a space. For example, to say "this is a test", you would type; tz-ih-s ih-z ah t-eh-s-t-t. This disk gives examples of how to say the cardinal numbers, the ordinal numbers, the letters of the alphabet, and over fifty different words.

SPEECH is easy to use, comes fully documented, and can teach your computer to talk like a parrot. AT and 386 users will need to slow their computers down to about 7.5 MHz in order to be able to understand the computer voice.

(PC-SIG Disk# 1668)

Special Requirements: *Internal computer speaker.*
Author Registration: *$29.95*

Stackey
by CtrlAlt Associates

STACKEY is a keyboard stuffer with natural syntax (F1 is F1) and lots of bells and whistles: hotkey, shift masks, scans Batutil is a batch file enhancer as a high order language; pop up a menu in a one line command: menus, user input, colors, large characters (BIGECHO), etc. Together they can be used to automate much of your computing. Includes on disk manual of over 200 pages and printed manual with registration. Registered users get free Compuserve signup and $15 credit.

(PC-SIG Disk# 2207)

Special Requirements: *None.*
Author Registration: *$30.00*
➤*ASP Member.*

Swap Shop
by Dale Botkin

SWAP SHOP is a collection of various programs used for swapping printer and communication port addresses electronically. No more resetting mechanical switches. Documentation and Assembly source code are included.

(PC-SIG Disk# 2380)

Special Requirements: *None.*
Author Registration: *$3.00 to $5.00.*

The SWAP Utilities
by Innovative Data Concepts

SWAP reduces the memory usage of four popular memory resident programs so you can use them even though you may have a shortage of RAM memory. Consisting of four separate utilities, SWAP will reduce Borland's SideKick and SideKick Plus memory usage to below 9,000 bytes each. Micro Logic's Tornado will need less that 8,000 bytes. Microlytic's GOfer will need less than 8,500 bytes.

The upshot is that you can squeeze more clout into your computer even though you may have an older PC with only 128K or 256K of RAM.

(PC-SIG Disk# 1883)

Special Requirements: *None.*
Author Registration: *$25.00 per utility.*
➤*ASP Member.*

Swapdos
by Innovative Data Concepts

With SWAPDOS, one DOS application may run another, even if both would normally not fit in memory at the same time. By copying base memory, used by the currently running application, to expanded memory/extended memory, or to a disk file, base memory needed by the application is freed up. The desired program is run before restoring the original environment.

Swap out single programs, multiple programs, resident programs, etc. The amount of extra memory gained by using SWAPDOS depends on the application(s) being swapped out. In general, all of the memory used by your program is available for use, minus about 3000 bytes.

If you use one or two main programs and wish to switch among them, or to switch to other programs, SWAPDOS is essential. If you only have 640K with no expanded or extended memory, it's indispensable!

(PC-SIG Disk# 2245)

Special Requirements: *None.*
Author Registration: *$25.00*
➤*ASP Member.*

Test Drive
by Micro Systems Development

TEST DRIVE is a floppy disk drive diagnostic utility for 5.25" 360K disk drives with many tests to ensure that your disk drive is in working order. This can help to alleviate data loss or damage to your diskettes.

As the drive is tested, important operating parameters are displayed on the screen. A spindle speed test and read/write test of the disk drive can be done with just this disk. The alignment, hysteresis, head azimuth and hub centering of your disk drive can be tested but these tests require a precision alignment disk that is available upon registration.

TEST DRIVE can indicate when your disk drives need cleaning and has a utility for use with a standard cleaning disk. It can perform continuous tests for certain adjustments on your drives and can test the general performance of the drive before and after any changes are made.

(PC-SIG Disk# 908)

Special Requirements: *None.*
Author Registration: *$50.00.*

Trash-It ✍
by RSE Inc.

Discover the ultimate protection against accidentally deleting important files. Instead of deleting the file, TRASH-IT moves it to a special "trash" subdirectory where you can easily recover it.

(PC-SIG Disk# 2391)

Special Requirements: *None.*
Author Registration: *$10.00.*

V7CURS
by clySmic

V7CURS is for anyone who owns a VGA card based on the V7VGA chipset, such as the FastWrite VGA or VRAM VGA and hates blinking cursors.

It exploits the non-blinking hardware cursor built into the V7VGA chipset by Video-7/Headland Technologies. It is a small TSR (memory- resident) program that turns off the blinking, leaving you with an XOR cursor. This mode shows what's underneath the cursor.

(PC-SIG Disk# 2234)

Special Requirements: *VGA with the V7VGA chip set.*
Author Registration: *None.*

Vector
by Matt Visser

Programmers — VECTOR inspects the interrupt vector table of your system and displays the vectors in human-readable form with some brief comments describing each interrupt. This is useful because some interrupts are not standardized and are difficult to interpret.

(PC-SIG Disk# 874)

Special Requirements: *360K RAM.*
Author Registration: *$10.00*

VFONT
by clySmic

Tired of the default VGA text-mode font? VFONT contains and loads replacement fonts for VGA systems. It includes two variations of a "modern" font, and a handwritten "scrawl" font.

The DOS version is a TSR (memory-resident) program that takes up approximately 4.5K of RAM, and works only in text modes. The OS/2 version calls the OS to request a new font, and works only in full-screen sessions.

The four fonts are modern solid-line, modern-double-line, scrawl-straight-line, and scrawl-scrawled-line. Modern is a pleasing, sans serif font. Scrawl is a handwritten looking "scrawled" font.

VFONT remains in place even if your software sets the video mode. This means the font won't go away as with some other font programs. The OS/2 version is saved and restored by the OS when switching between screen groups.

(PC-SIG Disk# 2234)

Special Requirements: *VGA.*
Author Registration: *None.*

VGAColor ✍
by DigiTec Software, Ltd.

VGACOLOR helps you to modify the standard color palettes of your VGA monitor. It was designed for those who wish to display different colors while in DOS, and to aid programmers in designing color schemes for their applications.

VGACOLOR provides several other functions, as well. Save your color modifications to a disk file, load a saved color description and, optionally, print a map of the individual color registers. A saved color description file can be loaded as a DOS command and even included in your AUTOEXEC.BAT file. Have many color description files? Change your colors to fit the type of work you are doing.

VGACOLOR prints a color modification report with information on the current state of the individual color registers — particularly useful for programmers who want to incorporate the colors into their own applications. Simply supply the appropriate hex values to the proper Bios routine to change the color and VGACOLOR takes advantage of Bios (Int 10H) for all manipulation of the color palettes and individual color registers.

VGACOLOR provides a separate utility program to change the foreground and background colors, getting away from the standard black and white DOS prompt. Add to your AUTOEXEC.BAT file and your colors will be set automatically whenever you start up your computer.

(PC-SIG Disk# 2576)

Special Requirements: *VGA*
Author Registration: *$20.00*

✍ = Updated Program
☆ = New Program

Virus Central ☆
by Alejandro L. Abello

Everyone should have some kind of virus detection program. The last thing you need is a virus in your system.

ViruScan is a favorite among power users and novices alike, but its lack of interface made it a little intimidating — until VIRUS CENTRAL came along.

VIRUS CENTRAL is a shell program that simplifies the use of ViruScan and CleanUp, both from McAfee Associates. The menu-driven environment eliminates the need to memorize command line parameters. It is ideally suited for locations that devote a computer to checking incoming media for virus infections (i.e., the computer lab of a college). The graphical user interface works well with a mouse, although keyboard use is equally pleasant. As an added bonus, VIRUS CENTRAL has a built-in screen-saver that clears the screen after a specified time.

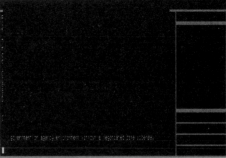
Virus Central (PC-SIG Disk #2552)

The single most powerful feature of VIRUS CENTRAL is its Clean Up function. As a disk is scanned, any infections detected are noted and placed in a queue. After the scan is completed, VIRUS CENTRAL executes CleanUp and passes the information stored in the queue to the program, effectively automating the process. This feature is invaluable for cleaning disks with multiple file infections.

(PC-SIG Disk# 2552)

Special Requirements: *512K RAM, CGA or EGA. A mouse is optional.*
Author Registration: *$25.00*

VMS40:286/386 w/extended memory ✍
by Fugue Software

This is a device driver that turns either a hard disk or a floppy disk into LIM4 expanded memory. It is a software emulation of the 28 function standard set forth in the Lotus/Intel/Microsoft Expanded Memory Standard (LIM/EMS) version 4.0. All of the EMS 4.0 functions that can be implemented through software are provided by VMS40, with the exception of the DMA functions included in the Alternate Map Register Set function (function 28).

The program is backwards compatible with software written for the earlier LIM 3.2 standard (courtesy of Lotus, Intel & Microsoft). It lets you specify which drive to use for expanded memory, and how much disk to reserve.

The trial version VMS40.240 restricts you to reserving no more than 240K for LIM memory, while the registered version VMS40.SYS allows you to reserve up to 32 megabytes.

Naturally, using a disk to simulate LIM memory is somewhat slower than having the appropriate hardware implementation, but it is also a lot cheaper! If you need to run big spreadsheets, or use Borland's standalone debugger to debug a really large program, and you cannot afford 2 megabytes of LIM memory, then VMS40 is your answer.

(PC-SIG Disk# 1957)

Special Requirements: *286/386 computer with extended memory*
Author Registration: *$25.00*

VPT
by clySmic

With this program, VGA or MCGA users can use the quarter-million (262,144) available VGA colors. It's interactive and easy to use. It has a graphic display — there are no "magic numbers" to type.

Set any text-mode attribute to any color out of the quarter-million and control the overscan (border) color (not available on MCGA systems). The colors "stick" with almost all programs. Load and save your favorite settings in color files, and use the program in a command-line mode (for batch files).

VPT operates in text mode and allows setting of any or all of the sixteen attributes available in text mode.

(PC-SIG Disk# 2234)

Special Requirements: *VGA.*
Author Registration: *$20.00*

WARP-TEN
by Software Brewing Company

"Cache in" on better speed and flexibility with WARP-TEN. WARP-TEN is a programmable disk cache for speeding up the relatively slow I/O that most applications perform with disk drives. Borrowing a technique from the world of mainframes and minicomputers, the basic idea is to use part of the PC's memory as buffers to store the more frequently used disk data. Thus, when your application calls for this data, the cache program speedily retrieves it, increasing the speed of your programs by an average of 25 percent.

WARP-TEN is a revolutionary product that recognizes that not all applications are equal in their disk access. To better utilize the caching concept, the author also provides a program (Warp-Din) that will de-install the disk cache, allowing the PC user to either regain all of WARP-TEN's memory for applications that don't need caching, or to respecify WARP-TEN with either more or fewer RAM buffers.

Warpstat, another program provided in this package, enables the user to check to see if the cache being used is optimal for the application that just ran. All these features allow the users to tailor the use of caching to fit their unique requirements.

(PC-SIG Disk# 2048)

Special Requirements: *Hard drive.*
Author Registration: *$20.00*

Within & Beyond DOS
by Sydex

TELEDISK is like a diskette FAX machine. Turns any diskette into a compressed DOS file, suitable for sending over a modem or network. Reconstruct an EXACT duplicate of the diskette from the image file. A nicely-windowed color operation. TELEDISK is great for those bootable diskettes or those with complex subdirectories. It even works with some "copy-protected" diskettes.

RAINDOS is a DOS device driver which provides an absolutely transparent way to read, write and format DEC Rainbow 100 DOS diskettes. Supports all DOS functions and requires a 1.2M diskette drive.

Eagle16 is another DOS device driver which provides an entirely transparent way to read, write and format Eagle 1600 DOS diskettes. Supports all DOS functions and requires a 1.2M diskette drive.

HP150.SYS is the DOS device driver which provides a completely transparent way to read, write and format Hewlett Packard HP150 diskettes. It also supports all DOS functions and requires a 1.2M diskette drive.

SHARP56 is another of our compatibility series. This is a DOS device driver which provides a totally transparent way to read, write and format Sharp 5600 series diskettes. Supports all DOS functions and requires a 1.2M diskette drive.

(PC-SIG Disk# 2357)

Special Requirements: *Modem for Teledisk. High density drives for the rest.*
Author Registration: *Teledisk $20.00   Raindos, Eagle16, HP150, & Sharp56 each $15.00*

ZZap
by Westcomp

ZZAP is a disk editor that can read, modify and write any sector on the disk, as well as any file by filename upon the disk — along the same lines as Norton's Utilities.

A 4,096-byte buffer is used to hold the information to be written to or read from the disk. Editing can be done on a byte-by-byte basis by entering the data in hex, decimal, octal or ASCII format. You can also add, copy, or exchange the data of the current buffer.

(PC-SIG Disk# 874)

Special Requirements: *360K RAM.*
Author Registration: *$30.00*

▼ ▼ ▼

The PC-SIG Encyclopedia of Shareware

✍ = Updated Program
☆ = New Program

Visually Impaired, Programs

Catcher *by CMD Data Services*

CATCHER is an interesting twist on an old theme. The object is to catch falling characters with a paddle at the bottom of the screen. The twist is the program was written for visually-impaired people and is designed for use with a speech synthesizer.

(PC-SIG Disk# 732)

Special Requirements: *Speech synthesizer.*
Author Registration: *None.*

Enable Reader Professional Speech System *by Enable Talking Software*

The ENABLE READER PROFESSIONAL SPEECH SYSTEM was written to improve computer access for the blind and visually-impaired, and is actually two programs in one.

The "Full Screen Speech Review System" is designed to let the visually-impaired use the wide selection of software written for MS-DOS compatibles. Now programs like Lotus 1-2-3 or dBASE are available to everyone.

The "Talking Tutorial Programmer's Aid" gives programmers access to many of the speech functions of the ENABLE READER to write talking tutorials for their software.

Several synthesizer language versions are included for the most popular synthesizers available. Among these are:

❏ Artic Technologies - speech board.
❏ Speech Plus - calltext 5050.
❏ Digital Equipment Corp. - dectalk.
❏ Street electronics - echo qp.
❏ Votrax, Inc. - Votalker ib., Votrax pss., Votrax pss/b.

(PC-SIG Disk#'s 674, 675, 676, 677)

Special Requirements: *Two floppy drives and synthesizer hardware.*
Author Registration: *None.*

Impaired Laser Font *by Daniel Ross*

IMPAIRED is a special soft font, for the HP LaserJet II, specifically designed for printing materials to be read by persons who suffer from severe visual impairment. The bold, proportionally spaced, uppercase characters print 7.5 lines per inch, with approximately 72 characters (maximum) per line. This type style provides maximum distinction between letters for easy recognition by individuals whose sight is limited.

IMPAIRED is extremely useful both for personal use, if your sight is waning, to still be able to prepare and read your own printed notes, reports etc.—and for those who are creating books or reference materials for others with visual impairment.

The complete source code, written in Microsoft C, is provided for modifying the font.

A recommended companion PC-SIG program is WORD PROCESSING FOR KIDS (PC- SIG disk #343), which features extra-large characters on the screen.

(PC-SIG Disk# 1223)

Special Requirements: *HP LaserJet II.*
Author Registration: *None.*

Listico *by Phillipe Rabergeau*

LISTICO is a small utility that displays Windows icons created with Icondraw. It displays icons alphabetically according to their icon names. This program makes it easier to find an icon in a large library of icons. Two sample icons and source code are included with the program.

(PC-SIG Disk# 2441)

Special Requirements: *EGA and Windows.*
Author Registration: *None.*

Tracker for the Visually Impaired
by CMD Data Services

TRACKER is a general-purpose income/expense tracking program written for the visually-impaired. The program is designed for use with a speech synthesizer, to vocalize information usually read from the screen. The documentation has internal help screens for each of the program's commands.

(PC-SIG Disk# 732)

Special Requirements: *Speech synthesizer.*
Author Registration: *$20.00*

▼ ▼ ▼

Windows Application

1000 Icons for Windows ☆   *collected by Michael E. Callahan*

What can be said about 1000 ICONS for Windows? If you want a full color icon for a particular application, you will probably find it here. Icons for hundreds of popular applications, games, utilities, and hardware are contained on this disk.

(PC-SIG Disk# 2779)

Special Requirements: *Windows.*
Author Registration: *None.*

200 Icons for Windows ✍

Wow! Here are 200 icons you can use with Windows! You'll find DOS prompts, faces, books, program names, trees, charts, graphs, and many other full color icons you can use to spruce up Windows 3.0. Changing old icons to new ones is a breeze. So dump out those boring monochrome icons that Windows gives you, and try some really vivid pictures that express your personality.

(PC-SIG Disk# 2442)

Special Requirements: *Windows 3.0*
Author Registration: *None.*

26 .BMP files for Windows ☆   *collected by Michael E. Callahan*

Twenty-six different, brightly colored .BMP files based on the Windows PAPER.BMP file.

(PC-SIG Disk# 2780)

Special Requirements: *Windows*
Author Registration: *None.*

Almanac ✍   *by Impact Software*

ALMANAC is a calendar/scheduler/information utility for Microsoft Windows. It provides traditional calendar displays in month and year format, as well as a popup desk set for day-to-day notes and schedules. Configuration files and overlays allow you to customize calendars for your business and personal needs.

An overlay is a set of data which provides ALMANAC with the information it needs to calculate the days events will occur on. The types of events ALMANAC will calculate include weekly, monthly, and annual events by day or date, as well as birthday, wedding anniversaries, and others. Up to ten overlays may be specified in a configuration file, and included are three sample files which define holidays for the United States, Canada, and Sweden.

In addition to specifying overlay files, ALMANAC auto-load modules allow you to configure options for calculating religious holidays (Christian and/or Jewish), phases of the moon, and calendar mode (Gregorian/Jewish). A built in database is used to determine your location so you can calculate the time and azimuth of the sunrise and sunset.

(PC-SIG Disk# 2457)

Special Requirements: *Windows 3.0*
Author Registration: *$34.95 - 59.95*

Aporia   *by NewTools Inc.*

APORIA brings even more of a Macintosh operating system to Windows, complete with trash can. At its most powerful, APORIA replaces Windows' Program Manager with a tool-laden shell. APORIA places file drawers onscreen; click on a drawer, and it shows you the contents (as icons). Click again, and the drawer closes, taking the icons with it. You can set up your own drawers and files. You can even get help by dragging an application over to the question mark icon.

(PC-SIG Disk# 2462)

Special Requirements: *Windows 3.0 and PKZIP, PC-SIG #1364.*
Author Registration: *$50.00*
➤*ASP Member.*

Applications for Microsoft Windows
by Wilson WindowWare

Personalize your Microsoft Windows environment with your own menus and submenus, arrange or stack open windows, close windows, iconize them, and hide windows by making them invisible. If that's not enough, you can browse files in your Windows environment and print out whatever you want.

This well-documented trio of microapplications makes Windows do it your way. With COMMAND POST, you easily add any number of menu and submenu items to the main MS-DOS Windows executive menu bar. Execution is only a mouse click away. COMMAND POST does a lot more than make it easy for you to start programs. It helps you get your work done faster and safer by reducing tedious manual steps. A single menu item can gather filenames and other information into listboxes for the user to choose from, perform arithmetic, parse strings, move and resize windows, read and write WIN.INI variables, read DOS environment variables, copy, move and delete files and much more.

While BROWSER cannot alter or edit files, you can display them in ASCII format. Or you can make a hex dump. A hide and seek feature lets users control the shown (displayable) and hidden lines of text.

APPLETS lets you put your windows where you want them. You can easily copy, rename, move and delete files with APPLETS.

(PC-SIG Disk# 1915)

Special Requirements: *EGA, hard drive, 286/386 PC, Microsoft Windows, and a mouse.*
Author Registration: *$49.95*
➤*ASP Member.*

Atmoids
by IBD GmBH

People with happy trigger fingers will love this game. ATMOIDS is a new Windows version of Asteroids. Your mission is simple, blast the boulders away until they get pulverized out of existence. Your trusty interstellar ship is guided with the cursor keys. This game will challenge even the most experienced players, since there is no hyper-space key to dodge out of the way at the last second.

(PC-SIG Disk# 2456)

Special Requirements: *Windows 3.0*
Author Registration: *$10.00*

BMP files #1 ☆
collected by Michael E. Callahan

Six .BMP files for Windows — Earth as seen from space, a surrealistic view of Jupiter and its moons, a moonscape, the moon with Earth rising, a picture of Saturn, and a lush forest scene.

(PC-SIG Disk# 2781)

Special Requirements: *Windows.*
Author Registration: *None.*

BMP files #2 ☆
collected by Michael E. Callahan

The second volume of .BMP files for Windows — A sharp-looking eagle with the US flag in the background, three Simpsons cartoons, four images from the Star Wars trilogy, and a waterfall.

(PC-SIG Disk# 2782)

Special Requirements: *Windows.*
Author Registration: *None.*

Checkers
by Gregory Thatcher

Nothing fancy about this one, it's just good old fashioned CHECKERS. But now you have a computer partner to help you pass an idle afternoon. The game can be played with either one player or two, and it has five levels of difficulty.

(PC-SIG Disk# 2455)

Special Requirements: *Windows 3.0*
Author Registration: *None.*

✍ = Updated Program
☆ = New Program

Chess for Windows ☆   *by Windows Consulting*

CHESS FOR WINDOWS — A simple, public domain chess program...for Windows. And that's where this program starts becoming attractive. Featuring four skill levels, with a hint feature that will suggest a move for you, CHESS FOR WINDOWS appeals to both the experienced and beginning players. But it's also for the novice C programmer. Source code is included, and modification of the program is encouraged by the author, provided his distribution agreement is followed.

(PC-SIG Disk# 2663)

Special Requirements: *Windows 3.0.*
Author Registration: *Public domain.*

Colorfix   *by Synergistic Enterprises*

COLORFIX is a "patcher" for Microsoft Windows EGA/VGA and similar screen drivers that will permit truer color reproduction in 64 color mode. Fixes "pinkish" reds and other off-color screen colors.

(PC-SIG Disk# 1663)

Special Requirements: *MS-Windows 1.0 or greater.*
Author Registration: *$40.00*

Command Post ✍   *by Wilson WindowWare*

COMMAND POST is a powerful file manager and custom menu system for Microsoft Windows 3.0 that lets you tailor your Windows-based workstations to your needs and preferences. The Text-based nature of COMMAND POST preserves screen real-estate, the batch file/basic-type language gives you unprecedented power in a Windows menu system.

COMMAND POST does a lot more than just make it easy to start programs. It gets your work done faster and more accurately by reducing tedious error-prone manual steps. A single COMMAND POST menu item can gather filenames and other information into listboxes for the user to choose from, perform arithmetic, parse strings, move and resize windows, read and write WIN.INI variables, read DOS environment variables; copy, move, and delete files, and more.

Command Post (PC-SIG Disk #2325)

Use COMMAND POST to turn your workstation into a power station!

(PC-SIG Disk# 2325)

Special Requirements: *Windows 3.0*
Author Registration: *$49.95*
➤ *ASP Member.*

Fireworks   *by Synergistic Enterprises*

FIREWORKS is a screen blanking utility for Microsoft Windows. When keyboard and mouse buttons are inactive for a user-specified length of time, the screen is blanked and simulated fireworks shoot off on the screen to let the user know the computer is still alive. In "active" mode (selecting the FIREWORK icon) the mouse cursor becomes a plane flying amongst the fireworks. The screen blank can also be blanked voluntarily using a hot-key.

(PC-SIG Disk# 1663)

Special Requirements: *MS-Windows 1.0 or greater.*
Author Registration: *$40.00*

GCP   *by Synergistic Enterprises*

GCP is a graphics conversion utility for Microsoft Windows. Converts to and from Windows Paint (both old and new formats), PC Paintbrush, CompuServe GIF, Macintosh MacPaint, Mac Startup screens and Windows clipboard bitmaps. Stretching, shrinking, inverting, dithering and cropping can also be performed using GCP.

(PC-SIG Disk# 1663)

Special Requirements: *MS-Windows 1.0 or greater.*
Author Registration: *$40.00*

Horse & YinYang
by Robert M. Curran

Here are more programs that look hip on your Windows display. HORSE places a galloping horse in a small window. Unlike Horse.tbk which appeared on a developers toolbox, HORSE does not even come close to putting strain the system. An interesting side note is that the original drawings used to create the horse date back to the 1800's. YINYANG draws a symbol, part yin-yang part floppy disk, and prints a koan from the book "The Zen of Programming."

And these two Windows programs won't set you back financially—they are both free.

(PC-SIG Disk# 2450)

Special Requirements: *Windows 3.0*
Author Registration: *None.*

Icon Draw
by Phillip B. Eskelin Jr.

Feeling a little limited by the simple icons on your Windows 3.0 screen? Now you can custom create your own 16-color icons to appear in Windows. And 11 pre-made icons will help get you started.

With ICONDRAW, you can make your own unique icons depicting the choices available from your particular windows environment. Creating new icons can be a snap, especially when using one of the 11 pre-made icons included to help get you started. Once a new icon is saved, you can change the icons on the Program Manager by using Windows "properties " command.

(PC-SIG Disk# 2441)

Special Requirements: *Windows 3.0*
Author Registration: *$15.00*

Klotz
by Wolfgang Strobl

KLOTZ is an interesting Tetris clone from Europe. As in the original Tetris, polygons fall from the top of your screen and it's your job to pack them neatly at the bottom before they stack up. It has 11 levels of play, optional multi-windowed displays, a look-ahead to the next piece, and even a statistical bar-line chart depicting fallen pieces. If you've never played this type of game, watch out, it's quite addicting.

(PC-SIG Disk# 2456)

Special Requirements: *Windows 3.0*
Author Registration: *None.*

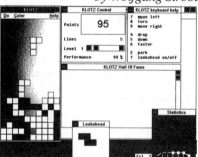
Klotz (PC-SIG Disk #2456)

Lander
by TMA

You're on the final approach one thousand meters above the moon, do you have what it takes to land the Lunar Excursion Module without creating another crater?

On this real-time simulation you must safely guide your lander with the mouse before you run out of fuel, or accumulate too much horizontal and vertical speed. You can change the settings for gravity, fuel, and thrust if you desire another level of difficulty.

(PC-SIG Disk# 2456)

Special Requirements: *None.*
Author Registration: *$15.00 for source code.*

Launch! ☆
by Wink Software

LAUNCH is a small Windows program that replaces the Windows Task Manager upon installation. New buttons can easily be added and old ones removed, without any help from the manual or the help screen.

LAUNCH is invoked by a double-click on the Windows background. This invokes the LAUNCH dialog box lined with upto 400 buttons for different programs. Clicking on one of these buttons starts up the application associated with the button.

✍ = Updated Program
☆ = New Program

LAUNCH starts programs relative to the current directory. This allows for starting different applications with different setups from multiple directories. This feature is significantly different from Windows Program Manager as the programs from LAUNCH are started from the current directory.

Intended for all WINDOWS users, LAUNCH serves as a utility that Windows forgot. It provides the quickest, most convenient access to DOS and WINDOWS programs in as little as three mouse clicks.

Special Requirements: *Windows 3.0*
Author Registration: *$30.00*

LessIsMore ☆   by R*D Applied Technologies

Windows multitasking can be a bit intimidating. But with LESSISMORE, even the unsophisticated can handle multitasking without much problem. This program manages simplicity of setup and use, and now anyone can do it. Switching between applications is done with Alt-Tab. Windows functions such as cut and paste are fully supported so that moving text, data, and graphics from screen to screen across applications is a breeze.

(PC-SIG Disk# 2628)

Special Requirements: *Windows 3.0.*
Author Registration: *$20.00*

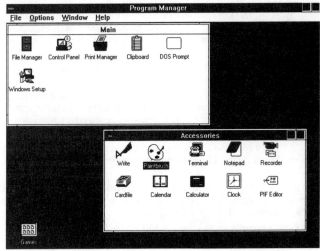

How Many Shareware Windows Products Could You Put in Here?

Mark30   by Kindlco Software Systems

Mark30 is a utility that marks old Windows applications so they will run under Windows 3.0 without the Windows 3.0 warning message. This utility does no checking of the application being marked, except to verify that it is a Windows application.

Many Windows 2.x application work fine under Windows 3.0, but many do not. If you have a Windows 2.x application that works under Windows 3.0, and you are tired of the annoying warning message Windows 3.0 gives you each time you run your program, Mark30 will save you that aggravation.

(PC-SIG Disk# 2461)

Special Requirements: *Windows 3.0*
Author Registration: *Up to user.*

MBW   by Robert Epps

Fractals generators are among the most popular shareware programs, and MBW is sure to become a hot item with Windows users. MBW creates fractals from a Mandelbrot set working out of its own window.

You can zoom in on any part of the image, and watch it form a new fractal, which you can save and use at a later time. Other options include color settings, iteration limits, scaling, and drawing extents.

If you have Windows and would like to see some neat fractal images, MBW is a must.

(PC-SIG Disk# 2450)

Special Requirements: *Windows 3.0*
Author Registration: *None.*

METZ Window Utilities ✍   by METZ Software

Metz Software has put together a package of Windows utilities that should appeal to wide spectrum of users who want to make their systems more manageable.

METZ TASK MANAGER (version 1.01) is a replacement for the Microsoft task list application. TASK MANAGER expands upon the task list functions providing a comprehensive set of tulities such as a screen blanker, file manager, customizeable tools menu, and more. PC Magazine Editors Choice (2/26/91) Registration $30.00

Metz Navigator (PC-SIG Disk #2273)

METZ DESKTOP MANAGER (version 3.21) is a Microsoft Windows application designed to provide you with a friendly menuing system plus several utilities. With DESKTOP you can easily create menus and sub-menus which directly access your applications and data (across directories and drives). Additional features such as customizeable screen blanker, windows arrangement functions, directory tree display, file finder, pint and shoot file management, and an automatic menu generator are also provided.

With DESKTOP MANAGER you can create menus and sub-menus which directly access your applications and data, across directories and drives. Registration $30.00

METZ DESKTOP NAVIGATOR (version 2.51) is a Microsoft Windows application designed to provide fast access to your drives, directories, and files. File and directory management functions are included as well. Additional features such as a customizable screen blanker, windows arrangement functions, and a file finder are also included. Registration $30.00

METZ PHONES (version 3.46) is a Microsoft Windows application designed for maintaining lists of names, phone numbers, and addresses. If you have a Hayes compatible modem, PHONES can dial the phone for you. Registration $15.00

METZ DIALER (version 2.22) is a pop-up, speed dialer which, when coupled with a Hayes compatible modem, provides a quick and convenient method of dialing phone numbers. A customizable pulldown menu allows you to add names and numbers you frequently call. Registration $10.00

METZ LOCK (version 1.52) is a security application for MICROSOFT WINDOWS. Lock can be used to prevent unauthorized use of your system while unattended. Registration $15.00

METZ RUNNER (version 1.2) is a utility which provides a quick method to run applications and files. Registration $10.00

METZ TIME (version 2.5) is a pop-up digital date and time display which placed anywhere on the screen. Registration $10.0

METZ FREEMEM (version 3.5) is a moveable digital display of free conventional and free expanded memory.

(PC-SIG Disk#'s 2273, 2605)

Special Requirements: *Windows*
Author Registration: *See program description.*

Monitor Saver ✍   by Moon Valley Software

The Windows environment is more fun to look at than DOS, but without this program the Windows display is likely to be burned into your monitor's phosphors forever. Monitor Saver is designed especially for Windows 3.0 with customizable delay times and network compatibility. The program can blank the screen, or fill it with a moving pattern after a period of keyboard inactivity.

(PC-SIG Disk# 2459)

Special Requirements: *Windows 3.0*
Author Registration: *$21.95*

New Paper
by Buttonware

Want to bring some excitement, or at least variety, into the hours you spend staring through Windows? This public domain program from Buttonware gives you a different background (.BMP) file each time Windows is started.

(PC-SIG Disk# 2461)

Special Requirements: *Windows 3.0*
Author Registration: *None.*
➤*ASP Member.*

Organize! 🖎
by Sing Cher Kwek

ORGANIZE! — an innovative, cost-effective PIM (Personal Information Manager) for Windows.

No matter how disorganized you are, this program can track all of your important projects without the complex and rigid control systems most PIMs use. Cluttered with unused functions, they steepen the learning curve unnecessarily. With ORGANIZE!, add new functions only as you need them. Learn as you go.

One of the easiest-to-use systems ever, ORGANIZE! looks and feels just like a diary. Flip pages like the real thing with binders that click open to insert more pages. The Word-in-Context system will manage all random AND structured personal information that you enter into the diary. You will never lose your way in this piece of software.

If you are looking for a program to help you record contacts, schedule appointments, track projects, or control random notes and ideas, this may be for you.

(PC-SIG Disk# 2320)

Special Requirements: *Windows 3.0, and EGA or VGA.*
Author Registration: *$35.00*

Paint Shop 🖎
by Jasc, Inc.

PAINT SHOP is a Windows program that will display, convert, alter, and print pictures using the file formats of TIF, GIF, WPG, BMP, PCX, MAC, IMG, PIC, and RLE. Altering includes stretch/shrink, trimming, dithering palette manipulation and more. Another feature of Paint Shop is screen capturing. The entire screen, just a portion of the screen or a specific window may be captured. Once captured, the user can treat the picture as any other picture, thus saving the picture to what ever format you want, instead of the format the program wants.

Other features include: Printing pictures, full clipboard support, an On-Line Help system and a user's manual. Viewing can be done in a window or full screen.

(PC-SIG Disk# 2447)

Special Requirements: *Windows 3.0*
Author Registration: *$29.00*
➤*ASP Member.*

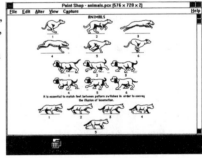

Paint Shop (PC-SIG Disk #2447)

Parents
by Nickleware

PARENTS makes collecting and organizing your genealogy easier. With the help of PARENTS, you will be able to easily gather, store, and view information about all of you ancestors, as well as your children and your children's children.

PARENTS allows you to enter and store vital information such as names, birth, marriage, death dates and places and more. All of this information can then be easily organized and related together to form your family tree. You will also be able to print the detailed information about any one of your ancestors as well as print your immediate tree.

(PC-SIG Disk# 2458)

Special Requirements: *Windows 3.0*
Author Registration: *$25.00*

Puzzle
by Paul Bechningham

This program is a sliding tile PUZZLE game that you can play with the mouse or keyboard. In order to complete a scrambled image, the player slides tiles up and down or sideways. The first tiles are easy to place, but as you get to the last tiles, it becomes harder. There are three levels of play to keep you interested, and new images can be imported to make new puzzles.

(PC-SIG Disk# 2455)

Special Requirements: *Windows 3.0*
Author Registration: *$5.00*

Screen Peace
by Anthony Anderson

SCREEN PEACE for Windows 3.0 not only blanks the monitor, but fills it with frills. Instead of a blank screen, you'll see animated fish eat each other onscreen. It contains 13 other graphic options, from the wavy lines to wobbling spheres. Other users have written their own animated sequences using a C compiler.

SCREEN PEACE lets users customize everything from the speed of the fish to the length of the delay before blanking. It also allows immediate blanking by pushing the mouse arrow into a corner. Another option tells Windows to boot up with fresh wallpaper each morning.

(PC-SIG Disk# 2461)

Special Requirements: *Windows 3.0*
Author Registration: *$10.00*

Wallmac
by Underware

If you are tired of the wallpaper files that come with Windows, check out these two new background screens that you can use to customize your desktop with, and even impress Mac users.

You get the original monochrome Macintosh™ background screen, and the newer color Mac II™, to use instead of the ribbons, paper, and other backgrounds that Windows offers you. These two BMP screens "look so realistic that you will find yourself reaching for the pull-down menus!"

(PC-SIG Disk# 2688)

Special Requirements: *Windows 3.0*
Author Registration: *$2.00*

Whiskers
by Number & Co

With Whiskers you can assign keystrokes to the middle and right mouse buttons. You could, for example, make the right button on the mouse be the DELETE key. For use with Windows 3.0.

(PC-SIG Disk# 2461)

Special Requirements: *Windows 3.0*
Author Registration: *$15.00*

WinBatch ✍
by Wilson WindowWare

WINBATCH brings the power of batch language programming to the Windows environment. Although WINBATCH can do everything that the familiar DOS batch language can do, WINBATCH's capabilities begin where the DOS batch language leaves off.

With more than a hundred functions, WINBATCH can:

❑ Run Windows and DOS programs
❑ Rearrange, resize, hide, and close windows
❑ Display information to the user in various formats
❑ Present scrollable file and directory lists
❑ Read and write files directly
❑ Make branching decisions based upon numerous factors
And much, much more.

❑ Send keystrokes directly to applications
❑ Run programs either concurrently or sequentially
❑ Prompt the user for any needed input
❑ Copy, move, delete, and rename files
❑ Copy text to and from the Clipboard
❑ Perform string and arithmetic operations

WINBATCH uses a logical "C-like" syntax, accessible to anyone with a minimal knowledge of programming, including DOS batch language programming. If you can write a .BAT file, you can write a WINBATCH file!

✍ = Updated Program
☆ = New Program

While offering immediate help to the novice, WINBATCH continues to reward the intermediate and experienced user with many advanced capabilities.

Whether you are creating batch files for others, or looking for a way to automate your own work and eliminate the drudgery of repetitive tasks, you will find WINBATCH to be a powerful, versatile, and easy-to-use tool.

(PC-SIG Disk# 2659)

Special Requirements: *Windows 3.0*
Author Registration: *$69.95*
➤*ASP Member.*

WinCheck ✍   *by Wilson WindowWare*

Wilson WindowWare proudly announces WINCHECK, an easy-to-use and attractive Windows 3.0 checkbook balancing program.

WINCHECK's purpose is to assist in balancing a personal checking and savings account. It can also print checks on virtually any pre-printed check form — both dot matrix and laser checks are supported. All data entered into the program can be exported into EXCEL compatible files for more sophisticated analysis and tax-time computations.

WINCHECK has an exceptionally attractive and easy-to-use interface. Checks and other transactions appear as 3-D dialog boxes with bitmapped backgrounds. Standard operations, such as writing a check or making a deposit, are performed by clicking on a 3-D iconic toolbox.

(PC-SIG Disk# 2658)

Special Requirements: *Windows 3.0*
Author Registration: *$39.95*
➤*ASP Member.*

WinEdit ✍   *by Wilson WindowWare*

WINEDIT is an ASCII text editor designed to be, first and foremost, a programmer's editor, with features to facilitate creating and maintaining program source code. With its ASCII file format, ability to edit files of almost unlimited size, and word processing features such as headers and footers, WINEDIT also serves as an effective "front end" for desktop publishers and word processors including PageMaker, Word For Windows, and Ventura Publisher.

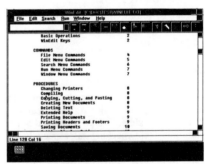

WinEdit (PC-SIG Disk #2657)

Features:

❑ Uses all available Windows memory to load up to 16MB of text files
❑ Multiple Document Interface allows an unlimited number of document windows
❑ Run your favorite compiler or other programming tool from within WINEDIT, monitor the compiler's output, review any warning or error messages
❑ Regular expressions can be used in Search and Replace operations for powerful text manipulation capabilities
❑ Full access to the Windows SDK Help and C 6.0 language Help by clicking on any SDK or C language keyword.
❑ Prints half-sized "two-up" pages side by side in landscape mode — ideal for source listings or early drafts of desktop publishing documents.
❑ Headers and footers. WINEDIT can place the document name, date, and time in the header or footer of any printout
❑ Easy to use. Online Help is always available. All major program features are available through the pulldown menus and dialog boxes. Most-used features have accelerator keys as well for lightning-fast operation
❑ Fast. One of WINEDIT's design goals is speed in all critical operations. WINEDIT loads large files quickly, updates and scrolls the screen instantly, and keeps up with the fastest typist

(PC-SIG Disk# 2657)

Special Requirements: *Windows 3.0*
Author Registration: *$59.95*
➤*ASP Member.*

Winfract (Fractint for Windows) ☆   *by Tyler Software*

WINFRACT is the Windows version of FRACTINT. WINFRACT plots and manipulates images of "objects" — actually sets of mathematical points — that have fractal dimension. Using integer math, these sets of points are generated by relatively simple calculations repeated over and over, feeding the results of each step back into the next, something computers can do very rapidly. WINFRACT lets you zoom into a small area created by the calculations to reveal intricate detail, from which you can assign colors to selected points and "animate" the images by quickly shifting those color assignments.

An advantage of WINFRACT over other fractal graphics programs is that, as formerly mentioned, it uses integer math, rather than the floating-point calculations. That means that you don't need a math coprocessor chip (aka floating-point unit or FPU), though it will recognize and automatically use an 80x87 chip if it's present.

WINFRACT works with many adapter and graphics modes from CGA to the 1024x768, 256-color 8514/A mode. Even "larger" images, up to 2048x2048x256, can be plotted to RAM, EMS, or disk: this bypasses the screen and allows you to create images with higher resolution than your current display can handle.

The program was born fast through an experiment in collaboration by Bert Tyler and many volunteers. The authors of this public domain program encourage further contribution of ideas to make FRACTINT even better than it already is: "speedy, versatile, and all-around wonderful."

(PC-SIG Disk# 2610)

Special Requirements: *Windows 3.0 and CGA or better.*
Author Registration: *Copyrighted Freeware.*

WinPost ☆   *by Eastern Mountain Software*

Use WINPOST to get rid of those Post-It notes on your monitor! Create and manage reminder notes in Microsoft WINDOWS with such features as: full print facility, search facility, alarm notes and numerous configuration parameters. Notes can be manipulated very easily. Move, Delete, Hide, or Display notes with a single keystroke or mouse operation. It automatically saves all data when you exit Windows.

(PC-SIG Disk# 2690)

Special Requirements: *Windows 3.0*
Author Registration: *$30.00*
➤*ASP Member.*

Wintris   *by Kipnis Enterprises*

WINTRIS is another Tetris-like game in which falling blocks must be rotated and dropped to form solid lines. This program has all the standard features; you can select the level, number of lines to begin with, speed up, slow down, sound, and music. All these features can be preset or changed on the fly. A unique feature of the game is "The Extended Set." The "Extended Set" is an extra set of block shapes not found on any other game. This feature is worth checking out, especially if you have become adept or bored with the same shapes which are prevalent in similar games.

(PC-SIG Disk# 2456)

Special Requirements: *Windows 3.0*
Author Registration: *$15.00*

Zip Manager 🖾   *by Moon Valley Software*

Zip Manager is a Windows 3.0 shell for files compressed using PKZIP, ARC, and LZH formats. It also gives you access to Vernon Buerg's LIST.COM program, McAffee's Virus SCAN program, and your favorite text editor—either DOS or Windows based. Zip Manager is an easy way to use these programs in Windows.

Zip Manager offers all of the available command line switches for PKZIP and PKUNZIP. By simply selecting the appropriate menu item, the user can easily set the program to store the path name with the Zip file, recurse sub-directories, retain the original Zip file date, etc.

Zip Manager makes it easy for even a novice to use the PKZIP programs in a simple point and shoot environment. Creating a Zip file is simply a matter of moving through a few dialog boxes, choosing the files to add to the zip file, and then clicking on OK to create it. The program gives the user complete control over every aspect of Zip file management.

The commenting of Zip files has never been easier. Zip Manager allows you to specify exactly how you would like to comment the file. It even allows you to comment an individual file contained in a large zip file simply by selecting the desired file. You are then asked to enter the comment for that file only. This is a feature that is offered by no other program.

(PC-SIG Disk# 2459)

Special Requirements: *Windows 3.0*
Author Registration: *$21.95*

▼ ▼ ▼

Wordprocessor and Text Utilities

Alchemy Desktop Publishing Utilities   *by Alchemy Mindworks Inc.*

If your desktop publishing efforts seem a little plain, spice them up with this collection of seven utilities for Xerox's Ventura Publisher!

GCAP imports charts, graphs, pictures or anything else in graphics mode that you want to use in desktop publishing. These files are written directly to disk, complete with compression and a suitable GEM/IMG file header. GCAP works with a CGA, EGA, or Hercules graphics card.

HP-SLASH hacks unwanted characters out of your soft fonts to create leaner, faster files. It works by creating a new soft font from an existing one but only includes the characters you want.

MAC2IMG converts standard MacPaint image files into GEM/IMG-compatible paint files, suitable for use with Ventura 1.1. MAC2PCX converts them to PC Paintbrush-compatible PCX files.

MCOPY is an enhanced COPY command to copy several files onto floppies. It sorts through the files to be copied and begins with the largest one that fits on a disk. It fills in the remaining space with smaller files to use as much of the floppy as possible. If there are still files to be copied when the disk is full, the program pauses and asks for another floppy. It then proceeds to fill that floppy as well. MCOPY also performs an authentic 16-bit CRC check on every file.

SCOOP lets your PC look at PC Paintbrush, MacPaint or GEM/IMG pictures.

VENTURA FONT MACHINE is a menu-driven front-end to create width tables for soft fonts used with LaserJet Plus compatible printers.

(PC-SIG Disk# 1360)

Special Requirements: *Xerox Ventura Publisher for some programs.*
Author Registration: *$5.00 each. $20.00 for source code.*

AnyWord   *by Packet Press*

ANYWORD is a text indexing and retrieval program consisting of two parts: Indexer which produces an index, and Finder which locates words in text. Like a book index, your text is untouched. All of the indexing information is put in a separate file, and your text files are not modified or rearranged in any way. This means you can experiment with ANYWORD as much as you want without the worry of making an inadvertent change to your text files.

You supply information about your files through the profile file, used by both Indexer and Finder. Some ANYWORD features:

❑ Searching by any word or combination of words
❑ Display of selected text
❑ Extraction of selected text into new files
❑ Searching with simple Boolean logic, AND - OR - NOT
❑ Searching with "wild cards", e.g., comput? for reference to computers, computing and so on
❑ Exit to DOS and return without disturbing selected text or search results
❑ Review of previous search results within a session
❑ View of all the words that have been indexed
❑ Automatic file location via the DOS PATH operation

ANYWORD is useful for locating simple information or combinations of text. It also extracts chunks of text into new files and allows browsing through a collection of files from any point within any file. You can page backward, forward, across files, to the beginning, to the end, etc.

(PC-SIG Disk# 1200)

Special Requirements: *Two floppy drives.*
Author Registration: *$35.00*

Armada Utilities
by Armada Software

A collection of PC utilities for use in wordprocessing, printer control, screen display and electronic music composition.

The utilities are:

❏ ALTPAGE lets you print on both sides of a page by splitting an ASCII file into two separate files while allowing you to specify the page-lengths.

❏ AUTHOR performs the functions of both ALTPAGE and PRINTIT while giving you a notepad, a quick text viewer, a typewriter emulator, a WordStar to ASCII converter, and a quick directory viewer.

❏ BOOTFIX and RB1000 give Tandy 1000 users means for speeding up the rebooting of their systems.

❏ CASE changes an ASCII or WordStar file into all upper- or lower-case characters.

❏ CASIOID generates a random text patch for the Casio CZ-101 or CZ-1000 synthesizer.

❏ CRLF converts the carriage return of an ASCII file into a carriage return plus a linefeed or vice versa.

❏ CRT31 changes the screen colors.

❏ CURSOR changes the size and blink rate of the cursor.

❏ DOCMAKER creates an executable .COM file from an ASCII file. You will be able to read an existing file and edit it, display the text and change the screen colors. Super fast display of single screens. Great for batch file use.

❏ FRQCNV4 prints musical staff paper, converts a frequency to the nearest musical note and vice versa and can change one key to another.

❏ FXPRNT is a set-up utility for an Epson-FX or Brother printer.

❏ MIDIPOP pops up tables showing a list of MIDI commands in hex and decimal for programming the MIDI synthesizer.

❏ PRINTIT is a companion file to ALTPAGE and page formatting printer which sets margins, lines per page, headers and page numbers.

❏ TSRMAKER, similar to DOCMAKER, can also retain the file in the background for a pop-up display when you want it.

(PC-SIG Disk# 1376)

Special Requirements: *CGA.*
Author Registration: *$20.00*

Asc2com
by MorganSoft

ASC2COM will take an ASCII format file of under 64K and turn it into one of five self-listing COM format files, each offering the user different features such as single line or page scrolling, printing, find, repeat find, help, an internal write to file, and even a "wide lister" allowing a width of up to 255 characters.

With ASC2COM, you can guarantee that vital information is communicated to your users. Your message (or copyright declaration) is much more difficult to alter and much, much more accessible to the user.

(PC-SIG Disk# 1948)

Special Requirements: *None.*
Author Registration: *$20.00*

Autonum ☆
by Linnell & Associates Ltd.

AUTONUM is a simple, useful program for assigning sequential numbers (seven digits max.) to such items as purchase orders, invoices, statements, checks, memos, and many other business forms. It works by using batch files to effectively automate the numbering process and reduce the possibility of repetitive errors.

(PC-SIG Disk# 1101)

Special Requirements: *A word processor.*
Author Registration: *$25.00 U.S., $30.00 Canadian*

AVScripter ✍
by Tom Schroeppel

If you write scripts that require separate audio and video columns, AVScripter is for you.

Unlike programs that graphically create two columns on your computer screen, AVScripter works with full-screen ASCII text files created with your word processor. Working with the whole screen, you see more text on the screen at one time, you don't have to continually jump back and forth from one column to the other, and you don't have to worry about keeping the appropriate audio and video lines opposite each other. AVScripter does it all for you, automatically.

Features include:

❏ Sends two-column output — single-spaced, double-spaced, or single-spaced video/double-spaced audio—to your printer, your screen, or a disk file, automatically syncing audio and video lines
❏ Allows variable-width audio and video columns
❏ Automatically numbers and renumbers your scenes and pages
❏ Looks for the best place to start each new page, then adds the appropriate "CONTINUED"s where necessary
❏ Automatically centers your title lines
❏ Prints a header line at the top of each page
❏ Permits you to switch between full-width lines and two-column format within your script
❏ Allows underlining anywhere, even in headers and title lines
❏ Sends printer commands to your printer
❏ Prints selected pages and multiple copies
❏ Chains files for processing
❏ Generates prompter/narrator scripts from the audio column.

(PC-SIG Disk# 1028)

Special Requirements: *A word processor capable of ASCII file output.*
Author Registration: *$40.00*

BIBLIO
by Donald G. Harbaugh

Writers, Students, Editors — BIBLIO will interest you.

BIBLIO selects references from a pre-existing text file with a list of bibliographic references. Each reference can have up to five labeled fields such as author, title, source, keywords, and notes. The number, length, or sequence of fields need not be the same for different references.

You can request selection of those references with a desired search phrase in a specified field. You can send the output of the selected records to the screen, printer or disk.

(PC-SIG Disk# 935)

Special Requirements: *None.*
Author Registration: *$15.00*
➤*ASP Member.*

Book ✍
by Robert Wallingford P.E

BOOK MEMO DISPLAY takes any ASCII text file and turns it into a computer book. Access any chapter, and any page in that chapter from the computer index. No more scrolling through long documents to find the section you want.

You provide the text file, this program converts it into a new file that is divided by chapters and pages. It also creates an index display that lists these chapters. When the index is displayed you can directly access any chapter with a single keystroke. You can display successive pages within a chapter with another keystroke. Move forward or backward through the pages, or go back to the index to change chapters.

To make your own "book" you will need a wordprocessor that makes ASCII files (most do).

(PC-SIG Disk# 1807)

Special Requirements: *None.*
Author Registration: *$7.00*

Breaker
by Don Rooney

BREAKER is a life-saving utility when you have a text file that is too large to fit in your wordprocessor. Invoke BREAKER and you are asked what file you want to break and how many lines each of your broken files will contain. The files are saved with any name you desire that has a sequentially added number attached to it for easy tracking.

Once you have worked with your broken files, put them back together again in the same fashion. A very easy program to use that should be in any person's utility library.

(PC-SIG Disk# 978)

Special Requirements: *None.*
Author Registration: *None.*

CAPBUF ✍   *by Cascoly Software*

CAPBUF is a memory resident program that lets you capture any text screen and save it for later processing or printing. It is quite useful for programs that do not otherwise provide means of printing their results. Use it for intermediate results of games, or collecting copies of messages while on a bulletin board. Remember that many elaborate program screens are line graphics. They too can be captured then brought into an ASCII editor. CAPBUF can be removed from memory once you are finished capturing screens. A second program, Filter, can be used to eliminate extra lines or line drawing characters (especially useful if your printer does not support these characters).

(PC-SIG Disk# 1958)
Special Requirements: *CGA.*
Author Registration: *$30.00*
➤*ASP Member.*

CleanUp ✍   *by Harry P. Calevas*

Remove those extra line feeds and blank lines from document files. Makes using Norton Commander or List so much easier.

(PC-SIG Disk# 1818)
Special Requirements: *CGA.*
Author Registration: *$15.00*

ConvDW ✍   *by CrossCourt Systems*

CONVDW converts IBM DisplayWrite 3 & 4 document files to ASCII.

IBM does not publish the file format for DisplayWrite, so CONVDW is one of the very few programs that can read DisplayWrite files. Create files that omit the soft returns and retain the tab characters. This format, very useful for importing to another word processor, is not available from within DisplayWrite.

CONVDW omits most page-formatting characteristics. For example, the left margin is not expanded to spaces, the top and bottom margins are not expanded to blank lines, and page breaks, headers, footers, and page numbering are omitted.

(PC-SIG Disk# 2346)
Special Requirements: *None.*
Author Registration: *$20.00*
➤*ASP Member.*

CopyFit-It   *by Gesture Sotware*

Copyfitting is the process of figuring out what typesetting format will make a text fit the space available for it in a layout. Try various typeface (or typefaces) from those available from your typesetter. COPYFIT-IT makes copyfitting faster and easier.

The essential data needed is the character count and the type size. COPYFIT-IT can calculate the height and number of lines for paragraphs. Determine the line length, the characters per line and number of characters in the line. This program can copyfit individual lines of type with the same or different type sizes, paragraphs, paragraphs and individual lines together, or long texts.

(PC-SIG Disk# 898)
Special Requirements: *None.*
Author Registration: *$54.00*

DCA Conversion for PC-Write   *by Quicksoft*

DCA CONVERSION climbs two mighty compatibility mountains and brings to the world of shareware solutions to problems IBM has long ignored. The biggest involves a duo of programs that convert text on IBM mainframe environments from EBCDIC to microcomputer ASCII. This allows mainframes to share files that were created with PC-Write. Likewise, PC-Write files can be converted to EBCDIC for the most part and sent to mainframes.

✍ = Updated Program
☆ = New Program

The same programs allow microcomputers using different wordprocessing programs to communicate. DCA CONVERSION lets PC-Write transfer files between any program that will accept DCA files. Many popular programs will accept DCA files including Ventura desktop publishing.

(PC-SIG Disk# 1295)

Special Requirements: *None.*
Author Registration: *$19.00*
➤*ASP Member.*

Doc Master   *by Pat Anderson*

DOC MASTER is a set of utilities for printing and viewing on-disk documentation files.

With READ, you can display a file on the screen and scroll through the text. WAIT makes the printer print only single sheets at a time. PRINT prints unformatted or partially-formatted ASCII text files. PRINT also lets you set the left margin, specify the lines per page, print a selected page-range, select a header with auto page numbering, and select either single-sheet or continuous-feed paper.

(PC-SIG Disk# 950)

Special Requirements: *A printer.*
Author Registration: *$10.00*
➤*ASP Member.*

DocuHelp   *by Cygnus Systems Development, Inc.*

DOCUMENTOR allows you to use your own documentation text file to create an on-line user's manual and an associated index file for that manual. Use it primarily as a display tool once the documentation files are created, or as a conversion tool for the documentation. Finally, create the index file to be used by the program.

When used as a display tool the program will window up on the lower portion of the screen and display the document which you have specified. You will also be able to use the index which you specified to go to various places in the document to provide an easy method for finding various places within the document. If you use the program with the index display option you will be able to add index descriptions and line numbers to the index file with only a few simple keystrokes.

When used as a conversion tool the program will convert a text file (which you create with your own wordprocessor or text editor) to a DOCUMENTOR file, which then can be used by the program to provide an on-line display tool for your document.

(PC-SIG Disk# 1820)

Special Requirements: *None.*
Author Registration: *$49.00*

Dovetail III   *by M.O. Embry*

DOVETAIL III merges a form letter with addresses from a mailing list and even addresses envelopes. It works with mailing lists and form letters written with WordStar, Easywriter or PerfectWriter. Source code is in BASIC and the executable program file is also included.

(PC-SIG Disk# 877)

Special Requirements: *Printer.*
Author Registration: *User determined.*

EasyEdit II   *by AsEditCo*

If you are looking for a strong text editor that works with plain ASCII files EASYEDIT II may be the answer for you. This program has many editing facilities and all the features you want in a wordprocessor, plu a way to configure the program to emulate other wordprocessors (WORDSTAR is the default).

Some of the features of this program are:

❑ LAN support
❑ Laser printer support
❑ Pull down menus with dialog boxes
❑ Word wrapping
❑ Save to disk at timed intervals

Wordprocessor and Text Utilities

❏ Indexed on-line help
❏ Macros
❏ 190 possible editor commands that you can customize to your liking.

The program is easy enough for beginners to use with the menu system, and more advanced users will like the power, speed, and the many ways to configure the program to suit their needs.

(PC-SIG Disk# 2274)

Special Requirements: *Hard drive or high density disk.*
Author Registration: *L20.00*

EasyEdit II (PC-SIG Disk# 2274)

EasyType   *by Advocate Enterprises, Ltd.*

EASYTYPE is the first and only typesetting program which directly translates wordprocessing files into the format of most typesetting systems, and some desktop publishing systems. In addition to a generic/ASCII mode which handles the standard ASCII files that are produced by most wordprocessors, EASYTYPE also offers special modes which directly translate codes unique to wordprocessing files created by industry leading WordPerfect and WordStar. With EASYTYPE, anyone familiar with wordprocessing can prepare basic typesetting files.

EASYTYPE is an intelligent translation program. Other programs translate wordprocessing files simply by removing characters which might confuse the typesetting program. They also turn all line endings into "hard" returns which must be individually removed by the typesetter. EASYTYPE is smart enough to truly translate word processing codes to typesetting codes. One-key macros are also supported by EASYTYPE, so unique file translations are easy to perform.

(PC-SIG Disk# 1664)

Special Requirements: *None.*
Author Registration: *$49.95*

The Editing Keypads   *by David Brender*

THE EDITING KEYPADS provides an organized collection of macros, which can be used individually or interactively, to augment PC-Write. PC-Write itself is unchanged. The basic idea here, which is quite simple, is to designate a variety of new access keys, with each access key reaching a keypad of new macros. This provides a quick two-key sequence for starting and running a host of spatially oriented macros. EKP uses 8 access keys to reach 30 new keypads and 1,234 macros.

A good example of the many macros found in THE EDITING KEYPADS is the "phrase keypad." This macro provides cursor motion, phrase by phrase. These "phrase" macros can move the cursor left or right through the text to the next punctuation mark or to successive punctuation marks.

There are lots of macros here. Select a few favorites and enjoy them. You will soon see from the documentation that the macros are organized in groups and laid out similarly on all keypads so that one can readily use lots of them, without having to remember too much. And, there are plenty of help screens.

(PC-SIG Disk# 1574)

Special Requirements: *PC-Write 3.0 or higher.*
Author Registration: *$10.00*

Elray Software Legal Disk Dictionary   *by Raymond J. Myers*

Legal secretaries - this software is just for you. The ELRAY SOFTWARE LEGAL DISK DICTIONARY lists 981 English and Latin legal terms and words to supplement the dictionaries in your word processors.

If you use Borland's Turbo Lightning, Microsoft Word, WordStar, PC Write, pfs:Write, XyWrite or another ASCII-literate word processor, these files can save you hours of look-up time. Bring your legal dictionary up to snuff while insuring that paperwork from your office is top quality.

(PC-SIG Disk# 1576)

Special Requirements: *Word processor.*
Author Registration: *$7.50*

🖛 = Updated Program
☆ = New Program

Every Other Page ✍

by William B. Anderson

EVERY OTHER PAGE paginates your text files so you can print on the front and back of pages while maintaining the proper text sequence. The program saves you paper, helps your documents fit into one binder, and gives your reports the look of printed books.

EVERY OTHER PAGE takes any text file and breaks it up into 56 lines per page, and into odd pages (1, 3, 5...) which are to be printed on one side and even pages (2, 4, 6...) which are printed on the other side. First, it prints the odd-numbered pages and when finished, prompts you to reverse the paper in the printer so the other side can be printed with the even-numbered pages.

(PC-SIG Disk# 1428)

Special Requirements: *Printer.*
Author Registration: *$40.00*

Executive Editor

by The League Group, Inc.

EXECUTIVE EDITOR is a text editor/freeform database that will handle as many 64K files within the database as disk space allows. EXECUTIVE EDITOR is perfect for the laptop user to retain key information, draft and store notes and memos, or maintain a diary of contacts.

EXECUTIVE EDITOR allows keyword search (exact and fuzzy search), multi- window editing, import-export (in ASCII), and supports over 50 keyboard editor commands — though only six or seven are needed for most uses. On-line help prompts you through all operations, making a manual redundant for all but extreme power users.

EXECUTIVE EDITOR is not intended as a replacement for your word processo (though it has more text handling capabilities than some), nor is it intended as a replacement for your database (though many databases would like to handle 64K fields!). EXECUTIVE EDITOR was written for it's programmer's own use, that is as a front end to a desktop publisher, and as a convenient storage facility for drafts and notes. Along the way to completing the program it was discovered that it is an ideal batch file editor, a handy researcher's notebook, and a perfect add-on to most laptop computers.

(PC-SIG Disk# 1829)

Special Requirements: *Hard drive.*
Author Registration: *$25.00*

EZCount

by Fred Mendenhall

Writers, secretaries, transcribers — Count the number of words in a standard ASCII file. Bells and whistles are minimal. It counts words and displays how much time the program took to count.

(PC-SIG Disk# 724)

Special Requirements: *None.*
Author Registration: *$10.00*

File Browser

by David O. Tinker

With FILEBROWSER, you can view the largest ASCII or WordStar files, and chop them down to size to fit your wordprocessor.

This menu-driven tool lets you access big files, view them on the screen, copy specific blocks and print to a designated device. You can read a screen at a time, jump back and forth within the file, or have the text automatically scroll. It provides a quick search function for locating a particular word or line of text in a file. A DOS shell is provided for easy access to an editor or wordprocessor, and the program offers on-line help and a well-written 20-page operations manual.

(PC-SIG Disk# 1398)

Special Requirements: *None.*
Author Registration: *$15.00*

Grab Plus with LaserLabel ✍

by Zpay Payroll Systems, Inc.

GRAB PLUS is a memory-resident utility that grabs an address typed with a word processor and immediately prints it.

While using your word processor, call the GRAB PLUS menu by pressing a selected hot key. A box appears which is placed around the address to be printed. Adjust the size of the box to accommodate the longest addresses. Edit the address before printing or type in a whole new address. GRAB PLUS also prints a default return address on the envelope. Once the address is printed, GRAB PLUS disappears, returning you to normal computer operation.

GRAB PLUS has a database that stores and organizes address information with easy access for printing. Mark groups of addresses to be printed at one time. Exchange data with other programs. GRAB PLUS is the program to grab if you want a quick and easy way to print nicely typed envelopes with your computer.

The LASERLABEL program was created to allow users of the GRAB PLUS Envelope Printer to turn their data files into a powerful label printing system. Use the data files from GRAB and print labels on your LaserJet, DeskJet, and other printers.

Use different label formats from Avery, as well as soft fonts for added impact. The program recognizes the tag fields of GRAB and will select by tags if you prefer. The LASERLABEL system comes with a sample set of soft fonts to show you how your labels can have a creative appearance for greater impact.

(PC-SIG Disk#'s 1145, 2567)

Special Requirements: *None.*
Author Registration: *$49.95*
➤*ASP Member.*

Index Maker ✍   *by Itasca Softworks*

Give your document files that professional touch — by adding an index. Creating an index to a document is a time-consuming process. INDEX MAKER can greatly reduce that investment of time by having your computer do the work. Load the file to be indexed, create a word list for the index, and sit back and watch. INDEX MAKER can index up to 500 words with a maximum of 50 page citations per word.

INDEX MAKER is menu-driven for ease of operation. Index word lists can be saved on disk and then imported when needed. Add or delete words from existing lists. Once the index has been created, it can be viewed on screen before being sent to the printer.

INDEX MAKER can also be used to locate key words as markers in large document files to find information quickly and easily.

(PC-SIG Disk# 2347)

Special Requirements: *DOS 3.0. Two drives and a printer recommended.*
Author Registration: *$45.00*

Intext Multilingual Wordprocessing   *by Intex Software Systems Intl., Ltd.*

Whether you're a linguist, translator, student, or work for a international company, you're going to be glad you heard about INTEXT. INTEXT is the first shareware word processor created for worldwide use.

Create documents in English and any of the following languages: Albanian, Arabic, Croatian, Danish, Dutch, Farsi, Finnish, French, Gaelic, German, Hebrew, Italian, Macedonian, Norwegian, Polish, Portuguese, Russian, Serbian, Spanish, Swedish, and Turkish.

INTEXT supports all the functions you would expect to find on a full function word processor: search-and-replace, text block commands, text formatting commands, etc. What makes it unique is that all the special characters and symbols for the languages are displayed on the screen and printed out on either Epson FX, LQ, or IBM Proprinter printer.

(PC-SIG Disk# 2281)

Special Requirements: *None.*
Author Registration: *$49.00*

JORJ ✍   *by Jorj Software Company*

Spell checkers are great to check spelling, but what do you do when you need to know the meaning of a word? Look it up in a book? You won't have to with JORJ, a computerized dictionary.

JORJ is a 58,000 word dictionary that can run as a stand-alone program or as a memory-resident utility inside your favorite word processor (or other program). If you don't know the spelling of a word or are unsure about its exact meaning, just pop-up JORJ. Type in the word and JORJ will display its spelling, the spelling of popular forms of the word (-ance, -ous, -ly, etc.), and its meaning. You don't need to know the correct spelling because

JORJ will take your phonetic spelling and find the correct word! If you type in "dayrigur," JORJ correctly answers with "de rigueur."

JORJ can even find related words. Scan for the word "president" and you'll get a list of presidents. Look up "planet" and get a list of the planets!

The next time you need to find a word, let JORJ do it!

(PC-SIG Disk#'s 2489, 2490)

Special Requirements: *Hard drive.*
Author Registration: *$30.00*

JORJ (PC-SIG Disk# 2489)

LetterWriter   *by Lightwave*

LETTERWRITER is a different kind of address manager — its specialty is mailmerge. You can keep address files full of different "kinds" of people; i.e., business acquaintances, friends, or relatives. You can sort these different files by first name, last name, or zip code, just as you would a more traditional database address manager.

But with LETTERWRITER you can also merge the database information into an ASCII document, such as a letter that has been created in a wordprocessor. In this way you can imbed names, phrases, or paragraphs into the body of a letter. And you can create form letters by simply typing out one letter you want to send to any number of different addresses and specifying those addresses. LETTERWRITER automatically prints a letter with each address. It can also print labels, envelopes, address books, and lots more.

(PC-SIG Disk# 719)

Special Requirements: *ASCII wordprocessor.*
Author Registration: *$39.00*

Maillist ✍   *by R.K. West Consulting*

MAILLIST is an easy-to-use mailing list manager that handles up to 99 separate lists. Prints labels (1- or 3-across), has automatic duplicate checking, search by any field, "sound alike" search, extra fields for user coding, quick find, pop-up notepad for each record, compare and combine lists, optional password protection, restore deleted records, change program defaults, and more. Simplicity and flexibility make MAILLIST perfect for both small businesses and personal use. Registration includes both MAILLIST and M-LABEL, MAILLIST's Clipper source code, and a printed manual.

(PC-SIG Disk# 1506)

Special Requirements: *460K RAM. A hard drive strongly recommended.*
Author Registration: *$39.00 (includes M-LABEL)*
➤**ASP Member.**

MDTS - Member and Donation Tracking System ✍   *by Tom&Cat DataMgmt Software*

MDTS is a database program for any church or non-profit organization to track members (mailing labels and telephone directories) and the pledges and actual donations by those members (member tax statements and internal analysis reports). It features numerous reports (A thru Z menu with some sub-menus), many of which (including mailing labels) permit user-defined selection criteria. Has 99 user-defined donation categories (Christmas toy drive, Building Mtce, any name you define) and up to ONE BILLION transactions. Bonus program (in a ZIP file) to extract data from any DBF file to an ASCII file. May have 26 (A-thru-Z) "SETS" of data files to have multiple years of information or several organizations in a directory.

(PC-SIG Disk# 1791)

Special Requirements: *384K RAM, and a hard drive.*
Author Registration: *$45.00; With Clipper source $100.00.*

MiniMax   *by The League Group, Inc.*

MINIMAX is a full featured text editor for use with database, desktop publishing, and spreadsheet programs. It is simple and fast, just what you need when making quick corrections your main program doesn't do well This text editor was created as a quick and easy alternative to bulky, complex programs.

Install MINIMAX and you can easily create ASCII text files of up to 64K length for inclusion in your database reports, spreadsheets, desktop publishing files, etc. MINIMAX can also create and edit batch files. MINIMAX includes multiple window editing (the number of windows is limited only by available memory) and file/block copying/importing.

(PC-SIG Disk# 1829)

Special Requirements: *None.*
Author Registration: *$25.00*

MMSORT & MMREPORT DOCS *by EWDP Software, Inc.*

MMSORT and MMREPORT are two utilities for sorting and creating reports and labels from data in FILEBASE database files and existing mailmerge files.

MMSORT sorts and provides for sort-merging mailmerge files on the basis of any numeric or character field, in ascending or descending order. Special sort features such as specific sorting on part of a field, character sorts and date sorts help to make a tedious job easier.

MMREPORT generates reports and labels for mailmerge files, and can also select records on the basis of field contents. Fields can be selectively printed from each record. When printing labels, you may print 1, 3 or 5 labels across, with optional multiple copies of each record. MMREPORT can also set up special print styles for printing.

(PC-SIG Disk# 1868)

Special Requirements: *None.*
Author Registration: *$15.00*

MorePerfick ✍ *by Simple Productions*

Here is a utility program WordPerfect fans should have. MOREPERFECT adds to the word processing program a new set of command keys in an ingenious arrangement. With a single keystroke, you can move the cursor or delete—by character, word, line, sentence, paragraph, or page— forward or backward—without moving your hands from the letter keys! MOREPERFECT can double your editing speed, yet it's easy to learn and use.

(PC-SIG Disk# 759)

Special Requirements: *WordPerfect 5.0, 5.1.*
Author Registration: *$15.00*

MSP Document Processing Utility *by The Nunnery Works Ltd.*

Writers — here's a useful addition to your library.

MSPANTOC reads a document you created on a wordprocessor and writes a new document, updated with:

❑ Assigned section, paragraph, figure, and table numbers
❑ Resolved cross references
❑ A table of contents
❑ A list of figures
❑ A list of tables

MSPANTOC is not a wordprocessor or an outline generator. It complements your existing wordprocessing package by providing the numbering and cross-reference features not available with many current wordprocessing packages. It works with WordStar, WordPerfect, or any other wordprocessor.

(PC-SIG Disk# 935)

Special Requirements: *None.*
Author Registration: *$35.00*

Multi-Merge *by David W. Meny*

MULTI-MERGE facilitates adding, editing, deleting, sorting, and printing information for later merging into your wordprocessing merge documents. Data can be sorted by name, company, zip, or two key fields you tailor to your own specifications. It is not a program meant to replace a wordprocessor, but rather to enhance it.

With MULTI-MERGE, you can manipulate your list, create your merge list, and then use your wordprocessor to merge the list with the wordprocessor's merge document. The program is easy to use and completely menu driven, but you do need to know your wordprocessor's merge functions and DOS to operate the program with facility.

(PC-SIG Disk# 1152)

Special Requirements: *512K RAM, two floppy drives, and an Epson-compatible printer.*
Author Registration: *$10.00*

MultiWord ☆   *by Digital Crypto*

There you are, speeding along on your favorite word processor when you suddenly realize that your latest sentence just doesn't sound right. You can either pull out your trusty thesaurus and flip the pages to find the perfect word or you can call MULTIWORD.

MULTIWORD is a electronic thesaurus with over 9000 main entries and more than 70,000 synonyms. Operate as a standalone or as a TSR.

MULTIWORD can be popped-up over your favorite word processors (Word Star, Galaxy Lite, or PC-Write) and allows you to find alternative words quickly.

(PC-SIG Disk# 2743)

Special Requirements: *None.*
Author Registration: *$24.95*

Neat Text Formatter   *by SEM Software*

NEAT reads in a standard ASCII file format created by most wordprocessors and writes a "formatted" file in output. Use NEAT and you can:
❑ Print multiple copies
❑ Begin and end on specified pages of a document
❑ Pause for single-sheet feeding
❑ Make room for your data during text formatting
❑ Include other text files up to a nested level of four
❑ Include merge fields from a second merge file.

NEAT also has font controls for double width, boldface, double strike, italics, two forms of underlining, letter-quality mode, headers and footers for every page, automatic page numbering in header or footer, even/odd page margin shifting, line centering, adjustable line spacing, and more.

(PC-SIG Disk# 1540)

Special Requirements: *Printer.*
Author Registration: *$15.00*

ParaSort   *by Chris DeGreet*

PARASORT will copy, sort and merge your ASCII OR dBASE files easily and quickly. Since most databases can export to ASCII, these files also can be sorted with PARASORT. It can use complex record selection criteria, including record and byte position on input and/or output, to select which records it will sort and merge. A special dBASE III interface enhances the program.

PARASORT can display the fields of the selected files on the screen, one page at a time, 20 fields per page. Specify which fields are key and in which sequence, and then choose the sorting order of each field. PARASORT can reformat the input file as it is read, skipping and limiting the input and/or output records, including or excluding dBASE header records. It will write the output records to one or more output files, formatting it as you wish.

Sort on ascending, descending and absolute values of keys. Convert fixed length records to variable length records and back again. PARASORT can eliminate duplicates or place them in an expected order, first, last, or don't care.

(PC-SIG Disk# 1858)

Special Requirements: *None.*
Author Registration: *$15.00*

PC-Browse   *by Quicksoft*

The PC's primary limitation has just been overcome! Finally you can be working in one application, and still have access to the information contained in all your other text files. Imagine you're working in your spreadsheet when you realize you need some information in a memo you wrote two days earlier. No need to exit your spreadsheet, just use PC- BROWSE to pop the old memo onto the top of your screen. Better still, PC-BROWSE will let you cut and paste part or all of that memo right into your spreadsheet — even though the original memo was written with your wordprocessor. Sounds incredible, and it is!

PC-BROWSE is a top notch software product from Quicksoft, the authors of famed PC-Write. As expected, PC-BROWSE is loaded with all the extras needed to optimize your use of this powerful tool. PC-BROWSE will let you search entire directories for a word or phrase, then view each file in that directory where the requested word or phrase occurs. Once you find what you were looking for, you're free to browse through the surrounding text.

Because PC-BROWSE can actually recognize the word at your cursor when activated, it has hypertext-style functionality never before possible on an overhead memory program requiring only 60K of RAM (3K if loaded into EMS). PC-BROWSE is so well designed, it can even remove itself from memory when you no longer need its unique skills, all without rebooting — now that's polished software.

The uses for PC-BROWSE are numerous: create on-line context-sensitive help files for any program, create study guides or customized dictionaries, compile a program with often used lines of code, write a telemarketing script with various categories of information, keep product literature handy and accessible by product number, features, or use. But most importantly, you will never have to exit your current application to go browse text files in an attempt to find additional data; PC-BROWSE will do it for you.

(PC-SIG Disk#'s 1670, 1671)
Special Requirements: *None.*
Author Registration: *$69.00 plus $5.00 shipping.*
➤*ASP Member.*

PC-Write Font Selector   *by Quicksoft*

FONT SELECTOR was written for PC-Write users with Hewlett Packard LaserJets and compatible printers. It enables them to select, with print controls within their text, the fonts built into the HP, the HP cartridge, and hundreds of commercially available soft fonts! It's a poor man's desktop publishing.

This program is a boon to graphic artists whose customers request a wide variety of type faces and sizes for their documents. Firms which generate their own documents will find their ability to create custom-looking documents is greatly enhanced.

FONT SELECTOR works by creating special print control files for each font you use. It also creates a download batch file that copies the soft fonts into the printer's memory. Simple control characters within PC-Write are then used to tag text.

(PC-SIG Disk# 1267)
Special Requirements: *Hard drive, LaserJet printer, and PC-Write.*
Author Registration: *$20.00*
➤*ASP Member.*

PC-Write Macros ✍   *by Simple Productions*

PC-WRITE devotees will enjoy a macro feast with this collection designed for shareware's most popular wordprocessor. You also get a mass of information and three tutorials to educate you on macros — their care and feeding.

PC-WRITE MACROS offers 100 special commands for PC-Write and helps you place them on the keys of your choice. You will gain greater power and convenience with many commands not found in PC-Write or any other wordprocessor. With PC-WRITE MACROS you can:

❏ "Grab" an address block from a letter and print it on an envelope.
❏ Reverse the video on your mono or single-color monitor so it shows dark text on a light background.
❏ Set up margins, ruler, spacing, all in an instant.
❏ Mark, delete, or transpose an entire sentence or paragraph witha single keystroke.
❏ Store deleted text in a special file, ready for retrieval at any time.
❏ Begin continuous printing with one stroke.

A choice of four versions of keyboard and keypad options are provided. You can load macros as you need them or keep them in memory to use again and again. You can load them singly or in groups.

(PC-SIG Disk# 1457)

Special Requirements: *PC-WRITE 3.0 or later.*
Author Registration: *$10.00*

PC-Write Macros, Volume 2 ✍   *by Simple Productions*

This program offers another 100 special commands for the popular word processing program PC-WRITE. Place them on the keys of your choice. With PC-WRITE MACROS, VOL. 2, you can;
❑ Speed up PC-WRITE.
❑ Call up a Notepad, for sending notes to printer or file.
❑ Convert your documents for WordPerfect or Macintosh.
❑ Instantly set up page formats for Elite fonts.
❑ Adjust page breaks to avoid splitting paragraphs.
❑ Triple-space in a double-spaced document.
❑ Experiment with a Dvorak keyboard.
❑ Test and install macros without leaving your document.
   And much, much more!

(PC-SIG Disk# 2285)

Special Requirements: *PC-Write 3.0.*
Author Registration: *$10.00*

PC-Write Pagemaker Import Filter   *by Quicksoft*

PC-WRITE PAGEMAKER IMPORT FILTER allows PC-Write users to transfer PC-Write documents into a Pagemaker environment while retaining most of the formatting.

(PC-SIG Disk# 1267)

Special Requirements: *Hard disk drive, PC-Write, and Pagemaker.*
Author Registration: *None.*
➤*ASP Member.*

Pen Pal ✍   *by Micro Data Assist*

Is it a mailmerging text editor that works great as an address manager? Or is it a super address manager for business or personal use that also automates mass correspondence? Or is it the perfect printing utility that lets you print Rolodex cards, envelopes, labels, and more a from the same program? It is all of these things and none the worse for being so versatile.

With PEN PAL you don't have to worry about getting your wordprocessor to talk to your database and vice versa. This is a truly integrated system that takes out the middleman. Even the ambitious beginner can be mass producing letters the first time through the program. You will find features that help you improve your correspondence, such as the ability to customize the salutation for each individual in your database. It is completely menu-driven for fast effective use and the screen design is easy to follow. You can save up to 99 different letters on file for future editing and use. The program even supports common database formats for easy data exchange into other programs should you need them.

Before you go to all the trouble of building a database/wordprocessing system and configuring it all for custom printing, consider PEN PAL. The work may already be done for you.

(PC-SIG Disk# 1570)

Special Requirements: *512K free RAM.*
Author Registration: *$25.00*

PRO-CR ✍   *by Gray Design Associates*

This is the world's first Optical Character Recognition program, which enables IBM-PC owners with scanners to scan text into editable ASCII text files, saving the effort of typing the text themselves. Features include:
❑ Reads 8 to 30 point mono and proportional fonts.
❑ No font selection required, just hit Start.

❑ Supports HP ScanJet directly.
❑ Supports other scanners via TIFF, compressed TIFF, and .PCX files.
❑ Selectable resolution, including 200 dpi (FAX), and 300 dpi.
❑ Preview and on-line correction modes with graphics adapter.
❑ Mis-recognition flagged with selectable character.
❑ Real-time viewing for text during processing.
❑ Includes both menu-driven and command line interface.
(PC-SIG Disk# 2269)

Special Requirements: *Scanner.*
Author Registration: *$42.00*
➤*ASP Member.*

ProIndex
by Elfring Soft Fonts

Writers, Students, Editors — PROINDEX lets you negotiate the most problem-filled part of writing a document or book: building the index.

PROINDEX saves you the trouble of having to handmark each and every word you want in your index. You simply provide a file of words listing the keywords you want to be in your index, and PROINDEX searches your document and marks all occurrences of those keywords. Works with any ASCII text file (as well as WordStar files).

(PC-SIG Disk# 977)

Special Requirements: *None.*
Author Registration: *$65.00*
➤*ASP Member.*

Quattro & 1-2-3 to WordPerfect
by Stephen Lowens

QWP makes life easier for editors and others who frequently incorporate spreadsheets into WordPerfect documents. QWP converts Lotus 1-2-3 (Versions 1A and 2.1) and Quattro (Versions 1.0 and 1.1) spreadsheet files into WordPerfect 4.2 files (readable by WordPerfect Versions 4.2 and above).

QWP allows column alignments to be maintained when the WordPerfect user wishes to incorporate a spreadsheet into a document formatted for a printer using proportional spacing. This offers an advantage over the commonly used technique of "printing" spreadsheets to an ASCII format disk file and importing them into WordPerfect, because the conversion process translates all tabs into a fixed number of spaces. QWP automatically calculates an appropriate tab format for each line, even as data types change.

Most users who are already familiar with Lotus 1-2-3 or Quattro and WordPerfect will find QWP's documentation adequate to get them started. However, they should be prepared to experiment a bit in order to produce exactly the results they want. This time will be repaid by eliminating hours reformatting or retyping a spreadsheet in order to align the columns.

The registration provisions are unusually generous, allowing a registered user to make an unlimited number of copies for all machines located at a single street address.

(PC-SIG Disk# 2002)

Special Requirements: *Lotus 1-2-3 or Quattro, and WordPerfect.*
Author Registration: *$25.00*

Qwik Help
by Advocate Enterprises, Ltd.

QTEXT turns your ordinary text files into standalone, instantly executable .COM program files. Any user can easily view their contents simply by typing the file's name — just like any other file ending with .COM. Screens pause where you want them until the you're ready to continue, at which point the screen clears and the next section is displayed.

QHELP transforms your text into a menu-driven environment. By a simple, one-word key at the head of the file, you determine whether the user will be offered the opportunity to print out the file in a professionally-formatted manner, complete with a header line containing useful information (page and section numbers, date of last file revision and title of your choice). You can also give your users the choice to display or print the entire file or only chosen sections. Files can be printed complete with a title and table of contents.

✐ = Updated Program
☆ = New Program

If you're the de facto "computer expert" for your family or office, preparing such files offers you the chance to thoughtfully provide your knowledge and advice in an organized, easily-used format.

(PC-SIG Disk# 2270)

Special Requirements: *None.*
Author Registration: *$39.95*

ReadIt
by Cobrasoft, Inc.

THE TEXT FILE READER (READIT) allows users to scroll, page, and print on-line documents. All commands are displayed on a horizontal menu bar. An intuitive interface provides a straightforward source for on-line help. READIT provides the means to distribute manuals, instructions, procedures and other documents, royalty free, to users with a wide range of computer experience. Users without wordprocessing experience can be brought "up to speed" in minutes.

Using READIT with your text file requires that text be prepared as shown in the documentation. Control over formatted printing and screen display is provided so documents come out looking professional — printer or screen.

(PC-SIG Disk# 1687)

Special Requirements: *None.*
Author Registration: *$20.00*

RefList
by Edward J. Shillitoe

REFLIST is an easy-to-use program that lets you create and format lists of references and bibliographies, — elements which are always a problem for the writer submitting material to a variety of publishing houses, each with its own specific requirements.

The truly unique feature of REFLIST is that once your paper has been written, it reformats your references into different user-defined formats. You can submit a paper to one publisher with the references in one format and then, with REFLIST, reformat the references to a different format expected by another publisher — all quickly and easily. In addition, REFLIST has instructions for quick integration into WordPerfect, PC-Write, or any ASCII-based wordprocessor.

(PC-SIG Disk# 231)

Special Requirements: *None.*
Author Registration: *$30.00*

SeekEasy
by Correlation Systems

SEEKEASY is a very easy-to-use, "flexible match" information- retrieval program which lets you search a text file for a character string and lists the "best matches" to your request in the order of match quality. It can do this even if the item found is not exactly what you requested, or has words in it that were not in your request, or doesn't use words spelled exactly the same way. Because of the flexibility of the program, it can be used for a multitude of uses, both for personal and business needs.

(PC-SIG Disk# 820)

Special Requirements: *None.*
Author Registration: *$30.00*

Shuffles
by Newline Products

Want to print on both sides of the paper? You could figure out how your file will be printed, break it up and feed the parts to your printer one at a time (and hope that you didn't make an error) — or — you can use SHUFFLES, a computerized collator.

SHUFFLES breaks your text file into chunks and rearranges them so your dot matrix, daisy wheel or laser printer can print on both sides of the paper without getting the page order messed up.

(PC-SIG Disk# 1312)

Special Requirements: *Two floppy drives.*
Author Registration: *$30.00*

Stripper
by Don Rooney

STRIPPER reads an input text file and produces an output file by replacing any control character visible. You have the option of deleting characters in the ASCII character set that are above 126, below 126, 126 only, below 32, above 32, delete spaces, or any combination in between.

(PC-SIG Disk# 978)

Special Requirements: *None.*
Author Registration: *None.*

SXU
by PTD Software Systems

Programmers — A utility for you called THE SELECT XTRAC UTILITY (SXU). SXU extracts selected sections of data files according to your specifications. It accepts any standard ASCII sequential files composed of character or numerical data.

The input file to SXU cannot have embedded control characters, except for normal print-control characters. SXU reads the input data file and creates an output extract file with the data between your specified start and end strings in the input data file.

SXU can extract data and append it to an already-existing extract file, and allows up to 32 different extracts from a single file at one time. On-line help and directions are included.

(PC-SIG Disk# 962)

Special Requirements: *320K RAM.*
Author Registration: *$15.00*

Text/File Handling Utility
by RT Computer Consultants

You've just finished the Great American Novel only to discover you've mispelled the name of a key historical figure. You can ask for your old job back or you can use HUNTMOD! Coming to your rescue, HUNTMOD searches out every mispelled name and replaces it with the correct one!

Or have you forgotten in which file(s) you wrote about a particular subject, or placed a valuable snippet of data? Let a companion program, HUNSTR, sniff them out. This program looks for phrases or names you indicate (up to 10 at a time), and tirelessly searches through all your files. When a match turns up, it records the names of specific file(s), and where in them it discovered which items of interest.

Other utilities in this set are small improvements to the DOS commands DEL and TYPE. QDEL deletes filenames listed on the command line from the specified directory or drive, but stops and queries first, "Do you really want to do this?" This gives you one last chance to avoid disaster. FVIEW lets you read text files the same way as TYPE, but also lets you view a screen at a time, automatically, without having to play rapid fire with the CONTROL-S command.

(PC-SIG Disk# 1404)

Special Requirements: *None.*
Author Registration: *$20.00*

TextCon ✍
by CrossCourt Systems

TEXTCON allows you to import ASCII files into your word processor without having to manually delete carriage returns, remove extra spaces, and generally reformat your documents.

Files can be imported with accurate paragraph breaks due to TEXTCON's intelligent paragraph recognition algorithms. No more manual deletion of hard returns. TEXTCON even works with difficult formats, such as fully nested, outline style and hanging indents. TEXTCON also removes excess spaces, blank lines, and headers and footers. TEXTCON can accept any form of ASCII file, including those transferred from Macintosh or UNIX, as well as WordStar.

(PC-SIG Disk# 2346)

Special Requirements: *None*
Author Registration: *$25.00*
➤*ASP Member.*

✍ = Updated Program
☆ = New Program

TextOut/5 ✍ *by CrossCourt Systems*

TEXTOUT/5 converts WordPerfect 5.0 and 5.1 document files to ASCII.

It improves upon WordPerfect's Text Out command, in both DOS Text and generic word processing formats. TEXTOUT/5 translates the entire document, including text, captions and equations from graphics boxes, as well as footnotes and endnotes — all items that WordPerfect ignores. TEXTOUT/5 can mark certain font attributes, such as underlining, in the ASCII file by using special characters. This is useful if you want to transfer the ASCII file to another word processor and restore the attributes.

(PC-SIG Disk# 2346)

Special Requirements: *None.*
Author Registration: *$20.00*
➤*ASP Member.*

Thesaur — A Thesaurus program *by Thesaur Plus*

Searching for the right word to say what you really mean? This computerized thesaurus should help you become both more stylish and concise (make that succinct!) in all your writing and prepared speeches.

Add panache to your letters, eloquence to your term papers, and a Phi Beta Kappa impact to your speaking endeavors by spending just few minutes with THESAUR. When you call up a word, you are provided an array of synonyms and related words. Set the pointer over your synonym of choice and you get a definition to confirm its aptness.

There are over 10,000 main words and close to 50,000 synomyms in THESAUR The program also allows you to add your own words as synomyms, and even delete words that you think are inappropriate.

(PC-SIG Disk# 1245)

Special Requirements: *None.*
Author Registration: *$20.00*
➤*ASP Member.*

Thesaur Plus *by Thesaur Plus*

THESAUR PLUS is a pop-up thesaurus, whenever you need a different word or a different shade of meaning than the word that comes to mind, pop-up THESAUR PLUS and get the word you wanted, but couldn't quite remember!

THESAUR PLUS was designed with simplicity in mind. You only need to remember your Hot-key (the key combination you use to pop THESAUR PLUS up over what you are doing now) to use the program!

You can look up the word at your cursor, or call the thesaurus and type a word to reference. With the registered version, if you don't like the synonyms THESAUR PLUS comes with, you can easily change them; allows full style editing with insert, overstrike, and delete.

(PC-SIG Disk# 1245)

Special Requirements: *Hard Drive.*
Author Registration: *$20.00*
➤*ASP Member.*

Vernon Buerg's List ☆ *by Vernon D. Buerg*

LIST lets you scroll up, down, left, and right through documentation or data files. Search for specific data. LIST uses wildcards to let you browse a series of related files with only one command. LIST also has hex display, screen wrap, strip high bits, split screen, rulers, and much more. Supports 43-line and 132-column modes on EGA. Prints files and has a phone dialer.

Other features include:
❏ If you have PKZIP, LHARC, and a hard drive, view contents of .ZIP, .ARC, and .LZH files (including self-extracting files)
❏ A small file management utility to copy, delete, rename, etc. Call your favorite text editor from this DIR listing
❏ Bookmark, DOS shell now callable from within the program
❏ Supports mice and LANs
❏ Paste data from the file being viewed to another file
❏ Execute programs from within LIST itself

LIST also has the ability to search a group of files for hex data or text strings, with one command.

Other niceties are the split-screen display, extensive documentation, and the 3-program setup. There are small, medium, and large versions included. Pick the one that has just enough features and a small enough .COM file size (from 9K to 20K) for you.

(PC-SIG Disk# 2565)
Special Requirements: *None.*
Author Registration: *$20.00*

Word Processing Preview System
by Chelsea-Skye, Inc.

See what your page layout looks like before you print your document. Experiment with different formatting options without printing a single page!

The WORD PROCESSING PREVIEWING SYSTEM (WPPS) gives you a picture of page layouts from any ASCII wordprocessor file. WPPS draws from one to 18 rectangular "pages" on your color display and then fills them with output to show you exactly how your document will look when printed. Repeating the operation, up to 18 pages at a time, is an invaluable tool for saving time and paper!

The previewer is especially useful when dealing with documents of 100 or more pages, and can quickly pay for itself in paper saved.

(PC-SIG Disk# 415)
Special Requirements: *CGA.(can't find author!)*
Author Registration: *$40.00*

The Wordsmith Newsletter Kit
by Wordsmith Document Design Inc.

The novice using Ventura Publisher without a great deal of typographical or page design experience can now design a complete newsletter. For the experienced user, the style sheets provide instant design, which may be quickly modified to suit a variety of needs. Eight chapter templates containing newsletter designs are included.

The WORDSMITH NEWSLETTER KIT manual outlines all procedures required to turn word processor files into a complete, attractive publication using the included style sheets and Ventura Publisher. It also provides a range of tools — for example, copyfitting techniques, dealing with writers, proofreading and Ventura speed tricks — that go outside the mandate of the layout software. The kit provides a total solution for the user's needs, linking the world of software with the traditions of printing and typography.

(PC-SIG Disk# 1974)
Special Requirements: *Ventura Desktop Publisher.*
Author Registration: *$29.95*

Writer's Heaven ✍
by Simple Productions

WRITER'S HEAVEN transforms the popular wordprocessing program PC-Write into one of the fastest and most efficient editing tools today.

WRITER'S HEAVEN, using PC-WRITE's own macro feature, grafts a unique keyboard structure onto PC-WRITE itself. The result is a wordprocessor that combines speed, power, simplicity, and ease of learning — a wordprocessor that brings on-screen editing significantly closer to the speed of thought. While most of the principal PC-WRITE command keys remain intact as an alternate command set, you can now edit text without ever moving your hands from the typewriter position, and you can do it faster than ever before.

(PC-SIG Disk# 759)
Special Requirements: *PC-Write V3.0.*
Author Registration: *$10.00*

▼ ▼ ▼

Wordprocessors, Education

The ECC Learning System for WordPerfect 5.1
by ECC Learning Systems

For classroom or private use, THE ECC LEARNING SYSTEM is a state-of-the- art disk-based tutorial for WordPerfect v5.1. Composed of 500 screens, it covers basic commands and provides exercises practicing those commands in a real look and feel simulation. A computer user can use the tutorial as a self-paced learning tool. A 200-page workbook comes with registration.

You are introduced to the computer, the disk operating system, the WordPerfect wordprocessor and learn to create and edit documents and how to use WordPerfect commands and menus. Starting with basic DOS commands and conventions, the tutorial runs through WordPerfect commands which teach in detail how to: set margins, set tabs, use tabs, use indents, center text, interpret the document screen, select a printer, print, edit a document by using delete, insert, move and block, use newspaper columns, perform math calculations, spell-check, use the thesaurus, and more.

(PC-SIG Disk#' 1338)

Special Requirements: *512K RAM.*
Author Registration: *$79.95*

▼ ▼ ▼

Wordprocessors, Text Editors, and Outliners

The "perfect" Editor ☆   *by Just Excellent Software, Inc.*

Is there any editor out there that is totally perfect? Maybe not, but THE "PERFECT" EDITOR is a great editor designed to facilitate the building and writing of many types of documents. With full mouse support, configuration of colors, and lots more, there are, of course, the typical word processing features: justification, word wrap, block operations, etc. And then there's tiling of up to 20 windows, cutting and pasting between windows, box graphics, and for the programmer, editing in either hex or ASCII, with PE automatically making the appropriate adjustments. With a whole range of excellent features and good documentation, THE "PERFECT" EDITOR is well worth the time to check out!

(PC-SIG Disk# 2776)

Special Requirements: *No special requirements.*
Author Registration: *$39.00*
➤ *ASP Member.*

BlackBeard   *by Blackbeard*

Programmers — here's an editor that can perform just about every task you'll need to have done. This is due to its windowing capacity (13!), work-horse text formatter, macro capabilites, and integral mouse driver. It works well for source code editing in structured languages such as Pascal, C, Fortran, etc.

While its primary use is for source code editing, it also has some wordprocessing features (reformats, centers, cut and paste, etc.) to ease your housekeeping/documentation chores.

(PC-SIG Disk# 611)

Special Requirements: *None.*
Author Registration: *$20.00*

Boxer Text Editing System ✍   *by David R. Hamel*

BOXER is a fast, fully-functional, text editor written by a software engineer that will appeal to experienced programmers. Since the program has an excellent user interface, even novices can utilize it quickly.

Features include:

❑ 512 level genuine UNDO command
❑ Full mouse support; close, resize, drag, and zoom on windows
❑ 43/50 line modes for EGA/VGA/MCGA
❑ Multiple files, multiple windows — limited only by RAM
❑ User-configurable color settings
❑ Twenty-six user-definable keystroke macros
❑ Online, indexed, context-sensitive Help system
❑ Issue commands from keyboard or pull-down menus
❑ Fast screen scrolling
❑ Search forward, backward, regular expressions

❑ Search & replace, globally or selectively or across all edited files
❑ Word processing support; reformat, pagination, headers/footers
❑ Block/line/columnar text marking — by keyboard or mouse
❑ Extensive block operations
❑ Locate "lost" files anywhere on disk
❑ Graphic drawing mode for drawing boxes and frames
❑ Select files from a pop-up file menu, or traverse directories

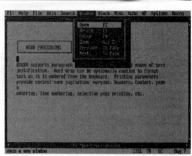

Boxer Text Editing System (PC-SIG Disk# 2629)

All these features would make this program a contender in its category, but BOXER goes one step further by providing these additional options:

❑ Multi-base pop-up ASCII chart
❑ Multi-base programmer's calculator
❑ Keystroke multiply
❑ Typewriter-style tab stops
❑ Automatic Save option
❑ Automatic Indent option
❑ Date/time/calendar displays

(PC-SIG Disk# 2629)

Special Requirements: *384K RAM, and high density or hard drive.*
Author Registration: *$35.00*
➤*ASP Member.*

CopyCon
by John Bean

COPYCON is a program designed to take the place of the DOS command "COPY CON" commonly used to create BATCH files. The program allows full screen editing of your file with line length of up to 80 characters. COPYCON also provides a number of "macro" keys to help make the process simpler. These macros include some of the common commands used in batch files (ie. echo, rem, etc.), as well as macro keys for all of the single and double-line graphics characters. This makes simple work of adding graphics boxes to your batch files. There are no block commands included, as this is not designed to be a full featured text editor, however there is a command to copy one line to another. The program is very easy to use and the documentation, although not really needed, is quite complete.

(PC-SIG Disk# 2029)

Special Requirements: *None.*
Author Registration: *$10.00*

E!
by Guy Lachance

E! is a powerful full-screen text editor. Its implementation has been driven by three keywords; quick, simple, and efficient. E! will allow you to edit as many files as your system memory can hold simultaneously. A "split screen" mode is available to see two different parts of a file on the same screen. Although E! is not a wordprocessor, it offers some functions you will rarely find in a text editor. E! has a versatile interface with DOS which makes it a valuable tool for both programmers and non-programmers alike. It edits and saves ASCII files but does not include any control characters in the text flow except if you insert them yourself. Support for a specific printer is not included, but you can add printer control characters in your text very easily.

E! is a professional level tool. It is highly configurable, allowing you to tailor it to your specific needs using profiles and macros. E! supports EGA 43 lines mode, VGA 50 lines mode, and a special 35 lines mode which is even more readable. The IBM 101T enhanced keyboard is also fully supported. E! has an abundance of built-in functions that can be grouped together to build macros and then saved in a macro file, to be used at any time during the editing process. You can even assign a macro to any key. E!'s configuration can be changed at any time by loading a new profile. You can have profiles for programming support, profiles adapted to program documentation editing, etc. When loading a file E! automatically expands tabs if this is specified in the main profile. The same option compresses blanks to tabs when saving edited files.

E! offers programming support by allowing you to compile any source file from within the editor without leaving it. Compiler detected errors can be retrieved from the compiler and E! will then point directly to the error in the source text.

✍ = Updated Program
☆ = New Program

E! supports full windowing. You can edit up to six files simultaneously on the same screen in separate windows. Also included in E! is a very convenient application programming interface (API) which allows you to write new functions and utilities using your usual programming language, such as C, Pascal, etc.

(PC-SIG Disk# 1615)

Special Requirements: *None.*
Author Registration: *$50.00*

E88 Text Editor
by Microsystems Research and Engineeri

The E88 TEXT EDITOR (E88) is a powerful, fully-functional text and programming editor completely written in Assembly language. It is both compact and extremely fast.

Rather than using complicated keyboard commands such as those commonly used in other editors or wordprocessors, E88 primarily uses single-keystroke commands. These make it more natural, logical, and easy to learn. File control and set-up functions are handled in a menu-driven command window and informational prompts make operation easy.

(PC-SIG Disk# 1102)

Special Requirements: *None.*
Author Registration: *$20.00*
➤*ASP Member.*

ESL Writer
by Richard Raker

ESL WRITER is a word processing program and four help programs especially designed for the writing student.

Help files are included for commands, punctuation, grammar, and revision and can be accessed from within the program or viewed from the outside.

ESL WRITER has a pull-down menu system for the most common editing commands, while other commands are described in detail in the command help file. Use your own printer control characters for print formats (e.g., underlining, italics, bold print, etc.), making ESL WRITER compatible with any printer.

INVISIBLE WRITER lets the user type without seeing the text, which can be brought to the screen with a single command. This helps writers concentrate on their thought processes and content, rather than grammar, punctuation, or spelling errors.

LISTER asks simple questions and provides ideas to help develop a topic and choose a thesis, and 1001 TOPICS contains 1,358 topics in twenty-one categories that are suitable for many different types of composition.

(PC-SIG Disk#'s 899, 900)

Special Requirements: *None.*
Author Registration: *$15.00 to $50.00*

EZX-Word ✍
by EZX Publishing

EZX-WORD is a full-function word processor that uses less than 100K of memory — perfect for laptops! EZX-WORD has common-sense, pull-down menus to help most users get up and running in minutes. Included are all of the standard features such as: multiple windows, on-line Help, headers/footers, search and replace, pagination, undo, adjustable margins, block commands, a spell checker, and more.

EZX-WORD doesn't have documentation. Don't worry. With the plain English menus and on-line Help, most users won't need any. Most popular printers and 43/50 line EGA/VGA displays are supported. Also great for single-drive computers.

(PC-SIG Disk# 2494)

Special Requirements: *None.*
Author Registration: *$49.00*

EZX-Word (PC-SIG Disk# 2494)

FILE!
by Financial Planning Consultants, Inc

"All I want is a simple text editor!" You got it — FILE! is a convenient text editor designed for editing small batch files, your CONFIG.SYS file, and your AUTOEXEC.BAT. Very few features to bother with, but enough: edit lines, delete lines, swap lines, and cripple (REM) a file line. Maximum file size to load and print is 100K. Ideal when using the phone to help a remote user revise critical batch files.

(PC-SIG Disk# 1893)

Special Requirements: *None.*
Author Registration: *$10.00*

Freeword
by Stilwell Software Products

FreeWord is a powerful and easy to use, menu-driven word processor. It is capable of right and left text justification; moving the cursor either by character, word, line, screen or page; searching a document for a word or phrase; and moving and copying blocks of text. FreeWord even permits printing in the background mode so that you can proceed with other work!

Features:

❑ Cursor movement by character, word, line, screen, page
❑ Move, copy, delete boxes
❑ Automatic formatting
❑ Forced page breaks supported
❑ Typewriter mode
❑ Search and replace
❑ Page breaks displayed on-screen

(PC-SIG Disk# 1084)

Special Requirements: *Two floppy drives.*
Author Registration: *$49.00*

Galaxy Lite (by Starlite) ✍
by Starlite Software Co.

Back by popular demand! This program was Galaxy 2.43, but Omniverse stopped distributing it when they released version 3. Starlite Software has released GALAXY LITE to continue to support those who prefer the older version of the program.

You get the best of both worlds: a choice of menu or quick keyboard commands for most functions. One is great for beginners, the other handy for vets who want to go faster. Mix and match command modes. The pull-down commands work so well, the user's guide can be used as a paperweight after a half hour's experience with the program.

Logically structured, GALAXY LITE boasts a short learning curve; its commands the result of research into how people use word processors. WordStar users love GALAXY because it understands WordStar commands and handles WordStar files. It allows you to print and edit at the same time, something that will save hours of time for most fulltime word crunchers. Macros are a snap, easy to develop and easier to use. The window system allows you to cut and paste between two files while the zoom feature can blow up either window to full screen size.

Galaxy Lite (PC-SIG Disk# 2318)

GALAXY LITE — Still one of the best word processors around.

(PC-SIG Disk#'s 2318, 7034)

Special Requirements: *None.*
Author Registration: *$30.00 in US, $40.00 International.*
➤*ASP Member.*

The PC-SIG Encyclopedia of Shareware ✍ = Updated Program
☆ = New Program

GEdit ☆
by Cat Creek Enterprises, Inc.

GEDIT is a powerful text editor designed for use by programmers and those providing technical support to multiple computer users. It is useful for writing source code and batch files; word processing; creating, maintaining, and repairing data files; recovering files from damaged diskettes; and exploring computer memory.

GEDIT provides all of the standard word processing functions such as formatting text; justification; automatic wordwrap; printing attributes such as bold, underline, italics, sub/superscript; user-defined attributes; and line drawing capabilities.

GEDIT supports an edit file size limited only by the available memory, up to 640K. Text files can have a preset or unlimited line length. Split-screen editing is possible for two files. Cut and paste columns. "Undo" an edit action. Edit in either 25 or 43/50 line mode on EGA/VGA monitors.

GEDIT differs from other word processors by keeping a running total of available memory as well as its ability to explore and edit memory segments and display hexdumps of files on disk and in memory. Compare two text files and append files in memory.

An additional feature is the ability of GEDIT to directly edit dBASE III and WordStar files.

(PC-SIG Disk# 2714)
Special Requirements: *320K RAM.*
Author Registration: *$50.00*

Jove
by Karl Gegenfurther

JOVE stands for Jonathan's Own Version of EMACS, the popular wordprocessor for programmers, used on mainframe computers. This PC version has all the wordprocessing functions of its mainframe relative, with some interactive PC niceties.

Experienced users will enjoy the convenience of using the same editor they use with UNIX. JOVE provides simple insertion and deletion, multiple buffers and files, virtually unlimited file size, on-line help, file encryption, and more. An extensive built-in macro command language and the complete C source code are also included for further customization. JOVE goes beyond EMACS, with a LISP programmers' mode, added document functions, and operating system interaction. On-disk documentation is backed up by a tutorial.

(PC-SIG Disk#'s 1429, 1430, 1454)
Special Requirements: *512K RAM.*
Author Registration: *None.*

KEDITOR
by Everygreen Automation Ltd.

Designed to edit source code files, KEDITOR makes the life of a programmer easier with its swift assembler language and versatile file manipulation capabilities. Lots of on-line help makes this source code editor a good choice regardless of what language you program in. KEDITOR offers language features enhancing its use with C, MASM, Turbo C, TASM, QuickBASIC, Turbo Pascal, Clipper, dBASE III+, dBASE IV, and Lotus 1-2-3.

Additionally, you get ASCII and scan code tables, BIOS addresses, DOS interrupts, word cross reference, and Hex conversion. Over 100 commands and subcommands give you the control to sort, show-only, program macros, shell to DOS, point and find next, and print a range of lines. Pick your commands in WordStar type, two letter mnemonics, or alias names of up to 10 letters. You even have the ability to cut and paste as you browse code.

(PC-SIG Disk#'s 1643, 1665)
Special Requirements: *None.*
Author Registration: *$49.95 (half price for students).*

Mega-Star
by Schmitt Software

This is a full-featured wordprocessor that has special abilities for programmers and persons who need to edit/examine numerous files.

MEGA-STAR features macros, pulldown menus with learn-as-you-go help, on-line help, 6 text windows that can be easily resized and zoomed, style sheets, read and writes standard ASCII, Logitech mouse support, and more.

This wordprocessor will impress you with its simplicity, yet win you with its power to work on several documents in different windows. And if you are programming, DOS is always available through a back door exit.

(PC-SIG Disk# 1766)
Special Requirements: *None.*
Author Registration: *$49.95*

Micro-EMACS
by Daniel Lawrence

MICRO-EMACS is the baby brother of the powerful mainframe wordprocessor EMACS. Experienced EMACS users will enjoy the convenience of using the same editor that they use on mainframes. This PC version has all the functions of its bigger relative, with some PC niceties like 43-line EGA mode.

MICRO-EMACS has several facilities that go beyond simple editing tasks like insertion and deletion. These include multiple buffers and files, virtually unlimited file size, on-line help, file encryption, wild card search/replace, and many modes of operation on files, such as read-only viewing, C-mode for programmers working on source code, or wrap-mode for documents. The system is extremely flexible due to an extensive built-in macro command language which lets the experienced user create or re-map any command. The complete C source code to the program is also provided.

EMACS is a two disk set, the second disk is #1455.

(PC-SIG Disk#'s 1431, 1455)

Special Requirements: *None.*
Author Registration: *None Specified.*

New York Edit
by Magma Software Systems

NEW YORK EDIT is a program editor, written by the author of NEW YORK WORD, containing a C-like macro programming language which can be used to extend the editor.

Sample macros are included and you can create other macros to define your own commands. Other features of interest to programmers are: multiple windows, column cut-and-paste, capturing DOS output, line marking, regular expression search and substitute, EGA support (forty-three-line display), and a keyboard remapper.

Up to 12 windows can be displayed simultaneously, with a different file in each window. You can enlarge any window to occupy the whole screen. Place bookmarks at various points in the document, and return to any point at any time. Scroll continuously up or down the document, with user-selectable scrolling speed. There are 10 buffers which you can use to temporarily store text. A configuration file is included to change the program parameters.

(PC-SIG Disk# 829)

Special Requirements: *None.*
Author Registration: *$39.95*

New York Word
by Magma Software Systems

NEW YORK WORD is a powerful word processor that allows split-screen editing, movement of text between windows, and creation of macros (to perform functions with just a few keystrokes), and footnotes. It also features automatic table of contents, automatic index generation, automatic hyphenation, and mail merge. This shareware package is more powerful than some retail word processors.

(PC-SIG Disk# 528)

Special Requirements: *Two floppy drives.*
Author Registration: *$45.00*

NOVA (formerly Galaxy) ☆
by Nova-1 Software

GALAXY has gone NOVA! Presenting a unique word processor that is easy to learn and use, yet has all the powerful conveniences today's user demands.

Features:

❏ A modern interface similar to Microsoft Windows and OS/2 Presentation Manager, using pull-down menus, dialog boxes, multiple windows, and supports a mouse and keyboard
❏ Work in up to ten windows on-screen at once
❏ Size, overlap, zoom any window to full screen in a single keystroke
❏ Logically-structured keyboard commands that are color-highlighted to help you learn shortcuts. Context-sensitive on-line Help

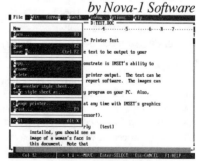

NOVA (PC-SIG Disk# 2582)

✍ = Updated Program
☆ = New Program

❏ Powerful editing features such as cut and pasting between documents, style sheets for easy consistent formatting — or create your own formats, and more!

❏ Headers and footers, micro-justification, and automatic reformatting

❏ Multiple fonts, proportional spacing, and laser printer support

❏ Edit files as large as eight megabytes, using EMS expanded memory or hard drive

(PC-SIG Disk# 2582)

Special Requirements: *400K RAM, and PKZIP. A hard drive recommended.*
Author Registration: *$79.95*

PC-Ted
by Melvin Clark

Programmers — A text editor written especially for you to enter and edit source code files.

PC-TED can process two files at the same time; has full horizontal- vertical screen editing; adjustable horizontal-vertical screen edit; file comparison; full find/replace functions; block commands; an ASCII table; and a DOS exit and command processor. Print files, encrypt files, and select a file to load from a directory list. Help screens are available.

(PC-SIG Disk# 898)

Special Requirements: *None.*
Author Registration: *$30.00*

PC-Type 🖎
by Buttonware

PC-TYPE II, Jim Button's new supercharged version of PC-TYPE, comes equipped to help you easily create impressive documents.

Not just a simple word processor anymore, PC-TYPE II is now equipped with all the standard word processing functions, with many advanced features. These include a Mail Merge that works hand-in-hand with PC-File databases, WordStar and ASCII files; a 100,000-word Spell Checker; and a "whoops" key to recover up to 15 lost or deleted lines. Automatically reformat files. You can even create multiple column, newspaper-style documents.

PC-Type II (PC-SIG Disk# 455)

Graph your data within PC-TYPE II by creating bar or pie charts and scatter diagrams. Multiple variables can be graphed and accumulated. Save up to 25 macros per file to eliminate repetitive keystrokes. An extensive on-line Help system provides all the support you need to produce professional work.

(PC-SIG Disk#'s 455, 681, 682, 2566)

Special Requirements: *Hard drive or two high-density floppy drives, and DOS 3.0.*
Author Registration: *$99.95*
➤*ASP Member.*

PC-Write 🖎
by Quicksoft

PC-WRITE is a wordprocessor with features and power that overshadow many commercial wordprocessing programs on the market. Advanced users and wordprocessing professionals will find the package very multi-faceted; it can accomplish virtually any task on almost any printer. While essentially an advanced program, thanks to a special tutorial and new help screens, beginners can be running the program in minutes.

PC-Write (PC-SIG Disk# 78)

PC-WRITE handles files that are as large as the available RAM memory in your computer. The program allows quick and easy access to the features that most wordprocessors include: cut-and-paste of blocks of text; headers and footers; automatic page numbering; editing multiple documents; bold type and other special text enhancements; a spell checker that lets you add words; and many others. Other features include: multiple-column layout; cut-and-paste of rectangular boxes of text; menus to help you select page layout and fonts; support of foreign language characters; and a feature that lets you use your computer like a typewriter.

PC-WRITE supports most printers (over 800) and includes special supports for laser printers, including Postscript. It also accepts most WordStar commands and converts WordStar files. The pop-up menus make most tasks easier and the user guide is included on-disk.

(PC-SIG Disk#'s 78, 627, 1235, 7050, 7403)

Special Requirements: *384K RAM.*
Author Registration: *$129.00*
➤*ASP Member.*

PC-Write Lite ✍   *by Quicksoft*

Here's a simpler version of Quicksoft's popular PC-Write wordprocessor. By removing some of the complexities of PC-Write, Quicksoft has tailored LITE to the needs of a different class of user. Since document files and most keyboard commands are the same in both LITE and full PC-Write, it's easy to move from one program to the other.

LITE is designed for laptop users, programmers, creative writers, students, and anyone else who may not need full PC-Write's advanced formatting features.

Some of the features that PC-WRITE LITE supports are:
❑ The same editing keys as PC-WRITE
❑ Block and box operations
❑ Search and replace
❑ Common ruler margins and controls   ❑ Standard spell-checking
❑ Basic page layout commands   ❑ Footnotes and auto-numbering
❑ Common typefaces and effects   ❑ New, simplified printing

PC-Write Lite (PC-SIG Disk# 2090)

Some of the features that PC-WRITE LITE doesn't support:
❑ Absolute measurements
❑ Ruler letters and dot commands
❑ Mail merge

PC-WRITE LITE can be used to create simple letters, memos, and articles, or to edit copy for later desktop publishing in an easy and efficient way. Since the program only needs 256K (without the speller) it's an ideal editor for laptops. This program is sure to become a favorite among people needing a quick and easy wordprocessor.

(PC-SIG Disk#'s 2090, 2091)

Special Requirements: *384K RAM (256K without speller).*
Author Registration: *$79.00 plus $5.00 shipping.*
➤*ASP Member.*

pEDIT ✍   *by Terry G. Muench*

PEDIT is a split-screen text editor that can edit up to four files at a single time. This is a text editor, not a word processor or desktop publisher and does not have features such as graphics or multiple fonts. It does, however, have options that programmers need; multiple buffers, split-screen editing, access to DOS, insert and overstrike modes and auto-indent, to name a few.

While the purpose of PEDIT is to create and edit text, it has some features normally associated with word processors such as settable margins and autowrapping text, text centering between defined margins, words (or parts of words) capitalized, lower-cased, or upper-cased. Paragraphs can be filled or reformatted to fit within existing margins.

PEDIT also supports definable keys, macros, autosave, recall/edit any previous command, DOS buffer, 43-line mode, and colors. A key feature of PEDIT is that the file being edited is stored entirely in memory, which makes accessing any part of the file very fast. Move from the top to the bottom of any buffer instantaneously. The size of the file being edited is limited only by the amount of available memory.

✍ = Updated Program
☆ = New Program

If you edit text files, such as computer programs, and want an extremely fast split-screen editor, then PEDIT is for you.

(PC-SIG Disk# 2352)

Special Requirements: *None.*
Author Registration: *$25.00*
➤*ASP Member.*

Phoenix Word
by Phoenix Business Systems

PHOENIX WORD PROCESSOR is a WordStar command compatible deluxe menu driven, multi-windowed wordprocessor. PHOENIX WORD provides an easy to use environment for wordprocessing and text editing. Unique features like built-in line drawing facilities and easy to use support for any printable ASCII characters make this editor outstanding for including ASCII graphics such as boxes and line separaters in your programs or documents. Great for making forms.

Depending on your computer's memory and video adapter you can have up to 8 windows on-screen. You can have the convenience of multiple views of any file or view different files in separate windows and copy blocks of text between them. Adjust the size of each window at the touch of a key!

Block functions include stream, line and column modes making block moves and copies extremely easy and flexible. PHOENIX WORD PROCESSOR fully supports Borland International's Turbo Lightning Spelling Checker and Thesaurus.

(PC-SIG Disk# 1770)

Special Requirements: *None.*
Author Registration: *$9.95*

Programmer's Editor
by Weidman Enterprises

PROGRAMMER'S EDITOR is a text editor primarily for programmers.

Many special functions are featured, such as: multiple files and windows, DOS file management and program execution, displayable ASCII table, ANSI control sequences, insertable control characters, a Hex and Decimal calculator, and a calendar. Extended ASCII characters can be used to produce boxes, charts and forms, math signs, and Greek characters. ANSI codes can control cursor movement, color, and other display attributes from within a text. This program has block commands, search-and-replace functions, auto indent, word wrap, and line commands.

You can execute commands by using a function key menu at the bottom line of the screen, or use control-key sequences from the keyboard. On-line help is available.

(PC-SIG Disk# 880)

Special Requirements: *Printer.*
Author Registration: *$35.00*

PTE
by The League Group, Inc.

PTE is a fast full-screen programmer's editor with Wordstar-like commands, a complete command menu, multiple windows (limited only by memory), and an "intelligent file finder." The editor includes all of the usual block commands, including copy to printer or file, block import and export, insert and delete, undo, autoindent, wordwrap, etc.

PTE may be entered from the command line or the menu. You don't even have to have the correct spelling of the file to be edited! PTE maintains a "directory" of each drive that it uses for fuzzy searching for filenames.

File size is limited only by memory, as are the number of auxiliary edit or import windows opened. PTE is intended for programmers, developers, and desktop publishers or anyone else looking to create ASCII files. It is suitable for all levels of users.

(PC-SIG Disk# 2259)

Special Requirements: *CGA. A hard drive is recommended.*
Author Registration: *$39.95*

QEdit Advanced
by SemWare

QEDIT is an extremely fast, easy-to-use, and fully-featured text editor for entering program code, letters, and small documents. Just load and go. And when loaded, QEDIT uses less than 56K of memory — perfect for those who want to use QEDIT in conjunction with other software (e.g., dBase, FoxBase, Paradox) and do not have a lot of free memory to spare.

A "pop-down" style menu system makes editing a snap. There is a help screen which can be modified by the user, and the keyboard is completely reconfigurable. The user can easily assign any QEDIT command to almost any key desired. Also, the keyboard can be configured to look like WordStar, Brief or other popular editors.

QEDIT is fully featured. Although QEDIT is fast and easy to use, it doesn't skimp on features. You still get all of the basic text editing features, plus many features found only on the more expensive editors. Edit dozens of files simultaneously, open up to eight windows, create macros with pause and keyboard recording, recover deleted text, and do line drawing. Files to edit cannot be larger than available memory.

(PC-SIG Disk# 1783)

Special Requirements: *None.*
Author Registration: *$44.00*
➤ *ASP Member.*

QIP - The Quick Information Processor   *by SORD Computer Corporation*

QIP is first and foremost a wordprocessor. If you are accustomed to using wordprocessors and text editors, you will find all the commands found in a good wordprocessor, such as marking and copying blocks, search and replace, etc. A few more pleasant surprises lie in wait for you in the form of features such as effects. Effects gives you easy and flexible control of both display colors and printout fonts.

QIP is also a table processor. Create tables, graphs or lists, large and small, anywhere in your document. These tables, graphs, or lists are managed along with your text to help you produce attractive reports, or to create large databases. More than that, QIP provides many powerful table processing functions, ranging from the simple extract and sort commands, to the enormously versatile update and calculation commands.

When you first start to use QIP, you'll probably view it as a wordprocessor, and experiment with its on-screen formatting, line drawing, color-processing, on-line help system, and printer control capabilities. As you start to work with tables, adding simple lists or charts to your reports, you'll see how all your data can be smoothly collated and updated. Before very long, you'll be using the more powerful table processing features to generate sales summaries, prepare work schedules, create form letters, or update stock lists. Ultimately, QIP may become your best tool for the most critical task of all — turning volumes of raw data into that essential element of modern life — useful information.

(PC-SIG Disk#'s 1477, 1478, 1479, 1480)

Special Requirements: *500K free memory, hard drive. 286 or faster computer recommended.*
Author Registration: *None stated.*

Ravitz Editor (RE) ✍   *by Cary Ravitz*

RAVITZ EDITOR is a powerful ASCII text editor bent towards the programmer but can be utilized for any text editing needs. RE makes great use of one- and two-key commands and supports a mouse. RE has all the basic commands of other text editors like edit, save, name, print, and quit, plus ones you're not used to, such as marking an area where you are going to do several functions.

❑ The line exclude function can be used to compress the view of a file by hiding lines that are low in the hierarchy of function (nice for programmers).
❑ The word wrap margin command is used to set the margins in the word wrap mode.
❑ Tab lets you specify what kind of tabs you want to use by choosing either of the two preset commands or one of the user set tab commands.
❑ There are flow functions that help you make the text look smooth by moving words in a set of lines or paragraphs.
❑ Three drawing modes are available to do basic single lines, double lines, and boxes.
❑ A find command that has several options to let you modify a search to find almost anything in a text.
❑ A change command complements the find command by being able to search and replace a string of text with another string of your choosing.
❑ You can put a line or group of lines in another order with the order lines command. Type in any existing line number less then 60000 and RE moves the cursor to it.
❑ Use one or two windows for viewing, letting you see the original and edited text at the same time.
❑ RE has a status line on the screen at all times, letting you know where you are and what you are doing.

❏ RE uses only standard memory and does not utilize any expanded or extended memory. Although RE does not use that extra memory, you can edit any number of files at the same time, subject only to memory limits.

THE RAVITZ EDITOR also comes with another program to enhance it called THE RAVITZ EDITOR PROFILE REFERENCE. This allows the user to configure RE's keyboard usage, default values, macros, menus, panels, and help text and assemble it into another complete stand-alone RAVITZ EDITOR. A complete Help feature is present at all times throughout the program.

All this and more is available from this 60K program.

(PC-SIG Disk# 2424)

Special Requirements: *None.*
Author Registration: *$25.00*
➤*ASP Member.*

RGB^TechWriter
by BA^EL Software

RGB^TECHWRITER is a wordprocessor specifically designed to fulfill the technical writing needs of engineers, scientists and students. Scientific notations, equations, and symbols not present on your keyboard are quickly available without the need for an extensive background in wordprocessing. Instead of displaying various arcane notes, it uses color to identify such things as superscripts, subscripts, and other symbolic information. This keeps your display relatively uncluttered and insures exact correspondence between screen and printer while allowing you to print complex equations and formulas.

The easy-to-use menu gives you access to all of the standard wordprocessing functions such as: headers and footers, page numbering, search and replace, line centering and justification, underlining and bold print, text-block movement, page-break control, and fractional line spacing. Written in assembly language, it's fast — able to handle typing speeds of up to 120 WPM. Individual files are limited to 62.8K characters, approximately 20 pages of printed material.

(PC-SIG Disk# 1368)

Special Requirements: *CGA, EGA, MCGA, or VGA.*
Author Registration: *$20.00*

RGB^TechWriter (PC-SIG Disk# 1368)

SageWords ✍
by Cosmic Annex Software

SAGEWORDS is a sophisticated and powerful wordprocessor whose advanced features may take some time to learn. However, for simple text entry, you are up and running as soon as you type SW.

The main menu choices are file, window, text, block, goto, search, options, and SageWords. Each of these has a pull-down submenu. File, for instance, has open, close, save, write to, print, get info, and quit. Many of the choices and options can be operated intuitively, and under the SageWords selection there is a help file which explains everything you may not be able to figure out yourself. There are also extensive instructions in the SW.BIN file.

This wordprocessor has a lot going for it. It can be used with ease for light-weight wordprocessing, and, with a little more time spent learning the commands and features, it can perform feats matching high- end products.

(PC-SIG Disk# 1170)

Special Requirements: *None.*
Author Registration: *$25.00*

Technical Editor ☆
by Superior Soft

TECHNICAL EDITOR is a programmer's editor that lets you edit any size file — text or binary. And it's FAST! TECHNICAL EDITOR has all the standard features you demand from any strong editor plus:
❏ 43/50 line EGA/VGA mode
❏ UNDO command
❏ Multi-screen AND multi-windows support
❏ Keystroke macros

❏ Redefinable commands

The OS/2 version and source code is available to registered users.

(PC-SIG Disk# 2526)

Special Requirements: *None.*
Author Registration: *$39.95*
➤*ASP Member.*

Visual Display Editor (VDE) ✍

by Eric Meyer

VDE is a small (47K), fast and powerful text editor. It can work with as little as 128K RAM. This makes it ideal for laptop computers with limited space.

This tough little text editor offers:

❏ Edits up to eight files at once; windows, compares, copies between them
❏ Wordwrap and reformat
❏ Append to existing file
❏ Margins, tabs and spacing control
❏ Various file modes: pure ASCII, Wordstar, WordPerfect, XYWrite, Word
❏ Block operations
❏ Find and replace
❏ Undelete functions
❏ Macro programs and programmable keys
❏ Full DOS utilities and subdirectory support
❏ WordStar compatibility
❏ Configurable options and more

Visual Display Editor (VDE) (PC-SIG Disk #1273)

VDE is fast. Written in 8086 assembler, it writes directly to video RAM (on PC compatibles) and operates entirely in memory with no disk access during editing. Speed is a factor that more cumbersome, full-featured programs overlook.

(PC-SIG Disk# 1273)

Special Requirements: *Printer.*
Author Registration: *$50.00*

W - The Note Writer ✍

by Infinity Data Products

Originally designed for use by handicapped persons, W - THE NOTE WRITER, is a quick and easy way for anyone to write a letter. No fancy frills, just type your letter (any number of pages), and print.

Like most word processors, W - THE NOTE WRITER, includes wordwrap, standard cursor movement commands, paragraph reformatting, printing, and document storage. But unlike most word processors, it stops there. No complex commands to get lost in, no fancy key combinations to press; just type and print. The perfect program for anyone who wants to dash off a quick letter or for someone who has trouble with the complex word processors or keyboards.

(PC-SIG Disk# 2460)

Special Requirements: *None.*
Author Registration: *$5.00*
➤*ASP Member.*

W-ED

by WyndhamWare

Dash off a letter, work on your poetry, or revise your Christmas list with this friendly program. W-ED is a small, fast, and intuitive editor and wordprocessor.

Simplicity of use was a major design criteria. The program is based on the premise that sequences of often-used functions are more productive than many obscure hard-to-remember and arbitrary commands. The commands are easy to remember. Create an ASCII file that can be printed or re-edited.

(PC-SIG Disk# 415)

Special Requirements: *None.*
Author Registration: *$39.95*

Word Fugue ✍

by *Fugue Software*

This a heavy duty wordprocessing program with an optional WordStar compatible interface. It's ideal for the touch typist, since there is no need to take your hands off the home row to activate any functions. Its features are extensive and include:

❑ Eight editing windows
❑ Context-sensitive help
❑ Pull-down menus
❑ Printer support that includes laser printers
❑ Generation of indexes and tables of contents.
❑ Macro facilities, the ability to record keystrokes, and a number of macro files for additional flexibility.
❑ Automatic reformatting of text
❑ Support of newspaper style columns, with word wrap and justification of each column. Column mode blocks that can be defined and copied, moved or deleted.
❑ Comprehensive monitor support — Mono, CGA, EGA or VGA or Hercules graphics.
❑ A DOS shell that permits the use of all DOS commands from within the program.
❑ A pop up calculator with 16 functions. The calculation result can be pasted into your text.
❑ Support for box and line drawing, with characters available at the press of a key.
❑ Optional on screen display of fonts and the ability to edit text with this mode operating (unlike WordStar).
❑ Printing with multiple headers and footers, including functions such as current date or time.

Hundreds of other sophisticated features are included such as insertion of current date or time (in different formats), the ability to mark changed text in the left hand margin, and offset page number on odd or even pages. Registered users get a 100,000-word dictionary and an updated program that will add or delete words from the dictionary.

The wordprocessor document files are ASCII text files, so there are no funny embedded characters and the files are WordStar compatible, so you can load them into any wordprocessor that reads WordStar files.

Apart from printer control strings, all formatting commands are by use of dot commands (. in column one) or embedded functions ({. }) in the text body.

(PC-SIG Disk#'s 1970, 1971)
Special Requirements: *640K RAM, and two floppy drive or a hard drive.*
Author Registration: *$65.00*

WordMaster

by *MasterWorks*

WordMaster is a full-function wordprocessor so easy to use you can be up and writing before ever reading the documentation. This is made possible by WordMaster's outstanding menu system. All the basic wordprocessing commands are included in it with online help to explain each command.

The excellent documentation offers clear explanations and examples of using the more sophisticated capabilities that have become standard in wordprocessors. The serious user will quickly be employing features that include: multiple fonts, time-saving macros, search and replace, cutting-and-pasting blocks of text on multiple documents, headers and footers, automatic page numbering, the ability to customize the working environment and much more.

These capabilities combined with its ease of use have prompted many to declare WordMaster superior to any other wordprocessor they have ever used — even top-of-the-line commercial products.

(PC-SIG Disk# 1686)
Special Requirements: *None.*
Author Registration: *$30.00*
➤*ASP Member.*

▼ ▼ ▼

Writing and Composition Aids

1001 Topics for Composition

by *Richard Raker*

1001 TOPICS FOR COMPOSITION is an educational aid to help you choose a topic for writing English compositions and essays. The program has 1,358 topics and 21 different categories to choose from.

Categories include personal reminiscences and reactions, familiar essay topics, sports, national and international news, science, the arts and entertainment, philosophy, education, specific literary topics, and more.

Besides having several different subject areas there are categories for different writing styles, such as comparison and contrast, persuasion, argumentative, exposition, and description. The program first presents a list of main categories and, once you indicate your general line of interest, several suggested topics are listed on the screen.

(PC-SIG Disk# 1088)

Special Requirements: *None.*
Author Registration: *$20.00*

Basic English   *by Louie Crew*

BASIC ENGLISH can tell you how many words in your poem or prose are on the magic list of 850 words scholars agree are simple and most understandable to the average reader. The program can flag words excluded from the magic list and is valuable for technical writers.

(PC-SIG Disk# 1181)

Special Requirements: *None.*
Author Registration: *$5.00*

Book Report   *by Richard Raker*

Arrange your thoughts and create the structure of your book report with this organizer.

BOOK REPORT asks several general questions to help you get started writing your book report. Questions concern the basic library information, the setting, the main character and supporting characters, the main scene, and your own feelings about and reactions to the book. The advantage is it organizes the basic information into simple categories that can be incorporated easily into your final report. Once finished, print or save the information in an ASCII text file.

(PC-SIG Disk# 1088)

Special Requirements: *None.*
Author Registration: *$20.00*

Cliche Finder &   *by R.K. West Consulting*

Faster than greased lightning, easy as pie, and more fun than a barrel of monkeys, CLICHE FINDER checks your writing for old, hackneyed, trite, and overused words and phrases. It examines your text files and creates a report listing the "cliches" found. Hundreds of cliches are supplied in the program's database, and you can add your own favorite "bad writing habits."

So don't delay another instant, grab a copy of this user friendly, easy-to-use, powerful, program that's guaranteed to have you up-and-running in seconds...and say goodbye to tired, worn out communication!

(PC-SIG Disk# 1525)

Special Requirements: *360K RAM.*
Author Registration: *$10.00*
➤*ASP Member.*

Congress-PCW   *by Groff Software*

Here, at last, all in one place and ready to use with your PC-Write mail merge features are titles, names, addresses, and phone numbers of hundreds of elected and appointed members of our government, both Federal and the State of California.

Simply type your letter and by using the mail merge features of PC-Write and the names and addresses supplied by this program you can make sure everyone will know how you feel.

The files in this directory were designed for use in PC-Write or ASCII compatible mail merge systems. Included in these lists are the Members of the U.S. Senate, Members of the House of Representatives, The President, his Cabinet and senior officials of Executive Branch, The Supreme Court and the Governors of the States. The equivalent offices in the State of California are also supplied, as well as the names and addresses of most of the Mayors and City Managers of the major cities in California.

(PC-SIG Disk# 1821)

Special Requirements: *PC-Write or an ASCII text editor.*
Author Registration: *$10.00*

Congress-WP
by Groff Software

Here, at last, all in one place and ready to use with WordPerfect's mail merge features are titles, names, addresses, and phone numbers of hundreds of elected and appointed members of our government, both Federal and the State of California.

Simply type your letter and by using the mail merge features of PC-Write and the names and addresses supplied by this program you can make sure everyone will know how you feel.

The files in this directory were designed for use in WordPerfect type mail merge systems. Included in these lists are the Members of the U.S. Senate, Members of the House of Representatives, The President, his Cabinet and senior officials of Executive Branch, The Supreme Court and the Governors of the States. The equivalent offices in the State of California are also supplied, as well as the names and addresses of most of the Mayors and City Managers of the major cities in California.

(PC-SIG Disk# 1822)
Special Requirements: *WordPerfect.*
Author Registration: *$10.00*

Creativity Package 🖎
by R.K. West Consulting

The CREATIVITY PACKAGE is a three disk creativity and idea generator. Disk one contains Thomas A. Easton's complete book, *Think Thunder! And Unleash Your Creativity*, a straightforward explanation of the nature of creativity and how to develop it. Disk two contains the program, THUNDER THOUGHT, a proven tool for computer-aided brainstorming, developing and refining ideas, particularly in the fields of creative writing and inventing. Disk three contains VERSIFIER, the amazing poetry writing program that works with the user's word selection to create fascinating free verse or haiku poetry. Considering that any one of these disks could be tremendously helpful in understanding and developing creative thinking, the effect of all three may be mind expanding! *Think Thunder!* can be read chapter by chapter on the computer screen or printed out. The book can encourage creative thinking with or without the use of THUNDER THOUGHT.

THUNDER THOUGHT works to facilitate the creative process by automating its initial stages. With it, you don't need to worry about how to come up with novel combinations of words, images, or ideas. THUNDER THOUGHT will do that for you, leaving you with the task of finding or recognizing sense in whatever combinations of words and ideas it produces. THUNDER THOUGHT offers a variety of approaches for this creative process including images, topical idea chaining, and other innovative ways to expand your idea bank.

VERSIFIER is a creativity-enhancement program for poets. The program combines words and phrases into several kinds of free verse and haiku, which you can then save and edit. To get started, both THUNDER THOUGHT and VERSIFIER come with a vocabulary. These lists can be modified or replaced to include your own words and thoughts. The program puts ideas together in ways you might not have thought of consciously, yet they are still your own ideas, expressed in your own words.

(PC-SIG Disk#'s 2075, 2076, 2077)
Special Requirements: *400K RAM.*
Author Registration: *$29.00*
➤*ASP Member.*

Do-It-Yourself Legal Forms
by New Ventures Enterprises

If you need a help creating a standard will, revocable living trust, or durable power of attorney, here is a quick, easy, and inexpensive alternative to a lawyer. Included are examples of common legal documents you can personalize for your own use. All of the SoftForm files on this diskette are ASCII files. They may be edited with a text editor or read into a wordprocessor.

Forms include:

❑ Copyright notice and registration form
❑ Estate Summary Sheet; Family and Financial
❑ Generic Last Will and Testament form
❑ Living Will form
❑ Simple checklist of administrator's duties
❑ Durable Power of Attorney form
❑ Revocable Living Trust forms

Do-It-Yourself Legal Forms (PC-SIG Disk# 1949)

❏ Revocation of a Revocable Living Trust
❏ Irrevocable Trust Agreement.

These forms were prepared according to current law and precedence. Nonetheless, laws vary with each state and change over time. These forms are to help you prepare your own legal documents, not a substitute for a lawyer.
(PC-SIG Disk# 1949)

Special Requirements: *None.*
Author Registration: *$20.00*

Form Letters
by Patomac Pacific Engineering, Inc.

Need to remind some of your customers to pay their bill? Have to turn someone down for credit? Would you like to send a thank you letter to a valued client?

These letters have already been written for you, along with 97 others in this collection of 100 boiler-plate business letters. See the file listing below for specifics. Tailor each to your individual needs by modifying with any standard ASCII wordprocessor.

Let FORM LETTERS do the work for you while you get down to business!
(PC-SIG Disk# 388)

Special Requirements: *None.*
Author Registration: *None.*

File Descriptions:

1LTSCHRA	Overdue account letters.
EMPLMNT	Job inquiry turn down letter.
5LTSCHRA	Overdue account letters.
4SLPYBS	Overdue account letters.
4LTSCHRA	Overdue account letters.
3SLPYBS	Overdue account letters.
3LTSCHRA	Overdue account letters.
2SLPYBS	Overdue account letters.
2LTSCHRA	Overdue account letters.
1SLPYBS	Overdue account letters.
INCOMPL	Letter of sales exchange.
INCMTXCO	Tax consultant sales mailer.
INACTVE	Inactive customer sales inquiry.
INACTVCS	Inactive customer status inquiry.
ILLHLTH	Ill health resignation letter.
ILL	Ill employee response letter.
HSPTYGFT	Hospitality gift thank you letter.
GVNGLTR	Cancel incorrect service charges.
GDCRDTST	Positive response to credit reference inquiry.
FURN	Furniture store grand opening.
FOLLWUP	Follow up to phone call when customer not in.
FNDSLMT	Turn down charity donation request.
FNDRSNG	Decline charity sponsorship request.
FLLWUP	Customer sales visit follow up letter.
FLLUPREP	Mailing list follow up letter.
EXPNSVGT	Return of an expensive gift from a client.
DTHOTHER	Death sympathy.
DLYDCRD	Delayed returned merchandise refund.
DLVRMTH	Delivery method error refund letter.
DCLDN	Dinner invitation turn down letter.
CSTMRTHS	Customer thank you letter.
CRVOUCH	Neutral response to credit reference inquiry.
CRDTSUSP	Response from supplier suspending credit.
CRDTSTND	Response from supplier turning down credit request.
CRDTRQST	Response from supplier granting credit request.
CRDTINFR	Request to supplier for a credit account.
COPLCY	Company policy denial of donation request.
COND	Sympathy letter for co-workers death.
COMPLNT	Incoming product variance notice.
CNCLCNTR	Certified letter canceling the order.
CMPLNTAD	Product defect and replacement request to supplier.

✍ = Updated Program
☆ = New Program

5SLPYBS		Overdue account letters.
CLLCTN		Request for bill due date extension.
CLAIMS		Response to complaint about employee behavior.
CHRGACCT		New charge account acceptance.
BSCLSD		Layoff notice.
BSAPPCTN		Credit account denial.
BNKDPST		Idle bank account inquiry.
BLLNGMST		Billing error.
BDRSK		Bad risk notice.
BDBHVR		Bad behavior notice.
BADCHK		Bad check notice.
APOLOGYC		Apology for incorrect collection letter.
AFTRSLSL		Proposal follow up.
AD		Information about this and other programs.
ACKNORDR		Acknowledge order.
ABSNTRCD		Attendance notice.
6SLPYBS		Overdue account letters.
INTROSLS		Sales introduction.
INJURY		Injury gift.
UNSATCRD		Negative response to credit reference inquiry.
THNKYOU		COD shipment denial, holding product for payment.
STMTER		Corrected statement cover letter.
STATEMNT		Correction for billing error.
SLSVLM		Salesman congratulation for landing a new account.
SLSLLPRD		Negative response to slow selling product return request.
SLSGRMTN		Sales agreement cancellation confirmation.
SLS		Mail inquiry response letter.
SHRTEPMT		Negative credit application response.
SERVCHRG		Service charge increase announcement.
SECYRCM		Positive response to employment reference.
RSMJOB		Resume cover letter.
RJCTREF		Negative response to employement reference.
RETRMNT		Retirement congratulations.
RESIGN		Resignation letter.
RESCHDLO		Request production schedule change.
REFUND		Wrong product refund.
REFRNCE		Positive response to company reference inquiry.
REFPR		Deny price discount request.
RECMMD		Neutral response to company reference inquiry.
QUESTNNR		Sample credit questionnaire.
PRSNLCRD		Credit line denial.
PRQUOTE		Request for quote.
PRPY		Credit denial.
PRINTLET	EXE	Program to print all the letters out to a prnter.
PRCRDT		Negative response to credit reference inquiry.
PRCRDIT		Order refusal due to bad credit history.
POSUNSTE		No position available response to job inquiry.
PMPTPMNT		Thank you for prompt credit account payments.
PERSCRE		Credit account offer mailer.
PERSCRDT		Incomplete credit application response.
ORDRCONF		Mail order request.
ORDRCNFR		Mail order request.
OPNACCT		Request for credit account.
NWCSTMR		New customer thank you.
NOINFRMT		Incomplete credit application response.
MSMTNG		Apology for missed meeting.
MNRNIMG		Gift return by civil court judge.
LTDLVY		Late delivery due to engraving.
JBDNWL		Christmas rush employee effort commendation letter.
LFINSRNC		Life insurance policy inquiry.
JBRSM		Job advertisement inquiry.

Govern-US

by Foundation for Infinite Survival

GOVERN-U.S. helps make your voice heard in Washington, D.C. If you belong to any organization lobbying or dealing with federal lawmakers, courts and executive agencies, or if you are the sort of citizen who writes his federal representatives, GOVERN-U.S. will prove an incredibly useful program.

You get a database of members of the House of Representatives and Senate along with key executive officers and members of the U.S. Supreme Court. Add to this a great search program to pick your targets by political party or otherwise. You also get templates for letters and envelopes that you can edit on your wordprocessor. A mail merge program makes sending out your letters a snap.

GOVERN-U.S. is a big program but it takes only about 45 minutes to learn. Suddenly you can extend your reach to everyone who counts in the U.S. capitol.

(PC-SIG Disk# 1666)

Special Requirements: *None.*
Author Registration: *$28.00*

Handwriting Analyst

by CIASA, Inc.

HANDWRITING ANALYST asks you several questions about a person's signature, and then produces a summary or detailed report on that person based on your responses.

Each report includes information on physical and material drives, intellectual style, personality traits, social behavior, and vocational implications. You can display on-screen, print, or write the report to a disk file. Save the answers to the questions for up to 20 signatures on the disk. The signature report of this program can be either a direct description of the person, or it can describe how that person wants others to see him.

You can attach up to 1200 characters of notation to an individual idea. A note stays with an idea as you move or copy it from one place to another. You can also export notes to your favorite wordprocessing program and format them any way you want.

Use IDEA TREE to create, structure, analyze and document reports, books, catalogs, projects and processes, business procedures, organizational structures, job analyses, database planning, system architecture . . .there's really no limit.

IDEA TREE installs painlessly and comes with in-depth documentation, drop down menus and clear tutorials. If you're interested in ideas and organizing ideas, you'll be interested in IDEA TREE.

(PC-SIG Disk# 1050)

Special Requirements: *Two floppy drives or a hard drive.*
Author Registration: *$29.95*

Idea Tree

by Mountain House Publishing Inc.

IDEA TREE is a unique brainstorming/organizing tool that lets you examine, expand and organize your thoughts on any subject. IDEA TREE lets you structure your ideas like a tree. Add ideas to the tree anywhere, then rearrange and reorganize them as you change your mind and new thoughts take shape. Focus on the development of one part of an idea by identifying related elements and making them into a separate tree. When you are finished, move or copy this new tree back into the original.

You can attach up to 1200 characters of notation to an individual idea. A note stays with an idea as you move or copy it from one place to another. You can also export notes to your favorite wordprocessing program and format them any way you want.

Idea Tree (PC-SIG Disk# 1888)

Use IDEA TREE to create, structure, analyze and document reports, books, catalogs, projects and processes, business procedures, organizational structures, job analyses, database planning, system architecture...there's really no limit.

IDEA TREE installs painlessly and comes with in-depth documentation, drop down menus and clear tutorials. If you're interested in ideas and organizing ideas, you'll be interested in IDEA TREE.

(PC-SIG Disk# 1888)

Special Requirements: *Two floppy drives or a hard drive.*
Author Registration: *$29.95*

     🖸 = Updated Program
     ☆ = New Program

Invent
by Louie Crew

INVENT helps you create beautiful metaphors from words that you supply to the program. You enter up to 40 words into each of the lists of nouns, verbs, adjectives and adverbs and then let the program do the work.

The program then quickly generates sentences, which you may use in your writing endeavors. You can request as many re-scramblings of the same data as you like.

(PC-SIG Disk# 1181)

Special Requirements: *None.*
Author Registration: *$7.00*

Mastery Learning: Grammar
by R. Allen Hackworth

MASTERY LEARNING: GRAMMAR collection teaches principles of English grammar and provides tests to measure one's understanding of basic grammar. These four disks cover a wide range of grammar issues all students should master. Each lesson has two parts: (1) a tutorial which teaches with clarity and brevity, and (2) drills which reinforce the concepts taught by the tutorials.

To generate more student interest and to make a more effective system, the disks are personalized. It is expected that each student has his or her own software. The first time a disk is used, the student enters information which is later used in the tutorial examples.

Identifying subjects and verbs, reviewing parts of speech, and the five basic English sentence patterns are covered on the first disk. The collection also explores clause types, sentence structures, punctuation, capitalization, pronoun case, metaphor and simile. Additional study sections include prefix and affix study, vocabulary study, and verbals.

Mastery Learning: Grammar (PC-SIG Disk#

(PC-SIG Disk#'s 1847, 1848, 1849, 1850)

Special Requirements: *None.*
Author Registration: *$9.95 per disk; $399.95 network or site.*

Names
by Geoffrey Kirk

NAMES makes unusual names for use by writers, game players, and just for fun!

The unusual names are created by a scheme similar to a random number generator. You specify how many names you want made. Names are stored in user-designated ASCII files at the rate of four names per line. Since many of the names can't be pronounced or are unusual spellings, you need to select usable names from those created. However, the program is easy, quick, and inexpensive. Even if only a few names in a hundred are usable, the seconds it takes to make them might prove this program helpful for certain users.

(PC-SIG Disk# 1102)

Special Requirements: *None.*
Author Registration: *$5.00*

Poetease
by Louie Crew

Roses are red, violets are blue, POETEASE will rhyme most anything for you!

POETEASE generates rhyming, consonant or assonant endings for poetry. One drawback: the program matches spelling only. Hence, POETEASE will not list 'liar' as a rhyme word for 'buyer.'

(PC-SIG Disk# 1181)

Special Requirements: *None.*
Author Registration: *$5.00*

Poetry Generator
by R.K. West Consulting

POETRY GENERATOR produces original poetry effortlessly: thousands of phrases, words, and several formats can be combined by random selection to form thousands of different poems. After the poem has been created, you can save it.

The program has a vocabulary of about 20,000 words. The words are organized into short phrases and combined into poems of four to 12 lines. There is very little punctuation inserted, so you can punctuate in whatever way yields individual interpretation. The poems do not always make sense, but such is sometimes the nature of poetry. In any case, the original poetry created is entertaining.

(PC-SIG Disk# 1166)

Special Requirements: *Hard drive.*
Author Registration: *$29.00*
➤*ASP Member.*

Readability Plus ✍ by Scandinavian PC Systems, Inc.

READABILITY PLUS is the ideal complement to any grammar checker, such as Grammatik or RightWriter.

Unlike grammar checkers, this program assumes that what it's been asked to analyze is mechanically correct. Rather than look for errors, it looks for sentences and words that aren't used appropriately for the writer's intended audience. Comparing the text to any of nine writing style models, READABILITY PLUS guides the writer in "aligning" the style of the draft with the style model chosen. For example, by using the magazine style model for company reports, writers can produce more interesting and easier-to-understand documents. READABILITY PLUS can read documents produced with WordPerfect, WordStar, Microsoft Word, and all ASCII (text) files.

(PC-SIG Disk# 2333)

Special Requirements: *None.*
Author Registration: *$25.00*

Styled/Stylist by Louie Crew

Writers — Analyze your writing style. Step back and take a cool look at how you do it.

STYLED and STYLIST chart word and letter patterns in ASCII text files to help you revise, analyze and compare your writing style. The programs only work with ASCII text files, but included on this disk is a utility program that converts any non-ASCII text file into ASCII format (this includes documents).

These two programs can save you time in your revisions and help improve your writing style. STYLED analyzes each text for word length, punctuation, syntax or nominalization. You can view a text file without leaving the program, and you can shell to DOS. STYLLIST does the same thing as STYLED, except that it records your long words, forms of "to be," and potential nominalizations in a disk file.

(PC-SIG Disk# 1181)

Special Requirements: *None.*
Author Registration: *$10.00*

THS English Tutorial by Tehillah Hills Software

THS ENGLISH TUTORIAL is an on-line textbook of English grammar and usage. Many of the lessons and examples have a Christian orientation.

Chapter One teaches the parts of speech: noun, pronoun, and adjective. Chapter Two teaches the other five parts of speech: verb, adverb, preposition, conjunction, and interjection. The parts of speech are defined according to their functions in sentences; examples are given; and exercises are provided, typically using passages taken from the Bible, for practice in identifying the parts of speech.

There are a variety of exercises that differ in degree of difficulty and type of skills applied. The computer checks the exercises and gives a list of correct answers beside the list of student answers for comparison. On creative exercises the computer offers the option of printing the exercises if a printer is available.

Extra exercises are included at the end of the table of contents in each part of speech.

The program runs from menus and on-screen instructions. There are a few footnotes for additional help. The footnotes can be reached from the menu screen in any part of speech.

(PC-SIG Disk#'s 1742, 1743)

Special Requirements: *None.*
Author Registration: *$12.00*

▼ ▼ ▼

SHAREWARE

MAGAZINE

The following pages provide reprints of features and other articles from the past four issues of *Shareware Magazine*. See the back section of this encyclopedia for a discount subscription offer.

This article was originally printed in the November/December 1990 issue of *Shareware Magazine.*

Starting With Shareware

Learning new programs can be frustrating, even for PC jocks. Here are shareware basics guaranteed to keep the beginner at the keyboard.

By Sherry Goldfisher

If you're a PC novice, chances are good your newly purchased hardware is begging for software. You've heard shareware is a good place to start—but that's the hard part. How and where to begin amidst the mind-boggling array of programs available? Don't be daunted! Once you know the basics of shareware, getting up and running is a breeze.

First, the cardinal rule of computing: Before you do anything else with your brand-new disk, make a backup copy. Once that's done, put the original in a safe place, and work off the backup.

Now, do a directory listing (type DIR) of the disk, but don't panic if you find only one or two files and you know most programs have more. Many shareware programs are archived (compressed) and packaged together into one large file to save disk space.

On the other hand, don't feel overwhelmed if you see a large listing of files. Most shareware programs come with a text file that contains installation and decompression instructions. This file may also list all files on the disk and their functions; it is usually called READ.ME, README.TXT, [PROGRAM NAME].DOC, or something similar. A filename with a .DOC or .TXT extension is usually a clue that a file contains information about starting the program. This file is generally in ASCII format (a standard code for representing characters, short for American Standard Code For Information Interchange), so you can access it from most word processors, or send it directly to a printer (Type COPY [filename] PRN). Some documentation in an executable, or .EXE file, might automatically output to a printer when you access the file.

Reading the documentation is crucial at this point, because it tells you how to proceed in installation or decompression. Don't skip it! Once you have the program installed, check for more documentation files by doing a DIR listing. Take a moment to print or read them. They may contain tutorials, reference manuals, or other material that will help you learn the program.

Now that you're ready to put that hardware to work, take a look at the following programs notable for their ease-of-use (but not necessarily unsophistication!).

Word Processor

Galaxy Lite is a powerful, but not overwhelming word processor. Formerly known as Galaxy 2.43, it includes basic formatting commands, a spell checker and global search/replace. It's completely menu-driven, although you can use keyboard shortcuts when you're comfortable with the program. As in WordPerfect, a blank screen appears upon entering. Press F10 and you'll be presented with a pop-up menu of choices. Help (F1) is available from this menu; there is also an extensive on-disk reference manual.

Because Galaxy Lite saves files in ASCII format, it's compatible with most other word processors. A mouse is optional.

Database

Database programs range from the simple to complex, and can be arranged to suit an endless number of tastes, from the banana label collector to the corporate VP. **Wyndfields** is easy to learn and use, but has more advanced features waiting once you're ready for them.

A pop-up menu bar at the top of the screen lists commands and their keyboard shortcuts. The program, which can be used with a mouse, includes extensive on-line help. A short combination reference manual/tutorial gets you started right away.

Functions include group totaling of columns, summaries of contents of database fields, and record counts. You can choose to be as broad or specific with a data field's format as you want. Record search criterion can range from one to multiple field searches. When you're ready, you can print reports and labels. The multiple report format gives you ample choice in viewing data.

Spreadsheet

Packed with commands and features, **As-Easy-As** is a spreadsheet that's powerful, yet easy for the novice to get calculating on. Upon opening the program, you're presented with a blank spreadsheet ready for formatting. Hit the "/" key for the main menu, from which you can set up the spreadsheet to your specifications.

Standard formulas and functions are supported. More advanced functions include macros, graphing, and x-y data regression. As-Easy-As is fully Lotus 1-2-3 compatible, and runs on any monitor. On-line help is included.

DOS Shell

A DOS "shell" helps you manipulate the DOS environment, protecting you from the dreaded drive ("A:\" or "C:\") prompts. With a DOS shell, you can execute DOS commands without memorizing them.

The Still River Shell is good for DOS beginners because it explains each function without making you wade through pages of documentation. You can display a graphic tree and drive and directory statistics, execute programs, and perform commands like copy, delete, and move—from file level to directory level. Still River is also capable of more advanced functions, like macros. A menu at the bottom of the screen displays available options.

Although the on-disk documentation that comes with the shell is long, it's thorough. If you want to get started quickly, there is a mini-tutorial within the main documentation that leads you through step-by-step demonstrations.

TreeView is recommended for more advanced beginners. While it does have on-line help, it's

rather lengthy, and because there are so many features and functions, it can be a little daunting to true novices.

A pop-up menu at the top of the screen lists commands. You can execute programs, move, copy, delete, tag/untag files and perform other DOS commands. You can also see a graphic tree display at any time—hence the name. Macros are available, and the program can be used with a mouse.

Communications

ProComm is a widely-used telecommunications program, for good reason. However, don't be intimidated by the blank screen that pops up when you first load it. Press ALT-F10 for help, and you're shown a full menu of commands. One of the first things you will want to do is hit ALT-S for the setup screen. You will need to know your modem's baud rate (the speed at which information is transferred), the setup of the destination service, and its phone number. Once you dial (ALT-D), ProComm lets you know the status of your call: CONNECTed or BUSY.

ProComm can save a telecommunication session; that is, keep a record of your on-line moves. Just toggle the OPEN/CLOSE log command. More advanced functions are also offered, like macros and a host mode for incoming calls. Although the on-line help screen is not broad, the reference documentation is.

Virus Checker

Computers can catch viral "infections" that may range from mild (such as adding space to your programs) to severe (crashing your system). **Viruscan**, **Clean-Up**, and **Virushield** are programs that search for, eradicate, and prevent viral attacks on a hard drive or floppy disks.

Viruscan will scan a selected volume for any of 134 known viruses and their 213 sub-strains, and note the virus and its identification number. Eradicate any viruses found with Clean-Up. Virushield is a memory-resident "watchdog" that keeps alert for any suspicious activity and notifies you. Validate can check software for signs of tampering—before you install it on your system.

These programs don't have on-line help, but their straightforward documentation is sufficient.

Make sure you read the documentation for each program **before** running them, though, or you may end up removing files inadvertently.

Paint/Draw

A painting and drawing program similar to older versions of MacPaint on the Macintosh, **Finger Paint** supports both mouse and keyboard interfaces; using both works best.

The function keys access a variety of functions such as freehand drawing, drawing circles, squares, pyramids, etc. Magnifying "Fatbits" enables you to edit pixel by pixel, and there are over 30 different fill patterns. All options are represented graphically in the bar on the left side of the screen. Once within a function, use the arrow keys to move the cursor, and the plus (+) key to "click" as you would with a mouse.

Finger Paint works on all monitor types. Although there is no on-line help, the on-disk documentation is enough to get you started, and it's fairly intuitive from there. Registered users get a program that converts the Finger Paint format into .PCX format, the standard many illustration and desktop publishing programs use.

We've just touched on the tip of the shareware iceberg. With innumerable programs, it can be difficult to choose which programs are just right for you. But since you can "try before you buy," take your time and practice until you find the programs that suit you best. ❏

Sherry Goldfisher is a computer enthusiast and freelance writer based in Capitola, California.

This article was originally printed in the November/December 1990 issue of *Shareware Magazine*.

Dr. File Finder's Personal Picks

Nobody Knows Shareware Like The Doctor. So What Programs Does He *Really* Use?

Mike Callahan

How you view a piece of software will depend on your point of view, your needs, and expectations you may not even be aware of consciously. In a telephone conversation with John Dvorak about the VDE editor, for example, we bantered excitedly back and forth about the "neat" things it could do. Another friend, however, didn't seem to share in our excitement and, instead, cited some features he thought were missing.

In discussing software programs I have tried to maintain my objectivity. All the programs mentioned are excellent. There is no one product that is the best in a category, since what is best will always depend on what you think is best.

MAKING A CAREER OUT OF SOFTWARE

Over the course of the last seven and a half years, much of my time has been dedicated to studying shareware as well as commercial software. This research has included finding, testing, and comparing programs that perform similar functions, as well as promoting the exceptional programs so people can be aware of them. This research has also involved visiting thousands of bulletin boards to determine what other users want or feel they need in a program. This information is passed on to numerous shareware programmers so new and better programs can be created, benefiting all of us. Since no one pays me, I consider my work to be as unbiased and honest as I can make it. I test programs thoroughly and I'm very proud that

computer users around the world have come to respect my opinions, particularly on shareware. In the course of reviewing programs, I am asked one question quite frequently: "What program do you use?"

Many people often want to know what shareware programs I use personally—which utilities, editor, communications program, and so on. If it happens that I don't use a certain type of program, people want to know which one I *would* use if I were going to use such a program. In a few instances, there are types of programs mentioned that I do not personally use. In these cases, I recommend the ones I would use based on features, ease of use, and so on. When it comes to good shareware, you have to decide for yourself which program is best for you.

APPLICATIONS PROGRAMS

This first section discusses application-type programs: communications, editors, databases, and so on. You'll recognize many of the programs I use, but some smaller ones are covered here for the first time.

Communications Program—Qmodem. Having tried all of the programs in the communications category, in my opinion Qmodem has the most solid internal file transfer protocols. This conclusion is based on testing and experience. Qmodem is a fine program that is constantly being improved by John Friel, who is dedicated to his program.

Many new features were added with the release of version 4.0 and still more with version 4.1.

Version 4.2 introduced internal Zmodem, the BEW (batch entry window) for doing uploads, dynamic configuration options, and complete on-line help. Since I'm a Qmodem alpha tester, I do know that Friel is steadily working toward the exciting release of Qmodem 5.

Editing Chores. For some time I have used QEdit by Sammy Mitchell because of its configuration capabilities. Unlike with other editors, you can define keys to be what you want them to be. It also has other excellent features including a built-in menu, column blocks, box drawing, multiple windows, and now even a TSR version. QEdit is a good, solid editor with features that most people want. I have used QEdit to work with thousands of notes and documents.

Another program I use is VDE by Eric Meyer. By default, VDE uses the WordStar command set. It is the only shareware editor that I have ever seen that can create double-spacing inside a document. I also like the fact that printing codes can easily be inserted into text so italics, bold, and underlining can be added. Instead of loading a word processor to add special touches to quick letters, I now use VDE, which has macros, windows, special formatting, and printing options.

Database—PC-File. After trying both commercial and shareware databases, I prefer PC-File, by ButtonWare. It is easy to use, supports a mouse, and provides a variety of options. PC-File allows users to perform quick and simple procedures or design a fancy input screen. PC-File is easy to use and gently guides you through the program.

Spreadsheet Programs. I have used and evaluated both commercial and shareware spreadsheets but at the present time have no need for a spreadsheet program. In the past I used As-Easy-As by Trius, which is simple to use yet filled with features. In many cases, the program can use Lotus .WKS templates that are often found on bulletin boards and commercial online networks. As-Easy-As can perform complex calculations and is fast.

Menu and Shell Programs. By nature I am not one to use a program with a menu or shell, although I recognize the usefulness of such programs. My experience with these programs was strictly from the standpoint of testing and

evaluating, but I never had either a menu or a shell program for personal use. After letting other people use my Northgate 386 computer on occasion, I have seen more of a need for a menu (*smile*). A good menu makes it easy for others to access programs while making it easy for you to keep them away from things you don't want them to access.

A good shell program can also be useful when working with large numbers of files. As noted in the course of the book, there are programs that are strictly menu programs, others that are strictly DOS shell programs, and a few that are a combination of each. To be fair, I'll tell which one I use in each of these three categories.

4DOS. 4DOS has many features missing from DOS. For example, 4DOS lets you see the names of files as they are deleted, giving you a chance to see if you deleted a file you hadn't intended to delete. You can also see if files are being copied or moved to where you want them to be moved.

The 4DOS "aliases" are spectacular, as are the enhanced batch file commands, built-in log function, and timer. You can also alter colors, create menus, and more. 4DOS picks up where DOS leaves off, giving you a complete package, including online help. If only half of its functions are used, you're still ahead, which is why I use it.

Menu Program—HDM IV. In the category of menu programs I like HDM IV by Jim Hass. It has a nice presentation, many configurable options, and usage logging. I appreciate its ability to run programs at designated times, making it very handy for optimizing drives while you're sleeping. HDM is fast, easy to use, and has good mouse support. The author is constantly improving the program and giving it more features. It is an excellent menu system for both home or business use. I have HDM IV running on two of my machines.

Shell Program—The Director. For a straight DOS shell program the modular approach of The Director, by Dan Baumbach, in my opinion provides the most flexibility. The main module, DL, is an excellent DOS shell. It's configurable, has mouse support, and offers all of the things that most people would want in a DOS shell. The small module, DB, is great for working in individual directories. For those times when I want an overview of everything on my system, the DA module provides that. The Director appears to have been carefully thought out and its author works to keep improving it. In one way or another, The Director is used on all my machines.

Menu and Shell—DCOM. On my frequently used Northgate 386, I use dCOM. The Directory Commander, or dCOM, by Dave Frailey, is the best possible combination of a shell and menu program. Because dCOM has its own powerful macro language, it's extremely flexible when creating menus. This makes it easy to set up menus that can be used by someone who knows nothing about computers. I can track usage with dCOM's logging abilities. Another likable feature is that you can lock anyone out of the shell functions, thus eliminating the possibility of someone logging in and accidentally wiping out a directory.

The power of the menus is astounding. The macro language lets you prompt for input, gives a list of possible selections, and much more. Since the functions have been carefully integrated, you can tag and move files one second and select an item off a menu the next. For my needs, dCOM provides everything in one great package.

Background Mail. In this busy world we often spend our time playing phone tag with one another. BackMail, by Alethic Software, has eliminated this problem for me by handling electronic mail and files. Friends and associates who also use BackMail can send me messages while I keep on working. You don't need a multi-tasking environment to take advantage of Back-Mail since it's designed to work in the background. You can pop into BackMail, read a message, write a quick reply, and go back to what you were doing while BackMail takes care of delivering your reply. If you leave your machine for awhile and a message comes in, you'll see the message "You have new mail" on the screen. It's a complete "point to point" mail system that is excellent for use among friends or in any business environment.

Personal Notes. For keeping notes or jotting down random thoughts, I use Notebook. You can keep multiple folders that can be password protected. Whenever a password is used, the folder is encrypted upon closing. You can even use it as a place to store your passwords for other files, so the only password you need remember is the one to access your Notebook folder (*smile*).

UTILITY PROGRAMS

Once again, the utility programs you use will be governed by the things you do. The utilities I use suit my needs the best, based on features and performance.

PSEARCH—For Finding Text in Files. There are times when I want to find text located within files and see the text in context. PSEARCH, by Norm Patriquin, suits my needs in this area. I can search multiple drives, look for multiple strings of text, all very quickly. PSEARCH can also be made to search the entire system, to do a case-sensitive search, and to exclude certain types of files. I've used PSEARCH for years, and it performs all the important search functions while retaining speed.

File Finding—DFF. For finding files quickly anywhere on my system, I use DFF by Dan Doman. I've tested and timed all of the other find programs and DFF is consistently faster. To be fair, DFF does [TK ITALICSnot] look inside packed files, which is one factor that slows down other utilities in the same category. On programs where this feature can be toggled off, DFF is still a bit faster. For a find utility that can look into packed files, the two fastest seem to be by Douglas Hay and NJFIND by Nifty James (Mike Blaszczak).

Compression Programs. It is difficult today to get by with just one of the file compression programs. My personal favorites are PKZIP and PKUNZIP by Phil Katz's PKWARE. The ZIP programs offer very good compression and excellent speed. I also keep PAK, by NoGate Consulting, for unpacking .PAK and .ARC files, and to create self-extracting (SFX) files. The same is true for LHarc, which I use to unpack .LZH files and occasionally for creating SFX files. I have a copy of the latest version of ZOO on a floppy disk just in case I have to unpack a .ZOO format file. For daily use, however, I use PKZIP and PKUNZIP.

Viewing Compressed Files—FV. To determine the contents of a compressed file, I use

Vern Buerg's FV (File View). FV is fast and tells you what program was used to pack the file. In addition, FV is used by LIST PLUS for the View-Arc function, so you can view the contents of packed files from within LIST PLUS.

Compressed Files—Viewing Documentation. For scanning the documentation of compressed files without having to unpack them, I use ZIPTV by Samuel Smith. ZIPTV lists the contents of a compressed file and allows you to read through the files. You can scan through READ.ME, .TXT, and documentation files without having to unpack a compressed file. In working with so many programs, I find this a particularly handy and timesaving program.

Keyboard Enhancer—KBFIX. To enhance a keyboard, I haven't found anything better than KBFIX by Skip Gelbrecht. KBFIX will increase the typematic rate, repeat rate, amount of delay, and more. KBFIX can adjust the function of the CAPS LOCK key, increase the size of the keyboard buffer, and be loaded into high memory. KBFIX is a solid utility that combines the functions of several utilities and still only uses about 2K of RAM. It does everything I need and does it well without compatibility problems.

Remind/Prompt Program—LCG/Remind. As a reminder to back up the hard disks, or for prompting me to load a program, I use LCG/Remind by the Levin Consulting Group. I like the way LCG/Remind displays its reminders and the information about my system it provides in conjunction with a reminder, such as how much disk space is free, percentage of files not backed up, and so on. If only 3 percent of the files on your system aren't backed up, for example, you may not want to take the time to do a full backup. LCG/Remind lets you make the choice.

Formatting Program—Format Master. For formatting disks of all sizes, I use Format Master by John Newlin and New-Ware. Format Master has an agreeable interface, is configurable, and formats 360K to 800K disks on a 1.2 meg drive. Other options include making a system disk, putting on a volume label, "cycling" a drive while you format several disks, and so on. Format Master works on a wide variety of machines, is

fast, has excellent error checking, and even has mouse support. Carefully programmed, Format Master is upgraded to keep pace with new BIOS and DOS versions.

DOS Command Editor—Anarkey. Anarkey 3.0, by Steve Calwas and Moderne Software, is an excellent DOS command line editor that offers AKAs and other features like command line completion and execution, a history buffer, and now, mouse support. It can also use EMS, which allows Anarkey to use almost no DOS RAM, while similar programs may use 10K to 12K or more.

Anarkey also lets you change the default command sequences, write the history buffer to a file, and more. From the standpoint of features and lack of RAM consumption, I feel that Anarkey 3.0 is the one to beat.

DOCTOR'S NOTE: You may have noticed what seems to be a contradiction. I stated earlier that I use 4DOS, which has aliases and now I've also said I use Anarkey, which has AKAs—in essence, the same thing. (Aliases, AKAs, and synonyms are commands that you define to carry out complex operations.) I generally test programs without the presence of 4DOS however, I still like to have my "aliases a la AKAs" on my system. Thus, when I remove 4DOS to test programs, I use Anarkey 4.0 to provide me with its AKA functions and DOS command line editing. When I reinstall 4DOS to test programs in its environment, I use the 4DOS alias feature. The alias file and the AKA file are nearly identical in content, but are formatted to meet the needs of the individual programs. You have to be flexible (*smile*).

Overall Utility—Professional Master Key. When it comes to editing disk sectors and individual program sectors, and erasing stubborn files, I use Professional Master Key (PMK) from Public Brand Software. I like PMK's interface and find it easy to use. It's also excellent for altering file attributes, undeleting files, and so on. I use PMK primarily for its Disk Edit and File Edit functions and occasionally to remove a file from my system.

Another part of the PMK package I use is the Full Screen File Sort, which puts files in a specified order on the disk and eliminates erased files through a command similar to:

CFS C:\/PACK

Once I've sorted the files in the root directory of drive C and have written the changes to disk, the directory is "packed." This means that all erased files have been removed.

List Plus. Vern Buerg's LIST is a program I've used for years. I really don't know how I'd get along without it. I use LIST for searching through documentation to find items in a hurry. Now, with LIST PLUS, I can delete the file when I'm finished, or move it off to another directory to examine later in more detail. When one considers that nearly every shareware program has documentation and other supplementary text files, I don't know how anyone can get by without a copy of LIST. It's excellent for finding information in any file by searching forward or backward. It can view files with high bit characters, filter out junk characters, and it has mouse support. Considering the volume of text I read each day, I can't imagine using DOS's TYPE command to do it. In my opinion, LIST is a must have utility.

General Printing—PPRINT. For printing with either the Panasonic KX-P1124 dot matrix printer or the Panasonic KX-P4450 laser printer, I use Norm Patriquin's PPRINT. This printing utility has so many options that Patriquin suggests you only bother learning the ones you need. You can format text to be printed, make it double-spaced, put the text in bold print, and much more. PPRINT may well be the best overall printing utility available supporting dot matrix and laser printers. Its flexibility is the reason I use it.

Keyboard Macros—NewKey. In creating keyboard macros, I use NewKey by Frank Bell and FAB Software. NewKey supports multicharacter macros, fixed fields, variable fields, pauses, and descriptions for each macro you define. NewKey is as powerful as any of the commercial macro programs and more powerful than any other shareware macro program. With three modules, you have your choice of features depending on how much RAM you have available.

NewKey has helped me create some spectacular macros. You can even call up macros from within batch files, which you can't do with any other macro program. NewKey is efficient and offers me everything I could want from a macro program.

Organization—The Folders System. When using PC-Write by Quicksoft, I use The Folders System written by Robert Allen. There is also a Folders interface for WordPerfect and Microsoft Word. What I like best about The Folders System is that I can enter a meaningful description for a new file. DOS filenames can be strange, especially if you try to give them some meaning. With The Folders System, I can enter something like "Letter to Lisa of 04/24/90 re:book" and never have to guess about the contents of a file. The Folders System has an easy-to-use format, keeps like files in individual folders of your choosing, and makes it easy to find exactly the file you want to work with. I've used the WordPerfect and Microsoft Word versions of The Folders System and both work very well. Programs like The Folders System can save you a lot of headaches when working with documents.

Screen Blanker—BURNOUT. To protect my monitor screens, I use BURNOUT. I like this program because, unlike most screen blankers, BURNOUT is a device driver that is loaded from the CONFIG.SYS file. Its parameters can be changed using a .COM file that comes with the package. This gives me flexibility—I can turn the blanker off, extend the time before the screen will blank, and so on.

For Sorting Data—SORTF. To sort the contents of files I use SORTF by Vern Buerg. SORTF is fast and allows for a wide range of sort criteria on many fields. SORTF will automatically prompt for an input filename and an output filename. It's the best sort program I've found thus far.

For Filling Diskettes—FILL. For getting the most from my floppy disks I use FILL, by Jean LaLonde, which fills each disk to its maximum capacity. FILL will calculate the space that a given number of files will require and then copy them to floppies so all the disk space is utilized. I often end up with disks that have 0 bytes free. Since I have so many programs in storage on floppies, it's important to me not to waste any space. FILL takes care of that for me and does a great job.

STACKEY. I use STACKEY, by Barry Simon and Rick Wilson, for a number of tasks including loading the keyboard buffer with keystrokes that I want passed to another program. With STACKEY I can insert pauses or delays and pass just about any keyboard key to a program. I can also halt the processing by pressing a hot key. STACKEY can reboot the computer and control the cursor, the EGA and VGA palettes, the length and tone of a beep, and much more. STACKEY does so many useful things that I can't describe them all here, but I use it on my machine many times a day to make my work easier.

SUMMING IT ALL UP

These are some of the shareware programs that are on my system. As mentioned earlier, the ones you decide to use will depend in part on your needs and on your own personal tastes. There are many excellent programs available in shareware, many of which you simply won't find in the commercial arena. Shareware programs provide good quality software at good prices. Now you know some of the shareware programs that I use. Take a good look at the abundance of quality programs that are available. Test and compare them. When you find those that meet your needs, remember to register them with their authors. ❑

Dr. File Finder, *known off-line as Mike Callahan, regularly accesses thousand of bulletin board systems and has been a major force in promoting many top shareware packages. This is an excerpt from his recently published book* **Dr. File Finder's Guide to Shareware** *(Osborne/McGraw-Hill).*

This article was originally printed in the March/April 1991 issue of *Shareware Magazine.*

Inexpensive Desktop Publishing Solutions

Shareware vs. Commercial Software

by William Harrel

It wasn't all that long ago that printers and publishers relied on expensive typesetting equipment to produce newsletters, brochures and other important documents. Small businesses and organizations had two choices: publish unsophisticated documents in-house using a typewriter, or pay expensive typesetting fees. But, like so many other tasks, the personal computer has changed all that. Today there is a third choice—desktop publishing.

Just what is desktop publishing? As with many aspects of the computer industry, the exact definition changes with technological advancements. In the beginning, when Aldus released the first copy of PageMaker software, desktop publishing was defined as simply setting text and graphics with a computer and a laser printer.

Today, desktop publishing includes sophisticated graphics creation, photograph touchup, slide preparation, four-color document preparation—the list goes on and on. This level of desktop publishing requires several different kinds of software and application-specific hardware. We here at The WRITE Desktop Publisher use a number of $400+ software packages, scanners, 23" high-resolution monitors and powerful 386 machines to produce sophisticated documents and other media.

Most small business and home computer users, however, have more modest needs—publishing relatively professional looking documents as cost-effectively as possible. Many users are simply looking for software that will merge text and graphics on the same page. And there are several desktop publishing software packages that will do just that, at a low cost.

Looking at the maze of low-end desktop publishing software—both shareware and commercial—*Shareware Magazine* decided to compare them to find out just which low-cost solutions delivered the best results. The WRITE Desktop took three shareware desktop publishing packages:

Asysta Consultants' **City Desk** 7.1 ($45),

XLEnt, Inc.'s **Typesetter PC** ($30), and

Rubicon Computer Labs, Inc.'s **Rubicon Publisher** 2.1 ($85),

and put them through their paces. Then we took three commercial desktop publishing packages:

Unison World's **NewsMaster II** ($60),

TimeWorks' **Publish It! Lite** ($60), and

Software Publishing Company's **First Publisher** 3.0 ($149),

and ran them. The results were interesting.

Do You Really Need DTP Software?

Before purchasing any software package, you should first evaluate your application and your equipment. There are many DTP jobs for which using a good word processor will suffice. In many cases, a high-end word processor such as the shareware product PC-Write will work better for you than most of these DTP packages. This is especially true if you have a laser printer, or will be doing final output on one. Where most of the DTP packages reviewed here are useful is getting the most out of your dot-matrix printer.

How We Tested These Programs

Each DTP package was evaluated in six categories. Some of the packages were stronger

than others in certain categories, but none ex-
celled in all six. The first test was installation,
how easily the software was to get up and running. The second category was interface, how
easy the software was to use. Next, the
software's compatibility with other programs
such as word processors and graphics programs
was evaluated. For the fourth test, customer support, we called each publisher to see what kind of
technical support they offered. Test five
evaluated how informative each package's
manual or documentation, and test six evaluated
output—how the printed page looked.

Installation

All but two products came with built-in install
programs that place the software either on your
hard disk or a working floppy. The two that
didn't, Typesetter PC and First Publisher, recommended a standard DOS COPY *.* to install the
necessary files. A drawback to this method is that
you often end up with unnecessary files gobbling
up precious disk space.

First Publisher copied a number of unnecessary
files to our hard disk, such as fonts and graphics.
It had a cumbersome printer and font installation
program that proved especially unclear when it
came to installing a PostScript printer.

Interface

WYSIWYG (What You See Is What You Get)
DTP software has been the industry standard for
some time. What this means is that the screen
representation looks exactly like what will come
rolling out of your printer. The benefit of
WYSIWYG is that it limits the number of
hardcopy drafts, thereby saving valuable production time. Professional desktop publishers go to
great expense to get true WYSIWYG. We at The
WRITE desktop spend thousands of dollars on
oversized, high-resolution monitors capable in
order to achieve WYSIWYG, but it's still not
exact.

Of the six programs reviewed, four claim
WYSIWYG interfaces. Typesetter PC is the only
shareware product that allows you to see your
page as you work. Rubicon Publisher comes with
a VGA preview that allows you to view your
page on screen before you print. None of these
products support anything close to true

WYSIWYG. However, all but City Desk—
which had no WYSIWYG at all—were clear
enough to give a fair idea how the printed document would look.

Part of our interface criteria was whether or not
the program had a tutorial. We found that all
three commercial programs walk the user
through the first publication. Typesetter PC has a
"Just Messing Around" section which adequately
acquaints the user with the program, and
Rubicon has several sample documents and a
number of style templates that get you going
quickly enough. City Desk, on the other hand,
leaves the user to his or her own devices.

Most of the products were easy to use. Only
City Desk and Rubicon Publisher, the two non-
WYSIWYG packages, were difficult to master.
Rubicon, which uses embedded tags and styles to
format text, requires some dedication to learn.
This package may be more suitable for setting
type for paste-up rather than publishing flyers
and other graphics-intensive documents.

An important factor in determining ease-of-use
was time—how quickly the user could get to the
printed page. Typesetter PC and First Publisher
took us from blank screen to printed page in the
least amount of time, and with the fewest number
of surprises.

Compatibility

DTP programs are of little worth if information
can't be imported other software. A disappoint-
ment to most of these packages was that they supported only standard ASCII text, and, in a couple
of cases, only one or two word processors.
Graphics support was even less common.

Usually, when a DTP package supports a certain word processor, some or all formatting—
tabs, bolds, italics, fonts, etc.—are imported with
the text. This saves the user from having to reformat text in the page layout program. Rubicon
and First Publisher both support popular word
processors. First Publisher, in particular, supported a variety of commercial word processors
excellently.

Rubicon, which, uses tags and styles, allows
typesetting via your word processor. Tag formatting is done within the word processor before exporting the file to ASCII. This process may seem

cumbersome, but the popular high-end Ventura Publisher works similarly. The use of tags and styles makes Rubicon more versatile than most of the other programs reviewed here.

All three commercial products came with a graphics library, and all three advertise additional graphics available at extra cost. Each of the commercial products also provided some kind of graphics editing. Only First Publisher imported graphics from other sources, such as paint programs TIFF files.

The shareware products' graphics support were mediocre. Typesetter PC does, however, have a built-in graphics editor. City Desk claims an optional TSR program called INSET that allows the user to place graphics in columns, but we were unable to get a copy. (We suspect there is a newer version of City Desk than the one we downloaded from PC-Link, but Asysta Consultants declined to send it to us.) A review we read said that Rubicon Publisher 2.1 had graphics support, but the documentation on our version mentioned nothing about graphics. Rubicon Computer Labs, Inc. did, however, stay up late several nights helping us review version 2.1, for which the documentation was incomplete. Failure to mention graphics support could have been an oversight.

All three commercial programs as well as Typesetter PC and City Desk provided screen capture utilities for "grabbing" graphics from other programs. Though screen captures are handy, the quality of the graphics depend on the quality of the monitor. This is especially true of TIFF and PCX grayscale photographs.

That none of the shareware products came with graphics libraries was unimportant. The graphics that came with NewsMaster and Publish It Lite! were not impressive. First Publisher's were better, but users can download some of the best computer graphics from local BBSs and Compuserve forums.

Customer Support

All three of the commercial products had adequate customer support. Software Publishing Company, whose First Publisher is the most expensive package of the six, seemed to have the most experienced support technicians. On the

Shareware side, City Desk publishers didn't want their product reviewed—in light of this, we can't comment on the support City Desk users receive. The publishers of Typesetter PC didn't return our calls, either. The publishers of Rubicon Publisher not only returned our calls promptly but were very helpful.

Documentation

Except for the confusion we experienced installing a printer and fonts with First Publisher, all three of the commercial products exhibited fair documentation. Of the shareware products, Rubicon's documentation is excellent. Since the Version 2.1 manual wasn't ready at the time of our review, we relied on documentation from an earlier release. Still, using this highly technical program was relatively easy.

The documentation that unzipped with City Desk is another story altogether. It rambled and went nowhere, mentioning bits and pieces of installation and use without any real cohesion. However, there is a typeset, complete manual available upon registration.

We were unable to get Typesetter PC's typeset manual. The documentation that came on the disk was thorough enough, and friendly—we could tell that the author had had a lot of fun with it. The author did forget to number the pages, which made reference difficult.

Output

Installation, ease-of-use and other criteria discussed thus far are important in any software program, but the real test of desktop publishing software is the printed page. Only two of these programs support laser printers—First Publisher and Rubicon Publisher. The Typesetter PC manual mentions future LaserJet and PostScript printer support, but we were unable to reach the publisher to find out if that had happened yet.

Most dot-matrix printers have very limited font capabilities, especially when it comes to larger fonts. Even if your dot-matrix printer does contain larger fonts, you're probably not happy with them.

Herein lies the benefit to most of these low-end DTP products—they provide proportional fonts in different styles and sizes for use with dot-matrix printers. (But these are not really fonts at all, not in the conventional DTP font outline sense. Actually, what the software does is instruct your printer to draw graphic fonts, just like any other graphic element on the page. What you end up with is often noticeably better than the normal typewriterlike fonts that came with your printer.)

All of the DTP products tout souped-up dot-matrix printer support, either on the packaging or somewhere in the documentation. But the problem with dot-matrix is low resolution, or dots per inch (dpi). The average dot-matrix prints at about 75 dpi. Two of the shareware products —Typesetter PC and Rubicon Publisher—have printer drivers that enhance resolution. Typesetter PC explains its resolution enhancement process in the documentation. As mentioned, we didn't have the latest copy of Rubicon's manual. Regardless, we were impressed with both products' dot-matrix output. The others produced nothing more noteworthy than what we'd seen come out of dot-matrix printers previously.

The two packages that do support laser printers, Rubicon and First Publisher, support both Laser-Jet-compatible and PostScript devices as well as a variety of softfonts. Rubicon comes with Laser-Jet-compatible serif and sans serif fonts in an array of sizes—which makes the product well worth the $85. (A spokesperson at Rubicon Computer Labs, Inc. says their surveys show that a vast majority of the shareware users who do own laser printers have LaserJets or compatibles.) These are probably all the softfonts you'll need for most print jobs. And if you have a PostScript printer, Rubicon supports all 35 standard Post-Script fonts.

First Publisher came bundled with Bitstream Fontware, a high-quality font product. The differences between Rubicon and First Publisher are many. The commercial product is suited to shorter documents such as mailers and flyers while Rubicon works well for creating newsletter galleys and type set for magazine paste-up. Both products will do either job adequately.

It's A Matter of Application

The purpose of this article is not to recommend one product over another, and that's a good thing. The weaknesses and strengths of each product leave programmers with ample ground-breaking space. As the user, you'll have to deter-

mine your DTP needs before choosing a product. Though the cost difference between most of these products is almost negligible, these days it's important that time is not wasted learning to use a product that will not meet your needs in the end.

DTP Supporting Shareware

Desktop publishers need more than just a page layout program to produce high-quality documents. The DTP software is just the hub of the craft. We pored over The PC-SIG Encyclopedia of Shareware and spent hours on Compuserve and some of our local BBSs to find shareware programs to enhance the products discussed in this article. Here are some ideas:

Graphics:

VGA Paint: You'll need a good paint program to create and edit graphics for your publications. We downloaded paint program after paint program. Most of them are not worth mentioning. Then we found this one. It is easy to use and produces high enough quality graphics for use with a screen capture utility. Registration fee: Unknown.

Cooper Graphics: This is a 17-disk clipart set of almost every symbol, flag and other graphic you can think of. These graphics are of at least as high a quality as the images included with the commercial packages talked about in this article. The graphics come in several different formats, including PCX, making them highly compatible with other products, including high-end DTP packages such as PageMaker. Registration fee: $6 per disk.

Dropcaps: This collection of ornate French capital letters is ideal for raised first letters in book chapters and for typesetting poetry. They are in PCX format, making them compatible for most applications. Registration fee: $15

Word Processing

PC-Write: This is an excellent word processor for creating text for your publications. It supports many of the high-end word processing features such as macros, headers and footers and spell checking. And it supports laser printers. For many documents this will be the only software you need. Registration fee: $99.

Fonts

Q-Font 1.5: A font editor, Q-Font allows you to create variations on existing fonts. You can enlarge, shrink slant and do all kinds of creative things to your typefaces. In many ways this package is comparable to the commercial product Z-Soft Softype for creating special-effect fonts. Registration fee: $80.

William Harrel is the owner-operator of the Ventura, California-based firm The WRITE Desktop Publisher. He is also a freelance writer who writes extensively about DTP applications. Harrel is currently working on two books: *Illustrated PageMaker 4.0* for WordWare Publishing, Inc., and *Publishing a Newsletter on Your PC*.

City Desk,

Rubicon Publisher, #2334, 2335, 2336, [SR], $89.00

Typesetter PC, #2167, 2168, 512K RAM, Hercules graphics or CGA and an Epson compatible printer

[commercial packages tested]

NewMaster II, Unison World (1321 Harbor Bay Parkway, Alameda, CA 94501 415/748-6680) [SR?]

Publish It Lite!, Timeworks, Inc., 444 Lake Cook Rd., Deerfield, IL 60015-4919 312/948-7626)

First Publisher, Software Publishing Corporation, P.O. Box 7210, Mountain View, CA 94039-7210 415/962-8910)

Once you become comfortable with your desktop publisher, you'll want to add a few extras. The following programs are available through the PC-SIG library:

Graphic Workshop eliminates the problem of image file format incompatibility when you need to juggle graphics. With Graphic Workshop it's possible to convert, view, print, dither, and halftone images from virtually any source: MACPAINT, VENTURA, PC PAINTBRUSH, .BMP, .TIFF, .WPG, and more. Features batch processing for multiple file conversion and expanded memory. Author registration: $35. (#2277)

Desktop Paint bypasses image file format conversion altogether; it operates in the native file formats of the most popular desktop publishing programs, including MACPAINT, VENTURA, and PC PAINTBRUSH. Desktop Paint allows you to create and edit pictures of any size and comes with EMS support. Requires a Microsoft-compatible mouse and driver; 640K memory recommended. Author registration: $35. (#2546)

CropGif (packaged with Graphic Workshop) works like a cut and paste program, allowing you to crop fragments from existing GIF files and assign them to new files, without the hassles of using complicated measurements. Requires Microsoft compatible mouse. Author Registration: $20. (#2277)

Stylize your desk top published documents with Qfont 1.5, a mouse-driven font editor that lets you shrink, enlarge, or slant any HP-compatible font. Create logos or new fonts with Qfont's built-in paint program. Author Registration: $80. (#2529)

This article was originally printed in the November/December 1990 issue of *Shareware Magazine*.

Holy Software!

Studying Scripture—Electronically

By Barry Brenesal

Mixing computer technology with the Judeo-Christian Bible may seem incongruous at first glance: a fusion of scientific technology at its most advanced, with a pre-computerized literary work speaking of things, by definition, immeasurable. The two would appear to have nothing in common, and juxtaposition only emphasizes this disparity: Moses coming down from Mt. Sinai bearing the Ten Commandments on a fax. Paul writing his letters to the Churches using an early edition of WordStar (CP/M version, of course). Born-again Bernoulli Boxes . . . .

But in fact, technology has encouraged the spread of established religion. The printing press made holy documents of both the Jewish and Christian faiths available to all at a reasonable price for the first time. Similarly, the electronic Bible (or "Bible database") does much to aid in-depth scriptural study. It combines simple and compound text retrieval with the search features of a concordance, and printing options that would have had Johannes Gutenburg confessing green envy to his parish priest.

If serious research is your goal, four such programs are available as shareware. All deliver good value. Choosing among them is a case of matching personal needs with the right set of features. We'll attempt to point you in the right direction.

On-Line Bible 3.0

This is venerable freeware, and serves an honorable function by making an electronic Bible available to all for study. Timely upgrades have kept it growing and responsive to user input. No matter the changes, however, the basic program shows its age in a few unsubtle ways, most clearly through a lack of internal text editing. The only notes you can take while viewing this database are pen-and-paper ones: there's no provision to jot down ideas on screen and move them into a file.

When you want to indulge in some computerized commentary, the program's solution is to invoke UED, a good text editor. (It comes bundled with the software.) Unfortunately, it's not integrated with the package, and that means you A) perform a search and export verses; B) exit the **On-Line Bible** and enter UED; C) call up your verse file and add notes; D) exit UED and re-enter the On-Line Bible; E) load in your verse file for viewing. Simple, eh?

And that hassle is really too bad, because this third major release of the On-Line Bible also includes a Greek lexicon. (It's one of the few electronic Bibles to offer this aid in comprehending the New Testament.) Access could be easier, perhaps something like "Position cursor over requested word, hit [ENTER]". Instead, you use [F5] to show all four-digit Strong reference numbers alongside nearly every word in the New Testament text, then hit [F4], and type in the particular number you want. The results display on an overlay screen rather than the main one: curious, since the scripture takes up only half a screen at any one time. Still, you can always write down the reference facts or save them to file.

The latter is one of the best aspects of the On-Line Bible. Without carefully reading the manual, however, you might never know that the grouped Print commands refer, not to a printer, but to the directional piping of contents. (On-screen help is context sensitive, but inadequate, usually no more than a line.) "Print Verses," for instance, is a laconic way of saying "You can perform a search, and send all the verses you find to a printer or filename of your choice." Other options allow you to include Strong's Koine Greek references, or exclude verses and save the text references, alone. Formatting controls of document and non-document mode and single or double-spaced lines are also available.

Another useful function lets you compile a list of verses and verse ranges for file export. Unfortunately, the list first has to be compiled outside the program and then imported—the absence of a text editor once again making itself felt.

The On-Line Bible's search facility is quick, and accepts a couple of parameters lacking in other databases under review. It can search for phrases, rather than just several keywords in a verse; this yields very specific results. The program also permits the Boolean A-NOT-B, excluding as well as including certain words from the search.

On-Line Bible 3.0 contains the Greek lexicon and King James Version (KJV) in its amended, 1760's form which corrects for non-standard spelling and typographical errors. The New International Version (NIV) is available for $40 from the programmer. If you don't mind dividing your study time into two completely separate operations, internal search-and-view and external editing, then this program probably will do quite well. But running it after trying out any of the other shareware Bibles is like viewing an antique car. You can certainly admire its meticulous attention to detail, but those modern amenities really count for a lot.

SeedMaster 2.0

An unusual program, **SeedMaster** combines some perceptive ideas about the computerized presentation of information with some decidedly unconventional ones about how people expect to access it.

The good news, first. SeedMaster has the best search facility of the four shareware biblical databases. If you merely want a particular, predefined passage, you can scroll through a list of scriptural books, enter chapter and verse, and instantly see the results. More difficult searches based on words and phrases are dispatched with equal speed. All results are shown simultaneous-ly, each reference with a line to itself on which the search material is highlighted. Book, chapter and verse are given in the left columns. Scroll to a particular line, hit [ENTER], and the screen temporarily displays that passage. Back out via [ESC], scroll again . . . well, you get the idea. It's a good one.

There are others. A case-sensitive switch. Hot-keyed search defining controls that let you isolate not merely books, but chapters and verses, as well. (As many as 26 search areas can be defined at once.) Up to three windows for viewing. Although not resizable, they're a handy option.

There's also a secondary word search, for those absent-minded moments when you can't remember how to spell, much less find, Elonbethhanan. You can scan SeedMaster's list of available words until the right selection appears.

This is the better of PC-SIG's databases offering the New International Version, rather than just the King James Version. It's an additional $30 from White Harvest Software, but easily worth the cost. Those scholars who worked under King James' instructions were guilty of both timidity and mistakes, but more so of many colloquialisms; they frequently squeezed several different Greek and Hebrew words into a single English one, losing various meanings in the process. The authors of the On-Line Bible noted with surprise (in itself, surprising) that the NIV contained approximately 2,500 more unique words than the KJV. All of which comes down to the fact that it's a lot harder to create a database from the NIV, because there are more distinct words to input, but it also provides a more accurate translation.

Arrayed against SeedMaster's positive value there's some formidable opposition, unfortunately. The on-line help is located in two external files, and takes time to load—and no matter how short a period of time that might be, if it's not instantaneous, it's too long. (You might try printing those files, HELP.1 and HELP.2.)

The documentation also spends too much time describing its different task modules (Commentary, Notepad, Grabber, Peek, etc.), their interrelationship and the sometimes duplicative commands that will (and won't) run from each, even to the point of including a small schematic diagram. The user only sees one basic screen, however: why bother confusing matters, if you're not running for public office?

Finally, the command structure is hampered by over-complexity. Consider one process, Seed-Master's "Grabber," which copies text to a buffer for future printout. [ALT+F4] starts the defining process in inverse video, and you have to scroll the cursor over the text you want to capture. (All of it. You can't scroll down 3 lines, say, and then hit a combination of keys to move over 65 columns. You have to walk that cursor every step of the way. Sloooowly.) Logically, repeating [ALT+F4] should signal the end of procedure, but it doesn't: [CTL+F4] does. And when you drop back to the notepad, the text isn't there, yet. You have to use [SHFT+F4] to fix it in place.

But concordance features rank very high in what most people want from an electronic Bible, and in that area this software beats the competition. Better still, by the time this article is out, White Harvest Software plans to have its next upgrade on the shareware market. While changes to the program itself will be minor, the author informs me that he's finished more Bible versions for purchase with the database, including several in English and one each in Spanish and Greek. Access will be interlinear: that is, if several Bibles are present when you request a reference, each version's text will be displayed simultaneously, alongside each other.

If you plan to use your biblical database on a regular basis and an elaborate interface won't bother you while learning its intricacies, Seed-Master's major strengths easily outweigh its quirkiness. Otherwise you may want to try it, but make room on your hard drive, as well, for Scripture.

Scripture 2.0

Gil Yoder's **Scripture** dates from 1989, and shows the substantial advance both our expectations of programming sophistication and the programming itself have taken in just a few years. The help screen uses hypertext to swing you from one relevant area to another, and a subject-oriented survey of all topics is displayed upon hitting [F1], twice. Moving to a particular verse is as easy as ^J, followed by the first few letters of the book, chapter and verse. Three dis-

play screens and an editing screen can be summoned, overlapped or hidden at any time, all accessible by toggling #1-4. A separate configuration file lets you move and color the individual screens, and issue a host of printer, search and text editor parameters. (Temporary changes for each session can be made from within the program.)

The software packages we've considered so far each have their virtues, but none can exactly be said to make the transfer of text to a point outside the program a simple matter. It's this ability to easily retrieve searched-for data and save it to file or printer that is the hallmark of this particular biblical database. The process is so simple, in fact, that once it's used, subsequent documentation proves largely superfluous.

Yoder seems to have grasped the poorly understood fact that it's more time-consuming to edit your verse choices before transcribing them, than afterwards, when they're all in one nice, neat file. Scripture allows you to automatically capture all references and texts from a search [F8], compile a list of verse references [F4], or decide whether to transfer each isolated verse as it is found [F7]. You can then backup, examine, and delete irrelevant material. The text editor displays similar thoughtfulness, responding to either arrow commands or the older Wordstar standards. There's even a Zoom feature [ALT+Z] that toggles the editor between its user-determined number of lines and full-screen mode.

Anyone who has read a Bible knows how time-consuming it is to lose your place. Scripture also allows the unlimited creation via [F6] of user-named files that act as bookmarks. Its search facility is rather more limited, though it handles (like the other databases) a common series of Boolean AND/OR operatives. It even goes Seed-Master one better in a single instance, hotkeying word searches on every letter. This means you can type in a few letters of the word you want, and watch the list scroll to the entry that meets your increasingly narrowing criteria.

But both SeedMaster and the On-Line Bible are much faster while searching. SeedMaster further accepts case-sensitive arguments and performs phrase searches; Scripture doesn't. The limitation of choosing words from a predefined list also means it can't search on a double word, which the On-Line Bible can.

This aside, Scripture's simple user interface, attractive screens, multiple verse viewing and excellent copying facility make it the biblical database of choice in PC-SIG's library. Note that their version of scripture only comes with the New Testament, but given the five or so megabytes of storage space required for the full Bible, this makes an excellent starting point. Those interested in pursuing the matter further can find both Yoder and his latest version of Scripture (OT included) on the Coalgate BBS (2400-14400 bps) at (408) 720-8326—which, by the way, is an excellent board, with no downloading restrictions.

WordWorker

WordWorker doesn't have a Greek lexicon like the On-Line Bible. It doesn't have Seed-Master's search features or interlinear options, and it doesn't boast Scripture's ease of use and copy controls. It doesn't even possess an Old Testament. It does have two special distinctions, though, which make it unique in the electronic Bible field: WordWorker can be activated as a TSR. And when you expand it within your favorite word processor or communications program, WordWorker can transfer displayed verses to your current file or directly on screen. Rather than containing a text editor, it remains contained within one.

Probably the importance of keeping its memory usage to a minimum (the kernel takes up 7K; when expanded, it requires about 256K) has kept this program relatively light on features. It can't print selected verses or even save a list, and there's no internal text editor. It does maintain a single internal bookmark, and the search system is based, like Scripture, on a word list. Boolean AND/OR searches are once again supported. All actions are instigated through the function keys, F1-F10, and (for once in this survey) their general contents is listed in a pair of lines at the bottom of the screen.

WordWorker's ability to go resident establishes a unique role for the program as an instantly accessible reference tool. It won't supplant any of the other electronic bibles presently available,

but as an adjunct to these for a special purpose it serves with distinction.

Forward into the Unknown

What does the future hold for developments in this field? By now, you may perceive a pattern among the preceding four reviews. Each Bible database has offered something distinctive, unduplicated by the others. The On-Line Bible includes a Greek lexicon and powerful search criteria. SeedMaster has the best search display, and several interlinear Bible versions. Scripture possesses the best on-line help, user interface and copying facility. Memory-resident WordWorker pops up inside other software, and directly exports text into word processors. Future Bible databases should begin with a combination of these factors.

It should continue with a review of the contemporary home computer, for computer hardware has always driven the software market. Relational databases and full-featured spreadsheets weren't really possible until 640K RAM become standard on most clones, and multitasking is a product of the newer technology which in turn breaks that very same 640K barrier.

Currently, the low price, relatively high performance and escalating sales of 386SX computers have prompted speculation they might be the home machines of the near future. Combine their megabytes of RAM and larger hard drives with faster access time to stored information—throw in the first Mac-oriented screen interface to conquer the PC public, Microsoft Windows 3.0—and an image begins to form. Although it's still hazy, the outlines may be those of the first icon-oriented electronic Bible.

It seems a perfect match. All the operations we've considered in four Bible databases (with the exception of note entry) can be performed quite well with a mouse. Some things might even be done better. Footnotes, for instance, could be embedded in a verse. Click on them, and zoom into the relevant information. Choose a symbol, and bring up all the names of commentators alongside every passage. Click on one, zoom out of the Bible, and into his text.

Don't expect this to happen anytime soon, although changes may occur sooner than you think. Would any of us have suspected back in 1980 that, 10 years later, we'd be sitting down before a keyboard to locate and print a dozen biblical quotations in 10 seconds, or view three different Bible versions alongside one another? Technology has a way of making fools of prophets.

Maybe Moses could have gotten a fax of the Ten Commandments, but preferred the direct route. He always *was* a little hasty . . . .   ❏

Barry Brenesal, a freelance writer based in Louisburg, North Carolina, has written for Personal Computing, Byte, PCResource, and Computer Shopper, among others.

Other Religious Shareware Programs

Revelation Tutorial (#1554-1555; AR $30): Not really a tutorial at all. The program asks multiple-choice questions of interpretation about the Book of Revelation and provides the author's opinion as to the appropriate answers.

Destiny and Daily Bread (#1327; AR none): Two separate programs. Daily Bread is a pleasant shadow-box display of scriptural quotes, chosen at random for meditation every day. Destiny is a text adventure game which employs symbolic concepts to illustrate a Christian message.

Problems (#1526; AR none): A collection of 59 subjects. Choosing a number brings up an individual chapter and verse for study.

Verse (#1511; AR none): A pleasant little program designed to display one particular Bible verse each day upon bootup. Other verses can be added or loaded in place of those present.

Scripture Memory (#1658; AR $38): No mnemonics are used to assist in the process of memorization; the program simply displays the verses you've chosen to the screen for study.

Bible Men (#781; AR $15): A well-designed program containing two games, one each for the Old and New Testaments. Two or three lines of a first-person description are entered, and the players must guess the correct identity. Each time the game is played, the characters are rescrambled.

This article was originally printed in the March/April 1991 issue of *Shareware Magazine*.

Dealing With the Virus Threat

Antivirus programs to defend your data.

by Pat Berry

Many of us live in dread a nasty virus will wipe out precious data. Fortunately, there's no need for distress. There are a number of commercial and shareware antivirus software programs to guard against assault. This article looks at one of each: Virex-PC, from Microcom Software Division, is available commercially, and ViruScan/Clean-Up/VShield is a shareware trio from McAfee Associates.

The Microcom package includes two components: VPCScan searches for viruses, removes them, and repairs infected files. Virex-PC, a memory-resident program, monitors your computer for suspicious activities that might be caused by a virus.

Each of the McAfee programs plays a different role in defending against viruses. ViruScan searches systems for viruses; Clean-Up removes viruses and repairs infected files; and VShield, a memory-resident program, prevents viruses from loading into memory.

Scanning Your System for Viruses

If you're just setting up virus defenses, your first concern is whether or not your system is already infected by a virus. Both antivirus packages include a program that scans your system for known viruses.

Memory. If your system is infected, the virus may be loaded into memory every time you turn on your computer. Both ViruScan and VPCScan can detect memory-resident viruses and report their presence. The safest way to deal with a resident virus is to turn off the computer and reboot from a floppy disk that you know is not infected.

(Make sure to turn off the power—some viruses are able to survive a Ctrl-Alt-Del reboot).

System areas. Some viruses infect the boot record or partition table of a disk. Microcom's VPCScan automatically checks the boot record and partition table for known viruses. McAfee included this capability in the VShield memory-resident program, which checks the boot record and partition table whenever it is loaded. VShield also scans the command interpreter (normally COMMAND.COM) and all hidden files on the disk.

Files. Viruses normally infect programs (.COM or .EXE files), but other files can contain viral code as well. The overlay files used by some applications may be affected, and, of course, any file could be a .COM or .EXE that has been renamed. The only way to be sure is to scan all of the files on a disk, but this is too time-consuming to do regularly. An effective virus detection program should be flexible, allowing you to scan all files, or just certain types.

Both packages do that, but McAfee's ViruScan is more flexible. By default, it checks only .COM and .EXE files, but provides command-line options for including overlays or all files. You can also use the overlay option to specify any other set of extensions you want.

Microcom's VPCScan offers two types of scans. By default, it checks .EXE, .COM, and overlays. A command-line option allows you to check all files. There is no way to check only programs.

Eradicating Viruses

Once a virus has been found in your system, it must be removed. There are several ways to accomplish this:

•Erase the infected file and replace it with a new copy from the original master disk or a safe backup. This is the best way, because it restores the file to its original state.

•Remove the virus and repair the infected file. This is not always possible; antivirus packages can only remove known viruses, and not all of those. The result is a version of the program that should work, but may not be identical to the original (the size or checksum may be different).

•Erase the infected file. If you don't have a master or backup copy of the program and your antivirus software can't repair it, the only way to get rid of the virus is to delete the infected file. This is a drastic action—like cutting off an infected limb to save your life—but at least it destroys the virus. Before doing this, contact the publisher of your antivirus package for assistance. They may be able to help you remove the virus without deleting the infected file.

Repair Or Erase? Microcom and McAfee handle virus eradication differently. Microcom's VPCScan program alerts you when it finds a virus, and offers the choice of removing the virus (if the virus is one that VPCScan knows how to remove), erasing the file, or leaving the file as is.

McAfee's ViruScan has an option to automatically delete infected files when it finds them, but it doesn't repair files. Instead, McAfee provides a separate remove-and-repair program called Clean-Up. When ViruScan detects a virus, it displays the name of the virus on your screen. You can then run Clean-Up, specifying the name of the virus to be removed. If Clean-Up can repair the infected file, it does; otherwise, the file is erased. Both VPCScan and Clean-Up overwrite deleted files to ensure that the virus can't be revived by undeleting the file.

Which Viruses Can Be Removed? Microcom states that the viruses VPCScan can remove account for over 90% of the infections in PC software. McAfee doesn't make a similar claim, although the documentation for ViruScan states that it can detect the ten viruses that account for

95% of reported infections. But comparison of the lists provided by both companies shows that McAfee's Clean-Up to be the clear winner. As Table 1 indicates, McAfee's product removes almost every virus that Microcom's does, and many more besides.

Preventing New Infections

It isn't enough to detect and remove the viruses that are already in your system. You also need to guard against new infections. Microcom and McAfee both provide ways to do this, using several different strategies.

Program Verification. When a virus infects a program, the program is always changed in some way. Usually the size of the program is increased, and the contents of the program is altered by the addition of the viral code. If you can detect these changes, you can identify infected programs before they have a chance to spread the virus.

One way to do this is to use the validation option of McAfee's ViruScan program. ViruScan can add a ten-byte validation code to each program that it checks. The next time you use ViruScan, the validation code is recomputed and compared to the one included in the file. If the two codes don't match, the program has been changed—probably by a virus. In addition to programs, ViruScan can create validation codes for the partition table, boot sector, and system files of a disk. These codes are stored in a hidden file in the root directory.

Microcom's package provides a similar capability. Any program can be "registered" with Virex-PC; this means that a checksum for that program is calculated and stored in the Virex-PC Protection File. When a registered program is executed, the memory-resident Virex-PC can recalculate the checksum and compare it to the one in the Protection File. If the two don't match, Virex-PC scans the file for viruses. Even if no viruses are found, Virex-PC warns you that the file has changed. Virex-PC also provides checksum protection of disk boot sectors.

Scanning Programs at Execution Time. McAfee's antivirus package includes a memory-resident program called VShield, which prevents infected programs from being loaded into memory. Whenever DOS tries to load a program, VShield scans it for viruses. If the program contains a virus, VShield refuses to allow DOS to load it. VShield can also check a program's validation code, if one has previously been created by ViruScan.

Monitoring System Activity. Viruses do their damage by formatting disks, overwriting files, and other destructive actions. If you stop the viruses from doing these things, you can prevent them from harming your system.

Virex-PC can do just that. The memory-resident Virex-PC program monitors activities on your system, and alerts you if an attempt is made to format a disk, an attempt is made to write directly to a disk (bypassing the usual DOS function calls), a program attempts to terminate and stay resident, or an attempt is made to run an unregistered program.

If the operation that triggered the alert is legitimate, you can allow it to continue. However, if the operation was unexpected, it may indicate the presence of a virus. You can then cancel the operation.

Virex-PC also allows you to write-protect and read-protect individual files or groups of files. You can tailor the Protection File to your individual needs, using wildcards and a list of exceptions. The overall security level can be adjusted to four settings, from "basic skill" to administrator, that govern the your options for responding to alerts and your ability to run unregistered programs. You can also select a password to prevent unauthorized people from changing the Virex-PC settings.

If multiple people use the same computer, you can create a separate Protection File and password for each user. At boot time, Virex-PC starts in password log-in mode, ensuring that the right Protection File is used for each person. Virex-PC can also record file operations and alerts in a log file, providing an audit trail for system security.

Virex-PC's system monitoring capabilities are powerful and flexible. By you taking advantage of them, you can create a customized computer security system that allows you to limit the ability of any program or person to harm or destroy your data.

Which One Do You Need?

Both packages are valuable weapons in the fight against computer viruses. To decide which one you should be using, consider the level of virus protection you need:

Basic Protection. At a minimum, you need to be able to scan your system for viruses and delete infected files. Both packages provide this capability, but McAfee's costs you much less. By registering only the ViruScan program, you can get a detect-and-delete tool for just $25.00.

Moderate Protection. To improve your virus defenses, you need two things: a tool for repairing virus-infected files, and a memory-resident watchdog program to catch viruses trying to invade your system. In the remove-and-repair category, McAfee's Clean-Up is the best choice. It removes more viruses than Microcom's program, and it costs only $35.00 to register.

The choice of memory-resident watchdog isn't clear-cut, since each program works differently. McAfee's VShield prevents infected programs from loading, while Microcom's Virex-PC watches for suspicious activities. Virex-PC is more flexible, allowing you to restrict some programs more than others. This flexibility should be balanced against its higher cost— $129.95, compared to $85.00 to register all three McAfee programs.

Maximum Protection. If you want the best possible virus defenses, you need Microcom's package. Virex-PC's ability to monitor your system is invaluable, since it prevents any program from deleting your files, going TSR, or even running without your permission. For users who need system security as well as virus protection, this product is perhaps the best choice. Used properly, it can protect against Trojan horse programs and user errors (such as accidentally formatting a disk) as well as viruses. But you need the McAfee package, too—it removes viruses that Microcom's program can't. Get them both.

The Bottom Line

Computer viruses are a threat to all of us. In light of that threat, competitive rivalry between commercial software and shareware makes little sense. In the war against computer viruses,

Microcom and McAfee are allies, not competitors. They're both fighting on the same side: yours. ❏

Pat Berry is a freelance technical writer who lives in Cary, North Carolina.

At right are the viruses which can be removed by each program.

VIRUS	MCAFEE	MICROCOM
1168		•
1260	•	
1280		•
1701	•	•
1704	•	•
4096	•	
Alabama	•	
Alameda	•	
Ashar	•	
Dark Avenger	•	
Data Crime		•
Data Lock	•	
Disk Killer	•	
EDV	•	
Fish	•	
Flip	•	
Fu Manchu		•
Ghost Balls		•
Icelandic	•	
Invader	•	
Jerusalem A	•	
Jerusalem B	•	•
Jerusalem D		•
Jerusalem E	•	•
Jerusalem/Israeli/PLO		•
Joshi	•	
Key Press	•	
Liberty		
MIX1		
Pakistani Brain	•	
Pay Day	•	
Ping Pong	•	•
Plastique	•	
Slow	•	
Stoned	•	•
Sun Day	•	•
Surviv03	•	
Taiwan	•	
V800	•	
VacSina	•	
Vienna	•	•
Violator	•	
Whale	•	
Yankee Doodle	•	
Zero Bug	•	

This article was originally printed in the July/August 1991 issue of *Shareware Magazine*.

Personal Information Managers

by Lonnie Brown

The Professor, the disorganized staff writer for the *Treetop Tattler*, appeared in the *"Shoe"* comic strip a few months back. He'd been infected with the spring cleaning bug. "I've got to get rid of all this excess paperwork," he thought. "I wonder if liposuction works on desks?"

Many of us come from the same School of Good Deskkeeping the Professor attended. The school motto: Clean desk, clean mind. Unfortunately, a clean desk for most of us is more of a daydream rather than a reality.

The right shareware can help get organized. No more searching for your day timer. No more flipping through an unruly rolodex. No more last minute shopping for birthday, holiday, or anniversary gifts. No more washing the penned notes from your palms. Personal Information Managers (PIMs for short) will bring order to the chaos of your daily office and personal life.

Shareware PIMs compare favorably with their commercial counterparts. They offer pop-up calendars, powerful search features to locate important words, dates, names or expense categories, alarms that summon you through your computer's speaker. Some PIMs not only keep track of your daily schedule, but also the schedules of your co-workers. PIMs can even track schedules of people over several departments. Still others offer features not available in commercial packages. One PIM, for instance, not only times long-distance calls but calculates the charges as soon as the call is completed.

Finding the PIM that fits your lifestyle is important; you're more apt to use the program daily, a key factor in your organizational success. And, of course, with shareware you can try several programs until you find the one that's right for you. Here's an overview of some of the offerings on the shareware circuit:

Ample Notice

Ample Notice and I have been together for more than a year now. I like it because it's easy to use and can print a To-Do list in a flea-sized type that easily slips into a shirt pocket.

Currently in its second version, Ample Notice was written by a North Carolina school teacher named Mark Harris and, as Harris notes in the manual, "is easier to use than to describe."

It features a pop-up alarm clock to alert you to appointments while you're working on something else at your computer (you determine how much advance notice the program gives you), and automatic transfer of outdated appointments or tasks to another file for follow-up. The program will also automatically mark events containing a similar string. For instance, if you enter all your daily expenses with "exp" as an extension, you can quickly pull them all together into one file at the end of the month. Ample Notice also allows scheduling for several people or for several categories.

When running, Ample Notice divides the screen into three sections. The left side of the screen shows the daily list of activities. An event which hasn't been assigned a specific date or time will appear in the "notes" section at the top of the list. Listed too are events you've marked with the "nag" feature. If a task due on a certain date isn't completed, it's moved into the notes section where it will appear daily until you take it out. Each item gets its own line, though more explanatory information can be typed if needed. The overflow shows up in another window in the lower right quadrant of the screen. In the quadrant above appears a monthly calendar.

With Ample Notice, it's not necessary to type in each date when entering an appointment. Simply press Ctrl-C, and the cursor moves to the current date. Use the arrow keys to find the date you want, hit enter, and the date is entered automatically. Pressing Alt-D places the current date in the proper field for the appointment.

Recurring appointments are also handled well. If, for example, you attend a company meeting every Monday at 10:30 a.m., enter, "!Mon 10:30 a.m. company meeting," and the appointment will appear on a list of chores every Monday. If your anniversary is Jan. 24 and you want a reminder a few days in advance, enter "!Jan. 2 ding Anniversary." For five days before the date, "Wedding Anniversary" will appear in the notes field as a reminder.

Ample Notice's printing feature works well with both 9- and 24- pin dot matrix printers. It's possible to print out a schedule in either list or calendar form.

Active Life

Sure, the registration fee is a little higher, but how many PIMs offer seven day a week, toll free technical support until as late as 9 p.m. eastern time? Active Life's publisher, 1Soft Corp., says version 1.2 has been eight years in the making. Registration carries with it a cross-license for DOS, Windows and OS/2 versions, so if you change systems, you don't have to buy another version of the program. A LAN/workgroup version is also available.

It's a massive program—the program needs 720K of combined disk space when running. It's so large, in fact, it can only run on laptops with either a hard drive or two floppy drives. But all this information is covered in the 65 page manual that includes an index. Good thing it has one, too. Active Life is loaded with features. The windows showing schedules, the pop-up calendar, and the notebook can be resized (even using the non-Windows environment).

Uncompleted items from one day can be automatically moved over to the next. If you have an item to add to your schedule that must be placed between appointments, Active Life will find the

first available time slot and fill it with the item. Alarms can be set to go off to alert you to upcoming appointments and meetings. Items in the calendar can be set to reccur once a week, twice a week, once a month or at any other frequency. If a recurring appointment isn't happening on one of its usual days, the item can be scratched for that one time. When items are begun, a clock can be started along with it. When the item is marked finished, the clock is stopped and the elapsed time is included with the completed item. It's a handy feature for billing clients. While you work with the program, items are automatically saved every 60 seconds. That way, if power fails, you lose only the last minute's work.

In terms of features, Active Life is the most complete program of the lot. Most users, however, will find it provides far more than their everyday needs.

ToDo

ToDo keeps a list of things to do and that's about the extent of the program. Each item or activity can be up to 38 letters long. That way, printouts will slip into your pocket or Day Timer. The to-do list can be up to 100 items long. As each event is entered, you'll be asked for the month and day. After that, you can assign each item a two-letter or letter-number priority and a two-letter code. Items are then sorted by date, priority and key.

If all you need is a simple list of things to be done, this program can handle it. Beyond that, seek out one of the other PIM's outlined here.

Flexical

Of all the programs mentioned here, Flexical probably offers the most eclectic collection of features. It is, as the title page notes, a "complete engagement calendar, address book with mailing system, with runner's and hiker's diary, and sunrise and sunset calculations." What more could a nineties executive ask for?

FlexiCal will print full-page schedule and annual calendars or datebooks in a booklet format that folds to 4.25 by 5.50 inches. Events are entered into the engagements calendar. Once you've marked an event as passed, it's saved to a journal file for later reference.

Almanac for Windows

Almanac, a calendar display program for Windows, includes small corner calendars for the next and previous months and keeps track of holidays and events (weekly, biweekly, monthly, etc.) as well as time spans (trips and vacations). Enter a birthday or wedding anniversary and Almanac will update it each year. For example, "Fred's 50th birthday" will be "Fred's 51st birthday" when next year rolls around.

A desktop function offers a scheduler, notepad, alarm clock, daily calendar and event viewer. Locations for anywhere in the world can be entered to provide sunset, sunrise and azimuths. The calendars also display phases of the moon.

Almanac schedules for up to ten people and allows for mixing and matching of events among those people scheduled.

TickleX

TickleX's strong point is its ability to handle schedules for many people across multiple departments. This is a serious program: It's a tickler, scheduler, calendar and to-do list. Produced by Integra Computing, it is a member of Manage-X Time & Billing, and may be used separately or in conjunction with those programs.

Aside from handling appointments, deadlines, trips, vacations, reminders, miscellaneous events and other tasks, TickleX handles schedules for employees across as many as 20 departments. And for fitting last-minute crisis meetings into a busy day, TickleX can search schedules and find vacant blocks of time. Events are entered as appointments, reminders, vacations, exercises, deadlines or "gotchas." TickleX can also be programmed to bring up regularly scheduled events, whether they meet on the last Thursday of the month or 14 days apart.

Other options include a beeper to remind you or other scheduled employees of upcoming appointments; the ability to see a six month calendar for any year in the next half century; weekly views of employee schedules; the ability to hunt for all scheduled items involving various employees and departments; printed calendars and printed schedules.

InView

InView isn't so much a scheduler as it is a project manager and coordinator. It's a bit like the hypercard concept used by Macintosh programs in that one word can pull up topic-related information.

The InView screen is divided into three parts: The top right side shows current time, date and alarm settings. Below are the active function keys and descriptions. The left two-thirds of the screen is taken up by the note pad window. It's the program's backbone, and provides a free-form way to link notes and projects. For instance, on the first page, you might set up several categories of projects, to-do list and contracts. By designating each as a "link" word, you can simply move the cursor to the desired word and press Enter. You'll immediately be taken to the page linked to that word.

InView can also search a directory or file for a key word and display a list of files containing the sought-after string. InView has a built-in calendar to list and display appointments, but it lacks the ability to track recurring events. It does its best work in the areas of integrating and launching applications, and in information management through its hyper-link function.

Any one of the programs mentioned here will help improve your productivity and efficiency. Settle on one that has the features you need, but doesn't have the frills you need to work around. Use the program daily, or you'll lose track quickly. Make sure the one you like will produce a print-out you can use. Armed with the right PIM, you too can lose the disorganizational blues.

Lonnie Brown, associate editor of *The Ledger* in Lakeland, FL, writes the computer column for *The New York Times Regional Newspaper Group*. He received the Software Publishers Association Best Computer News Reporting Award in 1989.

This article was originally printed in the May/June 1991 issue of *Shareware Magazine*.

Shareware Power Tools

Why Buy More Hardware When There's Shareware To Rev Up Your PC?

By Wayne N. Kawamoto

Most of us don't own—and can't afford—the latest and fastest computers. For those of us sauntering along with basic DOS on less than a 486-based speed demon, there are excellent software programs that will speed up and enhance your system's capability while greatly improving your computing efficiency. DOS does an adequate job, but shareware power tools can enhance its performance.

Since software costs a lot less than hardware upgrades, you can save money improving your system. And the shareware versions of these enhancements offer at least comparable capability at a lower cost than their commercial counterparts. If you've been pulling out your hair waiting for your computer or feeling that it doesn't do everything you need it to, you'll find some solutions here.

NEWKEY

One way to improve computing speed is to reduce keystrokes. A macro, a single keystroke that performs many commands, accomplishes this. With a macro, you can easily execute ten individual commands with one keystroke. Macros also prevent you from mistyping commands, reducing the chance of error.

Newkey is a terrific package that lets you create macros for DOS and other applications. With Newkey, you can customize your keyboard. Taking only 60K of RAM, Newkey is a RAM-resident program (resides in your computer's memory), ready at your command. You simply call it up, define a macro (a particular keystroke, e.g. Alt-Left Shift-F3), execute the steps you want it to perform, and save it. You can call up this macro anytime thereafter. Newkey also gives you a way to edit existing macros.

I created macros to start up different programs and execute commands in them. Through a Newkey macro, I call up my spreadsheet and have it load a specific file. It was also useful to make a daily "backup" macro that condensed all the steps into a single keystroke. Newkey is a real time-saver; when you get used to it, you'll wonder how you got along without it.

4DOS

You might feel the same way about 4DOS. 4DOS replaces DOS' command structure to give you enhanced capability. After loading the program, your DOS prompt will appear. But you'll have a whole new array of enhanced commands and features not offered by raw DOS.

With 4DOS, the Memory command generates a map to show you how much RAM you're using, and how much remains. 4DOS records your keystrokes and can search and execute earlier ones; helpful if you want to avoid rekeying tedious, complicated commands. It also reduces errors. While DOS gives you a meager eight characters to identify a file, 4DOS lets you describe a file with up to 40 characters.

Instead of using DOS' Type command to view the contents of your files, the List command lets you casually browse through an ASCII document as if you were using a word processor. You won't have to speed read or press Control-S to freeze the screen at just the right moment.

Other commands easily change file attributes, move files, and change your screen. Also, many of your familiar commands like Dir are improved under 4DOS to provide you with more information.

Some of you may be asking, "Why would I want to install a DOS enhancement with more confusing commands?" But, unlike DOS, 4DOS has a Help button. When you press "?" and Return, the program lists all its commands. And if you incorrectly enter a command, 4DOS shows you the correct format. On-screen help makes 4DOS easier to use than DOS, and you won't have to refer to the manual so frequently. I recommend 4DOS for its ability to make the DOS environment more powerful and keep you informed about your system.

ANARKEY

If you insist on using pure DOS, Anarkey can improve your efficiency. This program lets you edit DOS commands much like word processor functions do.

Anarkey also remembers past commands and stores them in a buffer. To retrieve them, type the command's first few letters and tell Anarkey to look for the most recent match. For example, if you originally typed in "copy A:\letters*.ltr c:\word\files\letter\," you could later execute this command simply by typing "A:\let." By saving keystrokes, Anarkey becomes a real asset.

SWAPDOS

How many times have you needed to look up something in your database while working in your word processing program? If you aren't using Windows or Desqview, it's necessary to save your file, quit the word processor, switch directories, call up the database, load the file, and then reverse every step to get back to where you were.

Some software has a "drop to DOS" feature that lets you exit your application to use another program. When you exit the second program, you should return to exactly where you left the first one. Unfortunately, what usually happens is that you exit the first program, but you don't have enough memory to run a second one.

SwapDOS can help. SwapDOS is a chaining utility that frees up RAM when you exit (drop to DOS) a program by saving to expanded memory, extended memory, or disk. SwapDOS lets you have most of your available RAM to run the second application. When you exit the second program, you return to the exact point where you left the first.

The program works quite well. Using SwapDOS, I easily chained several programs

that would not fit together normally in 640K of RAM. The chained programs included memory hogs like a sophisticated project manager, a word processor, an accounting program, and a spreadsheet. It certainly isn't multitasking, but it does give you a convenient way to switch among programs.

The only limitation is that you must use programs that can "drop to DOS." Also, it can take some time to save to disk if you have a slow computer. But the required time is still a lot less than what's needed to exit a program, start another, and return. If you want a low cost solution to access different programs, SwapDOS may be a good addition to your power toolbox.

ConFormat.If you're like me, you don't look forward to formatting an entire box of new disks, but can't bear to buy pre-formatted disks at a premium price. ConFormat, by Sydex, gives you a reasonable solution. You still have to format your disks with ConFormat, but this program will do it while you perform other tasks.

All you do with this program is run it and tell it to start formatting. Go back to what you were doing, and switch disks when the program prompts you. In fact, as I wrote the first draft of this article in my word processor, I formatted several 1.2MB floppy disks. With a registration fee of only $15, this program will pay for itself in a short time with the aggravation it saves.

RECONFIG

I constantly change my config.sys and autoexec.bat files. Whether it's to change the settings to accommodate some new software, load RAM-resident programs differently, or change startup applications, I constantly edit my configuration files with a text editor. I've often wished there were a way to select different booting configurations with the correct driver and buffers for the software I wanted to use.

Reconfig is a utility that lets you create, edit, and load different config.sys and autoexec.bat files in your root directory. Once you have a variety of these files, you may select any one of them to define your system, and the utility will reboot your computer. Reconfig is easy to use and the screen is logically structured.

DISK SPOOL AND SP.EXE

Do you get tired of waiting on your printer? I do, since I use the slow daisywheel printer that came with my first computer. With my printer, spoolers can save me a significant amount of time. A print spooler allows you to continue computing as you print by intercepting the data going to the printer and storing it either in RAM or on disk. Spoolers that work well are Disk Spool II, and SP.EXE of the Printer Utilities 4 disk.

SST

The speed at which your disk reads information is a factor in your computer's overall speed. And fragmentation of files affects disk-reading time. After many writes and deletes to your disk over time, files start to fragment, which spreads the information across the disk inefficiently and requires more read time. A disk optimizer can rearrange the files on your disk so that they are contiguous instead of fragmented. This will help your disk, and your computer, operate at its optimum speed.

One optimizer program, SST—The Seek Stopper, rearranges your drive to reduce fragmentation. However, the program comes with a word of caution. Although it performs the optimizing process faster than many similar programs in the market, it does not take the time to do the task as safely. Many programs buffer data to the disk during the reconfiguration so that you won't lose your data if power is interrupted. Because SST does not take such precautions, you must back up your disks before using it. SST is easy to use, and at $10 this program is a real bargain; far cheaper than comparable commercial programs. Just don't ignore its caveat when using it.

VMS40

If you use programs that need massive amounts of RAM and can access expanded memory, then you'll probably want expanded memory in your system. VMS40 is a low-cost software alternative, albeit a much slower one, to expensive hardware. Using space on your disk, this program will create 240K of expanded memory compatible with the common LIM 4 standard. I found this program worked flawlessly with programs that use expanded memory. It easily installs through your config.sys file and is a bargain at only $25.

PC KWICK

Another way to speed up your system is to use caching software. Normally, a program in use refers to disk. A cache allocates a portion of RAM to store the most recently read information on the chance that it will be used again. Since disk access time is relatively slow compared to RAM, you can see significant speed improvements with a cache depending on the software you're using.

PC Kwick, a caching program, is easy to use. Just type in the executable file and it's ready to go. This program requires about 200K of your basic 640K RAM. Yes, it is presumptuous not to offer the option to use expanded or extended memory, but you should still have about 360K of RAM to run applications, depending on your DOS version.

The basic registration fee is $19.95, but the manufacturer, Multisoft Corporation, offers other packages that do more (and cost more). Once you see the advantages of using a cache, you may want to reap the benefits of Multisoft's higher priced and more powerful packages.

You may not need to trade in your computer for a 33 MHz monster. After all, the right software can work wonders. If your computer is too slow, it's time to speed things up with low cost shareware tools. Now, you've got the power.

Wayne Kawamoto is an L.A.-based freelance writer whose articles have been published in a variety of national computer magazines.

Glossary

AI (Artificial Intelligence) Computers are pretty dumb, but programmers try to make them think like people. That's called artificial intelligence. For instance programmers create "expert systems" software that allows a computer to make a decision or draw a conclusion based on new information it is given and how it was programmed to "think" about that information. All AI programs in the PC-SIG Library are actually classified as expert sytems, which is a branch of AI.

Algorithm This is an optional operating system file that controls your screen display. For instance, it can tell your computer when to blank your screen or clear it. See your DOS manual for further information.

Application program Wordprocessors and spreadsheets are application programs. That means they were designed to carry out a specific task. The other kind of programs are system software. They hang around to make sure your computer, and the devices you hook up to it, go on working correctly while you switch from one application program to another.

Archive bit Whenever you store a file on a disk, your computer adds some bits of information to denote its status. One of the bits is called the archive bit. It's a handy thing if you are backing up files on your hard disk. The archive bit makes it possible for you to back up only those files that have been modified since the last time you backed your hard disk files up. If you have a large number of files, the archive bit can save you quite a lot of time. Sometimes, the term archive refers to anything you plan to store for a long time. The archive bit can't tell if files have been archived (squeezed); only if they have been backed up.

Archive/ARC To archive a file is to condense it so it will take up less storage space. When you see a filename like REPORT.ARC, the .ARC means the file has been archived. Sometimes, it consists of several files that have been condensed down to one file. Condensed files are called archived files. You must unarchive condensed files before you can run them on your computer. Shareware boasts excellent programs that compress and uncompress files such as PKXARC, ARC and PK-ZIP. This same process is sometimes referred to as squeezing or crunching.

ASCII (American Code for Information Exchange) ASCII is essentially the alphabet of your computer. This code is understood by most personal computers to represent 128 letters, characters, and numbers. Since it is a standard, it is a good way to exchange files between programs and between remote computers. Many wordprocessors store their files in ASCII format. Many other wordprocessors and databases can convert ASCII files for their own use. For instance, PC-WRITE stores files in ASCII format. WordPerfect, a commercial wordprocessor, can convert ASCII files for its own use.

Assembler/Assembly language Assembly is a "low level" computer programming language that is very close to the machine code a computer directly executes. Machine code or machine language consists of nothing but zeroes and ones which is all a computer can really understand. An assembler is a program which translates (assembles) assembly language programs into machine code. "High level" languages (BASIC and Pascal) have commands that are in English and must be compiled to get them down to zeroes and ones.

Asynchronous, synchronous communication Asynchronous communication is when bits of data are transmitted without requard to the speeds of the communicating devices. As with a slow computer communicating with a fast computer, the speed of the computer is not important in asynchronous communication. In synchronous communication, both communication devices must be operationing at the same speed or "sychronized." Sychronous communication is much quicker but asychronous communication communication lets different types of communications devices talk to each other.

Author Take command of your text files. AUTHOR takes large text files and splits them into files in page lengths you specify. Also contains notepad, text viewer, typewriter, and directory viewer.

AUTOEXEC.BAT Power up your computer and it immediately loads its operating system files. The next thing it does is look on the boot disk for the AUTOEXEC.BAT file. You don't have to have an AUTOEXEC.BAT but they can be helpful if you want the same commands carried out whenever your computer is first switched on. This is a batch file with those commands. For instance, you might have your AUTOEXEC.BAT prompt you for the time and date and then invoke your wordprocessor.

Backup, BACKUP Backup is a process of making copies of data and/or programs so you'll have them in case you destroy the original copy. Some programs are available that are designed to make this easier for you if you have a hard drive. BACKUP —with capitol letters — is a DOS command specifically designed for backing up hard disk files. See your DOS manual for information on the DSO BACKUP command.

BASIC (Beginner's All-Purpose Symbolic Instruction Code)   This popular computer programming language was designed in the 1960's at Dartmouth College by John Kemeny and Thomas Kurtz. BASIC was developed for teaching beginners how to program. In DOS, BASIC and BASICA are commands that call up BASIC interpreters. These interpreters can look at a program written in BASIC and make it work on your computer. In an IBM computer, the interpreter is stored in ROM. In compatibles, the BASIC command calls up an interpreter program stored on a disk.

BASICA, BASIC   These are both names for the BASIC interpreter stored in ROM in an IBM PC. If you own a compatible, you probably have a file called GW-BASIC on your DOS disk for the same purpose. Except for a few rare cases, it doesn't matter which you have.

Batch/.BAT   A batch file is a file or list of DOS commands that are executed one after another. The file extension .BAT denotes a batch file. Type in the filename of your batch file (without the extension), press ENTER, and your computer executes all the DOS commands in your batch file. These are handy tools for things like file management or starting up regular application programs. See your DOS manual for information.

Baud   Baud is an accepted measure of how fast information is transmitted. The baud rate measures bits per second. Normal telephone modems generally work at 300, 900, 1200 or 2400 baud.

BBS (Bulletin Board System)   A BBS is an electronic message center. Hardware and software work together to lets the computer to answer the phone and offer an electronic message service to many users. The BBS lets the users swap software programs and files. It is also known as a remote bulletin board system (RBBS) or an electronic bulletin board.

BIOS (Basic Input/Output System)   The part of the system that controls exchange of data between the computer processor, disk drives, and the keyboard and screen. In the early days of MS-DOS computers, different BIOS's were a primary reason for incompatibilities. In MS-DOS computers, BIOS routines are stored in a chip.

Bit   This term is short for binary digit and is really the key to understanding how computers work. A bit is the smallest piece of information used by a computer and actually the only thing it really understands. A bit is represented by either a zero or a one and that is determined by whether a spot on a magnetized disk is positively or negatively charged. Through a system of counting called binary, the computer can count to infinity even though it only knows two numbers, zero and one. It works much the same with our regular system of counting; we only have ten numbers but we can use them to count as high as we want.

Boot/Boot Disk   Booting is the act of powering up a computer system and loading the operating system. The computer reads the operating system software on the boot disk. A cold boot refers to powering up the whole system after turning off power. When you hit the Ctrl, Alt and Del keys at the same time, you warm boot your computer. That is, you invoke your DOS system without turning off the power to the computer.

Buffer   A buffer is memory, usually a small section of RAM, used for temporary storage. Sometimes data might be held in a buffer during data transfer. Other times, it might be held there while it is being manipulated by a database or other program.

Bug   A bug refers to an error in a program.

Bus   The bus is the wiring which constitutes the main communication path for data in a computer. It consists of parallel wires hooking the main processor, RAM memory, disk drives and all input-output devices together.

Byte   A byte is the number of bits a computer takes to represent a single character or word. Most computers combine eight bits to designate a letter of the alphabet or some other character. Remember, eight bits to a byte.

C   A very popular general-purpose computer programming language developed in the 1970's.

Cache   The act of storing data in RAM so your program won't need to read it from a slow device like a floppy disk every time it is needed. For instance, a program might load a large portion of a data file from a database into RAM so that the computer wouldn't pause to read the floppy disk each time the data is changed.

CAD (Computer Aided Design) Use of a computer to help engineers, architects or draftsmen design structures and devices and display their plans during the process. A CAD program allows a computer user to substitute graphics, light pens and mouses for pencils and paper.

CAM (Computer Aided Manufacturing) Use of a computer in a manufacturing process. Sometimes, CAD and CAM are combined for the term CADCAM.

CD ROM (Compact Disc Read-Only Memory) A method of computer data storage that uses light in the same way an audio compact disc does. A computer CD ROM disc looks identical to an audio CD. In fact, most computer CD players (sometimes called CD players) allow you to play audio CD's in them. CD's can only be read by a CD ROM player, not written to (thus the "read-only memory"). CR-ROM disc's hold a tremendous amount of information, 550 megabytes. In fact, the entire PC-SIG Library of shareware is available on one CD ROM disc.

Cell The space where a row and column in an electronic spreadsheet overlap is called a cell. Spreadsheet programs let you put data, descriptors, mathematical formulas or the results of computations in cells. Spreadsheets are often rated by the number of cells they contain.

CGA (Color Graphics Adaptor) A graphics hardware standard that enables an IBM compatible personal computer to display color and limited graphics. The CGA was designed for graphic applications like drawing programs and video games. The clarity is not as good as EGA (Enhanced Graphics Adapter) or Hercules graphics.

Clock A clock coordinates all activity within a computer. That's hard to do because an ordinary PC has a "clock speed" of about 4.77 megahertz or 4.77 million cycles per second. The clock, usually based on a quartz crystal, gives off regular pulses. Each time the clock pulses, switching activity can occur. Clock can also refer to the time of day set on your DOS Clock/Calendar.

Clock/Calendar A part of the DOS software which keeps the system date and time in a personal computer.

Clone A clone is anything which is an exact imitation of something else. For instance, IBM manufactured the IBM-PC personal computer and now many companies manufacture clones of that computer. Generally any software that will run on a IBM-PC will run on a clone. Even software can be cloned. Many clones of commercial software programs exist in shareware.

Code/Coding Code is what a programmer writes using a programming language. Code is a list of instructions that tell a computer what to do. Writing this code is called coding.

Colore COLORE lets you choose the colors your monitor will display when your system first boots up. You can select from 16 different colors for the foreground, background, and border of your monitor.

COM, EXE file extensions These are filename extensions which signify executable programs. A program is executed by typing its filename (without the extension) at a DOS prompt and pressing ENTER.

COM1, COM2 These are the names for the first and second communication ports on a computer. RS-232 is the term for the standard communication port connection. While other devices such as a mouse or printer may be attached, modems used for long distance communication are most often attached to communication ports.

Command Any DOS function typed at the keyboard. For example, COPY is a DOS command. It also refers to the word typed to invoke an application program.

Compiler A compiler is a program which converts source code written in a computer language such as C or Pascal into the machine language that is directly executed by the computer. Unlike an interpreter which only runs one line of a program at a time; the compiler first reads all of the code then stores it in a new "compiled" form. The complete compiled program can then be run without needing the compiler or an interpreter. Compilied programs operate at speeds as much as 10 times as fast as programs that use an interperter.

Compressed file A data file which has been condensed by an archive program to consume less disk space.

Concatenate To join two or more strings together. A string can be any set of consecutive, adjacent characters, but concatenation usually refers to the joining of two text or data files into one big long one.

CONFIG.SYS The CONFIG.SYS file is read by the computer when the computer is started. It tells the computer about the type of keyboard, the memory buffers and other elements of how the system is to be configured. See your DOS manual for more complete information.

Console A DOS term for your screen and keyboard.

Context-Sensitive Help   While operating a computer program, help documentation usually can be displayed on the screen by pressing a designated help key. Sometimes the help is general and may not refer to the particular task or part of the program you are working on. Help is considered context-sensitive when the help given is relevant and responsive to the task you are performing, and to the particular part of the program you are working on. Many shareware programs boast context- sensitive help.

Copyprotected   Software programs stored on a disk in a manner that prevents the programs or data from being copied or backed up in any normal way. Shareware disks are never copy protected so you can make all the backup copies you want.

CP/M (Control Program for Microcomputers)   An early operating system used by eight-bit personal computers before there was MS-DOS.

Crippleware   Some programs claiming to be shareware are actually missing integral parts of the program. The user cannot use all the functions of the program. For instance, the program might not print or save files to disk, making the program incomplete and possibly useless. These authors promise to provide the missing pieces upon payment of registration. PC-SIG has gone to great lengths to keep its library free of crippleware.

Cursor   CURSOR, for either monochrome or color, sets your cursor back to normal after some other program has changed it to a "blinkin blob."

Cursor   Change the size and speed of your DOS cursor to your liking.

Cut and Paste   In word processing, the movement of phrases, sentences and paragraphs within a file or between files. Every shareware wordprocessor lets you do things like snatching a sentence from the last paragraph of your letter and moving it wherever you want.

Daisy Wheel Printer   An impact printer with its characters located on the spokes of a rotating wheel. Images are made on paper when a hammer strikes a character, forcing it into an inked ribbon and against the paper. Graphics cannot be printed with a daisy wheel printer.

Data   Generally, data can refer to anything stored on disk. More specifically, data may refer only to the information used by an applications program and not the program itself. For example, you feed data into a spreadsheet.

dBase   The name of a succession of commercial database programs known as dBase II, dBase III+, etc. This relational database program is similar to the shareware program Wampum.

Debug, DEBUG   Debugging is the act of removing errors from a program. DEBUG is an MS-DOS utility used for that purpose. DEBUG lets programmers modify programs and data stored in binary or byte form. See your DOS manual for more information on DEBUG.

Decryption   Decoding or changing information from a secret code to a usable form.

Default   The default setting is the assumption a computer program makes unless given contrary information. For instance, your wordprocessor may assume a certain "default setting" on the page margins unless you tell it differently.

Delimit, Delimiter   To delimit is to establish limits or bounds by placing a marker to separate the beginning or end of a special part of a computer program or data file. A delimiter is the symbol or character used as a marker.

Demo   To demonstrate a product or program. Many shareware programs have demo modules that show you how they work.

Device   Any hardware connected to the CPU (central processing unit) of a computer such as disk drives, printers, tape drives, plotters, monitors, or modems.

Device Driver   A software program which informs a computer operating system how to communicate with a special device attached to it. These programs are installed by being referenced in the DOS CONFIG.SYS file.

DIF   DIF stands for Data Interchange Format and is one common format for data storage used by many databases and spreadsheets. Even if a program doesn't use DIF format as its normal storage structure, it can often convert to and from DIF format as a means of transferring data to other programs.

Directory, DIR   A list of computer files contained on a disk. The term also refers to the place on a disk where the list of files is stored. DIR is the DOS command that displays a disk directory.

Disk The actual magnetic wheel and its case on which a computer stores information. There are two main types: floppy disks and hard disks. Floppy disks are a removable media that can be inserted into a disk drive and read by the computer. Floppy disks come in two sizes, 5.25" and 3.5". Storage capacity varies from 360 kilobytes to 1.44 megabytes. A hard disk, also called a fixed disk, hard drive, or winchester drive, is a single unit of disk and disk drive manufactured together. Whereas floppy disks are easily removed and used in another computer, a hard disk is permanently mounted. Hard disks have far greater data storage capacity than floppy drives —usually over 20 megabytes — and are much faster.

Disk Drive The mechanical device used by a computer to read data from and write data to disks.

DOS (Disk Operating System) The collection of software routines which control the basic operations of a computer and makes it possible for a user to load and run other programs.

DOS Shell A DOS shell is a software program that lets users carry out many of the functions of DOS, but in a more manageable environment with help and DOS commands on the screen to guide you. Many software applications are including DOS shells as part of their programs so users can carry out DOS operations without leaving the application. In some instances, the phrase "shell to DOS" can mean that a program will send you to a DOS prompt to perform standard DOS operations while keeping the application running in the background. This "shell to DOS" function is more aptly described as a "DOS window."

Dot-matrix printer These fast, low-cost impact printers produce images by firing small, round pins against an inked ribbon to produce an image on paper. The impact of each pin produces a part of the image. Different pin patterns create different characters or images.

Download, Upload files To download is to take files from another remote computer such as a BBS. To upload files is to send files to another remote computer.

EGA (Enhanced Graphics Adaptor) A graphics hardware standard that displays in more colors and with higher resolution than the older CGA standard. An EGA monitor is required to take advantage of the EGA card. Some users found the first color standard, CGA, difficult to view for long periods of time because of the low resolution of letters and numbers. The higher resolution of the EGA standard solves this problem for many and makes more detailed pictures possible.

Electronic Mail A system which allows one person to type a document at a computer terminal and send it over telephone lines to a person at another terminal where it is stored until read. Also referred to as E- mail.

Encryption To convert information into a code so others cannot read it.

Entrap Trap the computer's game pieces before it traps you. Easier said than done.

EXE, COM file extensions These are filename extensions which signify executable programs. A program is executed by typing its filename (without the extension) at a DOS prompt and pressing ENTER.

Expansion slot (card slot) The slots are spaces within a computer's electronic circuit into which electronic circuit boards or "cards" can be quickly plugged. Expansion slots make it easy for people who want to add a modem, disk drive or other devices to their computer.

Expert system An expert system is a computer program that can draw rational conclusions about a particular problem or set of circumstances based on supplied information. Expert systems can be created for everything from troubleshooting machines, to recommending insurance policies, to diagnosing diseases. The system has a method for the user to interface with the program, such as a menu or a series of questions. A database — sometimes called a knowledge base — provides facts about the topic under consideration. An inference engine compares the "answers" or information provided by the user with the database and comes up with conclusions about the case.

Export Process of moving a data file from the format of one application to the format of another so the file can be processed by the second program.

Extension The characters of a filename following the period. Not all files have extensions, but for those that do the extension often reveals what kind of file it is. In the filename LETTER.TXT, the extension is TXT which tells you it's a text file.

FDate Instead of changing the date on your system so you can change the date on a file, use this file-date change utility.

Field The place where individual pieces of information are held in each record of a database. For example, in a database of people the information on each person makes up their record, but the name, address and phone number would each be stored in a separate field of that record.

File A file is a collection of interdependent information that is grouped together so it can always be found together. A file is also the unit that DOS usually works with. Files can be program files meaning they get your computer to do something. Files can be text files, such as a letter or a report. Files can be data files that store information for use by a program.

Filecomp Compare two ASCII text files for differences. All lines that are differen will be shown on screen and may be sent to your printer.

Filter A filter is a DOS program which intercepts information being sent to a device and modifies in some way then sends it on to the device. The term can also refer to the sorting of information, or the elimination of electronic noise on a line.

Font A font is a characteristic size and style that is uniform to a set of letters and numbers. Dot matrix printers can generally print in a number of different fonts with the help of different software programs available through The PC-SIG Library.

Format, FORMAT To format is to arrange information so it can be displayed or stored. For instance, wordprocessors let users format each page. FORMAT is a DOS command that lets you organize the magnetic storage area of a disk so your computer can store and find information on it.

FORTH Invented by Charles Moore in about 1970, Forth is a programming language considered to have very fast execution.

FORTRAN (FORmula TRANslator) A programming language developed by IBM in the 1950's designed to solve engineering and mathematical problems.

Freeware A misnomer for shareware. The software known as shareware or freeware is not in fact free, but needs to be purchased from the author if the user enjoys the benefits of a shareware program.

Gantt Chart A diagram that shows the schedule for a series of interrelated tasks. Such a chart is used primarily as a business scheduling tool. Gantt charts were in use before computers, but software has made them much more manageable.

Graphics Card/Graphics Adaptor A hardware device which allows a computer to process and display graphics as well as text. The devices normally are cards which fit into computer expansion slots. Examples are the CGA, EGA and Hercules graphics adapters.

GW-BASIC A BASIC interpreter that is the MS-DOS equivalent of BASIC or BASICA on the IBM PC. Most BASIC programs work with either interpreter.

Hardware The physical parts of a computer and its peripherals. Anything you can touch such as disk drives, keyboards, printers, etc.

Help, Help Screen The instructions or advice given by a program while the program is in operation. Sometimes help screens are an automatic part of the program operation. In other cases, help can be called by pressing a certain help key (many times F1).

Hercules Graphics Card A circuit board enabling a computer to display enhanced graphics on a monochrome monitor. Most graphic programs can work on either the actual Hercules card or a Hercules compatible card.

Hexadecimal A base-16 number system often used in computer software and hardware.

Hot key A key or combination of keys which will call up a memory-resident program when pressed.

I/O (Input/Output) Input is the information or data put into a computer for processing. Output is the information the computer generates by processing input data.

Icon An on-screen picture that represents a process or command. When an icon is singled out (usually with the "click" of a mouse) the command is executed or the process begins. For instance, a picture of a garbage can might represent the process of deleting. To delete a file you would identify the file then "click" on the garbage can to indicate you want to erase the file.

Input Data or information that is enter into a computer. Without some sort of input, a computer would just sit there.

Integrated software Integrated software combines several applications into one program. For instance, a program might be a wordprocessor, database, and spreadsheet all in one. An advantage of integrated software is it allows for free transfer of information from one application to another without leaving the program or reformatting the data. For example, you can take the raw data from a database program and shift it to your spreadsheet for mathematical processing, then move the results to your wordprocessor to use as part of a letter or report.

Interface   To connect two pieces of hardware or software so communication can occur. Interface can also refer to the connection itself.

Interpreter   A program which executes other programs by converting source code to machine language. An interpreter reads the program it executes one line at a time, immediately carrying out each instruction. Unlike a compiler which permanently converts source code to machine language, an interpreter does not convert the source code, only translates for one-time execution. Programs in the BASIC programming language require an interpreter for execution.

Joystick   A joystick is a manually-controlled device that lets a user move images and pointers around on a screen. The joystick has a vertical rod or handle which sticks out of a base. Movement of the handle "forward, back, and side to side" communicates positional information to a computer in much the same way a mouse does. Joysticks are used most often in video games.

K, Kilobyte   K is computer shorthand for kilobyte. A kilobyte is 1024 bytes. Computer memory or storage space is often measured in K or kilobytes. For instance, a 360K floppy disk would have room to store 360K, or 368,640 bytes of information. Sometimes memory and storage space are measured in megabytes, one million bytes.

Key Field   Many databases locate and sort the information they contain by key fields. For instance, a person may keep a record of friends in a database. The record might consist of one field containing each name and a second field containing phone numbers. A key field is the one by which a computer sorts or locates records. In the example, the name field would be an easy field for the computer to sort alphabetically or to locate the records of a particular friend. Thus, it would be designated a key field.

LAN (Local Area Network)   A group of nearby computers which are connected allowing them to share files and devices such as printers.

Language (programming)   A programming language is a unique set of words, phrases, and symbols that can be combined in a number of different ways to form instructions that a computer can understand. Like any language, a programming language has its own rules and conventions for combining those phrases, words, and symbols to write meaningful computer instructions. Low-level languages are very close to machine language, whereas high-level languages closely resemble standard English.

Laser Printer   A laser printer combines laser beam and copier technology to generate images and electrostatically transfer them to paper. Laser printers are noted for speed, quietness, the ability to print graphics and high print quality.

Letter Quality   Print quality equal in sharpness to the best typewriters.

LISP (LISt Processing)   LISP is an interpretive language developed during the early 1960's under the direction of John McCarthy at the Massachusetts Institute of Technology. Because it handles complex data structures with comparative ease, LISP is particularly useful in artificial intelligence applications.

Log On   To log on generally means to gain access to another remote computer system. It can also refer to the process of starting a certain application program, especially if starting the program requires some type of identification code without which the program will not be started.

Lotus 1-2-3   A commercial spreadsheet which originally set many standards for spreadsheet operation. Today there are numerous look-alike programs which function as well or better than Lotus 1-2-3, some of which are in the PC-SIG Library.

LPT1, LPT2   The names DOS gives to the first and second parallel printer ports.

Machine Language   Machine language is the binary language computers really understand and can execute directly. This language consists of ones and zeros, has neither grammar nor sentence structure, and usually can be understood only by the computer. Most programming languages are translated into machine language by a compiler or interpreter. The machine code or language output by a compiler is called object code.

Macros, Keyboard   A feature of many software programs, permitting a series of keystrokes to be combined into a single keystroke. For instance, someone might use the term "temporarily approved" repeatedly in wordprocessing. A macro would allow the user to type out the phrases by pressing one key. In programming, a macro is a user-defined abbreviation for one or more lines of code.

Mail Merge Process of combining a list of names and addresses from a database to a specific letter, document or report. Mail merge for instance would allow the names and addresses of different people to be printed at the correct location on mulitple copies of the same letter. This way each person would receive a personalized letter.

Memory-Resident A computer program which resides in memory after it has been run, so it can be instantly called up later. For instance, a user may be inputting data into an accounts payable program and invoke the memory-resident program by hitting a special "Hotkey." The memory-resident program might be a pop-up calculator that can be used as needed.

Menu, menu-driven A menu is a list of choices displayed on the screen that indicates all the alternatives a user has at a certain point in a software program. Programs which boast menus that let users quickly access different modules and options are said to be menu-driven.

Modem (MOdulator-DEModulator) A device which converts electrical pulses from a computer to signals suitable for transmission over mediums such as telephone lines, coaxial cables, microwaves, and fiber optics. The most common is the telephone modem, which allows remote computers to communicate by telephone line.

Modula-2 A programming language that stresses modular program design and was developed by Nichlaus Wirth in the 1970's to replace Pascal.

Mouse A small manual device which controls the position of an on-screen pointer. The movements of a mouse being rolled over a mouse pad correspond with the movements of the on-screen pointer. Buttons on a mouse allow the user to enter commands or grab and move data or images on the screen.

MS-DOS The Microsoft Corporation operating system devised for IBM compatible personal computers. This Disk Operating Software (DOS) allows the user to take control over the basic functions of their computer with plain- language commands. For most purposes it is almost identical to PC-DOS.

Multitasking The execution of more than one program at the same time on a single computer. During that time, the computer can switch from one program to the other. For instance, this might allow a user to be writing a letter with a wordprocessor while the computer is crunching spreadsheet numbers in the background.

NDOSedit An invaluable time saver that remembers a stack of previously issued commands. Allows scrolling through and editing of these commands.

Network A computer network consists of two or more interconnected computer systems, terminals and/or communication facilities. Computer networks can be either local or remote. A local-area network (LAN) connects several computers within several hundred feet of each other. LAN users can share databases, software, printers, hard disks and other peripherals. Remote networks which use common telephone lines for communication are called dial-ups. Some remote networks use radio, microwave or infrared waves for communications.

On-line system A system which directly connects terminals with a computer.

OS/2 An operating system for IBM AT and PS/2 computers to replace DOS. This new operating system permits multitasking and use of larger amounts of memory.

Output Device Hardware, such as the screen or printer, which can receive output generated by the CPU as a result of a software application.

Parity bit In data storage and communication, each byte has a bit which is used to check the data for accuracy.

Pascal A programming language developed by Niklaus Wirth in 1968. Using a structured syntax, Pascal forces a program to be organized. It was named after the French mathematician, Blaise Pascal.

Password Keep unwanted users off your system. Protect your computer with a password.

Path The route through directories and subdirectories to find a file. Also an MS-DOS command used to tell the operating system where to look for a program if it is in another directory.

PCjr An early IBM computer product that was designed and marketed to be one of the first "home" computers. It was a small IBM computer with 128K of RAM, a single disk drive, CGA, a cordless keyboard and a slot for a cartridges which contained programs.

Peripheral Hardware attached to a computer system such as a printer, hard disk, modem, etc. Anything that complements the CPU as either an input or output device.

Piping To cause the output of one software process to become the input of another. See your DOS manual for additional information.

Pitch The number of characters per inch in printing.

Plotter Computer peripheral which draws on paper with colored pens. The plotter holds the pen over the paper and receives signals from the CPU regarding where to draw and in what color. Many drawing and graphics programs support plotters.

Pop-up Program/Utility This is a memory-resident program or utility which can be used while operating a second program. When a "hotkey" is pushed, the program or utility pops onto the screen over the primary program.

Port, Serial, Parallel A port allows devices like printers and terminals to access and be accessed by a computer microprocessor. Electronically, a port is a wire connection to the bus, the main electronic pathway to the computer processor. A parallel port lets the microprocessor or the device transmit several bits at a time, with each bit travelling over a separate wire. A serial port limits data transmission one bit at a time over one wire.

Print Spooler See Spooler.

Program A series of statements and instructions which direct a computer to carry out a task.

Prompt A symbol such as **A** or **C** which appears on a computer screen to signal the user that the computer is ready to receive input. Also called the DOS prompt, the letter in the prompt indicates the default drive.

Protocol Rules or conventions for communicating between computer devices.

Public Domain The condition of being free of copyright or patent. Public domain software is free of charge.

RAM Random Access Memory. The main computer memory used for processing programs. RAM is only active when the computer is turned on; it loses its data when the computer is shut off. The amount of computer memory is typically measured in kilobytes of RAM (640K, etc.)

RAM disk A disk drive that is simulated with a computer's memory. Data can be written to or copied from a RAM disk just like any other disk drive. The advantage of a RAM disk is that access is faster than that of a magnetic disk. However, the RAM disk and data it is storing are lost when the computer is switched off. Also called a virtual disk.

RDIR A time-saving utility that will remove a subdirectory and all the files in it.

Registration, Shareware The process whereby a satisfied shareware user pays a required fee to the program author. Unlike most software sales, the payment is generally made after the user has tried out the program and decides he wants it. The support an author gives in return can range from none, to full printed documentation, telephone-based technical support, and notification of updates and upgrades. At times, the user also receives copies of the software which contain expanded features and capabilities in return for the registration fee. Registration can be construed as a license for a user to permanently use a shareware product within the terms of the registration.

Restore See Backup

Reverse Polish Notation See RPN (Reverse Polish Notation).

ROM (Read-Only Memory) This non-changeable computer memory is contained in chips and is retained when the computer is switched off or loses power.

Root Directory The main directory from which all subdirectories branch in a disk directory tree structure. It can be thought of as the trunk from which all the subdirectory branches stem.

Routine/subroutine A set of computer instructions designed to carry out a specific task. Usually a programmer will refer to a piece of programming as a routine or subroutine when it is one part of a larger program.

RPN, Reverse Polish Notation Polish notation is a way of writing algebraic expressions that tell which operations should be done first, without the need to use parentheses. Because the expressions are written in reverse order from what they would be using parentheses, it gained the name of Reverse Polish Notation. Engineers view it as a more intuitive way to solve problems and has been used on HP calculators. It was so named to honor its inventor, Jan Lukaisiewicz, whose name was difficult to pronounce.

Server A main computer on a network which provides services, such as data storage, for other computers on the network.

Shareware Software distributed freely with the understanding that users will pay a registration fee directly to the author if, after trying the software, they are satisfied with the program. Also called "user- supported software."

Site License A software license which allows the use of a computer program by many different people at a single site.

SNOBOL A little used programming language that specilizes in the processing of "strings" of data. It was developed by Bell Labs in the early 1960's.

Source Code The lines of programming language code that form a specific program. A compiler and/or an interpreter translates this source code into a machine language for direct execution by the computer. Some of the programs in the PC-SIG Library come complete with source code so programmers can make modifications to the program if desired.

Speech Synthesizer A combination of software and hardware which allows a computer to mimic human speech. Many visually handicapped people use the computer very effectively with the help of a speech synthesizer that can actually read the screen to them.

Spooler A spooler can refer to any software or hardware that intercepts and redirects computer information, but the term usually refers to a print spooler software for directing printer output to somewhere other than the printer. Most print spoolers set aside memory to quickly intercept printer output so you can return to your application while the memory continues to send output to the printer in the background.

Spreadsheet An electronic worksheet that uses the versatile metaphor of an accounting ledger, rows and columns, as a forum for all types of business management tasks. The most outstanding feature of a spreadsheet is that a user can set aside a cell (where a row and a column overlap) to be the calculated result of data that appears in other cells elsewhere on the spreadsheet. Then, as the other data changes, the calculated result is automatically updated. A spreadsheet allows a user to instantly see the effect of changing variables on other calculations.

String A sequence of characters, words or phrases which is treated as a single character by a program or utility. Any set of consecutive, adjacent characters, including spaces, can qualify as a string.

Subdirectory A separate place where files can reside which branches from the root directory or other subdirectory, usually on a fixed disk.

Synchronous, Asynchronous Communication See Asynchronous Communication

Telecommunications The science of communication by electric, electronic, or electromagnetic means.

Template Templates are individual organized formats that are created for extremely versatile software programs. For example, a spreadsheet can be used for any number of different tasks, from doing a payroll to keeping track of a student's educational costs. Each different use requires a different template. A tax template might set up the spreadsheet to do anyone's taxes, but the data you enter into the template will allow it to calculate your taxes. Templates for most programs can be created by the user, but often ready-made templates are available for popular programs.

Terminal A keyboard and CRT connected to a computer so a person can input and view data and instructions. A terminal is usually one of many hooked to a large powerful computer. Generally a PC is not a terminal, but software can be used to allow a PC to log on to a large computer and act as a terminal.

Terminal Emulation The act of a PC pretending it is a terminal by imitating the input/output of terminals. It can also refer to one type of terminal imitating the input/output of another type of terminal.

Text Editor A program that allows revision, repositioning and general editing of computer texts. A text editor generally has less formatting capabilities than a wordprocessor and may even edit only one line at a time. The line by line approach that text editors take is often very helpful for programmers.

Text File A document file which is stored in a universally accepted text format that can be displayed in conventional alphabet letters and/or numbers with the DOS command TYPE, or sent directly to the printer with the COPY command. Since shareware programs are usually distributed without any form of written documentation, text files are used to relay messages and instructions to the users.

Tree A common diagram of files on a hard disk which can be displayed graphically as a tree. The root directory is the trunk or base and the subdirectories resemble branches with individual files attached to them as leaves. See you DOS maunal for explanation of the DOS TREE command.

Trojan Horse A computer program that "pretends" to do one thing and really does something else. It may pose as a utility and when you run it it may erase files or format your hard disk. By acquiring software from a known source, you minimize your chancc of getting a Trojan Horse.

TSR See Memory-Resident.

Turbo C A popular version of the C programming language complete with compiler for the IBM PC. Sold by Borland International.

Turbo Pascal A popular version of the Pascal programming language complete with compiler for the IBM PC. Sold by Borland International.

Unarchive To uncompress or unsqueeze a file that has been stored in archived form to save space.

UNIX An operating system developed during the early 1970's by Bell Laboratories and generally used on larger multi-user systems.

Upload, Download To upload files is to send files to another remote computer. To download is to take files from another remote computer such as a BBS.

User Supported Software An older way of saying Shareware.

Virus A general term for any number of computer programs that can infect a computer by copying itself onto other disks or into other programs without the user knowing it. The virus then disrupts the computer operation by playing some sort of trick. Sometimes the trick can be malicious, sometimes a prank. PC-SIG guards against viruses by obtaining shareware programs directly from authors and keeping its systems insulated from outside software. Serious shareware users who are aware of the dangers of viruses find PC-SIG an excellent source for software.

Wild Card Two characters which can represent any character in the search for a filename. * represents any string of characters, while ? represents any single character. These wild card characters make it possible to manipulate groups of files by not specifying part or all of the filenames and extensions. See your DOS manual for further explanation.

Window An area of a screen set aside for a particular purpose such as a help window or menu. "Windowing" can refer to the process of going back and forth between two programs or between a program and DOS without exiting applications.

Word wrap In wordprocessing, the automatic positioning of the cursor on a new line when the preceding line has been filled. With wordwrap it is never necessary to hit the return key while typing until you come to the end of a paragraph.

WordPerfect A popular commercial wordprocessor.

Wordprocessor Any one of a category of programs which allows editing or manipulation of text. Wordprocessors can range from very simple programs that allow you to easily write letters, to complex programs that support multiple fonts, three-column formatting, and powerful text manipulation capabilities. As with most software, there is usually a trade-off between power and ease of use.

WordStar A commercial wordprocessing program.

Xmodem Protocols for transmitting files from one personal computer to another and detecting any transmission errors if they occur.

Ymodem Protocols for transmitting files from one personal computer to another and detecting any transmission errors if they occur. YMODEM is a faster protocol developed after Xmodem.

ALPHABETICAL INDEX

DISK NUMBER INDEX

For the Best in Shareware . . .

Order From Your Local

Following is a directory of our domestic and international PC-SIG authorized dealers to date.

Domestic dealers are listed alphabetically by state and city. International dealers are listed alphabetically by country and city.

Our authorized dealers carry the distinctive red-and-white insignia. PC-SIG disks have grey covers and have our logo on each label. For your protection, buy only from authorized PC-SIG dealers. We do not update or support non -PC-SIG disks.

For information concerning dealerships, contact Kim Washington at PC-SIG, 1030-D East Duane Ave., Sunnyvale, CA 94086. Or phone (408) 730-9291 FAX: (408) 730-2107

U.S.A.

ARIZONA:
RECYCLED MICRO
4312 East University Drive
Phoenix, AZ 85034
(602) 437-1413
SHO-TRONICS
1831 West Rosegarden Lane
Suite 10
Phoenix, AZ 85027
(602) 581-3008

CALIFORNIA:
COMPUTER SOLUTIONS
958 East Avenue
Chico, CA 95926
(916) 343-0204
ENTERTAINMENT UNLIMITED, INC.
P.O. Box 3728
Lake Isabella, CA 93240
(619) 379-3300
HOLMAN DATA PROCESSING
2210 5th Ave.
Oroville, CA 95965
(916) 533-5992
COMUPUTER HOME
9225 Mira Mesa Blvd.
San Diego, CA 92126
(619) 549-8402
STELLAR SOFTWARE

PRODUCTS
3989 Martin Drive
San Mateo, CA 94403
(415) 637-5535

COLORADO:
ENTERTAINMENT RENTALS, INC.
3050 W. Northern
Pueblo, CO 81005
(719) 566-0566

CONNECTICUT:
HIGH TECH SYSTEMS
138 Main St.
Kensington, CT 06037
(203) 828-9938

FLORIDA:
CONCEPT ONE MARKETING
7837 W. Sample Road, #108
Coral Springs, FL 33065
1(800) 940-2550
FLORIDA COMPUTER RESOURCES, INC.
3950 Confederate Point Road
Jacksonville, FL 32210
(904) 771-7422
CARRIBEAN COMPUTERS, INC.
1021 White St.
Key West, FL 33040
(305) 294-3500
COMPUTRAC
11 Miracle City Mall
Titusville, FL 32780
(407) 268-4355

GEORGIA:
LAWHORN ELECTRONICS
1013 Main St.
Perry, GA 31069
(912) 987-2306
ROME VIDEO & COMPUTER
2006 Redmond Circle
Rome, GA 30161
(404) 235-7843

HAWAII
GSC, INC. dba PC-LINK HAWAII
1154 Fort Street Mall
Suite 401
Honolulu, HI 96813
(808) 537-3073

ILLINOIS:
THE COMPUTER WORKS
2909 N. Water St.
Decatur, Il 62526
(217) 875-0844
T.G.T ENTERPRISES, INC.
664-A Meacham Road, #423
Elk Grove, IL 60007
(800) 562-0759
SOFTWARE CITY
334 W. North St.
Geneseo, IL 61254
COMPUTER DOCTOR
14634 South Pulaski
Midlothian, IL 60445
(312) 396-2300

INDIANA:
DAVE'S COMPUTER WORLD
109 West Third St.
Brookston, IN 47923
(317) 563-3504
COMPLETE COMPUTER WORKS
711 Hwy. 131
Clarksville, IN 47130
(812) 282-6926
BEST COM
319 N.W. 7th
Evansville, IN 47708
(812) 464-0022
THE LOGICAL CHOICE
1721-A Handball Lane
Indianapolis, IN 46260
(317) 251-9833

IOWA:
P.V. COMPUTER CENTER
2217 Thornwood
Le Claire, IA 52753
(319) 332-6229

KANSAS:
COMPUTECH
404 South Buffalo
Oberlin, KS 67749
(913) 475-3964

KENTUCKY
COMPUTER MANIA
8117-B Connector Drive
Florence Center
Florence, KY 41042
(606) 525-2525

LOUISIANA:
CHAUMONT & ASSOCIATES
805 Bayou Pines
Suite A
Lake Charles, LA 70601
(318) 478-8373

MARYLAND
COMPUTER ANALYSTS
12904 Buccaneer Road
Silver Spring, MD 20904
(301) 384-1998

MASSACHUSETTS
NORTHERN STAR
1280A Belmont Street
Suite 201
Brockton, MA 02401
(617) 456-7595

MICHIGAN:
DSL COMPUTER PRODUCTS
23906 Ford Road
Dearborn Heights, MI 48127
(313) 278-5940
LOAD-N-GO
18716 Grand River
Detroit, MI 48223
(313) 835-0782
SOFTWARE CITY
2845 Breton, S.E.
Grand Rapids, MI 49512
(616) 245-5653
AMITY COMPUTER CENTER
759 West Franklin St.
Jackson, MI 49201

(516) 778-77844
COMPUTER CONSIGNMENTS
5501 South Cedar St.
Lansing, MI 48911
(517) 394-4408
COMPUTER PLUS, INC.
39755 Garfield Road
Mount Clemens, MI 48044
(313) 286-6666
PS SOFTLINE
13690 Tyler
Detroit, MI 48227
(313) 356-1163

MISSOURI:
DATA SOLUTIONS
18 Northport Plaza
Hannibal, MO 63401
314-221-6308

NEVADA:
COMPUTER HOUSE
155 Glendale Ave., #14
Sparks, NV 89431
(702) 356-7216

NEW JERSEY:
QUIKTHINKING SOFTWARE
P.O. Box 66
Lindenwold, NJ 08021
(609)435-7848
TOMORROW'S TECHNOLOGY TODAY, INC.
21 Hawthorne Court
Maple Shade, NJ 08052
(609) 482-2517

NEW YORK:
CORBIT MICROSYSTEMS
40-4 Oser Ave.
Hauppauge, NY 11788
(516) 273-0051
COMPACT DISK PRODUCTS
272 Route 34
Aberdeen, NJ 07747
(212) 737-8400
COMPUTER SUPPLY
100 Seneca Ave.
Rochester, NY 14621
(716) 342-8140
CROMLAND, INC.
BNYDC, Bldg. 131, Room P
Flushing Ave. & Cumberland St.
Brooklyn, NY 11205
(718) 797-0100
LOVE AT FIRST BYTE
P.O. Box 702
Flushing, NY 11374
(718) 849-8741

NORTH DAKOTA:
Aqua Terra Software
2038 N. 2nd St.
Bismark, ND 56501

OHIO:
PC/ALTERNATIVES
3220 La Grange St.
Toledo, OH 43608
(419) 255-5303

PENNSYLVANIA:
WEIGOLD PRODUCTIONS
1209 Carlisle St.

Natrona Heights, PA 15065
(412) 224-7021
SOME HOLE IN THE WALL
6394 Castor Ave.
Philadelphia, PA 19149
(215) 533-1211
MEGABYTE
1527 Evans Ave.
Prospect Park, PA 19076
(215)522-0849
COMPUTER WURX
720 Main St.
Stroudsburg, PA 18360
(717) 424-2792

SOUTH CAROLINA:
*KRANTZ KOMPUTER
SYSTEMS*
1512 Anthony Dr.
W. Columbia, SC 29172
(803) 755-0793

TEXAS:
C.C. COMPUTER TIME
307 S. Staples
Corpus Christi, TX 78411
(512) 883-7368
COMPUTER CONTROLS, INC.
4303 N. Central
Dallas, TX 75205
(214) 521-2242
*TAYLORS TECHNICAL
BOOKSTORE*
5455 Belt Line Road
2nd Floor
Dallas, TX 75220
(214) 357-1700
WORD PROCESSING & MORE
333 North Belt, Suite #150
Houston, TX 77060
(713) 999-0713
*HOME & BUSINESS
COMPUTERS*
1863 N. Plano Road
Richardson, TX 75081
(214) 234-1228
*SPECIALTY COMPUTER
SYSTEMS, INC.*
13519 Nacogdoches
San Antonio, TX 78217
(512) 650-5331

VIRGINIA:
ASHLEY'S
7701 Timberlake Rd.
Old Kings Bldg.
Lynchburg, VA 24502
(804) 237-3823

WASHINGTON:
KORTEN'S INC.
1400 Commerce Ave.
Lonview, WA 98632
(206) 425-3400
ALFI NEWS
4427 Wallingford Ave. N.
Seattle, WA 98103
(206) 632-9390

WISCONSIN:
2ND BYTES
9721 West Greenfield Ave.
West Allis, WI 53214
(414) 774-1155

CANADA
*A P COMPUTER
GROUP LTD.*
5112 Whitemud Road
Edmonton, Alberta
CANADA T6H 5B1
(403) 436-2383
ENTERPRISE AUDOIR
212 2nd Ave.
Unit #3
Lae Etchemin, Quebec
CANADA G0R 1S0
(418) 625-1234
*MOUNTAINVIEW
DATAWORKS*
210-11180 Bridgeport Road
Richmond, B.C.
CANADA V6X 1T3
(604) 273-2930
OPTICAL STORAGE SYSTEMS
7 West 7th Ave., Suite 300
Vancouver, B.C.
CANADA V5Y 1L4
SUNSHINE SOFTWARE, INC.
102-1812 152nd Street
White Rock, B.C.
CANADA V4A 4N5
(604) 536-9666
MSF COMPUTERS, INC.
268 Breithaupt Street
Kitchner, Ontario
CANADA N2H 5H5
(519) 749-0374
DINSDALE INDUSTRIES
2032 Merivale Road
Ottawa, Ontario
CANADA K2G 1G6
1-800-561-2427 (CANADA)
(613)725-0661 (Ottawa/Carleton
area)
WATERLOO DATAPATH, INC.
119 University Ave. E.
Waterloo, Ontario
CANADA N2J 2W1
(519) 885-3553
*COMPUTER ACCESSORIES
PLUS*
6955 Lacordaire
Suite 302
Montreal, Quebec
CANADA H1T 2K5
(514) 255-2000
DESCOTEAUX STRECKO INC.
7168 Boulevard Pie 1X
Montreal, Quebec
CANADA H2A 2G4
(514) 944-4259

INTERNATIONAL

Note: In an effort to better serve our international customers, PC-SIG has set up the following distributors. For local service, please refer international orders to the distributor nearest you.

AUSTRALIA:
MANACCOM PTY. LTD.
1/9 Camford St.
Milton. Qld. 4064

AUSTRALIA
07 368 2366

AUSTRIA
*WISSENSCHAFTLICHE
BERATUNG fur
INFORMATIONSTECHNOLOGI*
ENJahnstrape 26/2
A-6020 Innsbruck
AUSTRIA
43 512 562253

BELGIUM:
*HA-VE
SYSTEEMTECHNOLOGIE NV*
Postelarenweg 2/2
2400 Mol
BELGIUM
014 31 69 34

BRAZIL:
MAPLE INFORMATICA LTDA.
Caixa Postal 54201
01296 Sao Paulo, SP
BRAZIL
55 11 825 9390

CANADA:
PC-SIG CANADA
800 Steeles Ave. W.
Suite B-10106
Thornhill, , Ontario
CANADA L4J 9Z9
(416) 512-7250

FINLAND:
OY SUOMEN MD-SYSTEMS AB
Eratie 3
02300 Espoo
FINLAND
0 801 9544

FRANCE:
AB CLUB
13 Rue Lacordaire
75015 Paris
FRANCE
1 45 75 50 78

GREECE:
I. FALDAMIS & SIA E.E.
Spirou Trikoupi 16 St.
Athens
GREECE 106 83
(013) 616-167

HONG KONG:
PANCHA BOOKS COMPANY
HiTech & Communications Ser.
Div.
Unit 903, Join In Comm. Ctr.
33 Lai Chi Kok Rd., Mongkok
HONG KONG
86 852 789 3941

ITALY:
ULTIMOBYTE EDITRICE
Via A Manuzio 15
Milan, ITALY 20124
392 6555 306 0

JAPAN:
OTC CORPORATION
Ikaida Bldg., 7th Floor
3-25-8 Hachoubori, Cho-ku
Tokyo
JAPAN 104
813 555 0640

MALAYSIA
*CBA OFFICE SYSTEMS SDN
BHD*
No. 6 Jalan SS19/1D, Subang Jaya
47500 Petalin Jaya
MALAYSIA
(603) 733-6388

MEXICO
MAINBIT S.A. de C.V.
Felix Cuevas #630 6to. Piso
Col. del Valle
03100 MEXICO, D.F.

THE NETHERLANDS:
MEGA-K PRODUCTS
Staten Bolwerk 44
2011mn Haarlem
THE NETHERLANDS
023 319 216

NEW ZEALAND:
*MANACCOM (NZ)
SHAREWARE (NZ)*
P.O. Box 90088
Victoria Street West
Auckland
NEW ZEALAND
09 3600 500

NORWAY:
PECE-SOFT
Oppsalveien 16f
0686 Oslo
NORWAY
472 270627

PORTUGAL:
COMPUTAR
Rua do Arsenal 25-A
Apartado 21.017
11096 Lisbon CODEX
PORTUGAL
351 1 54 32 85

SPAIN:
*SOFTWARE INTERNATIONAL
GROUP*
Sorzano 21, 1B
28043 Madrid
SPAIN
91 519 20 09

SWEDEN:
*OY SUOMEN MD-SYSTEMS
AB*
Eratie 3
02300 Espoo
FINLAND

THE UNITED KINGDOM:
PC-SIG UK
111-113 Wandsworth High St.
London SW18 4HY
ENGLAND
081 877 1103

WEST GERMANY:
KIRSCHBAUM
Kronau 15
D-8091 Emmering
WEST GERMANY
49 80 67 1220

EZ-FORMS LITE Create, fill-in, print, and revise all kinds of forms.
#6310 **$69.00**
PC-SIG Trial Disk #1202

EZ-FORMS EXECUTIVE This is EZ-FORMS LITE, plus: 101+ pre-designed forms and smart keys. Forms up to 248 columns by 132 lines, and more! Hard drive recommended.
#6309 **$129.00**
PC-SIG Trial Disk #404

EZ-FORMS LASER FONT SUPPORT PACK Ten downloadable soft fonts for the HP LaserJet Plus and Series II.
#6330 **$99.00**

EZ-FORMS LIBRARY FORMS PACK Over 450 forms for use with EZ-FORMS LITE or EXECUTIVE: general business, sales, management and personnel, home, property management, construction and genealogy.
#6329 **$119.00**

FASTBUCKS A completely menu-driven home-finance program that is easy to understand and operate. It handles personal checking and charge accounts and helps to create workable household budgets.
#6320 **$47.75**
PC-SIG Trial Disk #855, 1296

FILEBASE If you find your data needs constantly take you between your database and mail list style output (ASCII comma delimited format), FILEBASE is for you. It gives you database power yet stores files in mail list format.
#6381 **$30.00**
PC-SIG Trial Disk #2152

FILE EXPRESS 5.0 A database for both the novice and the professional user. Perform all standard database functions with ease and confidence. Version 5.0 is a major upgrade, adding 100 new features and basic relational capability.
#6354 **$99.00**
PC-SIG Trial Disks #287, 288, 1255, 2672

FINANCE MANAGER II - Getting Started and General Ledger This accounting package for "non-accountants" does your company's books and teaches you basic double entry bookkeeping.
#6348 **$49.95**
PC-SIG Trial Disk #151

FINANCE MANAGER II - Full Package This accounting package for "non-accountants" does your company's books and teaches you basic double entry bookkeeping. Contains: GL, AR, AP, PR, accounts reconciliation, and financial utilities. Can run on XT dual floppy systems.
#6454 **$219.70**
PC-SIG Trial Disk #151

FINANCIER PLUS Use FINANCIER PLUS to calculate amortization schedules when considering that big purchase. Schedules can be scrolled, printed, or stored in a file. Windows 3.0 compatible.
#6390 **$15.00**
PC-SIG Trial Disk #2492

FRACTAL GRAFICS FRACTAL GRAFICS is an easy and intuitive fractal drawing program anybody can use. It has on-line help and many examples to get you started. Begin to explore the world of fractals with a new and fascinating fractal drawing program!
#6385 **$59.00**
PC-SIG Trial Disk #2217

GALAXY LITE A fast memory-resident word processor with a choice of pull-down menus or quick keyboard commands. One's great for beginners, the other for vets who want to go fast.
#6384 **$30.00 U.S. $40.00 Intl.**
PC-SIG Trial Disk #2318

GRAB PLUS Capture an address while you're inside your word processor and print an envelope or label, complete with your return address.
#6376 **$49.95**
PC-SIG Trial Disk #1145,2567

GRAPHTIME A graph maker that generates scatter, pie, bar, step, 3D-blocks and 14 other graph formats. Lotus, Multiplan, dBase, and ASCII compatible.
#6331 **$49.95**
PC-SIG Trial Disks #669, 670

HDM IV: Hard Disk Menu System A hard disk menuing utility of the finest commercial quality in a shareware package. Access and execute up to 10,000 different programs with this utility.
#6335 **$50.00**
PC-SIG Trial Disk #631

LQ PRINTER UTILITY Your dot matrix printing can have a near-letter-quality look. Added on is a 400K print spooler. You can also create logos and modify character sets.
#6321 **$35.00**
PC-SIG Trial Disk #718

LOTTO PROPHECY A new and interesting lottery prediction program. It contains two prediction systems that work with any "pick 6" lottery.
#6372 **$15.00**
PC-SIG Trial Disk #1616

HARD DISK DIRECTOR Four programs which make up a complete hard disk menu and shell designed for speed and ease of use. Use your mouse to copy or move directories or files without entering a keystroke, or enter a few letters from the name of a directory and watch the shell find it for you.
#6373 **$35.00**
PC-SIG Trial Disk #1219

LOTUS LEARNING SYSTEM This interactive tutorial teaches beginners how to become proficient with a Lotus 1-2-3 spreadsheet. Does not require 1-2-3.
#6342 **$79.95**
PC-SIG Trial Disks #846, 947

MAHJONG Try this electronic version of the ancient Chinese game of skill and luck. Three levels of play from help for the beginner to challenge the expert.
#6374 **$30.00**
PC-SIG Trial Disk #641

MOREPERFECT Double your WordPerfect editing speed. With a single keystroke, you can move the cursor or delete — by character, word, line, sentence, paragraph, or page, without moving your hands from the letter keys.
#6382 **$45.00**
PC-SIG Trial Disk #759

MORSOFT CALCULATOR Here's a calculator built to use your computer's power. It can be used as an adding machine for up to 1,000 values, or used to multiply, divide and do trig functions in decimal or hexadecimal.
#6377 **$14.95**
PC-SIG Trial Disk #1831

ON-SIDE Turns and prints too wide spreadsheets, tables, or reports on any Epson dot-matrix printer.
#6357 **$19.95**
PC-SIG Trial Disk #1184

PAINLESS ACCOUNTING A full-featured accounting which is as easy to use as Dac Easy and more business oriented than Dac Easy Light. Made for small businesses looking for an inexpensive accounting program.
#6386 **$125.00**
PC-SIG Trial Disks #2059, 2060, 2061

PC-BROWSE Another PC limitation has just been overcome! Work in one application and still have access to all the information in your other text files.
#6369 **$69.00**
PC-SIG Trial Disks #1670, 1671

PC-CALC+ Powerful spreadsheet offers a 64 x 256 matrix, presentation graphics, and the ability to import Lotus 1-2-3 worksheets.
#6302 **$69.95**
PC-SIG Trial Disks #199, 1016, 1017

PC-CHART "Stock-broker-on-a-disk" helps you know when to buy or sell stocks and commodities.
#6378 **$99.00**
PC-SIG Trial Disk #1436

PC-DESKTEAM Pop-up desktop productivity tools — An appointment calendar, an alarm, a phone book with auto-dialer, DOS access, printer controls and a calculator. All there when and where you need them.
#6339 **$29.95**
PC-SIG Trial Disk #405

PC-FILE A flexible database with the unbeatable combination of ease of use, power and versatility. Requires 512K and a hard drive.
#6363 **$149.95**
PC-SIG Trial Disks #2082, 2083, 2084

PC-FOTO Print custom labels on your dot-matrix printer to identify your slides and photos. Includes pin-fed slide labels.
#6360 **$30.00**
PC-SIG Trial Disk #1040

PC-KEY-DRAW PC-KEY-DRAW combines the features of CAD, paint, slide show, desktop publishing, HP soft font editing (36 included), authoring language, and hypertext graphical database.
#6319 **$100.00**
PC-SIG Trial Disks #344, 345, 1032, 1124

PCLOAN 5 Amortization program loan calculator with pull-down menus and pop-up help screens designed by a banker. All schedules are stored on disk and can be recalled and modified. Negative amortization, change payment amount or interest or principal at any date and supports REGZ.
#6332 **$79.95**
PC-SIG Trial Disk #399

PC-JIGSAW PUZZLE 2.0 Draws a puzzle on the screen and then it shuffles the pieces. Can you put it back together? It includes 30 free jigsaw puzzles and PCX file support.
#6370 $15.00
PC-SIG Trial Disk #1558

PC-PAYROLL Computes company payroll and prints employees' checks, and required federal and state reports.
#6325 $95.00
PC-SIG Trial Disks #565, 1019

PC-POSTCARD Print and address custom postcards on your dot-matrix printer for sales announcements, invitations, and more. Includes pin-fed postcards.
#6361 $25.00
PC-SIG Trial Disk #1361, 2561

PC-TYPE Create impressive documents with this flexible wordprocessing program. Features such as on-line help, spell-checker, mail merge and keyboard macros combine to provide power for the most demanding user.
#6305 $99.95
PC-SIG Trial Disks #455, 681, 682, 2566

PC-WRITE LITE A simpler, easier, faster version of the word processor PC-WRITE. It requires less memory to run but remains file and keystroke compatible with PC-WRITE.
#6368 $79.00
PC-SIG Trial Disks #2090, 2091

PC-WRITE MACROS 100 advanced commands including an address grabber for envelope printing, reverse video, one key print start-up, instant page formatting, and more! Assign to keys of your choice.
#6314 $10.00
PC-SIG Trial Disk #1457

PC-WRITE The most popular wordprocessor of all! Full-featured, fast, friendly, and flexible. Columns, spell check, mail merge, micro-justify, and more!
#6345 $129.00
PC-SIG Trial Disks #78, 627, 1235

POINT AND SHOOT BACKUP/RESTORE Make fast, easy backups of your hard disk!
#6327 $35.00
PC-SIG Trial Disk #1188

POINT AND SHOOT HARD DISK MANAGER Manage all of the programs, files and directories on your hard drive with POINT & SHOOT.
#6326 $45.00
PC-SIG Trial Disk #930

POINT AND SHOOT HOME MANAGER Manage many details of operating a home — calculate bills and address the envelopes, track maintenance, generate to-do lists and much more!
#6328 $35.00
PC-SIG Trial Disk #940

PROSCAN Stop viruses in their tracks. PROSCAN scans diskettes, entire systems, and networked drives for 220 known viruses. It identifies the intruder, removes it, and often repairs damage to the system.
#6375 $89.95
PC-SIG Trial Disk #2095

PSEARCH Quickly locate any file by name or text the file contains! Search for files containing 1-5 strings or words. Look for filenames in .ARC, .ZIP, .LZH. Search algorithm is fast!
#6393 $20.00
PC-SIG Trial Disk #2313

SOFT87 SOFT87 is a memory resident math coprocessor emulator that emulates floating point calculations (80287, 802387) on your 286 or 386 computer. Cheap way to acquire math coprocessing capability.
#6392 $79
PC-SIG Trial Disk #2481

SPORTSBOOK A menu-driven bookie emulator. All necessary record-keeping is provided.
#6351 $59.95
PC-SIG Trial Disk #1132

THE STILL RIVER SHELL A file and directory management program and DOS interface to simplify your life. Cut down on time and keystrokes and get on with your computing. Top rated!
#6343 $39.00
PC-SIG Trial Disk #481

TREEVIEW Find your way around your own hard disk with this file maintenance system. Many powerful features include on-line help and command line macros.
#6455 $25.00
PC-SIG Trial Disk #1243

WILDCAT! BBS A new bulletin board system which even the relatively inexperienced user can set up and operate. Built-in security system.
#6340 $129.00
PC-SIG Trial Disks #745, 746

WORDPERFECT 5.0 LEARNING SYSTEM Interactive tutorial teaches beginners how to become proficient with WordPerfect 5.0. Does not require WordPerfect.
#6365 $79.95
PC-SIG Trial Disks #1338, 1339

WRITER'S HEAVEN Customize the popular word processing program PC-WRITE into one of the fastest and most efficient editing tools today.
#6364 $10.00
PC-SIG Trial Disk #759

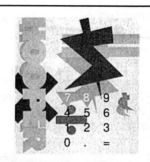

TAKIN' CARE OF BUSINESS A complete professional accounting system for non-accountants, improves on the top-rated FINANCE MANAGER II by increasing speed, number of transactions, and ease of use. 5- and 8-module packages available.
#6456 / #6457 $149 / $299
PC-SIG Trial Disk #2130, 2131

ZOOMRACKS Selected by *COMPUTE! Magazine*'s "Choice Award" as database of the year, 1989! Uses a hypercard approach.
#6347 $89.95
PC-SIG Trial Disks #1287, 1288

ZPAY3 A computer payroll system designed to eliminate professional accountants while giving you complete control over your own payroll.
#6388 $69.95
PC-SIG Trial Disks #2322, 2323

TIME TRACKER A professional's time-billing program that does it all — simply. Prints plain paper invoices and plenty of reports. Includes complete A/R.
#6315 $69.00
PC-SIG Trial Disk #825

Submission Tracking No. (if known): _____

Your Author ID# (if known): _____

Submission/Update Information Form

This form is a vital part of the review process and the primary source for marketing information that appears in SHAREWARE Magazine and our national advertisements-it must be kept current. Please fill out and return to PC-SIG, 1030 D East Duane Ave., Sunnyvale, CA 94086.

Program Title: _____

Submission's Version Number: _____

Author Information (if you are not the author please provide this information for both yourself and the author somewhere on this form):

Name _____ Company Name _____

Address _____

City _____ State_____ Zip _____

Phone, Day _____Eve _____

Please check one:

☐ I am the author of this shareware program and hereby authorize PC-SIG to distribute my new version of this program.

☐ The program above is, to the best of my knowledge, in the public domain and may be freely distributed.

☐ I wrote the above program and hereby place it in the public domain to be distributed freely.

☐ I am not the author but have provided his/her name and address so PC-SIG can contact him/her regarding submission of this shareware program.

Signature _____ Date _____